# The Baby Name Countdown

# The
# Baby Name
# Countdown

## 140,000
## Popular and Unusual Baby Names

## JANET SCHWEGEL

Da Capo
LIFE
LONG

A Member of the Perseus Books Group

*To Bryan and Allison, who continue to give this work
meaning, origin, and popularity.*

Copyright © by Janet Schwegel, 1988, 1990, 1996, 1997, 2001, 2008

Designed by Brent Wilcox
Set in 11 point Minion by the Perseus Books Group

Library of Congress Cataloging-in-Publication Data
Schwegel, Janet, 1959-
   The baby name countdown : 140,000 popular and unusual baby names /
Janet Schwegel. — 1st Da Capo Press ed.
      p.   cm.
   Includes bibliographical references (p.   ).
   ISBN 978-1-60094-036-1 (alk. paper)
   1. Names, Personal—Dictionaries.   I. Title.
   CS2377.S285 2008
   929.4'03—dc22

                                        2008007707

First Da Capo Press edition 2008

Published by Da Capo Press
A Member of the Perseus Books Group
www.dacapopress.com

Da Capo Press books are available at special discounts for bulk purchases in the United States by corporations, institutions, and other organizations. For more information, please contact the Special Markets Department at the Perseus Books Group, 2300 Chestnut Street, Suite 200, Philadelphia, PA 19103, or call (800) 810-4145, ext. 5000, or e-mail special.markets@perseusbooks.com.

1 2 3 4 5 6 7 8 9

DISCLAIMER
Please note: All governments and government branches who have supplied data for this book specifically disclaim responsibility for any misspellings, analyses, interpretations, or conclusions drawn from the data. As well, the publisher and author disclaim responsibility for any analyses, interpretations, or conclusions, and for any typographic, spelling, or arithmetic errors. Spelling, capitalization, and punctuation variations may occur due to the nature of database records.

# Contents

# Introduction

The best thing about *The Baby Name Countdown* is not that it contains over 140,000 given names, although it does. (In fact, the lists in Part 3, Popular and Unusual Names, contain 81,486 different names for girls and 58,310 different names for boys, for a total of 139,796. If you count the unique second names, the total is over 140,000.) What makes it great is that as well as providing a huge list of first names, *The Baby Name Countdown* tells you how often each name was used. Every name is accompanied by a number indicating its frequency of use per thousand babies. If there's no number, it's a one-in-a-million name. Of course, *The Baby Name Countdown* contains other information you'll find useful or interesting: the meanings and origins of popular names, lists of the most popular names by region of the United States and Canada, and tables that show how popularity of names changes over time.

Every name in this book is a name actually given to a baby in North America last year or the year before. These are not fabricated lists of names gleaned from research in a library but compilations of data from birth records. The data presented is based on birth records for 2.5 million children, over half of the 4.5 million babies born in a year in the United States and Canada.

## First-name basis

First names in North America are crucial. In the course of our daily lives, our last names are rarely used. Our friends, families, acquaintances, and even people who hardly know us—bank tellers, shop clerks, telephone solicitors, and so on—use our first names. In many instances when we introduce ourselves, we use only our first names.

Traditionally only people who knew you very well—family members or close friends—would call you by your first name. Over time in North America this custom of addressing familiars by their first names developed into informal address for a wide variety of people, including coworkers and supervisors, even religious leaders (for instance, one might call the local pastor Father Mike, assuming his name is Michael) and sometimes teachers of young children.

Many children call peers of their parents by first name rather than the more traditional Mrs. Friendlyperson. Some children, mine included, even call their own parents by their first names. I took care to refer to myself as Mommy and my husband as Daddy, but our daughter heard everyone else calling us Janet and Bryan, so she did too.

Children and young adults are normally referred to in North America by first names, so that's what they're accustomed to. As they mature, they may feel uncomfortable being called by the titles Mr. or Mrs. This is especially true if a woman kept her maiden name when she married. In that circumstance to be called Mrs. Husbandslastname is wrong. Since Mrs. is short for "Mister's", meaning belonging to the mister, being called Mrs. Maidenname isn't right either. It's simpler just to go by first name.

From familiarity to informality, the custom of using only first names is now becoming a security feature. Since one can't usually be uniquely identified by first name, more information about us can't be found if we divulge only our first name. When we provide our first name, we don't feel exposed to potential unwanted contact, but we appear friendly and open.

Conversely, while we seem to enjoy the anonymity of first names, many parents want a unique name for their child, something that sets them apart. Perhaps because of their increasing use as a person's sole name, more and more parents choose a name for their child that is unique or unusual, making their child more identifiable by first name only.

Although most children are given a popular name, the variety of popular names has increased. A century ago three-quarters of all children received a top 200 name. The following table charts the percentage of babies given one of the top 200 names in the United States over the last century. It shows a slow increase from 76% of babies receiving a popular name in the first decade, up to 80% in the 1940s. Then the percentages decrease until nowadays only 52% of babies have a popular name.

**Percentage of babies receiving a top 200 (popular) name**

| 1900s | 1910s | 1920s | 1930s | 1940s | 1950s |
|-------|-------|-------|-------|-------|-------|
| 76% | 76% | 77% | 78% | 80% | 80% |

| 1960s | 1970s | 1980s | 1990s | 2000s | |
|-------|-------|-------|-------|-------|---|
| 76% | 70% | 68% | 62% | 52% | |

An intriguing feature of naming in North America is that there are many more names for girls than for boys. This book contains approximately 81,500 different names for girls and 58,300 different names for boys. That's 40% more names for girls than for boys. On the other hand, while parents give girls a huge range of first names, their choices for middle names are not so varied. According to Gary Thompson, the state registrar for West Virginia, in 2006 "there were 1,879 distinct first names given to 10,682 males and 2,884 distinct first names given to 10,181 females. But when it comes to middle names, mothers tend to be more 'conservative' in their naming choice for female children than they do their male children. In 2006 in West Virginia, there were 2,366 distinct female middle names and 2,381 distinct male middle names."

In some ways, names change dramatically over time. In the 1950s the name Ashley was rare for a girl. A generation later, it was one of the most popular names given to baby girls. Many of the Ashleys' parents no doubt thought they were giving their girl an unusual name because when they were children, they didn't know any girls named Ashley. A few years after their babies were born, though, kindergarten classes sprouted Ashleys.

Some names that were almost unheard of 20 years ago are very popular today. For example, in 1985 the boys' name Ethan had a popularity rating of 1.9. Now it's the most popular name in western Canada and fourth overall in the U.S. and Canada with a popularity rating of 9.62. Another example is the girls' name Ava, which had a popularity of 0.1 in the mid-1980s but shot up to eighth place in the early 21st century with a popularity rating of 6.91.

Naming is influenced by many factors, such as social factors, like what our ancestors were named or what our peers are naming their children, and cultural sources such as television, film, and books. For example, the names Draco and Hermione, first names of characters in the Harry Potter book series, have increased in popularity over the last decade, from being almost unheard of in North America to having current popularities of .01 and .02 respectively. While low, these popularity ratings mean approximately 23 baby boys were named Draco last year and about 44 baby girls were named Hermione. Interestingly, over the last decade the name Harry has decreased slightly in popularity, from a rating of .21 in the mid-1990s to .15 today, showing that culture can affect a name's popularity in inexplicable ways. Like many trends, names seem to simply go in and out of fashion. For example, the name Tina rose from a rank of 488 in the first decade of the 1900s to 30th place in the 1960s and 1970s and has since fallen to a current rank of 709.

One of the ways that parents achieve singularity in their child's name is through spelling. Often parents choose or invent an unusual spelling for a well-known name. For example, I found 72 different spellings for the girl's name Abigail, which has a popularity rating of 7.27 per thousand girls when spelled that way, including Abagael, Abagail, Abagaile, Abagaiyle, Abagale, Abagayl, Abagayle, and so on, not to mention all the spelling variations for Abby.

Another spelling option is to add punctuation, an accent or an apostrophe. There were over 5,000 apostrophes in the boys' names and 8,000 in the girls' names. Many of these apostrophes were intended to be accents on the preceding or following vowel, but due to data processing limitations the accents were input as apostrophes. (Where it was clear that an apostrophe was an accent, such as after an e at the end of the name, I changed the apostrophe to appear as, for instance, é.)

Another way that parents achieve singularity in names is by using English words that aren't typically names. This is my favorite type of naming creativity. For instance, in the list of unusual names in Part 3 you'll find such surprises as Illusion, Tomorrow, and Matrix.

On the other hand, in some ways names don't change. Two decades ago Michael was the most popular name for boys, with a popularity rating of 32.37. One decade ago Michael was still the most popular name for boys, but its popularity rating had decreased to 19.47. Nowadays Michael is the third most popular name, with a popularity rating of 9.98. In other words, Michael has been a very popular name for decades.

In particular, from one year to the next the most popular names don't change greatly. Compare, for instance, the top 10 names in Florida in 2006, 2005, and 1995.

The top seven names for boys in Florida are unchanged from 2005 to 2006, and the eighth, ninth, and 10th most popular are the same three names in different order. In fact, seven of the top 10 names didn't change in the decade from 1995 to 2005. Similarly, in 2005 and 2006 the top five names for girls were the same names in slightly

### Popular boys' names in Florida

| 2006 | 2005 | 1995 |
|------|------|------|
| 1. Joshua | Joshua | Michael |
| 2. Michael | Michael | Christopher |
| 3. Anthony | Anthony | Joshua |
| 4. Christopher | Christopher | Brandon |
| 5. Jacob | Jacob | Austin |
| 6. Daniel | Daniel | Matthew |
| 7. Matthew | Matthew | Nicholas |
| 8. David | Alexander | Tyler |
| 9. Alexander | Nicholas | Daniel |
| 10. Nicholas | David | David |

### Popular girls' names in Florida

| 2006 | 2005 | 1995 |
|------|------|------|
| 1. Isabella | Emily | Ashley |
| 2. Emily | Isabella | Jessica |
| 3. Madison | Madison | Sarah |
| 4. Sophia | Emma | Emily |
| 5. Emma | Sophia | Samantha |
| 6. Ava | Ashley | Taylor |
| 7. Olivia | Samantha | Brittany |
| 8. Mia | Brianna | Amanda |
| 9. Hannah | Hannah | Alexis |
| 10. Brianna | Olivia | Kayla |

different order. The only real change in the top 10 list was replacing Samantha and Ashley with Ava and Mia. Three of the top 10 names in 1995 were still in the top 10 a decade later.

Another way that names don't change is in meaning and origin. The name Ashley, for example, comes from an English word meaning "from the ash tree meadow." The meaning and origin of Ashley is unchanging.

## The organization of this book

*The Baby Name Countdown* is divided into three main sections. Part 1, The Top Names, starts with lists of the 100 most popular first names for babies born recently in all of the United States and Canada and in particular regions of those countries. That's followed by lists of the 100 most popular names in the years 2001 to 2006 in the United States. As well, there's a chart of the 500 most popular names of the last century, showing the change in rank of each name over the ten decades from 1900 to 2006 in the United States. It's fascinating, not just for prospective parents, to note the rise and fall of a name over time.

Part 2, Popular Names with Popularity Ratings, Origins, and Meanings, is a listing of currently popular names along with their etymologies— their meanings and origins—as well as popularity ratings.

Part 3, Popular and Unusual Names with Popularity Ratings, is the heart of the book. It contains two lists—one for boys and one for girls—of 140,000 names recently given to 2.5 million babies in the U.S.A. and Canada, with a popularity rating for all but the rare names, which are those with a popularity rating less than .01.

## Using the popularity ratings

Popularity rating numbers indicate how many baby girls or boys per thousand were given that first name. For example, a popularity rating of 1.0 indicates that one of every thousand girls or boys born was given that first name. Although it doesn't sound like much, a name with a frequency of one per thousand is a fairly popular name. Similarly, a popularity rating of .10 indicates that one of every 10,000 baby girls or boys was given that name, and a popularity rating of .01 indicates that one of every 100,000 baby girls or boys was given that first name. In Part 3, Popular and Unusual Names with Popularity Ratings, names which do not have a popularity rating indicated are rare names with a frequency of less than one in 100,000. Often these names are one in a million, such as Rylicia or Dollarian.

#### Popularity ratings

| Rating | Frequency of use |
|---|---|
| 10.00 | One boy or girl out of 100 received this name |
| 1.00 | One girl or boy out of 1,000 received this name |
| .10 | One boy or girl out of 10,000 received this name |
| .01 | One girl or boy out of 100,000 received this name |
| No number | One in a million! Only one boy or girl out of more than 100,000 received this name |

The simplest way to understand popularity ratings is to view them relatively: the higher the number, the more popular the name. So, for instance, you can use the popularity ratings to choose the most popular spelling of a name.

But the ratings can also be multiplied or added. A name with a popularity rating of 2 is twice as popular as one with a rating of 1. So you could add up the popularity ratings for all the variant spellings of Christopher to find out whether it is actually more popular than Michael.

Popularity ratings indicate popularity per thousand boys or girls, but by moving the decimal places in the population and the popularity rating to the right or left, you can quickly calculate other statistical frequencies.

For example, the name Linda has a popularity of

|  | .25 | per 1,000 |
|---|---|---|

**which is equivalent to**

|  | .025 | per 100 |
|---|---|---|
|  | 2.5 | per 10,000 |
|  | 25 | per 100,000 |
| **and** | 250 | per 1,000,000. |

You can go further with the data in *The Baby Name Countdown* and estimate roughly how many children in any geographic location will receive a certain name.

Start with this fact: the birth rate in the United States is approximately 14 per thousand, meaning that for every thousand people in the population, 14 children are born in a year. In Canada the current birth rate is about 11 per thousand.

To calculate the approximate number of children that will be born in any location in the United States, multiply that location's population by .014 (14 divided by 1,000). For Canada multiply the location's population by .011.

Just over half, 51%, of babies are boys, so to calculate the approximate number of boys that will be born in any location in the United States, multiply that location's population by .00714. (That's 14 divided by 1,000 times .51.) For boys in Canada multiply the location's population by .00561.

Just under half, 49%, of babies are girls, so to calculate the approximate number of girls that will be born in any location in the United States, multiply that location's population by .00686. (That's 14 divided by 1,000 times .49.) For girls in Canada multiply the location's population by .00539.

The formula is

(1)  $b = g \times r$

where $b$ is the number of births, $g$ is the population of some location, and $r$ is:

.00714 for boys in the United States
.00686 for girls in the United States
.00561 for boys in Canada
.00539 for girls in Canada or
.014 for boys and girls combined in the United States or
.011 for boys and girls combined in Canada.

Once you know the number of children born in a year in a community, you can estimate how many might be given a certain name using the second formula:

(2)  $n = b \times p/1{,}000$

where *n* is the number of children who will receive a particular name, and *p* is the popularity rating of that name.

For example, I can estimate how many children will be named Linda this year in an American city with a population of about 800,000. First calculate the approximate number of girls that will be born.

(1)  $b = g \times .00686$
     $b = 800{,}000 \times .00686$
     $b = 5{,}488$

The popularity rating for the name Linda is .25. To estimate how many girls will be named Linda, use the second formula:

(2)  $n = b \times p/1{,}000$
     $n = 5{,}488 \times .25/1{,}000$
     $n = 1.372$

Based on current trends, one girl born in this city this year will be named Linda.

You could also estimate the frequency of use of a name among a population using the following formula:

(3)  $n = s \times p/1{,}000$

where *s* is the number of children in the sample.

For example, if I'm curious how many children might have the name Michael in a kindergarten class of 30 children in four or five years, I can plug values into formula (3) thus:

$s = 15$ [the number of boys expected in the class]
$p = 9.98$ [the popularity rating for Michael]
$n = s \times p/1{,}000$
$n = 15 \times 9.98/1{,}000$
$n = .1497$

In other words, I calculate that most kindergarten classes won't have a boy named Michael.

The point of these examples is that you can play with the popularity ratings to estimate a statistical likelihood of a certain number of children having a particular name in a particular place. (The term "statistical" reminds you that any calculations based on the data do not give you actual frequencies of use of names but estimated—or statistical—probabilities based on all of the data collected being summed together. Further, due to rounding and regional variations, these estimated probabilities are approximations.)

Fortunately for prospective parents searching for the perfect name for their baby, *The Baby Name Countdown* contains all the information needed to make the choice. It isn't enough to know what a name means or where it came from; you need to know how popular that name is. Whether you want to ensure your child is in synch with the times by giving her or him a popular name or you want your child's name to be unique, you'll find the names and popularity ratings you need in *The Baby Name Countdown*.

— *Janet Schwegel*
January 2008

# The Baby Name Countdown

# Part 1

# The Top Names

- The 100 most popular names by region
- The 100 most popular names in recent years
- The 500 most popular names in each decade of the last century

The number to the left of a name indicates its popularity rating: how frequently the name was used per thousand babies. For example, a popularity rating of 1.23 means that approximately one of every thousand girls or boys was given that name in a year.

# The Top 100 Girls' Names by Region

*Popularity ratings indicate usage per thousand baby girls.*

## United States and Canada

| | | | | | | | | | |
|---|---|---|---|---|---|---|---|---|---|
| 10.48 | Emily | 4.20 | Ella | 2.62 | Brooke | 2.10 | Trinity | 1.64 | Isabel |
| 9.50 | Emma | 4.13 | Lauren | 2.60 | Kaylee | 2.09 | Gabriella | 1.63 | Mariah |
| 8.76 | Madison | 4.10 | Taylor | 2.57 | Maria | 2.07 | Audrey | 1.61 | Jenna |
| 7.71 | Isabella | 4.02 | Hailey | 2.52 | Allison | 2.06 | Kimberly | 1.60 | Mary |
| 7.27 | Olivia | 3.87 | Anna | 2.51 | Megan | 2.01 | Gabrielle | 1.54 | Amelia |
| 7.27 | Abigail | 3.80 | Kayla | 2.44 | Zoe | 2.00 | Nicole | 1.51 | Arianna |
| 6.92 | Hannah | 3.66 | Victoria | 2.39 | Jennifer | 1.98 | Stephanie | 1.41 | Isabelle |
| 6.91 | Ava | 3.55 | Jasmine | 2.36 | Addison | 1.98 | Sara | 1.40 | Claire |
| 5.96 | Sophia | 3.53 | Jessica | 2.35 | Nevaeh | 1.93 | Brooklyn | 1.38 | Jada |
| 5.86 | Samantha | 3.29 | Sydney | 2.34 | Angelina | 1.91 | Evelyn | 1.37 | Rebecca |
| 5.76 | Ashley | 3.29 | Julia | 2.33 | Makayla | 1.88 | Vanessa | 1.35 | Valeria |
| 5.70 | Sarah | 3.02 | Savannah | 2.32 | Lillian | 1.88 | Paige | 1.33 | Aaliyah |
| 5.69 | Elizabeth | 2.96 | Lily | 2.28 | Faith | 1.88 | Riley | 1.32 | Caroline |
| 5.26 | Mia | 2.93 | Kaitlyn | 2.24 | Katelyn | 1.86 | Leah | 1.30 | Natalia |
| 5.26 | Grace | 2.90 | Alexandra | 2.22 | Mackenzie | 1.81 | Michelle | 1.29 | Amanda |
| 5.24 | Alexis | 2.90 | Morgan | 2.19 | Kylie | 1.77 | Haley | 1.26 | Jordan |
| 4.88 | Natalie | 2.86 | Katherine | 2.17 | Sofia | 1.74 | Jocelyn | 1.22 | Autumn |
| 4.78 | Alyssa | 2.81 | Destiny | 2.16 | Maya | 1.73 | Madeline | 1.20 | Melissa |
| 4.74 | Chloe | 2.77 | Rachel | 2.16 | Avery | 1.66 | Melanie | 1.19 | Gracie |
| 4.30 | Brianna | 2.63 | Alexa | 2.13 | Andrea | 1.64 | Ariana | 1.17 | Amy |

## New England

| | | | | | | | | | |
|---|---|---|---|---|---|---|---|---|---|
| 13.56 | Ava | 5.06 | Chloe | 3.33 | Morgan | 2.69 | Kaitlyn | 1.88 | Juliana |
| 12.57 | Isabella | 4.81 | Lauren | 3.31 | Sofia | 2.55 | Nicole | 1.86 | Rebecca |
| 12.38 | Emma | 4.61 | Katherine | 3.27 | Amelia | 2.53 | Nevaeh | 1.80 | Claire |
| 12.11 | Emily | 4.55 | Brianna | 3.25 | Maya | 2.52 | Jenna | 1.79 | Jennifer |
| 11.86 | Olivia | 4.48 | Victoria | 3.20 | Madeline | 2.43 | Gabrielle | 1.74 | Addison |
| 10.65 | Abigail | 4.45 | Natalie | 3.18 | Riley | 2.41 | Jillian | 1.64 | Margaret |
| 9.97 | Sophia | 4.29 | Gabriella | 3.15 | Angelina | 2.37 | Jasmine | 1.54 | Evelyn |
| 9.83 | Madison | 4.19 | Hailey | 3.11 | Mackenzie | 2.32 | Sara | 1.48 | Stephanie |
| 8.96 | Grace | 4.12 | Alyssa | 3.06 | Arianna | 2.30 | Katelyn | 1.34 | Eva |
| 8.13 | Hannah | 3.96 | Alexandra | 3.04 | Avery | 2.28 | Catherine | 1.29 | Mary |
| 7.78 | Julia | 3.91 | Kayla | 2.99 | Zoe | 2.28 | Isabel | 1.28 | Caitlin |
| 7.29 | Samantha | 3.88 | Lillian | 2.95 | Gianna | 2.27 | Alexa | 1.28 | Kathryn |
| 7.24 | Sarah | 3.78 | Brooke | 2.93 | Leah | 2.24 | Makayla | 1.25 | Julianna |
| 6.71 | Ella | 3.66 | Taylor | 2.92 | Savannah | 2.18 | Ariana | 1.22 | Jordan |
| 6.50 | Elizabeth | 3.56 | Molly | 2.84 | Allison | 2.15 | Amanda | 1.14 | Lucy |
| 6.05 | Mia | 3.50 | Charlotte | 2.84 | Paige | 2.15 | Kylie | 1.14 | Nora |
| 5.75 | Lily | 3.48 | Caroline | 2.83 | Isabelle | 2.13 | Audrey | 1.12 | Sadie |
| 5.47 | Anna | 3.42 | Megan | 2.81 | Sophie | 2.08 | Keira | 1.02 | Maria |
| 5.27 | Alexis | 3.42 | Sydney | 2.78 | Jessica | 2.07 | Destiny | 1.01 | Madelyn |
| 5.19 | Ashley | 3.37 | Rachel | 2.78 | Kaylee | 2.03 | Erin | 0.95 | Faith |

## Mid-Atlantic U.S.A

| | | | | | | | | | |
|---|---|---|---|---|---|---|---|---|---|
| 10.41 | Emily | 4.45 | Natalie | 3.04 | Lily | 2.27 | Faith | 1.55 | Catherine |
| 9.42 | Madison | 4.30 | Chloe | 3.02 | Maya | 2.24 | Lillian | 1.53 | Charlotte |
| 9.27 | Ava | 4.18 | Ella | 2.95 | Savannah | 2.16 | Rebecca | 1.52 | Addison |
| 9.16 | Isabella | 4.15 | Anna | 2.91 | Jasmine | 2.13 | Arianna | 1.42 | Katelyn |
| 8.58 | Emma | 3.97 | Victoria | 2.88 | Gabrielle | 2.11 | Caroline | 1.36 | Jordan |
| 8.43 | Olivia | 3.97 | Lauren | 2.82 | Nicole | 2.07 | Kaylee | 1.36 | Isabelle |
| 7.51 | Abigail | 3.96 | Taylor | 2.81 | Riley | 2.06 | Jennifer | 1.31 | Trinity |
| 7.39 | Sophia | 3.69 | Katherine | 2.80 | Sara | 2.05 | Jenna | 1.31 | Isabel |
| 6.92 | Sarah | 3.67 | Hailey | 2.79 | Mackenzie | 2.01 | Amanda | 1.23 | Haley |
| 6.39 | Samantha | 3.64 | Gabriella | 2.75 | Allison | 1.99 | Amelia | 1.22 | Adriana |
| 6.28 | Hannah | 3.63 | Alexandra | 2.75 | Alexa | 1.84 | Jayla | 1.20 | Autumn |
| 6.17 | Ashley | 3.61 | Jessica | 2.66 | Destiny | 1.84 | Keira | 1.17 | Danielle |
| 5.99 | Grace | 3.48 | Rachel | 2.63 | Megan | 1.77 | Ariana | 1.14 | Mary |
| 5.79 | Kayla | 3.35 | Angelina | 2.50 | Makayla | 1.74 | Kimberly | 1.13 | Gabriela |
| 5.62 | Elizabeth | 3.35 | Gianna | 2.40 | Madeline | 1.73 | Michelle | 1.13 | Evelyn |
| 5.36 | Mia | 3.25 | Morgan | 2.38 | Nevaeh | 1.72 | Stephanie | 1.08 | Melanie |
| 5.19 | Julia | 3.23 | Leah | 2.35 | Paige | 1.68 | Jada | 1.04 | Vanessa |
| 5.02 | Alexis | 3.17 | Brooke | 2.35 | Sofia | 1.66 | Aaliyah | 1.03 | Erin |
| 4.90 | Brianna | 3.12 | Kaitlyn | 2.33 | Zoe | 1.60 | Kylie | 1.02 | Claire |
| 4.79 | Alyssa | 3.06 | Sydney | 2.29 | Maria | 1.59 | Molly | 0.97 | Avery |

## Southeastern U.S.A.

| | | | | | | | | | |
|---|---|---|---|---|---|---|---|---|---|
| 11.05 | Madison | 4.14 | Jasmine | 2.95 | Katherine | 2.19 | Alexandra | 1.39 | Aubrey |
| 10.12 | Emily | 4.06 | Addison | 2.91 | Jada | 2.19 | Jennifer | 1.35 | Melanie |
| 9.43 | Emma | 4.05 | Destiny | 2.90 | Jessica | 2.16 | Aaliyah | 1.32 | Katie |
| 8.40 | Isabella | 4.01 | Ella | 2.69 | Nevaeh | 2.04 | Jordan | 1.30 | Jenna |
| 8.02 | Hannah | 4.01 | Kayla | 2.66 | Mary | 2.02 | Faith | 1.25 | Reagan |
| 7.33 | Abigail | 3.93 | Mia | 2.64 | Katelyn | 2.00 | Brooklyn | 1.25 | Angelina |
| 6.97 | Olivia | 3.92 | Lauren | 2.63 | Gabrielle | 1.97 | Layla | 1.20 | Mariah |
| 6.80 | Ava | 3.90 | Hailey | 2.59 | Mackenzie | 1.94 | Amelia | 1.18 | Michelle |
| 6.10 | Sarah | 3.90 | Natalie | 2.58 | Riley | 1.92 | Megan | 1.18 | Sofia |
| 5.93 | Elizabeth | 3.89 | Makayla | 2.56 | Jayla | 1.92 | Kimberly | 1.18 | Bailey |
| 5.56 | Chloe | 3.66 | Morgan | 2.55 | Maria | 1.90 | Leah | 1.15 | Vanessa |
| 5.53 | Anna | 3.50 | Victoria | 2.50 | Caroline | 1.85 | Gracie | 1.14 | Breanna |
| 5.51 | Alexis | 3.44 | Grace | 2.42 | Rachel | 1.69 | Autumn | 1.13 | Shelby |
| 5.27 | Ashley | 3.40 | Kaylee | 2.41 | Allison | 1.61 | Rebecca | 1.11 | Ariana |
| 5.00 | Taylor | 3.22 | Trinity | 2.36 | Brooke | 1.55 | Kennedy | 1.10 | Evelyn |
| 4.92 | Alyssa | 3.21 | Kaitlyn | 2.35 | Sara | 1.49 | Andrea | 1.08 | Audrey |
| 4.91 | Brianna | 3.21 | Sydney | 2.34 | Julia | 1.49 | Alexa | 1.06 | Mckenzie |
| 4.83 | Sophia | 3.11 | Lillian | 2.30 | Kylie | 1.47 | Gabriella | 1.05 | Skylar |
| 4.40 | Savannah | 3.05 | Lily | 2.26 | Zoe | 1.47 | Stephanie | 1.03 | Jocelyn |
| 4.29 | Samantha | 2.95 | Haley | 2.21 | Avery | 1.41 | Madeline | 1.02 | Nicole |

## Northcentral U.S.A.

| | | | | | | | | | |
|---|---|---|---|---|---|---|---|---|---|
| 10.92 | Emma | 4.55 | Lillian | 3.04 | Megan | 2.59 | Maya | 1.55 | Sara |
| 10.65 | Ava | 4.47 | Alyssa | 2.96 | Claire | 2.56 | Kylie | 1.55 | Jayla |
| 9.89 | Olivia | 4.46 | Taylor | 2.94 | Kaylee | 2.54 | Jenna | 1.51 | Haley |
| 9.84 | Emily | 4.39 | Hailey | 2.92 | Avery | 2.42 | Zoe | 1.50 | Molly |
| 9.10 | Madison | 4.21 | Ashley | 2.84 | Isabelle | 2.40 | Amelia | 1.48 | Sofia |
| 8.45 | Abigail | 4.19 | Mia | 2.83 | Makayla | 2.35 | Evelyn | 1.44 | Aaliyah |
| 8.35 | Isabella | 4.13 | Morgan | 2.79 | Audrey | 2.26 | Alexa | 1.40 | Kennedy |
| 7.87 | Hannah | 3.83 | Lily | 2.79 | Victoria | 2.16 | Destiny | 1.25 | Angelina |
| 7.83 | Grace | 3.79 | Sydney | 2.77 | Jasmine | 2.14 | Mariah | 1.22 | Jocelyn |
| 7.33 | Sophia | 3.73 | Nevaeh | 2.76 | Gabrielle | 2.05 | Trinity | 1.21 | Marissa |
| 6.68 | Elizabeth | 3.72 | Brianna | 2.73 | Rachel | 2.04 | Arianna | 1.15 | Jada |
| 6.20 | Ella | 3.49 | Julia | 2.72 | Jessica | 2.01 | Mya | 1.08 | Ariana |
| 6.10 | Alexis | 3.46 | Kayla | 2.70 | Riley | 1.95 | Aubrey | 1.03 | Layla |
| 5.75 | Samantha | 3.45 | Allison | 2.69 | Katherine | 1.92 | Autumn | 1.02 | Gianna |
| 5.60 | Chloe | 3.31 | Mackenzie | 2.68 | Gabriella | 1.79 | Lydia | 0.95 | Andrea |
| 5.42 | Addison | 3.29 | Savannah | 2.67 | Madeline | 1.75 | Maria | 0.92 | Jennifer |
| 5.20 | Natalie | 3.23 | Brooke | 2.64 | Katelyn | 1.67 | Mary | 0.88 | Alivia |
| 5.19 | Lauren | 3.15 | Brooklyn | 2.63 | Faith | 1.64 | Madelyn | 0.82 | Nicole |
| 4.84 | Anna | 3.10 | Paige | 2.62 | Leah | 1.61 | Isabel | 0.78 | Kendall |
| 4.71 | Sarah | 3.06 | Kaitlyn | 2.59 | Alexandra | 1.56 | Gracie | 0.76 | Charlotte |

## Southcentral U.S.A.

| | | | | | | | | | |
|---|---|---|---|---|---|---|---|---|---|
| 10.16 | Emily | 3.88 | Addison | 2.67 | Trinity | 2.24 | Sofia | 1.66 | Isabel |
| 8.61 | Madison | 3.83 | Jasmine | 2.67 | Nevaeh | 2.22 | Lily | 1.64 | Angela |
| 7.82 | Emma | 3.75 | Lauren | 2.66 | Makayla | 2.22 | Stephanie | 1.63 | Daniela |
| 7.51 | Mia | 3.57 | Hailey | 2.65 | Zoe | 2.21 | Gabriella | 1.63 | Briana |
| 7.18 | Isabella | 3.49 | Taylor | 2.64 | Kaitlyn | 2.12 | Leslie | 1.63 | Gabriela |
| 7.10 | Abigail | 3.45 | Destiny | 2.55 | Melanie | 2.07 | Natalia | 1.61 | Miranda |
| 6.41 | Hannah | 3.39 | Kayla | 2.53 | Brooklyn | 2.04 | Katelyn | 1.56 | Sara |
| 6.21 | Ashley | 3.35 | Andrea | 2.53 | Sydney | 2.03 | Allison | 1.53 | Ana |
| 6.03 | Ava | 3.33 | Alexa | 2.51 | Faith | 2.01 | Vanessa | 1.53 | Alondra |
| 5.60 | Natalie | 3.16 | Avery | 2.50 | Morgan | 1.92 | Ariana | 1.52 | Madeline |
| 5.52 | Alyssa | 3.10 | Savannah | 2.48 | Katherine | 1.92 | Aubrey | 1.41 | Amy |
| 5.25 | Elizabeth | 3.07 | Valeria | 2.43 | Alexandra | 1.86 | Michelle | 1.37 | Giselle |
| 5.11 | Samantha | 3.05 | Grace | 2.41 | Lillian | 1.79 | Julia | 1.33 | Daisy |
| 4.97 | Alexis | 3.01 | Maria | 2.38 | Angelina | 1.77 | Haley | 1.33 | Jazmin |
| 4.88 | Olivia | 2.96 | Anna | 2.35 | Mariah | 1.76 | Aaliyah | 1.33 | Nicole |
| 4.83 | Brianna | 2.95 | Kaylee | 2.33 | Evelyn | 1.74 | Jacqueline | 1.32 | Genesis |
| 4.83 | Chloe | 2.91 | Ella | 2.32 | Audrey | 1.73 | Valerie | 1.30 | Melissa |
| 4.62 | Victoria | 2.90 | Jessica | 2.32 | Brooke | 1.72 | Arianna | 1.28 | Mariana |
| 4.51 | Sophia | 2.87 | Kimberly | 2.30 | Kylie | 1.69 | Leah | 1.28 | Camila |
| 4.31 | Sarah | 2.85 | Jennifer | 2.27 | Jocelyn | 1.68 | Rachel | 1.27 | Diana |

## Central U.S.A.

| | | | | | | | | | |
|---|---|---|---|---|---|---|---|---|---|
| 12.85 | Emma | 4.68 | Lillian | 3.17 | Claire | 2.46 | Victoria | 2.02 | Destiny |
| 10.77 | Ava | 4.65 | Alyssa | 3.15 | Riley | 2.45 | Madeline | 2.01 | Mary |
| 10.69 | Madison | 4.54 | Avery | 3.11 | Nevaeh | 2.40 | Julia | 1.98 | Rylee |
| 9.40 | Emily | 4.54 | Hailey | 3.09 | Audrey | 2.38 | Zoey | 1.91 | Madelyn |
| 9.35 | Abigail | 4.30 | Sydney | 3.00 | Makayla | 2.35 | Jessica | 1.84 | Reese |
| 9.11 | Olivia | 4.24 | Morgan | 2.98 | Faith | 2.28 | Amelia | 1.83 | Autumn |
| 8.82 | Hannah | 4.18 | Brooklyn | 2.98 | Zoe | 2.27 | Kennedy | 1.70 | Ashlyn |
| 8.15 | Addison | 4.18 | Lily | 2.93 | Isabelle | 2.26 | Kayla | 1.66 | Maya |
| 7.68 | Alexis | 4.12 | Mia | 2.87 | Katelyn | 2.26 | Mariah | 1.60 | Lydia |
| 7.50 | Isabella | 3.96 | Allison | 2.87 | Katherine | 2.23 | Isabel | 1.39 | Lucy |
| 7.19 | Grace | 3.96 | Kaylee | 2.86 | Megan | 2.16 | Molly | 1.31 | Alexandra |
| 6.98 | Elizabeth | 3.81 | Sarah | 2.84 | Haley | 2.14 | Leah | 1.28 | Payton |
| 6.72 | Sophia | 3.62 | Ashley | 2.67 | Alexa | 2.14 | Maria | 1.17 | Breanna |
| 6.27 | Chloe | 3.61 | Paige | 2.64 | Gracie | 2.13 | Gabriella | 1.16 | Jennifer |
| 6.03 | Ella | 3.60 | Mackenzie | 2.64 | Jasmine | 2.11 | Kylee | 1.15 | Caroline |
| 5.68 | Anna | 3.40 | Kaitlyn | 2.63 | Gabrielle | 2.08 | Reagan | 1.13 | Evelyn |
| 5.55 | Taylor | 3.40 | Savannah | 2.59 | Rachel | 2.07 | Bailey | 1.07 | Katie |
| 5.48 | Lauren | 3.33 | Brianna | 2.58 | Aubrey | 2.06 | Peyton | 0.99 | Sara |
| 5.32 | Natalie | 3.29 | Brooke | 2.56 | Trinity | 2.05 | Shelby | 0.85 | Delaney |
| 5.28 | Samantha | 3.28 | Kylie | 2.48 | Jenna | 2.04 | Mya | 0.83 | Jordan |

## Midwestern U.S.A.

| | | | | | | | | | |
|---|---|---|---|---|---|---|---|---|---|
| 10.11 | Emma | 4.63 | Mia | 2.74 | Megan | 2.04 | Makayla | 1.49 | Aubrey |
| 8.31 | Emily | 4.50 | Taylor | 2.73 | Katelyn | 1.95 | Gracie | 1.49 | Jade |
| 7.83 | Abigail | 4.41 | Sarah | 2.72 | Jessica | 1.90 | Isabel | 1.49 | Mary |
| 7.72 | Hannah | 4.40 | Lily | 2.59 | Kaitlyn | 1.90 | Lucy | 1.46 | Mackenzie |
| 7.56 | Madison | 4.21 | Alyssa | 2.57 | Brianna | 1.87 | Leah | 1.39 | Madeline |
| 7.33 | Ava | 4.18 | Anna | 2.47 | Katherine | 1.86 | Ellie | 1.38 | Keira |
| 7.29 | Isabella | 4.09 | Natalie | 2.47 | Kylie | 1.86 | Kimberly | 1.33 | Gabriella |
| 7.27 | Olivia | 3.69 | Nevaeh | 2.47 | Victoria | 1.81 | Alexandra | 1.31 | Sadie |
| 6.63 | Grace | 3.64 | Savannah | 2.41 | Jasmine | 1.78 | Trinity | 1.30 | Haley |
| 6.39 | Elizabeth | 3.58 | Sydney | 2.40 | Julia | 1.76 | Maria | 1.30 | Mariah |
| 6.24 | Samantha | 3.56 | Lauren | 2.38 | Claire | 1.74 | Lydia | 1.30 | Melanie |
| 5.90 | Sophia | 3.54 | Morgan | 2.36 | Bailey | 1.67 | Faith | 1.29 | Autumn |
| 5.66 | Ella | 3.16 | Brooke | 2.30 | Kayla | 1.65 | Jennifer | 1.28 | Destiny |
| 5.57 | Alexis | 3.08 | Isabelle | 2.30 | Maya | 1.65 | Sierra | 1.28 | Sophie |
| 5.30 | Addison | 3.06 | Alexa | 2.26 | Audrey | 1.61 | Rylee | 1.27 | Angelina |
| 4.94 | Chloe | 3.00 | Kaylee | 2.19 | Amelia | 1.57 | Kylee | 1.22 | Jenna |
| 4.90 | Hailey | 2.97 | Paige | 2.19 | Evelyn | 1.55 | Vanessa | 1.13 | Jordan |
| 4.78 | Brooklyn | 2.87 | Lillian | 2.17 | Ashlyn | 1.54 | Kate | 1.12 | Arianna |
| 4.74 | Ashley | 2.87 | Rachel | 2.16 | Allison | 1.52 | Jocelyn | 1.12 | Aspen |
| 4.68 | Avery | 2.84 | Zoe | 2.15 | Riley | 1.50 | Sara | 1.08 | Zoey |

## Southwestern U.S.A. and Hawaii

| | | | | | | | | | |
|---|---|---|---|---|---|---|---|---|---|
| 10.64 | Emily | 4.29 | Olivia | 3.27 | Alexandra | 2.30 | Daniela | 1.82 | Briana |
| 9.63 | Isabella | 4.23 | Jessica | 3.09 | Leslie | 2.27 | Arianna | 1.81 | Adriana |
| 8.88 | Ashley | 4.12 | Valeria | 2.99 | Valerie | 2.26 | Angela | 1.78 | Sara |
| 8.78 | Mia | 4.03 | Sarah | 2.98 | Lauren | 2.26 | Kaitlyn | 1.75 | Jade |
| 7.87 | Samantha | 3.95 | Angelina | 2.93 | Natalia | 2.20 | Sydney | 1.73 | Camila |
| 7.28 | Natalie | 3.93 | Jennifer | 2.92 | Maya | 2.13 | Giselle | 1.68 | Megan |
| 6.80 | Sophia | 3.90 | Victoria | 2.87 | Ariana | 2.13 | Mariah | 1.65 | Amy |
| 5.93 | Emma | 3.77 | Chloe | 2.86 | Savannah | 2.13 | Daisy | 1.65 | Liliana |
| 5.45 | Ava | 3.70 | Jocelyn | 2.86 | Ella | 2.13 | Kaylee | 1.62 | Amanda |
| 5.42 | Madison | 3.66 | Hailey | 2.69 | Taylor | 2.12 | Gabriela | 1.59 | Mariana |
| 5.28 | Abigail | 3.66 | Vanessa | 2.66 | Isabel | 2.12 | Nevaeh | 1.51 | Kylie |
| 5.08 | Alyssa | 3.58 | Grace | 2.61 | Nicole | 2.04 | Jazmin | 1.47 | Esmeralda |
| 5.02 | Elizabeth | 3.58 | Stephanie | 2.61 | Julia | 2.03 | Allison | 1.47 | Karen |
| 4.85 | Jasmine | 3.57 | Kayla | 2.61 | Melissa | 2.01 | Zoe | 1.42 | Gianna |
| 4.85 | Brianna | 3.57 | Maria | 2.55 | Diana | 1.95 | Katelyn | 1.39 | Jasmin |
| 4.62 | Kimberly | 3.48 | Sofia | 2.44 | Jacqueline | 1.93 | Brooke | 1.38 | Genesis |
| 4.50 | Hannah | 3.44 | Michelle | 2.43 | Katherine | 1.93 | Faith | 1.36 | Crystal |
| 4.46 | Alexa | 3.43 | Evelyn | 2.38 | Audrey | 1.91 | Rachel | 1.34 | Guadalupe |
| 4.39 | Andrea | 3.33 | Destiny | 2.35 | Alondra | 1.90 | Gabriella | 1.32 | Fatima |
| 4.32 | Alexis | 3.31 | Melanie | 2.34 | Lily | 1.85 | Ruby | 1.29 | Karla |

## Northwestern U.S.A. and Alaska

| | | | | | | | | | |
|---|---|---|---|---|---|---|---|---|---|
| 10.29 | Emma | 4.27 | Lily | 2.74 | Kaitlyn | 2.28 | Maria | 1.67 | Katie |
| 8.98 | Emily | 4.18 | Ashley | 2.73 | Nevaeh | 2.26 | Riley | 1.66 | Lilly |
| 8.18 | Olivia | 3.90 | Anna | 2.67 | Brianna | 2.22 | Amelia | 1.60 | Haley |
| 8.01 | Madison | 3.87 | Alyssa | 2.67 | Faith | 2.22 | Katelyn | 1.47 | Eva |
| 7.90 | Ava | 3.49 | Addison | 2.65 | Megan | 2.15 | Gracie | 1.45 | Kimberly |
| 7.71 | Isabella | 3.49 | Jasmine | 2.65 | Rachel | 2.13 | Mackenzie | 1.45 | Stephanie |
| 7.40 | Abigail | 3.49 | Lauren | 2.62 | Madeline | 2.12 | Ruby | 1.44 | Gabrielle |
| 7.15 | Sophia | 3.45 | Sydney | 2.60 | Evelyn | 2.10 | Bailey | 1.41 | Sophie |
| 6.96 | Hannah | 3.41 | Lillian | 2.60 | Victoria | 2.09 | Alexa | 1.39 | Molly |
| 6.33 | Elizabeth | 3.33 | Kaylee | 2.54 | Isabelle | 2.06 | Jennifer | 1.36 | Aubrey |
| 5.89 | Grace | 3.25 | Savannah | 2.53 | Maya | 2.05 | Vanessa | 1.34 | Lydia |
| 5.81 | Natalie | 3.21 | Jessica | 2.49 | Claire | 2.01 | Trinity | 1.24 | Ellie |
| 5.73 | Samantha | 3.19 | Brooklyn | 2.48 | Paige | 1.97 | Naomi | 1.24 | Mya |
| 5.40 | Hailey | 3.00 | Audrey | 2.47 | Allison | 1.94 | Angelina | 1.24 | Rebecca |
| 5.26 | Chloe | 2.93 | Zoe | 2.40 | Sofia | 1.94 | Isabel | 1.24 | Zoey |
| 5.09 | Ella | 2.86 | Katherine | 2.38 | Avery | 1.93 | Rylee | 1.14 | Kate |
| 4.94 | Alexis | 2.81 | Alexandra | 2.37 | Kylie | 1.90 | Keira | 1.11 | Sara |
| 4.80 | Mia | 2.79 | Brooke | 2.35 | Makayla | 1.88 | Lucy | 1.10 | Mariah |
| 4.71 | Taylor | 2.79 | Kayla | 2.31 | Morgan | 1.70 | Jocelyn | 1.05 | Jordan |
| 4.51 | Sarah | 2.74 | Julia | 2.29 | Andrea | 1.68 | Gabriella | 0.86 | Nicole |

## Western Canada

| | | | | | | | | | |
|---|---|---|---|---|---|---|---|---|---|
| 12.11 | Emma | 4.30 | Brooke | 2.96 | Ashley | 2.12 | Mya | 1.72 | Amber |
| 11.77 | Emily | 4.15 | Mackenzie | 2.87 | Sara | 2.04 | Jade | 1.72 | Makayla |
| 9.88 | Ava | 4.09 | Rachel | 2.79 | Morgan | 2.01 | Katie | 1.68 | Abby |
| 9.61 | Madison | 4.07 | Sydney | 2.73 | Claire | 2.01 | Nevaeh | 1.64 | Annika |
| 9.38 | Hannah | 3.97 | Julia | 2.69 | Natalie | 2.01 | Sofia | 1.64 | Sienna |
| 8.73 | Olivia | 3.94 | Megan | 2.64 | Rebecca | 1.99 | Sadie | 1.62 | Marissa |
| 8.22 | Sarah | 3.88 | Avery | 2.48 | Jasmine | 1.97 | Trinity | 1.62 | Vanessa |
| 6.50 | Abigail | 3.76 | Kaitlyn | 2.48 | Kaylee | 1.95 | Summer | 1.59 | Kylie |
| 6.48 | Grace | 3.71 | Lauren | 2.45 | Nicole | 1.93 | Danielle | 1.53 | Payton |
| 6.13 | Samantha | 3.69 | Alyssa | 2.37 | Brianna | 1.93 | Maria | 1.49 | Kiera |
| 6.11 | Hailey | 3.61 | Keira | 2.37 | Mia | 1.91 | Sierra | 1.47 | Autumn |
| 6.04 | Ella | 3.57 | Alexis | 2.29 | Faith | 1.89 | Leah | 1.45 | Jennifer |
| 5.69 | Chloe | 3.57 | Jenna | 2.27 | Zoe | 1.87 | Georgia | 1.45 | Jordan |
| 5.54 | Isabella | 3.57 | Paige | 2.25 | Victoria | 1.85 | Angelina | 1.43 | Jada |
| 5.18 | Taylor | 3.55 | Anna | 2.22 | Amelia | 1.83 | Eva | 1.11 | Danica |
| 5.14 | Sophia | 3.48 | Kayla | 2.20 | Kate | 1.78 | Katherine | 1.03 | Addison |
| 4.97 | Elizabeth | 3.17 | Alexandra | 2.18 | Gabrielle | 1.76 | Madeline | 0.94 | Peyton |
| 4.87 | Brooklyn | 3.17 | Isabelle | 2.18 | Jordyn | 1.76 | Naomi | 0.92 | Amanda |
| 4.66 | Jessica | 3.06 | Lily | 2.18 | Katelyn | 1.74 | Alexa | 0.90 | Michelle |
| 4.64 | Maya | 3.06 | Sophie | 2.12 | Amy | 1.74 | Charlotte | 0.88 | Isabel |

## Central and Eastern Canada

| | | | | | | | | | |
|---|---|---|---|---|---|---|---|---|---|
| 15.78 | Emma | 4.75 | Jade | 3.16 | Alexis | 2.50 | Madeleine | 1.93 | Marianne |
| 13.28 | Sarah | 4.61 | Maya | 3.05 | Ella | 2.47 | Coralie | 1.91 | Claire |
| 12.75 | Emily | 4.29 | Ashley | 3.01 | Noemie | 2.42 | Ariane | 1.87 | Emy |
| 8.90 | Olivia | 3.98 | Gabrielle | 2.98 | Rosalie | 2.42 | Ava | 1.82 | Annabelle |
| 7.71 | Madison | 3.95 | Elizabeth | 2.97 | Anna | 2.41 | Oceane | 1.82 | Melissa |
| 6.87 | Hannah | 3.81 | Mackenzie | 2.89 | Kaitlyn | 2.40 | Amanda | 1.79 | Maika |
| 6.59 | Megan | 3.76 | Paige | 2.84 | Amy | 2.27 | Laurie | 1.77 | Erin |
| 6.50 | Jessica | 3.74 | Brianna | 2.84 | Vanessa | 2.25 | Avery | 1.77 | Faith |
| 6.42 | Julia | 3.72 | Hailey | 2.83 | Catherine | 2.24 | Natalie | 1.75 | Sierra |
| 5.74 | Victoria | 3.67 | Mia | 2.78 | Laurence | 2.23 | Amelia | 1.73 | Angelina |
| 5.71 | Chloe | 3.63 | Taylor | 2.74 | Alicia | 2.18 | Emilie | 1.71 | Maude |
| 5.51 | Abigail | 3.59 | Nicole | 2.72 | Camille | 2.17 | Maria | 1.70 | Lily |
| 5.37 | Lauren | 3.59 | Zoe | 2.72 | Jenna | 2.17 | Sofia | 1.69 | Amelie |
| 5.36 | Grace | 3.58 | Kayla | 2.68 | Florence | 2.14 | Juliette | 1.67 | Katherine |
| 5.14 | Rachel | 3.58 | Sophia | 2.64 | Brooke | 2.14 | Justine | 1.64 | Katelyn |
| 5.09 | Alexandra | 3.46 | Sophie | 2.64 | Sabrina | 2.10 | Leah | 1.61 | Bianca |
| 4.91 | Isabella | 3.43 | Sydney | 2.58 | Laura | 2.08 | Isabelle | 1.61 | Marie |
| 4.83 | Lea | 3.35 | Jasmine | 2.56 | Megane | 1.98 | Cassandra | 1.58 | Alexia |
| 4.83 | Samantha | 3.31 | Charlotte | 2.55 | Audrey | 1.95 | Elodie | 1.53 | Brooklyn |
| 4.76 | Alyssa | 3.28 | Rebecca | 2.53 | Mya | 1.95 | Morgan | 1.53 | Leanne |

# The Top 100 Boys' Names by Region

*Popularity ratings indicate usage per thousand baby boys.*

## United States and Canada

| | | | | | | | | | |
|---|---|---|---|---|---|---|---|---|---|
| 11.45 | Jacob | 6.49 | Samuel | 4.53 | Thomas | 3.20 | Charles | 2.20 | Brayden |
| 10.29 | Joshua | 6.44 | Logan | 4.40 | Mason | 3.20 | Luis | 2.12 | Cole |
| 9.98 | Michael | 6.33 | Benjamin | 4.40 | Aidan | 3.16 | Adam | 2.03 | Tristan |
| 9.62 | Ethan | 6.26 | Jonathan | 4.38 | Luke | 2.98 | Adrian | 2.03 | Dominic |
| 9.37 | Matthew | 6.16 | Christian | 4.37 | Gavin | 2.95 | Alex | 1.99 | Chase |
| 8.87 | Daniel | 6.12 | Dylan | 4.33 | Jordan | 2.85 | Nathaniel | 1.99 | Wyatt |
| 8.84 | Andrew | 5.67 | Gabriel | 4.30 | Isaiah | 2.76 | Eric | 1.83 | Miguel |
| 8.69 | William | 5.58 | Brandon | 4.29 | Robert | 2.73 | Brian | 1.78 | Liam |
| 8.43 | Anthony | 5.30 | Zachary | 4.23 | Isaac | 2.71 | Sean | 1.78 | Antonio |
| 8.40 | Christopher | 5.09 | Elijah | 3.91 | Jayden | 2.69 | Ian | 1.69 | Steven |
| 8.16 | Alexander | 4.85 | Jose | 3.72 | Cameron | 2.64 | Kyle | 1.65 | Carson |
| 7.91 | Joseph | 4.85 | Caleb | 3.71 | Jason | 2.62 | Carlos | 1.65 | Alejandro |
| 7.90 | David | 4.81 | Justin | 3.63 | Connor | 2.62 | Hayden | 1.65 | Jesse |
| 7.59 | Ryan | 4.80 | Jack | 3.57 | Owen | 2.60 | Xavier | 1.63 | Timothy |
| 7.19 | Nicholas | 4.76 | Angel | 3.55 | Hunter | 2.60 | Bryan | 1.59 | Caden |
| 7.09 | Tyler | 4.69 | Kevin | 3.52 | Aaron | 2.58 | Julian | 1.55 | Victor |
| 7.05 | James | 4.68 | Aiden | 3.52 | Lucas | 2.58 | Jesus | 1.51 | Jaden |
| 6.98 | Noah | 4.62 | Austin | 3.40 | Diego | 2.40 | Carter | 1.49 | Richard |
| 6.72 | Nathan | 4.58 | Evan | 3.38 | Landon | 2.33 | Sebastian | 1.44 | Kaden |
| 6.55 | John | 4.54 | Jackson | 3.26 | Juan | 2.23 | Jeremiah | 1.44 | Riley |

## New England

| | | | | | | | | | |
|---|---|---|---|---|---|---|---|---|---|
| 13.88 | Ryan | 8.30 | Aidan | 5.11 | Kyle | 3.53 | Jake | 2.18 | Jaden |
| 13.49 | Matthew | 8.29 | Samuel | 5.11 | Liam | 3.49 | Alex | 2.13 | Sebastian |
| 12.95 | Jacob | 8.08 | Dylan | 5.09 | Charles | 3.49 | Isaiah | 2.10 | Steven |
| 12.66 | Michael | 7.80 | Thomas | 5.06 | Sean | 3.46 | Cole | 2.09 | Luis |
| 12.34 | Nicholas | 7.79 | Noah | 5.00 | Jackson | 3.36 | Dominic | 1.99 | Cody |
| 11.20 | Andrew | 7.56 | Owen | 4.93 | Mason | 3.30 | Ian | 1.94 | Peter |
| 11.02 | William | 7.50 | Logan | 4.86 | Robert | 3.25 | Austin | 1.84 | Maxwell |
| 11.01 | Joseph | 7.38 | David | 4.82 | Justin | 3.09 | Brian | 1.82 | Bryan |
| 10.98 | Benjamin | 7.23 | Connor | 4.76 | Jason | 2.98 | Henry | 1.75 | Richard |
| 10.87 | Alexander | 7.23 | Zachary | 4.66 | Brandon | 2.86 | Xavier | 1.74 | Devin |
| 10.36 | John | 7.20 | Aiden | 4.51 | Kevin | 2.80 | Timothy | 1.72 | Vincent |
| 10.30 | Jack | 6.82 | Evan | 4.41 | Adam | 2.79 | Aaron | 1.70 | Edward |
| 10.18 | Tyler | 6.56 | Jonathan | 4.41 | Elijah | 2.74 | Isaac | 1.61 | Mark |
| 10.07 | Joshua | 6.49 | Cameron | 4.29 | Nathaniel | 2.69 | Angel | 1.54 | Shane |
| 9.98 | Anthony | 5.94 | Lucas | 4.26 | Jordan | 2.67 | Chase | 1.53 | Nolan |
| 9.83 | Christopher | 5.92 | Gabriel | 4.17 | Caleb | 2.60 | Brendan | 1.53 | Victor |
| 9.44 | Daniel | 5.73 | Jayden | 4.08 | Brady | 2.56 | Eric | 1.49 | Nicolas |
| 9.25 | James | 5.68 | Luke | 3.95 | Hunter | 2.48 | Julian | 1.47 | Carter |
| 9.18 | Ethan | 5.27 | Christian | 3.88 | Patrick | 2.30 | Tristan | 1.27 | Oliver |
| 8.78 | Nathan | 5.16 | Gavin | 3.75 | Colin | 2.21 | Jose | 1.25 | Landon |

## Mid-Atlantic U.S.A.

| | | | | | | | | | |
|---|---|---|---|---|---|---|---|---|---|
| 13.95 | Michael | 6.82 | Justin | 4.80 | Evan | 3.12 | Xavier | 2.26 | Jose |
| 11.98 | Matthew | 6.78 | Dylan | 4.61 | Connor | 3.02 | Alex | 2.06 | Sebastian |
| 10.95 | Joseph | 6.57 | Noah | 4.53 | Sean | 2.94 | Ian | 2.00 | Vincent |
| 10.92 | Ryan | 6.55 | Logan | 4.44 | Jordan | 2.93 | Liam | 1.92 | Cole |
| 10.62 | Joshua | 6.49 | Jonathan | 4.38 | Isaiah | 2.93 | Jeremiah | 1.91 | Henry |
| 10.55 | Jacob | 6.47 | Brandon | 4.37 | Gavin | 2.90 | Hunter | 1.91 | Tristan |
| 10.45 | Anthony | 6.05 | Jack | 4.04 | Austin | 2.80 | Steven | 1.73 | Carlos |
| 10.36 | Christopher | 5.94 | Aidan | 4.03 | Owen | 2.79 | Dominic | 1.73 | Luis |
| 10.21 | Daniel | 5.83 | Samuel | 4.01 | Lucas | 2.79 | Isaac | 1.64 | Brayden |
| 10.16 | Nicholas | 5.83 | Kevin | 3.95 | Mason | 2.58 | Angel | 1.56 | Diego |
| 9.12 | Andrew | 5.77 | Thomas | 3.82 | Charles | 2.56 | Julian | 1.54 | Hayden |
| 9.03 | Alexander | 5.70 | Jayden | 3.77 | Aaron | 2.56 | Jaden | 1.52 | Mark |
| 9.01 | John | 5.69 | Nathan | 3.70 | Jackson | 2.55 | Colin | 1.49 | Carter |
| 8.81 | William | 5.56 | Zachary | 3.63 | Brian | 2.54 | Chase | 1.42 | Wyatt |
| 8.72 | Ethan | 5.29 | Jason | 3.55 | Adam | 2.54 | Patrick | 1.31 | Devin |
| 8.23 | James | 5.11 | Elijah | 3.52 | Cameron | 2.46 | Bryan | 1.27 | Paul |
| 7.95 | David | 5.09 | Luke | 3.48 | Caleb | 2.41 | Richard | 1.26 | Jeremy |
| 7.92 | Tyler | 5.08 | Robert | 3.31 | Nathaniel | 2.38 | Timothy | 1.19 | Peter |
| 7.02 | Benjamin | 5.03 | Gabriel | 3.30 | Kyle | 2.35 | Jake | 1.19 | Adrian |
| 6.93 | Christian | 5.01 | Aiden | 3.18 | Eric | 2.26 | Landon | 1.14 | Kenneth |

## Southeastern U.S.A.

| | | | | | | | | | |
|---|---|---|---|---|---|---|---|---|---|
| 12.64 | William | 6.73 | Nicholas | 4.81 | Justin | 2.75 | Angel | 1.97 | Carter |
| 11.82 | Joshua | 6.66 | Elijah | 4.79 | Isaiah | 2.75 | Brian | 1.95 | Caden |
| 11.63 | Jacob | 6.58 | Caleb | 4.69 | Mason | 2.70 | Alex | 1.89 | Bryson |
| 10.79 | Christopher | 6.55 | Jackson | 4.69 | Thomas | 2.63 | Jaden | 1.84 | Richard |
| 10.41 | Michael | 6.20 | Samuel | 4.67 | Aiden | 2.62 | Chase | 1.82 | Diego |
| 9.76 | James | 6.20 | Brandon | 4.59 | Gavin | 2.61 | Nathaniel | 1.80 | Owen |
| 9.43 | Ethan | 6.12 | Landon | 4.40 | Charles | 2.59 | Bryan | 1.74 | Kaleb |
| 9.00 | Matthew | 5.94 | Jordan | 4.35 | Jeremiah | 2.58 | Eric | 1.69 | Adam |
| 8.22 | John | 5.78 | Austin | 4.01 | Luke | 2.54 | Juan | 1.60 | Sebastian |
| 8.06 | David | 5.70 | Ryan | 3.99 | Evan | 2.48 | Brayden | 1.54 | Ashton |
| 8.03 | Andrew | 5.60 | Gabriel | 3.80 | Jose | 2.47 | Sean | 1.54 | Adrian |
| 7.79 | Daniel | 5.56 | Dylan | 3.77 | Jason | 2.37 | Xavier | 1.45 | Blake |
| 7.78 | Noah | 5.47 | Robert | 3.65 | Connor | 2.30 | Ian | 1.37 | Preston |
| 7.68 | Tyler | 5.40 | Cameron | 3.60 | Hayden | 2.26 | Luis | 1.37 | Steven |
| 7.45 | Joseph | 5.34 | Nathan | 3.49 | Aidan | 2.25 | Devin | 1.29 | Seth |
| 7.41 | Christian | 5.24 | Benjamin | 3.30 | Lucas | 2.20 | Carlos | 1.27 | Kaden |
| 7.29 | Anthony | 5.04 | Zachary | 3.24 | Jack | 2.17 | Timothy | 1.23 | Jaylen |
| 7.19 | Alexander | 5.00 | Hunter | 3.16 | Isaac | 2.13 | Antonio | 1.22 | Bryce |
| 6.96 | Jonathan | 4.89 | Jayden | 3.15 | Aaron | 2.09 | Carson | 1.21 | Marcus |
| 6.80 | Logan | 4.83 | Kevin | 3.01 | Tristan | 2.02 | Wyatt | 1.17 | Julian |

## Northcentral U.S.A.

| | | | | | | | | | |
|---|---|---|---|---|---|---|---|---|---|
| 12.06 | Jacob | 6.68 | Jack | 5.01 | Connor | 3.49 | Kevin | 2.10 | Bryce |
| 10.73 | Ethan | 6.58 | Christopher | 5.00 | Aidan | 3.48 | Cole | 2.09 | Timothy |
| 9.73 | Andrew | 6.46 | Gavin | 4.96 | Christian | 3.44 | Ian | 2.07 | Liam |
| 9.69 | Michael | 6.44 | David | 4.75 | Lucas | 3.28 | Hayden | 2.05 | Riley |
| 9.37 | Alexander | 6.42 | Mason | 4.75 | Jonathan | 3.28 | Chase | 2.04 | Angel |
| 9.08 | Logan | 6.31 | John | 4.66 | Cameron | 3.26 | Alex | 2.03 | Julian |
| 8.99 | Joshua | 6.27 | Evan | 4.64 | Hunter | 3.15 | Carson | 2.01 | Jose |
| 8.74 | Noah | 6.20 | Dylan | 4.61 | Isaac | 3.04 | Dominic | 1.96 | Seth |
| 8.70 | Matthew | 6.11 | Aiden | 4.59 | Charles | 3.03 | Nathaniel | 1.91 | Parker |
| 8.60 | Joseph | 6.01 | Zachary | 4.45 | Isaiah | 3.01 | Jason | 1.84 | Henry |
| 8.40 | William | 5.97 | Owen | 4.38 | Thomas | 2.82 | Jeremiah | 1.68 | Eric |
| 8.15 | Tyler | 5.79 | Austin | 4.15 | Jordan | 2.66 | Brady | 1.64 | Nolan |
| 7.81 | Benjamin | 5.61 | Elijah | 4.12 | Robert | 2.53 | Blake | 1.54 | Devin |
| 7.76 | Anthony | 5.50 | Luke | 4.01 | Brayden | 2.40 | Xavier | 1.35 | Vincent |
| 7.76 | Nicholas | 5.46 | Jackson | 3.83 | Jayden | 2.37 | Sean | 1.32 | Cody |
| 7.58 | Ryan | 5.42 | Caleb | 3.81 | Aaron | 2.34 | Tristan | 1.21 | Maxwell |
| 7.45 | Nathan | 5.29 | Landon | 3.75 | Adam | 2.33 | Caden | 1.21 | Ashton |
| 7.35 | Daniel | 5.10 | Gabriel | 3.65 | Justin | 2.23 | Kaden | 1.19 | Diego |
| 7.06 | James | 5.06 | Carter | 3.53 | Kyle | 2.18 | Brian | 1.15 | Trevor |
| 6.80 | Samuel | 5.01 | Brandon | 3.52 | Wyatt | 2.15 | Colin | 1.13 | Antonio |

## Southcentral U.S.A.

| | | | | | | | | | |
|---|---|---|---|---|---|---|---|---|---|
| 10.76 | Jacob | 6.24 | Alexander | 4.49 | Isaac | 3.52 | Julian | 2.23 | Adam |
| 10.09 | Joshua | 5.89 | Diego | 4.49 | Jackson | 3.47 | Jason | 2.12 | Brian |
| 9.82 | Jose | 5.85 | Brandon | 4.44 | Luke | 3.43 | Hayden | 2.03 | Ricardo |
| 9.73 | Christopher | 5.80 | Nathan | 4.38 | Aaron | 3.40 | Miguel | 2.02 | Jesse |
| 9.01 | Daniel | 5.75 | Gabriel | 4.38 | Jordan | 3.26 | Xavier | 1.99 | Alexis |
| 8.91 | Ethan | 5.68 | Luis | 4.35 | Carlos | 3.25 | Jeremiah | 1.98 | Sean |
| 8.73 | Michael | 5.58 | Ryan | 4.30 | Mason | 3.22 | Alejandro | 1.93 | Fernando |
| 8.72 | David | 5.45 | Caleb | 4.23 | Robert | 2.95 | Thomas | 1.93 | Ivan |
| 7.99 | Matthew | 5.37 | Logan | 4.14 | Benjamin | 2.89 | Eric | 1.92 | Alan |
| 7.85 | Angel | 5.15 | Kevin | 4.11 | Austin | 2.82 | Jorge | 1.91 | Antonio |
| 7.81 | Christian | 5.14 | Isaiah | 4.11 | Jayden | 2.78 | Charles | 1.89 | Joel |
| 7.55 | Andrew | 5.12 | Elijah | 4.07 | Bryan | 2.77 | Alex | 1.87 | Hector |
| 7.50 | Anthony | 5.06 | Nicholas | 4.05 | Gavin | 2.65 | Nathaniel | 1.84 | Andres |
| 7.19 | Jonathan | 5.05 | Samuel | 4.02 | Zachary | 2.64 | Victor | 1.83 | Damian |
| 7.06 | Juan | 5.03 | Adrian | 3.73 | Aidan | 2.63 | Jack | 1.79 | Javier |
| 6.94 | William | 5.02 | Aiden | 3.70 | Evan | 2.56 | Caden | 1.79 | Francisco |
| 6.93 | Noah | 5.01 | Jesus | 3.62 | Hunter | 2.54 | Tristan | 1.72 | Cesar |
| 6.85 | Joseph | 4.99 | Dylan | 3.60 | Justin | 2.41 | Ian | 1.68 | Edgar |
| 6.61 | John | 4.94 | Landon | 3.59 | Sebastian | 2.33 | Eduardo | 1.68 | Manuel |
| 6.31 | James | 4.76 | Tyler | 3.57 | Cameron | 2.32 | Oscar | 1.56 | Cristian |

## Central U.S.A.

| | | | | | | | | | |
|---|---|---|---|---|---|---|---|---|---|
| 11.91 | Jacob | 6.60 | Matthew | 5.29 | Luke | 4.02 | Cooper | 2.57 | Henry |
| 10.65 | Ethan | 6.49 | Dylan | 5.27 | Christian | 3.97 | Caden | 2.41 | Dominic |
| 10.05 | Logan | 6.47 | Carter | 5.24 | David | 3.94 | Robert | 2.38 | Brady |
| 9.75 | Andrew | 6.40 | Hunter | 5.23 | Lucas | 3.63 | Aaron | 2.35 | Xavier |
| 9.30 | William | 6.26 | Aiden | 5.22 | Wyatt | 3.52 | Jayden | 2.31 | Kaleb |
| 8.91 | Alexander | 6.21 | John | 5.06 | Connor | 3.36 | Ian | 2.30 | Tristan |
| 8.68 | Noah | 6.07 | Nicholas | 4.79 | Aidan | 3.23 | Grant | 2.29 | Kevin |
| 8.22 | Michael | 6.03 | Anthony | 4.63 | Jonathan | 3.17 | Alex | 2.24 | Riley |
| 8.18 | Tyler | 6.02 | Jack | 4.42 | Brandon | 3.00 | Colton | 1.97 | Conner |
| 7.94 | Jackson | 6.02 | Ryan | 4.39 | Kaden | 2.99 | Parker | 1.81 | Jose |
| 7.76 | Joshua | 6.01 | Nathan | 4.35 | Blake | 2.97 | Justin | 1.80 | Bryce |
| 7.38 | Landon | 5.93 | Zachary | 4.34 | Carson | 2.94 | Levi | 1.77 | Brody |
| 7.35 | Joseph | 5.88 | Elijah | 4.25 | Cole | 2.90 | Kyle | 1.73 | Braden |
| 7.08 | Caleb | 5.83 | Owen | 4.25 | Hayden | 2.87 | Nathaniel | 1.56 | Jace |
| 7.02 | Mason | 5.72 | Gabriel | 4.23 | Cameron | 2.86 | Cody | 1.30 | Angel |
| 6.98 | Samuel | 5.68 | Isaac | 4.22 | Chase | 2.81 | Adam | 1.21 | Jeremiah |
| 6.89 | Benjamin | 5.51 | Evan | 4.17 | Thomas | 2.80 | Jason | 1.18 | Ayden |
| 6.69 | Gavin | 5.46 | Christopher | 4.14 | Charles | 2.74 | Preston | 1.18 | Jaden |
| 6.69 | James | 5.31 | Daniel | 4.08 | Isaiah | 2.70 | Seth | 1.09 | Dalton |
| 6.62 | Austin | 5.29 | Brayden | 4.06 | Jordan | 2.58 | Gage | 1.09 | Devin |

## Midwestern U.S.A.

| | | | | |
|---|---|---|---|---|
| 11.21 Jacob | 6.34 Gabriel | 4.67 Wyatt | 3.46 Ian | 2.10 Cody |
| 10.59 Ethan | 6.34 Isaac | 4.65 Evan | 3.45 Justin | 2.09 Tanner |
| 9.28 Joshua | 5.89 Jack | 4.62 John | 3.42 Diego | 2.07 Dominic |
| 8.79 Logan | 5.88 Aiden | 4.59 Carson | 3.42 Jayden | 2.01 Tristan |
| 8.63 Samuel | 5.87 Anthony | 4.40 Aidan | 3.19 Adam | 1.91 Jace |
| 8.02 Benjamin | 5.78 Nathan | 4.39 Christian | 3.07 Riley | 1.91 Jesus |
| 7.94 Alexander | 5.71 Gavin | 4.38 Thomas | 3.02 Luis | 1.82 Sean |
| 7.81 Noah | 5.62 Caleb | 4.29 Jonathan | 2.95 Charles | 1.77 Juan |
| 7.78 Andrew | 5.56 Christopher | 4.01 Kaden | 2.82 Alex | 1.76 Jaxon |
| 7.47 William | 5.48 Austin | 3.98 Brandon | 2.79 Kevin | 1.71 Seth |
| 7.31 Michael | 5.45 Dylan | 3.97 Hayden | 2.77 Aaron | 1.68 Preston |
| 7.22 Tyler | 5.39 Zachary | 3.82 Cole | 2.77 Blake | 1.59 Bryan |
| 7.12 Jackson | 5.32 Hunter | 3.79 Jordan | 2.77 Robert | 1.58 Spencer |
| 6.96 Joseph | 5.21 Elijah | 3.73 Cameron | 2.74 Chase | 1.57 Julian |
| 6.85 Mason | 5.19 Carter | 3.72 Angel | 2.67 Parker | 1.57 Xavier |
| 6.79 Matthew | 5.10 Landon | 3.72 Jose | 2.63 Jason | 1.55 Josiah |
| 6.78 Daniel | 4.93 Luke | 3.69 Brayden | 2.51 Caden | 1.53 Kaleb |
| 6.67 Ryan | 4.82 Owen | 3.60 Lucas | 2.38 Kyle | 1.52 Liam |
| 6.54 James | 4.76 Nicholas | 3.59 Isaiah | 2.36 Adrian | 1.52 Sebastian |
| 6.47 David | 4.71 Connor | 3.49 Cooper | 2.16 Ashton | 1.51 Trevor |

## Southwestern U.S.A. and Hawaii

| | | | | |
|---|---|---|---|---|
| 12.61 Daniel | 6.88 Adrian | 4.66 Elijah | 3.35 Jayden | 2.74 Alexis |
| 12.54 Anthony | 6.82 Juan | 4.54 Sebastian | 3.34 Oscar | 2.73 Fernando |
| 12.26 Angel | 6.81 Brandon | 4.54 Aiden | 3.32 Jorge | 2.72 Ricardo |
| 10.90 Jacob | 6.80 Ryan | 4.45 John | 3.27 Adam | 2.69 Xavier |
| 10.23 Jose | 6.74 Kevin | 4.37 Justin | 3.24 Ivan | 2.63 Omar |
| 10.21 David | 6.61 Gabriel | 4.37 Aaron | 3.22 Alex | 2.59 Antonio |
| 10.12 Joshua | 6.44 Noah | 4.28 Miguel | 3.11 Eric | 2.58 Kyle |
| 9.97 Andrew | 6.15 Isaac | 4.12 Alejandro | 3.09 Caleb | 2.53 Manuel |
| 9.47 Christopher | 5.79 Dylan | 4.08 Jason | 3.00 Nathaniel | 2.51 Cesar |
| 9.33 Michael | 5.71 Carlos | 4.03 Brian | 2.96 Austin | 2.50 Damian |
| 9.04 Matthew | 5.63 Nicholas | 3.90 Robert | 2.91 Dominic | 2.43 Andres |
| 8.67 Diego | 5.33 Isaiah | 3.90 Jordan | 2.91 Francisco | 2.32 Owen |
| 8.63 Jonathan | 5.25 Samuel | 3.87 Jack | 2.89 Mason | 2.31 Ian |
| 8.45 Alexander | 5.23 Tyler | 3.82 Aidan | 2.87 Jesse | 2.21 Giovanni |
| 8.16 Ethan | 5.09 William | 3.55 Victor | 2.87 Lucas | 2.17 Hector |
| 7.96 Joseph | 4.92 James | 3.47 Gavin | 2.85 Thomas | 2.01 Cristian |
| 7.91 Nathan | 4.89 Julian | 3.42 Luke | 2.82 Sean | 1.99 Vincent |
| 7.42 Christian | 4.88 Benjamin | 3.40 Zachary | 2.79 Jackson | 1.97 Richard |
| 7.17 Luis | 4.70 Bryan | 3.39 Eduardo | 2.77 Steven | 1.91 Edgar |
| 6.90 Jesus | 4.67 Logan | 3.38 Evan | 2.76 Alan | 1.78 Javier |

## Northwestern U.S.A. and Alaska

| | | | | | | | | | |
|---|---|---|---|---|---|---|---|---|---|
| 10.65 | Jacob | 6.37 | Ryan | 4.57 | Wyatt | 3.45 | Kaden | 2.63 | Cooper |
| 10.14 | Ethan | 6.33 | Joseph | 4.50 | Lucas | 3.40 | Justin | 2.61 | Jason |
| 9.24 | Alexander | 6.13 | Jack | 4.40 | Luke | 3.32 | Juan | 2.61 | Julian |
| 8.73 | Logan | 6.08 | Mason | 4.36 | Aidan | 3.30 | Aaron | 2.60 | Liam |
| 8.25 | Daniel | 5.99 | Isaac | 4.36 | Christian | 3.25 | Carson | 2.53 | Kyle |
| 8.20 | Andrew | 5.97 | Dylan | 4.32 | John | 3.22 | Ian | 2.46 | Tanner |
| 7.71 | Noah | 5.78 | Elijah | 4.03 | Connor | 3.12 | Tristan | 2.42 | Blake |
| 7.54 | Joshua | 5.76 | Christopher | 3.99 | Jayden | 3.08 | Cody | 2.36 | Preston |
| 7.47 | William | 5.60 | Austin | 3.91 | Angel | 3.07 | Charles | 2.30 | Caden |
| 7.38 | Michael | 5.60 | Jackson | 3.88 | Landon | 2.97 | Kevin | 2.11 | Colton |
| 7.35 | Samuel | 5.42 | Owen | 3.86 | Thomas | 2.91 | Jesus | 2.04 | Carlos |
| 7.07 | Benjamin | 5.38 | Caleb | 3.80 | Cameron | 2.89 | Alex | 1.82 | Levi |
| 6.94 | Tyler | 5.35 | Gavin | 3.77 | Jordan | 2.83 | Nathaniel | 1.65 | Ayden |
| 6.85 | Matthew | 5.03 | Evan | 3.76 | Hayden | 2.82 | Adrian | 1.52 | Timothy |
| 6.75 | Anthony | 4.89 | Isaiah | 3.72 | Brandon | 2.79 | Chase | 1.44 | Dominic |
| 6.72 | James | 4.81 | Hunter | 3.69 | Robert | 2.73 | Brayden | 1.40 | Brian |
| 6.68 | David | 4.73 | Nicholas | 3.65 | Cole | 2.73 | Henry | 1.40 | Josiah |
| 6.62 | Nathan | 4.72 | Zachary | 3.61 | Riley | 2.68 | Sean | 1.33 | Jesse |
| 6.56 | Aiden | 4.70 | Jonathan | 3.58 | Carter | 2.67 | Adam | 1.28 | Seth |
| 6.41 | Gabriel | 4.62 | Jose | 3.58 | Diego | 2.67 | Luis | 1.18 | Eric |

## Western Canada

| | | | | | | | | | |
|---|---|---|---|---|---|---|---|---|---|
| 15.54 | Ethan | 6.09 | Connor | 3.99 | Mason | 2.92 | John | 2.18 | Jonathan |
| 11.83 | Joshua | 5.97 | James | 3.92 | Luke | 2.90 | Jesse | 2.16 | Oliver |
| 10.77 | Matthew | 5.89 | Jack | 3.92 | Thomas | 2.78 | Anthony | 2.14 | Robert |
| 10.61 | Jacob | 5.85 | Lucas | 3.88 | Cameron | 2.66 | Chase | 2.08 | Kai |
| 9.25 | Logan | 5.85 | Tyler | 3.88 | David | 2.64 | Ryder | 2.08 | Levi |
| 9.09 | Noah | 5.71 | Aiden | 3.80 | Joseph | 2.62 | Aaron | 2.04 | Elijah |
| 8.99 | Liam | 5.45 | Cole | 3.76 | Ashton | 2.62 | Seth | 2.02 | Kaleb |
| 8.65 | Nathan | 5.21 | Andrew | 3.68 | Gabriel | 2.56 | Eric | 2.02 | Spencer |
| 7.71 | Alexander | 4.97 | Adam | 3.62 | Jackson | 2.50 | Parker | 2.00 | Cody |
| 7.31 | Nicholas | 4.83 | Riley | 3.58 | Caleb | 2.48 | Brody | 1.94 | Isaiah |
| 7.19 | Owen | 4.73 | Michael | 3.52 | Brandon | 2.48 | Marcus | 1.82 | Christian |
| 7.15 | Ryan | 4.63 | Zachary | 3.44 | Hayden | 2.40 | Jason | 1.82 | Jeremy |
| 6.89 | William | 4.51 | Justin | 3.38 | Kyle | 2.38 | Kaden | 1.78 | Brady |
| 6.83 | Carter | 4.37 | Aidan | 3.34 | Nolan | 2.34 | Jake | 1.72 | Charles |
| 6.69 | Dylan | 4.35 | Tristan | 3.30 | Carson | 2.28 | Landon | 1.72 | Colton |
| 6.59 | Austin | 4.29 | Jordan | 3.16 | Isaac | 2.28 | Nathaniel | 1.70 | Alex |
| 6.59 | Benjamin | 4.23 | Jayden | 3.14 | Wyatt | 2.26 | Dominic | 1.70 | Lukas |
| 6.51 | Evan | 4.11 | Brayden | 3.00 | Christopher | 2.26 | Rylan | 1.66 | Max |
| 6.41 | Daniel | 4.05 | Gavin | 2.96 | Ty | 2.20 | Kevin | 1.64 | Patrick |
| 6.37 | Samuel | 4.03 | Hunter | 2.94 | Tyson | 2.20 | Sean | 1.62 | Cohen |

## Central and Eastern Canada

| | | | | | | | | | |
|---|---|---|---|---|---|---|---|---|---|
| 14.01 | Jacob | 7.41 | Dylan | 5.02 | Logan | 3.34 | Alex | 2.05 | Jayden |
| 13.98 | William | 7.02 | Liam | 4.83 | Jack | 3.22 | Kevin | 1.96 | Loic |
| 12.40 | Samuel | 7.00 | Tyler | 4.70 | Jordan | 3.19 | Emile | 1.95 | Luca |
| 12.37 | Matthew | 6.86 | Andrew | 4.58 | Tristan | 3.13 | Aiden | 1.94 | Mason |
| 11.87 | Ethan | 6.85 | Adam | 4.55 | Vincent | 3.03 | Maxime | 1.94 | Patrick |
| 11.69 | Nathan | 6.64 | Lucas | 4.53 | Cameron | 2.98 | Caleb | 1.93 | Brayden |
| 11.09 | Joshua | 6.46 | David | 4.52 | Jonathan | 2.78 | Riley | 1.88 | Julien |
| 10.50 | Benjamin | 6.05 | Connor | 4.40 | Mathis | 2.75 | Carter | 1.88 | Philippe |
| 10.32 | Ryan | 5.98 | James | 4.39 | Brandon | 2.75 | Christian | 1.77 | Colin |
| 10.00 | Justin | 5.94 | Jeremy | 4.19 | Alexandre | 2.74 | Mathieu | 1.75 | Jake |
| 9.46 | Nicholas | 5.90 | Xavier | 3.93 | Raphael | 2.66 | Robert | 1.75 | Steven |
| 9.18 | Michael | 5.66 | Joseph | 3.89 | Simon | 2.46 | Gavin | 1.68 | Sean |
| 8.92 | Thomas | 5.52 | Evan | 3.87 | Charles | 2.46 | Hunter | 1.65 | Tommy |
| 8.72 | Zachary | 5.48 | Alexis | 3.87 | Kyle | 2.41 | Aaron | 1.62 | Matteo |
| 8.70 | Alexander | 5.35 | Aidan | 3.64 | Jason | 2.39 | Hayden | 1.59 | Spencer |
| 8.40 | Gabriel | 5.32 | Christopher | 3.61 | Isaac | 2.31 | Luke | 1.57 | Cody |
| 8.15 | Anthony | 5.26 | Nicolas | 3.51 | Cole | 2.28 | Nathaniel | 1.56 | Jesse |
| 8.07 | Daniel | 5.22 | Olivier | 3.45 | Eric | 2.25 | Jackson | 1.54 | Mitchell |
| 7.87 | Noah | 5.16 | Felix | 3.39 | John | 2.18 | Etienne | 1.52 | Carson |
| 7.43 | Owen | 5.06 | Antoine | 3.35 | Austin | 2.09 | Nolan | 1.51 | Guillaume |

# The Top 100 Girls' Names
# from the Years 2001 to 2006

About 35% of all girls received a top 100 name in 2006. The number to the left of the name indicates the number of times the name was given per thousand girls born.

| 2006 | | 2005 | | 2004 | | 2003 | | 2002 | | 2001 | |
|------|------|------|------|------|------|------|------|------|------|------|------|
| 10.14 | Emily | 11.60 | Emily | 12.34 | Emily | 12.78 | Emily | 12.39 | Emily | 12.69 | Emily |
| 9.05 | Emma | 9.85 | Emma | 10.67 | Emma | 11.30 | Emma | 11.03 | Madison | 11.22 | Madison |
| 8.83 | Madison | 9.48 | Madison | 10.18 | Madison | 10.04 | Madison | 9.52 | Hannah | 10.47 | Hannah |
| 8.62 | Isabella | 7.64 | Abigail | 7.95 | Olivia | 8.76 | Hannah | 8.37 | Emma | 8.37 | Ashley |
| 8.04 | Ava | 7.62 | Olivia | 7.69 | Hannah | 8.03 | Olivia | 7.91 | Alexis | 8.30 | Alexis |
| 7.41 | Abigail | 7.35 | Isabella | 7.61 | Abigail | 7.92 | Abigail | 7.77 | Ashley | 8.03 | Sarah |
| 7.32 | Olivia | 7.17 | Hannah | 7.41 | Isabella | 7.38 | Alexis | 7.75 | Abigail | 8.03 | Samantha |
| 6.86 | Hannah | 6.62 | Samantha | 7.10 | Ashley | 7.22 | Ashley | 7.46 | Sarah | 7.49 | Abigail |
| 6.39 | Sophia | 6.61 | Ava | 6.79 | Samantha | 7.00 | Elizabeth | 7.43 | Samantha | 7.47 | Elizabeth |
| 5.91 | Samantha | 6.45 | Ashley | 6.67 | Elizabeth | 6.90 | Samantha | 7.41 | Olivia | 7.07 | Olivia |
| 5.86 | Elizabeth | 6.14 | Sophia | 6.65 | Alexis | 6.84 | Isabella | 7.38 | Elizabeth | 7.04 | Jessica |
| 5.85 | Ashley | 6.14 | Elizabeth | 6.26 | Sarah | 6.82 | Sarah | 6.50 | Alyssa | 6.93 | Taylor |
| 5.69 | Mia | 5.80 | Alexis | 6.17 | Grace | 6.36 | Grace | 6.25 | Lauren | 6.73 | Emma |
| 5.32 | Alexis | 5.73 | Grace | 5.98 | Alyssa | 6.34 | Alyssa | 6.16 | Isabella | 6.71 | Alyssa |
| 5.24 | Sarah | 5.55 | Sarah | 5.39 | Sophia | 5.50 | Lauren | 6.11 | Grace | 6.47 | Lauren |
| 5.18 | Natalie | 5.29 | Alyssa | 4.94 | Lauren | 5.44 | Kayla | 6.03 | Jessica | 6.11 | Grace |
| 5.18 | Grace | 5.26 | Mia | 4.83 | Brianna | 5.26 | Brianna | 5.83 | Brianna | 6.01 | Kayla |
| 4.92 | Chloe | 5.21 | Natalie | 4.82 | Kayla | 5.19 | Jessica | 5.81 | Taylor | 5.96 | Brianna |
| 4.82 | Alyssa | 4.64 | Chloe | 4.79 | Natalie | 5.13 | Taylor | 5.72 | Kayla | 5.34 | Anna |
| 4.43 | Brianna | 4.54 | Brianna | 4.68 | Anna | 4.82 | Sophia | 5.25 | Anna | 5.21 | Megan |
| 4.36 | Ella | 4.48 | Lauren | 4.67 | Jessica | 4.69 | Anna | 4.95 | Victoria | 5.15 | Victoria |
| 4.07 | Taylor | 4.40 | Ella | 4.60 | Taylor | 4.60 | Victoria | 4.67 | Megan | 4.92 | Destiny |
| 4.05 | Anna | 4.38 | Anna | 4.30 | Chloe | 4.55 | Natalie | 4.58 | Sydney | 4.88 | Sydney |

| 2006 | | 2005 | | 2004 | | 2003 | | 2002 | | 2001 | |
|---|---|---|---|---|---|---|---|---|---|---|---|
| 4.03 | Lauren | 4.21 | Taylor | 4.28 | Hailey | 4.52 | Chloe | 4.51 | Rachel | 4.82 | Rachel |
| 4.00 | Hailey | 4.18 | Kayla | 4.27 | Ava | 4.44 | Sydney | 4.51 | Chloe | 4.53 | Jasmine |
| 3.89 | Kayla | 4.18 | Hailey | 4.18 | Jasmine | 4.37 | Hailey | 4.48 | Jasmine | 4.51 | Jennifer |
| 3.62 | Addison | 3.93 | Jessica | 4.14 | Sydney | 4.00 | Jasmine | 4.39 | Sophia | 4.47 | Julia |
| 3.62 | Victoria | 3.85 | Victoria | 4.07 | Victoria | 3.96 | Rachel | 4.32 | Jennifer | 4.47 | Isabella |
| 3.55 | Jasmine | 3.80 | Jasmine | 4.07 | Ella | 3.95 | Morgan | 4.27 | Morgan | 4.42 | Morgan |
| 3.35 | Savannah | 3.59 | Sydney | 3.65 | Mia | 3.88 | Megan | 4.23 | Natalie | 4.14 | Chloe |
| 3.26 | Julia | 3.43 | Julia | 3.60 | Morgan | 3.76 | Jennifer | 4.04 | Kaitlyn | 4.13 | Kaitlyn |
| 3.22 | Jessica | 3.30 | Destiny | 3.53 | Julia | 3.76 | Kaitlyn | 4.04 | Hailey | 4.08 | Natalie |
| 3.20 | Lily | 3.27 | Morgan | 3.45 | Kaitlyn | 3.70 | Julia | 4.03 | Julia | 4.07 | Hailey |
| 3.09 | Sydney | 3.17 | Kaitlyn | 3.40 | Rachel | 3.57 | Haley | 3.94 | Destiny | 4.05 | Haley |
| 3.08 | Morgan | 3.13 | Savannah | 3.33 | Katherine | 3.54 | Katherine | 3.77 | Haley | 3.98 | Katherine |
| 2.98 | Katherine | 3.09 | Katherine | 3.31 | Megan | 3.52 | Mia | 3.65 | Katherine | 3.95 | Nicole |
| 2.97 | Destiny | 3.07 | Alexandra | 3.27 | Alexandra | 3.45 | Destiny | 3.53 | Nicole | 3.62 | Sophia |
| 2.95 | Lillian | 3.00 | Rachel | 3.23 | Jennifer | 3.26 | Alexandra | 3.52 | Alexandra | 3.56 | Alexandra |
| 2.90 | Alexa | 2.95 | Lily | 3.21 | Destiny | 3.13 | Ava | 3.33 | Savannah | 3.52 | Amanda |
| 2.89 | Alexandra | 2.85 | Megan | 2.90 | Allison | 3.09 | Nicole | 3.23 | Maria | 3.51 | Mackenzie |
| 2.88 | Kaitlyn | 2.85 | Kaylee | 2.86 | Savannah | 3.05 | Savannah | 3.18 | Stephanie | 3.45 | Maria |
| 2.84 | Kaylee | 2.84 | Jennifer | 2.83 | Maria | 3.02 | Maria | 3.17 | Mackenzie | 3.41 | Savannah |
| 2.79 | Nevaeh | 2.80 | Angelina | 2.83 | Haley | 2.97 | Brooke | 3.17 | Mia | 3.34 | Stephanie |
| 2.73 | Brooke | 2.77 | Makayla | 2.83 | Mackenzie | 2.94 | Ella | 3.16 | Allison | 3.14 | Allison |
| 2.68 | Makayla | 2.74 | Allison | 2.82 | Brooke | 2.92 | Mackenzie | 3.12 | Jordan | 3.11 | Jenna |
| 2.64 | Allison | 2.70 | Brooke | 2.82 | Nicole | 2.91 | Allison | 3.10 | Amanda | 2.96 | Rebecca |
| 2.64 | Maria | 2.69 | Maria | 2.79 | Makayla | 2.87 | Paige | 2.87 | Jenna | 2.94 | Jordan |
| 2.60 | Angelina | 2.65 | Trinity | 2.78 | Trinity | 2.81 | Jordan | 2.79 | Faith | 2.91 | Andrea |
| 2.59 | Rachel | 2.53 | Lillian | 2.75 | Kylie | 2.79 | Stephanie | 2.77 | Makayla | 2.88 | Mary |
| 2.54 | Gabriella | 2.53 | Mackenzie | 2.69 | Kaylee | 2.78 | Faith | 2.77 | Paige | 2.83 | Gabrielle |
| 2.50 | Jennifer | 2.52 | Faith | 2.68 | Paige | 2.77 | Makayla | 2.75 | Mary | 2.81 | Amber |
| 2.49 | Avery | 2.51 | Sofia | 2.66 | Lily | 2.76 | Kylie | 2.71 | Brooke | 2.75 | Katelyn |
| 2.47 | Mackenzie | 2.49 | Riley | 2.66 | Faith | 2.71 | Kaylee | 2.67 | Katelyn | 2.73 | Faith |
| 2.44 | Zoe | 2.49 | Haley | 2.64 | Zoe | 2.66 | Jenna | 2.63 | Rebecca | 2.69 | Makayla |
| 2.41 | Riley | 2.42 | Gabrielle | 2.56 | Stephanie | 2.65 | Amanda | 2.59 | Andrea | 2.65 | Sierra |
| 2.41 | Sofia | 2.42 | Nicole | 2.55 | Jenna | 2.55 | Trinity | 2.59 | Madeline | 2.64 | Madeline |
| 2.38 | Maya | 2.41 | Kylie | 2.50 | Andrea | 2.53 | Zoe | 2.52 | Kaylee | 2.64 | Brooke |
| 2.37 | Kimberly | 2.39 | Katelyn | 2.46 | Riley | 2.51 | Katelyn | 2.50 | Michelle | 2.60 | Sara |
| 2.37 | Andrea | 2.39 | Zoe | 2.44 | Katelyn | 2.48 | Mary | 2.50 | Sara | 2.54 | Michelle |
| 2.34 | Megan | 2.39 | Paige | 2.41 | Angelina | 2.48 | Madeline | 2.47 | Zoe | 2.51 | Erin |
| 2.32 | Katelyn | 2.33 | Gabriella | 2.39 | Kimberly | 2.47 | Andrea | 2.45 | Kylie | 2.47 | Kimberly |
| 2.29 | Gabrielle | 2.33 | Jenna | 2.36 | Mary | 2.42 | Michelle | 2.42 | Sierra | 2.46 | Caroline |
| 2.29 | Trinity | 2.31 | Kimberly | 2.35 | Madeline | 2.41 | Rebecca | 2.42 | Kimberly | 2.42 | Danielle |

| 2006 | 2005 | 2004 | 2003 | 2002 | 2001 |
|------|------|------|------|------|------|
| 2.28 Faith | 2.28 Stephanie | 2.34 Leah | 2.40 Kimberly | 2.42 Aaliyah | 2.36 Vanessa |
| 2.25 Evelyn | 2.26 Alexa | 2.33 Lillian | 2.36 Sara | 2.39 Amber | 2.35 Zoe |
| 2.24 Kylie | 2.26 Avery | 2.33 Michelle | 2.29 Alexa | 2.36 Gabrielle | 2.34 Kaylee |
| 2.23 Brooklyn | 2.25 Andrea | 2.30 Amanda | 2.29 Gabrielle | 2.36 Caroline | 2.26 Trinity |
| 2.21 Audrey | 2.22 Leah | 2.21 Sara | 2.28 Caroline | 2.25 Vanessa | 2.21 Shelby |
| 2.19 Leah | 2.20 Madeline | 2.20 Sofia | 2.21 Lily | 2.23 Alexa | 2.20 Bailey |
| 2.13 Stephanie | 2.20 Nevaeh | 2.20 Jordan | 2.16 Vanessa | 2.22 Trinity | 2.19 Jacqueline |
| 2.13 Madeline | 2.18 Evelyn | 2.19 Alexa | 2.12 Angelina | 2.13 Danielle | 2.16 Paige |
| 2.07 Sara | 2.15 Maya | 2.19 Rebecca | 2.11 Riley | 2.10 Erin | 2.12 Autumn |
| 2.07 Jocelyn | 2.13 Mary | 2.18 Gabrielle | 2.11 Sierra | 2.08 Autumn | 2.11 Courtney |
| 2.04 Nicole | 2.09 Michelle | 2.16 Caroline | 2.04 Amber | 2.01 Shelby | 2.10 Melissa |
| 2.03 Haley | 2.07 Jada | 2.15 Vanessa | 2.01 Autumn | 2.01 Angelina | 2.02 Jada |
| 2.03 Paige | 2.07 Sara | 2.09 Gabriella | 2.00 Lillian | 1.98 Riley | 1.98 Angela |
| 2.02 Arianna | 2.01 Audrey | 2.00 Avery | 2.00 Gabriella | 1.98 Gabriella | 1.98 Mia |
| 2.01 Ariana | 2.00 Brooklyn | 1.98 Marissa | 1.99 Audrey | 1.97 Jada | 1.97 Alexa |
| 1.97 Vanessa | 1.99 Vanessa | 1.97 Ariana | 1.98 Jada | 1.94 Lily | 1.95 Marissa |
| 1.94 Michelle | 1.98 Amanda | 1.93 Audrey | 1.95 Erin | 1.91 Melissa | 1.89 Catherine |
| 1.92 Mariah | 1.93 Ariana | 1.92 Jada | 1.94 Leah | 1.91 Jacqueline | 1.89 Christina |
| 1.92 Amelia | 1.93 Rebecca | 1.90 Autumn | 1.92 Danielle | 1.90 Ava | 1.84 Claire |
| 1.91 Melanie | 1.92 Caroline | 1.86 Evelyn | 1.92 Isabel | 1.88 Angela | 1.83 Leslie |
| 1.91 Mary | 1.89 Amelia | 1.85 Maya | 1.91 Maya | 1.85 Bailey | 1.82 Gabriella |
| 1.91 Isabelle | 1.85 Mariah | 1.85 Jocelyn | 1.90 Ariana | 1.85 Isabel | 1.81 Mariah |
| 1.90 Claire | 1.79 Jordan | 1.81 Arianna | 1.89 Arianna | 1.83 Jade | 1.79 Laura |
| 1.89 Isabel | 1.79 Jocelyn | 1.79 Isabel | 1.85 Jocelyn | 1.82 Leah | 1.78 Leah |
| 1.86 Jenna | 1.78 Arianna | 1.79 Amber | 1.84 Evelyn | 1.81 Courtney | 1.77 Isabel |
| 1.79 Caroline | 1.75 Isabel | 1.77 Melanie | 1.84 Avery | 1.80 Ella | 1.75 Caitlin |
| 1.77 Valeria | 1.74 Marissa | 1.76 Diana | 1.82 Aaliyah | 1.79 Maya | 1.73 Alexandria |
| 1.77 Aaliyah | 1.74 Autumn | 1.74 Danielle | 1.81 Leslie | 1.78 Leslie | 1.73 Molly |
| 1.74 Aubrey | 1.70 Melanie | 1.73 Sierra | 1.78 Claire | 1.78 Jocelyn | 1.71 Ariana |
| 1.73 Jada | 1.67 Aaliyah | 1.73 Leslie | 1.76 Melanie | 1.77 Ariana | 1.70 Breanna |
| 1.70 Natalia | 1.63 Gracie | 1.72 Aaliyah | 1.76 Shelby | 1.76 Melanie | 1.70 Angelina |
| 1.69 Autumn | 1.59 Claire | 1.66 Erin | 1.75 Marissa | 1.73 Claire | 1.70 Kylie |
| 1.68 Rebecca | 1.59 Isabelle | 1.65 Amelia | 1.74 Melissa | 1.72 Lillian | 1.69 Aaliyah |
| 1.67 Jordan | 1.56 Molly | 1.65 Molly | 1.74 Sofia | 1.71 Christina | 1.68 Kathryn |
| 1.63 Gianna | 1.54 Mya | 1.65 Claire | 1.73 Bailey | 1.71 Evelyn | 1.66 Jade |
| 1.62 Jayla | 1.53 Diana | 1.64 Melissa | 1.70 Jacqueline | 1.68 Marissa | 1.65 Kelsey |
| 1.58 Layla | 1.53 Katie | 1.63 Bailey | 1.69 Molly | 1.67 Audrey | 1.65 Katie |

# The Top 100 Boys' Names
# from the Years 2001 to 2006

About 50% of all boys received a top 100 name in 2006. The number to the left of the name indicates the number of times the name was given per thousand boys born.

| 2006 | 2005 | 2004 | 2003 | 2002 | 2001 |
|---|---|---|---|---|---|
| 11.27 Jacob | 12.00 Jacob | 13.21 Jacob | 14.72 Jacob | 15.46 Jacob | 16.45 Jacob |
| 10.25 Michael | 11.05 Michael | 12.03 Michael | 13.46 Michael | 14.28 Michael | 15.01 Michael |
| 10.09 Joshua | 10.79 Joshua | 11.44 Joshua | 12.46 Joshua | 13.14 Joshua | 13.56 Matthew |
| 9.35 Ethan | 9.97 Matthew | 10.83 Matthew | 11.92 Matthew | 12.74 Matthew | 13.16 Joshua |
| 9.22 Matthew | 9.96 Ethan | 10.53 Ethan | 11.00 Andrew | 11.20 Ethan | 11.75 Christopher |
| 9.07 Daniel | 9.62 Andrew | 10.28 Andrew | 10.64 Ethan | 11.14 Andrew | 11.56 Nicholas |
| 8.97 Christopher | 9.37 Daniel | 9.93 Daniel | 10.59 Joseph | 11.07 Joseph | 11.34 Andrew |
| 8.96 Andrew | 9.01 Anthony | 9.58 William | 10.44 Daniel | 11.02 Christopher | 11.11 Joseph |
| 8.81 Anthony | 8.94 Christopher | 9.51 Joseph | 10.36 Christopher | 10.84 Nicholas | 10.60 Daniel |
| 8.60 William | 8.87 Joseph | 9.34 Christopher | 10.01 Anthony | 10.78 Daniel | 10.16 William |
| 8.32 Joseph | 8.85 William | 9.27 Anthony | 9.93 William | 10.18 William | 9.98 Anthony |
| 8.28 Alexander | 8.44 Alexander | 9.25 Ryan | 9.79 Nicholas | 9.91 Anthony | 9.76 David |
| 7.96 David | 8.40 Ryan | 8.77 Nicholas | 9.74 Ryan | 9.43 David | 9.75 Tyler |
| 7.48 Ryan | 8.39 David | 8.68 David | 9.23 David | 9.25 Tyler | 9.55 John |
| 7.42 Noah | 7.94 Nicholas | 8.49 Alexander | 9.03 Tyler | 8.97 Alexander | 9.26 Ryan |
| 7.36 James | 7.91 Tyler | 8.27 Tyler | 8.81 Alexander | 8.94 Ryan | 9.21 Zachary |
| 7.11 Nicholas | 7.47 James | 7.79 James | 8.54 John | 8.83 John | 9.09 Ethan |
| 7.05 Tyler | 7.32 John | 7.78 John | 8.38 James | 8.57 James | 9.05 Brandon |
| 6.91 Logan | 6.72 Jonathan | 7.05 Dylan | 7.82 Dylan | 8.42 Zachary | 8.62 James |
| 6.89 John | 6.68 Nathan | 6.93 Nathan | 7.72 Zachary | 8.24 Brandon | 8.46 Alexander |
| 6.56 Christian | 6.61 Samuel | 6.79 Jonathan | 7.57 Brandon | 7.84 Jonathan | 8.35 Dylan |
| 6.51 Jonathan | 6.59 Christian | 6.70 Brandon | 7.44 Jonathan | 7.54 Justin | 8.21 Justin |
| 6.47 Nathan | 6.45 Noah | 6.67 Samuel | 7.28 Samuel | 7.50 Dylan | 8.16 Jonathan |

| 2006 | 2005 | 2004 | 2003 | 2002 | 2001 |
|------|------|------|------|------|------|
| 6.24 Benjamin | 6.43 Dylan | 6.57 Christian | 6.99 Benjamin | 7.38 Christian | 7.81 Christian |
| 6.17 Samuel | 6.29 Benjamin | 6.55 Benjamin | 6.90 Christian | 7.36 Austin | 7.57 Austin |
| 6.00 Dylan | 6.28 Logan | 6.50 Zachary | 6.79 Justin | 7.36 Samuel | 7.48 Samuel |
| 5.77 Brandon | 6.03 Brandon | 6.24 Logan | 6.79 Nathan | 6.82 Benjamin | 7.25 Benjamin |
| 5.69 Gabriel | 5.91 Gabriel | 5.77 Jose | 6.56 Logan | 6.70 Nathan | 6.82 Noah |
| 5.45 Elijah | 5.71 Zachary | 5.64 Noah | 6.22 Gabriel | 6.57 Logan | 6.44 Logan |
| 5.27 Aiden | 5.61 Jose | 5.62 Justin | 6.16 Jose | 6.52 Jose | 6.40 Robert |
| 5.26 Angel | 5.38 Elijah | 5.54 Elijah | 5.88 Noah | 6.11 Noah | 6.40 Nathan |
| 5.25 Jose | 5.11 Angel | 5.47 Gabriel | 5.83 Kevin | 6.10 Gabriel | 6.38 Kevin |
| 5.00 Zachary | 5.09 Kevin | 5.35 Caleb | 5.81 Austin | 6.10 Kevin | 6.15 Thomas |
| 4.99 Caleb | 5.09 Jack | 5.32 Kevin | 5.78 Caleb | 6.08 Robert | 6.14 Jose |
| 4.95 Jack | 5.07 Caleb | 5.09 Austin | 5.64 Robert | 5.90 Caleb | 5.87 Cameron |
| 4.95 Jackson | 4.90 Justin | 5.05 Robert | 5.44 Thomas | 5.71 Thomas | 5.74 Hunter |
| 4.91 Kevin | 4.72 Austin | 4.97 Thomas | 5.29 Elijah | 5.63 Jordan | 5.65 Caleb |
| 4.78 Gavin | 4.72 Evan | 4.77 Connor | 5.13 Jordan | 5.61 Hunter | 5.52 Gabriel |
| 4.75 Mason | 4.71 Robert | 4.74 Evan | 5.01 Aidan | 5.24 Cameron | 5.46 Jordan |
| 4.71 Isaiah | 4.67 Thomas | 4.66 Aidan | 4.95 Cameron | 5.10 Kyle | 5.35 Kyle |
| 4.69 Austin | 4.66 Luke | 4.55 Luke | 4.93 Hunter | 5.08 Elijah | 5.14 Jason |
| 4.61 Evan | 4.56 Mason | 4.55 Jack | 4.87 Jason | 5.03 Jason | 4.82 Aaron |
| 4.58 Luke | 4.55 Aidan | 4.51 Angel | 4.82 Connor | 4.56 Jack | 4.33 Eric |
| 4.56 Aidan | 4.47 Jackson | 4.51 Jordan | 4.70 Evan | 4.55 Aaron | 4.33 Isaiah |
| 4.53 Justin | 4.41 Isaiah | 4.36 Isaiah | 4.64 Jack | 4.53 Isaiah | 4.21 Elijah |
| 4.51 Jordan | 4.35 Jordan | 4.34 Isaac | 4.63 Luke | 4.41 Luke | 4.20 Brian |
| 4.48 Robert | 4.35 Gavin | 4.29 Jason | 4.55 Angel | 4.26 Connor | 4.14 Isaac |
| 4.37 Isaac | 4.35 Connor | 4.26 Jackson | 4.43 Isaac | 4.20 Isaac | 4.13 Jack |
| 4.37 Landon | 4.24 Aiden | 4.22 Hunter | 4.40 Aaron | 4.14 Angel | 4.09 Connor |
| 4.37 Jayden | 4.22 Isaac | 4.21 Cameron | 4.40 Isaiah | 4.13 Jackson | 4.05 Luke |
| 4.33 Thomas | 4.01 Jason | 4.09 Mason | 4.36 Gavin | 4.09 Brian | 3.92 Adam |
| 4.02 Cameron | 3.99 Cameron | 4.09 Gavin | 4.33 Jackson | 4.02 Eric | 3.79 Luis |
| 3.94 Connor | 3.97 Hunter | 3.97 Aaron | 4.30 Kyle | 3.99 Mason | 3.77 Mason |
| 3.90 Hunter | 3.84 Jayden | 3.86 Juan | 3.93 Mason | 3.96 Juan | 3.77 Juan |
| 3.85 Jason | 3.84 Juan | 3.71 Kyle | 3.89 Juan | 3.92 Adam | 3.68 Charles |
| 3.81 Diego | 3.67 Charles | 3.62 Charles | 3.87 Eric | 3.75 Evan | 3.67 Evan |
| 3.75 Aaron | 3.62 Aaron | 3.55 Luis | 3.82 Charles | 3.73 Luis | 3.65 Sean |
| 3.73 Owen | 3.54 Lucas | 3.54 Adam | 3.82 Adam | 3.65 Charles | 3.53 Angel |
| 3.70 Lucas | 3.49 Luis | 3.47 Brian | 3.82 Brian | 3.56 Sean | 3.46 Carlos |
| 3.63 Charles | 3.35 Owen | 3.39 Aiden | 3.77 Luis | 3.52 Aidan | 3.46 Jackson |
| 3.61 Juan | 3.31 Landon | 3.39 Eric | 3.53 Sean | 3.52 Gavin | 3.36 Nathaniel |
| 3.60 Luis | 3.23 Diego | 3.28 Jayden | 3.38 Alex | 3.45 Alex | 3.35 Alex |
| 3.36 Adrian | 3.23 Brian | 3.23 Alex | 3.31 Nathaniel | 3.44 Nathaniel | 3.33 Steven |

| 2006 | | 2005 | | 2004 | | 2003 | | 2002 | | 2001 | |
|---|---|---|---|---|---|---|---|---|---|---|---|
| 3.08 | Adam | 3.18 | Adam | 3.20 | Sean | 3.29 | Bryan | 3.35 | Bryan | 3.32 | Cody |
| 3.08 | Julian | 3.13 | Adrian | 3.20 | Bryan | 3.21 | Ian | 3.33 | Carlos | 3.26 | Jared |
| 3.05 | Bryan | 3.12 | Kyle | 3.19 | Owen | 3.09 | Carlos | 3.22 | Jesus | 3.25 | Jesus |
| 3.03 | Alex | 3.12 | Eric | 3.18 | Lucas | 3.07 | Jesus | 3.22 | Ian | 3.24 | Timothy |
| 3.01 | Sean | 3.11 | Ian | 3.15 | Nathaniel | 3.04 | Adrian | 3.14 | Steven | 3.15 | Seth |
| 3.00 | Nathaniel | 3.10 | Nathaniel | 3.08 | Ian | 2.94 | Cole | 3.06 | Cole | 3.10 | Bryan |
| 2.97 | Carlos | 3.06 | Carlos | 3.07 | Jesus | 2.90 | Steven | 3.04 | Timothy | 3.08 | Ian |
| 2.96 | Jeremiah | 3.02 | Alex | 2.96 | Carlos | 2.86 | Lucas | 3.00 | Cody | 3.06 | Devin |
| 2.96 | Brian | 3.02 | Bryan | 2.91 | Adrian | 2.84 | Owen | 2.90 | Seth | 2.93 | Patrick |
| 2.95 | Hayden | 2.97 | Jesus | 2.79 | Diego | 2.83 | Aiden | 2.88 | Adrian | 2.92 | Richard |
| 2.93 | Jesus | 2.86 | Julian | 2.68 | Julian | 2.81 | Devin | 2.75 | Devin | 2.91 | Cole |
| 2.93 | Carter | 2.78 | Sean | 2.68 | Cole | 2.76 | Jayden | 2.72 | Lucas | 2.74 | Adrian |
| 2.86 | Sebastian | 2.76 | Carter | 2.58 | Ashton | 2.72 | Timothy | 2.71 | Blake | 2.73 | Trevor |
| 2.84 | Eric | 2.76 | Hayden | 2.53 | Jeremiah | 2.69 | Julian | 2.69 | Richard | 2.71 | Blake |
| 2.81 | Xavier | 2.69 | Jeremiah | 2.53 | Steven | 2.68 | Cody | 2.65 | Julian | 2.67 | Gavin |
| 2.81 | Brayden | 2.61 | Cole | 2.47 | Timothy | 2.62 | Blake | 2.61 | Patrick | 2.63 | Chase |
| 2.80 | Kyle | 2.57 | Brayden | 2.45 | Seth | 2.61 | Seth | 2.60 | Sebastian | 2.56 | Garrett |
| 2.80 | Ian | 2.50 | Wyatt | 2.45 | Chase | 2.59 | Dominic | 2.56 | Trevor | 2.52 | Sebastian |
| 2.66 | Wyatt | 2.43 | Chase | 2.45 | Devin | 2.58 | Jaden | 2.46 | Chase | 2.50 | Julian |
| 2.62 | Chase | 2.36 | Steven | 2.44 | Jaden | 2.55 | Diego | 2.45 | Dominic | 2.48 | Lucas |
| 2.57 | Cole | 2.33 | Timothy | 2.44 | Colin | 2.54 | Hayden | 2.45 | Jared | 2.40 | Mark |
| 2.53 | Dominic | 2.32 | Dominic | 2.42 | Cody | 2.52 | Xavier | 2.39 | Antonio | 2.40 | Antonio |
| 2.46 | Tristan | 2.31 | Sebastian | 2.39 | Landon | 2.51 | Richard | 2.38 | Jeremiah | 2.35 | Aidan |
| 2.29 | Carson | 2.28 | Xavier | 2.38 | Hayden | 2.50 | Chase | 2.35 | Jaden | 2.30 | Alejandro |
| 2.24 | Jaden | 2.25 | Jaden | 2.38 | Carter | 2.43 | Colin | 2.35 | Xavier | 2.30 | Miguel |
| 2.22 | Miguel | 2.20 | Jesse | 2.37 | Xavier | 2.42 | Carson | 2.35 | Miguel | 2.16 | Jeremy |
| 2.18 | Steven | 2.19 | Devin | 2.36 | Wyatt | 2.41 | Jeremiah | 2.24 | Jesse | 2.13 | Jesse |
| 2.17 | Caden | 2.19 | Seth | 2.31 | Dominic | 2.38 | Patrick | 2.21 | Garrett | 2.13 | Jeremiah |
| 2.16 | Kaden | 2.18 | Antonio | 2.30 | Richard | 2.34 | Antonio | 2.21 | Alejandro | 2.10 | Bryce |
| 2.14 | Antonio | 2.17 | Richard | 2.29 | Antonio | 2.31 | Sebastian | 2.14 | Mark | 2.01 | Xavier |
| 2.12 | Timothy | 2.17 | Miguel | 2.25 | Jesse | 2.29 | Miguel | 2.12 | Owen | 2.01 | Dakota |
| 2.11 | Henry | 2.12 | Colin | 2.23 | Blake | 2.28 | Jesse | 2.11 | Jeremy | 1.99 | Carson |
| 2.07 | Alejandro | 2.11 | Cody | 2.15 | Sebastian | 2.20 | Victor | 2.10 | Hayden | 1.98 | Victor |
| 2.06 | Blake | 2.09 | Alejandro | 2.14 | Miguel | 2.19 | Landon | 2.06 | Bryce | 1.98 | Kenneth |
| 2.04 | Liam | 2.06 | Caden | 2.12 | Jake | 2.19 | Jake | 2.01 | Diego | 1.97 | Dalton |
| 2.03 | Richard | 2.06 | Blake | 2.11 | Alejandro | 2.18 | Trevor | 2.01 | Riley | 1.96 | Colby |
| 2.02 | Devin | 2.03 | Carson | 2.10 | Patrick | 2.14 | Alejandro | 1.99 | Victor | 1.94 | Jake |

# The Top 500 Names—
# Rankings over the Last Century

As well as recording the change in popularity of first names over the last century and a bit, these lists give prospective parents ideas for names that were once popular but have gone out of fashion. Perhaps it's time for a revival!

Each year most babies—70% of the boys and 60% of the girls—receive a name in the top 500 rank of popularity.

## Girls' Names

The number to the left of the name is a popularity rating indicating the frequency of use per thousand baby girls born in the decades from the 1900s to the mid-2000s. A higher number represents greater popularity. For each decade in this time frame the **rank** of the name appears to the right of the name, a lower number meaning the name was more popular in that decade, 1 being the most popular.

| Pop. | Name | 1900s | 1910s | 1920s | 1930s | 1940s | 1950s | 1960s | 1970s | 1980s | 1990s | 2000s |
|---|---|---|---|---|---|---|---|---|---|---|---|---|
| 1.16 | Abigail | | | | | 854 | 654 | 615 | 317 | 150 | 50 | 5 |
| 0.74 | Ada | 85 | 110 | 154 | 196 | 244 | 331 | 445 | 627 | 962 | | 986 |
| 0.28 | Addie | 165 | 213 | 249 | 324 | 460 | 686 | | | | | |
| 0.30 | Adeline | 194 | 171 | 201 | 395 | 631 | | | | | | 620 |
| 0.33 | Adriana | | | | | | | 649 | 385 | 225 | 142 | 120 |
| 0.34 | Adrienne | 699 | 730 | 633 | 405 | 432 | 336 | 342 | 201 | 189 | 335 | 651 |
| 1.49 | Agnes | 37 | 46 | 68 | 134 | 229 | 372 | 612 | | | | |
| 0.57 | Alberta | 135 | 120 | 146 | 180 | 264 | 431 | 730 | | | | |
| 0.36 | Alexa | | | | | | | | | 465 | 116 | 68 |
| 0.99 | Alexandra | 728 | | | | 817 | 778 | 581 | 314 | 85 | 28 | 38 |
| 0.40 | Alexandria | | | | | | | | 893 | 231 | 81 | 117 |

| Pop. | Name | 1900s | 1910s | 1920s | 1930s | 1940s | 1950s | 1960s | 1970s | 1980s | 1990s | 2000s |
|------|------|-------|-------|-------|-------|-------|-------|-------|-------|-------|-------|-------|
| 1.39 | Alexis | | | | | 716 | 734 | 855 | 394 | 112 | 19 | 9 |
| 4.36 | Alice | 10 | 13 | 14 | 23 | 42 | 87 | 149 | 236 | 319 | 382 | 425 |
| 1.13 | Alicia | 750 | 641 | 384 | 329 | 298 | 240 | 170 | 83 | 45 | 79 | 133 |
| 0.50 | Alison | | | | | 689 | 347 | 259 | 134 | 107 | 152 | 246 |
| 1.21 | Allison | | | | | | 419 | 203 | 96 | 49 | 43 | 43 |
| 1.29 | Alma | 57 | 68 | 94 | 130 | 182 | 274 | 353 | 377 | 394 | 430 | 575 |
| 1.26 | Alyssa | | | | | | 923 | 395 | 89 | 23 | 13 | |
| 3.90 | Amanda | 205 | 269 | 387 | 534 | 477 | 400 | 206 | 17 | 3 | 7 | 47 |
| 1.82 | Amber | 970 | 907 | | | | 891 | 446 | 60 | 13 | 18 | 71 |
| 0.70 | Amelia | 152 | 168 | 211 | 251 | 293 | 386 | 431 | 411 | 254 | 207 | 119 |
| 3.47 | Amy | 196 | 244 | 284 | 356 | 331 | 136 | 35 | 2 | 16 | 61 | 113 |
| 0.90 | Ana | 359 | 286 | 212 | 153 | 156 | 186 | 201 | 182 | 164 | 131 | 139 |
| 2.08 | Andrea | 560 | 594 | 539 | 389 | 150 | 140 | 66 | 29 | 33 | 46 | 53 |
| 0.41 | Angel | | | | | | 792 | 469 | 179 | 167 | 163 | 121 |
| 3.42 | Angela | 212 | 195 | 247 | 246 | 175 | 106 | 21 | 7 | 27 | 73 | 101 |
| 0.43 | Angelica | | | 650 | 668 | 829 | | 704 | 278 | 151 | 99 | 160 |
| 0.62 | Angelina | 218 | 197 | 199 | 284 | 475 | 517 | 541 | 386 | 298 | 269 | 72 |
| 0.32 | Angie | 437 | 426 | 499 | 476 | 528 | 501 | 250 | 193 | 387 | 624 | 398 |
| 1.28 | Anita | 219 | 163 | 145 | 119 | 95 | 91 | 83 | 158 | 295 | 488 | 926 |
| 3.10 | Ann | 63 | 45 | 50 | 34 | 38 | 45 | 60 | 102 | 180 | 325 | 592 |
| 6.30 | Anna | 4 | 7 | 12 | 33 | 72 | 103 | 101 | 86 | 53 | 40 | 21 |
| 2.15 | Anne | 79 | 57 | 83 | 90 | 86 | 83 | 81 | 123 | 130 | 206 | 361 |
| 0.94 | Annette | 263 | 236 | 225 | 154 | 152 | 123 | 77 | 173 | 332 | 587 | 726 |
| 2.60 | Annie | 28 | 34 | 33 | 41 | 83 | 155 | 291 | 405 | 307 | 348 | 348 |
| 0.53 | Antoinette | 204 | 175 | 191 | 231 | 247 | 307 | 297 | 346 | 346 | 538 | |
| 0.31 | Antonia | 268 | 277 | 268 | 265 | 303 | 423 | 592 | 578 | 612 | 567 | 771 |
| 1.18 | April | | | | | 443 | 254 | 140 | 34 | 40 | 121 | 267 |
| 0.94 | Arlene | 334 | 196 | 128 | 69 | 111 | 170 | 263 | 407 | 515 | 744 | 866 |
| 3.96 | Ashley | | | | | | | 662 | 142 | 4 | 1 | 7 |
| 1.44 | Audrey | 176 | 127 | 72 | 78 | 145 | 165 | 204 | 258 | 191 | 165 | 84 |
| 0.40 | Autumn | | | | | | | | 345 | 205 | 127 | 80 |
| 0.46 | Ava | 456 | 557 | 561 | 643 | 769 | 438 | 692 | 962 | 926 | 745 | 33 |
| 0.32 | Bailey | | | | | | | | | 541 | 110 | 88 |
| 8.63 | Barbara | 143 | 85 | 18 | 3 | 3 | 6 | 22 | 73 | 153 | 296 | 601 |
| 1.72 | Beatrice | 44 | 38 | 54 | 108 | 159 | 257 | 377 | 547 | 643 | 828 | |
| 0.40 | Becky | | | | 661 | 260 | 151 | 141 | 195 | 419 | | |
| 0.32 | Belinda | | | | | 505 | 174 | 165 | 217 | 448 | 799 | |
| 0.30 | Bernadette | 416 | 408 | 356 | 386 | 240 | 271 | 287 | 426 | 555 | 891 | |
| 1.59 | Bernice | 67 | 42 | 45 | 91 | 160 | 263 | 384 | 628 | 990 | | |
| 1.71 | Bertha | 26 | 47 | 77 | 118 | 158 | 265 | 403 | 581 | 980 | | |
| 1.45 | Bessie | 32 | 56 | 86 | 137 | 216 | 375 | 610 | 926 | | | |
| 0.79 | Beth | 592 | 425 | 373 | 359 | 254 | 133 | 69 | 116 | 192 | 705 | |
| 0.44 | Bethany | | | | | | 742 | 502 | 210 | 98 | 118 | 190 |
| 6.91 | Betty | 92 | 44 | 4 | 2 | 11 | 35 | 104 | 244 | 434 | 779 | |
| 0.71 | Beulah | 77 | 93 | 143 | 233 | 329 | 707 | | | | | |

| Pop. | Name | 1900s | 1910s | 1920s | 1930s | 1940s | 1950s | 1960s | 1970s | 1980s | 1990s | 2000s |
|---|---|---|---|---|---|---|---|---|---|---|---|---|
| 2.23 | Beverly | 834 | 340 | 98 | 21 | 31 | 37 | 85 | 224 | 406 | 655 | |
| 0.30 | Bianca | | | | | | | | 635 | 207 | 112 | 169 |
| 0.64 | Billie | 403 | 260 | 144 | 117 | 166 | 259 | 332 | 261 | 473 | 864 | |
| 0.83 | Blanche | 58 | 79 | 140 | 229 | 400 | 557 | 999 | | | | |
| 0.54 | Bobbie | 578 | 437 | 245 | 124 | 165 | 234 | 310 | 266 | 362 | 712 | |
| 1.88 | Bonnie | 207 | 180 | 119 | 68 | 34 | 50 | 90 | 168 | 222 | 509 | |
| 0.50 | Brandi | | | | | | | 838 | 115 | 69 | 130 | 585 |
| 0.54 | Brandy | | | | | | | | 79 | 65 | 178 | 569 |
| 0.35 | Breanna | | | | | | | | | 329 | 90 | 108 |
| 3.04 | Brenda | | | | 301 | 27 | 18 | 20 | 54 | 114 | 123 | 207 |
| 0.41 | Briana | | | | | | | | 756 | 237 | 80 | 111 |
| 1.01 | Brianna | | | | | | | | 757 | 173 | 29 | 18 |
| 0.45 | Bridget | 381 | 666 | 913 | 837 | 803 | 407 | 228 | 152 | 169 | 194 | 294 |
| 1.75 | Brittany | | | | | | | | 518 | 20 | 6 | 155 |
| 0.39 | Brittney | | | | | | | | | 92 | 85 | 310 |
| 0.77 | Brooke | | | | | | | 751 | 197 | 86 | 56 | 46 |
| 0.51 | Caitlin | | | | | | | | 927 | 90 | 69 | 128 |
| 0.31 | Camille | 489 | 498 | 660 | 471 | 345 | 398 | 424 | 378 | 330 | 272 | 266 |
| 0.41 | Candace | | | | | 291 | 225 | 288 | 213 | 115 | 217 | 807 |
| 0.33 | Candice | | | | | 500 | 348 | 542 | 225 | 97 | 251 | 968 |
| 0.73 | Carla | | | | 450 | 235 | 138 | 82 | 119 | 185 | 295 | 452 |
| 1.87 | Carmen | 171 | 151 | 105 | 58 | 50 | 76 | 89 | 110 | 178 | 261 | 262 |
| 4.63 | Carol | 340 | 243 | 116 | 11 | 5 | 16 | 38 | 128 | 280 | 417 | 797 |
| 0.66 | Carole | | 876 | 503 | 98 | 60 | 203 | 282 | 682 | | | |
| 1.14 | Caroline | 130 | 149 | 173 | 186 | 209 | 304 | 202 | 205 | 155 | 92 | 69 |
| 3.20 | Carolyn | 223 | 174 | 127 | 30 | 12 | 25 | 56 | 114 | 162 | 222 | 397 |
| 1.61 | Carrie | 70 | 99 | 139 | 168 | 197 | 201 | 136 | 42 | 78 | 257 | 711 |
| 0.35 | Casey | | | | | | | | 310 | 99 | 122 | 303 |
| 0.81 | Cassandra | | | | | 486 | 322 | 208 | 154 | 60 | 66 | 142 |
| 4.35 | Catherine | 19 | 21 | 28 | 43 | 46 | 34 | 58 | 72 | 63 | 86 | 104 |
| 0.79 | Cathy | | | | | 169 | 52 | 76 | 215 | 558 | | |
| 0.39 | Cecelia | 187 | 191 | 235 | 293 | 263 | 337 | 511 | 881 | 981 | 756 | 719 |
| 0.56 | Cecilia | 185 | 211 | 232 | 249 | 236 | 268 | 329 | 389 | 347 | 277 | 271 |
| 0.41 | Celia | 167 | 203 | 257 | 288 | 322 | 367 | 481 | 645 | 556 | 658 | 656 |
| 0.73 | Charlene | 922 | 595 | 272 | 155 | 114 | 132 | 163 | 207 | 273 | 610 | |
| 1.77 | Charlotte | 96 | 83 | 80 | 73 | 63 | 117 | 160 | 204 | 294 | 284 | 178 |
| 0.74 | Chelsea | | | | | | | | 531 | 67 | 30 | 176 |
| 2.17 | Cheryl | | | | 624 | 44 | 19 | 28 | 80 | 196 | 671 | |
| 0.55 | Chloe | 533 | 620 | 915 | 732 | | | | | 600 | 146 | 24 |
| 2.40 | Christina | 278 | 323 | 349 | 400 | 256 | 181 | 75 | 16 | 19 | 36 | 109 |
| 3.16 | Christine | 137 | 124 | 124 | 129 | 55 | 30 | 27 | 22 | 48 | 101 | 315 |
| 0.49 | Christy | | | | | 761 | 314 | 222 | 71 | 149 | 444 | 959 |
| 1.20 | Cindy | | | | | 328 | 51 | 48 | 103 | 181 | 186 | 287 |
| 0.82 | Claire | 222 | 207 | 158 | 164 | 205 | 280 | 400 | 462 | 262 | 140 | 91 |
| 2.13 | Clara | 23 | 37 | 52 | 79 | 136 | 223 | 363 | 535 | 542 | 433 | 285 |

| Pop. | Name | 1900s | 1910s | 1920s | 1930s | 1940s | 1950s | 1960s | 1970s | 1980s | 1990s | 2000s |
|---|---|---|---|---|---|---|---|---|---|---|---|---|
| 0.69 | Claudia | 314 | 309 | 347 | 261 | 149 | 157 | 283 | 198 | 204 | 171 | 254 |
| 0.83 | Colleen | | 998 | 296 | 234 | 228 | 121 | 95 | 131 | 146 | 220 | 598 |
| 1.38 | Connie | 434 | 315 | 269 | 145 | 53 | 42 | 64 | 162 | 405 | 665 | |
| 0.87 | Constance | 247 | 212 | 156 | 122 | 109 | 126 | 229 | 434 | 407 | 743 | |
| 0.79 | Cora | 80 | 114 | 155 | 179 | 253 | 364 | 547 | 742 | 700 | 788 | 442 |
| 1.25 | Courtney | | | | | | | 596 | 132 | 37 | 20 | 102 |
| 0.29 | Cristina | 812 | 773 | 880 | 726 | 921 | 789 | 536 | 283 | 172 | 208 | 390 |
| 1.64 | Crystal | 550 | 553 | 759 | 867 | 563 | 296 | 157 | 36 | 21 | 60 | 158 |
| 3.48 | Cynthia | 407 | 406 | 357 | 198 | 48 | 11 | 10 | 31 | 64 | 103 | 197 |
| 0.85 | Daisy | 102 | 139 | 164 | 205 | 261 | 356 | 453 | 498 | 249 | 155 | 144 |
| 0.94 | Dana | | | 836 | 626 | 344 | 192 | 80 | 59 | 77 | 157 | 365 |
| 1.76 | Danielle | | | | | 928 | 735 | 238 | 46 | 25 | 22 | 77 |
| 1.09 | Darlene | | 542 | 244 | 100 | 80 | 71 | 92 | 238 | 466 | 628 | 981 |
| 1.43 | Dawn | | | 615 | 361 | 259 | 114 | 37 | 27 | 145 | 531 | |
| 0.67 | Deanna | | | | 271 | 187 | 247 | 133 | 120 | 160 | 183 | 401 |
| 0.87 | Debbie | | | | | 428 | 55 | 52 | 245 | 564 | 947 | |
| 3.52 | Deborah | 674 | 774 | 773 | 413 | 66 | 5 | 12 | 61 | 175 | 360 | 600 |
| 2.55 | Debra | | | | | 323 | 7 | 23 | 94 | 288 | 713 | |
| 0.48 | Della | 122 | 165 | 195 | 239 | 307 | 365 | 476 | 789 | | | |
| 0.76 | Delores | 737 | 366 | 153 | 64 | 110 | 182 | 315 | 651 | | | |
| 1.77 | Denise | | | 917 | 549 | 221 | 26 | 29 | 55 | 110 | 199 | 335 |
| 0.39 | Desiree | | | | | | 513 | 356 | 269 | 134 | 137 | 229 |
| 0.59 | Destiny | | | | | | | | 790 | 371 | 82 | 32 |
| 1.81 | Diana | 458 | 483 | 400 | 206 | 54 | 57 | 62 | 91 | 73 | 97 | 107 |
| 2.64 | Diane | | 726 | 459 | 113 | 22 | 17 | 39 | 125 | 242 | 485 | 927 |
| 0.48 | Dianne | | | | 313 | 107 | 120 | 200 | 501 | | | |
| 1.57 | Dolores | 228 | 140 | 51 | 20 | 92 | 176 | 285 | 502 | 808 | | |
| 4.42 | Donna | 392 | 278 | 113 | 22 | 16 | 10 | 8 | 67 | 217 | 461 | 743 |
| 0.80 | Dora | 87 | 122 | 133 | 172 | 224 | 293 | 346 | 449 | 716 | | |
| 3.55 | Doris | 72 | 36 | 8 | 13 | 45 | 102 | 183 | 414 | 683 | 973 | |
| 9.19 | Dorothy | 7 | 3 | 2 | 6 | 20 | 60 | 124 | 218 | 354 | 565 | 912 |
| 2.32 | Edith | 25 | 29 | 38 | 80 | 126 | 206 | 301 | 489 | 588 | 551 | 625 |
| 2.67 | Edna | 17 | 19 | 34 | 53 | 118 | 196 | 318 | 493 | 797 | | |
| 0.33 | Effie | 117 | 187 | 252 | 337 | 516 | 895 | | | | | |
| 1.18 | Eileen | 238 | 134 | 97 | 120 | 88 | 116 | 156 | 296 | 385 | 568 | 684 |
| 1.53 | Elaine | 364 | 190 | 84 | 52 | 47 | 82 | 143 | 267 | 349 | 454 | 634 |
| 2.09 | Eleanor | 65 | 31 | 29 | 49 | 122 | 267 | 404 | 637 | 748 | 599 | 309 |
| 0.32 | Elena | 410 | 393 | 391 | 464 | 419 | 463 | 442 | 412 | 360 | 329 | 218 |
| 9.82 | Elizabeth | 6 | 8 | 10 | 17 | 23 | 20 | 17 | 11 | 9 | 8 | 11 |
| 1.44 | Ella | 55 | 77 | 99 | 132 | 170 | 256 | 427 | 781 | 965 | 662 | 48 |
| 1.76 | Ellen | 78 | 86 | 101 | 101 | 70 | 79 | 117 | 252 | 264 | 226 | 485 |
| 0.32 | Eloise | 271 | 208 | 177 | 237 | 299 | 490 | 952 | | | | |
| 1.63 | Elsie | 35 | 43 | 67 | 109 | 190 | 360 | 567 | 845 | | | |
| 3.87 | Emily | 98 | 105 | 142 | 173 | 188 | 229 | 257 | 64 | 24 | 3 | 1 |
| 3.04 | Emma | 29 | 39 | 58 | 84 | 124 | 207 | 323 | 420 | 270 | 71 | 3 |

| Pop. | Name | 1900s | 1910s | 1920s | 1930s | 1940s | 1950s | 1960s | 1970s | 1980s | 1990s | 2000s |
|---|---|---|---|---|---|---|---|---|---|---|---|---|
| 1.12 | Erica | | | | | | 806 | 397 | 62 | 36 | 57 | 154 |
| 0.59 | Erika | | | | | | | 428 | 126 | 74 | 95 | 174 |
| 1.50 | Erin | | | | | | 446 | 217 | 41 | 28 | 48 | 81 |
| 0.48 | Erma | 157 | 145 | 162 | 197 | 279 | 440 | 735 | | | | |
| 0.30 | Ernestine | 300 | 250 | 210 | 226 | 273 | 384 | 582 | | | | |
| 0.33 | Essie | 160 | 181 | 214 | 276 | 406 | 661 | | | | | |
| 0.45 | Estelle | 124 | 123 | 175 | 279 | 431 | 708 | | | | | |
| 2.18 | Esther | 30 | 35 | 49 | 93 | 137 | 190 | 270 | 322 | 293 | 297 | 292 |
| 2.51 | Ethel | 12 | 22 | 41 | 81 | 144 | 239 | 471 | 890 | | | |
| 0.30 | Etta | 164 | 221 | 265 | 287 | 376 | 594 | 849 | | | | |
| 0.42 | Eula | 131 | 156 | 182 | 241 | 362 | 623 | | | | | |
| 0.64 | Eunice | 114 | 121 | 135 | 178 | 274 | 435 | 625 | 800 | 854 | 927 | |
| 1.84 | Eva | 39 | 53 | 69 | 105 | 151 | 187 | 226 | 300 | 311 | 349 | 192 |
| 3.94 | Evelyn | 34 | 11 | 13 | 31 | 61 | 98 | 142 | 209 | 224 | 205 | 92 |
| 0.53 | Faith | 767 | 596 | 540 | 351 | 365 | 339 | 338 | 392 | 355 | 176 | 50 |
| 0.68 | Fannie | 81 | 112 | 151 | 189 | 280 | 538 | 792 | | | | |
| 0.47 | Faye | 203 | 200 | 205 | 162 | 192 | 251 | 494 | 863 | | | |
| 0.47 | Felicia | 628 | 576 | 798 | 761 | 844 | 495 | 185 | 135 | 128 | 191 | 740 |
| 0.31 | Fern | 177 | 176 | 208 | 309 | 463 | 695 | | | | | |
| 0.55 | Flora | 110 | 130 | 161 | 211 | 277 | 422 | 599 | | | | |
| 3.07 | Florence | 11 | 14 | 22 | 59 | 135 | 272 | 420 | 661 | | | |
| 4.73 | Frances | 16 | 9 | 11 | 19 | 35 | 88 | 151 | 211 | 261 | 355 | 653 |
| 0.35 | Freda | 168 | 198 | 229 | 255 | 357 | 413 | 658 | 860 | | | |
| 0.31 | Gabriela | | | | | | | | 536 | 301 | 129 | 114 |
| 0.53 | Gabrielle | 977 | | | | | | 723 | 520 | 238 | 74 | 57 |
| 1.09 | Gail | 658 | 613 | 556 | 140 | 52 | 43 | 123 | 349 | 762 | | |
| 0.33 | Gayle | 910 | 764 | 736 | 267 | 164 | 158 | 281 | 579 | | | |
| 0.67 | Geneva | 170 | 115 | 117 | 148 | 233 | 350 | 519 | 665 | 703 | | |
| 0.81 | Genevieve | 109 | 80 | 111 | 201 | 326 | 549 | 626 | 537 | 417 | 539 | 419 |
| 1.02 | Georgia | 100 | 102 | 121 | 125 | 138 | 214 | 321 | 494 | 695 | 645 | 347 |
| 1.49 | Geraldine | 179 | 97 | 56 | 39 | 64 | 152 | 299 | 694 | 921 | | |
| 1.75 | Gertrude | 22 | 32 | 64 | 146 | 258 | 464 | 904 | | | | |
| 0.74 | Gina | | | | | | 900 | 227 | 73 | 89 | 121 | 189 | 468 |
| 2.78 | Gladys | 15 | 20 | 31 | 60 | 123 | 198 | 302 | 515 | 613 | 780 | |
| 0.58 | Glenda | | 836 | 638 | 200 | 97 | 127 | 198 | 329 | 653 | | |
| 2.61 | Gloria | 452 | 291 | 36 | 29 | 26 | 40 | 98 | 190 | 244 | 273 | 411 |
| 0.34 | Goldie | 126 | 172 | 228 | 348 | 589 | 844 | | | | | |
| 3.13 | Grace | 18 | 26 | 42 | 86 | 139 | 210 | 248 | 366 | 226 | 96 | 14 |
| 0.30 | Gracie | 318 | 322 | 295 | 295 | 424 | 523 | 757 | | | | 134 |
| 0.30 | Gretchen | 480 | 407 | 665 | 381 | 320 | 366 | 305 | 220 | 415 | 581 | 773 |
| 0.34 | Guadalupe | 419 | 470 | 326 | 399 | 342 | 401 | 491 | 400 | 390 | 230 | 253 |
| 0.67 | Gwendolyn | 320 | 257 | 218 | 188 | 147 | 134 | 188 | 311 | 516 | 682 | 623 |
| 0.52 | Hailey | | | | | | | | | 549 | 119 | 27 |
| 0.69 | Haley | | | | | | | | 810 | 212 | 49 | 39 |
| 1.86 | Hannah | 188 | 264 | 366 | 460 | 651 | 836 | 905 | 475 | 91 | 16 | 4 |

| Pop. | Name | 1900s | 1910s | 1920s | 1930s | 1940s | 1950s | 1960s | 1970s | 1980s | 1990s | 2000s |
|---|---|---|---|---|---|---|---|---|---|---|---|---|
| 0.70 | Harriet | 116 | 113 | 134 | 160 | 189 | 319 | 573 | | | | |
| 0.71 | Hattie | 74 | 111 | 149 | 199 | 257 | 441 | 789 | | | | |
| 2.18 | Hazel | 20 | 27 | 44 | 92 | 154 | 302 | 569 | 834 | | 854 | 639 |
| 2.68 | Heather | | | | | 585 | 381 | 127 | 8 | 10 | 38 | 195 |
| 0.66 | Heidi | | | | | 798 | 253 | 129 | 77 | 111 | 265 | 325 |
| 9.12 | Helen | 2 | 2 | 3 | 10 | 32 | 74 | 138 | 241 | 324 | 317 | 354 |
| 0.42 | Henrietta | 133 | 158 | 196 | 263 | 290 | 451 | 851 | | | | |
| 0.80 | Hilda | 91 | 103 | 132 | 170 | 201 | 297 | 429 | 575 | 814 | | |
| 0.97 | Holly | | | | | 426 | 183 | 132 | 58 | 59 | 114 | 256 |
| 0.40 | Hope | 522 | 431 | 388 | 474 | 471 | 418 | 317 | 246 | 356 | 223 | 168 |
| 1.48 | Ida | 41 | 55 | 79 | 127 | 174 | 284 | 398 | 598 | | | |
| 0.58 | Inez | 108 | 108 | 148 | 215 | 332 | 544 | 738 | | | | |
| 3.01 | Irene | 21 | 17 | 19 | 46 | 100 | 143 | 220 | 312 | 350 | 422 | 539 |
| 0.57 | Iris | 351 | 253 | 213 | 175 | 181 | 211 | 278 | 326 | 428 | 475 | 385 |
| 0.64 | Irma | 140 | 146 | 167 | 187 | 215 | 230 | 312 | 467 | 667 | 846 | |
| 0.73 | Isabel | 141 | 159 | 198 | 240 | 283 | 361 | 451 | 466 | 461 | 215 | 85 |
| 0.72 | Isabella | 312 | 382 | 477 | 702 | | | | | | 202 | 12 |
| 0.41 | Isabelle | 193 | 192 | 259 | 426 | 619 | 987 | | | | 440 | 110 |
| 0.31 | Iva | 151 | 199 | 250 | 277 | 483 | 737 | | | | | |
| 0.48 | Jackie | | 751 | 433 | 217 | 191 | 180 | 150 | 276 | 383 | 774 | |
| 2.20 | Jacqueline | 715 | 486 | 141 | 82 | 67 | 73 | 51 | 81 | 57 | 75 | 89 |
| 0.43 | Jacquelyn | | | 411 | 252 | 206 | 218 | 266 | 340 | 201 | 271 | 510 |
| 1.30 | Jamie | | | 959 | 1008 | 517 | 281 | 153 | 40 | 35 | 77 | 183 |
| 2.27 | Jane | 134 | 70 | 57 | 47 | 40 | 54 | 96 | 264 | 334 | 365 | 441 |
| 3.18 | Janet | 234 | 153 | 114 | 25 | 21 | 21 | 49 | 127 | 199 | 283 | 471 |
| 2.24 | Janice | 501 | 328 | 187 | 45 | 24 | 24 | 67 | 177 | 318 | 517 | 870 |
| 0.45 | Janie | 210 | 245 | 243 | 257 | 184 | 212 | 358 | 483 | 668 | 855 | |
| 1.05 | Jasmine | | | | | | | | 481 | 87 | 25 | 26 |
| 3.19 | Jean | 97 | 50 | 16 | 18 | 36 | 61 | 110 | 239 | 439 | 934 | |
| 1.04 | Jeanette | 197 | 137 | 136 | 103 | 120 | 156 | 178 | 206 | 268 | 401 | |
| 1.01 | Jeanne | 281 | 194 | 95 | 131 | 106 | 112 | 171 | 293 | 615 | | |
| 0.49 | Jeannette | 213 | 184 | 204 | 190 | 232 | 287 | 340 | 370 | 523 | | |
| 0.63 | Jenna | | | | | | | | 504 | 81 | 76 | 52 |
| 0.97 | Jennie | 69 | 81 | 122 | 191 | 281 | 326 | 393 | 337 | 384 | 683 | |
| 7.38 | Jennifer | | | | | 210 | 105 | 19 | 1 | 2 | 14 | 34 |
| 0.48 | Jenny | 566 | 614 | 484 | 415 | 392 | 292 | 265 | 133 | 152 | 266 | 413 |
| 5.16 | Jessica | 913 | 953 | | | 539 | 448 | 234 | 10 | 1 | 2 | 17 |
| 1.27 | Jessie | 61 | 67 | 93 | 136 | 202 | 315 | 468 | 438 | 247 | 267 | 472 |
| 1.01 | Jill | | | | | 484 | 207 | 110 | 61 | 57 | 122 | 527 |
| 0.35 | Jillian | | | | | | | | 439 | 113 | 158 | 140 |
| 0.98 | Jo | 869 | 622 | 258 | 96 | 62 | 72 | 184 | 363 | 784 | | |
| 3.12 | Joan | 360 | 206 | 60 | 7 | 25 | 47 | 112 | 350 | 543 | 866 | |
| 0.89 | Joann | | 789 | 286 | 77 | 77 | 131 | 164 | 265 | 478 | 841 | |
| 0.50 | Joanna | 573 | 570 | 451 | 349 | 324 | 403 | 298 | 187 | 137 | 174 | 249 |
| 1.19 | Joanne | | 703 | 236 | 56 | 56 | 84 | 122 | 212 | 423 | 706 | |

| Pop. | Name | 1900s | 1910s | 1920s | 1930s | 1940s | 1950s | 1960s | 1970s | 1980s | 1990s | 2000s |
|---|---|---|---|---|---|---|---|---|---|---|---|---|
| 0.37 | Jocelyn | | | | 951 | 999 | 515 | 584 | 401 | 277 | 147 | 94 |
| 0.39 | Jodi | | | | | | 425 | 146 | 105 | 218 | 603 | |
| 0.32 | Johanna | 235 | 297 | 424 | 481 | 444 | 568 | 534 | 330 | 259 | 436 | 449 |
| 0.35 | Johnnie | 291 | 242 | 202 | 213 | 230 | 353 | 577 | 968 | | | |
| 0.58 | Jordan | | | | | | | | | 198 | 52 | 56 |
| 2.44 | Josephine | 33 | 23 | 32 | 66 | 121 | 199 | 300 | 428 | 440 | 426 | 252 |
| 0.70 | Joy | 740 | 400 | 242 | 171 | 167 | 154 | 181 | 145 | 239 | 403 | 487 |
| 3.05 | Joyce | 390 | 237 | 65 | 12 | 19 | 31 | 87 | 221 | 424 | 609 | 734 |
| 1.51 | Juanita | 147 | 92 | 53 | 55 | 96 | 144 | 195 | 280 | 370 | 660 | |
| 2.60 | Judith | 448 | 383 | 293 | 40 | 8 | 33 | 97 | 255 | 395 | 481 | 593 |
| 2.06 | Judy | | 675 | 464 | 110 | 17 | 27 | 79 | 268 | 444 | 781 | |
| 2.87 | Julia | 45 | 40 | 62 | 97 | 105 | 128 | 113 | 129 | 88 | 59 | 31 |
| 2.49 | Julie | 530 | 517 | 483 | 311 | 140 | 44 | 18 | 20 | 51 | 125 | 244 |
| 1.27 | June | 266 | 106 | 46 | 54 | 119 | 163 | 276 | 587 | 886 | | |
| 0.68 | Kaitlyn | | | | | | | | | 234 | 51 | 35 |
| 0.45 | Kara | | | | | | | 360 | 144 | 105 | 138 | 240 |
| 4.89 | Karen | 929 | | | 141 | 15 | 8 | 3 | 24 | 80 | 128 | 156 |
| 0.43 | Karla | | | | | 459 | 252 | 189 | 240 | 219 | 197 | 193 |
| 0.35 | Kate | 236 | 330 | 531 | 753 | 792 | 931 | 754 | 423 | 216 | 299 | 171 |
| 0.54 | Katelyn | | | | | | | | | 194 | 62 | 54 |
| 3.64 | Katherine | 53 | 49 | 63 | 102 | 73 | 68 | 78 | 53 | 32 | 26 | 37 |
| 3.94 | Kathleen | 128 | 104 | 81 | 72 | 18 | 15 | 33 | 68 | 71 | 124 | 279 |
| 2.65 | Kathryn | 76 | 63 | 89 | 111 | 71 | 59 | 88 | 93 | 50 | 70 | 115 |
| 1.59 | Kathy | | | | 698 | 93 | 22 | 42 | 136 | 364 | 588 | 765 |
| 1.24 | Katie | 132 | 178 | 207 | 238 | 305 | 408 | 464 | 165 | 43 | 68 | 105 |
| 0.49 | Katrina | | | | | | 491 | 246 | 124 | 100 | 170 | 272 |
| 0.57 | Kay | 538 | 373 | 427 | 139 | 98 | 150 | 261 | 728 | | | |
| 1.49 | Kayla | | | | | | | 821 | 853 | 55 | 12 | 19 |
| 0.36 | Kaylee | | | | | | | | | 585 | 143 | 51 |
| 0.37 | Kelli | | | | | | 679 | 211 | 140 | 144 | 249 | 835 |
| 2.30 | Kelly | | | | | | 209 | 31 | 14 | 29 | 55 | 137 |
| 0.66 | Kelsey | | | | | | | | | 104 | 33 | 125 |
| 0.41 | Kendra | | | | | | 862 | 432 | 185 | 123 | 133 | 236 |
| 0.85 | Kim | | | | | 707 | 78 | 44 | 143 | 568 | | |
| 4.00 | Kimberly | | | | | 683 | 92 | 5 | 5 | 18 | 35 | 61 |
| 0.36 | Krista | | | | | | 727 | 349 | 148 | 127 | 182 | 503 |
| 1.06 | Kristen | | | | | 838 | 573 | 197 | 76 | 38 | 58 | 219 |
| 0.39 | Kristi | | | | | | 967 | 399 | 212 | 106 | 158 | 416 |
| 0.89 | Kristin | | | | | 577 | 427 | 159 | 75 | 42 | 111 | 412 |
| 0.66 | Kristina | | | | | 891 | 518 | 237 | 98 | 62 | 115 | 290 |
| 0.40 | Kristine | | | | | | 380 | 245 | 167 | 141 | 200 | 375 |
| 0.34 | Kristy | | | | | | 500 | 335 | 117 | 129 | 438 | |
| 0.35 | Krystal | | | | | | | 886 | 397 | 79 | 149 | 410 |
| 0.34 | Kylie | | | | | | | | 994 | 421 | 148 | 67 |
| 4.47 | Laura | 50 | 61 | 75 | 99 | 89 | 39 | 15 | 19 | 23 | 45 | 118 |

| Pop. | Name | 1900s | 1910s | 1920s | 1930s | 1940s | 1950s | 1960s | 1970s | 1980s | 1990s | 2000s |
|---|---|---|---|---|---|---|---|---|---|---|---|---|
| 2.16 | Lauren | | | | | 568 | 313 | 239 | 139 | 17 | 13 | 15 |
| 0.80 | Laurie | | | | 871 | 333 | 94 | 57 | 121 | 316 | 959 | |
| 0.29 | Laverne | 427 | 248 | 180 | 245 | 296 | 376 | 591 | | | | |
| 0.90 | Leah | 226 | 263 | 323 | 362 | 423 | 385 | 251 | 137 | 82 | 98 | 78 |
| 0.38 | Lee | 260 | 265 | 306 | 298 | 284 | 226 | 252 | 333 | 514 | | |
| 0.30 | Lela | 158 | 202 | 241 | 323 | 448 | 667 | 992 | | | | |
| 1.03 | Lena | 60 | 76 | 123 | 193 | 275 | 383 | 438 | 444 | 441 | 591 | 524 |
| 0.95 | Leona | 73 | 72 | 107 | 158 | 245 | 374 | 531 | 673 | | | |
| 1.30 | Leslie | 621 | 712 | 751 | 560 | 172 | 100 | 71 | 69 | 70 | 120 | 97 |
| 0.35 | Lila | 211 | 231 | 193 | 228 | 355 | 502 | 717 | | | | 516 |
| 3.21 | Lillian | 13 | 16 | 26 | 61 | 127 | 194 | 258 | 371 | 404 | 312 | 74 |
| 1.14 | Lillie | 56 | 75 | 100 | 128 | 171 | 301 | 492 | | | | 604 |
| 0.39 | Lily | 295 | 341 | 353 | 456 | 713 | 873 | 902 | | 705 | 326 | 66 |
| 7.50 | Linda | 327 | 338 | 324 | 95 | 2 | 2 | 7 | 63 | 133 | 224 | 403 |
| 0.61 | Lindsay | | | | | | | | 200 | 47 | 100 | 234 |
| 0.74 | Lindsey | | | | | | | | 328 | 44 | 64 | 131 |
| 4.70 | Lisa | | | | | 464 | 38 | 1 | 6 | 31 | 113 | 386 |
| 2.47 | Lois | 86 | 51 | 21 | 24 | 49 | 119 | 236 | 601 | | | |
| 0.58 | Lola | 112 | 135 | 166 | 195 | 268 | 377 | 646 | 861 | | | 584 |
| 0.30 | Lora | 262 | 310 | 385 | 416 | 461 | 342 | 232 | 325 | 552 | | |
| 0.31 | Lorene | 259 | 188 | 185 | 259 | 375 | 516 | 630 | | | | |
| 1.18 | Loretta | 115 | 117 | 130 | 88 | 108 | 139 | 176 | 308 | 616 | | |
| 1.62 | Lori | | | | | 881 | 81 | 16 | 35 | 140 | 490 | |
| 1.36 | Lorraine | 261 | 118 | 55 | 71 | 101 | 129 | 172 | 323 | 504 | 790 | |
| 0.38 | Lottie | 118 | 152 | 209 | 321 | 491 | 723 | | | | | |
| 2.80 | Louise | 24 | 18 | 25 | 42 | 84 | 146 | 273 | 614 | 973 | | |
| 0.33 | Lucile | 149 | 147 | 217 | 418 | 728 | | | | | | |
| 1.93 | Lucille | 49 | 30 | 40 | 85 | 142 | 236 | 497 | 865 | | | 950 |
| 1.18 | Lucy | 71 | 84 | 103 | 142 | 173 | 215 | 309 | 549 | 483 | 473 | 221 |
| 0.64 | Lula | 90 | 125 | 150 | 183 | 276 | 478 | 844 | | | | |
| 0.46 | Luz | 606 | 518 | 297 | 219 | 186 | 216 | 244 | 286 | 400 | 502 | 582 |
| 0.98 | Lydia | 111 | 167 | 188 | 167 | 162 | 175 | 235 | 285 | 232 | 190 | 132 |
| 0.39 | Lynda | | | | 486 | 115 | 162 | 213 | 484 | 780 | | |
| 0.91 | Lynn | 854 | 831 | 841 | 345 | 113 | 67 | 72 | 169 | 348 | 875 | |
| 0.30 | Lynne | | | | 448 | 180 | 164 | 210 | 555 | | | |
| 1.27 | Mabel | 27 | 60 | 115 | 212 | 372 | 747 | 911 | | | | |
| 0.44 | Mable | 146 | 142 | 170 | 230 | 334 | 620 | | | | | |
| 0.43 | Mackenzie | | | | | | | | | 525 | 106 | 44 |
| 1.01 | Madeline | 136 | 128 | 157 | 221 | 243 | 318 | 370 | 450 | 382 | 94 | 60 |
| 1.30 | Madison | | | | | | | | | 539 | 37 | 2 |
| 0.92 | Mae | 62 | 87 | 118 | 165 | 251 | 378 | 694 | | | | |
| 0.67 | Maggie | 104 | 154 | 190 | 244 | 339 | 524 | 663 | 542 | 328 | 263 | 194 |
| 0.32 | Makayla | | | | | | | | | | 180 | 49 |
| 0.60 | Mamie | 83 | 126 | 163 | 235 | 317 | 506 | 857 | | | | |
| 0.45 | Marcella | 229 | 179 | 171 | 227 | 301 | 334 | 412 | 497 | 642 | 868 | |

| Pop. | Name | 1900s | 1910s | 1920s | 1930s | 1940s | 1950s | 1960s | 1970s | 1980s | 1990s | 2000s |
|---|---|---|---|---|---|---|---|---|---|---|---|---|
| 0.73 | Marcia | 532 | 538 | 310 | 151 | 87 | 99 | 191 | 287 | 645 | | |
| 9.52 | Margaret | 3 | 4 | 5 | 8 | 14 | 23 | 54 | 101 | 95 | 107 | 127 |
| 0.40 | Margarita | 382 | 355 | 260 | 225 | 252 | 248 | 322 | 391 | 475 | 513 | 780 |
| 0.71 | Margie | 246 | 223 | 109 | 115 | 141 | 222 | 339 | 723 | | | |
| 0.82 | Marguerite | 82 | 82 | 125 | 204 | 269 | 320 | 513 | | | | |
| 4.33 | Maria | 59 | 69 | 61 | 38 | 39 | 36 | 32 | 26 | 41 | 42 | 42 |
| 0.38 | Mariah | | | | | | | | 898 | 586 | 78 | 95 |
| 1.07 | Marian | 119 | 90 | 71 | 104 | 163 | 204 | 362 | 668 | 722 | | |
| 0.34 | Marianne | 757 | 531 | 412 | 250 | 196 | 189 | 267 | 432 | 607 | | |
| 4.42 | Marie | 8 | 10 | 15 | 32 | 51 | 89 | 119 | 153 | 163 | 294 | 461 |
| 2.28 | Marilyn | | 539 | 88 | 16 | 29 | 56 | 139 | 263 | 359 | 462 | 537 |
| 1.64 | Marion | 54 | 48 | 47 | 89 | 148 | 238 | 392 | 663 | 959 | | |
| 0.54 | Marissa | | | | | | | 890 | 398 | 147 | 63 | 87 |
| 2.10 | Marjorie | 89 | 41 | 20 | 44 | 99 | 173 | 274 | 431 | 596 | | |
| 0.76 | Marlene | | | 842 | 63 | 112 | 149 | 253 | 361 | 433 | 463 | 527 |
| 0.53 | Marsha | | | | 419 | 117 | 104 | 209 | 253 | 562 | | |
| 3.87 | Martha | 31 | 25 | 24 | 26 | 30 | 46 | 93 | 163 | 209 | 289 | 455 |
| 29.26 | Mary | 1 | 1 | 1 | 1 | 1 | 1 | 2 | 15 | 34 | 41 | 55 |
| 0.33 | Maryann | 961 | 669 | 435 | 222 | 155 | 249 | 311 | 524 | 744 | | |
| 0.98 | Mattie | 68 | 88 | 104 | 144 | 198 | 349 | 597 | | | | 759 |
| 0.31 | Maude | 103 | 209 | 312 | 513 | 781 | | | | | | |
| 0.77 | Maureen | | 739 | 488 | 176 | 102 | 101 | 121 | 257 | 335 | 760 | |
| 0.81 | Maxine | 274 | 101 | 82 | 116 | 161 | 276 | 465 | | | | |
| 0.35 | May | 120 | 177 | 231 | 327 | 497 | 712 | | | | | |
| 2.10 | Megan | | | | | | 740 | 417 | 84 | 14 | 10 | 28 |
| 0.45 | Meghan | | | | | | | | 290 | 76 | 104 | 198 |
| 1.05 | Melanie | | | | | 348 | 172 | 114 | 56 | 83 | 109 | 98 |
| 0.65 | Melinda | | | | | 310 | 161 | 118 | 90 | 139 | 292 | |
| 3.74 | Melissa | 824 | 973 | | 917 | 513 | 160 | 34 | 3 | 7 | 27 | 90 |
| 0.38 | Melody | | | | | 393 | 213 | 192 | 214 | 245 | 381 | 314 |
| 0.33 | Mercedes | 336 | 290 | 299 | 305 | 403 | 520 | 683 | 724 | 495 | 187 | 324 |
| 0.35 | Meredith | | 920 | 731 | 625 | 504 | 531 | 472 | 180 | 157 | 229 | 333 |
| 0.46 | Mia | | | | | | | 500 | 485 | 403 | 227 | 36 |
| 1.08 | Michele | | | | | | 195 | 107 | 50 | 51 | 165 | 455 |
| 3.97 | Michelle | | | | | 304 | 96 | 9 | 4 | 12 | 31 | 64 |
| 4.34 | Mildred | 9 | 6 | 9 | 35 | 94 | 168 | 289 | 526 | 996 | | |
| 1.23 | Minnie | 43 | 66 | 106 | 143 | 204 | 359 | 616 | | | | |
| 0.47 | Miranda | | | | | | | 907 | 315 | 126 | 83 | 136 |
| 0.72 | Miriam | 173 | 150 | 160 | 209 | 231 | 232 | 269 | 344 | 321 | 287 | 282 |
| 0.42 | Misty | | | | | | | 415 | 78 | 103 | 471 | |
| 0.32 | Mollie | 162 | 232 | 321 | 429 | 511 | 713 | 858 | 777 | 590 | 508 | 668 |
| 0.72 | Molly | 378 | 352 | 416 | 390 | 377 | 344 | 307 | 186 | 108 | 93 | 103 |
| 1.26 | Monica | 514 | 439 | 523 | 417 | 359 | 178 | 86 | 45 | 58 | 84 | 206 |
| 0.38 | Monique | | | | | | 880 | 254 | 166 | 132 | 172 | 444 |
| 0.90 | Morgan | | | | | | | | 899 | 119 | 32 | 30 |

| Pop. | Name | 1900s | 1910s | 1920s | 1930s | 1940s | 1950s | 1960s | 1970s | 1980s | 1990s | 2000s |
|---|---|---|---|---|---|---|---|---|---|---|---|---|
| 0.45 | Muriel | 198 | 132 | 138 | 218 | 347 | 598 | | | | | |
| 0.34 | Myra | 303 | 298 | 304 | 275 | 249 | 262 | 351 | 554 | 631 | 804 | 997 |
| 1.25 | Myrtle | 40 | 58 | 92 | 157 | 272 | 560 | | | | | |
| 0.30 | Nadine | 551 | 301 | 253 | 254 | 315 | 312 | 354 | 525 | 662 | 761 | |
| 5.71 | Nancy | 125 | 100 | 66 | 9 | 7 | 9 | 26 | 74 | 116 | 153 | 263 |
| 0.84 | Naomi | 163 | 138 | 147 | 147 | 238 | 324 | 382 | 302 | 246 | 225 | 157 |
| 1.43 | Natalie | 391 | 296 | 251 | 269 | 371 | 338 | 187 | 108 | 54 | 53 | 22 |
| 0.44 | Natasha | | | | | | | 834 | 157 | 75 | 144 | 300 |
| 1.22 | Nellie | 48 | 62 | 91 | 135 | 222 | 380 | 652 | 971 | | | |
| 0.40 | Nettie | 113 | 160 | 216 | 278 | 378 | 652 | | | | | |
| 0.31 | Nichole | | | | | | | 895 | 159 | 106 | 233 | 693 |
| 2.84 | Nicole | | | | | 1006 | 881 | 186 | 12 | 8 | 17 | 41 |
| 0.75 | Nina | 154 | 164 | 184 | 194 | 242 | 241 | 296 | 335 | 213 | 255 | 250 |
| 0.76 | Nora | 95 | 148 | 178 | 207 | 239 | 235 | 306 | 379 | 401 | 464 | 353 |
| 2.00 | Norma | 155 | 119 | 37 | 28 | 65 | 115 | 162 | 235 | 377 | 532 | |
| 0.61 | Olga | 145 | 136 | 165 | 232 | 227 | 260 | 331 | 433 | 632 | 871 | |
| 0.42 | Olive | 106 | 133 | 203 | 341 | 675 | | | | | | |
| 1.34 | Olivia | 315 | 311 | 290 | 307 | 270 | 355 | 504 | 324 | 193 | 47 | 6 |
| 0.33 | Ollie | 148 | 193 | 237 | 264 | 405 | 645 | | | | | |
| 0.65 | Opal | 99 | 91 | 131 | 220 | 395 | 810 | | | | | |
| 0.32 | Ora | 159 | 182 | 240 | 283 | 402 | 571 | | | | | |
| 0.56 | Paige | | | | | | 988 | 449 | 479 | 255 | 65 | 59 |
| 2.87 | Pamela | | | 863 | 478 | 41 | 13 | 13 | 49 | 118 | 305 | 509 |
| 8.90 | Patricia | 287 | 170 | 30 | 5 | 4 | 3 | 6 | 32 | 61 | 126 | 295 |
| 0.75 | Patsy | 772 | 572 | 220 | 65 | 79 | 167 | 385 | 762 | | | |
| 0.34 | Patty | | | 413 | 210 | 203 | 195 | 199 | 591 | | | |
| 1.47 | Paula | 319 | 331 | 274 | 203 | 76 | 48 | 53 | 100 | 241 | 367 | 649 |
| 1.95 | Pauline | 52 | 33 | 39 | 76 | 130 | 220 | 314 | 453 | 673 | 885 | |
| 1.35 | Pearl | 36 | 54 | 90 | 156 | 267 | 415 | 618 | 997 | | | |
| 1.72 | Peggy | 325 | 272 | 129 | 36 | 43 | 53 | 108 | 251 | 637 | | |
| 0.47 | Penny | | | 656 | 183 | 147 | 105 | 202 | 675 | | | |
| 2.14 | Phyllis | 189 | 107 | 43 | 27 | 37 | 77 | 152 | 511 | | | |
| 0.66 | Priscilla | 357 | 304 | 227 | 214 | 146 | 224 | 290 | 289 | 174 | 196 | 307 |
| 0.39 | Rachael | 857 | 664 | 769 | | 991 | 989 | 619 | 216 | 117 | 132 | 304 |
| 2.92 | Rachel | 142 | 155 | 159 | 166 | 179 | 191 | 147 | 33 | 15 | 15 | 29 |
| 0.50 | Ramona | 309 | 262 | 206 | 161 | 225 | 200 | 227 | 406 | 723 | | |
| 3.79 | Rebecca | 161 | 169 | 176 | 169 | 68 | 29 | 40 | 13 | 22 | 24 | 58 |
| 0.32 | Rebekah | | | | | 940 | 766 | 712 | 273 | 161 | 156 | 220 |
| 1.02 | Regina | 182 | 186 | 189 | 253 | 185 | 135 | 84 | 109 | 187 | 377 | 606 |
| 0.91 | Renee | 842 | 715 | 490 | 377 | 265 | 130 | 74 | 88 | 120 | 232 | 454 |
| 0.98 | Rhonda | | | | | 340 | 75 | 46 | 92 | 303 | 853 | |
| 1.82 | Rita | 206 | 89 | 48 | 57 | 57 | 70 | 130 | 248 | 368 | 720 | |
| 1.07 | Roberta | 224 | 173 | 137 | 94 | 81 | 118 | 175 | 318 | 569 | | |
| 1.37 | Robin | | | | 957 | 294 | 49 | 36 | 70 | 131 | 308 | 887 |
| 0.29 | Robyn | | | | | 610 | 299 | 230 | 189 | 236 | 402 | 917 |

| Pop. | Name | 1900s | 1910s | 1920s | 1930s | 1940s | 1950s | 1960s | 1970s | 1980s | 1990s | 2000s |
|---|---|---|---|---|---|---|---|---|---|---|---|---|
| 1.44 | Rosa | 88 | 98 | 102 | 114 | 116 | 141 | 168 | 175 | 210 | 247 | 370 |
| 0.45 | Rosalie | 275 | 214 | 192 | 149 | 194 | 332 | 530 | 866 | 988 | | |
| 3.80 | Rose | 14 | 15 | 23 | 37 | 58 | 65 | 126 | 234 | 252 | 309 | 327 |
| 0.29 | Rosemarie | | 782 | 319 | 192 | 213 | 308 | 341 | 592 | 801 | | |
| 0.93 | Rosemary | 472 | 219 | 108 | 107 | 91 | 153 | 224 | 402 | 436 | 586 | 672 |
| 0.53 | Rosie | 175 | 166 | 168 | 174 | 214 | 275 | 473 | 734 | | | |
| 2.60 | Ruby | 42 | 24 | 27 | 48 | 104 | 179 | 294 | 362 | 380 | 264 | 179 |
| 6.97 | Ruth | 5 | 5 | 6 | 14 | 33 | 69 | 109 | 188 | 228 | 306 | 350 |
| 0.62 | Sabrina | | | | | | 406 | 241 | 130 | 125 | 89 | 138 |
| 0.63 | Sadie | 93 | 131 | 194 | 258 | 427 | 564 | 970 | | 617 | 347 | 196 |
| 0.34 | Sallie | 153 | 204 | 238 | 286 | 321 | 480 | 695 | | | | |
| 1.28 | Sally | 169 | 162 | 172 | 70 | 69 | 93 | 158 | 271 | 372 | 592 | 962 |
| 2.52 | Samantha | | | | | | | 272 | 107 | 26 | 5 | 8 |
| 4.61 | Sandra | | 942 | 606 | 50 | 6 | 12 | 11 | 39 | 94 | 168 | 283 |
| 0.34 | Sandy | | | | 849 | 266 | 246 | 166 | 275 | 336 | 484 | 823 |
| 2.29 | Sara | 129 | 116 | 126 | 133 | 131 | 166 | 161 | 50 | 30 | 44 | 65 |
| 5.76 | Sarah | 46 | 52 | 59 | 62 | 75 | 109 | 91 | 18 | 5 | 4 | 10 |
| 0.55 | Savannah | 720 | 803 | 927 | | | | | | 296 | 87 | 40 |
| 1.47 | Shannon | | | | | 566 | 357 | 125 | 21 | 39 | 72 | 222 |
| 3.72 | Sharon | | | 763 | 87 | 9 | 14 | 24 | 65 | 168 | 301 | 526 |
| 1.22 | Sheila | | | 452 | 182 | 85 | 64 | 59 | 118 | 240 | 530 | 815 |
| 0.69 | Shelby | | | | 266 | 350 | 503 | 568 | 372 | 312 | 39 | 93 |
| 0.34 | Shelley | | | | | 526 | 184 | 155 | 178 | 369 | | |
| 0.40 | Shelly | | | | | | 291 | 115 | 122 | 275 | 824 | |
| 0.29 | Sheri | | | | | 567 | 255 | 148 | 191 | 457 | | |
| 0.40 | Sherri | | | | | 520 | 208 | 94 | 170 | 450 | | |
| 1.13 | Sherry | | | | 370 | 103 | 66 | 55 | 95 | 300 | 795 | |
| 0.39 | Sheryl | | | | | 942 | 211 | 137 | 144 | 354 | 702 | |
| 4.52 | Shirley | 239 | 143 | 17 | 4 | 13 | 32 | 102 | 243 | 398 | 601 | 871 |
| 0.41 | Sierra | | | | | | | | | 297 | 88 | 76 |
| 0.44 | Sonia | 614 | 767 | 622 | 344 | 289 | 264 | 190 | 164 | 257 | 363 | 549 |
| 0.31 | Sonya | | | | | 510 | 590 | 455 | 177 | 147 | 291 | 654 |
| 0.82 | Sophia | 201 | 227 | 369 | 700 | 908 | 768 | 461 | 458 | 248 | 154 | 20 |
| 0.60 | Sophie | 121 | 109 | 174 | 401 | 722 | 967 | | | 838 | 370 | 145 |
| 0.72 | Stacey | | | | | | 442 | 106 | 47 | 93 | 298 | 774 |
| 0.82 | Stacy | | | | | | 421 | 111 | 38 | 72 | 328 | 643 |
| 1.08 | Stella | 66 | 64 | 112 | 181 | 212 | 311 | 456 | 640 | 879 | | 364 |
| 3.69 | Stephanie | 473 | 335 | 475 | 511 | 200 | 122 | 45 | 9 | 6 | 11 | 45 |
| 0.88 | Sue | 233 | 226 | 254 | 126 | 74 | 113 | 180 | 533 | 891 | | |
| 0.29 | Summer | | | | | | | | 305 | 223 | 164 | 149 |
| 5.71 | Susan | 156 | 185 | 219 | 121 | 10 | 4 | 4 | 28 | 96 | 240 | 514 |
| 0.59 | Susie | 107 | 144 | 181 | 243 | 234 | 273 | 350 | 562 | | | |
| 1.15 | Suzanne | 598 | 502 | 346 | 163 | 78 | 86 | 65 | 112 | 211 | 553 | |
| 0.67 | Sydney | | | | 791 | 657 | 791 | 947 | | 487 | 67 | 25 |
| 1.63 | Sylvia | 101 | 73 | 110 | 75 | 82 | 111 | 134 | 203 | 278 | 378 | 534 |

| Pop. | Name | 1900s | 1910s | 1920s | 1930s | 1940s | 1950s | 1960s | 1970s | 1980s | 1990s | 2000s |
|---|---|---|---|---|---|---|---|---|---|---|---|---|
| 0.65 | Tamara | | | | | 527 | 231 | 103 | 87 | 142 | 236 | 499 |
| 1.62 | Tammy | | | | | | 142 | 14 | 23 | 183 | 627 | |
| 0.57 | Tanya | | | | | 545 | 317 | 169 | 66 | 138 | 327 | 632 |
| 0.86 | Tara | | | | | | 522 | 233 | 43 | 52 | 141 | 311 |
| 1.33 | Taylor | | | | | | | | | 197 | 9 | 16 |
| 2.16 | Teresa | 195 | 228 | 200 | 208 | 134 | 28 | 25 | 48 | 124 | 228 | 409 |
| 0.70 | Terri | | | | | 374 | 95 | 63 | 146 | 325 | 827 | |
| 0.48 | Terry | | | 643 | 446 | 178 | 97 | 145 | 403 | 846 | | |
| 2.14 | Thelma | 38 | 28 | 35 | 67 | 143 | 237 | 391 | 711 | | | |
| 2.41 | Theresa | 94 | 96 | 76 | 74 | 90 | 41 | 43 | 82 | 135 | 256 | 551 |
| 1.66 | Tiffany | | | | | | | 320 | 44 | 11 | 34 | 150 |
| 1.46 | Tina | 488 | 609 | 649 | 712 | 407 | 125 | 30 | 30 | 109 | 333 | 709 |
| 0.49 | Toni | | | 866 | 576 | 220 | 169 | 154 | 184 | 229 | 303 | 688 |
| 0.59 | Tonya | | | | | | 434 | 120 | 52 | 166 | 575 | |
| 0.42 | Tracey | | | | | | 389 | 99 | 113 | 317 | 796 | |
| 1.22 | Tracy | | | | | 959 | 250 | 41 | 25 | 102 | 392 | 908 |
| 1.22 | Valerie | 654 | 533 | 525 | 302 | 176 | 85 | 70 | 97 | 84 | 136 | 161 |
| 1.16 | Vanessa | | | | | | 188 | 174 | 99 | 46 | 54 | 70 |
| 0.76 | Velma | 105 | 95 | 120 | 152 | 246 | 371 | 514 | | | | |
| 1.16 | Vera | 64 | 65 | 87 | 138 | 193 | 243 | 395 | 727 | | | |
| 0.58 | Verna | 123 | 129 | 152 | 184 | 262 | 346 | 507 | | | | |
| 1.20 | Veronica | 186 | 183 | 224 | 273 | 199 | 193 | 137 | 85 | 68 | 108 | 177 |
| 0.73 | Vicki | | | | 692 | 128 | 63 | 100 | 226 | 786 | | |
| 0.51 | Vickie | | | | 975 | 219 | 80 | 131 | 334 | | | |
| 2.30 | Victoria | 144 | 141 | 179 | 223 | 132 | 90 | 107 | 104 | 56 | 21 | 23 |
| 1.22 | Viola | 47 | 59 | 85 | 150 | 271 | 397 | 639 | | | | |
| 0.92 | Violet | 84 | 74 | 96 | 159 | 295 | 443 | 661 | | | | 482 |
| 4.73 | Virginia | 51 | 12 | 7 | 15 | 28 | 62 | 116 | 160 | 186 | 274 | 417 |
| 1.30 | Vivian | 127 | 78 | 73 | 112 | 129 | 148 | 221 | 380 | 491 | 330 | 245 |
| 1.80 | Wanda | 248 | 161 | 78 | 51 | 59 | 58 | 68 | 155 | 571 | | |
| 1.28 | Wendy | | | | | 250 | 108 | 47 | 37 | 136 | 258 | 293 |
| 0.45 | Whitney | | | | | | | 687 | 461 | 66 | 91 | 389 |
| 1.17 | Willie | 75 | 71 | 74 | 106 | 153 | 285 | 510 | | | | |
| 1.09 | Wilma | 139 | 94 | 70 | 83 | 133 | 233 | 439 | 743 | | | |
| 0.38 | Winifred | 166 | 157 | 183 | 280 | 379 | 659 | 1007 | | | | |
| 0.65 | Yolanda | 749 | 389 | 316 | 346 | 223 | 159 | 128 | 111 | 221 | 512 | |
| 0.31 | Yvette | | 761 | 694 | 780 | 587 | 340 | 173 | 233 | 323 | 443 | 742 |
| 0.91 | Yvonne | 289 | 321 | 215 | 123 | 125 | 124 | 135 | 176 | 287 | 435 | |
| 0.32 | Zoe | 710 | 928 | | 835 | | 981 | | | 853 | 193 | 63 |

# Boys' Names

The popularity rating to the left of the name indicates the frequency of usage per thousand baby boys born over the period from 1900 to 2006. A higher number represents greater popularity. For each decade in this time frame the **rank** of the name appears to the right of the name, a lower number meaning the name was more popular in that decade, 1 being the most popular.

| Pop. | Name | 1900s | 1910s | 1920s | 1930s | 1940s | 1950s | 1960s | 1970s | 1980s | 1990s | 2000s |
|---|---|---|---|---|---|---|---|---|---|---|---|---|
| 0.42 | A | 83 | 140 | 228 | 286 | 426 | 612 | 486 | 577 | 836 | | |
| 2.54 | Aaron | 193 | 208 | 218 | 274 | 279 | 232 | 132 | 36 | 32 | 31 | 49 |
| 0.49 | Abraham | 144 | 158 | 261 | 350 | 408 | 410 | 503 | 347 | 274 | 238 | 198 |
| 2.49 | Adam | 178 | 200 | 280 | 376 | 444 | 407 | 144 | 38 | 22 | 39 | 60 |
| 0.22 | Adolph | 156 | 185 | 281 | 406 | 640 | 734 | 827 | | | | |
| 0.83 | Adrian | 348 | 379 | 395 | 394 | 401 | 374 | 297 | 153 | 107 | 95 | 69 |
| 0.37 | Aidan | | | | | | | | | | 370 | 54 |
| 0.25 | Aiden | | | | | | | | | | 885 | 75 |
| 1.65 | Alan | 408 | 366 | 213 | 120 | 56 | 45 | 59 | 112 | 109 | 145 | 137 |
| 4.10 | Albert | 16 | 18 | 21 | 32 | 48 | 76 | 103 | 123 | 147 | 211 | 317 |
| 0.38 | Alberto | 404 | 488 | 411 | 360 | 341 | 311 | 288 | 236 | 213 | 219 | 272 |
| 0.22 | Alec | 968 | 954 | | | 997 | | 812 | 948 | 524 | 137 | 218 |
| 0.56 | Alejandro | 688 | 567 | 478 | 410 | 517 | 470 | 413 | 237 | 167 | 111 | 96 |
| 1.35 | Alex | 137 | 132 | 177 | 222 | 231 | 250 | 224 | 177 | 79 | 52 | 62 |
| 2.76 | Alexander | 101 | 99 | 141 | 188 | 199 | 212 | 204 | 102 | 48 | 24 | 16 |
| 0.29 | Alexis | | | | | | 933 | 594 | 355 | 255 | 182 | 135 |
| 0.26 | Alfonso | 341 | 348 | 310 | 301 | 357 | 357 | 389 | 416 | 392 | 440 | 520 |
| 2.09 | Alfred | 33 | 42 | 40 | 61 | 92 | 120 | 164 | 224 | 296 | 434 | 665 |
| 0.34 | Alfredo | 475 | 422 | 330 | 327 | 317 | 302 | 323 | 272 | 264 | 267 | 319 |
| 0.54 | Allan | 287 | 282 | 216 | 152 | 147 | 172 | 229 | 331 | 328 | 432 | 476 |
| 1.57 | Allen | 119 | 107 | 94 | 86 | 75 | 84 | 101 | 135 | 129 | 184 | 257 |
| 0.24 | Alonzo | 273 | 315 | 337 | 364 | 385 | 363 | 385 | 471 | 505 | 499 | 544 |
| 0.36 | Alton | 175 | 213 | 202 | 190 | 249 | 292 | 414 | 480 | 609 | 763 | |
| 1.18 | Alvin | 98 | 82 | 72 | 95 | 116 | 142 | 182 | 248 | 287 | 371 | 496 |
| 0.24 | Amos | 218 | 222 | 258 | 323 | 402 | 439 | 586 | 578 | 712 | 860 | |
| 0.52 | Andre | 969 | | 875 | 712 | 518 | 270 | 171 | 139 | 135 | 162 | 204 |
| 0.40 | Andres | 421 | 458 | 436 | 351 | 379 | 401 | 417 | 322 | 231 | 174 | 161 |
| 6.33 | Andrew | 40 | 46 | 57 | 71 | 86 | 67 | 38 | 28 | 13 | 6 | 5 |
| 0.42 | Andy | 343 | 332 | 396 | 383 | 370 | 289 | 226 | 231 | 262 | 253 | 206 |
| 1.34 | Angel | 361 | 288 | 192 | 145 | 128 | 146 | 149 | 129 | 110 | 93 | 45 |
| 0.47 | Angelo | 207 | 165 | 175 | 243 | 322 | 290 | 315 | 362 | 317 | 348 | 270 |
| 7.19 | Anthony | 43 | 35 | 42 | 46 | 44 | 30 | 22 | 22 | 20 | 18 | 12 |
| 1.49 | Antonio | 118 | 136 | 133 | 135 | 157 | 170 | 141 | 81 | 74 | 82 | 88 |
| 0.43 | Archie | 127 | 150 | 169 | 211 | 257 | 342 | 459 | 570 | 892 | | |

| Pop. | Name | 1900s | 1910s | 1920s | 1930s | 1940s | 1950s | 1960s | 1970s | 1980s | 1990s | 2000s |
|------|------|-------|-------|-------|-------|-------|-------|-------|-------|-------|-------|-------|
| 0.37 | Armando | 591 | 437 | 388 | 404 | 329 | 288 | 296 | 243 | 219 | 240 | 247 |
| 0.84 | Arnold | 116 | 97 | 100 | 113 | 150 | 208 | 250 | 454 | 554 | 590 | 928 |
| 4.35 | Arthur | 14 | 16 | 19 | 28 | 36 | 56 | 99 | 126 | 178 | 243 | 337 |
| 0.27 | Arturo | 660 | 627 | 451 | 422 | 423 | 341 | 332 | 326 | 281 | 282 | 296 |
| 0.23 | Aubrey | 242 | 247 | 277 | 288 | 360 | 440 | 536 | 647 | 663 | 777 | |
| 0.30 | August | 138 | 194 | 256 | 335 | 450 | 560 | 734 | 793 | 922 | 788 | 640 |
| 1.70 | Austin | 237 | 258 | 292 | 357 | 434 | 528 | 562 | 382 | 96 | 23 | 30 |
| 0.88 | Barry | | | 846 | 216 | 79 | 75 | 84 | 157 | 243 | 485 | 926 |
| 0.66 | Ben | 88 | 116 | 160 | 176 | 223 | 264 | 304 | 334 | 437 | 520 | 552 |
| 3.41 | Benjamin | 64 | 73 | 88 | 124 | 130 | 126 | 131 | 42 | 31 | 30 | 25 |
| 0.38 | Bennie | 213 | 180 | 189 | 185 | 213 | 291 | 390 | 549 | 654 | | |
| 0.29 | Benny | 513 | 444 | 299 | 197 | 197 | 246 | 345 | 452 | 634 | 793 | 920 |
| 1.59 | Bernard | 71 | 50 | 47 | 64 | 102 | 131 | 175 | 238 | 324 | 480 | 758 |
| 0.28 | Bert | 160 | 198 | 243 | 275 | 351 | 383 | 498 | 682 | | | |
| 0.99 | Bill | 255 | 191 | 91 | 66 | 81 | 136 | 137 | 342 | 664 | 963 | |
| 0.22 | Billie | 928 | 449 | 174 | 169 | 336 | 505 | 573 | 746 | | | |
| 2.29 | Billy | 770 | 329 | 48 | 20 | 41 | 69 | 74 | 84 | 140 | 255 | 426 |
| 0.59 | Blake | | | | | 783 | 462 | 376 | 332 | 119 | 85 | 85 |
| 0.58 | Bob | 443 | 345 | 138 | 89 | 122 | 225 | 199 | 583 | 947 | | |
| 1.79 | Bobby | | | 135 | 26 | 49 | 77 | 79 | 98 | 134 | 249 | 427 |
| 0.39 | Brad | | | | | 554 | 185 | 159 | 127 | 192 | 443 | 756 |
| 1.35 | Bradley | 834 | 939 | 684 | 442 | 271 | 122 | 75 | 58 | 54 | 79 | 159 |
| 0.29 | Brady | 886 | 711 | 957 | | 948 | 685 | 638 | 388 | 294 | 199 | 136 |
| 3.22 | Brandon | | | | | | 726 | 379 | 54 | 18 | 12 | 19 |
| 0.37 | Brendan | | | | | | 679 | 448 | 293 | 190 | 133 | 139 |
| 0.64 | Brent | | | | 797 | 323 | 209 | 127 | 85 | 99 | 183 | 389 |
| 0.71 | Brett | | | | | | 271 | 135 | 96 | 78 | 106 | 216 |
| 5.47 | Brian | | | | 324 | 113 | 35 | 16 | 8 | 16 | 36 | 56 |
| 1.99 | Bruce | 236 | 182 | 137 | 87 | 40 | 32 | 48 | 133 | 177 | 318 | 478 |
| 1.72 | Bryan | 482 | 762 | 615 | 537 | 347 | 150 | 65 | 47 | 51 | 56 | 64 |
| 0.23 | Bryant | 850 | 842 | 731 | 886 | 704 | 492 | 349 | 320 | 246 | 278 | 324 |
| 0.39 | Bryce | | | 732 | 826 | 804 | 669 | 614 | 383 | 242 | 139 | 105 |
| 0.45 | Byron | 250 | 245 | 252 | 253 | 230 | 233 | 234 | 244 | 257 | 343 | 497 |
| 0.45 | C | 75 | 149 | 255 | 313 | 465 | 633 | 342 | 447 | 670 | | |
| 0.88 | Caleb | 869 | | | | | | | 405 | 143 | 57 | 35 |
| 1.07 | Calvin | 199 | 167 | 83 | 127 | 129 | 116 | 145 | 187 | 187 | 194 | 221 |
| 0.94 | Cameron | | | | | | 607 | 440 | 250 | 124 | 53 | 39 |
| 3.89 | Carl | 20 | 24 | 26 | 29 | 39 | 48 | 60 | 94 | 116 | 204 | 359 |
| 1.76 | Carlos | 222 | 234 | 182 | 147 | 136 | 114 | 93 | 60 | 64 | 58 | 65 |
| 0.30 | Carlton | 315 | 286 | 250 | 263 | 286 | 260 | 316 | 371 | 412 | 578 | 977 |
| 0.28 | Carroll | 229 | 237 | 222 | 195 | 243 | 385 | 528 | 847 | | | |
| 0.29 | Carson | 679 | 574 | 656 | 728 | 607 | 735 | 804 | 721 | 543 | 337 | 100 |
| 0.30 | Carter | 646 | 643 | 720 | 660 | 576 | 624 | 679 | 722 | 720 | 326 | 97 |
| 0.50 | Casey | | 763 | | | 889 | 453 | 398 | 147 | 84 | 120 | 249 |
| 1.01 | Cecil | 70 | 71 | 87 | 116 | 154 | 219 | 300 | 431 | 489 | 778 | |

| Pop. | Name | 1900s | 1910s | 1920s | 1930s | 1940s | 1950s | 1960s | 1970s | 1980s | 1990s | 2000s |
|---|---|---|---|---|---|---|---|---|---|---|---|---|
| 0.31 | Cesar | | | | 750 | 608 | 546 | 467 | 286 | 244 | 177 | 168 |
| 1.15 | Chad | | | | | 1,000 | 557 | 177 | 30 | 55 | 127 | 316 |
| 16.12 | Charles | 6 | 7 | 5 | 6 | 7 | 10 | 17 | 23 | 34 | 43 | 58 |
| 1.22 | Charlie | 60 | 66 | 73 | 104 | 131 | 188 | 247 | 296 | 351 | 456 | 377 |
| 0.48 | Chase | | | | | | | | 809 | 171 | 98 | 80 |
| 1.10 | Chester | 65 | 54 | 71 | 130 | 156 | 221 | 305 | 373 | 560 | 840 | |
| 0.70 | Chris | 323 | 508 | 510 | 501 | 239 | 128 | 61 | 109 | 333 | 451 | 387 |
| 1.62 | Christian | 297 | 434 | 603 | 617 | 621 | 392 | 253 | 117 | 90 | 33 | 23 |
| 9.22 | Christopher | 333 | 349 | 385 | 367 | 155 | 49 | 20 | 2 | 2 | 2 | 6 |
| 2.94 | Clarence | 18 | 23 | 29 | 45 | 80 | 112 | 172 | 222 | 278 | 489 | 699 |
| 0.25 | Clark | 294 | 309 | 357 | 289 | 290 | 294 | 324 | 579 | 564 | 630 | 750 |
| 0.84 | Claude | 73 | 88 | 106 | 137 | 165 | 230 | 318 | 467 | 624 | 977 | |
| 0.72 | Clayton | 174 | 163 | 167 | 192 | 233 | 253 | 272 | 229 | 168 | 167 | 189 |
| 1.48 | Clifford | 63 | 59 | 64 | 83 | 104 | 119 | 160 | 221 | 249 | 508 | 883 |
| 0.48 | Clifton | 197 | 161 | 179 | 198 | 217 | 243 | 291 | 283 | 319 | 631 | 982 |
| 0.59 | Clinton | 203 | 188 | 186 | 209 | 245 | 249 | 249 | 167 | 156 | 320 | 718 |
| 1.24 | Clyde | 59 | 64 | 69 | 91 | 123 | 174 | 262 | 394 | 527 | 766 | |
| 1.24 | Cody | | | | | | 856 | 639 | 239 | 61 | 26 | 73 |
| 0.44 | Cole | | | | | | | 998 | 715 | 270 | 112 | 71 |
| 0.46 | Colin | | | | 813 | 488 | 479 | 394 | 271 | 165 | 131 | 106 |
| 0.27 | Collin | | | | | 950 | | 891 | 587 | 338 | 154 | 143 |
| 0.28 | Colton | | | | | | | | | 456 | 122 | 132 |
| 0.63 | Connor | | | | | | | | | 515 | 71 | 47 |
| 0.23 | Conrad | 289 | 326 | 297 | 250 | 335 | 405 | 542 | 610 | 586 | 661 | 735 |
| 0.82 | Corey | | | | | | 593 | 256 | 72 | 65 | 74 | 195 |
| 0.26 | Cornelius | 211 | 272 | 311 | 316 | 432 | 432 | 490 | 400 | 409 | 565 | 855 |
| 0.58 | Cory | | | | | | 626 | 341 | 100 | 73 | 103 | 306 |
| 1.43 | Craig | 1005 | 846 | 707 | 439 | 126 | 53 | 45 | 56 | 82 | 193 | 422 |
| 0.22 | Cristian | | | | | | | | | 561 | 166 | 151 |
| 1.46 | Curtis | 148 | 123 | 118 | 112 | 103 | 86 | 78 | 97 | 104 | 169 | 303 |
| 0.36 | Dakota | | | | | | | | | 548 | 81 | 120 |
| 1.61 | Dale | 225 | 142 | 90 | 62 | 62 | 51 | 71 | 151 | 236 | 381 | 560 |
| 0.29 | Dallas | 372 | 336 | 316 | 282 | 321 | 382 | 463 | 418 | 336 | 294 | 345 |
| 0.35 | Dalton | 809 | 584 | 506 | 569 | 602 | 736 | 920 | | 673 | 110 | 134 |
| 0.23 | Damian | | | | | | 849 | 605 | 299 | 331 | 230 | 171 |
| 0.28 | Damon | | | 933 | 815 | 662 | 553 | 281 | 144 | 349 | 310 | 311 |
| 0.63 | Dan | 184 | 205 | 187 | 165 | 134 | 130 | 155 | 349 | 516 | 802 | |
| 0.27 | Dana | 583 | 723 | 628 | 635 | 294 | 183 | 215 | 267 | 390 | 663 | |
| 9.22 | Daniel | 56 | 55 | 44 | 40 | 22 | 19 | 18 | 11 | 6 | 7 | 7 |
| 1.34 | Danny | | | 545 | 217 | 59 | 44 | 58 | 95 | 144 | 218 | 289 |
| 0.82 | Darrell | 647 | 399 | 265 | 153 | 137 | 95 | 100 | 142 | 197 | 340 | 547 |
| 0.45 | Darren | | | | | | 539 | 107 | 128 | 183 | 222 | 323 |
| 0.43 | Darryl | | | | 509 | 258 | 195 | 96 | 259 | 229 | 372 | 651 |
| 0.30 | Daryl | | | 675 | 461 | 285 | 189 | 179 | 208 | 316 | 606 | 934 |
| 0.35 | Dave | 256 | 314 | 386 | 268 | 172 | 197 | 193 | 485 | 721 | | |

| Pop. | Name | 1900s | 1910s | 1920s | 1930s | 1940s | 1950s | 1960s | 1970s | 1980s | 1990s | 2000s |
|------|------|-------|-------|-------|-------|-------|-------|-------|-------|-------|-------|-------|
| 18.28 | David | 29 | 30 | 22 | 11 | 6 | 5 | 2 | 4 | 5 | 11 | 13 |
| 0.87 | Dean | 334 | 231 | 162 | 134 | 153 | 107 | 88 | 183 | 271 | 319 | 373 |
| 0.36 | Delbert | 230 | 181 | 172 | 166 | 246 | 333 | 424 | 598 | 878 | | |
| 3.16 | Dennis | 227 | 204 | 181 | 74 | 20 | 21 | 40 | 62 | 97 | 173 | 280 |
| 0.99 | Derek | | | | | 806 | 347 | 167 | 76 | 53 | 73 | 148 |
| 0.63 | Derrick | | | | | | 308 | 158 | 87 | 83 | 149 | 242 |
| 0.61 | Devin | | | | | | | 517 | 298 | 130 | 72 | 79 |
| 0.30 | Devon | | | | | | | 738 | 478 | 240 | 128 | 166 |
| 0.27 | Dewey | 192 | 262 | 208 | 242 | 288 | 394 | 533 | 611 | 894 | | |
| 0.32 | Diego | 860 | | | | 1001 | 918 | 884 | 669 | 407 | 242 | 82 |
| 0.25 | Dillon | | | | | | | | | 385 | 115 | 196 |
| 0.58 | Dominic | 327 | 239 | 288 | 395 | 414 | 390 | 371 | 258 | 209 | 146 | 92 |
| 0.33 | Dominick | 277 | 235 | 274 | 343 | 431 | 446 | 470 | 508 | 402 | 306 | 227 |
| 1.07 | Don | 216 | 171 | 110 | 57 | 87 | 115 | 146 | 247 | 360 | 607 | |
| 9.03 | Donald | 51 | 20 | 10 | 7 | 12 | 14 | 25 | 44 | 67 | 125 | 256 |
| 0.30 | Donnie | | 925 | 848 | 296 | 182 | 178 | 240 | 279 | 457 | 691 | |
| 0.22 | Donovan | 973 | 880 | 849 | 701 | 826 | 802 | 591 | 435 | 414 | 251 | 194 |
| 2.85 | Douglas | 200 | 154 | 112 | 72 | 30 | 28 | 30 | 52 | 76 | 151 | 318 |
| 0.29 | Drew | | | | | 598 | 429 | 402 | 359 | 188 | 178 | 211 |
| 0.63 | Duane | 716 | 440 | 178 | 119 | 140 | 140 | 140 | 200 | 377 | 692 | |
| 0.93 | Dustin | | | | | | | 625 | 113 | 45 | 66 | 201 |
| 0.35 | Dwayne | | | 734 | 490 | 387 | 257 | 130 | 181 | 259 | 403 | 608 |
| 0.44 | Dwight | 270 | 300 | 294 | 255 | 173 | 152 | 219 | 300 | 388 | 538 | 943 |
| 1.23 | Dylan | | | | | | | | 392 | 193 | 37 | 22 |
| 0.32 | E | 94 | 166 | 328 | 443 | 738 | 704 | 534 | 650 | 925 | | |
| 2.55 | Earl | 27 | 31 | 31 | 44 | 72 | 111 | 163 | 210 | 288 | 486 | 834 |
| 0.41 | Earnest | 208 | 168 | 152 | 186 | 214 | 285 | 397 | 473 | 616 | | |
| 1.29 | Eddie | 126 | 122 | 107 | 92 | 78 | 96 | 114 | 169 | 214 | 286 | 379 |
| 1.08 | Edgar | 78 | 86 | 101 | 146 | 186 | 247 | 286 | 269 | 207 | 147 | 173 |
| 0.41 | Edmund | 153 | 146 | 165 | 227 | 262 | 300 | 386 | 517 | 717 | 879 | |
| 0.51 | Eduardo | 592 | 585 | 538 | 433 | 430 | 349 | 301 | 226 | 194 | 121 | 126 |
| 9.25 | Edward | 9 | 8 | 9 | 12 | 18 | 23 | 29 | 40 | 57 | 80 | 127 |
| 1.88 | Edwin | 55 | 53 | 56 | 77 | 100 | 105 | 125 | 148 | 162 | 164 | 179 |
| 0.29 | Elbert | 202 | 174 | 198 | 236 | 328 | 441 | 561 | 707 | | | |
| 0.28 | Eli | 351 | 351 | 371 | 492 | 583 | 587 | 654 | 415 | 344 | 345 | 183 |
| 0.25 | Elias | 353 | 445 | 502 | 424 | 473 | 584 | 575 | 448 | 372 | 342 | 209 |
| 0.75 | Elijah | 370 | 361 | 334 | 417 | 457 | 519 | 663 | 481 | 292 | 118 | 38 |
| 0.29 | Ellis | 191 | 209 | 225 | 279 | 308 | 365 | 516 | 679 | 771 | 956 | 816 |
| 1.37 | Elmer | 36 | 45 | 60 | 115 | 178 | 283 | 407 | 536 | 752 | 683 | 779 |
| 0.27 | Emanuel | 260 | 330 | 329 | 391 | 494 | 520 | 558 | 484 | 318 | 361 | 291 |
| 0.34 | Emil | 117 | 144 | 214 | 283 | 452 | 644 | 666 | 883 | | | |
| 0.22 | Emilio | 335 | 424 | 393 | 381 | 427 | 468 | 602 | 567 | 495 | 366 | 315 |
| 0.24 | Emmanuel | | | | | | 850 | 708 | 532 | 203 | 202 | 181 |
| 0.29 | Emmett | 165 | 192 | 239 | 304 | 383 | 459 | 592 | 769 | 981 | 855 | 642 |
| 0.34 | Enrique | 477 | 438 | 333 | 336 | 326 | 353 | 362 | 288 | 266 | 250 | 250 |

| Pop. | Name | 1900s | 1910s | 1920s | 1930s | 1940s | 1950s | 1960s | 1970s | 1980s | 1990s | 2000s |
|---|---|---|---|---|---|---|---|---|---|---|---|---|
| 4.14 | Eric | 254 | 427 | 487 | 317 | 159 | 74 | 27 | 14 | 21 | 29 | 57 |
| 0.28 | Erick | 905 | | | | | 752 | 388 | 273 | 253 | 198 | 185 |
| 0.67 | Erik | 976 | | | | 784 | 489 | 187 | 91 | 89 | 108 | 165 |
| 2.57 | Ernest | 26 | 33 | 37 | 51 | 67 | 92 | 129 | 171 | 222 | 382 | 600 |
| 0.26 | Ernesto | 706 | 512 | 426 | 331 | 386 | 364 | 367 | 307 | 307 | 332 | 343 |
| 0.30 | Ervin | 205 | 199 | 193 | 258 | 338 | 369 | 461 | 595 | 841 | 889 | |
| 1.23 | Ethan | | | | | | 954 | 633 | 346 | 234 | 60 | 9 |
| 2.86 | Eugene | 49 | 40 | 25 | 24 | 51 | 83 | 118 | 162 | 226 | 390 | 573 |
| 0.92 | Evan | 481 | 510 | 547 | 553 | 567 | 483 | 331 | 274 | 92 | 67 | 48 |
| 0.75 | Everett | 86 | 93 | 109 | 158 | 195 | 267 | 322 | 441 | 549 | 568 | 555 |
| 0.22 | Felipe | 484 | 479 | 368 | 369 | 371 | 408 | 434 | 377 | 406 | 401 | 443 |
| 0.61 | Felix | 149 | 155 | 176 | 170 | 206 | 231 | 255 | 246 | 310 | 338 | 384 |
| 0.50 | Fernando | 529 | 501 | 387 | 318 | 320 | 263 | 290 | 216 | 191 | 160 | 155 |
| 1.36 | Floyd | 50 | 62 | 58 | 80 | 120 | 175 | 244 | 323 | 469 | 798 | |
| 0.35 | Forrest | 179 | 186 | 219 | 262 | 314 | 359 | 481 | 475 | 530 | 355 | 968 |
| 2.34 | Francis | 37 | 34 | 35 | 50 | 71 | 102 | 157 | 218 | 260 | 353 | 501 |
| 0.99 | Francisco | 164 | 164 | 155 | 148 | 169 | 198 | 196 | 155 | 126 | 123 | 150 |
| 7.43 | Frank | 8 | 9 | 12 | 16 | 21 | 34 | 44 | 65 | 91 | 152 | 225 |
| 0.88 | Franklin | 167 | 137 | 139 | 75 | 127 | 160 | 194 | 249 | 279 | 356 | 466 |
| 3.01 | Fred | 19 | 25 | 34 | 34 | 53 | 99 | 138 | 242 | 391 | 619 | |
| 0.44 | Freddie | 478 | 320 | 227 | 156 | 151 | 194 | 268 | 350 | 424 | 610 | |
| 1.83 | Frederick | 62 | 56 | 62 | 70 | 74 | 88 | 115 | 137 | 201 | 315 | 436 |
| 0.35 | Fredrick | 464 | 298 | 260 | 256 | 226 | 227 | 289 | 264 | 382 | 528 | 801 |
| 1.18 | Gabriel | 429 | 377 | 358 | 407 | 435 | 387 | 313 | 114 | 87 | 68 | 33 |
| 0.56 | Garrett | 683 | 682 | 855 | 697 | 571 | 566 | 474 | 311 | 141 | 86 | 101 |
| 0.22 | Garry | | | | | 413 | 191 | 161 | 299 | 432 | 593 | |
| 4.43 | Gary | 747 | 677 | 525 | 47 | 14 | 12 | 26 | 48 | 80 | 170 | 313 |
| 0.45 | Gavin | | | | | | | 598 | 533 | 337 | 208 | 55 |
| 0.81 | Gene | 399 | 226 | 111 | 67 | 99 | 159 | 190 | 308 | 443 | 704 | |
| 0.24 | Geoffrey | | | | | 372 | 279 | 282 | 212 | 210 | 369 | 836 |
| 11.71 | George | 4 | 6 | 6 | 8 | 15 | 25 | 33 | 49 | 72 | 105 | 138 |
| 2.83 | Gerald | 120 | 83 | 45 | 21 | 26 | 46 | 62 | 104 | 175 | 269 | 460 |
| 0.34 | Gerard | 415 | 291 | 266 | 246 | 218 | 202 | 257 | 390 | 526 | 675 | |
| 0.26 | Gerardo | 863 | 943 | 825 | 819 | 663 | 562 | 330 | 301 | 267 | 225 | 237 |
| 0.94 | Gilbert | 121 | 105 | 105 | 106 | 139 | 158 | 191 | 253 | 280 | 428 | 583 |
| 0.85 | Glen | 146 | 125 | 122 | 126 | 144 | 132 | 150 | 241 | 361 | 557 | 986 |
| 1.59 | Glenn | 102 | 90 | 80 | 84 | 83 | 68 | 72 | 168 | 230 | 410 | 674 |
| 1.11 | Gordon | 122 | 92 | 81 | 79 | 107 | 135 | 185 | 281 | 368 | 521 | 743 |
| 0.28 | Grady | 257 | 220 | 237 | 248 | 309 | 388 | 495 | 574 | 796 | 832 | 589 |
| 0.55 | Grant | 288 | 283 | 300 | 339 | 344 | 313 | 303 | 282 | 189 | 140 | 140 |
| 0.36 | Greg | | | | | 297 | 163 | 105 | 215 | 465 | 773 | |
| 3.33 | Gregory | 497 | 502 | 375 | 319 | 66 | 26 | 23 | 29 | 46 | 70 | 180 |
| 0.62 | Guy | 125 | 145 | 163 | 187 | 208 | 166 | 195 | 327 | 474 | 653 | 914 |
| 0.31 | H | 97 | 173 | 332 | 456 | 726 | 778 | 509 | 708 | | | |
| 0.25 | Harley | 253 | 256 | 267 | 297 | 398 | 530 | 669 | 711 | 587 | 429 | 467 |

| Pop. | Name | 1900s | 1910s | 1920s | 1930s | 1940s | 1950s | 1960s | 1970s | 1980s | 1990s | 2000s |
|---|---|---|---|---|---|---|---|---|---|---|---|---|
| 4.83 | Harold | 15 | 13 | 14 | 19 | 28 | 64 | 102 | 160 | 251 | 411 | 598 |
| 0.28 | Harrison | 338 | 304 | 347 | 414 | 475 | 563 | 694 | 823 | 436 | 231 | 207 |
| 3.86 | Harry | 13 | 19 | 23 | 36 | 52 | 89 | 142 | 203 | 290 | 388 | 530 |
| 0.97 | Harvey | 81 | 91 | 93 | 102 | 121 | 207 | 283 | 428 | 614 | 991 | |
| 0.29 | Hayden | 802 | 741 | | | 938 | | | | 983 | 207 | 89 |
| 0.73 | Hector | 557 | 547 | 415 | 224 | 171 | 162 | 162 | 145 | 142 | 150 | 188 |
| 5.02 | Henry | 10 | 12 | 18 | 25 | 35 | 58 | 97 | 118 | 133 | 143 | 111 |
| 2.05 | Herbert | 32 | 39 | 36 | 55 | 98 | 139 | 207 | 284 | 421 | 623 | |
| 1.32 | Herman | 45 | 52 | 70 | 96 | 145 | 203 | 273 | 361 | 521 | 782 | |
| 0.61 | Homer | 91 | 103 | 115 | 161 | 242 | 361 | 524 | 724 | | | |
| 0.48 | Horace | 133 | 128 | 143 | 194 | 229 | 301 | 471 | 670 | 849 | | |
| 2.83 | Howard | 30 | 26 | 28 | 38 | 54 | 85 | 124 | 196 | 323 | 561 | 725 |
| 0.54 | Hubert | 131 | 117 | 123 | 157 | 227 | 328 | 501 | 599 | 865 | | |
| 0.67 | Hugh | 108 | 111 | 127 | 143 | 184 | 234 | 312 | 461 | 677 | 803 | 868 |
| 0.72 | Hunter | 776 | 778 | 938 | | 939 | 813 | 896 | 834 | 342 | 78 | 40 |
| 0.81 | Ian | | | | 999 | 813 | 619 | 378 | 158 | 85 | 69 | 66 |
| 0.41 | Ira | 134 | 162 | 196 | 230 | 238 | 280 | 381 | 498 | 640 | | |
| 0.32 | Irvin | 181 | 183 | 199 | 271 | 339 | 442 | 549 | 760 | 691 | 513 | 643 |
| 0.46 | Irving | 113 | 114 | 150 | 277 | 416 | 498 | 673 | 795 | 806 | 696 | 913 |
| 0.99 | Isaac | 171 | 197 | 203 | 260 | 269 | 322 | 383 | 211 | 154 | 102 | 50 |
| 0.62 | Isaiah | 777 | 630 | 601 | 583 | 619 | 700 | 1002 | 734 | 308 | 116 | 43 |
| 0.24 | Ismael | | 728 | 432 | 302 | 303 | 372 | 449 | 385 | 367 | 331 | 327 |
| 0.31 | Israel | 416 | 522 | 485 | 421 | 364 | 376 | 395 | 278 | 301 | 264 | 229 |
| 0.67 | Ivan | 196 | 184 | 194 | 213 | 295 | 275 | 284 | 245 | 208 | 165 | 131 |
| 1.43 | J | 35 | 57 | 63 | 100 | 176 | 255 | 180 | 198 | 276 | 725 | |
| 4.18 | Jack | 41 | 29 | 17 | 18 | 37 | 57 | 106 | 161 | 176 | 113 | 41 |
| 0.43 | Jackie | | | 341 | 125 | 142 | 168 | 254 | 312 | 512 | 757 | |
| 0.56 | Jackson | 498 | 404 | 437 | 487 | 495 | 662 | 862 | 668 | 493 | 175 | 51 |
| 3.81 | Jacob | 96 | 126 | 173 | 234 | 283 | 329 | 344 | 83 | 35 | 5 | 1 |
| 0.38 | Jaime | | 997 | 633 | 462 | 367 | 295 | 245 | 185 | 195 | 214 | 262 |
| 0.52 | Jake | 262 | 312 | 323 | 479 | 484 | 630 | 751 | 453 | 225 | 117 | 103 |
| 31.81 | James | 3 | 3 | 3 | 2 | 1 | 2 | 4 | 5 | 7 | 13 | 18 |
| 0.40 | Jamie | | | | | 779 | 436 | 258 | 77 | 157 | 270 | 536 |
| 0.90 | Jared | | | | | | | 520 | 115 | 58 | 59 | 93 |
| 4.81 | Jason | 717 | 707 | 667 | 679 | 563 | 420 | 87 | 3 | 11 | 45 | 42 |
| 0.46 | Javier | | | | 891 | 585 | 406 | 259 | 164 | 159 | 144 | 157 |
| 0.98 | Jay | 234 | 216 | 191 | 154 | 135 | 103 | 90 | 122 | 184 | 260 | 336 |
| 0.25 | Jayden | | | | | | | | | | 758 | 74 |
| 0.59 | Jeff | 320 | 448 | 481 | 468 | 260 | 134 | 55 | 204 | 428 | 744 | |
| 1.05 | Jeffery | | | | | 312 | 87 | 47 | 70 | 100 | 203 | 388 |
| 4.54 | Jeffrey | | | | 619 | 89 | 24 | 10 | 15 | 30 | 55 | 142 |
| 0.61 | Jeremiah | 472 | 652 | 548 | 571 | 612 | 600 | 729 | 159 | 106 | 157 | 84 |
| 1.99 | Jeremy | | | | | 981 | 740 | 368 | 24 | 28 | 47 | 107 |
| 0.97 | Jerome | 204 | 147 | 124 | 101 | 118 | 117 | 152 | 175 | 211 | 349 | 531 |
| 3.39 | Jerry | 180 | 169 | 108 | 23 | 19 | 31 | 41 | 63 | 114 | 192 | 282 |

| Pop. | Name | 1900s | 1910s | 1920s | 1930s | 1940s | 1950s | 1960s | 1970s | 1980s | 1990s | 2000s |
|---|---|---|---|---|---|---|---|---|---|---|---|---|
| 2.31 | Jesse | 68 | 77 | 89 | 110 | 115 | 127 | 139 | 69 | 49 | 50 | 95 |
| 0.73 | Jessie | 139 | 124 | 126 | 151 | 188 | 237 | 270 | 270 | 227 | 298 | 440 |
| 1.21 | Jesus | 233 | 240 | 166 | 160 | 175 | 204 | 192 | 132 | 93 | 76 | 67 |
| 0.92 | Jim | 157 | 177 | 158 | 98 | 88 | 124 | 111 | 319 | 538 | 834 | |
| 0.72 | Jimmie | 258 | 210 | 131 | 73 | 114 | 186 | 252 | 343 | 461 | 636 | |
| 1.52 | Jimmy | 624 | 498 | 211 | 63 | 46 | 72 | 81 | 105 | 138 | 205 | 278 |
| 3.14 | Joe | 38 | 38 | 33 | 27 | 38 | 60 | 64 | 110 | 179 | 234 | 329 |
| 1.25 | Joel | 336 | 352 | 303 | 181 | 143 | 129 | 104 | 73 | 69 | 107 | 123 |
| 0.23 | Joey | | | | | 600 | 296 | 227 | 227 | 268 | 420 | 511 |
| 34.18 | John | 1 | 1 | 2 | 3 | 3 | 4 | 3 | 6 | 9 | 14 | 17 |
| 0.37 | Johnathan | | | | | | | 506 | 289 | 131 | 132 | 175 |
| 0.73 | Johnnie | 155 | 121 | 103 | 123 | 149 | 201 | 274 | 316 | 472 | 697 | |
| 1.66 | Johnny | 359 | 229 | 147 | 76 | 50 | 55 | 69 | 86 | 118 | 163 | 241 |
| 0.79 | Jon | | | 805 | 208 | 132 | 123 | 86 | 99 | 166 | 272 | 395 |
| 3.60 | Jonathan | 631 | 708 | 583 | 459 | 216 | 141 | 82 | 33 | 17 | 21 | 21 |
| 0.29 | Jonathon | | | | | | 643 | 570 | 268 | 151 | 158 | 284 |
| 1.43 | Jordan | | 850 | 660 | 703 | 983 | 663 | 628 | 330 | 62 | 28 | 37 |
| 0.78 | Jorge | | 641 | 399 | 310 | 234 | 226 | 181 | 136 | 108 | 100 | 115 |
| 4.22 | Jose | 80 | 95 | 65 | 52 | 47 | 47 | 43 | 35 | 37 | 32 | 31 |
| 16.69 | Joseph | 5 | 5 | 7 | 10 | 13 | 13 | 12 | 12 | 10 | 10 | 8 |
| 5.22 | Joshua | 487 | 557 | 639 | 732 | 644 | 548 | 346 | 25 | 4 | 4 | 3 |
| 2.40 | Juan | 111 | 115 | 96 | 85 | 95 | 98 | 91 | 59 | 59 | 51 | 53 |
| 0.76 | Julian | 195 | 201 | 197 | 233 | 299 | 325 | 365 | 295 | 198 | 134 | 76 |
| 0.52 | Julio | 298 | 296 | 276 | 220 | 225 | 261 | 275 | 207 | 220 | 187 | 255 |
| 0.59 | Julius | 105 | 113 | 148 | 231 | 276 | 330 | 400 | 423 | 394 | 470 | 385 |
| 0.23 | Junior | | 469 | 146 | 205 | 354 | 496 | 681 | 927 | 883 | 827 | 639 |
| 3.46 | Justin | 662 | 666 | 618 | 682 | 590 | 514 | 320 | 39 | 12 | 17 | 27 |
| 0.22 | Kaleb | | | | | | | | | 552 | 223 | 118 |
| 0.66 | Karl | 142 | 175 | 238 | 189 | 190 | 169 | 156 | 225 | 232 | 391 | 648 |
| 2.14 | Keith | 422 | 254 | 151 | 128 | 105 | 42 | 34 | 46 | 66 | 124 | 254 |
| 0.40 | Kelly | 549 | 571 | 598 | 507 | 413 | 211 | 126 | 166 | 250 | 476 | |
| 0.23 | Kelvin | | | | | | | 356 | 233 | 254 | 285 | 288 | 410 |
| 7.41 | Kenneth | 47 | 27 | 20 | 15 | 16 | 16 | 21 | 31 | 47 | 61 | 112 |
| 0.24 | Kenny | | | | | 517 | 301 | 258 | 228 | 376 | 322 | 387 | 475 |
| 0.33 | Kent | 937 | 872 | 678 | 347 | 219 | 165 | 169 | 294 | 363 | 637 | 987 |
| 0.23 | Kerry | | | | | 905 | 340 | 205 | 178 | 309 | 417 | 657 | |
| 5.32 | Kevin | | | | 830 | 444 | 185 | 27 | 14 | 13 | 23 | 25 | 32 |
| 0.30 | Kirk | | | | | 924 | 422 | 180 | 153 | 213 | 303 | 517 | |
| 0.28 | Kristopher | | | | | | | 670 | 184 | 136 | 209 | 341 |
| 0.41 | Kurt | 437 | 757 | 806 | 623 | 366 | 173 | 128 | 190 | 237 | 421 | 790 |
| 2.17 | Kyle | 718 | 780 | 772 | 669 | 650 | 318 | 176 | 90 | 29 | 22 | 46 |
| 0.46 | L | 110 | 134 | 156 | 206 | 296 | 431 | 432 | 638 | 905 | | |
| 0.48 | Lance | | | | | 612 | 319 | 241 | 165 | 140 | 146 | 232 | 267 |
| 0.29 | Landon | | | | | 906 | | | 629 | 355 | 259 | 91 |
| 4.19 | Larry | 401 | 327 | 209 | 33 | 11 | 18 | 35 | 57 | 94 | 200 | 320 |

| Pop. | Name | 1900s | 1910s | 1920s | 1930s | 1940s | 1950s | 1960s | 1970s | 1980s | 1990s | 2000s |
|---|---|---|---|---|---|---|---|---|---|---|---|---|
| 0.27 | Laurence | 244 | 242 | 247 | 278 | 252 | 278 | 391 | 597 | 696 | | |
| 3.22 | Lawrence | 34 | 37 | 38 | 37 | 29 | 41 | 67 | 101 | 150 | 227 | 353 |
| 1.54 | Lee | 74 | 84 | 86 | 78 | 94 | 109 | 116 | 130 | 149 | 279 | 540 |
| 0.34 | Leland | 217 | 207 | 195 | 221 | 240 | 321 | 453 | 552 | 595 | 726 | 879 |
| 1.52 | Leo | 44 | 47 | 55 | 88 | 148 | 184 | 269 | 339 | 431 | 446 | 293 |
| 1.17 | Leon | 89 | 87 | 77 | 90 | 112 | 145 | 202 | 230 | 309 | 461 | 505 |
| 2.24 | Leonard | 48 | 44 | 39 | 53 | 64 | 90 | 122 | 170 | 233 | 373 | 562 |
| 1.51 | Leroy | 82 | 65 | 52 | 56 | 90 | 137 | 183 | 263 | 345 | 553 | 820 |
| 0.87 | Leslie | 93 | 109 | 117 | 136 | 125 | 153 | 206 | 275 | 448 | 733 | |
| 1.18 | Lester | 54 | 60 | 78 | 114 | 146 | 182 | 248 | 351 | 478 | 749 | |
| 0.39 | Levi | 281 | 343 | 403 | 445 | 513 | 573 | 705 | 451 | 202 | 168 | 163 |
| 1.17 | Lewis | 72 | 68 | 82 | 103 | 119 | 176 | 235 | 280 | 350 | 455 | 617 |
| 1.34 | Lloyd | 69 | 58 | 61 | 81 | 108 | 157 | 208 | 313 | 419 | 649 | |
| 0.91 | Logan | 765 | 732 | 807 | | | | | 688 | 200 | 63 | 29 |
| 0.57 | Lonnie | 173 | 212 | 224 | 182 | 161 | 156 | 203 | 240 | 362 | 581 | |
| 0.29 | Loren | 302 | 278 | 244 | 238 | 241 | 304 | 333 | 424 | 473 | 658 | |
| 0.31 | Lorenzo | 331 | 393 | 331 | 361 | 382 | 340 | 325 | 353 | 311 | 293 | 310 |
| 3.26 | Louis | 21 | 22 | 30 | 43 | 55 | 80 | 108 | 143 | 161 | 217 | 288 |
| 0.30 | Lowell | 267 | 232 | 207 | 167 | 237 | 332 | 423 | 749 | | | |
| 0.60 | Lucas | | | 738 | 836 | | | 851 | 266 | 120 | 101 | 68 |
| 1.98 | Luis | 245 | 203 | 154 | 118 | 111 | 108 | 94 | 68 | 60 | 46 | 59 |
| 0.85 | Luke | 388 | 441 | 473 | 573 | 586 | 585 | 384 | 228 | 112 | 94 | 44 |
| 0.58 | Luther | 107 | 110 | 129 | 179 | 220 | 299 | 441 | 538 | 599 | | |
| 0.42 | Lyle | 206 | 176 | 168 | 177 | 211 | 256 | 358 | 495 | 546 | 884 | |
| 0.33 | Lynn | 304 | 280 | 321 | 235 | 162 | 206 | 319 | 539 | 866 | | |
| 0.23 | M | 154 | 233 | 335 | 412 | 539 | 651 | 485 | 449 | 665 | | |
| 0.26 | Mack | 214 | 225 | 248 | 244 | 280 | 398 | 487 | 689 | 874 | | |
| 0.36 | Malcolm | 283 | 230 | 235 | 229 | 267 | 319 | 359 | 406 | 403 | 289 | 469 |
| 1.36 | Manuel | 100 | 104 | 95 | 108 | 117 | 147 | 161 | 141 | 132 | 138 | 167 |
| 0.64 | Marc | | | | 974 | 263 | 149 | 113 | 89 | 139 | 226 | 304 |
| 0.29 | Marco | 1015 | | | | 753 | 611 | 428 | 256 | 245 | 185 | 190 |
| 0.24 | Marcos | 829 | 966 | 712 | 595 | 625 | 523 | 457 | 333 | 293 | 235 | 246 |
| 1.01 | Marcus | 291 | 353 | 389 | 397 | 373 | 254 | 201 | 75 | 68 | 84 | 114 |
| 0.74 | Mario | 349 | 277 | 263 | 267 | 278 | 214 | 198 | 138 | 111 | 136 | 174 |
| 0.60 | Marion | 130 | 118 | 113 | 138 | 198 | 269 | 392 | 501 | 798 | | |
| 6.31 | Mark | 194 | 215 | 226 | 199 | 57 | 9 | 6 | 18 | 33 | 49 | 104 |
| 0.54 | Marshall | 183 | 178 | 185 | 201 | 196 | 242 | 302 | 305 | 282 | 323 | 372 |
| 1.90 | Martin | 66 | 79 | 84 | 94 | 93 | 78 | 70 | 108 | 127 | 142 | 197 |
| 1.71 | Marvin | 104 | 75 | 53 | 48 | 84 | 104 | 123 | 173 | 218 | 283 | 346 |
| 0.59 | Mason | 626 | 606 | 591 | 613 | 716 | 925 | 770 | 543 | 341 | 119 | 52 |
| 0.36 | Mathew | 455 | 439 | 495 | 745 | 698 | 558 | 372 | 220 | 153 | 189 | 273 |
| 7.14 | Matthew | 168 | 159 | 180 | 225 | 205 | 100 | 36 | 10 | 3 | 3 | 4 |
| 0.93 | Maurice | 106 | 101 | 119 | 133 | 180 | 223 | 197 | 179 | 185 | 284 | 374 |
| 0.87 | Max | 87 | 106 | 132 | 149 | 203 | 266 | 363 | 393 | 261 | 186 | 164 |
| 0.30 | Maxwell | 458 | 474 | 761 | 790 | 817 | 1,000 | 959 | 929 | 366 | 176 | 133 |

| Pop. | Name | 1900s | 1910s | 1920s | 1930s | 1940s | 1950s | 1960s | 1970s | 1980s | 1990s | 2000s |
|---|---|---|---|---|---|---|---|---|---|---|---|---|
| 1.74 | Melvin | 85 | 61 | 50 | 54 | 73 | 97 | 133 | 192 | 241 | 350 | 412 |
| 0.26 | Merle | 238 | 206 | 212 | 218 | 349 | 443 | 634 | 944 | | | |
| 0.25 | Micah | | | | | | | 718 | 302 | 224 | 229 | 172 |
| 20.99 | Michael | 39 | 43 | 49 | 35 | 9 | 1 | 1 | 1 | 1 | 1 | 2 |
| 0.72 | Micheal | | 607 | 571 | 512 | 187 | 94 | 112 | 116 | 155 | 228 | 357 |
| 1.10 | Miguel | 278 | 284 | 210 | 172 | 163 | 177 | 168 | 119 | 105 | 88 | 90 |
| 1.14 | Mike | 182 | 139 | 188 | 203 | 82 | 82 | 49 | 217 | 476 | 583 | 629 |
| 0.27 | Miles | 376 | 389 | 410 | 474 | 485 | 424 | 464 | 600 | 339 | 292 | 223 |
| 0.99 | Milton | 84 | 76 | 85 | 121 | 152 | 190 | 246 | 357 | 485 | 569 | 730 |
| 0.80 | Mitchell | 350 | 279 | 313 | 359 | 251 | 148 | 148 | 199 | 122 | 89 | 191 |
| 0.66 | Morris | 90 | 98 | 128 | 173 | 209 | 259 | 357 | 511 | 643 | 936 | |
| 0.22 | Moses | 295 | 305 | 317 | 342 | 381 | 438 | 553 | 483 | 518 | 650 | 486 |
| 0.30 | Myron | 274 | 244 | 232 | 226 | 281 | 305 | 352 | 438 | 591 | 745 | |
| 2.30 | Nathan | 140 | 138 | 229 | 269 | 292 | 244 | 189 | 50 | 41 | 40 | 26 |
| 1.17 | Nathaniel | 266 | 211 | 183 | 200 | 204 | 224 | 241 | 152 | 81 | 77 | 63 |
| 0.30 | Neal | 360 | 370 | 315 | 298 | 254 | 235 | 266 | 328 | 364 | 570 | |
| 0.56 | Neil | 322 | 318 | 254 | 175 | 170 | 171 | 211 | 194 | 217 | 347 | 568 |
| 0.55 | Nelson | 223 | 202 | 205 | 191 | 194 | 215 | 232 | 260 | 256 | 297 | 428 |
| 4.17 | Nicholas | 132 | 112 | 130 | 162 | 141 | 144 | 147 | 51 | 19 | 8 | 10 |
| 0.34 | Nick | 241 | 219 | 201 | 264 | 306 | 297 | 276 | 366 | 563 | 768 | 804 |
| 0.35 | Nicolas | 564 | 609 | 523 | 532 | 570 | 544 | 616 | 408 | 235 | 172 | 141 |
| 0.97 | Noah | 280 | 354 | 408 | 494 | 529 | 608 | 610 | 344 | 205 | 90 | 28 |
| 0.26 | Noel | 433 | 410 | 458 | 340 | 331 | 368 | 354 | 297 | 330 | 425 | 445 |
| 0.26 | Nolan | 593 | 579 | 496 | 452 | 502 | 570 | 696 | 589 | 400 | 276 | 170 |
| 1.88 | Norman | 76 | 51 | 43 | 41 | 69 | 113 | 143 | 235 | 346 | 525 | 864 |
| 0.56 | Oliver | 135 | 130 | 153 | 204 | 255 | 350 | 482 | 434 | 429 | 376 | 236 |
| 0.41 | Omar | 845 | 622 | 688 | | 865 | 800 | 564 | 201 | 170 | 148 | 146 |
| 0.29 | Orlando | 597 | 541 | 499 | 508 | 440 | 336 | 251 | 251 | 254 | 312 | 367 |
| 0.37 | Orville | 145 | 133 | 161 | 228 | 350 | 503 | 787 | 945 | | | |
| 1.33 | Oscar | 57 | 81 | 104 | 139 | 183 | 217 | 238 | 189 | 169 | 130 | 119 |
| 0.45 | Otis | 147 | 153 | 171 | 193 | 215 | 272 | 337 | 462 | 611 | 836 | |
| 0.34 | Otto | 99 | 152 | 241 | 346 | 486 | 602 | 739 | | | | |
| 0.53 | Owen | 226 | 241 | 257 | 276 | 324 | 418 | 512 | 459 | 423 | 313 | 78 |
| 0.32 | Pablo | 325 | 367 | 287 | 285 | 327 | 366 | 396 | 379 | 332 | 324 | 290 |
| 0.24 | Parker | 619 | 769 | 969 | | | | | | 547 | 216 | 124 |
| 3.35 | Patrick | 114 | 156 | 142 | 107 | 58 | 40 | 32 | 37 | 38 | 44 | 86 |
| 8.77 | Paul | 17 | 14 | 13 | 14 | 17 | 17 | 19 | 27 | 40 | 64 | 121 |
| 0.85 | Pedro | 159 | 179 | 149 | 142 | 166 | 187 | 188 | 180 | 173 | 180 | 220 |
| 0.27 | Percy | 158 | 214 | 245 | 280 | 361 | 422 | 526 | 614 | 944 | | |
| 0.45 | Perry | 220 | 218 | 242 | 259 | 228 | 179 | 210 | 338 | 418 | 498 | 786 |
| 0.29 | Pete | 235 | 224 | 233 | 241 | 273 | 331 | 361 | 503 | 667 | | |
| 3.40 | Peter | 46 | 48 | 59 | 59 | 42 | 39 | 42 | 55 | 63 | 87 | 145 |
| 2.08 | Philip | 77 | 78 | 75 | 69 | 60 | 66 | 85 | 88 | 86 | 161 | 283 |
| 1.63 | Phillip | 198 | 187 | 164 | 117 | 76 | 79 | 68 | 74 | 71 | 129 | 233 |
| 0.48 | Preston | 282 | 267 | 284 | 303 | 318 | 354 | 343 | 314 | 247 | 197 | 144 |

| Pop. | Name | 1900s | 1910s | 1920s | 1930s | 1940s | 1950s | 1960s | 1970s | 1980s | 1990s | 2000s |
|---|---|---|---|---|---|---|---|---|---|---|---|---|
| 0.51 | R | 92 | 127 | 184 | 237 | 394 | 487 | 293 | 325 | 488 | | |
| 0.69 | Rafael | 246 | 252 | 215 | 168 | 181 | 213 | 212 | 176 | 172 | 196 | 230 |
| 3.41 | Ralph | 23 | 21 | 24 | 30 | 45 | 62 | 109 | 186 | 272 | 448 | 666 |
| 0.75 | Ramon | 190 | 195 | 144 | 132 | 160 | 196 | 216 | 188 | 221 | 254 | 335 |
| 0.96 | Randall | 576 | 486 | 493 | 352 | 133 | 61 | 66 | 124 | 148 | 265 | 532 |
| 0.28 | Randolph | 364 | 383 | 381 | 379 | 232 | 199 | 279 | 386 | 536 | 790 | |
| 1.49 | Randy | | | | 931 | 158 | 33 | 39 | 79 | 102 | 179 | 294 |
| 0.50 | Raul | 1020 | 564 | 305 | 245 | 212 | 228 | 243 | 195 | 196 | 201 | 243 |
| 1.51 | Ray | 67 | 70 | 66 | 65 | 96 | 121 | 151 | 234 | 277 | 393 | 570 |
| 5.58 | Raymond | 22 | 15 | 16 | 17 | 23 | 37 | 46 | 66 | 77 | 109 | 184 |
| 0.57 | Reginald | 301 | 365 | 314 | 311 | 236 | 151 | 134 | 172 | 212 | 275 | 457 |
| 0.28 | Rene | 577 | 588 | 438 | 386 | 374 | 320 | 267 | 261 | 297 | 321 | 444 |
| 0.33 | Rex | 326 | 253 | 272 | 232 | 235 | 216 | 294 | 457 | 580 | 750 | 969 |
| 0.71 | Ricardo | 722 | 593 | 471 | 393 | 311 | 210 | 174 | 134 | 117 | 114 | 149 |
| 15.02 | Richard | 25 | 17 | 8 | 5 | 5 | 7 | 8 | 16 | 27 | 41 | 81 |
| 0.35 | Rick | | | | | 275 | 110 | 136 | 317 | 442 | 633 | |
| 0.26 | Rickey | | | | | 334 | 125 | 217 | 364 | 373 | 655 | |
| 1.00 | Ricky | | | | | 247 | 50 | 53 | 131 | 137 | 220 | 340 |
| 0.35 | Riley | 400 | 442 | 509 | 620 | 480 | 666 | 803 | 799 | 471 | 188 | 108 |
| 29.76 | Robert | 7 | 4 | 1 | 1 | 2 | 3 | 5 | 7 | 8 | 20 | 34 |
| 0.67 | Roberto | 790 | 594 | 278 | 207 | 207 | 192 | 184 | 149 | 145 | 156 | 199 |
| 0.23 | Roderick | 737 | 661 | 528 | 480 | 418 | 293 | 260 | 252 | 327 | 503 | 691 |
| 1.20 | Rodney | 499 | 431 | 283 | 163 | 109 | 73 | 52 | 78 | 160 | 224 | 396 |
| 2.44 | Roger | 209 | 135 | 92 | 42 | 25 | 38 | 51 | 93 | 163 | 257 | 403 |
| 0.70 | Roland | 151 | 129 | 114 | 129 | 164 | 218 | 261 | 340 | 397 | 562 | 731 |
| 0.23 | Roman | 342 | 359 | 382 | 543 | 628 | 603 | 597 | 430 | 434 | 368 | 259 |
| 5.82 | Ronald | 252 | 172 | 98 | 13 | 10 | 15 | 24 | 45 | 70 | 135 | 232 |
| 0.89 | Ronnie | | | | 178 | 68 | 81 | 110 | 156 | 228 | 339 | 534 |
| 0.30 | Roosevelt | 185 | 297 | 275 | 196 | 244 | 310 | 456 | 621 | 656 | | |
| 0.49 | Ross | 219 | 227 | 264 | 261 | 248 | 245 | 263 | 265 | 174 | 258 | 565 |
| 3.16 | Roy | 24 | 32 | 32 | 39 | 43 | 63 | 95 | 120 | 180 | 299 | 448 |
| 0.64 | Ruben | 379 | 347 | 251 | 214 | 200 | 181 | 200 | 178 | 182 | 181 | 219 |
| 0.48 | Rudolph | 129 | 148 | 134 | 184 | 250 | 303 | 419 | 581 | 732 | 986 | |
| 0.25 | Rudy | 627 | 662 | 383 | 294 | 282 | 284 | 314 | 341 | 384 | 439 | 577 |
| 0.31 | Rufus | 172 | 190 | 200 | 251 | 307 | 389 | 483 | 653 | 973 | | |
| 2.35 | Russell | 53 | 49 | 54 | 68 | 70 | 65 | 56 | 80 | 113 | 213 | 347 |
| 3.94 | Ryan | | | | | | 622 | 242 | 26 | 14 | 15 | 14 |
| 0.29 | Salvador | 467 | 423 | 304 | 322 | 337 | 355 | 421 | 335 | 300 | 300 | 338 |
| 0.41 | Salvatore | 201 | 170 | 170 | 215 | 264 | 309 | 334 | 411 | 479 | 586 | 667 |
| 1.03 | Sam | 58 | 69 | 99 | 131 | 168 | 236 | 278 | 380 | 467 | 408 | 452 |
| 4.05 | Samuel | 31 | 41 | 46 | 60 | 61 | 71 | 83 | 61 | 52 | 35 | 24 |
| 3.66 | Scott | 406 | 412 | 454 | 441 | 177 | 36 | 15 | 17 | 39 | 75 | 202 |
| 1.88 | Sean | | | | | 931 | 335 | 76 | 41 | 42 | 42 | 61 |
| 0.35 | Sebastian | 594 | 552 | 578 | 687 | 799 | | 789 | 697 | 510 | 215 | 83 |
| 0.32 | Sergio | | | | 642 | 666 | 482 | 420 | 276 | 199 | 159 | 192 |

| Pop. | Name | 1900s | 1910s | 1920s | 1930s | 1940s | 1950s | 1960s | 1970s | 1980s | 1990s | 2000s |
|---|---|---|---|---|---|---|---|---|---|---|---|---|
| 0.70 | Seth | 670 | 654 | 810 | 981 | 771 | 554 | 452 | 174 | 95 | 96 | 77 |
| 0.84 | Shane | | | | | | 450 | 205 | 64 | 75 | 91 | 147 |
| 0.25 | Shannon | | | | | 968 | 715 | 264 | 106 | 258 | 572 | 821 |
| 0.32 | Shaun | | | | | | 733 | 347 | 146 | 121 | 296 | 381 |
| 1.38 | Shawn | | | | | 992 | 324 | 77 | 34 | 56 | 92 | 156 |
| 0.28 | Sherman | 247 | 243 | 240 | 254 | 291 | 315 | 411 | 474 | 608 | 1009 | |
| 0.68 | Sidney | 115 | 94 | 125 | 174 | 193 | 248 | 309 | 437 | 480 | 505 | 693 |
| 0.30 | Simon | 210 | 269 | 336 | 400 | 443 | 551 | 557 | 446 | 386 | 352 | 252 |
| 0.52 | Spencer | 412 | 475 | 486 | 419 | 407 | 448 | 401 | 287 | 181 | 97 | 130 |
| 2.25 | Stanley | 52 | 36 | 41 | 58 | 63 | 70 | 120 | 182 | 248 | 394 | 545 |
| 4.41 | Stephen | 95 | 89 | 120 | 109 | 24 | 20 | 28 | 32 | 36 | 48 | 125 |
| 1.33 | Steve | 161 | 120 | 157 | 183 | 85 | 59 | 54 | 163 | 223 | 329 | 463 |
| 5.95 | Steven | 382 | 313 | 302 | 257 | 31 | 11 | 11 | 19 | 24 | 34 | 70 |
| 0.39 | Stuart | 394 | 333 | 318 | 265 | 192 | 200 | 186 | 345 | 320 | 512 | 961 |
| 0.34 | Sylvester | 177 | 193 | 206 | 239 | 265 | 314 | 393 | 540 | 610 | | |
| 0.34 | Tanner | | | | | | | | 888 | 352 | 104 | 117 |
| 0.50 | Taylor | 578 | 633 | 668 | 665 | 800 | 793 | 865 | 585 | 152 | 62 | 193 |
| 0.48 | Ted | 224 | 257 | 204 | 155 | 167 | 193 | 214 | 354 | 537 | 940 | |
| 0.31 | Terrance | | | | 615 | 284 | 239 | 265 | 206 | 206 | 285 | 446 |
| 0.33 | Terrence | | | 1012 | 436 | 222 | 222 | 237 | 209 | 239 | 334 | 549 |
| 2.05 | Terry | 650 | 611 | 501 | 150 | 32 | 29 | 37 | 71 | 125 | 233 | 383 |
| 1.69 | Theodore | 42 | 63 | 67 | 82 | 101 | 118 | 154 | 193 | 215 | 277 | 307 |
| 13.46 | Thomas | 12 | 11 | 11 | 9 | 8 | 8 | 9 | 21 | 25 | 27 | 36 |
| 0.39 | Tim | 994 | 953 | 873 | 627 | 224 | 143 | 92 | 352 | 835 | | |
| 4.97 | Timothy | 284 | 378 | 378 | 249 | 65 | 22 | 13 | 20 | 26 | 38 | 72 |
| 1.31 | Todd | | | | | 467 | 167 | 31 | 43 | 103 | 248 | 513 |
| 0.88 | Tom | 123 | 151 | 140 | 122 | 97 | 138 | 121 | 369 | 618 | 858 | |
| 0.95 | Tommy | 568 | 409 | 217 | 105 | 77 | 106 | 119 | 165 | 238 | 305 | 370 |
| 1.31 | Tony | 228 | 157 | 159 | 171 | 138 | 93 | 50 | 82 | 123 | 195 | 300 |
| 0.30 | Tracy | 922 | 828 | 1013 | 644 | 560 | 298 | 117 | 197 | 455 | 579 | |
| 1.40 | Travis | 659 | 454 | 450 | 315 | 359 | 384 | 225 | 53 | 44 | 54 | 154 |
| 0.66 | Trevor | | | | | | | 416 | 202 | 115 | 65 | 94 |
| 0.31 | Tristan | | | | | | | | 966 | 275 | 153 | 109 |
| 1.04 | Troy | 290 | 228 | 230 | 240 | 266 | 265 | 57 | 67 | 128 | 155 | 238 |
| 2.42 | Tyler | | | | | | 759 | 469 | 214 | 50 | 9 | 15 |
| 0.37 | Tyrone | | | | 759 | 310 | 220 | 173 | 150 | 216 | 346 | 518 |
| 1.10 | Vernon | 112 | 80 | 68 | 93 | 124 | 155 | 209 | 285 | 356 | 614 | 999 |
| 2.07 | Victor | 79 | 67 | 79 | 97 | 91 | 91 | 89 | 92 | 88 | 83 | 102 |
| 1.84 | Vincent | 103 | 74 | 76 | 111 | 106 | 101 | 73 | 103 | 98 | 99 | 116 |
| 0.66 | Virgil | 109 | 100 | 116 | 144 | 201 | 277 | 338 | 464 | 689 | | |
| 0.56 | W | 61 | 119 | 220 | 295 | 460 | 568 | 348 | 444 | 681 | | |
| 0.37 | Wade | 309 | 292 | 319 | 345 | 332 | 252 | 218 | 223 | 305 | 396 | 521 |
| 0.62 | Wallace | 141 | 131 | 97 | 140 | 179 | 251 | 356 | 505 | 725 | | |
| 5.34 | Walter | 11 | 10 | 15 | 22 | 27 | 52 | 80 | 107 | 158 | 245 | 342 |
| 1.19 | Warren | 136 | 102 | 51 | 99 | 110 | 133 | 170 | 233 | 283 | 418 | 509 |

| Pop. | Name | 1900s | 1910s | 1920s | 1930s | 1940s | 1950s | 1960s | 1970s | 1980s | 1990s | 2000s |
|------|------|-------|-------|-------|-------|-------|-------|-------|-------|-------|-------|-------|
| 2.07 | Wayne | 150 | 108 | 74 | 49 | 33 | 43 | 63 | 111 | 186 | 330 | 579 |
| 0.35 | Wendell | 347 | 238 | 231 | 223 | 210 | 238 | 280 | 399 | 517 | 700 | |
| 1.08 | Wesley | 152 | 143 | 136 | 159 | 174 | 164 | 166 | 125 | 101 | 126 | 186 |
| 0.31 | Wilbert | 249 | 196 | 190 | 210 | 268 | 345 | 430 | 601 | 932 | | |
| 0.54 | Wilbur | 124 | 96 | 121 | 180 | 253 | 409 | 491 | 776 | | | |
| 0.27 | Wilfred | 186 | 189 | 221 | 270 | 375 | 466 | 572 | 830 | 958 | | |
| 0.25 | Will | 162 | 275 | 353 | 368 | 455 | 559 | 590 | 528 | 573 | 616 | 529 |
| 0.68 | Willard | 128 | 85 | 102 | 141 | 189 | 287 | 373 | 529 | 890 | | |
| 27.26 | William | 2 | 2 | 4 | 4 | 4 | 6 | 7 | 9 | 15 | 19 | 11 |
| 3.33 | Willie | 28 | 28 | 27 | 31 | 34 | 54 | 98 | 121 | 164 | 263 | 462 |
| 0.41 | Willis | 163 | 141 | 145 | 202 | 256 | 358 | 489 | 617 | 711 | | |
| 0.34 | Wilson | 263 | 160 | 268 | 272 | 293 | 360 | 436 | 466 | 486 | 454 | 500 |
| 0.35 | Woodrow | | 72 | 282 | 321 | 313 | 465 | 632 | 800 | | | 0 |
| 0.30 | Wyatt | 794 | 989 | | | | 744 | 857 | 672 | 571 | 190 | 99 |
| 0.38 | Xavier | | | | | | 846 | 601 | 489 | 263 | 141 | 87 |
| 2.25 | Zachary | | | | | | 509 | 455 | 154 | 43 | 16 | 20 |

# Part 2

# Popular Names

*with Popularity Ratings, Origins, and Meanings*

The most popular names for girls and boys along with a
popularity rating indicating frequency of use per thousand babies,
origin of the name, and meaning of the name.

# Popular Girls' Names

*Popularity ratings indicate usage per thousand baby girls.*

## Popularity rating • Name • Origin and meaning

| | | | | |
|---|---|---|---|---|
| 1.75 | Aaliyah | *Arabic* sublime, exalted; *Hebrew* ascend | 0.25 | Ainsley | *Scottish* from one's own meadow |
| 0.12 | Abagail | *Hebrew* father of joy | 0.17 | Aisha | *African* life |
| 0.18 | Abbey | *Hebrew* father of joy | 0.13 | Aiyana | *Native American* eternal blossom |
| 0.18 | Abbie | *Hebrew* father of joy | | | |
| 0.25 | Abbigail | *Hebrew* father of joy | 0.57 | Alaina | *Irish* fair, beautiful |
| 0.80 | Abby | *Hebrew* father of joy | 0.77 | Alana | *Irish* fair, beautiful |
| 7.45 | Abigail | *Hebrew* father of joy | 0.23 | Alanna | *Irish* fair, beautiful |
| 0.11 | Abigale | *Hebrew* father of joy | 0.50 | Alayna | *Irish* fair, beautiful |
| 0.16 | Abigayle | *Hebrew* father of joy | 0.16 | Aleah | *Arabic* high, exalted; *Persian* God's being |
| 0.15 | Ada | *English* prosperous, happy; *Hebrew* an ornament | 0.30 | Alejandra | *Greek* defender of mankind |
| 3.16 | Addison | *English* son of Adam | 0.14 | Alena | *Greek* a torch, light |
| 0.10 | Addisyn | *English* son of Adam | 0.19 | Alessandra | *Greek* defender of mankind |
| 0.20 | Addyson | *English* awesome | 2.78 | Alexa | *Greek* defender of mankind |
| 0.21 | Adeline | *French* noble, kind | 3.17 | Alexandra | *Greek* defender of mankind |
| 1.38 | Adriana | *Latin* dark one; rich | 0.96 | Alexandria | *Greek* defender of mankind |
| 0.71 | Adrianna | *Latin* dark one; rich | 0.89 | Alexia | *Greek* defender of mankind |
| 0.11 | Adrienne | *Latin* dark one; rich | 5.38 | Alexis | *Greek* defender of mankind |
| 0.10 | Aileen | *Irish* form of Helen; *Gaelic* light bearer | 0.21 | Alexus | *Greek* defender of mankind |
| | | | 0.39 | Alice | *German* noble; *Greek* truthful |
| 0.12 | Aimee | *French* from *Latin* beloved | 0.94 | Alicia | *German* noble; *Greek* truthful |

| 0.23 | Alina | *Polish and Russian* bright, beautiful |
|---|---|---|
| 0.12 | Alisa | *German* noble; *Greek* truthful |
| 0.26 | Alisha | *German* noble; *Greek* truthful |
| 0.47 | Alison | *German* noble; *Greek* truthful |
| 0.29 | Alissa | *German* noble; *Greek* truthful |
| 0.54 | Alivia | *Latin* olives |
| 0.15 | Aliya | *Arabic* high, exalted; *Persian* God's being |
| 0.52 | Aliyah | *Hebrew* to ascend, to go up |
| 0.11 | Aliza | *Hebrew* joyful |
| 0.60 | Allie | *Greek* defender of mankind; *German* noble; *Greek* truth |
| 2.64 | Allison | *German* noble; *Greek* truthful |
| 0.18 | Ally | *Greek* defender of mankind; *German* noble; *Greek* truth |
| 0.49 | Allyson | *German* noble; *Greek* truthful |
| 1.21 | Alondra | *Spanish* variant of Alexandra defender of mankind |
| 0.13 | Alycia | *German* noble; *Greek* truthful |
| 0.29 | Alyson | *German* noble; *Greek* truthful |
| 4.82 | Alyssa | *Greek* logical one |
| 2.01 | Amanda | *Latin* worthy of love |
| 0.15 | Amani | *Arabic* aspiration |
| 0.21 | Amara | *Greek* unfading or eternal beauty |
| 0.20 | Amari | *African* immortal |
| 0.54 | Amaya | *Japanese* night rain |
| 1.30 | Amber | *French* amber |
| 2.18 | Amelia | *Latin* work |
| 0.24 | Amelie | *Latin* work |
| 0.13 | Amina | *Arabic* security |
| 0.20 | Amira | *Arabic* a princess; *Hebrew* speech |
| 0.11 | Amiya | *English* beloved |
| 0.13 | Amiyah | *English* beloved |
| 1.60 | Amy | *Latin* beloved |
| 0.23 | Amya | *English* beloved |

| 1.05 | Ana | *Greek* resurrection |
|---|---|---|
| 0.15 | Anabelle | Anna + Belle |
| 0.14 | Anahi | *Armenian* goddess of the moon |
| 0.18 | Anais | *Hebrew* one of grace, gracious |
| 0.46 | Anastasia | *Greek* resurrection |
| 0.18 | Anaya | *Polish and Slavic* grace |
| 2.41 | Andrea | *Greek* valiant, strong, courageous; *Latin* womanly |
| 0.98 | Angel | *Latin* angelic |
| 1.53 | Angela | *Latin* angelic |
| 0.44 | Angelica | *Latin* angelic |
| 2.84 | Angelina | *Latin* angelic |
| 0.10 | Angeline | *Latin* angelic |
| 0.16 | Angelique | *Latin* angelic |
| 0.21 | Angie | *Latin* angelic |
| 0.24 | Anika | *Hebrew* gracious |
| 0.43 | Aniya | *Polish and Slavic* grace |
| 0.56 | Aniyah | *Polish and Slavic* grace |
| 0.17 | Ann | *Hebrew* gracious |
| 4.54 | Anna | *Italian, German, Russian* forms of *Hebrew* one of grace, gracious |
| 0.12 | Annabel | Anna + Belle |
| 0.13 | Annabella | Anna + Belle |
| 0.74 | Annabelle | Anna + Belle |
| 0.16 | Annalise | Anna + Lise |
| 0.33 | Anne | *Hebrew* gracious |
| 0.30 | Annie | *Hebrew* gracious |
| 0.39 | Annika | *Hebrew* gracious |
| 0.24 | Ansley | *English* from the meadow |
| 0.11 | Antonia | *Latin* priceless |
| 0.24 | Anya | *Hebrew* gracious |
| 0.25 | April | *Latin* open |
| 0.12 | Arabella | *Germanic* eagle, heroine; lovable; beautiful altar |
| 0.15 | Aria | *Greek* warlike |
| 1.99 | Ariana | *Greek* most holy |
| 0.21 | Ariane | *Greek* most holy |

| | | |
|---|---|---|
| 1.92 | Arianna | *Greek* most holy |
| 0.58 | Ariel | *Hebrew* likeness of God |
| 0.20 | Arielle | *Hebrew* likeness of God |
| 0.13 | Aryanna | *Hindi* noble |
| 0.11 | Ashanti | *Ghanaian* power and victory |
| 0.40 | Ashlee | *English* from the ash tree meadow |
| 0.21 | Ashleigh | *English* from the ash tree meadow |
| 5.90 | Ashley | *English* from the ash tree meadow |
| 1.29 | Ashlyn | *English* from the ash tree pool |
| 0.39 | Ashlynn | *English* from the ash tree pool |
| 0.11 | Ashton | *English* from the ash tree farm |
| 0.39 | Asia | *Greek* resurrection |
| 0.23 | Aspen | *English* aspen |
| 0.20 | Athena | *Greek* wisdom |
| 0.18 | Aubree | *French* blond ruler; elf ruler |
| 1.60 | Aubrey | *French* blond ruler; elf ruler |
| 0.13 | Aubrie | *French* blond ruler; elf ruler |
| 2.28 | Audrey | *English* noble strength |
| 0.10 | Aurelie | *Latin* gold |
| 0.36 | Aurora | *Latin* daybreak |
| 2.04 | Autumn | *Latin* autumn |
| 6.97 | Ava | *Latin* birdlike |
| 2.66 | Avery | *French* blond ruler; elf ruler |
| 0.13 | Aya | *Hebrew* bird |
| 0.14 | Ayana | *Hindi* innocent being; *Swahili* beautiful flower |
| 0.22 | Ayanna | *Hindi* innocent being; *Swahili* beautiful flower |
| 0.26 | Ayla | *Hebrew* oak tree |
| 0.15 | Bailee | *English* fortification; *English/French* public official, person in charge |
| 1.65 | Bailey | *English* fortification; *English/French* public official, person in charge |
| 0.17 | Barbara | *Latin* stranger |
| 0.22 | Baylee | *English* fortification; *English/French* public official, person in charge |
| 0.18 | Beatrice | *Latin* she who makes others happy |
| 0.59 | Bella | *Latin* beauty |
| 0.55 | Bethany | *Greek and Latin* house of figs |
| 0.70 | Bianca | *Italian* white |
| 0.11 | Brandi | *Dutch* brandy |
| 0.12 | Brandy | *Dutch* brandy |
| 0.11 | Breana | *Irish* strong |
| 1.39 | Breanna | *Irish* strong |
| 0.31 | Brenda | *English* firebrand |
| 0.37 | Brenna | *Irish* raven |
| 0.11 | Bria | *Latin* from the boundary line; *Latin* from England |
| 1.32 | Briana | *Irish* strong |
| 4.41 | Brianna | *Irish* strong |
| 0.36 | Bridget | *Irish* strong |
| 0.28 | Brielle | *French* region noted for its cheese |
| 0.22 | Britney | *Latin* from England |
| 0.41 | Brittany | *Latin* from England |
| 0.18 | Brittney | *Latin* from England |
| 2.71 | Brooke | *English* brook |
| 2.61 | Brooklyn | a borough of New York |
| 0.55 | Brooklynn | a borough of New York |
| 0.22 | Bryanna | *Irish* strong |
| 0.10 | Bryn | *Welsh* hill, mound |
| 0.34 | Brynn | *Latin* from the boundary line |
| 0.68 | Cadence | *Latin* rhythm |
| 0.71 | Caitlin | *Greek* pure |
| 0.71 | Caitlyn | *Greek* pure |
| 0.16 | Cali | *English, Irish* lark |
| 0.38 | Callie | *Greek* beautiful |
| 0.43 | Cameron | *Scottish* crooked nose |
| 0.99 | Camila | *Latin* young attendant |

| | | |
|---|---|---|
| 0.57 | Camille | *Latin* young attendant |
| 0.14 | Campbell | *Gaelic* crooked mouth |
| 0.59 | Camryn | *Scottish* crooked nose |
| 0.10 | Candace | *Greek* glittering white, incandescent |
| 0.22 | Cara | *Irish* friend |
| 0.10 | Carina | *Latin* keel |
| 0.15 | Carissa | *Latin* charity |
| 0.17 | Carla | *French* little and womanly |
| 0.16 | Carlee | *French* little and womanly |
| 0.23 | Carley | *French* little and womanly |
| 0.18 | Carlie | *French* little and womanly |
| 0.69 | Carly | *French* little and womanly |
| 0.40 | Carmen | *Latin* a song |
| 0.27 | Carolina | *French* little and womanly |
| 2.13 | Caroline | *French* little and womanly |
| 0.23 | Carolyn | *French* little and womanly |
| 0.12 | Carrie | *French* little and womanly; *Latin* strong and womanly; *French* song of joy |
| 0.32 | Casey | *Irish* brave |
| 0.75 | Cassandra | *Greek* not believed |
| 0.79 | Cassidy | *Irish* clever, quick one |
| 0.14 | Cassie | *Greek* not believed |
| 0.13 | Catalina | *Spanish* form of *Greek* pure |
| 1.52 | Catherine | *Greek* pure |
| 0.10 | Cayla | *Greek* pure, virginal |
| 0.18 | Cecelia | *Latin* blind |
| 0.36 | Cecilia | *Latin* blind |
| 0.26 | Celeste | *Latin* heavenly |
| 0.15 | Celia | *Latin* blind |
| 0.11 | Chana | *Hebrew* graceful |
| 0.12 | Chanel | *English* channel |
| 0.16 | Charity | *Latin and Greek* charity, loving |
| 0.18 | Charlie | *French* little and womanly |
| 0.11 | Charlize | *French* little, womanly |
| 1.51 | Charlotte | *French* little and womanly |
| 0.11 | Chasity | *Latin* pure |
| 0.18 | Chaya | *Hebrew* life |

| | | |
|---|---|---|
| 0.76 | Chelsea | *English* a port |
| 0.13 | Chelsey | *English* a port |
| 0.19 | Cheyanne | *American Indian* tribal name |
| 0.87 | Cheyenne | *American Indian* tribal name |
| 4.86 | Chloe | *Greek* blooming green bird |
| 1.04 | Christina | *Greek* a Christian, anointed one |
| 0.27 | Christine | *Greek* a Christian, anointed one |
| 0.77 | Ciara | *Irish* black |
| 0.26 | Cierra | *Irish* black |
| 0.24 | Cindy | *Greek* moon |
| 2.03 | Claire | *Latin* clear, bright |
| 0.66 | Clara | *Latin* clear, bright |
| 0.16 | Clare | *Latin* clear, bright |
| 0.14 | Clarissa | *Greek* most brilliant |
| 0.31 | Claudia | *Latin* lame |
| 0.13 | Cloe | *Greek* blooming green bird |
| 0.14 | Colleen | *Irish* girl |
| 0.30 | Cora | *Greek* maiden |
| 0.21 | Coralie | *Latin* coral from the sea |
| 0.15 | Corinne | *Greek* maiden |
| 0.92 | Courtney | *French* from the king's court |
| 0.16 | Cristina | *Greek* a Christian, anointed one |
| 0.80 | Crystal | *Greek* brilliant glass |
| 0.40 | Cynthia | *Greek* moon |
| 1.12 | Daisy | *Old English* eye of the day |
| 0.59 | Dakota | *American Indian* tribal name |
| 0.26 | Dana | *Latin* bright, pure as day; from Denmark |
| 0.10 | Dania | *Hebrew* God is my judge |
| 0.23 | Danica | *Slavic* morning star |
| 1.33 | Daniela | *Hebrew* God is my judge |
| 0.30 | Daniella | *Hebrew* God is my judge |
| 1.42 | Danielle | *Hebrew* God is my judge |
| 0.17 | Danika | *Slavic* morning star |
| 0.10 | Danna | *English* light as the day |
| 0.20 | Daphne | *Greek* laurel tree |
| 0.13 | Daphnee | *Greek* laurel tree |
| 0.10 | Dayana | *Scandinavian* light |
| 0.16 | Dayanara | origin unknown |

| | | | | | |
|---|---|---|---|---|---|
| 0.23 | Deanna | *Latin* divine | 0.17 | Elodie | *Greek* shore, plain, marsh |
| 0.17 | Deborah | *Hebrew* a bee | 0.16 | Eloise | *Greek* hale, complete |
| 0.10 | Deja | *French* already, before | 0.14 | Elsa | *German* noble one |
| 0.76 | Delaney | *Irish* offspring of the challenger | 0.10 | Elsie | *Danish* form of Elsa: noble one |
| 0.12 | Delilah | *Hebrew* brooding | 0.16 | Elyse | *Hebrew* God's oath |
| 0.19 | Denise | *Greek* from Dionysius, god of wine and drama | 0.25 | Emely | *German* industrious |
| | | | 0.29 | Emerson | *English* son of Emery |
| 0.12 | Desirae | *French* to crave | 0.34 | Emilee | *German* industrious |
| 0.30 | Desiree | *French* to crave | 0.25 | Emilia | *German* industrious |
| 0.18 | Destinee | *French* destiny | 0.42 | Emilie | *German* industrious |
| 0.10 | Destiney | *French* destiny | 10.56 | Emily | *German* industrious |
| 0.10 | Destini | *French* destiny | 9.57 | Emma | *Greek* grandmother |
| 3.07 | Destiny | *French* destiny | 0.14 | Emmalee | *German* industrious |
| 0.10 | Devon | *Irish* poet; *English* from Devon | 0.16 | Emy | *Latin* beloved |
| 0.35 | Diamond | *Latin* precious stone | 0.71 | Erica | *German* honorable ruler |
| 1.46 | Diana | *Latin* divine | 0.62 | Erika | *German* honorable ruler |
| 0.17 | Dominique | *French* belonging to the Lord | 1.54 | Erin | *Irish* peace |
| 0.15 | Dulce | *Latin* agreeable | 0.65 | Esmeralda | *Spanish* emerald |
| 0.16 | Dylan | *Welsh* the sea | 0.10 | Essence | *American* perfume |
| 0.39 | Eden | *Hebrew* delight | 0.50 | Esther | *Persian* a star |
| 0.10 | Edith | *Old English* rich gift | 0.21 | Estrella | *Latin* star |
| 0.10 | Eileen | *Greek* a torch, light | 1.16 | Eva | *Latin* life |
| 0.25 | Elaina | *Greek* a torch, light | 0.10 | Evangeline | *Greek* like an angel |
| 0.16 | Elaine | *Greek* a torch, light | 0.29 | Eve | *Latin* life |
| 0.51 | Eleanor | *Greek* a torch, light | 2.19 | Evelyn | *Celtic* pleasant |
| 0.58 | Elena | *Greek* a torch, light | 2.36 | Faith | *English* fidelity |
| 0.36 | Eliana | *Hebrew* God has answered me | 0.68 | Fatima | *Arabic* a daughter of Muhammad |
| 0.16 | Elisa | *Hebrew* God's oath | | | |
| 0.33 | Elisabeth | *Hebrew* God's oath | 0.11 | Felicia | *Latin* happy |
| 0.57 | Elise | *Hebrew* God's oath | 0.14 | Felicity | *Latin* happy |
| 0.42 | Eliza | *Hebrew* God's oath | 0.11 | Fernanda | *German* to make peace, to be bold |
| 5.83 | Elizabeth | *Hebrew* God's oath | | | |
| 4.30 | Ella | *Old English* beautiful fairy maiden | 0.37 | Fiona | *Celtic* white |
| | | | 0.24 | Florence | *Latin* blooming |
| 0.21 | Elle | *English* light | 0.13 | Frances | *French* free |
| 0.19 | Ellen | *Greek* a torch, light | 0.25 | Francesca | *French* free |
| 0.10 | Elliana | *Hebrew* God has answered me | 0.10 | Frederique | *German* peace, king, ruler |
| 0.94 | Ellie | *English*: short form of English names beginning with El- | 1.50 | Gabriela | *Hebrew* God is my strength |
| | | | 2.34 | Gabriella | *Hebrew* God is my strength |

| | | |
|---|---|---|
| 2.79 | Gabrielle | *Hebrew* God is my strength |
| 1.07 | Genesis | *Latin* birth, origin, descent |
| 0.31 | Genevieve | *Celtic* white wave |
| 0.45 | Georgia | *Latin* farmer |
| 0.11 | Gia | *Italian* God's grace |
| 0.13 | Giana | *Italian* God is gracious |
| 1.71 | Gianna | *Italian* form of Jane: *Hebrew* gracious, merciful |
| 0.15 | Gillian | *Latin* young; *Greek* soft-haired, youthful |
| 0.18 | Gina | *Latin* queen |
| 0.13 | Giovanna | *Italian* form of Jean: *Hebrew* gracious, merciful |
| 1.10 | Giselle | *German* pledge; hostage |
| 0.20 | Gloria | *Latin* glory |
| 5.38 | Grace | *Latin* grace, agreeable, pleasantness |
| 0.13 | Gracelyn | *German* graceful as a waterfall; quiet and shy |
| 1.89 | Gracie | *Latin* grace of God |
| 0.18 | Greta | *Greek* pearl |
| 0.15 | Gretchen | *German* form of Margaret: *Greek* a pearl |
| 0.57 | Guadalupe | *Spanish* reference to St. Mary of Guadalupe; *Arabic* valley of wolf |
| 0.18 | Gwendolyn | *Welsh* white |
| 0.18 | Hadley | *Old English* heath-covered meadow |
| 0.28 | Hailee | *Scottish* hero |
| 4.12 | Hailey | *Scottish* hero |
| 0.12 | Hailie | *Irish* hero |
| 0.23 | Haleigh | *Scottish* hero |
| 2.46 | Haley | *Scottish* hero |
| 0.10 | Halie | *Scottish* hero |
| 0.30 | Halle | *Scottish* hero |
| 0.27 | Hallie | *Scottish* hero |
| 0.15 | Hana | *Hebrew* gracious |
| 0.52 | Hanna | *Hebrew* gracious |

| | | |
|---|---|---|
| 6.97 | Hannah | *Hebrew* gracious |
| 0.29 | Harley | *Old English* hare meadow |
| 0.32 | Harmony | *Latin* complete peace |
| 0.15 | Harper | *English* harp player |
| 0.15 | Haven | *Old English* safe place |
| 0.27 | Hayden | *Teutonic* hedged hill |
| 0.57 | Haylee | *Scottish* hero |
| 0.10 | Hayleigh | *Scottish* hero |
| 0.58 | Hayley | *Scottish* hero |
| 0.24 | Haylie | *Scottish* hero |
| 0.19 | Hazel | *Old English* hazel tree or nut |
| 0.36 | Heather | *English* a heath, a plant |
| 0.45 | Heaven | heaven |
| 0.34 | Heidi | *German* noble, kind |
| 0.32 | Helen | *Greek* a torch, light |
| 0.23 | Helena | *Greek* a torch, light |
| 0.10 | Hillary | *Latin* cheerful |
| 0.43 | Holly | *English* holly |
| 0.81 | Hope | *English* trust, faith, hope |
| 0.10 | Iliana | *Greek* brilliant, resplendent |
| 0.29 | Imani | *Arabic* believer |
| 0.23 | India | the name of the country as a first name |
| 0.11 | Ingrid | *Old Norse* a hero's daughter |
| 0.13 | Irene | *Greek* peace |
| 0.23 | Iris | *Greek* rainbow |
| 1.87 | Isabel | *Spanish* consecrated to God |
| 0.18 | Isabela | *Spanish* consecrated to God |
| 0.11 | Isabell | *Spanish* consecrated to God |
| 7.90 | Isabella | *Spanish* consecrated to God |
| 2.12 | Isabelle | *Spanish* consecrated to God |
| 0.16 | Isis | *Egyptian* earth or throne, goddess of nature |
| 0.11 | Itzel | *Basque* variant of Amparo: *Spanish* protection |
| 0.36 | Ivy | *English* ivy |
| 0.31 | Izabella | *Spanish* consecrated to God |
| 0.12 | Jacey | invented name, possibly from initials J and C |

| | | | | | |
|---|---|---|---|---|---|
| 0.12 | Jaclyn | *Hebrew* to supplant | 0.16 | Jazmyn | *Persian* jasmine |
| 1.48 | Jacqueline | *Hebrew* to supplant | 2.41 | Jenna | *Arabic* small bird |
| 0.11 | Jacquelyn | *Hebrew* to supplant | 2.60 | Jennifer | *Welsh* white, fair |
| 2.18 | Jada | *Spanish* jade, a precious stone | 0.21 | Jenny | *Welsh* white, fair |
| 1.75 | Jade | *Spanish* jade, a precious stone | 3.67 | Jessica | *Hebrew* God's grace |
| 0.43 | Jaden | *Hebrew* God has heard | 0.20 | Jessie | *Hebrew* God's grace |
| 0.46 | Jadyn | *Hebrew* God has heard | 0.11 | Jewel | *Latin* jewel, joy |
| 0.23 | Jaelyn | *American* bird of light | 0.81 | Jillian | *Latin* young; *Greek* soft-haired, youthful |
| 0.12 | Jaelynn | *American* bird of light | | | |
| 0.18 | Jaida | *Spanish* jade | 0.10 | Jimena | *Spanish* heard |
| 0.25 | Jaiden | *Hebrew* God has heard | 0.30 | Joanna | *Hebrew* gracious, merciful |
| 0.16 | Jaidyn | *Hebrew* God has heard | 2.08 | Jocelyn | *German* supplanted, substituted |
| 0.12 | Jakayla | origin unknown | 0.10 | Joelle | *Hebrew* the Lord is winning |
| 0.10 | Jaliyah | *English* a gift from God | 0.21 | Johanna | *Hebrew* gracious, merciful |
| 0.53 | Jamie | *Hebrew* supplanter | 0.13 | Jolie | *French* pleasant, happy |
| 0.10 | Jana | *Hebrew* gracious, merciful | 1.92 | Jordan | *Hebrew* descending |
| 0.15 | Janae | *Hebrew* gracious, merciful | 0.84 | Jordyn | *Hebrew* descending |
| 0.24 | Jane | *Hebrew* gracious, merciful | 0.15 | Jorja | *English* phonetic variant of Georgia: *Latin* farmer |
| 0.23 | Janelle | *Hebrew* gracious, merciful | | | |
| 0.16 | Janessa | *Hebrew* gracious, merciful | 0.20 | Joselyn | *German* supplanted, substituted |
| 0.13 | Janet | *Hebrew* gracious, merciful | 0.56 | Josephine | *Hebrew* he shall increase |
| 0.28 | Janiya | *Hebrew* God is gracious | 0.48 | Josie | *Hebrew* he shall increase |
| 0.16 | Janiyah | *Hebrew* God is gracious | 0.11 | Joslyn | *German* supplanted, substituted |
| 0.81 | Jasmin | *Persian* jasmine | 0.21 | Joy | *Latin* joy |
| 3.63 | Jasmine | *Persian* jasmine | 0.12 | Joyce | *Latin* joyous |
| 0.10 | Jasmyn | *Persian* jasmine | 0.12 | Judith | *Hebrew* of Judah |
| 0.10 | Jaycee | *American* J + C | 3.44 | Julia | *Greek* soft-haired, youthful |
| 0.46 | Jayda | *Spanish* jade, a precious stone | 0.67 | Juliana | *Greek* soft-haired, youthful |
| 0.60 | Jayden | *English* green gemstone | 0.62 | Julianna | *Greek* soft-haired, youthful |
| 1.38 | Jayla | *Arabic* charity | 0.21 | Julianne | *Greek* soft-haired, youthful |
| 0.10 | Jaylee | origin unknown | 0.42 | Julie | *Greek* soft-haired, youthful |
| 0.15 | Jaylin | *American* bird of light | 0.14 | Juliet | *Greek* soft-haired, youthful |
| 0.10 | Jaylyn | *American* bird of light | 0.32 | Juliette | *Greek* soft-haired, youthful |
| 0.15 | Jaylynn | *English* gaius, a bird in the crow family; *English* blue jay | 0.25 | Julissa | *Latin* Jupiter, God the Father |
| | | | 0.19 | Justice | *Latin* just, honest |
| 0.14 | Jazlyn | *American* a flower in the olive family; waterfall | 0.30 | Justine | *Latin* just, honest |
| | | | 0.36 | Kadence | *Latin* rhythmic |
| 1.09 | Jazmin | *Persian* jasmine | 0.25 | Kaelyn | *Arabic* beloved |
| 0.36 | Jazmine | *Persian* jasmine | 0.14 | Kaia | *Greek* earth |

| 0.15 | Kaila | *Arabic* beloved |
|---|---|---|
| 0.19 | Kailee | *Arabic* beloved |
| 0.49 | Kailey | *Arabic* beloved |
| 0.21 | Kailyn | *Arabic* beloved |
| 0.40 | Kaitlin | *Greek* pure, unsullied |
| 3.01 | Kaitlyn | *Greek* pure, unsullied |
| 0.21 | Kaitlynn | *Greek* pure, unsullied |
| 0.12 | Kaiya | *Aboriginal* a type of spear |
| 0.26 | Kaleigh | *Sanskrit* energy |
| 0.20 | Kaley | *Sanskrit* energy |
| 0.19 | Kali | *Sanskrit* energy |
| 0.10 | Kallie | *Sanskrit* energy |
| 0.42 | Kamryn | *English* spiritual one |
| 0.46 | Kara | *Danish* form of Katherine: *Greek* pure, unsullied |
| 0.87 | Karen | *Danish* form of Katherine: *Greek* pure, unsullied |
| 0.37 | Karina | *Latin* a keel |
| 0.11 | Karis | *Greek* grace |
| 0.17 | Karissa | *Greek* beloved |
| 0.67 | Karla | *French* little and womanly |
| 0.17 | Karlee | *French* little and womanly |
| 0.12 | Karley | *French* little and womanly |
| 0.13 | Karli | *French* little and womanly |
| 0.15 | Karlie | *French* little and womanly |
| 0.11 | Karly | *French* little and womanly |
| 0.17 | Kasey | *Irish* brave |
| 0.21 | Kassandra | *Greek* not believed |
| 0.26 | Kassidy | *Greek* not believed |
| 1.13 | Kate | *Greek* pure, unsullied |
| 2.31 | Katelyn | *Greek* pure, unsullied |
| 0.43 | Katelynn | *Greek* pure, unsullied |
| 0.10 | Katharine | *Greek* pure, unsullied |
| 3.00 | Katherine | *Greek* pure, unsullied |
| 0.35 | Kathleen | *Greek* pure, unsullied |
| 1.02 | Kathryn | *Greek* pure, unsullied |
| 0.10 | Kathy | *Greek* pure, unsullied |
| 1.55 | Katie | *Greek* pure, unsullied |
| 0.17 | Katlyn | *Greek* pure, unsullied |
| 0.57 | Katrina | *Greek* pure, unsullied |
| 0.15 | Kaya | *Hopi Indian* my elder sister little |
| 0.17 | Kayden | *Arabic* friend, companion |
| 0.33 | Kaydence | *Latin* rhythmic |
| 3.92 | Kayla | *Hebrew* a crown, a laurel |
| 0.11 | Kaylah | *Hebrew* a crown, a laurel |
| 2.78 | Kaylee | *Hebrew* a crown, a laurel |
| 0.48 | Kayleigh | *Hebrew* a crown, a laurel |
| 0.17 | Kayley | *Hebrew* a crown, a laurel |
| 0.11 | Kayli | *Hebrew* a crown, a laurel |
| 0.38 | Kaylie | *Hebrew* a crown, a laurel |
| 0.26 | Kaylin | *Hebrew* a crown, a laurel |
| 0.15 | Kaylyn | *Hebrew* a crown, a laurel |
| 0.15 | Kaylynn | *Hebrew* a crown, a laurel |
| 0.11 | Keely | *Gaelic* beautiful one |
| 1.09 | Keira | *Irish* dark, black |
| 0.75 | Kelly | *Irish* warrior |
| 0.81 | Kelsey | *Scottish* from the ship island |
| 0.15 | Kelsie | *Scottish* from the ship island |
| 0.16 | Kendal | *Celtic* ruler of the valley |
| 1.13 | Kendall | *Celtic* ruler of the valley |
| 0.60 | Kendra | *English* knowledgeable |
| 0.14 | Kennedi | *Irish* royal |
| 1.56 | Kennedy | *Irish* royal |
| 0.15 | Kenya | *Hebrew* horn (of an animal); *Russian* short form of Innokenti |
| 0.19 | Kenzie | *Scottish* the fair one |
| 0.32 | Kiana | *American* soft |
| 0.14 | Kianna | *Irish* ancient |
| 0.81 | Kiara | *Irish* little dark one |
| 0.41 | Kiera | *Irish* dark, black |
| 0.19 | Kierra | *Irish* dark, black |
| 0.27 | Kiersten | *Greek* a Christian, anointed one |
| 0.30 | Kiley | *Irish* handsome; *Western Australian Aboriginal* curled, stick or boomerang |
| 2.44 | Kimberly | *English* chief, ruler |

| | | | | | |
|---|---|---|---|---|---|
| 0.19 | Kimora | origin unknown | 1.55 | Leslie | *English* meadowlands |
| 0.51 | Kira | *Persian* sun | 0.13 | Lesly | *English* meadowlands |
| 0.36 | Kirsten | *Greek* a Christian, anointed one | 0.33 | Lexi | *Greek* protector of men |
| 0.15 | Krista | *Greek* a Christian, anointed one | 0.18 | Lexie | *Greek* defender of mankind |
| 0.33 | Kristen | *Greek* a Christian, anointed one | 0.17 | Lia | *Hebrew* to be weary |
| 0.17 | Kristin | *Greek* a Christian, anointed one | 0.13 | Liana | *English* from the meadow |
| 0.32 | Kristina | *Greek* a Christian, anointed one | 0.14 | Libby | *Hebrew* consecrated to God |
| 0.18 | Krystal | *Greek* brilliant glass | 0.21 | Liberty | *Latin* freedom |
| 0.11 | Kya | *African* season's beginning | 0.28 | Lila | *Hindi* free, playful will of God |
| 0.67 | Kyla | *Irish* handsome | 0.22 | Lilian | *Latin* lily |
| 1.14 | Kylee | *Irish* handsome | 0.91 | Liliana | *Latin* lily |
| 0.32 | Kyleigh | *Irish* handsome | 2.85 | Lillian | *Latin* lily |
| 2.30 | Kylie | *Irish* handsome; *Western Australian Aboriginal* curled, stick or boomerang | 0.15 | Lilliana | *Spanish* purity and beauty |
| | | | 0.22 | Lillie | *English* flower |
| | | | 0.92 | Lilly | *Latin* lily |
| 0.75 | Kyra | *Greek* lord or god | 3.04 | Lily | *Latin* lily |
| 0.28 | Lacey | *Latin* cheerful | 0.13 | Lina | *Latin* temptress |
| 0.21 | Laci | *Latin* cheerful | 0.25 | Linda | *Spanish* pretty |
| 0.11 | Lacie | *Latin* cheerful | 0.50 | Lindsay | *English* the camp near the stream |
| 0.51 | Laila | *Hebrew* dark beauty | | | |
| 0.15 | Lainey | *English* light | 0.70 | Lindsey | *English* the camp near the stream |
| 0.26 | Lana | *Latin* woolly | | | |
| 0.21 | Laney | *English* path, roadway | 0.22 | Lisa | *Hebrew* God's oath |
| 0.13 | Lara | *Latin* shining; famous | 0.13 | Litzy | origin unknown |
| 0.18 | Larissa | *Latin* cheerful | 0.15 | Livia | *Latin* the olive tree |
| 0.99 | Laura | *Latin* laurel | 0.21 | Lizbeth | *Hebrew* God's oath |
| 0.12 | Laurel | *Latin* laurel | 0.25 | Logan | *Middle English* a felled tree |
| 4.23 | Lauren | *Latin* laurel | 0.35 | Lola | *Spanish* little woman |
| 0.23 | Laurence | *Latin* laurel | 0.19 | London | *English* fierce ruler of the world |
| 0.21 | Laurie | *Latin* laurel | 0.11 | Lorelei | *German* alluring song |
| 0.27 | Lauryn | *Latin* laurel | 0.12 | Lorena | *Latin* laurel |
| 1.32 | Layla | *Arabic* dark as night | 0.31 | Lucia | *Latin* light |
| 0.56 | Lea | *Hebrew* to be weary | 0.13 | Lucille | *English* light |
| 2.34 | Leah | *Hebrew* to be weary | 1.05 | Lucy | *Latin* light |
| 0.12 | Leanna | *English* from the meadow | 0.13 | Luna | *Latin* the moon |
| 0.18 | Leanne | *English* from the meadow | 0.10 | Luz | *Latin* light |
| 0.37 | Leila | *Arabic* dark as night | 1.54 | Lydia | *Greek* from Lydia |
| 0.25 | Leilani | *Hawaiian* heavenly child | 0.10 | Lyla | *English* from the island |
| 0.26 | Lena | *Latin* temptress | 0.14 | Lyric | *Greek* a lyre |

| | | | | | |
|---|---|---|---|---|---|
| 0.19 | Macey | origin unknown | 0.10 | Maren | *English* sea of bitterness |
| 0.15 | Maci | origin unknown | 1.26 | Margaret | *Greek* a pearl |
| 0.23 | Macie | origin unknown | 2.77 | Maria | *Latin, French, Italian, Spanish, Swedish* sea of sorrow |
| 2.86 | Mackenzie | *Irish* son of the wise leader | | | |
| 0.58 | Macy | *African American* name | 1.89 | Mariah | *Hebrew* sea of sorrow |
| 0.34 | Madalyn | *Greek* a high tower | 0.20 | Mariam | *Arabic* form of Mary |
| 0.11 | Madalynn | *Spanish* woman from Magdala | 1.02 | Mariana | *English* combination of Mary and Ann |
| 0.27 | Maddison | *English* son or daughter of Matthew or Maude | 0.13 | Marianna | *English* combination of Mary and Ann |
| 0.58 | Madeleine | *Greek* a high tower | 0.20 | Marianne | *English* combination of Mary and Ann |
| 2.17 | Madeline | *Greek* a high tower | | | |
| 1.50 | Madelyn | *Greek* a high tower | 0.32 | Marie | *Latin, French, Italian, Spanish, Swedish* forms of Mary: *Hebrew* sea of sorrow |
| 0.19 | Madelynn | *Spanish* woman from Magdala | | | |
| 0.21 | Madilyn | *Greek* a high tower | | | |
| 8.98 | Madison | *English* son or daughter of Matthew or Maude | 0.13 | Marilyn | *Hebrew* descendants of Mary |
| | | | 0.10 | Marin | *French* sailor |
| 0.30 | Madisyn | *English* son or daughter of Matthew or Maude | 0.26 | Marina | *Latin* the sea |
| | | | 0.29 | Marisa | *Latin* the sea |
| 0.29 | Madyson | *English* son or daughter of Matthew or Maude | 0.18 | Marisol | *Spanish* sunny sea |
| | | | 1.67 | Marissa | *Latin* the sea |
| 0.18 | Maeve | *Irish* intoxicating, she who makes drink | 0.11 | Maritza | *Arabic* blessed |
| | | | 0.12 | Marlee | *Greek* a high tower |
| 0.71 | Maggie | *Greek* a pearl | 0.23 | Marley | *Greek* a high tower |
| 0.22 | Maia | *Old English* kinswoman; *Middle English* maiden | 0.18 | Martha | *Aramaic* a lady; sorrowful |
| | | | 2.40 | Mary | *Hebrew* sea of sorrow |
| 0.15 | Maika | *Japanese* child of Mai | 0.11 | Maryam | *Arabic* variant of Mary: bitter |
| 0.10 | Makaila | *American* who is like God | 0.12 | Mathilde | *Greek* battle maid |
| 2.72 | Makayla | *American* who is like God | 0.12 | Mattie | *Aramaic* a lady; sorrowful |
| 0.12 | Makena | *African* happiness | 0.14 | Maude | *Teutonic* heroine |
| 0.69 | Makenna | *African* happiness | 0.13 | Maura | *Latin* dark |
| 0.70 | Makenzie | *Irish* son of the wise leader | 2.69 | Maya | *Latin* great |
| 0.10 | Maleah | origin unknown; beautiful young woman | 0.20 | Mckayla | *Irish* who is like God |
| | | | 0.67 | Mckenna | surname used as first name |
| 0.22 | Malia | *Hawaiian* form of Mary: *Hebrew* sea of sorrow | 1.10 | Mckenzie | surname used as first name |
| | | | 0.13 | Meadow | *American* field of flowers |
| 0.71 | Mallory | *French* armor mailed | 0.16 | Meagan | *Greek* a pearl |
| 0.10 | Mandy | *Latin* lovable | 2.93 | Megan | *Greek* a pearl |
| 0.20 | Mara | *Hebrew* bitter | | | |

| | | | | | |
|---|---|---|---|---|---|
| 0.22 | Megane | *Greek* a pearl | 1.69 | Natalia | *Latin* to be born |
| 0.60 | Meghan | *Greek* a pearl | 5.02 | Natalie | *Latin* to be born |
| 2.00 | Melanie | *Greek* black, dark appearance | 0.12 | Nataly | *Latin* to be born |
| 0.13 | Melany | *Greek* black, dark appearance | 0.10 | Natalya | *Latin* born on Christmas day |
| 0.21 | Melina | *Greek* a song | 0.47 | Natasha | *Latin* to be born |
| 1.56 | Melissa | *Greek* a bee, honey | 0.15 | Nathalie | *Latin* to be born |
| 0.13 | Melodie | *Greek* a melody | 0.16 | Nayeli | origin unknown |
| 0.34 | Melody | *Greek* a melody | 2.46 | Nevaeh | heaven spelled backwards |
| 0.31 | Mercedes | *Latin* reward, payment | 0.25 | Nia | *Welsh* figure in *Irish* legend |
| 0.33 | Meredith | *Welsh* protector of the sea | 2.46 | Nicole | *Greek* victory of the people |
| 5.39 | Mia | *Italian* mine, my | 0.48 | Nina | *Spanish* girl |
| 0.10 | Miah | *Italian* mine, my | 0.22 | Noelle | *Latin* Christmas |
| 0.11 | Micah | *Hebrew* who is like God | 0.10 | Noemi | *Hebrew* beautiful |
| 0.42 | Michaela | *Hebrew* who is like God | 0.25 | Noemie | *French* variant of Naomi: pleasantness |
| 2.17 | Michelle | *Hebrew* who is like God | | | |
| 0.16 | Mikaela | *Hebrew* who is like God | 0.51 | Nora | *Greek* light |
| 0.97 | Mikayla | *Hebrew* who is like God | 0.27 | Norah | *Greek* light |
| 0.10 | Mila | *Russian* loved by the people | 0.10 | Nya | *Swahili* lustrous; goal, purpose |
| 0.10 | Mira | *Slavonic* the famous one | 0.30 | Nyla | *Greek* from the river Nile |
| 0.22 | Miracle | miracle | 0.20 | Oceane | *Greek* ocean |
| 1.06 | Miranda | *Latin* strange, wonderful | 0.12 | Oceanne | *Greek* ocean |
| 0.39 | Miriam | *Hebrew* sea of sorrow | 7.45 | Olivia | *Latin* olive |
| 0.14 | Mollie | *Irish* sea of sorrow | 2.83 | Paige | *English* child, young |
| 1.79 | Molly | *Irish* sea of sorrow | 0.12 | Pamela | *Greek* all honey |
| 0.39 | Monica | *Greek* solitary; *Latin* advisor | 0.20 | Paola | *Latin* small |
| 0.10 | Monique | *Greek* solitary; *Latin* advisor | 0.61 | Paris | *French* place name |
| 0.11 | Montana | *Spanish* mountain; place name used as a first name | 0.13 | Parker | *English* keeper of the park |
| | | | 0.17 | Patience | *French* endurance |
| 3.39 | Morgan | *Welsh* edge of the sea | 0.24 | Patricia | *Latin* of noble descent |
| 1.88 | Mya | *Danish and Swedish* short form of Maria | 0.13 | Paulina | *Latin* small |
| | | | 0.95 | Payton | *Latin* village warrior |
| 0.17 | Myah | *Italian* mine, my | 0.22 | Penelope | *Greek* type of duck or goose noted for red stripes |
| 0.10 | Myriam | *Hebrew* sea of sorrow | | | |
| 0.59 | Nadia | *French, Slavic* hope | 0.13 | Perla | *Latin* bone |
| 0.10 | Naima | *Arabic* to be contented | 1.23 | Peyton | *Latin* village warrior |
| 0.27 | Nancy | *Hebrew* gracious | 0.29 | Phoebe | *Greek* the shining |
| 1.07 | Naomi | *Hebrew* beautiful, pleasant | 0.10 | Phoenix | *Greek* dark red |
| 0.20 | Natalee | *French* birthday | 0.50 | Piper | *English* flute player |

| | | | | |
|---|---|---|---|---|
| 0.18 | Precious | precious | 0.86 | Sabrina | *Latin* from the boundary line |

0.18 Precious   precious

0.22 Presley   *English* priests field

0.11 Princess   princess

0.17 Priscilla   *Latin* from ancient times

0.20 Quinn   *Old English* queen

0.33 Rachael   *Hebrew* a female sheep

2.91 Rachel   *Hebrew* a female sheep

0.22 Raegan   *Celtic, Old French* royal

0.11 Raina   *Old German* mighty

0.16 Raquel   *Hebrew* a female sheep

0.30 Raven   *English* like a raven

0.13 Rayna   *Yiddish* pure, clean

1.22 Reagan   *Celtic, Old French*, royal

2.11 Rebecca   *Hebrew* to tie, to bind

0.48 Rebekah   *Hebrew* to tie, to bind

0.81 Reese   *Welsh* enthusiastic

0.26 Regan   *Latin* queen

0.15 Regina   *Latin* queen

0.21 Renee   *French* to be born again

0.14 Rhiannon   *Welsh* a mythological witch, nymph, goddess

2.50 Riley   *Irish* valiant

0.10 Riya   *Spanish* river

0.18 Rosa   *Latin* rose

0.29 Rosalie   Rose + Lee

0.50 Rose   *Latin* rose

0.10 Roselyn   *French* red haired

0.11 Rosemary   Rose + Mary

0.17 Rowan   *English* tree with red berries

1.26 Ruby   *French* ruby

0.30 Ruth   *Hebrew* friendship

0.20 Ryan   *Irish* little king

0.13 Ryann   *Irish* little king

1.45 Rylee   *German, Dutch* a small stream; *Irish* valiant

0.35 Ryleigh   *Irish* island meadow

0.34 Rylie   *German, Dutch* a small stream; *Irish* valiant

0.86 Sabrina   *Latin* from the boundary line

0.93 Sadie   *Hebrew* princess, noble

0.33 Sage   *Latin* wise

0.12 Saige   *Latin* wise

0.14 Salma   *Spanish* divine protector

6.01 Samantha   *Aramaic* the listener

0.30 Samara   *Hebrew* ruled by God

0.10 Samira   *Arabic* entertaining companion, amusing

0.13 Sanaa   *Swahili* work of art, beauty

0.27 Sandra   *Greek* defender of mankind

0.16 Saniya   origin unknown

0.13 Saniyah   *Arabic* resplendence, brilliance

2.10 Sara   *Hebrew* princess, noble

5.76 Sarah   *Hebrew* princess, noble

0.15 Sarai   *Hebrew* quarrelsome

0.33 Sasha   *Russian* form of Alexandra: *Greek* defender of mankind

0.10 Savana   *Spanish* barren

0.15 Savanah   *Spanish* barren

0.50 Savanna   *Spanish* barren

3.09 Savannah   *Spanish* barren

0.30 Scarlett   *English* bright red color

0.47 Selena   *Greek* moon

0.12 Selina   *Greek* moon

0.39 Serena   *Latin* peaceful

0.86 Serenity   *Latin* serene, tranquil

0.34 Shania   *English* God is gracious

0.18 Shaniya   *Grenadian* pretty as a blossom

0.40 Shannon   *Irish* small; wise

0.18 Sharon   *Hebrew* a plain

0.37 Shayla   *Irish* from the fairy fort

0.10 Shaylee   *Celtic* fairy princess

0.13 Shayna   *Hebrew* beautiful

0.10 Shea   *Hebrew* asked for

1.44 Shelby   *English* from the ledge estate

0.10 Sherlyn   origin unknown

0.11 Shyann   *American Indian* tribal name

| | | |
|---|---|---|
| 0.14 | Shyanne | *American Indian* tribal name |
| 0.32 | Sidney | *French* from the city of St. Denis |
| 0.10 | Siena | *Italian* earth colored |
| 0.52 | Sienna | *Italian* earth colored |
| 1.35 | Sierra | place name; *Irish* black |
| 0.19 | Simone | *Hebrew* one who hears |
| 0.10 | Sky | *English* sky |
| 0.29 | Skye | *Arabic* water giver; *Scottish* surname |
| 0.20 | Skyla | *English* sky, sheltering |
| 1.13 | Skylar | *Dutch* a shelter |
| 0.36 | Skyler | *Dutch* a shelter |
| 2.67 | Sofia | *Greek* wisdom |
| 0.15 | Sonia | *Slavic and Russian* form of Sophia: *Greek* wisdom |
| 6.10 | Sophia | *Greek* wisdom |
| 1.55 | Sophie | *Greek* wisdom |
| 0.11 | Stacy | *Irish* form of Anastasia: *Greek* resurrection |
| 0.56 | Stella | *Latin* star |
| 2.28 | Stephanie | *Greek* crown |
| 1.06 | Summer | *English* summer |
| 0.18 | Susan | *Hebrew* a rose, a lily |
| 0.12 | Sydnee | *French* from the city of St. Denis |
| 3.37 | Sydney | *French* from the city of St. Denis |
| 0.23 | Sylvia | *Latin* forest |
| 0.21 | Tabitha | *Greek, Aramaic* a gazelle |
| 0.36 | Talia | *Hebrew* dew; *Greek* blooming |
| 0.11 | Taliyah | *Hebrew* lamb |
| 0.19 | Tamara | *Hebrew* palm tree |
| 0.18 | Tamia | origin unknown |
| 0.18 | Tania | *Slavic* fairy queen |
| 0.11 | Taniya | *Slavic* fairy queen |
| 0.11 | Tanya | *Slavic* fairy queen |
| 0.31 | Tara | *Arabic* a measurement; *Aramaic* to throw, carry |
| 0.27 | Taryn | *Arabic* a measurement; *Aramaic* to throw, carry |
| 0.45 | Tatiana | *Slavic* fairy queen |
| 0.35 | Tatum | *Anglo Saxon* cheerful |
| 0.10 | Tatyana | *Slavic* fairy queen |
| 0.11 | Taya | *English* tailor |
| 0.10 | Tayler | *English* tailor |
| 4.20 | Taylor | *English* tailor |
| 0.28 | Teagan | *Welsh* beautiful |
| 0.20 | Teresa | *Greek* to reap |
| 0.17 | Tess | *Greek* to reap |
| 0.52 | Tessa | *Greek* to reap |
| 0.16 | Thalia | *Greek* bloom, muse of comedy |
| 0.15 | Theresa | *Greek* to reap |
| 0.20 | Tia | *Greek* princess |
| 0.26 | Tiana | *Greek* princess |
| 0.17 | Tianna | *Greek* princess |
| 0.17 | Tiara | *Latin* crown |
| 0.62 | Tiffany | *Latin* trinity |
| 0.12 | Tina | *Greek* Christian |
| 0.31 | Tori | *Japanese* bird |
| 2.60 | Trinity | *Latin* three in one |
| 0.16 | Trista | *Latin* melancholy |
| 0.13 | Tyler | *Middle English* a tiler of roofs |
| 0.16 | Tyra | *Scandinavian* one who does battle |
| 0.24 | Valentina | *Latin* strong and healthy |
| 1.90 | Valeria | *Latin* to be strong |
| 1.40 | Valerie | *Latin* to be strong |
| 2.18 | Vanessa | *Greek* butterfly |
| 0.56 | Veronica | *Latin* true image |
| 3.77 | Victoria | *Latin* victorious |
| 0.33 | Violet | *Old French* little purple flower |
| 0.23 | Virginia | *Latin* pure, virgin |
| 0.42 | Vivian | *Latin* alive |
| 0.12 | Viviana | *Latin* alive |
| 0.20 | Wendy | *English* a created name that first appeared in the book "Peter Pan" |
| 0.22 | Whitney | *English* from the white island |

0.25 Willow       *English* from the willow tree,        0.14 Yesenia    *Arabic* flower
                  noted for its grace and pliancy        0.12 Zara       *Hebrew* eastern brightness
0.12 Ximena       *Greek* a heroine; *Hebrew* he         0.13 Zaria      *Arabic* beauty and light
                  heard                                  0.10 Zariah     *Arabic* beauty and light
0.11 Yadira       origin unknown                         2.51 Zoe        *Greek* life
0.27 Yasmin       *Persian* jasmine                      1.35 Zoey       *Greek* life
0.22 Yasmine      *Persian* jasmine                      0.17 Zoie       *Greek* life

# Popular Boys' Names

*Popularity ratings indicate usage per thousand baby boys.*

## Popularity rating • Name • Origin and meaning

| | | | |
|---|---|---|---|
| 3.57 | Aaron | *Hebrew* to sing, to shine, to teach or a mountain, enlightened; *Arabic* a messenger | |
| 0.12 | Abel | *Hebrew* breath, evanescence | |
| 0.40 | Abraham | *Hebrew* father of the multitude | |
| 0.10 | Abram | *Hebrew* exalted father | |
| 3.40 | Adam | *Hebrew* earth, man of the red earth; *Phoenician* man, mankind | |
| 0.16 | Adan | *Irish* warmth of the home | |
| 0.13 | Addison | *Old English* son of Adam | |
| 0.39 | Aden | *Irish* noble | |
| 3.40 | Adrian | *Greek* rich; *Latin* black, dark | |
| 0.10 | Adrien | *French* Adrian | |
| 0.16 | Ahmad | *Arabic* the most praised | |
| 0.18 | Ahmed | *Arabic* most highly praised | |
| 4.45 | Aidan | *Irish* warmth of the home | |
| 4.74 | Aiden | *Irish* warmth of the home | |
| 1.60 | Alan | *Celtic* harmony, peace | |
| 0.20 | Albert | *French* noble, bright | |
| 0.14 | Alberto | *French* noble, bright | |
| 0.34 | Alec | *Greek* helper of mankind, protector of man | |

| | | | |
|---|---|---|---|
| 2.25 | Alejandro | *Greek* helper of mankind, protector of man | |
| 2.99 | Alex | *Greek* helper of mankind, protector of man | |
| 8.01 | Alexander | *Greek* helper of mankind, protector of man | |
| 0.35 | Alexandre | *Greek* helper of mankind, protector of man | |
| 1.90 | Alexis | *Greek* helper of mankind, protector of man | |
| 0.10 | Alexzander | *Greek* helper of mankind, protector of man | |
| 0.12 | Alfredo | *Old English* elfin counselor | |
| 0.39 | Ali | *Arabic* greatest | |
| 0.10 | Alijah | *Hebrew* God is lord | |
| 0.14 | Allan | *Celtic* harmony, peace | |
| 0.33 | Allen | *Celtic* harmony, peace | |
| 0.16 | Alvin | *German* beloved by all | |
| 0.18 | Amari | *African* immortal | |
| 0.28 | Amir | *Arabic* prince; *Punjabi* wealthy; king's minister | |
| 0.16 | Anderson | *Greek* manly, courageous | |

| | | | |
|---|---|---|---|
| 0.48 | Andre | *Greek* manly, valiant, courageous, strong | |
| 1.28 | Andres | *Greek* manly, valiant, courageous, strong | |
| 8.68 | Andrew | *Greek* manly, valiant, courageous, strong | |
| 0.48 | Andy | *Greek* manly, valiant, courageous, strong | |
| 5.38 | Angel | *Italian* messenger | |
| 0.35 | Angelo | *Greek* angel, a messenger or a saintly person | |
| 8.52 | Anthony | *Greek* flourishing; *Latin* worthy of praise | |
| 0.46 | Antoine | *Greek* flourishing; *Latin* worthy of praise | |
| 2.11 | Antonio | *Greek* flourishing; *Latin* worthy of praise | |
| 0.13 | Ariel | *Hebrew* lion of God | |
| 0.10 | Arjun | *Indian* one of the Pandavas | |
| 0.19 | Armando | *Old German* army man | |
| 0.24 | Arthur | *Gaelic* a rock, noble, lofty, hill | |
| 0.13 | Arturo | *Spanish* and *Italian* form of *Gaelic* a rock, noble, lofty, hill | |
| 0.39 | Asher | *Hebrew* blessed, happy | |
| 1.83 | Ashton | *Old English* one who lives at the ash-tree farm | |
| 0.10 | August | *Latin* exalted and sacred | |
| 4.68 | Austin | *Latin* majestic, dignity; form of August | |
| 0.58 | Avery | *Old English* leader of the elves | |
| 0.18 | Axel | *Hebrew* father of peace | |
| 0.10 | Aydan | *Irish* warmth of the home | |
| 1.28 | Ayden | *Irish* warmth of the home | |
| 0.16 | Bailey | *English* fortification; *English/French* public official, person in charge | |
| 0.18 | Beau | *English* handsome | |

| | | | |
|---|---|---|---|
| 0.15 | Ben | *Hebrew* son of my right hand | |
| 6.39 | Benjamin | *Hebrew* son of my right hand | |
| 0.23 | Bennett | *Latin* little blessed one | |
| 0.19 | Billy | *English* resolute protector | |
| 0.11 | Blaine | *Irish* thin, lean | |
| 2.10 | Blake | *English* white | |
| 0.16 | Bobby | *German* bright fame | |
| 0.12 | Boston | *English* the capital city of Massachusetts, U.S.A. | |
| 1.14 | Braden | *English* a broad lea, a meadow | |
| 0.84 | Bradley | *English* a broad lea, a meadow; *English* from the broad river crossing | |
| 1.56 | Brady | *English* broad island | |
| 0.12 | Bradyn | *English* from the broad valley | |
| 0.32 | Braeden | *English* a broad lea, a meadow | |
| 0.13 | Braiden | *English* a broad lea, a meadow | |
| 0.19 | Branden | *Irish* a raven; *English* a sword | |
| 5.63 | Brandon | *Irish* a raven; *English* a sword | |
| 0.60 | Braxton | *Anglo Saxon* Brock's town | |
| 0.18 | Brayan | *Celtic* strong; *Irish* strength, virtue | |
| 3.05 | Brayden | *English* a broad lea, a meadow | |
| 0.27 | Braydon | *English* a broad lea, a meadow | |
| 0.26 | Braylon | *American* meaning unknown | |
| 0.86 | Brendan | *Irish* a raven; *English* a sword | |
| 0.31 | Brenden | *Irish* a raven; *English* a sword | |
| 0.17 | Brendon | *Irish* a raven; *English* a sword | |
| 0.39 | Brennan | *Irish* a raven; *English* a sword | |
| 0.11 | Brennen | *Irish* a raven; *English* a sword | |
| 0.17 | Brent | *Irish* a raven; *English* a sword | |
| 0.43 | Brett | *Celtic* a Breton, a native of Brittany | |
| 2.97 | Brian | *Celtic* strong; *Irish* strength, virtue | |
| 0.41 | Brock | *Gaelic* a badger | |
| 0.18 | Brodie | *Irish* ditch | |
| 0.95 | Brody | *Irish* ditch | |

| | | | | | |
|---|---|---|---|---|---|
| 0.16 | Bruce | *English* from the brushwood thicket | 0.36 | Chance | *Old English* secretary to the throne |
| 3.04 | Bryan | *Celtic* strong; *Irish* strength, virtue | 0.25 | Chandler | *Old English* candlemaker |
| 0.22 | Bryant | *Celtic* strong; *Irish* strength, virtue | 3.79 | Charles | *English* manly, strong; *German* farmer |
| 1.66 | Bryce | *English* son of Rice; *Welsh* form of Price, son of the ardent one | 0.29 | Charlie | *English* manly, strong; *German* farmer |
| 0.11 | Brycen | *English* son of Rice; *Welsh* form of Price, son of the ardent one | 2.67 | Chase | *English* the hunt, hunter |
| | | | 0.17 | Chris | *Greek* Christ bearer |
| 0.96 | Bryson | *Welsh* son of Bryce | 6.23 | Christian | *Greek* Christ bearer |
| 0.13 | Byron | *Old French* from the cottage | 8.11 | Christopher | *Greek* Christ bearer |
| 0.29 | Cade | *Irish* spirit of battle | 0.10 | Clay | *English* a town built upon clay land |
| 2.28 | Caden | *Old English* round | 0.54 | Clayton | *English* a town built upon clay land |
| 0.30 | Caiden | *Gaelic, English* battle | 1.87 | Cody | *English* a cushion |
| 0.10 | Cale | *English* bold | 0.22 | Cohen | *German* brave |
| 5.02 | Caleb | *Hebrew* a dog, faithful, bold one | 0.47 | Colby | *Old English* from the black farm |
| 0.52 | Calvin | *Latin* bald | 2.97 | Cole | *English* cola miner; *Latin* a man who farms cabbage |
| 0.46 | Camden | *Old English* dweller in the winding valley | 0.11 | Coleman | *English* cola miner; *Latin* a man who farms cabbage |
| 4.29 | Cameron | *Celtic* bent nose | 1.90 | Colin | *Irish* child; *Celtic* a cub, whelp; short form of Nicholas: victory |
| 0.10 | Camren | *Irish* crooked nose | | | |
| 0.22 | Camron | *Celtic* bent nose | 0.80 | Collin | *Irish* child; *Celtic* a cub, whelp; short form of Nicholas: victory |
| 0.23 | Carl | *English* manly, strong; *German* farmer | 0.15 | Colten | *Old English* from the dark town |
| 3.01 | Carlos | *English* manly, strong; *German* farmer | 1.25 | Colton | *Old English* from the dark town |
| 2.41 | Carson | *English* son of the family on the marsh | 1.28 | Conner | *Irish* wise aid |
| | | | 4.49 | Connor | *Irish* wise aid |
| 3.35 | Carter | *Old English* cart driver | 0.17 | Conor | *Irish* wise aid |
| 0.35 | Casey | *Celtic* valorous; *Irish* brave | 1.50 | Cooper | *Old English* barrel maker |
| 0.11 | Cash | *Slavic* man at peace | 0.34 | Corbin | *Latin* the raven |
| 0.51 | Cayden | *Gaelic* fighter spirit of battle | 0.53 | Corey | *Latin* a helmet, from the hollow |
| 0.18 | Cedric | *Old English* chieftain | 0.24 | Cory | *Latin* a helmet, from the hollow |
| 1.24 | Cesar | *Latin* long-haired | 0.16 | Craig | *Celtic* from the crag or rugged rocky mass |
| 0.27 | Chad | *Celtic* battle or warrior; *English* warlike | | | |
| | | | 1.30 | Cristian | *Greek* Christ-bearer |

| | | |
|---|---|---|
| 0.41 | Curtis | *Latin* an enclosure, court; *English* courteous |
| 0.14 | Cyrus | *Persian* sun |
| 1.02 | Dakota | *American Indian* friend |
| 0.25 | Dallas | *Old English* from the waterfall |
| 0.88 | Dalton | *Old English* dweller in the town in the valley |
| 1.45 | Damian | *Greek* divine power or fate |
| 0.61 | Damien | *Greek* divine power or fate |
| 0.14 | Damion | *Greek* divine power or fate |
| 0.32 | Damon | *Greek* tamer |
| 0.18 | Dane | *Norse* inhabitant of Denmark |
| 8.86 | Daniel | *Hebrew* God is my judge |
| 0.27 | Danny | *Hebrew* God is my judge |
| 0.32 | Dante | *Latin* enduring |
| 0.13 | Darian | *Anglo-Saxon* dear, darling; *Persian* wealthy, king |
| 0.34 | Darius | *Greek* wealthy |
| 0.11 | Darrell | *English* beloved; *English* a grove of oak trees |
| 0.26 | Darren | *English* a small, rocky hill |
| 7.67 | David | *Hebrew* beloved |
| 0.12 | Davin | *Scandinavian* brilliance of the Finns |
| 0.17 | Davion | *English* beloved |
| 0.21 | Davis | *Old Scottish* son of the beloved son of David |
| 0.58 | Dawson | |
| 0.16 | Dayton | *Middle English* day town; bright cheerful town |
| 0.10 | Deacon | *Greek* messenger |
| 0.22 | Dean | *English* head, leader; *English* from the valley |
| 0.12 | Deandre | *French* prefix De + Andre |
| 0.30 | Declan | *Irish* a man of prayer |
| 0.16 | Demetrius | *Greek* belonging to Demeter, the *Greek* god of fertility |
| 0.32 | Dennis | *English* from *Latin and Greek*, wild, frenzied |

| | | |
|---|---|---|
| 0.82 | Derek | *English* from *German* Hrodrich, famous ruler |
| 0.10 | Derick | *English* from *German* Hrodrich, famous ruler |
| 0.38 | Derrick | *English* from *German* Hrodrich, famous ruler |
| 0.11 | Deshawn | origin unknown derived from John, gracious gift from God |
| 0.16 | Desmond | *Old English* kindly protector |
| 0.12 | Devan | *Irish* poet; *English* place name |
| 0.13 | Deven | *Irish* poet; *English* place name |
| 1.91 | Devin | *Irish* poet; *English* place name |
| 0.71 | Devon | *Irish* poet; *English* place name |
| 3.79 | Diego | *Spanish* form of James: held by the heel, supplanter |
| 0.53 | Dillon | *Irish* faithful |
| 2.59 | Dominic | *Latin* belonging to or pertaining to God |
| 0.49 | Dominick | *Latin* belonging to or pertaining to God |
| 0.11 | Dominik | *Latin* belonging to the Lord |
| 0.37 | Donald | *Irish* brown stranger, world ruler |
| 0.63 | Donovan | *Irish* dark warrior |
| 0.19 | Dorian | *Celtic* stranger |
| 0.27 | Douglas | *Celtic* gray; *Scottish* from the dark water |
| 0.42 | Drake | *Latin* dragon |
| 0.11 | Draven | origin unknown |
| 0.63 | Drew | *English* sturdy; *Welsh* wise, short form of Andrew |
| 0.13 | Duncan | *Scottish* dark-skinned warrior |
| 0.48 | Dustin | *English* brown, stone, the brown rock quarry |
| 0.10 | Dwayne | *Irish* little and dark |
| 5.94 | Dylan | *Welsh* the sea |
| 0.29 | Easton | *English* east town |
| 0.17 | Eddie | *English* happy guardian |

| | | |
|---|---|---|
| 1.10 | Edgar | *Old English* prosperous spearman |
| 0.11 | Edouard | *English* happy guardian |
| 1.64 | Eduardo | *English* happy guardian |
| 0.97 | Edward | *English* happy guardian |
| 0.58 | Edwin | *English* rich friend |
| 1.06 | Eli | *Hebrew* on, up, high |
| 0.55 | Elias | *German and Dutch* form of Elijah: *Hebrew* Jehovah is God |
| 5.15 | Elijah | *Hebrew* Jehovah is God |
| 0.10 | Elisha | *Hebrew* God is salvation |
| 0.32 | Elliot | *English* modern form of Elijah |
| 0.22 | Elliott | *English* modern form of Elijah |
| 0.30 | Emanuel | *Hebrew* God is with us |
| 0.12 | Emerson | *Old English* son of the industrious leader |
| 0.24 | Emile | *Latin* flattering |
| 0.10 | Emiliano | *Spanish, Italian* form of Roman family name Aemilianus |
| 0.21 | Emilio | *Latin* flattering |
| 0.57 | Emmanuel | *Hebrew* God is with us |
| 0.12 | Emmett | *Old German* hardworking and strong |
| 0.20 | Enrique | *Spanish* form of Henry: *German* ruler of an estate |
| 3.03 | Eric | *Norse* honorable ruler |
| 0.41 | Erick | *Norse* honorable ruler |
| 0.43 | Erik | *Norse* honorable ruler |
| 0.11 | Ernesto | *English* earnest |
| 0.16 | Esteban | *Spanish* form of Steven: *Greek* a crown |
| 9.71 | Ethan | *Hebrew* strong, firm |
| 0.16 | Etienne | *French* form of Stephen: *Greek* a crown |
| 4.49 | Evan | *Welsh* form of John, young warrior |
| 0.15 | Everett | *English* strong as a boar |
| 0.31 | Ezekiel | *Hebrew* strength of the Lord |

| | | |
|---|---|---|
| 0.26 | Ezra | *Hebrew* strength |
| 0.18 | Fabian | *Latin* bean grower |
| 0.11 | Felipe | *Greek* a lover of horses |
| 0.54 | Felix | *Latin* fortunate |
| 1.33 | Fernando | *Spanish* form of *Old German* world venturing |
| 0.16 | Finn | *Irish* fair |
| 0.19 | Francis | *Latin* free man, *French* man |
| 1.36 | Francisco | *Latin* free man, *French* man |
| 0.36 | Frank | *Latin* free man, *French* man |
| 0.17 | Franklin | *English* free landowner |
| 0.23 | Frederick | *German* peace, king, ruler |
| 5.73 | Gabriel | *Hebrew* God is my strength, devoted to God |
| 0.12 | Gael | name for Celtics of Scotland, Ireland, and the Isle of Man |
| 1.15 | Gage | *French* a pledge, a pawn |
| 0.10 | Garret | *English* to watch; with a mighty spear |
| 1.09 | Garrett | *English* to watch; with a mighty spear |
| 0.27 | Gary | *English* a spear bearer, a warrior |
| 4.42 | Gavin | *Welsh* little hawk |
| 0.10 | Gavyn | *Scottish* white hawk |
| 0.92 | George | *Greek* a farmer, a tiller of the soil |
| 0.13 | Gerald | *English* a warrior; *Latin* spear ruler |
| 0.15 | Gerardo | *Old English* brave with a spear |
| 0.10 | Gianni | *Italian* God is gracious |
| 1.28 | Giovanni | *Italian* form of John: Jehovah has been gracious |
| 0.16 | Grady | *Gaelic* famous |
| 0.23 | Graham | *Latin* a grain; *English* the gray home |
| 1.05 | Grant | *English* to give, to assure; *English* great |

| | | | |
|---|---|---|---|
| 0.40 | Grayson | *Old English* son of the local bailiff | |
| 0.57 | Gregory | *Greek* vigilant; *Latin* watchman, watchful | |
| 0.11 | Greyson | *English* bailiff's son | |
| 0.47 | Griffin | mythological animal with body of a lion and head and wings of an eagle | |
| 0.11 | Guillaume | *French* form of William: resolute protector | |
| 0.12 | Gunnar | *Norse* battle army | |
| 0.11 | Gunner | *Norse* battle army | |
| 0.17 | Gustavo | *Old Norse* staff of the Goths | |
| 0.11 | Hamza | *Arabic* strong or strength, lion cub | |
| 0.16 | Harley | *Old English* from the meadow of the hare | |
| 0.10 | Harold | *Scottish* army ruler; *English* soldier | |
| 0.51 | Harrison | *English* Harry's son; *Old English* son of the army man | |
| 0.15 | Harry | *Scottish* army ruler; *English* soldier, short form of Harold | |
| 0.10 | Hassan | *Arabic* handsome | |
| 3.12 | Hayden | *Old English* from the hedged hill | |
| 1.21 | Hector | *Greek* steadfast | |
| 2.08 | Henry | *German* ruler of an estate | |
| 0.22 | Holden | *Old English* a valley | |
| 0.35 | Hudson | *English* son of the hooded man | |
| 0.22 | Hugo | *German and Dutch* form of Hugh: intelligence | |
| 4.23 | Hunter | *Old English* a huntsman | |
| 2.74 | Ian | *Scottish* form of John | |
| 0.15 | Ibrahim | *Arabic* form of Abraham: *Hebrew* father of the multitude | |
| 4.27 | Isaac | *Hebrew* he will laugh | |
| 4.42 | Isaiah | *Hebrew* God is my salvation | |

| | | |
|---|---|---|
| 0.23 | Isiah | *Hebrew* God's helper |
| 0.19 | Ismael | *Hebrew* God will laugh |
| 0.32 | Israel | *Hebrew* soldier of the Lord |
| 0.13 | Issac | *Hebrew* he will laugh |
| 1.64 | Ivan | *Russian* form of John, grace |
| 0.14 | Izaiah | *Hebrew* God is my salvation |
| 0.10 | Jabari | *African* fearless |
| 0.76 | Jace | *American* J + C |
| 4.85 | Jack | short form of Jacob; nickname for John |
| 4.46 | Jackson | *Old English* son of Jack |
| 11.25 | Jacob | *Hebrew* one who holds back another, supplanter |
| 2.21 | Jaden | *Hebrew* God has heard |
| 0.19 | Jadon | *Hebrew* God has heard |
| 0.47 | Jaiden | *Hebrew* God has heard |
| 0.16 | Jaime | *Spanish* form of James |
| 1.54 | Jake | *Hebrew* one who holds back another, supplanter |
| 0.47 | Jakob | *Hebrew* one who holds back another, supplanter |
| 0.50 | Jalen | *American* supplanter, light |
| 0.15 | Jamal | *Arabic* a camel, beauty |
| 0.10 | Jamar | origin unknown |
| 0.17 | Jamari | *French* warrior |
| 0.17 | Jamarion | *African, American* handsome |
| 7.12 | James | *English* form of Jacob, held by the heel, supplanter |
| 0.17 | Jameson | son of James |
| 0.13 | Jamie | *English* form of Jacob, held by the heel, supplanter |
| 0.15 | Jamison | son of James |
| 0.91 | Jared | *Hebrew* to descend, descendent, one who rules |
| 0.12 | Jarrett | *Hebrew* to descend, descendent, one who rules |
| 0.12 | Jase | origin unknown |
| 3.77 | Jason | *Greek* healer |
| 0.15 | Jasper | *Old French* stone |

| | | |
|---|---|---|
| 1.14 | Javier | *Spanish* owner of the new house |
| 0.21 | Javon | *Biblical* Javan is son of Japheth |
| 0.57 | Jaxon | *English* God has been gracious |
| 0.22 | Jaxson | *English* God has been gracious |
| 0.24 | Jay | *English* gaius, a bird in the crow family; *English* blue jay |
| 0.17 | Jayce | *American* J + C |
| 3.95 | Jayden | *Hebrew* God has heard |
| 0.17 | Jaydon | *Hebrew* God has heard |
| 0.82 | Jaylen | *American* supplanter, light |
| 0.16 | Jaylin | *American* supplanter, light |
| 0.14 | Jaylon | *American* supplanter, light |
| 0.29 | Jayson | *Greek* healer |
| 0.19 | Jeffery | *English* gift of peace |
| 0.85 | Jeffrey | *English* gift of peace |
| 2.94 | Jeremiah | *Hebrew* appointed by Jehovah, God will uplift |
| 0.10 | Jeremie | *Hebrew* appointed by Jehovah, God will uplift |
| 1.61 | Jeremy | *Hebrew* appointed by Jehovah, God will uplift |
| 0.19 | Jermaine | *Middle English* sprout, a bud |
| 0.19 | Jerome | *English* of holy name |
| 0.29 | Jerry | *German* spear warrior |
| 2.17 | Jesse | *Greek* wealthy, a gift, God exists |
| 0.11 | Jessie | *Greek* wealthy, a gift, God exists |
| 3.25 | Jesus | *Hebrew* God will help |
| 0.11 | Jett | *Hebrew* excellence, abundance, riches |
| 0.28 | Jimmy | *English* form of Jacob, held by the heel, supplanter |
| 0.15 | Joaquin | *Hebrew* God will establish |
| 0.13 | Joe | *Hebrew* Jehovah adds |
| 1.24 | Joel | *Hebrew* God is willing, Jehovah is the Lord |
| 0.18 | Joey | *Hebrew* Jehovah adds |
| 0.10 | Johan | *Hebrew* God is gracious |

| | | |
|---|---|---|
| 6.62 | John | *Hebrew* Jehovah has been gracious |
| 0.60 | Johnathan | *Hebrew* Jehovah has been gracious |
| 0.15 | Johnathon | *Hebrew* Jehovah has been gracious |
| 0.32 | Johnny | *Hebrew* Jehovah has been gracious |
| 0.16 | Jon | *Hebrew* Jehovah has been gracious |
| 0.72 | Jonah | *Hebrew* dove |
| 0.25 | Jonas | *Hebrew* the doer |
| 6.32 | Jonathan | *Hebrew* Jehovah has been gracious |
| 0.29 | Jonathon | *Hebrew* Jehovah has been gracious |
| 4.37 | Jordan | *Hebrew* to descend |
| 0.10 | Jordon | *Hebrew* to descend |
| 1.75 | Jorge | *Spanish* form of George: *Greek* a farmer, a tiller of the soil |
| 5.30 | Jose | *Hebrew* Jehovah adds; *Spanish* for Joseph |
| 7.77 | Joseph | *Hebrew* Jehovah adds |
| 10.39 | Joshua | *Hebrew* Jehovah saves |
| 1.09 | Josiah | *Hebrew* Jehovah supports |
| 0.31 | Josue | form of Joshua |
| 3.72 | Juan | *Spanish* form of John: *Hebrew* God has been gracious |
| 0.15 | Judah | *Hebrew* praised |
| 0.30 | Jude | *Latin* praised |
| 3.09 | Julian | *Greek* soft haired, light bearded |
| 0.23 | Julien | *Greek* soft haired, light bearded |
| 0.27 | Julio | *Spanish* form of Julius: *Greek* youthful and downy-bearded; *Latin* the god Jupiter |
| 0.24 | Julius | *Greek* youthful and downy bearded |
| 0.20 | Justice | *Latin* from the virtue named Justice |

| | | |
|---|---|---|
| 4.86 | Justin | *Latin* just, upright |
| 0.19 | Kade | *Scottish* from the wetlands |
| 2.11 | Kaden | *Arabic* friend of companion |
| 0.13 | Kadin | *Arabic* friend of companion |
| 0.42 | Kai | *Hawaiian* ocean; *Welsh* keeper of the keys |
| 0.43 | Kaiden | *Celtic* warrior |
| 1.66 | Kaleb | *Hebrew* a dog, faithful, bold one |
| 0.37 | Kameron | *Celtic* bent nose |
| 0.10 | Kareem | *Arabic* noble, exalted |
| 0.11 | Karl | *German* form of Charles: *English* manly, strong; *German* farmer |
| 0.12 | Karson | *English* son of Carr |
| 0.11 | Kasey | *Celtic* valorous; *Irish* brave |
| 0.46 | Kayden | *Arabic* friend, companion |
| 0.11 | Keagan | *Irish* small; fiery |
| 0.25 | Keaton | *English* one who comes from Ketton |
| 0.57 | Keegan | *Irish* little and fiery |
| 0.13 | Keenan | *Gaelic* little ancient one |
| 0.36 | Keith | *Gaelic* the wind; *Welsh* from the forest |
| 0.15 | Kellen | *German* surname |
| 0.17 | Kelvin | *English* a friend or lover of ships |
| 0.10 | Kendall | *Old English* from the bright valley |
| 0.11 | Kendrick | *Irish* son of Henry; *English* royal ruler |
| 1.33 | Kenneth | *Scottish* comely, handsome; *English* royal oath |
| 0.16 | Kenny | *Scottish* comely, handsome; *English* royal oath |
| 4.82 | Kevin | *Gaelic* handsome, beautiful |
| 0.16 | Khalil | *Arabic* friend |
| 0.17 | Kieran | *Irish* little and dark skinned |
| 0.14 | Kobe | *Hungarian* held by the heel |
| 0.17 | Kody | *English* a cushion |
| 0.12 | Kolby | *Old English* from the black farm |
| 0.11 | Kole | *English* cola miner; *Latin* a man who farms cabbage |
| 0.12 | Kolton | *Old English* from the dark town |
| 0.17 | Kristian | *Greek* Christ bearer |
| 0.21 | Kristopher | *Greek* Christ bearer |
| 0.10 | Kyan | *African American* little king |
| 3.22 | Kyle | *Gaelic* a hill where the cattle graze |
| 0.35 | Kyler | *American* surname |
| 0.10 | Lamar | *Latin* from the sea |
| 0.33 | Lance | *Latin* a light spear; *German* land |
| 0.55 | Landen | *English* long hill |
| 4.40 | Landon | *Old English* from the long hill |
| 0.31 | Lane | *Old English* from the narrow road |
| 0.23 | Larry | *Latin* a laurel, a crown |
| 0.20 | Lawrence | *Latin* a laurel, a crown |
| 0.11 | Layne | *Old English* from the narrow road |
| 0.10 | Lee | *English* field, meadow |
| 0.20 | Leland | *Old English* from the meadowland |
| 0.48 | Leo | *Latin* lion |
| 0.17 | Leon | *Greek* form of Leo, lion; *French* lionlike |
| 0.12 | Leonard | *English* form of *German*, strong as a lion |
| 0.35 | Leonardo | *English* form of *German*, strong as a lion |
| 1.29 | Levi | *Hebrew* joined to, attendant upon; *Hebrew* joined in harmony |
| 0.12 | Lewis | *Welsh* lionlike, lightning |
| 2.60 | Liam | *Irish* form of William: *English* resolute protector; *English* to bind, tie |

| | | |
|---|---|---|
| 0.25 | Lincoln | *Old English* from the settlement by the pool |
| 6.32 | Logan | *English* a felled tree; *Irish* from the hollow |
| 0.14 | Loic | origin unknown |
| 0.27 | Lorenzo | *Spanish and Italian* form of Lawrence: a laurel, a crown |
| 0.35 | Louis | *English* famous in battle |
| 0.39 | Luca | *English* light |
| 3.94 | Lucas | *English* light |
| 3.63 | Luis | *English* famous in battle |
| 0.10 | Luka | *English* form of *Latin* Lucius: light |
| 0.50 | Lukas | *English* form of *Latin* Lucius: light |
| 4.42 | Luke | *English* form of *Latin* Lucius: light |
| 0.38 | Maddox | *Welsh* son of the patron |
| 1.10 | Malachi | *Hebrew* angel |
| 0.17 | Malcolm | *Arabic* a dove |
| 0.41 | Malik | *Arabic* king; angel, divine messenger; *Punjabi* lord or master |
| 1.28 | Manuel | form of Emanuel: *Hebrew* God is with us |
| 0.16 | Marc | *Latin* warlike; *Italian* form of Mark |
| 0.36 | Marco | *Latin* Mars, warlike |
| 0.23 | Marcos | *Latin* Mars, warlike |
| 1.50 | Marcus | *Latin* Mars, warlike |
| 0.40 | Mario | *Latin* warlike; *Italian* form of Mark |
| 1.20 | Mark | *Latin* warlike; *Italian* form of Mark |
| 0.12 | Markus | *Latin* warlike; *Italian* form of Mark |
| 0.10 | Marlon | *English* little falcon |
| 0.14 | Marquis | *Old French* a nobleman |
| 0.20 | Marshall | *English* steward, horse keeper |

| | | |
|---|---|---|
| 0.41 | Martin | *English* warlike; *Latin* akin to Marcus |
| 0.20 | Marvin | *Old English* famous friend |
| 4.46 | Mason | *English* a mason, a worker in stone |
| 0.31 | Mateo | *Hebrew* gift of God |
| 0.30 | Mathew | *Hebrew* gift of God |
| 0.16 | Mathias | *Hebrew* gift of God |
| 0.21 | Mathieu | *Hebrew* gift of God |
| 0.32 | Mathis | origin unknown |
| 0.23 | Matteo | *Hebrew* gift of God |
| 9.46 | Matthew | *Hebrew* gift of God |
| 0.19 | Maurice | *Latin* dark skinned |
| 0.13 | Mauricio | *Spanish* form of Maurice: *Latin* dark skinned |
| 0.11 | Maverick | *American* wildly independent |
| 0.92 | Max | *Latin* great, most excellent |
| 0.13 | Maxim | *Latin* great, most excellent |
| 0.22 | Maxime | *Latin* great, most excellent |
| 0.14 | Maximilian | *Latin* great, most excellent |
| 0.20 | Maximus | *Irish* greatest |
| 1.08 | Maxwell | *Latin* great, most excellent |
| 0.24 | Mekhi | origin unknown |
| 0.17 | Melvin | *Gaelic* polished chief |
| 0.93 | Micah | *Hebrew* who is like God |
| 10.08 | Michael | *Hebrew* who is like God |
| 0.20 | Micheal | *Hebrew* who is like God |
| 2.39 | Miguel | *Hebrew* who is like God |
| 0.10 | Mikael | *Hebrew* who is like God |
| 0.49 | Miles | *Latin* a warrior, a soldier |
| 0.61 | Mitchell | *Hebrew* who is like God |
| 0.26 | Mohamed | *Arabic* praised |
| 0.14 | Mohammad | *Arabic* praised |
| 0.14 | Mohammed | *Arabic* praised |
| 0.12 | Moises | *Spanish* form of Moses: *Greek* drawn from the water |
| 0.29 | Morgan | *Celtic* one who lives near the sea |
| 0.13 | Moses | *Greek* drawn from the water |

| | | | | |
|---|---|---|---|---|
| 0.12 | Moshe | *Polish* drawn out of the water | 0.38 | Payton |
| 0.12 | Muhammad | *Arabic* praised | | |
| 0.33 | Myles | *Latin* a warrior, a soldier | 0.27 | Pedro |
| 0.25 | Nasir | *Arabic* the helper, the supporter | 0.99 | Peter |
| 6.78 | Nathan | *Hebrew* he gave | 1.05 | Peyton |

0.12 Moshe — *Polish* drawn out of the water
0.12 Muhammad — *Arabic* praised
0.33 Myles — *Latin* a warrior, a soldier
0.25 Nasir — *Arabic* the helper, the supporter
6.78 Nathan — *Hebrew* he gave
0.21 Nathanael — *Hebrew* he gave
0.10 Nathanial — *Hebrew* he gave
2.99 Nathaniel — *Hebrew* he gave
0.17 Nehemiah — *Hebrew* the Lord's comfort
0.12 Neil — *English* a champion
0.18 Nelson — *Gaelic* son of Neal
7.06 Nicholas — *Greek* victory of the people
0.28 Nickolas — *Greek* victory of the people
1.24 Nicolas — *Greek* victory of the people
0.27 Nikolas — *Greek* victory of the people
7.05 Noah — *Hebrew* rest, peace
0.13 Noel — *English* to be born, the Nativity, born at Christmas
1.30 Nolan — *Irish* famous, noble
0.59 Oliver — *Latin* an olive tree
0.38 Olivier — *French* form of Oliver: an olive tree
1.31 Omar — *Arabic* long life, first son, highest, follower of the Prophet
0.10 Omari — *Arabic* full of life and prosperity
0.13 Omarion — origin unknown
0.12 Orion — *French* the Orient, the East, where the sun rises
0.17 Orlando — *English* from the pointed land
1.77 Oscar — *Old Norse* divine spearman
4.00 Owen — *Welsh* variation of Eugene, well born
0.18 Pablo — *Spanish* form of Paul: *Latin* small
1.56 Parker — *Old English* guardian of the park
1.81 Patrick — *Latin* a patrician, a person of noble descent
1.06 Paul — *Latin* small

0.38 Payton — *Old English* from the estate of the warrior
0.27 Pedro — *Spanish* form of Peter
0.99 Peter — *Greek* a rock
1.05 Peyton — *Old English* from the estate of the warrior
0.32 Philip — *Greek* a lover of horses
0.14 Philippe — *Greek* a lover of horses
0.37 Phillip — *Greek* a lover of horses
0.17 Phoenix — *Greek* dark red
0.13 Pierce — *Anglo French* form of Peter
0.14 Porter — *Latin* door guard
1.41 Preston — *English* from the priest's estate
0.28 Quentin — *Latin* fifth; *Old English* from the estate of the queen
0.15 Quincy — *Old French* from the estate of the fifth son
0.40 Quinn — *Irish* wise
0.13 Quintin — *Latin* fifth
0.18 Quinton — *Latin* fifth
0.34 Rafael — *Spanish* form of Raphael: *Hebrew* God has healed
0.14 Ramon — *Spanish* form of Raymond: *English* wise protection
0.11 Randall — *English* superior protection; *English* shield wolf
0.26 Randy — *English* superior protection; *English* shield wolf
0.38 Raphael — *Hebrew* God has healed
0.18 Raul — *French* form of Randolph: *Old English* shield wolf
0.11 Ray — *English* wise protection
0.53 Raymond — *English* wise protection
0.25 Reece — *Old Welsh* rash, ardent
0.17 Reed — *English* red haired
0.22 Reese — *Old Welsh* rash, ardent
0.13 Reginald — *Old English* powerful and mighty
0.21 Reid — *English* red haired

| | | | | | |
|---|---|---|---|---|---|
| 1.32 | Ricardo | *English* powerful, rich ruler | 0.39 | Sawyer | *Middle English* one who works with a saw |
| 2.06 | Richard | *English* powerful, rich ruler | | | |
| 0.19 | Ricky | *English* powerful, rich ruler | 0.52 | Scott | *English* Scotsman |
| 2.11 | Riley | *German, Dutch* a small stream; *Irish* valiant | 2.90 | Sean | *Irish* form of John |
| | | | 2.98 | Sebastian | *Greek* venerable |
| 0.15 | River | *Latin* large stream of water | 0.11 | Sebastien | *Greek* venerable |
| 4.21 | Robert | *German* bright fame | 0.27 | Sergio | *Italian* form of Serge: *Latin* attendant |
| 0.28 | Roberto | *German* bright fame | | | |
| 0.15 | Rocco | *English* a rock | 2.05 | Seth | *Hebrew* garment, appointed; *Syrian* appearance |
| 0.18 | Rodney | *English* from the island clearing | | | |
| | | | 0.84 | Shane | *Irish* form of John |
| 0.10 | Rodrigo | *Spanish and Italian* form of Roderick: famous ruler | 0.25 | Shaun | *Irish* form of John |
| | | | 0.89 | Shawn | *Irish* form of John |
| 0.16 | Roger | *English* famous, noble warrior | 0.10 | Sheldon | *English* protected kill |
| 0.14 | Rohan | *Hindi* saddlewood | 0.24 | Silas | *Latin* forest dweller |
| 0.44 | Roman | *Latin* a person from Rome | 0.72 | Simon | *Latin* he heard |
| 0.10 | Romeo | *Latin* of the Romans | 0.10 | Sincere | origin unknown |
| 0.42 | Ronald | *Scottish* wise, judicious | 0.18 | Skylar | *Dutch* a shelter |
| 0.13 | Ronan | *Irish* little seal | 0.43 | Skyler | *Dutch* a shelter |
| 0.12 | Ronnie | *Scottish* wise, judicious | 0.19 | Solomon | *Hebrew* man of peace |
| 0.10 | Rory | *Irish* red king | 0.92 | Spencer | *English* steward, administrator, butler |
| 0.10 | Ross | *English* woods, meadow; *English* red; *Scottish* headland | | | |
| | | | 0.14 | Stanley | *English* a stony meadow |
| 0.24 | Rowan | *English* tree with red berries | 0.86 | Stephen | *Greek* a crown |
| 0.15 | Roy | *English* king | 2.36 | Steven | *Greek* a crown |
| 0.21 | Ruben | *Hebrew* behold, a son | 0.17 | Talan | origin unknown |
| 0.22 | Russell | *English* red | 0.13 | Talon | *French, English* nails or claws |
| 7.67 | Ryan | *Irish* little king | 1.27 | Tanner | *English* leather worker |
| 0.38 | Ryder | *Middle English* to clear land | 0.21 | Tate | *American Indian* windy |
| 0.12 | Ryker | *Dutch* rich, powerful ruler | 0.50 | Taylor | *English* tailor |
| 0.42 | Rylan | *English* dweller on hill where rye is grown | 0.19 | Terrance | *Latin* smooth |
| | | | 0.16 | Terrell | *German* belonging to Thor; martial |
| 0.10 | Sage | *Latin* wise | | | |
| 0.10 | Salvador | *Latin* to be saved | 0.12 | Terrence | *Latin* smooth |
| 0.18 | Sam | *Hebrew* God has heard | 0.22 | Terry | *Latin* smooth |
| 6.56 | Samuel | *Hebrew* God has heard | 0.40 | Theodore | *Greek* divine gift |
| 0.27 | Santiago | form of Saint Diego: held by the heel, supplanter | 4.45 | Thomas | *Hebrew* a twin |
| | | | 2.33 | Timothy | *Greek* to honor God |
| 0.14 | Saul | *Hebrew* asked for | 0.14 | Titus | *Greek* to honor |

| | | | | | |
|---|---|---|---|---|---|
| 0.17 | Tobias | *Hebrew* goodness of God | 0.15 | Wade | *English* to wade; from the river crossing |
| 0.17 | Toby | *Hebrew* the Lord is good | 0.22 | Walker | *Old English* one who cleans and thickens cloth |
| 0.12 | Todd | *English* fox | | | |
| 0.13 | Tomas | *Hebrew* a twin | 0.22 | Walter | *German* powerful warrior |
| 0.28 | Tommy | *Hebrew* a twin | 0.13 | Warren | *English* preserver, defender |
| 0.26 | Tony | short form for Anthony: *Greek* flourishing; *Latin* worthy of praise | 0.11 | Waylon | *English* from the land by the road |
| 0.13 | Trace | *Greek* harvester | 0.11 | Wayne | *English* a way; wagoner |
| 0.76 | Travis | *Latin* crossroads | 0.71 | Wesley | *English* the west meadow |
| 0.37 | Trent | *Latin* torrent | 0.21 | Weston | *English* from the western estate |
| 0.74 | Trenton | *Latin* torrent | 0.15 | Will | *English* resolute protector |
| 0.10 | Trevon | *English* fair town | 8.77 | William | *English* resolute protector |
| 1.27 | Trevor | *Celtic* prudent | 0.14 | Willie | *English* resolute protector |
| 0.48 | Trey | *Middle English* third born | 0.17 | Wilson | *Old German* son of William |
| 2.47 | Tristan | *Celtic* tumult, noise; *Welsh* sorrowful | 2.83 | Wyatt | *Old French* form of Guy: *English* a guide; *Hebrew* valley |
| 0.27 | Tristen | *Celtic* tumult, noise; *Welsh* sorrowful | 0.39 | Xander | *Greek* protector of men |
| 0.13 | Tristin | *Celtic* tumult, noise; *Welsh* sorrowful | 2.81 | Xavier | *Arabic* bright |
| | | | 0.10 | Yahir | origin unknown |
| 0.13 | Triston | *Celtic* tumult, noise; *Welsh* sorrowful | 0.19 | Zachariah | *Hebrew* the remembrance of the Lord |
| 0.47 | Troy | *Irish* foot soldier | 5.35 | Zachary | *Hebrew* the remembrance of the Lord |
| 0.39 | Tucker | *Old English* one who fulled, teased, and burled cloth | 0.18 | Zachery | *Hebrew* the remembrance of the Lord |
| 0.74 | Ty | *British* a house | 0.36 | Zackary | *Hebrew* the remembrance of the Lord |
| 6.96 | Tyler | *English* maker of tiles | | | |
| 0.10 | Tyrell | *German* belonging to Thor; martial | 0.17 | Zackery | *Hebrew* the remembrance of the Lord |
| 0.14 | Tyrone | *Greek* sovereign; *Irish* land of Owen | 0.10 | Zakary | *Hebrew* the remembrance of the Lord |
| 0.57 | Tyson | *English* firebrand | 0.30 | Zander | *English* defender of mankind |
| 0.10 | Uriel | *Hebrew* powerful light of God | 0.44 | Zane | form of John: *Hebrew* Jehovah has been gracious |
| 2.10 | Victor | *Latin* victor, conqueror | | | |
| 2.06 | Vincent | *Latin* victor, conqueror | 0.35 | Zion | *Hebrew* highest point |

# Part 3

# Popular and Unusual Names

*with Popularity Ratings*

Parentheses after a name contain its popularity rating, which is the frequency of use per thousand baby girls or boys born. Names without numbers have a popularity rating of less than .01. In other words, fewer than one in 100,000 baby girls or baby boys received that name. Many of these names are one in a million or are unique in North America.

# Girls' Names—The Complete List

142,044 names

*Popularity ratings indicate usage per thousand baby girls.*
*Rare names with usage lower than one in 100,000 have no popularity rating numbers.*

| ~ A ~ | A'brasha | A'isha | A'keele | A'laizhua | A'lexus | A'mariae |
|---|---|---|---|---|---|---|
| | A'breal | A'ishah | A'keia | A'lajah | A'lexxsus | A'mariah |
| A | A'bree | A'iyana | A'keidra | A'lajha | A'leyah | A'mariana |
| A Janae | A'breia | A'iyona | A'keila | A'lajia | A'lia | A'marianna |
| A Jayne | A'breon | A'iyonna | A'kela | A'lana | A'liah | A'marie (0.01) |
| Á Keira | A'byanah | A'ja | A'kelsa | A'lani | A'liajah | A'mariea |
| A Lasiah | A'caria | A'jae | A'keria | A'lasheina | A'lice | A'mariona |
| A Leah | A'chaunte | A'jah | A'kerria | A'lasia | A'licia | A'mariya |
| Á Livia | A'cyere | A'jahni | A'keviah | A'latia | A'lisa | A'mariyah |
| A Mahri | A'daejah | A'jahyna | A'keyla | A'laura | A'livia | A'marrah |
| A Marie | A'daishia | A'janae | A'khiya | A'laya | A'livya | A'marrie |
| Á Merie | A'dayah | A'janée | A'khiyah | A'layasia | A'liyah | A'marya |
| A Mya | A'daysha | A'janett | A'kia | A'layga | A'llanah | A'mauri |
| A Niyah | A'dayshia | A'jayceya | A'kierah | A'layhna | A'llatin | A'mauri-Gianni |
| A Nya | A'dejah | A'jayda | A'kira | A'layla | A'lona | A'maya |
| A Shonti | A'destiny | A'jeria | A'kirrya | A'layna | A'lonnah | A'mayah |
| A Tianna | A'deysiah | A'jhané | A'kiya | A'laysha | A'lonnie | A'mayha |
| A Zada Lynn | A'dia | A'jhia | A'kiyah | A'layshaona | A'lora | A'mayya |
| A'agracia | A'dianna | A'jiah | A'kizha | A'laysia | A'lya | A'meea Jinaee |
| A'ahmariel | A'dream | A'jinay | A'kyah | A'layzha | A'lyiah | A'meisha |
| A'alaiya | A'dreana | A'joenae | A'kyia | A'layzia | A'lyvia | A'mela |
| A'alayh | A'dreyonna | A'jordan | A'kyla | A'lazha | A'mahni | A'mere |
| A'alaysia | A'drianna | A'jori | A'kyra | A'lea | A'maia | A'meria |
| A'aliyah | A'driell | A'joyah | A'kyrah | A'leah | A'maiah | A'merical |
| A'amiajh | A'drionna | A'kaia | A'lacious | A'leaya | A'maiya | A'merika |
| A'areana | A'dryanna | A'kaijanai | A'ladryn | A'leayah | A'maiyah | A'metrius |
| A'ariah | A'erin | A'kaila | A'lahna | A'lechia | A'maja | A'mia |
| A'aryona | A'hisha | A'kailah | A'laijah | A'leeyan | A'mani | A'miah |
| A'asaiyah | A'hmariona | A'kayiah | A'laila | A'leigha | A'mara | A'miaya |
| A'ayanni | A'honisty | A'kayla | A'laisa | A'lejah | A'maree | A'miayah |
| A'blessing | A'ionnah | A'keela | A'laisha | A'leshia | A'mari (0.01) | A'miayh |
| A'blesyn | A'isatu | A'keelah | A'laiyah | A'lexia | A'maria | A'milian |

| | | | | | | |
|---|---|---|---|---|---|---|
| A'mille | A'niah-Romayne | A'saundra | A'yanni | Aahniya | Aalaya | Aáliyah |
| A'millia | A'niaya | A'saundra'ya | A'yasho | Aahriannie | Aalayah (0.01) | Aaliyah- |
| A'millian | A'niece | A'sautriun | A'yauna | Aahryiyah | Aalayla | Aaliyah (1.75) |
| A'milliyon | A'nielyha | A'senath | A'yesha | Aaíjah | Aalayna | Aaliyah |
| A'mira | A'nieyah | A'shadieeyah | A'yona | Aailah | Aalaysha |    Heavenly |
| A'miracle | A'nihya | A'shae | A'yonna | Aaileah | Aalaysia | Aaliyaha |
| A'mirah | A'nijae | A'shah | A'yonnah | Aailiyah | Aalayzia | Aaliyahana |
| A'miriyah | A'nijah | A'shala | A'yunna | Aaillyah | Aale'yah | Aaliyah-Angela |
| A'mirra | A'nijia | A'shana | A'zaiah | Aailyah | Aaleah | Aaliyahellie |
| A'mirrah | A'nika | A'shantay | A'zaira | Aaina | Aaleeany | Aaliyah-Riana |
| A'mirror | A'nila | A'sharia | A'zareeah | Aaira | Aaleehaane | Aaliyah-Teta |
| A'mirycal | A'nireiah | A'shauney | A'zareyah | Aairieal | Aaleeiyah | Aaliyal |
| A'miya (0.01) | A'nis | A'shawnie | A'zari | Aairona | Aaleeya | Aaliyan |
| A'miyah (0.01) | A'nisia | A'shawnti | A'zaria (0.01) | Aaisha | Aaleeyah | Aaliyana |
| A'moni | A'nivea | A'shayla | A'zariah (0.01) | Aáisha | Aaleia | Aaliyarah |
| A'monica | A'nivyah | A'shea | A'zariyah | Aaishah | Aaleigh | Aaliyaria |
| A'moray | A'niy | A'shelle | A'zariyan | Aaiyana | Aaleigha | Aaliyeh |
| A'morning | A'niya (0.02) | A'shia | A'zarriah | Aaiyanna | Aaleighia | Aaliyha (0.01) |
| A'mouré | A'niyah (0.02) | A'shiana | A'zarriyah | Aaiyla | Aaleijah | Aaliyyah |
| A'mya (0.03) | A'niyha | A'shira | A'zaughania | Aaiza | Aaleina | Aasiyah |
| A'myah (0.01) | A'niyia | A'shirya | A'zaurionna | Aaizlynn | Aaleiyah | Aalizah |
| A'myerical | A'niylah | A'shoria | A'zayah | Aajah | Aalena | Aalliyah (0.01) |
| A'myia | A'nnika | A'shreah | A'zeriah | Aajane | Aalexie | Aalliyha |
| A'myiah | A'ny | A'shuna | A'zha | Aajiah | Aalexiyah | Aallyah |
| A'myila | A'nya (0.01) | A'shya | A'zhanae | Aajinelle | Aaleya | Aalona |
| A'mylah | A'nyah (0.01) | A'shyah | A'zhane | Aakailya | Aaleyah (0.01) | Aalonnie |
| A'myrical | A'nyia | A'shyia | A'zhara | Aakanksha | Aaleyha | Aalonzah |
| A'myyah | A'nyiah | A'shyiah | A'zhariah | Aakasha | Aaleysia | Aaltje |
| A'nadyia | A'nyjah | A'shyla | A'ziah | Aakayla | Aalia | Aalya |
| A'naejah | A'nyjai | A'shyra | A'ziana | Aakeira | Aaliah (0.01) | Aalyah (0.01) |
| A'naeya | A'nyla | A'siyah | A'ziya | Aakeisha | Aaliahy | Aalycia |
| A'nahjae | A'nylah | A'skyah | A'ziyah | Aakhieljah | Aaliana | Aalydia |
| A'naija | A'nyra | A'sohntea'a | A'zori | Aakifah | Aalianah | Aalyeah |
| A'naisha | A'nyre | A'sonte | A'zoria | Aakilyah | Aalianna | Aalyha |
| A'naiya | A'nysha | A'stajah | A'zura | Aakira | Aaliayah | Aalyiah (0.01) |
| A'naiyha | A'precious | A'sya | Aabha | Aákira | Aaliayh | Aalyja |
| A'naja | A'quirea | A'tariyah | Aabrielle | Aakirah | Aaliayha | Aalyna |
| A'najah | A'qyra | A'taylor | Aadi | Aakiyha | Aalicia | Aalysa |
| A'najiana | A'rabia | A'taysha | Aadilah | Aakycea | Aalicya | Aalysah |
| A'naka | A'rae | A'teria | Aadison | Aal'jah | Aalicyah | Aalysha |
| A'nari | A'raven | A'teyah | Aadome | Aala | Aalieah | Aalysia |
| A'nariah | A'ray'ia | A'treal | Aadra | Aalaá | Aaliegha | Aalyssa |
| A'naya | A'raya | A'trinidé | Aadya | Aalaiah | Aalieyah | Aalyvia |
| A'nayah | A'reon | A'tysha | Aaema | Aalaijah | Aalija | Aalyza |
| A'nayasia | A'reyanna | A'veeuna | Aaenia | Aalailah | Aalijah | Aamadi |
| A'naylah | A'riah | A'veyonna | Aafiyah | Aalaiya | Aalilyah | Aamaiya |
| A'nayzha | A'rielle | A'viana | Aafreen | Aalaiyah | Aalirah | Aamana |
| A'nehya | A'rika | A'vianna | Aahana | Aálaizha | Aalise | Aamani |
| A'neria | A'riya | A'vionna | Aaheli | Aalajah | Aalisia | Aamani-Merie |
| A'neye'a | A'riyah | A'yahna | Aahliya | Aalam | Aalissa | Aamara |
| A'ngelia | A'riyana | A'yana (0.01) | Aahmyah | Aalana | Aalivia | Aamarah |
| A'nia | A'rmoni | A'yani | Aahmyyah | Aalanah | Aaliya (0.01) | Aamari |
| A'niah | A'rya | A'yanna | Aahna | Aalavia | Aaliyaah | Aámaricanna |

| | | | | | | |
|---|---|---|---|---|---|---|
| Aamarius | Aanshi | Aarlynn | Aathira | Abbe | Abbye | Abhilasha |
| Aámariya | Aanvi | Aarna | Aatianna | Abbee | Abbygael | Abhinaya |
| Aamaya | Aanya (0.01) | Aarohi | Aatika | Abbegail (0.01) | Abbygaelle | Abhishri |
| Aambria | Aanyah | Aaron (0.01) | Aatiqa | Abbegale | Abby-Gail | Abhitha |
| Aameerah | Aanyiah | Aaronasha | Aatiyana | Abbegayle | Abbygail (0.05) | Abi |
| Aamena | Aanyjah | Aaronay | Aaudi | Abbella | Abbygaile | Abiageal |
| Aamera | Aanyla | Aaronette | Aauna | Abbeni | Abbygal | Abiah |
| Aamiah | Aanylah | Aaroni'a | Aaunyae | Abberly | Abbygale (0.02) | Abiail |
| Aamiiya | Aanyree | Aaronique | Aava | Abbey (0.18) | Abbygayle (0.01) | Abianca |
| Aamillian | Aanysia | Aaronnia | Aavashirley | Abbey Anna | Abbygayle | Abianju |
| Aamina | Aanyssa | Aaronzandr | Aavion | Abbey-Gail | Catherine | Abianna |
| Aaminah | Aar'niyah | Aarrianna | Aaya | Abbeygail | Abby-Jewel | Abiaun |
| Aamira | Aar'zah | Aarshi | Aayah | Abbeygale | Abby-Kate | Abibatou- |
| Aamiracle | Aara'niya | Aarshitha | Aayana | Abbeygayle | Abbylane | Khadija |
| Aamirah | Aaraleigh | Aarsy | Aayanna | Abbey-Jo | Abbylee | Abie |
| Aamiyah | Aaralin | Aarthi | Aayden | Abbey-Lee | Abbylene | Abiebatu |
| Aamiyla | Aaralyn (0.02) | Aarti | Aayla | Abbgail | Abbylin | Abiegail |
| Aamna | Aaralynn | Aartie | Aaylah | Abbi (0.01) | Abby-Lynn | Abiegal |
| Aamnah | Aaralynne | Aarushi (0.01) | Aayleah | Abbie (0.18) | Abbylynn | Abiela |
| Aamoni | Aarathi | Aarushi Singh | Aayliah | Abbie Mckenna | Abby-Rae | Abieliz |
| Aamoreanna | Aareal | Aary'onis | Aayona | Abbiegail (0.01) | Abby-Rose | Abiella |
| Aamya | Aaren | Aarya | Aáyonia | Abbiegal | Abcde | Abier |
| Aamyah | Aarenna | Aaryah | Aayonika | Abbiegale | Abcidee | Abigael (0.03) |
| Aamyria | Aareona | Aaryana | Aayumi | Abbiegayle | Abdianys | Abigaelle (0.01) |
| Aan | Aaresa | Aaryanna | Aayushi | Abbigael | Abdul | Abigail (7.45) |
| Aana | Aareyana | Aaryel | Aazarria | Abbigail (0.25) | Abeeha | Abigail Carol |
| Aanae | Aaria | Aaryka | Aazeen | Abbigail Marie | Abeer | Ann |
| Aanaisa | Aariah | Aaryn (0.01) | Ab'zarria | Abbigaile | Abegael | Abigail |
| Aanandi | Aáriah | Aaryuna | Aba | Abbigal | Abegail (0.01) | Daniellen |
| Aanayah | Aarial | Aarzu | Aba Akwoa | Abbigale (0.05) | Abegale | Abigail Jo |
| Aanchal | Aarian | Aasha | Abagael | Abbigayl | Abegayle | Abigail Karol |
| Aanestee | Aariana | Aashaé | Abagail (0.12) | Abbigayle (0.02) | Abegial | Abigail Leila |
| Aangelique | Aarianna | Aáshaili | Abagaile | Abbi-Kristé | Abelia | Abigail Nacole |
| Lucia | Aarica | Aashi | Abagaiyle | Abbillyne | Abella | Abigail Noelle |
| Aangi | Aarieal | Aashia | Abagale (0.01) | Abbilongo | Abellah | Abigaile (0.01) |
| Aani | Aarieana | Aashiyana | Abagayl | Abbilyn | Abena | Abigail-Grac |
| Aania | Aarika | Aashka | Abagayle (0.01) | Abbishai | Abenaa | Abigaill |
| Aaniah | Aarilyn | Aashna (0.01) | Abagayll | Abbot | Abeni (0.01) | Abigaille |
| Aanick | Aarin | Aashni | Abagil | Abbott | Aber | Abigail-Lynn |
| Aaniece | Aarinae | Aashraya | Abagyle | Abbreonna | Aberdeen | Abigail- |
| Aánijah | Aarini | Aashrita | Abaigael | Abbrey | Aberleen | Magdalena |
| Aanijhá | Aarion | Aashritha | Abaigail | Abbriana | Aberly | Abigail- |
| Aanika | Aariona (0.01) | Aashvi | Abaigeal (0.01) | Abbrianna | Abery | Margaret |
| Aanisah | Aarionanna | Aáshyiahi | Abak | Abbrianya | Abethany | Abigail- |
| Aa-Niya | Aarionna | Aashyla | Abang | Abbriel | Abey | Masengu |
| Aaniya | Aaris | Aasia | Abanie | Abbriela | Abeygail | Abigail-Shirley |
| Aániya | Aarissa | Aasiah | Abany | Abbrielle | Abgela | Abigal (0.01) |
| Aániyah | Aariyah | Aasis | Abb | Abbry | Abhaa | Abigale (0.11) |
| Aaniyah (0.02) | Aariyana | Aasiya | Abbagail (0.02) | Abbsalaat | Abheri | Abigale Julie |
| Aanna | Aariyannah | Aasiyah (0.01) | Abbagaile | Abbsidy | Abhia | Elise |
| Aanniya | Aariyonna | Aastha (0.01) | Abbagale | Abby (0.80) | Abhideep | Abigale-Marie |
| Aanole | Aarkeria | Aasya | Abbagayle | Abby Gail | Abhigna | Abigali |
| Aanosti | Aarlin | Aateyah | Abbaigaelle | Abbyanne | Abhijna | Abigayil |

| | | | | | | |
|---|---|---|---|---|---|---|
| Abigayl | Abrabella | Abronia | Acelis | Adaesha | Adalin | Adarah |
| Abigayle *(0.16)* | Abraham | Abrosia | Acelyn | Adaeze | Adalina | Adarea |
| Abigayle G | Abraia | Abrum | Acelynn *(0.01)* | Adah *(0.02)* | Adalind | Adaria |
| Abigayle Marie | Abrana | Abryana | Acesa | Adah Evely | Adaline *(0.02)* | Adarie |
| Abigayle-Rhea | Abrany | Abryanna | Acey | Adai | Adalis | Adarrah |
| Abigeal | Abrár | Abryannah | Achai | Adaia | Adalise | Adarriel |
| Abigel | Abrar *(0.01)* | Abryell | Achaia | Adaiah | Adalisia | Adarsh |
| Abigia | Abraya | Abryella | Achaiah | Adaijah | Adalisse | Adasena |
| Abigial | Abrea | Abryona | Achal | Adaila | Adalis-Tamara | Adasha |
| Abigil | Abreale | Abryonna | Achan | Adailya | Adaliyah | Adasia |
| Abigil's | Abreana | Absara | Achayo | Adaimys | Adaliz | Adaska |
| Abiging | Abreanah | Absera | Achia | Adain | Adallie | Adason |
| Abihail | Abreanna | Absidy | Achiara | Adair *(0.01)* | Adaly | Adassa |
| Abijah | Abree | Abuk | Achla | Adaira | Adalya | Adasyn |
| Abijetli | Abreea | Aby | Achli | Adaire | Adalye | Adau |
| Abileini | Abreeah | Abyan | Achol *(0.01)* | Adais | Adalyn *(0.04)* | Adaugo |
| Abilena | Abregella | Abybatou | Achonce | Adaisha | Adalyne | Adavee |
| Abilene *(0.01)* | Abrenna | Abydalahi | Achsa | Adaishya | Adalynn *(0.02)* | Adaya |
| Abilgail | Abreona | Abygael *(0.01)* | Achsah | Adaiya | Adalynne | Adayah |
| Abiliene | Abreonna | Aby-Gaelle | Achta | Adaizah | Adalyz | Adayisha |
| Ability | Abrey | Abygaelle *(0.01)* | Achyle | Adaja | Adam | Adayja |
| Abilyn | Abri | Abygail *(0.05)* | Acia | Adajah | Adama | Adayjah |
| Abimsha | Abria *(0.01)* | Abygal | Acie | Adajha | Adamari *(0.03)* | Adayla |
| Abinaya | Abriah | Abygale *(0.01)* | Acillia | Adajia | Adamarie | Adaysa |
| Abinee | Abrial | Abygayl | Acinoret | Ada-Kathryn | Adamariely | Adaysha |
| Abington | Abriale | Abygayle | Acire | Adala | Adamaris *(0.03)* | Adayshia |
| Abinoor | Abrialia | Abyni | Ackeelah | Adalai | Adamariz | Adaysia |
| Abiola | Abriana *(0.05)* | Abyshalin | Aconiya | Adalaide | Adamary *(0.01)* | Adaziah |
| Abiona | Abrianna *(0.07)* | Abyssinia | Acord | Adalaina | Adamarys | Adbianna |
| Abir | Abrianna | Acacia *(0.04)* | Acoya | Adalay | Adamay | Adcharapon |
| Abir Nour El | Bobbiejo | Acadia *(0.02)* | Acoyia | Adale | Adamayis | Adchsaya |
| Houda | Abriannah | Acalia | Acree | Adaleah | Adamie | Adda |
| Abira | Abrianne | Acantha | Acsanaille | Adalee | Adamina | Addaleigh |
| Abirami | Abriauna | Acara | Actavya | Adaleen | Adamis | Addalene |
| Abisha | Abricha | Acarianna | Acuria | Adaleena | Adamris | Addaley |
| Abishai | Abrie *(0.01)* | Acasha | Acxel | Adaleesa | Adan | Addalina |
| Abishana | Abrieana | Acashala | Acyl | Adaleeya | Adana | Addallee |
| Abivarni | Abriel *(0.01)* | Acasia | Ada *(0.15)* | Adalei | Adanaya | Addalyn |
| Abiya | Abriel Lat | Acayla | Ada Georgia | Adaleia | Adanely | Addalynn *(0.01)* |
| Abiyah | Abriella *(0.01)* | Acayshua | Ada Lynn | Adaleida | Adanhi | Addalyse |
| Abjini | Abrielle *(0.04)* | Acaysia | Ada Mae | Adaleigh | Adani | Addaniey |
| Ablessen | Abrielli | Accacia | Ada'ja | Adaleine | Adania | Addason |
| Ablessyn | Abrienne | Accalia | Ada-Anne | Adalena | Adanija | Addelai |
| Abnashi | Abriey | Accalya | Adaara | Adalene | Adaniris | Addelin |
| Abnee | Abrigail | Accashia | Adabel | Adalenea | Adanna | Addeline |
| Abneet | Abril *(0.05)* | Accoria | Adabell | Adaley | Adannaya | Addelyn *(0.01)* |
| Abneris | Abrina | Aceann | Adacha | Adali | Adanya | Addelyne |
| Abnie | Abriona | Acee | Adacyn | Adalia *(0.02)* | Adanyzha | Addelynn |
| Abnit | Abrionna | Acel | Adadiah | Adaliah | Adaobi | Adderley |
| Abogail | Abriya | Acelee | Adadrionna | Adalian | Adaora | Addesa |
| Abok | Abriyah | Aceleigh | Adaea | Adalicia | Adar | Addesen |
| Abony | Abriyana | Acelia | Ada-Elaina | Adalid | Adara *(0.02)* | Addeson |
| Abra | Abriyannah | Acelin | Adaelle | Adalie | Adara Shay | Addessa |

Addey
Addi
Addiad
Addiana
Addicca
Addie *(0.07)*
Addie-Belle
Addiemae
Addienna
Addileigh
Addiley
Addiline
Addilyn *(0.01)*
Addilynn
Addilynne
Addis
Addisan
Addisen *(0.02)*
Addison *(3.16)*
Addison Ging
Addison-Grace
Addisson
Addisyn *(0.10)*
Addisynn
Addisynne
Addler
Addlyn
Addrianna
Addrita
Addy *(0.01)*
Addy-Lane
Addycen
Addycus
Addye
Addyline
Addys
Addysan
Addysea
Addysen *(0.01)*
Addysin
Addyson *(0.20)*
Addyson-Renee
Addysun
Addysyn
Adea
Adeana
Adeanna
Adeanne
Adebelle
Adedolapo
Adedoyin
Adee
Adeen

Adeena
Adeeyi
Adeigh
Adeine
Adeja
Adel *(0.01)*
Adela *(0.03)*
Adelae
Adelaene
Adelah
Adelai
Adelaida *(0.01)*
Adelaide *(0.09)*
Adelaine
Adelan
Adelay
Adelaya
Adelayda
Adèle
Adele *(0.07)*
Adelea
Adele-Anne
Adelei
Adeleigh
Adelen
Adelena
Adelene
Adeleni
Adelenn
Adelfa
Adelheid
Adeli
Adelia *(0.01)*
Adelianne
Adelice
Adelicia
Adelie *(0.01)*
Adelin
Adelina *(0.04)*
Adelina-Maria
Adelind
Adelinda
Adelinde
Adeline *(0.21)*
Adeline-
    Theodora
Adelisa
Adelita
Adeliz
Adell
Adella *(0.01)*
Adelle *(0.02)*
Adelle-Marie

Adellia
    Madeleine
Adellyn
Adely
Adelya
Adelyn *(0.07)*
Adelyne
Adelynn *(0.03)*
Adelynne
Ademi
Aden *(0.01)*
Adena *(0.01)*
Adené
Adeola
Adera
Aderinola
Aderinsola
Aderola
Aderonke
Aderrica
Aderynna
Adesire
Adesja
Adesola
Adessa
Adesuwa
Adesyn
Adetokunbo
Adetutu
Adewonuola
Adex
Adey
Adeyla
Adhara
Adhel
Adhifah
Adhira
Adhithi
Adhiti
Adhvika
Adhya
Adi
Adia *(0.05)*
Adiah
Adiaha
Adialis
Adia-Lyn
Adian
Adiana *(0.01)*
Adianelys
Adianet
Adianez
Adianna

Adiannie
Adiany
Adiba
Adicia
Adiela
Adieny
Adiesly
Adigail
Adikuor
Adila
Adileena
Adileh
Adilen
Adilene *(0.03)*
Adileni
Adilenny
Adileny
Adilia
Adilyn
Adilynn
Adimar
Adin
Adina *(0.04)*
Adinaa
Adinah
Adine
Adinna
Adiolina
Adira
Adiranna
Adis
Adisen *(0.01)*
Adison *(0.09)*
Adisson
Adiston
Adisyn *(0.03)*
Adisyne
Adisynne
Adita
Adithi
Adithri
Aditi *(0.04)*
Aditri
Adiya
Adiyah
Adiyala
Adiza
Adja
Adja Fatou
Adja Seybatu
Adjani
Adjaratou
Adjoa

Adjoba Julianie
Adjoni
Adjriana
Adjuke
Adla
Adlai
Adlea
Adlee
Adleigh
Adleigh-Mae
Adlen
Adler
Adley *(0.01)*
Adliani
Adlianna
Adlih
Adlin
Adlina
Adline
Adlyn
Admi
Admira
Admire
Adna *(0.01)*
Adnan
Adnayris
Adnelys
Adneri
Adona
Adonai
Adonais
Adoncia
Adondria
Adonia
Adoniah
Adonica
Adonikah
Adonna
Adonya
Adonys
Ador
Adora *(0.01)*
Adora Rose
Adoracion
Adore
Adoree
Adori
Adoria
Adorian
Adorra
Adorrie
Adorya
Adr'yanna

Adra
Adrain
Adraina
Adrair
Adraya
Adrayanna
Adrea
Adream
Adreamia
Adrean
Adreana *(0.01)*
Adreanna *(0.02)*
Adréannah
Adreanne
Adreaunna
Adreem
Adreena
Adrehna
Adreiana
Adreinn
Adrena
Adreoanna
Adreona
Adreonna
Adreyana
Adreyanna
Adrhia
Adri
Adri'aunna
Adria *(0.04)*
Adrialisse
Adrialy
Adrialys
Adrian *(0.06)*
Adriana *(1.38)*
Adriana Camila
Adriana Lucia
Adriana May
Adrianae
Adrianah
Adrianalis
Adrianana
Adriane *(0.01)*
Adriania
Adrianie
Adrianise
Adriann
Adrianna *(0.71)*
Adriannah
    *(0.01)*
Adriannah
    Emily
Adriannal

Adrianne *(0.04)*
Adrianne
    Nicoleg
Adriannia
Adrianona
Adriany
Adrianyna
Adrianys
Adriauna *(0.01)*
Adriaunna
Adriawna
Adrie
Adrieana
Adrieanna *(0.01)*
Adrieauna
Adriel *(0.01)*
Adriele
Adriell
Adriella
Adrielle *(0.01)*
Adrielys
Adrien *(0.01)*
Adriena
Adrienah
Adriene *(0.01)*
Adrienna
Adrienne *(0.11)*
Adrienne Liqi
Adrieonna
Adrieyanna
Adrijauna
Adrilia
Adrina
Adrinae
Adrinenne
Adrion
Adriona *(0.01)*
Adrionna *(0.02)*
Adriorria
Adrisa
Adrisela
Adrishaliz
Adrita
Adrith
Adriuna
Adriunna
Adriunnah
Adriyah
Adriyana
Adriyanna
Adriyanna-
    Monet
Adriyaunna

| | | | | | | |
|---|---|---|---|---|---|---|
| Adriyen | Aebria | Aeriella | Afifeh | Agnes (0.02) | Ahajah | Ahkiya |
| Adriyna | Aebrie | Aeries | Afina | Agnes Ann | Ahala | Ahlaeah |
| Adrjana | Aeda | Aerika | Afnaan | Agnesa | Ahalia | Ahlaina |
| Adron | Aedan | Aerin (0.01) | Afnan | Agnese | Ahalil | Ahlainna |
| Adronnia | Aeden | Aeriona | Afra | Agness | Ahaluyni | Ahlam (0.01) |
| Adry'ana | Aedreanna | Aerionah | Afrah | Agnice | Ahalya | Ahlana |
| Adrya | Aedyhn | Aerionia | Afreen | Agnus | Ahana | Ahlani |
| Adryahna | Aedyn | Aerionna | Afreena | Agrionna | Ahanna | Ahlantis |
| Adryan | Aeelyn | Aeriqa | Africa | Agrippina | Ahava | Ahlaya |
| Adryana (0.01) | Aeesha | Aeris (0.02) | Africanus | Agueda | Ahavah | Ahlayah |
| Adryann | Aeilani | Aerith | Afrida | Aguil | Ahayla | Ahlayjia |
| Adryanna (0.01) | Aeiragon | Aerius | Afrienque | Agulria | Ahbigail | Ahlaysha |
| Adryauna | Aeire | Aeriyana | Afrin | Agurrhock | Ahbrahim | Ahlaysia |
| Adryawna | Aeireona | Aeriyonna | Afsana | Agustina (0.01) | Ahbrianna | Ahlea |
| Adryenna | Aeiress | Aeroine | Afsara | Ah' Bria Ra | Ahdaiyah | Ahleah |
| Adryona | Aeisha | Aerolynn | Afsha | Ah'breyona | Ahdhessiah | Ahlece |
| Adryonna | Aeja | Aerrianna | Afshaan | Ah'jia | Ahdia | Ahleea |
| Adsiri | Aejhiyana | Aerris | Afshan | Ah'kalah | Ahdiayh | Ahleeah |
| Adual | Aela | Aerryn | Afsheen | Ah'kieyah | Ahdom | Ahleema |
| Aduke | Aelan | Aerwyn | Afsuhn | Ah'kya | Ahdriana | Ahleeya |
| Adut | Aeleen | Aerya | Aftab | Ah'kyra | Ahdyah | Ahleia |
| Advaita | Aelia | Aeryal | Aftan | Ah'lailah | Aheen | Ahleigha |
| Advenia | Aeliana | Aeryel | Aften | Ah'laya | Ahemiyat | Ahleighcia |
| Advienne | Aelicity | Aerylana | Afton (0.02) | Ah'leira | Ahiena | Ahleina |
| Advika | Aelina | Aeryn (0.03) | Aftyen | Ah'licia | Ahieshyrenia | Ahleksis |
| Advithi | Aelisabeth | Aeryn Reese | Aftyn | Ah'liyah | Ahijah | Ahlena |
| Adwiyianna | Aella | Aerynn | Afua | Ah'lyria | Ahilin | Ahlexis |
| Adwoa | Aelwyn | Aeschlinn | Afuwa | Ah'lyss | Ahilyn | Ahlexiz |
| Adwyn | Aelyn | Aesha | Agam | Ah'lyssa-Rayne | Ahimsa | Ahleyah |
| Ady | Aemandeep | Aeshah | Agametochi | Ah'marionya | Ahinara | Ahlia |
| Ady'zeona | Aemelia | Aeslyn | Aganilah | Ah'maya | Ahisma | Ahliria |
| Adya | Aemilia | Aetheldred | Agape | Ah'mayze | Ahixa | Ahliva |
| Adyan | Aemy | Aetienne | Agapé | Ah'meina | Ahiya | Ahlivia |
| Adyanna | Aenea | Aeujeami | Agapi | Ah'mere | Ahizel | Ahliya |
| Adycen | Aenia | Aeva (0.01) | Agata | Ah'modesty | Ahja'rae | Ahliyah |
| Adylan | Aenicia | Aeviel | Agatha (0.01) | Ah'mya | Ahjae | Ahlola |
| Adylene | Aenrieta | Aevryn | Agathe (0.02) | Ah'naria | Ahjah | Ahlona |
| Adylenn | Aera | Aewyn | Agatte | Ah'nia | Ahjahli | Ahlonna |
| Adyline | Aeralie | Aeysha | Agdriauna | Ah'niya | Ahjahnae | Ahlonnah |
| Adylyn | Aeralyn | Aeyssa | Ageeda | Ah'niyae | Ahjaleah | Ahloura |
| Adylynn | Aerawyn | Aezlinn | Ageil | Ah'niyah | Ahjanae | Ahlya |
| Adymin | Aerayonna | Aezlynn | Agejenay | Ah'nyla | Ahjané | Ahlyanee |
| Adyn | Aeress | Afaaf | Agel | Ah'nyrian | Ahjanelle | Ahlyia |
| Adys | Aerial (0.01) | Afaf | Agela | Ah'rayna | Ahjareece | Ahlysa |
| Adysan | Aeriale | Afaya | Aggie | Ah'rianna | Ahjeauna | Ahlyvea |
| Adysen (0.01) | Aerian | Afeefa | Aggy | Ah'rieya | Ahjeiza | Ahmaia |
| Adysin | Aeriana (0.01) | Afeera | Agigail | Ah'sharia | Ahjey | Ahmajah |
| Adyson (0.08) | Aerianha | Afefa | Agina | Ah'shiya | Ahjina | Ahmajai |
| Adysonne | Aerianna (0.01) | Affaf | Aglae | Ah'shyrie | Ahjunae | Ahmajene |
| Adysun | Aerica | Affina | Aglaee | Ah'vionce | Ahkeelah | Ahmalia |
| Adysyn | Aericca | Affinity | Aglarainna | Ah'zanae | Ahkelah | Ahmani |
| Adyxalis | Aerieana | Afia | Agma-Michel | Ah'zyler | Ahkia Stella | Ahmara |
| Aebi | Aeriel (0.01) | Afifa | Agner | Ahaad | Ahkiriah | Ahmarah |

| | | | | | |
|---|---|---|---|---|---|
| Ahmareann | Ahnalisa | Ahriyana | Ai'yonna | Aijah | Ailissha | Ainslea |
| Ahmari *(0.01)* | Ahnalyse | Ahryah | Ai'zarrianna | Aijahlon | Ailiyah | Ainslee *(0.01)* |
| Ahmaria | Ahnanyia | Ahryanna | Aia | Aijahnae | Ailleagan | Ainsleigh |
| Ahmariah | Ahnasia | Ahryanne | Aiah | Aijalin | Aillin | Ainsley *(0.25)* |
| Ahmarree | Ahnastacia | Ahryiele | Aiana | Aijalon | Ailsa | Ainsli |
| Ahmathyah | Ahnawake | Ahryona | Aianna | Aijia | Ailyah | Ainslie *(0.01)* |
| Ahmatiana | Ahnayah | Ahsaunta | Aiat | Aijia-Ari | Ailym | Ainsly |
| Ahmaune | Ahnayee | Ahsean'j | Aiba | Aika | Ailyn *(0.01)* | Ainul |
| Ahmauri | Ahne | Ahsees | Aibha | Aikam | Ailyna | Mardhiyan |
| Ahmawanya | Ahnee | Ahsha | Aibhleen | Aïka-Milka | Ailyne | Ainy |
| Ahmaya | Ahnesia | Ahshaily | Aibhlin | Aikaterini | Ailynn | Ainye |
| Ahmber | Ahnesti | Ahshanay | Aibreann | Aikayla | Ailyona | Ainy-Love |
| Ahmea | Ahnesttii | Ahsharia | Aicha *(0.03)* | Aiken | Ailysh | Aíofe |
| Ahmeena | Ahnesty | Ahshawnti | Aicha-Rym | Aiko *(0.01)* | Aima | Aiona |
| Ahmeerah | Ahney | Ahsia | Aicha-Walo | Aikum | Aimal | Aione |
| Ahmeesha | Ahni | Ahsley | Aicia | Aïla | Aimani | Aionna |
| Ahmelia | Ahni'ya | Ahsley Jitsel | Aida *(0.07)* | Aila *(0.01)* | Aimarose | Air'ra |
| Ahmeraka | Ahnia | Ahtaya | Aida Malvina | Ailah | Aime | Aira Grace |
| Ahmeyia | Ahnica | Ahtiahna | Aidaangelica | Ailahchante | Aimeé | Airabella |
| Ahmi | Ah-Nijah | Ahtsiri | Aidah | Ailaina | Aimée | Airal |
| Ahmielle | Ahnika | Ahtum | Aidaina | Aila-Jai | Aimee *(0.12)* | Airaleana |
| Ahmii | Ahnikah | Ahtviri | Aidalee | Ai-Lan | Aimee-Elizabeth | Airalyh |
| Ahmina | Ahnisa | Ahtym | Aidaleydi | Ailani *(0.02)* | Aimeelee | Airalyn |
| Ahminah | Ahnistee | Ahtziri *(0.01)* | Aidalina | Ailanie | Aimee-Lee | Airalynah |
| Ahmiracle | Ahnisty | Ahtziry | Aidan *(0.05)* | Ailanthus | Aimee-Rae | Airam |
| Ahmirah | Ahniya *(0.01)* | Ahtzyri | Aidangelly | Ailany | Aimée-Rae | Airamee |
| Ahmirah-Jholie | Ahniyah | Ahunnika | Aida-Thiam | Ailanys | Aimelya | Airanisha |
| Ahmirey | Ahnjala | Ahuva *(0.01)* | Aidden | Ailathyna | Aimen | Airanna |
| Ahmiya | Ahnna | Ahva | Aide | Ailayah | Aimey | Airauna |
| Ahmiyah | Ahnná Claire | Ahvae | Aidé | Ailbe | Aimie *(0.01)* | Airawen |
| Ahmni | Ahnnaesti | Ahvey | Aide Maria | Aileana | Aimiya | Airazona |
| Ahmoi | Ahnnaka | Ahviana | Aidee | Ailee | Aimmen | Aireal |
| Ahmonee | Ahnnaleise | Ahwin | Aideen | Aileen *(0.10)* | Aimy | Aireale |
| Ahmoni | Ahnoni | Ahyana | Aiden *(0.05)* | Aileena | Aimy Lee | Aireana |
| Ahmonshay | Ahnteya | Ahyani | Aidenrose | Aileesha | Aimya | Aireanna *(0.01)* |
| Ahmoon-Rah | Ahnya | Ahyashah- | Aidia | Ailen | Aimynn | Aireauna |
| Ahmora | Ahnyah | Ahmath | Aidreana | Ailena | Aimyra | Airee'ona |
| Ahmoria | Ahnye | Ahylin | Aidree | Ailene *(0.01)* | Aina | Aireka |
| Ahmuni | Ahnyia | Ahyonna | Aidrian | Ailenis | Ainara | Airel |
| Ahmya *(0.01)* | Ahnyka | Ahza | Aidriana | Aileny | Ainath | Airelle |
| Ahmyah | Ahnysty | Ahzadara | Aidya | Ailey *(0.01)* | Ainayat | Airelys |
| Ahmyia | Ahnyya | Ahzahria | Aidyen | Aili *(0.01)* | Aindra | Airen |
| Ahmyra | Ahona | Ahzareiah | Aidyn *(0.01)* | Ailia | Aindrila | Aireona *(0.01)* |
| Ahmyrah | Ahonesty | Ahzhane | Aiereionna | Ailiana | Áine | Aireonna |
| Ahmyriaha | Ahreéa | Ahziah | Aierheanna | Ailianna | Aine *(0.01)* | Aires |
| Ahna | Ahri | Ai | Aiesah | Ailidh | Ainesey | Aireyana |
| Ahna Marie | Ahria | Ai Khuyen | Aiesha | Ailie | Aingeal | Aireyanah |
| Ahnabelle | Ahriana | Ai Ling | Aighlee | Ailill | Aingelise | Aireyanna |
| Ahnae | Ahrianna | Ai'juah | Aigner | Ailimn | Ainhoa | Aireyonna |
| Ahnaija | Ahriel | Ai'yana | Aihnoa | Ailin | Ainiya | Aireyunna |
| Ahnaka | Ahriella | Ai'yanna | Aiireal | Ailinh | Ainjinae | Airi |
| Ahnalea | Ahrim | Ai'yauna | Aija *(0.01)* | Ailis | Ainniarys | Airia |
| Ahnaleigha | Ahritzi | Ai'yona | Aija'nae | Ailish *(0.01)* | Aino | Airiahna |

| | | | | | | |
|---|---|---|---|---|---|---|
| Airiana (0.01) | Aisha Lizbeth | Aiwa | Ajainay | Ajianna | Akee'llah | Akhayla |
| Airianna | Aisha-Celia | Aixa (0.01) | Ajaira | Ajionne | Akeela | Akhia |
| Airica | Aishadeep | Aiy Anna | Ajaisha | Ajiya | Akeeláh | Akhila |
| Airicka | Aishah (0.01) | Aiy'ana | Ajak | Ajla (0.01) | Akeelah (0.04) | Akhira |
| Airieanna | Aishah Jeanny | Aiya | Ajala | Ajmaani | Akeelaha | Akhirra |
| Airiel | Aishakhyah | Aiyah | Ajalae | Ajmal | Akeelha | Aki |
| Airielle | Aishanti | Aiyahna | Ajalatue | Ajonai | Akeeli | Aki'lah |
| Airies | Aishat | Aiyana (0.13) | Ajali | Ajsa | Akeema | Akia |
| Airika | Aishatou | Aiyanah | Ajalia | Ajsha | Akeena | Akiachu |
| Airilee | Aishe | Aiyani | Ajalie | Ajunea | Akeer | Akiah |
| Airily | Aishi | Aiyanna (0.06) | Ajalon | Ajure | Akeera | Akiana |
| Airin | Aishia | Aiyanna Aaliyah | Ajalona | Ajva | Akeerah | Akianna |
| Airiona | Aishleen | Ciara | Ajana | Ajza | Akeeva | Akiaya |
| Airionna | Aishlinn | Aiyannah | Ajanae (0.01) | Ajzah | Akeeviah | Akiea |
| Airis | Aishlynn | Aiyauna | Ajanai | Aka | Akeeymah | Akiera (0.01) |
| Airlea | Aishna | Aiyaunah | Ajanay | Akacia | Akeidra | Akiereona |
| Airlia | Aishwarya (0.01) | Aiyda | Ajané | Akadia | Akeila | Akihya |
| Airn | Aishwinder | Aiydan | Ajanea | Akaeira | Akeilah | Akiko |
| Airolyn | Aisia | Aiyhunna | Ajaneá | Akahsa | Akeili | Akila |
| Airreal | Aisiah | Aiykiera | Ajanee | Akai | Akeira | Akilah (0.02) |
| Airreana | Aisiana | Aiyla | Ajanga | Akaiah | Akeisha | Akilee |
| Airreanna | Aiskel | Aiylin | Ajani | Akaila | Akela (0.01) | Akili |
| Airreanne | Aisleigh | Aiyna | Ajania | Akaisha (0.01) | Akelah | Akilianna |
| Airrell | Aislen | Aiyona | Ajanjot | Akaiya | Akeley | Akilina |
| Airreon | Aislenn | Aiyoni | Ajanna | Akaiyah | Akelia | Akima |
| Airrieonna | Aisley | Aiysia | Ajaria | Akal | Akeliah | Akimlione |
| Airse | Aislin (0.01) | Aiza | Ajariah | Akal Dev | Akella | Akimmy |
| Airulan | Aisling (0.01) | Aizah | Ajasia | Akala | Akellis | Akina (0.01) |
| Airus | Aislinn (0.04) | Aizelyn | Ajauna | Akalah | Akemi | Akinia |
| Airy | Aislyn (0.02) | Aizja | Ajaya | Akam | Akemi Lynn | Akinyi |
| Airyal | Aislynn (0.03) | Aizlinn | Ajaye | Akane | Akenhiio | Akira (0.07) |
| Airyana | Aislynne | Aizlyn | Ajayla | Akanksha | Akenya | Akirah |
| Airyanna (0.01) | Aisone | Aizlynn | Ajaylah | Akansha | Akera | Akire |
| Airyannah | Aissa | Aizsoni | Ajayna | Akari | Akeri | Akirea |
| Airyannia | Aissata (0.01) | AJ | Ajaysia | Akarie | Akeria | Akiria |
| Airyn | Aissatou (0.01) | Aj'anae | Ajazia | Akarya | Akeriah | Akiriah |
| Airyona | Aissatou Kane | Aja (0.04) | Ajdina | Akasha (0.03) | Akeriauna | Akiriya |
| Airyonia | Aisstau | Aja'nae | Ajea | Akashah | Akerria | Akirra |
| Airyonna | Aisulu | Aja'nique | Ajeetha | Akasha-Madison | Akesia | Akisa |
| Airys | Aiswarya | Ajaah | Ajelet | Akasia | Akessa | Akisha |
| Aisa | Aisyah | Ajae'lyn | Ajena | Akausha | Aketthia | Akita |
| Aisabella | Aitana | Ajaguta | Ajene | Akaya | Aketzali | Akiva |
| Aisah | Aithao | Ajah (0.02) | Ajeya | Akayaha | Aketzalli | Akivah |
| Aisaleg | Aitza | Ajah Agnes | Ajha | Akaycia | Aketzally | Akiyá |
| Aisata | Aiuanna | Ajahca | Ajhae-Maria | Akaydia | Akeya | Akiya (0.01) |
| Aisatou | Aiva (0.01) | Ajahia | Ajhani | Akayh | Akeyla | Akiya'h Nevae'h |
| Aisatu | Aivah | Ajahly | Ajharia | Akayha | Akeylah | Akiyah (0.01) |
| Aisceln | Aivee | Ajahna | Ajhia | Akayla (0.01) | Akeyleeha | Akiyana |
| Aisela | Aivery | Ajahnay | Aji | Akaylah | Akeyma | Akiyra |
| Aish | Aivree | Ajai | Ajia | Akaylin | Akeymah | Akiyrria |
| A-Isha | Aivry | Ajaia | Ajiah | Akaysha | Akeyra | Akkice |
| Aisha (0.17) | Aivvary | Ajaiah | Ajian | Akayvia | Akhasha | Akkili |
| Aisha Dorethy | Aivy | Ajaicia | Ajianaye | Akayzia | Akhaya | |

| | | | | | | |
|---|---|---|---|---|---|---|
| Akmcyak | Al'isha | Alaghia | Alana (0.77) | Alara (0.01) | Alayciana | Alaza |
| Akora | Al'janaih | Alahna (0.02) | Alana Belle | Alaralynn | Alaydyn | Alazae |
| Akosha | Al'janeria | Alahni | Alana Erica | Alariah | Alayeh | Alazah |
| Akosia | Al'keirra | Alahnia | Alana Marie | Alarica | Alayeha | Alazaha |
| Akosua | Al'keria | Alahnna | Alana | Alariss | Alayha | Alazai |
| Akota | Al'kerria | Alahnys | Meleululani | Alariya | Alayhia | Alazandra |
| Akout | Al'ladaya | Alahya | Alanah (0.05) | Alarra | Alayhna | Alazay (0.01) |
| Akovia | Al'laysha | Alai | Alanah Ilean | Alarria | Alayia (0.01) | Alazha |
| Akoya | Al'lazae | Alaia | Alanahjean | Alarrionna | Alayiah | Alazia |
| Akpene | Al'lazayia | Alaiah | Alana-Jasmine | Alarryia | Alayijah | Alba (0.02) |
| Akram | Al'leah | Alaida | Alana-Marie | Alary | Alayiji | Albana |
| Akrisala | Al'lonna | Alaija | Alana-Rae | Alaryana | Alayisha | Albane |
| Akrystaire | Al'lyn | Alaijah (0.01) | Alana-Shay | Alaryn | Alayj'ah | Albaney |
| Aksa | Al'miyah | Alaijha | Alanca | Alasah | Alayja (0.01) | Albani |
| Aksanti | Al'naya | Alaika | Alancia | Alasandra | Alayjah | Albanie |
| Aksaya | Al'shalon | Alaila | Alanda | Alasha | Alayjia | Albany (0.01) |
| Akshadaa | Al'shanti | Alailah | Alandea | Alashawnee | Alayla (0.01) | Albareli |
| Akshara | Al'sharia | Alaimy | Alandis | Alashia | Alaylah | Albatool |
| Akshaya | Al'taevia | Alaina (0.57) | Alandra (0.01) | Alasia (0.02) | Alayna (0.50) | Alberly |
| Akshita | Al'takaria | Alaina Daisy | Alandrea | Alasianna | Alayna Mone | Alberlyn |
| Akshitha | Al'taniyah | Alainah (0.01) | Alandreia | Alaska (0.01) | Alayna-Adel | Albernya |
| Aku Mireille | Al'ziah | Alaine | Alandria | Alaskah | Alaynah (0.01) | Albert |
| Akua | Ala | Alainee | Alandrio | Alaskka | Alayne | Alberta (0.01) |
| Akuah | Ala'a | Alaines | Alandryah | Alason | Alaynee | Albertina |
| Akual | Ala'avion | Alainey | Alane | Alasqa | Alayni | Albina |
| Akuch | Ala'eh | Alainia | Alanea | Alassandra | Alaynia | Albony |
| Akuch-Charle | Ala'ja | Alainna | Alaney | Alathea | Alaynie | Albreah |
| Akum | Ala'vee | Alainya | Alani (0.08) | Alathia | Alaynna (0.01) | Albree |
| Akumu | Ala'zhah | Alaira | Alania | Alatia | Alaynnah | Albrey |
| Akunnamaka | Alaa (0.01) | Alairah | Alanie | Alauna (0.01) | Alayra | Albreyona |
| Akuoit | Alaa Norihane | Alaire | Alanii | Alaunah | Alaysah | Albrianna |
| Akuot | Alaaysia | Alairia | Alanis (0.04) | Alaunna | Alayseiah | Alcatraz |
| Akura | Alaba | Alaisha (0.01) | Alaniz | Alaura (0.02) | Alaysha (0.03) | Alcee |
| Akuya | Alabama | Alaisia | Alanna (0.23) | Alauralynn | Alayshia (0.01) | Alcira |
| Akwasia | Alacia | Alaisjah | Alanna Mar | Alauria | Alayshiah | Aldamily |
| Akwata | Alacie | Alaixa | Alannah (0.08) | Alavay | Alayshja | Aldana |
| Akya | Alacie Lisi | Alaiya | Alanni | Alavia | Alaysia (0.04) | Aldaysia |
| Akyia | Saniko | Alaiyah (0.01) | Alannie | Alawi | Alaysiah | Aldejeda |
| Akyiah | Alacoque | Alaiza | Alannis | Alawna | Alaysianna | Aldemy |
| Akyjah | Alaczandra | Alaja | Alanny | Alawnya | Alaysie | Alden (0.01) |
| Akylah | Aladrain | Alajah (0.01) | Alannys | Alaxandria | Alaysja | Aldeniraquel |
| Akyra | Aladrien | Alajandria | Al-Anood | Alay Ja | Alayssa | Aldia |
| Akyrah | Aladrienne | Alajane | Alanoud | Alay'jah | Alayssia | Aldina |
| Akyree | Aladrine | Alajha | Alanta | Alaya (0.05) | Alaythia | Aldora |
| Al | Alae | Alajia | Alantá | Alaya Fernande | Alayva | Aldrea |
| Al Anisa | Alaeja | Alajiah | Alante | Alayah (0.05) | Alayyah | Aldria |
| Al Shari'ah | Alaejah | Alajiona | Alantha | Alayah Mar | Alayz'ja | Aldriona |
| Al'ashia | Alaena (0.01) | Alajyah | Alantis | Alayai | Alayza | Ale'jah |
| Al'breiona | Alaesha | Alak | Alany | Alayaja | Alayzaih | Ale'yah |
| Al'dajha | Alaeshea | Alakiir | Alanya | Alayana | Alayzha | Ale'zah |
| Al'daysha | Alaesia | Alala | Alanyia | Alayanna | Alayzia | Alea (0.04) |
| Al'eciah | Alaeyah | Alan | Alanys (0.01) | Alayasia | Alayziah | Aleacia |
| Al'ina | Alaezha | A-Lana | Alanza | Alaycia | Alaz'jah | |

| | | | | | | |
|---|---|---|---|---|---|---|
| Aleaciea | Aleécia | Aleily | Alendria | Alessandra | Alexandra Eve | Alexeya |
| Aleacya | Aleecia (0.01) | Aleina | Alene | (0.19) | Alexandra | Alexha |
| Aleada-Marie | Aleedia | Aleinah | Aleneiza | Alessandra | Isabell | Alexhai |
| Aleafia | Aleeha | Aleiram | Aleni | Maria | Alexandra Kim | Alexi (0.03) |
| Aleah (0.16) | Aleeia | Aleisa | Alenia | Alessandra | Alexandra Marie | Alexiá |
| Aleaha | Aleelah | Aleisha (0.02) | Aleniah | Marowie | Alexandra Pier | Alexia (0.89) |
| Aleah-Mirel | Aleemah | Aleisha Meriam | Alenis | Alessaundra | Alexandra- | Alexia Corra |
| Aleahy | Aleen | Aleishka | Alenka | Alessia (0.06) | Amber | Alexiah (0.01) |
| Aleahya | Aleena (0.09) | Aleisia | Alenna | Alessia-Maria | Alexandra-Kyra | Alexia-Irina |
| Aleajah | Aleenah | Aleithia | Aleny | Alessondra | Alexandra-Lia | Alexiakay |
| Aleana (0.01) | Aleenamarie | Aleiya | Alenya | Alesya | Alexandre | Alexia-Lenora |
| Aleanah | Aleenarose | Aleiyah | Alenyz | Aleta | Alexandréa | Alexiana |
| Aleandra | Aleene | Aleiza | Alenzia | Aletha | Alexandrea | Alexiane |
| Aleandra- | Aleera | Aleja | Aleona | Alethea (0.01) | (0.07) | Alexianie |
| Bernice | Alees | Alejah | Aleora | Aletheia (0.01) | Alexandriá | Alexiann |
| Aleanna | Aleesa (0.01) | Alejandra (0.30) | Alera | Alethia | Alexandria | Alexianna |
| Alearsi | Aleese | Alejandria | Alerah | Alethya | (0.96) | Alexianna Angel |
| Aleasa | Aleesea | Alejandrina | Alerey | Aletris | Alexandriah | Alexianne |
| Alea-Sarah | Aleesha (0.01) | Alejandro | Aleri'a | Aletta | Alexandria- | Alexiano |
| Alease | Aleesha-Keysha | Alejondra | Aleria | Alette | Lynne | Alexias |
| Aleasha | Aleesia | Alek | Aleriane | Aletza | Alexandriana | Alexia-Skye |
| Aleasia | Aleeya (0.01) | Aleka | Alerice Grace | Alevia | Alexandrie | Alexica |
| Aleatha | Aleeyah (0.01) | Alekah | Alerika | Alex (0.09) | Alexandriea | Alexice |
| Aleathea | Aleeza (0.01) | Alekis | Aleris | Alex'a | Alexandrine | Alexicia |
| Aleaya | Aleezay | Aleksa (0.01) | Alerjandra | Alex'cia | (0.01) | Alexie (0.03) |
| Aleayah | Aleezeh | Aleksandra | Alerra | Alex'ya | Alexandriya | Alexie |
| Alec | Aleeziah | (0.02) | Alerrah | Alex'zia | Alexandrya | Christiane |
| Aleca | Alefe | Aleksandreia | Alerry | Alexa (2.78) | (0.01) | Alexie Faith |
| Aleccandra | Alegiance | Aleksandria | Alerus | Alexa Alicia | Alexandryea | Alexie'auna |
| Alece | Alegna | Aleksey | Alesa | Alexa Christina | Alexane (0.02) | Alexiea |
| Alecea | Alegria | Aleksi | Alesandra (0.01) | Alexa Grace | Alexanjria | Alexieana |
| Aleceia | Aleha | Aleksia | Alesasia | Alexa Rey | Alex-Ann (0.01) | Alexies |
| Alechia | Alehtza | Aleksis | Alese | Alexabel | Alexann (0.01) | Alexina (0.01) |
| Alecia (0.03) | Aleia (0.02) | Aleksys | Aleseandra | Alexa-Brooke | Alexanna | Alexine |
| Aleciah | Aleiah (0.01) | Aleksyss | Aleseanna | Alexagail | Alex-Anne | Alexiney |
| Aleciana | Aleice | Alekszandria | Aleseya | Alexah (0.01) | Alexanne (0.04) | Alexiona |
| Alecion | Aleicia | Alektra | Alesha (0.02) | Alexahi | Alexanria | Alexionna |
| Alecktra | Aleida (0.01) | Alekxandra | Alesha Anita | Alexah-Jo | Alexany | Alexious |
| Alecsis | Aleidah | Alekya | Aleshanee | Alexaira | Alexaria | Alexis (5.38) |
| Alectra | Aleidy | Alekza | Aleshanee | Alexakai | Alexaris | Alexis Angeli |
| Alecxandra | Aleidys | Alekzandra | Magena | Alexalee | Alexas (0.01) | Alexis Nicole |
| Alecxia | Aleigh (0.01) | Alela | Lakota | Alexalis | Alexaundri | Alexis Quantasia |
| Aleczandra | Aleigha (0.06) | Aleli | Aleshia (0.01) | Alexa-Loudwina | Alexay | Alexis Taegan M |
| Aleczandrea | Aleighia | Alem | Aleshka | Alexa-Loulouse | Alexcea | Alexis Tu Nhi |
| Aleczia | Aleighn Marie | Alema | Alesi | Alexamarin | Alexcee | Alexisa |
| Aleda | Bra | Alemarys | Alesia (0.02) | Alexana | Alexcia (0.02) | Alexis-Dee |
| Alee (0.01) | Aleighya | Alemi | Alesiah | Alexander (0.02) | Alexciana | Alexis-Grace |
| Alee Shaunté | Aleiha | Alemia | Alesie | Alexandera | Alexcis | Alexis-Jo |
| Aleea (0.01) | Aleihs | Alena (0.14) | Alesiya | Alexanderia | Alexe | Alexiss |
| Aleeah (0.01) | Aleijah | Alena Caresse | Aleska | (0.01) | Alexea (0.01) | Alexisse |
| Aleeana | Aleika | Alenah | Aleson | Alexandia | Alexee | Alexius (0.02) |
| Aléeca | Aleila | Alenay | Alesondra | Alexandiama | Alexeia | Alexiya |
| Aleece | Aleilah | Alencia | Alessa (0.01) | Alexandra (3.17) | Alexes (0.01) | Alexiyah |

Alexiyona
Alexiz
Alexmarie
Alex-Marie
Alexnadra
Alexondra
Alexs
Alexsa (0.01)
Alexsandra (0.02)
Alexsandrea
Alexsandri
Alexsandria
Alex-Sarah
Alexseah
Alexsey
Alexsha
Alexsia (0.01)
Alexsis (0.01)
Alexson
Alexssa
Alexsus
Alexsys
Alexus (0.21)
Alexusin
Alexus-Megan
Alexuz
Alexx
Alexxa (0.01)
Alexxia
Alexxie
Alexxis (0.01)
Alexxiz
Alexxus
Alexy (0.01)
Alexya (0.01)
Alexyah
Alexya-Jade
Alexyanne
Alexyia
Alexys (0.07)
Alexys Rose
Alexysis
Alexys-Marie
Alexyss (0.01)
Alexyz
Alexza
Alexzah
Alexzahs
Alexzanderia
Alexzandra (0.01)
Alexzandrea

Alexzandri
Alexzandria (0.02)
Alexzandriah
Alexzavia
Alexzeena
Alexzia
Alexziah
Alexzya
Aley
Aleya (0.02)
Aleyah (0.02)
Aleyana
Aleyasia
Aleyce
Aleycha
Aleycia
Aleyda (0.01)
Aleydis
Aleydy
Aleyha
Aleyia
Aleyla
Aleyna (0.01)
Aleynahsi
Aleysa
Aleyse
Aleysha
Aleyshka
Aleysia
Aleyx
Aleyzia
Aleza
Alezah
Alezandra
Alezandrea
Alezha
Alfa
Alfi
Alfira
Alfreda
Algieria
Alham
Alhana
Alheli
Alhona
Alhonna
Ali (0.08)
Ali'anua
Ali'hana
Ali'yah
Alia (0.08)
Aliah (0.04)

Aliah Sarah
Aliaha
Aliahna
Aliahy
Alia-Ines
Aliajona
Aliana (0.06)
Alianah
Aliandra
Aliane
Alianet
Aliani
Alianis
Aliann
Alianna (0.02)
Alianna
  Cansandra
Alianne
Aliannys
Aliany
Alianys
Alia-Rose
Aliayah
Aliaza
Alibbia
Alic
Alica
Aliccia
Alice (0.39)
Alicea (0.01)
Alice-Ann
Alicecelis
Aliceia
Alice-Joair
Alicel
Alicemaday
Alicen (0.01)
Aliceona
Alice-Saveya
Aliceson
Alicesun
Alice-Vict
Alicia (0.94)
Alicia Jane
Alicia
  Joannamaria
  Margorie
  Marlenakari
  Kaylani
  Giovannaleigh
Alicia Marie
Alicia-Addison
Alicia-Breana

Alicia-Felicite
Aliciah
Aliciahmonae
Alicia-Idaly
Alicia-Lee
  Kamylle
Aliciam
Aliciana (0.01)
Alicianah
Aliciane
Alicianna
Alicianne
Aliciara
Alicia-Renae
Alicia-Rose
Aliciea
Alicira
Alicja
Alicya (0.01)
Alicya Helena
Alicyana
Alicyanna
Alicyn (0.01)
Alida (0.01)
Alidale
Alidia
Alidreah
Alie (0.01)
Alie Hadassah
Aliea
Alieaniz
Aliecia
Alieen
Aliegh
Aliegha
Aliehia
Aliejah
Aliely
Alie-Mae
Aliena
Alienor
Alieonya
Aliera
Aliesa
Aliese
Aliesh
Aliesha
Aliesia
Aliesjha
Aliette
Aliexna
Alieyah
Alieyanna

Alieyna
Alieza
Alifa
Ali-Faith
Aliha
Aliha Marb
Alihauna
Alihya
Alijah (0.01)
Alijahh
Alijahliz
Alijanae
Alijandra
Alijea
Alijeleyah
Alijha
Alijia
Alijiah
Alijoy
Alika
Alikah
Ali-Kay
Alikay
Aliksandra
Alila
Alilah
Alilia
Alillah
Alillyah
Alilyonna
Alima
Alimah
Alimar
Alimata
Alimma
Alin
Alina (0.23)
Alina Leanna
Alina Ruth
Alina T
Alinah
Alinayzjah
Alincy
Alinda
Aline (0.01)
Aline Pootida
Alinea
Aline-Kim
Alinna
Alinta
Aliona
Alionna
Alira

Aliria
Aliriea
Aliriyah
Alirose
Alis
Alisa (0.12)
Alisa Nalene
Alisabella
Alisabeth
Alisabethe
Alisah
Alisa-Mae
Alisa-Mich
Alisana
Alisandra (0.01)
Alisandy
Alisciana
Alisdaire
Alisé
Alise (0.02)
Alisea
Alisebeth
Alisee
Alisen
Alisette
Alisha (0.26)
Alishae
Alishah
Alishai
Alishamiya
Alishan
Alishba (0.01)
Alishia (0.01)
Alishieah
Alishka
Alishua
Alishya
Alishyia
Alisia (0.03)
Alisianna
Alisica
Alisin
Alisity
Alison (0.47)
Alison Maya
Alisonne
Alissa (0.29)
Alissah
Alissande
Alissandra
Alissandrya
Alissane
Alisse

Alisset
Alissey
Alissia (0.01)
Alissia Kayl
Alissie
Alisson (0.01)
Alisson Jade
Alissondra
Alissya
Alissyah
Alissyn
Alissynn
Alista
Alistair
Alistaire
Alisten
Alistor
Alisun
Alisya
Alisyah
Alisyana
Alisyia
Alisyn (0.01)
Alita (0.01)
Alithea
Alithia
Alitia
Alittia
Alitza
Alitzel
Alitzet
Alivea (0.01)
Aliveah
Aliveya
Alivia (0.54)
Alivia Leigh
Aliviah (0.01)
Alivian
Aliviana
Alivianna
Aliviya
Aliviyah
Alivya
Alivya Rose
Alix (0.02)
Alixa
Alixana
Alixandera
Alixandra (0.01)
Alixandrea
Alixandree
Alixandria
Alixandrya

| | | | | | | |
|---|---|---|---|---|---|---|
| Alixe | Alizé | Allanna | Allenaya | Alliesandra | Allorah | Allyza |
| Alixea | Alize (0.04) | Allannah (0.01) | Allene | Alliese | Allori | Allyzon |
| Alixia | Alizéa | Allany | Allenessa | Alliesha | Allorie | Allyzza |
| Alixie | Alizea (0.01) | Allara | Allenia | Allieson | Alloyria | Alma (0.09) |
| Alixis | Alizeah | Allarie | Allenie | Alliezabeth | Allura (0.01) | Almadaliz |
| Alixis-Moné | Alizée | Allason | Allenna | Alli-Kay | Allure | Almadelia |
| Alixsandra | Alizee (0.01) | Allasondra | Allenniah | Allin | Allurea | Almairis |
| Alixza | Alizee-Ann | Allassandra | Allenta | Allina | Alluria | Almaleah |
| Alixzandrea | Alizeh | Allasten | Allera | Allina Joy | Ally (0.18) | Almanique |
| Aliya (0.15) | Alizette | Allasun | Alleria | Allinah | Ally Cecelia | Almara |
| Aliyaa | Alizey | Allasyn | Allery | Allinee | Allya | Almarelis |
| Aliyaah | Alizeya | Allaughna | Allesandra | Alliona | Allyah (0.01) | Almarely |
| Ali-Yah | Alizia | Allaunnah | Alleson | Allira | Allyana | Almarie |
| Aliyah (0.52) | Aliziah | Allaura | Allessandra | Allis | Ally-Anna | Almarihanna |
| Aliyaha | Alizlexani | Allawna | Allessendra | Allisa | Allyanna | Almasia |
| Aliyan | Alizon | Allayah | Allessia | Allisan | Allyannah | Almayassa |
| Aliyana (0.01) | Alizsa | Allayana | Allexandriea | Allisandra | Allyce | Almaz |
| Aliyanah | Alizsha | Allayjah | Allexia | Allisen | Allycia | Almedina |
| Aliyanna | Alizz | Allayla | Allexis (0.01) | Allisha | Allyciah | Almeira |
| Aliyannah | Alizza | Allayna (0.01) | Allexus | Allishya | Allydra | Almendra |
| Aliyce | Alizze | Allaynah | Allexys | Allisia | Allye | Almeta |
| Aliyciah | Aljanea | Allazaya | Alley (0.02) | Allisin | Allyeha | Almetta |
| Aliye | Aljeanae | Allbri | Alleya | Allison (2.64) | Allyia | Almia |
| Aliyha | Aljerneria | Alle | Alleya Helena | Allison Ha | Allyiah | Almina |
| Aliyhia | Alji | Allea | Alleyah | Allison Jo | Allyiahmarie | Almira (0.01) |
| Aliyiah | Aljowah | Alleah | Alleyan | Allison Trina | Allyissia | Almita |
| Aliylta | Aljydah | Alleaha | Alleycea | Allisondra | Allyma | Almonie |
| Aliym | Alka | Alleana | Alleycia | Allissa (0.02) | Allyn | Almudena |
| Aliyna | Alkayed | Alleaona | Alleyna | Allissah | Allyna | Almya |
| Aliyonna | Alkayla | Allecia | Alleyni | Allissia | Allynda | Alnasha |
| Aliyrah | Alkee | Allectra | Alli (0.06) | Allisson | Allyne | Alnashia |
| Aliyshia | Alkeisha | Allee (0.02) | Allia | Allisson- | Allys | Alnaya |
| Aliysia | Alkinoey | Alleece | Alliah (0.01) |   Camille | Allysa (0.02) | Alneasha |
| Aliyuana | Alla | Al-Leena | Alliaha | Allista | Allysah | Alnishia |
| Aliyyah | Allah | Alleena | Alliahna | Allisundria | Allysan | Alniva |
| Aliza (0.11) | Allahna | Alleene | Alliahnna | Allisyn (0.01) | Allysandra | Alo |
| Alizabelle | Allahnah | Alleesha | Alliajh | Allivia | Allyse (0.01) | Aloaha |
| Alizabeth (0.02) | Allaija | Allegra (0.01) | Alliana | Allix | Allysen (0.01) | Alock |
| Alizabith | Allaijah | Allegresse | Alliance | Alliya | Allysen-Elian- | Alodie |
| Alizae (0.01) | Allaina | Allegria | Alliann | Alliyah (0.05) |   Eva | Alofamoni |
| Alizah (0.01) | Allaira | Alleha | Allianna | Alliyah Leira | Allysha | Alogan |
| Alizaia | Allaire | Alleigh (0.01) | Alliauna | Alliyah Malaysia | Allyshia | Aloha |
| Alizandra | Allaisja | Alleigha | Allica | Alliyia | Allysia (0.01) | Alohna |
| Alizandria | Allamjit | Alleina | Allicea | Allizaya | Allysin | Alohnie |
| Alizani | Allan | Alleinna | Allicia | Allizayah | Allyson (0.49) | Alois |
| Alizara | Allana (0.02) | Alleisha | Allicyn | Allizei | Allysoon | Aloisa |
| Alizaraya | Allanah (0.02) | Alleluh | Allidje | Allizey | Allyssa (0.08) | Aloise |
| Alizay (0.01) | Allanah-Vianie | Allen | Allie (0.60) | Allona | Allyssia | Aloma |
| Alizaya | Allanaja | Allena (0.01) | Allieanna | Allonah | Allysson | Alomdra |
| Alizaye | Allana-Marie | Allenae | Alliee | Allondra | Allysta | Alona (0.04) |
| Alizayh | Allanee | Allenah | Alliegh | Allonia | Allysun | Alonah (0.01) |
| Alizbeth | Allaney | Allenaih | Allie-Jo | Allonna | Allyvia | Aloncia |
| Alizcelie | Allanis | Allenavia | Alliena | Allora | Allyx | Alonda |

| | | | | | | |
|---|---|---|---|---|---|---|
| Alondra (1.21) | Altijha | Alycia Anne | Alysa Marie | Alyssandre | Alyzza | Amairis |
| Alondrea | Altin | Alycia Zaria | Alysabeth | Alyss-Ann | Alzain | Amairy |
| Alondria | Altisha | Alyciah | Alysah | Alyssas | Alzina | Amaiya (0.02) |
| Alonee | Alton | Alycia-Kokho | Alysan | Alyssa-Taylor | Alzirea | Amaiya Yvette |
| Aloni | Altonisjah | Alyciana | Alysandra | Alysscia | Alzora | Amaiyah (0.01) |
| Alonia | Altrina | Alycianna | Alysandria | Alyssea | Am'briell | Amaiyah- |
| Alonie | Altwaniece | Alycia-Rose | Alys-Ann | Alyssia (0.08) | Am'myiah |    Monet |
| Alonis | Alual | Alyciea | Alysanne | Alyssia | Ama | Amaiyee |
| Alonjé | Alucia | Alycyn | Alysaundra |    Shontavious | Ama'lia | Amaja |
| Alonna (0.03) | Aluel | Alyczandra | Alysbeth | Alyssiana | Amaal | Amajae |
| Alonnah | Aluko | Alyda | Alyscia | Alyssia-Rebecca | Amaana | Amajah |
| Alonsjae | Aluna | Alydia (0.01) | Alyse (0.05) | Alysson (0.01) | Amaanat | Amajan |
| Alontaé | Alunda | Alyea | Alyseana | Alysssa | Amaara | Amajané |
| Alonya | Alundria | Alyeah | Alyseia | Alyssum | Amabel | Amajasti |
| Alonza | Alunna | Alyecia | Alysen | Alysta | Amachi | Amajé |
| Alonzaia | Aluong | Alyeriyah | Alysha (0.06) | Alysun | Amada | Amajha |
| Alonziana | Alura (0.01) | Alyesha | Alysha Janie | Alythia | Amadaleen | Amajiah |
| Alora (0.06) | Aluryonna | Alyesia | Alysha-Faith | Alytris | Amadalia | Amajyah |
| Alora Dannin | Aluxas | Alyeska | Alyshah | Alyvea | Amadalla | Amaka |
| Alorah | Aluxia | Alyessa | Alysha-Lynn | Alyveah | Amadaysha | Amakelech |
| Alori | Alva | Alyette | Alyshea | Alyvia (0.08) | Amadea | Amal (0.03) |
| Aloria | Alvadeli | Alyeza | Alysheva | Alyviah | Amadee | Amala |
| Aloriah | Alvalon | Alyha | Alyshia (0.01) | Alyviana | Amadi | Amalah |
| Alorianna | Alvannie | Alyhanna | Alyshiah | Alyvia-Skye | Amadia | Amalea |
| Alorra | Alvera | Alyhia | Alysia (0.05) | Alyvma | Amadion | Amalee |
| Alorrianna | Alvi'ya | Alyia | Alysiah | Alyvvia | Amadis | Amalexia |
| Alory | Alvia | Alyiah (0.02) | Alysiah-Rae | Alyvya | Amadora | Amaleyah |
| Aloura | Alvie | Alyisa | Alysiana | Alyvyah | Amady | Amali |
| Alove | Alvina | Alyissa (0.01) | Alysiani | Alyx (0.01) | Amadys | Amalia (0.07) |
| Aloynna | Alvinia | Alyizzia | Alysin | Alyxandra (0.01) | Amaeli | Amaliah |
| Aloysia | Alviona | Alyjah | Alysium | Alyxandria | Amaelle | Amálie |
| Alpana | Alvita-Jayne | Alyjiah | Alyson (0.29) | Alyxea | Amaeya | Amalie (0.01) |
| Alpha | Alviyana | Alyla | Alysonne | Alyxia | Amaezin | Amalielcka |
| Al-Rabab | Alwen | Alylah | Alyss | Alyxis | Amahirany | Amalija |
| Alriel | Aly (0.01) | Alylia | Alyssa (4.82) | Alyxsa | Amahni | Amalin |
| Alsatia | Aly'assia | Alymarie | Alyssa Jean | Alyxzah | Amahra | Amaliyah |
| Alsesta | Aly'yah | Alyn (0.01) | Alyssa Lee | Alyxzandrea | Amahri | Amaliz |
| Alsha | Alya (0.01) | Alyna (0.01) | Alyssa Marie | Alyza (0.01) | Amahriah | Amallia |
| Al-Shiniah | Alyaa | Alynah | Alyssa Maya | Alyzabeth | Amahrrin | Amaly |
| Alssya | Alyah (0.01) | Alyncia | Alyssa Michelle | Alyzah | Amai | Amalya |
| Alston | Alyahna | Alynda | Alyssa-Ann | Alyzandra | Amai'yah | Amalyia |
| Alsy | Alyahys | Alyne | Alyssa-Arame | Alyze | Amaia (0.02) | Amalyie |
| Alta (0.01) | Alyana (0.01) | Alynn | Alyssabeth | Alyzea | Amaiah | Amalyn |
| Altaevyah | Alyanah | Alynna | Alyssah (0.01) | Alyzeah | Amaija | Amalyssa |
| Altagracia | Alyani | Alynne | Alyssa-Hope | Alyzee | Amailé | Amama |
| Altajah | Alyania | Alynza | Alyssa-Jade | Alyzeh | Amailee | Amamda |
| Altanique | Alyanna (0.01) | Alyona (0.01) | Alyssa-Jai | Alyzhanay | Amaily | Aman |
| Alte'onna | Alyasia | Alyonna | Alyssa-Lee | Alyzia | Amaira | Amana |
| Altesa | Alyce (0.02) | Alyra | Alyssa-Lynn | Alyziah | Amairah | Amanae |
| Althaea | Alycea | Alyria | Alyssamae | Alyzibeth | Amairani | Amanah |
| Althea (0.03) | Alyceia | Alyric | Alyssa-May | Alyzisha | Amairany | Amanat |
| Althea Bernadhe | Alycen | Alys (0.01) | Alyssandra | Alyzon | Amaire | Amancay L |
| Altia-Meta | Alycia (0.13) | Alysa (0.08) |    (0.01) | | | Amanda (2.01) |

| | | | | | | |
|---|---|---|---|---|---|---|
| Amanda Isabella | Amareana | Amarissa | Amaura | Amberlie | Ambyre | Amelia Sum-Yit |
| Amanda K | Amareé | Amarita | Amauri (0.01) | Amberlin | Ambyrlyn | Amelia-Angela |
| Amanda Lynn | Amaree (0.01) | Amarius | Amauria | Amberlis | Amdije | Amelia-Anne |
| Amanda-Bea | Amareéa | Amariya (0.01) | Amaurianna | Amberlise | Amea | Amelia-Grace |
| Amanda-Grace | Amareh | Amariyah (0.01) | Amauriel | Amberlito | Ameah | Ameliah |
| Amandah | Amareia | Amariyana | Amauriyah | Amberliz | Amea-Lorianah | Amelia-Kamwanya |
| Amandalee | Amareli | Amariyanna | Amaurry | Amberly (0.04) | Amear | Amelian |
| Amanda-René | Amarelis | Amariyna | Amaury | Amberlyn (0.01) | Amearh | Ameliana |
| Amandeep | Amarelyz | Amariyona | Amauryana | Amberlynn | Ameaya | Ameliane |
| Amandine | Amareni | Amariz | Amauryia | Ambernesé | Amechia | Ameliane-Amour |
| Amandolin | Amareona | Amarjot | Amay | Amber-Rose | Amedea | Amelianne |
| Amandra | Amareonna | Amarosa | A-Maya | Ambiance | Amee | Amelica |
| Amanee | Amareyah | Amarra (0.01) | Amaya-Angel | Ambica | Ameeha | Amèlie |
| Amaní | Amarha | Amarrah | Amaya (0.54) | Ambika | Ameen | Amélie (0.02) |
| Amani (0.15) | Amarhaé | Amarre | Amayah (0.03) | Ambir | Ameena (0.01) | Amelie (0.24) |
| Amania | Amarhua | Amarri | Amaya-Kai | Ambiyo | Ameenah | Amelie Ashley |
| Amanie | Amarí | Amarria | Amaya-Lee | Ambra | Ameenna | Amelie Eve |
| Amanii | Amari (0.20) | Amarriah | Amaya-Marie | Ambraih | Ameera (0.02) | Amelie Jandriel |
| Amanise | Amari'onnah | Amarrie | Amayelle | Ambrale | Ameerah (0.02) | Amelie-Azul |
| Amanjot | Amari'yana | Amarriea | Amayelle-Talla | Ambralyn | Ameeriah | Amelie-Rose |
| Amanni | Amariá | Amarrionna | Amayia | Ambrasia | Ameet | Amelina |
| Amanpreet | Amaria (0.05) | Amarriya | Amayiah | Ambraysha | Ameeya | Ameline |
| Amant | Amaria Tytiona | Amarrod | Amaylah | Ambre | Ameeyah | Amelis |
| Amanta | Amariah (0.03) | Amarta | Amaylia | Ambrea | Ameia (0.01) | Ameliya |
| Amanthis | Amarian | Amaru | Amayra | Ambreana | Ameiah | Amelle |
| Amanti | Amariana (0.02) | Amarya | Amayralis | Ambreanah | Ameica | Amellia (0.01) |
| Amantí | Amarianna | Amaryá | Amayrani | Ambreanna | Ameicia | Amelliah |
| Amany | Amarianna Tacari | Amaryah | Amayrany | Ambreeda | Ameila | Amellya |
| Amanye | Amariaunah | Amaryana | Amayza | Ambreellé | Ameilia | Amelmeriah |
| Amar | Amaricka | Amarye | Amaz | Ambreia | Ameilja | Amely (0.01) |
| Amar'ria | Amarié | Amaryi | Amaza | Ambreis | Ameillia | Amelya (0.02) |
| Amara (0.21) | Amarie (0.03) | Amaryia | Amazalie | Ambrelle | Ameillya | Amelyah |
| Amara-Bynaé | Amarie Kandrall | Amarykis | Amazen | Ambrey | Ameilyah | Amelyane |
| Amarach | Amariea | Amarylis | Amaziah | Ambreyah | Ameina | Amelyann |
| Amarachi | Amariell | Amaryllis | Amazing | Ambria (0.02) | Ameir | Amely-Anne |
| Amarachukwu | Amarih | Amaryn | Amba | Ambriah | Ameirah | Amelye |
| Amarae | Amarihia | Amaryona | Ambar (0.01) | Ambriana | Ameiya | Amelys |
| Amaraé | Amarii | Amarys | Ambellina | Ambrianix | Ameka | Amen |
| Amaraeyana | Amariia | Amarysa | Amber (1.30) | Ambrianna | Amekia | Amena (0.01) |
| Amarah (0.01) | Amarili | Amaryus | Amber Dee | Ambrie | Amel | Amenah |
| Amarahliz | Amarilis (0.01) | Amason | Amber Lee | Ambriel | Amel El Donia | Amenaide |
| Amaraiah | Amarillis | Amastasia | Amber Lynn | Ambrielle | Amela | Amenda |
| Amaralee | Amarillo | Amaszha | Amber Rey | Ambrin | Ameleah | Amenia |
| Amaralis | Amarily | Amatallah | Amber Tam | Ambriona | Amelee | Ameniah |
| Amarani | Amarilys | Amath | Amberia | Ambrionna | Ameleon | Amenta Uahmet |
| Amaranta | Amariona (0.01) | Amatista | Amberian | Ambriyon | Ameli | Amentykas |
| Amaranth | Amarionna | Amatrani | Amber-Jade | Ambrocia | Amélia | Amer |
| Amaray | Amaris (0.05) | Amatul | Amberlea | Ambrosette | Amelia (2.18) | Amera (0.01) |
| Amard | Amarisa | Amatulah | Amber-Lee | Ambrosia (0.01) | Amelia Jean | Amerae |
| Amardia | Amarise | Amatullah | Amberlee (0.01) | Ambrosia Angel | Amelia Kay Lynn | Amerah |
| Amare | Amarisee | Amaunet | Amberleigh | Ambry | Amelia Killa | Amerakis |
| Amaré | Amaris-Myzella | Amaunie | Amberlen | Ambryn | Amelia Rae | |
| Amarea | | Amauny | Amberley (0.01) | Ambur | | |

Amerakiss
Ameralie
Ameralys
Amere
Amereia
Amerelle
Amereya
Ameri
Ameria *(0.01)*
Ameriah
Amerial
Ameriana
Ameriauna
America *(0.09)*
America An
Americal
Americas
Americis
Americis May
Americle
Americus *(0.01)*
Amerié
Amerie *(0.03)*
Amerika
Amerikiss
Amerikyiah
Amerine
Ameris
Amerish
Ameriya
Ameriyah
Amerlee
Amerra
Amerria
Amerricas
Amerryce
Amery *(0.01)*
Ameryka
Amerykah
Ameryn
Ameryoni
Ames
Amesha
Amesiali
Amesika
Amethyst *(0.02)*
Ametria
Amey
Ameya
Améya
Ameyah
Ameyan
Ameyia

Ameylah
Ameynah
Ameza
Ami *(0.02)*
Ami'en
Amia *(0.05)*
Amiah *(0.05)*
Amialee
Amianna
Amiary
Amiaya
Amiayh
Amiayia
Amica
Amice
Amici
Amicia
Amidy
Amie *(0.03)*
Amie-Baoan
Amiee *(0.01)*
Amiel
Amiela
Amiela
Elizabeth
Amiella
Amielle
Amiera
Amierah
Amierra
Amigia
Amihya
Amiia
Amiiah
Amiira
Amiiya
Amija
Amijah
Amijilay
Amika
Amil
Amila
Amilea
Amileah
Amilee
Amileigh
Amilia *(0.02)*
Amilian
Amiliana
Amilianna
Amilie
Amiline
Amilka

Amilleah
Amillia
Amilliana
Amillianna
Amillion
Amillionna
Amilliya
Amilliyon
Amillya
Amillyah
Amiluah
Amily
Amilya *(0.01)*
Amilyah
Amilyan
Amilyia
Amilyn
Amilyona
Amin
Amina *(0.13)*
Amina A
Amina-Andrea
Aminadade
Aminah *(0.02)*
Aminat
Aminata *(0.04)*
Aminata Mimi
Aminata-Tina
Aminatou
Cherif
Aminatta
Aminda
Amineh
Aminetou
Amingo
Aminyah
Amir
Amir'eana
Amirá
Amira *(0.20)*
Amira-Carla
Amiracle *(0.01)*
Amiracle C
Amirae
Amirah *(0.08)*
Amirald
Amiranay
Amira-Sarai
Amirat
Amire
Amireanna
Amiree
Amirelis

Amirelyz
Amireya
Amiri
Amiria
Amiriana
Amiricah
Amiricole
Amiriona
Amiriya
Amir-Nikyla
Amiro
Amirra
Amirrah *(0.01)*
Amirral
Amirria
Amirriya
Amirya
Amisadai
Amisaday
Amisha *(0.01)*
Amishaday
Amishi
Amislediz
Amissa
Amit
Amita
Amitai
Amithi
Amithiste
Amithy
Amithyst
Amitis
Amitoj
Amitra
Amity *(0.01)*
Amiyá
Amiya *(0.11)*
Amiyae
Amiyah *(0.13)*
Amiya-Mildred
Amiyan
Amiyea
Amiyha
Amiyja
Amiyya
Amizadai
Amjot
Amlika
Amma
Ammaarah
Ammani
Ammanilla
Ammar

Ammara
Ammariah
Ammarie
Ammarreah
Ammena
Ammerisa
Ammi
Ammie
Ammielle
Ammishaddai
Ammn
Ammy
Amna *(0.02)*
Amnah
Amne
Amneet
Amneh
Amneris
Amnestiey
Amnesty
Amodisy
Amodrae
Amoire
Amol
Amoldeep
Amolia
Amolika
Amollia
Amom
Amondria
Amoné
Amonee
Amoni *(0.02)*
Amonie
Amonimarie
Amonni
Amonnie
Amontanise
Amonte
Amonti
Amony
Amonyae
Amór
Amor *(0.01)*
Amora *(0.01)*
Amora Jade
Amorae
Amorah
Amorás
Amoré
Amore *(0.01)*
Amoreá
Amoree

Amoreena
Amorelli
Amorese
Amorette
Amori
Amoriah
Amorie
Amoriey
Amorin
Amorina
Amorinayae
Amoriya
Amoriyah
Amorosa
Amorriyana
Amory
Amos
Amou
Amounia
Amour
Amoura
Amouri
Amouria
Amoy
Amoya
Amparo
Ampelia
Ampnecia
Amra
Amran
Amreen
Amreese
Amreet
Amreh
Amrei
Amren
Amri
Amrie
Amri-Joelle
Amrin
Amrit *(0.01)*
Amrita *(0.01)*
Amritdeep
Amrith
Amritha
Amrithasai Silst
Amritleen
Amritpreet
Amruta
Amrutha
Amry
Amryn
Amrynn

Amsley Denise
Amtoj
Amtul
Amtus Subour
Amudharani
Amukta
Amuktha
Amulet
Amulya
Amun
Amunet-Ka
Amuni
Amunique
Amuria
Kawanna
Amurianna
Amy *(1.60)*
Amy Amanda
Amy Ann
Amy Desneiges
Amy Florence
Amy Jo
Amy Tam
Amy'rr
Amyá
Amya *(0.23)*
Amyaa
Amya-Ariana
Amyah *(0.04)*
Amyaih
Amyala
Amyalee
Amy-Ann
Amy-Ann Renee
Amy-Ashley
Amyel
Amyele
Amy-Elizabeth
Amyelle
Amy-Grace
Amyha
Amyia *(0.01)*
Amyiah *(0.01)*
Amyisha
Amy-Jade
Amy-Jane
Amy-Jin
Amy-Jo
Amykka
Amykkah
Amyla *(0.01)*
Amyle
Amy-Lee

| | | | | | | |
|---|---|---|---|---|---|---|
| Amylee | Ana Clara | Anacarolina | Anaheeta | Anaixa | Analia (0.01) | Ana-May |
| Amylee-Ann | Ana Cristina | Anaceli | Anahei | Anaixly | Analicia (0.02) | Ana-Melina |
| Amylen | Ana Fernanda | Anacelia | Anahelena | Anaiya (0.03) | Analie | Anamika |
| Amylia (0.01) | Ana Florentina | Anacely | Anahi (0.14) | Anaiyah (0.01) | Analiece | Anamilena |
| Amyliah | Ana Gabriela | Ana-Cesili | Anahia | Anaiyla | Analiese (0.03) | Anamitra |
| Amylie | Ana Isabel | Ana-Christina | Anahid | Anaiz | Analiesia | Anamta |
| Amy-Lynn | Ana Isabella | Anacia | Anahis | Anaizja | Analiesse | Anan |
| Amylynn | Ana Jully | Anaclaire | Anahit | Anaja | Analilia | Ananada |
| Amyna | Ana Kaoru | Anaclaudia | Anahita (0.01) | Ana-Jade | Analis (0.01) | Anand |
| Amyni | Ana Karen | Anacorina | Anahjé | Anajae | Analisa (0.02) | Ananda (0.01) |
| Amy-Nicole | Ana Laura | Ana-Cristina | Anahlea | Anajah (0.01) | Analise (0.05) | Ananda Jot |
| Amyra (0.01) | Ana Leeah | Anacristina | Anahleesah | Anajaraye | Analisia | Anandi |
| A-Myracle | Ana Leigh | Anadalay | Anahli | Anajeá | Analiss | Anani |
| Amyrah | Ana Lilia | Anadea | Anahlia | Anajiah | Analissa | Anania |
| Amyrakle | Ana Lisa | Anadeli | Anahy (0.01) | Anajjah'waah | Analisse | Ananiah |
| Amyre | Ana Lucia | Anadia | Anahya | Anajshare | Analita | Ananiese |
| Amyria | Ana Luiza | Anadialyn | Anahyia | Anaka | Analivia | Ananilda |
| Amyriah | Ana Lusia | Anadya | Anahys | Anakah | Analiya | Ananirobee |
| Amyrillas | Ana Maria | Anadyah | Anaí | Anakaren | Analiyah | Anansi |
| Amy-Rosalie | Ana Marie | Anae (0.01) | Anai (0.02) | Anakarina | Analiz (0.01) | Anantpreet |
| Amyrra | Ana Marija | Anaea | Anaia (0.01) | Anakarla | Analiza | Anantya |
| Amysia | Ana Pilar | Anaee | Anaiah (0.02) | Anakia | Analize | Ananya (0.05) |
| Amystique | Ana Raphaela | Anaeja | Anaica | Ana-Kim | Analleli | Ananyaa |
| Amythyst | Ana Rita | Anaejah | Anaid | Anakim | Anallely | Ana-Paula |
| Amyzhané | Ana Rosa | Anael (0.01) | Anaida | Anakin | Ana-Lois | Anara |
| Amzi | Ana Rosi | Anaele | Anaie | Ana-Kym | Analucia | Anarah |
| An | Ana Sofia | Anaeli | Anaii | Anala | Analuisa | Anareen |
| An'asia | Ana Teodora | Anaeliese | Anaija | Analah | Analvisa | Anareidy |
| An'astajah | Ana Teressa | Anaelise | Anaijah | Analaubra | Analy | Anareli |
| An'drea | Ana Zuleika | Anaeliz | Anaijyah | Analaura | Analya | Anarelis |
| An'dria | Anaahat | Anaëlle | Anaika | Analaya | Analyah | Anarely |
| An'ishia | Anab | Anaelle (0.01) | Anaila | Analaysia | Analyce | Anarelys |
| An'iya | Anabarbara | Anaely | Anaile | Anale | Ana-Lycia | Anarha |
| An'keria | Ana-Beatrice | Anaesia | Anailys | Analea | Analycia | Anarí |
| An'kyera | Anabel (0.08) | Anaester | Anaira | Analeah | Analyese | Anari (0.01) |
| An'niya | Anabela | Anaeve | Anairam | Analease | Analyiah | Anaria |
| An'talayah | Anabelen | Ana-Eve | Anairis | Analecia | Analyn | Anariah |
| An'tanajah | Anabel-Jade | Anaeya | Anairis | Analee (0.01) | Analynn | Anarie |
| An'tanasia | Anabell (0.01) | Anafely | Ana-Is | Analeesa | Analys | Anariyah |
| An'tazsia | Ana-Bella | Anafernanda | Anaïs | Analeese | Analysa | Anarosa |
| An'tonikah | Anabella (0.06) | Anafrancis | Anais (0.18) | Analeez | Analyse (0.01) | Anarria |
| An'tyana | Ana-Belle | Anagabriel | Anais Chloe | Analei | Analysia | Anasah |
| An'unique | Anabelle (0.15) | Anagabriela | Anais Davda | Analeia | Analysiya | Anasaria |
| An'ya | Anabelle Andrea | Anageliz | Anais Yasmine | Ana-Leigh | Analyssa (0.01) | Anasette |
| An'yae | Anabelleoine | Anagely | Anaisa | Analeigh (0.01) | Analyz | An-Asha |
| An'yah | Anabeth | Anagha | Anaisabel | Analeigha | Analyze | Anasha |
| An'yia | Anabeti | Ana-Gloria | Ana-Isabel | Analeise | Anam | Anasheay |
| Ana (1.05) | Anabexis | Anagrace | Anaise | Analeiss | Anamae | Anashia |
| Ana Beatriz | Anab-Fatima | Anagret | Anaisha | Analena | Ana-Maria | Anashija |
| Ana Carolina (0.01) | Anaca | Anah | Anaishja | Analene | Anamaria (0.01) | Anashley |
| Ana Carolina (0.01) | Anacamila | Anah'reya | Anaisia | Analese | Anamarie (0.01) | Anashya |
| Ana Celia | Anacaren | Anahaim | Anaisjia | Analessa | Anamaris | Anasia (0.02) |
| | Anacarla | Anahee | Anaisse | Anali (0.01) | Anamary | Anasia'lee |
| | | | Anaistan | | | |

| | | | | | | |
|---|---|---|---|---|---|---|
| Anasija | Anataya | Anayzha | Andisten | Andree-Ann | Andromeda | Aneko |
| Anasja | Anathalia | Anazao | Andjela | Andree-Anne | Andromida | Anel |
| Anasjia | Anaum | Anazia | Andolena | Andrée-Anne | Andronika | Anéla |
| Ana-Sofía | Anaundra | Anazja | Andonia | Andreeka | Andronisha | Anela (0.02) |
| Anasofia | Anauri | Anbelle | Andora | Andreen | Andrya | Anele |
| Anasol | Anautica | Anber | Andra (0.01) | Andreia | Andrya Skye | Aneleigh |
| Ana-Sophia | Anavah | Anberlyn | Andra Maria | Andreianna | Andryah | Aneli |
| Anasophia | Anavai | Anbiya | Andra'nique | Andreighauna | Andy | Anelia |
| Anasseh | Anavay | Anbreá | Andra'nyla | Andreina | Andyn | Aneliese |
| Anassia | Anavelisa | Anbria | Andraeana | Andreína | Aneah | Aneliesse |
| Anastaca | Anavey | Anbriana | Andrah | Andreita | Anealise | Anelina |
| Anastacia (0.05) | Anavi | Ancaria | Andra-Lee | Andreiya | Aneasia | Anelis |
| Anastaciya | Anavia | Ancelin | Andraly | Andreka | Anecia (0.01) | Anelise (0.01) |
| Anastacyia | Anavictoria | Anchal | Andralyn | Andrel | Anee | Anelisse |
| Anastaisa | Anawake | Anchelle | Andra-Maria | Andrena | Anee'ya | Aneliz |
| Anastaisha | Anaxa | Anchranesha | Andras | Andrénay | Aneea | Aneliza |
| Anastaisia | Anay (0.01) | Ancieona | Andraya (0.01) | Andrenayzia | Aneecia | Anelize |
| Anastaisya | Anaya (0.18) | Ancika | Andrayana | Andrenna | Aneeia | Anella |
| Anastaja | Anaya Patricia | Ancilla | Andre | Andreonna | Aneeka | Anellah |
| Anastajah | Anaya-Angela | Ancora | Andreá | Andresha | Aneekah | Anelle |
| Anastajia | Anayad | Anda-Gabriela | Andréa | Andressa | Aneela | Anelliana |
| Anastasha | Anayah (0.03) | Andaira | Andrea (2.41) | Andreuanna | Aneeqa | Anellie |
| Anastashia | Anayahjade | Andaleese | Andrea Del Carmen | Andreus | Anees | Anellise |
| Anastasia (0.46) | Anayalyse | Andalicia | Andrea Esther | Andrew | Aneesa (0.02) | Anelsy |
| Anastasiah | Anayanci | Andalyn | Andrea Michaela | Andrewnique | Aneesah | Anely |
| Anastasia-Lynne | Anayas | Andania | Andrea Noele | Andréya | Aneesha | Anelya |
| Anastasie | Anayca | Andariel | Andrea'le | Andreya (0.01) | Aneeshia | Anelym |
| Anastasija | Anayeli (0.03) | Andawen | Andrea-Alexandra | Andreyah | Aneesia | Anelys |
| Anastasiya (0.01) | Anayelic | Ande | Andreah | Andréyah | Aneessa | Anelyse |
| Anastasja | Anayelie | Andea | Andrea-Jade | Andreyana | Aneeta | Aneres |
| Anastassia | Anayelli | Andee (0.01) | Andrealiz | Andreyauna | Aneeve | Aneri |
| Anastasya | Anayely | Andel | Andrealyn | Andreyeena | Aneeya | Aneriya |
| Anastaszia | Anayhi | Andeline | Andrea-Maria | Andreyonne | Aneeza | Aneriyah |
| Anastaysha | Anayi | Andella | Andreana (0.01) | Andri | Anei'ya | Aneroly |
| Anastaysia | Anayia | Andellow | Andreane | Andria (0.02) | Aneia | Anerrá |
| Anastayzia | Anayiah | Andelynn | Andreann | Andriah | Aneiamarie | Anesa (0.01) |
| Anastaza | Anayis | Andenashia | Andreanna (0.01) | Andriana (0.01) | Aneiarra | Anesah |
| Anastazha | Anayise | Anderea | Andreanna Jenelle | Andriana-Isabella | Aneice | Anescia |
| Anastazia (0.01) | Anayiz | Anderiah | Andréanne | Andriani | Aneigia | Anesheniu |
| Anastazja | Anayj'ah | Anderse | Andreanne (0.02) | Andrianna (0.01) | Aneila | Aneshia |
| Anastazzja | Anayjah | Andersen | Andreas | Andrianne | Aneira | Aneshka |
| Anastin | Anayka | Anderson (0.01) | Andreauna | Andrianonna | Aneisa | Anesia |
| Anaston | Anayla | Andi (0.03) | Andrecia | Andrice | Aneisah | Anesiah |
| Anastusia | Anayniah | Andi Jo | Andree | Andriel | Aneise | Anessa (0.03) |
| Anastyn | Anayris | Andia | Andrée | Andrijah | Aneisey | Anessah |
| Anasuya | Anays | Andie (0.05) | Andreea | Andrika | Aneisha | Anestasia |
| Anasya | Anaysha | Andie Marie | | Andrina | Aneisia | Anestazya |
| Anasyn | Anaysia (0.01) | Andile | | Andriuna | Aneissa | Anesti |
| Anat | Anaysse | Andilyn | | Andriunna | Aneiysa | Anestin |
| Anata | Anayulisa | Andi-Mae | | Andriyah | Aneizha | Anesya |
| Anatalia | Anayvia | Andi-Marie | | Andriyona | Aneka | Anet |
| Anatasaisa | Anayya | Andina | | | Anekae | Anete |
| | Anayza | Andini | | | Anekah | Aneth |

Anetha
Anetra
Anetreya
Anett
Anetta
Anette (0.01)
Aneva
Anevaeh
Anevay
Aneve
Anexie
Anexys
Aneya
Aneyah
Aneysha
Aneysia
Anezka
Anfal
Anfal Moubaraka
Anfessa
Anfisa
Angailica
Angal
Angalea
Angaleana
Angaleha
Angaleina
Angalena
Angalenna
Angali
Angalie
Angalina
Angalique
Angalyn
Angavis
Ange
Ange-Desiree
Angeel
Angeer
Angeili
Angejolie
Angel (0.98)
Angel Aaliyaha
Angel Arco
Angel Chey
Angel La'sha
Angel Lea
Angel Mareeka
Angel Marie
Angel Naki
Angel Rosa
Angel Shanik

Angel'lina
Angela (1.53)
Angela Grace Linly
Angela Jiahan
Angela Sophia
Angela-Maria
Angelan
Angelana
Angelann
Angelanne
Angelay
Angelaya
Angel-Dawn
Angele
Angelea (0.01)
Angeleah (0.01)
Angeleana
Angelee (0.01)
Angeleea
Angeleen
Angeleena
Angeleigh
Angeleigha
Angeleina
Angeleis
Angelek
Angeleka
Angel-Elizabeth
Angelena (0.04)
Angelene
Angeles (0.03)
Angelesha
Angelestrella
Angeleta
Angeleyse
Angelez
Angeli (0.01)
Angeli'a
Angelia (0.04)
Angelia-Anne
Angeliah
Angelic (0.01)
Angélica
Angelica (0.44)
Angelica Marie
Angelice
Angelicia
Angélie
Angelie (0.03)
Angeliegh
Angeliena
Angelies

Angeliesh
Angelieth
Angelik (0.01)
Angelika (0.03)
Angelike
Angeliki
Angelin
Angelina (2.84)
Angelina Dan
Angelina Sheila
Angelinah
Angelina-Kameah
Angelina-Mae
Angelina-Rae
Angelina-Rose
Angeline (0.10)
Angeline Julieth
Angelinee
Angelinna
Angelinne
Angelino
Angeliq
Angeliqué
Angelique (0.16)
Angelique Sophie
Angelique-Desiree
Angeliques
Angelis (0.01)
Angelisa (0.01)
Angelise (0.02)
Angelisha
Angeliss
Angelissa
Angelisse (0.01)
Angelita (0.01)
Angelius
Angelivette
Angelixa
Angeliyah
Angel-Iyauanna
Angeliz
Angeliza
Angelize
Angel-Joy
Angell
Angella
Angel-Lalelei
Angelle (0.01)
Angel-Lea

Angellea
Angelleah
Angel-Leah
Angellee
Angellen
Angellena
Angelli
Angellia
Angel-Liana
Angellica
Angel-Lin
Angellina (0.01)
Angellisa
Angelly
Angel-Lyn
Angellyna
Angellynn
Angel-Lynn
Angellys
Angelmarie
Angelrose
Angelus
Angeluz
Angely (0.02)
Angelyc
Angelyce
Angelyk
Angelyka
Angelymar
Angelyn (0.01)
Angelyna (0.01)
Angelynah
Angelyne
Angelynn
Angelynna
Angelynne
Angelyque
Angelys
Angelyse
Angelyss
Angelyssa
Angelzay
Angenaya
Angeni
Angenie
Angeniece
Angenise
Angenlika
Ange-Noella
Angerilis
Angery
Angesha
Angeuna

Anggy
Anghelia
Anghelina
Angher
Angi
Angie (0.21)
Angie Marie
Angiela
Angielee
Angie-Leila
Angielina
Angielis
Angieliz
Angielyn
Angie-Nayelli
Angiery
Angil
Angila
Angilea
Angileah
Angilee
Angilese
Angilica
Angiline
Angina
Anginae
Anginya
Angiolina
Angiriah
Anglasha
Angle (0.01)
Anglea
Anglena
Anglin
Anglina
Anglique
Angolina
Angowa
Angria-Yemalla
Angsumalee
Angui
Anguil
Angy
Angyliah
Anh
Anh Phuong
Anh Thi
Anh'janell
Anhel
Anhelica
Anhely
Anhelyna
Anhjay

Anh-Linh
Anh-Tam
Anh-Thi
Anhthi
Anh-Thu
Anhthu
Ani (0.02)
Ani'jah
Ani'yah
Ania (0.04)
Aniah (0.05)
Aniaha
Aniajah
Aniajeshia
Anialyn
Aniarelis
Aniary
Anias
Aniaya (0.01)
Aniayah
Anibel
Anibelea
Anibell
Anibeth
Anica (0.01)
Anicah
Anicca
Anice-Yvonne
Anicham
Anichelle
Anichka
Anicia
Anick
Anicka
Anicya
Anides
Anie'ya
Aniea
Anieca
Anieja
Aniek
Aniela (0.01)
Anielka
Aniella
Anielle
Anieria
Aniesa
Aniesha
Aniesia
Aniessa
Anieya
Anieyah
Anigha

Anigye
Anihaya
Anihja
Anihya
Aniila
Aniiya
Aniiyah
Anija (0.01)
Anijah (0.03)
Anijan
Anijha
Anijzah
Anik
Anika (0.24)
Anika Nylah
Anika-Ayanna
Anikah
Anika-Lynn
Ani-Kamille
Anikaua
Anike
Anikha
Anikim
Anikka
Aniko
Anila (0.01)
Anilah
Anilaya
Anilee
Anilem
Anilet
Aniley
Anilou
Anilya
Anilyn
Ani-Maria
Anina
Aninda
Anine
Aninka
Aninsley
Anipier
Aniqa
Anique
Anira
Anirah
Anires
Anirie
Anis
A-Nisa
Anisa (0.07)
Anisah (0.01)
Anïse

Anise *(0.01)*
Anisette
Anish
Anisha *(0.04)*
Anisha-Anna
Anisha-Rose
Anishatou
Anishe
Anishea
Anishka
Anishtah
Anisia
Anisiana
Anisjah
Anislee
Anisleydi
Anislyer
Anissa *(0.05)*
Anisse
Anissia
Anistasha
Anistasia
Anistee
Anisten
Anistey
Anistin
Aniston *(0.02)*
Anisty
Anistyn
Anisya
Anita *(0.09)*
Anita Sevastia
Anitarose
Anitaya
Anitoneti
Anitra
Anitria
Anitriah
Anitsa
Anitza
Anivea
Anixa
Aniy'yah
Aniyá
Aniya *(0.43)*
Aniya Juanit
Aniya Nikayla
Aniya'h
Aniyaah
Aniya-Claire
Aniyah *(0.56)*
Aniyah
Diamoniqu

Aniyaha
Aniyahh
Aniyahn
Aniyah-Veronica
Aniyalis
Aniyan
Aniyeah
Aniyha
Aniyia
Aniyiah
Aniyja
Aniyjah
Aniyla
Aniylah
Aniyra
Aniysha
Aniyus
Aniyyah
Aniza
Anizette
Anja *(0.05)*
Anja Mary
Anjahi
Anjahlai
Anjahlina
Anjail
Anjalea Marie
Anjaleah
Anjalee
Anjali *(0.09)*
Anjalie
Anjalina
Anjaliya
Anjana
Anjanaa
Anjanae
Anjanette
Anjani
Anjanise
Anjaylee
Anjeanete
Anjeanetta
Anjel
Anjela *(0.01)*
Anjelah
Anjelay
Anjelena
Anjeli
Anjelia
Anjelica *(0.01)*
Anjelicia
Anjelie
Anjelika

Anjelina *(0.01)*
Anjeline
Anjelique
Anjelise
Anjelisia
Anjelita
Anjella
Anjelle
Anjellica
Anjelyce
Anjelyna
Anjelyss
Anjenique
Anjeska
Anjewel
Anjewl
Anjhinay
Anjhy'lee
Anjie
Anjil
Anjila
Anjili
Anjilinna
Anjini
Anjli
Anjoel
Anjolaoluwa
Anjolee
Anjolena
Anjoli
Anjolia
Anjolie *(0.01)*
Anjolina
Anjolique
Anjou
Anjoulise
Anjoyel
Anju
Anjule
Anjulene
Anjuli
Anjulie
Anjulina
Anjun
Anjyyah
Anke
Ankita
Ankitha
Anlana
Anlei
Anlil
Anllelina
Anllely

Anlly
Anlyah
Anlyn
Anmarie
Anmerose
Anmoalpreet
Anmol *(0.01)*
Anmool
Anmy
Anmya
Ann *(0.17)*
Ann Elise
Ann Emma
Ann Felix
Ann Frederique
Ann Haden
Ann Joly
Ann Marie
    *(0.01)*
Ann Mei
Ann Nicole
Ann Sophie
Ann Sophy
Ann'ashia
Ann'tonia
Anna *(4.54)*
Anna Adalissa
Anna Annie
Anna Bella
Anna Belle
Anna Carolin
Anna Carolina
Anna Cathe
Anna Cecilia
Anna Christine
Anna Clair
Anna Claire
Anna Clara
Anna Eve
Anna Grace
    *(0.01)*
Anna Graci
Anna Isabel
Anna Julia
Anna Kate
Anna Kathe
Anna Kathr
Anna Kym
Anna Laeticya
Anna Lucille
Anna Luiza
Anna Lydia
Anna Mae

Anna Maria
    *(0.01)*
Anna Marianik
Anna Marie
    *(0.01)*
Anna Mariya
Anna Mary
Anna Maude
Anna Rae
Anna Reese
Anna Sofia
Anna-Abakar
Anna-Alexandra
Annabel *(0.12)*
Annabela
Annabele
Annabell *(0.03)*
Annabella *(0.13)*
Anna-Belle
Annabelle *(0.74)*
Annabelle
    Christina
Annabelle
    Marie-Jo
Annaberly
Annabeth *(0.01)*
Annablle
Anna-Britta
Anna-Brook
Annacatherine
Anna-Christina
Anna-Clair
Anna-Claire
Annaclaire
Annadely
Annadora
Annael
Annaele
Annaeli
Annaelisa
Annaelise
Annaelle
Anna-Eve
Annafaith
Anna-Gabrielle
Annagail
Annagayle
Anna-Giulia
Anna-Grace
Annagrace
Annah *(0.02)*
Annah Isabel
Annah Joy

Annah Marie
Annahi
Annahis-Mahika
Annahita
Annah-Lee
Annahy
Annaica
Annaick
Annaijah
Annaika
Annaira
Annais
Annaise
Annaisha
Annaitza
Anna-Jaelle
Annajo
Annajoe
Annaka *(0.01)*
Anna-Karen-
    Nina
Anna-Kate
Anna-Kay
Annakay
Anna-Kaye
Anna-Kim
Annakim
Annakiya
Annalara
Anna-Laura
Annalaura
Annalavisa
Annalayne
Annalaysia
Annalea *(0.01)*
Annaleagh
Annaleah *(0.01)*
Anna-Leasa
Anna-Lee
Annalee *(0.03)*
Annaleea
Annaleeah
Annaleece
Annaleese
Annalei
Anna-Leigh
Annaleigh *(0.01)*
Annaleigha
Annaleis
Annaleise *(0.01)*
Anna-Lena
Annalena
Annalesa

Annalese *(0.01)*
Annalesia
Annalesse
Annaley
Annali
Annalia *(0.01)*
Annalice
Annalicia *(0.01)*
Annalie *(0.01)*
Annaliece
Annalies
Annaliesa
Annaliese *(0.07)*
Annaliess
Annaliesse
Annaliet
Annalieze
Anna-Liisa
Annalina
Annaline
Annalis
Anna-Lisa
Annalisa *(0.04)*
Anna-Lise
Annalise *(0.16)*
Annalisia
Anna-Lissa
Annalissa
Annalisse
Annaliya
Annaliyah
Annaliz
Annaliza
Annalize
Annallese
Anna-Lubov
Annalucia
Annaluse
Annaly
Annalyce
Annalyese
Annalyiah
Annalyn *(0.01)*
Annalynn *(0.01)*
Annalynne
Annalysa
Annalyse *(0.02)*
Annalysia
Annalyssa
Annalysse
Annalyze
Anna-Mae
Annamae

| | | | | | | |
|---|---|---|---|---|---|---|
| Anna-Maelle | Annastazij | Anne-Barbara | Annelies | Annette (0.06) | Annika Wambli | Ann-Marie |
| Annamaree | Annastee | Annebel | Anneliese (0.08) | Annevaeh | Annika | (0.01) |
| Anna-Maria | Anna-Stella | Annebella | Anneliesia | Anneya | Winifred | Annmarie |
| Annamaria | Annaston | Annebelle | Anneliesse | Anneyah | Annikah | (0.03) |
| (0.02) | Annastyn | Anne-Catherine | Annelis | Ann-Frederic | Annikia | Annmarin |
| Anna-Marie | Annasue | Annecha | Annelisa | Ann-Frederick | Annikka | Annmary |
| (0.01) | Annatronett | Anne-Charlie | Annelisabeth | Ann-Frederik | Annikki | Annmerie |
| Annamarie | Annave | Anne-Charlotte | Ann-Elise | Ann-Frederique | Anniko | Annola |
| (0.03) | Anna-Veronika | Anne-Chloe | Anne-Lise | (0.01) | Annilyn | Annora (0.01) |
| Anna-Marielle | Anna-Victoria | Anne-Christie | Annelise (0.06) | Ann-Gabrielle | Annilyse | Annquaneisha |
| Annamary | Annavie | Annecia | Annelisee | Anngalinia | Annina | Annrayia |
| Anna-Maude | Annay | Anne-Clara | Anneliz | Anngel | Annira | Ann-Rosalie |
| Annamay | Annaya | Annecy | Ann-Elizabeth | Anngela | Annis | Ann-Sara |
| Annamiah | Annayah | Annedee | Annelize | Anngelica | An-Nisa | Ann-Sarah |
| Annamiek | Annaye | Annee | Annell | Anngelie | Annisa | Ann-Sidney |
| Annan | Annayha | Anne-Elizabeth | Annella | Anngelina | Annise | Annslee |
| Annangel | Annayi | Anne-Elyzabeth | Annella Rose | Anngeline | Annisha | Annsleigh |
| Annani | Annaysha | Anneesa | Annelle | Ann-Haven | Annissa | Annsley (0.01) |
| Anna-Nicole | Annayuan | Anne-Esther | Anne-Louise | Anni | Annissia | Annsofia |
| Annaniya | Ann-Berrie | Anne-Flavie | Annelys | Annia | Annistacia | Ann-Sophie |
| Annanya | Annbriella | Anne-Florence | Annelyse | Annia De Jesus | Annisten | (0.02) |
| Anna-Paige | Ann-Catherine | Anne-Frederick | Anne-Marie | Anniah | Anniston (0.02) | Annsophie |
| Annaraye | Anndee | Anne- | (0.03) | Annibel | Annistyn | Ann-Talbot |
| Annarayne | Anndelyn | Frederique | Annemarie | Annibell | Annita | Anntanasia |
| Annareesa | Anndi | (0.01) | (0.02) | Annibelle | Anniya (0.01) | Anntasia |
| Annari | Anndie | Anne-Gabrielle | Anne-Marie | Annica (0.01) | Anniyah (0.01) | Ann-Taylor |
| Annaria | Anndilande | Annegeliyah | Rebecca | Annice | Anniyyah | Anntisha |
| Annarin | Anndra | Anneida | Anne-Mary | Annicet | Annjaleah | Anntoinette |
| Annarita | Anndraya | Anneisa | Annemary | Annick (0.01) | Annjelika | Anntonella |
| Anna-Rose | Anndrea | Anne-Isabelle | Annemiek | Annie (0.30) | Annjelina | Annum |
| Annarose | Anndreia | Anneisha | Ann-Emilie | Annie Lizzie | Ann-Jessica | Annwyn |
| Anna-Sarah | Anndriana | Anneishia | Anne-Mya | Heather | Annjolea | Anny (0.01) |
| Annasaria | Anndrianna | Anneishka | Anneriah | Anniea | Annjolena | Annya |
| Annasen | Anndronica | Anne-Julia | Anne-Rose | Annie-Claude | Annjoliyah | Annyah |
| Annashey | Anne (0.33) | Anne-Julie | Annesa | Anniegrace | Annjoly | Annyce |
| Annasia | Anne Catherine | (0.01) | Anne-Sarah | Annie-Kim | Annjulie | Anny-Elizabeth |
| Anna-Simone | Anne Darby | Anne-Justine | Annese | Anniel | Ann-Julie | Annyka |
| Anna-Sofia | Anne Flavie | Anneka (0.01) | Annesia | Annie-Laure | Ann-Katrine | Annymae |
| Annasofia | Anne | Annekatherine | Annesley | Anniell | Ann-Kelly | Anny-Pier |
| Annason | Frederique | Anneke (0.02) | Anne-Soleil | Anniemae | Ann-Laure | Annysa |
| Anna-Sophia | Anne Laurie | Anne-Kristy | Anne-Sophia | Annie-Marie | Ann-Laurence | Annyssa |
| Annasophia | Anne Marie | Annel | Anne-Sophie | Annie-Pier | Ann-Laurie | Annyston |
| Annastacia | (0.01) | Annela | (0.06) | Annierya | Ann-Lee | Annyxia |
| Annastaisa | Anne Soleil | Anne-Laetitia | Anness | Annigail | Annlee | Ann-Yzobel |
| Annastaisha | Anne Sophie | Annelaina | Annessa | Anniina | Annleigh | Anodyne |
| Annastan | (0.01) | Anne-Laurence | Annessia | Annijah | Annlesica | Anoi'pua Hiilan |
| Annastasha | Annea | Anne-Laurie | Annestasha | Annijuliet | Annley-Coralie | Anola |
| Annastashia | Anne-Alise | Anneleace | Annestesia | Annik | Ann-Li | Anoma |
| Annastasia | Anne-Aliya | Annelease | Annet | Annika (0.39) | Ann-Lori | Anon |
| (0.02) | Anneamie | Annelee | Annete | Annika Liv | Ann-Lorie | Anona |
| Annastavia | Anne-Audree | Anneleise | Anneth | Annika Mabel | Ann-Lory | Anonda |
| Annastaysia | Anne-Aurelie | Anneli | Annett | Annika Mahlia | Annlyn | Anonnie |
| Anna-Stazi | Anne-Aurora | Annelie | Annetta | | Ann-Margaret | |

| | | | | | | |
|---|---|---|---|---|---|---|
| Anoop | Ansya | Antelecia | Antoinique | Antreace | Anuon | Anyelic |
| Anoosha | Ant'anasia | Antelia | Antoinyah | Antrecia | Anupama | Anyelina |
| Anooshey | Ant'kivia | Antenise | Antomaya | Antreise | Anupreet | Anyessa |
| Anooshka | Ant'nasia | Anteria | Antonae | Antrice | Anupriya | Anyha |
| Anora | Ant'taesha | Anterica | Antonaeja | Antricia | Anuradha | Anyi |
| Anorah | Ant'tinaesha | Anterria | Antonaja | Antrinette | Anureet | Anyia (0.02) |
| Anoryea | Anta'noshia | Anterriana | Antonasia | Antronece | Anusaga | Anyiah (0.01) |
| Anosha | Jaylee | Anterricka | Antonaya | Antronique | Anusha (0.02) | Anyicia |
| Anosia-Lyne | Antaizya | Antesha | Antonecia | Anttanaya | Anushka (0.01) | Anyih |
| Anotiyae | Antalayah | Antha | Antoneise | Anttonella | Anushkaa | Anyis |
| Anouchka | Antalaysia | Anthania | Antoneisha | Anttria | Anushree | Anyja |
| Anouck | Antaliyah | Anthea | Antonela | Antuanette | Anushri | Anyjah |
| Anouk (0.02) | Antamille | Anthonay | Antonella (0.02) | Antunette | Anuska | Anyka |
| Anouksha | Antanae | Anthoneá | Antonello | Anturnett | Anuujin | Anyla (0.02) |
| Anoukyane | Antanaisha | Anthonella | Antonelly | Antwainé | Anvalie | Anylah |
| Anouluck | Antanaja | Anthoneshall | Antonely | Antwanae | Anveigh | Anyliah |
| Anousha | Antanajah | Anthonette | Antonesé | Antwanasia | Anvesha | Anyng |
| Anoushka (0.01) | Antanasha | Anthonin | Antonesia | Antwanette | Anvi | Any-Pier |
| Anouska | Antanasia | Anthony (0.01) | Antonet | Antwania | Anvita (0.01) | Anyrah |
| Anovale | Antanay | Anthonyc | Antonette | Antwanique | Anvitha | Anyriah |
| Anovalean | Antanaysha | Anthoula | Antonetty | Antwanise | Anwaar | Any-Rose |
| Anovia | Antanazha | Anthya | Antoneya | Antwanisha | Anwar | Anysa |
| Anqelique | Antaneak | Anthynee | Antoniá | Antwaniya | Anwasha | Anysha |
| Anqi | Antaneece | Anti'niya | Antónia | Antwaniyah | Anwen | Anyshia |
| Anquaneisha | Antaneesha | Antigone | Antonia (0.11) | Antwanya | Anwita | Anysia |
| Anquinette | Antanese | Antigoni | Antoniah | Antwanyia | Anwitha | Anysiah |
| Anra | Antanesha | Antigony | Antonia-Maria | Antwauna | Anwyn | Anyssa (0.01) |
| Anreesha | Antanesia | Antija | Antonica | Antwayja | Anxhela | Anyssia |
| Anreet | Antanette | Antiliyah | Antoniea | Antwinae | Any | Anystazia |
| Anri | Antaniá | Antimayra | Antonietta | Antwnyai | Any'jah | Anyuta |
| Anria | Antania (0.01) | Antinet | Antoniette | Antwonique | A-Nya | Anyuta-Laurita |
| Anrich | Antaniah | Antinia | Antonika | Antwonisha | Anyá | Anyya |
| Anrit | Antanilya | Antinie | Antonina | Antwoniya | Anya (0.24) | Anyzia |
| Anroop | Antanine | Antiniya'h | Antonine | Antwuaneka | Anya Lina | Anzal |
| Ansal | Antaniya | Antiona | Antonio | Antwunasia | Anyaa | Anzané |
| Ansaria | Antaniyah | Antionae | Antonique | Antwunyce | Anyae | Anzarria |
| Ansharaneka | Antanyah | Antionett | Antonise | Antynette | Anyah (0.03) | Anzel |
| Ansharaye | Antanye | Antionette | Antonisha | Antyonise | Anyah-Ashley | Anzell |
| Anshika | Antaria | (0.01) | Antonishe | Anty-Sallay | Anyai | Anzhel |
| Anshious | Antarria | Antionia | Antoniya | Antyshia | Anyais | Anzie |
| Anshra | Antashay | Antioniya | Antóniyah | Anu | Anyalese | Anziya |
| Anshrah | Antashia | Antiqueshia | Antonline | Anuh | Anyalie | Anzlee |
| Anshu | Antasia (0.01) | Antiya | Antonnette | Anuhea (0.01) | Anyalisse | Anzley |
| Anshula | Antastasia | Antiyana | Antonya | Anuja | Anya-Marie | Anzsa |
| Ansi | Antavia | Antje | Antoria | Anujin | Anyaniah | Aohna |
| Anslea | Antaviha | Antoinella | Antoria Oc | Anula | Anyanka | Aoi |
| Anslee (0.01) | Antaya | Antoineque | Antorious | Anulekha | Anycia | Aoibhe |
| Ansleigh (0.01) | Antayah | Antoinese | Antoryia | Anum | Any-Claude | Aoibheann |
| Ansley (0.24) | Antayeah | Antoinet | Antranae | Anumeet | Anye | Aoibheil |
| Anslie | Antaysia | Antoinett | Antranasia | Anumitha | Anyea | Aoibhgreine |
| Anson | Antayvia | Antoinette | Antraniece | Anunaya | Anyeah | Aoibhinn |
| Ansonia | An-Tazia | (0.05) | Antranise | Anuncia | Anyeh | Aoife (0.02) |
| Anstianasia | Anteeshia | Antoinette Cole | Antrea | Anuoluwadamisi | Anyeli (0.01) | Aolani |

| | | | | | | |
|---|---|---|---|---|---|---|
| Áolani | Aquazá | Aracelli | Arashdroanel | Ardaejah | Areiana | Arey |
| Aolannie | Aqueen | Aracelly | Arati | Ardajah | Areianna | Areya |
| Aolany | Aquela | Aracely (0.06) | Araura | Ardelia | Areicy | Areyah |
| Aolanys | Aqueria | Aracelys | Aravella | Ardella | Areiel | Areyana |
| Aomalbanan | Aquetzalli | Arachana | Aravis | Ardelle | Areigha | Areyanna |
| Aonesty | Aquila | Aradhana | Araviszia | Arden (0.05) | Areika | Areyli |
| Λonyaé | Aquilah | Aradhna | Arawen | Ardiana | Areil | Areyon |
| Aotad | Aquilat | Aradia | Arawyn | Ardielee | Arein | Areyona |
| Aoua | Aquilia | Aradonna | Arax | Ardil-Zera | Areina | Areyonah |
| Aowyn | Aquilla | Aradyn | Araxi | Ardin | Areion | Areyonna |
| Aowynn | Aquina | Araeanna | Aray | Ardine- | Areionna | Areysi |
| Apaarajita | Aquinna | Araelia | Araya (0.04) |   Pardonee | Areisi | Areyuanna |
| Apache | Aquinnah | Araena | Araya Beth | Ardis | Arek | Areyunna |
| Apala | Aquiriá | Araeya | Arayah (0.01) | Ardita | Arela | Arezo |
| Aparaajita | Aquista | Araeyah | Araydia | Ardreanna | Arelayn | Arfa |
| Aparna | Ar'destinee | Araezha | Arayea | Ardriana | Areli (0.04) | Arfida |
| Apeksha | Ar'keilah | Arah | Arayia | Ardyn | Areli Yasmin | Argelia |
| Aphia | Ar'keria | Arahbella | Arayiah | Are'aun | Arelia | Argelinda |
| Aphrodite | Ar'mani | Arahelys | Arayjiah | Are'nayjhia | Arelis (0.01) | Argy |
| Apiphani | Ar'mauni | Arahis | Araylee | Are'nyhia | Arelise | Argyl |
| Apishaa | Ar'moni | Araiana | Arayli | Are'ona | Areliz | Arhema |
| Apolinar | Ar'monni | Arailya | Arayna | Are'onna | Arella | Arheya-Hope |
| Apollonia | Ar'mya | Araina | Arayveia | Are'ya | Arelle | Arhianna |
| Apolonia | Ar'najah | Araix | Arazeli | Are'yanah | Arelli | Arhya |
| Aponi | Ar'nella | Araiya | Arazely | Areaba | Arelly | Ari (0.01) |
| Apoorva | Ar'niyah | Araiza | Arbani | Arealya | Arellya | Ari'anna |
| Appeline | Ar'nyiah | Arajah | Arbany | Arean | Arellys | Ari'ei |
| Apple (0.01) | Ar'nyjah | Arakai | Arbella | Areana | Arely (0.08) | Ari'monie |
| Apple-Madisyn | Ar'reinna | Aralee | Arbiona | Areanah | Arelya | Ari'onna |
| Apreia | Ar'reonna | Aralese | Arbra | Areane | Arelys | Ari'yanah |
| Aprele | Ar'reyana | Aralhya | Arbreon | Areanna (0.01) | Areme | Ari'yanna |
| Aprell | Ar'rhana | Aralie | Arbrielle | Areanna Halee | Aremi | Ari'yona |
| Apria | Ar'riel | Aralyn (0.02) | Arbryonna | Areanne | Aremily | Ari'yonn |
| Apriel | Ar'shunti | Aralynn (0.01) | Arcadia | Areany | Aren | Ari'yonna |
| April (0.25) | Ar'teria | Aram | Arcatreona | Areasia | Arena | Aria (0.15) |
| April Alicia | Ar'yiona | Aramea | Arceira | Areaunna | Arene | Ariabella |
| Aprile | Ar'zhanae | Arameli | Arceli | Arechavaleta | Arenessa | Ariaceli |
| Aprincess | Ara (0.01) | Aramenah | Arcelia | Arecyli | Areon | Ariacna |
| Apryl (0.01) | Arabel | Arami | Arcellya | Aree | Areona | Ariaczy |
| Apryle | Arabela | Aramia | Archana | Areea | Areonia | Ariadna (0.02) |
| Apsara | Arabelia | Aramis | Archee | Areeba | Areonice | Ariadne (0.01) |
| Apsley | Arabell | Arana | Archelle | Areebah | Areonna | Ariae |
| Apurva | Arabella (0.12) | Aranai | Archer | Areeha | Areouna | Ariael |
| Apurvaa | Arabellah | Aranda | Archi | Areej | Arere'll | Ariah (0.04) |
| Aputi Judith | Arabella-Joisce | Aranelis | Archianne | Areely | Areria | Ariahana |
| Aqari | Arabelle (0.01) | Aranessa | Archie | Areen (0.01) | Aresa | Ariahla |
| Aqiila | Arabia | Arania | Archielia | Areena | Aretae | Ariahlise |
| Aqquujaq | Aracele | Arantxa | Archisha | Areeonna | Arete | Ariahna (0.01) |
| Aqsa | Araceli (0.09) | Arantza (0.01) | Archita | Areesha | Aretta | Ariahnna |
| Aqua | Aracelia | Aranza | Arcia | Areeyanna | Aretzi | Ariahtna |
| Aquara | Aracelie | Araschuna | Arcina | Areeyona | Areughna | Arial (0.01) |
| Aquarius | Aracelis | Araseli | Arctura | Areia | Arev | Arializ |
| Aquayla | Araceliy | Arasely | Arcyana | Areial | Arewyn | Arialy |

| | | | | | | |
|---|---|---|---|---|---|---|
| Ariam | Aribah | Arieyah | Arismel | Arkei'rea | Arlisia | Armiyah |
| Ariame | Aribella | Arieyana | Arismelix | Arkema | Arlissa | Armonea |
| Ariamelix | Aribreauna | Arieyanna | Arisneidy | Arkeria | Arlivia | Armonee |
| Ariammys | Arica (0.01) | Arieyauna | Arison | Arkevia | Arliya | Armoni (0.02) |
| Arian (0.01) | Aricel | Arieyonna | Ariss | Arkeya | Arliz | Armoni Makayla |
| Ariana (1.99) | Aricela | Arieyonnah | Arissa (0.04) | Arkheyz | Arlly | Armonia |
| Ariana Candice | Ariceli | Arifa | Arissa-Noele | Arkhya | Arlonna | Armonie |
| Ariana Rose | Aricelli | Arige | Arista | Arkia | Arly | Armonii |
| Arianah (0.01) | Aricelly | Ariha | Aristea | Arkisa | Arlyah | Armoniy |
| Arianaisab | Aricely | Arihana | Aristeia | Arkrista | Arlyn | Armontasha |
| Ariana-Isabel | Aricia | Arihanna | Aristine | Arlaina | Arlynn | Armonte |
| Arianaliz | Aricka | Ariiana | Aristotle | Arlana | Arlyssia | Armony |
| Arianaly | Arie (0.02) | Arij | Arisvel | Arlanni | Armaan | Armya |
| Arianalyn | Arie'anna | Arija | Arit | Arlaysia | Armada | Armyea |
| Ariandra | Arie'onna | Arijana | Aritza | Arleah | Armaghan | Armyyah |
| Ariane (0.21) | Arie'yauna | Arijandra | Ariuna | Arleahna | Armahnni | Arna |
| Ariane May | Ariea | Arijha | Ariunia | Arlee | Armala | Arnaaz |
| Arianell | Arieah | Arika (0.02) | Arius | Arleen (0.01) | Armalie | Arnae |
| Arianella | Arieal (0.01) | Arikcely | Arixamairanny | Arleena | Arman | Arnai |
| Ariani | Arieana (0.01) | Arikka | Ariya (0.02) | Arleene | Armanda | Arnaja |
| Arianis | Arieanna (0.02) | Arikza | Ariyaan | Arleeyah | Armandina | Arnasia |
| Arianjeliz | Arieauna | Arilis | Ariyaé | Arleigh | Armane | Arnavia |
| Ariann | Ariel (0.58) | Arillana | Ariyah (0.02) | Arleigha | Armanee | Arnaya |
| Ari-Anna | Ariela (0.03) | Arilyn (0.01) | Ariyahl | Arlem | Armaneé | Arnaysha |
| Arianna (1.92) | Ariele | Arima I'onyae | Ariyan (0.01) | Arlen | Armaní | Arnaz |
| Arianna Imani | Arieli | Ari-Marie | Ariyaná | Arlena | Armáni | Arndra |
| Arianna Marie | Arielis (0.01) | Arin (0.02) | Ariyana (0.05) | Arlene (0.04) | Armani (0.08) | Arne'tas |
| Ariannah (0.01) | Arielisse | Arina | Ariyanah | Arlenis | Armanie | Arnecia |
| Ariannah Kao | Ariell | Arine | Ariyanh | Arlenne | Armanii | Arneet |
| Mee See | Ariella (0.08) | Aringwa | Ariyani | Arleny | Armaniti | Arneisha |
| Ariannalis | Ariellah | Arinna | Ariyann | Arlesia | Armanti | Arnela |
| Arianna-Rose | Arielle (0.20) | Arion (0.01) | Ariyanna (0.04) | Arlet (0.01) | Armany | Arnelis |
| Arianné | Arielle Jai | Ariona (0.02) | Ariyel | Arlete | Armaree | Arnell |
| Arianne (0.09) | Arielle Kennedy | Arionan | Ari-Yele | Arleth (0.05) | Armari | Arnesa |
| Arianne Helsy | Ariellis | Arione | Ariyelle | Arlethe | Armaria | Arnescia |
| Arianne Jean | Arielyn | Ari-Onna | Ariyhana | Arlett | Ar-Marna | Arnese |
| Arianne-Sophie | Arielys (0.01) | Arionna (0.05) | Ariyl | Arlette (0.02) | Armarni | Arneshia |
| Ariannette | Arielyse | Arionnah | Ariyoana | Arletty | Armauni | Arnesia |
| Ariannh | Arien | Arionne | Ariyon | Arlety | Armaya | Arneya |
| Arianni | Ariena | Arionnha | Ariyona (0.01) | Arley | Armeen | Arni |
| Ariannon | Ariena Elizabeth | Arionnia | Ariyonah | Arli | Armeia | Ar-Nia |
| Arianny | Ariene | Aris (0.01) | Ariyonná | Arlibeth | Armela | Arniaya |
| Arianny's | Arienna | Arisa | Ariyonna (0.01) | Arlicia | Armeliss | Arnie |
| Ariannys | Arienne | Arisai | Ariyonnia | Arlida | Armelle | Arniecia |
| Ariany | Arienne Therese | Arisandi | Ariyuana | Arlie (0.01) | Armena | Arniesha |
| Arianya | Arieny | Arisbeidy | Arizbel | Arliette | Armenia | Arnija |
| Arias | Arieon | Arisbet | Arizbeth | Arlin | Armesia | Arnijah |
| Ariauna (0.01) | Arieona | Arisbeth (0.01) | Arize | Arlina | Armiah | Arnineveh |
| Ariaunia | Arieonah | Arisdely | Arizona (0.01) | Arline | Armida | Arnisea |
| Ariaunna | Arieonna (0.01) | Arisel | Arjanna | Arlined | Armin | Arnisha |
| Ariaunnah | Aries (0.02) | Arisha | Arkatya | Arlington | Armina | Arnyliaa |
| Ariaya | Ariett | Arisia | Arkaysia | Arlinn | Arminda | Aroha |
| Ariba | Arietta | Arislgydi | Arkeelah | Arlisha | Armita | Arok |

Aron
Aronhiahawe
Aroniah
Aronicia
Aronika
Aronna
Aronranksy
Aroosa
Arora
Aroura
Aroush
Arowa-Mim
Arowyn
Arowynn
Arpan
Arpita
Arquielys
Arra
Arrabella
Arrah
Arralee-Este
Arrathy
Arraya
Arrayah
Arrayh
Arre'yonna
Arrea
Arreana
Arreanna
Arreion
Arreis
Arrelia
Arrena
Arreon
Arreonna
Arria
Arriah
Arrian
Arriana (0.02)
Arriana Angela
Arriané
Arrianna (0.03)
Arrica
Arricka
Arrie
Arriel
Arriella
Arrielle
Arrington
Arriona
Arrione
Arrionna
Arrionte

Arrisa
Arrissa
Arrissie
Arritt
Arriuna
Arrius
Arriya
Arriyah
Arriyana
Arriyiah
Arrolee
Arron
Arrow
Arry'l
Arrya
Arryana
Arryani
Arryanna
Arryannah
Arryawna
Arrybella
Arryce
Arryelle
Arryona
Arryonna
Arrysohn
Arsalie
Arseima
Arsema
Arsenal
Arsenia
Arsh
Arsha
Arshae
Arshanti
Arshdeep
Arshea
Arshek
Arshe-Mah
Arsheyra
Arshi
Arshia
Arshita
Arshiya
Arshpreet
Arshveer
Arsine
Art'teaonna
Arta
Artai'sha
Artaija
Artanique
Artasia

Artatyana
Artavia
Artayshia
Artchai
Arteana
Artel-Tomilla
Artemis
Artemisa
Artemisia
Arteona
Arteria
Arteshia
Arthi
Arthika
Arthurine
Artia
Artianna
Artie
Artierra
Artimisha
Artina
Artiste
Artrice
Artriná
Arturo
Artwanijah
Aruai
Arub
Aruba
Aruna
Arunata
Arundathi
Arundeep
Arundel
Arunima
Arusha
Arushi (0.01)
Arviet
Arvionne
Arvoniee
Arwa (0.01)
Arwaa
Arwen (0.04)
Arwin
Arwyn (0.01)
Arwynn
Ary
Ary'ana
Ary'anna
Ary'onna
Arya (0.03)
Arya'nna
Aryaah

Aryadevi
Aryah (0.01)
Aryahana
Aryahna
Aryahnna
Aryaki
Aryal
Aryam
Aryan (0.01)
Aryana (0.09)
Aryanah (0.01)
Aryane (0.01)
Aryani
Aryann
Aryanna (0.13)
Aryannah (0.01)
Aryanne (0.01)
Aryauna
Aryca
Arycah
Arycelli
Arydai
Aryeal
Aryeana
Aryeanna
Aryejah
Aryel
Aryele
Aryell
Aryella
Aryelle
Aryena
Aryenna
Aryenne
Aryeri
Aryhana
Aryi
Aryia
Aryiah
Aryiana
Aryianna
Aryion
Aryissa
Aryka
Arykah
Arykerica
Aryl
Arylise
Aryn (0.01)
Arynn
Arynton
Aryon
Aryona (0.01)

Aryonna (0.01)
Aryonne
Arys
Arysa
Aryssa (0.01)
Aryssia
Aryssta
Arysta
Aryyah
Aryzan
Aryzona
Arz
Arzaliya
Arzelia
Arzen
Arzo
Arzu
As'atay
As'ja
As'jah
Asa (0.01)
Asab
Asabea
Asabel
Asabi
Asaciah
Asah
Asaiah
Asaira
Asaisha
Asalah
Asaleah
Asalee
Asaliah
Asalla
Asana
Asani
Asante
Asantewa
Asanti
Asaria
Asasia
Asauda
Asaundi
Asaunti
Asaya
Asayah
Asayriah
Asaysha
Asbah
Asbel
Asbriel
Ascha

Aschelyn
Aschertyn
Aschley
Aschly
Asdrelle
Aseanni
Aseel
Aseera
Asees
Asela
Aselin
Aselis
Asena
Asenatta
Aseneth
Asenka
Asercet
Aseret
Asfa
Asfi
Ash
Ash'lyn
Ash'sha
Asha (0.08)
Asha'i
Ashaejha
Ashaela
Ashaelee
Ashah
Ashai
Ashaia
Ashaila
Ashairi
Ashaja
Ashaki
Ashal
Ashala
Ashalee
Ashalei
Ashaley
Ashalina
Asha-Lynn
Ashalynn
Ashan'tia
Ashana
Ashanale
Ashanay
Ashani
Ashanna
Ashanni
Ashanta
Ashante (0.01)
Ashantee

Ashantí
Ashanti (0.11)
Ashantia
Ashantie
Ashantii
Ashanty (0.01)
Ashara
Asharah
Ashari (0.01)
Asharia (0.01)
Asharie
Ashariya
Asharrah
Asharria
Asharyah
Ashauna
Ashauni
Ashauntae
Ashaunté
Ashaunti
Ashauntí
Ashaunty
Ashaurrion
Ashawana
Ashawna
Ashawnee
Ashawnta
Ashawnté
Ashawnti
Ashay
Ashaya
Ashayah
Ashayla (0.01)
Ashayna
Ashbee
Ashby (0.01)
Ashcraft
Ashden
Ashdon
Ashdyn
Ashe
Ashe'laya
Ashea
Ashearha
Asheleigh
Asheley
Ashelie
Ashelin
Ashelle
Ashely (0.01)
Ashelyn (0.01)
Ashelyne
Ashelynn

| | | | | | | |
|---|---|---|---|---|---|---|
| Ashelynne | Ashlene- | Ashmeen | Ashylne | Asjoat | Assiatou- | Ataja |
| A-Sheonna | Emeletta | Ashmeet | Ashylnn | Asjwomu | Massayon | Atajia |
| Asher | Ashlenn | Ashmi | Ashyra | Aska | Assir | Atalaya |
| Ashera | Ashley *(5.90)* | Ashmin | Ashyrah | Askiyah | Assitan | Atalia |
| Asherah | Ashley Atziry | Ashmina | Ashyya | Aslan | Assiya | Ataliah |
| Asheton | Ashley Kim | Ashmita | Asiá | Aslee | Assiyah | Atalie |
| Asheya | Ashley Zaray | Ashmy | Asia *(0.39)* | Asleerose | Assmae | Atallah |
| Asheyla | Ashleyann | Ashna *(0.01)* | Asia Amauri | Asleiram | Assouline | Atalya |
| Ashgan | Ashleyanna | Ashnah | Asia'nay | Aslel | Assriel | Atalyah |
| Ashi'onna | Ashley-Anne | Ashni | Asia'nieya | Asleny | Asstan | Atara |
| Ashia *(0.01)* | Ashley-Djamilia | Ashnitha | Asiaa | Asley | Assunta | Atarah |
| Ashiah | Ashley-Dolores | Ashonni | Asia-Brianne | Aslhey | Assya | Atari |
| Ashian | Ashley-Jayden | Ashonti | Asiah *(0.02)* | Asli | Assyria | Atasha |
| Ashiana | Ashley-Jewel | Ashoori | Asia-Lee | Aslie | Astacianna | Atasia |
| Ashianna | Ashley-Kate | Ashpreet | Asialee | Aslin | Astaria | Atavia |
| Ashijia | Ashley-Marie | Ashriel | Asialena | Aslinn | Astarra | Ataya |
| Ashika *(0.01)* | Ashleymariv | Ashrita | Asia-Li | Asliyah | Astashia | Atayah |
| Ashilah | Ashley-Michelle | Ashritha | Asia-Marie | Asly | Astasia | Atayeveona |
| Ashilei | Ashleyn | Ashriya | Asiana | Aslyn *(0.01)* | Astella | Atayviana |
| Ashira | Ashley-Nora | Ashtain | Asianai | Aslynn | Aster | Ateanna |
| Ashiri | Ashleyona | Ashtan | Asiané | Asma *(0.03)* | Astera | Ateeanonya |
| Ashita | Ashley-Reid | Ashtaynne | Asianic | Asma'a | Astha *(0.01)* | Ateekah |
| Ashiya | Ashleyrose | Ashten *(0.01)* | Asianna *(0.01)* | Asmaa *(0.02)* | Asti | Atenas |
| Ashiyah | Ashleyy | Ashtin *(0.01)* | Asiauna | Asmaa Sawsan | Astin | Ateria |
| Ashiyana | Ashli *(0.01)* | Ashtine | Asiayana | Asmae | Aston | Aterra |
| Ashjanae | Ashliana | Ashton *(0.11)* | Asiayanna | Asmah | Astou | Aterria |
| Ashjnae | Ashlie *(0.02)* | Ashton Wyn | Asija | Asmaou | Astra | Athaena |
| Ashka | Ashliee | Ashtra | Asijah | Asmara | Astra Nicole | Athalee |
| Ashke | Ashlin *(0.04)* | Ashtrid | Asila | Asmarii | Astraea | Athalia |
| Ashkiah | Ashlinda | Ashtyn *(0.05)* | Asilee | Asmi | Astrea | Athaliah |
| Ashla | Ashline | Ashtyn-Grace | Asilynn | Asmira | Astrid *(0.07)* | Athalie |
| Ashlahn | Ashling | Ashtynn | Asima | Asmita | Astrid Ariadna | Athan |
| Ashlan | Ashlinn | Ashtynne | Asin | Asmo | Astrondria | Athanasia |
| Ashland *(0.01)* | Ashlinne | Ashuanti | Asinae | Asondiya | Astryd | Athasia |
| Ashlann | Ashliyah | Ashuna | Asireanna | Aspa | Asucena | Athea |
| Ashle | Ashliyn | Ashunti | Asitu | Aspen *(0.23)* | Asude | Atheana |
| Ashlé | Ashlley | Ashvi | Asiya *(0.01)* | Aspin | Asuka | Atheena |
| Ashlea *(0.01)* | Ashlly | Ashvita | Asiyah *(0.01)* | Aspn | Asurim | Atheenah |
| Ashleah | Ashloy | Ashviya | Asiyhah | Aspyn *(0.02)* | Asusena | Athela Grace |
| Ashleanne | Ashly *(0.07)* | Ashwaak | Asiyyah | Asra | Asuzena | Atheleisia |
| Ash-Lee | Ashlyana | Ashwaq | Asja | Asraa | Aswan | Athen |
| Ashlee *(0.40)* | Ashlye | Ashwariya | Asjad | Asrar | Aswane | Athena *(0.20)* |
| Ashlee Ann | Ashlyl | Ashwika | Asjae | Asrelia | Asya *(0.03)* | Athenia |
| Ashlee M E | Ashlyn *(1.29)* | Ashwina | Asjah | Asriel | Asyah | Athenn |
| Ashleen | Ashlynd *(0.01)* | Ashwinameera | Asjahnay | Asrutha | Asyha | Athenni |
| Ashleerose | Ashlyne *(0.01)* | Ashwini | Asjahnii | Assa | Asyia | Athessa |
| Ashleey | Ashlynn *(0.39)* | Ashy'la | Asjanae | Assal | Asyiah | Atheylia |
| Ashlei *(0.01)* | Ashlynn Kayley | Ashya | Asjanaya | Assala | Asylan | Athiang |
| Ashleia | Ashlynne *(0.02)* | Ashyah | Asjayah | Assani | Asyria | Athina |
| Ashleigh *(0.21)* | Nicole | Ashybrianne | Asjha | Assata *(0.01)* | Asyriah | Athina Paulina |
| Ashleigh-Sage | Ashlynne | Ashyia | Asjhana | Assel | Asyza | Athira |
| Ashlen *(0.01)* | Ashlyyn | Ashyla | Asji'anna | Assia | Aszani | Athisaya |
| Ashlend | Ashmara | Ashyln | Asjia | Assiatou | Ataejah | Athsiri |

| | | | | | | |
|---|---|---|---|---|---|---|
| Athyna | Attiana | Aubreanna | Aubryonna | Audrey Anna | Audyn | Aumoi |
| Athzary | Attianna | Aubreauna | Auburn (0.01) | Audrey Anne | Audyssee | Aumoni |
| Athziri | Attia-Tul-Hai | Aubreaunna | Aubury'ana | Audrey Maude | Augande | Aumora |
| Athziry | Attica | Aubree (0.18) | Aubyn | Audrey Maxim | Auganei | Aumya |
| Ati | Attira | Aubreeana | Auceane | Audrey Qiao | Augest | Aun'drea |
| Atia | Attisa | Aubrei | Auceanne | Audrey Victoria | August (0.03) | Aun'yale |
| Atiah | Attiya | Aubreie | Aucerann | Audreya | Augusta (0.01) | Auna (0.01) |
| Atiaja | Attori | Aubreigh (0.01) | Auchia'a | Audrey-Alexie | Augustah | Aunabella |
| Atiana (0.01) | Attoria | Aubreila | Audam | Audreyana | Augustina | Aunaia |
| Atianah | Attouria | Aubreiona | Audbria | Audrey-Ann | Augustine | Auna-Lee |
| Atianna (0.01) | Attrina | Aubretta | Aude (0.01) | (0.04) | Auhdra | Aunalee |
| Atifahuda | Atumm | Aubreuna | Aude-Gabrielle | Audreyann | Auhmya | Aunallie |
| Atijahnea | Ature | Aubrey (1.60) | Audelie | Audrey-Anna | Auhnice | Aunastasia |
| Atika | Atyana | Aubrey Ann | Audelina | Audreyanna | Auigail | Aunaysia |
| Atikaa | Atyanna | Aubrey Auna | Auden | (0.01) | Aujaé | Aundi |
| Atilliana | Atyia | Aubreyah | Audessa | Audrey-Anne | Aujah | Aundra |
| Atira | Atyse | Aubreyana | Audi | (0.04) | Aujalay | Aundraiana |
| Atissan | Atzahyrah | Aubreyanna | Audia | Audreyanne | Aujanae | Aundranae |
| Atisyn | Atzai | Aubrey-Jo | Audiana | Audrey-Eve | Aujanay | Aundraya |
| Ativah | Atzel | Aubrey-Lee | Audianna | Audrey-Jade | Aujanee | Aundre'a |
| Atiya | Atzhiri | Aubreylyn | Audim | Audrey-Lillian | Aujanet | Aundrea (0.02) |
| Atiyana | Atzhiry | Aubri (0.02) | Audisy | Audrey-Maude | Aujani | Aundreana |
| Atiyanna | Atzin | Aubria | Audiyonna | Audreyonna | Aujaray | Aundreas |
| Atiyyah | Atziri | Aubriana (0.02) | Audjenea | Audrey-Pier | Aujaye | Aundreya |
| Atlana | Atziry (0.01) | Aubrianah | Audlaluk | Audrey-Precillia | Aujene | Aundria |
| Atlaneci | Au'bri | Aubriane | Audon Milante | Audrey-Rose | Aujia | Aundriana |
| Atlanta (0.01) | Au'brionna | Aubriann | Audra (0.07) | Audri (0.01) | Aujianna | Aundrielle |
| Atlantis (0.01) | Au'janay | Aubrianna | Audrah | Audria | Aujinay | Aundrya |
| Atlee | Au'janea | (0.04) | Audralyn | Audria Marie | Aujinee | Auneria |
| Atley (0.01) | Au'keila | Aubriannah | Audray-Ann | Audriana (0.03) | Aujoni | Aunesha |
| Atly | Au'keira | Aubrianne | Audre | Audriane | Auki | Aunesti |
| Atong | Au'miracle | Aubriauna | Audrea | Audriann | Aukia | Aunestie |
| Atonyé | Au'mya | Aubrie (0.13) | Audreaina | Audrianna | Aukiya | Aunesty |
| Atoosa | Au'nahya | Aubriegh | Audreana | (0.04) | Aulani | Aungelique |
| Atorhia | Au'naja | Aubriel | Audréane | Audriauna | Aulbany | Aunica |
| Atorria | Au'niya | Aubriella | Audreane (0.01) | Audriaunna | Aulbré | Aunicca |
| Atoyria | Au'nyah | Aubrielle | Audreanna | Audrie (0.02) | Aulbreauna | Aunika |
| Atqiya | Au'reyunae | Aubrienda | Audréanne | Audrieauna | Aulbrey | Aunikah |
| Atravia | Au'zaria | Aubrienne | Audreanne | Audriel | Aulexsia | Aunima |
| Atrem | Aubany | Aubriey | (0.01) | Audrielle | Aulie | Aunistee |
| Atreona | Aubbr'ie | Aubrin | Audreaona | Audrina (0.01) | Aulise | Aunisti |
| Atreonna | Aube | Aubrionna | Audreauna | Audrionna | Aulissa | Aunisty |
| Atreya | Auben-Grace | Aubriyah | Audrée (0.01) | Audriy | Aulonna | Auniya |
| Atreyi | Aubin | Aubriyonna | Audree (0.02) | Audriyana | Aulora | Aunjalé |
| Atrianna | Aubori | Aubry (0.02) | Audree-Ann | Audriyanna | Aulyvia | Aunjalea |
| Atriona | Aubra | Aubryana | Audrei | Audron | Aumani | Aunjanae |
| Atrisa | Aubrae | Aubryanna | Audreiana | Audry (0.01) | Aumari | Aunjoli |
| Atryana | Aubraina | Aubrye | Audrena | Audryana | Aumariya | Aunna |
| Atsaruaq | Aubrayanna | Aubryella | Audreona | Audryanna | Aumaya | Aunnah |
| Attalie | Aubré | Aubryn | Audreonia | Audryn | Aumbria | Aunnaleah |
| Attalissa | Aubre (0.01) | Aubrynn | Audreonna | Audryonna | Aumerie | Aunnalee |
| Attarria | Aubrea | Aubrynne | Audrey (2.28) | Audum | Aumilya | Aunnani |
| Attaya | Aubreana | Aubryona | Audrey Ann | Audun | Aumnia | Aunnika |

Aunterial-
Alexandria
Auntesy
Aunusha
Aunya
Aunyá
Aunyae
Aunye
Aunyee
Auphelie
Auquella
Aur'miah
Aura *(0.02)*
Aura'jae
Auraelea
Auraleanna
Aura-Lena
Auralie
Aurane
Auraya
Aurayliah
Aurbenia
Aure
Aurea
Aureana
Aureanna
Aureanne
Auree
Aureilia
Aurelia *(0.03)*
Aurelianne
Aurelie *(0.10)*
Aurelie-Maria
Aurelienne
Aurelio
Aurellie
Aurely *(0.01)*
Aurelya
Aurely-Ann
Aurelye
Auren
Aureya
Aureyiana
Auri
Auri'ana Anitra
Auria
Aurian
Auriana
Auriane
Aurianna *(0.01)*
Aurianne
Auriauna
Aurieanna

Auriel *(0.01)*
Aurie-Lee
Aurielle *(0.01)*
Aurihs
Aurika
Auril
Auriol
Auriona
Aurionna
Auris
Aurisela
Aurita
Auriyana
Aurni
Auroa
Auroara
Aurora *(0.36)*
Aurora Anne
Aurorabelle
Aurorah
Aurora-Jean
Auroralea
Aurorarose
Aurore
Aurpa
Aurri
Aurriaunna
Aurryanna
Aurterika
Aury
Aury'ea
Auryana
Auryanna
Auryannah
Ausa
Ausha
Aushanae
Aushanique
Ausharie
Aushaté
Aushaundra
Aushenay
Aushianna
Aushyia
Ausia
Ausiata
Ausley
Aussane
Austan
Austeja
Austen
Austin *(0.03)*
Austina

Austine
Austra
Australia
Austyn *(0.03)*
Austynn
Austynne
Autajah
Autavia
Auterviah
Autiana
Autianna
Autium
Autmn
Automn
Auttum
Auttumn
Autum *(0.03)*
Autuman
Autume
Autumé
Autumm
Autummay
Autummn
Autumn *(2.04)*
Autumn Maria
Ann
Autumn Rain
Autumn Rose
Autumne
Autumn-Jai
Autumn-Jewels
Autumn-Marie
Autumn-Mirakle
Autumnn
Autumn-Rose
Autumn-Taylor
Autum-Rain
Autyana
Autym
Autymn
Auvia
Auvianna
Auxmary
Auytumn
Auzalei
Auzilie
Auzilon
Auzzieahna
Av'eon
Av'ionna
Av'rie
Ava *(6.97)*
Ava Grace

Ava Grayce
Ava Izabel
Ava Jade
Ava Josianne
Ava Lynn
Ava Maria
Ava Marie
Ava Nicole
Ava Ray
Ava Rebecca
Ava Rei
Ava Rose
Ava Symone
Avaani
Avabella
Ava-Belle
Ava-Caroline
Ava-Daeh
Avadah
Avadar
Avadaun
Avadon
Avae
Ava-Elizabeth
Avaery
Ava-Faith
Avagail
Avagale
Ava-Grace
Avagrace
Avah *(0.04)*
Avahlyn
Avah-Lynn
Avahni
Avahnnah
Avahry
Availia
Avaisha
Avaiya
Ava-Jade
Ava-Jane
Avajra
Avala
Avalayne
Avalea
Ava-Lee
Avalee *(0.01)*
Ava-Leigh
Avaleigh
Avalena
Avalene
Avalesca
Avaley

Avalie
Avaliese
Avaliliana
Avalin
Avalina
Avalinè
Ava-Lisa
Avalla
Avallina
Avalon *(0.03)*
Avalondria
Ava-Lyn
Avalyn *(0.01)*
Avalyne
Ava-Lynn
Avalynn
Avamae
Ava-Mae
Ava-Marie
Avamarie
Avamarina
Avan'elle
Avana
Avanee
Avanell
Avanelle
Avangela
Avangeleen
Magdalen
Avangelina
Avangeline
Avangline
Avani *(0.03)*
Avanna
Avannah
Avannika
Avante
Avantika
Avaon
Avaree
Avaree-
Elisabeth
Avareigh
Ava-Rene
Avarey
Avarí
Avari *(0.01)*
Avaria
Avarie *(0.02)*
Avariella
Avarielle
Avarielys
Avari-Nicole

Avariy
Avaruby
Avary *(0.03)*
Avasa
Ava-Sky
Avatara
Avaya *(0.01)*
Avayah
Avbrill
Ave
Avé
Ave'ian
Ave'yanna
Aveah
Aveanna
Avee
Aveen
Aveena
Avegayle
Aveherra
Aveigh
Aveilya
Avejah
Avela
Avelee
Aveleen
Aveleigh
Avelina *(0.01)*
Aveline
Avelinn
Avell
Avellaná
Avelyn *(0.01)*
Avelyna
Avelynn
Aven *(0.01)*
Avena
Avenelle
Avenlea
Aveon
Aveona
Aveonna
Aveonnia
Aveonya
Avera
Averae
Averail
Averee *(0.01)*
Avereia
Averella
Averey
Averi *(0.08)*
Averi'el

Averia
Averian
Averiana
Averianna
Averie *(0.08)*
Averiel
Averil
Averiona
Averionna
Averlene
Averona
Averri
Avery *(2.66)*
Averyanna
Averyauna
Averyelle
Averyl
Averyon
Averyonna
Avery-Rae
Avesha
Avette
Avey
Aveya
Aveyah
Aveyaunna
Aveyonce
Aveyonna
Avhani
Avi *(0.01)*
Avia *(0.01)*
Avia'nna
Aviah
Aviahna
Avian
Aviana *(0.03)*
Avianah
Aviance
Avianiea
Avianna *(0.03)*
Avianne
Avianni
Aviaonna
Aviary
Aviauna
Aviay
Avie
Avieanna
Aviegayle
Aviel
Aviella
Avielle
Aviena

| | | | | | | |
|---|---|---|---|---|---|---|
| Avienda | Avondale | Avyonce | Ayaan | Aydan *(0.01)* | Aylaniah | Aynialah |
| Aviendha | Avondia | Avyonna | Ayaanna | Aydelin | Aylanies | Aynnteris |
| Avieon | Avonlea | Avyonnce | Ayaat | Ayden *(0.05)* | Aylanna | Aynslee |
| Avieona | Avonlee | Avys | Aya-Faith | Aydia | Aylaynah | Aynsleigh |
| Avier Tyshera | Avonleigh | Avyukta | Ayah *(0.07)* | Aydiah | Aylea | Aynsley *(0.01)* |
| Aviera | Avonly | Awa *(0.02)* | Ayahna | Aydin | Ayleah | Aynslie |
| Avigael | Avonna | Awa-Bilan | Ayahnah | Aydreanna | Ayleana | Aynur |
| Avigaid | Avonni | Awash | Ayahni | Aydria | Aylee | Ayodele |
| Avigail *(0.02)* | Avony'ce | Awbrey | Ayahnie | Aydrial | Ayleen *(0.02)* | Ayofemi |
| Avigailda | Avori | Awiagina | Ayaila | Aydriannah | Ayleen Monserat | Ayoka |
| Avigale | Avorie | Awien | Ayairis | Aydrienne | Aylen |    Olubunmi |
| Avigayil | Avory | Awna | Ayaisha | Aydyn | Aylena | Ayokemi |
| Avigayl | Avoryanna | Awndrea | Aya-Ishraq | Aydynn | Aylene | Ayomide |
| Avigeya | Avra | Awnesty | Ayak Victoria | Aye'janaye | Aylessa | Ayomikun |
| Avihana | Avre'auna | Awnica | Ayaka | Aye'yanna | Aylet | Ayona *(0.01)* |
| Avila | Avree | Awnna | Ayala | Ayeah | Ayli Anahi | Ayonah |
| Aviles | Avreen | Awnor | Ayala Josephine | Ayeasha | Aylia | Ayonna *(0.01)* |
| Avilia | Avreet | Awnya | Ayalah | Ayedrianne | Ayliah | Ayonnah |
| Avilis | Avreigh | Awo | Ayame | Ayeelen | Aylie | Ayonnie |
| Avilynn | Avreiona | Awog | Ayamey | Ayeesha | Ayliene | Ayooluwa |
| Avin | Avrey *(0.01)* | Awok | Ayan *(0.01)* | Ayeisha | Aylijyah | Ayoto Allah |
| Avina | Avreyanna | Awteana | Ayana *(0.14)* | Ayela | Aylin *(0.07)* | Ayou |
| Avinashdeep | Avri | Awtum | Ayana'h | Ayelen *(0.01)* | Ayline | Ayozieuwa |
| Avineet | Avria | Awtumn | Ayanah | Ayelet | Aylisa | Ayra |
| Avinoor | Avriana | Awuok | Ayanami | Ayeli | Aylish | Ayralyn |
| Avion | Avrianna *(0.01)* | Awura | Ayane | Ayelin | Aylissa | Ayrana |
| Aviona | Avriannah | Awut | Ayani | Ayelishka-Bel | Ayliza | Ayrashe |
| Avionah | Avrie *(0.01)* | Axa | Ayania | Ayen | Aylla | Ayre |
| Avionce | Avriee | Axana | Ayaniah | Ayerabella | Aylona | Ayreana |
| Avionia | Avriel | Axary | A-Yanna | Ayeriona | Ayloni | Ayreanna |
| Avionna *(0.01)* | Avriella | Axel | Ayanna *(0.22)* | Ayesa | Aylssa | Ayrelia |
| Avionne | Avrielle | Axelle | Ayannah *(0.01)* | Ayesha *(0.05)* | Aylyene | Ayren |
| Avireet | Avril *(0.03)* | Axl | Ayanni | Ayeva | Aylyn | Ayreona |
| Avis | Avrile | Axtyn | Ayannia | Ayiahhah | Ayma | Ayreonna |
| Avishai | Avrill | Axymya | Ayanti | Ayiana *(0.02)* | Ayman | Ayress |
| Avishi | Avrina | Axyria | Ayantu | Ayianna *(0.01)* | Aymara | Ayreyonia |
| Avital *(0.01)* | Avry *(0.01)* | Axzyre | Ayari | Ayih | Ayme | Ayriah |
| Aviv | Avryanna | Ay Kiara | Ayary | Ayilin | Aymee | Ayrial |
| Aviva *(0.02)* | Avryelle | Ay'briyuna | Ayas | Ayina | Aymiah | Ayrian |
| Avivah | Avryl | Ay'jah | Ayasani | Ayinna | Aymin | Ayriana *(0.01)* |
| Aviya | Avvie | Ay'kayln | Ayasha | Ayisah | Aymisha | Ayrianna *(0.01)* |
| Aviyanna | Avvin | Ay'nari | Ayat *(0.01)* | Ayisat | Aymyrrea | Ayriauna |
| Avjaut | Avy *(0.01)* | Ay'nesha | Ayat Safeiah | Ayisha *(0.01)* | Ayn | Ayrie |
| Avleen | Avy'on | Ay'rianna | Ayato | Ayjah | Aynalysa | Ayriel |
| Avlin | Avya | Ay'sha | Ayatullah | Aykerquia | Aynara | Ayrieona |
| Avlyn | Avyana | Ay'sha-Monet | Ayauna | Aykhia | Aynaz | Ayrieonna |
| Avlynn | Avyanna | Ay'sia | Ayaunna | Ayla *(0.26)* | Aynecia | Ayries |
| Avnee | Avyanne | Aya *(0.13)* | Aybrie | Ayla-Abigail | Ayneira | Ayrika |
| Avneek | Avyiana | Aya Bahja | Aybuke | Aylah *(0.01)* | Aynelise | Ayrin |
| Avneet *(0.02)* | Avylon | Aya Dorsaf | Ayca | Ayla-Marie | Aynett | Ayrion |
| Avni | Avyn | Aya't | Aycedes | Aylan | Ayni | Ayriona |
| Avoiana | Avynn | Ayaa | Aycie | Aylana *(0.01)* | Aynia | Ayris |
| Avona | Avyonah | Ayaah | Ayda *(0.01)* | Aylanah | Ayniah | Ayrissen |

| | | | | | | |
|---|---|---|---|---|---|---|
| Ayrita | Ayzelin | Azamarie | Azeria | Azlee | Azyria | Bahina |
| Ayrlei | Ayzha | Azameria | Azeriah | Azlen | Azytiana | Bahiyah |
| Ayro | Ayzia | Azan | Azerika | Azley | Azza | Bahiyyah |
| Ayron | Ayziah | Azana | Azerria | Azlia | Azzareya | Bahiyyeh |
| Ayryn | Ayzlan | Azandria | Azeyanna | Azlin | Azzareyah | Bahja |
| Aysa | Ayzlei | Azanet | Azha | Azlinn | Azzaria | Bahjo |
| Aysah | Ayzlyn | Azanina | Azhaar | Azlyn *(0.01)* | Azzariah | Bahozhoni |
| Ayse | Az'jahnique | Azara | Azhah | Azlyne | Azzarreya | Bai |
| Aysegul | Aza | Azarae | Azhanae | Azlynn *(0.01)* | Azzarys | Baiely |
| Aysel | Azaara | Azaraé | Azhannaé | Azmarie | Azzaya | Baihjae |
| Aysha *(0.03)* | Azabell | Azarah | Azhar | Azmariyah | Azzereya | Baija |
| Ayshawnie | Azabria | Azare | Azharia | Azmené | Azziah | Baije |
| Ayshia | Azadria | Azarea | Azhary | Azmina | Azziana | Baijea |
| Ayshia-Marie | Azaeleia | Azareah | Azhe'ra | Aznii | Azzira | Baila *(0.03)* |
| Aysia *(0.04)* | Azaeli | Azaree | Azi'ana | Azona | Azzka | Bailay |
| Aysiah | Azaelia | Azareeyah | Azia *(0.01)* | Azorah | Azzure | Bailea |
| Aysiana | Azaeliah | Azareia | Aziah *(0.01)* | Azori | Azzureya | Bailee *(0.15)* |
| Ayslin | Azah | Azarel | Aziah Rose | Azoria | | Bailei |
| Ayssandra | Azahara | Azari | Aziahnai | Azoriah | | Baileigh *(0.03)* |
| Aysten | Azahra | Azaria *(0.08)* | Azianna | Azoryona | | Bailey *(1.65)* |
| Ayten | Azahrea | Azaria-Ann | Aziara | Azoza | ~ B ~ | Baili |
| Aytiana | Azahree | Azariah *(0.05)* | Aziayah | Azra *(0.01)* | | Bailie *(0.01)* |
| Aytza | Azahria | Azariana | Azier | Azrael | B. Hope | Baillee |
| Ayuana | Azahrri | Azariea | Azillia | Azrah | B'arry | Baillie |
| A-Yuanna | Azaia | Azariya | Azina | Azraiel | B'elana | Baily *(0.01)* |
| Ayuko | Azailyah | Azariyah *(0.01)* | Azinwi | Azreaha | B'elanna | Bailye |
| Ayumi | Azaira | Azarrea | Azion | Azria | B'ianca | Bailyn |
| Ayuna | Azairah | Azarriah | Azira | Azrianna | B'treyonna | Baine |
| Ayunna | Azaireal | Azarriyah | Azirah | Azriel *(0.01)* | B'yonka | Baisa |
| Ayuong | Azajah | Azarya | Azire | Azriela | Ba'lena | Baishali |
| Ayusha | Azala | Azaryon | Aziriah | Azriell | Baala | Baiya |
| Ayushi *(0.01)* | Azale | Azauni | Azita | Azriella | Baallani | Bakayla |
| Ayva *(0.03)* | Azalea *(0.04)* | Azavia | Aziya | Azrielle | Babanpreet | Bakhsish |
| Ayvah *(0.01)* | Azalea Darcel | Azaya | Aziyah *(0.01)* | Azrina | Babette | Bakya |
| Ayvelynn | Azaleah | Azayda | Aziyana | Azsa | Babi | Bala Sivani |
| Ayven | Azalee | Azayia | Aziza *(0.01)* | Azsha | Babitha | Balasa |
| Ayverée | Azaleea-Marie | Azaylah | Azizah | Aztlali | Babiy | Balbina |
| Ayvette | Azaleia | Azaylia | Azizaryic | Azucena *(0.01)* | Bacilia | Baldeep |
| Ayvia | Azaleigh | Azaylla | Azize Naz | Azul *(0.01)* | Badriah | Baleigh *(0.02)* |
| Ayviana | Azaleya | Azayra | Azizza | Azullema | Badriya Safia | Baleria |
| Ayvindana | Azalfa | Azaysha | Azja | Azumi | Badur | Balery |
| Ayvre | Azalia *(0.01)* | Azaytah | Azjah | Azura | Baejwoke | Baley |
| Ayvree | Azaliah | Azayvya | Azjana | Azurae | Baela | Balianna |
| Ayvri | Azaliah Mae | Azbikahleyann | Azjaneah | Azure *(0.01)* | Baelen | Balie |
| Ayvrie | Azalianna | Azeezah | Azjannie | Azuree | Baeli | Baliey |
| Ayvyonna | Azalie | Azelea | Azjei | Azurie | Baha | Balinda |
| Ayya | Azalinn | Azel-Hana | Azjhia | Azurliz | Bahaja | Baljot |
| Ayyah | Azaliya | Azelia | Azjhion | Azusena | Bahar | Balkis |
| Ayyan | Azalya | Azelie | Azjia | Azya | Baharia | Balle |
| Ayyi | Azalyah | Azelin | Azka | Azyah | Bahati | Balloo |
| Ayyultuz | Azalyn | Azeneth | Azlan | Azyaiah | Baheya | Balmonte |
| Ayza | Azalynn | Azera | Azland | Azyhia | Bahia | Balneet |
| Ayzaria | Azalyse | Azeri | Azlayah | Azyiah | Bahiah | Balpreet |
| | | | | | Bahijah | |

Balqees
Balqiis
Balqis
Balqisa
Balreen
Balreet
Balveen
Balynn
Bambalina
Bana
Banan
Banein
Banen
Banesa
Banessa
Baneza
Bangning
Bani
Baniah
Banija
Banin
Banisha
Banks
Bannan
Bannelly
Bannesa
Banraz
Banu
Banyan
Banyja
Banyu
Bao
Bao Bai
Bao Thanh
  Christine
Bao Tran
Bara'ah
Baraa
Barabara
Barabra
Barakah
Baran
Bara-Serene
Barath
Barbara (0.17)
Barbara Alice
Barbara
  Johanna
Barbara Rachel
Barbarann
Barbaranna
Barbee
Barbiann

Barbie (0.02)
Barbra
Barbreanna
Barbriel
Barclay
Bari
Baria
Bariah
Barirah
Barit
Barjona
Barker
Barné
Barni
Baronica
Barran
Barratou
Barrett (0.01)
Barretta
Barrette
Barrie
Barry
Barsny
Bartley
Barton
Barwaqo
Basa Lat
Ba-Safiramedina
Bascha
Basha
Bashabee
Bashana
Basheba
Bashiah
Bashie
Bashira
Bashirah
Bashra
Bashua
Basia
Basila
Basim
Basimah
Basma
Basmah
Basmala
Basmallah
Bassha
Bassmala
Basya (0.01)
Bates
Bathia
Bathsada

Bathsheba
Batool
Batoul (0.01)
Batoule
Batsheva
Batu
Batul
Batule
Batulla
Batya
Batzion
Bauer
Baughman
Baxley
Bay
Baya
Bayaan
Bayan (0.01)
Bayane
Baydan
Bayden
Baydriana
Baye
Bayee
Bayeza
Bayinah
Bayla (0.01)
Baylan
Bayle
Baylea
Bayleann
Baylece
Baylee (0.22)
Baylee-Ann
Baylei
Bayleigh (0.04)
Bayleighann
Baylen
Bayley (0.01)
Bayli
Baylie (0.04)
Bayliegh
Baylin
Baylisa
Baylla
Baylor (0.01)
Baylsan
Bayly
Baylyn
Baysia
Bayvin
Bayyajah
Bayyinah

Bazahyah
BB
Be'asia
Be'la
Be'lia
Be'lla
Be'nequia
Be'renee
Béa
Bea (0.01)
Bea Mariz
Bea'mariah
Beactrice
Beaja
Bea-Laurice
Beall
Beanca
Beanica
Beanie
Beany
Beata
Beatrace
Beatrice (0.18)
Beatrice
  Byabula
Beatrice-Rose
Beatris
Beatrix (0.02)
Beatríz
Beatriz (0.05)
Beatriz Anabeli
Beatryz
Beatta
Beau
Beaudlyne
Beautesha
Beautiful (0.01)
Beautifull (0.01)
Beautifullskhiye
Beauty
Bebe (0.01)
Beberli
Becca (0.02)
Becca-Lynn
Beckah
Becka-Lyn
Beckett
Beckham
Becki
Becky (0.02)
Becsy
Beczaida
Beda Fernanda

Beddgilene
Bede
Bedelia
Bedginie
Beela
Beenti
Beerat
Begonia
Behechta
Behencya-
  Mevida
Behishta
Behla
Beibhinn
Beicy
Beidaly
Beighjah
Beighlee
Beila
Beilen
Beilin
Beillez
Beimnet
Beitris
Bejewel
Bejia
Bejthara
Beka
Bekah
Bekka
Bekken
Bela
Belae
Belana
Belande
Belanice
Belanie
Belcy
Belén
Belén
Belen (0.03)
Beliani
Belicia (0.01)
Believe
Belin
Belina
Belinda (0.08)
Belisiana
Belissa
Beliz
Beliza
Beljot
Belkis

Bell
Bella (0.59)
Bella Leilani
Bella Louvisa
Bella Rose
Bella Stephanie
Bella'rae
Belladiem
Belladonna
Bella-Grace
Bellagrace
Bellah
Bellalize
Bellaluna
Bella-Mae
Bellamina
Bellamy (0.01)
Bellanira
Bella-Rose
Bellarose
Bellasan
Bellaveyon
Bellazara
Belldandy
Belle (0.06)
Belle Ann
Belle Belize Nila
Belle Rose
Bellea
Belleanie
Belledona
Belle-Shia
Bellina
Bellini
Bellona
Bellorna
Bellstarr
Belmary
Belnilsa
Beloved
Beloved-Mi'bella
Belovely
Belqui
Belquin
Belsy
Belynda
Belytha
Bemi
Ben Nita
Ben'iya
Bena
Bená
Benadetta

Benae
Benaysay
Bency
Bendania
Bene
Benedetta
Benedicta
Benedicte
Benedicte-Lara
Beneisha
Benelli
Benet
Bengelyne
Bengi
Beniah
Benicia
Benisha
Benisse
Benita
Benite
Benitez
Benitha
Beniyah
Benjamia
Benjamin
Benna
Bennet
Bennett (0.01)
Bennette
Bennie
Bennita
Benniya
Benthana
Bentje
Bentlee
Bentleigh
Bentley (0.01)
Bentli
Bentlie
Bently
Bentu
Benyanna
Benyde
Benyoncé
Benysha
Benzia
Benzie
Beonca
Beonica
Beonka
Ber'daijsa
Ber'nasia
Berachah

| | | | | | | |
|---|---|---|---|---|---|---|
| Berakah | Bernaisha | Betaniya | Betisha | Beyoncé | Bianett | Bilqiis |
| Beratrice | Bernalene | Betanya | Betsabe | Beyonce *(0.02)* | Bianey | Bilquis |
| Beray | Bernalie | Betbirai | Betsabe-Zaray | Beyonka | Bianka *(0.03)* | Bina |
| Berdena | Bernally | Betchina | Betsaida | Beyonka-Averee | Bianka Roxanne | Binal |
| Berdine | Bernalys | Betcy | Betsey | Beyza | Biankiannette | Binaventura |
| Berea | Bernandie- | Betdzay | Betsiri | Beza | Biankka | Binayshee |
| Beredice |   Narkide | Beth *(0.03)* | Betsy *(0.04)* | Bezaley | Biankov-Rose | Bindu |
| Bereket | Bernarda | Beth Ann | Betsy Allyson | Bezawit | Bianna | Bineeta |
| Berelean | Bernardina | Beth Kimberly | Betsye | Bhagveer | Biannca | Bingjing |
| Berenciana | Bernaria | Bethaida | Betsylynn | Bhagyashree | Bianney | Binh Giang |
| Berengere | Bernelle | Bethalyn | Betthy | Bhakti | Bianni | Binta |
| Berenice *(0.03)* | Bernice *(0.01)* | Bethan | Bettie | Bhan | Biata | Binti |
| Berenise | Bernide | Bethanea | Bettina | Bhargavi | Biatrice | Bintou |
| Berenith | Bernie | Bethanee | Betty *(0.05)* | Bharghavi | Bibechana | Bintouamy |
| Bereniz | Berniesha | Bethaney | Betty Ann | Bhavagna | Bibhusika | Bintu |
| Berenize | Berniya | Bethani | Betty Jean | Bhavana | Bibi | Bioleta |
| Berfina | Berniyah | Bethanie *(0.02)* | Betty Lou | Bhavanjot | Bibiana *(0.01)* | Bioluwatife |
| Bergan | Bernnie Jean | Bethanii | Bettyann | Bhavi | Bibiane | Bioly-Karissa |
| Bergell | Berny | Bethaniya | Bettye | Bhavika | Bibianie | Bionca *(0.01)* |
| Bergen | Beronica | Beth-Ann | Bettylou | Bhavishya | Bibianna | Bioncaa |
| Bergetta | Berra | Bethann | Bety | Bhavkiran | Bibyana | Bioncia |
| Berghan | Berray | Bethanne | Betzabe | Bhavna | Bielka | Bipasha |
| Bergyn | Berrin | Bethannie'ann | Betzabeth | Bhavnoor | Biftu | Biraharna |
| Beri | Berry | Bethanny | Betzaida *(0.01)* | Bhavreet | Bigail | Birch |
| Beria | Berryann | Bethany *(0.55)* | Betzaira | Bhavya | Bihamta | Birdy |
| Beril | Bersabel | Bethany Brooke | Betzalda | Bhavyasree | Bijal | Bireyma |
| Berit *(0.01)* | Berseli | Bethany-Emma | Betzali | Bhavyasri | Bijou | Birgit |
| Berkaylah | Bershawna | Bethea | Betzanarai | Bhoomi | Bika | Birgitta |
| Berkeley *(0.02)* | Berta | Bethel *(0.01)* | Betzayda | Bhoomika | Bilad | Birhan |
| Berkely | Bertha *(0.01)* | Bethelany | Betzayra | Bhreagh | Bilal | Biriaha |
| Berkenya | Berthaniah | Bethelle | Betzhy | Bhriceydi | Bilan | Biridana |
| Berklee | Berthe | Betheney | Betzi | Bhumi | Bilashia | Biridiana |
| Berkleigh | Bertie | Betheny | Betzy *(0.01)* | Bhuvi | Bilaya | Birka |
| Berkley *(0.03)* | Bertilia | Bethia | Beulah | Bi'jahnae | Bilen | Birydiana |
| Berkli | Bertille | Bethine | Beutiful | Bi'unca | Bilges | Birzayit |
| Berlancia | Bertsuany | Bethlehem | Bevalee | Bi'zari | Bili Jose | Bisan |
| Berlange | Bertyana | Bethlin | Bevan | Biabina | Bilie | Bishara |
| Berlin *(0.01)* | Bertyann | Bethlisa | Beverley | Biak | Bilise | Bisma |
| Berlince | Bervaly | Bethlyne | Beverley-Ann | Bian | Billee | Bismah |
| Berlinda | Beryl | Bethmari | Beverly *(0.04)* | Biana | Billeigh | Bisola |
| Berline | Besaida | Bethony | Beverly-Ann | Bianay | Billi | Bissane |
| Berline-Luz | Besan | Bethsabe | Bevie | Bianca *(0.70)* | Billiah | Bissette |
| Berly | Beshkar | Bethsaida | Bevin | Bianca Isabel | Billianna | Bithaniya |
| Berlyn *(0.01)* | Besiana | Bethsey | Bevinn | Bianca Lee | Billie *(0.04)* | Bithiah |
| Berlyne | Besma | Bethya | Bexlei | Bianca- | Billie Jo | Bitia |
| Berlynn | Bess | Bethzabel | Beya |   Ginabella | Billie Maye | Bity |
| Bermuda | Bessann | Bethzabeth | Beyanca | Bianca-Isabelle | Billie Nevaeh | Bitzy |
| Berna | Bessi | Bethzaida | Beycel | Biancan | Billie-Marie | Biuma-Noamie |
| Bernadett | Bessie | Bethzayda | Beyda | Biancaris | Billie-Rose | Bivian |
| Bernadette | Bessy | Bethzi | Beyla | Biancha | Billy | Biviana |
|   *(0.03)* | Bet | Bethzxeidy | Beyle | Biancia | Bilmary | Biyanca |
| Bernadine | Betale | Bethzy *(0.02)* | Beyleigh | Biancka | Bilnyia | Biyani |
| Bernae | Betania | Betina | Beyonca *(0.01)* | Biandi | Bilqees | Bjorna |

| | | | | | | |
|---|---|---|---|---|---|---|
| Blace | Blescin | Bobbye | Boyeresa | Braelyne | Branaugh | Brantleigh |
| Blackcey | Bless (0.01) | Bobetta | Br'ia | Braelynn (0.02) | Branay | Brantley (0.01) |
| Blackwell | Blessed | Bobygirl | Br'niya | Brae-Ounce | Branda | Branwen |
| Blaike | Blessella | Bodaysha | Br'nohja | Braeshel | Brandaesia | Branwyn |
| Blaiklee | Blessen | Bodhi | Br'shiya | Braeton | Brandajah | Branya |
| Blaiklyn | Blessencce | Bodhicea | Br'yon | Bragetna | Brandalyn | Branyce |
| Blaine (0.01) | Blessin | Bodie | Br'yonna | Braha | Brandalynn | Braona |
| Blair (0.04) | Blessin | Bodoor | Bra | Brahambinde | Branda-Nae | Brasaya |
| Blaire (0.01) | Kaylonda | Boe | Bra'dasia | Braidee | Brandashia | Brasen |
| Blaise | Blessin' | Boede | Bra'kailah | Braiden | Brandazia | Brashaé |
| Blaize | Blessing (0.02) | Boey | Bra'lyn | Braidey | Brande | Brashawna |
| Blake (0.02) | Blessing- | Bogdana | Bra'naye | Braidyn | Brandee (0.01) | Brashaya |
| Blakelee | Cheng'isiwe | Boglarka | Bra'niya | Braie | Brandeja | Brashel |
| Blakelei | Blessing-Rose | Boglárka | Bra'niyah | Brailea | Branden | Brashley |
| Blakeleigh | Blessyn | Bok | Bra'shae | Brailee | Brandey | Brasinn |
| Blakeley | Blesyn | Bokoum | Bracen | Braileen | Brandi (0.11) | Braslin |
| Blakeli | Bleu | Bolade | Bracey | Braileigh | Brandi Jo | Brateria |
| Blakelie | Blia | Bolanle | Bracha (0.03) | Brailen | Brandi Lyn | Braunna |
| Blakely (0.03) | Blige | Boluwatife | Braci | Brailenn | Brandi'anna | Braveena |
| Blakelyn | Blima (0.01) | Bona | Bracie | Brailey (0.01) | Brandia | Brawnwyn |
| Blakeria | Blimy (0.01) | Bond | Bracy | Brailin | Brandice | Braxie |
| Blakleigh | Bliss (0.01) | Bondie | Bradee | Braily | Brandie (0.01) | Braxten |
| Blakley | Blondine | Boneicea | Braden (0.01) | Brailyn | Brandilee | Braxtin |
| Blaklie | Bloom | Bongkem | Bradey | Brailynn | Brandilin | Braxton (0.01) |
| Blakyn | Bloor | Bonica | Bradi | Brailynne | Brandis | Braxtyn |
| Blanca (0.06) | Blossom | Bonita (0.01) | Bradie | Brainna | Brandisha | Bray |
| Blanca Idaliz | Blu | Bonna | Bradilyn | Braislee | Brandon | Braya (0.01) |
| Blanche (0.01) | Blu Elizabeth | Bonnie (0.07) | Bradin | Braisly Ju | Brandy (0.12) | Brayan |
| Blanche- | Blue | Bonnie Ava | Bradlee | Braison | Brandya | Brayanna |
| Eleonore | Bluejean | Bonnie Kate | Bradleigh | Braith | Brandyce | Brayaunna |
| Blandina | Bluma | Bonnilyn | Bradley | Brajasia | Brane | Braycee |
| Blandine | Bly | Bonntte | Bradlie | Brakenna | Brane'ja | Braycen |
| Blandy | Blyth | Bonny | Brady (0.01) | Brakia | Branee | Braydee |
| Blane | Blythe (0.02) | Booker | Bradyn (0.01) | Brakiyah | Braneisha | Braydeen |
| Blaney | Bo (0.01) | Booklyn | Bradynn | Braleena | Branesha | Brayden (0.02) |
| Blanflore | Boadicea | Booyoowakhuq | Brae | Bralei | Branijah | Braydi |
| Blanka | Bobbee-Jules | Bopasoreya | Braeden | Braleigh (0.01) | Bra-Nijaia | Braydin |
| Blanly | Bobbi (0.03) | Bophae | Braedi | Braleighann | Braniya (0.01) | Braydn |
| Blaque | Bobbi Jo | Bora | Braedon | Bralene | Braniyah | Braydon |
| Blayke | Bobbi Joe | Borelie | Braedy | Braley (0.01) | Braniyah | Braydyn |
| Blayne | Bobbie (0.03) | Borin | Braedyn | Bralie | Tanyetta | Brayella |
| Blayr | Bobbie Jo | Boston (0.01) | Braedynn | Bralyn | Braniyzha | Brayla |
| Blayre | Bobbie Sue | Bostyn | Braegan | Bralynn | Brankia | Braylan |
| Blayze | Bobbieann | Bothaina | Braelee | Bramley | Branna | Brayle |
| Blaze | Bobbie-Jean | Bouakeo | Braelei | Bran Dynne | Brannagh | Braylee (0.03) |
| Blazey | Bobbie-Lee | Bounna | Braeleigh | Bran'yea | Brannaya | Brayleigh |
| Bleighlah | Bobbie-Noel | Boupha | Braelene | Bran'yell | Branndy | Braylen (0.01) |
| Blein | Bobbie-Skyy | Bousso | Braeli | Brana | Brannea | Braylene |
| Blen | Bobbi-Jo | Bouthaina | Braelie | Branae | Branneka | Brayley |
| Blenda | Bobbijo | Bowen | Braelin | Branah | Brantasia | Braylie |
| Blenita | Bobbilee | Bowie | Braely | Branairah | Brantina | Braylin (0.01) |
| Blerta | Bobbi-Lyn | Bowyn | Brae-Lyn | Branariya | Brantiya | Braylinn |
| Bles | Bobby | Boye | Braelyn (0.08) | Branasia | Brantlee | Brayln |

| | | | | | | |
|---|---|---|---|---|---|---|
| Braylon | Bre'onka | Breannie | Breeasia | Breighten | Brendee-Jo | Breonica |
| Braylyn *(0.01)* | Bre'onna *(0.01)* | Breannon | Breeauna | Breighton | Brendi | Breonie |
| Braylynn *(0.01)* | Bre'ontaviya | Breannyn | Bree-Ayna | Breijah | Brendle | Breonna *(0.07)* |
| Braylynne | Bre'onyi | Breannynn | Breece | Breilee | Brendolyn | Breonnah |
| Braynon | Bre'shanti | Breanté | Breedelle | Breily | Brendon | Breonne |
| Brayon | Bre'yana | Breantinic | Breegan | Breilyn | Brendy | Breony |
| Brayonna | Bre'yanna | Breanya | Breejah | Breina | Brenedyn | Breosha |
| Brayounah | Bre'yanne | Breaonna | Breelan | Breindy | Brenee | Brerica |
| Brayton | Bre'yel | Breasana | Breelee | Breionna | Breneé | Bresaida |
| Brayzhane | Bre'yhana | Breashae | Breeleigh | Breiya | Brenette | Brescias |
| Brayziana | Bre'yon | Breashia | Breeley | Brejenae | Brenica | Breseis |
| Brazil | Bre'yonah | Bre-Asia | Breeli | Brekendria | Brenijah | Bresenda |
| Brazille | Bre'yonna | Breasia *(0.01)* | Breelie | Brekka | Breniqua | Breseyda |
| Brazyah | Bre'yonnie | Breasya | Breella | Brekyn | Breniya | Bre-sha |
| Brazyl | Breá | Bre-Auna | Breelle | Brela | Breniyah | Breshae |
| Bre | Brea *(0.05)* | Breauna *(0.02)* | Bréelle | Brelan | Brenjha | Breshana |
| Bré | Breacia | Breaunna *(0.01)* | Breely | Breland | Brenla | Breshanae |
| Bre Anna | Breaelle | Breawna | Breelyn *(0.01)* | Brelayna | Brenlanne | Breshauna |
| Bre Asia | Breagh | Breayannah | Breelynn | Brelee | Brenlea | Breshay |
| Bre Essenz | Breagha | Breaysia | Breena *(0.01)* | Breleigh *(0.01)* | Brenlee | Breshayln |
| Bré Jah | Breah *(0.01)* | Breaze | Bree-Niyah | Brelen | Brenleigh | Breshea |
| Bre Yona | Breahanna | Breaziah | Breeona | Brelin | Brenley | Breshon |
| Bre'ahja | Breahn | Breazshia | Breeonna | Brelle | Brenlie | Breshuna |
| Bre'aja | Breahna *(0.01)* | Brec | Breera | Brelyiah | Brenn | Bresia |
| Bre'ajh | Breaira | Breca | Bree-Sum | Brelyn *(0.01)* | Brenna *(0.37)* | Breslynn |
| Bre'ana | Breaisa | Brecca | Breetania | Brelynn *(0.01)* | Brennaann | Bresnia |
| Bre'anah | Breaisha | Breceis | Breeyahneae | Bren | Brennah | Bresyda |
| Bre'ann | Breajah | Breceiss | Breeyana | Brena *(0.01)* | Brennalyn | Bret |
| Bre'anna *(0.01)* | Breajza | Brechelle | Breeyonna | Brenadi | Brennan *(0.02)* | Brethany |
| Bre'ara | Brealle | Breckann | Breez | Brenae | Brennda | Bretly |
| Bre'ari | Breallie | Brecken | Breeze *(0.01)* | Brenah | Brennen | Brett *(0.01)* |
| Bre'aria | Breallyn | Brecklyn | Breezea | Brenai | Brennley | Bretta |
| Bre'ashia | Brealyce | Breckyn | Breezeida | Brenajah | Brennya | Brettany |
| Bre'asia *(0.01)* | Brealyn | Bredanna | Breezi | Brenann | Brennyn | Brette |
| Bre'asijah | Brean | Bredka | Breezie | Brenasia | Brent | Brettlyn |
| Bre'auna | Breana *(0.11)* | Bree *(0.09)* | Breezy | Brenay | Brentasia | Bretton |
| Bre'aunnah | Breanah | Bree Ann | Bregetta | Brenayah | Brentlea | Brettyn |
| Bre'jhnae | Breanda | Bree Anna | Bregette | Brency | Brentleigh | Bretyn |
| Bre'jhnaé | Breangela | Bree'ana | Bregyt | Brenda *(0.31)* | Brentley | Breuanna |
| Bre'kayla | Breani | Breea *(0.01)* | Brehan | Brenda Lee | Brently | Breuarah |
| Bre'keiyah | Bre-Ann | Bree-Ah | Brehanna | Brenda-Ambre | Breny | Breuna |
| Bre'nae | Breann *(0.04)* | Breeah | Brehily | Brenda-Esmeralda | Brenya | Breunna *(0.01)* |
| Bre'naysia | Bre-Anna | Breeahna | Brehna | Brendajo | Brenyesha | Brevie |
| Bre'ne | Breanna *(1.39)* | Breeair | Brehnna | Brenda-Lee | Brenynn | Brevyn |
| Bre'nee | Breanna Nicole | Breean | Brei | Brendalee | Brenzel | Brexton |
| Bre'nique | Breannah *(0.01)* | Breeana *(0.01)* | Breia | Brendaliz | Brenzlee | Brey |
| Bre'niya | Breanna-Lynn | Bree-Ann | Breiana | Brendaly | Brenzley | Breya *(0.01)* |
| Bre'niyah | Breannan | Breeann | Breianna | Brendalyn | Breohna | Breyah |
| Bre'nya | Breanna-Nico | Bree-Anna | Breigh | Brenda-Lynn | Breon | Breyahna |
| Bre'nyah | Breannarose | Breeanna *(0.03)* | Breighan | Brendan | Breona *(0.02)* | Breyan |
| Bre'nyja | Breanne *(0.05)* | Breeannah | Breighana | Brenda-Sandra | Breonah | Breyan'a |
| Bre'ona | Breanne Casey | Bree-Anne | Breighann | Brendaya | Breoni | Breyana *(0.02)* |
| Bre'onda | Breannia | Breeanne | Breighlynn | | Breonia | Breyana-Ann |

Breyane
Breyanna (0.01)
Breyannah
Breyawna
Breyel
Breyelle
Breyer
Breyhana
Breylee
Breylin
Breyline
Breylyn
Breyon
Breyona
Breyonca
Breyonce
Breyonia
Breyonna (0.01)
Breyonnah
Breyunna
Breyza
Brez'hee
Brezayda
Breze
Brezhanae
Breziah
Brezlynn
Brezy
Bri
Bri Anna
Bri Ayzha
Bri'ajah
Bri'ajanae
Bri'an
Bri'ana
Bri'anna
Bri'arie
Bri'asia
Bri'asja
Bri'ayl
Bri'jhia
Bri'kiria
Bri'nya
Bri'onna
Bri'ontais
Bri'ya
Bri'yana
Bri'yanah
Bri'yanna
Briá
Bria (0.11)
Bria Eleanor
Bria'hna

Bria'na
Briaa
Briah (0.01)
Briahana
Briahna (0.02)
Briaisa
Briajah
Briajurilianda
Brialle
Brian
Briana (1.32)
Briana Lak
Briana Skye
Brianah
Briana-Laura
Briana-Martin
Briananna
Brianca (0.01)
Brianda
Briane
Briania
Brianica
Brianisha
Brianka
Bri-Ann
Briann (0.01)
Brianna (4.41)
Brianna El
Brianna Faith
Brianna Lynn
Brianna-Claudet
Briannah (0.03)
Briannaliz
Briannan
Brianne (0.09)
Brianni
Briannia
Briannie
Briannna
Briannon
Brianny (0.01)
Briannyn
Brianti
Briany
Briar (0.02)
Briara
Briar-Rose
Briarsha
Briasha
Briashia
Briasia (0.01)
Briauna (0.02)

Briaunna (0.01)
Briaura
Briawna
Briayelle
Briaysia
Briazia
Brice (0.01)
Briceida (0.01)
Briceila
Bricel
Briceshana
Briceth
Briceyda
Briceylla
Brichela
Bricia
Brickell
Briclynn
Bridey
Bridgain
Bridget (0.36)
Bridget Mary
Bridget Rose
Bridgete
Bridgeth
Bridgett (0.02)
Bridgette (0.07)
Bridghaite
Bridgid
Bridgit (0.01)
Bridgitte
Bridie
Brie (0.03)
Brie'ana
Brie'anna
Brie'unna
Brie'yana
Brie'yanna
Briea
Brieah
Brieahna
Brieahyna
Brieal
Brieana (0.01)
Brie-Ann
Brieann
Brie-Anna
Brieanna (0.03)
Brieannah
Brieanne
Brieasia
Briee
Briegan

Briel
Briela
Brielan
Brieland
Briele
Brielee
Brieley
Briell
Briella (0.03)
Briellah
Brielle (0.28)
Briellei
Brielyn
Brielynn
Brie-Lynne
Briena
Brienasia
Brienna (0.01)
Brienne (0.01)
Brieona
Brieonna
Brier
Briera
Briere
Briesez
Brietta
Brieyana
Briezja
Briget
Brigett
Brigetta
Brigette (0.01)
Brigette-Marie-
Josee
Briggett
Briggette
Briggitte
Brighid
Brighten
Brightni
Brighton (0.01)
Brigid (0.04)
Brigida
Brigit (0.01)
Brigitta
Brigitte (0.02)
Brigney
Brihana
Brihanna
Brihyanna
Briia
Briiana
Briiane

Briiona
Bri-Jai
Brijanee
Brijourne
Briklyn
Brilee (0.01)
Brileigh
Briley (0.08)
Brilie
Brilli
Brilliant
Brillit
Brilye
Brilyn
Brilynn (0.01)
Brilynne
Brima
Brin (0.01)
Brina (0.01)
Brinae
Brinaisha
Brinaya
Brinayia
Brinaysja
Brinda
Brindy
Brinea
Briney
Bring
Briniyha
Brinkley (0.01)
Brinkly
Brinlea
Brinlee (0.02)
Brinleigh
Brinley (0.09)
Brinli
Brinly
Brinn
Brinna
Brinnly
Brinsley
Brintey
Brintlee
Brintley
Brinton
Brinyah
Briohny
Brion
Briona (0.02)
Brionah
Briondra
Brione

Brioni
Brionie
Brionna (0.08)
Brionna-Simone
Brionne
Brionni
Briony
Briquelle
Brisa (0.06)
Brisa Guadalupe
Brisa Jasmin
Brisaida
Brisalinda
Brisamar
Brisanna
Brisareli
Brisayda
Brisca
Brisceyda
Brischell
Briseas
Briseida (0.03)
Briseidy
Briseis (0.02)
Briselia
Brisely
Brisen
Brises
Brisey
Briseyda (0.02)
Brisha
Brishae
Brishan
Brishanna
Brishauna
Brishiya
Brisia
Brisis
Briski
Brisli
Brisna
Brisny
Brissa (0.01)
Brisseida
Brisselda
Brissell
Brisseyda
Brissia
Brisstal
Brista
Bristal
Bristin
Bristoe

Bristol (0.01)
Bristyn
Brisza
Brit
Brita
Britain
Britaney
Britani (0.01)
Britanie (0.01)
Britanni
Britanny (0.01)
Britany (0.05)
Britany-Eve
Britany-Kim
Briteney
Britessani
Britget
Brithani
Brithanie
Brithanny
Brithany (0.01)
Brithcel
Brithney
Britian
Britin
British
Britisha
Britlee
Britley
Britlyn
Britnea
Britnee
Britney (0.22)
Britney-Ngo
Britni (0.01)
Britnie
Britny (0.01)
Britreyunna
Britt
Britt'nique
Britta (0.01)
Brittain
Brittainee
Brittan
Brittane
Brittaney
Brittani (0.01)
Brittania
Brittanie
Brittanna
Brittanny
Brittany (0.41)
Brittany-Celia

| | | | | | | |
|---|---|---|---|---|---|---|
| Brittany-Lynn | Brnaya | Brooklee | Bry'anne | Brylei | Bryse | Byreanna |
| Brittenie | Brnlee | Brooklei | Bry'asia | Bryleigh (0.04) | Bryseda | Byron |
| Britteny | Brnyia | Brookleigh | Bry'auna | Brylen | Bryseida | Byue |
| Britthanie | Brnysia | Brooklein | Bry'najha | Bryley | Bryseis | |
| Brittia | Brock | Brooklen (0.01) | Bry'onna | Bryli | Brysen | |
| Brittian | Brodi | Brookley | Bry'yona | Brylie (0.02) | Bryson | ~ C ~ |
| Brittiana | Brodie | Brooklien | Bry'zeria | Brylin | Brysonn | |
| Brittianni | Brody (0.01) | Brooklin (0.03) | Brya | Bryly | Bryssa | (Ciala) Skyla |
| Brittin | Brodyn | Brooklinn | Bryah | Brylyn | Brystal (0.01) | C Anne |
| Brittleigh | Broegan | Brookllyn | Bryahna | Brylynn | Brystalmae | C Laire |
| Brittlynn | Brogan | Brooklon | Bryail | Brylynne | Brystol | C Niyah |
| Brittna | Brogyn | Brookly | Bryan | Bryn (0.10) | Brysyn | C'amia |
| Brittnay (0.01) | Brohm | Brooklyen | Bryan Nick | Bryn Elizabeth | Brytanie | C'ana |
| Brittne | Bronagh | Brook-Lyn | Bryan'tae | Bryna (0.01) | Brytany | C'ani |
| Brittnee | Bronicka | Brooklyn (2.61) | Bryana (0.07) | Brynadee | Brytasia | C'anna |
| Brittnei | Brontë (0.01) | Brooklynd | Bryana-Curtish | Brynae | Bryte | C'ara |
| Brittney (0.18) | Bronwen (0.01) | Brooklyne | Bryanah | Brynah | Bryten | C'arah |
| Brittney Ayanna | Bronwyn (0.04) | (0.01) | Bryanalyzz | Brynautica | Brythanie | C'daysiah |
| Brittneysue | Bronwynn | Brooklyn-H | Bryanda | Bryndalyn | Brytiera | C'era |
| Brittni | Brook (0.07) | Brook-Lynn | Bryané | Bryndle | Brytney | C'errya |
| Brittniann | Brook Lee | (0.01) | Bryani | Bryne | Brytni | C'essence |
| Brittnie | Brook'lyn | Brooklynn | Bryann (0.01) | Bryniah | Brytnie | C'leshia |
| Brittny | Brookasia | (0.55) | Bryanna (0.22) | Bryniya | Bryton | C'lina |
| Britton (0.01) | Brooké | Brooklynne | Bryanna Su | Brynja | Bryttan | C'liyah |
| Brittyn (0.01) | Brooke (2.71) | (0.04) | Bryannah (0.01) | Brynlea | Bryttani | C'mere |
| Britza | Brooke Ann | Brooklynn-Rae | Bryannalys | Brynlee (0.07) | Bryttany | C'milya |
| Briuna | Brooke Lyne | Brooklynn- | Bryanne (0.01) | Brynleigh | Bryttni | C'niya |
| Briunceé | Brooke Lynn | Raine | Bryannette | Brynley (0.01) | Bryza | C'onna |
| Briunna | Brooke Nevaeh | Brookmere | Bryannie | Brynli | Budhivali | C'riyah |
| Brixey | Brooke Noelle | Brooks (0.01) | Bryannon | Brynlie | Budour | C'terra |
| Brixi | Brooke'lynne | Brookynn | Bryant | Brynlin | Buetifull | C'yahna |
| Brixton | Brooke-Alexis | Broqueza | Bryar | Brynly | Buhlebenkosi | C'yahni |
| Briya | Brookel | Brougen | Bryar Lee | Brynlyn | Alishia | C'yani |
| Briyah | Brookelan | Brou-Jennyfer | Bryasia | Brynn (0.34) | Buil | C'yanna |
| Briyana (0.01) | Brookelenn | Brownleigh | Bryauna | Brynna (0.04) | Bunnie | C'yonnie |
| Briyani | Brookelin | Brownley | Bryce (0.04) | Brynnae | Buola | Ca Lia |
| Briyania | Brookelle | Broyianna | Brycee | Brynndelyn | Burgandi | Ca Nya |
| Briyanna (0.01) | Brookellyn | Brrendi | Bryceleigh | Brynne (0.04) | Burgany | Ca'deja |
| Briyannah | Brooke-Lyn | Bru'shawna | Brycelin | Brynnen | Burgundy | Ca'iynanna |
| Briyari | Brookelyn | Brucha (0.01) | Brycelyn | Brynnja | Burhana | Ca'leah |
| Briyelle | (0.07) | Bruchy (0.01) | Brycen | Brynnlee | Burjea | Ca'lecionna |
| Briyit | Brookelyn Rylee | Brucie | Brycena | Brynn-Leigh | Burke | Ca'leyah |
| Briyith | Brookelyne | Bruna (0.01) | Brycie | Brynnley | Buse | Ca'lia |
| Briyona | Brooke-Lynn | Brundith | Bryden | Brynnly | Buse-Nergiz | Ca'licia |
| Briyonna | (0.01) | Brunella | Brydgette | Brynn-Marie | Bushra (0.01) | Ca'lin |
| Briyonnah | Brookelynn | Brunia | Bryea | Brynoshay | Buthaina | Ca'lyciah |
| Briza (0.01) | (0.05) | Brunita | Bryeli | Bryona | Butterfly | Ca'lyiah |
| Brizane | Brooke-Lynne | Brunna | Bryelin | Bryonah | Buva Esther | Ca'mari |
| Brizeida | Brookelynne | Brunnie | Bryelle (0.01) | Bryoni | By'yanna | Ca'marie |
| Brizeiry | Brookes | Bruwaah | Bryer | Bryonna (0.02) | Byanca | Ca'mariya |
| Brizeyda | Brookin | Brween | Brylan | Bryonni | Byanka | Ca'mauri |
| Brizia | Brooklan | Bry'ana | Brylea | Bryony | Bydirah | Ca'maya |
| Brizni | Brookland | Bry'annah | Brylee (0.09) | Bryre | Byhalia | Ca'mayra |

| | | | | | | |
|---|---|---|---|---|---|---|
| Ca'miya | Cadence (0.68) | Caeton | Caillin | Caitriona | Caleigha | Calixa |
| Ca'miyah | Cadence Ayanna | Caezaria | Caily | Caitryn | Caleiya | Calixta |
| Ca'mora | Cadens | Cafflene | Cailyn (0.08) | Caity | Calen | Caliya |
| Ca'mya | Cadense | Cagney | Cailynn (0.01) | Caityln | Calene | Caliyah (0.02) |
| Ca'myah | Cadey | Caharey | Caimbree | Caitylyn | Calesha | Caliyha |
| Ca'myia | Cadi | Cahill | Caimen | Caivriona | Caley (0.04) | Caliyia |
| Ca'myiah | Cadiance | Cahlaya | Caimile | Caiya | Caleya | Calla (0.03) |
| Ca'myra | Cadie (0.01) | Cahmya | Caindaja | Caiyanna | Caleyah | Calla Lily |
| Ca'nai | Cadience | Cahri | Cainey | Caiyla | Caley-Anne | Calla-Bryn |
| Ca'naijah | Cadin | Cahushee | C-Aira | Caja | Calezia | Callaghan |
| Ca'naria | Cadince (0.01) | Cai | Caira (0.01) | Cakaiya | Calgora | Callah |
| Ca'nija | Cadison | Cai'aire | Cairene | Cakiyah | Cali (0.16) | Callahan (0.01) |
| Ca'nila | Cadon | Cai'la | Cairi | Cal'la'jah | Cali Mina | Callaina |
| Ca'niya | Cady (0.02) | Cai'lyn | Cairin | Cal'lisa | Calia | Callaisha |
| Ca'niyria | Cadye | Caia | Cairis | Cala | Caliah | Callan (0.01) |
| Ca'ny | Cady-Lynn | Caianny | Cairli | Calaeya | Caliana | Callathreal |
| Ca'nyiah | Cadyn (0.01) | Caicee | Cairo | Calah | Calianna | Callaway |
| Ca'shauna | Cadynce | Caicos | Cairys | Calahan | Calianne | Calle |
| Ca'shea | Cadynn | Caidan | Caisa | Calais | Calicia | Callea |
| Ca'viyah | Cae'dence | Caidance | Caisha | Calajah | Calico | Callee (0.01) |
| Ca'yanna | Caea | (0.01) | Caisley | Calajsia | Calico-Jean | Callee Ann |
| Ca'zaria | Caeana | Caiden (0.01) | Caison | Calamity | Calidia | Calleigh (0.03) |
| Ca'ziyah | Caecilia | Caiden Marie | Cait | Calandra | Calie (0.02) | Calleja |
| Caaliyah | Caedah | Caidenca | Caitalyn | Calani | Caliea | Callen (0.01) |
| Caalyn | Caedan | Caidence (0.03) | Caitelinn | Calansia | Calie-Ann | Calley (0.01) |
| Caasi | Caedance | Caiden-Marie | Caitelyn | Calantha | Caliece | Calli (0.05) |
| Caaz | Caeden | Caidha | Caithlin | Calasia | Caliegh | Callia (0.01) |
| Cabela | Caedence | Caidie | Caithlyn | Calaway | Caliese | Calliah |
| Cabella | Caedon | Caidy | Caitie | Calay | Caliesyn | Callian |
| Cabot | Caedyn | Caidyn (0.01) | Caitilin | Calaya | Calieyah | Calliana |
| Cabreah | Caedynce | Caidynce | Caitilyn | Calayah | California | Calliann |
| Cabria | Cael | Caiera | Caitlan | Calaysia | Caligrace | Callidora |
| Cabrina | Caela | Caija | Caitland | Calberta | Calila | Callie (0.38) |
| Cabrini | Caelan (0.01) | Caila (0.01) | Caitlee | Calcily | Caliliana | Callie Ann |
| Cabryn | Caelee | Cailah | Caitlen | Calder | Calin | Callie Jo |
| Cacee | Caeleigh | Cailan | Caitlene | Cale (0.01) | Calina (0.01) | Callieanne |
| Cacey | Caelen | Caile | Caitli N | Calea | Calinda | Calliegh |
| Cache | Caeley (0.01) | Cailea | Caitlin (0.71) | Caleah | Calindria | Callie-Joy |
| Caché | Caeli (0.01) | Caileane | Caitlinn | Calease | Caline | Callihan |
| Cachet | Caelie | Cailee (0.02) | Caitlyn (0.71) | Caleb | Caliope | Callilah |
| Cacilia | Caelin (0.01) | Caileen | Caitlyn | Calebe | Calipha | Calliope (0.01) |
| Cadaja | Caelinn | Caileigh (0.01) | Elizabeth | Caleby | Calis | Callisa |
| Cadalina | Caeliy | Cailen | Caitlyn-Alyssia | Calece | Calisa | Callisandra |
| Cadan | Caely | Cailey (0.06) | Caitlyn-Connie | Caledonia | Calise (0.01) | Callise |
| Cadance (0.04) | Caelyn (0.05) | Caili | Caitlynd | Caledra | Calisen | Callissa |
| Cadarrion | Caelynn | Cailie | Caitlyne | Calee | Calisha | Callista (0.03) |
| Cadayzhia | Caendra | Cailin (0.04) | Caitlyn-Marie | Caleecia | Calissa (0.01) | Callisto |
| Caddie-Jack | Caenna | Cailinda | Caitlynn (0.07) | Caleen | Calissia | Calliya |
| Cade | Caer | Cailinn | Caitlynne | Caleesta | Calista (0.07) | Calliyah |
| Cadee (0.01) | Caera | Cailleigh | Caiton | Caleeyah | Calistria | Calliyan |
| Cadelyn | Caerdwean | Caillenn | Caitriana | Caleia | Cali-Trining | Calloway |
| Cadelynne | Caesen | Cailliah | Caitrin | Caleiah | Calix | Cally (0.01) |
| Caden (0.03) | Caetlin | Caillie | Cáitrin | Caleigh (0.08) | | |

| | | | | | | |
|---|---|---|---|---|---|---|
| Callyn | Camaron | Camera | Camniekay | Candaice | Cansas | Caralin |
| Callyna | Camarria | Cameran (0.04) | Camon | Candance | Cantara | Caralina |
| Callyr | Camaryn | Cameren (0.01) | Camora (0.01) | Candela | Cantewastewi | Caraline (0.01) |
| Callysta | Camauria | Camereon | Camorah | Candelaria | Canyia | Caralyn (0.01) |
| Calmiya | Camaya (0.01) | Camerin | Camorahh | Candence | Canyiá | Caralyne |
| Calneshia | Camaylia | Cameron (0.43) | Camourah | Candess | Canyon | Cara-Lynn |
| Calnisha | Camayrn | Cameron-Eliz | Campbell (0.14) | Candi | Cao Thuy | Caralynn |
| Caloni | Cambaro | Cameronique | Campbelle | Candiace | Caoilainn | Cara-Marianna |
| Calonnie | Cambel | Camerria | Camra | Candi-Anne | Caoilfíonn | Caramia |
| Caloren | Cambell (0.01) | Cameryn (0.05) | Camran | Candias | Caoilin | Caranye |
| Calvi | Cambelle | Camerynn | Camree | Candice (0.06) | Caoilinn | Carataleala |
| Calviana | Camber | Camesha | Camreen | Candida | Caoimhe | Carcelyn |
| Calvin | Camberlie | Camey | Camren (0.01) | Candide | Caoline | Carcionna |
| Calvina | Cambre | Cami (0.03) | Camrey | Candie | Caollin | Cardae |
| Calvinaí | Cambrea | Camia | Camri (0.01) | Candis (0.01) | Capella | Cardajia |
| Calviona | Cambree (0.02) | Camiah | Camria | Candiss | Capley | Cardasia |
| Calvonna | Cambreia | Camie (0.01) | Camrie | Candler | Caprecia | Cardeja |
| Calyah | Cambreigh | Camiel | Camrin | Candra | Caprese | Cardie |
| Calyan | Cambrey | Camielle | Camr-Morgan | Candrian | Capresha | Cardin |
| Calyce | Cambri (0.01) | Camil | Camron (0.01) | Candus | Capri (0.01) | Cardina |
| Calye | Cambria (0.03) | Camila (0.99) | Camry (0.01) | Candy (0.02) | Capria | Cardine |
| Calyie | Cambriah | Camila Marie | Camrya | Candya | Caprial | Cardyne |
| Calylah | Cambrian | Camile | Camryn (0.59) | Candyce (0.01) | Capriana | Carea |
| Calyn (0.01) | Cambridge | Camilha | Camrynn (0.01) | Candyel | Capriauni | Careah |
| Calynn | Cambrie (0.01) | Camilia (0.01) | Camrynne | Candyn | Caprice (0.02) | Caree |
| Calypso | Cambrielle | Camilie | Camryon | Candyse | Caprie | Careen |
| Calyse | Cambry | Camill | Camy | Cane'sha | Caprieca | Careena |
| Calyssa | Cambrya | Camilla (0.09) | Camya (0.01) | Caneek | Caprienne | Carein |
| Calysta (0.01) | Cambryn | Camilla Joanne | Camyah | Canei | Capril | Careleena |
| Calystah | Cambrynn | Camillah | Camyha | Caneisha | Capritta | Careli |
| Calysto | Camby | Camilla-Valerie | Camyia | Canela | Capriya | Carelle |
| Cam'ree | Camden (0.04) | Camille (0.57) | Camyiah | Caneliz | Capryce | Carelys |
| Cam'ron | Camdin | Camille Andree | Camyla | Canelly | Capucine | Carem |
| Cam'ryen | Camdon | Camille-Athena | Camylah | Caneshia | Car'lyse | Caren (0.01) |
| Cam'ryn | Camdyn (0.04) | Camille-Hazel | Camylle | Canesse | Car'mari | Carena |
| Camaea | Cameia | Camillia | Camyr | Cania | Car'mell | Carence |
| Camaily | Cameiá | Camily | Camyra | Caniecya | Car'mika | Carene |
| Camaira | Cameilla | Camilyah | Camyria | Canihya | Car'nya | Carene-Laure |
| Camaiya | Cameisha | Camira | Camyrn | Canija | Car'nyia | Carenisha |
| Camani | Cameka | Camirah | Camyya | Canijah | Car'reona | Carenzie |
| Camara (0.01) | Camela | Camiria | Cana | Canila | Car'tiyana | Carera |
| Camarah | Camelah | Camiron | Canaa | Canisha | Cara (0.22) | Carerra |
| Camaren | Camelia (0.02) | Camirra | Canaan | Caniya | Cara Luisa | Caressa (0.01) |
| Camareonn | Cameliah | Camiya (0.01) | Canai | Caniyah (0.01) | Cara Mia | Caresse |
| Camari (0.02) | Camelie | Camiyah (0.01) | Canan | Caniyla | Cara-Ann | Carey |
| Camaria (0.01) | Cameline | Camlyn | Canann | Canlena | Carabella | Careyann |
| Camariah | Camella | Camma | Canaria | Canna | Caradan | Careylin |
| Camariana | Camelle | Cammeron | Canary | Cannaday | Caragh | Cari (0.01) |
| Camarianna | Camellia | Cammi (0.01) | Canaush | Cannady | Carah | Caria |
| Camarie | Camelliah | Cammie (0.01) | Canaya | Canni | Caralea | Cariah |
| Camarieyah | Camelya | Cammille | Canayah | Cannice | Caralee | Carianalyz |
| Camariona | Camelye | Cammryn | Canayla | Cannon | Caraleena | Cariann |
| Camariyah | Cameo | Cammy (0.01) | Candace (0.10) | Canon | Caraleigh | Carianna |

Carianne
Carianyeli
Caribbean
Caricha
Caridad
Carigan
Carih
Carilyn
Carilyne
Carimah
Carime
Carin
Carina (0.10)
Carine
Cariness
Carinna
Carinne
Caris (0.02)
Carisa (0.01)
Carisha
Carisia
Carisma
Cariss
Carissa (0.15)
Carisse
Carissmarie
Carista
Carisya
Carita
Caritina
Caritza
Cariuna
Cariya
Ca-Riyah
Cariyauna
Cariyonna
Carizma
Carl
Carla (0.17)
Carla Lanell
   Beth
Carla Sama
Carlaeona
Carla-Loriane
Carlana
Carlania
Carlariea
Carla-Rose
Carlasha
Carlashia
Carlasia
Carlay
Carlayshia

Carlaysia
Carle
Carlé
Carlea
Carlean
Carlecia
Carleda
Carlee (0.16)
Carleen
Carleena
Carlei
Carleigh (0.08)
Carleight
Carleisha
Carlella
Carlena (0.01)
Carlene (0.01)
Carlene Allyissa
Carlenne
Carlesha
Carleshia
Carlesia
Carletta
Carley (0.23)
Carley Jo
Carleyanne
Carley-Jane
Carleysia
Carli (0.09)
Carli Rose
Carlia
Carliah
Carliana
Carli-Ann
Carlianna
Carli-Anne
Carlianys
Carlie (0.18)
Carlie Tif
Carliee
Carliegh
Carlie-Jane
Carliena
Carliessa
Carlieth
Carliey
Carlin (0.01)
Carlina (0.01)
Carlincea
Carline
Carlini
Carlinn
Carlisa

Carlise
Carlisha
Carlisia
Carlisle
Carlissa
Carlisse
Carlita
Carlitta
Carliya
Carliyah
Carliyha
Carllana
Carllee
Carllie
Carllynn
Carlneshia
Carloine
Carlos
Carlota
Carlotta
Carlotta Amalia
Carlriyana
Carlson
Carltonaja
Carltyn
Carly (0.69)
Carly Jo
Carly Rose
Carlya
Carlyah
Carlyale
Carlyce
Carlye (0.01)
Carlyn (0.01)
Carlyna
Carlyne
Carlynn
Carlyse
Carlysia
Carlysica
Carlyssa
Carma (0.01)
Carma-Jo
Carman
Carmani
Carmarey
Carmaria
Carmarys
Carmaylis
Carmea
Carmel (0.01)
Carmela (0.03)
Carmelia

Carmelina
   (0.01)
Carmelinda
Carmelita (0.01)
Carmell
Carmella (0.04)
Carmelle
Carmellia
Carmellina
Carmello
Carmelyn
Carmen (0.40)
Carmen Brecze
Carmen-
   Angelise
Carmen-
   Brianna
Carmencita
Carmenica
Carmenlita
Carmenynez
Carmi
Carmiah
Carmichael
Carmie
Carmiliah
Carmilina
Carmin
Carmina (0.01)
Carmindy
Carmine
Carmisha
Carmiya
Carmody
Carmon
Carmondie
Carmoni
Carmoní
Carmory
Carmyn (0.01)
Carmynn
Carnaisha
Carnaiya
Carnajah
Carnaya
Carnecia
Carneicia
Carnel
Carnelli
Carnellia
Carnesha
Carney
Carnijah

Carnisha
Carniya
Carniyah
Caro
Carol (0.09)
Carol Ann
Carol Anne
Carola
Carolain
Carolane (0.02)
Carol-Ann
   (0.01)
Carolann
Carol-Anne
Carolanne
   (0.01)
Carole (0.01)
Carole Anne
Carole-Ann
Carole-Anne
Caroleen
Caroleena
Carolena
Carolene
Caroletta
Carolie
Caroliena
Carolin
Carolina (0.27)
Carolina Faye
Carolina Isabel
   Sanchez
Carolina Rose
Caroline (2.13)
Caroline Hailey
Caroline-Rose
Carolinn
Carol-Jane
Caroljean
Carolyn (0.23)
Carolyna
Carolyne (0.01)
Carolynn (0.01)
Carolynne
Caron
Caronnie
Carr
Carra
Carralyne
Carreira
Carrena
Carreon
Carrera

Carressa
Carria
Carriahnna
Carriann
Carrianna
Carribbean
Carrie (0.12)
Carrie Jo
Carriea
Carrie-Ann
Carrieann
Carrie-Anne
Carrie-Jo
Carriella
Carrielynn
Carrietta
Carrigan (0.02)
Carrilyn
Carrin
Carrine
Carrington
   (0.03)
Carrini
Carrir
Carrisa
Carrison
Carrissa
Carrol
Carroline
Carroll
Carrollyn
Carry
Carryn
Carsan
Carsen (0.01)
Carsha
Carsie
Carsin
Carson (0.06)
Carsten
Carston
Carsyn (0.04)
Carter (0.04)
Carteria
Cartezia
Cartiana
Cartiyah
Carvin
Cary
Cary-Anne
Caryanne
Caryea
Caryl

Carylee
Caryliana
Caryn (0.01)
Caryna
Caryne
Carynn
Carys (0.06)
Carys-Anne
Caryse
Caryss
Caryssa
Caryvette
Casadie
Casady
Casana
Casandra (0.06)
Casara
Casca
Cascada
Cascayde
Casche't
Cascie
Casdyn
Case'ya
Casee
Casei
Caselie
Caselyn
Casen
Casey (0.32)
Casey Chau
Casey Lynn
Casey Sue
Caseyn
Cash
Cash'ae
Casha
Casha'mona
Cashae
Cashai
Cashalie
Cashawn
Cashawndra
Cashé
Cashelle
Cashia
Cashion
Cashmere
Cashmeré
Cashmere-
   Saughnassie
Cashonda
Cashsaí

| | | | | | |
|---|---|---|---|---|---|
| Casi (0.01) | Cassidy (0.79) | Caterinne | Catie (0.01) | Caydynce | Caytlynne | Ceashia |
| Casia | Cassidy Danya | Caterra | Catience | Cayelin | Cayton | Ceasia |
| Casiana | Cassidy Jo Ann | Catey | Catilin | Cayenna | Caytriana | Ceason |
| Casidee | Cassidy-Hally | Cateyn | Catilyn | Cayenne | Caytron | Ceaudy |
| Casidy | Cassidy-Lynn | Cathalene | Catiya | Cayetana | Cayzia | Ceaundra |
| Casie (0.01) | Cassie (0.14) | Cathaline | Catlin (0.01) | Cayetlin | Cazani | Ceaunnie |
| Casimira | Cassie-Anne | Catharina | Catlinh | Caygen | Cazea | Ceaveon |
| Casin | Cassiel | Catharine | Catlyn | Cayla (0.10) | Caziya | Ceazia |
| Casiphia | Cassina | Cathelina | Catlynn | Caylaa | Cazjin | Cebele |
| Casity | Cassini | Catherin | Catori (0.01) | Caylah (0.01) | Cazlen | Cece |
| Casja | Cassiope | Catherina | Catoria | Caylan | Cazmeina | Cecee |
| Casjah | Cassiopee | Catherine (1.52) | Catra | Caylani | CC | Ceceilia |
| Caslyn | Cassiopeia | Catherine | Catrena | Caylas | Ce Ce | Ceceilla |
| Casmere | (0.01) | Elizabeth | Catrianna | Cayle (0.01) | Cé Nautica | Ceceilya |
| Casmyn | Cassitty | Catherine | Catrin | Caylea | Ce'airra | Ceceionna |
| Cason | Cassity | Kayonia | Catrina (0.03) | Caylee (0.08) | Ce'aja | Cecela |
| Casondra | Cassius | Catherine Rose | Catrine | Cayleeana | Ce'andra | Cecelia (0.18) |
| Casonna | Casslyn | Catherine Zhin- | Catriona (0.01) | Cayleen | Ce'arra | Cecelia Joy |
| Cass | Cassondra | Lin | Catryna | Cayleh | Ce'asia | Cecelya |
| Cassadee | (0.01) | Catherine- | Cattarina | Caylei | Ce'deja | Cecess |
| Cassadi | Cassy (0.01) | Amelia | Catti-Bree | Cayleigh (0.02) | Ce'irah | Ceci |
| Cassadie | Casta | Catherine- | Cattie | Caylen | Ce'lina | Cecially |
| Cassadra | Castalia | Elizabeth | Catty | Caylene | Ce'liyah | Cecie |
| Cassady (0.01) | Castella | Catherine-Eve | Caty | Cayley (0.02) | Ce'mar | Cecila |
| Cassandra (0.75) | Casuela | Catherine- | Catyia | Cayli (0.01) | Ce'mayah | Cécile |
| Cassandra Chloe | Casyia | Melvina | Catyria | Cayliana | Ce'naiyah | Cecile (0.01) |
| Cassandrah | Casyn | Catherine-Reilly | Catzia | Caylie (0.02) | Ce'nasia | Cecilemarie |
| Cassandranicole | Cat | Catherine- | Causey | Caylin (0.03) | Ce'nieyah | Ceciley |
| Cassandre (0.03) | Catalena | Yutong | Cauthen | Cayliss | Ce'niya | Cecilia (0.36) |
| Cassandre Daina | Catalia | Catherinne | Cautrina | Caylissa | Ce'niyah | Cecilia |
| Cassandrea | Catalina (0.13) | Cathern | Cauyenne | Cayliy | Ce'nyah | Amankwa |
| Cassandre- | Catalla | Catheryn (0.01) | Cavasia | Caylon | Ce'oani | Cecilia Maria |
| Eugenie | Catalyn | Catheryne | Cavelle | Cayly | Ce'omas | Ceciliah |
| Cassandriana | Catana | Cathi | Cavilla | Caylyn | Ce'oni | Cecilianne |
| Cassara | Catara | Cathia | Cavin | Caylynn | Ce'renity | Cecille |
| Cassaundra | Catarena | Cathie | Cavins | Caylynn Nevaeh | Ce'yanna | Cecillee |
| Cassdan | Catarina (0.02) | Cathleen (0.01) | Caya | Caylynne | Ce'yonie | Cecillia |
| Cassedy | Catarzyna | Cathlin | Cayana | Cayman | Ce'yonna | Cecily (0.03) |
| Cassee | Catavia | Cathlyn | Cayce (0.01) | Caymen | Ceaira (0.01) | Cecilya |
| Cassetia | Cate (0.04) | Cathlynn | Caycee | Caymin | Ceairas | Cecrect |
| Cassey (0.01) | Cateilyn | Cathrin | Caycie | Cayna | Ceairra (0.01) | Cecret |
| Casshay | Catelin | Cathrine (0.01) | Caydah | Cayndence | Cealan | Cecy |
| Casshea | Cateline | Cathrinelunie | Caydan | Cayni | Cean | Cecylia |
| Cassi (0.01) | Catelyn (0.04) | Cathryn (0.04) | Caydance (0.01) | Cayona | Ceana | Ced |
| Cassia (0.02) | Catelynn | Cathryn Kaku | Cayde | Caysee | Ceane | Cedaia |
| Cassiah | Catelynne | Cathryna | Caydee | Caysen | Ceanha | Cedalia |
| Cassiana | Catera | Cathrynne | Caydei | Caysha | Ceanna (0.01) | Cedar (0.01) |
| Cassiane | Cateri | Cathy (0.03) | Cayden (0.04) | Caysi | Ceara (0.01) | Cedejah |
| Cassiddy | Cateria | Cathyrn | Caydence (0.06) | Caysia | Cearra | Cedella |
| Cassidee (0.01) | Caterin | Cati | Caydin | Caysie | Cearrah | Cedena |
| Cassidey | Caterina (0.02) | Catia (0.01) | Caydnce | Caytlee | Cearstan | Cederika |
| Cassidi (0.01) | Caterine | Catianna | Caydra | Caytlin | Cearstin | Cedjrionna |
| Cassidie (0.01) | Caterinna | Caticia | Caydrian | Caytlyn | Ceasha | Cedkeriah |

| | | | | | | |
|---|---|---|---|---|---|---|
| Cedona | Celee | Celis | Ceona | Cesiah | Cha'nelle | Chaidinae |
| Cedra | Celeena | Celisa | Ceonna | Cesilia | Cha'niya | Chaielle |
| Cedrea | Celeia | Celise | Ceonni | Cesilie | Cha'niyah | Chailey |
| Cedreanna | Celeiah | Celissa | Ceonoia | Cesily | Cha'nya | Chailyn (0.01) |
| Cedrenna | Celeina | Celissia | Ceonyah | Ceslie | Cha'nyan | Chaima |
| Cedrese | Celelity | Cella | Cephora | Cessana | Cha'raya | Chaina |
| Cedriah | Celena (0.01) | Celladora | Cequoia | Cessna | Cha'rhonda | Chaina-Jade |
| Cedrianna | Celene | Cellest | Cequoyah | Cesylia | Cha'riel | Chainey |
| Cedricka | Celeni | Cellina | Cera (0.01) | Ceterra | Cha'risma | Chaini |
| Cedrieana | Celes (0.01) | Cellise | Ceraiya | Cetirria | Cha'rrell | Chainiee |
| Cedriyanna | Celesea | Celma | Ceraya | Cevaejion | Cha'trice | Chaira |
| Cedtoria | Celesley | Celmi | Cerayla | Cevanah | Cha'voynna | Chairish |
| Cee | Celess | Celsey | Cerbie | Cevanna | Chaahat | Chaise |
| Cee'annaka | Celest (0.01) | Celtie-Rae | Cerelia | Cevaya | Chaances | Chaisen |
| Ceejaye | Celesta | Celya | Cerem-Elmas | Ceve | Chabeli | Chaislyn |
| Ceely | Céleste | Celyane | Ceren | Cevilla | Chabelli | Chaiston |
| Ceequan | Celeste (0.26) | Celymarie | Cerena (0.01) | Cevin | Chabely | Chaisty |
| Cee-Wun | Celeste | Celyn | Cerene | Cevyn | Chablis | Chaitanya |
| Cehcily | Jullianna | Celyne | Cerenitee | Cey'arieah | Chabraya | Chaiya |
| Ceialah | Celeste Sofia | Celynn | Cereniti | Ceyani | Chabrya | Chaiyah |
| Ceianna | Celeste-Odalis | Celynndra | Cerenitie | Ceyanna | Chacayla | Chakai |
| Ceidya | Celest-Eugenie | Celyse | Cerenity (0.01) | Ceyanni | Chachira | Chakariah |
| Ceila | Celestia (0.01) | Celysie | Cerent'a | Ceyarra | Chaci | Chakayla |
| Ceileigh | Celestial | Celysse | Ceres | Ceyda | Chacie | Chakeira |
| Céili | Celestianna | Celzey | Ceresmy | Ceydee | Chad | Chakeria |
| Ceili (0.01) | Celestina (0.01) | Cemarea | Cereza | Ceydi | Chadaisia | Chakira |
| Ceilia | Celestine (0.01) | Cemelia | Cerhiya | Ceyera | Chadalyn | Chakiyah |
| Ceilidh | Celeyah | Cemia | Ceri | Ceyli | Chaday | Chakrika |
| Ceilin | Celeyse | Cemiya | Ceriah | Ceyliana | Chade | Chakyia |
| Ceinie | Celi | Cena | Ceridwen | Ceylin | Chaderne | Chakyla |
| Ceinwyn | Celia (0.15) | Cenaa | Ceridwyn | Ceylone | Chadi | Chakyra |
| Ceiona | Celiane | Cenaida | Cerina | Ceyona | Chadia | Chakyrah |
| Ceioni | Celiann | Cenaii | Cerine | Ceyonnie | Chadsity | Chakythia |
| Ceira | Celianna | Cendia | Ceriniti | Ceyphora | Chady | Chalaieja |
| Ceirra (0.01) | Celianne | Cendrine | Cerinity | Ceyrrah | Chadyn | Chalaine |
| Ceirrin | Celica | Cendy | Cerise | Cezanne | Chae | Chalea |
| Ceirsten | Celicia | Cenecia | Ceroara | Cézanne | Chae-Hee | Chaleah |
| Ceiwyn | Celiciana | Cenedra | Cerrah | Ch Nyiah | Chaela | Chalece |
| Cejay | Celie | Ceniah | Cerra-Kay | Ch'kara | Chaelee | Chalecia |
| Cejaya | Celiegh | Ceniiya | Cerrena | Ch'khiya | Chaeley | Chalee |
| Cekaijah | Celiene | Cenilia | Cerria | Ch'loe | Chaeli (0.01) | Chaleigh |
| Cekeria | Celika | Cenise | Cerridwen | Ch'nyia | Chaelin | Chalexus |
| Cekhia | Celilia | Cenita | Cerridwyn | Cha'da | Chaella | Chaley |
| Celaya | Celin | Ceniya | Cerrina | Cha'diamond | Chaelsi | Chaleyah |
| Celby | Celina (0.09) | Ceniyah | Cerstin | Cha'kae | Chaelynn | Chaliah |
| Celda | Célina-Hélène | Cenna | Ceryana | Cha'kayla | Chaena | Chalice |
| Celdyn | Celina-Marie | Cennedy | Cerye | Cha'kerria | Chaerin | Chalina |
| Cele | Celindia | Cenobia | Ceryne | Cha'kiya | Chahak | Chalinda |
| Celebrian | Celine (0.08) | Cenora | Cerys | Cha'mar | Chahat | Chalino |
| Celebrity | Celine | Censarity | Cesar | Cha'miah | Chahra | Chalis |
| Celece | Cassandrae | Censory | Ceseleigh | Cha'michae | Chai | Chalisa |
| Celecia | Celines | Cenyah | Cesi | Cha'miya | Chai'ayre | Chalise |
| Celeda | Celiona | Ceola | Cesia (0.01) | Cha'nell | Chaia | Chalisha |

| | | | | | | |
|---|---|---|---|---|---|---|
| Chaliyah | Chance (0.01) | Chaniah | Chantelle (0.02) | Chardajah | Charitye | Charlesse |
| Chalize | Chancela | Chanice | Chanteria | Chardan | Charitza | Charleston |
| Challi | Chancellar | Chanickza | Chanterria | Chardana | Chariya | Charlet |
| Chalondra | Chances Janyla | Chanida | Chanteshia | Chardanae | Chariz | Charleta |
| Chalonzia | Chancey | Chanie | Chantey'aria | Chardannay | Chariza Pauleen | Charlette |
| Chaltu | Chancie | Chaniece | Chanthavi | Chardanne | Charizma | Charley (0.05) |
| Chaly | Chancina-Marie | Chaniiya | Chantia | Chardasha | Charjonney | Charley-Anna |
| Chalyn | Chanclynn | Chanijah | Chantiah | Chardé | Charkala | Charley-Beth |
| Chalynn | Chancy | Chanise | Chantilly | Charde'vion | Charkendra | Charlez |
| Chalysa | Chanda | Chanitey | Chantol | Chardecia | Charkeria | Charleze |
| Chalyssa | Chandana | Chanity | Chantra | Charderra | Charkia | Charli (0.04) |
| Cham | Chandani | Chaniva | Chantrell | Chardey | Charkin'la | Charlia |
| Chamael | Chandé | Chaniya (0.02) | Chantrija | Chardon | Charla (0.01) | Charliane |
| Chamara | Chandell | Chaniyah | Chany (0.02) | Chardoney | Charlai | Charliann |
| Chamari | Chandelle | Chaniyyah | Chanya | Chardonnay | Charlaine | Charlianna |
| Chamaria | Chandelyn | Chanlee | Chanyah | Chardonnee | Charlamagne | Charlianne |
| Chamarra | Chandhini | Chanler | Chanybel | Chardren'a | Charlatan | Charlice |
| Chamaya | Chandini | Chanley | Chanyce | Charee | Charlayé | Charlicea |
| Chamberlain | Chandlar | Chanlier | Chanydre | Chareese | Charlazia | Charlié |
| Chambrazia | Chandle | Chanmony | Chanyel | Chareka | Charle | Charlie (0.18) |
| Chamce | Chandler (0.06) | Channa | Chanyia | Charel | Char-Lea | Charlie Ella |
| Chameli | Chandlier | Channah | Chanylaah | Charell | Charlea (0.01) | Charlie Rose |
| Chamelia | Chandni | Channel | Chanyse | Chareta | Charleah | Charlie-Ann |
| Chamere | Chandon | Channell | Chanytel | Chari | Charlea-Jo | Charlie-Anne |
| Chamhya | Chandra (0.01) | Channelle | Chanz | Chariana | Charlease | Charlie-Ella |
| Chami | Chandre | Channery | Chaoli | Charianna | Charlecia | Charlie-Frederique |
| Chamia | Chandrea | Channey | Chaosity | Charidel | Charlee (0.09) | Charlie-Jane |
| Chamiah | Chandree | Channie | Chapel | Charidy | Charlee Rose | Charlie-Joe |
| Chamiia | Chandreya | Channing (0.02) | Chapin | Chariel | Charlee-Ann | Charlie-Maude |
| Chamille | Chandria | Channitra | Chappell | Chariely | Charlee-Anne | Charlie-May |
| Chamillia | Chandrika | Channon | Chappelle | Chariety | Charleen | Charliene |
| Chamira | Chanea | Channtell | Chaprece | Charifma | Charleena | Charlie-Rose |
| Chamiya | Chaneal | Channy | Chaquona | Charill | Charleene | Charlies |
| Chamiyah | Chanedra | Chanpreet | Char'lejua | Chariotte | Charleese | Charliese |
| Chamon | Chaneil | Chanpuchana | Char'lese | Charis (0.03) | Charleez | Charliesia |
| Chamoni | Chaneise | Chansadie | Char'lize | Charisa | Charlei | Charli-Madelynn |
| Champagne | Chánel | Chanta | Char'meyka | Charish | Charleigh (0.03) | Charlin |
| Chams Addoha | Chanel (0.12) | Chantal (0.03) | Char'myia | Charisima | Charleize | Charlina |
| Chamya | Chanel-Grace | Chantale | Char'nia | Charisma (0.05) | Charlekeytha | Charline (0.01) |
| Chamyah | Chanel-Jale-Ayse | Chantall | Char'resse | Chariss | Charlemagne | Charlisa |
| Chan | Chanell (0.01) | Chantalle | Chara (0.01) | Charissa (0.01) | Charlena | Charlise (0.02) |
| Chan'niyah | Chanelle (0.04) | Chantal-Lynn | Chara-Angele | Charisse | Charlene (0.07) | Charlisha |
| Chan'tasia | Chanelly | Chantana | Charai | Charisse Nicole | Charlene Florentine | Charlisia |
| Chana (0.11) | Chanely | Chantashia | Charale | Charisten | Charles | Charlissa |
| Chanadia | Chanera | Chanté | Charanpreet | Charita | Charlesanna | Charlisse |
| Chanae | Chanesha | Chante (0.01) | Charaun | Charitee | Charlese | Charlissia |
| Chanah (0.01) | Chaney (0.01) | Chante'a | Charaya | Charitha | Charlesetta | Charlita |
| Chanarius | Chanez | Chantee | Charcey | Chariti | Charlesey | Charlix |
| Chanariyah | Chang | Chantel (0.03) | Charcy | Charitie | Charlesha | Charliyah |
| Chanay | Changkuoth | Chanteleina | Charda | Chariti-Elizabeth | Charlesia | Charliz |
| Chanayah | Chani (0.01) | Chanteli | Chardae | Charity (0.16) | Charlesity | Charlizé |
| Chanayse | Chania | Chantell | Chardaé | Charity-Dawn | Charlessai | |
| Chanazia | | Chantell Elyka | Chardai | | | |

Charlize (0.11)
Charlize-Joelle
Charlotte (1.51)
Charlotte Elizabeth
Charlotte Jane
Charlotte Kyla
Charlotte Lowell
Charlotte Luz
Charlotte-Alix
Charlotte-Anne
Charlotte-Emilie
Charlsea
Charlsey
Charlsi
Charlsie
Charlstyn
Charly (0.02)
Charly-Ann
Charlycaye
Charlye
Charly-Maya
Charlyn
Charlyne
Charlynn
Charlyse
Charm
Charma
Charmail
Charmaine (0.01)
Charmane
Charmantine
Charmari
Charmaria
Charme
Charmelika
Charmeria
Charmesha
Charmi
Charmia
Charmine
Charmisa
Charmiss
Charmiya
Charmonique
Charmony
Charmya
Charmyhia
Charnae
Charnaeh

Charnaja
Charnavia
Charnay
Charnayá
Charnaye
Charne
Charnee
Charneka
Charnell
Charnelle
Charney
Charnia
Charnice
Charniece
Charnise
Charnisha
Charnita
Charniya
Charnvir
Charo
Charol
Charolette
Charonda
Charra
Charral
Charree
Charrell
Charry
Charshay
Chartaysia
Chartonya
Charu
Charyn
Chasadi
Chasadie
Chasady
Chasaya
Chascity
Chase (0.05)
Chasee
Chasely
Chaselyn
Chaselynn
Chasey
Chasia
Chasiana
Chasidie
Chasidy (0.01)
Chasina
Chasisty
Chasitee
Chasiti
Chasití

Chasitie
Chasity (0.11)
Chaska
Chaslon
Chaslyn
Chasmitha
Chasney
Chassadi
Chassedi
Chassetty
Chassiddy
Chassidi
Chassidy (0.02)
Chassie
Chassilynn
Chassiti
Chassity (0.01)
Chastain
Chastely
Chasti
Chastidy
Chastin
Chastity (0.02)
Chastney
Chasya
Chasydi
Chatae
Chatavia
Chatelaine
Chaterra
Chaterrica
Chatherine
Chatianna
Chatuan
Chatyla
Chatyvia
Chau
Chauchondria
Chaudae
Chaunacee
Chaunasha
Chaunce
Chauncey
Chaunci
Chauncy
Chaunee
Chaunessey
Chaunsai
Chauntasia
Chaunte
Chauntea
Chauntel
Chaurita

Chautel
Chava (0.03)
Chava Toba
Chavae
Chavai
Chavalah
Chavaya
Chavé
Chavel
Chavela
Chaveleh
Chaveli
Chavelle
Chavely
Chaveona
Chavi
Chavia
Chavie
Chaviya
Chavon
Chavonne
Chavoun
Chavy
Chawanda
Chay'ne
Chaya (0.18)
Chaya Mushka
Chaya Yitty
Chayah
Chayan
Chayane
Chayanna
Chayanne
Chayce (0.01)
Chayil
Chayili
Chayill
Chayla
Chayland
Chaylee (0.01)
Chaylen
Chaylene
Chayli
Chaylie
Chaylyn
Chayma
Chaymaa
Chayna
Chaynce
Chaynee
Chaynei
Chaynne
Chaypin

Chayse (0.02)
Chayton
Chaz'ney
Chaza
Chazany
Chaza-Rae
Chaziah
Chazie
Chazity
Chazlee
Chazlyn
Chazlynn
Chazmin
Chazmine
Chazmyn
Chazney
Chazoria
Chazy-Lee
Che
Ché
Che'lynn
Che'nita
Chea Sophir
Chea Sophirly
Chealeigh
Chealselyn
Chealsey
Chealsie
Cheanna
Chebet
Chebria
Chechnia
Checota
Chedin
Cheelai
Cheelye
Cheevua
Chehalis
Cheila
Cheily
Cheinefl
Chekayla
Chela
Chelacy
Chelan
Chelanda
Chelbi
Chelbie
Chelby
Chelce
Chelcee
Chelcey
Chelci

Chelcie
Chelcy
Cheley
Chelisa
Chelise
Cheliya
Chella
Chellby
Chellie
Chellse
Chellsea
Chellsie
Chelora
Chelsa
Chelsae
Chelse
Chelsea (0.76)
Chelsea Korenna-Rosa
Chelsea Lynn
Chelsea Morgan
Chelsea Pat
Chelsea-Amber
Chelsea-Ardma
Chelsea-Marie
Chelsea-May
Chelsea-Melodie
Chelsea-Rae
Chelsee (0.01)
Chelsei
Chelseigh
Chelser
Chelsey (0.13)
Chelsey Nicole
Chelseyna
Chelsey-Stephany
Chelsi (0.01)
Chelsia
Chelsie (0.06)
Chelsie-Elizabeth
Chelsse
Chelsy (0.01)
Chelsy-Ann
Chelsye
Chelsylyne
Cheltsie
Chely
Chelya
Chelys
Chelyza
Chelzie

Chemayra
Chemen
Chemerah
Chemere
Chemicka
Chemiyah
Chen Yu
Chenae
Chenai
Chenarya
Chenaya
Chenayder
Chendal
Chendra
Chendyl
Chene
Chené
Chenea
Chenee
Chenel
Cheneldine
Chenele
Chenell
Chenelle
Cheney
Cheneya
Cheneyah
Cheng
Chengyeng
Chenia
Chenielle
Chenika
Chenille (0.01)
Chenin
Chenissa
Cheniya
Cheniyah
Chennill
Chenoa (0.01)
Chenoah
Chenowa
Chensie
Chenyanne
Chenyao
Chenyrai
Chenyze
Chenzira
Chepchirchir
Cher
Cher'ron
Cheradin
Cherai
Cheray

| | | | | | | |
|---|---|---|---|---|---|---|
| Cherdi | Cherri | Chevelle *(0.02)* | Chezney | Chila | Chion | Chloe-Deann |
| Cherea | Cherrie | Chevelle-Kelly | Chezni | Chilai | Chionna | Chloeé |
| Cherease | Cherrilyn | Chevelyne | Chezny | Chilali | Chipo | Chloee *(0.03)* |
| Cheree | Cherrish *(0.01)* | Chevi | Chezza | Childers | Chiquera | Chloe- |
| Cherell | Cherrissa | Chevilyn | Chhavi | Chilena | Chiquita | Frederique |
| Cherelle | Cherrlin | Chevon | Chhaya | Chiloe | Chiquivia | Chloe-Jade |
| Cheresa | Cherry *(0.01)* | Chevonne | Chhrzat | Chiloh | Chireene | Chloé-Jayde |
| Cheresh | Cherub | Chevryn | Chi | Chilota | Chireyona | Chloe-Kate |
| Chereyona | Cherubim | Chevy | Chí Liyah | Chilton | Chirine | Chloe-Lynn |
| Cheri | Cherwinna | Chevy-Lynn | Chi'kayla | Chilynn | Chirome | Chloemaé |
| Cheriah | Chery'she | Chevyón | Chi'quita | Chimaie | Chirsten | Chloe-Mari |
| Cheriana | Cheryalann | Chewane | Chia | Chimaree | Chisam | Chloe-Nadya |
| Cherianne | Cheryally | Chey Anne | Chia Shi | Chimay | Chisato | Chloeona |
| Cherickey | Cheryl *(0.03)* | Chey'tajah | Chiada | Chimdindu | Chise | Chloe-Quin |
| Cheridan | Cherylann | Cheyaen | Chiaki | Chime | Chisom | Chloeva |
| Cheriden | Cherylin | Cheyan | Chialeen | Chime'nora | Chistany | Chloey *(0.02)* |
| Cheridyn | Cherylynn | Cheyane | Chialia | Chimere | Chistin | Chloeye |
| Cherie *(0.01)* | Cherysh | Cheyann *(0.02)* | Chiamaa | Chimuanya | Chitkala | Chloi |
| Cherielle | Cherysse | Cheyanna *(0.01)* | Chiamaka | China *(0.01)* | Chito | Chloie *(0.02)* |
| Cheriena | Chesa | Cheyanné | Chi-An | Chinaka | Chivia | Chlok |
| Cherif | Chesalon | Cheyanne *(0.19)* | Chian | Chinara | Chiwen | Chlolee |
| Cherika | Chesed | Cheyannia | Chiana | Chinasa | Chiwin | Chlora |
| Cheril | Chesidy | Cheye | Chiane | Chinasaokwu | Chiyana | Chlorissa |
| Cherilyn | Cheska | Cheyeane | Chiangna | Chinasia | Chiyanne | Chloye |
| Cherilynn | Cheslee | Cheyeanna | Chiann | Chinaza | Chiyanné | Choice |
| Cherise *(0.01)* | Chesleigh | Cheyeanne | Chianna | Chinazo | Chiye'anne | Cholé |
| Cherise-Belle | Chesley | Cheyene *(0.01)* | Chianne | Chinazyiá | Chizara | Chole *(0.02)* |
| Cherish *(0.08)* | Chesly | Cheyenee | Chiará | Chinchana | Chizoba | Cholena |
| Cherisha | Cheslyn | Cheyenna *(0.01)* | Chiara *(0.07)* | Chine | Chkyria | Cholie |
| Cherisse | Chesna | Cheyenne | Chiashee | Chineda | Chles | Choloé |
| Cherita | Chesnay | *(0.87)* | Chiasokam | Chinela | Chlo | Chonice |
| Cherith *(0.01)* | Chesnea | Cheyenne Faith | Chiau | Chinella | Chloa | Chonnya |
| Cheriti | Chesnee | Cheyenne Lee | Chibuzo | Chinelo | Chloah | Chontrelle |
| Cherity | Chesnei | Cheyenne O | Chicago | Chineme | Chlöe | Chora |
| Cherkara | Chesney *(0.05)* | Cheyenne | Chidalu | Chinenye | Chlöe *(0.01)* | Choral |
| Cherkeita | Chesni | Samatha | Chidera | Chinera | Chloé *(0.07)* | Chorlotte |
| Cherlande | Chesnie *(0.01)* | Cheyira | Chideraa | Chinesha | Chloe *(4.86)* | Chosen |
| Cherlene | Chesny | Cheyisha | Chidiebere | Chini | Chloe Anna | Chosyn |
| Cherlicia | Chessa *(0.01)* | Cheyla *(0.01)* | Chidimma | Chiniah | Chloe Ashley | Choyce |
| Cherlie | Chessa-Lynn | Cheyleigh | Chido | Chiniya | Chloe Ciera | Cho-Youn |
| Cherline | Chessie | Cheylene | Chidochashe | Chinmayi | Chloe Denise | Chreasia |
| Cherlisa | Chestiny | Cheylyn | Chidra | Chinna | Chloe Gabrielle | Chriche |
| Cherloula | Chestionia | Cheymarie | Chiely | Chinnu | Chloe Jane | Chrijaya |
| Cherly | Chesyca | Cheynay | Chifundo | Chinonye | Chloe Janelle | Chrinasia |
| Cherlyn | Chetana | Cheyne | Chigozie | Chinonyelum | Chloe Mae | Chriniyah |
| Cherlyne | Chetanna | Cheynea | Chigozirim | Chinoye | Chloé Miá | Chris |
| Chermaine | Chetettee | Cheynelle | Chihiro | Chinue | Chloe Taylor | Chris'kianna |
| Chermyia | Cheuk Men | Cheynere | Chih-Yu | Chinwe | Chloe'ann | Chris'sha |
| Cherokee *(0.02)* | Chevalle | Cheynetria | Chika | Chinwendu | Chloe-Alexis | Chris'shia |
| Cheroki | Chevaughn | Cheynne | Chikaora | Chinweotuto | Chloe-Anais | Chris'tiana |
| Cherokie | Chevay | Cheza | Chikhyia | Chinya | Chloe-Ann | Chrisa |
| Cherolee | Chevela | Chezekah | Chikita | Chinyra | Chloe-Anne | Chrisaelle |
| Cheron | Chevell | Chezlee | Chikondi | Chioma *(0.01)* | Chloeaunna | Chrisalia |

| | | | | | | |
|---|---|---|---|---|---|---|
| Chrisalyn | Chrisovalantou | Christell | Christiney | Chrysta | Chylie | Ciamaya |
| Chrisalyne | Chrissa | Christella | Christini | Chrystal (0.01) | Chylinae | Cian |
| Chrisangela | Chrissaunna | Christelle (0.02) | Christinn | Chrystale | Chylynn | Ciana (0.03) |
| Chrisanique | Chrisshona | Christelle- | Christinna | Chrystalyn | Chyme | Cianai |
| Chrisanne | Chrisshylia |   Meghri | Christion | Chrystaza | Chymikiya | Ciandra |
| Chrisasia | Chrisshyra | Christen (0.02) | Christiona | Chrystell | Chyna (0.03) | Cianelliz |
| Chrisaun | Chrissia | Christena | Christione | Chrystelle Gaile | Chyna Del | Ciang |
| Chrisaundra | Chrissie | Christene | Christionn | Chrystene | Chynah | Ciani (0.03) |
| Chrisaunna | Chrissilie | Christene'a | Christis | Chrystianna | Chynajah | Cianie |
| Chriscaria | Chrisstoria | Christeona | Christivi | Chrystina | Chyna-Noel | Cianna (0.06) |
| Chriscianna | Chrissy (0.01) | Christeria | Christi-Yani | Chrystine | Chyncee | Cianne |
| Chriscionna | Christ'shuwna | Christerra | Christiyon | Chryston | Chynece | Ciannee |
| Chrisdan | Christa (0.07) | Christha | Christjaylie | Chuazong | Chynelle | Cianni (0.02) |
| Chrisden | Christabel | Christhana | Christjian | Chuba | Chynesa | Ciannie |
| Chrisee | Christabel- | Christhele | Christlin |   Uzoamaka | Chynna | Cianta |
| Chriselda |   Francisca | Christi (0.01) | Christlynn | Chueka | Chynna-Renaé | Ciante |
| Chrisha | Christabella | Christi'ana | Christofili | Chunpriya | Chynne | Ciany |
| Chrishae | Christabelle | Jaden | Christol | Chunshower | Chynya | Ciará |
| Chrishana | Christacia | Christi'auna | Christony | Chuqing | Chynzie | Ciara (0.77) |
| Chrishanna | Christah | Christia | Christophe | Churié | Chyonia | Ciara Marie |
| Chrishauna | Christain | Christiamah | Christopher | Churmire | Chyonna | Ciara-Anisa |
| Chrishawna | Christajah | Christian (0.04) |   (0.01) | Chuyang | Chyra | Ciarabel |
| Chrishay | Christa-Jane | Christiana | Christorpher | Chy | Chyrell | Ciarah (0.01) |
| Chrishayla | Christal (0.02) |   (0.08) | Christtal Angel | Chy'anne | Chyriae | Ciara-Lee |
| Chrishell | Christ-Al | Christianae | Christy (0.06) | Chy'keira | Chyrish | Ciaralee |
| Chrishelle |   Keishya | Christianana | Christy'anna | Chy'meira | Chysschynn- | Ciaralis |
| Chrishia | Christalea | Christiane | Christyal | Chy'na |   Charl | Ciara-Marie |
| Chrishiya | Christalie |   (0.01) | Christyana | Chy'naae | Chythra | Ciari |
| Chrishonda | Christalina | Christianna | Christyanna | Chyabelle | Chytiera | Ciaria |
| Chrishuna | Christaljade |   (0.02) | Christyanne | Chyala | Ci'ahra | Ciarimar |
| Chrishya | Christalle | Christianne | Christyauna | Chyan | Ci'andrea | Ciarra (0.05) |
| Chrishyah | Christalley | Christiaun | Christyiana | Chyane | Ci'anna | Ciarrah |
| Chrishyra | Christaly | Christiauna | Christyle | Chyani | Ci'auna | Ciarstin |
| Chrisiáh | Christalyn | Christie (0.02) | Christylee | Chyann (0.02) | Ci'aunna | Ciasha |
| Chrisian | Christalynn | Christienne | Christyn (0.01) | Chyanna | Ci'khiayah | Ciasi |
| Chrisiana | Christa-Maria | Christieon | Christyna | Chy-Anne | Ci'mya | Ciasia |
| Chrisitian | Christan | Christil | Christyon | Chyanne (0.04) | Ci'naya | Ciasiab |
| Chrisiyah | Christana | Christin (0.02) | Christyona | Chyanne-Marie | Ci'nethia | Ciayr |
| Chrisiyone | Christanna | Christina (1.04) | Christyonna | Chyara | Ci'nya | Cibo |
| Chrislaine | Christanni | Christina | Chrisy | Chyde | Ci'nyah | Cicada |
| Chrisland | Christany |   Bianca | Chrisyana | Chye | Ci'nyia | Cicari |
| Chrislane | Christar | Christina | Chrisyn | Chyeann | Ci'onnie | Ciceley |
| Chrislin | Christasia |   Elizabeth | Chryjada | Chyenne (0.01) | Ci'oveonie | Cicelia |
| Chrislove | Christavia | Christina Irish | Chrysamei | Chyhanna | Cia | Cicely (0.01) |
| Chrislyan | Christayiah | Christina Joan | Chrysanna | Chykaria | Ciá | Cici |
| Chrislyn (0.01) | Christazia | Christina | Chrysh | Chykieda | Ciaara | Cicilia |
| Chrislynn | Christeah |   Suzanne | Chrysilis | Chyla | Ciadra | Cicily |
| Chrismane | Christeana | Christinaabigail | Chrysla | Chylah | Ciahi | Ciclale |
| Chrismarie | Christee | Christina-Rae | Chrysler | Chylee | Ciahlynn | Ciclali |
| Chrismarleen | Christeena | Christine (0.27) | Chrysoula | Chyleigh | Ciahnna | Ciclaly |
| Chrismene | Christel (0.01) | Christine Jenn | Chryssa | Chyler | Ciaina | Ciclee |
| Chrisnalie | Christela | Christine-Joyce | Chryssoula | Chyli | Cialah | Cidasha |
| Chrisneshia | Christele | Christinemarie | Chrysstal | Chylicia | Cialeigh | Cidilee |

Cidnee
Cidnei
Cidney *(0.01)*
Cidnie
Cidra
Cieara *(0.01)*
Ciearra
Ciearre
Ciel
Ciela
Cielle
Cielo *(0.02)*
Cieloceleste
Ciena *(0.01)*
Cienna *(0.03)*
Ciera *(0.09)*
Cierah
Ciera-Lee
Cierci
Cierr
Cierra *(0.26)*
Cierra Dawn
Cierrah
Cierralyn
Cierrea
Cierria
Ciersten
Cierstin
Ciin
Cikerria
Cilee
Cilena
Cileste
Ciley
Cileyah
Cilia
Cilla
Cilyn
Cimarron
Cimirah
Cimona
Cimone
Cimyiah
Cimyrah
Cinamon
Cinara
Cinaya
Cinayla
Cinceer
Cincelle
Cincere
Cinceria
Cincira

Cincu
Cindel
Cindelle
Cinderella
Cindi *(0.01)*
Cindy *(0.24)*
Cindy Crilly
Cindy-Furaha
Cindy-Trang
Cineva
Cing
Cinia
Ciniah
Ciniya
Ciniyah
Cinna
Cinnamon
*(0.01)*
Cinnia
Cinniyah
Cinobia
Cinquetta
Cinsearé
Cinseride
Cintha
Cinthia *(0.03)*
Cinthya *(0.02)*
Cintia
Cintoria
Cintra
Cintya
Cinyah
Cinyia
Cinyon
Cinyya
Ciomara
Ciona
Cionee
Cioni
Cionna
Cionne
Cionnie
Cipriana
Cira *(0.01)*
Cirar
Ciraya
Circe
Circi
Cire
Ciré
Cireena
Cirely
Cirenity

Ciria
Ciriah
Cirleth Sulay
Cirli
Cirsten
Ciryá
Cisne
Cisse
Cita
Citabria
Cithlally
Cithlaly
Citiera
Citlahli
Citlalhi
Citlalhy
Citlali *(0.04)*
Citlalic
Citlalit
Citlalith
Citlalli *(0.01)*
Citlallit
Citlally
Citlaly *(0.03)*
Cityra
Ciuk
Civanah
Ciya
Ciyanda
Ciyanna
Ciyanni
Ciyara
Ciyera
Ciznné
CJ
Ckloe
Ckristell
Cla'mya
Claiborne
Claida
Clair *(0.01)*
Claira *(0.03)*
Claire *(2.03)*
Claire Nicole
Clairece
Claireese
Claire-Marie
Clairemarie
Clairenthi
Clairese
Clairessa
Clairice
Clairissa

Clairlyn
Clairrisa
Clairyssa
Clalynn
Clamoni
Clamya
Clancy
Clar'ricka
Clara *(0.66)*
Clara Ann
Clara Grace
Clara Jane
Clara Marie
Clara Maude
Clara Rose
Clarabella
Clarabelle
Clara-Eve
Clara-Ève
Clarafaye
Clara-Fee
Clarah
Clara-Lily
Clara-Maude
Claramay
Clara-Michele
Claranique
Clara-Rose
Clare *(0.16)*
Clareece
Claren
Clarencia
Claressa
Clareta
Claretta
Clari
Claribel
Claribella
Claribeth
Clarice *(0.01)*
Claricia
Clarie
Clarimar
Clarinda
Clarinizia
Claris
Clarisa *(0.01)*
Clarise
Clarismar
Clarissa *(0.14)*
Clarisse *(0.01)*
Clarisse-Masoka
Clarissia

Clarita
Claritta
Clarity
Claritza
Clarivel
Clariza
Clarizza
Clark
Clark Sandra
Clarke
Clarrisa
Clarry
Clary
Clary Lucia
Clarymary
Claryssa
Classic
Classie
Clatie
Claubel
Clauchelle
Eunika
Claudaia
Claudaja
Claudee
Claudel
Claudele
Claudelle
Claudette
Claudgena
Claudi Sam
Claudia *(0.31)*
Claudia Ireland
Claudiana
Claudiane
Claudia-Yole
Claudie *(0.01)*
Claudie-Rose
Claudine
Claudio
Claudionna
Claudiyah
Claudy
Claudya
Clausonge
Claxton
Claynisha
Clayra
Clayre
Clayryss
Clayton
Cle'zanae
Clea *(0.01)*

Cle-Ana
Cleanne
Clear
Clearah
Cleausha
Cledeja
Cledis
Cleia
Cleigh
Clella
Clemari
Clemariya
Cleme
Clemence
*(0.02)*
Clementina
Clementine
*(0.02)*
Clements
Clemmesia
Clemmie
Cleny Jessenia
Cleo *(0.02)*
Cleofas
Cleona
Cleondre
Cleone
Cleopatra
Cleophee
Cleora
Cleoria May
Louise
Clera
Clertina
Clesarah
Cleshay
Clevondria
Clhoe
Clhoie
Clif'tizur
Cliffishawan
Cliftanique
Clinesha
Clinique
Cliniyah
Clinnique
Clintashia
Clintia
Clintorya
Clio
Clisedia
Clismary
Clista

Cliyah
Cloa
Clodagh
Clodie *(0.01)*
Clodine
Cloé *(0.01)*
Cloe *(0.13)*
Cloee *(0.01)*
Cloei
Cloerae
Cloey *(0.05)*
Clohee
Clohi
Cloi
Cloia
Cloie *(0.02)*
Clora
Cloriesa
Clorinda
Clorissa
Clotaisa
Clotilde
Cloud
Cloudia
Cloui
Clovella
Clover *(0.02)*
Clovie
Clowey
Clowie
Clowye
Cloye
Cloyie
Cly'tajah
Clydine
Clynthia
C-Mone
Cmoniela
Cniyah
Cnydra
Coachman
Coada
Coalie
Cobi
Cobielea
Coby
Cochesia
Coco *(0.02)*
Cocoa
Cocoanna
Cocoro
Coco-Summe
Coda

| | | | | | | |
|---|---|---|---|---|---|---|
| Codee | Colteria | Contearia | Coraly-Jade | Corey (0.01) | Cornaye | Cortese |
| Codi (0.01) | Colton | Contess | Coralyn | Coreyana | Cornecyia | Cortez |
| Codie | Coltrane | Contessa (0.01) | Coralyne | Coreym | Corneilia | Cortezza |
| Codoleeza | Columba | Cony | Coralynn | Coreyona | Corneise | Cortia |
| Cody | Columbia | Conyia | Coralys | Coreyonna | Corneisha | Cortiria |
| Coe-Coe | Colvin | Conzuelo | Corarose | Coreyunna | Cornelia | Cortlin |
| Coeurvlyne | Coma | Cookie | Corayma | Cori (0.03) | Cornella | Cortlyn |
| Cóeyae | Comaiyah | Cooper (0.02) | Corazzon | Coria | Cornesha | Cortlynn |
| Coffey | Comfort | Copeland | Corban | Coriah | Corniah | Cortnee |
| Cogan | Comoni | Copper | Corbett | Coriahn | Cornielia | Cortney (0.03) |
| Cohen | Comrada | Cor'daja | Corbey | Corian | Cornisha | Cortni |
| Cohreena | Con'najha | Cor'daye | Corbin | Coriana | Corniya | Cortnie |
| Coila | Conasiah | Cor'lysha | Corbinia | Coriandra | Corniyah | Cortny |
| Coizele | Concepcion | Cor'mani | Corbyn | Coriane | Corona | Corvannah |
| Coker | Concetta | Cor'naisha | Corbynn | Corianna | Corra | Cory (0.01) |
| Coknodeya | Conchita | Cor'nayleah | Cordaejah | Coriannah | Correen | Corya |
| Colasia | Concianna | Cor'neisha | Cordaija | Corianne | Corren | Coryahn |
| Colbey | Condesa | Cor'neliyah | Cordaishá | Coriawna | Correy | Coryauna |
| Colbi | Condoleezza | Cor'niya | Cordaiza | Corie (0.01) | Corri | Coryeanna |
| Colbie | Condy | Cor'tanay | Cordajah | Corie-Ann | Corrianna | Coryelle |
| Colby (0.02) | Coniah | Cor'teja | Cordasia | Coriel | Corrie (0.01) | Coryn (0.01) |
| Coldia | Conlee | Cora (0.30) | Corday | Corien | Corrienn | Coryne |
| Cole | Conleigh | Cora Linn | Cordayja | Coriena | Corrieonda | Corynn (0.01) |
| Coleen | Conley | Cora Mae | Cordayshia | Cori-Lynn | Corrieonna | Corynne |
| Coleeta | Connar | Cora-Ann | Cordeasha | Corimichelle | Corrigan | Cosby |
| Colesha | Connell | Corabella | Cordee | Corin (0.01) | Corrin (0.01) | Cosette (0.02) |
| Colette (0.04) | Connelly | Corabelle | Cordélia | Corina (0.03) | Corrina (0.03) | Coshiela |
| Coley | Conner (0.01) | Corae | Cordelia (0.06) | Corine (0.01) | Corrine (0.03) | Cosie |
| Colia | Connie (0.02) | Coraellen | Cordelia Jad | Corinn | Corrinna | Cosima |
| Coliana | Connie-Jean | Cora-Emily | Cordell | Corinna (0.01) | Corrinne | Cossette |
| Colin | Conniya | Corah | Cordella | Corinne (0.15) | Corrissa | Costa |
| Coline | Connleigh | Corahleigh | Cordellia | Corinthia | Corriyah | Costalee |
| Colisa | Connor (0.01) | Coraima | Cordesha | Corinthian | Corruna | Costanza |
| Colista | Conny | Corajayne | Cordey'ja | Corissa (0.01) | Corryn (0.01) | Coti |
| Colita | Connye | Corajean | Cordia | Corjh'a | Corryne | Cotia |
| Colleen (0.14) | Conquisha | Coral (0.06) | Cordie | Corlaiyah | Corshaé | Cottia |
| Colleena | Consepcion | Coralani | Cordillia | Corlancyia | Corshell | Coumba |
| Collejah | Conshara | Cora-Lee | Cordney | Corlea | Corshey | Countess |
| Collett | Consquslia | Coralee | Cordoves | Corleasha | Corsondra | Couper |
| Colletta | Constadina | Corali | Corea | Corlecia | Corta'ja | Courali |
| Collette | Constance | Coralia | Coreal | Corleen | Cortaeja | Courie |
| Colli | (0.07) | Coralie (0.21) | Corean | Corlene | Cor-Tajea | Courielle |
| Collianna | Constancia | Coralie-Farah | Coreen | Corley | Cortana | Cournazhia |
| Collier | Constantina | Coralie-Maya | Coreena | Corli | Cortarra | Cournecya |
| Colline | Constantine | Coralie-Rose | Coreleah | Corlie | Cortasha | Courniya |
| Collissa | Constanza | Coraline | Corelianne | Corlyn | Cortasia | Courson |
| Collyn | (0.01) | Coraline | Corelie | Corlynn | Cortasja | Courtasia |
| Colomba | Constanza- | Mikuen | Corellie | Cormaija | Cortavia | Courtaysia |
| Colombe | Isabel | Coralis | Coren | Cormariah | Cortaysha | Courtenay |
| Colonia | Constynae | Corally | Corena | Cormariee | Cortaysia | Courtenee |
| Colours | Consueala | Coraly (0.01) | Corenna | Cormesha | Cortazia | Courteney |
| Colson | Consuela | Coralyane | Coreshia | Cormiya | Corteazia | Courteny |
| Colsyn | Consuelo (0.01) | Coralye | Coretta | Cornasia | Corterius | Courtett |

| | | | | | | |
|---|---|---|---|---|---|---|
| Courtland | Creshyiah | Cristan | Crystaja | Curnik | Cydnee *(0.01)* | Cynaa |
| Courtley | Cressen | Cristana | Crystal *(0.80)* | Curran | Cydnei | Cynaea |
| Courtlin | Cressida | Cristany | Crystal-Brianna | Currisa | Cydney *(0.04)* | Cynai |
| Courtlyn *(0.01)* | Cressie | Cristel | Crystalie | Curry | Cydni | Cynara |
| Courtlynn | Creyanna | Cristelle | Crystaline | Cursten | Cyeirra | Cynaria |
| Courtnay | Cricia | Cristen *(0.01)* | Crystall | Curstin | Cyeisha | Cyncere |
| Leeshann | Cricket | Cristhal | Crystallynn | Curtajia | Cyelisha | Cyndal |
| Courtnee | Crickett | Cristi | Crystal- | Curtavia | Cyen | Cyndara |
| Courtney *(0.92)* | Criestin | Cristian *(0.01)* | Minhnguyet | Curtesea | Cyenna | Cynde |
| Courtney | Crimson *(0.01)* | Cristiana *(0.01)* | Crystalyn | Curtira | Cyenne | Cyndee |
| Elizabeth | Crinesha | Cristiane | Crystalynn | Curtisha | Cyera | Cyndeja |
| Courtney | Criosa | Cristiané | Crystan | Curtlin-Marie | Cyeria | Cyndel |
| Gavriela | Cris'tion | Cristianna | Crystel | Curtsten | Cyerra | Cyndi |
| Courtney-Rose | Crisalis | Cristiauna | Crystelle | Cusha | Cyhelle | Cyndia |
| Courtni | Cris-Anna | Cristie | Crysten | Cushele | Cyiera | Cyndy |
| Courtnie | Crisanne | Cristin *(0.01)* | Crysti | Cuteera | Cyierah | Cynea |
| Courtny | Crisbel | Cristina *(0.16)* | Crystian | Cuyler | Cyila | Cynedra |
| Couryanna | Criscia | Cristina | Crystianna | Cy | Cyisha | Cyneyia |
| Cova | Crisdion | Jacqueline | Crystina | Cy'amani | Cyla | Cyni |
| Covington | Criseah | Cristina-Isabel | Crystine | Cy'anna | Cylah | Cyní |
| Covonn | Crisell | Cristina-Maria | Crystionna | Cy'ashia | Cylea | Cynia |
| Cownga | Crisella | Cristinamaria | Crystle | Cy'briyonnia | Cylee *(0.01)* | Cyniah *(0.01)* |
| Cowther | Criselli | Cristine | Crystlyn | Cy'corra | Cyleena | Cyniece |
| Coyleasha | Crishay | Cristionna | Crystyle | Cy'enna | Cyleerae | Cynijah |
| Coynesha | Crishonda | Cristiya | Crystyna | Cy'kiria | Cyleigh | Cynjae |
| Cozette | Crishya-Liz | Cristlin Janellea | Csenia | Cy'kiyah | Cylena | Cynnae |
| Cozinaé | Crishyra | Cristy | Csilla | Cy'kyia | Cylene | Cynnarra |
| Cra'lyreia | Crisi | Cristyn | Cu'koyia | Cy'terria | Cylese | Cynncere |
| Crace | Crisia | Cristyna | Cu'mariea | Cy'yonna | Cylia | Cynnia |
| Craig | Crisily | Crisyaris | Cu'maya | Cyaira | Cyliane | Cynteria |
| Craigen | Crisinda | Criszel | Cu'niyah | Cyan *(0.01)* | Cylie *(0.01)* | Cynteriah |
| Crainiyah | Crisiya | Criz'stal | Cue | Cyana | Cylie-Ann | Cynterria |
| Crea | Crisleny | Crockett | Cui Bing | Cyane | Cylin | Cynthair |
| Creadince | Crisleydi | Cronin | Cuiaira | Cyanea | Cyllan | Cyntheria |
| Creanna | Crisly | Crucita | Cuiying | Cyani | Cylle | Cynthia *(0.40)* |
| Creaze | Crislyn | Crump | Culeeya | Cyann | Cyllia | Cynthia Ann |
| Crecence | Crislynn | Crus | Culissia | Cyanna *(0.01)* | Cylyce | Cynthialee |
| Crechka | Crismairy | Crusita | Culture | Cyanne | Cymantha | Cyntiah |
| Cree *(0.01)* | Crisna | Cruz | Culver | Cyanni | Cymara | Cynyia |
| Creeann | Crissa | Cruzita | Cumandá | Cyara | Cymaria | Cynyonna |
| Creeanna | Crisslyn | Crymson | Cummingham | Cyarah | Cymbeline | Cyomara |
| Creed | Crissmis | Crysandra | Cur Sharae | Cyarra | Cymbre | Cyonia |
| Creedance | Crissy | Crysanna | Cur'leah | Cyauni | Cymbrie | Cyonie |
| Creedence | Crist | Crysany | Cur'myria | Cyaurh | Cymera | Cypress |
| Creek | Crist'yana | Crysbet | Cur'shay | Cybel | Cymetria | Cypriane |
| Cree-Lee | Crista *(0.01)* | Cryselle | Cur'taja | Cybelle | Cymiah | Cyra *(0.01)* |
| Creighton | Cristabel | Crysha | Cur'tasia | Cybil | Cymone | Cyrafina |
| Crelia | Cristabella | Cryshana | Cura | Cyble | Cymonne | Cyrah |
| Creosha | Cristal *(0.09)* | Cryshelle | Curajis | Cybrina | Cymorah | Cyrai |
| Crescencia | Cristalia | Cryshonna | Curbee | Cycilia | Cymoria | Cyre |
| Crescentia | Cristaliz | Cryssa | Curiah | Cyd | Cymric | Cyreena |
| Cresha | Cristal-Maria | Crysta *(0.01)* | Curiya | Cydia | Cyn'cear | Cyren |
| Creshona | Cristalyn | Crystaisha | Curmaya | Cydne | Cyn'terria | Cyrena |

| | | | | | | |
|---|---|---|---|---|---|---|
| Cyrene | D'ajana | D'azia | D'naja | D'yani | Da'jonet | Da'miria |
| Cyreniti | D'ajanae | D'azja | D'najah | D'yanna | Da'ju | Da'mirica |
| Cyrenity | D'alastone | D'charvyana | D'najia | D'yaun | Da'juhonna | Da'miya |
| Cyreonna | D'alayzia | D'earah | D'nalya | D'yavion | Da'kara | Da'miyah |
| Cyria | D'alexandra | D'earra | D'naria | D'yiara | Da'kari | Da'miyana |
| Cyriah | D'aliyah | D'eira | D'nasia | D'ymon | Da'kariya | Da'moni |
| Cyriana | D'amanti | D'ejanera | D'nay | D'ymonasia | Da'kayla | Da'monyea |
| Cyrien | D'amaris | D'elosha | D'nayjah | D'ymond | Da'kera | Da'morriah |
| Cyrii | D'ana | D'emoni | D'nayre | D'yniah | Da'kerria | Da'moya |
| Cyrilla | D'anasia | D'era | D'nayzha | D'zaria | Da'kesha | Da'mya (0.01) |
| Cyrina | D'andra | D'erica | D'nazhay | D'zire | Da'keya | Da'myah |
| Cyrine | D'andrea | D'erricka | D'nazia | D'ziyah | Da'kezionna | Da'myia |
| Cyrine Narjes | D'andria | D'errika | D'nejah | D'zyah | Da'kijah | Da'myla |
| Cyrinna | D'angel | D'eryka | D'neyah | D'zyire | Da'kirah | Da'nae |
| Cyrinthia | D'angela | D'essence | D'neyjah | Da | Da'kiyah | Da'naejah |
| Cyrs' Derria | D'angelee | D'ette | D'nia | Da J La | Da'kota | Da'naesia |
| Cyrstin | D'angeline | D'eziya | D'nijae | Da Kyja | Da'kyia | Da'naeya |
| Cyteriell | D'ani | D'hani | D'nijah | Da Min | Da'kyla | Da'nahjah |
| Cythlaly | D'ania | D'ionaya | D'niya | Da Nea | Da'kyliah | Da'naijah |
| Cytlali | D'aniah | D'itti | D'niyah | Da Shanna | Da'la | Da'naisha |
| Cytnhia | D'aniya | D'jai | D'nya | Da Shanti | Da'laney | Da'naja |
| Cyvi-Lauren | D'ann | D'janaeh | D'nyah | Da'ahna | Da'lani | Da'najah |
| Czahraa | D'anna (0.01) | D'jarra | D'nyia | Da'aja | Da'lasha | Da'najia |
| Czaria | D'annamarie | D'jhene | D'nysia | Da'asia | Da'lasia | Da'nalya |
| Czarina | D'ara | D'jonai | D'ondra | Da'bri | Da'layisha | Da'naria |
| Czarina | D'arah | D'juana | D'onnee | Da'cariya | Da'layna | Da'nasha |
|   Norbezita | D'archeena | D'kaila | D'onvion | Da'chyna | Da'laysia | Da'nasia |
| Czenzi | D'ari | D'kaiya | D'oralee | Da'coreyia | Da'layzia | Da'nasiah |
| | D'aria | D'kayda | D'ovion | Da'corya | Da'leah | Da'nata |
| | D'ariea | D'kayla | D'ozjanae | Da'coyia | Da'lia | Da'nay |
| | D'ariel | D'kendalyn | D'pree | Da'daisha | Da'liliah | Da'naya |
| **~ D ~** | D'arin | D'kyra | D'reginique | Da'ijah | Da'lisha | Da'nayah |
| D | D'arnaesia | D'laneigh | D'seanna | Da'ja | Da'liyah | Da'nayja |
| D Ajah | D'arrian | D'laney | D'sha | Da'jada | Da'lon'a | Da'nayla |
| D Amare | D'aryl | D'laysia | D'shaelyn | Da'jae | Da'mahnii | Da'naysha |
| D Ana | D'ashanea | D'liyah | D'shani | Da'jah | Da'maiya | Da'naysia |
| D Asia | D'ashia | D'lyla | D'shanti | Da'jahnae | Da'mani | Da'neah |
| D Avionne | D'asia (0.02) | D'mahni | D'shaunna | Da'jahnai | Da'mara | Da'nee |
| D Aysia | D'asianna | D'maia | D'shaunti | Da'jajuan | Da'mari | Da'neisha |
| D Azya | D'asiya | D'maiya | D'shawnee | Da'janae | Da'maria | Da'nely |
| D Nayah | D'asya | D'marayana | D'shermya | Da'janaye | Da'mariana | Da'nesha |
| D Viyne | D'aubrey | D'mauria | D'shila | Da'jane | Da'mariyah | Da'neva |
| D Zhanae | D'aundria | D'maya | D'shiyah | Da'janee | Da'marriyah | Da'neyah |
| D' | D'aunsty | D'mayah | D'shuna | Da'janique | Da'maya | Da'nezia |
| D' Anna | D'ausia | D'mayia | D'siree | Da'jaunae | Da'meaka | Da'nia |
| D'ahazanae | D'aviana | D'miaya | D'talia | Da'jeana | Da'mecia | Da'niah |
| D'ahvion | D'ayala | D'miyah | D'tavia | Da'jhanae | Da'mia | Da'nicia |
| D'aijah | D'aydra | D'miyreonna | D'tonya | Da'jhane | Da'mia Lou | Da'nijah |
| D'aijha | D'aynn Jynn | D'monae | D'vaya | Da'jhanique | Da'miah | Da'nijha |
| D'airah | D'ayoshia | D'mya (0.01) | D'vianna | Da'jionna | Da'mijah | Da'nita |
| D'aisha | D'aysa | D'nae | D'vine | Da'jiya | Da'mion | Da'nivea |
| D'aja | D'ayzha | D'nai | D'vinity | Da'johna | Da'mira | Da'niya (0.01) |
| D'ajah | D'azhai | D'naisha | D'vorah | Da'jonea | Da'miracle | Da'niyah (0.01) |

| | | | | | | |
|---|---|---|---|---|---|---|
| Da'niyia | Da'yahna | Dacotah | Daemani | Dahecha | Daiah | Daimyne |
| Da'nya | Da'yana | Dacoto | Daena | Dahens | Daian | Daina *(0.01)* |
| Da'nyah | Da'yani | Dacyrah | Daenerys | Dahesha | Daiana | Dainah |
| Da'onna | Da'yanna | Dade | Daennah | Dahiana | Daianara | Daine |
| Da'osha | Da'zaeonna | Daderianna | Daeonie | Dahika | Daiandra | Dainelis |
| Da'querria | Da'zaria | Dadiola | Daeonna | Dahila | Daianna | Dainery |
| Da'quoya | Da'zarreya | Dadlishaa | Daeonnah | Dahirah | Daiannah | Dainijah |
| Da'riah | Da'zayah | Dadne | Daesha *(0.01)* | Dahisha | Daiany | Daintry |
| Da'riahana | Da'zhanae | Dadreanna | Daeshanea | Dahissa | Daica | Daiona |
| Da'riana | Da'zhia | Dadreon | Daeshanel | Dahja | Daicy | Daionna |
| Da'ryiah | Da'zhon | Dae J Anai | Daesharia | Dahjae | Daidreyonna | Dair |
| Da'sani | Da'zia | Dae Janae | Daeshauna | Dahkeya | Daidriana | Daira *(0.01)* |
| Da'sha | Da'zire | Dae'briel | Daeshawn | Dahlak | Daigyania | Dairam |
| Da'shanique | Da'zygheona | Dae'ja | Daeshawna | Dahlen | Daija *(0.03)* | Daire |
| Da'shanna | Da'zyre | Dae'janae | Daeshawnae | Dahlia *(0.07)* | Daijah *(0.02)* | Daireanna |
| Da'shantay | Daaimah | Dae'janielle | Daeshonna | Dahlia-Sarah | Daijah' | Dairelis |
| Da'shanti | Daaisha | Dae'lashae | Daesia | Dahlila | Daijahnna | Dairely |
| Da'shaquenise | Daaliyah | Dae'onii | Daessha | Dahlilah | Daijai | Dairianys |
| Da'sharail | Daana | Dae'preea | Daeton | Dahlya | Daija-Lyn | Dairielle |
| Da'shari | Daania | Dae'shalae | Daevanie | Dahlylah | Daijana | Dairin |
| Da'sharia | Daanya | Dae'viona | Daevena | Dahna | Daijha | Dairish Leeah |
| Da'shaunti | Daasia | Daea | Daevinee | Dahna'sia | Daijhe | Dairiz |
| Da'shawna | Dabiana | Daeanne | Daevis | Dahnae | Daiji | Dairyn |
| Da'shawndra | Dabney | Daecin | Dae-Yanna | Dahnelah | Daijiona | Dairza |
| Da'shaylyn | Dabney-Grace | Daedrian | Daeyona | Dahnesa | Daijreana | Dais'aiya |
| Nayana | Dabo | Daedrianna | Daeyouna | Dahnija | Daila | Daisa |
| Da'shayyah | Daborah | Daegan | Daezanee | Dahnyah | Dailamarie | Daisee |
| Da'sheana | Dabria | Daeja *(0.01)* | Dafany | Dahomy | Dailana | Daisey |
| Da'sheona | Dabrielis | Daejah | Dafarie | Dahrea | Dailani | Daishá |
| Da'shia | Dacara | Daejahnaye | Daffani | Dahsha | Dailee | Daisha *(0.04)* |
| Da'shi-Niera | Dacarion | Daejahni | Daffney | Dahsom | Daileen | Daishah |
| Da'shya | Dacarley | Daejas | Dafina | Dahsyar | Dailen | Daishaleez |
| Da'shyliah | Dace | Daejea | Dafna | Dahvion | Dailene | Daishalie |
| Da'siona | Dacee | Daejha | Dafne *(0.01)* | Dahyra | Daileny | Daishamar |
| Da'siyah | Dacey | Daejia | Dafne Giovanna | Dahyshana | Dailey | Daishana |
| Da'tionna | Dachaun | Daejsha | Dafnee | Dai | Dailiann | Daishanee |
| Da'trell | Dacheca | Daekira | Dafney | Dai Auna | Dailin | Daishauna |
| Da'trice | Dachelie | Daelan | Dafni | Dai'ja | Dailis | Daishaunaé |
| Da'vajah | Dachelle | Daelee | Dafnie | Dai'jah | Dailisha | Daishaundria |
| Da'varriea | Dachely | Daelen | Dafny | Dai'jana | Dailoni | Daishawnna |
| Da'via | Dachia | Daelene | Dagan | Dai'jha | Daily | Daisheonia |
| Da'viana | Dachyea | Daeli | Dagen | Dai'jona | Dailyn *(0.01)* | Daisheyoncia |
| Da'vianna | Daci | Daelin | Dagmawit | Dai'juana | Dailynn | Daishia |
| Da'viere | Dacia *(0.01)* | Daelisse | Dagne | Dai'kira | Daimarion | Daisi |
| Da'vieyona | Daciana | Daelle | Dagnna | Dai'mariana | Daime | Daisia |
| Da'vina | Dacianelle | Daelonni | Dagny *(0.01)* | Dai'monika | Daimein | Daisiana |
| Da'vine | Dacie | Daely | Dagrea | Dai'sha | Daimely | Daisie |
| Da'vion | Dackota | Daelycia | Dah'jea | Dai'sheyunna | Daimelys | Daisimay |
| Da'vionna | Dacne | Daelyn *(0.01)* | Dah'nija | Dai'yahna | Daimeona | Daisja |
| Da'visha | Dacoda | Daelyne | Dahab | Dai'yonna | Daimiani | Daisjah |
| Da'viya | Dacole | Daélynn | Dahabo | Dai'zasky | Daimond | Daismary |
| Da'vonn | Dacoria | Daelynn *(0.01)* | Dahae | Dai'zhauna | Daimya | Daissy |
| Da'vonna | Dacota | Daelynne | Daha-Lee | Daia | Daimyn | Daisy *(1.12)* |

| | | | | | | |
|---|---|---|---|---|---|---|
| Daisy Julliana | Dajari | Daksha | Dale'sya | Dalissa | Damaneisha | Damiah |
| Daisy Mae | Dajaria | Dakshayani | Dalea | Dalita | Damaneshia | Damiaha |
| Daisy May | Dajas'von | Dakya | Daleccia | Daliya | Damani *(0.01)* | Damiana *(0.01)* |
| Daisy Michelle | Daje | Dakyia | Daleela | Daliyah *(0.01)* | Damanique | Damiani |
| Daisy Vanessa | Dajenae | Dakyiah | Daleen | Daliza | Damanjot | Damianna |
| Daisya | Dajeona | Dakyla | Dalei | Dalizabeth | Damanpreet | Damiaya |
| Daisy-Ann | Dajhaniya | Dal'ya | Daleiah | Dallalee | Damara *(0.01)* | Damicka |
| Daisyray | Dajia | Dala | Daleisha | Dallana | Damarea | Damiecia |
| Daisziana | Dajia'nique | Dalaceia | Dalejah | Dallanara | Damareia | Damieniesha |
| Daiton | Dajiah | Dalai | Dalelena | Dallani | Damares | Damieona |
| Daiya | Dajiana | Dalai'jah | Dalemyne | Dallas *(0.06)* | Damareya | Damiera |
| Daiyaana | Dajianne | Dalaiah | Dalen | Dallas-Anna | Damari *(0.01)* | Damierah |
| Daiyana | Dajin | Dalaila | Dalena | Dallee | Damaria *(0.01)* | Damilie |
| Daiyon | Dajionae | Dalailah | Dalendria | Dalleh | Damariah | Damilola |
| Daiyonna | Dajionaé | Dalaina | Dalene | Dallen | Damariana | Damina |
| Daiysa | Dajionshae | Dalainey | Dalesha | Dallia | Damarie | Daminica |
| Daizah | Dajohna | Dalainy | Daleth | Dallie | Damarieonna | Damion |
| Daizee | Dajon | Dalaisha | Daletrayza | Dallis *(0.01)* | Damariona | Damique |
| Daizelle | Dajona | Dalaizah | Dalexa | Dally | Damarionna | Damira |
| Daizha *(0.01)* | Dajonna | Dalal | Daley | Dallyn | Damaris *(0.09)* | Damirah |
| Daizhana | Dajonnah | Dalan | Daleya | Dallys | Damariss | Damire |
| Daizhanae | Dajouria | Dalana | Daleyney | Dalma | Damariya | Damireana |
| Daizhanai | Dajsha | Dalancey | Dalhia | Dalnesha | Damariz | Damirrah |
| Daizi | Dakaejah | Dalanda | Dali | Dalona | Damarrion | Damirre |
| Daiziana | Dakaicia | Dalandeep | Dalia *(0.08)* | Dalonda | Damary | Damisela |
| Daizie | Dakaila | Dalandis | Dalia Mae | Dalorecy | Damarys | Damita |
| Daizjah | Dakailyn | Dalanee | Daliah *(0.01)* | Dalshea | Damasha | Damiya *(0.01)* |
| Daizlynn | Dakalluh | Dalaney *(0.01)* | Daliala | Dalsy | Damaya *(0.01)* | Damiyae |
| Daizuki | Dakara | Dalani | Daliana | Dalton | Damayah | Damiyah *(0.01)* |
| Daizy *(0.01)* | Dakarai | Dalanie *(0.01)* | Daliane | Daltonee | Damayanti | Damiyana |
| Daizya | Dakari | Dalanna | Dalianie | Daltyn | Damayi | Damonae |
| Daja *(0.01)* | Dakaria | Dalannie | Dalianis | Dalunee | Damayia | Damone |
| Daja'nique | Dakarri | Dalansea | Dalianna | Daly | Damea | Damonee |
| Daja'onna | Dakaya | Dalasha | Dalianne | Dalya *(0.01)* | Dameani | Damoni |
| Da-Jah | Dakayla *(0.01)* | Dalasia | Dalianny | Dalyah | Dameara | Damonica |
| Dajah *(0.02)* | Dakaylah | Dalastone | Dalice | Dalyana | Dameashea | Damonie |
| Dajaha | Dakayta | Dalatrice | Dalicha | Dalyane | Damecka | Damonique |
| Dajahna | Dakeira | Dalay'jay | Dalicia | Dalyann | Dameicia | Damor |
| Dajahnae | Dakerria | Dalaya | Dalie | Dalyce | Dameika | Damoria |
| Dajah-Nay | Dakevia | Dalaygana | Daliela | Dalyd | Dameisha | Damoya |
| Dajahnique | Dakia | Dalayia | Dalienis | Dalyla | Dameisy | Damy'jah |
| Dajaleya | Dakiah | Dalayla | Dalijah | Dalylha | Dameona | Damya *(0.02)* |
| Dajalyse | Dakiera | Dalayna *(0.01)* | Dalila *(0.03)* | Dalymar | Damera | Damyah |
| Dajana | Dakiya | Dalayne | Dalilah *(0.01)* | Dalyn | Dameria | Damyai |
| Dajanae *(0.01)* | Dakiyah | Dalaynee | Dalili | Dalynise | Damerious | Damyala |
| Dajanara | Daknyca | Dalayni | Dalin | Dalynn | Dameriya | Damyanna |
| Dajanee | Dakoda *(0.01)* | Dalaynie | Dalina | Dalynne | Dameriyah | Da-Myia |
| Dajaneek | Dakohta | Dalaysha | Dalinda | Dalys | Damerriah | Damyia |
| Dajaneque | Dakota *(0.59)* | Dalayshia | Daline | Dalysha | Damesha | Damyiah |
| Dajanik | Dakotah *(0.02)* | Dalaysia | Dalisa | Damaiah | Dametria | Damyla |
| Dajaniqu | Dakotah Jo | Dalayza | Dalise | Damaiya | Dami | Damyra |
| Dajanique | Dakota-Marie | Dalaziah | Dalisha | Damaly | Dami'a | Dan |
| Dajaree | Dakotis | Dale | Dalisia | Daman | Damia *(0.01)* | Dan'eis |

| | | | | | | |
|---|---|---|---|---|---|---|
| Dan'kyrah | Danalin | Daneica | Daniaya | Danijah | Dannaija | Danyaris |
| Dan'najash | Danalli | Daneijah | Danica (0.23) | Dani-Jean | Dannaka | Danyca |
| Dan'yelle | Danaly | Daneijia | Danica | Danijha | Dannalee | Danycka |
| Dana (0.26) | Danalyce | Daneil | Gabriellel | Danijiah | Dannalynn | Danyeal |
| Dana Isabel | Dana-Nhatanh | Daneille | Danica Joy | Danik | Dannan | Danyeall |
| Dana Siclaly | Danara | Daneisha | Danica Mikayla | Danika (0.17) | Dannay | Danyeila |
| Dana'ja | Danarah | Daneishka | Danicah | Danika-Lee | Danneka | Danyel (0.01) |
| Dana'jha | Danaria | Daneisi | Danicha | Danikha | Dannelle | Danyela |
| Dana'sha | Danarielle | Danejah | Danicia | Danikka | Dannely | Danyele |
| Danaca | Danasha | Daneli | Danicka | Danilea | Dannetta | Danyeli |
| Danaé | Danashia | Danelia | Danida | Danilee | Dannette | Danyeliz |
| Danae (0.07) | Danasia (0.03) | Danelis | Danie | Danille | Dannezzia | Danyell |
| Danae" | Danataly | Danell | Danie Stephanie | Danilo | Danni (0.01) | Danyella |
| Danaea | Danaviea | Danella | Daniece | Danilya | Dannia | Danyelle (0.02) |
| Danaee | Danay | Danelle (0.01) | Danieckqua | Danimar | Dannica (0.01) | Danyellys |
| Danaeh | Danay'sha | Danelli | Danie-Eve | Daniqa | Dannie | Dany-Eve |
| Danaeja | Danaya (0.01) | Danelly | Danieja | Da-Nique | Danniegirl | Danyia |
| Danaejah | Danayah | Danely | Daniel (0.01) | Danira | Dannie-Jo | Danyiala |
| Dànaëjah | Danayara | Danelys | Daniela (1.33) | Danirah | Danniella | Danyja |
| Danaelle | Danaye | Danemaima | Daniela Aurora | Danis | Dannielle (0.01) | Danyjah |
| Danaerika | Danayha | Danera | Daniela Idalina | Danisa | Dannielly | Danyka (0.01) |
| Danaeshia | Danayiah | Danery | Daniela Maria | Danisah | Dannika (0.01) | Danykah |
| Dana-Eve | Danayja | Danerys | Daniela Nicole | Danise | Dannisha | Danyka-Taylor |
| Danaeya | Danayjah | Danesa | Daniela Zaira | Danisha (0.01) | Danniya | Dany-Kim |
| Danah (0.01) | Danayjha | Danesha | Daniela-Itzel | Danisher | Dannon | Danyla |
| Danah Janine | Danayla | Danesha-Marie | Danielar | Danishia | Danny | Danyliah |
| Danahai | Danaylia | Daneshia | Daniele | Danisley | Dannyela | Dany-Liane |
| Danahe | Danaysha | Danesia | Danielia | Danissa | Dannyelle | Danyna |
| Danahi | Danayshia | Danessa (0.01) | Danielice | Danisse | Dannyn | Danysha |
| Danai | Danaysia | Danessia | Daniell | Danissha | Dannysha | Danyshia |
| Danaiah | Danaysiah | Danesya | Daniella (0.30) | Danissia | Danory | Danyssa |
| Danaija | Danazah | Danesys | Daniella Barbar | Danita | Danouchee | Danzey |
| Danaijah | Danazhia | Daneth | Daniellah | Danitha | Dansia | Dao |
| Danaijha | Danazja | Danett | Danielle (1.42) | Danitra | Dantaja | Daola |
| Danaique | Danazjah | Danette | Danielle | Danitrias | Dantavia | Daomely |
| Danaisa | Dance | Daneya | Antonett | Danitsa | Dante | Daonna |
| Danaisha | Dancy | Daneyli | Danielle Dung | Danity | Danterricka | Daovong |
| Danaisia | Dandrea | Daneysa | Danielle Helen | Danitza | Danthy | Daoyun |
| Danaisy | Dandreka | Daneyshailene | Danielle Maricia | Daniya (0.02) | Dantreana | Dapanga |
| Danait | Dandria | Daneysi | Daniellee | Daniyah (0.02) | Dantrianna | Daphanee |
| Danaiya | Dane | Danez | Danielli | Daniyan | Dantrielle | Dapheca |
| Danaiye | Dane'ah | Daneza | Danielly | Daniyerria | Danunca | Daphene |
| Danaizá | Dane'-Jia | Dangeli | Daniellynn | Danizya | Danusia | Daphenie |
| Danaj'a | Danea | Danh | Daniellys | Danjanaé | Danwa | Dapheria |
| Danaja | Daneá | Danhaee | Daniels | Danjela Jo | Dany | Daphine |
| Danajah | Daneali | Dani (0.03) | Daniely | Danlee | Dany'a | Daphiney |
| Danajai | Danecia | Dania (0.10) | Danielys | Danleigh | Danya (0.03) | Daphna |
| Danajha | Danee | Daniah | Danieria | D-Anna | Danyae | Daphné |
| Danajiah | Daneea | Dania-Kim | Daniese | Danna (0.10) | Danyael | Daphne (0.20) |
| Danajshia | Daneelia | Daniale | Daniesha | Danna Paola | Danyah | Daphne Alexia |
| Danaka | Daneen | Danialiss | Danieshia | Dannae | Danyaja | Daphne Paulina |
| Danalee | Daneenya | Danialys | Danieyia | Dannaë | Danyale | Daphne-Alyson |
| Danali | Daneetria | Daniane | Danija | Dannah | Danyanara | Daphnée |

| | | | | | | |
|---|---|---|---|---|---|---|
| Daphnee (0.13) | Darcell | Darilin | Darnaja | Darriqa | Dasany | Dasia (0.05) |
| Daphnee-Alexandra | Darcelle | Darilyn | Darnasia | Darris | Dasaundria | Dasiah |
| Daphnee-Tiffany | Darcey | Darin | Darnayah | Darrith | Dash | Dasian |
| Daphney (0.01) | Darchanell | Darina | Darne'ja | Darriya | Dashá | Dasianette |
| Daphni | Darci (0.01) | Darinah | Darneisha | Darriyah | Dasha (0.03) | Dasinia |
| Daphnie (0.01) | Darcia | Darine | Darnela | Darriyn | Dasha'nae | Dasiy |
| Daphnie-Rose | Darcie | Darinel | Darneliz | Darry'lle | Dashae | Dasiya |
| Daphnny | Darcy (0.03) | Darines | Darnell | Darryell | Dashaé | Dasja |
| Daprincia | Darden | Darinesha | Darnella | Darryen | Dashaeyla | Dasjah |
| Daquana | Darea | Darinie | Darnelle | Darryett | Dashah | Dasmien |
| Daquandae | Dareana | Darinise | Darnencha | Darryl | Dashaia | Dassine |
| Daquarriah | Dareea | Darion | Darnesha | Darryll-Anne | Dashaira | Dastan |
| Daquasha | Dareein | Dariona | Darneshia | Darrylneik | Dashaiya | Dastany |
| Daquilla | Dareen | Darione | Darnisha | Darryn | Dashala | Dasteni |
| Daquinna | Dareenka | Darionna | Darnisia | Darsea | Dashanae | Dasyani |
| Daquisha | Dareese | Daris | Darnjahnae | Darsey | Dashanai | Datanael |
| Dar'narius | Darehini | Darissa | Daronika | Darshana | Dashandra | Datavia |
| Dar'nasja | Dareisy | Darithe | Darplin | Darshawn | Dashanique | Datera |
| Dar'neisha | Dareka | Daritsa | Darquasia | Darshawna | Dashanna | Datia |
| Dar'neria | Dareli | Darius | Darquella | Darshell | Dashanti | Datielle |
| Dar'niyah | Darelis | Dariusha | Darra | Darshini | Dashara | Dationa |
| Dar'nyla | Darelys | Dariya | Darra'leigh | Darsie | Dashari | Datjtona |
| Dar'reyle | Darena | Dariyah | Darra-Ann | Darsilynn | Dasharra | Datne |
| Dar'sha | Dareonna | Dariyan | Darrah (0.01) | Darsy | Dasharyaei | Daton |
| Dara (0.03) | Dareth | Dariyana | Darraiel | Darvani | Dashauna | Datori |
| Daraeno | Darh'ia | Dariyanna | Darreale | Darvinae | Dashawn | Datrice |
| Darah (0.01) | Daria (0.06) | Dariyona | Darreca | Darviona | Dashawna | Datricia |
| Daraheinka | Dariah | Dariyonna | Darrelis | Darvy | Dashawne | Datsha-Itayetsi |
| Daraiel | Darializ | Darja | Darrelle | Darwens | Dashawnna | Daubrey |
| Daraijah | Daria-Maria | Darla (0.02) | Darrell-Lynn | Darwin | Dashay | Daucen |
| Daraila | Darian (0.02) | Darlarhea | Darrellyn | Darwon | Dashaya | Daujiah |
| Daraishkaly | Dariana (0.03) | Darle | Darrelnahja | Darya (0.01) | Dashayion | Daulie |
| Darajha | Dariana-Ilinca | Darleen (0.01) | Darrelyn | Daryah | Dashayla | Daultana |
| Daralie | Dariane | Darleene | Darreonna | Daryan | Dashayna | Daun |
| Daralis | Dariann | Darlen | Darreya | Daryana | Dashell | Daunay |
| Daralyn | Darianna (0.01) | Darlene (0.03) | Darria | Daryanne | Dashena | Daunne |
| Daramarie | Darianne | Darlene-Maria | Darriah | Daryean | Dasheonna | Dauphne |
| Darani | Darianny | Darlenis | Darrian | Daryeon | Dashia (0.01) | Daura |
| Daranii | Dariany | Darlenne | Darriana | Daryeve | Dashielle | Dauria |
| Daranziah | Dariashia | Darlin | Darrianna | Daryien | Dashira | Dausha |
| Darara | Dariasia | Darlina | Darriasha | Daryl | Da-Shiya | Dav'eanna |
| Daravattey | Darice | Darline | Darriasia | Darylinn | Dashley | Dav'rielle |
| Daravia | Darieal | Darling | Dartensia | Daryll | Dashly | Dava |
| Daray | Darie-Anne | Darlinne | Darrica | Darylyn | Dashmarie | Dava'yah |
| Darbee | Dariel | Darlissa | Darriell | Darymar | Dashona | Davae |
| Darbey | Dariela | Darlita | Darrielle | Daryn (0.01) | Dashoni | Davah |
| Darbi | Darielix | Darllene | Darrien | Darynne | Dashton | Davahy |
| Darbie | Darieliz | Darlyn (0.01) | Darrienne | Daryona | Dashuna | Davaia |
| Darby (0.06) | Darielle (0.01) | Darlynn | Darrika | Daryonna | Dashy'ra | Davaja |
| Darbye | Dariely | Darlynna | Darrinay | Darytsa | Dashya | Davalyn |
| Darcee | Darielys | Darmyra | Darrineisha | Darzhane | Dashyia | Davalynn |
| Darcel | Darien (0.01) | Darnae | Darriona | Dasani (0.02) | Dashyla | Davan (0.01) |
| | Darienne | Darnaishia | Darrionna | Dasaniana | Dashyra | Davana |

| | | | | | |
|---|---|---|---|---|---|
| Davanee | Davilyn | Dawneisha | Dayana Isabel | Dayjah | Dayoni | Dazahnique |
| Davanise | Davin | Dawnele | Dayana Pao | Dayjahne | Dayonia | Dazahria |
| Davanna | Davina (0.02) | Dawnette | Dayanah | Dayjanae | Dayonna (0.01) | Dazaiya |
| Davannah | Davinah | Dawnie | Dayanaira | Dayjaniya | Dayra (0.01) | Dazalyn |
| Davany | Davinder | Dawnlea | Dayanara (0.16) | Dayjenik | Dayrana | Dazani |
| Davarra | Davinderjit | Dawn-Marie | Dayanara Anymi | Daykaila | Dayrayshja | Dazaray |
| Davasia | Davine (0.01) | Dawnn | Dayanarah | Daykota | Dayrelis | Dazaria |
| Davaya | Davinee | Dawn-Nicole | Dayanare | Dayla (0.02) | Dayrelys | Dazaria Amir |
| Dave'yonna | Daviney | Dawntá | Dayanari | Daylah | Dayren | Dazaun'a |
| Daveah | Davinity | Dawntae | Dayanaris | Daylan | Dayri | Dazee |
| Davease | Davinna | Dawntashia | Dayanary | Daylanna | Dayriah | Dazeha |
| Daveen | Davion | Dawnya | Dayane | Dayle (0.01) | Dayriel | Dazenae |
| Daveena | Daviona | Dawnyale | Dayanella | Daylean | Dayrin | Dazey |
| Daveeta | Davionah | Dawnyel | Dayanera | Daylee | Dayris | Dazha |
| Daveigh | Davionia | Dawnyell | Dayaneris | Dayleeia | Dayse | Dazhelyn |
| Davelynn | Davionna (0.01) | Dawresa | Dayanes | Dayleen | Daysea | Dazhia |
| Davena | Davionne | Dawsey | Dayanette | Dayleigh | Daysha (0.02) | Dazi |
| Davendria | Daviony | Dawson (0.01) | Dayani | Daylen | Dayshalie | Dazia |
| Daveney | Davis (0.01) | Dawsyn | Dayanis | Daylene | Dayshana | Daziah |
| Daveni | Davita | Daxani | Dayanna (0.02) | Dayleonna | Dayshia | Daziana |
| Davenia | Daviya | Day'ahna | Dayannah | Dayley | Dayshmarie | Daziannah |
| Davenna | Daviyah | Day'ja | Dayannara | Dayli | Dayshona | Dazie |
| Daveny | Daviyana | Day'jah | Dayanne | Daylia | Dayshonna | Dazier |
| Daveona | Daviyanah | Day'jaiona | Dayanni | Daylian | Dayshunia | Dazirah |
| Daveshia | Daviyanna | Day'janay | Dayany | Daylie | Daysi (0.01) | Dazisa |
| Davetta | Daviyhana | Day'jialyn | Dayaris | Daylin (0.02) | Daysia (0.01) | Daziya |
| Davey | Daviyona | Day'le | Dayasia | Daylisha | Daysie | Daziyah |
| Daveyana | Davlin | Day'naisha | Dayauna | Daylon | Daysiemae | Dazja |
| Daveyon | Davona | Day'nija | Dayaunah | Daylona | Daysi-Maria | Dazjah |
| Daveyonna | Davonna | Day'niyah | Dayavian | Dayloni | Daysin | Dazlyn |
| Davi | Davonni | Day'onna | Dayawna | Daylydia | Daysja | Dazmyn |
| Davi'neyshia | Davonny | Day'ranec | Daybria | Daylynn (0.01) | Dayssia | Dazrielle |
| Davi'ona | Davonya | Day'sha | Dayce | Daymalesha | Daysy | Dazsa |
| Davi'onna | Davoyna | Day'shia | Daycee | Daymani | Dayten | Dazsha |
| Davia (0.01) | Davria | Day'sia | Dayci | Daymara | Dayton (0.01) | Dazunique |
| Daviah | Davy | Day'vonna | Daycia | Daymaris | Daytona (0.01) | Dazure |
| Davian | Davy'ana | Day'zha | Daydream | Daymiah | Daytriana | Dazurnae |
| Daviana (0.01) | Davyna | Daya (0.01) | Daydreana | Daymone'a | Daytzy | Dazy |
| Davianah | Davyon | Dayaa | Daydriah | Daymyia | Dayunistie | Dazya |
| Davianie | Dawa Yangi | Dayaana | Daydrianna | Dayna (0.05) | Dayunna | Dazzaree- |
| Davianna (0.01) | Dawanda | Dayah | Daydrieawna | Daynah | Dayva | Destiny |
| Daviannah | Dawanee | Dayahna | Dayeana | Daynalees | Dayvana | Dazzatie |
| Daviasia | Dawanyah | Dayahvion | Dayeli | Daynalese | Dayveeda | Dazzlyn |
| Daviauna | Dawauna | Dayailyn | Dayenne | Daynara | Dayvelisse | Dazzmine |
| David | Daweana | Dayali | Dayeonna | Daynasia | Dayvia | De |
| Davida (0.01) | Dawinsky | Dayalis | Dayera-Miliane | Dayne | Dayvn | De Angel |
| Davidia | Dawiska | Dayaliz | Dayerlin | Daynelis | Dayvonnie | De Angela |
| Davie | Dawn (0.05) | Dayami (0.01) | Dayheni | Daynia | Dayya | De Angelina |
| Daviegh | Dawn Angel | Dayamy | Dayiah | Daynisha | Dayzah | De Angelo |
| Daviera | Dawn Jade | Dayan | Dayija | Daynyia | Dayzanae | De Anna |
| Davihana | Dawn Marie | Dayana (0.10) | Dayijahnae | Daynyzhia | Dayzanell | De Anyah |
| Davika | Dawna | Dayana | Dayinna | Dayona | Dayzha | De Asha |
| Davilia Tanisse | Dawnae | Alejandra | Dayja (0.01) | Dayonah | Dayziah | Dé Ashia |

| | | | | | | |
|---|---|---|---|---|---|---|
| De Asia | De'auria | De'mariya | De'quasha | Deajana | Deaverin | Decmbr |
| Dé Asia | De'auveon | De'marya | De'quasia | Deajha | Deavonne | Decora |
| De Janae | De'avion | De'mauria | De'raya | Deajia | Deavonnie | Decorah |
| De Khyra | De'avionna | De'maya | De'reasha | Dealan | Deawnna | Dedawn |
| De Leon | De'aysa | De'metriah | De'rhaya | Dealyce | Deaxia'naya | Dedee |
| De Lia | De'azah | De'mia | De'riah | Deamonie | Deayla | Dedra |
| De Marria | De'azha | De'miah | De'riya | Dean'a | Deayra | Dedrianna |
| De Mora | De'breona | De'minee | De'ryah | Deana (0.02) | Deaysa | Dedrionna |
| De Naija | De'calah | De'mitria | De'saraye | Deandra (0.02) | Deaysah | Dee |
| De Riya | De'carieasia | De'miyah | De'shawn | Deandra | Deaysia | Dee Dee |
| Dé Zhiyah | De'coreya | De'moni | De'shawna | Dolores | Deazanae | Dee'andrea |
| De Ziniah | De'iijah | De'monkerria | De'shay | De-Andrea | Deaziah | Dee'asia |
| De'aashia | De'ja (0.01) | De'mornay | De'shayla | Deandrea (0.01) | Deba | Dee'onna |
| De'ahja | De'jah | De'mya (0.01) | De'shianeé | Deandres | Debanhi | Deeanah |
| De'aija | De'jahnae | De'myah | De'shuntae | Deandria | Debanie | Deeane |
| De'aijah | De'jahnay | De'myiah | De'shyla | Deandriah | Debany | Deeann |
| De'aira | Nachel | De'myra | De'simber | Deanesha | Debbie (0.01) | Deeanna (0.01) |
| De'airra | De'jahnique | De'myria | De'sire | Deangela | Debbieretta | Deeara |
| De'airrah | De'janae | De'nai | De'tahjiona | Deangeliz | Debborah | Deeba |
| De'aisa | De'janai | De'naisha | De'tazia | Deanglis | Debbra | Deeda |
| De'aisha | De'janay | De'naisia | De'traycia | Deanicka | Debby | Deedee |
| De'aivia | De'janell | De'naj | De'vauna | Deann | Debera | Deedra |
| De'aja | De'janelle | De'najah | De'viana | Deanna (0.23) | Debora (0.02) | Deegan |
| De'ajah | De'janna | De'najhzea | De'vion | Deanna Maria | Debora-Esther | Deeinn |
| De'ajia | De'jayah | De'najia | De'yanna | Deanndra | Deborah (0.17) | Deejah |
| De'amani | De'jira | De'nariel | De'yauna | Deanne (0.01) | Debra (0.04) | Deejinae |
| De'ambria | De'jonea | De'nasia | De'yonna | Deannea | Debrah | Deeka |
| De'amontay | De'jonier | De'nausia | De'yonnis | Deanni | Debranna | Deekendreiah |
| De'ana | De'juh | De'nay | De'zariyah | Deannia | Debraylee | Deeksha |
| De'andrea | De'kayla | De'naya | De'zhane | Deannie | Debreana | Deelan |
| De'andreia | De'keira | De'nayah | De'zire | Deanny | Debrena | Deelay |
| De'andria | De'kiera | De'nayla | De'ziya | Deanza | Debreona | Deelda |
| De'angela | De'kiria | De'nazia | De'ziyah | Dearia | Debreya | Deelicia |
| De'anna (0.01) | De'kiya | De'neshia | De'zyna | Dearie | Debria | Deelila |
| De'arah | De'koda | De'nevea | Dea (0.01) | Deasare | Debriah | Deem |
| De'aria | De'kya | De'neya | Dea Kindle | Deasha | Debrianna | Deema (0.01) |
| De'ariana | De'lady | De'nicha | Deaaryonna | Deashia | Debrionah | Deemah |
| De'arrionn | De'laija | De'nira | Deacota | Deasia (0.04) | Debrionna | Deemecia |
| De'asa | De'laja | De'nireya | Deadra | Deasia'arnee | Debrionne | Deemelda |
| De'ashia | De'lajha | De'nisha | Deadrah | Deasjanae | Debryn | Deemirenna |
| De'ashya | De'lana | De'niya | Deaglan | Deastiny | Decandus | Deena (0.02) |
| De'asia (0.04) | De'lannii | De'nya | Deah | Deasy | Decari | Deenah |
| De'asiah | De'lany | De'nyjah | De-Aija | Deatany | Decariah | Deenia |
| De'asialé | De'lashawnta | De'nyla | Deaija | Deauna | Decarlos | Deenoshka |
| De'asya | De'lasia | De'nyrica | Deaira | Deaurae | Decatur | Deepa |
| De'aubrey | De'laysha | De'nysia | Deairra | Deausa | Decayla | Deepali |
| De'auja | De'lonna | De'ondrea | Deairrika | Deaushawney | December (0.01) | Deepika |
| De'aujanae | De'lores | De'onie | Deaisha | Deauveon | Decerie | Deepinder |
| De'aujanah | De'majae | De'oriona | Deaizja | Deava | Dechara | Deepnoor |
| De'aujané | De'mani | De'oshanaj | De-Aja | Deavan | Decien | Deepthi |
| De'aundra | De'marah | De'oviana | Deaja | Deavean | Decirek | Deepti |
| De'aundria | De'mari | De'ovion | Deajah (0.01) | Deaven | Declan | Deera |
| De'aunevah | De'mariee | De'preanna | Deajah Raleena | Deaveon | Declyn | Déere |

Deesa
Deesca
Deesha
Deestiny
Deethi
Deevah
Deewa
Deeya
Deeyah
Deezire
Defne *(0.01)*
Dega
Degan
Degarya
Dehjah
Dehlia
Dehyani
Dei'aja
Deiah
Deianarra
Deiandra
Deianira
Deianna
Deiara
Deiauna
Deibi
Deicy
Deidra *(0.01)*
Deidre *(0.01)*
Deidrea
Deihanna
Deihasia
Deija
Deijah
Deijahna
Deijanae
Deila
Deilenys
Deily
Deilyn
Deimireilis
Deimy
Deina
Deinaba
Deinalys
Deion
Deiona Ann
  Arnell
Deiondra
Deionna
Deirdra
Deirdrah
Deirdre *(0.01)*

Deirdri
Deiri
Deirra
Deisha
Deisi
Deisialies
Deisree
Deissy
Deisy *(0.03)*
Deitra
Deizy
Dej
Dejá
DéJa
Deja *(0.10)*
Dejá Niqua
Deja Ranee
Deja'rae
Dejaa
Dejah *(0.02)*
Dejahnae
Dejahnay
Dejahue
Dejahyria
Dejalei
Dejalina
Dejalise
Deja-Marie
Dejana
Dejanace
Dejanada
Deja-Nae
Dejanaé
Dejanae *(0.01)*
Dejanaeh
Dejanahe
Dejanara
Dejanay
Deja-Ne
Dejanelle
Dejaney
Dejani
Dejaniera
Dejanique
Dejanira
Dejanna
Deja-Raye
Dejasearah
Dejean
Dejhana
Dejia
Dejiah
Dejiang

Dejianna
Dejohna
Dejon
Dejonai
Dejonay
Dejreanna
Dejsha
Deka
Dekaiaa
Dekaiha
Dekailah
Dekaiyah
Dekalya
Dekayla
Dekeidra
Dekera
Dekere
Dekeyia
Dekhaia
Dekhila
Dekhilah
Dekilia
Dekiya
Deklyn
Dekorah
Dekota
Dekylah
Dekyra
Del'mia
Del'miyah
Del'monnie
Del'nisha
Del'rayeshia
Dela
Dela'ja
Delace
Delacey
Delacroix
Delacy
Deladis
Delahny
Delaiah
Delaila
Delailah
Delaina *(0.01)*
Delaine
Delainey *(0.03)*
Delainna
Delainy
Delaiya
Delana *(0.02)*
Delanah
Delancey

Delancy
Delande
Delandra
Delandria
Delane
Delanea
Delanee
Delanei
Delaneny
Delaney *(0.76)*
Delani *(0.02)*
Delanie *(0.06)*
Delanis
Delanna
Delannie
Delany *(0.01)*
Delanye
Delanys
Delara
Delaram
Delasia
Delaston
Delaury
Delaveen
Delawaynne
Delaya
Delayah
Delayiah
Delayla
Delayna *(0.01)*
Delayne
Delaynee
Delayni
Delaynia
Delaynie *(0.01)*
Delayza
Delcena
Delchona
Delcie
Delcy
Deldre
Dele
Delea
Deleah
Deleana
Delece
Delecia
Delee
Deleeha
Deleesa
Deleia
Deleilah
Delena

Delenn
Delerie
Delexus
Deleyne
Delfee
Delfina *(0.01)*
Delfinia
Delfyna
Delia *(0.08)*
Delia Stephanie
Deliah *(0.01)*
Delialah
Deliana
Delianna
Deliany
Delicia *(0.01)*
Delicity
Delijah
Delika
Delila *(0.02)*
Delilah *(0.12)*
Deliliah
Delillah
Delima
Delimar
Delin
Delina *(0.01)*
Delinda
Deling
Delis
Delisa
Delisha
Delisia
Delissia
Deliyah
Deliz
Deljinder
Dell
Della *(0.03)*
Dellafay
Dellah
Dellahia
Dellana
Dellaney
Dellanie
Dellina
Dellnasia
Dellney
Dellya
Delmara Lee
Delmaris
Delmary
Delmi

Delmichelle
Delmika
Delmy
Delnay
Delondria
Deloni
Delonni
Delonnie
Delontae
Delora
Deloras
Delores *(0.01)*
Deloris
Delphia
Delphine *(0.05)*
Delphyne
Delquevia
Delry
Delsey
Delsie
Delsin
Delsy
Delta *(0.01)*
Delunays
Delvanna
Delyla
Delylah
Delyliah
Delylla
Delynnda
Delyssa
Delyssia
Delyza
Delyzanet
Delzha
Dema
Demaia
Demaishon
Demaja
Demajay
Deman
Demara
Demareya
De-Mari
Demari
Demaria *(0.01)*
Demariah
Demarian
Demariana
Demarie
Demarien
Demaris
Demarius

Demariya
Demariyah
Demariyea
Demarra
Demarraye
Demarriah
Demarrihanna
Demarris
De-Mauria
Demauria
Demaya
Demayah
Deme'ya
Demeah
Demechia
Demecia
Demeeka
Demeisha
Demeria
Demeriah
Demeriauna
Demerica
Demerie
Demerria
Demeryia
Demesha
Demetra *(0.01)*
Demetrah
Demetrasia
Demetre'yonna
Demetrea
Demetri
Demetria *(0.03)*
Demetriana
Demetrifana
Demetriona
Demetris
Demetriua
Demetriunna
Demetriyana
Demetrya
Demeya
Demí
Demi *(0.04)*
Demi Lee
Demia
Demiah
Demiana
Demicka
Demie-Anne
Demietriah
Demii
Demilade

| | | | | | | |
|---|---|---|---|---|---|---|
| Demillia | Denaly | Denija | Denosh | Dereen | Derrington | Deshanell |
| Demionna | Denalyn | Denijah | Density | Derek | Derriona | Deshania |
| Demiracle | Denaria | Denika | Denver *(0.01)* | Dereka | Derrionna | Deshanté |
| Demiria | Denaryia | Denilah | Denyah | Derenique | Derrisha | Deshanti |
| Demirra | Denarys | Denilda | Denyce | Derenza | Derrissa | Deshara |
| Demita | Denasha | Denilssa | Denyla | Dereonna | Derriyah | Deshari |
| Demitah | Denashia | Denim | Denylah | Deresa | Derronda | Deshaun |
| Demitra | Denasia *(0.01)* | Denina | Denym | Dereyana | Derry'iana | Deshauna |
| Demitria | Denay | Denine | Denyra | Dereyanna | Derryauna | Deshaunte |
| Demitry | Denaya | Denira | Denyse | Dereyona | Dervana | Deshauntis |
| Demiya | Denayah | Denis | Denysha | Dereyonna | Dervla | Deshautae |
| De-Miyah | Denaysha | Denisa | Denyssa | Dergina | Derya | Deshaviya |
| Demiyah | Denaysia | Denise *(0.19)* | Denza | Deria | Deryn | Deshavyonna |
| Demmi | Denayzhia | Denise Ann | Denzia | Deriana | Derys | Deshawn |
| Demmy | Denazia | Denise Marielle | Deohnie | Derianna | Des'mariah | Deshawna |
| Demonica | Denaziah | Deniseia | Deojhanic | Derica | Des'nee | Deshawnae |
| Demonika | Dency-Andrea | Denise-Jacque | Deon | Dericia | Des'tani | Deshawnna |
| Demontayvia | Denea | Denisha *(0.01)* | Deona *(0.01)* | Dericka | Des'tynie | Deshawnti |
| Demonyia | Deneá | Denishea | Deondra | Derieana | Des'zyre | Deshay |
| Demoshea | Deneasha | Denishia | Deondrea | Derika | Desa | Deshaye |
| Demri | Denecia | Deniss | Deondria | Derine | Desaine | Deshayla |
| Demrie | Denee | Denisse *(0.04)* | Deoni | Deriona | Desani | Deshazo |
| Demtria | Deneez | Denisslian | Deonicah | Derionna | Desara Dahiyha | Deshea |
| Demya *(0.01)* | Deneia | Denisty | Deonionica | Derise | Desarae *(0.01)* | Deshira |
| Demyah | Deneicia | Denitra | Deonna *(0.02)* | Deristhi | Desarai | Deshiya |
| Demye | Deneile | Deniya *(0.01)* | Deonni | Deriunna | Desaray *(0.01)* | Deshjia |
| Demyia | Deneilybeth | Deniyah | Deonnie | Deriya | Desaraya | Deshna |
| Demyjah | Deneisha | Deniyiah | Deonquasha | Deriyah | Desaré | Deshonda |
| Demyla | Denelle | Deniz | Deonte | Deriyana | Desarea | Deshonna |
| Demyra | Deneria | Denize | Deontranie | Deriyanna | Desaree | Deshontay |
| Den'nisha | Denesha | Denizja | Deonviana | Derlande | Desarie | Deshundra |
| Dena *(0.02)* | Deneshia | Denizlea | Deonya | Derli | Desbah | Deshunna |
| Denaé | Denesia | Denna | Deop | Derlin | Dese'ray | Deshunti |
| Denae *(0.02)* | Denesie | Dennae | Deora | Deronye | Deseanna | Deshy'rionna |
| Denaea | Denetra | Dennaria | Deounka | Derrah | Desely | Deshya |
| Denaee | Denetress | Dennasia | Deovian | Derranae | Desera | Deshyra |
| Denaejah | Denetria | Dennay | Deovion | Derreal | Deserae *(0.01)* | Desi |
| Denaesha | Deneva | Dennaya | Dephaney | Derrecka | Deserai | Desiah |
| Denaija | Denevia | Dennayjah | Dephne | Derreyona | Deseray | Desian |
| Denaijah | Deneya | Denné | Deqa | Derri'ana | Deserea | Desianna |
| Denaisa | Deni | Dennia | Dequala | Derriah | Deseree | Desiaray |
| Denaisha | Denia *(0.01)* | Dennica | Dequandre | Derrian | Desereé | Desiderata |
| Denaiya | Deniah | Dennie | Dequasha | Derriana | Deserey | Desier |
| Denaizja | Denibe | Denniela | Dequesha | Derrica | Deseria | Desierra |
| Denaja | Denica | Dennika | Dequisha | Derricca | Deserrae | Design |
| Denajae | Denice | Dennis'ha | Dequita | Derrick | Deserray | Desinnie |
| Denajah | Denicha | Dennisa | Der | Derricka | Desha | Desinty |
| Denajah' | Denicia | Dennise *(0.01)* | Der'kiearah | *(0.01)* | Deshae | Desiny |
| Denajha | Deniece | Dennisha | Der'rihanna | Derrickann | Deshaé | Desira |
| Denajia | Deniella | Denny | Deralyn | Derriea | Deshaila | Desiraé |
| Denali *(0.02)* | Denielle | Dennyce | Deranar | Derriel | Deshaina | Desirae *(0.12)* |
| Denalia | Deniese | Dennyne | Derayshia | Derrika | Deshana | Desiraha |
| Denalie | Denieya | Dennyse | Dereck | Derrinesha | Deshanay | Desirai |

| | | | | | | |
|---|---|---|---|---|---|---|
| Desiray *(0.01)* | Dessirrae | Destiny Tehya | Devaeh | Devona | Deyci | Dezeraye |
| Desiraye | Dessy | Destiny-Ann | Devahuti | Devona Shontal | Deycy | Dezerea |
| Desiré | Desta | Destinyann | Devainna | Devondria | Deydy | Dezeree |
| Desire *(0.03)* | Destane | Destiny-Divin | Devan *(0.03)* | Devonia | Deyiliah | Dezeriaha |
| Desire Nicole | Destané | Destinyi | Devanee | Devonicka | Deyja | Dezerray |
| Desirea *(0.01)* | Destanee *(0.01)* | Destiny-Jean | Devaney | Devonie | Deyjah | Dezhá |
| Desireah | Destaney | Destiny-Joi | Devani | Devonique | Deyli | Dezhané |
| Desireé | (0.01) | Destiny-Marie | Devanie | Devonna | Deylin | Dezhirae |
| Desirée | Destani *(0.02)* | Destinyn | Devann | Devonnah | Deymalie | Dezi |
| Désirée | Destanie *(0.02)* | Destiny- | Devanny | Devonne | Deymi-Locia | Dezi'rah |
| Desireé *(0.02)* | Destanni | Ntumba | Devanshi | Devonnie | Deyna | Deziah |
| Desiree *(0.30)* | Destannie | Destiny-Rose | Devansya | Devonteria | Deyona | Deziaha |
| Desireé Jo | Destany *(0.05)* | Destinystar | Devanta | Devontria | Deyonce | Deziana |
| Desiree Lee | Destene | Destonee | Devany *(0.01)* | Devora *(0.02)* | Deyondra | Dezier |
| Desireigh | Desteney | Destoni | Devaria | Devorah *(0.03)* | Deyoniah | Dezinae |
| Desirhea | Desteni | Destra | Devaro | Devorah- | Deyonna | Dezira |
| Desiriee | Desteny *(0.01)* | Destriana | Devawna | Crystal | Deyonnah | Dezirae *(0.02)* |
| Desirray | Desti'ni | Destry | Devayani | Devorreia | Deyonne | Dezirah |
| Desirre | Destian | Desttiny | Devaylin | Devota | Deyri | Dezirai |
| Desislava | Destiana | Destuhni | Deveigh | Devotion | Deyse | Deziray |
| Desiya | Destimy | Desty'ne | Deven | Devra | Deysha | Deziraye |
| Desiyah | Destin *(0.01)* | Destyn | Deveni | Devvyn | Deysi *(0.01)* | Deziré |
| Desjanay | Destina | Destynasia | Devenshire | Devy | Deysia | Dezire *(0.01)* |
| Desjeanta | Destinae | Destyne | Deveny Ann | Devylah | Deysie | Dezirea |
| Deslyn | Destinay | Destynee *(0.01)* | Deveona | Devyn *(0.08)* | Deysy | Dezirée |
| Desma | Destiné | Destyni *(0.01)* | Devi | Devyne | Deyton | Deziree *(0.02)* |
| Desmarae | Destine *(0.01)* | Destynie | Devian | Devyn-Lee | Deyysi | Dezirie |
| Desmariah | Destineé | Destyny | Deviana | Devynn *(0.01)* | Deyzha | Deziya |
| Desmarie | Destinée | Desymber | Devianna | Devynne | Dez'er'rea | Deziyah |
| Desmarria | Destinee *(0.18)* | Desyn | Devika *(0.01)* | Dewan | Dez'marie | Dezja |
| Desmeana | Destineeh | Desyonna | Devilla | Dex'terra | Dezah E'l | Dezjae |
| Desmia | Destinei | Desyre | Devin *(0.09)* | Dexaria | Dezamiya | Dezlyn |
| Desmonae | Destinese | Desyree | Devina | Dexian | Dezamya | Dezmari |
| Desneiges | Destiney *(0.10)* | Deszeray | Devinah | Dexire | Dezarae *(0.01)* | Dezmariah |
| Desola | Destiney-Lynn | Deszerei | Devin- | Dexteria | Dezarai | Dezmin |
| Desorray | Destini *(0.10)* | Detarshea | De'shaun | Dextiney | Dezaray *(0.01)* | Dezmiyana |
| Despina | Destini'jo | Detavioné | Devine | Dey'ja | Dezaraya | Dezmon |
| Despoina | Destinia | Detona | Devinee | Dey'leana | Dezarayae | Dezmyrah |
| Desraia | Destinie *(0.03)* | Detoria | Devini | Deyairah | Dezaraye | Deznin |
| Desray Anne | Destinii | Detorri | Devinie | Deyaisa | Dezarea | Dezonnee |
| Desriee | Destinique | Detra | Devinity | Deyalith | Dezarey | Dezrae |
| Desrieé | Destinniyiah | Detria | Devinne | Deyana | Dezari | Dezrayh |
| Dessa *(0.01)* | Destinny | Detrice | Deviny | Deyanae | Dezaria | Dezreona |
| Dessarae | Destinty | Detrie | Devion | Deyanee | Dezariah | Dezrihanna |
| Dessaray | Destiny *(3.07)* | Detronnesha | Deviona | Deyaneira | Dezarie | Dezsaray |
| Desseray | Destiny Ann | Deuangela | Devira | Deyaneyra | Dezariya | Dezsirae |
| Dessi | Destiny | Deunna | Devisi | Deyanira | Dezariyah | Dezstynie |
| Dessie | Beyonce | Dev | Devita | (0.01) | Dezarya | Deztanee |
| Dessie Mae | Destiny Lee | Dev'ani | Devlin | Deyanis | Dezden | Deztany |
| Dessielena | Destiny Lyn | Dev'veona | Devlyn | Deyanna | Dezekiah | Deztiné |
| Dessire | Destiny Re | Deva | Devlynne | Deyaret | Dezené | Deztinee |
| Dessiré | Destiny Ré | Devada Ash | Devna | De-Yauna | Dezerae | Deztiney |
| Dessiree | Destiny Ressey | Devae | Devon *(0.10)* | Deyavna | Dezeray | Deztini |

| | | | | | | |
|---|---|---|---|---|---|---|
| Deztiny | Dhymond | Diamondnez | Dianymarie | Dihannel | Dilyn | Diona |
| Deztynee | Di Angelie | Diamone | Dianza | Dihj'zierra | Dilynda | Dionasia |
| Deztyney | Di Leyxa | Diamoneyqua | Diara | Dihlyla | Dilynn | Dionce |
| Dezyrae | Di'amani | Diamoni | Diaralyz | Dihya | Dima | Dioncee |
| Dezyre | Di'andrea | Diamonique | Diaraye | Dijana | Dimaia | Diondra |
| Dezyria | Di'arrah | (0.01) | Diariata | Dijeauna | Dimara | Diondria |
| Dezza | Di'asia | Diamonnde | Diariatou | Dijonae | Dimari | Dione |
| Dezzarae | Di'jah | Diamya | Diario | Dijonay | Dimaya | Dioni |
| Dezzirae | Di'mae | Diamyn | Diariyata | Dikila | Dimena | Dionica |
| Dezzman | Di'mon | Dian | Diarra | Dikilah | Dimend | Dionicia |
| Dezzray | Di'mond | Diana (1.46) | Diarre | Diksha | Dimiah | Dionie |
| Dh'ryai | Di'moniq | Diana Lourdes | Diary | Dilan | Dimira | Dionisia |
| Dhadiza | Di'nayshia | Diana Maria | Diasha | Dilana (0.01) | Dimitra | Dionisio |
| Dhae'lynn | Di'niya | Diana- | Diasia | Dilani | Dimitroula | Dionna (0.03) |
| Dhaeyonna | Di'or | Esmeralda | Dia-Theresa | Dilanni | Dimond | Dionna Jade |
| Dhakirah | Di'zari | Dianah | Diavani | Dilanur | Dimonde | Dionnah |
| Dhalia | Dia (0.01) | Diana-Karen | Diavanna | Dilara | Dimonque | Dionne (0.01) |
| Dhalie | Dia'nna | Dianali | Diavega | Dilara-Edanur | Dimore | Dionni |
| Dhalis | Diadely | Diana-Marisol | Diavian | Dilaya | Dimpal | Dionnie |
| Dhalya | Diah | Dianamary | Diaviane | Dilayla | Dimya | Dionysia |
| Dhana | Diaira | Dianara | Diavion | Dilayni | Dimyn | Dionyssia |
| Dhanalakshmi | Diaja | Dianca | Diavohan | Dilcia | Dina (0.07) | Dior (0.02) |
| Dhani | Di-Ajah | Diance Nijai | Diavonna | Dilcy | Dinaann | Diora |
| Dhanika | Diajah | Diandra | Diavvian | Dileen | Dinae | Diore |
| Dhannie | Diajhane | Diandraly | Diawna | Dileinys | Dinah (0.01) | Diorea |
| Dhannon | Diaka | Diane (0.07) | Diaya | Dilenzia | Dinahlynn | Dioselin |
| Dhanya | Diakher | Diane'qua | Diayonna | Dilia | Dinah-Maurie | Dioselyne |
| Dhara (0.01) | Dialikatou | M'lindaleesia | Diaz | Diliahna | Dinali | Diosmary |
| Dharaya | Diamané | Dianel | Dibora | Diliana | Dinalie | Dioulde |
| Dharia | Diamani | Dianeli | Cristhyne | Dililah | Dinasty | Diouna |
| Dharini | Diamann | Dianelis | Dicey | Dilis | Dinaya | Dipali |
| Dharla | Diamantae | Dianelly | Dickel | Diljaan | Dinayjah | Diplai |
| Dharma (0.01) | Diamante | Dianely | Didiana | Diljot | Dinea | Dipree |
| Dharmendra | Diamantina | Dianelys | Diedra | Dilkeerit | Dineaste | Dipta |
| Dharzhae | Diamara | Dianeris | Diedrah | Dilkush | Dinedra | Dira |
| Dhatri | Diamaris | Diane-Shawna | Diedre | Dillan | Dineiciya | Diretha |
| Dhawan | Diameka | Dianet | Diem | Dillanna | Dineisha | Dirian |
| Dhaya | Diameliz | Dianette | Diem My | Dillen | Dinejia | Disha (0.01) |
| Dhe'lanee | Diamelys | Dianey | Dieme | Dillian | Dinesh | Dishawni |
| Dheaven | Diamend | Dianeysha | Diemhanh | Dillin | Dineshia | Dishell |
| Dhelena | Diamon | Diangellis | Diem-Mi | Dillon (0.01) | Dinia | Dishika |
| Dhestini | Diamonaijha | Diangely | Dieneba | Dillya | Diniah | Dishyah |
| Dheysy | Diamond (0.35) | Diani | Dieneka | Dillyn | Dinora | Disire |
| Dhiksha | Diamond Em | Dianie | Dienesha | Dillynne | Dinorah | Disney |
| Dhirinita | Diamond | Dianique | Dienisbel | Dilma | Dinoreisy | Divani |
| Dhiya | Takiara | Diann | Dieonna | Dilnaz | Dinosha | Divany |
| Dhoha Elislam | Diamond | Dianna (0.04) | Dierah | Dilondra Merae | Dinya | Diveah |
| Dhrithi | Te'marie | Dianna Marjorie | Dierra | Dilpreet | Diocelin | Diveena |
| Dhriti | Diamond | Adriano | Diesiah | Dilraj | Diodely | Divena |
| Dhruvi | Yvonne | Dianna-Gra | Dieula | Dilrose | Diogenae | Divi |
| Dhurshanie | Diamond- | Dianne (0.01) | Digna | Dilveer | Dioja | Diviana |
| Dhvani | J'monei | Diannea | Digness | Dilylah | Dion | Divina (0.01) |
| Dhye'sienna | Diamondly | Dianni | Dihanalis | Dilyliah | | Divine (0.02) |

Divine
  Lalouange
Divine-Alexia
Divini
Divinia
Divinity (0.01)
Divinna
Diviny
Divita
Divjot
Divleen
Divneet
Divonna
Divora
Divya (0.03)
Divyani
Divyn
Divyne
Diwata
Dixee
Dixianna
Dixie (0.05)
Dixita
Dixon
Diya (0.08)
Diyae
Diyalaksha
Diyamond
Diyana
Diyani
Diyanna
Diyonne
Diziyah
Djaida
Djaide
Djala
Djamila
Djamilah
Djamilatou
Djaney
Djassi
Djazya
Djedje
Djeina
Djeinaba
Djemila
Djeneba
Djenita
Djenn Hershley
Djenna
Djesmineda
Djessa
Djiana

Djienaba
D-Juandolyn
Djunie
  Franchelle
Dkalia
Dkalyn
Dkayla
Dkhia
Dlache
Dlaysiah
Dmarri
Dmarya
Dmonyie
Dnaisha
Dnasia
Dne'jia
Dniya
D-Niyah
Doaa
Doan Nancy
Doanh Dahlia
Doda
Dodger
Doga
Doha
Doireann
Dokata
Dolce
Dolcemia
Dolci
Doldgie
Doli
Dollia
Dollie
Dollilah
Dolly
Dollya
Dollyane
  Uapukunis
Dolma
Dolon
Dolorah
Dolorean
Dolores (0.01)
Dolveig
Domaneeck
Domani
Domanic
Domenica (0.01)
Domenique
Domienick'deizre
Dominae
Domineé

Domineeck
Domineique
Dominga
Dominia
Dominic (0.01)
Dominica (0.01)
Dominick
Dominik
Dominika
Dominike
Domininque
Dominiq
Dominiqué
Dominique
  (0.17)
Dominique
  Angel
Dominiquez
Domino
Dominque
  (0.01)
Domiyana
Domiyanah
Domna
Domneak
Domnica
Domnikka
Domonic
Domonicque
Domonik
Domoniq
Domonique
  (0.01)
Domyferth
Don
Don'ajah
Don'asia
Don'naisa
Don'naisha
Don'nasia
Don'nay
Don'naysha
Don'nesha
Don'shya
Don'tajah
Don'tasia
Don'yae
Don'yalle
Dona
Donae
Donae'jha
Donaeisha
Donaejia

Dona-Gabriella
Donahi
Donahsia
Donailyahi
Donaisha
Donaja
Donajh
Donald
Donalda
Donalyn
Donara
Donasha
Dónashia
Donashja
Donasia
Donastey
Donatela
Donatella
Donatha
Donay
Donaysa
Donaysha
Donaysja
Donaziah
Doneashia
Donee
Doneisha
Donelda
Donelia
Donell
Donelle
Donesha
Donetria
Donetta
Donia (0.01)
Donica
Donice
Doniell
Doniella
Donielle
Doniesha
Donika
Donila
Donillia
Donilyn
Doninique
Donisha (0.01)
Donita
Donitia
Doniya
Donjae
Donjanae
Donjanay

Donjanie
Donjerna
Donjhanae
Donkaysia
Donmonique
Donna (0.09)
Donna Faye
Donna Jean
Donnae
Donnaé
Donnaisha
Donnakay
Donnalee
Donnamarie
Donnarria
Donnasha
Donnashia
Donnasia
Donnasue
Donnavin
Donnavya
Donnaya
Donnecia
Donnell
Donnella
Donnelle
Donnelly
Donnesha
Donnetta
Donnia
Donnica
Donniesha
Donnisha
Donnita
Donniya
Donniyah
Donnyshia
Donovan
Donquinay
Donshonaye
Dontae
Dontaesha
Dontanna
Dontarika
Dontashia
Dontasia
Dontavia
Dontaya
Dontaysah
Dontayvia
Dontaza
Donté
Donte'sha

Dontera
Donteria
Donterria
Donteysha
Dontiera
Dontoria
Donya (0.01)
Donyada
Donyae
Donyaé
Donyale
Donye
Donyé
Donyea
Donyee
Donyeih
Donyel
Donyell
Donyelle
Dor
Dor'keta
Dora (0.04)
Dora Maame
Dorah
Doralicia
Dorama
Dorana
Dorathea
Dorathy
Dorcas (0.01)
Doreanna
Doreen
Doreena
Dorelis
Dorenda
Dorene
Doreonna
Doreshia
Doretha
Doretta
Dori (0.01)
Doria
Doriah
Doriam
Dorian (0.01)
Doriane (0.01)
Doriane-Mianda
Doriangelys
Doriann
Dorianna
Dorianne (0.01)
Dorice
Dorie

Doriece
Doriela
Dorielle
Dorikah
Dorinda-Elise
Doris (0.03)
Dorisann
Dorisbeth
Dorisca
Doriselda
Dorismar (0.01)
Dorissa
Dorita
Doritha
Dorleen
Dorlene
Dorley
Dorlisa
Dornasia
Dornecia
Doron
Doronit
Dorota
Dorotea
Dorotee
Dorothea (0.01)
Dorothea Maria
Dorothee (0.01)
Dorothie
Dorothy (0.08)
Dorottya
Dorra
Dorrie
Dorris
Dorsa
Dorthey
Dorthia
Dorthie
Dorthy
Dorvelie
Dorvena
Dory
Doryane
Doryann
Doryanne
Doshanie
Dossie
Dosya
Dotianna
Dotri
Dottie
Doua
Douaa

Douachee
Douce-Melodie
Doug'ja'na
Dougkevia
Douglas
Dougless
Doulsina
Dounia
Dounia-Nawell
Dounya
Dove
Dovey
Dovie
Dovieanna
Dovie-Rhea
Dowee
Doyinsola
Doykeria
Dr'iona
Dr'onna
Dra'nilayh
Dra'niya
Dra'nyhia
Drac
Dracey
Dracie
Dradaya
Draegon
Draeshawna
Draevynne
Dragyn
Draia
Draiona
Drake
Drakkona
Draley
Drashae
Drasti
Draven
Dravlyn
Dravyn
Drayah
Drayaunna
Drayonna
Drayton
Drazel
Dré Onna
Dre'anna
Dre'kayla
Dre'naya
Dre'niya
Dre'ona
Dre'onna

Dre'onnah
Dre'seanna
Dre'unna
Dre'vionna
Dre'yonna
Drea (0.01)
Dreah
Dreahna
Dreaira
Dreaiunna
Dreaka
Drealinear
Dream (0.02)
Dreama (0.01)
Dreamalynn
Dreamer
Dreamera
Dreamnoel
Dreams
Drean
Dreana
Dreane
Dreanna
Dreanne
Drechelle
Dreeanna
Drejuana
Drekeya
Dreli
Dremyah
Drendalin
Dreneisha
Dreniyah
Drenusha
Dreona
Dreonna
Dreraya
Dresden
Dreviona
Drew (0.08)
Drewann
Drewe
Dreya
Dreyá
Dreyah
Dreyahna
Dreyanna
Dreygen
Driana
Drianna
Drielle
Driem
Drihanna

Drinen
Drisana
Drishti
Dristi
Drithi
Drose
Dru (0.02)
Dru'niyah
Drucilla
Drue
Druscilla
Druselita
Drusilla
Druvi
Dryden
Dshawna
Dshawnjua
Dtamanie
Dua
Duaa
Duabci
Duache
Duachi
Duachung
Duanayzia
Duanelys
Duang
Duangdtawa
Duarijah
Dublin
Duchealla
Duchnah
Duha
Duice-Magd
Dujana
Dukeyna
Dulaney
Dulce (0.15)
Dulce Maria
Dulcea
Dulcebeth
Dulcekarel
Dulcemaria
Dulcey
Dulcie
Dulcina
Dulcinea
Duleiny
Duline
Dulse
Dumarri
Dun'neka
Dunah

Dunia (0.01)
Duniya
Duniyah
Dunja
Dunneane
Dunnia
Dunya
Duong
Duraina
Durant
Duree-Aden
Dureti
Durga
Durgallah
Durienne
Durkadin
Durre
Durre'una
Duru
Dustashyia
Dustee
Dusti
Dustin
Dustina
Dusty (0.01)
Dustyn
Dusty-Storm
Dutchess
Duwameer
Duwania
Duwyne
Dvailyn
Dvyne
Dwa'nae
Dwala
Dwanna
Dwayna
Dwehnyonorh
Dwele
Dwivoni
Dwynae
Dxyah
Dy'ana
Dy'ashiana
Dy'asia
Dy'asiah
Dy'hasia
Dy'honesti
Dy'min
Dy'mon
Dy'monay
Dy'mond
Dy'mondann

Dy'nanjho
Dy'nastee
Dy'nasty
Dy'neka
Dy'niyah
Dy'nyle
Dy'rionna
Dy'ziya
Dyahatou
Dyamand
Dyami
Dyamon'
Dya-Mond
Dyamond (0.02)
Dyamonique
Dyamune
Dyan
Dyana (0.01)
Dyanada
Dyanahi
Dyanali
Dyanara
Dyanarra
Dyandra
Dyanela
Dyani (0.01)
Dyania
Dyanises
Dyann
Dyanna (0.01)
Dyasia
Dybresha
Dycee
Dydrah
Dyemond
Dyerra
Dyiana
Dyionna
Dyjon
Dykeira
Dykeria
Dykota
Dykotah
Dylan (0.16)
Dylan Summer
Dylana
Dylane
Dylanie
Dylann
Dylanna
Dylanne
Dylaysia
Dylen

Dylena
Dylhyla
Dyliah
Dylin
Dyllan
Dyllas
Dylyn
Dymen
Dymin
Dymon
Dymonasia
Dymond (0.02)
Dymonde
Dymonik
Dymonique
Dymphine
Dymphna
Dymund
Dymynd
Dymyra
Dyna
Dynaisa
Dynaisha
Dynaja
Dynali
Dynalis
Dynaliz
Dynasia
Dynastee
Dynasti (0.01)
Dynastie
Dynastii
Dynasty (0.03)
Dynazty
Dyneajah
Dynera
Dynesha
Dynessa
Dynestee
Dynesti
Dynesty
Dynezty
Dynezz
Dyniah
Dynisha
Dyomnd
Dyondrea
Dyone
Dyshani
Dyshawn
Dyshayla
Dyshell
Dyshira

Dysiah
Dystani
Dystini
Dystinie
Dytie'ra
Dyuthi
Dyvine
Dyzairea
Dz
Dzejlana
Dzenana
Dzenita
Dzifa
Dzoay
Dzyier

## ~ E ~

E
É
E Lia
E Myaha
E Naisha
E Niyah
E.Anya
E'ana
E'ban
E'desia
E'dwiyana
E'ianni
E'janay
E'kira
E'kiriya
E'laena
E'layah
E'laylah
E'laysha
E'layshia
E'laysia
E'lexiona
E'lisa Mcchelle
E'lisha
E'lonté
E'lyce
E'magine
E'mane
E'mani
E'mari
E'mauria
E'maya
E'mere
E'mese

| | | | | | | |
|---|---|---|---|---|---|---|
| E'mia | Eadon | Ebanie | Edalys | Edlin | Eelatsoii | Eianalicia |
| E'miah | Eadyn | Ebany | Edan | Edlyn | Eeleah | Eibhlin |
| E'mireyonna | Eahdi | Ebba | Edana | Edlyn Lilianna | Eelee | Eicia |
| E'miyah | Eaira | Ebba-Paige | Edanaz | Edlyna | Eelin | Eicies |
| E'mmia | Eajah | Ebbe | Edanda | Edman | Eellandria | Eiden |
| E'mmya | Eaknoorjit | Ebbianne | Edanna | Edmanie | Eeman | Eidra |
| E'mon | Eakum | Ebbie | Edashia | Edmayole | Eemonie | Eidy |
| E'moni | Eala | Ebby | Edaysia | Edmon | Eenawahs | Eiesha |
| E'monie | Ealessandra- | Ebelen | Edazia | Edna *(0.03)* | Eenroi | Eiet |
| E'monni | Mari | Ebelin | Edden | Edna Mae | Eesha *(0.01)* | Eighmey |
| E'mori | Ealiana | Ebeline | Edderia | Ednacia | Eeshal | Eigne |
| E'muree | Ealise | Ebelyn | Eddie | Ednah | Eeshani | Eija |
| E'mya | Ealiyah | Ebemidayo | Eddreana | Ednaysia | Eesten | Eijah |
| E'nailey | Ealiza | Eben | Eddy | Edneisha | Eeva | Eijana |
| E'naiya | Ealy | Ebene | Edee | Ednijah | Eeva-Liisa | Eijée |
| E'naja | Eamonni | Ebeney | Edelin | Edniya | Eeveeya | Eika |
| E'najah | Eanya | Ebere | Edeline | Edom | Effia | Eila |
| E'nasha | Earin | Eberilda | Edelis | Edona | Effie *(0.01)* | Eilaf |
| E'nashah | Earionna | Eberle | Edelmira | Edreana | Effort | Eilan |
| E'nasia | Earleeisha | Eberlee | Edelyn | Edremmene | Efma | Eiland |
| E'navia | Earlene | Ebilin | Edem Nicole | Edrianna | Efraimia | Eile |
| E'nayja | Earlisha | Ebise | Eden *(0.39)* | Edrice | Efrat | Eileah |
| E'nayjah | Earlissa | Ebonae | Eden Ellerie | Edrik | Efrata | Eilecia |
| E'nayshja | Earllasia | Ebonee | Edena | Edrina | Efrem | Eiledh |
| E'necia | Earlmarria | Eboney | Eden-Maya | Edsha | Efrosini | Eilee |
| E'neisha | Earlyanna | Eboni *(0.02)* | Eden-Monais | Edsiguery | Efstathia | Eileen *(0.10)* |
| E'nijah | Earneese | Ebonie *(0.01)* | Eden-Rose | Edu | Eftyhia | Eileen Faith |
| E'niya | Earnestine | Eboniquie | Ederlin | Eduaniry | Efua | Eileen Tracy |
| E'niyah | Earon | Ebonnie | Edgelynn | Eduarda *(0.01)* | Efua Essawah | Eileena |
| E'nnyia | Earth | Ebony *(0.06)* | Edgna | Eduardo | Eg'ypt | Eileenna |
| E'nya | Earth-Deneal | Ebrecia | Edhit | Eduvijes | Egan | Eileigh |
| E'nyah | Eashanie | Ebrina | Edhna | Edvin | Eghosasere | Eilene |
| E'nyaw | Eashvir | Ebru | Edi | Edvonica | Egich | Eiley |
| E'nyia | Easia | Ebyan | Ediah | Edward | Eglan | Eiliana |
| E'nyja | Easterwood | Ebyn | Ediana | Edwardsen | Egra | Eilidh |
| E'nyya | Eastin | Ecatarina | Edianad | Edweige | Egypt *(0.05)* | Eilie |
| E'owyn | Eastlan | Ecaterina | Edianiz | Edwige | Egyptian | Eilin |
| E'reisha | Easton | Eccence | Ediany | Edwin | Ehlaina | Eilir |
| E'reshia | Eastyn | Ece | Edidiong | Edwina *(0.01)* | Ehlam | Eilis |
| E'riel | Eastynn | Ece Yaren | Edie *(0.02)* | Edwyn | Ehlana | Eilish |
| E'riyah | Eather | Eceil | Edie-Raine | Edwyne | Ehlena | Eiliya |
| E'rozjha | Eaton | Echo *(0.02)* | Ediht | Edye | Ehlonna | Eilla |
| E'ryha | Eava | Echo Jayde | Edilia | Edyliz | Ehonna | Eilley |
| E'shanti | Eavah | Echoe | Edin | Edyn *(0.01)* | Ehralyn | Eily |
| E'shayla | Eavan | Eckly | Edina | Edyta | Ehren | Eilyn |
| E'sia | Eavann | Ecko | Edison | Edythe | Ehrengton | Eilynn |
| E'taige | Eaven | Ecstacy | Edisto | Edzaria | Ehrianne | Eima |
| E'tavia | Eavie | Ed'kerria | Edit | Edziah | Ehrin | Eimaan |
| E'ticia | Eavon | Ed'mariea | Edita | Ee | Ehryka | Eiman |
| E'zariah | Eazila | Ed'zariah | Edith *(0.10)* | Eeara | Ehsan | Eimani |
| E'zoria | Eb'briel | Edaja | Edith Stephany | Eedyn | Ehssan | Eimi |
| Eadaoin | Ebalyn | Edaleina | Edleweiss | Eeeva | Ei | Eimiliz |
| Eadlin | Ebanehita | Edalia | Edlie | Eelajah | Eian | Eimiy |

| | | | | | | |
|---|---|---|---|---|---|---|
| Eimy | Ela (0.02) | Elarie | Elease | Elenita | Elexyas | Elidavoncile |
| Eira | Ela Andrea | Elasa | Eleasia | Eleniz | Elexys | Elide |
| Eiranasha | Ela'na | Elasah | Eleaunah | Elenna | Eleydi | Elide Gabriella |
| Eireanna | Elaena | Elasha | Eleccia | Elenne | Eleyna | Elidelkys |
| Eireen | Elaf | Elasia | Elecia | Elenny | Eleyna Madeline | Elidia |
| Eiren | Elah | Elaudie | Elecktra | Elenor | Eleysha | Elidia |
| Eirena | Elahn | Elaura | Electra (0.01) | Elenorah | Elfa | Guadalupe |
| Eiress | Elahna | El-Ayanna | Electria | Elenore | Elfee-Maya | Elie (0.01) |
| Eirian | Elaie | Elayjah | Elecxion | Eleny | Elfie | Elie-Ann |
| Eirianne | Elaija | Elayjha | Eledina | Eleona | Elfin | Elieanna |
| Eirin | Elaijah | Elayna (0.06) | Eleece | Eleonor | Elfrieda | Elie-Anne (0.01) |
| Eirinn | Elain | Elaynah | Eleeka | Eleonora | Elgin | Eliel |
| Eirlys | Elaina (0.25) | Elayne | Eleen | Eleonore (0.02) | Elhaam | Elienai |
| Eiryonna | Elainah | Elaynna | Eleena | Eleora | Elhame | Elienna |
| Eirys | Elaina-Mae | Elaysha | Eleesa | Eleorah | Elhan | Elienora |
| Eisabel | Elaine (0.16) | Elaysia | Eleesha | Elephteria | Elhana | Elie-Rose |
| Eisabella Jayde | Elainea | Elazia | Eleeysiae | Eleri | Elheyna | Eliese |
| Eisha (0.01) | Elaineah | Elba | Eleeza | Elerin | Elhonei | Eliesser |
| Eisland | Elainelee | Elbetal | Eleftheria | Elesa | Eli | Elietta |
| Eisley | Elainey | El-Bethel | Elegance | Elescha | Elia (0.03) | Eliette |
| Eithne | Elaini | Elbia | Eleice | Elese | Eliadna | Elif (0.01) |
| Eiyena | Elainie | Elcee | Eleidi | Elesea | Eliah (0.01) | Elifnaz |
| Eiyyanna | Elainna (0.01) | Elchana | Eleidy | Elesha | Elian | Eligia |
| Eizabella | Elainneise | Elcy | Eleigh | Eleshea | Eliana (0.36) | Eliha |
| Ej Lynne | Elainy | Elda (0.01) | Eleigha | Elesia | Eliana Jea | Eliina |
| Eja | Elaira | Eldai | Eleighana | Elessa | Elianah | Eliis |
| Ejanayah | Elaisha | Eldana | Eleighanna | Elesse | Eliana-Rose | Elijah (0.01) |
| Ejaniyyah | Elaiya | Eldasia | Eleijah | Elessia | Eliandra | Elijane |
| Ejept | Elaiynebeth | Eldena | Eleina | Eleta | Éliane | Elijanna |
| Ekampreet | Elaiza | Eldiana | Eleiona | Eleticia | Eliane (0.07) | Elijiah |
| Ekani | Elaja | Eldina | Eleis | Eletra | Eliangni | Elika |
| Ekaterena | Elajah | Eldonnesha | Eleisha | Eletta | Eliani | Elilia |
| Ekaterina (0.01) | Elampourni | Eldora | Eleisia | Elette | Elianie | Elimar |
| Ekaterini | Elan | Eldriana | Eleison | Elettra | Elianis | Elimarie |
| Ekatherina | Élan | Eldy | Eleka | Elexa (0.01) | Elianise | Elimelen |
| Ekco | Elana (0.08) | Eldy-Ninoska | Elekera | Elexas | Elianna (0.05) | Elimelise |
| Ekemini | Elanah | Ele'na | Eleksys | Elexciana | Eli-Anne | Elin (0.01) |
| Ekin | Elanda | Elea | Elektra (0.02) | Elexcis | Elianne (0.02) | Eliná |
| Ekira | Elandra | Eleah | Elen | Elexes | Eliany | Elina (0.03) |
| Ekjot | Elandria | Eleaisha | Elena (0.58) | Elexia | Elia-Rose | Elinah |
| Ekko | Elanee | Eleajiah | Elena Dora | Elexiah | Elias | Eline |
| Ekman | Elaney | Eleana (0.01) | Elena Kaithlin | Elexiauna | Eliauna | Elink |
| Eknahrri | Elani (0.01) | Eleanah | Elena Pastory | Elexiella | Eliazbeth | Elinor (0.01) |
| Eknoor | Elania | Eleane | Elena Shania | Elexious | Elibeth | Elinore |
| Eko | Elanie | Eleanna | Elenae | Elexis (0.04) | Elica | Eliona |
| Ekram | Elanizja | Eleanor (0.51) | Elena- | Elexiss | Eliccia | Elionae |
| Ekseer | Elanna (0.01) | Eleanor | Marguerite | Elexius | Elice | Elionnah |
| Ekta | Elannah | Branwen | Elena-Maria | Elexsia | Elicia (0.02) | Eli-Opal |
| Ekysjha | Elannia | Eleanor Celeste | Elenette | Elexsis | Eliciah | Eliora |
| El | Elanor (0.01) | Eleanora (0.01) | Eleni (0.04) | Elexus (0.01) | Eliciana | Eliot (0.01) |
| El'janique | Elanora | Eleanore (0.01) | Elenia | Elexxys | Elicianna | Eli-Rose |
| El'jriana | Elara | Eleanyse | Eleni-Claire | Elexy | Elida (0.01) | Elis |
| El'riyonna | Elaria | Eleasa | Elenie | | Elidainys | Elis Saray |

Elisa *(0.16)*
Elisaa
Elisabel
Elisabelle
Elisabet *(0.01)*
Élisabeth
Elisabeth *(0.33)*
Elisabetta
Elisabith
Elisah
Elisama
Elisamai
Elisa-Marie
Elisamarie
Elisana
Elisanda
Elisandra
Elisanne
Elisapi
Elisapie
Elisa-Rae
Elisavet
Elisaveta
Eliscia
Élise
Elise *(0.57)*
Elise Andrea
Elisea
Elisebeth
Elisee
Elisella
Eliseo
Elisha *(0.07)*
Elisha Maria
Elishaba
Elishadie
Elisha-Grace
Elishah
Elisha-Kakanga
Elisha-Mae
Elisheva *(0.01)*
Elishevah
Elishia
Elishka
Elisia *(0.02)*
Elisiahna
Elisiana
Eliska
Elisol
Elissa *(0.09)*
Elissar
Elisse
Elissel

Elissia
Elissya
Elissyana
Elisua
Elita
Elitta
Elive
Elivia *(0.01)*
Elivier
Elivira
Elixandra
Elixsi
Eliya
Eliyah *(0.01)*
Eliyahna
Eliyana
Eliyanna
Eliyse
Eliysia
Eliz
Eliza *(0.42)*
Eliza Jane
Eliza Marie
Eliza Therese
Eliza-Anne
Elizabed
Elizabel
Elizabella
Elizabelle
Elizabess
Elizabet
Elizabeta
Eliza-Beth
Elizabeth *(5.83)*
Elizabeth Ann
Elizabeth Elena
Elizabeth
  Evalyne
Elizabeth Grace
Elizabeth
  Ngocat
Elizabeth Rose
Elizabeth-Ann
Elizabethann
Elizabeth-Anne
Elizabeth-Marie
Elizabeth-
  Nycole
Elizabeth-
  Prestod
Elizabeth-Sarai
Elizabeth-
  Victoria

Elizabith
Elizah
Elizaida
Eliza-Kate
Elizamariah
Elizandra
Elizangel
Elizanna
Elizaveta
Elizbeth
Elize
Élize
Elizebeth *(0.01)*
Elizela
Elizeth
Eliziaunna
Elizibeth
Elizmarie
Elizzabeth
Elizzbeth
Elizzet
Eljana
Eljanae
Eljesa
Elkanah
Elke
Elki
Ella *(4.30)*
Ella Aliese
Ella Anne
Ella Clare
Ella Franscine
Ella Jo
Ella M
Ella Marie
Ella Rose
Ella Shae
Ellabay
Ellabelle
Ella-Bleu
Ellablue
Ella-Catherine
Ellacyn
Elladah
Ellaena
Ellagence
Ella-Grace
Ellagrace
Ellah *(0.01)*
Ellaheh
Ellahiqa
Ellahna
Ellaina *(0.01)*

Ellaine
Ellaira
Ellaka
Ella-Kate
Ellakate
Ellalena
Ella-Mae
Ellamae
Ella-Marie
Ellamarie
Ella-Maude
Ella-May
Ellamy
Ellan
Ellana
Ellana Leigh
Ellanah
Ellandra
Ellania
Ellanie
Ellannah
Ellanor *(0.01)*
Ellanora
Ellanore
Ellaq
Ella-Rae
Ellarae
Ellaree
Ellareen
Ellarie
Ellarose
Ellary
Ella-Sandra
Ellashani
Ellason
Ellasyn
Ellavy
Ellawyn
Ellawynn
Ellaxandra
Ellaya
Ella-Yanna
Ellaycia
Ellayna
Ellaysha
Ellbie
Ellé
Elle *(0.21)*
Elle Mae
Elle Marie
Ellea
Elleah
Elleana

Elleann
Elleanna
Elleanor
Elleanore
Ellecia
Elleciyanna
Ellee *(0.01)*
Elleeana
Elleen
Elleese
Ellegra
Elleiana
Elleigh
Elleighana
Elleina
Elleke
Elle-Mae
Elle-Mcgin
Ellen *(0.19)*
Ellen Ann
Ellena *(0.01)*
Ellenah
Ellenia
Ellenor
Ellenora
Ellenore
Elleonia
Eller
Ellerie
Ellery *(0.05)*
Ellesheva
Ellesie
Elleson
Ellest
Ellette
Ellewyn
Ellexa
Ellexiah
Elley
Elleyna
Elli *(0.03)*
Ellia *(0.01)*
Elliah
Elliahna
Elliana *(0.10)*
Elliana Celeste
Ellianah
Elliandra
Ellianet
Ellianna *(0.03)*
Ellianne
Elliat
Ellice

Ellicia
Ellicianna
Ellida
Éllie
Ellie *(0.94)*
Ellie Ann
Ellie Marcella
Ellie'anna
Ellieana
Ellie-Ann
Ellieanna
Ellieblue
Ellie-Elle
Ellie-Hannah
Ellie-Jade
Ellie-Mae
Ellieora
Ellierose
Elliet
Elliette
Elliiot
Ellijanna
Ellina
Ellington
Ellinor
Ellinshua
Elliona
Ellionah
Ellionna
Elliot *(0.03)*
Elliott *(0.02)*
Elliotte
Ellis *(0.03)*
Ellisa *(0.01)*
Ellisabeth
Ellisandra
Ellise *(0.01)*
Ellisema
Ellisen
Ellisha
Ellishah
Ellishiah
Ellisia
Ellison *(0.04)*
Ellissa
Elliston
Ellisya
Ellisyn
Ellita
Ellivia
Elliyah
Elliza
Elliza-Eve

Elllie
Elloise
Ellon
Ellona
Ellora
Elloree
Ellorie
Ellory
Ellsa
Ellsah
Ellsey
Ellsie
Ellura
Elly *(0.04)*
Ellya
Ellyana *(0.01)*
Ellyandra
Elly-Ann
Ellyanna *(0.01)*
Ellyauna
Ellyce
Ellyette
Ellyn
Ellynn
Ellynor
Ellyot
Ellys
Ellysa
Ellysania
Ellyse
Ellysha
Ellyshia
Ellysia
Ellysn
Ellyson
Ellyssa *(0.01)*
Ellyza Jade
Elma *(0.01)*
Elmani
Elmaya
Elmedina
Elmeena
Elmer
Elmina
Elmira
Elna
Elnora
Eloa
Eloane
Elodia
Élodie
Elodie *(0.17)*
Elodie-Lorie

| | | | | | | |
|---|---|---|---|---|---|---|
| Elodie-Rosanne | Elsiana | Elydianis | Em'rie | Emanuela | Emele | Emersyn (0.04) |
| Elody (0.01) | Elsie (0.10) | Elyiana | Ema (0.05) | Emanuella | Emelee | Emery (0.07) |
| Elodye | Elsiemarie | Elyishia | Ema'lee | Emanuelle | Emelena | Emese |
| Eloe | Elsie-May | Ely-Jade | Emaan (0.01) | Emany | Emeli (0.01) | Emgy |
| Elohy | Elspeth (0.01) | Elyka | Emadelys | Emara | Emeli Anah | Emi (0.01) |
| Eloik | Elssy | Elyla | Emadgen | Ema-Rae | Emelia (0.09) | Emia |
| Eloina | Elsy (0.01) | Elymar | Emae | Emarae | Emeliana | Emiah |
| Eloisa (0.01) | Elsye | Ely-Maude | Emagyn | Emaralyse | Emelic | Emiaj |
| Eloïse | Eltanese | Elyn | Emah | Emarea | Emelie (0.02) | Emialia |
| Éloïse | El-Tinukemiwa | Elyna | Emahni | Emaree | Emeliina | Emica |
| Eloise (0.16) | Eltis | Elyne | Emaijah | Emaretta | Emelin (0.01) | Emice |
| Eloiza | Eltzy | Elynne | Emaily | Emari | Emelina | Emicka |
| Eloize | Elura | Elynnor | Emaja | Emaria | Emelinda | Emie (0.03) |
| Elon | Eluvia | Elynor | Emajen | Emariah | Emeline (0.01) | Emie-Anne |
| Elona (0.01) | Eluvielle | Elynore | Emajhé | Emarie (0.01) | Emelisa | Emie-Jeanne |
| Elonda | Eluzai | Elyonna | Emalayne | Emariel | Emelisabel | Emie-Rose |
| Eloni | Elva (0.01) | Elyra | Emalaysha | Emarilys | Emelisse | Emigh |
| Elonna | Elvena | Elyria | Emalea | Emariona | Emelly (0.01) | Emiika |
| Elonnah | Elvera | Elys Milagro | Emaleah | Emaris | Emely (0.25) | Emiily |
| Elonnie | Elvesta | Elysa (0.02) | Ema-Lee | Emariya | Emely's | Emijade |
| Elony | Elvia (0.01) | Elysabelle | Emalee (0.07) | Emariyah | Emelya | Emika |
| Elora (0.04) | Elvida | Elysabeth (0.01) | Emalee-Jo | Emariz | Emelyn (0.02) | Emiko (0.01) |
| Elora-Dannan | Elvina | Elysanne | Emalei | E-Marjay | Emelynn | Emila |
| Elorah | Elvina- | Elysant | Emaleigh (0.02) | Emary | Emem | Emilce |
| Elorie |    Rifkhatovna | Elysdee | Emaleigh Jean | Emaryn | Emer | Emile |
| Elory | Elvira (0.01) | Élyse | Emaleigha | Emaya | Emera | Emilea (0.01) |
| Elouise | Elvitia | Elyse (0.16) | Emalene | Emaye | Emerald (0.05) | Emileah |
| Elowen | Elvla | Elysea | Emaleth | Emaysa | Emerald | Emi-Lee |
| Elowyn | Elwaat | Elyseia | Emaley | Ember (0.06) |    Sunshine | Emilee (0.34) |
| Eloxia | Ely (0.01) | Elysha (0.01) | Emali | Ember-Brooks | Emeraldmay | Emileen |
| Eloysa | Elya | Elysia (0.03) | Emalia (0.01) | Emberley | Emeraude | Emilei |
| Elpida | Elyabelle | Elysiann | Emalie (0.01) | Emberli |    (0.01) | Emileigh (0.02) |
| Elriana | Elyadah | Elysis | Emaliee | Emberlie | Emeraude Lea | Emilena |
| Elricheca | Elya-Kim | Elyska | Emalina | Emberline | Emercyn | Emilene |
| Elrika | Elyan | Elyss | Emaline (0.02) | Emberlinne | Emeree | Emileny |
| Elroi | Elyana (0.01) | Elyssa (0.08) | Emallie | Emberly | Emerey | Emiley (0.03) |
| Elsa (0.14) | Elyane (0.01) | Elyssah | Emaly (0.01) | Emberlyn | Emergaid | Emili (0.03) |
| Elsabea | Elyane Rose | Elysse (0.01) | Emalyn | Emberlynn | Emergy | Emilia (0.25) |
| Elsah | Elyaness | Elyssia (0.01) | Emalyne |    (0.01) | Emeri | Emiliah |
| Elsaie | Elyani | Elytza | Emalynn | Embre | Emeriald | Emiliana (0.01) |
| Elsa-Laurie | Ely-Ann | Elytze | Emamichelle | Embree | Emeribeth | Emiliane |
| Elsalee | Elyann | Elyvia | Eman (0.02) | Embrelin | Emerica | Emilianna |
| Elsalynn | Elyanna (0.01) | Elyza (0.01) | Emane | Embria | Emerie (0.01) | Emilianne |
| Elsbeth | Elyannah | Elyzabeth | Emanee | Embriah | Emerika | Emilianys |
| Else | Elyanne (0.01) | Elyzah | Emaney | Embrianna | Emeril | Émilie |
| Elsee | Elyannie | Elyza-Star | Emaní | Embrii | Emerill | Emilie (0.42) |
| Elsey | Elyara | Elyzzabeth | Emani (0.06) | Embry | Emerise | Emilie Laura |
| Elsha | Elyce | Elza | Emani Larae | Embyr-Lee | Emerlee | Emilie Thao Vy |
| Elshaday | Elycia | Elzabeth | Emanie | Eme Lillyth | Emerleysha | Emilie-Ann |
| El-Shaddai | Elyciah | Elzada | Emaniela | Emefa | Emerly | Emilie-Anne |
| Elshaddai | Elyciana | Elzahra | Emanise | Emeka | Emersen (0.01) | Emiliee |
| Elshadye | Elyda | Elzie | Emanize | Emel | Emersin | Emilie-Maude |
| Elsi | Elydia | Elzora | Emanni | Emelda | Emerson (0.29) | Emilija |

| | | | | | | |
|---|---|---|---|---|---|---|
| Emilin | Emily-Rose | Emmaann | Emmalene | Emmaree | Emmilya | Emri-Kate |
| Emiline | Emilyrose | Emma-Anne | Emmalenn | Emmari | Emmly | Emry |
| Emilise | Emilyse | Emma-Astri | Emmaley | Emmariah | Emmlyann | Emryanna |
| Emilissa | Emima | Emma-Cathe | Emmali | Emmarie (0.01) | Emmma | Emry-Elizabeth |
| Emiliy | Emime | Emma-Clair | Emmalia | Emmarita-Nikol | Emmonie | Emrys |
| Emiliya | Emina | Emma-Claire | Emmalie (0.01) | Emma-Rose | Emmonline | Emsley |
| Emiliz | Eminah | Emmacolman | Emmaliene | Emmarose | Emmpreet | Emslie |
| Emille | Emine | Emmad | Emmaliese | Emmarsyn | Emmri | Emuna |
| Emillee | Eminet | Emmadale | Emmalin | Emmary | Emmy (0.09) | Emunah |
| Emilleigh | Emiola | Emma-Delphine | Emmalina | Emmasara | Emmye | Emuni |
| Emilli | Emira | Emmae | Emmaline | Emmauni | Emmylea | Emy (0.16) |
| Emillia | Emir-Ari | Emma- | (0.04) | Emmaus | Emmy-Leigh | Emy Ann |
| Emillianna | Emirelys | Elizabeth | Emmalisa | Emmaya | Emmylou | Emy Rose |
| Emillie | Emiret | Emma-Eve | Emmalise | Emmazel | Emna | Emya (0.01) |
| Emilly (0.02) | Emireth | Emma-Gayle | Emmaliya | Emme (0.02) | Emna-Beya | E-Myah |
| Emilly Hellen | Emirsen | Emmagen | Emmaliz | Emmelan | Emnet (0.01) | Emyah |
| Emilu | Emirson | Emmagene | Emmallee | Emmelean | Emogen | Emydouce |
| Émily | E-Miya | Emmagin | Emmalou | Emmelene | Emogin | Emye Jane |
| Emily (10.56) | Emiya | Emmagine | Emma-Louise | Princess | Emon | Paskale |
| Emily Alexis | Emiyah | Emma-Grace | Emmaly (0.01) | Emmeli | Emone | Emyha |
| Emily Alisha | Em-Jai | (0.01) | Emmalye | Emmelia | Emonee | Emyhia |
| Emily Ann | Emjay | Emmagrace | Emmalyn (0.02) | Emmelin | Emoney | Emyia |
| Emily Eliz | Emli | Emmah (0.02) | Emmalyne | Emmeline | Emoní | Emyiah |
| Emily Elizabeth | Emliea | Emmaiya | Emma-Lynn | (0.02) | Emoni (0.02) | Emy-Jade |
| Emily Elvira | Emlyn | Emma-J | Emmalynn | Emmellise | Emonie (0.01) | Emyjae |
| Emily Gabriela | Emma (9.57) | Emma-Jane | (0.01) | Emmely | Emonni | Emylah |
| Emily Grace | Emma Ann | Emma-Jayne | Emmalynne | Emmelyn | Emonnie | Emyle |
| Emily Nicole | Emma Anne | Emma-Jean | Emmalys | Emmera | Emontí | Emy-Lee |
| Emily Rachel | Emma Camille | Emmajean | Emmamae | Emmerald | Emony | Emylee (0.01) |
| Emily Ria | Emma Corazon | Emma-Jeanne | Emma-Maria | Emmerey | Emoree | Emyleigh |
| Emily Rose | Emma Danie | Emma-Jo | Emma-Marie | Emmeri | Emori | Emylene |
| Emily S | Emma Denika | Emmajo | Emma-May | Emmerie | Emorie | Emylia |
| Emily Vanessa | Emma Grace | Emma-Kate | Emman | Emmersen | Emorria | Emyliane |
| Emily Victoria | Emma Grayce | Emmakate | Emmane | Emmerson | Emory (0.03) | Emylianne |
| Emilyah | Emma Jean | Emma-Kathe | Emmanet | (0.03) | Emory Quinn | Emylie |
| Emilyana | Emma Jo | Emma-Katheri | Emmani | Emmersun | Emperatris | Emylise |
| Emily-Andrea | Emma Kate | Emmakay | Emma-Nicole | Emmersyn | Emperess | Emy-Lou |
| Emily-Ann | Emma Kay | Emmale | Emmanna | Emmery | Emperesse | Emylou |
| Emilyann | Emma Lee | Emma-Lea | Emmanuel | Emmet | Emperia | Emyrald |
| Emilyanna | Emma Leigh | Emmalea (0.01) | Emmanuela | Emmette | Empress (0.01) | Emyreth |
| Emily-Anne | Emma Liegh | Emma-Lee | (0.01) | Emmey | Empress | Emy-Rose (0.01) |
| Emilyanne | Emma Lou | (0.01) | Emmanuella | Emmi (0.02) | Jahseandra | Emyrson |
| Emilya-Sarah | Emma Lynn | Emmalee (0.14) | (0.01) | Emmie (0.04) | Empris | Emyyah |
| Emily-Clarissa | Emma Madison | Emma-Lei | Emmanuelle | Emmii | Empryess | En'dyia |
| Emily-Elizabeth | Emma Marie | Emmalei | (0.04) | Emmika | Empryss | Ena |
| Emily-Grace | Emma Paige | Emmaleia | Emmanuelle La | Emmilee | Emra | Enaara |
| Emily-Jane | Emma Rose | Emma-Leigh | Fleche | Emmilene | Emree | Enaelle |
| Emily-Jean | Emma Ruth | (0.01) | Emmanuellle | Emmiley | Emrey | Enahya |
| Emily-Malu | Emma Ryan | Emmaleigh | Emmanya | Emmilie | Emri | Enaiha |
| Emily-Maria | Emma'lee | (0.02) | Emmara | Emmilina | Emria | Enaija |
| Emilyn (0.01) | Emma'leigh | Emmaleis | Emma-Rae | Emmilly | Emrickka | Enaisha |
| Emilynda | Emma'lynn | Emmalen | Emmarae | Emmilou | Emrie (0.01) | Enaja |
| Emilynn | Emma'nae | Emmalena | Emma-Ray | Emmily (0.01) | Emrika | Enajaé |

| | | | | | | |
|---|---|---|---|---|---|---|
| Enaly | England | Enslie | Eralyn | Ericcia | Eriqa | Ershla |
| Enam | English | Ensly | Eralys | Ericellie | Eris (0.01) | Ersida |
| Enana | Engoleth | Entela | Eran | Erich | Erisa | Ersily |
| Enara | Enia | Enuri | Erandi | Ericha | Erissa | Erva |
| Enashia | Eniah | Envi | Erandy | Ericia | Eriuna | Erwa |
| Enasia | Enialex | Envionna | Erashawn | Ericka (0.06) | Eriyah | Eryan |
| Enatano | Eniaya | Envy | Erblina | Ericka Melissa | Eriyana | Eryana |
| E-Navi'ah | Enibokun | Envyia | Ercy | Ericse | Eriyanna | Eryanna |
| Enaya | Enica | Enxhi | Erebecca | Erie | Eriyannah | Eryca |
| Enayah | Enice | Enya (0.01) | Ereionna | Erie'yanna Ali | Eriyauna | Erycea |
| Enchrina | Enid | Enyah | Erelyn | Erieal | Eriyel | Eryckah |
| Enda | Enidmarie | Enyce | Erelys | Erieanna | Eriyelle | Eryel |
| Endea | Enihyah | Enyche | Erem | Eriel (0.01) | Eriyona | Eryiona |
| Endeaver | Enijah | Enye | Eremi | Erielle | Eriyonna | Eryka (0.02) |
| Endelie | Eninaja | Enyia | Eremiah | Erielys | Erjona | Erykah (0.01) |
| Ender | Eniola | Enyius | Eren | Erien | Erlande | Eryn (0.06) |
| Endi | Eniolanimi | Enyjah | Erena | Erieona | Erlinda | Eryn Nycole |
| Endia (0.01) | Enirah | Enyola | Erendida | Eries | Erline | Eryne |
| Endiah | Eniree | Enyonam | Erendira | Eriesia | Erliz | Erynn (0.02) |
| Éndiah | Enisa | Enysah | Erenisa | Erik | Erma (0.01) | Erynne |
| Endie | Enise | Enyssa | Eres | Erika (0.62) | Ermanie | Eryona |
| Endigo | Enisha | Enza | Ereshka | Erika Ashley | Ermeli | Erys |
| Endiya | Enisia | Eolanta | Eresina | Erika Lorraine | Ermelinda | Erysse |
| Endiyah | Enith | Eolie | Eressea | Erikah | Ermica | Erza |
| Endline | Eniya (0.01) | Eona | Ereuna | Erika-Josslyne | Ermioni | Esa |
| Endora | Eniyah (0.01) | Eonia | Erez | Erika-Kelsey | Erna | Esabel |
| Endrelie | Eniyia | Eonna | Ereza | Erikakenyahta | Ernaysha | Esabela |
| Endsley | Enjoli | Eonni | Erfa | Erikan | Ernecia | Esabella |
| Endurance | Enjolie | Eonshana | Ergysthanie | Eriketi | Erneshia |    (0.01) |
| Endy | Enlla | Éowyn | Eri'anah | Erikha | Ernesta Marie | Esabelle |
| Endya (0.01) | Enma | Eowyn (0.02) | Eri'asia | Erikia | Ernestina | Esanty |
| Endyah | Enmaline | Ephany | Eri'nai | Erikkah | Ernestine | Esbeida |
| Endyiah | Enmeisinei | Epherata | Eri'yonna | Eriksre | Ernie | Esbeidy |
| Eneasha | Enmily | Ephrata | Eriahnna | Erilyn | Erniece | Esbeiry |
| Enedelia | Enn | Epifania | Eriajah | Erimell | Erniya | Esbeyde |
| Enedin | Enna | Epipany | Erial | Erin (1.54) | Erniyah | Esbeydi |
| Enedys | Ennah | Epiphany | Erialys | Erin Eliza | Erotisse | Esbheidi |
| Eneece | Ennasence | Epona | Erian | Erin Larissa | Erreeze | Escalin |
| Eneida | Enndya | Eponine | Eriana (0.01) | Erina | Erriale | Escarlet |
| Eneli | Ennea | Eppie | Erianna (0.02) | Erinaejah | Erriana | Escarleth |
| Enelis | Ennely | Epryincez | Eriannah | Erinasia | Errica | Escarlett |
| Eneliz | Ennocence | Eqra | Erianthe | Erindy | Erricka | Escencia |
| Eneque | Enochlynna | Equeria | Eriasia | Erini | Errika | Esela |
| Enerel | Enola (0.01) | Equilla | Eriauna | Erinn (0.01) | Errin | Eselda |
| Enerida | Enolla | Er Maya | Eribelys | Erinna | Errion | Esella |
| Enesa | Enora | Er'nya | Eric | Erinne | Errionna | Esenia |
| Enevi | Enorah | Er'yuan | Erica (0.71) | Erin-Xinyu | Erriyon | Ese-Osa |
| Eneydy | Enrelin | Era (0.01) | Erica Marie | Erion | Erron | Eseosa |
| Enfinity | Enrica | Era Ty'nikkiwa | Ericah | Eriona | Errow | Esha (0.03) |
| Engelina | Enrika | Erabelle | Ericajo | Erionah | Erryiana | Eshaa |
| Engelle | Ensia | Erác | Erica-Lynn | Erionna (0.01) | Erryn | Eshaal |
| Engelyn | Ensleigh | Erácya | Ericarose | Erionne | Errzarieya | Eshal (0.01) |
| Engi | Ensley (0.01) | Eralee | Ericca | Erioyana | Ersheen | Eshana |

| | | | | | |
|---|---|---|---|---|---|
| Eshane | Esperanza | Estephany | Ethnee | Eumayah | Evalee | Evangelyn |
| Eshani | *(0.09)* | *(0.01)* | Ethney | Eumeisha | Evalena | Evangiline |
| Eshaya | Esperlyne | Ester *(0.03)* | Ethnie | Eun | Evalene | Evanglyn |
| Eshea | Esperoniza | Esterline | Ethny | Euneshia | Evalese | Evani |
| Eshell | Espn | Esteyli | Etianna | Eunhae | Evali | Evania |
| Eshera | Espyn | Estfania | Etienna | Euniaya | Evalicia | Evanice |
| Eshita | Esra | Esthefani | Etienne | Eunice *(0.03)* | Evalienna | Evanie |
| Eshmeet | Essance | Esthefania | Etiona | Eunice Jane | Evalin | Evanjelina |
| Eshnoor | Essani | Esthefanny | Etiyana | Eunice Ju | Evalina *(0.01)* | Evanjilyn |
| Eshonica | Esse | Esthefany | Etnamyna | Eunicet | Evaline | Evanka |
| Eshpreet | Essence *(0.10)* | Esthel | Etni | Euniecia | Evalinn | Evanlee |
| Eshroop | Essence | Esthela | Etrulia | Eunique *(0.01)* | Evalis | Evann |
| Eshveer | Aumyree | Esther *(0.50)* | Etsubdenk | Eunise | Evaliz | Evanna |
| Eshyia | Essenia | Esther-Anne | Etta *(0.01)* | Eunisela | Eva-Luna | Evanne |
| Esia | Essense | Estheranne | Etta Grace | Eunisha | Evaly | Evanniesse |
| Esienl | Essia | Esther-Victoria | Etti | Eunitra | Evalyce | Evanny |
| Esilena | Essie | Estie | Ettienne | Eunive | Evalyn *(0.03)* | Evans |
| Esinam | Essience | Estifpani | Etty *(0.01)* | Euniya | Evalyna | Evanthea |
| Eslaam | Essilee | Estin | Eu'nique | Euniyah | Evalyn-Louise | Evanthia |
| Esli | Essynce | Estoria | Eucini | Eunji | Evalynn *(0.01)* | Evany |
| Eslin | Esta | Estrella *(0.21)* | Eudokia | Eunjin | Evalynne | Eva-Rose |
| Esly | Estacey | Estrella Anahi | Eudora | Euodia | Evalyse | Evarose |
| Eslyn | Estafani | Estrellea | Eudy Nequita | Euphemia | Evalyz | Evarya |
| Esma | Estafany | Estrellita *(0.01)* | Euge'onia | Euriah | Evamaria | Evasia |
| Esmae | Estaijjah | Estreya | Eugena | Euricka | Eva-Marie | Evaskye |
| Esmael | Estashia | Estrianna | Eugenah | Eurlee | Evamarie | Eva-Symone |
| Esmaralda | Estecia | Esttefany | Eugenane | Euronica | Evan *(0.03)* | Evaye |
| Esmé | Estee | Esty *(0.01)* | Eugene | Euronn | Evana *(0.01)* | Evbelin |
| Esme *(0.02)* | Estée | Estyni | Eugenia *(0.01)* | Europe | Evander | Evdokia |
| Esmee | Estefana | Esu | Eugenia- | Eurriah | Evane | Éve |
| Esmelda | Estefane | Esugen | Zowana | Eurykah | Evanee | Ève |
| Esmelisa | Estefani *(0.04)* | Esykya | Eugenie *(0.02)* | Eusebia | Evanelly | Eve *(0.29)* |
| Esmerai | Estefanía | Esynce | Eugenie- | Eustina | Evanely | Eve Marie |
| Esmeralda | Estefania *(0.04)* | Eszter | Gracielle | Euvelyn | Evanescence | Evea |
| *(0.65)* | Estefanie | Etaliah | Eugenie-La | Euzzela | Evanessa | Eveah |
| Esmeralda | Estefanni | Etaly | Fleche | Éva | Evaney | Evealiz |
| Angelica | Estefanny | Etania | Eugenielle | Eva *(1.16)* | Evangalyna | Eveana |
| Esmerallda | Estefany *(0.04)* | Etaya | Eugeny | Eva Anne | Evangel | Eveanlee |
| Esmerally | Estefanya | Etayne | Euginia | Eva Jakaylee | Evangela Marie | Evee |
| Esmerelda | Estefhany | Eternal | Euicenia | Eva Jasmine | Evangelea | Eve- |
| Esmerilda | Esteisy | Eterniti | Eujin | Eva Jayne | Evangeleah | Emmanuelle |
| Esmerin | Estela *(0.01)* | Eternity *(0.01)* | Eukelia | Eva Lisa | Evangeleen | Eve-Gabrielle |
| Esmi | Estelie | Eternyti | Eula | Eva Tallulah | Evangelena | Eveiona |
| Esmira | Estella *(0.07)* | Etha | Eulaenee | Eva-Belin | Evangelene | Eve-Julie |
| Esmirna | Estelle *(0.04)* | Ethan *(0.01)* | Eulala | Evabelle | Evangelia *(0.01)* | Evel |
| Esmma | Estelma | Ethar | Eulalea | Evadne | Evangelica | Eve-Laurence |
| Esosa | Estely | Ethel *(0.01)* | Eulalia *(0.01)* | Evadney | Evangelie | Eve-Lea |
| Esparanza | Estepfani | Ethel May | Eulalie | Evagelia | Evangelina | Evelee |
| Esparonza | Estephane | Ether | Eulani | Evageline | *(0.04)* | Eveleen |
| Espen | Estephani | Ethiopia | Eulashia | Evah | Evangéline | Evelena |
| Esperance | Estephania | Ethly | Eulia | Evah-Moonlight | Evangeline | Evelene |
| Esperanez | Estephanie | Ethne | Eulogia | Eva-Jean | *(0.10)* | Evelesse |
| Esperansa | *(0.01)* | Ethnea | Eumaria | Evaleasia | Evangelisa | Evelia |

Evelice
Evelie
Eveliina
Evelin (0.08)
Evelina (0.02)
Evelinda
Evéline
Eveline (0.01)
Evelino
Evelisa
Evelise
Evelisse
Eveliz
Evellyn
Eve-Lorie
Evely
Evelyn (2.19)
Evelyn Iris
Evelyn Jane
Evelyna
Évelyne
Evelyne (0.04)
Eve-Lynn
Evelynn (0.05)
Evelynna
Evelynne
Evelyze
Eve-Mahee
Eve-Mari
Eve-Marie (0.03)
Evemarie
Evena
Evenelle
Evenese
Evenie
Evening
Evenli
Evennie
Evenon
Eveny
Eveona
Ever (0.01)
Ever'lesia
Everdina
Evereóna
Evereonna
Everest
Everett
Everetta
Everette
Everiauna
Everica
Everie

Everlee
Everley
Everley-Jean
Everly (0.01)
Everney
Everson
Every
Everyonna
Eves-Marie
Eve-Sophie
Eve-Stephani
Evet
Evett
Evette
Evey
Evgenia
Evi
Evi'yanna
Evia
Evian
Eviana
Evianna
Evie (0.07)
Eviee
Evien
Evie-Rose
Evillyan
Evily
Evilynn
Evin
Evinne
Eviona
Evionna
Evionnia
Evita (0.01)
Evita-Judith
Evlyn
Evlynn
Evnka
Evodie
Evon
Evona
Evondee
Evone
Evoney
Evoni
Evonna
Evonnah
Evonne
Evonta
Evony
Evrianna
Evrilena

Evrim
Evrist
Evryana
Evryle
Evvie
Evy (0.01)
Evyana
Evyannie
Evy-Darenne
Evyenia
Evyette
Evyline
  Jennavev
Evyllin
Evylyn
Evylynn
Evylyse
Evyn (0.01)
Evyni
Evynn
Evynne
Evyon
Ewa
Ewan
Ewelina
Ewly
Ewura Akua
Exania
Exaviana
Exiah
Exilia
Exiquia
Exira
Exsis
Exsomiah
Extasy
Exzilian
Ey Sence
Ey'myia
Eya
Eyagelia
Eyahna
Eyahni
Eyala
Eyanah
Eyanalys
Eyanbert
Eyanee
Eyanla
Eyanna
Eybe
Eyden
Eydie

Eygpt
Eyhania
Eyjada
Eykta
Eyla
Eylav
Eylee
Eyleen
Eyli
Eylin
Eylinne
Eylissa
Eylissea
Eylsa
Eyman
Eymani
Eymbyr
Eymi
Eymma
Eyndia
Eyoka
Eyona
Eyonna
Eyota
Eyppro
Eyre
Eyrin
Eyrin-Maarie
Eyriona
Eyslin
Eyva
Eyvette
Eza
Ezabel
Ezabela
Ezabella
Ezabellah
Ezabelle
Ezaniyah
Ezaraih
Ezarea
Ezaria
Ezarria
Ezayara
Ezaysiah-Lynn
Ezekielly
Ezequiel
Ezerai
Ezeri
Ezgi
Ezginur
Ezia
Eziekala

Ezinia
Ezinma
Ezinne
Ezirya
Ezmarelda
Ezme
Ezmea
Ezmeralda
Ezmerelda
Ezra (0.02)
Ezrah
Ezralynn
Ezraylia
Ezreiona
Ezri
Ezrie
Ezriella
Ezrielle
Ezrille
Ezrin
Ezry
Eztefani
Ezza
Ezzynce

~ F ~

F
Fa'heema
Fa'isah
Fa'naja
Faadumo
Faakirah
Faatima
Faatimah
Faatimah As-
  Salifi
Fabbiana
Fabiana (0.02)
Fabiana
  Valentina
Fabianca
Fabianna
Fabie
Fabiencka
Fabienne
Fabienne-
  Corane
Fabiha
Fabiola (0.03)
Fabiolah
Fabiona

Fabiyanna
Fabjona
Fable
Fabriana
Fabriela
Fachynia
Facia
Fadda
Fadhi
Fadia
Fadiila
Fadila
Fadilah
Faduma
Fadumo (0.01)
Fadumo Sahro
Fadumo Sirad
Fadwa
Fadya
Fadymath
Fae
Faedra Fionna
Faelan
Faelynn
Faeryn
Faeth
Fafali
Fagou
Fah'kira
Faharia
Fahia
Fahima
Fahma
Fahmia
Fahmida
Fahn
Faiesha
Faiga (0.01)
Faige
Faigie
Faigy (0.05)
Faihaa
Failyn
Faina
Faiqa
Fair
Faira
Fairen
Fairley
Fairli
Fairlyn
Fairyane
Fairyn

Faisa
Faisha
Faisia
Faith (2.36)
Faith Angel
Faith Ann
Faith Breanne
Faith Madison
Faithalyn
Faith-Ann
Faithann
Faithanna
Faithanne
Faithany
Faith-Danielle
Faithe
Faithful
Faithfull
Faithfulness
Faith-Lee
Faithlin
Faithlyn
Faith-Lynn
Faithlynn
Faith-Madison
Faith-Veronique
Faith-Victoria
Faiza (0.02)
Faizah
Fajar
Fajr
Fakhariea
Fakiya
Fal
Falak
Falan
Falasteen
Falda
Faleen
Faleisha
Falena
Falencia
Falene
Faleona
Falesoa
Falicia
Falicity (0.01)
Falika
Falina
Faline
Falisha
Falisity
Fallan

Fallan Antonayah
Fallingstar
Fallon *(0.05)*
Falloy Mae
Fallyn *(0.01)*
Fallynn
Falon *(0.01)*
Falycia
Falyn *(0.01)*
Falynne
Fama
Famah
Famata
Fancie
Fancy
Fandazhia
Fanecia
Fanery
Fanette
Fania
Fanijha
Fanilou
Fannie *(0.05)*
Fanny *(0.03)*
Fanon
Fansainey
Fanta *(0.02)*
Fantaisha
Fantaja
Fantasee
Fantasha
Fantashia
Fantasia *(0.04)*
Fantasia Treasure
Fantasias
Fantasie
Fantaysia
Fantisa
Fany
Fanya
Faolynne
Fara
Faraday
Faradja-Sarah
Farafoluwa
Farah *(0.03)*
Farah-Nour
Faraji
Farazanah
Fardausa
Fardosa

Fardowsa
Fardoza
Fardusa
Fareen
Fareeza
Faren
Farendy
Farha
Farhaanah
Farhana
Farhannah
Farhin
Farhina
Farhiya
Farhiyo
Fari'ah
Faria
Fariah
Farida *(0.01)*
Faridah
Faridat
Fariha
Faris
Farishta
Farithat
Fariya
Fariza
Farjeha
Farkunda
Farniyan
Faro-Dawn
Faron
Farra
Farrah *(0.04)*
Farrah Rai
Farraha
Farrah-Fe
Farran
Farren
Farrin
Farrington
Farris
Farron
Farryn
Fartun
Farva
Farwah
Farya
Faryal
Faryn
Farzan
Farzana
Farzin

Farzinah
Faseeha
Fatala
Fatama
Fate
Fateemah
Fatema *(0.01)*
Fatemah
Fatemeh
Fatemeh Alzahara
Faten
Fatha
Fathi
Fathia
Fathieh
Fathima
Fathiya
Fatia
Fatiha
Fatilaria
Fatim
Fatima *(0.68)*
Fatima Alzhraa
Fatima Andrea
Fatima Elisha
Fatima Sarai
Fatima Zahra
Fatima-Anais
Fatima-Asma
Fatimah *(0.02)*
Fatimah Shawnday
Fatima-Hame
Fatimata
Fatimatou
Fatima-Zahra
Fatima-Zohra
Fatime
Fatimetou
Fatine
Fatisha
Fatma *(0.01)*
Fatma Asya
Fatma-Ezzahra
Fatmagul
Fatmah
Fatmanur
Fatmata
Fatmeh
Fatou *(0.01)*
Fatoudiop
Fatouma

Fatoumata *(0.04)*
Fatoumatou
Fatoumatta
Fatou-Rehema
Fatra
Fatu
Fatuma
Fatumah
Fatumata
Fatyma
Faustina *(0.01)*
Faustine
Faustyna
Fauve
Favee
Favela
Faven
Faviana
Favieelie
Favin
Faviola
Favor
Favour
Fawn
Fawna
Fawziyah
Fay *(0.01)*
Faybrianna
Faye *(0.05)*
Faye Carol
Faye-Ella
Fayel
Fayelynn
Faye-Michelle
Fayeth Elizabeth
Fayette
Fayha
Fayka
Fayla
Fayla-Dawn
Faylee
Fayleigh
Faylin
Fayonna
Fayrose
Fayrouz
Faysia
Faysiah
Fayt
Faytasia
Fayte

Fayth *(0.04)*
Faythe *(0.01)*
Fayunei
Fazayl
Fazeela
Fazeelah
Fazilat
Fe
Feanix
Feather
Febe
Febriana
Feddrah
Fedelia
Fedelina
Fedena
Fedenia
Federica
Fedjina
Fedkalzahraa
Fedleine
Fedline
Fedlyne
Fedora
Fedra
Fedrina
Fee
Feelar
Feelixe
Feenie
Feeriel
Fehdi
Feigel
Feigy
Fei-Xia
Feiyah
Feker
Fekir
Felaney
Felecia *(0.01)*
Felecitas
Felecity
Feleisha
Felianna
Felianne
Felica
Felicciana
Felice
Felicety
Felicia *(0.11)*
Felicia Ann
Felicia Emily
Feliciana

Felicidade
Felicie
Felicita
Felicitas
Felicite
Felicitee
Feliciti
Feliciti-Love
Felicity *(0.14)*
Felicityl
Felicya
Felie
Felin
Felina
Felini
Felipa
Felisa
Felisha *(0.01)*
Felisha-Velle
Felisia
Felisita
Felista
Felixane
Felix-Anne
Felixanne
Felixe
Felixias
Felixita
Feliz
Feliza
Feliziana
Fellara
Felony
Felya
Felycia
Felynn
Femarie
Femi
Femina
Feminique
Femma
Fena
Fenanda
Fenani
Fenella
Fenet
Feng
Fenia
Fenicia
Fenique
Fenix
Fenley
Fenlie

Fenna
Fennanola
Fenya
Feona
Feonyx
Fer'anishia
Ferdanda
Ferdaws
Ferdoos
Ferdosa
Ferhia
Ferial
Feriel
Ferity
Ferlyn
Fermina
Fern
Fernadette
Fernaja
Fernanda *(0.11)*
Fernandamaria
Fernando
Feroza
Ferquaylah
Ferra
Ferrara
Ferrari
Ferrell
Ferris
Ferry
Ferryn
Ferseis
Fershy
Feryi
Fethiye
Fetisha
Feven
Fey
Feyce
Feyde
Feyisope
Feylin
Feyona
Feyvleen
Feyza
Fhalan
Fia
Fiaavaé
Fiala
Fialeta
Fiama
Fiana
Fianna

| | | | | | | |
|---|---|---|---|---|---|---|
| Fibi | Fionnoula | Florence- | Fortuna | Francis (0.01) | Fre'daijah | Frenchesca |
| Fibiana | Fionnuala | Emilie | Fortunata | Francisca (0.01) | Fred'neshia | Frencheski |
| Fida | Fiora | Florence- | Annabella | Francisca | Fred'nica | Frenchetta |
| Fidan | Fiorela | Kapela | Forum | Ashantia | Freda (0.01) | Frenesha |
| Fidela | Fiorella (0.02) | Florencia (0.01) | Foster | Francisco | Freda-Mia | Frenesi |
| Fidelia | Fiorenza | Florentia | Fotini | Francise | Fredashia | Freniyah |
| Fidelina | Firdaws | Florentina | Fouashe | Francis-Morgan | Fredazha | Freshelle |
| Fidelite | Firdous | Florenza | Fountae | Francoise | Freddreanna | Freshta |
| Fidji | Firdousi | Floresita | Fowler | Françoise | Frederic | Fressia |
| Fields | Firdows | Florgisel | Fox | Francoise | Frederica | Freya (0.03) |
| Fieona | Fire | Flori | Fradel (0.01) | Victoria | Frederick | Freyah |
| Fiera | Firestar | Floria | Fradisha | Francy | Fredericka | Freyda |
| Fife | Firrah | Floriana | Frady (0.01) | Francys | Fredericke | Freyja (0.01) |
| Fifer | Fischer | Floriane | Fraida | Francysse | Frederik | Frhaanah |
| Fifi | Fisher | Florianne | Fraidy | Franiah | Frederika | Frida (0.04) |
| Filicity | Fitztasia | Floribel | Fran | Franiariz | Frederike (0.01) | Friday |
| Filisicia | Fiyaanah | Floriberta | Fran'da'yan | Franice | Frédérique | Frideriki |
| Fillipia | Fiza (0.01) | Floricel | Franangely | Franisa | Frederique | Frieda |
| Filloreta | Fizza | Floridalma | Franca | Franjelina | (0.10) | Frisnir |
| Filmarie | Flabia | Florie | Franccesca | Franjell | Frederyke | Fritzcilia |
| Filomena | Flannery (0.01) | Floriemay | Francceska | Frankee | Fredeshanai | Fritzi |
| Filoula | Flaurance | Florina | Francci | Frankeria | Fredjhnia | Fritzie |
| Filsan | Flaurie | Florinda | France | Franki | Fredlen | Fronie |
| Fimisokan | Flavia | Florine | Franceli | Frankia | Fredlynn | Frosina |
| Fin | Flaviana | Floris | Francelia | Frankie (0.04) | Fredreka | Froukje |
| Fina | Flavie (0.03) | Florisatala | Francelis | Frankie | Fredreonna | Fruma |
| Finalashea | Flechelle | Florita | Francella | Katherine | Fredreshay | Fryanda |
| Findlay | Flechere | Flormaria | Francelys | Frankie-May | Fredri'onna | Fucshia |
| Fineli | Fleecy | Florsita | Frances (0.13) | Franklin | Fredriana | Fumi |
| Finely | Fletasia | Flortasia | Francesa | Franmely | Fredriania | Fumiyo |
| Finesse | Fletcher | Flory-Ann | Francesca (0.25) | Franny | Fredrica | Funminiyi |
| Finja | Fleur | Flotricia | Francesco | Fransheca | Fredricka | Funteisha |
| Finlay (0.01) | Fleur-Ange | Flourencia | Franceska | Franshesca | Fredrika | Furaha-Safi |
| Finlee | Fleur-Anne | Flower | Francess | Fransheska | Fredriona | Fushia |
| Finleigh | Fleurdemay | Floy | Francessa | Franshezka | Fredriqua | Futoh |
| Finley (0.08) | Flor (0.05) | Flynn | Frances-Saige | Franshica | Fredriuna | Fuyuka |
| Finliegh | Flor De Angel | Foai | Francesse | Fransi | Fredronia | Fy'kirah |
| Finn | Flor Maria | Folasade | Franchelle | Fransis | Fredtina | Fyath |
| Finna | Flora (0.05) | Folashade | Franchellie | Frantasia | Fredvieve | Fyn |
| Finnah | Floralie | Follesha | Franchesca | Frantia | Freeanna | Fynlee |
| Finnian | Florance | Foluwasade | (0.03) | Frantxa | Freeara | Fynleigh |
| Finnleigh | Florane | Fonda | Franchesica | Frantzceska | Freeda | Fynn |
| Finnley (0.01) | Floranne | Fondjahnique | Francheska | Franyelys | Freeda-Louve | Fynnlee |
| Finola | Flore | Fong | (0.02) | Franzce Dana | Freedom (0.01) | Fynnlie |
| Finthuja J | Flore Nidi | Fontaine | Francheski | Franzelle | Freemya | Fyore |
| Fion | Flore-Anne | Fontana | Franchessca | Franzi | Freicia | |
| Fion Winghei | Floreasha | Fontasia | Franchestca | Franzie | Freida | |
| Fiona (0.37) | Floree Ann | Forcynthia | Francia | Franziska | Freidy | ~ G ~ |
| Fionah | Florela | Forever | Francie | Franzmarie | Freja | |
| Fionai | Florelba | Forniah | Francielli | Frasni | Frely | G'airra |
| Fionay | Florella | Foronda | Francina | Fraya | Frema | G'ajanae |
| Fionna | Florence (0.24) | Forrest | Francine (0.02) | Frayda | Fremeria | G'alena |
| Fionnah | Florence Justine | Forsythia | Francine Jolie | Frayleni | Frenche | G'amani |

| | | | | | | |
|---|---|---|---|---|---|---|
| G'anna | Gabreanna | Gabrielle- | Gaiane | Gamilett | Gariana | Gayathri |
| G'aria | Gabreel | Eugenie | Gaige | Gamze | Garianna | Gayatri |
| G'asia | Gabreella | Gabrielle- | Gail | Gana | Gariela | Gayla |
| G'ihanna | Gabreelle | Genevieve | Gailchanda | Ganale | Garielle | Gayle (0.01) |
| G'kiya | Gabreial | Gabriellen | Gaile | Ganalita | Garilynn | Gayleen |
| G'maya | Gabreiell | Gabriellia | Gailya | Ganelle | Garina | Gaylen |
| G'nae | Gabreil | Gabriello | Gaita | Ganeria | Garisha | Gaze |
| G'naria | Gabreila | Gabrielly | Gaitlyn | Ganesha | Gariunna | Gbemisola |
| G'niah | Gabreille | Gabriellys | Gakiya | Ganessa | Gariyanna | Ge Miya |
| G'nilaeh | Gabrelilla | Gabriely | Gakiyla | Ganika | Garkeesha | Ge Tosja |
| G'niyah | Gabrella | Gabrien | Gakyra | Ganila | Garland | Ge'ahnette |
| G'oni | Gabrelle | Gabrieshka | Gakyung | Ganitta | Garmalyne | Ge'arikka |
| G'onna | Gabrellia | Gabrijela | Gal | Ganiya | Garmesha | Ge'aunae |
| G'onnah | Gabrey | Gabrila | Gala (0.01) | Ganya | Garner | Ge'kaylia |
| G'oyna | Gabreylla | Gabrille | Galabriel | Ganyah | Garnet | Ge'lisa |
| G'ustyce | Gabriah | Gabrillia | Galadriel | Gao | Garnett | Ge'miya |
| Ga Eul | Gabriaile | Gabrionna | Galadriella | Gao Hli | Garnycia | Ge'naria |
| Ga'briella | Gabrial (0.01) | Gabriyale | Galadrielle | Gao Houa | Garren | Ge'niah |
| Ga'liyah | Gabriall | Gabriyell | Galamarie | Gao Ia | Garrett | Ge'niyah |
| Ga'miracle | Gabriana | Gabryal | Galanne | Gao Nou | Garrianna | Ge'nya |
| Ga'nasia | Gabriane | Gabryalla | Galataya | Gao Sue | Garrin | Ge'onna |
| Ga'nya | Gabrianna | Gabryel | Galatea | Gao Zhong | Garrison | Ge'quoia |
| Ga'nyah | (0.01) | Gabryela | Galatia | Gaochee | Garriyonna | Ge'tahra |
| Ga'nyia | Gabriayla | Gabryele | Galaxie | Gaoger | Garsha | Ge'vaeh |
| Ga'riyah | Gabrieal | Gabryell | Galaxy | Gaohmong | Garshiya | Gea |
| Gaayatri | Gabriel (0.05) | Gabryella (0.01) | Galaya | Gaojah | Gary | Geahnna |
| Gabanna | Gabriel Eleanor | Gabryella-Jaide | Gale | Gaojee | Garyanna | Gean |
| Gabbey | Gabriela (1.50) | Gabryelle (0.01) | Galeicia | Gaojia | Garyanne | Geana |
| Gabbi | Gabriela Maria | Gabryellia | Galen | Gaojou | Garyel | Geanah |
| Gabbiana | Gabriela Maria | Gabrylle | Galena | Gaojoua | Garylen | Geanara |
| Gabbie | Db | Gaby (0.01) | Galexia | Gaokia | Garyn | Geanell |
| Gabbreil | Gabriela Rubi | Gaby Denni | Galhia | Gaonou | Gashly | Geanellys |
| Gabbrella | Gabriela-Anaeli | Gabyangel | Gali | Gaonuli | Gasiah | Geaniyah |
| Gabbrialla | Gabriela-Nataly | Gaby-Licia | Galia | Gaorii | Gasmin | Geanna |
| Gabbriela | Gabrièle | Gacia | Galiana | Gaoshialia | Gaspar | Geanny |
| Gabbriell | Gabriele (0.02) | Gadgina | Galianna | Gaoshoua | Gatheroot | Geatane |
| Gabbriella | Gabrielia | Gaebriela | Galicia | Gaozhi | Gatlin | Geavonna |
| Gabbrielle | Gabriell (0.01) | Gaeda | Galilea (0.04) | Gara | Gaurangi | Gecktter |
| Gabbryanna | Gabriella (2.34) | Gael | Galileah | Garaibella | Gauri (0.01) | Gedaly |
| Gabby | Gabriella Marie | Gaela | Galilee | Garam | Gauryama | Gedatli |
| Gabereille | Gabriella Tifany | Gaele | Galina | Garance | Gaven | Gedline |
| Gaberelle | Gabriellah | Gaelen | Gallegos | Garbiella | Gavianna | Gee Gee |
| Gaberial | Gabriella-Marie | Gaella | Galliane | Garbrielle | Gavin (0.01) | Gee May |
| Gabi | Gabriellanne | Gaelle (0.02) | Gally | Garcelle | Gavina | Geehan |
| Gabie | Gabriella-Rose | Gaelyn | Gallyan | Garcia | Gavraelle | Geena (0.01) |
| Gabiela | Gabrielle (2.79) | Gaeta | Gally-Anne | Garcie | Gavriela | Geeta |
| Gabiella | Gabrielle Alexis | Gaetana | Gally-Samantha | Gardenia | Gavriella | Geethanjali |
| Gable | Gabrielle Marie | Gagan | Galvia | Gardith | Gavrielle | Geethika |
| Gabraella | Ling | Gagandeep | Galya | Gardner | Gavry | Geetika |
| Gabray'l | Gabrielle Th | Gaganpreet | Galyani | Gareonna | Gavryayla | Geeyah |
| Gabreaila | Gabrielle-Ann | Gahiesha | Galylea | Garette | Gavyn | Gege |
| Gabreal | Gabrielle- | Gaia (0.01) | Galynn | Gargi | Gaya | Gehida |
| Gabrealla | Audrey | Gaia-Maude | Gameelah | Gari'onna | Gayanthika | Gehna |

Geidiht
Geili
Geionni
Geisha
Geiya
Gela
Gelahana
Geleeyah
Gelen
Gelila
Gelina
Gelis
Gelisa
Gelise
Gelissa
Geliyah
Geliyaha
Gelsey
Gelsy
Gema *(0.01)*
Gemaris
Gemeyah
Gemikalyn
Gemily
Gemin
Gemini *(0.01)*
Geminia
Geminis
Gemiyah
Gemma *(0.07)*
Gemma-Gevara
Gemyah
Gemyia
Gen'asia
Gena *(0.01)*
Genae
Genaisia
Genarosa-Velici
Genasee
Genasis
Genavee
Genaveve
Genavieve *(0.01)*
Genaviv
Genavive
Genaya
Genayah
Gendi
Gene
Gené
Genea
Genean
Geneane

Genearia
Genecia
Genecis
Geneen
Geneice
Geneira
Geneissa
Geneli
Genella
Genelle
Generosity
Generria
Genesa
Genese
Genesee
Geneshia
Genesi
Genesiis
Genesis *(1.07)*
Genesis-
   Marialena
Genesis-Mariana
Genessa
Genessis *(0.01)*
Genessis-
   Zuhaila
Genesys
Geneva *(0.06)*
Geneve
Genevese
Genevette
Genevie
Genevieva
Geneviève *(0.01)*
Genevieve *(0.31)*
Genevieve-Marie
Genevieve-Odile
Genevive
Genevra
Genevyeve
Genevyra
Genexis
Genia
Genicha
Genie
Geniese
Geniess
Genieva
Genieve
Genifer
Genika
Genika-Marie
Genina

Genine Mae
Genique
Genise
Genises
Genisis
Genisses
Genisus
Genitia
Geniva
Genive
Genivea
Geniveve
Genivi
Genivieve
Genixa
Geniya *(0.01)*
Geniyah
Genna *(0.01)*
Gennacy
Gennaleigh
Gennasee
Gennasis
Gennavive
Genna-Vive
Genneises
Gennelle
Gennesa
Gennesis
Gennessy
Genneva
Gennica
Gennifer
Gennika
Genny
Gennyce
Genoa
Genoea
Genoia
Genova
Genoveva
Genovieve
Genre
Gentel
Gentiane
Gentijana
Gentri
Gentry *(0.01)*
Genuia
Geny
Genya
Genyea
Genylah
Genysis

Genyva
Geolee
Geona
Geonna
Geor'kiyah
Geor'vonta
Geordee
Geordyn
Georga
Georgann
Georganna
George
Georgea
Georgeanná
Georgeanne
Georgegina
Georgeianna
George-Jeanna
Georgena
Georgenae
Georgetta
Georgette
Georgia *(0.45)*
Georgia Lynn
Georgia-Ann
Georgia-Lee
Georgia-May
Georgian
Georgiana
   *(0.01)*
Georgianna
   *(0.02)*
Georgiarae
Georgiauna
Georgie
Georgina *(0.02)*
Georgina
   Adeana
Georgy-Anne
Geori
Georiana
Georkayla
Georli
Georliyah
Geormaya
Georniya
Geornori
Geovana
Geovanna
Geovanni
Geovany
Ger'kihjah
Ger'kya

Ger'miah
Ger'niyla
Ger'shyah
Gera
Gerah'niyah
Geraine
Gerajanae
Geral
Gerald
Geralda
Geraldi
Geraldina
Geraldine *(0.03)*
Geraldine-
   Clarence
Geraldy
Geralyn
Geralynn
Geralys
Gerarna
Gerda
Gerdany
Gerdi
Gereni
Geresa
Geri
Geriah
Geriann
Gerielle
Gerijo
Gerika
Gerilon
Gerilyn
Gerilynne
Geriyah
Gerkyhia
Gerlalicia
Gerline
Gerlineda
Germallolys
Germalys
Germarielis
Germeane
Germina
Germiya
Germonie
Germyia
Gernaya
Gernaye
Gernee
Gernei
Gernia

Gerniya
Geronah
Gerrayah
Gerrelle
Gerri
Gerria
Gerriah
Gerryiah
Gersanni
Gershiya
Gerta
Gertie
Gertrude *(0.01)*
Gertrudis
Gerty
Gervenia-Pearl
Gery
Geryann
Geryanna
Gerzie
Gesami
Gesana
Gesaria
Geselle
Gesenelly
Gesenia
Gessel
Gessellier
Gessica
Gessy
Geta
Getruda
Getsel
Getsemani
Getsemany
Getzemany
Geulah
Geum
Gevalia
Gevevieve
Gevyn
Geydy
Geyhonee
Geyleen
Geysel
Gezelin
Gezelle
Geziyah
Gha'naye
Ghadeer
Ghadir
Ghaida
Ghalia

Ghati
Ghazal
Ghazala
Ghazaleh
Gheed
Gheena
Gheg
Ghemyini
Ghenesis
Ghenessy
Gheonie
Ghianna
Ghida
Ghiechelle
Ghina
Ghiseidi
Ghislaine
Ghislane
Ghislene
Ghita
Ghyanna
Ghyslaine
Ghzal
Gi'niya
Gia *(0.11)*
Gia Bella
Gia Denise
Gia-Angie
Giacomina
Giada *(0.02)*
Giada-Jaden
Giadanna
Giah
Giahna
Giahnie
Gialanni
Gialena
Giamani
Giamarie
Giamaris
Giamille
Gian
Giana *(0.13)*
Gianabrook
Gianaleze
Gianalys
Giana-Renée
Giandra
Gianel Madison
Gianelis
Gianella *(0.01)*
Gianelle
Gianelli

| | | | | | |
|---|---|---|---|---|---|
| Gianelly | Gicel | Ginelix | Gisbelle | Giyah | Glenna | Gold'ann |
| Gianellys | Gicell | Ginelle | Giseel | Giyonnah | Glennaejah | Golda |
| Gianerys | Gicella | Ginelly | Gisel (0.02) | Gizabeth | Glennariah | Goldberry |
| Gianessa | Gicelle | Ginelsa | Gisela (0.02) | Gizel | Glenneshia | Golden (0.01) |
| Giangely | Gid | Ginely | Giseld | Gizele | Glenniyua | Goldie (0.01) |
| Giani | Giearra | Ginelys | Gisèle | Gizell | Glenntajah | Goldsheng |
| Gianiece | Gielinn | Ginette | Gisele (0.03) | Gizella | Glenn-Teh | Goldy (0.02) |
| Gianina (0.01) | Gifti | Gineva | Gisele Fernanda | Gizelle (0.01) | Glennya | Goldyn |
| Gianise | Gifty | Ginevieve | Giselis | Gizem | Gleny | Golsa |
| Giann | Gigi (0.01) | Ginevra | Gisell (0.01) | Gizzel | Glenyiah | Gonnia |
| Gianna (1.71) | Gilana | Ginger (0.05) | Gisella (0.01) | Gizzele | Glerisbeth | Gonzalo |
| Gianna Eleen | Gilari Enr | Ginger-Lee | Gisellé | Gizzelle | Glerysbeth | Gopiga |
| Gianna Lhuna | Gilbianis | Gini | Giselle (1.10) | Gjoa | Gleske | Gopika |
| Gianna Ysabelle | Gilda | Ginia | Giselle De La | Glacia | Glidera | Gordan |
| Giannah | Gildeng | Ginipher | Giselle Ma | Glacie | Glinda | Gordana |
| Giannais | Gilead | Giniyah | Giselle-Maria | Glacy | Glindi | Goretti |
| Giannalis | Gilesa | Ginna | Giselli | Gladis (0.01) | Gloqowe'j | Gorga |
| Gianna-Marie | Gileyska | Ginni | Gisely | Gladisha | Glori | Gorgeous |
| Gianne | Gili | Ginny (0.01) | Giselys | Gladiss | Gloria (0.20) | Gorgie |
| Gianneli | Gilian | Ginou | Gislaine | Gladness | Gloria Grace | Gorkavia |
| Giannely | Giliana | Gintry | Gisseel | Gladyanna | Gloria Mary | Gorlhia |
| Gianni (0.03) | Gillary | Giny | Gissel (0.01) | Gladybetzy | Gloriah | Gorska |
| Gianni Nya | Gilleandry | Ginya | Gissela | Gladyce | Gloriana | Gotouf |
| Giannie | Gilleen | Ginyah | Gissele | Gladyne | Glorianis | Goufrane |
| Giannina | Gillian (0.15) | Ginylah | Gissell | Gladys (0.03) | Gloriann | Gouia |
| Giannis Alex | Gilliana | Gioia (0.01) | Gisselle (0.07) | Glaidja | Glorianna | Goundo |
| Giannishka | Gilliane | Giomarie | Gissellee | Glaidmar | Gloria-Rachel | Gouri |
| Giannisse | Gillianne | Giona | Gissellet | Glaisa | Gloribeth | Gowri |
| Giannoula | Gilliany | Gioni | Gisselly | Glaismarie | Gloricarmen | Gowthami |
| Gianny | Gillie | Gionna (0.01) | Gistina | Glaivis | Gloriconny | Goyette |
| Gianonna | Gillien | Giordana | Giszelle | Glamoura | Glorie | Grabiela |
| Giany | Gillyan | Giordana Jessica | Gita | Glareh | Glorimar | Grabriela |
| Giao Ngoc | Gillyanne | Giorgi | Gitana | Glarelis | Glorious | Graccie |
| Giara | Gilma | Giorgia | Gitane | Glarpherah | Gloriyasia | Grace (5.38) |
| Giasseling | Gilmary | Giorgina | Gitanjali | Glaysheus | Glory (0.01) | Grace Amisa |
| Giavana | Gilouna Ludovie | Giovana (0.01) | Githmi | Glebhyz | Glory-Ann | Grace Ann |
| Giavanna (0.06) | Gilyane | Giovanina | Gitika | Glee | Gloryanne | Grace Anne |
| Giavanna Grace | Giman Awaste | Giovanna (0.13) | Gitta | Gleidy | Glorymar | Grace Charlotte |
| Giavanni | Gimena | Giovanna Betina | Gittel (0.01) | Gleisy | Gloryona | Grace Elizabeth |
| Giavanti | Gimiah | Giovanni | Gitty (0.03) | Glena | Glydel | Grace Ellen |
| Giavaughn | Gina (0.18) | Giovanny | Gitzel | Glenajah | Glynnith | Grace Katherine |
| Giavauna | Gina Lee | Giovina | Giulia (0.04) | Glenajaha | Glynns | Jord |
| Giavona | Gina Marie | Giovonna | Giuliana (0.06) | Glency | Glystin | Grace Kathrine |
| Giavoni | Ginabella | Giovonni | Giulianna (0.01) | Glenda (0.02) | Gmommy | Grace Leah |
| Giavonna (0.01) | Ginae | Giowri | Giuliannah | Glendaliz | Gnaya | Grace Lynn |
| Giavonnah | Ginai | Giralis | Giulianne | Glendalize | God'andi | Grace Nadia |
| Giavonne | Ginaliz | Giralys | Giulietta | Glendi | God'iss | Grace Natalia |
| Giavonni | Ginamaria | Girasol | Giulliana | Glendoria | Goddess | Grace Susanne |
| Giawndra | Ginan | Girdielene | Giulya | Glendy | Godiva Lois | Grace'xiomaris |
| Giaynah | Ginaovaline | Girija | Givea | Gleneva | Godsenta | Grace-Alynn |
| Gibraelle | Ginaveve | Girisha | Given | Glenia | Goff | Grace-Ann |
| Gibria | Ginavieve | Girland | Giverny | Glenis | Gohmee | Graceann (0.01) |
| Gibson | Ginel | Girlie | Givonna | Glenmary | Goiri | Graceanna |

| | | | | | | |
|---|---|---|---|---|---|---|
| Grace-Anne | Gracieanna | Graycen *(0.01)* | Gretta *(0.02)* | Guerrero | Gurnasib | Gwendylan |
| Graceanne | Graciee | Grayci | Grettel | Guervely | Gurneer | Gwendyline |
| Grace-Avona | Graciela *(0.04)* | Graycie *(0.01)* | Grettell | Gugulethu | Gurneesh | Gwendyn |
| Grace-Catherine | Graciela Ann | Graycin | Grettsy | Guilia | Gurneet *(0.01)* | Gweneal |
| Graced | Gracieliin | Graydee | Grevi | Guilian | Gurnia | Gwenen |
| Gracee *(0.03)* | Graciella *(0.01)* | Grayden | Grey *(0.01)* | Guiliana | Gurnoor | Gweneth *(0.01)* |
| Gracee-Ann | Gracielle | Graylen | Greyce | Guilianna | Gurparsad | Gwenevere |
| Grace-Elizab | Gracie-Mae | Graylin | Greysen Mercy | Guiliaunna | Gurpinder | Gwenevieve |
| Graceful | Graciemay | Graylisha | Greyshmari | Guillane | Gurpreet | Gwenhwyfar |
| Gracel | Gracilyn | Graylyn | Greysi | Guillianee | Gurpriya | Gwenith |
| Graceland | Gracin *(0.01)* | Graysen *(0.02)* | Greyson *(0.01)* | Guinavier | Gurroop | Gwenivere |
| Gracelin | Gracina | Grayshia | Greyssy | Guinevere | Gurseert | Gwenna |
| Gracelind | Gracine | Grayson *(0.06)* | Greyting | (0.02) | Gurshaan | Gwenndalynn |
| Graceline | Gracious | Graysyn | Greyxis | Guinivere | Gursheen | Gwenneth |
| Gracella | Graclyn | Grayton | Gricelda | Guinn | Gursimar | Gwennyth |
| Gracellen | Graclynn | Grazia | Grier | Guinnella | Gursimran | Gwentarya |
| Gracellyn | Gracy *(0.02)* | Graziana | Griffaen | Guirlande | Gurveen | Gwenyth *(0.05)* |
| Graceloyes | Gracye | Grazianna | Griffin | Guisel | Gurver | Gwenyth Hope |
| Gracelun | Gracyela | Graziella | Griffith | Guiselle | Gurvir | Gwyn *(0.01)* |
| Gracely | Gracyella | Grazzia | Griffyn | Guity | Gusherae | Gwynalynn |
| Gracelyn *(0.13)* | Gracylen | Greacy | Grimanesa | Gul Hayat | Gushyrria | Gwyndalyn |
| Gracelynd | Gracymae | Greanlee | Grisel | Gulgina | Gussianna | Gwyndolyn |
| Gracelyne | Gracyn *(0.08)* | Grechyn | Griselda *(0.03)* | Guliana | Gustel | Gwyneth *(0.07)* |
| Grace-Lynn | Gracyne | Grecia *(0.02)* | Griseliz | Gulsahara | Guusje | Gwynith |
| Gracelynn | Gracynn | Greenlea | Grisha | Gulsheen | Guylendria | Gwynn |
| (0.04) | Grady | Greenlee *(0.01)* | Grisi | Gulsu | Guynesha | Gwynna |
| Gracelynna | Grae | Greenlee-Bay | Grisselda | Guneet | Guy-Rodly | Gwynneth |
| Gracelynne | Graecee | Greenleigh | Grisselle | Guneev | Gwen *(0.05)* | Gwynnevere |
| Grace-Manuela | Graecyn | Greenley *(0.01)* | Gritzel | Gunit | Gwena | Gwynnyth |
| Gracen *(0.04)* | Graelyn | Greenliegh | Gryffin | Gunner | Gwenalex | Gy'iana |
| Graces-Anna | Graham | Greenly | Gryphan | Gunnit | Gwenann | Gya |
| Gracesen | Graice | Greer *(0.02)* | Gryphon | Gunreet | Gwenashley | Gyanee |
| Graceson | Graicyn- | Gregoria | Guadalajara | Gurarpan | Gwenaveere | Gyanna |
| Gracesyn | Tambree | Gregory | Guadalope | Gurbani | Gwenavere | Gyansagara |
| Gracey *(0.07)* | Grainne | Greicy | Guadalupe | Gurdeep | Gwenavyre | Gychena |
| Gracey Jo | Graisen | Greilyan | (0.57) | Gurgia | Gwenda | Gyiani |
| Graceyn | Graison | Greisi | Guadelupe | Gurgina | Gwendalin | Gykiah |
| Graci *(0.05)* | Graisyn | Greisy | Guadulupe | Gurikam | Gwendaline | Gyleisa |
| Graci Lynne | Grant | Grenesha | Guangwe | Gurjeena | Gwendalyn | Gyliliana |
| Gracia *(0.01)* | Granuaile | Gresa | Zsabelle | Gurjeet | (0.01) | Gyllian |
| Gracian | Granvaile | Greshely | Guatelupe | Gurjeevan | Gwendalyne | Gymila |
| Graciana | Grasea | Greta *(0.18)* | Gudalupe | Gurjina | Gwendalynn | Gynara |
| Gracianna | Grashanae | Greta Cynthia | Gudi | Gurjiya | Gwendalynne | Gyonna |
| Gracianne | Grasie | Greta Marie | Gueda | Gurjot | Gwendelyn | Gypsee |
| Gracibel | Grasiela | Gretchen *(0.15)* | Guenevere | Gurkiran | Gwendolen | Gypsie |
| Gracie *(1.89)* | Grasyn | Gretchin | Guenevieve | Gurkiranjot | Gwendoline | Gypsy |
| Gracie Ann | Gratielle | Gretchka | Guenievre | Gurkirat | Gwendollyn | Gyselle |
| Gracie Eliza | Gray | Gretchyn | Guenivere | Gurleen *(0.03)* | Gwendolyn | Gysiaha |
| Gracie Elizabeth | Gray Marga | Gretel | Guenna | Gurman | (0.18) | Gyueun |
| Gracie Jayne | Grayce *(0.04)* | Grethe | Guerdyanard | Gurmandeep | Gwendolynn | Gyu-Yeon |
| Gracie Jo | Grayce | Grethel | Guerjai | Gurmeen | Gwendolynne | Gyzelle |
| Gracie-Ann | Margaret | Grethell | Guerlenda | Gurnaaz | Gwendul | Gyzelle Kay |
| Gracieann | Graycee *(0.01)* | Gretlian | Guerline | Gurnain-Kaur | Gwendy | Gzer |

## ~ H ~

| | | | | | | |
|---|---|---|---|---|---|---|
| H | Hadasa | Haela | Haileigh *(0.02)* | Haizy | Halen *(0.01)* | Hallie *(0.27)* |
| H'elena | Hadasha | Haeleah | Hailey *(4.12)* | Haja | Halen Ammarrie | Hallieann |
| H'evanlee | Hadassa *(0.01)* | Haelee | Hailey Ann | Haja Yasin | Halena *(0.01)* | Halliey |
| H'lindsay | Hadassah *(0.05)* | Haeleigh | Hailey Jade | Hajamariama | Halex | Hallis |
| H'uriayya | Hadaya | Haeley | Hailey Kaj | Hajar *(0.01)* | Haley *(2.46)* | Hallulejeah |
| Ha Linh | Hadden | Haeli | Hailey Marie | Hajara | Haley Abbygail | Hally *(0.01)* |
| Ha Neul | Haddessah | Haelie | Hailey Mei | Hajaratu | Haley Brooke | Hallye |
| Ha Neul Magalie | Haddie | Haeli-Jolynn | Hailey Mickenzief | Hajare | Haley Grace | Hallyson |
| Ha'ani | Haddlea | Haelli | Hailey-Ann | Hajdia Dalanda | Haley Han | Halo |
| Ha'dia | Haddlee | Haellie | Haileyanne | Hajean | Haley Jade | Halona |
| Ha'layia | Hade | Haely | Hailey-Autumn | Hajer | Haley Mae | Halonah |
| Ha'layjah | Hadeel *(0.01)* | Haelyn | Hailey-Brooke | Hajir | Haley' | Halsey |
| Ha'nia | Hadeh | Haeven | Hailey-Grace | Hajirah | Haleyann | Halsie |
| Ha'rhiya | Haden | Haevyn | Hailey-Jean | Hajjah | Haleyanna | Halston |
| Ha'seannaa | Hadessa | Haewon | Hailey-Mae | Hajna | Haley-Jade | Haltie |
| Ha'vanna | Hadey | Haezel | Hailey-Rae | Hajr | Haleymaria | Haluca |
| Ha'vaughnya | Hadez | Hafeezah | Haili *(0.02)* | Hajra | Haleys | Haluh |
| Ha'ven | Hadia | Hafida | Hailie *(0.12)* | Hajrah | Hali *(0.02)* | Haly |
| Haadiya | Hadiatou | Hafisa | Hailiea | Hajrija | Halia *(0.01)* | Halya |
| Haala | Hadichahon | Hafiza | Hailie-Ann | Hakeemah | Haliana | Halycia |
| Haamilee | Hadil | Hafsa *(0.02)* | Hailie-Daniella | Hakiima | Halianna | Halyn *(0.01)* |
| Haania | Hadile | Hafsaah | Hailiee | Hakima | Halianne | Halynn |
| Haanya | Hadill | Hafsah *(0.01)* | Hailies | Hakimah | Halice | Halyssa-Heidy |
| Haarika | Hadiya *(0.01)* | Hagan | Hailiey | Hakirah | Halie *(0.10)* | Hamani |
| Haasaanah | Hadiyah | Hagar | Hailiy | Hakua | Haliee | Hamanpreet |
| Habaiah | Hadiyo | Hagen | Haille | Hala *(0.01)* | Haliegh *(0.01)* | Hamberlyn |
| Habamia | Hadiyyah | Hager Ayma | Haillee | Halaena | Haliey | Hamda |
| Habbas | Hadja | Hahnah | Hailley | Halah | Haligh | Hamdi *(0.01)* |
| Habeeba | Hadjar | Hai | Haillie *(0.01)* | Halaia | Hali-Kathr | Hamdisa |
| Haben | Hadjer | Hai Quyen | Hailly | Halaina | Halima *(0.02)* | Hameema |
| Habiba *(0.01)* | Hadjia-Sira | Haida | Haily *(0.04)* | Halaiyah | Halimah | Hamerti |
| Habibaa | Hadlea | Haidan | Hailyanna | Ha-Lan | Halima-Manar | Hamia Fallen |
| Habibah | Hadlee *(0.01)* | Haide | Hailye | Halana | Halimat | Hamida |
| Habibatu | Had-Leigh | Haidee | Hailyn *(0.01)* | Halania | Halimatou | Hamilee |
| Habibeh | Hadleigh *(0.01)* | Haiden *(0.02)* | Hailynne | Halasha | Halime | Hamiley |
| Habigael | Hadley *(0.18)* | Haidence | Haiqa | Halaya | Halimo | Hamioi |
| Habinette | Hadli | Haidi | Haisa | Halaydea | Halina | Hamisini |
| Habisa | Hadlie | Haidin | Haisha | Halayla | Halina-Lee | Hamna |
| Habon | Hadly | Haidley | Haisley | Halayna | Haliwie | Hamnah |
| Haboon | Hadn | Haidy | Haisya | Halaynna | Haliya | Hamonee |
| Habsa | Hady | Haidyn *(0.02)* | Haiti | Hale | Haliyah | Hamony |
| Habun | Hadya | Haifa | Hai-Ting | Halea | Haliymah | Hampton |
| Hachen | Hadyia | Haigen | Haiven | Haleah | Halla | Hamsa |
| Hadachelle | Hadyn *(0.01)* | Haighlee | Haivenly | Haleé | Hallé | Hamsini |
| Hadaijah | Hadynn | Haila | Haivery | Halee *(0.04)* | Halle *(0.30)* | Hamya |
| Hadar | Hae | Hailan | Haivyn | Haleema *(0.01)* | Hallee *(0.02)* | Han |
| Hadara | Hae'vin | Haile *(0.01)* | Haiwan | Haleena | Halleigh | Han Lindsey |
| Hadarah | Haeden | Hailea *(0.01)* | Haiya | Haleha | Hallelujah | Han Lu |
| Hadas | Haedy | Haileah | Haiyle | Halei *(0.01)* | Hallewyn | Han'nah |
| Hadas | Haedyn | Hailee *(0.28)* | Haiylee | Haleigh *(0.23)* | Halley *(0.03)* | Hana *(0.15)* |
| Hadas'sah | Haegen | Haileebeth | Haiyven | Haleigha | Halli *(0.01)* | Hanaa *(0.01)* |
| | Haeilie | Hailee-Jade | | Haleigh-Si | Hallianna | Hanaa Ali |
| | Hael | Hailei *(0.01)* | Haiziyna | Haleiya | | Hanaan |

| | | | | | | |
|---|---|---|---|---|---|---|
| Hanade | Hannah | Hanny | Harlan | Harmoney | Haruna | Hattiana |
| Hanadi | Corinne | Hannya | Harlea | (0.01) | Harva'jja | Hattie (0.03) |
| Hanah (0.03) | Hannah Gem | Hanovi | Harleanna | Harmoni (0.03) | Harvalee | Hatty |
| Hanah-Eve | Hannah Grace | Hanoyva | Harlee (0.07) | Harmonica | Harveen | Haunah |
| Hanahgayle | Hannah Hien- | Hansel | Harlee Rae | Harmonie (0.03) | Harveer | Haunalyn |
| Hanais | Khanh | Hansika | Harlee-Jo | Harmonii | Harvest | Hava |
| Hana-Kay | Hannah Jane | Hansini | Harleen (0.02) | Harmony (0.32) | Harvieleisha | Havah |
| Hanalei | Hannah Jo | Hanul | Harleey | Harmony-Rain | Harvir | Havahna |
| Hanan (0.03) | Hannah K | Hanwen | Harlei | Harmony-Rose | Harvira | Hava-Leah |
| Hanane | Hannah Marie | Hany | Harleigh (0.04) | Harmorni | Harwa | Havan |
| Hanano | Hannah | Hanya | Harleigh-Rae | Harmyni | Hasana | Havana (0.01) |
| Hanaya | Paulette | Hanyah | Harlem | Harnaz | Hasanaat | Havanah |
| Hancock | Hannah Rae | Hanzenia | Harlene | Harneet (0.01) | Hasanah | Havana-Sky |
| Hande | Hannah Rose | Hanzli | Harleth | Harni | Haschabna | Havanna (0.01) |
| Handrea | Hannah Sofia | Haoua | Harley (0.29) | Harnoor (0.02) | Haset | Havannah |
| Hane | Hannah Sophia | Haoulatou | Harley Jo | Haromis | Hashanna | Havannha |
| Haneefah | Hannaha | Happi | Harleyann | Haroshni | Hashawnia | Haveen |
| Haneen (0.01) | Hannahbah | Happy | Harleyia | Haroula | Hashli | Haven (0.15) |
| Hanefa | Hannah-Belle | Hapsatou | Harleyquinn | Harparneet | Hashly | Haven Jae |
| Haneiyah | Hannah- | Haque | Harley-Shae | Harper (0.15) | Hashuni | Havilah |
| Hanelis | Elizabethe | Har | Harli (0.01) | Harper Danielle | Hasie | Haviland |
| Hanessy | Hannah-Grace | Har'mony | Harlie (0.04) | Harpriya | Hasina | Havin |
| Hanetou | Hannahh | Harakem | Harliee | Harpuneet | Hasini | Havishka |
| Hang Minh | Hannah-Isabelle | Harbhajan | Harli-Kay | Harri | Hasitha | Havlyn |
| Hangatu | Hannah-Jane | Harbor | Harlina | Harriet (0.02) | Hasiyah | Havona |
| Hanh | Hannah-Jayne | Harbour | Harlington | Harris | Hasley | Havva |
| Hani | Hannahjo | Hardi | Harlo | Harrisann | Hasna | Havyn (0.01) |
| Hania | Hannahlaine | Hardin | Harloew | Harrisen | Hasnaa | Hawa (0.03) |
| Haniah | Hannah-Lee | Hardiya | Harlow | Harrison | Hasraat | Hawah |
| Hania-Yohaira | Hannahleigh | Hardy | Harlowe | Harrleyn | Hasreen | Hawaii |
| Haniela | Hannah-Leigh | Haredo | Harly | Harryca | Hasret | Hawanatu |
| Hanifa | Hannah-Lillie | Hareena | Harlye | Harsha | Hassaanah | Hawani |
| Hanifah | Hannah-Marie | Hareni | Harlyn | Harshaan | Hassan | Haweeya |
| Hanifa-Tallah | Hannah-Mary | Hargun | Harmaline | Harsharan | Hassanah | Hawi |
| Han-In | Hannah-Nicole | Harianna | Harman | Harshi | Hassania | Hawley |
| Hanine | Hannah-Rachel | Harika | Harmandeep | Harshia | Hassena | Hawly |
| Hanita | Hannah-Rose | Hariklia | Harmani | Harshika | Hasset | Hawo |
| Haniya (0.01) | Hannah-Talia | Harin I | Harmanie | Harshini | Hassete | Hawon |
| Haniyah | Hannah- | Harina | Harmanjit | Harshita | Hassiba | Hawraa |
| Haniyyah | Vladisla | Harini (0.01) | Harmannat | Harshitha | Hassidy | Hawwa |
| Hanley | Hannaly | Harit | Harmanpreet | Harshjot | Hassnah | Hay |
| Hanlie | Hannamae | Harjan | Harmaya | Harsiga | Hasty | Hay'lee |
| Hanlon | Hannan (0.01) | Harjas | Harmeen | Harsimar | Hasya | Haya (0.01) |
| Hanmo | Hannaniah | Harjashan | Harmeera | Harsimran | Hataya | Hayaad |
| Hanna (0.52) | Hanna-Rose | Harjeen | Harmen | Harsimret | Hataysa | Hayah |
| Hanna Joy | Hannay | Harjoban | Harminder | Harsimrn | Hatena | Hayam |
| Hanna Kathleen | Hannea | Harjot (0.01) | Harmini | Hartland | Hateya | Hayana |
| Hanna Marie | Hanneen | Harkhushi | Harmon | Hartlee | Hathairathana | Hayasen |
| Hanna-Beth | Hannen | Harkiran | Harmone | Hartleigh | Hatixhe | Hayat (0.01) |
| Hanna-Faith | Hannia (0.01) | Harkirat | Harmoneé | Hartley | Hatlyn | Hayatt |
| Hannagh | Hannie | Harkiren | Harmónee | Hartlie | Hatteras | Haydan |
| Hannagrace | Hannity | Harkirt | Harmonee | Harttley | Hatti | Hayde |
| Hannah (6.97) | Hannon | Harkomal | (0.01) | Haruka | Hattia | Haydee (0.01) |

Hayden *(0.27)*
Hayden Raine
Haydi
Haydin
Haydn *(0.01)*
Haydon
Haydrian
Haydyn
Hayes
Haygen
Hayiad
Hayim
Hayla *(0.01)*
Haylah
Hayle *(0.02)*
Haylea *(0.01)*
Hayleah
Hayleanah
Hayleann
Haylee *(0.57)*
Haylee Marie
Haylee-Fay
Hayleen
Hayleeonna
Haylee-Rose
Haylei *(0.02)*
Hayleigh *(0.10)*
Hayleii
Haylen *(0.01)*
Hayley *(0.58)*
Hayli *(0.03)*
Hayliana
Haylie *(0.24)*
Haylie My-
  Uhuyen
Haylieana
Haylie-Jade
Haylim
Haylin
Haylix
Haylle
Hayllie
Hayln
Hayly
Haylyn
Haylynn
Hayne
Haynes
Hayse
Haysha
Hayslie
Ha-Yunie
Hayvah

Hayvan
Hayveann
Hayven *(0.01)*
Hayvin
Hayvn
Hayzel
Hayzen
Hayzes
Hayzlynn
Hazal
Hazaley
Hazel *(0.19)*
Hazel Rheneé
Hazelelizabeth
Hazell
Hazelle
Hazel-Marie
Hazeltine
Hazel-Victoria
Hazely
Hazelyn
Hazel-Yohani
Hazen
Hazera
Haziah
Hazina
Hazle
Hazley
Hazra
Hazy
Hazyel
Hazyl
Hazyll
Hazzel
Hea Ven
Heaany
Headan
Heala
Healy
Heartley
Heather *(0.36)*
Heather-Li
Heatherly
Heavan
Heavanly
Heaven *(0.45)*
Heaven
  Carnation
Heaven Lyvae
Heaven'
Heavengrace
Heaven-Gracie
Heavenlai

Heaven-Lee
Heavenlee
Heaven-Lei
Heaven-Leigh
Heavenleigh
Heavenley
Heavenli
Heavenlie
Heavenly *(0.05)*
Heavenlyn
Heaven-Lynn
Heavenn'
Heaven-Nadir
Heavensent
Heavenwise
Heavenz
Heavin
Heavlyn
Heavnli
Heavon
Heavun
Heavyn *(0.02)*
Heavynn
Heavynn-Leigh
Heba *(0.01)*
Hebatullah
Hebe
Hebelyn
Hebriona
Hecate
Hechiel
Hector
Hedaia
Hedaya
Hedayah
Hedi
Hedit
Hedy
Hedya
Hee
Hee Joo
Hee Jung
Heeba
Heela
Heema
Heena
Heer
Hefziba
Heide
Heidee
Heidey
Heidi *(0.34)*
Heidi Abigael

Heidie
Heidi-Giselle
Heidrun
Heidry
Heidy *(0.04)*
Heidynn
Heighton
Heiji
Heilee
Heilin
Heily
Heilyn
Heimi
Heiress
Heiris
Heirmala
Heiry
Heivie
Heivy
Heiyin
Heizel Ann
Hélaina
Helaina *(0.02)*
Helaine
Helainna
Helan
Helana *(0.01)*
Helania
Helanie
Helayna *(0.01)*
Heldana
Heleana
Heleanaure
Heleen
Heleena
Heleine
Helem
Helen *(0.32)*
Helen Patricia
Helen Stephanie
Helena *(0.23)*
Helena-Maria
Helené
Hélène
Helene *(0.02)*
Helene Kate
Helenia
Helenita
Helenn
Helen-Ruth
Helen-Sophia
Heleny
Helesha

Heley
Heleyna
Helga
Heli
Helia
Heliade
Helicie
Helin
Helina
Helisa
Helizabeh
Hellary
Hellen *(0.01)*
Hellien
Hellyka
Heloisa
Heloise *(0.01)*
Heloysa
Helsa
Helsy
Hely
Helya
Helyne
Helysee
Helyssa
Hema
Hemaiya
Hemani
Hemen
Hemi
Hemmi
Hemy
Hen'drijuana
Hena
Henacie
Henacy
Hend
Hendi
Hendra
Hendrix
Henedi
Henesis
Henessis
Henessy
Henezy
Henika
Henissy
Henleigh
Henley *(0.01)*
Henlie
Henliee
Henna *(0.01)*
Hennasee

Hennasey
Hennassy
Hennd
Hennesey
Hennessey
Hennessie
Hennessy *(0.01)*
Hennetha
Hennicee
Hennyah
Henriane
Henrietha
Henrietta
Henriette
Henriette M.
  Artur
Henriette-Geny
Henry
Henry'unia
Henschen
Hensley
Henya
Hephziah
Hera
Hera Athena
Herada
Heran
Herandhy
Herandi
Herane
Herani
Herberttinay
Herbphearia
Herbretta
Herdenna
Herenia
Herika
Herleine
Herlinda
Herline
Hermani
Hermayonni
Hermela
Hermelinda
Hermella
Hermia
Hermiany
Hermila
Herminia
Hermione *(0.02)*
Hermionne
Hermiony
Hermon

Hermonie
Hernandez
Herneasha
Hernestina
Hernijah
Herniyah
Hero
Heron
Herran
Herreet
Herrizen
Herroop
Herserit
Hershena
Hervena
Herzion
Heslie
Hester
Hetanshi
Hetvi
Hevegn
Heven
Hevin
Hevn
Hewan
Heyde
Heydee
Heydi *(0.01)*
Heydy
Heylee
Heyleigh
Heylen
Heyli
Heylie
Heylinne
Heylis
Heylix
Heynni
Heyre
Heysell
Heyven
Heyzyll
Hezakia
Hezakiha
Hezekiah
Hezekirah
Hi'ilani
Hiahni
Hiawayi
Hiba *(0.04)*
Hibah
Hibak
Hibaq

| | | | | | | |
|---|---|---|---|---|---|---|
| Hibat Arrahman | Hillaya | Hoatien | Honeisha | Houda | Hunny | Hyllari |
| Hibatallah | Hillery | Hocelyn | Honest | Houda-Amal | Hunter *(0.09)* | Hylton |
| Hibatollah | Hilse | Hoda | Honestee | Housseinatou | Hunterose | Hyma |
| Hibatou Allah | Hilty | Hodan | Honesti *(0.01)* | Houston | Huntlee | Hyneka |
| Hibba *(0.01)* | Himaal | Hodane Saad | Honestie | Howard | Huntley | Hyojin |
| Hibo | Himaani | Hodasa | Honesty *(0.04)* | Howunique | Huntter | Hypatia |
| Hibris | Himani *(0.01)* | Hodaya | Honey *(0.03)* | Hozhoni | Huntyr | Hysheemah |
| Hidalia | Himasri | Hodman | Honey-Arlene | Hridaya | Huong | Hyson |
| Hidaly | Hime | Hodo | Hong | Hridya | Hureeya | Hyun |
| Hidanielis | Himeeka | Hofsa | Hong Tri | Hrudya | Huriya | Hyun Al |
| Hidaya | Himeka | Hogla | Hong-Vy | Hsiang-Yi | Husaina | Hyunjhee |
| Hidayyah | Himiani | Hoi | Honisty | Hsiao-Ting | Husan Preet | |
| Hidtzayana | Hina | Holden | Honna | Hsin | Hushi | |
| Hidy | Hinal | Holeigh | Honna-Lee | Hsiou-Chin | Huslen | ~ I ~ |
| Hiedi | Hinaya | Holi | Honneiah | Hu'riyyah | Husna | |
| Hien | Hind | Holiday | Honney | Hua | Husnia | I |
| Hiermon | Hinda *(0.01)* | Hollan | Honoka | Hubert | Hussa | I Anna |
| Hiero | Hindy *(0.02)* | Holland *(0.03)* | Honor *(0.01)* | Huckslee | Hutton | I Nya |
| Hifada | Hinke | Hollander | Honorae | Huda *(0.02)* | Huwaida | I Shari |
| Hifza | Hionia | Hollanne | Honorah | Hudah | Huyana | I. Marina |
| Hija | Hira *(0.01)* | Holle | Honoria | Hudaya | Huyen Nhu | I'airea |
| Hijrah | Hirais | Hollee *(0.01)* | Honorina | Hudrine | Nicole | I'ana |
| Hikma | Hiree | Holleigh | Honorine | Hudson *(0.01)* | Huyen-Tran | I'ann |
| Hikmah | Hiroko | Hollen | Honour | Hudsyn | Hven | I'aonia |
| Hikmat | Hirra | Holley *(0.01)* | Hooda | Hudzyn | Hvlwe-Este | I'asia |
| Hikmo | Hisalda | Holley-Ann | Hoodo | Hue Man | Hwa-In | I'carole |
| Hila | Hisela | Holli *(0.02)* | Hoor | Hufsa | Hy'jahnae | I'dris |
| Hilah | Hiskia | Holliday | Hooria | Hugh | Hyacinth | I'esha |
| Hilaire | History | Hollie *(0.04)* | Hooriya | Hugo | Hyacinthe | I'honor |
| Hilal | Hitha | Holliegh | Hope *(0.81)* | Hui | Hyacinth-Grace | I'jah |
| Hilan | Hitika | Hollin | Hope Chastity | Huimei | Hyam | I'janae |
| Hilani | Hitsel | Hollis *(0.01)* | Hopealika | Hui-Shan | Hyat | I'janai |
| Hilari | Hiwot | Hollisa | Hopelynn | Huishu | Hyatt | I'jaynea-Nicole |
| Hilaria | Hiya | Hollisha | Hopemaria | Huiyoun | Hyba | I'jeerah |
| Hilarie | Hiyaa | Hollister | Hope-Marie | Hulannu | Hyca | I'karah |
| Hilary *(0.07)* | Hiyabel | Holly *(0.43)* | Hope-Querene | Hulee | Hydaya | I'keiah |
| Hilcia | Hiyam | Holly Ruby | Horacetta | Hulya | Hydea | I'kenya |
| Hilda *(0.02)* | Hiyumi | Hollybrook | Horane | Hulyessha | Hydee | I'kera |
| Hildaliz | Hizabelly | Hollyday | Horiyah | Humaira | Hydi | I'keria |
| Hilde | Hizabo | Holly-Marie | Horizon | Humayara | Hydia | I'keriah |
| Hildelisa | Hlee | Hollyn *(0.01)* | Horreyarnna | Humayra | Hydie | I'kerria |
| Hildie | Hleema | Hollynn | Hortencia | Humayraa | Hye | I'keyrah |
| Hileigh | Hlijah | Hollywood | Hortense | Humayrah | Hyerim | I'leia |
| Hilery | Hlina | Holmarline | Hosanna *(0.01)* | Hummaira | Hyeryn | I'lynae |
| Hiley | Hlis | Holmes | Hosannah | Humna | Hye-Sue | I'mani |
| Hiliana | Hluas Ntxhee | Holt | Ho-See | Humyra | Hyjah | I'maní |
| Hilianex | Hmonique | Holy | Hoshebelle | Hunah | Hyla | I'mari |
| Hilit | Hnueda | Holyn | Hosmaira | Huné Jane | Hylah | I'mirra |
| Hilkeja | Hoa | Homira | Hossain | Huner | Hylayna | I'miya |
| Hillard | Hoang | Honami | Hotatian | Huniecha | Hylene | I'muneik |
| Hillaree | Hoang Bao | Honay'jha | Houa | Hunley | Hyley | I'nailyne |
| Hillari | Ngoc | Honda | Houa Der | Hunni | Hylie | I'nasia |
| Hillary *(0.10)* | Hoanglam | Honei | Houashi | Hunnie | Hylii | I'naya |

I'nayah
I'nayjah
I'nesha
I'neshia
I'niya
I'niyah
I'nya
I'onna
I'rica
I'sha
I'shakia
I'shana
I'shayia
I'sheondra
I'shya
I'talia
I'toria
I'yahna
I'yahnie
I'yana (0.01)
I'yanah
I'yani
I'yanna (0.01)
I'yannah
I'yannia
I'yhani
I'yianna
I'yona
I'yonesti
I'yonna
I'yonnah
I'zanaijah
I'zaria
I'zariyia
I'zarrea
I'zhariyah
I'zhaya
I'zona
Ia
Ia'yona
Iaana
Iahia
Iaisha
Iakohat Ti Io
Iakonerahtakatste
Ialah
Ialicia
Ialiyah
Iamani
Iamhia-Passion
Ian
Iana (0.01)
Ianca

Iandra
Ianina
Ianis
Ianiya
Ianna (0.01)
Iannah
Iantha
Iany
Ianyanna
Ianzaginai
Iara
Iaroya
Iasbel
Iasbela
Iashia
Iashja
Iasia
Iasmi
Iassaha
Iasya
Iavae
Iayana
Iayanna
Iayasha
Iayna
Iayona
Iayonnie
Iba
Ibadete
Ibania
Ibeht
Ibeliset
Iben
Ibeth
Ibis
Ibri
Ibryanna
Ibtihal
Ibtisam
Iceis
Iceis Breeya
Iceiss
Icela
Iceley
Icelina
Icely
Icese
Icesis
Icess
Icez
Ichelle
Icia
Iciani

Icie
Icis (0.01)
Icisann
Icses
Icsis
Icsys
Icy
Icy'sis Karmella
Icyes
Icyis
Icyonna
Icysis
Icyss
Ida (0.03)
Idaayu
Idadlia
Idalena
Idali
Idalia (0.01)
Idaliana
Idalin
Idalis
Idaliz
Idaly (0.01)
Idalya
Idalys
Idamarie
Idamis
Idan
Idania
Idanya
Idara
Ida-Rose
Iday
Idayah
Idayanna
Idaysia
Ide
Ideashua
Idefix
Idella
Idellia
Idhaly
Idia
Idianaliz
Idieh
Idielys
Idil
Idman
Idolina
Idolydia
Idy (0.01)
Ieasha

Ieesha
Ieisha
Ielena
Ielexus
Iemima
Ieonna
Iera
Iesha (0.02)
Ieshea
Ieshia
Ieshie
Ieslen
Ieva
Iewerahente
Ieyahnna
Ieyonnia
Ieysha
Ifah
Ifeanyi
Ifeanyichukwu
Ifechi
Ifedayo
Ifeoluwa
Ifeoluwa Ruth
   Moradeke
Ifeoma
Ifetayo
Ifeyinwa
Iffat
Iffet
Ifrah
Ifray
Ifunanya
Ifunaya
Igena
Ignacio
Ignazia
Igsel
Iguewa Celia
Igusti
Ihesa
Ihiekelumma
Ihsane
Ihsene
Iiayanna
Iilayah
Iiman
Iina
Iivyonna
Ijá
Ija'nna
Ijae
Ijah

Ijahnay
Ijahné
Ijan Aiyah
Ijanae
Ijaraya
Ijaya
Ijé
Ijeoma
Ijin
Ijinay
Ijonae
Ijunaé
Ijynae
Ijzhaleiz
Ika
Ikaijah
Ikaika
Ikaja
Ike'isha
Ikea
Ikeasha
Ikeia
Ikeile
Ikendra
Ikeoluwapo
Ikerah
Ikerria
Ikhasijah
Ikhbal
Ikhlas
Ikhlasse
Ikhlaygia
Ikhra
Ikia
Ikierra
Ikjot
Ikma
Iknoop
Iknoor
Ikraa
Ikraam
Ikraan
Ikram (0.01)
Ikrame
Ikran
Ikriyah
Ikroop
Iksha
Ikyeanna
Ikyrrah
Ila (0.02)
Ilaejah
Ilah

Ila-Hart
Ilaijah
Ilaisaane
Ilaisanne
Ilakkiya
Ila-Mae
Ilamay
Ilana (0.04)
Ilani
Ilanie
Ilanize
Ilannie
Ilara
Ilari
Ilaria
Ilaria-Misha
Ilaron
Ilary
Ila-Tsahi
Ilayah
Ilayah Yimearah
Ilayda
Ilayna
Ilda
Ildanita
Ildelisa
Ildised
Ileah
Ileana (0.01)
Ileanis
Ileannah
Ileanne
Ilee
Ileen
Ileena
Ileene
Ileeyah
Ileigha
Ileina
Ileiram
Ileiyah
Ilem
Ilena
Ilene (0.01)
Ilenia
Ilenne
Ilesecia
Ilexia
Iley
Ileyah
Ilhaan
Ilham
Ilhan (0.01)

Ilhem
Ili
Ilia
Iliah
Ilialna
Iliana (0.10)
Iliana-Marie
Ilianara
Ilianetzy
Iliani
Ilianis
Ilianiz
Ilianna
Ilianne
Ilianny
Iliany
Ilicia
Ilie
Ilieana
Ilijsha
Ilily
Ilinah
Ilinca
Iliona
Iliriana
Ilisa
Iliyah
Iliyana
Iliyonna
Ilizebeth
Ilke
Ilkim
Ilknur
Illa
Illabelle
Illah
Illana
Illanie
Illeana (0.01)
Illeany
Illenea
Illia
Illiana (0.01)
Illianna
Illini
Illiyana
Illona
Illusion
Illyana
Illyanna
Illyleanna
Illyria
Illyse

| | | | | | | |
|---|---|---|---|---|---|---|
| Illyssa | Imane-Lina | Imoan | Inaya-Shakeira | Indyanna | Innocence | Iracema |
| Ilo | Imani (0.29) | Imoen | Inayiris | Indyia | Innonence | Irah |
| Iloa | Imani Rejane | Imogen (0.02) | Inayja | Indyonah | Inoha | Iraiana |
| Ilona (0.01) | Imania | Imogene | Inazianna | Indyra | Inseeya | Iraima |
| Iloni | Imanie | Imohni | Inazsna | Ineabelle | Insherah | Irais |
| Ilori | Imani-Janih | Imojin | Inbal | Ineesha | Inshira | Irais Del |
| Ilsa | Imanilee | Imone | Inbar | Ineke | Insiya | Carmen |
| Ilsah | Imanni | Imonee | Inca | Inelda | Insley | Iraiza |
| Ilse (0.01) | Imany | Imoni | Inci | Ineliz | Intaisha | Iraj |
| Ilsette | Imanya | Imonie | Indabelle | Inés | Intan | Iram |
| Ilwaat | Imaobong | Imonitie | Indah | Inesha | Integrity | Iran |
| Ilwad | Imara | Imonni | Inde'a | Ines (0.04) | Intisar | Irana |
| Ily (0.01) | Imarah | Imony | Inde'an | Iness | Inuyasha | Irandy |
| Ilyana (0.01) | Imarhi | Imori | Indea | Inessa (0.01) | Invee | Iranelly |
| Ilyanda | Imari (0.02) | Imperial | Indeeyah | Inesse | Invi | Irania |
| Ilyanna | Imaria | Impress-Livity | Indegul | Inez (0.01) | Inya | Iraniallis |
| Ilyea | Imarie | Impreza | Indeia | Ineza | Ioana | Irannikia |
| Ilyha | Imaris | Impryss | Independent | Infiniti | Ioanna | Iranpreet |
| Ilyiunique | Imarri | Imrath | Inder | Infinity (0.01) | Iola | Irany |
| Ilynna | Imauri | Imrie | Indera | Inga (0.01) | Iolaijhia | Irasema |
| Ilyrah | Imauriz | Imrrah | Inderpreet | Ingaborg | Iolana | Iratze |
| Ilyria | Imaya | Imsaal | Indeya | Inge-Marie | Iolanda Agata | Irayma |
| Ilyrika | Imayah | Imunike | Indhya | Ingerlise | Iona (0.01) | Ire |
| Ilysa | Imayen | Imunique | Indi | Ingiete | Ionae | Ire'lynn |
| Ilyse | Imeisha | Imya | Indi'yah | Ingina | Ionah | Ire'ona |
| Ilysha | Imela | Imyah | India (0.23) | Inglesh | Ione | Irea |
| Ilyssa (0.01) | Imelda | Imzal | India Arianna | Ingmarie | Ioné | Irean |
| Ilyssia | Imelia | In'asia | Indiah | Ingred | Ionee | Ireanna |
| Ilze | Imen | In'deya | India-Jay | Ingri | Ionesti | Ireauna |
| Im'unique | Imena | Ina (0.01) | India-Marie | Ingrid (0.11) | Ionesty | Iree |
| Ima | Imene | Inaara | Indiana (0.01) | Ingrid Rose | Ioni | Ireida |
| Ima'jaunay | Imeria | Inaaya (0.01) | Indianess | Ingrid Rub | Ionia | Irel |
| Imaan (0.01) | Imeshia | Inace | Indiann | Ingris | Ionie | Irelan |
| Imaani | Imgred | Inacia | Indianna | Ingrit | Ionika | Ireland (0.09) |
| Imaelle | Imi | Inaé | Indianté | Ingry | Ionna | Irelen |
| Image | Imiera | Inah | Indiayauna | Iniah | Iora Rafique | Irelin |
| Imagen | Imilee | Inaijah | Indica | Iniaha | Iosef | Irelyn (0.01) |
| Imagery | Imilia | Inaissa | Indie (0.01) | Inika | Iotstharatenion | Irelynd |
| Imagin | Imin | Inajah | Indieya | Iniko | Iowa | Irelynn (0.01) |
| Imagine | Imira | Inanna | Indigo (0.02) | Inioluwa | Iowah | Irelynne |
| Imahn | Imirah | Inara (0.02) | Indika | Inis | Ipek | Irem |
| Imahni | Imisya | Inarah | Indiqua | Inity | Ipsita | Iren |
| Imaiah | Imiya | Inari | Indira (0.02) | Iniya | Iptisam | Irena (0.01) |
| Imaira | Imiyah | Inas | Indiria | Iniyaa | Iqan | Irene (0.13) |
| Imairaliz | Immacolata | Ina-Serene | Indiya (0.01) | Iniyah | Iqbal | Irenea |
| Imala | Immajin | Inasha | Indiyah | Injena | Iqlas | Irenis |
| Imalis | Immani | Inasia | Indra | Inji | Iqra (0.01) | Irenyana |
| Imaly | Immanuella | Inass | Indulekha | Injiasen | Iqraa | Ireoluwa |
| Iman (0.06) | Immiyah | Inasse | Indwanai | Inna | Iquira | Ireona |
| Imana | Immogen | Inavejunée | Indy | Innaya | Ira | Ireonna |
| Imane (0.02) | Immoni | Inaya (0.01) | Indya (0.02) | Innazia | Iraca | Ireonnee |
| Imane-Faiza | Imo | Inayah (0.01) | Indya-Miliani | Innea | Iracel | Ireri |

| | | | | | | |
|---|---|---|---|---|---|---|
| Ires | Irsa | Isabellea | Isckra | Ishwarya | Ismeray | Isysis |
| Iresha | Irulan | Isabelle-Anne | Isdalys | Isia | Ismya | Isyss (0.02) |
| Irey | Irum | Isabelle-Kettely | Isebella | Isiabella | Isna | Isys-Sophia |
| Irfaa | Irupe | Isabelli | Isel | Isianna | Isobeal | Iszabella |
| Iriah | Irva | Isabellia | Isela (0.02) | Isibeal | Isobel (0.03) | Iszabelle |
| Irialys | Irvika | Isabelly | Iselda | Isibealla | Isobella (0.01) | Iszaiha |
| Iriana | Irvin | Isabeya | Iselena | Isibelle | Isobelle | Isziah |
| Iriani | Irvionna | Isable | Iselie | Isidora | Isoiza | Ita |
| Irianis | Iry | Isabrella | Iselin | Isidra | Isoki | Ita'ley |
| Irianna | Iryna | Isadora (0.03) | Iseliya | Isidro | Isola | Itáá |
| Iriannie | Iryonna | Isae | Isella | Isielia | Isolde | Itaf |
| Iriany | Irys | Isaela | Iselle | Isika | Isolina | Italéi |
| Iridia | Isa | Isai'nah | Iselys | Isis (0.16) | Isrá | Italey |
| Iridian | Isa'acia | Isaiah | Iser | Isis Princess | Isra (0.01) | Itali |
| I-Rie | Isaac (0.01) | Isairy | Iseult | Isis-Katiana | Israa | Italia (0.01) |
| Irie (0.01) | Isabael | Isajlla | Isha (0.05) | Isismoon | Israe | Italia-Michelle |
| Irie-Ann | Isabal | Isa-Joy | Isha Chris | Isiss | Israea | Teresa |
| Irieona | Isabe'l | Isalen | Ishaani | Isiz | Israel (0.01) | Italica |
| Irihanna | Isabeau | Isalena | Ishaba | Isja | Israelya | Italie |
| Irilkha | Isabecca | Isaleoneli | Ishae | Isjah | Israth | Italivi |
| Irina (0.01) | Isabel (1.87) | Isaliah | Ishaie | Iskra | Israyel | Italy (0.01) |
| Iringo | Isabel Caridad | Isaline | Ishaleigh | Isla (0.03) | Isreal | Italya |
| Irini | Isabel Frances | Isamar (0.01) | Ishamely | Isla Mae | Isreya | I-Tanna |
| Iris (0.23) | Isabel Helena | Isamariela | Ishana (0.01) | Islady | Isrianna | Itari |
| Irisa | Isabela (0.18) | Isamary | Ishanayna | Islam | Isriel | Itasia |
| Irisah | Isabelah | Isana | Ishane | Islamyaat | Isryll | Itaski |
| Irisbella | Isabele | Isanayáh | Ishani | Island | Issa | Itati |
| Irisbelsy | Isabeli | Isanet | Ishaniaé | Islay | Issabel | Itcel |
| Irisbeth | Isabelita | Isania | Ishanie | Isleana | Issabela | Itcha |
| Irisdelia | Isabell (0.11) | Isarah | Ishanpreet | Isleigh | Issabell | Iteoluwakishi |
| Irisela | Isabell Rose | Isarahi | Ishara | Isleimy | Issabella (0.02) | Ither |
| Irisette | Isa-Bella | Isareli | Ishay | Islem | Issabelle | Ithiel |
| Irish (0.01) | Isabella (7.90) | Isaria | Ishdeep | Isleta | Issatou | Ithyary |
| Irisha | Isabella Aliyah | Isariah | Ishhara | Isley | Issavella | Ithzel |
| Irislet | Isabella Carrie | Isaris | Ishi | Islie | Issayanna | Itiana |
| Irislissa | Isabella Fai | Isaro | Ishia | Islynn | Isseth | Itoria |
| Irismar | Isabella I | Isata | Ishika (0.01) | Ismaelis | Isshiah | Itoro |
| Irissa | Isabella Joa | Isatou | Ishita | Ismaella | Isshiyah | Itsallana |
| Irit | Isabella Joy | Isatu | Ishitha | Ismaelle | Issi | Itsel |
| Iritza | Isabella Maria | Isauela | Ishmaela | Ismah | Issie | Itsi |
| Iriyah | Isabella Marie | Isaura | Ishmaella | Ismahaan | Issis | Itteonnia |
| Irlanda | Isabellah | Isaurua | Ishmani | Ismahan | Issis-Ivaney | Ittzel |
| Irlande | Isabella-Lily | Isavela | Ishmeet | Ismaiah | Issobell | Itxclari |
| Irlean | Isabella-Lynn | Isavella | Ishna | Ismailin | Issra | Itxel |
| Irma (0.02) | Isabella-Marie | Isay | Ishnoort | Ismaline | Issybelle | Ityauna |
| Irmani | Isabella-Rosina | Isayani | Ishpreet | Ismaris | Istahil | Itza |
| Irmary | Isabelle (2.12) | Isaydy | Ishtar | Ismary | Isy | Itzaida |
| Irmya | Isabelle Anne | Isbaella | Ishtar Aset | Ismat | Isyabella | Itzairy |
| Irmyah | Isabelle De | Isbella | Ishveen | Ismaya | Isyabellah | Itzalyn |
| Irnisa | Grandi | Iscah | Ishwa | Ismelda | Isyiah | Itzamary |
| Iroha | Isabelle Lynn | Ischa | Ishwak | Ismenia | Isyis | Itzari |
| Iromy | Isabelle Simone | Ischama | Ishwarpreet | Ismerai | Isys (0.01) | Itzayanna |

| | | | | | | |
|---|---|---|---|---|---|---|
| Itzbel | Iveshia | Ivyregina | Iyeh | Izaira | Izzily | J'lah |
| Itzeh | Ivet | Ivy-Rose | Iyesha | Izalena | Izzy | J'laylia |
| Itzel (0.11) | Iveth | Ivyuna | Iyesis | Izalia | | J'lee |
| Itzell | Ivett | Ivyunia | Iyette | Izalie | | J'leigh |
| Itzelle | Ivette (0.03) | Ixa | Iyia | Izaliyah | ~ J ~ | J'lesha |
| Itzia | Ivette-Sage | Ixaly | Iyiana | Izallana | | J'liyah |
| Itziar | Ivey (0.03) | Ixcel | Iyisha | Izamar | J | J'lyn (0.01) |
| Itzmari | Ivi | Ixchel | Iyla | Izamara | J Lynn | J'lynn (0.01) |
| Itzy | Ivia | Ixchell | Iyleigh | Izara | J Marie | J'lyssa |
| Itzyana | Iviana | Ixel | Iyllin | Izarah | J Mia | J'mariya |
| Itzyhar | Ivianna | Ixelyn | Iymaan | Izaraya | J Monnie | J'maya |
| Iulia | Iviannah | Ixia | Iynaja | Izarene | J Nih | J'meah |
| Iustina | Ivianzet | Ixmucane | Iyolah | Izarya | J Yawna | J'mecoh |
| Iv | Ivie (0.01) | Ixonia | Iyon'na | Izaura | J' La | J'meriah |
| Iv'esha | Iviee | Ixtzel | Iyona (0.01) | Izavella | J' Shaelea | J'meya |
| Iva (0.02) | Ivie-Kate | Ixuri | Iyonah | Izaya | J'ada | J'mila |
| Ivah | Ivieoghene | Ixziara | Iyone | Izebel | J'adore | J'miracle |
| Ivairis | Iviona | Iy'onna | Iyonia | Izebell | J'ae | J'miyah |
| Ivaldina | Ivionna | Iy'ronni | Iyonica | Izebella | J'alayha | J'mya |
| Ivalee | Iviria | Iya | Iyonna (0.03) | Izel | J'ali'anna | J'myah |
| Ivalisse | Ivis | Iya'nna | Iyonnah | Izela | J'alijiah | J'myia |
| Ivana (0.05) | Iviyan | Iyah | Iyonnie | Izellah | J'alin | J'myra |
| Ivanah | Ivnoor | Iyahana | Iyontha | Izelle | J'aliyah | J'nae |
| Ivanaliz | Ivoire | Iyahna | Iyriel | Izeryah | J'anice | J'nai |
| Ivane | Ivon | Iyahnna | Iyrullan | Izet | J'aniya | J'nareia |
| Ivangelina | Ivona | Iyamisamar | Iysis (0.01) | Izetta | J'aniyah | J'navia |
| Ivania | Ivonae | Iyan | Iyslin | Izette | J'anna | J'nay |
| Ivanis | Ivonna | Iyana (0.09) | Iyssis | Izhar | J'anni | J'naye |
| Ivanity | Ivonne (0.02) | Iyanah (0.01) | Iyuana | Izhiya | J'ara | J'nayshia |
| Ivanivelisse | Ivonni | Iyanah | Iyuanah | Izia | J'arriena | J'neisha |
| Ivanka | Ivonti | Ahmathah | Iyuannah | Iziana | J'asia | J'nia |
| Ivanna (0.02) | Ivorey-Rose | Iyandra | I-Yunna | Izibella | J'auna | J'niah |
| Ivanna Dalay | Ivori (0.01) | Iyanelli | Iyunna | Izir | J'ayla | J'nique |
| Ivannah | Ivoriana | Iyani | Iyuuna | Iziz | J'cynda | J'niya (0.01) |
| Ivanni | Ivorie (0.01) | Iyaniah | Iyyona | Izlette | J'deon | J'niyah (0.01) |
| Ivanova | Ivory (0.04) | Iyanla | Iza | Izlynn | J'doria | J'nya |
| Ivany | Ivoryah | I-Yanna | Izabaila | Izna | J'dyn | J'nyah |
| Ivaree | Ivoryana | Iyanná | Izabel (0.05) | Izobel | J'ela | J'nyia |
| Ivaruth | Ivoryanna | Iyanna (0.09) | Izabela (0.02) | Izreal | J'hmyra | J'nyrah |
| Ivayona | Ivoryona | Iyannah (0.01) | Izabele | Iztel | J'honari | J'nyya |
| Ived | Ivree | Iyannia | Izabell (0.02) | Iztli | J'jira | J'ona |
| Ivee | Ivrit | Iyanuoluwa | Izabella (0.31) | Izuaned | J'kaila | J'rah |
| Iveigh | Ivy (0.36) | Iyari | Izabellah | Izy | J'kayla | J'ronica |
| Ivelice | Ivy'unna | Iyarri | Izabelle (0.06) | Izyria | J'kea | J'ryan |
| Ivelin | Ivy-Aliya | Iyasha | Izabelle- | Izza | J'keia | J'ryn |
| Ivelis | Ivyana | Iyauna | Angélique | Izzabela | J'khaurea | J'shanti |
| Ivelissa | Ivyann | Iyaunna | Izabellia | Izzabella (0.02) | J'khia | J'sharron |
| Ivelisse (0.01) | Ivyanna | Iyawna | Izable | Izzabelle (0.01) | J'kira | J'shea |
| Ivelys | Ivyee | Iyawnah | Izadora | Izzadora | J'kiria | J'shuná |
| Iveon | Ivyhailyn | Iyces | Izaelle | Izzah | J'kouriah | J'siyah |
| Iverson | Ivyjaden | Iye'aunna | Izah | Izzahbella | J'kya | J'taiyah |
| Ivery | Ivyona | Iyecis | Izahora | Izzebella | J'kyla | J'tayea |
| Iveryana | Ivyonna | Iyeda | Izaiah | Izzi | J'la | J'veahna |

| | | | | | | |
|---|---|---|---|---|---|---|
| J'yani | Ja'bria (0.01) | Ja'hirah | Ja'kiera | Ja'leeyah | Ja'mashion | Ja'myala |
| J'yaniya | Ja'briah | Ja'hiya | Ja'kira | Ja'leigha | Ja'mauni | Ja'myarose |
| J'yonna | Ja'briana | Ja'hlysa | Ja'kirah | Ja'leiyah | Ja'mauria | Ja'myhia |
| J'zelle | Ja'brielle | Ja'hnae | Ja'kiriana | Ja'len | Ja'may | Ja'myia |
| J'zhana | Ja'briya | Ja'hyra | Ja'kirryia | Ja'lencia | Ja'maya (0.01) | Ja'myiah |
| J'zndrea | Ja'brya | Ja'hyria | Ja'kiryah | Ja'leonna | Ja'mayia | Ja'myla |
| Já | Ja'caija | Ja'ida | Ja'kivia | Ja'leria | Ja'mayne | Ja'myra |
| Ja (0.01) | Ja'carie | Ja'iria | Ja'kiya (0.01) | Ja'lesha | Ja'meah | Ja'myya |
| Ja 'Miracle | Ja'cayla | Ja'iyah | Ja'kiyah (0.01) | Ja'lexious | Ja'mearriy | Ja'nae (0.01) |
| Ja Anna | Ja'cayrria | Ja'kai | Ja'kiyla | Ja'lexis | Ja'mecia | Ja'naeya |
| Ja Da | Ja'ce | Ja'kaijha | Ja'kiylah | Ja'lexus | Ja'meciana | Ja'nai |
| Já Daisy | Ja'cedra | Ja'kaiya | Ja'kiyrha | Ja'leyah | Ja'meece | Ja'naihya |
| Ja Hillera | Ja'cee | Ja'kala | Ja'klya | Ja'lia | Ja'mees | Ja'naija |
| Ja Honest | Ja'charah | Ja'kalya | Ja'kobi | Ja'liah | Ja'meinah | Ja'nair |
| Ja Il | Ja'chelle | Ja'kara | Ja'koryous | Ja'lianna | Ja'meirium | Ja'naisha |
| Ja Kasia | Ja'chia | Ja'kararia | Ja'koy | Ja'liaya | Ja'meirra | Ja'naishia |
| Ja Kayla | Ja'chyia | Ja'karia | Ja'kryi | Ja'lin | Ja'meka | Ja'naishja |
| Ja Kaylia | Ja'cinta | Ja'kaseyon | Ja'kryia | Ja'lisa | Ja'mela | Ja'naiya |
| Ja Keria | Ja'cobi | Ja'kasia | Ja'ky | Ja'lisha | Ja'melia | Ja'naja |
| Ja Kkara | Ja'cora | Ja'kaya | Ja'kya | Ja'lisia | Ja'mella | Ja'najah |
| Ja Kya | Ja'cori | Ja'kayah | Ja'kyah | Ja'lisiah | Ja'meria | Ja'najia |
| Ja Laija | Ja'coria | Ja'kayla (0.03) | Ja'kye | Ja'lissia | Ja'meriah | Ja'naree |
| Ja Lynn | Ja'coya | Ja'kaylan | Ja'kyia | Ja'livia | Ja'merica | Ja'naria |
| Ja Mary | Ja'cree | Ja'kaylin | Ja'kyiah | Ja'liya | Ja'merria | Ja'narius |
| Ja Mia | Ja'csariah | Ja'kayln | Ja'kyialia | Ja'liyah (0.01) | Ja'mesa | Ja'narria |
| Ja Miya | Ja'cyla | Ja'kecia | Ja'kyla | Ja'liyha | Ja'mese | Ja'nashia |
| Ja Mya | Ja'cynthia | Ja'keda | Ja'kyli | Ja'liyiah | Ja'mesha | Ja'nasia (0.01) |
| Ja Myra | Ja'da | Ja'keena | Ja'kyra | Ja'lonia | Ja'meshia | Ja'nasiah |
| Ja Na'ya | Ja'dae | Ja'keijha | Ja'kyra (0.01) | Ja'lyiah | Ja'metria | Ja'nasja |
| Ja Nae | Ja'daisia | Ja'keira | Ja'kyrra | Ja'lyn | Ja'metriya | Ja'naté |
| Ja Nasia | Ja'daiyah | Ja'kelia | Ja'kyrrah | Ja'lynn | Ja'mia (0.01) | Ja'nauseai |
| Ja Niyah | Ja'dashia | Ja'kenya | Ja'kyva | Ja'lynn-Angelica | Ja'miah | Ja'navia |
| Ja Niyha | Ja'dayah | Ja'kera | Ja'la | Ja'lyric | Ja'miecia | Ja'nay |
| Ja Nya | Ja'dayla | Ja'kercia | Ja'lah | Ja'lyssa | Ja'miera | Ja'naya (0.01) |
| Ja Quita | Ja'daysha | Ja'keria | Ja'lahni | Ja'lyssia | Ja'mijha | Ja'nayah |
| Ja Ryah | Ja'deci | Ja'keriya | Ja'laia | Ja'mae | Ja'mika | Ja'naye |
| Ja Shun | Ja'den | Ja'kerria | Ja'laisha | Ja'maga | Ja'mika | Ja'nayia |
| Ja Shya | Ja'denn | Ja'kerrya | Ja'lashia | Ja'mahi | Ja'milah | Ja'nayla |
| Ja Syah | Ja'derrick | Ja'keva | Ja'lasia | Ja'maiya | Ja'miley | Ja'naysa |
| Ja Ziah | Ja'dia | Ja'kevia | Ja'lasiah | Ja'maka | Ja'milyah | Ja'naysia |
| Ja'adea | Ja'diamond | Ja'keya | Ja'laun | Ja'mara | Ja'mira | Ja'nayveah |
| Ja'aia | Ja'dora | Ja'keyia | Ja'launa | Ja'mari | Ja'miracle | Ja'nayzah |
| Ja'aisha | Ja'driana | Ja'khaiya | Ja'laya | Ja'maria | Ja'mirical | Ja'nazia |
| Ja'aliyah | Ja'driania | Ja'khara | Ja'layah | Ja'mariah | Ja'mirrah | Ja'nazja |
| Ja'ariyonna | Ja'dyn | Ja'khayia | Ja'layiah | Ja'mariona | Ja'misha | Ja'nazjha |
| Ja'asia | Ja'eden | Ja'kheria | Ja'layoh | Ja'mariuna | Ja'miya (0.01) | Ja'nea |
| Ja'asiania | Ja'el | Ja'khia | Ja'laysha | Ja'mariya | Ja'miyah (0.01) | Ja'necia |
| Ja'asiel | Ja'ell | Ja'khiya | Ja'laysia | Ja'marjauna | Ja'moni | Ja'neesha |
| Ja'aunna | Ja'eriona | Ja'khya | Ja'laysis | Ja'marri | Ja'monica | Ja'neisha |
| Ja'branda | Ja'frandrea | Ja'khyla | Ja'lea | Ja'marriah | Ja'morria | Ja'neja |
| Ja'braya | Ja'hai | Ja'kia | Ja'leah | Ja'marya | Ja'muriel | Ja'neka |
| Ja'breia | Ja'hara | Ja'kiah | Ja'leayannah | Ja'maryah | Ja'mya (0.05) | Ja'nekia |
| Ja'brena | Ja'hiaya | Ja'kiaya | Ja'leecia | Ja'marylin | Ja'myah | Ja'nell |

| | | | | | | |
|---|---|---|---|---|---|---|
| Ja'nelle | Ja'nylah | Ja'shiyah | Ja'zell | Jabsiry | Jacionna | Jackyelis |
| Ja'nelly | Patrickia | Ja'shontae | Ja'zharia | Jabyah | Jacire | Jackylen |
| Ja'nese | Ja'nylia | Ja'shrae | Ja'zhyia | Jac'kireah | Jaciya | Jackyln |
| Ja'nesha | Ja'nyne | Ja'shunti | Ja'zia | Jacalyn *(0.01)* | Jaciyanna | Jackziry |
| Ja'neshia | Ja'nysha | Ja'shya | Ja'ziaa | Jacalynne | Jack | Jaclyn *(0.12)* |
| Ja'nesiyah | Ja'nyshia | Ja'shyra | Ja'ziah | Jacanee | Jack'ya | Jaclynn *(0.01)* |
| Ja'nessa | Ja'ona | Ja'shyrra | Ja'ziaha | Jacara | Jackaline | Jaclynne |
| Ja'nessia | Ja'onie | Ja'siah | Ja'zinaya | Jacaranda | Jackalinn | Jaclyn-Nichole |
| Ja'ney | Ja'onna | Ja'sire | Ja'zire | Jacari | Jackalyn | Jacob *(0.01)* |
| Ja'neya | Ja'onni | Ja'siya | Ja'ziya | Jacaria | Jackalynn | Jacoba |
| Ja'nhiya | Ja'pashia | Ja'siyah | Ja'ziyah | Jacarie | Jackcel | Jacobi |
| Ja'nia *(0.01)* | Ja'qualah | Ja'skyyia | Ja'ziyaha | Jacariya | Jackciry | Jacobiah |
| Ja'niah *(0.01)* | Ja'quan | Ja'sya | Ja'zyia | Jacarla | Jackee | Jacoby |
| Ja'niaha | Ja'quarius | Ja'syla | Jaada | Jacarri | Jackelene | Jacole |
| Ja'niaja | Ja'quashia | Ja'taijah | Jaade | Jacasia | Jackelin *(0.01)* | Jacolynn |
| Ja'niaya | Ja'quasia | Ja'taisha | Jaahsel | Jacaycia | Jackeline *(0.04)* | Jacora |
| Ja'niayah | Ja'quavia | Ja'tashia | Jaaily | Jacayla | Jackelinne | Jacoreana |
| Ja'niayh | Ja'quisia | Ja'tavia | Jaala | Jacaylah | Jackelline | Jacoria |
| Ja'nice | Ja'quita | Ja'taya | Jaalah | Jacaylyn | Jackelyn *(0.02)* | Jacorrah |
| Ja'niece | Ja'quoia | Ja'tayah | Jaalicia | Jacci | Jackelyne | Jacorrieyah |
| Ja'niesha | Ja'quorea | Ja'teara | Jaaliyah | Jaccity | Jackelynn | Jacovia |
| Ja'nieva | Ja'rae | Ja'telah | Jaáln | Jace *(0.01)* | Jackencia | Jacoya |
| Ja'niha | Ja'rahjanay | Ja'teria | Jaalynn | Jace'y | Jacki | Jacqeline |
| Ja'niiyah | Ja'riah | Ja'terriah | Jaan | Jacedes | Jackia | Jacqilyn |
| Ja'nijza | Ja'riana | Ja'tiania | Jaana | Jacee *(0.02)* | Jackiana | Jacqise |
| Ja'nika | Ja'rielle | Ja'tiya | Jaanaaniy | Jacel | Jackie *(0.03)* | Jacqleen |
| Ja'nillal | Ja'riya | Ja'tiyah | Jaanvi | Jacelin | Jackie Lee | Jacqlynn |
| Ja'nilya | Ja'riyah | Ja'toddjah | Jaanya | Jacelyn *(0.02)* | Jackielin | Jacqua |
| Ja'nilyia | Ja'rya | Ja'tonie | Jaaratullah | Jacelynn *(0.01)* | Jackie-Lynn | Jacqualine |
| Ja'nique | Ja'ryah | Ja'toria | Jaas | Jacelynne | Jackiera | Jacqualyn |
| Ja'nise | Ja'ryha | Ja'torria | Jaasia | Jacelys | Jackilah | Jacqualynn |
| Ja'nita | Ja'ryiah | Ja'tyra | Jaatea | Jacenda | Jackilin | Jacquasia |
| Ja'niva | Ja'sade | Ja'tyus | Jaayla | Jacenia | Jackirah | Jacque |
| Ja'nivia | Ja'saih | Ja'vae | Jaaylahi | Jacenta | Jackiya | Jacquela |
| Ja'niya *(0.07)* | Ja'sandra | Ja'varia | Jaazania | Jacenyia | Jackleen | Jacqueleen |
| Ja'niyah *(0.06)* | Ja'sanova | Ja'vaya | Jaazaniah | Jaceonna | Jacklen | Jacquelin *(0.02)* |
| Ja'niyas | Ja'seanna | Ja'veah | Jaazeil | Jacey *(0.12)* | Jacklin | Jacquelina |
| Ja'niyha | Ja'sha | Ja'veair | Jaaziah | Jachai | Jackline | Jacqueline |
| Ja'niylah | Ja'shae | Ja'veal | Jaazinia | Jachelle | Jacklyn *(0.06)* | *(1.48)* |
| Ja'nohn | Ja'shanna | Ja'veonna | Jaba | Jachiyah | Jacklyne | Jacqueline |
| Ja'norah | Ja'shanti | Ja'viaya | Jabari | Jaci *(0.06)* | Jacklyn-Marie | Delrayo |
| Ja'nya *(0.02)* | Ja'shareia | Ja'vina | Jaboa | Jacia | Jacklynn *(0.01)* | Jacquelinee |
| Ja'nyah *(0.01)* | Ja'shari | Ja'von | Jabrayah | Jaciah | Jacklynne | Jacquelinne |
| Ja'nyda | Ja'shauna | Ja'vonna | Jabraysia | Jacie *(0.07)* | Jackna | Jacquella |
| Ja'nyea | Ja'shawn'tee | Ja'vonne | Jabrea | Jacieah | Jackolynn | Jacquelyn *(0.11)* |
| Ja'nyha | Ja'shawna | Ja'voria | Jabri | Jacielle | Jackquasha | Jacquelyn- |
| Ja'nyhia | Ja'shawnna | Ja'ya | Jabria *(0.01)* | Jacilyn | Jackquelin | Christy |
| Ja'nyia | Ja'shayah | Ja'yiona | Jabriah | Jacinda *(0.01)* | Jackqueline | Jacquelyne |
| Ja'nyiah | Ja'shayla | Ja'zara | Jabrielle | Jacinta *(0.01)* | Jackqulin | Jacquelynn |
| Ja'nyijah | Ja'shell | Ja'zareiah | Jabriya | Jacinth | Jacksen | *(0.01)* |
| Ja'nyjah | Ja'shelle | Ja'zaria | Jabriyah | Jacintha | Jackson *(0.01)* | Jacquelynne |
| Ja'nyla *(0.01)* | Ja'shiah | Ja'zariah | Jabryah | Jacinthe *(0.01)* | Jackson Chol | Jacqueria |
| Ja'nylah | Ja'shiya | Ja'zauria | Jabryia | Jaciona | Jacky *(0.01)* | Jacques |

| | | | | | | |
|---|---|---|---|---|---|---|
| Jacqui | Jadalyn (0.01) | Jadeleen | Jadira | Jae'riel | Jaeli | Jaeyoung |
| Jacquice | Jada-Lynn | Jadeliah | Jadirah | Jae'shae | Jaeliana | Jaezlynn |
| Jacquiline | Jadalynn (0.01) | Jadelin | Jadis | Jae'vianni | Jaelie | Jaffa |
| Jacquilyn | Jadalynne | Jadelinn | Jadison | Jae'vonna | Jaelin (0.01) | Jafon |
| Jacquinlyn | Jadalys | Jadelisa | Jadiyah | Jae'yana | Jaelinh | Jagaira |
| Jacquita | Jadalysse | Jadeliz | Jadlen | Jae'za-Kaiya | Jae-Linn | Jagbir |
| Jacquiuna | Jada-Marie | Jadelon | Jadliene | Jaeana | Jaelinn | Jagdeep |
| Jacquline | Jadan (0.01) | Jadelyn (0.03) | Jadlin | Jaeandrea | Jaelisa | Jageiry |
| Jacqulinn | Jadania | Jadelyne | Jadlyn | Jaeani | Jaelise | Jagger |
| Jacqulyn | Jada-Nicole | Jade-Lynn | Jadnerys | Jaeanna | Jaelisse | Jagianna |
| Jacqulyn Elizabeth | Jadanis | Jadelynn (0.02) | Jadon | Jaeasia | Jaelisyah-Lyn | Jagjot |
| | Jadann | Jadelynne | Jadora | Jae-Auna | Jaelizzaih | Jaglin |
| Jacqulyne | Jadareese | Jade-May | Jadori | Jaecee | Jaella | Jagvir |
| Jacquoline | Jadaria | Jaden (0.43) | Jadorie | Jaeceiri | Jaëlle | Jah'air |
| Jacsan | Jadashia | Jaden Des' | Jadra | Jaeces | Jaelle (0.01) | Jah'asia |
| Jacson | Jadasia | Jadence | Jadrah | Jaecey | Jaelle-Magdalie | Jah'ayla |
| Jacy (0.03) | Jada-Skyy | Jadenlee | Jadreona | Jaeci | Jaelly | Jah'brie |
| Jacylin | Jadassa | Jaden-Marie | Jadrian | Jaecia | Jaely | Jah'dae |
| Jacylyn | Jadaya | Jadenn | Jadrien | Jaecie | Jaelyn (0.23) | Jah'haria |
| Jacyn | Jadayah | Jaden-Skye | Jadrionna | Jaeda (0.05) | Jaelyn May | Jah'kari |
| Jacyna | Jadazia | Jade-Olivia | Jads | Jaedah (0.01) | Jaelyne | Jah'keriyah |
| Jacynda | Jadda | Jadera | Jadsia | Jaedalyn | Jae-Lynn | Jah'kia |
| Jacynte | Jaddah | Jaderia | Jadus | Jaedan | Jaelynn (0.12) | Jah'kira |
| Jacynth | Jaddalyne | Jaderiah | Jady | Jaeda-Somone | Jaelynne | Jah'kirah |
| Jacynthe | Jadden | Jaderricka | Jadya | Jaeden (0.02) | Jaelysa | Jah'kyla |
| Jacynthia | Jaddiah | Jaderynn | Jadyen | Jaedence | Jaemarie | Jah'lanna |
| Jacyra | Jadé | Jadesha | Jadyn (0.46) | Jaedian | Jaeme | Jah'lay |
| Jadá | Jade (1.75) | Jadess | Jadyn Jám | Jaedin | Jaemease | Jah'lea |
| Jada (2.18) | Jade Esmeralda | Jadeth | Jadyne | Jaedo | Jaemy | Jah'licia |
| Jada Alekxis | Jade Julia | Jadevia | Jadynn (0.01) | Jaedon | Jaena | Jah'lisa |
| Jada'lynn | Jade Ling | Jade-Viktorya | Jadyra | Jaedyn (0.06) | Jaenah | Jah'maine |
| Jadaá | Jade Lynne | Jadey | Jadzia | Jaedynn | Jaenee | Jah'metria |
| Jadaan | Jade Mona | Jadeyasha | Jadziah | Jaeghan | Jaeneisha | Jah'mia |
| Jada-Chea | Jade'rein | Jadeyn (0.01) | Jae (0.01) | Jaeisha | Jaenesa | Jah'miracle |
| Jadae | Jade-A | Jadeynne | Jae Hee | Jael (0.03) | Jaenisha | Jah'mirra |
| Jadah (0.04) | Jadea (0.01) | Jadi | Jae Izha | Jaela (0.03) | Jaenna | Jah'miyah |
| Jadah'li | Jadeah | Jadia | Jae Lyne | Jae-Lah | Jaenyce | Jah'miyha |
| Jadai | Jadea-Lyn | Jadiah | Jae Lynn | Jaelah | Jae-Onna | Jah'myia |
| Jadaia | Jade-Amy | Jadiahna | Jae'a | Jaelan | Jaeonna | Jah'nae |
| Jada-Imani | Jadean | Jadiamond | Jae'acesis | Jaelana | Jaeralyn | Jah'nalia |
| Jadaisha | Jade-Analy | Jadianna | Jae'ana | Jaelani | Jaerla | Jah'nasia |
| Jadaiya | Jadeanjali | Jadice | Jae'da | Jaelani Janae | Jaerlyn | Jah'nasya |
| Jadaiyah | Jadeann | Jadie (0.01) | Jae'dha | Jaele | Jaesa | Jah'nay |
| Jadaka | Jade-Ceinwen | Jadieah | Jae'dyn | Jaelee | Jaesah | Jah'naya |
| Jadalecia | Jaded | Jadielee | Jae'kira | Jaeleen | Jaeseana | Jah'nee |
| Jadalee | Jadee | Jadielis | Jae'l | Jaelei | Jaesia | Jah'neia |
| Jada-Leigh | Jadeh | Jadielyn | Jae'la | Jae-Leigh | Jaevette | Jah'neiah |
| Jadalin | Jadeha | Jadien | Jae'lee | Jaeleigh | Jaevin | Jah'netta |
| Jadalis | Jadeiliyah | Jadika | Jae'leigha | Jaeleigha | Jaevyn | Jah'ni |
| Jadalisse | Jadeily | Jadin (0.02) | Jae'liyn | Jaelen | Jaeya | Jah'niah |
| Jadaliz | Jadein | Jadina | Jae'lyn | Jaelene | Jaeyanna | Jah'nira |
| Jadalize | Jadeiona | Jadince | Jae'lynn | Jaelene Al | Jaeyce | Jah'nisha |
| Jadaly | Jadeize | Jadine | Jae'onna | Jaeley | Jaeyeon | Jah'niya |

| | | | | | | |
|---|---|---|---|---|---|---|
| Jah'nya | Jahida | Jahmila | Jahquay | Jai'dyn | Jaideep | Jailewa |
| Jah'nyah | Jahideni | Jahmirah | Jahraya | Jai'la | Jaidelle | Jailey |
| Jah'nyia | Jahija | Jahmiya | Jah-Rhe | Jai'lee | Jaiden *(0.25)* | Jaileyn |
| Jah'tyler | Jahilibeth | Jahmonica | Jahria | Jai'len | Jaiden Rae | Jaili |
| Jah'tyra | Jahira *(0.01)* | Jahmya | Jahriya | Jai'lyan | Jaidence | Jailia |
| Jah'zaire | Jahirah | Jahmyla | Jahsacha | Jai'lyn | Jaidene | Jailiang |
| Jahaada | Ja-Hiriah | Jahn'yce | Jahsenda | Jai'lynn | Jaidenn | Jailie |
| Jahaai | Jahiya | Jahna | Jahsene | Jai'lynne | Jaiden-Rose | Jailin |
| Jahadonai | Jahiyah | Jahnae | Jahsenya | Jai'maya | Jaiden-Sky | Jai-Lin |
| Jahaida | Jahkala | Jahnaé | Jahserie | Jai'nasia | Jaides | Jailine |
| Jahaira *(0.01)* | Jahkayah | Jahnai | Jahsiyah | Jai'nele | Jaidi | Jailinn |
| Jahairi | Jahkayla | Jahnalis | Jahsmari | Jai'nyia | Jaidin *(0.01)* | Jailinne |
| Jahairiz | Jahkevia | Jahnaria | Jahsolinn | Jai'ona | Jaidlyn | Jailla |
| Jahala | Jahkirah | Jahnasia | Jahstasia | Jai'onna | Jaidlynn | Jailya |
| Jahaliayah | Jahkiyah | Jahnavi | Jahstyce | Jai'quana | Jaidra | Jai-Lyn |
| Jahan | Jahkobi | Jahnay | Jahtalia | Jai'rah | Jaidy | Jailyn *(0.08)* |
| Jahana | Jahkya | Jahnaya | Jah-Vanah | Jai'riah | Jaidylise | Jailyne |
| Jahanii | Jahkyra | Jahnaye | Jahvia | Jai'ryah | Jaidyn *(0.16)* | Jai-Lynn |
| Jahanna | Jahla | Jahnazia | Jahya | Jai'sha | Jaidyn Ayanthi | Jailynn *(0.03)* |
| Jahaqira | Jahlaal | Jahne | Jahyden | Jai'via | Jaidyn Elizabet | Jailynne |
| Jahara | Jahlani | Jahné | Jahydi | Jai'vonna | Jaidyn Jannae | Jailys |
| Jaharam | Jahlasha | Jahnea | Jahyia | Jai'ya | Jaidynn | Jaimaly |
| Jahari | Jahlaya | Jah-Neila | Jahyie | Jai'yah | Jaidys | Jaime *(0.09)* |
| Jaharria | Jahlea | Jahnel | Jahyra | Jai'yana | Jaieda | Jaime Ebeth |
| Jahasia | Jahleah | Jahnesia | Jahzahnya | Jai'yanna | Jaiedin | Jaime Erin |
| Jahayle | Jahleana | Jahnessa | Jahzara | Jaia *(0.01)* | Jaiedyn | Jaimee *(0.01)* |
| Jahaylea | Jahleea | Jahnessiah | *(0.03)* | Jaiaa | Jaiela | Jaimeeyona |
| Jahayra | Jahlees | Jahnet | Jahzarah | Jaiah | Jaielle | Jaimelyn |
| Jahazee | Jahleeyah | Jahnetta | Jahzaralynn | Jaiana | Jaiera | Jaime-Lynne |
| Jahazel | Jahleise | Jahni | Jahzarra | Jaianna | Jaihanna | Jaimes |
| Jahaziah | Jahleitra | Jahní | Jahzarri | Jaianni | Jaihshaea | Jaimesen |
| Jahazie | Jahleya | Jahnia | Jahzeal | Jaiasia | Jaiida | Jaimeson |
| Jahazielle | Jahlia | Jahniah | Jahzeel | Jaiaya | Jaijer | Jaimesyn |
| Jahbre | Jahliah | Jahnica | Jahzeira | Jaicee *(0.01)* | Jaikaiya | Jaimie *(0.02)* |
| Jahbria | Jahlise | Jahniece | Jahzel | Jaicenya | Jaikerriah | Jaimilee |
| Jahcare | Jahlive | Jahniel | Jahzelle | Jaicey | Jaikia | Jaimilyz |
| Jahceline | Jahlivya | Jahnila | Jahzera | Jaici | Jaikiya | Jaimy |
| Jahcenya | Jahliya | Jahnina | Jahzia | Jaid | Jaikylar | Jaimya |
| Jahda | Jahliyah | Jahnisa | Jahzira | Jaida *(0.18)* | Jailá | Jaimz |
| Jahdai | Jahly | Jahnissa | Jahzlen | Jaidaah | Jaila *(0.04)* | Jaina *(0.03)* |
| Jahdan | Jahlya | Jahniya *(0.01)* | Jahzlyn | Jaidaci | Jailah *(0.01)* | Jainaia |
| Jahdani | Jahlyn | Jahniyah | Jahzrah | Jaidah *(0.01)* | Jailan | Jaine |
| Jahdaya | Jahlynn | Jahnne | Jahzya | Jaidaiya | Jailaya | Jainee |
| Jahdehya | Jahlyssa | Jahnosha | Jai *(0.01)* | Jaidalynn | Jailayah | Jaineen |
| Jahdell | Jahmaya | Jahnvi | Jai Li | Jaida-Marie | Jaile | Jaineisa |
| Jahdia | Jahmeeka | Jah-Nya | Jai Lia | Jaidan *(0.02)* | Jaileah | Jaineris |
| Jaheara | Jahmeelay | Jahnya | Jai Lynn | Jaidanese | Jailee *(0.01)* | Jainia |
| Jaheily | Jahmeiah | Jahnyah | Jai Quira | Jaidden | Jaileen *(0.01)* | Jainie |
| Jahel | Jahmelia | Jahnyah-Rose | Jai'ana | Jaiddie | Jaileigh | Jainiyiah |
| Jahelynn | Jahmeria | Jahnyce | Jai'ara | Jaiddyn | Jaileiyah | Jainna |
| Jahia | Jahmesha | Jahnyia | Jai'asia | Jaide *(0.01)* | Jailen | Jainny |
| Jahiah | Jahmia | Jahnyla | Jai'ciya | Jaidean | Jailene *(0.01)* | Jainya |
| Jahicis | Jahmiah | Jahonna | Jai'da | Jaidee | Jailenne | Jainyn |

Jaiona
Jaionae
Jaionna
Jaiosha
Jaipreet
Jair
Jaira
Jairah
Jairet
Jairi
Jairika
Jairin
Jairy
Jairyana
Jaisa
Jaisa Bron
Jaisaiyah
Jaisean
Jaisen
Jaisey
Jaisha
Jaishaliz
Jaishmar
Jaisley
Jaislie
Jaissiri
Jaitrinity
Jaitza
Jaiveonna
Jaiviona
Jaivonna
Jaiya (0.01)
Jaiyah
Jaiyaisja
Jaiya-Lea
Jaiyana
Jaiyda
Jaiye
Jaiyell
Jaiyla
Jaiylah
Jaiyona
Jaizalee
Jaizell
Jaizion
Jaizmyn
Jaizy
Jajbaat
Jak'eria
Jak'iyah
Jakada
Jakaeja
Jakaela

Jakahra
Jakai (0.01)
Jakaida
Jakaila
Jakailah
Jakailee
Jakaisha
Jakaiya
Jakaiyah
Jakala
Jakalah
Jakale
Jakalia
Jakalin
Jakaly
Jakalyn
Jakara
Jakareia
Jakari
Jakaria
Jakariah
Jakariyah
Jakarma
Jakarria
Jakasha
Jakashya
Jakatlyn
Jakaya
Jakayah
Jakayia
Ja-Kayla
Jakayla (0.12)
Jakayla Yolani
Jakaylah
Jakaylia
Jakaylyn
Jakayra
Jakaysha
Jakciry
Jake
Jakeara
Jakeda
Jakeelah
Jakeem
Jakeema
Jakeen'ma
Jakeia
Jakeiah
Jakeida
Jakeilei
Jakeira (0.01)
Jakeirah
Jakeithia

Jakelia
Jakelin (0.01)
Jakeline
Jakell
Jakelya
Jakelyn
Jakenya
Jakenzie
Jakera
Jakera Essence
Jakerah
Jakerauhnna
Jakeria (0.01)
Jakeriah
Jakerian
Jakerra
Jakeshia
Jakessa
Jakevia
Jakeya
Jakeyah
Jakeyla
Jakeyra
Jakhaela
Jakhaia
Jakhayla
Jakhi
Jakhia (0.01)
Jakhila
Jakhiya
Jakhya
Jakhyi
Ja-Kia
Jakia
Jakiah (0.01)
Jakiaya
Jakicia
Jakiera
Jakila
Jakilah
Jakira (0.01)
Jakirah
Jakireya
Jakireyona
Jakiria
Jakiriah
Jakirra
Jakirrah
Jakisha
Jakita
Jakiya (0.02)
Ja-Kiyah
Jakiyah (0.02)

Jakiyha
Jakiyia
Jakiyra
Jakiyrah
Jakkirah
Jaklyn
Jakob
Jakobi
Jakobie
Jakoda
Jakora
Jakoreyia
Jakoria
Jakoriea
Jakotda
Jakovia
Jakquelyn
Jakson
Jakya (0.01)
Jakyah
Jakyia
Jakyiah
Jakyirah
Jakyla (0.01)
Jakylah
Jakyra (0.01)
Jakyrah
Jakyri
Jakyria
Jakyriah
Jakyrii
Jakyya
Jakzi
Jal
Jalá
Jala (0.02)
Jala'zhah
Jalaa
Jalacea
Jalacey
Jaladia
Jalae
Jalaelah
Jalaeyah
Jalah (0.01)
Jalai'zjah
Jalaila
Jalaina
Jalaine
Jalaisha
Jalaisiah
Jalaiya
Jalaiyah

Jalaiyha
Jalajah
Jalajia
Jalana
Jalandra
Jalani
Jalanie
Jalanise
Jalann
Jalanna
Jalany
Jalasha
Jalasia
Jalasiah
Jalasrial
Jalaun
Jalay
Jalayá
Jalaya (0.02)
Jalayah (0.01)
Jalayasia
Jalayih
Jalayla
Jalayna
Jalayne
Jalaynna
Jalayshia
Jalaysia (0.01)
Jale'ah
Jale'ya
Jalea (0.01)
Jaleah (0.03)
Jaleaha
Jaleahney
Jaleana
Jalearya
Jaleata
Jaleaya
Jaleayah
Jalece
Jalecia
Jalecsia
Jalee (0.01)
Jaleea
Ja-Leeah
Jaleeah
Jaleece
Jaleeia
Jaleel
Jaleela
Jaleelah
Jaleen
Jaleena

Jaleene
Jaleesa (0.01)
Jaleesa
Elizabeth
Jaleese
Jaleesha
Jaleeya
Jaleeyah
Jaleeza
Jaleh
Jaleia (0.01)
Jaleiah
Jaleigh (0.01)
Jaleigha (0.01)
Jaleiha
Jaleika
Jaleina
Jaleisa
Jaleisia
Jaleiyah
Jaleka
Jalen (0.02)
Jalena (0.01)
Jalenda
Jalene (0.01)
Jalene-Victoria
Jalenid
Jalenis
Jaleria
Jalesa
Jalesah
Jalese
Jalesha
Jalesia
Jalessa
Jalexa
Jalexcia
Jalexi
Jalexia
Jalexie
Jalexis
Jalexiya
Jalexus
Jalexy
Jaley (0.01)
Jaleya (0.01)
Jaleyah
Jali
Jalia (0.02)
Jaliah (0.01)
Jalian
Jalianna
Jalice

Jalicia (0.01)
Jalicsa
Jalid
Jalie (0.01)
Jalieei
Jalieen
Jalieha
Jaliehya
Jaliene
Jalienne
Jaliese
Jaliha
Jalika
Jalikatu
Jalila
Jalilyah
Jalin (0.01)
Jalina (0.01)
Jalind
Jalinda
Jalindria
Jaline
Jalirah
Jalisa (0.03)
Jalisah
Jalisha
Jalisicia
Jalissa (0.04)
Jalisse
Jalitzy
Jalivia
Jalixet
Jaliya (0.01)
Jaliyaa
Jaliyah (0.10)
Jaliyh
Jaliyha
Jaliyiah
Jaliza
Jalizah
Jalizmar
Jallana
Jalle
Jalleni
Jallenis
Jallisa
Jallissa
Jallissya
Jalloh
Jalna
Jalon
Jalona
Jalonee

| | | | | | | |
|---|---|---|---|---|---|---|
| Jalonna | Jamalet | Jameciah | Jamesyn | Jamika | Jamita | Jana (0.10) |
| Jalonnie | Jamani (0.01) | Jamee (0.01) | Jameszyah | Jamil | Jamiya (0.04) | Jana'i |
| Jaloris | Jamanie | Jameela | Jametra | Jamila (0.03) | Jamiyah (0.03) | Jana'zjah |
| Jalyce | Jamara | Jameelah | Jamey (0.01) | Jamila-Amira | Jamiyha | Janacia |
| Jalycia | Jamarah | Jameemarie | Jameya | Jamilah (0.01) | Jamiyra | Janadya |
| Jalyese | Jamarea | Jameera | Jameyl | Jamilca | Jamizeona | Janaé (0.01) |
| Jalygsa | Jamarean | Jameerah | Jami (0.03) | Jamile | Jamme | Janae (0.15) |
| Jalyiah | Jamari (0.01) | Jameese | Jami'cia | Jamilee | Jammie | Janae Sable |
| Jalyin | Jamaria (0.02) | Jameetrice | Jami'ya | Jamileh | Jammily | Janaea |
| Jalyla | Ja-Mariah | Jameia | Jamia (0.05) | Jamilet (0.01) | Jammira | Janaee |
| Ja-Lyn | Jamariah (0.01) | Jameica | Jamiah (0.04) | Jamileth (0.01) | Jamna | Janaeh |
| Jalyn (0.09) | Jamarian | Jameice | Jamiahia | Jamilett | Jamonae | Janaei |
| Jalyna | Jamariana | Jameika | Jamiaya | Jamilette | Jamoni | Janaela |
| Jalyncia | Jamariayna | Jameilah | Jamiayah | Jamilex | Jamonica | Janaesha |
| Jalynda | Jamarie | Ja-Meisha | Jamice | Jamilia | Jamonie | Janaesia |
| Jalyndria | Jamariona | Jameisha | Jamicha | Jamilian | Jamora | Janaeya |
| Jalyne | Jamarionna | Jameiyani | Jamicia | Jamilie | Jamorra | Jana-Gabrielle |
| Ja-Lynn | Jamariya | Jameka | Jamie (0.53) | Jamilka | Jamouria | Janah |
| Jalynn (0.08) | Jamariyha | Jamela (0.01) | Jamie Bell | Jamilla | Jamry | Janahvi |
| Jalynne | Jamarrajakri | Jamelah | Jamie Danielle | Jamillah | Jamy | Janaí |
| Jalyric | Jamarrea | Jamelia | Jamie Heeseo | Jamille (0.01) | Jamy'a | Janai (0.04) |
| Jalyrika | Jamarrí | Jamelie | Jamie Lynn | Jamilleth | Jamy'iah | Janaia (0.01) |
| Jalysa | Jamarria | Jamella | Jamie Nicole | Jamillethe | Ja-Mya | Janaia-Amani |
| Jalyse | Jamarriae | Jamellida | Jamie Ursula | Jamilya | Jamya (0.07) | Janaiah |
| Jalyseia | Jamary | Jamely | Jamie'cia | Jamilyn | Jamyah (0.01) | Janaidaliz |
| Jalysia | Jamarya | Jamequa | Jamie'ka | Jamilynn | Jamyce | Janaiha |
| Jalyssa (0.02) | Jamarys | Jamera (0.01) | Jamiea | Jamin | Jamye | Samone |
| Jalyssia | Jamasha | Jamereail | Jamie-Ann | Jamina | Jamyha | Janaii |
| Jalyza | Jamasia | Jameriá | Jamie-Claire | Jaminah | Jamyi | Janaija |
| Jalyzia | Jamasyn | Jameria (0.02) | Jamiee | Jamine | Jamyia (0.01) | Janaijah |
| Jama | Jamauria | Jameriah | Jamie-Fay | Jamiolette | Jamyiah (0.01) | Janaijha |
| Jama'yah | Jamaurya | Jamerial | Jamieka | Jamionna | Jamyilaah | Janail |
| Jamaad | Jamay | Jamerica | Jamiela | Jamira (0.01) | Jamyis | Janaila |
| Ja-Mae | Ja-Maya | Jameril | Jamie-Lea | Jamiracle | Jamyla (0.01) | Janaina |
| Jamae | Jamaya (0.03) | Ja-Meriona | Jamie-Lee | Jamirah (0.01) | Jamylah | Janai-Nichel |
| Jamaelé | Jamayah | Jamerixe | Jamielee | Jamiral | Jamy-Lee | Janaira |
| Jamaelle | Jamayia | Jameriya | Jamie-Leigh | Jamire | Jamylett | Janairy |
| Jamai | Jamayla | Jamerra | Jamieliz | Jamirelys | Jamylkah | Janais |
| Jamaia | Jamaylah | Jamerrah | Jamie-Ly | Jamiria | Jamynat | Janaisa |
| Jamaiah | Jamaylia | Jamerrial | Jamielyn | Jamirika | Jamyne | Janaisha |
| Jamaia-Rae | Jamayra | James | Jamie-Lynn | Jamiriyia | Jamyra (0.01) | Janaiya |
| Jamaica (0.01) | Jamayshia | Jamesa | Jamielynn | Jamirka | Jamyrah | Janaiyah |
| Jamaija | Jamayyah | Jamescia | Jamiera | Jamirrah | Jamyre | Janaiye |
| Jamaique | Jambri | Jamese | Jamierah | Jamirriah | Jamyréeona | Janaiz |
| Jamaira | Jame | Jamesen | Jamie- | Jamirya | Jamyria | Janaj |
| Jamairah | Jamé | Jamesha (0.01) | Samantha | Jamiryah | Jamyriah | Janaja |
| Jamairer | Jame're | Jameshia (0.01) | Jamiese | Jamisa | Jamyriaua | Janajah |
| Jamairh | Jamea | Jamesia | Jamiesha | Jamisan | Jamyya | Janajia |
| Jamaishia | Jameah | Jamesica | Jamieson | Jamisen | Ja-Myyah | Janaka |
| Jamaiya | Jameanesa | Jamesina | Jamiezon | Jamisha | Jamyzia | Janala |
| Jamaiyah | Jameanne | Jameson (0.01) | Jamiiayanna | Jamison (0.03) | Jamzya | Janalee |
| Jamaizah | Jamearia | Jamessa | Jamiiyah | Jamisyah | Jan | Janali |
| Jamajah | Jamecia (0.01) | Jamessia | Jamijah | Jamisyn | Jan'dez | Janalis |

| | | | | | | |
|---|---|---|---|---|---|---|
| Janalise | Jandika | Janelliz | Janeyyah | Janilah Lynette | Janne | Janurie |
| Janalls | Jandin | Janelly (0.02) | Janez | Janilca | Jannease | Janvi |
| Janalyn | Jandresia | Janellys | Janeze | Janile | Janneka | Janvier |
| Janalys | Jandy | Janely (0.01) | Janferson | Janilee | Janneli | Jany |
| Janalyse | Jane (0.24) | Janelyn | Janhavi | Janilet | Jannelie | Ja-Nya |
| Janan | Janea (0.02) | Janelys (0.01) | Janhvi | Janilynn | Janneliz | Janyá |
| Janandeliz | Janeah | Janelyse | Janhya | Janina (0.01) | Jannelize | Janya (0.04) |
| Janani (0.01) | Janeaka | Janelyz | Jani (0.01) | Janine (0.02) | Jannell | Ja-Nyah |
| Janarah | Janeal | Janemarie | Jani'a | Janing | Jannelle (0.01) | Janyah (0.01) |
| Janaria | Janean | Janen | Jani's | Janique | Jannelly | Janyasia |
| Janaris | Janeana | Janene | Jani'ya | Janira (0.01) | Jannellyz | Ja-Nyce |
| Janariya | Janeanah | Janera | Jania (0.04) | Jani-Rae | Jannely | Janyce |
| Janariyah | Janeasia | Janeria | Jania Ya | Janirah | Jannelys | Janycia |
| Janascia | Janebatson | Janerica | Janiah (0.09) | Janiriha | Jannesia | Janyck |
| Janasee | Janece | Janerieh | Janiahya | Janis (0.01) | Jannet (0.01) | Janye |
| Janasha | Janeceia | Janeris | Janiana | Janisa | Jannete | Janyelle |
| Ja-Nashia | Janecia | Janerra | Janiasia | Janise (0.01) | Janneth | Janyia (0.01) |
| Janashia | Janée | Janery | Janiaya | Janisha | Jannethe | Janyiah (0.01) |
| Janasia (0.03) | Janee (0.01) | Janes | Janiayah | Janissa | Jannett | Janyka |
| Janassa | Janeea | Janes'a | Janic | Janisse | Jannetta | Janyla (0.01) |
| Janassi | Jane-Emily | Janesa | Janica | Janissia | Jannette | Janylah |
| Janasya | Janeen | Janese | Janicé | Janita | Janney | Janylee |
| Janaueria | Janeesa | Janesey | Janice (0.08) | Janithsay | Janni | Janylene |
| Janaula | Janeese | Janesha | Janice Mutoni | Janithzy | Jannia | Janyne |
| Janautica | Janeeva | Janeshia | Janicea | Janitza | Janniah | Janyra |
| Janavia | Janefield | Janesia | Janice-Ciela | Janitzy | Jannice | Janyrah |
| Janay (0.02) | Janei | Janesis | Janice-Lynn | Janiva | Jannick | Janyse |
| Janay'ja | Janeice | Janeska | Janicesia | Janivea | Jannie (0.01) | Janysha |
| Janaya (0.07) | Janeicia | Janessa (0.16) | Janicia | Janivya | Janniece | Janysia |
| Janayah (0.01) | Janeick | Janessah | Janick | Ja-Niya | Jannieh | Janyssa |
| Janayalin | Janeil | Janesse | Janicka | Janiya (0.28) | Jannifer | Janyza |
| Janaye | Janeili | Janesta | Janicya | Ja-Niyah | Jannika | Janzlee |
| Janayha | Janeise | Janet (0.13) | Janie (0.09) | Janiyah (0.16) | Jannine | Janzmin |
| Janayia | Janeisha | Janet Lynn | Janie Rose | Janiya-Tameia | Jannique | Jaomy |
| Janayla | Janeisy | Janet' | Janiece (0.01) | Janiydis | Jannisha | Jaoniaha |
| Janaymarie | Janeja | Janeth (0.03) | Janiecia | Janiyha | Jannishana | Jaosha |
| Janayra | Janel (0.01) | Janethe | Janielis | Janiyia | Jannitzy | Jaovian |
| Janaysa | Janelda | Janetlie | Janiell | Janiza | Janniya | Japan |
| Janaysea | Janelee | Janetssa | Janielle | Janja | Jannjill | Japkirit |
| Janaysha | Janelex | Janett | Janiellys | Janki | Janny | Japleen |
| Janayshia | Janeli | Janetta | Janiera | Janlee | Janny-Rose | Japmann |
| Janaysia | Janelie | Janette (0.02) | Janiesa | Janlinka | Janolia | Japnaa |
| Janayvia | Janelis (0.01) | Janettly | Janieya | Janmarie | Janon | Japnaam |
| Janaza | Janeliz (0.01) | Janetza | Janieyah | Janmeet | Janorrica | Japneet |
| Janazia | Janell (0.02) | Janetzi | Janihya | Janna (0.03) | Janou | Japneet Kaur |
| Jancey | Janella | Janetzy | Janii | Janna Amina | Jansen | Japnoor |
| Jancy | Janelle (0.23) | Janeva | Janiia | Jannaci | Jansi | Japonica |
| Jandailace | Janelle Dalcin | Janexis | Janijah | Jannae | Jansyn | Jappat |
| Jande | Janelli | Janey (0.01) | Janik | Jannah (0.02) | Jantasia | Japrashia |
| Jandelianne | Janellice | Janeya | Janika | Jannaira | Jantel | Japriest |
| Jandeliz | Janellie | Janeysa | Janikaa | Jannat | January (0.01) | Japrincess |
| Jandelys | Janellis | Janeysha | Janila | Jannate | Janubian | Japsimran |
| Jandery | Janellise | Janeyshka | Janilah | Jannay | Ja-Numri | Jaqairia |

| | | | | | | |
|---|---|---|---|---|---|---|
| Jaqauri | Jaraisa | Jariayah | Jarrian | Jasemine | Jasica | Jasmein |
| Jaqaushia | Jaraiyah | Jarica | Jarriana | Jasenah | Jasie | Jasmelia |
| Jaqoia | Jaralines | Jarice | Jarryn | Jasenia | Jasiel | Jasmelyn |
| Jaqu'aisa | Jaralise | Jarie | Jarryshia | Jasennya | Jasiemar | Jasmen (0.01) |
| Jaquacia | Jarallys | Jariel | Jarsie | Jasenya | Jasilyn | Jasmene |
| Jaquajha | Jaralyn | Jarieli | Jarte | Jasey | Jasimin | Jasmia |
| Jaqualah | Jaralyssa | Jarielis | Jarumi | Jasey Lynn | Jasimine | Jasmianna |
| Jaqualla | Jaramy | Jariellyz | Jarumy | Jaseyla | Jasimyn | Jasmien |
| Jaqualyn | Jaray | Jarielys | Jarvey | Jasgun | Jasin | Jasmiere |
| Jaquan | Jaraya | Jarihana | Jarvia | Jasha | Jasina | Jasmili |
| Jaquanda | Jarayah | Jarika | Jarvionna | Jashá | Jasinda | Jasmily |
| Jaquanna | Jarayia | Jarilee | Jarvisha | Jashaiya | Jasira | Jasmin (0.81) |
| Jaquara | Jardaisha | Jarilisse | Jaryah | Ja-Shalyn | Jasirah | Jasmina (0.01) |
| Jaquaria | Jardann | Jarilyn | Jarylis | Jashandeep | Jasiri | Jasmince |
| Jaquashia | Jarden | Jarilys | Jaryn | Jashanjot | Jasirie | Jasminda |
| Jaquavia | Jareah | Jarimar | Jarys | Jashanpreet | Jasiya | Jasminé |
| Jaquay | Jareakeona | Jarin | Jarysmar | Jashante | Jasiyah | Jasmine (3.63) |
| Jaquaya | Jarecci | Jarina | Jas | Jashanti | Jasjeet | Jasmine Honey |
| Jaquazzeá | Jareccy | Jarincka | Jas'alynn | Jashanty | Jaskamal | Jasmine Love |
| Jaque'ja | Jarect | Jarines | Jas'lyn | Jashanvir | Jaskeert | Jasmine Lynn |
| Jaquela | Jared | Jarineth | Jasa | Jashaquonn | Jaskiran | Jasmine Marie |
| Jaquelin (0.04) | Jarek | Jarinette | Jasahre | Jashara | Jaskirat | Jasmine Nicole |
| Jaquelina | Jareli | Jaris | Jasai | Jashari | Jaslee | Jasmine |
| Jaqueline (0.09) | Jarelin | Jarisalee | Jasaiveia | Jasharie | Jasleen (0.04) | Oceanne |
| Jaquelinne | Jarelis | Jarisely | Jasaiyra | Jashariya | Jasleene | Jasmine Re'nae |
| Jaquelyn (0.01) | Jareliz | Jarisha | Jasalyn | Ja-Shary | Jasleigh | Jasmine Taylor |
| Jaquelynn | Jarelli | Jarisleidi | Jasalynn | Jashary | Jaslen | Jasminea |
| Jaquera | Jarely (0.01) | Jarismery | Jasamaine | Jashauna | Jasli | Jasmine-Angela |
| Jaqueria | Jarelyn | Jarissa | Jasamea | Jashawna | Jaslian | Jasminee |
| Jaquetta | Jarelys | Jarissa Jamy | Jasamine | Jashay | Jaslin | Jasmine-Hien |
| Jaquia | Jareni | Jarisza | Jasana | Jashayla | Jasline | Jasmine-Laure |
| Jaquie | Jareny | Jarithza | Jasandra | Jashé | Jasliyn | Jasmine- |
| Jaquira | Jaresha | Jaritsa | Jasanee | Jashe'unna | Jasllyn | Michelle |
| Jaqulin | Jaretsy | Jaritza (0.01) | Jasani | Jasheenia | Jaslon | Jasmine- |
| Jaqulyn | Jarett | Jaritzy | Jasanjot | Jashell | Jaslyn (0.04) | Rebecca |
| Jaquoia | Jarettzia | Jarivette | Jasanne | Jashia | Jaslyne | Jasmini |
| Jaquora | Jaretxy | Jariya | Jasanveer | Jashira | Jaslynn (0.02) | Jasminne |
| Jaquoria | Jaretza | Jariyah (0.01) | Jasaria | Jashiya | Jaslynne | Jasmiya |
| Jaquoya | Jaretzi | Jarizeth | Jasaya | Jashiyá | Jasma 'Rhea | Jasmon |
| Jaquria | Jaretzy (0.01) | Jarla | Jasdeep | Jashley | Jasmaine | Jasmond |
| Jaqyria | Jarexi | Jarlissa | Jasdip | Jashly | Jasman | Jasmonica |
| Jar'kesia | Jarexy | Jarlyn | Jase | Jashona | Jasmane | Jasmonie |
| Jar'lae | Jarey | Jarmani | Jaseci | Jashonte | Jasmanpreet | Jasmun |
| Jar'miyah | Jarhec | Jarmara | Jasee | Jashonti | Jasmari | Jasmune |
| Jar'vanah | Jarheia | Jarmyia | Jaseirys | Jashuna | Jasmarie | Jasmyaine |
| Jara (0.01) | Jarhiyah | Jarodaye | Jasel | Jashyrah | Jasmatae | Jasmylex |
| Jaracca | Jari | Jarolyn | Jaselen | Jasi | Jasmayne | Jasmyn (0.10) |
| Jarae | Jaria | Jarorika | Jaselin | Jasia | Jasmeauna | Jasmyne (0.04) |
| Jaraeya | Jariah (0.02) | Jarrah | Jaselle | Jasiah (0.01) | Jasmeen (0.01) | Jasmynn (0.01) |
| Jarah (0.01) | Jarian | Jarren | Jasely | Jasiana | Jasmeena | Jasmynne |
| Jarahka | Jarianna | Jarret | Jaselyn | Jasianna | Jasmeet | Jasnaam |
| Jarai | Jariatu | Jarriah | Jaselynn | Jasiaya | Jasmeily | Jasneet |

| | | | | | | |
|---|---|---|---|---|---|---|
| Jasney | Jatareia | Javalynn | Jawnie | Jayanuka | Jayda-Necla | Jaykaria |
| Jasnoor (0.01) | Jatarra | Javani | Jaxan | Jayasia | Jaydarae | Jaykayla |
| Jasode | Jatasia | Javanna | Jaxen | Jayauna | Jayde (0.07) | Jaykia |
| Jason | Jatavia | Javanni | Jaxie | Jaybrianna | Jaydea | Jaykyrrah |
| Jasona | Jataya | Javanta | Jaxielyz | Jaybriel | Jaydee (0.01) | Jay-La |
| Jasonae | Jatayá | Javaria | Jaxirit | Jayce (0.01) | Jaydeen | Jaylá |
| Jasonia | Jatayah | Javariah | Jaxiry | Jaycea | Jaydely | Jayla (1.38) |
| Jasonna | Jatayia | Javarian | Jaxon | Jayceallena | Jaydelyn | Jayla Ann |
| Jasper (0.01) | Jatayla | Javarla | Jaxsen | Jay-Cee | Jaydelyse | Jayla Rae |
| Jaspreet (0.01) | Jatazja | Javauna | Jaxsin | Jaycee (0.10) | Jayden (0.60) | Jaylaa |
| Jaspreunna | Jatelyn | Javaya | Jaxson | Jaycelie | Jayden | Jayla-Arye |
| Jasprit | Jaterralyn | Javayaa | Jaxxy | Jaycelyn | Mercedes | Jaylah (0.07) |
| Jaspriya | Jaterria | Javayah | Jaxyn | Jaycelynn | Ferrer | Jaylaha |
| Jasreen | Jaterrica | Javeah | Jay | Jaycelynne | Jaydence | Jaylaine |
| Jasreet | Jatha | Javeanna | Jay Johnna | Jaycen | Jaydene | Jayla-Lee |
| Jassalyn | Jathusha | Javeena | Jay Lianna | Jaycey | Jayden-Paige | Jaylaliz |
| Jassamine | Jathy | Javelis | Jay Val | Jayci (0.02) | Jaydeonna | Jayla-Marie |
| Jassanique | Jathzire | Javelle | Jay'a | Jaycie (0.05) | Jaydess | Jaylan (0.01) |
| Jassany | Jathziry | Javen | Jay'ah | Jayciee | Jaydha | Jaylana |
| Jasselyn | Jatia | Javenai | Jay'airrah | Jaycielyn | Jaydi | Jaylani |
| Jassenia | Jatieria | Javeona | Jay'da | Jaycilla | Jaydie | Jaylanie |
| Jassiah | Jatisa | Javeonna | Jay'dann | Jaycilyn | Jaydien | Jaylann |
| Jassiann | Jatiya | Javeria | Jay'dyn | Jaycin | Jaydin (0.02) | Jaylannis |
| Jassidi | Jatna | Javeyah | Jay'la | Jayclen | Jaydince | Jaylany |
| Jassidy | Jatoia | Javi'ya | Jay'laa | Jaycln | Jaydison | Jayla-Rose |
| Jassie | Jatori | Javia (0.01) | Jay'lah | Jaycob | Jaydius | Jayle |
| Jassie-Leigh | Jatoria | Javiah | Jay'leen | Jaycy | Jaydlin | Jaylea |
| Jassity | Jatouria | Javian | Jay'len | Jayd (0.01) | Jaydn (0.01) | Jayleah |
| Jassly | Jatura | Javiana | Jay'lyn | Jaydá | Jaydon (0.01) | Jayleahna |
| Jassman | Jatyaha | Javiance | Jay'maya | Jayda (0.46) | Jaydra | Jaylean |
| Jassmine (0.01) | Jatyea | Javianlis | Jay'niah | Jayda Alexis | Jaydra-Ariahna | Jayleana |
| Jassney | Jatyia | Javianna | Jay'nijah | Jayda Lynn | Jaydy | Jayleanna |
| Jassoni | Jatyn | Javiera | Jay'onah | Jayda-Amyra | Jaydyn (0.02) | Jay-Lee |
| Jassyra | Jatzary | Javion | Jay'onna | Jaydacee | Jaydyss | Jaylee (0.10) |
| Jastell | Jatziry | Javiona | Jay'veonha | Jaydah (0.02) | Jaye | Jaylee Marilyn |
| Jastiny | Jau'cori | Javita | Jaya (0.07) | Jaydaha | Jaye'lynne | Jaylee'ann |
| Jastyn | Jauclyn | Javlyn | Jaya Essence | Jaydain | Jayeden | Jayleeana |
| Jasubi | Jauda | Javon | Jayadevi | Jaydalin | Jayelee | Jayleece |
| Jasundeep | Jauna | Javon Na | Jayah | Jaydalis | Jayelique | Jayleen (0.09) |
| Jasveera | Jaunesha | Javona | Jayah-Lynn | Jaydalisse | Jayelle | Jayleena |
| Jasvir | Jauneyte | Javonae | Jayalakshmi | Jayda-Liz | Jayelyn | Jayleene |
| Jasyah | Jauni | Javoni | Jayalaxmi | Jaydaliz | Jayelyne | Jaylei |
| Jasylin | Jauniqué | Javonna | Jayalice | Jayda-Louise | Jayelynn | Jayleigh (0.02) |
| Jasyma | Jauronika | Javonni | Jayana (0.01) | Jaydaluv | Jayemariyah | Jayleis |
| Jasyn | Jauzlin | Javonnica | Jayanah | Jaydalyn | Jayenissa | Jayleiyona |
| Jasynn | Javada | Javonté | Jayana-Lilly | Jayda-Lynn | Jayger | Jaylem |
| Jaszanara | Javadia | Javonya | Jayani | Jaydalynn | Jayiara | Jaylen (0.06) |
| Jaszmin | Javae | Javyn | Jayanna (0.01) | Jayda-Marie | Jayida | Jaylena |
| Jaszmine | Javaeh | Jawaher | Jayannah | Jaydamarie | Jayiden | Jaylene (0.09) |
| Jataiya | Javahla | Jawana | Jayanne | Jaydan (0.01) | Jayilah | Jaylenn |
| Jatajha | Javahn | Jawharah | Jayanni | Jaydana | Jayita | Jaylese |
| Jatara | Javalene | Jawilette | Jayanti | Jaydance | Jayka | Jaylesha |

| | | | | | | |
|---|---|---|---|---|---|---|
| Jaylesse | Jaymeelynn | Jaysha | Jazalyn *(0.01)* | Jazion | Jazmin-Vaneza | Jazzimae |
| Jaylet | Jayme-Lee | Jayshalin | Jazalynn | Jaziona | Jazmira | Jazzira |
| Jayley | Jayme-Lyn | Jayshanna | Jazalynne | Jazira | Jazmire | Jazzirra-Gloveia |
| Jayleyah | Jaymen | Jayshonna | Jazamine | Jazira Christelle | Jazmis | Jazziry |
| Jayleyana | Jaymera | Jaysia | Jazanae | Jazirianna | Jazmn | Jazzlien |
| Jayli *(0.01)* | Jaymes | Jaysie | Jazanail | Jazive | Jazmond | Jazzlin |
| Jaylia *(0.01)* | Jaymi *(0.01)* | Jaysina | Jazani | Jaziya | Jazmun | Jazzlun |
| Jayliah | Jaymie *(0.01)* | Jayslin | Jazania | Jaziyah | Jazmyn *(0.16)* | Jazzlyn *(0.03)* |
| Jayliam | Jaymienne | Jayslyn | Jazaniah | Jaziyha | Jazmyn Kora | Jazzlyne |
| Jayliana | Jaymijlah | Jayson | Jazara | Jazleen | Jazmyne *(0.08)* | Jazzlynn *(0.01)* |
| Jaylianie | Jaymin | Jaysonna | Jazaray | Jazleigh | Jazmyne Renee | Jazzlynne |
| Jaylianna | Jaymlin | Jaytilreya | Jazaria *(0.01)* | Jazlein | Jazmynn *(0.01)* | Jazzmaine |
| Jaylice | Jayms | Jaytionnah | Jazariah | Jazlen | Jazmynne | Jazzman |
| Jaylie *(0.01)* | Jaymye | Jaytta | Jazarionna | Jazlena | Jazmyra | Jazzmare |
| Jaylin *(0.15)* | Jayna *(0.06)* | Jayunna | Jazariyah | Jazlene | Jazney | Jazzmarie |
| Jaylina | Jaynae | Jayvani | Jazarria | Jazli | Jazní | Jazzmeire |
| Jayline *(0.01)* | Jaynah | Jayven | Jazavia | Jazlí | Jaznye | Jazzmen |
| Jaylinn *(0.01)* | Jaynaja | Jayvian | Jazaya | Jazlin *(0.01)* | Jazoria | Jazzmeyre |
| Jaylise | Jaynalee | Jayvin | Jazayla | Jazline | Jazreal | Jazzmilly |
| Jaylissa | Jaynalis | Jayvionna | Jazayra | Jazliyn | Jazrina | Jazzmin *(0.02)* |
| Jaylisse | Jayne *(0.02)* | Jayviouna | Jazbee | Jazlymarie | Jazsmen | Jazzmina |
| Jaylissia | Jaynea | Jayvonia | Jazcitty | Jazlyn *(0.14)* | Jazsmin | Jazzmine *(0.02)* |
| Jaylix | Jaynee *(0.01)* | Jayvonii | Jazden | Jazlyn Rae | Jazsmine | Jazzmon |
| Jayliyah | Jaynell | Jayvonna | Jazdyn | Jazlyn-Areli | Jazsmynn | Jazzmone |
| Jayliza | Jaynelle | Jayza | Jazeil | Jazlyne | Jazulea | Jazzmyn *(0.01)* |
| Jayllene | Jaynelly | Jayzalee | Jazeira | Jazlynn *(0.06)* | Jazya | Jazzmyne *(0.01)* |
| Jayllie | Jaynes | Jayzell | Jazel | Jazlynne | Jazyana | Jazzmynn |
| Jayln | Jaynese | Jayzlin | Jazele | Jazman | Jazyrea | Jazzni |
| Jaylnn | Jaynesha | Jayzmen | Jazelia | Jazmarae | Jazyris | Jazznoor |
| Jaylon | Jayneshia | Jayzmin | Jazelin | Jazmare | Jazz | Jazzrah |
| Jaylond- | Jaynex | Jayzn | Jazell | Jazmariah | Jazz Maine | Jazzrealla |
|   Alexandria | Jayni | Jayzonae | Jazelle *(0.02)* | Jazmarie | Jazz Myn | Jazzy |
| Jaylonnie | Jaynia | Jayzshia | Jazelyn | Jazmariyah | Jazza | Jcee |
| Jaylye | Jayniah | Jaz | Jazemine | Jazmary | Jazzabel | Jc-Lyn |
| Jay-Lyn | Jaynice | Jaz' | Jazen | Jazme | Jazzalin | JD |
| Jaylyn *(0.10)* | Jaynie | Jaz'ara | Jazenne | Jazmea | Jazzalyn | Jdeinaah |
| Jaylyne | Jaynise | Jaz'brielle | Jazera | Jazmeen | Jazzalynn | Jdia |
| Jaylynn *(0.15)* | Jaynisse | Jaz'lyn | Jazhaun | Jazmeenah | Jazzanna | Jdiahly |
| Jaylynne | Jayniyah | Jaz'maira | Jazia | Jazmein | Jazzarey | Jdnatasha |
| Jaylyz | Jaynna | Jaz'mayne | Jaziah | Jazmelee | Jazzarian | Jdoria |
| Jayma | Jaynyzha | Jaz'mel | Jazibe | Jazmelle | Jazzary | Je Ahnee |
| Jaymalyn | Jayona *(0.01)* | Jaz'mine | Jaziel | Jazmely | Jazze'onna | Je Kayla |
| Jaymar | Jayonah | Jaz'myn | Jazielaine | Jazmen *(0.01)* | Jazzel | Je T'aime |
| Jaymara | Jayonce | Jaz'rell | Jaziera | Jazmenne | Jazzell | Je'a |
| Jaymari | Jayonna *(0.02)* | Jaza | Jaziha | Jazmia | Jazzelle | Je'anna |
| Jaymarie | Jayonne | Jazael | Jazihya | Jazmiere | Jazzelynn | Je'da |
| Jaymason | Jayra | Jazaeri | Jazilin | Jazmilla | Jazzemin | Je'den |
| Jayme *(0.05)* | Jayrenid | Jazaher | Jazilyn | Jazmin *(1.09)* | Jazzia | Je'dyn |
| Jayme Lee | Jaysa *(0.01)* | Jazahria | Jazilynn | Jazmina | Jazzibell | Je'kalyia |
| Jaymecia | Jaysa'lena | Ja-Zahriya | Jazime | Jazmine *(0.36)* | Jazzibelle | Je'keria |
| Jaymee *(0.02)* | Jaysalyn | Jazale | Jazimen | Jazmini | Jazzie | Je'kira |
| Jaymee Mahina | Jayse | Jazalea | Jazimin | Jazminn | Jazzilyn | Je'kisia |
| Jaymeeann | Jayseline | Jazaline | Jazin | Jazminne | Jazzilynn | Je'kiyyah |

| | | | | | | |
|---|---|---|---|---|---|---|
| Je'lah | Jeane | Jeanny | Jehann | Jeleah | Jemina | Jenan |
| Je'lia | Jeanea | Jeantazyah | Jehan-Sofia | Jelecia | Jeminat | Jenani |
| Je'licia | Jeanee | Jeany | Jehenna | Jeleise | Jemirah | Jenann |
| Je'lina Lynn | Jeanel | Jeanya | Jehereli | Jelen | Jemiya | Jenarah |
| Kaye | Jeanelia | Jeavon | Jehieli | Jelena (0.01) | Jemiyha | Jenaria |
| Je'linn | Jeanell | Jebri | Jehira | Jelenys | Jemma (0.02) | Jenascia |
| Je'lyn | Jeanelle | Jebria | Jehna | Jelexis | Jemny | Jenasha |
| Je'lynn | Jeanellie | Jecara | Jehnaya | Jeley | Jemy | Jenasi |
| Je'mia | Jeanely | Jecayla | Jehnna | Jelianie | Jemya | Jenasia |
| Je'miyah | Jeane-Marie | Jecelle | Jehovana | Jelina | Jemyah | Jenasie |
| Je'more | Jeanentte | Jechelle | Jehzleen | Jelisa (0.01) | Jemyia | Jenasis |
| Je'myah | Jeanesha | Jecica | Jeida | Jelisbeth | Jemylah | Jenason |
| Je'naeci | Jeaneska | Jecilie | Jeidah | Jelise | Jen | Jenasys |
| Je'nasiah | Jeanett | Jecillia | Jeidaliz | Jelissa (0.01) | Jen'nycia | Jenaven |
| Je'nay | Jeanetta | Jecine | Jeidalyn | Jelisse | Jena (0.06) | Jenaveve |
| Je'neiyce | Jeanette (0.03) | Jecolia | Jeiden | Jelitza | Jena Bray | Jenavie |
| Je'niya | Jeaneviere | Jecoliah | Jeidi | Jell | Jena Bri | Jenavieve (0.01) |
| Je'niyah | Jeanevyia | Jecora | Jeidy | Jellani | Jenaan | Jenay |
| Je'novelli | Jeania | Jeda | Jeilany | Jellinette | Jenaba | Jenaya (0.02) |
| Je'nya | Jeaniah | Jedah | Jeileen | Jellymichell | Jenabelle | Jenayah |
| Je'nyia | Jeanice | Jedai | Jeili | Jellysha | Jenaca | Jenaysha |
| Je'nyiaah | Jeanie (0.01) | Jedaiah | Jeillyn | Jelonia | Jenacey | Jenaysia |
| Je'nyiah | Jeanielyn | Jedalie | Jeily | Jelsea | Jenacie | Jenazhia |
| Je'riah | Jeanin | Jedda | Jeilyn | Jelsey | Jenacis | Jencelly |
| Je'taysha | Jeanine (0.01) | Jeden | Jeilyss | Jeludy | Jenacy | Jenchia |
| Je'teria | Jeaniqua | Jedi | Jeimi | Jelyann | Jenada | Jency |
| Je'vaeh | Jeanise | Jediah | Jeimy (0.01) | Jelyn | Jenaé | Jencyn |
| Je'vair | Jeanith | Jedidiah | Jeina | Jelysa | Jenae (0.02) | Jencynn |
| Je'vonna | Jeanlix | Jediona | Jeine | Jelyssa | Jenae'a | Jendaesha |
| Je'zaria | Jean-Marie | Jedriany | Jeinesha | Jema | Jenaea | Jendalyn |
| Jeadah | Jeanmary | Jee-Ae | Jeirany | Jemara | Jenaesia | Jendasa |
| Jeainna | Jeanna (0.01) | Jeelin | Jeiry | Jemarah | Jenah | Jendaya |
| Jealine | Jeannae | Jeen | Jeishalian | Jemariah | Jenahlise | Jendayah |
| Jealyn | Jeanne (0.09) | Jeena | Jeishaly | Jemaya | Jenai | Jendayi |
| Jeamella | Jeanne Alexie | Jeenat | Jeisli | Jember | Jenaia | Jene |
| Jean (0.03) | Jeanne D'arc | Jeenette | Jeisly | Jemeela | Jenaica | Jené |
| Jean Christophe | Jeanne Marie | Jeenetzy | Jeisy | Jemelis | Jenaiyah | Jene Jah |
| Jean Marie | Emma | Jeesa'niya | Jekalyn | Jemema | Jenaka | Jenea (0.01) |
| Jean'niyria | Jeanne-Amaruk | Jeesue | Jekara | Jemera | Jenalee | Jenean |
| Jeana (0.01) | Jeanne-Eloise | Jeevan | Jekarria | Jemesia | Jenaleigh | Jeneba |
| Jeana Marie | Jeanne-Helene | Jeevani | Jekayla | Jemia | Jenalena | Jeneda |
| Jeanae | Jeannel | Jeevanpal | Jekaylah | Jemiah | Jenali | Jenedith |
| Jeanah | Jeannelle | Jeevika | Jekera | Jemiaya | Jenalis | Jenee |
| Jeanahlyn | Jeannely | Jeeya | Jekiyah | Jemijah | Jenalise | Jenée |
| Jeanaja | Jeanne- | Jefertine | Jelaci | Jemilines | Jenaliz | Jeneela |
| Jeanaline | Marguerite | Jeffiniya | Jelaina | Jemilla | Jenallise | Jeneen |
| Jeanalisse | Jeannette (0.01) | Jeffmilys | Jelaney | Jemily | Jenaly | Jeneesa |
| Jeanaliz | Jeannettie | Jeffrey | Jelani | Jemilyana | Jenalya | Jenefer |
| Jeanalla | Jeannettxi | Jeffreyona | Jelanie | Jemima (0.01) | Jenalyn | Jenei |
| Jeanalyz | Jeannice | Jeffrine | Jelany | Jemima | Jenalyne | Jeneida |
| Jeanavieve | Jeannie (0.01) | Jefthlynn | Jelayah | Emmanuel | Jenalyse | Jeneigh |
| Jeanaysia | Jeannielee | Jeh | Jelayni | Jemimah | Jenalyz | Jeneil |
| Jeandra | Jeannine (0.01) | Jehan | Jelaysia | Jemimma | Jenamae | Jeneisha |

Jeneishely
Jeneisy
Jeneiva
Jeneiza
Jenel
Jenelis
Jeneliz
Jenell (0.01)
Jenella
Jenelle (0.01)
Jenelly
Jenely
Jenensa
Jeneria
Jenery
Jenesa
Jenese
Jenesea
Jenesi
Jenesie
Jenesis (0.03)
Jenessa (0.03)
Jenessa-
  Joulianna
Jenessa-Lee
Jenessy
Jenesus
Jenesy
Jenesyss
Jenetta
Jenette
Jeneva
Jenevee
Jenevieve (0.01)
Jenevive
Jenevy
Jeneya
Jeneyah
Jeneyda
Jeneysha
Jeni
Jeni'ah
Jenia (0.01)
Jeniah (0.01)
Jenibel
Jenibelle
Jenica (0.01)
Jenice
Jenicka
Jenickah
Jenidy
Jeniece
Jenieya

Jenifer (0.06)
Jeniffer (0.02)
Jeniffert
Jenika (0.01)
Jenilca
Jenilee
Jenilyn
Jenilynn
Jenin
Jenina
Jenine
Jenipher
Jenisa
Jenise (0.01)
Jenisha
Jenishka
Jenisis
Jenison
Jenissa
Jenisse
Jenita
Jenitza
Jenive
Jeniven
Jenivieve
Jeniya (0.01)
Jeniyah (0.01)
Jeniz
Jenkins
Jen-Li
Jenling
Jenna (2.41)
Jenna Lee
Jenna Lynn
Jennabea
Jennabel
Jennabell
Jennabelle
Jennabeth
Jennae
Jennaeve
Jennafer
Jennafur
Jennah (0.02)
Jennai
Jennaive-Nation
Jenna-Jo
Jenna-Joy
Jenna-Judith
Jenna-Kate
Jennale
Jennalece
Jenna-Lee

Jennalee (0.01)
Jennalei
Jennaleigh
Jennaleise
Jennali
Jennalise
Jennalyn
Jenna-Lynn
Jennalynn
Jennalyse
Jenna-Maria
Jenna-Marie
Jennamarry's
Jennan
Jenna-Rae
Jennarae
Jennaray
Jennassy
Jennasy
Jennat
Jennaveve
Jennaviere
Jennavieve
  (0.01)
Jennavive
Jennay Marie
Jennaya
Jenne
Jennea
Jenneca
Jennefer
Jenneice
Jenneise
Jennel Rhaine
Jennelle
Jennelle-Asta
Jennely
Jennesha
Jennesis
Jennessa (0.01)
Jennessee
Jennessis
Jennesy
Jennesys
Jennett
Jennette
Jenneva
Jennevie
Jenney
Jennfier
Jenni (0.01)
Jennia
Jennializ

Jenni-Ann
Jennica (0.01)
Jennice
Jennici
Jennie (0.04)
Jenniel
Jennie-Rose
Jennifer (2.60)
Jennifer
  Isabelle
Jennifer Mary
Jennifer
  Roxanna
Jennifer Shur
  Nin
Jennifer-Olivia
Jenniffer
Jennigaelle
Jenniina
Jennika (0.01)
Jennikah
Jennileth
Jenniliz
Jennille
Jennilyn
Jennin
Jennine
Jennipher
Jennis
Jennisa
Jennise
Jennisen
Jennisha
Jennisse
Jennixa
Jennsen
Jennste
Jenny (0.21)
Jenny Lee
Jenny Tran
Jennya
Jennyah
Jenny-
  Aleksandra
Jennyfer (0.02)
Jennyfur
Jennyka
Jennyla
Jenny-Lee
Jennylee-Kate
Jennylie
Jennyliz
Jenny-Roxanne

Jennyse
Jenomar
Jenora
Jenovia
Jenoviyah
Jensa
Jense
Jensen (0.02)
Jensis
Jenski
Jensy
Jensyn
Jensynn
Jentai
Jentasia
Jente
Jentri
Jentrie
Jentry
Jenusha
Jeny
Jenya
Jenyá
Jenyah
Jenyaha
Jenyce
Jeny-Eve
Jenyia
Jenylette
Jenyrose
Jenzae
Jenzel
Jeonaliz
Jeonna
Jeorja
Jeorjena
Jeorjia
Jequayla
Jer'kaylah
Jer'keriah
Jer'leiah
Jer'liaja
Jer'maya
Jer'miah
Jer'miyah
Jer'mya
Jer'myra
Jer'niah
Jer'niya Dasani
Jer'quasha
Jer'reka
Jer'riyah
Jera

Jerada
Jeraldi
Jeraldin
Jeraldine
Jeraldy
Jeraldyn
Jerali
Jeraline
Jeralyn
Jeralyne
Jeralynn
Jerann
Jerawyn
Jeraya
Jercasia
Jerchel
Jeré
Jerea
Jeree
Jereé
Jereen
Jereisy
Jereka
Jerekah
Jereline
Jerelyn
Jeremajeney
Jeremi
Jeremia
Jeremiah
Jeremicah
Jeremie
Jeremy
Jeremya
Jeremyiah
Jeressica
Jereya
Jerhmani
Jeri (0.01)
Jeri Beth
Jeri Lynn
Jeriah
Jeriann
Jerica (0.02)
Jericah
Jericha
Jericho
Jericka (0.01)
Jericlay
Jerie
Jeriel-Tuzolana
Jerika (0.01)
Jerikah

Jeriko
Jerilin
Jerilyn
Jerilyne
Jerilynn
Jeri-Lynn
Jerimia
Jerinne
Jerionna
Jerious
Jerirose
Jerise
Jerissa
Jerisse
Jeriuanna
Jeriyah
Jerkia
Jerkyia
Jerkyla
Jerkysha
Jerlana
Jerleah
Jerlenda
Jerliah
Jerlicia
Jerline
Jerliyah
Jerlyn
Jermaica
Jermaijah
Jermaine
Jermaisha
Jermaiyah
Jermaneé
Jermani
Jermany
Jermaria
Jermariah
Jermariya
Jermariyah
Jermaya
Jermayah
Jermaysha
Jermeariah
Jermecya
Jermeeka
Jermeisha
Jermela
Jermelah
Jermera
Jermeria
Jermeriah
Jermerri

| | | | | | | |
|---|---|---|---|---|---|---|
| Jermes | Jerrette | Jesa | Jesly | Jessena | Jessmy | Jetzibeth |
| Jermesha | Jerreyah | Jesabella | Jeslyann | Jessenia (0.03) | Jessnia | Jeul |
| Jermeshia | Jerri (0.01) | Jesaida | Jeslyn (0.03) | Jessenya | Jessny | Jeulz |
| Jermeya | Jerria | Jesalene | Jeslyn Marie | Jessetta | Jessona | Jeurielys |
| Jermia | Jerriah | Jesalin | Jeslyn-Krystyn | Jessey | Jesstina | Jevae |
| Jermiah | Jerriahna | Jesaline | Jeslynn | Jessi (0.03) | Jesstyn | Jevai |
| Jermicia | Jerriana | Jesaliz | Jesmari | Jessia | Jessy (0.02) | Jeveah |
| Jermienia | Jerrica (0.02) | Jesalyn | Jesmenda | Jessiah | Jessy Quezel | Jeviana |
| Jermika | Jerricka | Jesani Liz | Jesmery | Jessiana | Jessy-Ann | Jeviya |
| Jermila | Jerrika | Jesara | Jesmi | Jessibel | Jessyca (0.01) | Jeviyah |
| Jermilyah | Jerri-Lyn | Jesbeth | Jesmin | Jessibell | Jessye | Jevon |
| Jermini | Jerrilyn | Jes-C | Jesminder | Jessica (3.67) | Jessyka | Jew'lea |
| Jermiracle | Jerrilynn | Jescena | Jesmine | Jessica Kiana | Jessykah | Jew'ora |
| Jermiria | Jerrin | Jescenia | Jesni | Jessica Shiffon | Jessylynn | Jewel (0.11) |
| Jermirriah | Jerrina | Jesci | Jesnoor | Jessica Victori | Jessyman | Jewelanna |
| Jermirryah | Jerriona | Jescolyn | Jesou | Jessica-Andrea | Jesta | Jewelee |
| Jermiya | Jerrionna | Jesel | Jess | Jessica-Benita | Jestacia | Jeweleighanna |
| Jermiyah | Jerrisa | Jesela | Jessa (0.04) | Jessica-Emily | Jestina | Jewelia (0.01) |
| Jermiyah' | Jerri-Shawnda | Jesell | Jessabella | Jessicah | Jestine | Jeweliana |
| Jermonie | Jerrissa | Jeselle | Jessabelle | Jessica-Jayell | Jestinie | Jeweliann |
| Jermya (0.01) | Jerritza | Jeselle Andrea | Jessah | Jessica-Kembou | Jestiny | Jewelianna |
| Jermyah | Jerriyah | Jesely | Jessalea | Jessica-Louise | Jestlene | Jeweliauna |
| Jermyia | Jerryana | Jeselyn | Jessalina | Jessicalynn | Jesunifemi | Jewelie |
| Jermyilia | Jerryn | Jesenia (0.01) | Jessalyn (0.04) | Jessie (0.20) | Jesus (0.01) | Jewelieana |
| Jermyla | Jersea | Jesenya | Jessalyne | Jessie Lea | Jesusita | Jewelina |
| Jermyrria | Jersee | Jesgoid | Jessalynn (0.01) | Jessie Ray | Jesuslyn | Jewelionna |
| Jernaee | Jersei | Jesha | Jessalynne | Jessieca | Jesvin | Jewelisa |
| Jernahria | Jerseigh | Jeshay | Jessamen | Jessie-Kate | Jesy | Jeweliza |
| Jernaya | Jersey (0.09) | Jeshayna | Jessamine | Jessie-Lou | Jesyca | Jewell (0.02) |
| Jernazia | Jershayla | Jeshli | Jessamyn | Jessiendra | Jesyka | Jewelle |
| Jerne | Jershon | Jeshua | Jessana | Jessieona | Jesyree | Jewellee |
| Jernee | Jersi | Jesi | Jessanie | Jessika (0.03) | Jesziah | Jewellin |
| Jerneii | Jersie (0.01) | Jesia | Jessarah | Jessikah | Jesziyah | Jewellyn |
| Jernesha | Jersy | Jesiah | Jessaria | Jessilea | Jet | Jewels (0.01) |
| Jerney | Jerusalem | Jesialis | Jessaya | Jessileigh | Jeta | Jewels-Sameera |
| Jerniah | Jerusalen | Jesica (0.02) | Jesse (0.05) | Jessilyn (0.01) | Jeterrica | Jewely |
| Jernie | Jerusalyn | Jesica Yaslin | Jessea | Jessilynn | Jeterrius | Jewelya |
| Jerniece | Jeruscha | Jesicka | Jesseca | Jessimae | Jetesa | Jewelye |
| Jerniesha | Jerusha | Jesi-Dawn | Jessecca | Jessimar | Jetirreca | Jewelyn |
| Jerniya | Jerushah | Jesika | Jessee | Jessimay | Jetlyane | Jewelynn |
| Jerniyah | Jeryca | Jesikah | Jessee Makaya | Jessimen | Jetlyn | Jewelz |
| Jeronda | Jeryce Nicole | Jesikah-Faithe | Jesse-Jane | Jessina | Jetsy | Jewleigha |
| Jeronique | Jeryiah | Jesilyn | Jessel | Jessinee | Jett | Jewleoná |
| Jerra | Jeryka | Jesina | Jessela | Jessire | Jetta (0.02) | Jewlia |
| Jerrae | Jeryn | Jesiree | Jessele | Jessiyah | Jetta-Ann | Jewlionna |
| Jerrah | Jerzee (0.01) | Jesisca | Jesse-Lee | Jesslan | Jettie | Jewlissa |
| Jerran | Jerzetta | Jesiskya | Jesseli | Jesslee | Jettona | Jewliuna |
| Jerray | Jerzey (0.01) | Jesiyah | Jesselin | Jessley | Jetzabel | Jewlya |
| Jerreah | Jerzi | Jeskaly | Jesseliz | Jesslin | Jetzalis | Jewlyana |
| Jerreayona | Jerzie (0.01) | Jesleana | Jessely | Jessly | Jetzany | Jewlyanna |
| Jerresha | Jerziee | Jesleane | Jesselyn | Jesslyn (0.01) | Jetzay | Jewlz |
| Jerrett | Jerzy | Jesleen | Jesselynn | Jesslynn | Jetzel | Jexeannia |
| Jerretta | Jes | Jesley | Jessen | Jessmarie | Jetzemani | Jexsiarys |

| | | | | | | |
|---|---|---|---|---|---|---|
| Jeyada | Jezzabell | Jhania | Jhonae | Jianna Cloe | Jilitza | Jimika |
| Jeyana | Jezzel | Jhaniah | Jhonnae | Jianni | Jil-Kel | Jimilia |
| Jeyarajia | Jezzey | Jhaniya | Jhordan | Jiaqi | Jill *(0.05)* | Jimira |
| Jeyce | Jezzy | Jhaniyah | Jhordyn | Jiaqi-Jasmine | Jillaney | Jimirah |
| Jeyd | Jh'ganna | Jhannet | Jhorian | Jiaunah | Jillayne | Jimishia |
| Jeyda | Jh'mya | Jhanvi | Jhosaline | Jiawei | Jillean | Jimiya |
| Jeyddi | Jh'neyla | Jhanyl | Jhoselin | Jiawen | Jilleann | Jimmauria |
| Jeydi | Jh'niya | Jhareht | Jhoseline | Jiaxi | Jillena | Jimmeellia |
| Jeydy | Jh'ordan | Jharet | Jhoselyn | Jia-Xue | Jillene | Jimmi |
| Jeyhna | Jha'miryca | Jharetta | Jhoslyn | Jiayah | Jilleyn | Jimmia |
| Jeyla | Jha'na | Jhatoria | Jhossabeth | Jiayang | Jillian *(0.81)* | Jimmie |
| Jeyleis | Jhaada | Jhaven | Jhosselin | Jia-Yi | Jilliana *(0.01)* | Jimmirah |
| Jeyli | Jhachrista | Jhaviana | Jhourney | Jiayi | Jillian-Cailey | Jimmiya |
| Jeylin | Jhada | Jhayan | Jhourni | Jiaying | Jilliane | Jimmyla |
| Jeylinette | Jhadai | Jhayda | Jhovanka | Jichele | Jilliann | Jimya |
| Jeyling | Jhadaya | Jhaydah | Jhovanna | Jicielle | Jillianne | Jimyah |
| Jeyllen | Jhade | Jhaydann | Jhustiena | Jida-Idil | Jillie | Jimyra |
| Jeymi | Jhadyn | Jhayla | Jhvaisja | Jidapa | Jillien | Jimysha |
| Jeymilin | Jhaedyn | Jhazmyn | Jhy'naiyah | Jidayasia | Jillienne | Jin |
| Jeymy | Jhaela | Jhazsmine | Jhyla | Jidelissa | Jillissa | Jin Blayze |
| Jeyna | Jhaelyn | Jhe'kayla | Jhyneya | Jie | Jilliyan | Jina *(0.01)* |
| Jeyna-Jayne | Jhai'lyn | Jhe'nyria | Ji | Jielka | Jilliyn | Jinaleez |
| Jeyneliz | Jhaid | Jhe'yda | Ji'kaiyah | Jiena | Jillyan | Jinan |
| Jeyrasani | Jhaida | Jhemilly | Ji'mecya | Jieni | Jillyann | Jinandi |
| Jeyriannette | Jhaiden | Jhene | Ji'mya | Jientry | Jillyn | Jinane |
| Jeysa | Jhaidyla | Jheneia | Ji'naria | Jiera | Jilneshai | Jinave |
| Jeysi | Jhaiesyn | Jhenelle | Ji'nayshia | Jiesalea | Jilyan | Jindpreet |
| Jeytsun | Jhakea | Jheneya | Ji'neahl | Jieva | Jilyanna | Jindveer |
| Jezabel | Jhakya | Jhenia | Ji'rah | Jiffany | Jilyenne | Jinea |
| Jezabella | Jhakyiah | Jheniah | Ji'teana | Jiggi | Jilyian | Jineen |
| Jezabelle | Jhalah | Jheraldin | Ji'terrius | Jihaan | Jilyssa | Jineily |
| Jezali | Jhalena | Jherika | Ji'yea | Jihad | Jim | Jinelle |
| Jezalyn | Jhalhea | Jheryanne | Ji'ymeria | Jihan | Jim'mariya | Jinelly |
| Jezannah | Jhalia | Jheryll Sophia | Ji'ziah | Jihane | Jim'maya | Jinely |
| Jezaria | Jhalin | Jhesnnyn | Jia *(0.03)* | Jihla | Jim'meka | Jinette |
| Jezariah | Jhaliya | Jhessica | Jia Belle Safeeya | Jihlian | Jim'milla | Jing |
| Jezayah | Jhalyah | Jheyana | Jia Xin | Jikayla | Jim'mya | Jinger |
| Jezayla | Jhalyla | Jhia | Jia Yi | Jikirra | Jimaeya | Jingya |
| Jezebel | Jhamaiya | Jhimere | Jiah | Jikissia | Jimah | Jingzhuo |
| Jezebell | Jhameria | Jhineye | Jiahan | Jil | Jimal | Jini |
| Jezell | Jhamilet | Jhingkie | Jiahna | Jila | Ji-Mari | Jinivie |
| Jezelle | Jhamori | Jhishae | Jiahnse | Jilaina | Jimariya | Jiniyah |
| Jezellya | Jhamya | Jhiya | Jiahua | Jilan | Jimaya | Jinna |
| Jezeyna | Jhana | Jhiyah | Jiali | Jilayne | Jimberly | Jinnalee |
| Jezika | Jhanai | Jhkayla | Jialynn | Jilena | Jimecia | Jinnet |
| Jezleyn | Jhanaiya | Jhmiya | Jiana | Jilene | Jimelia | Jinny |
| Jezlin | Jhanasia | Jhmyra | Jianca | Jileny | Jimena *(0.10)* | Jinolla |
| Jezlyn | Jhane | Jhnya | Jiane | Jilia | Jimenna | Jinwoo |
| Jezlynn | Jhané | Jhnyia | Jianesys | Jilian *(0.01)* | Jimesha | Jiomma |
| Jezmin | Jhanel | Jhoana *(0.01)* | Jianey | Jiliane | Jimi | Jionna |
| Jezmyn | Jhanelsy | Jhoanna | Jiang | Jilianne | Jimiah | Jiordan |
| Jezreel | Jhanely | Jho-Hannah | Jianilyne | Jiliany | Jimidee | Jiovanna |
| Jezyah | Jhani | Jhomoni | Jianna *(0.02)* | Jilina | Jimieka | Jiovanni |

| | | | | | | |
|---|---|---|---|---|---|---|
| Jip | Jlea | Jo'shae | Joban | Jo-Dawn | Joella (0.01) | Johana (0.05) |
| Jipsy | Jleigh | Jo'sia | Jobandeep | Joddi | Jo-Elle | Johanah |
| Jira | Jlona-Jzolda | Jo'vanna | Jobanna | Jodean | Joëlle | Johandria |
| Jirah | Jluanie | Jo'zavia | Jobany | Jodeci | Joelle (0.10) | Johane |
| Jiraya | J-Lyn | Joa'nescha | Jobeth | Jodee | Joelle Elise | Johani |
| Jireh (0.01) | Jlyne | Joada | Jobi | Jodey | Joelleen | Johanie |
| Jireh Ann | J-Lynn | Joadan | Jobina | Jodi (0.04) | Joellen | Johanna (0.21) |
| Jireheli | Jlynn | Joah | Jobinpreet | Jodi Lee | Joellene | Johanna Nicole |
| Jirehiah | Jme | Joahanna | Jocabed | Jodica | Joelle-Reese | Johanna- |
| Jirehly | J-Miyah | Joahnna | Jocalin | Jodie (0.02) | Joellie | Celestine |
| Jirehmina | Jmiyah | Joakee | Jocalyn | Jodie-Jeanne | Joellyn | Johannah |
| Jireth | Jmya | Joaleah | Jocalynn | Jodilee | Joellynn | (0.02) |
| Jirzell | Jmyra | Joalian | Jocara | Jodinae | Joely (0.01) | Johannalis |
| Jiscia | Jnae | Joalie | Jocasta | Jody (0.01) | Joelyn | Johanne |
| Jisel (0.01) | Jnia | Joaly | Jocee | Jody Anna | Joelynn | Johanni |
| Jisela | Jnique | Joalycia | Jocelan | Joe | Joelys | Johannie Alyssa |
| Jisele | Jniya | Joan (0.03) | Jocelin (0.02) | Joe Lee | Joelyssa | Johanny |
| Jisell | Jnya | Joan Catherine | Joceline (0.01) | Joe'lle | Joelysse | Johannye |
| Jisella | Jo | Joan Eliza | Jocelly | Joe'niyah | Joemi | Johany |
| Jiselle (0.01) | Jo Alyssa | Joana (0.05) | Jocellyn | Joe'nyiah | Joemy | Johari |
| Jisette | Jo Dee | Joanah | Jocelyn (2.08) | Joe'quandreah | Joemya | Joharia |
| Jisiya | Jo Hannah | Joanalesse | Jocelyn Hope | Joe'seionna | Joenaja | Joheiris |
| Jislane | Jo Irene | Joana-Pierre | Jocelynann | Joe'toria | Joenelly | Johethea |
| Jisleidy | Jo Lyanne | Joane | Jocelyne (0.02) | Joealie | Joeng So | Johhanna |
| Jislynn | Jo Nasia | Joaneliz | Jocelynn (0.05) | Joeanna | Joequeshia | Johie |
| Jismely | Jo'anna | Joangely | Jocelynne | Joeanne | Joeryn | Johleea |
| Jisoo | Jo'anne | Joani | Jocelynvan | Joebea | Joesalynn | Johlene |
| Jisseidy | Jo'cheryl | Jo-Anie | Jocelys | Joece | Joeselena | John (0.01) |
| Jissel | Jo'connie | Joanie (0.05) | Jocenia | Joeci | Joesia | John'keria |
| Jissell | Jo'ella | Joanier | Joceyln | Joedaya | Joesie | John'nae |
| Jissella | Jo'elz | Joanis | Jochabed | Joee | Joesy | John'naysia |
| Jisselle | Jo'hann | Joanita | Jochebed | Joeeha | Joetaisha | John'ta |
| Jissellie | Jo'hyra | Joanliz | Jochelle | Joee-Jade | Joetta | Johna (0.01) |
| Jitoyria | Jo'keria | Joanly | Jochima | Joehana | Joette | Johnacyé |
| Jitranan | Jo'kyira | Joanmarie | Joci | Joei | Joewanna | Johnaé |
| Jivan | Jo'lanna | Joann (0.02) | Jocie | Joeida | Joey (0.05) | Johnae (0.01) |
| Jivanny | Jo'laysia | Jo-Anna | Jocilyn | Joei-Madisen | Joey Alyxa | Johnai |
| Jivany | Jo'lee | Joanna (0.30) | Jocilynn | Joeisha | Joey Kay | Johnaija |
| Jiya (0.02) | Jo'leigha | Joanna Eliza | Joclyn (0.01) | Joel | Joey Lynn | Johnaisia |
| Jiyun | Jo'liyah | Joannah | Joclynn | Joela | Joeydy | Johnaja |
| Jizarriah | Jo'mari | Joanne (0.05) | Jocobia | Joele | Joeye | Johnajan |
| Jizel | Jo'mecya | Joannett | Jocrlyn | Joelea | Joey-Lynn | Johnalynn |
| Jizela | Jo'mira | Joanni | Jocyleen | Joelee | Joga | Johnara |
| Jizele | Jo'nae | Jo-Annie | Jocylen | Joelene | Joh'nea | Johnasha |
| Jizella | Jo'nah | Joannie (0.02) | Jocylin | Joelesa | Joh'nerrica | Johnasia |
| Jizelle | Jo'naiya | Joannise | Jocylnn | Joeli | Joh'ni | Johnathan |
| Jizma | Jo'nasia | Joannmarie | Jocylyn | Joelia | Joh'nia | Johnatta |
| Jizzele | Jo'nay | Jo-Anny | Joda | Joeliana | Joh'niah | Johnay |
| Jjolexys | Jo'necia | Joanny (0.01) | Jodaliz | Joelianne | Johaana | Johnayah |
| Jkaela | Jo'necionna | Joany (0.01) | Jodalyz | Joelie | Johahna | Johnayce |
| Jkayla | Jo'nerah | Joaquina | Jodana | Joelimar | Johainy | Johnaye |
| Jkirrya | Jo'nesha | Joasia | Jo-Dane | Joeline | Joha-Kym | Johnaysia |
| Jkyiah | Jo'nitta | Joayn | Jodanna | Joeliz | Johally | Johnazia |

Johnchea
John-Curtis
Johndalyn
Johnece
Johnecia
Johnee
Johnelle
Johnese
Johnesha
Johnessa
Johnetta
Johnette
Johni
Johnia
Johniah
Johnica
Johnice
Johnie
Johniece
Johnilyn
Johniq
Johniqua
Johnise
Johnisha
Johnisia
Johniya
Johniyia
Johnjalyn
Johnkeria
Johnlyn
Johnna *(0.03)*
Johnnae
Johnnaé
Johnnaija
Johnnay
Johnnaya
Johnnea
Johnnee
Johnneisha
Johnneshia
Johnnessa
Johnni
Johnnie
Johnniel
Johnnika
Johnni-Rae
Johnnisha
Johnniya
Johnny
Johnnya
Johnnyah
Johnnye
Johnsie

Johntaya
Johntaysia
Johntayza
Johnte'ja
Johntisha
Johnyah
Johnyea
Johnyia
Johnyla
Johnylah
Johnyra
Johoanna
Lynn
Johonna
Johonnii
Johora
Johrdan
Johrdon
Johrnee
Johslyne
Johvana
Johzlyn
Joi *(0.03)*
Joi'nasia
Joi'onna
Joia
Joiah
Joice
Joice Nathalia
Joiche
Joidyn
Joie *(0.02)*
Joiegh Love
Joielle
Joienette
Joiey
Joileny
Joilyn
Joilynn
Joi-Marie
Joinny
Joionna
Joious
Joirdyn
Joiriah
Joismary
Joix De Vivre
Jo-Jean
Jokasta
Jokenlee
Jokerra
Jokhia
Jokia

Jokira
Jola
Jolaina
Jolaine
Jolan
Jolanda
Jolane
Jolani
Jolanie
Jolany
Jolaya
Jolaynah
Jolea *(0.01)*
Jolean
Joleanna
Jolecia
Jolee *(0.04)*
Joleen *(0.01)*
Joleena
Jolei
Joleigh *(0.01)*
Joleigha
Joleil
Jolena *(0.01)*
Jolène
Jolene *(0.07)*
Joleniciya
Jolenis
Jolenna
Jolenni
Joleta
Jolete
Joleth
Jolett
Jolette *(0.03)*
Joley
Joli
Jolia
Joliah
Joliana
Joliane *(0.01)*
Joliann
Jolianna
Joli-Anne
Jolianne *(0.01)*
Jolicia
Jolié
Jolie *(0.13)*
Joliea
Jolieann
Jolie-Anne
Joliegh
Jolie-Lan

Joliene
Jolie-Sariyah
Joliet
Joliett
Joliex
Joliey
Jolimal
Jolin *(0.01)*
Jolina *(0.01)*
Jolinda
Joline *(0.01)*
Joliona
Jo-Lisa
Jolisa
Jolise
Jolissa *(0.01)*
Jolita
Jolitza
Joliyah
Jollet
Jollette
Jollie
Jollitta
Joly
Jolyan
Jolyane *(0.01)*
Jolyann
Joly-Anne
Jolyanne *(0.01)*
Jolyeann
Jolyève
Jolymar
Jolyn *(0.01)*
Jolyna
Jolyne
Jo-Lynn
Jolynn *(0.01)*
Jo-Lynne
Jolynne
Jolynnza
Jomabelle
Jomalizz
Jomaly
Jomana
Jomara
Jomaree
Jomari
Jomarie
Jomarilys
Jomaris
Jomariz
Jomarley
Jomary

Jomayra
Jomelys
Jomery
Jomirrah
Jomishka
Jomya
Jon'aiya
Jon'ajia
Jon'aysia
Jon'esia
Jon'ilyah
Jon'lexxus
Jon'mesha
Jon'nae
Jon'nahia
Jon'najah
Jon'neicia
Jon'nhai
Jon'nyce
Jon'quanvia
Jon'renay
Jon'shay
Jona
Jonadeli
Jonaé
Jonae *(0.01)*
Jonaesha
Jonafel-Marie
Jonah
Jonai
Jonairis
Jonairys
Jonaisha
Jonala
Jonalee
Jonalice
Jonalyn
Jonalynn
Jonalys
Jonaria
Jonarra
Jonasha
Jonasia
Jonathan
Jonathon
Jonay
Jonaya
Jonaye
Jonaysha
Jonaysia
Jonazia
Jondasia
Jondelynn

Jon-Drea
Jone'a
Jonece
Joneciah
Jonee
Jonei
Joneida
Joneisha
Jonelee
Jonelis
Jonelle
Jonelley
Jonelli
Jonelys
Jones
Jonese
Joneshia
Jonessa
Jonet
Jonette
Jonevia
Joneyah
Joni *(0.01)*
Joni Monique
Jonia
Joniah
Jonica
Jonie
Joniel
Joniessa
Jonique
Jonise
Jonisha
Joniya
Joniylah
Jonjanika
Jonmarie
Jonmereia
Jonna *(0.01)*
Jonnae
Jonnah
Jonnaleigh
Jonnashji
Jonnasia
Jonnaysia
Jonnea
Jonneiry
Jonnese
Jonnesha
Jonnesia
Jonnetta
Jonni
Jonnia

Jonniah
Jonnie
Jonniece
Jonnique
Jonnirae
Jonnise
Jonnisha
Jonniya
Jonor
Jonquitta
Jontae
Jontaisa
Jontasia
Jontavia
Jontay
Jonterria
Jonvieve
Jonya
Jonyah
Jonye
Jood
Joori
Joplin
Jora
Jorae
Jorah
Jorain
Joralie
Jorane
Joranna
Jorany
Jorcina
Jorclen
Jorda
Jordaan
Jordace
Jordae
Jordaé
Jordahn
Jordain
Jordaina
Jordan *(1.92)*
Jordan Mackenzie
Jordan Schmitt
Jordana *(0.02)*
Jordanah
Jordance
Jordane *(0.01)*
Jordangabriella
Jordan-Janai
Jordanlee
Jordan-Mae

| | | | | | | |
|---|---|---|---|---|---|---|
| Jordann (0.01) | Jorja-Jai | Joseene | Joshaline | Josleydy | Jotoria | Jovonnah |
| Jordanna | Jorjalynn | Josefa | Joshalyn | Joslin (0.01) | Jotprakash | Jovonray |
| Jordannah | Jorjay | Josefa-Antonia | Joshalynn | Josly | Jotroop | Jovvanna |
| Jordanne | Jorji | Josefene | Joshana | Joslyen | Jotti | Jovy |
| Jordany | Jorjia (0.01) | Josefin | Joshanna | Joslyhn | Joudly-Ann | Jowah |
| Jordanya | Jorjya | Josefina (0.02) | Joshany | Joslyin | Jouhara | Joweese |
| Jordayn | Jorlennys | Josefine | Joshauna | Joslyn (0.11) | Joule | Joy (0.21) |
| Jordayna | Jormyla | Josei | Joshe | Joslyne | Joulian | Joy Claudia |
| Jordee | Jorrdynne | Joselda | Joshelin | Joslynn (0.04) | Jouliane | Joy Love |
| Jordelle | Jorri | Joselee | Joshelyn | Joslynne | Joulin | Joya (0.01) |
| Jorden (0.02) | Jorriah | Joseleen | Joshia | Josmalyn | Joumana | Joyae |
| Jordenn | Jorryn | Joselena | Joshianna | Josmarie | Jounessa | Joyahna |
| Jordeyn | Jorwina | Joselia | Joshigey | Josmeri | Jourdan (0.01) | Joyann |
| Jordi | Jory | Joselien | Joshita | Josmire | Jourdane | Joyanna |
| Jordiana | Joryan | Joselin (0.04) | Joshiya | Josoline | Jourdn | Joyanne |
| Jordias | Jorybel | Joselina | Joshiyla | Josophia | Jourdyn (0.01) | Joyashri |
| Jordice | Jorylliam | Joselind | Joshlene | Josophine | Jouri | Joyaylee |
| Jordin (0.02) | Joryn | Joseline (0.04) | Joshliana | Josphine | Journe | Joybeliz |
| Jordine | Jorynn | Joselinne | Joshlimar | Joss (0.01) | Journeé | Joy-Beth |
| Jordis (0.02) | Josa'lyn | Joselle | Joshlin | Jossalin | Journee (0.02) | Joybeth |
| Jordis-Deanna | Josa'rae | Josellen | Joshlyn (0.01) | Jossalyn | Journei | Joyce (0.12) |
| Jordn | Josabella | Josellin | Josh-Lynn | Jossalynn | Journeigh | Joyce Ann |
| Jordna | Josafina | Joselly | Joshlynn (0.01) | Jossarit | Journey (0.09) | Joyceann |
| Jordon (0.01) | Josalan | Joselourdes | Joshua (0.01) | Josselin (0.01) | Journey | Joyce-Crystal |
| Jordus | Josaleen | Josely | Joshuné | Josseline (0.01) | Kailenne | Joycee |
| Jordy | Josalene | Joselyn (0.20) | Joshylin | Josselyn (0.03) | Journey Niaisa | Joycefene |
| Jordyan | Josalin | Joselyne (0.01) | Josi (0.01) | Josselynn | Journi | Joyce-Jean |
| Jordyn (0.84) | Josaline | Joselynn (0.01) | Josia | Josselynne | Journie (0.01) | Joyce-Keycha |
| Jordyne | Josalline | Joselynne | Josiaah | Jossi | Jouslynn | Joycelain |
| Jordyn-Leah | Josalyn (0.03) | Joselys | Josiah (0.01) | Jossie | Jovan | Joyceline |
| Jordynn (0.03) | Josa-Lynn | Josenae | Josiahnn | Jossiemarie | Jovana (0.01) | Joycelyn (0.01) |
| Jordynne | Josalynn (0.01) | Joseph | Josiane (0.01) | Jossilin | Jovana-Maria | Joycelyne |
| Joresa Mae | Josalynne | Josepha | Josiann | Jossilyn | Jovanda | Joycelynn |
| Jorey | Josanna | Josephene | Josianna | Jossilynn | Jovanelly | Joycey |
| Jorge | Josanne | Josephi | Josianne (0.01) | Josslin | Jovani | Joyci |
| Jorgi | Josaphine | Josephia | Josie (0.48) | Jossline | Jovania | Joycie |
| Jorgia (0.01) | Josaunna | Josephin | Josie Marie | Josslyn (0.02) | Jovanica | Joyclin |
| Jorgia-Layne | Josbely | Josephina (0.02) | Josie-Ann | Josslyne | Jovanka | Joyclyn |
| Jorgie | Joscalyne | Josephine (0.56) | Josielean | Josslynn | Jovanká | Joydan |
| Jorgya | Joscelin | Josephine Marie | Josie-Lee | Jossmaire | Jovann | Joydin |
| Jori (0.01) | Joscelyn (0.02) | Josephine Rose | Josieline | Jostalyn | Jovanna (0.01) | Joye |
| Joria | Joscelyne | Josephine- | Josie-Mae | Josten | Jovannia | Joyé |
| Jorialis | Joscelynn | Juliette | Josie-Rose | Jostyn | Jovantasia | Joyeaux |
| Jorian | Joscey | Josephyne | Josiey | Josue | Jovaria | Joyel |
| Joriana | Joscilynn | Josepine | Josihya | Josverany | Jovey | Joyelise |
| Jorianna | Jose | Joserah | Josilin | Josy | Jovi | Joyell |
| Jorie (0.01) | Josealeen | Josett | Josilyn (0.02) | Josyali | Jovia | Joyelle |
| Jorikah | Josealine | Josetta | Josilynn | Josyane | Joviale | Joyenne |
| Jorion' | Joseanna | Josette (0.01) | Josimar | Josyanne | Jovianna | Joyful |
| Jorisbel | Josecelina | Josette-Lynelle | Josina | Josylyn | Jovie (0.01) | Joyia |
| Jorja (0.15) | Josee (0.01) | Josey (0.03) | Josiphena | Josylynn | Jovine | Joyita |
| Jorja Grace | Josée (0.01) | Josh | Josleaun | Josynia | Jovon | Joyla |
| Jorjah | Josee-Anne | Joshae | Joslene | Joteshwar | Jovona | Joylaine |

| | | | | | | |
|---|---|---|---|---|---|---|
| Joyleen | Ju'naysia | Judi | Julayah | Julialy | Julie-Pier (0.01) | Julizbeth |
| Joyli | Ju'niya | Judie | Julayne | Julialyha | Julie-Rose | Julizeth |
| Joylin | Ju'niya Omarion | Judiel | Jule | Julia-Maria | Juliesa | Julizza |
| Joylinn | Ju'nyia | Judit | Julea | Julian (0.02) | Julie-Soleil | Jullet |
| Joylyn | Jua'nay | Judite | Juleah | Julian'ie | Juliet (0.14) | Jullia |
| Joylynn | Juadalupe | Judith (0.12) | Juleahna | Juliana (0.67) | Julieta (0.03) | Jullian |
| Joy-Mai | Juairiah | Judith Ann | Juleala | Juliana Amparo | Juliete | Julliana (0.01) |
| Joynae | Juajia | Judlen | Julean | Juliana Faith | Julieth (0.01) | Julliane |
| Joyner | Juali | Judlie | Juleanna | Juliana Teresa | Juliet-Marie | Jullianna |
| Joyon | Juamayla | Judly | Julee (0.01) | Julianah | Julietta | Jullianne |
| Joyondra | Juan | Judy (0.06) | Julee Anna | Juliana-Rae | Juliette (0.32) | Julliate |
| Joyous | Juan Shae | Judy Yan Jy | Juleeane | Juliane (0.02) | Juliette Ann | Jullie |
| Joyriana | Juan'sha | Judyann | Juleeann | Julianette | Juliette B | Jullieanna |
| Joysalyn D | Juana (0.06) | Judyeliz | Juleen | Juliania | Juliette | Jullies |
| Joyse | Juana'key | Judy-Kaelle | Juleeza | Julianice | Gabrielle | Julliette |
| Joyus | Juanalisia | Judymar | Juleidi | Julianis | Juliette-Marie | Jullisa |
| Joyvera | Juanda | Judy-Megane | Juleigh | Julianit | Julieve | Jullissa |
| Joz'lynne | Juaneisha | Judyth | Juleil | Juliann (0.02) | Juliexza | Jullissia |
| Jozalyn | Juaneyliz | Judyzairy | Juleimy | Julianna (0.62) | Julie-Yan | Julliza |
| Jozalynn | Juanida | Judzia | Juleiny | Julianna Nichol | Julieyanna | Jullya |
| Jozaria | Juanita (0.03) | Juel | Juleisy | Juliannah | Julieza | Jullynna |
| Joze | Juanita | Juelian | Julena | Juli-Anne | Julimar | Jullysa |
| Jozee (0.01) | Ednamae | Juell | Julene | Julianne (0.21) | Julimarie | Julnelle |
| Jozelyn | Juanita Rose | Juellyn | Juleni | Julianne | Julina | Julura |
| Jozelynn | Juanitta | Juelz | Julenyjicel | Annabelle | Juline | July |
| Jozette | Juaniya | Juhae | Juleona | Juliannee | Juliness | Julya |
| Jozey | Juanna | Juhana | Jules (0.01) | Juliannette | Julinnia | Julyana |
| Jozi | Juannys | Juhe | Julesa | Julianni | Juliona | Julyandria |
| Jozie (0.02) | Juanta | Juhi (0.01) | Julessa | Juliannie | Julione | Julyane |
| Jozilyn | Juary | Juhlyiah | Juleuna | Julianny | Julionna | July-Angell |
| Jozlin | Juazlyn | Juhnina- | Juleydi | Juliansy | Juliryss | July-Ann |
| Jozlyn (0.02) | Jubaleigh | Shaunte | Juleyiah | Juliany | Julisa (0.03) | Julyann |
| Jozlyne | Juberney | Juhree | Julez | Julianys | Julisbeth | Julyanne |
| Jozlynn (0.01) | Jubilee (0.02) | Juhstysse | Juli | Juliauna | Julise | Julyannette |
| Jozn | Jubilo | Juhsuan | Juli Ann A | Juliaunna | Julisha | Julye |
| Joznaé | Jubith | Juice | Juli'yah | Julicia | Julisia | Julyette |
| Jozy | Jucel Theresa | Juila | Julia (3.44) | Julie (0.42) | Julisiyah | Julyn |
| Jozzlin | Judaea | Juilana | Julia Anne | Julie Anne | Julissa (0.25) | Julysa |
| Jozzlynn | Judah | Juilanna | Julia Elsianne | Julieana | Julisselle | Julyssa |
| Jr'maria | Judai | Juile | Julia Gia-Kim | Julie-Ann | Julissia | Jumaana |
| Jream | Judaiah | Juileatt | Julia Helene | Julieann (0.01) | Julita | Jumaanah |
| Jreeym | Judarra | Juilyn | Julia Laurence | Julie-Anna | Julitta | Jumai |
| Jrewkayla | Juddy | Juitza | Julia Marie | Julieanna (0.01) | Julitza | Jumana |
| Jreyme | Jude (0.01) | Jukiah | Julia Rose | Julie-Anne | Juliusa | Jumanah |
| Jsheri | Judea | Jukipa | Julia Sophia | (0.01) | Juliveth | Jumanna |
| Jswa | Judeah | Jukya | Julia-Anne | Julieanne (0.01) | Julixa | Jumaria |
| Ju | Jude-Anne | Jukyiah | Juliaedith | Julieannic | Juliya | Jumeira |
| Ju' Nyla | Judelene | Julacia | Juliagene | Julie-Frederique | Juliyah | Jumera |
| Ju'keria | Judenie | Julacy | Juliah | Julien | Juliyana | Jumiyah |
| Ju'layah | Judera | Julana | Juliahn | Juliena | Juliyanna | Jummerbee |
| Ju'lecia | Judeson | Julane | Juliahna | Julienna | Juliza (0.01) | Jumya |
| Ju'lisa | Judeyliz | Julaya | Julia-Lourdes | Julienne | Julizabeth | Jumyasha |

Juna
Junabel
Junalee
June (0.03)
Juneceia
June-Eliza
Juneia
Juneily
Junelily
Junell
Junella
Junelyn
Junelys
Junelyse
Junesha
Junesia
Junetta
Jung
Junia
Junie
Juniper (0.02)
Junisha
Junita
Juniya
Juniyah
Junna
Junnessy
Junnia
Juno
Junsi
Junsida
Junup
Junya
Junyana
Junyia
Junylah
Jupjeet
Jupneet
Jur'ne
Juraesha
Jurashia
Jureidi
Jurely
Juri
Juriah
Jurianna
Juricely
Juridia
Juridiana
Juriel
Juritzi
Juritzy

Jurneé
Jurnée
Jurnee (0.02)
Jurnee Dwan
Jurneey
Jurney
Jurni
Jurnie
Juronica
Jury
Jurzee
Jus'tina
Jusaia
Juscella
Jusciven
Juselys
Jushona
Jusilet
Juslene
Jusline
Jusneet
Jussette
Jussiah
Jussinia
Just
Just'us
Justasia
Justaya
Juste
Justeen
Justena
Justene
Justess
Justia
Justiana
Justica
Justice (0.19)
Justice
  Alexandrea
Justice-Tyreé
Justiene
Justilyn
Justin (0.01)
Justina (0.05)
Justine (0.30)
Justine Zoe
Justine-Lara
Justinia
Justis
Justise
Justiss
Justley

Justus (0.01)
Justyce (0.02)
Justyce Allenia
Justyce-Arqué
Justycelynee
Justyna
Justyne
Justyne Alexia
Juuann
Juuy'aay
Juvania
Juveria
Juveryona
Juvette
Juvia
Juviany
Juvielle
Juvisah
Juvitce
Juwaireyah
Juwairiah
Juwairiyah
Juwairiyyah
Juwan
Juwaria
Juwariyah
Juwell
Juweria
Juweriya
Juyoung
Juzaiah
Juzelle
Juziyah
Juztice
Jvionna
Jwalyanne-
  Guadalupe
Jwan
Jxequnia
Jy'aira
Jy'aire
Jy'ariel
Jy'asia
Jy'brya
Jy'da
Jy'dae
Jy'kashia
Jy'kaya
Jy'keria
Jy'liyah
Jy'naria
Jy'naya

Jy'niha
Jy'nyah
Jy'quanae
Jy'rah
Jy'terrica
Jyah
Jyalyne
Jyana
Jyani
Jyanna
Jyara
Jyaria
Jyaritza
Jyasia
Jychera
Jyhana
Jyhanna
Jyhe'l
Jyhonnie
Jykera
Jykeria
Jykerria
Jykeya
Jykia
Jyla
Jylai
Jyleahla
Jyleemia
Jylese
Jylian
Jylianne
Jylie
Jylisecia
Jyllian
Jyllyan
Jylonne
Jylynn
Jymariah
Jyna
Jynarah
Jynasia
Jynel
Jynelli
Jynesha
Jynesis
Jynessa
Jynia
Jyniah
Jynira
Jynirah
Jynita
Jynneh

Jynngher-Darcy
Jyonna
Jyoti
Jyra
Jyrah
Jyreka
Jyrnee
Jyromy

## ~ K ~

K
K Leigh
K Mari
K Ti
K.C.
K' Lee
K'aliyah
K'anayah
K'anna
K'awna
K'ayonta
K'aysha
K'chelle
K'chiya
K'cia
K'hari
K'imya
K'jada
K'la
K'lailani
K'lani
K'lanna
K'lea
K'leah
K'lean
K'lee
K'lei
K'leigh
K'lene
K'londa
K'lonie
K'lyah
K'lyn
K'lynne
K'mi
K'Mia
K'miyah
K'monte
K'mya
K'myla

K'myra
K'naisa
K'nea
K'niyah
K'noah
K'nya
K'nyiah
K'ondrea
K'oside
K'riah
K'ryn
K'sea
K'ssyah
K'teria
K'tiannie
K'vionna
K'vontranique
K'wastanaya
K'yana
K'yauna
K'yhana
K'yiana
K'yona
K'yuna
K'zaira
Ka
Ká
Ka Lecia
Ka Lijah
Ka Mya
Ka Nece
Ká Nijha
Ka Nya
Ká Nylah
Ka'chyna
Ka'daijah
Ka'daja
Ka'daysha
Ka'daziah
Ka'dedré
Ka'dejah
Ka'derrah
Ka'drea
Ka'hiya
Ka'janea
Ka'jhirah-Ifa
Ka'jona
Ka'laha
Ka'laia
Ka'laijah
Ka'laya
Ka'layh

Ka'layshia
Ka'leah
Ka'leara
Ka'lecia
Ka'leesha
Ka'leigh
Ka'lesha
Ka'leyah
Ka'lia
Ka'lijiah
Ka'lise
Ka'lisha
Ka'lissa
Ka'liya
Ka'liyah
Ka'lliyanna
Ka'lyce
Ka'lyn
Ka'lyna
Ka'maia
Ka'mara
Ka'mare
Ka'mareyah
Ka'mari (0.01)
Ka'maria
Ka'marie
Ka'mariya
Ka'marra
Ka'marrie
Ka'marya
Ka'mauri
Ka'maya
Ka'meriyhia
Ka'mia
Ka'miah
Ka'miaya
Ka'mii
Ka'mill
Ka'mira
Ka'miya
Ka'miyah
Ka'moni
Ka'monie
Ka'mora
Ka'morah
Ka'mouri
Ka'mya (0.01)
Ka'myah
Ka'myia
Ka'myra
Ka'myri
Ka'nahya

| | | | | | | |
|---|---|---|---|---|---|---|
| Ka'naija | Ka'zariya | Kacy (0.03) | Kadida | Kaelah (0.01) | Kafia | Kahlise |
| Ka'najah | Ka'zha | Kacyn | Kadidia | Kaelan (0.01) | Kagan | Kahliya |
| Ka'nariah | Ka'zia | Kacyra | Kadie (0.03) | Kaelana | Kagey | Kahlyn (0.01) |
| Ka'nasia | Ka'ziah | Kada | Kadieann | Kaelani | Kaghan | Kahlynn |
| Ka'naya | Ka'ziyah | Kadacia | Kadieja | Kaelanny | Kagina | Kahlys |
| Ka'nayah | Kaadeigh | Kadaijah | Kadience | Kaelary | Kah'dir | Kahmaje |
| Ka'nayha | Kaajal | Kadaisa | Kadiera | Kaelayla | Kah'leese | Kahmani |
| Ka'nedia | Kaalee | Kadaisaná | Kadija (0.01) | Kaelbi | Kah'liah | Kahmara |
| Ka'neja | Kaaliyah | Kadaisha | Kadijah | Kaeldra | Kah'lisha | Kahmaree |
| Ka'nia | Kaaliyah- | Kadalina | Kadijatu | Kaele | Kah'liyah | Kahmari |
| Ka'niah |   Lionelly | Kadan | Kadin (0.01) | Kaelea | Kah'mya | Kahmaria |
| Ka'nijah | Kaaly | Kadance (0.03) | Kadince (0.01) | Kaeleah | Kah'niah | Kahmawriay |
| Ka'nilia | Kaandis | Kadaria | Kadison | Kaelee (0.01) | Kah'nyia | Kahmaya |
| Ka'niya (0.01) | Kaarina | Kadasia | Kadiya | Kaelei | Kahaira | Kahmia |
| Ka'niyah | Kaasaundra | Kadayja | Kadlyn | Kaeleigh (0.02) | Kahalynn | Kahmiah |
| Ka'niyah (0.01) | Kaashvi | Kadaysha | Kadra | Kaelen | Kahana | Kahmil |
| Ka'nya | Kaatya | Kadaysia | Kadreah | Kaeley (0.01) | Kaharra | Kahmilia |
| Ka'nyah | Kaavya | Kaddence | Kadrena | Kaeli (0.03) | Kahazea | Kahmiya |
| Ka'nyaiha | Kaavyasri | Kaddi | Kadria | Kaeliana | Kahbrea | Kahmiyah |
| Ka'nyelah | Kaaylah | Kaddijatou | Kadriana | Kaelianna | Kahci | Kahmora |
| Ka'nyia | Kabao | Kade | Kadrien | Kaelie (0.01) | Kahdiana | Kahmryn |
| Ka'nyjah | Kabella | Kadebra | Kadrin | Kaeliegh | Kaheem | Kahmunique |
| Ka'nyla | Kabie | Kadee (0.01) | Kady (0.02) | Kaelin (0.06) | Kaheen | Kahmya |
| Ka'nyra | Kabira | Kadeem | Kadyence | Kaelinn | Kahijah | Kahmyah |
| Ka'nysia | Kabita | Kadee-Nicole | Kady-Jo | Kaelle | Kahila | Kahna |
| Ka'praisha | Kabray | Kadeer | Kadyn (0.04) | Kaelob | Kahina | Kahnaiya |
| Ka'rea | Kabre | Kadein | Kadynce (0.01) | Kaeloni | Kahja | Kahniya |
| Ka'reysha | Kabreonna | Kadeja | Kadynn | Kaelonnah | Kahkee | Kahniyah |
| Ka'riah | Kabreya | Kadejha | Kadynse | Kaely (0.01) | Kahla | Kahnyla |
| Ka'rianna | Kabreyia | Kadek | Kadyona | Kaely Jo | Kahla Aasiyah | Kaho |
| Ka'risma | Kabri | Kadelyn | Kae'dynce | Kaelyn (0.25) | Kahlan (0.01) | Kahra |
| Ka'sandra | Kabria | Kadelynn | Kae'la | Kaelyne | Kahlani | Kahrae |
| Ka'sarra | Kabrie | Kaden (0.04) | Kae'osha | Kaelynn (0.04) | Kahlaya | Kahrema |
| Ka'saundra | Kabriela | Kadena | Kaeanna | Kaelynne | Kahlayjah | Kahren |
| Ka'seem | Kabriella | Kadence (0.36) | Kaecie | Kaelynn-Grace | Kahle | Kahria |
| Ka'shante | Kabrienne | Kadens | Kaeda | Kaemani | Kahlea (0.01) | Kahrijah |
| Ka'shari | Kabriyah | Kadenze | Kaedance | Kaena (0.01) | Kahleah | Kahrin |
| Ka'shawna | Kabrya | Kadera | Kaede | Kaenna | Kahlee | Kahrma |
| Ka'shay | Kabryna | Kaderica | Kaedence (0.01) | Kaeris | Kahleemah | Kahryne |
| Ka'shira | Kacee (0.01) | Kaderra | Kaedenze | Kaery | Kahleeya | Kahryssa |
| Ka'shirie | Kacela | Kadesh | Kaedia | Kaesha | Kahlei | Kahsahlia |
| Ka'shiya | Kacelyn | Kadesha | Kaedin | Kaeshla | Kahleia | Kahshay |
| Ka'shyra | Kacey (0.07) | Kadesia | Kaedince | Kaesler | Kahlen (0.02) | Kahshi |
| Ka'siya | Kache | Kadessa | Kaedyn (0.01) | Kaetlin | Kahlene | Kahteirra |
| Ka'tara | Kaché | Kadey (0.01) | Kaedynce | Kaetlyn | Kahler | Kahtrena |
| Ka'terra | Kachina | Kadeyn | Kaegan | Kaetlynn | Kahlesha | Kahtyeri'na |
| Ka'tia | Kaci (0.08) | Kadi | Kaehla | Kaetriana | Kahli | Kahunna |
| Ka'tianna | Kacia | Kadia | Kae-Ilani | Kaetty | Kahlia (0.01) | Kahyla |
| Ka'tiya | Kaciah | Kadiana | Kaejah | Kaety | Kahliah | Kahzeya |
| Ka'tourha | Kaciana | Kadiance | Kael | Kaetyn | Kahliana | Kahziya |
| Ka'yanni | Kacie (0.07) | Kadiann | Kaela (0.05) | Kaevin | Kahlie | Kai (0.05) |
| Ka'yauna | Kacin | Kadiatou (0.01) | Kaela Cristel | Kaevionna | Kahlin | Kai Con |
| Ka'zaria | Kacsy | Kadiatu | Kaela Leanne | Kaeyla | Kahlina | Kai Mira |

| | | | | | | |
|---|---|---|---|---|---|---|
| Kai Suri | Kaihla | Kailian | Kairy | Kaitym | Kalamie | Kaleigha (0.01) |
| Kai_ | Kaihlyn | Kailiana | Kaisa (0.01) | Kaityn | Kalamity | Kaleigh-Alexa |
| Kai'ja | Kaija (0.01) | Kailianne | Kaise | Kai-Tzu | Kalan | Kaleighanne |
| Kai'la | Kaija-Eun | Kailie (0.02) | Kaisei | Kaiulani | Kalana (0.01) | Kaleighn |
| Kai'liyah | Kaijah | Kailiegh | Kaisey | Kaiya (0.12) | Kalancea | Kaleigh-Renea |
| Kai'lyn | Kai-Jai Nichelle | Kailiga | Kaisha (0.01) | Kaiyah (0.01) | Kalandra | Kaleighya |
| Kai'marei | Kaijay | Kailin (0.01) | Kaisira | Kaiyana | Kalani (0.03) | Kaleiha |
| Kai'ya | Kaijé | Kailine | Kaisiya | Kaiyanni | Kalania | Kaleila |
| Kai'yana | Kaijee | Kailinn | Kaisja | Kaiyee | Kalanit | Kaleinah |
| Kai'yera | Kaikilani-Kahali | Kailiyah | Kaislyn | Kaiyia | Kalanite | Kaleiona |
| Kaia (0.14) | Kail | Kaille | Kaislynn | Kaiyin | Kalany | Kaleis |
| Kaia Mackenzi | Kaila (0.15) | Kaillie | Kaissy | Kaiyla | Kalanyia | Kaleisha |
| Kaiah (0.01) | Kaila-Eve | Kaillny | Kaita | Kaiyle | Kalashia | Kaleiyah |
| Kaiaire | Kailah (0.01) | Kailly | Kaitaia | Kaiylie | Kalashya | Kal-El |
| Kaia-Madison | Kailan | Kailoni | Kaite | Kaiyn | Kalasia | Kalema |
| Kaiana | Kailana | Kailonna | Kaitelyn | Kaiyon | Kalawya | Kalen (0.01) |
| Kaiani | Kailane | Kaily (0.02) | Kaitelynn | Kaja | Kalaya (0.01) | Kalena (0.02) |
| Kai-Ann | Kailani (0.02) | Kailyana | Kaiten | Kajai | Kalayah | Kalencia |
| Kaianna | Kailanie | Kailyda | Kaith | Kajal | Kalayanee | Kalene |
| Kaianne | Kailany | Kailye | Kaithleen | Kajanae | Kalayia | Kaleolani |
| Kaiara | Kailayia | Kailyn (0.21) | Kaithlyn | Kajarisha | Kalayla | Kalesa |
| Kaiashia | Kaile | Kailyna | Kaithlynn | Kajatu | Kalayna | Kalescia |
| Kaibre | Kailea | Kailyn-Aliyah | Kaitie | Kajayanna | Kalayshia | Kalese |
| Kaicee | Kaileah | Kailyne | Kaitilyn | Kajha | Kalaysia | Kalesha |
| Kaici | Kailean | Kailynn (0.05) | Kaitlan (0.01) | Kajia | Kaldara | Kaleshia |
| Kaida (0.01) | Kai-Lee | Kailynne | Kaitland | Kajin | Kaldriann | Kalesia |
| Kaidalyn | Kaileé | Kailyr | Kaitlann | Kajiya | Kale (0.01) | Kalestoe |
| Kaidan | Kailee (0.19) | Kailysa | Kaitlaynd | Kajla | Kalea (0.04) | Kaley (0.20) |
| Kaidance (0.01) | Kailee-Anna | Kailyssa | Kaitlee | Kajmiray | Kaleace | Kaley Lynn |
| Kaidashia | Kailee-Jaye | Kaimalino | Kaitleen | Kajsa | Kaleah (0.03) | Kaleya |
| Kaide | Kaileen | Kaimberlyn | Kaitlen | Kajsiab | Kaleaha | Kaleyah |
| Kaiden (0.03) | Kaileena | Kaimea | Kaitlenn | Kakayla | Kalealani | Kaleyonna |
| Kai-Dence | Kaileey | Kaimee | Kaitlin (0.40) | Kakenya | Kaleanna | Kali (0.19) |
| Kaidence (0.04) | Kai-Lei | Kaimi | Kaitlin Diane | Kal'daija | Kaleb | Kalia (0.05) |
| Kaideynce | Kailei (0.01) | Kaimia | Kaitlind | Kala (0.02) | Kalecia | Kaliah (0.03) |
| Kaidin | Kaileigh (0.04) | Kaina (0.01) | Kaitlinn | Kalaalee | Kalee (0.03) | Kali-Alexandra |
| Kaidince | Kaileigha | Kaina-Suzy | Kaitly | Kalacia | Kalee Ana | Kaliana (0.01) |
| Kaidis | Kaileih | Kainath | Kaitlye | Kalae | Kaleea | Kaliandra |
| Kaidlyn | Kailen (0.01) | Kainen | Kaitlyn (3.01) | Kalaeh | Kaleeanne | Kaliann |
| Kaidren | Kailene | Kainey | Kaitlyn A | Kalaesia | Kaleece | Kalianna |
| Kaidrie | Kailey (0.49) | Kainia | Kaitlyn Ann | Kalagee | Ka-Leeia | Kalianne |
| Kaidy | Kailey Erica | Kainijah | Kaitlynd | Kalah | Kaleel | Kaliany |
| Kaidyn (0.02) | Kailey Jo | Kainos | Kaitlyne | Kalahamsa | Kaleela | Kalia-Rose |
| Kaidynce (0.01) | Kailey Robynne | Kaiona | Kaitlynmarie | Kalahni | Kaleelah | Kaliayah |
| Kaidynn | Kailey Tamara | Kaira (0.03) | Kaitlynn (0.21) | Kalaia | Kaleema | Kalice |
| Kaidynz | Kaileya | Kairah | Kaitlynn B | Kalaiah | Kaleen | Kalicia |
| Kaidys | Kaileyahna | Kairee | Kaitlynne (0.01) | Kalaijah | Kaleena (0.01) | Kalidja |
| Kaiel | Kaileyana | Kairi (0.04) | Kaitrin | Kalaila | Kaleese | Kalidria |
| Kaielle | Kaileyann | Kairie | Kaitriona | Kalaina | Kalei (0.03) | Kalie (0.05) |
| Kaige | Kailey-Anne | Kairigan | Kaitryn | Kalaiyah | Kaleia | Kalieana |
| Kaigen | Kailey-Madison | Kairington | Kaitty | Kalajae | Kaleiah | Kalieanne |
| Kaighen | Kai-Li | Kairon | Kaity | Kalajia | Kaleigh (0.26) | Kaliec |
| Kaighley | Kaili (0.03) | Kairra | Kaityln | Kalam | Kaleigh Jayn | Kaliece |

| | | | | | | |
|---|---|---|---|---|---|---|
| Kaliee | Kaliyha | Kaloni Samoya | Kamahni | Kamayá | Kamera | Kamini |
| Kaliegh (0.01) | Kaliyssa | Kalonna | Kamahya | Kamaya (0.02) | Kameran (0.01) | Kamira (0.01) |
| Kalienah | Kalke | Kalonnie | Kamaia | Kamayah | Kameren | Kamirah (0.01) |
| Kaliese | Kalkidan | Kaloria | Kamaila | Kamayia | Kameri | Kamiraha |
| Kaliey | Kalla | Kalou | Kamaiya | Kamayla | Kameria | Kamiran |
| Kalieya | Kallah | Kalsan | Kamaiyah | Kambel | Kameriah | Kamire |
| Kalifah | Kallan | Kalsey | Kamajanee | Kambell | Kamerin | Kamiree |
| Kalifornia | Kallasandra | Kaltoum | Kamakila | Kambelle | Kameron (0.05) | Kamiren |
| Kalijah | Kalle | Kaltrin | Kamala | Kamber | Kamerra | Kamiria |
| Kali-Jo | Kallea | Kaltrina | Kamalani | Kamberly | Kamery | Kamirrah |
| Kalik | Kallee (0.01) | Kaltun | Kamaleimahie | Kamberlynn | Kameryah | Kamiryn |
| Kalika | Kalleeann | Kalvarie | Kamali | Kambili | Kameryn (0.03) | Kamisa |
| Kalil | Kallei | Kalviyana | Kamalia | Kamble | Kamesha | Kamise |
| Kalila | Kalleigh | Kalvunick | Kamalpreet | Kambrea | Kametrece | Kamissa |
| Kalila-Ameerah | Kalle-Marie | Kaly (0.01) | Kamalvir | Kambrean | Kametria | Kamiya (0.03) |
| Kalilah | Kallen | Kalya | Kamalynn | Kambree (0.01) | Kamey | Kamiyah (0.03) |
| Kalima | Kallena | Kalyaanee | Kamand | Kambri | Kameyl | Kamiyan |
| Kalimah | Kalley (0.01) | Kalyah | Kamani | Kambria (0.01) | Kami (0.03) | Kamiyha |
| Kalin (0.02) | Kalli (0.04) | Kalyana | Kamanjit | Kambriah | Kami'cah | Kamiyra |
| Kalina (0.04) | Kallianna | Kalyane | Kamar | Kambrian | Kamia (0.02) | Kamlee |
| Kalinda | Kalli-Anne | Kalyani | Kamara (0.03) | Kambriana | Kamia Molly | Kamleen |
| Kalindi | Kallianne | Kalyanne | Kamarae | Kambrie (0.01) | Kamiah (0.01) | Kamly |
| Kalindie | Kalliauna | Kalyca | Kamarah | Kambriel | Kamiaha | Kamlyn |
| Kaline | Kallie (0.10) | Kalyce | Kamare | Kambry | Kamie | Kammand |
| Kalinn | Kallihan | Kalye | Kamarea | Kambryanna | Kamiele | Kammarah |
| Kaliopi | Kallijo | Kalyesha | Kamaree | Kambryn | Kamielle | Kammen |
| Kaliroy | Kallin | Kalyha | Kamareeah | Kambyl | Kamien | Kammi |
| Kalirrah | Kallina | Kalyhanna | Ka-Mareeia | Kamden (0.01) | Kamiera | Kammie |
| Kalis | Kalliope | Kalyiah | Kamarí | Kamdyn (0.02) | Kamiesha | Kammoni |
| Kalisa | Kalliopi | Kalyjah | Kamari (0.05) | Kamea (0.01) | Kamijah | Kammy |
| Kalise (0.01) | Kallise | Kalyla | Kamariá | Kameah | Kamijha | Kamnysha |
| Kalisha (0.01) | Kallissa | Kalylah | Kamaria (0.04) | Kameal | Kamijsha | Kamoira |
| Kalisia | Kallista (0.01) | Kalyn (0.08) | Kamariah | Kameel | Kamika | Kamona |
| Kalisiya | Kallisti | Kalyna | Kamarian | Kameelah | Kamil | Kamoni |
| Kaliska | Kallisto | Kalyne | Kamariana | Kameerah | Kamila (0.06) | Kamonne |
| Kalispell | Kallita | Kalynn (0.03) | Kamarie | Kameika | Kamilah (0.03) | Kamonni |
| Kalissa (0.01) | Kallitaya | Kalynna | Kamariea | Kameil | Kamile | Kamoora |
| Kalista (0.03) | Kallitsa | Kalynne | Kamariha | Kameila | Kamilee | Kamor |
| Kalisya | Kalliyah | Kalypso | Kamarii | Kameile | Kamilei | Kamora (0.04) |
| Kalita | Kalliyan | Kalyse | Kamarionna | Kameira | Kamileon | Kamorah |
| Kaliunna | Kalliyana | Kalysha | Kamariya | Kameisha | Kamiley | Kamorea |
| Kalix | Kally (0.01) | Kalysia | Kamariyae | Kameka | Kamili | Kamoree |
| Kalixia | Kallye | Kalyssa (0.01) | Kamariyah | Kameko | Kamilia | Kamori |
| Kaliyá | Kallyn | Kalysse | Kamaron | Kamel | Kamiliyah | Kamoria |
| Kaliya (0.01) | Kallynn | Kalysta (0.01) | Kamarra | Kamela | Kamill | Kamoriah |
| Ka-Liyah | Kallysa | Kalyxia | Kamarrah | Kamelen | Kamilla (0.01) | Kamorra |
| Kaliyah (0.09) | Kallysta | Kam | Kamarri | Kamelia | Kamillah | Kamorri |
| Kaliyaha | Kalneisha | Kam'ren | Kamarria | Kamelia Rose | Kamille (0.04) | Kamorry |
| Kaliyan | Kal-Nicia | Kam'ryn | Kamary | Kamelie | Kamillie | Kamoryia |
| Kaliyana | Kalon | Kama | Kamaryana | Kamella | Kamilly | Kamouya |
| Kaliyanah | Kalona | Kamadia | Kamaryn | Kamen | Kamillya | Kampbell |
| Kaliyani | Kalondrea | Kamafo | Kamauria | Kamena | Kamilya | Kampten |
| Kaliyh | Kaloni | Kamahli | Kamaurie | Kameo | Kamilyah | Kamra |

| | | | | | | |
|---|---|---|---|---|---|---|
| Kamran | Kanaisa | Kaneishia | Kanna | Kapri (0.01) | Kareen | Karianna (0.01) |
| Kamree | Kanaisha | Kaneith | Kannady | Kapria | Kareena (0.02) | Karianne |
| Kamrée | Kanaja | Kaneitha | Kannaka | Kaprice (0.01) | Kareenah | Kariauna |
| Kamren (0.01) | Kanajah | Kanek | Kannet | Kapui | Kareese | Kariba |
| Kamrey | Kanak | Kanen | Kannika | Kara (0.46) | Kareiea | Karibbean |
| Kamreyana | Kanala | Kanequa | Kanniyah | Kara Marie | Kareigh | Karice |
| Kamri | Kanan | Kanera | Kannon | Kara'lynn | Karel | Karicesa |
| Kamria | Kananda | Kaneria | Kanoe | Kara-Ann | Kareli | Karid |
| Kamrie (0.01) | Kanani (0.01) | Kanesha | Kanoelani | Karaann | Karelie | Karie |
| Kamrin (0.01) | Kanaria | Kaneshia | Kanon | Kara-Beth | Karelie-Jude | Kariel |
| Kamrinne | Kanarie | Kaness | Kanong | Karadee | Karelis | Karielle |
| Kamron | Kanariona | Kanessa | Kanonn | Karadyn | Karelle | Kariely |
| Kamry (0.01) | Kanasha | Kanethia | Kanosha | Karagan | Karely (0.01) | Karielys |
| Kamrya | Kanashia | Kaneva | Kanoshia | Karagen | Karelyn | Kariemah |
| Kamryn (0.42) | Kanasia | Kaneysha | Kanosyia | Karagyn | Karelyne | Karigan (0.01) |
| Kamryn'nicole | Kanay | Kang | Kanryne | Karah (0.03) | Karem | Karighen |
| Kamryne | Kanaya | Kang Youn | Kansas (0.02) | Karaha | Karen (0.87) | Karijah |
| Kamrynn (0.01) | Kanayah | Kangana | Kantashia | Karahgan | Karen Arely | Karileigh |
| Kamrynne | Kanayia | Kangong | Kantchianna | Karahgen | Karen Dahiana | Kariliz |
| Kamsberly | Kanayjah | Kani | Kanti | Karajean | Karen Guad | Karilou |
| Kamura | Kanchan | Kani Jah | Kanto Fitia | Kara-Joe | Karen Jazmin | Karilyn |
| Kamuria | Kanda | Kani'jah | Kantrice | Karalee | Karena (0.01) | Karilyne |
| Kamvir | Kandace (0.02) | Kani'ya | Kanvas | Kara-Lei | Karena Nicole | Karilynn |
| Kamy | Kandal | Kani'yah | Kanya (0.01) | Karaleigh | Karencia | Karim |
| Kamy'a | Kandalaria | Kania (0.01) | Kanyah | Karalen | Karene | Karima (0.01) |
| Kamya (0.05) | Kandalin | Ka-Niah | Kanyah-Jean | Karalena | Karen-Elaine | Karimah |
| Kamyah (0.01) | Kanddy | Kaniah (0.01) | Kany-Ange | Karalie | Kareni | Karimar |
| Kamyia | Kande | Kaniaja | Kanyawee | Karalin | Karen-Luane | Karimata |
| Kamyiah (0.01) | Kandé | Kaniayh | Kanyia | Karalina | Karenn | Karimé |
| Kamyl | Kande'shus | Kanice | Kanyiah | Karaline (0.01) | Karenna | Karime (0.02) |
| Kamyla | Kandence | Kanie | Kanyjah | Karalinn | Karensa | Karimey |
| Kamylah | Kandi | Kanielle | Kanyl | Karalyn (0.01) | Karentin | Karimi |
| Kamylia | Kandice (0.02) | Kaniesha | Kanyla | Karalyne Joyce | Karenton | Karin (0.01) |
| Kamyll | Kandie | Kaniga | Kanylah | Kara-Lynn | Karessa | Karina (0.37) |
| Kamylle | Kandis | Kanija | Kanyon | Karalynn (0.01) | Karessma | Karina De Fatima |
| Kamyra (0.01) | Kandra | Kanijae | Kanysha | Karamae | Kareti | Karina-Maria |
| Kamyrah | Kandy | Kanijah | Kanyshia | Karamia | Karew | Karina-Marie |
| Kamyralee | Kandyce | Kanika | Kanyzia | Karamias | Karey | Karine (0.01) |
| Kamyran | Kandymarie | Kanila | Kao | Karamjot | Kareyanna | Karington |
| Kamyri | Kandyss | Kanina | Kaohtaw | Karan | Kareyna | Karingtyn |
| Kamyria | Kanea | Kanirrah | Kaolin | Kara-Nicole | Karhina | Karinn |
| Kamyrn | Kaneah | Kanisha | Kaona | Karawan | Kari (0.06) | Karinna (0.01) |
| Kamyron | Kanece | Kanishka | Kaonna | Karay | Kari'ana | Karinne |
| Kamysha | Kanee | Kanissa | Kaonou | Karaya | Kari'yae | Karintha |
| Kamysta | Kaneea | Kanita | Kaori (0.01) | Karcy | Karia | Karionna |
| Kamytra | Kaneeka | Kanivia | Kaosheng | Karcyn | Kariah | Karira |
| Kan Tan Chee | Kaneesha | Kaniya (0.06) | Kaoutar | Kardaiza | Kariaha | Karis (0.11) |
| Kan'asia | Kaneeshah | Kaniyah (0.03) | Kaouthar | Kare | Karian | Karisa (0.01) |
| Kana | Kaneeshia | Kaniyen | Kapesa | Kareah | Kariana (0.01) | Karise |
| Kanae | Kaneia | Kaniyna | Kapona | Kareanna | Kariane | Karisha |
| Kanag | Kaneija | Kaniysha | Kappy | Karee | Karianie | Karishma (0.01) |
| Kanah | Kaneillia | Kaniz | Kaprece | Kareema (0.01) | Kariann | Karishmeh |
| Kanaia | Kaneisha | Kankanit | Kapresha | Kareemah | | |

Karisia
Karisma (0.02)
Karismah
Karismé
Karis-Perpetuel
Kariss
Karissa (0.17)
Karissa Lola
Karissah
Karissa-Lynn
Karissas
Karisse
Karissma
Karista
Karisten
Karitza
Kariya
Kariyah
Karizma (0.01)
Karizmah
Karizmia
Karla (0.67)
Karla Mae
Karla Ruby
Karladalay
Karla-Lorena
Karlana
Karla-Sofia
Karlayijah
Karle
Karlea
Karleah
Karlee (0.17)
Karleea
Karlee-Grace
Karlee-Jo
Karleen
Karleena
Karlei
Karleigh (0.06)
Karleisha
Karlena
Karlene
Karlese
Karletta
Karley (0.12)
Karli (0.13)
Karlia
Karliana
Karliann
Karlice
Karlicia
Karlie (0.15)

Karliegh
Karliene
Karlin
Karlina
Kar-Ling
Karlissa
Karlisse
Karlita
Karliya
Karliyah
Karlize
Karllise
Karlonya
Karlota
Karlotta
Karly (0.11)
Karly-Anne
Karlye (0.01)
Karlyee
Karlyle
Karlyn (0.01)
Karlynn
Karlyta
Karma (0.09)
Karmadee
Karmah
Karman (0.01)
Karmari
Karmel
Karmela
Karmella (0.01)
Karmen (0.05)
Karmesha
Karmia
Karmia Elaina
Karmiah
Karmila
Karmille
Karmin
Karminna
Karmisha
Karmon
Karmoni
Karmonie
Karmya
Karmyla-La'shay
Karmyn (0.01)
Karmyndy
Karmyni
Karmynn

Karna
Karnania
Karnay
Karneisha
Karneithea
Karnellia
Karnesha
Karneysha
Karnvir
Karo
Karol (0.03)
Karol Daisy
Karol Paulina
Karolan
Karolane (0.01)
Karol-Ann
Karolann
Karolanne (0.01)
Karoleena
Karolena
Karolin
Karolina (0.02)
Karoline (0.01)
Karoll
Karolyn (0.01)
Karolyna
Karolyne
Karolynn
Karolynne
Karon
Karra
Karragan
Karrah (0.01)
Karre
Karrera
Karreuna
Karri
Karriah
Karrie
Karrigan
Karrigen
Karrighan
Karrigon
Karrin
Karringten
Karrington (0.01)
Karris
Karrisa
Karrisah
Karrissa
Karrla

Karrsen
Karryé
Karseana
Karsen (0.01)
Karsin
Karson (0.02)
Karstin
Karstyn
Karsyn (0.06)
Karsynn
Karter (0.01)
Kartessa
Karthigaa
Karthika
Karthy
Kartia
Kartika
Karuna
Karunya
Kary
Karya
Karyah
Karyahna
Karyane
Kary-Ann
Karyann
Karyanna-Khala
Karyanne
Karyell
Karyl
Karyla
Karyll
Karylle
Karylynn
Karyme (0.01)
Karyn (0.01)
Karyna (0.01)
Karynne
Karynton
Karys (0.02)
Karysa
Karysma
Karyss
Karyssa (0.01)
Karyzma
Kasa
Kasadie
Kasady
Kasai
Kasalyn
Kasalynn
Kasandera
Kasandra (0.05)

Kasandra L
Kasandria
Kasani
Kasanndra
Kasanny
Kasara
Kasaty
Kasaundra
Kasayna
Kascidy
Kascity
Kase
Kaseana
Kasedey
Kasedi
Kasee
Kaseena
Kasella
Kaselyn
Kaselynn
Kasen
Kasenya
Kaser
Kasey (0.17)
Kasey-Anne
Kash
Kasha (0.01)
Kashadriauna
Kashaedria
Kashai
Kashala
Kashana
Kashanna
Nikema
Kashanti
Kashara
Kashauna
Kashawnra
Kashay
Kashaya
Kashchelle
Kashé
Kashelah
Kashema
Kashf
Kashfi
Kashi
Kashia (0.01)
Kashifa
Kashika
Kashira
Kashish
Kashius

Kashiya
Kashlen
Kashlin
Kashmeera
Kashmeere
Kashmer
Kashmere
Kashmir
Kashmira
Kashmire
Kashong
Kashshay
Kashvi
Kashya
Kashydeua
Kashyla
Kasi (0.01)
Kasia (0.02)
Kasiae
Kasiah (0.01)
Kasianna
Kasidee
Kasidi
Kasidie
Kasidy (0.01)
Kasie (0.01)
Kasiegha
Kasima
Kasin
Kasithy
Kasiti
Kasity
Kasiurys
Kasiya
Kasiyah
Kasleen
Kaslin
Kaslyn
Kasman
Kasmira
Kasmyne
Kason
Kasondra
Kassadee
Kassadey
Kassadi
Kassadie
Kassady
Kassandra (0.21)
Kassandra-Marie

Kassandre-Alys
Kassarina
Kassarra
Kassaundra
Kassedy
Kassey
Kassi (0.01)
Kassia (0.01)
Kassia Jade
Kassiah
Kassiana
Kassiane
Kassiddy
Kasside
Kassidee
Kassidey
Kassidi (0.01)
Kassidie
Kassidy (0.26)
Kassie (0.04)
Kassiedy
Kassiera
Kassilyn
Kassinda
Kassionna
Kassiopee
Kassira
Kassiti
Kassity
Kassiyah
Kassondra
Kassy (0.01)
Kassya
Kassydi
Kastazia
Kastena
Kastin
Kasturi
Kastyn
Kasumi
Kasuni
Kasy
Kasyanne
Kasye
Kasyn
Kat
Kata
Katahana
Kataia
Kataleana
Katalena
Katalia
Katalin (0.01)

Katalina (0.03)
Katalina Alexandra
Katalina-Krystal
Kataliya
Katalyna
Katana (0.01)
Katance
Katanna
Katara
Katara-Skye
Katarene
Katarin
Katarina (0.09)
Katarina-Isabel
Katarinia
Katarra
Kataryn Anahlysse
Kataryna
Katarzyna
Katasia
Kataveya
Katawna
Katawna-Sue
Kataya
Katayah
Katayoun
Kate (1.13)
Kate Alycia
Kate Chloe
Kate Lynn
Kate Shawina Ashley
Katearia
Katee
Kate-Edouardine
Kateena
Kateia
Katektb
Katelaine
Katelan
Kateland
Katelee
Kateleen
Katelen
Katelend
Kateley
Katelian
Katelien
Katelijne
Katelin (0.09)

Katelina
Kateline
Kate-Linn
Katelinn
Katellyn
Katelon
Kately
Kate-Lyn
Katelyn (2.31)
Katelyn Ann
Katelyn Rose
Katelynd
Katelyne (0.01)
Katelyn-Mary
Kate-Lynn (0.01)
Katelynn (0.43)
Katelynn-Ann
Katelynne (0.02)
Katelynn-Grace
Katen
Katence
Katera
Kateri (0.02)
Kateri Rose
Kateria
Kateriana
Katerin (0.01)
Katerina (0.08)
Katerina-Maria
Katerine (0.01)
Katerini
Katerinne
Katerra
Katerria
Katerris
Kateryn
Kateryna
Kateryne
Katey (0.01)
Kateyanne
Kathalean
Kathaleen
Kathaleeya
Kathalena
Kathaleya
Kathalina
Kathalina Andrea
Kathan
Kathareeya
Katharin

Katharine (0.10)
Katharine Dianne
Katharyn (0.01)
Kathe
Katheen
Katheleen
Katheline
Kathellyn
Kathely
Kathelyn
Kathelynn
Kathereen
Katherene
Katheri Andrea
Katherin (0.02)
Katherina (0.01)
Kàtherine
Katherine (3.00)
Katherine Ann
Katherine Rebecca
Katherine Tatiana
Katherinee
Katherine-Olivia
Katherine-Patricia
Katherine-Rose
Katherinne
Kathern
Katheryn (0.04)
Katheryn Ann
Katheryna
Katheryne (0.01)
Katherynne
Kathi
Kathia (0.01)
Kathia Selena
Kathiana
Kathianna
Kathie (0.01)
Kathileeya
Kathilyn
Kathiria
Kathlanna
Kathlean
Kathlee
Kathleen (0.35)
Kathleen Huyen

Kathleen Marlene
Kathleen-Scarlet
Kathlene
Kathleyn
Kathlin
Kathlyn (0.01)
Kathlyne
Kathlynn
Kathreeya
Kathren
Kathrene
Kathrène
Kathrima-Jane
Kathrin
Kathrina
Kathrine (0.03)
Kathryen
Kathryn (1.02)
Kathryn Rose
Kathryna
Kathryne (0.01)
Kathryn-Isobel
Kathrynn
Kathrynne
Kathy (0.10)
Kathy Gisele
Kathya (0.01)
Kathyana
Kathy-Anne
Kathyra
Kathyria
Kathyrn
Kathysha
Kati (0.01)
Katia (0.05)
Katiah
Katiana (0.01)
Katiane
Katiann
Katianna
Katianne
Katie (1.55)
Katie Ann
Katie Jo
Katiea
Katieann
Katieanne
Katieauna
Katiebelle
Katiegrace
Katie-Jane

Katie-Jo
Katie-John
Katielyn
Katie-Lynn
Katielynn
Katiemae
Katiemarie
Katiera
Katie-Rose
Katierose
Kati-Lee
Katilin
Katiliya
Katilyn (0.02)
Katilynn (0.01)
Katina (0.01)
Katio
Katirah
Katiree
Katis
Katiushka
Katiuska
Katiya
Katiyanna
Katiyyah
Katja (0.01)
Katjana
Katjanna
Katlee
Katleen
Katleigh
Katlen
Katlin (0.03)
Katly
Katlyn (0.17)
Katlyne (0.01)
Katlynn (0.05)
Katlynne
Katona
Katonah
Katonya
Katora
Katorah
Katori
Katoria
Katorriah
Katrazina
Katreen
Katreena
Katrell
Katrelle
Katrena
Katria

Katrian
Katriana
Katriane
Katrianna
Katrice
Katricia
Katriel (0.01)
Katrielle
Katriena
Katrin (0.01)
Katrina (0.57)
Katrina Ann
Katrina Marie
Katrina-Rose
Katrine (0.01)
Katrine-Emily
Katrinelle
Katrinette
Katrinha
Katrinia
Katrisha
Katriya
Katrizia
Katryana
Katryina
Katryn
Katryna (0.02)
Katryna-Rose
Katryne
Katsuak
Katsya
Kattalena
Kattalin
Kattey-Kay
Katti
Kattie (0.01)
Kattiria
Kattlin
Kattorria
Katty
Katum
Katura
Katurah
Katuria
Katuriaunyia
Katy (0.06)
Katya (0.02)
Katyah
Katyana
Katyann
Katyanna
Katyayani
Katyce

Katye
Katyin
Katylynn
Katynce
Katyrina
Katyska
Kauai
Kaucia
Kauhnilaiyah
Kauilani
Kauiya
Kaulini
Kaulyn
Kaunah
Kaur
Kauraly
Kauriell
Kausha
Kaushiki
Kausie
Kauthar
Kauther
Kava
Kavana
Kavarea
Kavaria
Kavaughni
Kaveah
Kaveiona
Kaveona
Kavera
Kaveri
Kavina
Kavindi
Kavineeta
Kavinmiga
Kavinya
Kavionia
Kavisha
Kaviya
Kavla
Kavleen
Kavneet
Kavonna
Kavya (0.01)
Kavyadharshini
Kavyasri
Kavyona
Kawai
Kawaia
Kawaii
Kawani
Kawanzus

| | | | | | | |
|---|---|---|---|---|---|---|
| Kawena | Kaycee (0.06) | Kayelah | Kayla-Lea | Kayleen (0.06) | Kaylin (0.26) | Kayonia |
| Kawia | Kaycen | Kayelee (0.01) | Kayla-Lynn | Kayleena | Kaylin Elize | Kayonica |
| Kawsar | Kaycey | Kayeleen | Kayla-Mae | Kaylee-Rae | Kaylina | Kayonna (0.01) |
| Kawtar (0.01) | Kayci | Kayeleigh | Kayla-Marie | Kayleh | Kaylincz | Kayonza |
| Kawthar | Kayciann | Kayelene | Kaylamel | Kaylei (0.04) | Kaylind | Kayori |
| Kawther | Kaycie (0.02) | Kayelin | Kaylan (0.04) | Kayleiana | Kaylinda | Kayra (0.01) |
| Kaxine | Kayd | Kayell | Kaylana (0.01) | Kayleice | Kayline | Kayrah |
| Kaxiyah | Kayda (0.01) | Kayeln | Kayland | Kay-Leigh | Kaylinn | Kayrie |
| Kaxoriyah | Kaydalee | Kayelyn | Kaylandra | Kayleigh (0.48) | Kaylinna | Kayrissa |
| Kay (0.02) | Kaydan | Kaye-Lynn | Kaylani (0.02) | Kayleigh-Ann | Kaylis | Kayriya |
| Kay Ana | Kaydance (0.04) | Kayelynn | Kaylanie | Kayleighanna | Kaylisa | Kaysa |
| Kay Emma | Kaydann | Kayelynne | Kaylann | Kayleignonia | Kaylisha | Kaysah |
| Kay Lynn | Kaydanze | Kayemyn | Kaylanne | Kaylein | Kaylissa | Kaysandra |
| Kay Shaunna | Kayde | Kayen | Kaylanni | Kayleina | Kaylissie | Kayse |
| Kay'anah | Kaydee (0.02) | Kayenat | Kaylany | Kayleis | Kaylla | Kaysea |
| Kay'anna | Kaydee-Ann | Kayenna | Kayla-Rayne | Kaylen (0.09) | Kaylle | Kaysee |
| Kay'anna-Vashé | Kaydelynn | Kayenta | Kayla-Sherise | Kaylena (0.01) | Kayllly | Kaysen |
| Kay'la | Kayden (0.17) | Kayera | Kayla-Tamar | Kaylene (0.02) | Kayln (0.01) | Kaysey |
| Kay'lah | Kaydenc | Kayesha | Kaylayla | Kaylenid | Kaylnn | Kaysha (0.01) |
| Kay'lauria Tei'shailia | Kaydence (0.33) | Kayetlin | Kayle (0.05) | Kayleona | Kaylon | Kayshaly |
| Kay'lee | Kaydence Jaylin | Kayfli | Kaylea (0.05) | Kayler | Kaylona | Kayshawna |
| Kay'len | Kaydence Lee | Kaygan | Kayleah (0.01) | Kaylesha | Kaylond | Kayshela |
| Kay'lonni | Kaydence-Elisia | Kaygen | Kayleaha | Kayleta | Kayloni | Kaysheri |
| Kay'onna | Kaydene | Kayhlen | Kayleaire | Kaylex | Kaylonia | Kayshi'ana |
| Kay'tia | Kaydens | Kayia | Kaylean | Kayley (0.17) | Kaylonie | Kayshia |
| Kay'veonna | Kaydense | Kayiah | Kayleana | Kayleyona | Kaylonna | Kayshla |
| Kay'viona | Kaydenze | Kayianna Marie | Kayleanah | Kaylfen | Kaylonnie | Kayshlee |
| Kaya (0.15) | Kaydes | Kayilah | Kayleann | Kaylha | Kaylor | Kaysi |
| Kaya Ann | Kaydey | Kayin | Kayleanna | Kayli (0.11) | Kayly (0.01) | Kaysia |
| Kaya Shea | Kaydi (0.01) | Kayinda | Kayleanna-Louise | Kayli Alysee | Kaylyany | Kaysiara |
| Kayah (0.01) | Kaydiance | Kayingga | Kayleanne | Kayli Ann | Kaylyn (0.15) | Kaysie (0.01) |
| Kayajah | Kaydie | Kayiona | Kayleauna | Kaylia (0.01) | Kaylyne | Kaysin |
| Kayan | Kaydience | Kayisha | Kayleb | Kayliah | Kaylynn (0.15) | Kaysle |
| Kayana (0.01) | Kaydin (0.01) | Kayjah | Kay-Lee | Kayliam | Kaylynne (0.01) | Kaysley |
| Kayandra | Kaydince | Kay-Jah Lyn | Kaylee | Kaylian | Kaylynnzah | Kayson |
| Kayandria | Kaydis | Kayjayne | Kayleé | Kayliana (0.01) | Kaylyse | Kayssa |
| Kayani | Kaydn | Kayjulena | Kaylee (2.78) | Kayliane | Kaymaen | Kaysyn |
| Kayanie | Kaydnce | Kayjunette | Kaylee Abigail | Kayliani | Kayman | Kayte |
| Kayanna (0.01) | Kaydon | Kay-Kay | Kaylee Jade | Kayliann | Kaymariah | Kayteanna |
| Kayannah | Kaydra | Kayl | Kaylee May | Kaylianna | Kayme | Kaytee |
| Kayara | Kaydree | Kaylá | Kaylee-Ann | Kaylianne | Kaymen | Kaytelin |
| Kayari | Kaydrianna | Kayla (3.92) | Kayleeann | Kaylice | Kaymie | Kaytelyn |
| Kayaunna | Kaydyn | Kayla Marie | Kaylee-Faith | Kaylie (0.38) | Kaymin | Kaytelynn |
| Kaybre | Kaydynce (0.01) | Kayla Mira | Kayleeh | Kaylie Shawna | Kaymon | Kaythleen |
| Kaybreana | Kaydys | Kayla Rose | Kaylee-Hanna | Kaylieah | Kayna | Kayti |
| Kaybree | Kaye | Kaylaa | Kaylee-Jade | Kaylieana | Kaynat | Kaytie |
| Kaybri | Kayedance | Kaylaah | Kaylee-Jo | Kayliegh (0.01) | Kayneia | Kaytin |
| Kaybrie | Kayeden | Kayla-Angela | Kaylee-Joe | Kaylie-Jade | Kaynorra | Kaytin-Alexis |
| Kaybrielle | Kayedon | Kayla-Ann | Kayleela | Kaylie-Jo | Kayo | Kaytlan |
| Kayce (0.02) | Kayedyn | Kaylae | Kaylee-Lynn | Kaylie-Sirvart | Kayode | Kaytlann |
| Kay-Cee | Kayejah | Kaylah (0.11) | Kaylee-Mae | Kayligh | Kayomi | Kaytleen |
| Kayceé | Kayela | Kaylahn | Kaylee-Marie | Kaylihanna | Kayon | Kaytlen |
| | | Kayla-Joel | | Kaylijo | Kayona (0.01) | Kaytlie |

| | | | | | | |
|---|---|---|---|---|---|---|
| Kaytlin (0.04) | K-Dence | Ke'india | Ke'shyra | Kealani | Keasana | Keelah |
| Kaytlinn | Kdence | Ke'jhane | Ke'vaja | Kealee | Keaseana | Keelahn |
| Kaytlyn (0.03) | Kdynee | Ke'la | Ke'vaughn | Kealeigh | Keasha | Keelan |
| Kayt-Lynn | Ke Ajah | Ke'lasha | Ke'via | Kealey | Keasia (0.01) | Keele |
| Kaytlynn (0.02) | Ke Arra | Ke'laysia | Ke'vionna | Keali | Keasjah | Keeleah |
| Kaytlynne | Ke Asia | Ke'lia | Ke'viyona | Kealie | Keating | Keelee |
| Kayton | Ké Daijah | Ke'liyah | Ke'vonda | Kealoha | Keatley | Kee-Leigh |
| Kaytona | Ke Shai | Ke'maiya | Ke'vonne | Kealsy | Keaton (0.01) | Keeleigh |
| Kaytra | Ke Shuang | Ke'mani | Ke'yana | Kealy | Keauhoukaua | Keeleiy |
| Kaytria | Ke'adra | Ke'marah | Ke'yani | Kealya | Keauna | Keele-Jade |
| Kaytriel | Ke'aerria | Ke'mari | Ke'yanna | Kealyn | Keaunah | Keeler |
| Kayura | Ke'ahja | Ke'maria | Ke'yari | Keamber | Keaundra | Keeley (0.07) |
| Kayveonna | Ke'aija | Ke'mariah | Ke'yla | Keana (0.02) | Keaundrea | Keeli (0.01) |
| Kayviah | Ke'aijah | Ke'mauria | Ke'yona | Keanah | Keaune | Keelia |
| Kayvian | Ke'aira (0.01) | Ke'maya | Ke'yone | Keanda | Keaunna | Keeliana |
| Kayvianna | Ke'airra | Ke'mayria | Ke'yonna | Keandra (0.01) | Keaunsha | Keelie (0.01) |
| Kayvoni | Ke'aisha | Ke'miah | Ke'yonnah | Keandrea | Keaunya | Keelin (0.02) |
| Kaywon | Ke'aja | Ke'miaya | Ke'yontis | Keandreia | Keava | Keely (0.11) |
| Kayzeannah | Ke'aja Shawnae | Ke'miece | Ke'yosha | Keandria | Keavondra | Keelya |
| Kayzjah | Ke'ajah | Ke'mijiah | Ke'zaia | Keangel | Keaya | Keelyanne |
| Kayzlin | Ke'ajohne | Ke'miya | Ke'zandria | Keani | Keayala | Keelye |
| Kaz'ara | Ke'alah | Ke'monie | Ke'zaria | Keanilyzl | Keaylah | Keelyn (0.01) |
| Kazandra | Ke'amanti | Ke'mora | Ke'ziance | Keanna (0.04) | Keayona | Keelynn |
| Kazanea | Ke'amber | Ke'morah | Ke'ziyah | Keannah | Keayra | Keemara |
| Kazara | Ke'ana | Ke'mya | Kea | Keanna-Jean | Keayrah | Keemari |
| Kazari | Ke'andrea | Ke'myria | Keaarah | Keanna-Mae | Keazha | Keemie |
| Kazaria | Ke'anish | Ke'myrianna | Keadence | Keannice | Keazia | Keemorah |
| Kazarieyah | Ke'anna | Ke'naja | Keadria | Keante | Kebraea | Keemyah |
| Kazayah | Ke'anté | Ke'nayah | Keadryn | Keanu | Kebryana | Keena (0.01) |
| Kazden | Ke'arah | Ke'nia | Keadyn | Keanua | Keceirra | Keenan |
| Kazel | Ke'ari | Ke'niah | Keaera | Keaolani | Kecharrea | Kee-Nila |
| Kazeryn | Ke'aria | Ke'niya | Keagan (0.02) | Keaona | Kechette | Keenyah |
| Kazh Maraya | Ke'arie | Ke'niyah (0.01) | Keagen | Keara (0.07) | Kecialle | Keenyari |
| Kazhia | Ke'arra | Ke'nya | Keaghan | Kearah (0.01) | Keddy | Keeper |
| Kazi | Ke'arrah | Ke'nyhla | Keagonna | Kearany | Kedeja | Keera (0.01) |
| Kazia | Ke'arshae | Ke'nyia | Keagyn | Keari | Kedelin | Keerah |
| Kaziah | Ke'arya | Ke'nyjah | Keah | Kearia | Kedenia | Keerat |
| Kazimiera | Ke'ashaunti | Ke'ojah | Keahanne | Keariana | Kedest | Keerin |
| Kazire | Ke'ashia | Ke'ondra | Keahna | Kearice | Kedhija | Keerstan |
| Kaziya | Ke'asia (0.02) | Ke'ontae | Keahrie | Kearin | Kee'ayla | Keersten |
| Kaziyah | Ke'asya | Ke'osha | Keairá | Kearney | Keeana | Keerstin |
| Kazlan | Ke'auja | Ke'perra | Keaira (0.02) | Kearowline | Keeanna | Keerstyn |
| Kazone | Ke'aujah | Ke'saunnie | Keairah | Kearra (0.01) | Keeara | Keertana |
| Kazonnie | Ke'aujonea | Ke'seantee | Keairra | Kearsey | Keearah | Keerthana |
| Kazumi | Ke'auree | Ke'shae | Keaisa | Kearsly | Keeara-Lynn | Keerthanyaa |
| Kazuri | Ke'avia | Ke'shantia | Keaisha | Kearsta | Keeasia | Keerthi |
| Kazya | Ke'ayla | Ke'shara | Keaja | Kearstan | Keedra | Keerthi Yazhini |
| Kazziah | Ke'azia | Ke'shaunna | Keajá | Kearsten (0.01) | Keefer | Keerti |
| Kazzian | Ke'daijah | Ke'shaunté | Keajah | Kearstin (0.02) | Keegan (0.03) | Keesha |
| Kazzie | Ke'dasia | Ke'shawna | Keajanae | Kearston (0.01) | Keegann | Keesha'lynn |
| KC | Ke'era | Ke'sheanna | Keala (0.01) | Kearstyn (0.01) | Keeghan | Keeshia |
| Kclaila | Ke'etta | Ke'shundra | Kealana | Kearsyn | Keeiry | Keeta |
| Kdance | Ke'ila | Ke'shya | Kealanei | Kearyand | Keela | Keetin |

| | | | | | | |
|---|---|---|---|---|---|---|
| Keetyn | Keiaira | Keilee | Keionya | Keitra | Keldri | Kella |
| Keeva | Keiairah Hope | Keileen | Keiora | Keityn | Keldriuna | Kellah |
| Keevah | Keiaisha | Keilei | Keirá | Keiunna | Kele | Kellan |
| Keevia | Keiaja | Keileigh | Keira (1.09) | Keiva | Kelea | Kellanie |
| Keevonna | Keiajah | Keiley (0.01) | Keirah (0.01) | Keivea | Kelechi | Kell-Ann |
| Keeya | Keialah | Keili | Keiraia | Keivianna | Kelecia | Kellcie |
| Keeyah | Keiana (0.02) | Keilian | Keira-Leigh | Keivionya | Keleeanna | Kelleah |
| Keeyana | Keiandra | Keiliani | Keira-Lynn | Keivona | Kelei | Kellee |
| Keeyanah | Keiani | Keiliauna | Keiran (0.01) | Keivonnia | Keleiah | Kelleena |
| Keeyla | Keianna (0.01) | Keilidh | Keirdin | Keiya | Keleicia | Kelleigh |
| Keeyona | Keiantea | Keilie | Keiren | Keiyah | Keleigh (0.01) | Kellen |
| Keezaidra | Keiara (0.02) | Keilin | Keiri | Keiyala | Keleila | Kellena |
| Kegen | Keiarah | Keilisa | Keiriana | Keiyana | Keleis | Keller |
| Keghan | Keiari | Keilla | Keirka | Keiyanai | Kelela | Kelley (0.03) |
| Keglovic | Keiaria | Keiller | Keirra (0.01) | Keiyani | Kelena | Kelley Anne |
| Kegri | Keiarra (0.01) | Keilley | Keirria | Keiyanna | Kelendria | Kelleyah |
| Kegyn | Keiasha | Keilly (0.01) | Keirsdyn | Keiyera | Kelerra | Kelley-Ann |
| Keh'mani | Keiasia | Keiloni | Keirsen | Keiylei | Kelesa | Kelli (0.06) |
| Kehana | Keiauna | Keilotta | Keirstan | Keiymari | Keley | Kelli'ona |
| Kehaulani | Keibreonna | Keily (0.03) | Keirsteen | Keiyona | Keli | Kellia |
| Kehinde | Keidi | Keilyn (0.01) | Keirstein | Keiyonna | Kelia (0.01) | Kelliah |
| Kehley | Keidin | Keilynn | Keirsten (0.03) | Kejien | Keliah | Kelliane |
| Kehlie | Keidra | Keilys | Keirstin (0.01) | Kejmarie | Keliana | Kellie (0.06) |
| Kehlin | Keidris | Keima | Keirstine | Ke-Jun | Keliane (0.01) | Kellie-Anne |
| Kehmari | Keiera | Keimara | Keirston | Kekoa | Keliani | Kelliena |
| Kehona | Keigan | Keimare | Keirstyn (0.01) | Kel'c | Kelianne | Kelli-Jo |
| Kei | Keigh-Leanne | Keimaya | Keirstynn | Kela | Kelicia | Kellijo |
| Kei Lay Shia | Keighley | Keimelys | Keiry (0.01) | Kelaiah | Kelie | Kellimarie |
| Kei'aijah | Keighly | Keimesha | Keiryn | Kelainy | Keliegh | Kellin |
| Kei'ajah | Keighlynn | Keimiah | Keiseana | Kelaisha | Kelies | Kellina |
| Kei'ana | Keightlyn | Keimiyja | Keisha (0.05) | Kelan | Kelijah | Kelli-Raé |
| Kei'ara | Keightlynn | Keimya | Keishai | Kelana | Kelila | Kellis |
| Kei'archa | Keih'ara | Keimyan | Keishaly | Kelandria | Kelilah | Kellisa |
| Kei'arrah | Keihana | Keimyn | Keishanna | Kelaney | Kelile-Sarai | Kellise |
| Kei'asia | Keiiwana | Keimyra | Keisharia | Kelani | Kelin | Kellita |
| Kei'asja | Keijauna- | Keina | Keishauna | Kelanie | Kelina | Kellly |
| Kei'auni |   Treasure-Lea | Keinauia | Keishia | Kelany | Kelis (0.04) | Kellsee |
| Kei'azha | Keiko | Keinia | Keishla | Kelarrah | Kelisa | Kellsey |
| Kei'era | Keila (0.05) | Keinija | Keishley | Kelasya | Kelise (0.01) | Kellsi |
| Kei'lah-Al | Keila Marie | Keinina | Keishly | Kelaya | Kelisha | Kellsie (0.01) |
| Kei'mani | Keila Sakura | Kei-Niya | Keishlyan | Kelayce | Kelisiti | Kellsy |
| Kei'marri | Keilah (0.01) | Keiniyah | Keishona | Kelayla | Kelisiyah | Kelly (0.75) |
| Kei'miyah | Keilan | Keinly | Keishsean | Kelbi | Keliss | Kelly Ann (0.01) |
| Kei'moni | Keilana (0.01) | Keinya | Keishunna | Kelbie | Kelissa | Kellya |
| Kei'nhiya | Keilaney | Keinyia | Keishya | Kelbree | Kelisse | Kelly-Alice |
| Kei'nyjha | Keilani (0.02) | Keiojha | Keisi | Kelby (0.01) | Kelitia | Kellyan |
| Kei'tasha | Keilani Lanette | Keiona | Keissy | Kelcea | Keliva | Kellyane (0.01) |
| Kei'yajah | Keilanie | Keiondra | Keisy | Kelcee (0.01) | Keliyah | Kelly-Ange |
| Kei'yonna | Keilanna | Keioni | Keita | Kelcey (0.01) | Keliyonna | Kelly-Ann (0.07) |
| Keia | Keilany | Keionia | Keitasia | Kelci (0.01) | Kelizah | Kellyann (0.02) |
| Keiaela | Keilary | Keionna (0.01) | Keith | Kelcie (0.02) | Kelize | Kellyanna |
| Keiah | Keilayah | Keionne | Keithy | Kelcy (0.01) | Kelizha | Kelly-Anne |
| Keiahrra | Keilea | Keionni | Keiton | Kelden | Kell |   (0.03) |

| | | | | | | |
|---|---|---|---|---|---|---|
| Kellyanne *(0.01)* | Kelvina | Kemmani | Kenayah | Kendranique | Keniston | Kenneddey |
| Kellyce | Kelvinnia | Kemmari | Kenaylah | Kendrann | Kenithia | Kennedee |
| Kellydara | Kely | Kemonaye | Kenayria | Kendre | Kenitra | Kennedei |
| Kellye | Kelya | Kemoni | Kenaysha | Kendrea *(0.01)* | Keniya *(0.01)* | Kennedey |
| Kellyece | Kelyane *(0.01)* | Kemonie | Kenayshia | Kendreana | Keniyah *(0.02)* | Kennedi *(0.14)* |
| Kellykim | Kelyann | Kemora *(0.01)* | Kenaysia | Kendrece | Keniyia | Kennedie *(0.01)* |
| Kellylynn | Kelyha | Kemorah | Kenda *(0.01)* | Kendreia | Keniyya | Kennedra |
| Kellyn *(0.01)* | Kelyla | Kemoria | Kendace | Kendreiah | Kenja | Kennedy *(1.56)* |
| Kellynn | Kelylah | Kemorra | Kendahl *(0.01)* | Kendreka | Kenjali | Kennedy Ta |
| Kelly-Rae | Kelyn | Kemosia | Kendaija | Kendri | Kenjameka | Kenneila |
| Kellyrose | Kelynn | Kemota | Kendaisha | Kendria | Kimari | Kenneriea |
| Kellyshia | Kelyse | Kemoura | Kendajah | Kendrick | Kenji | Kennerly |
| Kellyyn | Kelysha | Kemper | Kendajia | Kendrionna | Kenjra | Kennesea |
| Kelmary | Kelyssa | Kempley | Kendak | Kendrix | Kenkara | Kennesey |
| Kelona | Kelzea | Kemya | Kendal *(0.16)* | Kendy | Kenlea | Kennesha |
| Kelowna | Kem'ori | Kemyah | Kendalin | Kendyl *(0.08)* | Kenlee *(0.01)* | Kenney |
| Kelress | Kema | Kemyja | Kendall *(1.13)* | Kendyle | Kenlei | Kennia *(0.01)* |
| Kelsa | Kemah | Kemyjah | Kendall Anne | Kendyll *(0.02)* | Kenleigh *(0.01)* | Kenniah |
| Kelsay | Kemahni | Kemyni | Kendall Lisa | Kendylle | Kenlessia | Kennice |
| Kelse | Kemaia | Kemyra | Kendall-An | Kendyn | Kenley *(0.03)* | Kennidee |
| Kelsea *(0.04)* | Kemala | Kemyriah | Kendall-Claire | Keneah | Kenli | Kennidi |
| Kelseay | Kemaley | Ken'asha | Kendalle | Kenecia | Kenlie | Kennidie |
| Kelsee *(0.01)* | Kemalie | Ken'asia | Kendalleah | Kenedee | Kenlin | Kennidra |
| Kelsei | Kemani *(0.01)* | Ken'daja | Kendall-Elise | Kenedi *(0.01)* | Kenlly | Kennidy |
| Kelseigh | Kemar'ra | Ken'dreya | Kendallyn | Kenedie | Kenly *(0.01)* | Kennie |
| Kelsen | Kemara | Ken'esha | Kendallynn | Kenedy *(0.01)* | Kenlyn | Kennis |
| Kelsey *(0.81)* | Kemari | Ken'iayh | Kendal-Nichole | Keneese | Kenlynn | Kennise |
| Kelshey | Kemaria | Ken'janiya | Kendalyn *(0.01)* | Keneesia | Kenmaria | Kennisha |
| Kelsi *(0.06)* | Kemarie | Ken'naria | Kendalynn | Keneicia | Kenmiah | Kennisson |
| Kelsi-Ann | Kemariya | Ken'nyia | Kendaria | Keneigha | Kenna *(0.09)* | Kenniya |
| Kelsie *(0.15)* | Kemarria | Ken'yannia | Kendasia | Keneisha | Kennadee | Kenniyah |
| Kelsieanne | Kemauria | Ken'yona | Kendea | Kenese | *(0.01)* | Kennlee |
| Kelsiee | Kemaya *(0.01)* | Ken'yorrie | Kendejah | Kenesha | Kennadi *(0.02)* | Kennley |
| Kelsilyn | Kemayla | Kena | Kendel *(0.01)* | Kenessa | Kennadie | Kennli |
| Kelslynn | Kember | Kenadae | Kendele | Kenetra | Kennady *(0.02)* | Kennon |
| Kelson | Kemberly *(0.01)* | Kenade | Kendell *(0.02)* | Kengeornay | Kennae | Kennoni |
| Kelspeth | Kemberlyn | Kenadea | Kendelle | Kenhiyah | Kennaé | Kennsie |
| Kelsy *(0.02)* | Kembrial | Kenadee *(0.02)* | Kendellin | Keni | Kennah | Kennunique |
| Kelsy Jared | Kemely | Kenadi *(0.01)* | Kendelyn | Kenia *(0.04)* | Kennahdi | Kenny |
| Kelsye | Kementari | Kenadie *(0.02)* | Kendelyne | Keniah | Kennaija | Kennya |
| Kelsyn | Kemerly | Kenady *(0.01)* | Kendelynn | Kenian | Kennalyn | Kennyah |
| Kelta | Kemia | Kenae | Kenderly | Keniana | Kennamer | Ramono |
| Keltee | Kemiah | Kenahjah | Kendi *(0.01)* | Kenidee *(0.01)* | Kennasia | Kennyasha |
| Keltie | Kemijah | Kenai | Kendin | Kenidi *(0.01)* | Kennay | Kennyiah |
| Keltrice | Kemille | Kenaija | Kendle *(0.01)* | Kenidy | Kennaya | Kenosha |
| Keltsy | Kemina | Kenais'ya | Kendlee | Kenielys | Kennberli | Kenra |
| Kelty | Kemiojo | Kenaiya | Kendlyn | Keniesha | Kenndal | Kensdiana |
| Keltzie | Kemira | Kenajah | Kendra *(0.60)* | Kenijha | Kenndda | Kensey *(0.01)* |
| Kelvanna | Kemirah | Kenarea | Kendra'lyn | Kenika | Kenndey | Kenshaina |
| Kelví | Kemistry | Kenaria | Kendrah | Kenila | Kenndi | Kenshundra |
| Kelvia | Kemiya | Kenasia | Kendra-Lee | Kenique | Kenndralin | Kensi |
| Kelvin | Kemiyah | Kenay | Kendralyn | Kenise | Kenndy | Kensie |
| | Kemiyia | Kenaya | Kendralynn | Kenisha *(0.01)* | Kennecise | Kensingten |

Kensington *(0.02)*
Kenslee *(0.01)*
Kensleigh
Kensley *(0.03)*
Kensley-Grace
Kensli
Kenslie
Kensly
Kenslynn
Kensy
Kentaira
Kentaizya
Kentake
Kentani
Kentasia
Kentavia
Kentaysia
Kentazia
Kenteria
Kentesa
Kentia
Kentionie
Kentlee
Kently
Kentoria
Kentorria
Kentraves
Kentreya
Kentya
Kentzler
Kenunique
Keny
Keny'jah
Kenya *(0.15)*
Kenyada
Kenyae
Kenyah
Kenyail
Kenyaisha
Kenyale
Kenyalee
Kenyana
Kenyanna
Kenyari
Kenyasia
Kenyata
Kenyatia
Kenyatta *(0.01)*
Kenyce
Kenydra
Kenyera
Kenyetta

Kenyha
Kenyia
Kenyon
Kenyona
Kenyonna
Kenysha
Kenyzjah
Kenza *(0.02)*
Kenza Samour
Kenzariah
Kenzariha
Kenze
Kenzee *(0.01)*
Kenzey
Kenzi *(0.02)*
Kenzie *(0.19)*
Kenzie Gra
Kenzington
Kenzle
Kenzleigh
Kenzley
Kenzli
Kenzlie
Kenzliegh
Kenzly
Kenzy
Kenzye
Keoana
Keojinny
Keolani
Keomi
Keon
Keona *(0.03)*
Keona Lani
Keonae
Keondra *(0.01)*
Keone
Keónese
Keoni
Keonia
Keonica
Keonna
Keonna-Lorai
Keonnia
Keonte
Keora
Keorey
Keori
Keória
Keosha
Keowin
Keowyn
Kephra

Kera *(0.03)*
Keragan
Keraghyn
Kerah
Kerahya
Keral
Keralei
Kerali
Keralyn
Keranisha
Keratin
Kerdasha
Kerdley
Kered
Keredith
Kerelle
Kerem
Keren *(0.02)*
Keren Kalubi
Kereny
Kerenza
Kereonda
Kereston
Keri *(0.03)*
Keri'yana
Keria *(0.01)*
Keriah
Keriana
Keriann
Kerianna
Keriauna
Keriaunna
Keribel
Kerigan
Kerik
Kerilou
Kerilyn
Kerin
Kerina
Kerine
Kerington
Kerinn
Kerinne
Keriona
Keris
Kerisly
Kerissa
Keriston
Keristyn-Janai
Kerith
Keriton
Keriyana
Keriyanna

Kerizma
Kerlande
Kerlda
Kerline
Kerlyana
Kerlyn
Kermesha
Kermina
Kermyla-Phalon
Kermyrah
Kerra *(0.01)*
Kerragan
Kerragen
Kerragyn
Kerrah
Kerrani
Kerri *(0.02)*
Kerri Lynn
Kerria
Kerrian
Kerri-Ann
Kerriann
Kerri-Anne
Kerrianne
Kerrica
Kerri-Daynae
Kerridwen
Kerrie
Kerrielle
Kerriery
Kerriey
Kerrigan *(0.03)*
Kerri-Lynn
Kerrin
Kerrina
Kerringten
Kerrington *(0.01)*
Kerringtyn
Kerrion
Kerris
Kerrissa
Kerrisyn
Kerry *(0.03)*
Kerryana
Kerry-Ann
Kerryann
Kerryn
Kersey
Kershie
Kerslly
Kerstein
Kersten

Kerstian
Kerlande
Kerstin *(0.02)*
Kerstyn *(0.01)*
Kersuze
Kerubo
Kerwine
Kerwing
Keryane
Keryanne
Keryia
Keryn
Keryna
Kerynsa
Keryson
Kerysten
Kes
Kesa
Kesandra
Kesanet
Kesar
Kesha *(0.01)*
Keshaila
Keshanti
Keshara
Keshauna
Keshaunna
Keshawna
Ke-Shawnna
Keshaya
Keshayla
Keshayous
Keshell
Keshia *(0.01)*
Keshima
Keshira
Keshiyah
Keshona
Keshuna
Keshundra
Keshunti
Keshvi
Kesi
Kesi'leigh
Kesia
Kesiah
Kesiley
Keslan
Kesley
Keslie
Kesly
Keslyn
Keslynn
Kesnyra

Kesonja
Kessa *(0.01)*
Kessah
Kessalyn
Kesseley
Kessia
Kessiah
Kessid
Kessie
Kesslor
Kesslyn
Kessya
Kessy-Ann
Kestin
Kestyn
Kesya
Keszia
Keta
Ketaki
Ketarria
Keteline
Ketenia
Ketevan
Kethleen
Kethyna
Ketilyieen
Ketirah
Ketki
Ketleen
Ketlene
Ketlyne
Ketoria
Ketrasia
Ketsia
Kettlie
Kettya
Ketura
Keturah *(0.02)*
Keturah-Anne
Ketzel
Ketzia
Keuna
Keundra
Keundranae
Keundria
Keunna
Keura
Kev'iana
Keva
Kevae
Kevalyn
Kevalynn
Kevan

Kevani
Kevanna
Kevannah
Kevaria
Kevayah
Kevelyn
Keven
Keveona
Kevi'yae
Kevia
Keviahna
Keviana
Kevien
Keviera
Kevin
Kevina
Kevinnia
Keviona
Kevionna
Keviontae
Keviyah
Keviyana
Keviyanna
Kevna
Kevona
Kevonna *(0.01)*
Kevonya
Kevra
Kevyahna
Kexin
Key
Key'ahrah
Key'ajani
Key'ana
Key'andrea
Key'anna
Key'ara
Key'ariel
Key'ashia
Key'asia
Key'chawnna
Key'chelle
Key'era
Key'honesti
Key'mairia
Key'miya
Key'myia
Key'niyah
Key'nsha
Key'ona
Key'vayea
Keya *(0.01)*
Keyadria

Keyah
Keyahja
Keyahjah
Keyahna
Keyaijah
Keyaira *(0.01)*
Keyairah
Keyairah-
  Aalliyah
Keyairra
Keyaisha
Keyala
Keyalah
Keyama
Keyamiah
Keyamonie
Keyamya
Keyana *(0.02)*
Keyana Esthe
Keyanah
Keyandra
Keyandrah
Keyandrea
Keyangeli
Keyanha
Keyani
Keyanie
Key-Anna
Keyanna *(0.03)*
Keyannah
Keyanni
Keyanté
Keyar
Keyara *(0.03)*
Keyarah
Keyaraha
Keyare
Keyaren
Keyarha
Keyari
Keyaria
Keyariah
Keyarie
Keyarra
Keyarrah
Keyasha
Keyasia *(0.01)*
Keyauna
Keyaunah
Keyaunna
Keyauntay
Keyausha
Keyavae

Keyawna
Keyazsha
Keybreona
Keydan
Keydi
Keydra
Keydy
Keyeda
Keyemani
Keyera *(0.01)*
Keyerah
Keyerra
Keygan
Keyhara
Keyia
Keyiana
Keyila
Keyiona
Keyionna
Keyira
Keyirah
Keyiyah
Keyjuannae
Keyla *(0.06)*
Keylaila
Keylandrea
Keylani
Keylanie
Keylanis
Keylannis
Keyle
Keylea
Keylee *(0.03)*
Keylei
Keyleigh
Keyley
Keyli *(0.01)*
Keyliah
Keyliane
Keylianna
Keylie
Keylin *(0.01)*
Keylina
Keyline
Keylis
Keylla
Keyllie
Keyly
Keylyn
Keylynn
Keyma
Keymani
Keymar'ree

Keymara
Keymaria
Keymariah
Keymarie
Keymariya
Keymarya
Key-Maya
Keymaya
Keymia
Keymiah
Keymoni
Keymonie
Keymora
Keymorah
Keymyd
Keyna
Keynacha
Keynajah
Keynari
Keynia
Keyniá
Keyniah
Key-Nija
Keynijah
Keynny
Keynu
Keynyah
Keyona *(0.02)*
Keyonah
Keyonal
Keyoncé
Keyondra
Keyondriah
Keyoni
Keyonia
Keyonia Ch
Keyonie
Keyonis
Keyonna
  *(0.03)*
Keyonni
Keyonnie
Keyonta
Keyora
Keyosha
Keyoshjana
Keyoshyia
Keyounce
Keyounia
Keyovia
Keyra *(0.01)*
Keyri
Keyrili

Keyrimar
Keyrstin
Keyry
Keysa
Keyschla
Keysha *(0.01)*
Keyshauna
Keyshe
Keyshia *(0.01)*
Keyshjanell
Keyshla
Keyshlamarie
Keyshona
Keyshonda
Keyshonna
Keyshy'ra
Keysiah
Keysie
Keytana
Keyth
Keyturah
Keyty
Keyuna
Keyundra
Keyunnyah
Keyvia
Keyvon
Keyvonna
Keyyonnie
Keyzariah
Keyziah
Keyziya
Kezah
Kezaiya
Kezayah-
  Adelaide
Kezia *(0.01)*
Keziah *(0.04)*
Keziona
Keziyah
Kezley
Kezra
Kezshuna
Kezzia
Kezziah
Kh'amyia
Kh'mari
Kh'miyah
Kh'mya
Kh'nasia
Kha'bria
Kha'lia
Kha'liah

Kha'liyah
Kha'mani
Kha'miyah
Kha'mya
Kha'myiah
Kha'nzia
Kha'shira
Kha'terra
Khabirah
Khaciah
Khadacha
Khadafi
Khadajza
Khadedra
Khadee
Khadeeja
Khadeejah
Khadeijah
Khadeja
Khadejah
Khadence
Khadesia
Khadia
Khadian
Khadidiatou
Khadidja
Khadidjatou
Khadiesja
Khadija *(0.04)*
Khadijah *(0.03)*
Khadijatou
Khadijatul
Khadijetou
Khadijo
Khadiya
Khadiza
Khadjiah
Khadra
Khadro
Khadyn
Khaelyn
Khahish
Khai
Khai'dra
Khaila
Khailand
Khaileah
Khailee
Khaileeh
Khailen
Khailiyah
Khaing
Khaira

Khairen
Khairya
Khaita
Khala
Khalae
Khalahari
Khalaiya
Khalan
Khalani
Khalaya
Khalaysia
Khalea
Khaleah
Khalece
Khaled
Khalee
Khaleema
Khaleeya
Khaleh
Khalehla
Khaleigh
Khaleigha
Khaley
Khaleya
Khaleyah
Khaley-Shai
Khali *(0.01)*
Khalia *(0.02)*
Khaliah *(0.01)*
Khalicia
Khalie
Khaliha
Khalihah
Khalil
Khalilah
Khalimah
Khalin
Khalique
Khalis
Khalisah
Khalise
Khalista
Khaliya
Khaliyah *(0.01)*
Khallia
Khalliah
Khalliyah
Khaloni
Khalsa
Khalyn
Khalysa
Khalyse
Khalyssa

Khalysta
Khamalah
Khamaly
Khamani
Khamanii
Khamara
Khamara Skye
Khamarah
Khamare
Khamarea
Khamari *(0.01)*
Khamaria
Khamarri
Khamaryah
Khamaya
Khameela
Khameil
Khamia
Khamil
Khamilah
Khamile
Khamillah
Khamirah
Khamiyah
Khammy
Khamoni
Khamora
Khamphout
Khamya
Khamyha
Khanari
Khandace
Khandi
Khandise
Khanedi
Khanh Doan
Khanh-An
Khanhhan
Khania
Khaniece
Khanijah
Khanisha
Khaniya
Khaniyah
Khannickaah
Khanthamalee
Khany'iah
Khanya
Khanyae
Khanysha
Khaqmari
Khara
Khardanaya

| | | | | | | |
|---|---|---|---|---|---|---|
| Kharen | Khayyirah | Khiley | Khristina | Khymora | Kiaena | Kianne |
| Khari | Khe'lyn | Khilyn | Khristine | Khynia | Kiah (0.04) | Kianni |
| Khariah | Kheaira | Khimauni | Khristo | Khyra (0.01) | Kiaha | Kiannie |
| Kharina | Kheayra | Khinya Monquie | Khristyana | Khyral | Kiahna (0.01) | Kianny |
| Kharis | Khedidja | Khira | Khrylyssa | Khyran | Kiahny | Kianti |
| Kharisa | Khedijah | Khirah | Khrystal | Khyriana | Kiahra | Kianu |
| Kharisma | Khei-Ann | Khirey | Khrystian | Khyrra | Kiahrra | Kiany |
| Kharismah | Kheir | Khirra | Khrystina | Khyrsten | Kiahya | Kianyliz |
| Khariz | Kheira | Khiya (0.01) | Khrystyna | Ki | Kiahzha | Ki-Ara |
| Kharla | Khelcee | Khiyan | Khudija | Kí Ajana | Kiailah | Kiara (0.81) |
| Kharlee | Khelse | Khiyana | Khush | Ki Ara | Kiaira | Kiara Cloeh |
| Kharley | Khelsea | Khiyonah | Khush Deep | Ki Aura | Kiaire | Kiara Jane |
| Kharli | Khelsey | Khiyone | Khushali | Ki'aina | Kiairra | Kiara La's |
| Kharlie | Khemani | Khiyra | Khushbir | Ki'ajha | Kiaisa | Kiarah (0.02) |
| Kharma (0.01) | Khemir | Khloé | Khushboo | Ki'andria | Kiajah | Kiara-Jane |
| Kharmani | Khemistry | Khloe (0.09) | Khushdeep | Ki'ann | Kiajiah | Kiaraleas |
| Kharmany | Khendal | Khloee | Khushi (0.02) | Ki'anna | Kiala | Kiara-Lee |
| Kharmella | Khendle | Khloey (0.01) | Khushleen | Ki'ara | Kiala-Jo | Kiaralee |
| Kharmen | Khendra | Khloi | Khushmann | Ki'arah | Kialee | Kiaralis |
| Kharmin | Khenlei | Khloie | Singh | Ki'arie | Kialeigh | Kiaraliz |
| Kharmn | Khennariya | Khmari | Khushmeet | Ki'arra | Kialey | Kiara-Lynn |
| Kharunyaa | Khennedi | Khmyrah | Khushmin | Ki'asia | Kiali | Kiaralys |
| Kharya | Khenya | Khmyree | Khushnoor | Ki'ayshia | Kia-Lillian | Kiaramari |
| Kharyss | Khenzie | Khoa | Khushpreet | Ki'liyah | Kialyn | Kiaran |
| Khashya | Khepera Maa | Khobi | Khuyen | Ki'mairah | Kialynn | Kiaré |
| Khashyra | Kheri | Khola | Khy | Ki'marrea | Kiam | Kiarey |
| Khasira | Khessence | Khole | Khy'liah | Ki'monnie | Kiamani | Kiarha |
| Khasmere | Kheta | Khonephet | Khya | Ki'mora | Kiamara | Kiari |
| Kha-Tam | Kheya | Khonstynce | Khyaira | Ki'morra | Kiamarie | Kiaria |
| Khathy | Kheyanna | Khora | Khyaiza | Ki'mya | Kiamarra | Kiarilys |
| Khatia | Kheyla | Khoralie | Khyara | Ki'myrah | Kiamonni | Kiarla |
| Khatibah | Khi'azhijah | Khori | Khyarra | Ki'nari | Kiamya | Kiarra (0.06) |
| Khatira | Khi'rika | Khoria | Khyelle | Ki'nasia | Kian | Kiarrah |
| Khatrica | Khi'yonnia | Khoriana | Khyia | Ki'niah | Kiana (0.32) | Kiarrah-Dashé |
| Khatrina | Khia (0.01) | Khory | Khyila | Ki'nieya | Kiana Lee | Kiarra-Jade |
| Khatrina Sarah | Khiabette | Khorya | Khyirra | Ki'niyah | Kianah | Kiarri |
| Khatro | Khiah | Khouloud | Khyjah | Ki'ona | Kianaliz | Kiarstin |
| Khawlah | Khiaira | Khounridy | Khyjayah | Ki'onna | Kiana-Marie | Kiarya |
| Khaycia | Khiala | Khouri | Khyla (0.01) | Ki'robin | Kia-Nashay | Kiaryn |
| Khayden | Khiana | Khourtney | Khylanni | Ki'sara | Kiandra (0.01) | Kiasha |
| Khaydence | Khiandre | Khowla | Khyle | Ki'shay | Kiandria | Ki-Asia |
| Khayla (0.01) | Khianna | Khrishauna | Khylee | Ki'tiona | Kianeris | Kiasia (0.01) |
| Khaylah | Khiannon | Khrisla | Khyleena | Ki'yanii | Kianessa | Kiasiah |
| Khaylan | Khiara | Khrislen A | Khylei | Ki'yarra | Kiani | Kiatyanna |
| Khaylee | Khiarah | Khrislyn | Khyleigh | Ki'yonna | Kianily | Kiauna (0.01) |
| Khaylen | Khiari | Khrismah | Khyler | Ki'zera | Kianjohnay | Kiaundra |
| Khayli | Khiarra | Khrismar | Khyli | Kia (0.01) | Kiann | Kiaunna |
| Khaylia | Khi-Ase | Khrista | Khylia | Kia'jah | Kianna (0.14) | Kiaura |
| Khaylin | Khiila | Khristeayahnah | Khylianna | Kiaalleah | Kianna | Kiavaahda |
| Khaylyn | Khila | Khristee | Khylie | Kiaara | Marguerite | Kiavier |
| Khayra | Khilah | Khristen | Khyll | Kiabeh | Kiannah | Kiavion |
| Khayro | Khilea | Khristia | Khylynn | Kiada | Kiannalee | Kiavitl |
| Khaysia | Khilee | Khristian | Khymaurii | Kiadrey | Kianndra | Kiaya (0.01) |

| | | | | | | |
|---|---|---|---|---|---|---|
| Kiayana | Kienndra | Kiersty | Kileen | Kimaura | Kimiah | Kimyada |
| Kiayanna Ane | Kientez | Kierstyn *(0.05)* | Kilei | Kimaya *(0.01)* | Kimie | Kimyah |
| Kiayla | Kienya | Kierstynn | Kileigh *(0.01)* | Kimayah | Kimie-Ann | Kimyatta |
| Kiayona | Kieona | Kiersyn | Kiley *(0.30)* | Kimbarly | Kimiesha | Kimyni |
| Kiayr | Kieona-Cashay | Kiertstern | Kiley Jae | Kimber *(0.03)* | Kimiko | Kimyra |
| Kiayra | Kieora | Kierya | Kileyana | Kimberely | Kimily | Kimyri |
| Kiaza | Kiera *(0.41)* | Kieryn | Kileyann | Kimberlain | Kimilya | Kimyriah |
| Kiazah | Kiera Lucia | Kiesha | Kili | Kimberle | Kimimela | Kin'deja |
| Kiazia | Kieragen | Kieshamaria | Kilian | Kimberlee | Kimimila | Kin'qua |
| Kibbie Theresa | Kierah *(0.01)* | Kieshia | Kiliane | (0.02) | Kimira | Kina *(0.01)* |
| Kibi | Kiera-Joy | Kiesli | Kilianne | Kimberleigh | Kimisha-Ann | Kinadee |
| Kibra | Kieraleigh | Kiesse | Kilie | Kimberley | Kimiya | Kinady |
| Kicsely | Kieralin | Kieu | Kiliey | (0.04) | Kimiyah | Kinaiya |
| Kida | Kieran *(0.02)* | Kiev | Kilikia | Kimberley-Joan | Kimiyha | Kinaly-Alsey |
| Kidada | Kierann | Kieva | Ki-Litta | Kimberli *(0.01)* | Kimjot | Kinana |
| Kidarrah | Kierany | Kieve | Kiliyah | Kimberlie | Kimla | Kinawin |
| Kidden | Kiera-Rae | Kième | Killasandra | Kimberlin | Kimlie | Kinaya |
| Kide | Kierce | Kieya | Killee | (0.01) | Kim-Ly | Kinberly |
| Kiden | Kiercy | Kieyah | Killian | Kim-Berly | Kimlynn | Kincade |
| Kidest | Kierden | Kieyamirah | Killiann | Kimberly *(2.44)* | Kimmara | Kinda |
| Kie'aria | Kierdrah | Kieyla | Killianna | Kimberly Alexa | Kimmaya | Kinda Lynn |
| Kie'asia | Kierdyn | Kieza | Killyane | Kimberly Danay | Kimmberlie | Kindajah |
| Kieahra | Kiere | Kifah | Killy-Ann | Kimberly Jade | Kimmel | Kindal |
| Kieandra | Kieren | Kiflyn | Kilmora | Balza | Kimmery | Kindale |
| Kieanna | Kiereona | Kighya | Kilmyla | Kimberly Koyi | Kimmi | Kindall *(0.01)* |
| Kieara *(0.01)* | Kieres | Kiha | Kilonna | Kimberly Nicole | Kimmia | Kindalyn |
| Kiearah | Kieria | Kihana | Kiloran | Kimberlyann | Kimmie | Kindel |
| Kiearra | Kieriae | Kihanna | Kilorin | Kimberlyn | Kimmora | Kindell |
| Kieasia | Kicrik | Kihara | Kilty | (0.02) | Kimmy | Kindle |
| Kieaunna | Kierin | Kihlee | Kilynn *(0.01)* | Kimberly- | Kimmya | Kindlelynn |
| Kieayla | Kierith | Kiira | Kim *(0.08)* | Niphaphone | Kimmyah | Kindness |
| Kiefer | Kierland | Kiishea | Kim'mya | Kimberlynn | Kimnya | Kindra *(0.01)* |
| Kiegan | Kierlyn | Kiiux | Kima | Kimble | Kimoni | Kindrea |
| Kieghly | Kiernan *(0.01)* | Kijana | Kimahja | Kimbolyn | Kimonie | Kindred |
| Kiehali | Kiernen | Kijia | Kimaia | Kimbra | Kimorá | Kindrinna |
| Kiehlie | Kierney | Kiki | Kimaily | Kimbralynn | Kimora *(0.19)* | Kindsey |
| Kiela | Kierra *(0.19)* | Kikilola | Kimaley | Kimbre | Kimorah | Kindsy |
| Kielain | Kierrah | Kiko | Kim-Alicia | Kimbrel | Kimora-Lee | Kindyl |
| Kielan | Kierralynn | Kikyo | Kimaly | Kimbrell | Kimore | Kineret |
| Kielar | Kierria | Kil'mari | Kimana | Kimbreya | Kimorea | Kinesa |
| Kiele *(0.01)* | Kierris | Kila *(0.01)* | Kim-Anh | Kimbriel | Kimori | Kinesha |
| Kielee | Kiersa | Kilah *(0.01)* | Kimanh | Kimbrley | Kimoria | King'yada |
| Kieleigh | Kiersley | Kilaiyah | Kimani *(0.01)* | Kimbry | Kimorra | Kinga |
| Kieley | Kierslyn | Kilan | Kimanni | Kimburly | Kimory | Kingiya |
| Kieliee | Kierson | Kilani | Kimara *(0.01)* | Kimeasha | Kimoya | Kingllana |
| Kielley | Kiersta | Kilanna | Kimarah | Kimeisha | Kimpreet | Kingsley |
| Kielly | Kierstan *(0.01)* | Kilara | Kimaraha | Kimera | Kimri | Kingston |
| Kiely *(0.01)* | Kiersteen | Kilari | Kimari | Kimesa | Kimsey | Kiniah |
| Kielynn | Kierstein | Kilay | Kimaria | Kimesha | Kimsin | Kinidi |
| Kiemelia | Kiersten *(0.27)* | Kile | Kimarie | Kimeyasa | Kimverli | Kinisaasie |
| Kiena | Kierstin *(0.07)* | Kilea *(0.01)* | Kimariya | Kim-Frederique | Kimy | Kinisha |
| Kieneace | Kierstine | Kileah | Kimarra | Kimi | Kimya *(0.01)* | Kiniya |
| Kienna | Kierston *(0.01)* | Kilee *(0.03)* | Kimarria | Kimia | Kimya Naomi | Kiniyah |

Kinlagh
Kinlea
Kinlee (0.01)
Kinlei
Kinleigh (0.01)
Kinley (0.06)
Kinlie
Kinly
Kinlye
Kinmaurie
Kinnadi
Kinnady
Kinnedi
Kinneret
Kinney
Kinnik
Kinnley
Kinsea
Kinsely
Kinsey (0.08)
Kinshassa
Kinsie
Kinslee (0.01)
Kinslei
Kinsleigh
Kinsley (0.09)
Kinsli
Kinslie
Kinsly
Kintasha
Kinyá
Kinyell
Kinyeta
Kinyi
Kinyya
Kinza
Kinzayda
Kinzee
Kinzetta
Kinzey
Kinzi
Kinzidee
Kinzie (0.01)
Kinzlee
Kinzley
Kinzlie
Kinzly
Kinzton
Kinzy
Kio
Kiojha
Kiokiane
Kiomara

Kiomari
Kiombee
Kiomi
Kiona (0.02)
Kionah
Kiondra
Kiónee
Kioni
Kionna (0.01)
Kiora
Kiori
Kiota
Kiowa
Kiproleen
Kira (0.51)
Kira Rose
Kira Skye
Kirah (0.02)
Kira-Lee
Kira-Liana
Kiralyn
Kira-Mackenzie
Kira-Matthew
Kiran (0.02)
Kirana
Kirandeep
  (0.01)
Kiranjeet
Kiranjot
Kiranpreet
Kiranvir
Kirat
Kiratpreet
Kirbey
Kirbie
Kirbilyn
Kirby (0.01)
Kire
Kiré
Kirean
Kireane
Kiree
Kireiana
Kirely
Kirennoor
Kireonna
Kiresten
Kirezi
Kiri
Kiria
Kiriah
Kiriaki
Kirializ

Kirian
Kirie
Kirin
Kirishnavi
Kirissa
Kiristen
Kirit
Kirithika
Kirka
Kirklyn
Kirklynn
Kirn
Kirna
Kirpa
Kirra (0.04)
Kirrah
Kirshell
Kirshona
Kirsi
Kirsta
Kirstan
Kirstein
Kirsten (0.36)
Kirsten
  Danniellb
Kirsten Zoey
Kirsten-Haylee
Kirsten-Ioanna
Kirstey
Kirsti
Kirstian
Kirstie
Kirstin (0.05)
Kirstina
Kirston
Kirsty
Kirstyn (0.01)
Kirstynn
Kirt
Kirtana
Kirthana
Kirthi
Kirthika
Kirti
Kirtlyn
Kirtya
Kiru
Kiruschnapillai
Kiruththika
Kirya
Kiryaona
Kiryn
Kiryna

Kisa
Kisani
Kiseiki
Kisha (0.01)
Kishae
Kishairia
Kishalund
Kishama
Kishana
Kishania
Kishanna
Kishanti
Kishina
Kishmala
Kishonti
Kishora
Kishori
Kiska
Kisla
Kissa
Kissel
Kissimmee
Kissy
Kistany
Kistena
Kit
Kita
Kita Etzu
Kitala
Kitalyn
Kitana (0.01)
Kitani
Kitanna
Kitanya
Kitara
Kitavalia
Kitaviah
Kitcia
Kitharina
Kitiana
Kitiara
Kitoria
Kitrin
Kitrina
Kitriyah
Kittana
Kitterra
Kittiara
Kittie
Kitt-Tanya
Kitty
Kitzia
Kitzya

Kiv'zharia
Kiva
Kivana Lynnae
Kively
Kivrin
Kivvaq
Kiwa
Kiwi
Kiya (0.06)
Kiyaa
Kiyaannii
Kiyah (0.03)
Kiyahna
Kiyahnna
Kiyale
Kiyana (0.02)
Kiyanah
Kiyani
Kiyania
Kiyanna (0.01)
Kiyanna
  Keimone
Kiyanni
Kiyannie
Kiyara
Kiyarah
Kiyarra
Kiyaura
Kiyawna
Kiyela
Kiye-Laiye
Kiyesha
Kiyez
Kiyilah
Kiyla
Kiylah
Kiylea
Kiylee
Kiyleh
Kiylei
Kiylie
Kiymaah
Kiyo
Kiyoana
Kiyoko
Kiyomi
Kiyona
Kiyonna
Kiyora
Kiyoshi
Kiyra
Kiyrah
Kiyre

Kiyreanna
Kiyumi
Kiyva
Kiyvona
Kizah
Kizhara
Kiziah
Kiziyah
Kizmet
Kizziah
Kizzie
Kjari
Kjera
Kjersten
Kjersti
Kjestina
Kjirsten
Klahasna
Klahree
Klahrissa
Klair
Klaira
Klairé
Klaire (0.01)
Klandre
Klara (0.02)
Klara Liese
Klarah
Klarel
Klaresa
Klaricya
Klarissa (0.01)
Klarista
Klarke
Klarysa
Klaryssa
Klashay
Klashia
Klaske
Klassic
Klaudia (0.01)
Klea
Kleah
Kleanna
Kleho
Kleiauna
K-Leigh
Kleo
Kler
Klhoe
Klhoie
Kliera
Klinque

Kliya
Kliyana
Kloé
Kloe (0.07)
Kloe Ann
Kloee (0.01)
Kloee Marie
Kloeigh
Kloey (0.05)
Klohye
Kloi
Kloie (0.02)
Kloreen
Klorisa
Klorresa
Kloryssa
Klover
Klovir
Klowie
Kloye
Kloyee
Klyia
Klyne
Klynn
Kmaia
Kmara
Kmari
Kmiya
Kmya
Kmyia
Kna'shante
Knai
Knajaiana
Knari
Knariah
Knea
Knia
Knight
Knightlyn
Kniyah
  Danielle
Knoelle
Knole
Knowwell
Kny'iar
Knyah
Knylah
Ko
Koa
Koala
Koan
Kobee
Kobi

| | | | | | | |
|---|---|---|---|---|---|---|
| Kobie | Komya | Koriana | Korvia | Krali | Krishanne | Kristany |
| Koby | Komyra | Korianna | Kory | Kraly | Krishara | Kristasia |
| Kochana | Konatsu | Korie (0.01) | Korya | Kramer | Krishauna | Kristasiah |
| Koda | Konika | Korielle | Koryanna | Krashaunda | Krishawti | Kristeanna |
| Kodee | Konner | Kori-Elle | Koryanne | Kraven | Krishay | Kristeena |
| Kodi (0.02) | Konneya | Korii | Korye | Kraysten | Krishena | Kristeine |
| Kodie | Kaydence | Korilynn | Koryhn | Kreanna | Krishenda | Kristel (0.01) |
| Kodi-Rae | Konnie | Korin (0.01) | Koryin | Kree | Krishma | Kristel Joselyn |
| Kody | Konrot | Korina (0.01) | Koryn (0.01) | Kree Skye | Krishna | Kristela |
| Koelii | Konstance | Korine | Koryne | Kreedence | Krishnaa | Kristell |
| Koen | Konstantina | Korinn | Korynn | Kreesha | Krishonda | Kristelle |
| Koey | Konsuelo | Korinna | Korynne | Kreeyaah | Krishtiana | Kristen (0.33) |
| Koh | Kontessica | Korinne | Koryundah | Kreiston | Krishtika | Kristena (0.01) |
| Kohana | Konztance | Korionna | Kosette | Kreshanna | Krishya | Kristenadia |
| Kohl | Koolonna | Kori-Rose | Koshielia | Kreshawna | Krishyra | Kristeon |
| Kohle | Kooper | Korissa | Koshvi | Kreshna | Krisi | Kristern |
| Kohlub | Kora (0.03) | Kóriya | Kosi | Kreshona | Krisiela | Kristeuana |
| Kohnstence | Korae | Koriyanna | Kosisochukwu | Kreshunna | Krisiliy | Kristhal |
| Kohnwirya | Korah (0.01) | Koriyea | Kosorochi | Kreslie | Krisily | Kristhana |
| Kohral | Korahlie | Korlee | Kostantina | Kressa | Krisitna | Kristhel |
| Koi (0.01) | Koraima | Korleece | Kota | Kressley | Krisley | Kristhine |
| Koinonia | Koral (0.01) | Kormasa | Koti | Kresta | Krisly | Kristhyn |
| Koisha | Kora-Lee | Korn | Kotich | Kreston | Krislyn (0.01) | Kristi (0.03) |
| Kojo | Koralee | Kornaya | Kotie | Kretell | Krislynn | Kristia |
| Koko | Kora-Lee Yuxie | Kornya | Koto | Kri'shauna | Krisma | Kristi-Ahyna |
| Kokomi | Koralei | Korona | Kotoe | Kri'toria | Krismari | Kristialys |
| Kolada | Koraleigh | Korpo | Kotoko | Krianna | Krismariel | Kristian (0.02) |
| Kolaia | Koralie (0.02) | Korra | Koumba | Kricheliz | Krisnee | Kristian B |
| Kolbee | Koraly (0.02) | Korrall | Koura | Kricket | Krissa (0.01) | Kristi-Ana |
| Kolbi | Koralyn | Korren | Kouri | Krickett | Krissalyn | Kristiana (0.02) |
| Kolbie | Koralynn | Korren Taneil | Kourtlyn | Krickit | Krissel | Kristiane |
| Kolby (0.01) | Koralys | Korri | Kourtlynn | Krimson | Kris-Shawna | Kristiann |
| Kolbye | Koran | Korria | Kourtnee | Krina | Krissheima | Kristianna |
| Koleigh | Korayma | Korriah | Kourtnei | Krinza | Krisshyla | (0.01) |
| Koliane | Korban | Korrie | Kourtney (0.06) | Kripa | Krissia | Kristianne |
| Kolie | Korbyn | Korrin (0.01) | Kourtni (0.01) | Kris | Krissie | Kristianni |
| Kolle | Kordai | Korrina | Kourtnie | Kris'ceona | Krisslyn | Kristiaun |
| Kollean | Kordellya | Korrine | Kourtny | Kris'tara | Krissty | Kristiauna |
| Kolleen | Korea | Korrinne | Koury | Krisalee | Krissy | Kristie (0.01) |
| Kollin | Korede | Korrtney | Kousso | Kris-Ali | Krissyah | Kristieanna |
| Kolsey | Koree | Korryn | Kouther | Krisalyn (0.01) | Krista (0.15) | Kristien |
| Kolya | Koreena | Korshea | Kova | Krisalynn | Kristah | Kristiina |
| Komal (0.01) | Korei | Kortez | Koveyiah | Krisandra | Kristain | Kristilynn |
| Komaldeep | Korel | Kortlyn | Kovi | Krisanne | Kristal (0.01) | Kristin (0.17) |
| Komali | Koren | Kortlynn | Kowsar | Krisanta | Kristalee | Kristin Marie |
| Komalpreet | Korena | Kortnee | Kowyn | Krisari | Kristaliz | Kris-Tina |
| Komalveer | Korene | Kortneigh | Koy | Krisayda | Kristal-Rose | Kristina (0.32) |
| Komara | Koresa | Kortney (0.04) | Koya | Krischelle | Kristalyn | Kristina-Kristen |
| Komel | Korey (0.01) | Kortni (0.01) | Koyah | Kriscia | Kristalynn | Kristine (0.06) |
| Komia | Korhal | Kortnie | Koye | Krisha (0.01) | Kristan (0.01) | Kristing |
| Komisha | Kori (0.06) | Kortny | Koyuki | Krishanda | Kristana | Kristinia |
| Komkan | Kori'ona | Korto | Kozmelina | Krishandra | Kristanie | Kristiona |
| Komora | Korian | Korttnee | Krachelle | Krishanna | Kristanna | Kristionna |

Kristis
Kristiyona
Kristjana
Kristlyn
Kristlynn
Kriston
Kristriauna
Kristrin
Kristten
Kristy (0.03)
Kristy Ana
Kristyan
Kristyana
Kristy-Ann
Kristyannah
Kristy-Anne
Kristyl
Kristyn (0.02)
Kristyna
Kristyne
Kristyon
Kristyona
Krisylvia
Krisynthia
Krisztina
Krithi
Krithiga
Krithigaa
Krithika
Kriti
Kritika
Kriya
Krizian
Kriztianity
Kriztiene
Krizzia
Kroi
Kronic
Krorza
Krosten
Krsna
Kruiz
Krupa
Krushi
Kruti
Kry'shia
Krya
Krymson
Kryn
Krys
Krysa
Krysanne
Kryscella

Krysel
Kryselle
Krysha
Kryshana
Kryshelle
Krysia
Kryslin
Kryslyn
Kryslynn
Kryssalynn
Kryssie
Krysta (0.03)
Krystabella
Krystah
Krystal (0.18)
Krystal Alea
Krystalee
Krystalin
Krystall
Krystalle
Krystallo
Krystal-Lynn
Krystallynn
Krystalyn
Krystalynn
Krystanna
Kryste
Krystel (0.01)
Krystele
Krystell
Krystelle (0.01)
Krysten (0.01)
Krystene
Krysti
Krystia
Krystian
Krystiana
Krystin (0.01)
Krystina (0.01)
Krystinah
Krystine
Krystion
Krystiyonna
Krystle
Krystol
Kryston
Krysttal
Krystyana
Krystyn
Krystyna
Kryuna
Kryzelle
Ksan

Ksena
Kseneya
Ksenia
Kseniya
Ksenya
K-Sha
Kshema
Kshipra
Kshuf
Kstie
Ku'niaya
Ku'tent
Kuantashia
Kubera
Kubra
Kucen
Kuei
Kuetatshesh
Kuiera
Kulani
Kulia
Kuliyah
Kulnoor
Kulraj
Kulsoom
Kulsum
Kulthoom
Kumaiah
Kumari
Kumaura
Kumba
Kumije
Kumite
Kumkum
Kumorah
Kumru
Kunakyla
Kunthira
Kuntumie
Kura
Kuranda
Kurdistan
Kuresha
Kuriana
Kuristan
Kurizma
Kurniyah
Kurra
Kurrina
Kursta
Kursten
Kurstin (0.01)
Kurstyn

Kurtlan
Kurtlyn
Kuruova
Kurzieria
Kushi
Kushmanda
Kushnoor
Kushur
Kusonah
Kustam
Kusum
Kutemba
Kutenai
Kuuipo
Kuullee
Kvitoslava
Kwa'merias
Kwai-Daja
Kwamecia
Kwan'tavia
Kwanice
Kwashonna
Kwateria
Kwaya'tsiiq'kwe
Kwayera
Kween
Kweli
Kwila
Kwincy
Kwinn
Kwyn
Kwyncee
Ky
Ky Ra
Ky Shanna
Ky Zha
Ky'aira
Ky'aisa
Ky'ana
Ky'anna
Ky'ara
Ky'asia (0.01)
Ky'aunna
Ky'bresha
Ky'dae
Ky'era
Ky'eshia
Ky'iah
Ky'irea
Ky'laney
Ky'lea
Ky'ledja
Ky'lee

Ky'lynn
Ky'mah
Ky'mani
Ky'mari
Ky'miah
Ky'mora
Ky'mya
Ky'najaha
Ky'nilah
Ky'ondra
Ky'onna
Ky'rale
Ky'riona
Ky'seanna
Ky'taveonn
Ky'una
Ky'unja
Ky'ya
Ky'yanna
Ky'yanna Aalon
Ky'yuna
Ky'zha
Kya (0.11)
Kyabi
Kyah (0.04)
Kyahna
Kyaija
Kyair
Kyaira (0.01)
Kyairah
Kyaire
Kyairra
Kyairriona
Kyala
Kyale
Kyalee
Kyaleigh
Kyalie
Kyamari
Kyamerah
Kyan (0.01)
Kyana (0.03)
Kyanah
Kyanah Shaye
Kyanah-Belle
Kyana-Rae
Kyandra
Kyani
Kyanie
Kyann (0.01)
Ky-Anna
Kyanna (0.03)
Kyannah

Kyanna-Rose
Kyanne
Kyar
Kyara (0.06)
Kyaraeliz
Kyarah
Kyara-Jane
Kyaraliz
Kyariah
Kyarie
Kyaris
Kyarra
Kyasi
Kyasia (0.01)
Ky-Asia Alexus
Kyatalin
Kyaudreea
Kydance
Kyden
Kydreiona
Kydreuna
Kye
Kye Aunna
Kye'masjhi
Kye'onna
Kyea
Kyeanna
Kyeesha
Kyeighh
Kyeisha
Kyel
Kyela
Kyelee
Kyelei Rhea
Kyeleigh
Kyeli
Kyelia
Kyelin
Kyella
Kyelle
Kyemani
Kyemontay
Kyemoria
Kyeniah
Kyenna
Kyer
Kyer'ah
Kyera (0.01)
Kyerra (0.01)
Kyerrah
Kyerrha
Kyersten
Kyerstin

Kyesha
Kyfong
Kygeri'a
Kyhana
Kyhara
Kyhlee
Kyhlie
Kyhlis
Kyhra
Kyi Mari
Kyi'azsia
Kyia (0.01)
Kyiah
Kyialyn
Kyiana
Kyiarra
Kyierinn
Kyierra
Kyihana
Kyila
Kyilee
Kyilei
Kyilenna
Kyiona
Kyira
Kyirah
Kyisha
Kyja
Kyjah
Kyl'ae
Kyla (0.67)
Kylaa
Kylaah
Kylah (0.08)
Kylaiah
Kyla-Mai
Kyla-Marie
Kylamay
Kylan (0.01)
Kylana
Kylanai
Kylandra
Kylani
Kylar (0.01)
Kylar Join
Kylarae
Kylari
Kylarria
Kylashia
Kylayah
Kylcee
Kyle (0.01)
Kylea (0.02)

Kyleah (0.01)
Kyleaha
Kylecia
Kylee (1.14)
Kylee Celeste
Kyleea
Kyleeah
Kylee-Ann
Kyleeann
Kyleeia
Kylee-Jo
Kyleen (0.01)
Kyleen Patricia Ferrer
Kyleena
Kyleene
Kylee-Rae
Kyleerose
Kylei (0.01)
Kyleigh (0.32)
Kyleigh Ann
Kyleigh Anna
Kyleigha
Kyleigh-Ann
Kyleigh-Dawn
Kylen
Kylena
Kylene (0.01)
Kylenn
Kyleonna
Kyler (0.02)
Kylera
Kylese
Kylette
Kyley (0.02)
Kyli (0.02)
Kylia (0.01)
Kyliah
Kyliaha
Kyliana (0.01)
Kyliane
Kylianna
Kyliannah
Kylianne
Kyliauna
Kylicia
Kylie (2.30)
Kylie Anne
Kylie Lynn
Kylie Zabrina
Kylie-Alyssa
Kylie-Ana
Kylie-Ann

Kylie-Anne
Kylieanny
Kylieayn
Kyliece
Kyliecia
Kyliee
Kyliegh (0.01)
Kylie-Jo
Kylie-Lynn
Kylien
Kyliera
Kylierae
Kyliey
Kylii
Kylijahnea
Kylil
Kylima
Kylin (0.02)
Kylina
Kyline
Kylinn
Kylip
Kylis
Kylise
Kyliss
Kyliya
Kyliyah
Kyllah
Kylli
Kylliane
Kyllie
Kyllie-Anne
Kylnia
Kyloni
Kyly
Kylyann
Kyly-Anne
Kylye
Kylyn (0.01)
Kylynn (0.01)
Kylynne
Kym
Kymaira
Ky-Mani
Kymani
Ky-Mani-Nishay
Kymara
Kymaree
Kymari
Kymaria
Kymariah
Kymarra
Kymayra

Kymbal
Kymber (0.01)
Kymberely
Kymberlee (0.01)
Kymberley
Kymberli
Kymberlin
Kymberly (0.01)
Kymberlyn
Kymbreelyn
Kymbreona
Kymbri
Kymbrie
Kymeisha
Kymiah
Kymiaha
Kymille
Kymion
Kymirra
Kymirriya
Kymis
Kymkecia
Kymlee
Kymmaya
Kymmeria
Kymon
Kymoni
Kymor
Kymora (0.01)
Kymorah
Kymoree
Kymori
Kymoria
Kymrie
Kymtraniece
Kymyrah
Kyn'yaja
Kyna
Kynacia
Kynade
Kynadee
Kynadi
Kynaiya
Kynala
Kynara
Kynasia
Kynayzya
Kynda
Kyndahl
Kyndal (0.05)
Kyndale
Kyndalinn

Kyndall (0.06)
Kyndel
Kyndele
Kyndell (0.01)
Kyndelle
Kyndl
Kyndle (0.01)
Kyndra (0.03)
Kyndrah
Kyndra-Lee
Kyndralee
Kyndslee
Kyndyll
Kyndzie
Kynedi
Kyneshia
Kynia
Kyniah
Kynijah
Kynlea
Kynlee (0.01)
Kynleigh
Kynley
Kynli
Kynlie
Kynna
Kynnade
Kynnadi
Kynnadie
Kynnady
Kynnan
Kynnedi (0.01)
Kynnedie
Kynnedy
Kynnidi
Kynnydy
Kynsie
Kynslee
Kynslei
Kynsley
Kynyk
Kynzee
Kynzey
Kynzi
Kynzie
Kynzley
Kyocha
Kyoko
Kyomi
Kyona
Kyondalyss
Kyondra
Kyonna

Kyori
Kyra (0.75)
Kyra Angela
Kyra Eliabeth
Kyrae
Kyrah (0.04)
Kyraha
Kyraih
Kyra-Jade
Kyra-Kay
Kyralee
Kyra-Leigh
Kyralia
Kyra-Lynn
Kyran (0.01)
Kyranyiah
Kyra-Suki
Kyre
Kyrea
Kyree
Kyreen
Kyreena
Kyrell
Kyren
Kyrena-Isabella
Kyrene
Kyreon
Kyrha
Kyri
Kyria (0.01)
Kyriae
Kyriah
Kyriaki
Kyriana
Kyriandra
Kyri-Ann
Kyrianna
Kyrie (0.02)
Kyrieeleison
Kyrielle
Kyrie-Mae
Kyrien
Kyrieon
Kyrie-Saria
Kyrin
Kyrina
Kyrinne
Kyrn
Kyrra
Kyrrah
Kyrrapearl
Kyrriah
Kyrrin

Kyrsta
Kyrstan
Kyrsten (0.02)
Kyrstin (0.02)
Kyrstyn
Kysee
Kysha
Kyshanna
Kyshauna
Kyshia
Kyshunn
Kysia
Kyslian
Kyson
Kyssira
Kytaja
Kytana
Kyteara
Kyterreian
Kytianna
Kytierya
Kytilin
Kytlyn
Kytonia
Kytt
Kyu
Kyungmi
Kyungmin
Kyurari
Kyveli
Kyya
Kyyonnah
Kyzareirre
Kyzha
Kyzhaira
Kyzira
Kzariah
Kzena

~ L ~

L' Sanlia
L'adia
L'eslie
L'kai
L'larry
L'naya
L'niyah
L'nyah
L'oren
L'raina
L'rhya

L'shaiylah
L'shiylah
L'siri
L'vena
L'yonna
L'zariah
La
Lá
La Chaja
La Chona
La Erika
La Hira
La Jae
Lá Karié Onna
La Kayla
La Kia
La Kya
La La
La Maya
La Meya
La Miracle
La Miya
La Naeh
La Najaha
La Nessa
La Neyah
La Nica
Lá Niya
La Niyah
La Nyah
La Quera
La Rin
La Sha Niqua
La Shayla
La Shea
La Tasia
La'airel
La'airy
La'aisa
La'aja
La'ajah
La'ashiana
La'asia
La'asisa
La'auna
La'breeia
La'bresha
La'brianna
La'briya
La'candrace
La'caria
La'carol
La'cary

| | | | | | | |
|---|---|---|---|---|---|---|
| La'chae | La'kala | La'myra | La'princia | La'teeyanha | Labriea | Lacyie |
| La'chance | La'kasja | La'myyah | La'qasia | La'teria | Labriya | Lacyn |
| La'chanta | La'kaya | La'na | La'qavia | La'terrica | Labrya | Lacynthia |
| La'charia | La'kayla | La'nae | La'quarious | La'tia | Lacaisha | Ladaeja |
| La'chasity | La'kaylah | La'nae'ja | La'quasia | La'tianna | Lacassia | Ladaijá |
| La'chay | La'kaylen | La'naesha | La'quincia | La'tikah | Lacaya | Ladaijah |
| La'chayre | La'keashia | La'nai | La'rae | La'tisha | Lacayla | Ladaisha |
| La'chelsea | La'keirra | La'naire | La'raeya | La'tonjua | Lace | Ladaiya |
| La'cher | La'keisha | La'naisa | La'ray | La'toria | Lacea | Ladaja |
| La'cheryl | La'kendra | La'naiya | La'rayah | La'toya | Lacee (0.01) | Ladajae |
| La'chevy | La'kenya | La'naiyah | La'riah | La'treasia | Lacee-Ann | Ladajah |
| La'chrisha | La'keria | La'naja | La'riana | La'treasure | Lacefield | Ladamiana |
| La'christian | La'keriana | La'najah | La'roxie | La'trice | Lacei | Ladan |
| La'chyna | La'kerria | La'naria | La'ryia | La'trina | Lacelia | Ladariuna |
| La'ciera | La'kesha | La'narvia | La'ryjai | La'tyra | Lacesia | Ladarra |
| La'coria | La'kevia | La'nasha | La'sepia | La'vara | Lacette | Ladasha |
| La'coya | La'keya | La'nasia | La'shae | La'vaya | Lacey (0.28) | Ladashia |
| La'crisa | La'khya | La'nasiah | La'shaela | La'veah Alaz | Lacey Allana | Ladava |
| La'daiya | La'kia | La'nautia | La'shai | La'veda | Lacey Ann | Ladavia |
| La'daja | La'kira | La'nautica | La'shanda | La'vesha | Lacey Bethzabet | Ladaya |
| La'dajah | La'kiriya | La'navia | La'shanti | La'vie | Laceylynn | Ladaysha |
| La'dariaja | La'kiya | La'naya | La'shauna | La'vondra | Laceyrae | Ladayshea |
| La'dariona | La'kiyah | La'nayah | La'shawn | La'vondria | Lache | Ladayshia |
| La'dasha | La'kori | La'nayjia | La'shawna | La'vone | Laché | Ladaysia |
| La'dasia | La'kresha | La'naysha | La'shay | La'vonna | Lachelle | Ladazia |
| La'dasmeonnia | La'kya | La'naysia | La'shaya | La'zadia | Lacheryl | Ladea |
| La'davia | La'kycha | La'nazah | La'shea | La'zaia | Lachionna | Ladeana |
| La'daviyah | La'kye | La'nee | La'shedria | La'zaria | Lachlaine | Ladeena |
| La'dawn | La'kyia | La'nehya | La'shinena | La'zariah | Lachlan | Ladeja |
| La'dayshia | La'kyla | La'neice | La'shiya | La'zariana | Lachlyn | Ladelle |
| La'dazia | La'kyra | La'neicia | La'shonda | La'zariyah | Lachristia | Laderia |
| La'dazya | La'kyrah | La'nhia | La'shondra | La'zeria | Lachya | Laderica |
| La'dedra | La'la | La'nia | La'shonti | Laaibah | Laci (0.21) | Ladestany |
| La'dedria | La'lah | La'niah |   Zanberia | Laalah | Lacia | Ladestiny |
| La'deja | La'magiana | La'niaya | La'shyia | Laamore | Laciann | Ladia |
| La'desha | La'maiya | La'niayeh | La'shyrah | Laangel | Lacianne | Ladicea |
| La'diamond | La'mareiana | La'nieya | La'sija | Laáreshia | Lacie (0.11) | Ladijjsha |
| La'drea | La'mariya | La'niiah | La'sjiah | Laarionna | Lacie Anna | Ladis |
| La'duntaun | La'maryen | Ladna | La'sonja | Laarni Lorraine | Lacie Raelene | Ladna |
| La'dysha | La'maya | La'nina | La'taja | Laashanti | Lacie-Lynn | Ladonica |
| La'erica | La'meka | La'niqua | La'tana | Laasia | Lacienna | Ladonna |
| La'erykah | La'mera | La'nisha | La'taria | Laasya | Lacilyn | Ladonnie |
| La'faye | La'metriah | La'nissa | La'tasha | Labecca | Lacimae | Ladonya |
| La'hiya | La'meyah | La'niva | La'tashia | Labella | Lacina | Ladoria |
| La'jade | La'mia | La'niya (0.01) | La'tashuja | Labelle | Lacoda | Ladrea |
| La'jaedan | La'miah | La'niyah (0.01) | La'tasia | Labeverly | Lacora | Ladrita |
| La'jaya | La'miracle | La'niyha | La'tasija | Labiba | Lacoria | Lady |
| La'jayceah | La'miria | La'nya (0.01) | La'tavia | Laboni | Lacorya | Lady Annasia |
| La'jazlyn | La'mya (0.01) | La'nyah | La'tavionnia | Labradyn | Lacoya | Lady Desteny |
| La'jhada | La'myah | La'nyia | La'taviyah | Labranjernekia | Lacquelyn | Lady Kezia |
| La'juria | La'mycah | La'nysha | La'tay | Labraya | Lacretia | Lady Willow |
| La'kahya | La'myia | La'paris | La'tayveana | Labre'a | Lacshana | Lady-Carol |
| La'kaila | La'myka | La'preciaus | La'tayvia | Labria | Lacy (0.09) | Ladymar |

| | | | | | | |
|---|---|---|---|---|---|---|
| Lae Lonnie | Lahkiyah | Lailanee | Lajadda | Lakeithia | Lakki-Marie | Lali |
| Lae'lani | Lahmya | Lailani (0.01) | Lajae | Lakeiya | Lakkyn | Lalia |
| Lae'llani | Lahna (0.01) | Lailany | Lajai'ah | Lakeiyah | Laklyn | Laliah |
| Laeh | Lahna Mae | Lailee | Lajaida | Lakeland | Laklynn | Lalianna |
| Laekyn | Lahney | Lailee-Onee | Lajala | Lakelin | Lakoda | Lalicea |
| Lael (0.01) | Lahrae | Laileh | Lajanna | Lakely | Lakota (0.02) | Laliftu |
| Laela (0.02) | Lahree | Laileigh | Lajay | Lakelyn (0.01) | Lakotah | Lalina |
| Laelah | Lahsa | Laileionna | Lajaya | Lakelynn | Lakourtney | Lalique |
| Laelana | Lahtia | Lailena | Lajayah | Laken (0.05) | Lakresha | Lalisha |
| Laelani | Lahyla | Lailennie | Lajayda | Lakencya | Lakria | Lalita |
| Laelanni | Lai | Lailiana | Lajayla | Lakendall | Lakrissa | Laliyah |
| Laelany | Lai'la | Lailie | Lajeris | Lakendra | Lakshitha | Lalla |
| Laelia | Lai'una | Lailissa | Lajerrica | Lakendrah | Lakshmi (0.01) | Lalla Sara |
| Laelie | Lai'yanah | Lailla | Lajhai | Lakendria | Lakshmimanasa | Lallah |
| Laella | Laia | Lailoni | Lajuan | Lakenley | Lakshpreet | Lallesca |
| Laelonnie | Laiah | Lailonie | Lajyria | Lakenndaurra | Lakshya | Lally |
| Laena | Laiani | Lailonnie | Lakaia | Seaheir | Laksmi | Lalohni |
| Laenie | Laiauna | Lailyana | Lakaila | Lakenya (0.01) | Lakuri | Lalon |
| Laethitia | Laiba (0.01) | Lailye | Lakaira | Lakenzie | Lakurioua | Lalona |
| Laethycia | Laice | Lailyn | Lakaiya | Lakeria (0.01) | Lakwanta | Laloni |
| Laetia | Laicha | Lailynne | Lakalian | Lakerra | Lakya | Lalonie |
| Laeticia (0.02) | Laicie | Laima | Lakalle | Lakesha | Lakyah | Lalou |
| Laëtitia | Laida | Laimah | Lakariah | Lakeshia | Lakyelah | Laly Marie |
| Laetitia (0.03) | Laiden | Lain | Lakashia | Laketrice | Lakyeriana | Lama (0.01) |
| Laetitia Wabana | Laiela | Laina (0.03) | Lakasia | Lakeva | Lakyha | Lamai |
| Laeyla | Laienose | Laine (0.03) | Lakata | Lakevia | Lakyia | Lamaiah |
| Laeza Sarah | Laighla | Lainee (0.01) | Lakaura | Lakeya | Lakyla | Lamaiya |
| Lafae | Laighton | Laineigh | Lakauree | Lakeyah | Lakylah | Lamaja |
| Lafaye | Laiha | Lainelle | Lakaya | Lakeyia | Lakylon | Lamajai |
| Lafayette | Laihl | Lainey (0.15) | Lakayah | Lakeysha | Lakyn (0.01) | Lamancia |
| Lafia | Laijia | Lainey Jo | Lakaycie | Lakeysia | Lakynn | Lamar |
| Lafieanna | Laika (0.01) | Laingley | Lakayiah | Lakhia | Lakyra (0.01) | Lamara |
| Lagan | Laikan | Laini | Lakayla (0.02) | Lakia | Lakyrah | Lamaranna |
| Lagar | Laiken (0.02) | Lainie (0.01) | Lakaylah | Lakiah | Lakyria | Lamarche Adam |
| Lagena | Laikin | Lainise | Lakaylyne | Lakiara | Lala Malak | Lamarea |
| Lagina | Laiklyn | Lainne | Lakaysha | Lakicia | Lala'isa | Lamareana |
| Lagrace | Laikyn (0.01) | Lainnie | Lakayzha | Lakiera | Lalaeha | Lamari |
| Lah'niiah | Laila (0.51) | Lainny | Lake | Lakiesha | Lalah | Lamaria (0.01) |
| Lahaela | Laila Aaliyah | Lainy | Lake'ysha | Lakieya | Lalaina | Lamariah |
| Lahaila | Laila Bint A | Laionia | Lakea | Lakiia | Lalani | Lamariana |
| Lahaina | Laila Chri | Laira | Lakecha | Lakijah' | Lalania | Lamarie |
| Lahana | Laila Symone | Laisa | Lakecia | Lakin (0.02) | Lalany | Lamariea |
| Lahanna | Lailaa | Laisha (0.04) | Lakedra | Lakina | Lalayna | Lamarionna |
| Laharah | Laila-Ann | Laishauna | Lakeesha | Lakinzie | Lalayne | Lamariya |
| Lahari | Laila-Elisa | Laissa | Lakeeyah | Lakira | Laleahyna | Lamariyah |
| Laharmony | Lai-Lah | Laitha | Lakeia | Lakiriyah | Laleen | Lamarja |
| Lahayla | Lailah (0.05) | Laithia | Lakeicia | Lakish | Laleigh | Lamarra |
| Lahee | Lailaha | Laiya | Lakeiea | Lakisha | Laleinia | Lamarrea |
| Laheiress | Lailah-Sofia | Laiyah | Lakeija | Lakita | Lalelei | Lamarreya |
| Lahela | Laila-Marie | Laiyhanna | Lakeila | Lakiya | Lalena | Lamarria |
| Lahiana | Lailamease | Laiyla | Lakeilla | Lakiyah | Lalesia | Lamarya |
| Lahib | Laila-Mia | Laiza | Lakeiria | Lakiyya | Laleya | Lamaryah |
| Lahkia | Lailana | Lajada | Lakeisha (0.01) | Lakken | Lalhmangaihi | Lamaryana |

| | | | | | | |
|---|---|---|---|---|---|---|
| Lamasajor | Lamysia | Lancy | Laniaja | Lanyla | Laraiha | Larissa Elie |
| Lamauria | Lan | Landeigh | Lani-Ann | Lanyra | Laraine | Larissah |
| Lamay | Lana *(0.26)* | Landen | Laniasha | Lanysia | Laraiyah | Larita |
| Lamaya | Lana Isabelle Th | Landi | Laniaya | Lanyyah | Laralee | Laritta |
| Lamayah | Lana Whitney | Landieliz | Lanice | Laoise | Laralyn | Laritza |
| Lamayha | Lanadja | Landina | Lanicia | Laoiseach | Laramie | Larixsa |
| Lamea | Lanae *(0.01)* | Landis | Lanie *(0.06)* | Laonna | Laranesha | Larixza |
| Lameana | Lanaea | Landon *(0.01)* | Lanieca | Laora | Laraney | Lariya |
| Lamecia | Lanaejah | Landrea | Laniece | La-Osha | Larato | Lariyah |
| Lameeka | La-Naesha | Landree *(0.01)* | Laniée | Laparis | Laravious | Lariyia |
| Lameerah | Lanagsha | Landrey | Lanielle | Lapeachtra | Laray | Lark |
| Lamees | Lanah *(0.01)* | Landri | Laniese | Lapeno | Laraya | Larkaja |
| Lameisha | Lanai *(0.01)* | Landria | Lanija | Laperrio | Larayna | Larke |
| Lameka | Lanaia | Landrie | Lanijah | Laporsha | Laraynah | Larken |
| Lameria | Lanaija | Landrigan | Lanijia | Laportia | Larealeigh | Larkin *(0.01)* |
| Lamerria | Lanaijah | Landry *(0.02)* | Lanika | Lapraya | Lareb | Larkyn *(0.01)* |
| Lamesha | Lanaisha | Landsey | Lanina | Laprecious | Laree | Larnesia |
| Lameshia | Lanaiya | Landy | Laninya | La-Precious | Lareece | Larochel |
| Lametria | Lanaiyah | Landyn *(0.01)* | Lanique | Lapree | Lareesa | Laronda |
| Lamia *(0.01)* | Lanaizona | Lane *(0.03)* | Lanisa | Laprincia | Lareese | Laronica |
| Lamiah *(0.01)* | Lanaja | Lanea | Lanise | Lapromyce | Larehna | Larosa |
| Lamiaya | Lanajah | Laneah | Lanisha | Laqaya | Lareija-Anne | Laroyia |
| Lamicah | Lanajha | La-Neasia | Lanissa | Laquanda | Lareika | Larra |
| Lamicha | Lanajia | Laneatra | Lanita | Laquasha | Lareily | Larrabee |
| Lamicheal | Lanajie | Lanecia | La-Niya | Laquaun | Lareina *(0.01)* | Larrae |
| Lamika | Lanajna | Lanee *(0.01)* | Laniya *(0.03)* | Laquavia | Lareissia | Larraeah |
| Lamikeka | Lanakila | Laneena | Laniyah *(0.04)* | Laquay | Larell | Larrah |
| Lamilah | Lanalea | Laneese | Laniyah Rheona | Laqueca | Laren | Larraine |
| Lamilliyona | Lana-Marie | Laneetrice | Laniyce | Laqueendra | Larena | Larrann |
| Lamira | Lan-Anh | Laneice | Laniyha | Laqueesha | Larencia | Lar-Rasia |
| Lamiracle | Lanardrea- | La-Neice | Lanna *(0.01)* | Laqueireon | Larenz | Larraye |
| Lamirrah | Arijah | Laneisha | Lannae | Laquesha | Lareona | Larree |
| Lamis | Lanaria | Laneiya | Lannah | Laquicia | Laresa | Larresha |
| Lamita | Lana-Rose | Laneleigh | Lannai | Laquinya | Laressa | Larriauna |
| Lamiya *(0.01)* | Lanarra | Lanema | Lannee | Laquisha | Laressia | Larrica |
| Lamiyah *(0.01)* | Lana-Salam- | Lanera | Lanni | Laquita | Lareyna | Larrin |
| Lamiyranna | Amil | Lanesha | Lannie | Laquitta | Largo | Larrinn |
| Lammii | Lanasha | La-Nesha | Lannisha | Laquoia | Larha | Larriondra |
| Lamoni | Lanashia | Lanessa | Lanniyah | Laquwayj | Larhiyyah | Larrionna |
| Lamonica | Lanasia *(0.01)* | Lanessha | Lanora | Lar | Laria | Larrisa |
| Lamonie | Lanasiah | Lanette | Lantvia | Lar'nesia | Lariah *(0.01)* | Larrisha |
| Lamont | Lanaura | Laney *(0.21)* | Lanvy | Lar'ryona | Lariana | Larrissa |
| Lamontika | Lanay | Laneya | Lany'a | Lara *(0.13)* | Larianna | Larriya |
| Lamonxiaron | Lanaya *(0.01)* | Lange | La-Nya | Lara Gabrielle | Lariaya | Larry |
| Lamy | Lanayah | Langely | Lanya *(0.01)* | Lara Sofia | Larica | Larry'asia |
| Lamyá | Lanayea | Langleigh | La-Nyaa | Lara-Aude | Laricha | Larryn |
| Lamya *(0.03)* | Lanayga | Langley *(0.01)* | Lanyah *(0.01)* | Larabeth | Lariea | Larrysa |
| Lamyah | Lanayia | Langston | Lanyhia | Larae *(0.01)* | Larinda | Larsen |
| Lamyaih | Lanaysia | Lani *(0.03)* | Lanyi | Larae'ya | Laris | Larson |
| Lamyia *(0.01)* | Lanazia | Lani'ah | Lanyia *(0.01)* | Larah | Larisa *(0.02)* | Laryah |
| Lamyra | Lanazia Marie | Lania *(0.02)* | Lanyiah | Larai | Larisha | Laryen |
| Lamyria | Lanazzja | Laniaah | Lanyijah | Laraib | Lariss | Laryia |
| Lamyrical | Lance | Laniah *(0.01)* | Lanyjah | Laraih | Larissa *(0.18)* | Laryiah |

| | | | | | | |
|---|---|---|---|---|---|---|
| Laryn | Lashell | Latara | Latifa | Latyana | Laurance | Laurenza |
| Larysa | Lashelle | Lataricka | Latifah | Latyirah | Laura-Ndaye | Lauretta |
| Laryssa *(0.01)* | Lashema | Latasha *(0.01)* | Latilya | Latyra | Laurane *(0.01)* | Laurette |
| Laryssa Isabell | Lashem- | Latashia | Latina *(0.01)* | Latyrieana | Lauranie | Laurha |
| Lasadia | Shamayen | Latasia *(0.01)* | Latisha *(0.01)* | Latyseau | Laurann | Lauri |
| Lasahra | Lashena | Latatianna | Latishia | Laubental | Lauranna | Lauri'ann |
| Lasaia | Lasheree | Latatyana | Latisia | Laudia | Lauranne *(0.01)* | Lauria |
| Lasallie | Lashia | Lataujanese | Latisia Ivanna | Laudy | Laurasia | Lauriana |
| Lasandra | Lashiontea | Lataun | Latitia | Lauea | Laura-Sofia | Laurianahi |
| Lasannies | Lashira | Latavea | Lativia | Laueriana | Laure *(0.01)* | Lauriane *(0.03)* |
| Lasara | Lashiya | Latavia *(0.02)* | Latiya | Laughlin | Laure Andree | Laurianna |
| Lasariah | Lashlee | Lataviona | Latiyana | Launa *(0.01)* | Laure Briana | Laurianne |
| Lasaunja | Lashley | Latavya | Latomyala | Launa-Marie | Laure-Anne | *(0.07)* |
| Laschell | Lashon | Latawna | Latona | Laundriann | Laureanne | Laurianne Alice |
| Lasha | Lashona | Latay | Latondress | Launie | Laureen | Lauribel |
| Lashá | Lashonda *(0.01)* | Lataya | Latonya | Launiysha | Laurel *(0.12)* | Lauribeth |
| Lashae *(0.01)* | Lashondra | La-Tayah | Latoria *(0.01)* | Lauphlyn | Laurel Lynn | Lauric |
| Lashai | Lashondria | Latayah | Latorian | Laur'a | Scarlett | Lauricha |
| Lashana | Lashonti | Lataye | Latoriania | Laura *(0.99)* | Laurel Victoria | Laurie *(0.21)* |
| Lashanda | Lashora | Latayesia | Latorie | Laura Anne | Laureli | Laurie Ann |
| Lashanna | Lashuna | Latayia | Latorria | Laura Ashley | Laurelia | Laurie Eve |
| Lashanta | Lashundra | Lataysha | Latorya | Laura Beth | Laurelie | Laurie Gabrielle |
| Lashante | Lashya | Lataysia | Latosha | Laura Christine | Laurelin | Laurie M |
| La-Shanté | Lashyia | Latayvia | Latoya *(0.01)* | Laura Dawn | Laureline | Laurie-Ange |
| Lashanté | Lashyiah | Latazhia | Latoz'janae | Laura Elena | Laurell | Laurie-Ann |
| Lashantee | Lasiah | Late'ya | Latracia | Laura Rachel | Laurelle | *(0.01)* |
| Lashanti *(0.01)* | Lasina | Lateasa | Latravia | Laura-Ann | Laurellee | Laurieann |
| Lashara | Lasiyah | Lateaya | Latrea | Laura-Edna | Laurely | Laurie-Anne |
| Lashari | Laskye | Latecia | Latrece | Lauraetta | Laurelye | *(0.02)* |
| Lasharia | Lasonja | Lateesh | Latreese | Laura-Florence | Laurelynn | Laurie-Claude |
| Lashaun | Lasonya | Lateesha | Latrel | Laura-Gabrielle | Lauren *(4.23)* | Laurie-Eve |
| Lashauna | Lassie | Latefee | Latrese | Laura-Gisele | Lauren Ashley | Laurie-Jade |
| Lashaundra | Lastacia | Latehya | Latressa | Laura-Grac | Lauren Clay | Laurie-Jeanne |
| Lashaunta | Lastarr | Lateisha | Latresse | Laurah | Lauren Evelyn | Lauriel |
| Lashaunti | Lastarria | Laterean | Latrevia | Lauraine | Lauren Frances | Laurielle |
| Lashauta | Lastenia | Lateria | Latrice *(0.02)* | Laura-Kate | Lauren Mae | Laurielle Kelly |
| Lashavia | Lastundierra | Laterica | Latricia | Laural | Laurena-Lamia | Laurie-Maude |
| Lashawn | Lasya | Laterra | Latrina | Laura-Lee | Lauren- | Laurie-Pier |
| Lashawna | Lasyah | Laterrerica | Latrinitie | Lauralee | Alessandra | Laurieve |
| Lashawnda | Lataejah | Laterrica | Latrinity | Laurenca | Laurence *(0.23)* | Laurin |
| Lashawndra | Lataevia | Latesha | Latris | Lauraleigh | Laurence- | Laurine |
| Lashawnee | Latagia | Latessa | Latrisha | Laurali | Noemie | Laurisha |
| Lashawnte | Latahvia | Latevia | Latrisha Eve | Lauralie *(0.01)* | Laurencia | Laurissa |
| Lashawnti | Latailya | Lathan | Phyllis | Lauraline | Laurene | Laurita |
| Lashay *(0.01)* | Lataiya | Lathika | Latristan | Lauralou | Lauren-Kate | Lauritza |
| Lashaya | Latajah | Lati | Latrivia | Lauraly | Lauren-Mar | Laurnea |
| Lashayla *(0.01)* | Latajha | Latia *(0.01)* | Latroya | Lauralye | Laurenne | Laurneidj |
| Lashayna | Lataliya | Latiah | Latsanyvone | Lauralyn | Lauren-Paris | Laurneshia |
| Lashayne | Latanisha | Latiana | Lattie | Laura-Lynn | Laurens Nicole | Laurren |
| Lashe | Latanya | Latianna | Lattu | Laura-Maude | Laurensia | Laurrie |
| Lasheavia | Latanya Leann | Laticia | La-Tya | Lauramay | Laurent | Laury *(0.02)* |
| Lasheena | Latanza | Latiera | Latyah | Lauran | Laurenys | Laury Ann |
| La-Shell | Lataoya | Latiesha | Latyalei | Laurana | | |

| | | | | | | |
|---|---|---|---|---|---|---|
| Laury Gabrielle Mya | La-Vera | Layal (0.01) | Laylette | Lazayda | Le'maya | Leaf |
| Lauryane | Lavera | Layalapri | Layli | Lazharia | Le'mya | Leaffa |
| Laury-Ann (0.01) | Laverda | Layalee-Jamila | Laylia | Lazia | Le'nadia | Lea-Frederique |
| Lauryann | Laverna | Layali | Layliani | Laziah | Le'naé | Leagh |
| Laury-Anne | Laverne | Layan (0.01) | Laylin | Lazirah | Le'naja | Leagha |
| Lauryanne | Laverta | Layana | Laylionna | Laziya | Le'nasia | Léah |
| Laurye | Laveya | Layanah | Laylla | Lazriah | Le'nasijan | Leah (2.34) |
| Lauryel | Laveyia | Lay-Ann | Layloni | Lazuli | Le'naya | Leah Kim |
| Laury-Kate | Laveyndar | Layanna | Laylonie | Le | Le'neiya | Leah Marie |
| Lauryl | Lavianna | Layanne | Laylou | Le Ana | Le'niesha | Leah Svetlana |
| Lauryn (0.27) | Lavie Joyce | Layara | Laymir | Le Andra | Le'niyah | Leaha |
| Lauryne | Lavilaine | Layce | Layna (0.04) | Le Ann | Le'niyyah | Leaha Loree |
| Laurynn | Lavilla | Laycee (0.01) | Laynah | Le Asia | Le'nya | Leahana |
| Lauryon | Lavin | Layci | Laynai | Lé Jend | Le'nyia | Leahanna |
| Lauryssa | Lavina (0.01) | Laycie | Layne (0.04) | Le Quest | Le'nyja | Leahanne |
| Laury-Virginie | Lavinia | Laydan | Laynee (0.02) | Le Ran | Le'ondria | Leah-Blanche |
| Lausane | Lavinnya | Laydi | Laynera | Le Ynia | Le'onie | Leah-Brooke |
| Lausanne | Laviona | Layel | Layney | Le'aani | Le'onna | Leaheila |
| Lauvia | Lavish | Layeska | Layni (0.01) | Le'aija | Le'quest | Leah-Kaye |
| Lava | Laviyah | Layia | Laynie (0.03) | Le'aira | Le'riah | Leahmel |
| Lavada | Lavleen | Layila | Laynie-May | Le'aisha | Le'roysha | Leahn |
| Lavaeh | Lavon | Layine | Layniyahra | Le'aisya | Le'shay | Leahna |
| Lavanah | Lavonda | Layionna | Laynne | Le'ajah | Le'tasia-Soriyah | Leahne |
| Lavance | Lavoni | Laykan | Laynnie | Le'ana | Le'teisha | Leahnette |
| Lavanda | Lavonna | Layke | Laynyana | Le'andra | Le'trel | Leahnna |
| Lavander | Lavonndra | Layken (0.01) | Layohne | Le'andrea | Le'vayah | Leah-Sjmone |
| Lavaniya | Lavonne | Laykin | Layoncye | Le'aniah | Le'yona | Leaijah |
| Lavanna | Lavontane | Layklei | Layonia | Le'anna | Le'yonna | Leailany |
| Lavannah | Lavonya | Laykyn | Layonna | Le'anna-Jean | Le'zaria | Leaira |
| Lavanya | Lavonye | Layla (1.32) | Layra | Le'anni | Le'zariya | Leairreonna |
| Lavarah | Lavrielle | Layla Anne | Laysa | Le'aona | Le'ziyahe | Leairya |
| Lavarea | Lawanda | Laylaa | Laysha (0.01) | Le'ara | Leá | Leaisa |
| Lavaria | Lawhitley | Layla-Grace | Laytissia | Le'asia (0.01) | Léa | Leaja |
| Lavariana | Lawina | Layla-Grey | Layton | Le'audra | Lea (0.56) | Leajade |
| Lavariya | Lawna | Lay-Lah | Layvon | Le'auja | Lea Alena | Lea-Jade |
| Lavarrea | Lawonda | Laylah (0.05) | Layyana | Le'auna | Lea Emilia | Leajah |
| Lavasia | Lawren (0.01) | Laylaha | Layyin | Le'ayshia | Lea Isabelle | Lea-Jeanne |
| Lavasyah | Lawrence | Laylah-Rai | Layza | Le'aysia | Lea Maude | Leakim |
| Lavaughnica | Lawrencia | Layla-Jade | Lazadeah | Le'ayzia | Lea Pier | Lea-Kim |
| Lavauna | Lawrene | Layla-Kay | Lazaire | Le'azionna | Lea Rose | Leala (0.01) |
| Lavay | Lawrynn | Layla-Lyn | Lazalya | Le'brayah | Lea Shuni | Lealanie |
| Laváy | Lawshana | Layla-Mae | Lazandria | Le'bryana | Leaa | Lealanna |
| Lavechia | Lawson (0.01) | Laylana | Lazara | Le'dacia | Lea-Angelique | Lealany |
| Laveda | Laxia | Laylanee | Lazarea | Le'dream | Lea-Ann | Lealeanna |
| Laveeda | Laxmi | Laylani (0.01) | Lazaree | Le'jour | Leaann | Leama |
| Laveen | Lay La | Laylanie | Lazareia | Le'khya | Lea-Anna | Lea-Mai |
| Laveena | Lay On | Laylé | Lazareya | Le'kira | Leaanna | Lea-Marie |
| Lavelle | Lay'annia | Laylee | Lazaria (0.01) | Le'l | Leacadia | Lea-Maude (0.01) |
| Lavena | Laya (0.02) | Layleighona | Lazariah | Le'lah | Lea-Catherine | Lea-Maxime |
| Lavendar | Layaal | Layleiona | Lazarriyah | Le'lani | Leadya | Lean |
| Lavendar | Layaan | Layleisha | Lazashanay | Le'liana | Lea-Elizabeth | Leana (0.03) |
| Lavender (0.01) | Layah (0.01) | Laylen | La-Zaviona | Le'mahya | Leaette | Leana Renee |
| | Layahna | | Lazay | Le'maurie | Lea-Eve | |

Leanah
Leandra (0.04)
Leandrah
Leandre
Leandrea
Leandrea
  Tinahia
Léane
Leane (0.06)
Leanelies
Leaney
Leangel
Leangela
Leanh
Leanie
Léanie
Le-Ann
Leann (0.05)
Le-Anna
Leanna (0.12)
Leannah
Leannan
Leanndra
Léanne
Leanne (0.18)
Leanne Denise
Leannette
Leanni
Leannie
Leannka
Leanny
Leanora
Leansy
Leanté Nefertit
Leanuh
Leanye
Leanza
Leaoma
Lear
Leara
Learia
Learic
Lea-Rose (0.03)
Learose
Learra
Leasha
Leashansky
Leashia
Leasia (0.01)
Leasiah
Leasija
Lea-Sophie
Leasyjiah

Leatha
Leati
Leaticia
Leatisha
Leaton
Leatrice
Leattea
Leaun
Leaunna
Leaura
Leauyna
Leaveny
Leavesther
Leaya
Leayah
Leayja
Leaysia
Leazjah
Lebrianna
Lebron
Lechelle
Lechina
Lechrista
Lecia
Lecole
Lecy
Leda
Ledaea
Ledawn
Leddi
Ledia
Ledif
Ledis
Lediya
Ledrezia
Ledya
Ledynn
Lee (0.01)
Lee Ann
Lee Anna
Lee Naya
Lee Sandra
Lee Yannia
Lee'aijza
Lee'al
Lee'anna
Lee'annah
Lee'asia
Lee'shel
Lee'yah
Leea
Leeah (0.01)
Leeaha

Leeahnna
Leeaira
Lee-Amanda
Leeana (0.01)
Leeanah
Leeandra
Leeani
Leeanie
Lee-Ann (0.01)
Leeann (0.04)
Leeanna (0.03)
Lee-Anne
Leeanne (0.01)
Leeannette
Leeara
Leeasia
Leeauna
Leeaundra
Leeazia
Leechelle
Lee-Danté
Lee-Han
Leehe
Leehee
Leeia
Leeian
Leeidah
Leela (0.02)
Leelah
Leelai
Leelee
Leella
Leelo
Leeloo
Leelou
Lee-Loup
Leelynn
Leemauria
Leen (0.01)
Leena (0.05)
Leenah
Leenaja
Leena-Jose
Leeniah
Leeona
Leeonia
Leeor
Leeora
Leeosha
Leera
Leesa
Leesia

Leesly
Leesulee
Leeta
Leetia
Leetta
Leetzy
Leeva
Leevi
Leeya (0.01)
Leeyah (0.01)
Leeyanis
Leeyanna
Leeza
Leezshania
Le-Fei
Legacee
Legaceé
Legaci
Legacine
Legacy
Legend
Leggee-Ann
Legina
Legna
Leha
Lehana
Lehanett
Lehany
Leh-Azah
Leheimiah
Lehiret
Lehla
Lehna
Lehonor
Lehua
Lehyla
Lehyla-
  Cymonne
Lei
Lei'ashia
Lei'asya
Lei'la
Lei'lani
Lei'launi
Lei'loni
Leia (0.09)
Leia Anishka
Leia Brona
Leia Joy
Leia Rose
Leiactria
Leia-Eve
Leiah (0.01)

Leiahna
Leiajanay
Leialani
Leialoha
Leian
Leiana
Leianajoy
Leiann
Leianna (0.01)
Leianne
Leiannette
Leiara
Leiarah
Leiarra
Leiauna
Leiba
Leica
Leickah
Leida
Leidi
Leidy (0.01)
Leigh (0.02)
Leigh Ann
Leigh Anna
Leigh Anne
Leigh Anyaha
Leigha (0.07)
Leighady
Leighah-Rhei
Leighaja
Leighana
Leighandra
Leighandrea
Leigh-Ann
Leighann (0.01)
Leigh-Anna
Leighanna
  (0.01)
Leighanne
Leigh-Anne
Leighara
Leighasia
Leighavae
Leighden
Leighel
Leighla (0.01)
Leighla-Ann
Leighlanni
Leighley
Leighlin
Leighlyn
Leighlynn
Leighta

Leightesha
Leighton (0.01)
Leihlanie
Leijla
Leika
Leikle
Leila (0.37)
Leila Angel
Leila-Christine
Leilah (0.02)
Leilai
Leila-Levi
Leilana
Leiland
Lei-Lani
Leilani (0.25)
Leilanie (0.01)
Leilanikuuipo
Leilaniluz
Leilanni
Leilanny
Leilany (0.01)
Leilanys
Leila-Rose
Leilena
Leili
Leilia
Leiliam
Leiliana
Leilianis
Leilonee
Leiloni
Leiloni-
  Michelleg
Leilonnie
Leilou
Leily
Leilya
Leilyn
Leilynd
Leilynn
Leilynne
Leimarie
Leimy
Leina (0.01)
Leinaly
Leini
Leiona
Leiporshia
Leira
Leisa
Leisan
Leisel

Leisha
Leishah
Leishka
Leishla
Leisli
Leita
Leith
Leiticia
Leivi
Leiya
Leiyah
Lejay Marie
Lejla (0.01)
Lejon
Lekai
Lekaiah
Lekaiya
Lekam'ryn
Lekasha
Lekaylynne
Lekendra
Lekeri
Lekha
Lekhana
Lekia
Lekicha
Lekiesha
Leko
Lekseea
Leksi
Leksie
Lekysha
Lela (0.04)
Lela Rae
Lelah (0.01)
Lelaina
Leland
Lelani
Lelanie
Lelaquoy
Lele
Leleana
Lelia (0.02)
Lelian
Leliani
Lelienna
Lella
Lello
Leloni
Leloz
Lelu
Leluia
Lely

| | | | | | |
|---|---|---|---|---|---|
| Lelyana | Leneya | Leola | Leraysia | Leslik | Lettie | Lexie *(0.18)* |
| Lelyane | Leni *(0.01)* | Leomary | Lerena | Leslit | Letty | Lexie-Ann |
| Lelynd | Le-Nia | Leomy | Leresa | Leslly | Lettzy | Lexiee |
| Lema | Lenia | Leon | Leriah | Lesly *(0.13)* | Letzy | Lexie-Jean |
| Lemareae | Leniah | Leon'dra | Lerin | Leslye | Leuna | Lexii |
| Lemaya | Leniaya | Leona *(0.06)* | Lerise | Leslyie | Leunamme | Lexi-Lyn |
| Lemdith | Lenice | Leonai | Lerissa | Leslyn | Leura | Lexi-Lynn |
| Lemman | Lenigha | Leonarda | Leroya | Leslynn | Levaeh | Lexine |
| Lemonik | Lenijah | Leonary | Leryah | Lesna | Levana | Lexington *(0.01)* |
| Lemorria | Leni-Jeanette | Leonaunna | Leryka | Lessa | Levanah | Lexis *(0.06)* |
| Lemya | Lenikah | Leonda | Les'shayla | Lessie | Levanee | Lexiss |
| Lemyah | Lenina | Leondra *(0.01)* | Lesa | Lessle | Levani | Lexly |
| Lemyiah | Lenique | Leondria | Lesaria | Lesslee | Levanna | Lexmarie |
| Len | Lenise | Leone | Lescia | Lessley | Leven | Lexos |
| Lena *(0.26)* | Lenisse | Leonee | Lesdy | Lesslie | Leverne | Lexsey |
| Lena Eutrula | Lenita | Leonela *(0.01)* | Leselerne | Lessly | Levi | Lexsis |
| Lena Marie | Leniya | Leonelly's | Lesette | Lestajah | Leviah | Lexsy |
| Lenae | Lenka | Leonetra | Lesha | Lestaria | Levie | Lextyn |
| Lenai | Lenna | Leong | Leshai | Lestie | Levin | Lexus *(0.08)* |
| Lenaia | Lennah | Leoni | Leshal | Lestreonna | Levina | Lexuz |
| Lenaiah | Lennan | Leonica | Leshaunik | Lesunyah- | Levis | Lexxi |
| Lenaj | Lenna-Rose | Léonie | Donnashia | Kaylah | Leviticus | Lexxie |
| Lenaja | Lennasia | Leonie *(0.07)* | Leshay | Lesvia | Levitikus | Lexxus *(0.01)* |
| Lenajah | Lennaya | Leonila | Leshaye | Leta | Levity | Lexxy |
| Lenajia | Lenneisha | Leonise | Leshayla | Letalia | Levy | Lexy *(0.04)* |
| Lenali | Lennell | Leonita | Leshayne | Letavia | Lewis | Lexya |
| Lenamarie | Lenni | Leonna *(0.01)* | Leshe | Letayla | Lewisa | Lexye |
| Lenanya | Lenniah | Leonnah | Leshea | Letaysia | Lewneil | Lexyee |
| Lenasia | Lennice | Leonnett | Lesheena | Letcely | Lex | Lexyn |
| Lenaya *(0.01)* | Lennisha | Leonnie | Leshelle | Leteisha | Lexa *(0.02)* | Lexyne |
| Lenayah | Lennon *(0.01)* | Leonor | Leshia | Letha | Lexah | Lexynton |
| Lenaye | Lennox | Leonora *(0.01)* | Lesia | Lethia | Lexana | Lexys |
| Lenayha | Lenny | Leonorah | Lesianne Ilie | Lethicia | Lexandra | Lexysmarie |
| Lenayjah | Lennyia | Leony | Lesile | Lethrenn | Lexane | Lexzary |
| Lency | Lennys | Leonye | Lesiya | Lethycia | Lexani | Lexzee |
| Lency Debora | Lenora *(0.01)* | Leopoldine | Lesl | Lethyl | Lexanie | Lexzis |
| Lendina | Lenore *(0.01)* | Leora *(0.01)* | Les-Lee | Lethzy | Lexanne | Leya *(0.01)* |
| Lendsay | Lenoria | Leorah | Leslee *(0.01)* | Leti | Lexanny | Leyah *(0.01)* |
| Lendsey | Lenox | Leósha | Leslee-Ayne | Letica | Lexany | Leyana |
| Lendsy | Lensey | Le-Oshe | Lesleigh | Leticia *(0.09)* | Lexas | Leyanda |
| Lene | Lensie | Leota | Lesley *(0.07)* | Leticia Taina | Lexee *(0.01)* | Leyandra |
| Lené | Lensie Allyah | Leotra | Lesleyann | Leticya | Lexeni | Leyanie |
| Lenea | Lensley | Leovette | Lesleygail | Letisha | Lexey | Leyanna |
| Leneah | Lentoria | Leozha | Lesli *(0.03)* | Letisia | Lexheille | Leyannah |
| Leneáh | Leny | Lepeka | Lesli Rosalin | Letissia | Lexi *(0.33)* | Leyasa |
| Lenease | Lenya | Lepha | Lesliany | Letitia | Lexi Jane | Leyaunna |
| Lenece | Lenyiah | Leprecious | Leslie *(1.55)* | Letizia | Lexia *(0.01)* | Leyda |
| Lenecia | Lenzi | Lepreya | Leslie Alison | Letoya | Lexiana | Leydalis |
| Lenee | Lenzie *(0.01)* | Leqa'nette | Leslie Anabeth | Letreese | Lexiane | Leyden |
| Lenejah | Lenzy | Lequayla | Leslieann | Letricia | Lexiann | Leydi *(0.01)* |
| Lenell | Leo | Lequlia | Leslie-Anne | Letsy | Lexi-Anna | Leydis |
| Lenesha | Leoany | Lera | Leslie-Mae | Letti | Lexianna | Leydith |
| Lenetta | Leocadia | Lerah | Lesliet | Letticia | Lexibella | Leydl |

| | | | | | | |
|---|---|---|---|---|---|---|
| Leydy | Liabella | Libbi | Lielit | Lileiny | Lilikoi | Lillianah |
| Leyi | Liadh | Libbie (0.01) | Liella | Liley | Lili-Mai | Lillian-Alexis |
| Leyla (0.07) | Liah (0.01) | Libby (0.14) | Lielou | Lili (0.04) | Lili-Marguerite | Lillian-Dawn |
| Leyla Rebecca | Liahna | Libby Ann | Lielt | Lili Ann | Lili-Marie | Lilliane |
| Leylah | Liajia | Libby-Kate | Lien | Lili Rose | Lili-Maude | Lillian-Faith |
| Leylani | Liakadja | Libby-Lu | Liena | Lilia (0.08) | Lili-May | Lillian-Mai |
| Leylanie | Lialah | Libee | Lienna | Lilia Martha | Lilimay | Lillian-Marie |
| Leylannie | Lialisse | Libertea | Liepa | Lilia-Feriel | Lilin | Lilliann (0.01) |
| Leylany | Liallieyanna | Libertee Ann | Lierra | Liliah | Liliokolany | Lillianna (0.06) |
| Leyle-Ann | Liam | Liberti | Liesbeth | Liliahna | Liliona | Lillianna Mary |
| Leyli | Liamar | Libertie | Liesel (0.01) | Lili-Alaya | Lili-Pier | Kathryn |
| Leylia | Liamm | Liberty (0.21) | Liesha | Lilian (0.22) | Lili-Rose (0.02) | Lilliannah |
| Leylian | Lian | Liberty-Anne | Liesl (0.01) | Lilian Grace | Lilirose | Lillianne (0.01) |
| Leylin | Liana (0.13) | Liberty-Faith | Liesse | Liliana (0.91) | Lilis | Lilliany |
| Leylou | Liana Mikayla | Liberty-Jo | Liezel | Liliana Catalina | Lilisa | Lilliawna |
| Leymary | Lianae | Libiashley | Liezl | Liliana Maria | Lilisbeth | Lilliayn |
| Leymet | Liana-Jade | Libni | Lifes Harmony | Lili-Anabelle | Lili-Stella | Lillibelle |
| Leyna (0.03) | Lianaly | Libny | Ligaya | Lilianah | Lilit | Lillibeth |
| Leynaliz | Lianalynn | Libra | Lightful | Liliana-Maria | Lilith (0.05) | Lillica |
| Leyni | Lianarra | Licah-Mari | Lihanna | Liliana-Marie | Liliya (0.01) | Lillie (0.22) |
| Leyona | Liana-Suy | Licelia | Li-Huai | Liliana-Monique | Liliyah | Lillie Ann |
| Leyonce | Liandra | Licenel | Liina | Liliane (0.02) | Lilja | Lillie Jo |
| Leyonna | Liandsy | Licet | Liisa | Lilianet | Liljean | Lillie May |
| Leysha | Liane | Licha | Liiyah | Lilianette | Lilkeysha | Lillie-Ann |
| Leysli | Lianet | Lichel | Lijah | Liliani | Lilla (0.01) | Lillieanna |
| Leyton | Lianette | Lichelle | Likando | Liliania | Lillah | Lillieannah |
| Leyvi | Liangeliz | Lici | Likeisha | Lilianie | Lillana | Lillieanne |
| Lezabella | Liani (0.01) | Licia | Likhitha | Lilianis | Lillani | Lillie-Arianna |
| Lezah | Lianisse | Licole | Lila (0.28) | Liliann | Lille | Lillieauna |
| Lezina | Lianka | Liczy | Lila Mae | Lilianna (0.08) | Lillean | Lillie-Cla |
| Lez-Lee | Liann | Lida (0.01) | Lilac | Liliannah | Lillee (0.01) | Lillie-Grace |
| Lezlee | Lianna (0.03) | Lidaya | Lilah (0.09) | Lili-Anne | Lilleean | Lilliejo |
| Lezley | Liannah | Liddiah | Lilah-Mai | Lilianne (0.02) | Lilleeana | Lillie-Mae |
| Lezli | Li-Anne | Liddy | Lilah-Rose | Lilianne Divine | Lilleeann | Lillien |
| Lezlie | Lianne | Lidelvi | Lilaina | Lilianohealani | Lilleigh | Lillienne |
| Lezly (0.01) | Liannet | Lidenia | Lila-Lea | Liliany | Lillemor | Lilliesa |
| Lhaissa-Nomie | Liannette | Lidia (0.05) | Lila-Lynn | Liliauna (0.01) | Lilleona | Lillieth |
| Lhakiyah | Lianni | Lidiana | Lilann | Lilibeth | Lilleth | Lillijana |
| Lhana | Liannie | Lidiya | Lilanna | Lili-Charlotte | Lilley | Lillimary |
| Lhasa | Lianny | Lidney | Lilas | Lilico | Lilleyen | Lillin |
| Lhea | Liannys | Lidoine | Lilas Clara | Lilie (0.01) | Lilli (0.05) | Lillineika |
| Lhela | Liany | Lidya | Lilath | Lilieana | Lillia (0.03) | Lilliona |
| Lhiann | Lianya | Lidyanniz | Lila-Yasmina | Lilien | Lillia Jane | Lillirose |
| Li | Lianys | Lidyea | Lilayla | Lili-Frederique | Lilliah | Lillis |
| Li Landra | Lianysha | Lidzey | Lileah | Lilija | Lilliam | Lillise |
| Li'airah | Liaokuo | Liebah | Lileanna | Lili-Jade | Lillian (2.85) | Lillith (0.01) |
| Li'ana | Liarys | Liedewij | Lilee (0.01) | Lilijade | Lillian Ann | Lilliun |
| Li'ania | Liasia | Liegha | Lilee-Ann | Lili-Jane | Lillian Doussou | Lillix |
| Li'mya | Liat | Lieimeliz | Lileeanne | Lilijane | Lillian Faye | Lilly (0.92) |
| Li'quavia | Liaylah | Liel | Lileeonna | Lilika | Lillian Ma | Lilly Ann |
| Li'rosella | Liba | Liela | Lileidy | Lili-Kate | Lillian Scarlett | Lilly Anne |
| Li'taezia | Libagail | Lielani | Lileigh | Lilike | Lillian Ulani | Lilly Claire |
| Lia (0.17) | Libbey | Lielany | Lileighan | | Lilliana (0.15) | Lilly Edda |

| | | | | | | |
|---|---|---|---|---|---|---|
| Lilly Grace | Lilya Mariam | Lilyruth | Lindse | Linsdey | Lisany | Liticia |
| Lilly Jo | Lilya'nna | Lily-Soleil | Lindsee | Linsey (0.03) | Lisbet (0.01) | Litisha |
| Lillyahna | Lilyain | Lima | Lindsey (0.70) | Linshan | Lisbeth (0.03) | Litka |
| Lillyan (0.04) | Lilyan (0.04) | Limairy | Lindsey-Victoria | Linsy | Lisbettee | Litsy |
| Lillyana (0.01) | Lilyana (0.07) | Limani | Lindsi | Linton | Lisbon | Littiana |
| Lillyanah | Lilyana Maricela | Limarie | Lindsie (0.01) | Linzee | Liseana | Lityana |
| Lillyandra | Lilyanah | Limavi | Lindsley | Linzey | Lise-Arielle | Litzamarie |
| Lillyane | Lilyandra | Limea | Lindssay | Linzi | Lise-Kyria | Litze |
| Lilly-Ann | Lilyane | Limna | Lindsy (0.01) | Linzie | Liseli | Litzel |
| Lillyann (0.01) | Lilyanena | Limny | Lindy (0.02) | Linzy (0.01) | Lisella | Litzi (0.01) |
| Lilly-Anna | Lilyanette | Limyanna | Lindzee | Liomary | Liselle | Litzie |
| Lillyanna (0.02) | Lily-Angel | Limyra | Lindzey | Liona | Lisely | Litzuly |
| Lillyannah | Lilyani | Lin (0.01) | Lindzi | Lionela | Liseri | Litzy (0.13) |
| Lilly-Anne | Lily-Ann (0.01) | Lin Najah | Lindzie | Lionna | Liset | Litzy Sherlyn |
| Lillyanne (0.01) | Lilyann (0.02) | Lin Shan | Lindzy | Lionnasia | Liseth (0.01) | Litzzie |
| Lillyauna | Lilyanná | Lin'dessia | Line | Lionnie | Lisett | Liu |
| Lillyaunha | Lilyanna (0.04) | Lin'nya | Line'sha | Lionora | Lisette (0.04) | Liv (0.03) |
| Lillybelle | Lilyannah | Lina (0.13) | Lineeyah | Lior | Lisha | Livalynn |
| Lillybeth | Lily-Anne (0.01) | Lina Paola | Linet | Liora (0.01) | Lishaly | Livana |
| Lillye | Lilyanne (0.01) | Linae'ja | Lineth | Lipaz | Lishania | Livanet |
| Lillyean | Lilyauna | Linaewen | Lineth Mhaye | Lipika | Lisi | Livea |
| Lillyen | Lilyaunna | Linah | Linette (0.01) | Lirane-Talia | Lisianne | Liveah |
| Lillyian | Lilybelle | Lina-Hadile | Ling | Liraz | Lisle | Liveleen |
| Lillyin | Lilybeth | Lina-Jolie | Lingyi | Liri | Lismari | Livia (0.15) |
| Lillyinn | Lilycatherine | Linariah | Linh (0.01) | Liria | Lismarie | Liviane |
| Lillyn | Lily-Dawn | Linaye | Linhmieu | Liric | Lismary | Livianna |
| Lillynn | Lilye | Lincoln (0.01) | Liniya | Liriel | Lisomarys | Livia-Rose |
| Lillyona | Lilyen | Linda (0.25) | Liniyah | Lirio | Lison | Livie |
| Lillyonna | Lilyeve | Linda Abig | Lin-Jada | Lirissa | Lissa | Livija |
| Lilly-Rose | Lily-Frederic | Linda Edoh | Link | Lirit | Lissadell | Livinder |
| Lillyth | Lilygrace | Linda Mae | Linka | Lis | Lissalynn | Livingston |
| Lilo | Lily-Jade | Lindabriannica | Linkyn | Lis Beidi | Lissandra | Livinia |
| Lilou (0.01) | Lily-Jeanne | Linda-Kay | Linlee | Lisa (0.22) | Lissayda | Liviya |
| Lilou-Rose | Lily-Kai | Linda-Sango | Linley (0.01) | Lisa Adebukonla | Lissel | Liviyah |
| Lilsecilia | Lily-Kate | Linde | Linmey | Lisa Marie | Lisset (0.01) | Livjot |
| Lilsy | Lily-Kim | Lindee | Linn | Lisa Mikuan | Lissete | Livvie |
| Lilu | Lily-Lyn | Linden (0.01) | Linna | Lisa Quynh | Lisseth | Livvy |
| Lilvana | Lily-Mae | Lindey | Linnae | Lisa-Ange | Lissett | Livyana |
| Lily (3.04) | Lily-Mai | Lindhay | Linnaea | Lisabeth | Lissette (0.02) | Liwá |
| Lily Alyn | Lilymarie | Lindi (0.01) | Linnaija | Lisa-Christine | Lissi | Liwaam |
| Lily Ana | Lily-Maude | Lindie | Linnara | Lisagi | Lissie | Liwanag |
| Lily Ann | Lily-May | Lindjana | Linnea (0.06) | Lisairy | Lissy | Liwv |
| Lily Anna | Lilymay | Lindle | Linnet | Lisa-Jane | Listilynn | Lixandra |
| Lily Annique | Lilyme | Lindler | Linnette | Lisa-Lou | Lisuer | Lixi |
| Lily Elise | Lilyn | Lindley | Linneya | Lisa-Marie | Lisve | Lixie-Anne |
| Lily Ellen | Lilynn | Lindly | Linny | (0.01) | Lisvet | Lixin |
| Lily Grace | Lilynova | Lindmary | Linnyia | Lisamarie | Lisvette | Lixsi |
| Lily Mai | Lily-Oceane | Lindora | Linnzi | Lisa-Mary | Lisvi | Lixy |
| Lily Rose | Lilyona | Lindsae | Linor | Lisandra (0.01) | Lisyani | Lixzy |
| Lily Sophia | Lilyonna | Lindsay (0.50) | Linoshka | Lisangela | Lita (0.02) | Liya (0.02) |
| Zenab | Lilypearl | Lindsay Kaye | Linoy | Lisangelly | Litali | Liyah (0.02) |
| Lily'ana | Lily-Rose (0.02) | Lindsay Yu | Linsay | Lisania | Litara | Liyana |
| Lilya (0.01) | Lilyrose | Lindsday | Linsday | Lisann | Lithika | Liyanna |

| | | | | | | |
|---|---|---|---|---|---|---|
| Liyhounane | Lizy | Lluvia Itzel | Lois (0.02) | Lonnie | Loreley | Lori-Kim |
| Liyla | Lizze | Llyric | Loivia | Lonnique | Loreli | Lorilee |
| Liz (0.04) | Lizzeida | Lma | Loiwe | Lonnisha | Lorelie | Lorilei |
| Liz Beth | Lizzely | Lmani | Loize | Lonny | Lorelle | Lorilei-Mai |
| Liza (0.04) | Lizzet | Loa | Lojian | Lonryia | Lorellei | Lorilie |
| Lizabell | Lizzete | Loadz | Lojine | Lonya | Lorellie | Lorilou |
| Lizabeth (0.01) | Lizzeteh | Loagen | Lokadia | Lonzia | Lorely | Lorilyn |
| Liza-Charlyne | Lizzeth (0.01) | Loagin | Lokeya | Looee | Lorelys | Lorimay |
| Lizaily | Lizzette | Loana | Lola (0.35) | Loona | Lorem Andrea | Lorin (0.01) |
| Lizandra | Lizzi | Loane | Lola Isidora | Loquaca | Louisse | Lorina |
| Lizanerys | Lizzie (0.03) | Loane-Elidia | Lolah | Lor Li | Lorén | Lorinda |
| Lizania | Lizzie Louisa | Loang | Lola-Jane | Lor'en | Loren (0.06) | Loring |
| Liz-Annabelle | Lizzieann | Loanis | Loleanna | Lora (0.03) | Lorena (0.12) | Loriniya |
| Lizara | Lizzy | Lo-Ann | Lolek | Lora Czen | Lorenae | Loris |
| Liza-Reis | Lizzyana | Loann | Loleta | Lora Lee | Lorence | Lorisa |
| Lizaret | Ljiljana | Loanna | Loli'ana | Lorae | Lorene (0.02) | Lorisha |
| Lizarria | Ljubica | Loanne | Lolietta | Lorah | Lorenia | Lorissa |
| Lizas | Lkada | Loany | Lolita (0.01) | Lorahlye | Lorenna | Loriyah |
| Liz-Ashley | Lladira | Loanys | Lolla | Loraine | Lorenza (0.01) | Lormani |
| Lizavia | Llajaira | Lobna | Lollie | Lorainna | Lorenzy Marine | Lorna (0.02) |
| Lizbe | Llakeeva | Lochelynne | Lollita | Loral | Loretta (0.03) | Lorne |
| Lizbeht | Llaken | Lochlan | Lolly | Loralai | Lori (0.08) | Lornna |
| Lizbelly | Llamilet | Lochlyn | Lolonna | Loralee | Lori Ann | Lorraina |
| Lizbet (0.01) | Llana | Lochlynn | Loma | Lora-Lei | Loriah | Lorraine (0.03) |
| Lizbeth (0.21) | Llanet | Lochlynne | Lomie | Loralei (0.02) | Loriana | Lorraine-Jean |
| Lizbett | Llani | Locie | Lon'naja | Lorali | Loriane (0.01) | Lorraine-Lydia |
| Lizbeydi | Llaquili | Lockey | Lona (0.01) | Loralie (0.01) | Loriani | Lorran |
| Lizbraide | Llareli | Locklynn | Lonaé | Loraly | Lorianie | Lorrayne |
| Lizchizedek | Llayna | Locktavia | Lonashia | Loralye (0.01) | Lori-Ann | Lorrellie |
| Lizde | Lleily | Loden | Lonasia | Loralyn | Loriann | Lorren |
| Lizea | Lleni | Lodia | Lonay | Loran (0.01) | Lorianna (0.01) | Lorrick |
| Lizedth | Llera | Lody | Lonaya | Lorance | Lori-Anne | Lorrie |
| Lizeete | Lleralin | Loee | Lonayah | Loranda | Lorianne (0.01) | Lorrinda |
| Lizeht | Llesiram | Loendy | Londen | Lorane | Loriasia | Lorrissa |
| Lizet (0.01) | Llewellyn | Loewen | Londin | Lorann | Lorie (0.05) | Lorry |
| Lizete | Llewelyn | Logahn | London (0.19) | Loranna | Lorie Ann | Lorry-Ann |
| Lizeth (0.05) | Lleykan | Logan (0.25) | Londya | Loranny | Lorie Dang-Thu | Lorryann |
| Lizett (0.01) | Lleylin | Logan Carrie | Londyn (0.04) | Loraya | Lorie Pier | Lorryn |
| Lizette (0.05) | Lleymi | Logane | Londynn | Lorayna | Lorie-Anna | Lory (0.01) |
| Lizhania | Llia | Logann (0.01) | Lonelle | Lordes | Lorie-Anne | Lory Ann |
| Lizhelle | Lliah | Loganne | Lonelli | Lordina | (0.01) | Loryana |
| Lizi | Lliana | Logen | Long | Lore | Lorie-Eve | Loryane |
| Lizianne | Llianay | Loghan (0.01) | Loni | Loreal | Lorie-Jeanne | Lory-Ann (0.01) |
| Liziris | Lli-Maud | Logyn | Lonie | Loreana | Lorie-Kim | Loryann |
| Lizmairy | Llolet | Logynn | Lonita | Loreanna | Lorielay | Lory-Anne |
| Lizmari | Lloryn | Lohan | Lonna (0.01) | Loredana | Lorielle | Loryanne |
| Lizmarie | Lloyce | Lohen | Lonnae | Loreen | Lorie-Michele | Lory-Jade |
| Lizmary (0.01) | Lloyd | Lohgan | Lonnah | Loreena | Lorien (0.01) | Loryn (0.01) |
| Lizneidy | Lloydeja | Loica | Lonnaja | Loreese | Lorienne | Lorynn |
| Lizseth | Llubianna | Loicka | Lonnasiah | Lorel | Lori-Eve | Lorynne |
| Lizvet | Llulisa | Loida | Lonneese | Lorelai (0.06) | Lorieve | Losanna |
| Lizveth | Llurani | Loijah | Lonnesha | Loreleí | Lorième | Lótaji |
| Lizvette | Lluvia (0.01) | Loika | Lonni | Lorelei (0.11) | Lorig | Lothlorien |

| | | | | | | |
|---|---|---|---|---|---|---|
| Lo-Ting | Lounishka | Lovinya | Lucette | Ludivina | Lulani | Lus |
| Loton | Loupecine | Lovish | Lucha | Ludivine | Lulanni | Lusalery |
| Lotoya | Louraine | Lovnaaz | Luchiana | Lud-Marie | Lulany | Lusclarita |
| Lottie (0.01) | Lourdemia | Lovonna | Luci (0.02) | Ludmia | Lule | Lusdary |
| Lottiegrace | Lourdemicka | Lovroop | Lucia (0.31) | Ludmila | Lulia | Lusero |
| Lotus (0.01) | Lourden | Lovyanne | Lucia-Alejandra | Ludmir | Lulianna | Lusey |
| Lotuz | Lourdes (0.05) | Lowell | Luciana (0.07) | Ludnie | Lulie | Lusi |
| Lou (0.01) | Lourdes De Prin | Lowen | Luciani | Ludovica | Lulit | Lusia |
| Lou Moya | Lourdess | Lowry | Lucianna (0.01) | Vittoria | Lullianna | Lusianna |
| Lou'taja | Lourdine | Lowyn | Luciannah | Ludrica | Lulov | Lusirelia |
| Louana | Lourdmia | Loyalty | Lucianne | Ludvika | Lulu (0.01) | Lusmari |
| Louana T | Lourdy | Loyda | Lucie (0.05) | Ludwika | Lulua | Lutanda |
| Louane | Lourelai | Loydie | Lucie-Gabrielle | Lueanne | Lulya | Lutchina |
| Lou-Ann | Louren | Loyette | Lucien | Luella (0.02) | Luma | Luthea |
| Louann | Lourina | Loyrilli | Luciena | Luetta | Lumari | Luthetis |
| Lou-Anna | Loursenie | Ltoria | Lucienda | Luh Putu | Lumaris | Luthien |
| Louanna | Louseney | Lu'mikha | Lucienna | Luhani | Lumena-Malika | Lutraya |
| Lou-Anne | Louve | Lua | Lucienne (0.01) | Luigina | Lumina | Luula |
| Louanne | Louvear | Lua Ryah | Lucila | Luisa (0.04) | Lun'don | Luuley |
| Louasia | Louvenia | Lualani | Lucile (0.01) | Luisa Fernanda | Luna (0.13) | Luv |
| Loubett | Louvenya | Luamia | Lucilida | Luisa Gabriela | Luna Isis | Luv'li |
| Loubna | Lovay | Luana (0.02) | Lucill | Luisa-Fernanda | Luna Rose | Luv'ly |
| Lou-Dayjah | Love (0.01) | Luane | Lucilla | Luisana | Luna Valentina | Luv'v |
| Loudeen | Love Elizabeth | Luann | Lucille (0.13) | Luisellys | Lunabella | Luvaeh |
| Loudeniveka | Love'ella | Luanna | Lucin | Luishayra | Lunabelle | Luvasia |
| Loudgee | Loveah | Luanna Marie | Lucina | Luisina | Lunaca | Luveah |
| Louella (0.01) | Loveanna | Luanne | Lucinda (0.04) | Luissa | Luna-Francesca | Luvenna |
| Louetta | Loveday | Luansian | Lucine | Luiya | Luna-Isabelle | Luvia |
| Lou-Eve | Lovee | Luany | Lucinta | Luiyina | Luna-Maia | Luvilia |
| Lougina | Loveiel | Luaralyn | Luciswann | Luiza (0.01) | Lunari | Luvinnia |
| Louidgena | Lovejoy | Luaren | Lucita | Luizanyi | Luna-Valentina | Luvrielys |
| Louis | Love-Lee | Lubabah | Lucius | Lujain (0.01) | Lunay | Luvy |
| Louisa (0.05) | Loveleen | Lubna | Lucja | Lujaine | Lunaya | Luwam |
| Louisa Nellie | Lovelene | Lubvea | Luckaila | Lujan | Lunayla | Luwamna |
| Louisanne | Lovelie | Luc'ia | Luckita | Lujane | Lundan | Lux |
| Louise (0.03) | Loveline | Luca (0.02) | Lucknacha | Lujayn | Lunden | Luxcie |
| Louise Xi | Lovell | Lucabella | Lucky | Lujue'la | Lundin | Luxi |
| Louise-Anne | Lovella | Lucas | Lucrecia | Luka (0.01) | Lundyn (0.01) | Luxie |
| Louise-Elizabeth | Lovely (0.01) | Lucaya | Lucretia | Lukah | Lundynh | Luxshiya |
| Louis-Felix | Lovemika | Lucca | Lucrezia | Lukaima | Lune | Luxury |
| Louisiana | Lovena | Lucchese | Lucx | Lukalu | Lunetta | Luya |
| Louiza | Loveneet | Luccia | Lucy (1.05) | Lukas | Lunja | Luyanda |
| Loujaine | Lovenia | Lucciana | Lucy Adams | Luke | Lunna | Luyeisy |
| Loujane | Lovepreet | Lucea | Lucyanna | Lukenya | Lupita (0.03) | Luyen |
| Loujayne | Lovett | Lucean | Lucyanne | Lukeria | Luquisha | Luz (0.10) |
| Loukia | Lovette | Lucelia | Lucyle | Luki | Lur'yce | Luz Geraldine |
| Loukya | Lovey | Lucellia | Lucy-Lee | Lukia | Lura | Luz Jamie |
| Loulou | Lovey Sarah | Lucely | Lucy-Maria | Lukiana | Lurdes | Luz Maria |
| Lou-Mai | Loviana | Lucena | Lucynda | Lukuncia | Luriah | Luz Marie |
| Lou-Mya | Lovie | Lucenda | Lud Nicka | Lul | Lurianny | Luz Nayeli |
| Louna | Lovin | Lucera | Ludian | Lula (0.01) | Lurissah | Luzbey |
| Lounise | Lovina (0.01) | Lucerito | Ludimila | Lulaila | Lurlene | Luzbilinda |
| | Loviniese | Lucero (0.04) | Ludine | Lulandile | Lurvi | Luzdary |

| | | | | | | |
|---|---|---|---|---|---|---|
| Luzenda | Lybertie | Lykayla | Lynaashia | Lyneia | Lynnkyia | Lyrik (0.01) |
| Luzhane | Lyberty | Lykiera | Lynae (0.01) | Lynelle (0.01) | Lynnlea | Lyrin |
| Luzia | Lybi | Lyla (0.10) | Lynae Felice | Lynellen | Lynnlee | Lyriq |
| Luziana | Lycette | Lyla Jewel | Lynah | Lynese | Lynnley | Lyrique |
| Luzie | Lychelle | Lylaanne | Lyna-Kim | Lynesha | Lynnlie | Lyris |
| Luzita | Lycia | Lylabeth | Lyna-Ngone | Lynessa | Lynn-Mariane | Lyryk |
| Luzmari | Lycretia | Lylah (0.02) | Lyna-Racha | Lynet | Lynn-Marie | Lys |
| Luzmaria | Lyda | Lylan | Lynashia | Lyneta | Lynnorea | Lysa |
| Luzmelinda | Lydaya | Lylauni | Lynasia | Lynetee | Lynn-Rose | Lysabeth |
| Luzmia | Lyddia | Lylee | Lyna-Sonya | Lyneth | Lynnsay | Lysaida |
| Luzmila | Lyddie | Lyleigh | Lynaya | Lynetta | Lynnsey | Lysaiiha |
| Lwnha | Lydeah | Lyli | Lynciemae | Lynette (0.02) | Lynnsi | Lysandra (0.01) |
| Ly | Lydell Maywood | Lylia | Lyncoln | Lynia | Lynnsie | Lysandra Amely |
| Ly Deja | Lydera | Lylia-Amina | Lynda (0.02) | Lyniah | Lynnsley | Lysandre |
| Ly Myia | Lydeyiah | Lylia-Keshan | Lyndaja | Lynica | Lynnze | Lysandree |
| Ly'ana | Lydia (1.54) | Lylian | Lyndall | Lynice | Lynnzee | Lysange |
| Ly'anna | Lydia Anne | Lyliana | Lynda-Lucy | Lyniece | Lynnzi | Lysann |
| Ly'asia | Lydia | Lyliane | Lyndan | Lynija | Lynnzie (0.01) | Lysanne |
| Ly'asiah | Qirniulaut | Lylianis | Lyndasia | Lynijah | Lynorya | Lysbeth |
| Ly'asis | Lydia Rose | Lyliann | Lyndazia | Lynise | Lynrosa | Lysella |
| Ly'dian | Lydia-Anne | Lylianna | Lynde | Lyniya | Lynsay | Lyset |
| Ly'esha | Lydiacarilissbeth | Lylianne | Lyndea | Lynlea | Lynsea | Lyseth |
| Ly'le | Lydia-Damaris | Lyliany | Lyndee (0.01) | Lynlee (0.01) | Lynsee | Lysett |
| Ly'naja | Lydia-Eve | Lylie | Lyndell | Lynleigh | Lynsey (0.03) | Lysette |
| Ly'nazia | Lydia- | Lylie-Rose | Lyndelynn | Lynley (0.01) | Lynsi | Lysha |
| Ly'niah | Gebremdhin | Lylla | Lynden (0.01) | Lynli | Lynsia | Lyshawn |
| Lya (0.01) | Lydiah | Lyllee | Lyndesy | Lynlie | Lynsie | Lyshmariz |
| Lyaba | Lydia-Louise | Lylli | Lyndey | Lynn (0.04) | Lynsley | Lysiah |
| Lyah | Lydian | Lylliahna | Lyndi | Lynn Marie | Lynyra | Lysiana |
| Lyahnize | Lydiana | Lyllian (0.01) | Lyndia | Lynna | Lynyvy | Lysiane |
| Lyaila | Lydiann (0.01) | Lylliana | Lyndie | Lynnae | Lynzay | Lysianne |
| Lyaiza | Lydianna | Lyllianne | Lyndley | Lynnaé | Lynze | Lysmar |
| Lyala | Lydia-Rose | Lyllie | Lyndon | Lynnann | Lynzea | Lyssa |
| Lyan | Lydie | Lyllien | Lyndra-Jazmine | Lynnasia | Lynzee | Lyssandra |
| Lyana (0.01) | Lydie-Onna | Lylou | Lyndrea | Lynnaya | Lynzey | Lyssandre |
| Lyanah | Lydieth | Lylou Brigantia | Lyndsay (0.04) | Lynnda | Lynzi (0.01) | Lyssia |
| Lyandra | Lydiya | Lyly | Lyndsaye | Lynndale | Lynzie (0.01) | Lyta |
| Lyane | Lydmila | Lyly Rose | Lyndsea | Lynndan | Lynzy | Lyticia |
| Lyanet | Lyela | Lylyane | Lyndsee | Lynn-Dereka | Lyoka | Lytina |
| Lyanette | Lyeleighah | Lyly-Anne | Lyndsey (0.09) | Lynndi | Lyonelle | Lytzi |
| Lyanie | Lyella | Lyly-France | Lyndsey Grace | Lynndie | Lyonna | Lytzia |
| Lyann | Lyeric | Lyly-Rose | Lyndsi | Lynne (0.01) | Lyonnie | Lytzy |
| Lyanna (0.01) | Lyerika | Lymajiah | Lyndsie (0.01) | Lynnea (0.01) | Lyra (0.02) | Lyubov |
| Lyannah | Lyeshia | Lyman | Lyndsy | Lynneah | Lyrasha | Lyudmila |
| Lyanne | Lygia | Lymarie | Lyndy | Lynnell | Lyrehc | Lyvana |
| Lyanni | Lyia | Lymaris | Lyndzee | Lynnelle | Lyri | Lyvia (0.02) |
| Lyarianna | Lyiah | Lymeika | Lyndzey | Lynnesy | Lyria | Lyviah |
| Lyat | Lyiicia | Lymirah | Lyndzie | Lynnette (0.01) | Lyriani | Lyviane |
| Lyaunna | Lyillie | Lyn | Lyndzy | Lyn-Nevaeh | Lyric (0.14) | Lyviann |
| Lyba | Lyinetshka | Lyn'dashia | Lyne | Lynnia | Lyric' | Lyvie-Ann |
| Lybah | Lyisha | Lyn'derica | Lynea | Lynniah | Lyrica | Lyvnia |
| Lybelle | Lyjayla | Lyn'iah | Lyneah | Lynniah Karyl | Lyrical | Lyvonne |
| Lyberti | Lykajsiab | Lyna (0.02) | Lyneé | Lynnishia | Lyrick | Lyza |

| | | | | | | |
|---|---|---|---|---|---|---|
| Lyzah | Má Laiya | Ma'kya (0.01) | Ma'shaila | Maata | Macenzie (0.01) | Mackenlee |
| Lyza-Jane | Ma Niyah | Ma'kyah | Ma'shaion | Maaya | Macenzy | Mackenley |
| Lyzandra | Ma'at | Ma'kyia | Ma'sharee | Maayan | Macey (0.19) | Mackenly |
| Lyzet | Ma'ayan | Ma'kyiah | Ma'sharia | Mabel (0.03) | Macha | Mackenna (0.07) |
| Lyzetta | Ma'caria | Ma'kyjah | Ma'shiyah | Mabelle | Machaela | Mackennah |
| Lyzette | Ma'chala | Ma'kyla | Ma'shyiah | Mabinty | Machaeli | Mackennzy |
| Lyzeyra | Ma'dashia | Ma'kyler | Ma'siya | Mable | Machali | Mackensay |
| Lyzzi | Ma'dia | Ma'kyrah | Ma'syiah | Mabrey | Machara | Mackensey |
| | Ma'eani | Ma'kyria | Ma'taiyah | Mabri | Machayla | Mackensi |
| | Ma'hajah | Ma'kyya | Ma'taja | Mabroka | Mache | Mackensie |
| **~ M ~** | Ma'hali | Ma'laddia | Ma'tasia | Mabruka | Macheala | (0.01) |
| | Ma'halia | Ma'laija | Ma'taya | Mabry (0.01) | Machella | Mackensy |
| M | Ma'harmony | Ma'laisha | Ma'tayla | Mac | Machelle (0.01) | Mackenze |
| M A | Ma'highya | Ma'laiysha | Ma'yana | Mac Kenzie | Machenna | Mackenzea |
| M Amaya | Ma'hiya | Ma'lasha | Ma'yea | Macaela | Machenzie | Mackenzee |
| M J Jennifer | Ma'hogni | Ma'lashia | Ma'zaria | Macaiah | Macheya | (0.01) |
| M_Shka | Ma'isha | Ma'layah | Ma'zhae | Macaila | Machia | Mackenzey |
| M'aliaha | Ma'jies | Ma'layia | Maab | Macailah | Machiah | Mackenzi (0.03) |
| M'aliyah | Ma'jiha | Ma'layiah | Maácah | Macailyn | Machila | Mackenzie |
| M'cayla | Ma'kaelah | Ma'layishi | Maadhusri | Macaiya | Maci (0.15) | (2.86) |
| M'cya | Ma'kaila | Ma'layla | Maaeen | Macala | Maciah | Mackenzie Lynn |
| M'halla | Ma'kailyn | Ma'laysia | Maahi | Macalah | Macianna | Mackenzie Rae |
| M'kai | Ma'kala | Ma'lea | Maahika | Macalaigh | Macie (0.23) | Mackenziel |
| M'kaijah | Ma'kalah | Ma'leah | Maahk | Macaley | Macie Jayne | Mackenzie-Lynn |
| M'kaiyah | Ma'kalya | Ma'leea | Maahum | Macallan | Macie Mich | Mackenzien |
| M'kala | Ma'kalynn | Ma'leighia | Maaidah | Macalynn | Macieana | Mackenzie-Ruth |
| M'kaya | Ma'kamri | Ma'leijza | Maaika | Macambria | Macieanne | Mackenzine |
| M'kayla (0.01) | Ma'kay-A | Ma'lia | Maaike | Macanda | Maciel | Mackenzy (0.02) |
| M'kaylah | Ma'kayla (0.04) | Ma'lijah | Maakor | Macara | Macienze | Mackenzye |
| M'kennah | Ma'kaylah | Ma'liyah (0.01) | Maakyah | Macarena (0.01) | Macier | Mackerria |
| M'kenzee | Ma'kaylia | Ma'lon | Maaliyah | Macari | Macii | Mackey |
| M'kenzie | Ma'kayshia | Ma'lonna | Maaly | Macaria | Macilyn | Mackeynzie |
| M'kiya | Ma'kayvia | Ma'lyiah | Maalyah | Macariya | Macinzie | Mackie |
| M'kiyah | Ma'keeyliah | Ma'najah | Maame | Macartney | Maciva | Mackinlee |
| M'kya | Ma'kendra | Ma'nasiah | Maame Akua | Macarya | Maciyaha | Mackinley |
| M'kyah | Ma'kenize | Ma'niaya | Maana | Macasiiyakae | Mackaila | Mackinna |
| M'kyle | Ma'kenzie | Ma'nijah | Maanami | Macaul | Mackailyn | Mackinnie |
| M'laysia | Ma'khaiya | Ma'nique | Maanasa | Macaya | Mackanzie-Mai | Mackinnon |
| M'lee | Ma'khala | Ma'niya | Maanavi | Macayala | Mackayah | Mackinsey |
| M'lunyia | Ma'khea | Ma'niyah | Maanha | Macayla (0.03) | Mackayla (0.02) | (0.01) |
| M'lynn | Ma'khia | Ma'nyah | Maani | Macaylah | Mackaylan | Mackinsie |
| M'mah | Ma'khiya | Ma'nyia | Maania | Macayle | Mackaylea | Mackinsy |
| M'rald | Ma'khize'ana | Ma'nyriel | Maanini | Maccie-Cla | Mackaylee | Mackinze (0.01) |
| M'ryah | Ma'khya | Ma'nysia | Maansi | Mace | Mackaylie | Mackinzee |
| M'taya | Ma'khyra | Ma'raya | Maant | Macedo | Mackaylla | Mackinzie (0.02) |
| M'uriah | Ma'kia | Ma'recia | Maanvi | Macee (0.02) | Mackaylyn | Mackinzy |
| Ma | Ma'kiah | Ma'reedah | Maanya | Macelaine | Mackeili | Mackira |
| Ma Ann | Ma'kierah | Ma'rerika | Maari | Macelyn | Mackemey | Mackirin |
| Ma Asia | Ma'kilah | Ma'rhonda | Maariyah | Macelynn | Mackena | Mackiya |
| Ma Diere | Ma'kinzi | Ma'riah | Maarya | Macen | Mackendra | Mackiyah |
| Ma Kahia | Ma'kiya (0.01) | Ma'rian | Maasai | Macenzae | Mackendrick | Macklyn |
| Má Kayelynn | Ma'kiyah | Ma'riyah | Maasiyah | Macenzee | Mackenize | Mackyenze |
| Ma Kayla | Ma'kiyla | Ma'rya | Maat | Macenzi | Mackenizee | Mackynsi |

| | | | | | | |
|---|---|---|---|---|---|---|
| Mackynzi | Madalin (0.01) | Maddison (0.27) | Madelyn (1.50) | Madisin | Madlyn (0.01) | Maedyn |
| Mackynzie | Madalina | Maddison-Paige | Madelyne (0.03) | Madision | Madlynn | Maee-Lee |
| Maclain | Madaline (0.02) | Maddisun | Madelynn (0.19) | Madison (8.98) | Madnan | Maegan (0.05) |
| Maclaine | Madalinn | Maddisyn (0.01) | Madelynne | Madison Agnes | Mado | Maeganne |
| Maclairyn | Madallyn | Maddisynn | (0.03) | Madison Aneise | Madolin | Maegen |
| Maclaren | Madalon | Maddix | Madena | Madison Ann | Madoline | Maegen Frances |
| Maclay | Madalun | Maddlyn | Maderiyah | Madison Anne | Madolyn (0.01) | Maeggan |
| Maclean | Madalyn (0.34) | Maddox (0.02) | Madesen | Madison Ar | Madonna | Maeghan (0.01) |
| Maclellan | Madalyn-Cath | Maddux | Madesha | Madison Dana | Madora | Maeghann |
| Maclyn | Madalyne (0.01) | Maddy (0.01) | Madesyn | Joy | Madreeka | Maegwin |
| Macoi | Madalynn (0.11) | Maddyn | Madgalena | Madison Isabella | Madrica | Maegyn |
| Macon | Madalynne | Maddysin | Madge | Madison Isabelle | Madrid | Maehren |
| Macoya | (0.01) | Maddyson (0.01) | Madgelen | Madison Jade | Madson | Maei |
| Macrae | Madam | Maddyx | Madgie | Madison | Maduson | Maeka |
| Macreena | Madan | Madea | Madhavi | Kahliyah | Madyan | Maekalah |
| Macrena | Madanna | Madecyn | Madhumita | Madison Kylie | Madycyn | Maekayla |
| Macrina | Madasan | Madee | Madhumitha | Madison Lee | Madyerson | Maekayliegh |
| Macrina Sassa | Madasen | Madeena | Madhupreetha | Madison Paige | Shanane | Maeke |
| Ma-Cubieona | Madasin | Madegan | Madhura | Madison Sasha | Madygan | Maekia |
| Macy (0.58) | Madason | Madeiline | Madhuri | Madison | Madylan | Maekyn |
| Macy-Ann | Madasyn (0.01) | Madeira | Madi | Shawnie | Madylen | Mael |
| Macyhah | Maday | Madelaina | Madi'ali | Madison Starr | Madylin (0.01) | Maela (0.01) |
| Macyiah | Madayson | Madelaine (0.02) | Madia | Madisonelizabet | Madylyn | Maelan |
| Macyla | Madchen | Madelane | Madiah | Madison- | Madylynn | Maelani |
| Macylah | Maddagen | Madelayne | Madiam | Elizabeth | Madyn | Maelat |
| Macyn (0.01) | Maddalana | Madelein | Madicela | Madison-Le | Madyna | Maele |
| Macynn | Maddalena | Madeleine (0.58) | Madicella | Madison-Lee | Madysan | Maelea |
| Macynna | Maddaline | Madeleine | Madicyn | Madison- | Madysen (0.06) | Mae-Lee |
| Macyquinn | Maddalyn | Vanessa | Madie | Michèle | Madysin (0.01) | Maelee (0.01) |
| Mada | Maddalynn | Madelen | Madielynn | Madisonn | Madyson (0.29) | Maeleen |
| Madacyn | Maddasin | Madelena | Madieson | Madison-Paige | Madysson | Maeleigh |
| Madaejah | Maddax | Madelene (0.01) | Madigan (0.02) | Madison-Rose | Madysun | Maelen |
| Madaelynne | Maddecyn | Madeley | Madighan | Madissen | Madyux | Maeley |
| Madagen | Maddee | Madeliene | Madiha | Madisson (0.01) | Madyx | Maeli (0.01) |
| Madahi | Maddeline | Madelijn | Madihah | Madisson | Madziyonna | Maelia |
| Madai | Maddelyn (0.01) | Madelijne | Madilen | Joanna | Mae (0.07) | Maelie (0.05) |
| Madailein | Maddelynn | Madelilne | Madilena | Madisson-Zenab | Mae Lea | Maelin |
| Madailyn | Madden (0.01) | Madelin (0.03) | Madiline | Madissyn | Mae Lei | Maella (0.01) |
| Madaket | Maddeson | Madelina | Madilinn | Madissynn | Mae'kale | Ma-Elle |
| Madalaine | Maddesyn | Madeline (2.17) | Madilon | Madisun (0.01) | Mae'nosh | Maëlle |
| Madalana | Maddex | Madeline Jo | Madily | Madisyen | Maea | Maelle (0.04) |
| Madalayna | Maddey | Madeline Joy | Madilyn (0.21) | Madisyn (0.30) | Maeann | Maelle Leyticia |
| Madalee | Maddi (0.01) | Madeline Mae | Madilyn Marie | Madisyne | Maeanna | Maelli |
| Madaleen | Maddi Jo | Madelinn | Madilyne | Madisynn (0.01) | Maebeline | Maellie |
| Madaleena | Maddicyn | Madelinne | Madi-Lynn | Madisynne | Maebrey | Maelly (0.01) |
| Madalein | Maddie (0.05) | Madelins | Madilynn (0.07) | Madita | Maebrie | Maellya |
| Madaleine | Maddiesyn | Madelis | Madilynne | Madix | Maebry | Maellys |
| Madalen | Maddigan | Madelissa | Madilynn-Mae | Madiya-Louise | Maeby | Maelonna |
| Madalena (0.01) | Maddilon | Madellenn | Madina (0.01) | Madiyson | Maecey | Maely (0.01) |
| Madalene (0.01) | Maddilyn | Madelline | Madinah | Madjiguene | Maeci | Maelya |
| Madalenn | Maddilynn | Madellyn | Madisan | Laye | Maecie | Maelye |
| Madali | Maddin | Madelon | Madisann | Madkeda | Maecy | Maelyn (0.01) |
| Madalie | Maddisen (0.01) | Madelon Rose | Madisen (0.09) | Madline | Maedean | Mae-Lynn |

| | | | | | | |
|---|---|---|---|---|---|---|
| Maelynn | Magally | Maggié | Mahasin | Mahimasai | Mahra | Maiella |
| Mae-Lys | Magaly (0.04) | Maggie (0.71) | Mahaska | Mahin | Mah-Raja | Maielle |
| Maelys | Magalye | Maggie Mae | Mahathi | Mahina | Mahreen | Maigan |
| Maelyss | Magan (0.01) | Maggie-Malu | Mahati | Mahin-Kaur | Mahreya | Maigane |
| Maemi Auri | Magane | Maggie-Rae | Mahauna | Mahira | Mahri | Maigen |
| Maena | Magann | Maggin | Mahawa | Mahirah | Mahriah | Maighan |
| Maena-Anyssa | Magaret | Maggy (0.01) | Mahaya | Mahita | Mahrian | Mai-Ha |
| Maeonna | Magaretha | Maghaly | Mahayanni | Mahite | Mahriana | Maiingan |
| Maera | Magda | Maghen | Mahayla (0.02) | Mahitha | Mahrlena | Maija (0.01) |
| Maerakie | Magdala | Magi | Mahaylah | Mahiya | Mahron | Maijani |
| Maerek | Magdalaina | Magic | Mahayleah | Mahiyah | Mahta | Maijayah |
| Maeren | Magdalaine | Magie | Mahaylee | Mahjabin | Mahtaya | Maijue |
| Maeri | Magdalana | Magnavox | Mahaylia | Mahjabin | Mahum | Mai-K |
| Maeron | Magdalayna | Magnelia | Mahbuba | Yesmin | Mahwash | Maïka |
| Maerose | Magdaleia | Magnin | Mahdia | Mahkaela | Mahwish | Maika (0.15) |
| Maeryn | Magdalen (0.01) | Magnolia (0.02) | Mahdis | Mahkaila | Mahya | Maika Day |
| Maesa | Magdalena | Magnolian | Mahdiya | Mahkalah | Mahyka | Maika Mahee |
| Maesane | (0.09) | Magracia | Mahea | Mahkayla | Mahzabeen | Maikachia |
| Maesen | Magdalena | Maguire | Maheah | Mahkenna | Mai (0.02) | Maika-Dalianne |
| Maesha | Yoland | Magun | Mahecha | Mahkenzie | Maí Frances | Maikael |
| Maeshayla | Magdalene | Maguy | Mahée | Mahkhyah | Mai Han | Maika-Loise |
| Maeson (0.01) | (0.05) | Mah'julie | Mahee (0.01) | Mahki | Mai Joy | Maikayla |
| Maessie | Magdalina | Mah'kayla | Maheen (0.01) | Mahkija | Mai Khanh | Maikaylinn |
| Maesyn | Magdaline | Maha (0.02) | Mahee-Sebel | Mahkiya | Kathleen | Maikeiya |
| Maesynne | Magdaly | Mahagany | Maheida | Mahkiyah | Mai Ly | Maikelyn |
| Maetinee | Magdalyce | Mahagony | Maheik | Mahkya | Mai Zong | Maikiah |
| Ma-Eva | Magdalyn (0.01) | Mahagonymarie | Maheja | Mahkyla | Mai'angel | Maiko |
| Maéva | Magdalyna | Mahaila | Mahek (0.01) | Mahlan | Mai'jor | Maikya |
| Maeva (0.07) | Magdalynn | Mahailah | Maheka | Mahlani | Mai'kayla | Maikyjah |
| Maeva Elise | Magdalys | Mahailey | Mahela | Mahlay | Mai'shey | Maikyla |
| Maeva Stella | Magdelana | Mahaileya | Mahelat | Mahlayzha | Maïa | Maikyn |
| Maevah | Magdeleine | Mahaily | Mahelate | Mahleah | Maia (0.22) | Maila |
| Maeva-Malaika | Magdelena | Mahak | Mahe-Lee | Mahler | Maiah (0.01) | Mailah |
| Maeve (0.18) | Magdelene | Mahakpreet | Maheli | Mahlet | Maialen | Mai-Lan |
| Maeven | Magdelin | Mahala (0.02) | Mahelia | Mahli | Maialie | Mailan |
| Maevree | Magdelina | Mahala Alexis | Mahelie (0.01) | Mahlia | Mai-Anh | Mailanee |
| Maevy | Magdeline | Mahalah | Mahelondri | Mahlon | Mai-Ann | Mai-Lani |
| Maevyn | Magdelyn | Mahaleigh | Mahelt | Mahloni | Mai-Anne | Mailani |
| Maewenn | Magdelynn | Mahalet | Mahely | Mahni | Maiar | Kanohea |
| Maewyn | Magdilynn | Mahaley (0.01) | Mahenee | Mahnoor (0.01) | Maiara | Mailay |
| Maeya | Magdlena | Mahali | Maheva (0.01) | Maho | Maiaysia | Mailayah |
| Maeyel | Magdolna | Mahalia (0.01) | Maheva Woberte | Mahogani | Maibelyn | Maile (0.03) |
| Maeyla | Magdylan | Mahalie | Maheva-Soleil | Mahogany | Maica | Maile Aloha |
| Maezee | Magee | Mahaljita | Mahfuza | (0.03) | Maicee | Mailea |
| Maezie | Magely | Mahallee | Mahher | Mahogany- | Maicey | Mailee |
| Maezy | Magen (0.01) | Mahalley | Mahi (0.01) | Adore | Maicie | Mailee Patricia |
| Mafalda | Magena | Mahalliah | Mahia-Kim | Mahoghany | Maicy | Maileen |
| Maftuna | Magency | Mahalya | Mahik | Mahogny | Maida (0.01) | Mailei |
| Magalee | Magenta | Maham | Mahika (0.01) | Mahogony | Maidah | Mailen |
| Magalene | Maggaly | Mahar | Mahikan | Mahonna | Maidelin | Mailena |
| Magali (0.02) | Maggee | Maharani | Mahila | Mahoua-Bah | Maiden | Mailene |
| Magalie (0.08) | Maggey | Maharene | Mahili | Mahouna | Maider | Mailey (0.01) |
| Magalie Rosalie | Maggi | Mahari | Mahima | Mahpara Yesmin | Maieda | Maili (0.01) |

| | | | | | | |
|---|---|---|---|---|---|---|
| Mailie | Maisen | Majandra | Makailee | Makayelah | Maken | Makheyla |
| Mailin | Maisey *(0.01)* | Majanique | Makailey | Ma-Kayia | Makena *(0.12)* | Makhi |
| Mailiyah | Maisha | Majarai | Makailla | Makayia | Makena Eve | Makhia *(0.03)* |
| Maille | Maisi | Majaye | Makaily | Makayka | Makena Noelle | Makhiah |
| Mailley | Maisie *(0.05)* | Majayla | Makailyn | Makayla *(2.72)* | Makenah | Makhila |
| Mailodie | Maisley | Majd | Makailynn | Makaylah *(0.07)* | Makenda | Makhila-Xandrea |
| Mai-Ly | Maislynn | Majda | Makaira | Makayla-Lee | Makendra | |
| Maily *(0.01)* | Maison *(0.01)* | Majdolaine | Makaitlynn | Makayla-Lynn | Makenece | Makhile |
| Mailyn | Maissa | Majdouline | Makaiya | Makaylan | Makenia | Makhira |
| Mailynn | Maissam | Majeeda | Makaiyah | Makayla-Rae | Makenize | Makhiya |
| Maily-Rose | Maissane | Majeisa | Makaiyla | Makaylas | Makenlee | Makhiyah |
| Mailys | Maissee | Majenna | Makala *(0.06)* | Makayle | Makenleigh | Makhuna |
| Maima | Maissie | Majenta | Makalah *(0.03)* | Makaylea | Makenley | Makhya |
| Maime | Maisy *(0.02)* | Majesstic | Makalay | Makaylee *(0.03)* | Makenlie | Mákhya |
| Maimiellia | Maisyn | Majesta | Makalee | Makayleigh | Makenly | Makhyia |
| Maimo | Maita | Majestic | Makaleigh | Makaylen | Makenna *(0.69)* | Makhyla |
| Maimoona | Maitae | Majestie | *(0.01)* | Makayli | Makennah | Makhyra |
| Maimouna *(0.01)* | Maite *(0.02)* | Majestiqq | Makaley *(0.01)* | Makaylia *(0.01)* | *(0.01)* | Maki |
| Maimuna | Maitea | Majesty *(0.01)* | Makaley-Jo | Makaylie *(0.01)* | Makennzie | Makiá |
| Maina *(0.02)* | Maitee | Maji | Makali | Makaylin *(0.01)* | Makensei | Makia *(0.01)* |
| Maine | Maithilee | Majiah | Makalia | Makaylla | Makensey | Makiah *(0.05)* |
| Mainhia | Maithili | Majik | Makaliah | Makaylnd | Makensi | Makiahfaith |
| Mainichi | Maithy | Majka | Makalie | Makaylyn | Makensia | Makiah-Lee |
| Maintxhee | Maiti | Majken | Makalinn | Makaylynn | Makensie *(0.01)* | Makialah |
| Maioree | Maitlan | Majorie | Makallah | Makaysha | Makensley | Makiálee |
| Maiory | Maitlyn | Majorretta | Makallie | Makaysia | Makenya | Makiaya |
| Maira *(0.02)* | Maitreya | Maka | Makalya *(0.01)* | Makazhiney | Makenza | Makida |
| Maira-Ahmed | Maitreyi | Maka'la | Makalyn *(0.01)* | Makda | Makenzae | Makielah |
| Mairah | Maiven | Maka'yá | Makalyn-Brooke | Make'la | Makenze *(0.01)* | Makien |
| Mairan | Maivys | Makaden | Makalynn | Makea | Makenzee *(0.02)* | Makienze |
| Maira-Nayeli | Maiwenn | Makadyn | Makana | Makeala | Makenzei | Makiera |
| Mairani | Maiy | Makae | Makani | Makeanne | Makenzey | Makieya |
| Mairany | Maiya *(0.05)* | Makaedyn | Makanna | Makeazie | Makenzí | Makighlee |
| Maire *(0.01)* | Maiyah | Makaela *(0.03)* | Makanzie | Makeba | Makenzi *(0.05)* | Makiiya |
| Mairead *(0.01)* | Maiyaka | Makaelie | Makao | Makebra | Makenzie *(0.70)* | Makila *(0.01)* |
| Maireade | Maiyer | Makaelin | Makara *(0.01)* | Makeda *(0.01)* | Makenzlie | Makilah |
| Mairen *(0.01)* | Maiyin | Makaelyn | Makari | Makedah | Makenzy *(0.02)* | Makilee |
| Maireni | Mai-Ying | Makaeo | Makarian | Makeeda | Makenzye | Makiley |
| Mairenis | Maiza | Makaeta | Makarie | Makeemah | Makenzzye | Makilynn |
| Mairenn | Maizah | Makaeyla | Makarrah | Makeena | Makesha | Makimmak |
| Mairhga | Maize | Makahia | Makarria | Makehla | Maketia | Makinah |
| Mairi | Maizee | Makahja | Makasha | Makeia | Makeya | Makindra |
| Mairim | Maizen | Makahla | Makasho | Makeiah | Makeyla | Makindree |
| Mairin *(0.01)* | Maizey | Makahlia | Makasia | Makeighia | Makeylah | Makinlee *(0.01)* |
| Mairo | Maizie *(0.01)* | Makahyla | Makasiah | Makeila | Makeylee | Makinlei |
| Mairwen | Maizy *(0.01)* | Makai | Makatylan | Makeilah | Makhailah | Makinley *(0.01)* |
| Mairy | Maja *(0.03)* | Makaia | Makaulah | Makeisha | Makhal | Makinli |
| Mairyn | Majada | Makaiah | Makaviya | Makeiya | Makhala | Makinly |
| Mais | Majae | Makaidea | Makaya *(0.01)* | Makele | Makhalia | Makinna *(0.01)* |
| Maisa | Majae'ya | Makaidyn | Makayah | Makell | Makharia | Makinsay |
| Maise | Majaia | Makail | Makaycia | Makelle | Makhaya | Makinsey *(0.01)* |
| Maisee | Majaiden | Makaila *(0.10)* | Makayda | Makellen | Makhayla | Makinsy |
| | Majanael | Makailah *(0.01)* | Makayden | Makelsie | Makhena | Makinze |

| | | | | | | |
|---|---|---|---|---|---|---|
| Makinzee | Makynze | Malak (0.07) | Malayshia | Malenys | Maliqu'a | Mallorey |
| Makinzey | Makynzee | Malak Firdaous | Malaysiá | Malerano E | Maliqué | Mallori (0.02) |
| Makinzi | Makynzey | Malaka | Malaysia (0.07) | Maleri | Malisa | Mallorie (0.05) |
| Makinzie (0.01) | Makynzi | Malakah | Malaysiah | Malerie (0.01) | Malise | Mallory (0.71) |
| Makinzy | Makynzie (0.01) | Malakai | Malayssia | Malesia | Malisha | Mally |
| Makinzzy | Makyra | Malaki | Malayyah | Maletha | Malishea | Malogi |
| Makir | Makyrah | Malakiha | Malayzia | Maletra | Malissa (0.01) | Maloire |
| Makira | Makyria | Malakuljenan | Malaz | Malexa | Malitha | Malone |
| Makisha | Makysha | Malan | Malazja | Maley | Malivia | Maloni |
| Makishi | Makyviah | Malana (0.01) | Malda | Maleya | Maliya (0.02) | Malonna |
| Makita | Mala | Malanah | Maldonado- | Maleyah | Maliyah (0.08) | Malora |
| Makiya (0.06) | Mala Kham | Malaney | Zamo | Maleyna | Maliyahh | Maloree |
| Makiyah (0.06) | Malaak | Malani (0.01) | Maldred | Maleysia | Maliyan | Malori (0.01) |
| Makiye | Malaak Ida | Malania (0.01) | Malea (0.04) | Maleyua | Maliyha | Malorie (0.05) |
| Makiyiah | Malachi | Malanie | Maleah (0.10) | Mali (0.01) | Maliyia | Malorie Shayna |
| Makiyla | Malachia | Malanna | Maleaha | Ma-Lia | Maliyyah | Malorrie |
| Makiylah | Malacia | Malanni | Maleaka | Maliá | Malize | Malory (0.02) |
| Makiylia | Malack | Malany | Maleana | Malia (0.22) | Malizia | Malorye |
| Makkaylah | Maladie | Malaree | Maleanna | Maliah (0.03) | Malka (0.07) | Malou |
| Makkenzie | Malady | Malarie (0.01) | Maleaya | Maliaka | Malka Pearl | Malthilde |
| Maklaine | Malae | Malarry | Maleca | Maliana | Malkia | Malu |
| Makliyah | Malaea | Malary | Maleda | Mali-Anais | Malkia-Dafani | Malulani |
| Mako | Malaejah | Malasha | Malee | Maliat | Malkiya | Malvika |
| Makoiya | Malaela | Malashia | Maleea | Maliayha | Malkolmx | Malvina |
| Makomborero | Malaena | Malasia (0.01) | Maleeah | Malica | Malky (0.03) | Maly |
| Makonahey | Malaesha | Malassia | Maleece | Malicia | Mallak | Malya |
| Makrae | Malah | Malaurie | Maleeha | Malie (0.01) | Mallaney | Malyah |
| Maky'la | Malaha | Malaury | Maleehah | Maliea | Mallarie | Malyan |
| Makya (0.02) | Malahanie | Malavika | Maleeka | Maliegha | Mallary | Malycia |
| Makyah (0.01) | Kalaniea | Malay | Maleena (0.01) | Malieka | Mallary-Marie | Malyciabella |
| Makye | Malai | Malaya (0.07) | Maleenia | Maliela | Mallasia | Malyea |
| Makyeyale | Ma-Laia | Malaya Jordan | Maleeya | Maliena | Mallavika | Malyia |
| Makyha | Malaia | Malaya Sahara | Maleeyah | Malieta | Mallaya | Malyiah |
| Makyi | Malaiah | Malaya- | Malei | Malieya | Malle | Malyisha |
| Makyia | Malaieja | Consuelo | Malei'ah | Maliha (0.01) | Malleana | Malyjah |
| Makyiah | Malaigha | Malayah (0.01) | Maleia (0.01) | Maliheh | Malleia | Malyka (0.01) |
| Makyilah | Malaijah | Malayasia | Maleiah | Maliika | Malleigh | Malyn |
| Makyla (0.05) | Malaijha | Malayeka | Maleigh | Malija | Malleine | Malyna |
| Makyla Lá | Malaika (0.02) | Malayia | Maleigha (0.02) | Malijah | Sapphir | Malynda |
| Makylah (0.01) | Malaila | Malayiah Nicole | Maleighya | Malik | Mallen | Malynn |
| Makylea | Malaina (0.01) | Malayika | Maleihny | Malika (0.04) | Mallerie | Malynte |
| Makylee | Malaine | Malayja Ny | Maleika-Lee | Malikah | Mallery | Malyshia |
| Makyler | Malainy | Malayjah | Maleina | Malikka | Malley (0.01) | Malyssa |
| Makyliah | Malaisa | Malayjha | Maleine | Malikqua | Malli | Malyssia |
| Makylie | Malaisha | Malayjiah | Maleiyah | Malikwah | Mallia | Malystryx |
| Makylin | Malaiya | Malayka | Malejah | Malila | Mallicent | Malyun |
| Makylla | Malaiyah | Malayla | Malek | Malin | Mallie (0.01) | Mam |
| Makymbri | Malaizsha | Malaylah | Maleka | Malina (0.03) | Mallika | Mam Kumba |
| Makyna | Malaja | Malaymia | Malena (0.05) | Malinah | Mallina | Mama Aissata |
| Makynlee | Malajah | Malayna (0.04) | Malendra | Malinda (0.05) | Mallisa | Mamah |
| Makynli | Malajha | Malayne | Malene | Maline | Malliyah | Mamalak |
| Makynlie | Malajia | Malayni | Malenie | Malini | Mallony | Maman |
| Makynna (0.01) | Malajisa | Malaysha | Malenna | Malinna | Malloree | Mamdiara |

| | | | | | | |
|---|---|---|---|---|---|---|
| Mame | Mandie (0.01) | Manmaya | Maquaisha | Mar'tyasia | Marayna | Marchley |
| Mame Penda | Mandilynn | Manmeet | Maque'la | Mar'zae | Maraysia | Marci (0.01) |
| Mamie (0.01) | Mandolin | Mann | Maque'la | Mar'ziya | Marazia | Marcia (0.02) |
| Mamijola | Mandoline | Mannar | Maquila | Mara (0.20) | Marbel | Marcia Cassidy |
| Mamme-Chie | Mandolyn | Mannat | Maquita | Mara Stephana | Marbella (0.01) | Marciana |
| Mamtaz | Mandon | Mannatpreet | Maquyyah | Marabel | Marbelly | Marciara |
| Man'a | Mandryn | Manndee | Maqyah | Marabelle | Marc'ia | Marcida |
| Mana | Mandy (0.10) | Mannisha | Mar | Marabeth | Marcaela | Marcie (0.01) |
| Manaahel | Mandysha | Manniyah | Mar Khiya | Maracela | Marcaelus | Marciel |
| Manaal | Manea | Mannusha | Mar Taisha | Marae | Marcaia | Marcilana |
| Manada | Maneejae | Manoah | Mar'chealah | Maraea | Marcaila | Marcile |
| Manae | Maneesa | Manola | Mar'ciah | Mara-Elena | Marcaisa | Marcina |
| Manahil | Maneet | Manolya | Mar'eianna | Maraeli | Marcaizah | Marckailla |
| Manai | Maneetveer | Manon (0.01) | Mar'ih | Maraely | Marcaja | Marco |
| Manaii | Maneeza | Manouane | Mar'jayah | Maragdaly | Marcanna | Marcquilla |
| Manail | Maneija | Manouchca | Mar'kaiya | Marah (0.03) | Marc-Antoine | Marcuetta |
| Manaja | Manekha | Manoush | Mar'kala | Marahyah | Marcari | Marcy (0.01) |
| Manaji | Manel | Manoya | Mar'kaya | Maraia | Marcarie | Mardel |
| Manaka | Manelle | Manpreet | Mar'kayah | Maraiah | Marcasia | Mardelis |
| Manal (0.02) | Manesa | Manraj | Mar'kaylah | Maraina | Marcayha | Mardena |
| Manale | Manessah | Manreen | Mar'kaysha | Marais | Marcayla | Mardi |
| Manami | Manette | Manreet (0.01) | Mar'keelah | Maraiza | Marcayle | Mardnisha |
| Manana Treseda | Maney | Manrit | Mar'keiah | Maraja | Marcé | Mardochee |
| Manar (0.01) | Mangianna | Manroop | Mar'keria | Mara-Jade | Marcede | Mare'a |
| Manare | Manha | Mansha | Mar'keriya | Marajade | Marcedes | Marea |
| Manariya | Manhattan | Mansi | Mar'kesha | Marajah | Marcediez | Maredith |
| Manasa | Manheer | Mansura | Mar'keyantis | Marajsha | Marcel | Maree |
| Manasi | Mania | Manu | Mar'keyshia | Marala | Marcela (0.03) | Mareea |
| Manasia | Maniah | Manuela (0.03) | Mar'kia | Maralea | Marcela | Mareena |
| Manasiah | Ma-Niaha | Manuelita | Mar'kila | Maralee | Alexandra | Mareesa |
| Manasvi | Mani-Anais | Manuella | Mar'kirra | Maralie | Marcelina (0.01) | Marehai |
| Manasvini | Maniece | Manveen | Mar'kiya | Maralin | Marcelinadelia | Mareike |
| Manaswini | Maniesha | Manveer | Mar'kyla | Maralise | Marceline | Mareina |
| Manat | Manijah | Manvi | Mar'layzia | Maralisha | Marcell | Mareisha |
| Manatpreet | Manijha | Manvir | Mar'lecia | Maralyn | Marcella (0.07) | Marek |
| Manayah | Antanae | Manvita | Mar'lexia | Maram | Marcella Lynn | Mareka |
| Manda | Manika | Manya (0.01) | Mar'liyah | Maram- | Marcellas | Marel |
| Mandalay | Manikasai | Manyah | Mar'lonna | Joumana | Marcelle | Marela |
| Mandale | Maninder | Manyaira | Mar'lun | Marana | Marcellina | Mareli |
| Mandalena | Maninush | Manyla | Mar'nae | Maranachel | Marcena | Marelin |
| Mandalene | Maniriah | Manzikella | Mar'nayah | Maranatha | Marcenzhi | Marelis |
| Mandalin | Manisha (0.01) | Manzo | Mar'neisha | Maranda (0.06) | Marceuna | Marella |
| Mandalyn | Manishka | Mao | Mar'nique | Marangeli | Marceydees | Marelly |
| Mandana | Manit | Maoko | Mar'quashia | Marangely | March | Marellyn |
| Mandara | Maniyá | Maoli | Mar'quaysha | Marania | Marchá | Marellyse |
| Mandarah | Maniya (0.01) | Maona | Mar'qura | Maranitza- | Marchaé | Marely |
| Mandee | Maniyah (0.01) | Maony | Mar'sha | Noemie | Marcha-Isabelle | Marelya |
| Mandeep | Maniyan | Maor | Mar'shay | Maranjalie | Marché | Marelym |
| Mandela | Maniyya | Maori | Mar'shelle | Maranyely | Marchela | Marelyn |
| Mandeline | Maniziah | Maple | Mar'sheunt | Marashellie | Marchelle | Mareme |
| Mandelyne | Manjari | Mapple | Mar'teenia | Marasiah | Marchely | Mareme Racine |
| Manderley | Manjot | Mapy | Mar'tesha | Maraya (0.01) | Marchet | Maren (0.10) |
| Mandi (0.02) | Manleen | Maquaila | Mar'tricia | Marayah (0.01) | Marchey | Marena (0.01) |

Marenah
Marenna
Mareny
Mareona
Maresa
Maresha
Maressa (0.01)
Maret
Mareta
Marett
Maretta
Mareuna
Mareunna
Marey
Mareyah
Mareyhana
Mareyiah
Mareyli
Margad
Margaina
Margalit
Margam
Margaret (1.26)
Margaret Annette
Margaret Jean
Margaret-Ann
Margaret-Anne
Margaret-C
Margaret-Dora
Margarete
Margaretha
Margarethe
Margaret-May
Margaretta
Margarette
Margarey
Margari
Margarit
Margarita (0.05)
Margarite
Margartia
Margaux (0.02)
Margeaux
Margen
Margené
Margenea
Margeolene
Margery
Margherita
Margia
Margie (0.01)

Margo (0.03)
Margorie
Margot (0.05)
Margret (0.01)
Margreta
Margrette
Margriana
Margrita
Margueret
Marguerite (0.06)
Marguerite Laura
Marguerite Tatiana
Marhiya
Marhiyah
Mari (0.04)
Mari Jane
Mari Kelis
Mari Yah
Mari'a
Mari'asia
Mari'auna
Mari'yawna
María
Maria (2.77)
Maria Alexandra
Maria Alic
Maria Angelica
Maria Angely
Maria Anita
Maria Aurelia
Maria Belen
Maria Camila
Maria Christina
Maria Clara
Maria D
Maria De Jesus
Maria De Los Angeles
Maria De Los Angles
Maria Dejesus
Maria Del Carmen
Maria Del Rayo
Maria Eduanda
Maria Eduarda (0.01)
Maria Elena
Maria Esther
Maria Fernanda

Maria Franchesca
Maria Gabriela
Maria Guad
Maria Guadalupe
Maria Guil
Maria Ileana
Maria Isabel
Maria Isabella
Maria Ivana
Maria Jose
Maria Katherine George
Maria Luisa
Maria Magdalena Cremade
Maria Mercedes
Maria Oceana
Maria Paula
Maria Pilar
Maria Rita
Maria Sabina
Maria Salma
Maria Sele
Maria Sophia
Maria Victoria
Maria Zelfa
Maria'jose
Maria'lessia
Maria-Alejandra
Maria-Alexandra
Maria-Angelica
Maria-Angelina
Mariabelen
Mariacarmen
Mariacecilia
Mariaceleste
Mariachiara
Maria-Clara
Mariaclara
Mariadalys
Maria-Daniela
Maria-Delmar
Mariaelena
Mariaemilia
Mariaesther
Maria-Fernanda
Mariafernanda
Maria-Gabriela
Mariah (1.89)
Mariah Caileen

Mariah Gayle
Mariah Lee
Mariah Richelle
Mariaha
Mariahana
Mariahjace
Mariah-Lee
Mariah-Mae
Mariahna
Mariahya
Maria-Ignacia
Mariainez
Maria-Jane
Mariajoeli
Maria-Jose
Mariajosé
Mariajose (0.01)
Mariakim
Mariala
Mari-Alandra
Marialaura
Maria-Lea
Maria-Lee
Marialee
Maria-Lena
Marialena
Maria-Leticia
Mariali
Maria-Lila
Maria-Lisa
Marialisa
Marializ
Mariallys
Maria-Luisa
Maria-Luiza
Marialy
Marialys
Marialyz
Mariam (0.20)
Mari-Ama
Mariama (0.03)
Mariama Dalanda
Mariam-Die'lo
Mariame
Mariame Dalanda
Maria-Mercedes
Mariamercedes
Maria-Mirabela
Mariam-Mercy
Mariamu
Maria-Muskan

Marian (0.05)
Marian Lindsay
Mariana (1.02)
Mariana Alexandra
Mariana Carme
Mariana-Alexandra
Marianah
Marianahi
Marianaliz
Maria-Nathalie
Mariand
Mariandre
Mariane (0.03)
Marianela
Marianelis
Marianet
Mariange
Mariangel
Mariangela
Mariangeli
Mariangelis
Mariangeliz
Mariangely
Mariangelyz
Mariangie
Marianie
Mariann (0.01)
Marianna (0.13)
Mariannah
Marianne (0.20)
Marianne Louna
Marianne Rose
Marianne-Josee
Marianne-Nour
Mariannne
Marianny
Marianthi
Mariantonia
Mariany
Marianyely
Marianys
Maria-Nzuzi-Gracia
Mariapaula
Maria-Paz
Maria-Rain
Mariarosa
Mariasha
Mariasia
Maria-Teresa-De Jesus

Maria-Theresa
Mariatu
Mariaude
Mariauna
Maria-Victoria
Mariavictoria
Mariay
Maribel (0.09)
Maribela
Maribell
Maribella
Maribelle
Maribeth (0.01)
Maric'a
Marica
Maricah
Maricarmen (0.01)
Marice
Maricel
Maricela (0.02)
Mariceli
Maricelis
Maricella
Maricellyn
Maricely
Marichka
Maricia
Maricielo
Marick
Marickyah
Maricle
Mariclode
Maricruz (0.01)
Maricsa
Marida
Maridel
Maridiann
Maridouce
Marie (0.32)
Marie Alice
Marie Anna
Marie Anne
Marie Arianna
Marie Christine
Marie Danie
Marie Denise
Marie Elizabeth
Marie Ester
Marie Eve
Marie Fee
Marie Francesca
Marie Helene

Marie Jeanne
Marie Josee
Marie Justine
Marie Laure
Marie Laurence
Marie Lizette
Marie Lou
Marie Louise
Marie Meleena
Marie Nadia
Marie Neige
Marie Norah
Marie Paule
Marie Pier
Marie Pierre
Marie Rachelle
Marie Rose
Marie Soleil
Marie Sophie
Mariea
Marie-Andree
Marie-Ange (0.02)
Marie-Angelis
Marieangelis
Marie-Ann
Marieann
Marie-Anna
Marie-Anne (0.01)
Marie-Annick
Marie-Annie
Marie-Aude
Marie-Audrey
Mariebel
Marie-Belle
Mariebelle
Marie-Blanche
Marie-Carmelle
Marie-Catherine
Marie-Céleste
Marie-Chantal
Marie-Charlotte
Mariechen
Marie-Christcia
Marie-Christine
Marie-Claire
Marie-Clara
Marie-Claude
Marie-Clemence
Mariecruz
Marieda
Marie-Dahlia

| | | | | | | |
|---|---|---|---|---|---|---|
| Marie-Douce | Marielena | Marie-Pascale | Mariko | Marinna | Marit | Marjolaine |
| Marie-Elisabeth | Marieli | Marie-Perle | Mariksa | Mariohna | Marita | *(0.01)* |
| Marie-Elizabeth | Marielis | Marie-Philip | Marila | Mariola | Marites | Marjoleen |
| Marie-Elle | Marie-Lisa | Marie-Philipe | Marilan | Marion *(0.05)* | Maritessa | Marjolène |
| Marie-Emmanuelle | Marieliz | Marie-Pier *(0.03)* | Marilea | Mariona *(0.01)* | Marithe | Marjolie |
| Marie-Esther | Mariell | Mariepier | Marilee *(0.01)* | Ma-Rionna | Marithza | Marjoreni |
| Marie-Ève | Mariella *(0.04)* | Marie-Pierre | Marilena | Marionna *(0.01)* | Maritsa *(0.01)* | Marjori |
| Marie-Eve *(0.03)* | Mariella Renee | Marier | Marilene | Marionnah | Maritshell | Marjorie *(0.05)* |
| Marie-Evelyne | Marielle *(0.04)* | Marie-Rose *(0.01)* | Marileysis | Mariouna | Maritssa | Marjorie Joi |
| Marie-Fay | Marielle Sofia | Marierose | Marili *(0.01)* | Marioxi | Maritt | Marjorine |
| Marie-Fee | Marielly | Marie-Rose Antonia | Mariliane | Maripaz | Maritza *(0.11)* | Marjory |
| Marie-Felix | Mariellyn | Mariesa | Marilia-Romane | Maripier | Maritzabel | Markada |
| Marie-Florence | Mariellyz | Mariesha | Marilie *(0.01)* | Mariposa | Maritzha | Markaela |
| Marie-France | Marie-Logan | Marie-Sol | Mariliegh | Mariqutta | Marium | Markaihla |
| Marie-Frederique | Marie-Lou *(0.01)* | Mariesol | Marilin | Marirrosi | Mariunah | Markala |
| Marie-Gabrielle | Marie-Louisa | Marie-Soleil *(0.05)* | Marilinda | Maris *(0.02)* | Marivel | Markalie |
| Marie-Genevieve | Marie-Louise | Marie-Sophie | Mariline | Marisa *(0.29)* | Marivilla | Markania |
| Marie-Hélène | Marie-Loup | Marieta | Marilise | Marisabel | Marixa | Markasha |
| Marie-Isabelle | Marie-Luce | Marie-Therese | Mariliss | Marisabela | Mariya *(0.03)* | Markasia |
| Marie-Jacob | Marie-Lune *(0.01)* | Marietou | Mariliz | Marisah | Mariyah *(0.07)* | Markavia |
| Marie-Jade *(0.01)* | Marie-Ly | Marietta *(0.01)* | Marilla | Marisa-Lynn | Mari-Yah | Markaya |
| Marie-Jane | Mariely *(0.01)* | Mariette | Marilorence | Marisca | Mariyahna | Markaylá |
| Mariejane | Marie-Lyne | Marieva | Mari-Lou | Marisela *(0.02)* | Mariyalee | Markayla *(0.04)* |
| Marie-Jeanne *(0.02)* | Marielyne | Marieve | Marilou *(0.09)* | Mariselda | Mariyam | Markaylah |
| Marie-Joe | Marie-Lys | Mariève | Mariloue | Marisele | Mariyama | Markaysha |
| Marie-Joelle | Marielys | Marie-Venus | Marilouise | Mariseli | Mariyana | Markeda |
| Marie-Jose | Marielyz | Marie-Wabania | Mariloup | Marisella | Mariyay | Markedia |
| Marie-Josee | Mariem | Marieya | Marilu | Mariselys | Mariyeah | Markee |
| Marie-Joseph | Marie-Madeleine | Marifer | Marilune | Marisette | Mariyela | Markeela |
| Marie-Julia | Marie-Mai | Marigny | Mariluz | Marisha | Mariyh | Markeema |
| Marie-Julie | Marie-Maud | Marigona | Marily *(0.01)* | Marishah | Mariyha | Markeesa |
| Marieka | Marie-Maude *(0.01)* | Marigrace | Marilyn *(0.13)* | Marishka | Mariyonna | Markeesia |
| Marie-Kate | Marie-Maxim | Marigza | Marilyn-Day | Marisia | Mariyza | Markeil |
| Marie-Kayle | Marie-Maxime | Marih | Marilyne | Marisiana | Mariza *(0.01)* | Markeirria |
| Marieke | Marie-May | Mariha | Marilynn *(0.01)* | Mariska *(0.02)* | Marizah | Markeish |
| Marie-Kim | Marieme | Marihelen | Marilys | Mariska Simone | Marizol | Markeisha |
| Marie-Kym | Marie-Michele | Marihicks | Marilyza | Marisleidy | Marizul | Markeiya |
| Mariel *(0.02)* | Marie-Michèle | Marihyona | Marim | Marisol *(0.18)* | Marizza | Markeiyah |
| Mariel Joy | Marie-Michelle | Marija | Marimar | Marisol Opal | Marjae | Markeja |
| Mariela *(0.09)* | Marien | Marijah | Marin *(0.10)* | Marisola | Marjahnna | Markel |
| Marie-Laurance | Mariena | Marijané | Marina *(0.26)* | Marisoleil | Marjan | Markela |
| Marie-Laure | Marie-Nadia | Marijane *(0.01)* | Marina-Dawn | Marisol-Uliela | Marjana | Markell |
| Marie-Laurence *(0.02)* | Marie-Najet | Marijke | Marinah | Marison | Marjane-Kadidja | Markella |
| Mariele Victoriac | Mariene | Marijose | Marinarose | Mariss | Marjan-E-Khadijah | Markenna |
| Marie-Lea | Marie-Neige | Marik | Marinda *(0.01)* | Marissa *(1.67)* | Marjani | Markenya |
| Marie-Lee *(0.01)* | Marieni | Marika *(0.06)* | Marindia | Marissa Jiliane | Marjannah | Markenyah |
| Marielen | Marienne | Marikah | Marine *(0.02)* | Marissa Noelle | Marjany | Markenzie |
| | Marie-Noel | Marikarla | Marinel | Marissalyn | Marjaria | Markeria |
| | Marie-Noelle *(0.01)* | Marikate | Marinelly | Marissa-Nishawn | Marjery | Markerra |
| | | | Marinely | Marissia | Marjie | Markesha |
| | | | Marinelys | Marista | Marjolain | Markeshia |
| | | | Marinette | Maristella | | Marketa |
| | | | Marinn | | | Markeva |

| | | | | | | |
|---|---|---|---|---|---|---|
| Markeya | Marleena | Marlynn | Marquez | Marsally | Martanah | Marvianna |
| Markeyia | Marleene | Marlys | Marquia | Marsavya | Martasia | Marvin |
| Markeysha | Marleeya | Marlyse | Marquicia | Marsaylees | Martavia | Marvolous |
| Markeyvia | Marlei | Marlyshia | Marquila | Marsden | Martaya | Marwa *(0.04)* |
| Markhia | Marleigh *(0.03)* | Marlythsa | Marquira | Marsea | Marteene | Marwah |
| Markhyah | Marleina | Marmiracle | Marquis | Marseille | Martela | Marwa-Yasmine |
| Markia *(0.02)* | Marlem | Marna | Marquise | Marsela | Martele | Marwen |
| Markiah | Marlen *(0.03)* | Marnaé | Marquisha | Marselena | Martena | Marwo |
| Markie | Marlena *(0.03)* | Marnay | Marquishia | Marselina | Marteria | Marwury |
| Markie Lee | Marlene *(0.08)* | Marnayya | Marquissa | Marsella | Martessa Anatae | Mary *(2.40)* |
| Markiecia | Marlenee | Marnee | Marquita *(0.01)* | Marsenia | Martha *(0.18)* | Mary Adelle |
| Markiee | Marleni *(0.01)* | Marnesha | Marquitta | Marsha *(0.01)* | Martha Ash | Mary Agnes |
| Markiesha | Marlenis | Marney | Marqula | Marsha'ne | Martha-Glen | Mary Alice |
| Markieshia | Marlenne | Marni | Marqwasia | Marshaé | Marthakay | Mary Ann *(0.01)* |
| Markila | Marlenny | Marniah | Marra | Marshae *(0.01)* | Marthalee | Mary Ann Emily |
| Markinsy | Marlennys | Marnie *(0.01)* | Marrah | Marshal | Marthaline | Mary Anna |
| Markira | Marleny | Marniece | Marraya | Marshala | Marthy-Gemima | Mary Anne |
| Markiria | Marlenys | Marniecia | Marre'oni | Marshalee | Marti | Mary Barbara |
| Markisha | Marlesha | Marnika | Marren | Marshalina | Marti'yana | Mary Beth |
| Markissia | Marlessa | Marnique | Marresa-Grace | Marshanea | Martiana | Mary Bradley |
| Markita *(0.01)* | Marlette | Marnisha | Marresha | Marshanette | Martice | Mary Case |
| Markiya | Marlexis | Marnita | Marret | Marsha-Nichole | Martie | Mary Cathe |
| Markiyah | Marley *(0.23)* | Marnitra | Marretje | Marshanti | Martien | Mary Catherine |
| Markley | Marleymae | Marniyah | Marri | Marshaun | Martika | Mary Charl |
| Marktavia | Marleyna | Maroi | Marriah | Marshawna | Marti-Leigh | Mary Charlotte |
| Markyia | Marleza | Marolena | Marriam | Marshawney | Martin | Mary Claire |
| Markyla | Marli *(0.02)* | Marom | Marrian | Marshay *(0.01)* | Martiná | Mary Clare |
| Markyrah | Marliana | Maron | Marrianna | Marshaya | Martina *(0.07)* | Mary Drue |
| Marla *(0.02)* | Marlicia | Marone | Marrie | Marshayla | Martine *(0.01)* | Mary Elena |
| Marlah | Marlie *(0.02)* | Maroua | Marriea | Marshé | Martinique | Mary Elise |
| Marlaila | Marlies | Marq'aella | Marriela | Marsheá | Martiya | Mary Eliza |
| Marlaina *(0.01)* | Marliese | Marqalisa | Marriiyah | Marsheala | Martiza | Mary Elizabeth |
| Marlaisha | Marlin *(0.01)* | Marqasha | Marrina | Marsheara | Martrese | Mary Ella |
| Marlaja | Marlina *(0.01)* | Marqi | Marrion | Marsheeda | Martrianna | Mary Ellen |
| Marlajah | Marlina-Maya | Marqia | Marrionna | Marshel | Martrice | Mary Emma |
| Marlan | Marlinda | Marquah | Marrisa | Marshell | Marty | Mary Erin |
| Marlana *(0.01)* | Marline | Marquaisha | Marrison | Marshella | Martyna | Mary Faith |
| Marlandrea | Marlisa | Marquasha | Marrissa *(0.01)* | Marshelle | Maruquita | Mary Frances |
| Marlann | Marlise | Marquashia | Marrit | Marshia | Marva | Mary Gail |
| Marlasia | Marlisha | Savaria | Marron | Marshunte | Marvá | Mary Grace |
| Marlat | Marlissa | Marquasia | Marrssa | Marshyia | Marvat | *(0.01)* |
| Marlay | Marlize | Marquattia | Marry | Marsiana | Marveda | Mary Grays |
| Marlay'ja | Marlo *(0.01)* | Marquayla | Marryam | Marsida | Marvel | Mary Grayson |
| Marlayja | Marlonda | Marquee | Marry-Ann | Marsieli | Marvela | Mary Hannah |
| Marlayna *(0.01)* | Marlott | Marqueira | Marryann | Marstena | Marveli | Mary Helen |
| Marlaynie | Marlow | Marqueja | Marryeá | Marston | Marveline | Mary Iris |
| Marlaysha | Marlowe | Marquela | Marryn | Marta *(0.02)* | Marvella | Mary Jane |
| Marlaysia | Marly *(0.02)* | Marquelle | Marryum | Martaisha | Marvely | *(0.02)* |
| Marlea | Marlyasia | Marquesha | Marsade's | Martaja | Marvelynn | Mary Jayne |
| Marleah | Marlycia | Marquessia | Marsadie | Martajah | Marvenous | Mary Jo |
| Marlee *(0.12)* | Marlyn *(0.01)* | Marquetta | Josiphene | Martajé | Marvese | Mary Jordan |
| Marleea | Marlyn's | Donae | Marsailles | Martalisa | Marveya | Mary Kate |
| Marleen | Marlyne-Myriam | Marquette | Marsali | Martana | Marveyuna | *(0.01)* |

| | | | | | | |
|---|---|---|---|---|---|---|
| Mary Kather | Maryann Catherine | Mary-Faith | Marylena | Maryssa (0.02) | Masira | Matelynn |
| Mary Katherine | Maryanna (0.01) | Maryfer | Marylene | Marysue | Masiya | Materrika |
| Mary Kathryn | Maryannabelle | Maryfrances | Marylie (0.01) | Mary-Therese | Masiyah | Mateya (0.01) |
| Mary Katlin | Mary-Anne | Mary-Francis | Marylin | Marytherese | Maslin | Mateyah |
| Mary Kay | Maryanne (0.02) | Mary-Gabrielle | Marylina | Marytza | Mason (0.05) | Mateyis |
| Mary Kim | Maryanté | Mary-Gae | Maryline | Marytzza | Mason-Elizabeth | Mathaba |
| Mary Lee | Maryauna | Marygile | Marylisa | Maryum (0.01) | Masonja | Mathalie |
| Mary Louise | Marybel | Mary-Grace | Maryliz | Maryuri | Masooma | Mathangi |
| Mary Loup | Marybell | Marygrace (0.01) | Maryllis | Maryurie | Massa | Mathani |
| Mary Luz | Marybelle | Mary-Holla | Maryloise | Maryury | Masseily | Mathea |
| Mary Lynn | Mary-Bess | Maryia | Mary-Lou | Maryvel Abigail | Massey | Mathelyn |
| Mary Madison | Mary-Beth | Maryiah | Marylou (0.03) | Maryxa-Taina | Massiah | Mathena |
| Mary Magdelena | Marybeth (0.01) | Maryian | Mary-Louise | Maryzabella | Massie | Mathews |
| Mary Margaret | Mary-Blanche | Maryiana | Maryloup | Marzareiah | Massiel | Mathia |
| Mary Marth | Marybrooke | Maryianna | Marylue | Marzena | Massilia | Mathiea |
| Mary Michael | Marycal | Maryiona | Marylune | Marzhae | Massilon | Mathilda (0.01) |
| Mary Robbins | Marycarmen | Mary-Jade | Marylyn | Marziah | Massiny | Mathilde (0.12) |
| Mary Rutledge | Mary-Caroline | Mary-Jael | Mary-Lynn | Marzialucia | Massylia | Mathilde-Berthe |
| Mary Selena | Mary-Catherine | Maryjan | Marylynn | Marziya | Masuma | Mathisen |
| Mary Silatigui | Maryce | Mary-Jane (0.01) | Marym | Marzjay | Masya | Mathumetha |
| Mary Streeter | Marycelis | Maryjane (0.02) | Mary-Makenzie | Marzjonae | Masyn (0.01) | Mathurishika |
| Mary Talley | Mary-Christine | Maryjayn | Marymar | Masa | Mata | Mathusha |
| Mary Teresa | Maryciela | Mary-Jean | Mary-Mckin | Masaeda | Mataea | Mathusija |
| Mary Therese | Mary-Clair | Maryjo | Mary-Michal | Masama | Mataeya | Mathuya |
| Mary Virginia | Mary-Claire | Maryjoe | Maryn (0.04) | Masani | Matai | Mathy |
| Mary'a | Maryclaire | Maryjose | Maryna | Masayá | Mataia | Mathylde |
| Mary'angel | Mary-Clare | Maryjosephine | Maryne | Mascey | Mataiya | Mathys |
| Mary'auna | Maryclare | Maryjoyce | Marynella | Masea | Matalee | Mathysse |
| Mary'mah | Mary-Claude | Maryjoyner | Marynez | Masee | Matalen | Mati |
| Marya (0.01) | Mary-Claura | Mary-K | Marynn | Maseerah | Matalie | Matia (0.01) |
| Mary-Addison | Marycle | Maryka (0.01) | Maryonia | Masen | Matalin | Matiah |
| Maryah (0.02) | Mary-Cooke | Mary-Kate (0.01) | Maryonna | Masey | Matalyn | Matiasha |
| Maryahna | Marycruz | Marykate (0.01) | Maryori | Masha (0.01) | Matalyne | Matigan |
| Maryaj | Marydawn | Mary-Katheri | Maryorie | Mashaal | Matalynn | Matika |
| Mary-Alan | Marye-Christine | Mary-Katherine | Maryorit | Mashae | Matana | Matilda (0.05) |
| Mary-Alex | Maryela | Marykatherine | Maryory | Mashael | Matanya | Matilde (0.01) |
| Mary-Alexi | Mary-Elisabeth | Mary-Katheryn | Mary-Pier | Mashaim | Matasha | Matilee |
| Maryalice | Mary-Elise | Mary-Kathleen | Mary-Rebecca | Mashal | Matasia | Matiley |
| Mary-Allen | Mary-Eliza | Mary-Kathrine | Mary-Renee | Mashawna | Matason | Matillda |
| Mary-Allys | Mary-Elizabe | Mary-Kathryn | Maryreya | Mashayia | Mataya (0.02) | Matilyn (0.01) |
| Maryam (0.11) | Mary-Elizabeth (0.01) | Marykathryn | Maryrose | Mashayla (0.01) | Matayah | Matilynn |
| Maryam Riad | Maryelizabeth | Marykay | Maryryan | Mashaylynn | Matayha | Matina |
| Maryama (0.01) | Maryella | Mary-Keely | Marysa (0.01) | Mashell | Matayia | Matisen |
| Maryame | Maryelle | Mary-Kendall | Marysan | Mashelle | Matayla | Matison |
| Maryan (0.01) | Maryellen (0.01) | Mary-Kensley | Mary-Savanna | Mashiya | Mataysha | Matisse |
| Maryana | Maryellie | Marylane | Mary-Scott | Mashiyah | Matayvia | Matisyn |
| Maryane | Maryem | Mary-Layne | Maryscott | Mashyia | Matdison | Matjea |
| Mary-Ange | Maryema | Mary-Lee | Maryse | Masiah | Matea (0.01) | Matlyn |
| Maryange | Mary-Emma | Marylee (0.01) | Marysha | Masie | Mateena | Matojah |
| Maryangel | Maryetta | Maryleigh | Maryshia | Masiel | Mateja | Matondo-M'eloheeka |
| Mary-Anikah | Maryeve | | Maryska | Masielle | Matejka | Matrinette |
| Mary-Ann (0.01) | | | Marysol (0.01) | Masilya | Matelyn | |
| Maryann (0.04) | | | Mary-Soleil | Masin | | |

| | | | | | | |
|---|---|---|---|---|---|---|
| Matrona | Mau'riah | Maurissia | May Munah | Maybella | Mayilaya | Maynetre |
| Matson | Maud | Mauriyah | Amatullah | Maybelle | Mayim | Mayola |
| Mattaea | Maude (0.14) | Mauriye | May Sarah | Maybelline | Mayka (0.01) | Mayoni |
| Mattali | Maude Alyson | Maurkita | Maya (2.69) | Maybree | Maykala | Mayowa |
| Mattalie | Maude- | Maurnaya | Maya Aisha | Maybrey | Maykalah | Mayra (0.06) |
| Mattalyn | Alexandra | Maurnisha | Maya Angelique | Maybritt | Maykayla | Mayra-Liz |
| Mattalynn | Maude-Elise | Maurquicia | Maya Caterina | Mayce (0.01) | Maykaylee | Mayran |
| Mattaya | Maude-Emile | Maury | Maya Jade | Maycee (0.02) | Maykeline | Mayrani |
| Mattéa | Maude-Emilie | Maurya | Maya Jo | Maycey | Maykhala | Mayrav |
| Mattea (0.03) | Maude-Evelyne | Mauryana | Maya Lee | Mayci (0.01) | Maykila | Mayre |
| Matteah | Maude- | Mauryayla | Maya Maite | Maycia | May-Kler | Mayree |
| Mattee | Frederique | Maurysa | Maya Mujany | Maycie (0.02) | Mayla (0.01) | Mayreli |
| Mattel | Maudella | Mausi | Maya Toddy | Maycin | Maylah | Mayrelis |
| Mattelin | Maude-Sophie | Mausie-Ann | Maya Virginia | Maycle | Maylana | Mayrena |
| Matteline | Maudie | Mave | Maya-Anabelle | Mayco | Mayland | Mayreni |
| Mattelyn | Maudist | Mavelyn | Maya-Camille | Maycy | Maylasia | Mayrette |
| Mattelynn | Maudreann | Mavenee | Maya-Christina | Mayda | Maylaza | Mayrim |
| Matterson | Maui | Maveric | Mayah (0.04) | Maydali | May-Lea | Mayrin |
| Mattey | Maulana | Maverick | Maya-Jade | Maydelid | Maylea | Mayrit |
| Matteya | Mauna | Mavi | Mayaka | Maydelin | Maylee (0.01) | Maysa (0.01) |
| Matthania | Maur'kevia | Mavie | Mayakim | Maydely | Mayleen | Maysane |
| Matthea | Maura (0.13) | Mavis | Mayalain | Mayden | Mayleena | Maysann |
| Matthew | Maurah | Mavourneen | Mayalea | Maydeni | Mayleigh | Mayse |
| Matthia | Mauralise | Mavrick | Maya-Lee | Maydine | Maylen (0.01) | Maysem |
| Matti (0.01) | Maur-Asia | Mawaahib | Mayalena | Maydson | Maylena | Maysen (0.01) |
| Mattia | Maureen (0.03) | Mawada | Maya-Lily | Maye | Maylene | Maysha |
| Mattias | Maureena- | Mawaddah | Mayalin | Mayeaux | Maylenia | Maysi |
| Matticlaire | Adelina | Mawata | Maya-Lissette | Mayeila | Maylesa | Maysie |
| Mattie (0.12) | Mauren | Mawuena | Mayalou | Mayel | Mayley | Mayson (0.02) |
| Mattie Isa | Maurena | Max | Maya-Lydia | Mayela | Mayli | Mayssa |
| Mattie-Joe | Mauri | Maxandre | Mayalynn | Mayeli | Maylia | Maysun |
| Mattie-Mae | Mauriah | Maxca | Maya-Maria | Mayeline | Mayliah | Maysyn |
| Mattilé | Mauriahana | Maxely | Mayamu | Mayelis | Mayliann | Mayte (0.02) |
| Mattilyn (0.01) | Mauriana | Maxence | Mayan | Mayelynn | Maylie (0.01) | Maytinee |
| Mattilynn | Maurianna | Maxene | Mayana | Mayerli | Maylie-Ann | Maytolla |
| Mattina | Maurica | Maxianna | Mayangay | Mayerli Betzaida | Maylilly | Maytriona |
| Mattingly | Mauricea | Maxie | Mayani | Mayerlin | Maylin (0.01) | Mayu |
| Mattisan | Mauriceya | Maxilynn | Mayanic | Mayerling | Maylina | Mayu Jamie |
| Mattisen | Mauricia | Maxim (0.05) | May-Ann | Mayeva | Maylinda | Mayukhi |
| Mattison (0.03) | Maurie | Maxim G | Mayann | Mayflor | Mayline | Mayuko |
| Mattisyn | Maurie Anadia | Maxima | Mayanna | Mayfrostina | Maylisa | Mayumi |
| Mattix | Maurin | Maxime (0.03) | Mayannah | Maygan (0.01) | Mayllina | Mayura |
| Mattlyn | Maurin'a | Maximiana | May-Anne | Maygane | Maylodie | Mayurie |
| Mattox | Maurine | Maximilienne | Mayanne | Mayganne | Maylon | Mayva |
| Matty | Maurinia | Maximina | Mayar | Mayge | Maylorie | Mayzee |
| Mattye | Maurinya | Maxine (0.04) | Mayara | Maygen (0.01) | Maylyma | Mayzi |
| Mattyline | Maurioanna | Maxra | Maya-Rae | Mayghan | Maylyn | Mayzie |
| Matty-Lynn | Maurionca | Maxum | Mayari | Mayha | Maylynn | Mazaya |
| Mattyson | Maurisa | Maxwell | Maya-Rose | Mayhgen | Mayme | Mazayic |
| Maty | Maurisha | Maxx | Maya-Soleil | Mayi | Maymouna | Mazden |
| Matya | Maurissa | Maxym (0.01) | Mayauna | Ma-Yia | Maymuna | Maze |
| Matyson | Maurissa- | Maxyme | Mayazeli | Mayia | Mayna | Mazee |
| Matysse | Mariah | May (0.04) | Maybel | Mayian | Maynet | Mazel |

| | | | | | | |
|---|---|---|---|---|---|---|
| Mazey | Mckailee | Mckenna (0.67) | Mckinzey | Mead | Meckenzy | Megan Angel Snow |
| Mazhara | Mckaileigh | Mckennah | Mckinzi | Meadelin | Meckilla | Megan Isabelle |
| Mazi | Mckailey | Mckenney | Mckinzie (0.02) | Meadhbh | Meckinze | Megan Laura |
| Mazie (0.02) | Mckaine | Mckenny | Mckinzy | Meado | Meda | Megan Patricia |
| Mazinaiy | Mckaitlin | Mckennzie | Mckinzye | Meadoe | Medariah | Mégane |
| Mazli | Mckala | Mckensey | Mckiyah | Meadoh | Medea | Megane (0.22) |
| Mazlyn | Mckalea | Mckensi | Mcklynn | Meadow (0.13) | Medeau | Megane Laurence |
| Mazy | Mckalee | Mckensie (0.01) | Mckree | Meadowe | Medeja | Megane Mia |
| Mazzalyn | Mckaleigh | Mckensley | Mckyla | Meadow-Lynn | Medelin | Megane-Jennyka |
| Mazzara | Mckalen | Mckensy | Mckylee | Meadreya | Medelisabel | Megan-Elizabeth |
| Mazzarine | Mckaley | Mckenxie | Mckynlee | Meagan (0.16) | Medha (0.01) | Megan-Isabel |
| Mazzi | Mckali | Mckenze | Mckynna | Meagan Christine | Medha Manogya | Meganlue |
| Mazzia | Mckaliah | Mckenzee (0.01) | Mckynsi | Meaganne | Medhini | Meg-Ann (0.01) |
| Mazzie | Mckalyn | Mckenzey (0.01) | Mckynzee | Meagan-Victoria | Mediesha | Megann (0.01) |
| Mazzy (0.01) | Mckalyn Hope | Mckenzi (0.03) | Mckynzi | Meagen | Medina (0.01) | Meg-Anne |
| Mbali | Mckalynn | Mckenzia | Mckynzie | Meagham | Medine | Meganne (0.02) |
| Mbia | Mckamy | Mckenzie (1.10) | Mckyrra | Meaghan (0.07) | Mediyma | Megan-Theresa |
| Mbia Theresa | Mckartnee | Mckenzie Carolyn | Mclain | Meaghanne | Medjina | Megdelyn |
| Mc (0.01) | Mckay (0.01) | Mckenzie L | Mclaren | Meaghen | Medjine | Megen |
| Mc Kailyn | Mckaya | Mckenziea | Mclaurin | Meaghin | Medj-Sephora | Meggan (0.01) |
| Mc Kenley | Mckayah | Mckenziee | Mclean | Meagin | Medjune | Meggane |
| Mc Kenna | Mckayda | Mckenzlee | Mcluann | Meagne | Medora | Meggie (0.04) |
| Mc Kenzie | Mckayden | Mckenzley | Mcmanuel | Meagyn | Medorae | Megglyne |
| Mcarra | Mckayla (0.20) | Mckenzy (0.01) | Mcnally | Meah (0.04) | Medori | Meggy (0.01) |
| Mccaffery | Mckaylah | Mckenzye | Mcrae | Meahnaj | Medow | Meggye |
| Mccailah | Mckayla-Leu | Mckenzyee | Mcrea | Meaira | Medrith | Megha (0.01) |
| Mccaitlyn | Mckaylan | Mckhiya | MD | Meairra | Mee | Meghaan |
| Mccall | Mckayleah | Mckiah | Me | Mealis | Meeah | Meghan (0.60) |
| Mccarley | Mckaylee | Mckiley | Me'arah | Meame | Meegan (0.01) | Meghana (0.01) |
| Mccarthy | Mckayleigh | Mckina | Me'asha | Meana | Meeghan | Meghanareddy |
| Mccartney | Mckaylie | Mckindra | Me'cole | Meandryne | Meegwin | Meghane |
| Mccary | Mckaylin | Mckinlay | Me'iiah | Meane | Meeka | Meghane Nichole |
| Mccauley | Mckechnie | Mckinlea | Me'jazia | Meann | Meeka Lenaj | Meghann |
| Mccaulley | Mckeeley | Mckinlee | Me'kailah | Meanne | Meeka-Alexianne | Meghen |
| Mccaylen | Mckeena | Mckinleigh | Me'kayla | Meara (0.02) | Meekah | Meghna (0.01) |
| Mcclary | Mckeilin | Mckinley (0.07) | Me'kayla-Ann | Mearria | Meekness | Megi |
| Mcclean | Mckelee | Mckinli | Me'kenzie | Measha | Meela | Megia |
| Mccord | Mckell | Mckinlie | Me'khiah | Measia | Meelah | Megie Jackie |
| Mccoy | Mckella | Mckinly | Me'kyah | Measiah | Meeleigh | Megumi |
| Mccrae | Mckellan | Mckinna | Me'laysia | Meava | Meena (0.02) | Megwon |
| Mccullough | Mckelle | Mckinnah | Me'lea | Meaya | Meenakshi | Megy |
| Mccyah | Mckellyn | Mckinney | Me'liyah | Meba | Meera (0.03) | Megyn |
| Mccyrah | Mckelvey | Mckinnlee | Me'oncia | Mebbie | Meerab | Meh'quira |
| Mcgill | Mckena | Mckinnley | Me'orah | Meblinda | Meesha | Meh'yonna |
| Mcgowan | Mckenah | Mckinnzie | Me'ron | Mecaela | Meeshah | Meha |
| Mcgraw | Mckenda | Mckinsey (0.01) | Me'ryah | Mecca (0.01) | Meeya | Mehak (0.01) |
| Mchaley | Mckendra | Mckinsie | Me'shalle | Mechaela | Meezee | Mehakdeep |
| Mchaney | Mckendyll | Mckinsley | Me'shoundr | Mechelle | Meg (0.02) | Mehaketv |
| Mckadie | Mckenize | Mckinsy | Me'yana | Meciah | Megaelle | Mehakpreet |
| Mckaela | Mckenlee | Mckinze | Me'yauney | Meciya | Mégan | |
| Mckai | Mckenley | Mckinzee | Me'yonna | Meckensie | Megan (2.93) | |
| Mckaila | Mckenlie | | Mea (0.04) | Meckenzie | Megan Alcinoe | |
| Mckailah | Mckenly | | Meabe | | | |

| | | | | | | |
|---|---|---|---|---|---|---|
| Mehakveer | Meilia | Mekensey | Melani (0.03) | Meleigha | Melisia | Melodie D |
| Mehal | Meilie | Mekensize | Melania (0.03) | Meleisha | Melissa (1.56) | Melody (0.34) |
| Mehanaz | Meilillany | Mekenzi | Mélanie (0.01) | Melek | Melissa | Melody B |
| Mehar (0.01) | Mei-Lin | Mekenzie (0.02) | Melanie (2.00) | Meleka | Alessandra | Melody June |
| Mehayla | Meilin | Mekhala | Melanie | Melena (0.01) | Melissa | Melodye |
| Meheeka | Meiling | Mekhayla | Elizabeth | Melenie | Elizabeth | Melodyfaith |
| Mehek | Meily | Mekhi | Melanie | Melenny | Melissa-Christy | Meloika |
| Meher (0.01) | Meilyn | Mekhia (0.01) | Georgette | Meleny | Melissa-Ngoya | Meloise |
| Meherin | Meina | Mekhiah | Melanie Heval | Meleri | Melisse | Melondy |
| Mehgan | Meira (0.01) | Mekhijah | Melanie Lan | Melery | Melissia | Meloney |
| Mehin | Meirakal | Mekhila | Melanie Nata | Melesse | Melita | Meloni |
| Mehkinzie | Meiran | Mekhiya | Melanie-Andrea | Meleya | Melitza | Melonia |
| Mehkiyah | Meisha | Mekiah | Melaniee | Meleyka | Meliya | Melonie (0.01) |
| Mehkwan | Meishell | Mekiah-Lee | Melanies | Meli | Meliyah | Melony (0.01) |
| Mehlani | Meisner | Mekiala | Melanise | Melia (0.05) | Meliza | Melora |
| Mehlika | Meissa | Mekiayla | Melaniya | Meliah | Melizahishia | Melorie |
| Mehma | Meital | Mekieyah | Melanna | Melian F | Melizandre | Melorra |
| Mehnaaz | Meive | Mekila | Melanni | Meliana | Melizza | Melory |
| Mehr | Meixi | Mekinezé | Melannia | Meliane (0.01) | Meljania | Melosa |
| Mehrael | Meiyauna | Mekinley | Melannie | Meli-Ann | Mella | Melriyah |
| Mehreen | Meiying | Mekinzee | Melanny (0.01) | Meliann | Mella'kya | Melsha |
| Mehrin | Meiyu | Mekinzie | Melany (0.13) | Melianne (0.01) | Melladee | Meltem |
| Mehrish | Mejenskah | Mekiya | Melany | Melicia | Mellady | Meltia |
| Mehrsa | Mejienah | Mekiyah | Alexandra | Melicya | Mellaina | Meltini |
| Mehsa | Mejra | Mekka | Melanye | Melida | Mellana | Meltrice |
| Mehsne | Meka | Meklit | Melany-Miseth | Melidy | Mellani | Melva |
| Mehtaab | Mekada | Mekya | Melanys | Melie | Mellanie (0.01) | Melvarria |
| Mehtab | Mekaela | Mekyah | Melaris | Melie-Anne | Mellany | Melvashia |
| Mehvish | Mekaelah | Mekyla | Melasha | Melie-Rose | Mellena | Melvasia |
| Mei (0.01) | Mekaelyn | Mel | Melasia | Meliha | Melleny | Melveanna |
| Mei Lee | Mekah | Mel'lashia | Melat | Melijade | Melliah | Melvin |
| Mei Lie | Mekai | Mela | Melaudy | Melika (0.01) | Mellie | Melvina |
| Mei'asia | Mekaila | Meladi Nalani | Melawnie | Melike | Mellila | Melvina |
| Mei'lin | Mekailah | Meladie | Melaya | Melilla | Mellina | Shauntea |
| Mei'yah | Mekailla | Melaed | Melayah | Melillani | Mellion | Melvinaysia |
| Meia | Mekailyn | Melaena | Melayna (0.01) | Mélina | Mellisa (0.01) | Melviona |
| Meiah | Mekaiyla | Melaenna | Melaysa | Melina (0.21) | Mellise | Melvona |
| Meighan | Mekala | Melah | Melaysha | Melina-Chance | Mellissa | Melvonna |
| Meiha | Mekalah | Melahrini | Melayzia | Melina- | Mellody | Melya |
| Meijin | Mekalya | Melaiah | Melchora | Elizabeth | Mellodye | Melyah |
| Meika (0.01) | Mekaya | Melaina (0.02) | Melda | Melinah | Mellony | Melyan |
| Meikayla | Mekayla (0.01) | Melaine | Meldane | Melinda (0.07) | Melly | Melyana |
| Meike | Mekaylah | Melainia | Meldina | Meline | Melly-Jade | Melyane |
| Meikesha | Mekdalawit | Melaisha | Melé | Melinie | Mellyssa | Mélyane |
| Meiki | Mekeida | Melaiyah | Mele'na | Melinna | Mellyzandre | Melyanie |
| Meiko | Mekel | Melajah | Melea (0.01) | Melis | Melnasia | Mely-Ann |
| Meila | Mekelet | Melak | Meleah (0.01) | Melisa (0.05) | Melneisha | Melyann |
| Meilahn | Mekelit | Melakyi | Meleana | Melisande | Melodee | Melyanne |
| Meilani | Mekena | Melana (0.01) | Meleane | Melisanne | Melodey | Melyda |
| Meilee | Mekendyn | Melanah | Meleanie | Melisant | Melodi | Melyka |
| Meileen | Mekenli | Melanee | Meleena (0.01) | Melise | Melodia | Melyna (0.02) |
| Meileighca | Mekenna (0.01) | Melaney (0.01) | Meleia | Melisende | Mélodie | Melynda |
| Meili | Mekennly | Melangell | Meleiah | Melisha | Melodie (0.13) | Melynn |

| | | | | | |
|---|---|---|---|---|---|
| Melynna | Meradith | Merdaydeez | Merissa *(0.02)* | Mersadize | Meshiah | Mezmaria |
| Melysa | Meraiah | Mereah | Merit | Mersadys | Meshun | Meztli |
| Melysane | Meraina | Merebeth | Meriwether | Mersaede | Mesiku | Meztly |
| Melyssa *(0.01)* | Meral | Meredith *(0.33)* | Meriya | Mersah | Mesinna | Mhairi |
| Melyssan | Meralee | Meredyth | Merlanda | Mersaides | Mesiyah | Mhari |
| Melyssandre | Meraliz | Meredythe | Merldley | Mersaidez | Mesly | Mhelody |
| Melyzane | Meralys | Merekal | Merle | Mersais | Mesmerai | Mhina |
| Memengwa | Meranda *(0.02)* | Merelin | Merlena | Mersaydeez | Messaia | Mhiranda |
| Memoree | Merandia | Merelis | Merli | Mersaydes | Messiah *(0.01)* | Mhorgan |
| Memorie | Merari *(0.02)* | Merelyn | Merlin *(0.01)* | Mersaydez | Messiane | Mhyah |
| Memory *(0.01)* | Meraris | Meren | Merlinda | Mersayus | Messina | Mhyrica |
| Memphis *(0.01)* | Merary | Merennah | Merlise | Mersedez | Mesyia | Mi Amor |
| Memree | Meraya | Meresa | Merlly | Mersheá | Meta | Mi Angel |
| Memuna | Merayah | Mere-Thérèse | Merlot | Mert | Metabelle | Mi Chaela |
| Memunatu | Merazhia | Mereya | Merloucy-Jane | Mertani | Metekiya | Mi Chaja |
| Mena *(0.01)* | Mercaddiez | Meri | Merly | Merva | Methila | Mi Ji |
| Menaa | Mercadeas | Meria | Merlyn | Merve | Methuli | Mi Kaija |
| Menaal | Mercadee | Meriah | Merlyne | Merveille | Methzybel | Mi Khiah |
| Menah | Mercadees | Meriah Faith | Meroma | Mervense | Metta | Mi Kyelah |
| Menaka | Mercades *(0.01)* | Meriam *(0.01)* | Meron | Merwa | Mette | Mí Layah |
| Menashia | Mercades | Merian | Merra | Mer-Xskalaysia | Metthea | Mi Thao |
| Mende | Lucille | Meriana | Merredith | Mery | Metzli | Mi Yana |
| Mendi | Mercadez | Meribah | Merriam | Mery Jane | Metzly | Mi Yane |
| Mendoza | Mercadies | Merica | Merribeth | Meryah | Metztli | Mi Yonte |
| Guzman | Mercadyz | Meridath | Merrice | Meryam | Metztlie | Mi'a |
| Mendy | Mercayde | Meriden | Merrick *(0.01)* | Meryam | Metztly | Mi'ahjah |
| Mendy Carole | Merce | Merideth | Merrie | Hibatallah | Meutiaaswila | Mi'ajah |
| Meneu | Mercea | Meridian | Merri-Elisabeth | Meryem *(0.01)* | Mevane | Mi'ajia |
| Meng Ting | Merceades | Meridith *(0.01)* | Merrielle | Meryk | Mevavi | Mi'alenn-I |
| Meng Xing | Merceadys | Meridth | Merriem | Meryl *(0.01)* | Mexi | Mi'ana |
| Mengzhu | Merceas | Meridyth | Merrigan | Merylie | Mextic-Metci | Mi'angel |
| Menija | Mercedas | Meriel | Merrik | Meryliz | Meya *(0.02)* | Mi'angela |
| Menina | Mercede | Meriella | Merrill | Meryll | Meyah *(0.01)* | Mi'anna |
| Menisha | Mercedee | Merielle | Merrin | Meryl-Lyn | Meyara | Mi'ari |
| Meniyah | Mercedekay | Meriem *(0.01)* | Merris | Meryn | Meyaunni | Mi'aria |
| Menji | Mercedes *(0.31)* | Meriem-Doudja | Merrissa | Meryssa | Meydelin | Mi'ashia |
| Mennah | Mercedes Jo | Merieme | Merrissa-Marie | Meryt | Meyer | Mi'asia |
| Mennya | Mercedese | Meriem-Razane | Merrit | Meryum | Meygan *(0.01)* | Mi'asiah |
| Mennyah | Mercedez *(0.02)* | Merien Amina | Merritt *(0.01)* | Merzedz | Meygane | Mi'auna |
| Menooha | Mercedi | Merietta | Merry | Mesa | Meygangrace | Mi'auni |
| Menrite | Mercedies | Merika | Merry-Jane | Mesaiya | Meyika | Mi'auntay |
| Menucha | Mercee | Merikls | Merryjayne | Mesange | Meykinna | Mi'cayla |
| Menyawnia | Mercehdez | Merilee | Merryjoy | Mescha | Meylei | Mi'dream |
| Menyon | Mercella | Merilin | Merryn | Meschon | Meylin | Mi'dynasti |
| Menzie | Mercer | Merill | Merryscot | Mesdean | Meyling | Mi'ejah |
| Meohmie | Merceylees | Merilyn | Merryum | Mesha | Meylissia | Mi'hyest |
| Meosha | Merci | Merin | Mersadeez | Meshal | Meyona | Mi'kaejah |
| Mephew | Mercia | Merina | Mersades | Meshari | Meyri | Mi'kaja |
| Meprise | Mercie | Meris | Mersadez | Meshayan'na | Meyrin | Mi'kala |
| Mequéla | Mercina | Merisa *(0.01)* | Mersadi | Meshayla | Meyshalee | Mi'kayah |
| Mera | Mercinda | Merisah | Mersadie | Meshell | Meytal | Mi'kayjah |
| Merab | Mercy *(0.04)* | Merisan | Mersadies *(0.01)* | Meshelle | Mezan | Mi'kayla *(0.01)* |
| Meracle | Merczaydes | Merisha | Mersadiez | Mesheyla | Meziah | Mi'keira |

| | | | | | | |
|---|---|---|---|---|---|---|
| Mi'kel | Miachael | Mia-Rose | Micalynn | Michalene | Michenna | Micky |
| Mi'kela | Mia-Emily | Miarrah | Micari | Michaley | Michenzi | Mickyela |
| Mi'kerria | Mia-Estrella | Mia-Sara | Micaya | Michali | Micheria | Mickyle |
| Mi'keyah | Miafaye | Mia-Sarah | Micayah | Michalina | Michia | Micole |
| Mi'khaya | Miagabriela | Mia-Saron | Micayala | Michaline | Michigan | Micyah |
| Mi'khia | Miah (0.10) | Miasha | Micayaly | Michall | Michiko | Midalia |
| Mi'khila | Miah Rose | Miashia | Micayella | Michalla | Michiya | Midestiny |
| Mi'kilyia | Miahta | Miasia | Mi-Cay-La | Michallea | Michiyah | Midian |
| Mi'kira | Mia-Isabella | Mia-Sophie | Micayla (0.04) | Michallie | Michkia | Midnight |
| Mi'kiya | Miaja | Miasya | Micayla-Ann | Michal-Michelle | Michlynn | Midori (0.01) |
| Mi'kiyah | Mia-Jane | Mia-Taline | Micaylah | Michalyn | Michole | Midxisi |
| Mi'kya | Miaje | Mia-Tilar | Micaylee | Michalynn | Michon | Midya |
| Mi'kyala | Miakayla | Miauna | Micaylie | Michanda | Michsha | Mie |
| Mi'kyiah | Miakaylia | Miaunna | Micca | Michanti | Michyia | Mieasha |
| Mi'kylah | Mia-Kelly | Miaya | Miccah | Micharia | Michyla | Mieashia |
| Mi'lan | Miaki | Miayah | Micgracious | Michay | Miciah | Mieawna |
| Mi'leana | Mia-Kim | Miayana | Micha (0.01) | Michaya | Miciaha | Miechelle |
| Mi'lee | Miakoda | Miayonah | Micha'iah | Michayela | Miciyah | Mieka |
| Mi'lyana | Miakota | Miaysia | Michaala | Michayla (0.01) | Mickaela | Miekayle |
| Mi'lyrah | Miala | Miazha | Michae | Miché | Mickaella | Mieke |
| Mi'nayjah | Miale | Mic Kaila | Michaea | Micheal | Mickaelle | Miekka |
| Mi'neisha | Mialeigh | Mic'keyia | Michael (0.02) | Micheala (0.01) | Mickaellya | Mieko |
| Mi'niel | Mialena | Mic'zaria | Michael An | Michealla | Mickailey | Miel |
| Mi'nooshkah | Mialexandra | Mica (0.01) | Michaela (0.42) | Michecoe | Mickal | Miela |
| Mi'shawna | Miali | Mica'iah | Michaela Love | Micheel | Mickala | Mielani |
| Mi'-Treasure | Miali Rosie | Micaecha | Michaela Munroe | Michel (0.01) | Mickalena | Mielchama |
| Mi'unique | Mialien | Micaela (0.07) | Michaela-Grace | Michel'le | Mickalynne | Mieldrean |
| Mi'yana | Mialou | Micaela Gabrielle | Michaelah | Michela (0.01) | Mickaya | Mielé |
| Mi'yani | Mialuna | Micaela-Angelica | Michaelea | Michelda | Mickayla (0.02) | Mièle |
| Mi'yanna | Mialyese | Micaella | Michaeleen | Michele (0.05) | Mickaylah | Mielie |
| Mi'yauna | Mialyn | Micah (0.11) | Michaelena | Michele Monique | Mickaylea | Miella |
| Mi'yona | Mia-Lynn | Micah Ellis | Michaeli | Michelena | Mickaylee | Mielle |
| Mi'yonna | Mialynn | Micah Racquel | Michaelie | Michelia | Mickeelah | Mienelle |
| Miá | Mia-Maria | Micaha | Michaella (0.01) | Michelina | Mickela | Miera |
| Mia (5.39) | Mia-Martina | Micah-Ann | Michaëlle | Michelina Antoinette | Mickell | Mierae |
| Mia Angelina | Mia-Maude | Micahela | Michaelle (0.01) | Micheline | Mickella | Miericle |
| Mia Bella | Mia-Melina | Micahila | Michael-Marie | Michell (0.01) | Mickelle | Mierna |
| Mia Chenna | Miami | Micahla | Michaelyn (0.01) | Michell'a | Mickelyn | Miesah |
| Mia Elena | Miamor | Micahlyn | Michaeya | Michella | Mickenah | Miesha (0.01) |
| Mia Elizabeth | Miamormara | Micahya | Michaeyla | Michellé | Mickenna | Mietreya |
| Mia Jade | Miana (0.01) | Micahyah | Michah | Michelle (2.17) | Mickenzie | Miette |
| Mia Jaylen | Mianay | Micaiah (0.02) | Michaiah (0.01) | Michelle Stephanie | Mickenzy | Mieyel |
| Mia Katherine | Miandrea | Micaila | Michaila | Michelled | Mickenzye | Mie-Yonna |
| Mia Yuzelmi | Mianeliz | Micailah | Michaila-Mae | Michelleda | Mickey | Migan |
| Mia'aisha | Miangel (0.01) | Micailee | Michaiyla | Michelle-Nataly | Mickhail | Migdaleez |
| Mia'anjel | Miangelina | Micaiyah | Michal (0.01) | Michellie | Mickhaila | Migdalia |
| Mia'francesca | Miani | Micajah | Michala (0.01) | Michelly | Mickiayah | Migdaliz |
| Mia'lanay | Miania | Micala | Michala Kioreen | Michelogue | Mickie | Migdelina |
| Mia'luna | Mianna (0.01) | Micalah | Michalea | Michelynn | Mickinna | Miggie |
| Mia-Alexandra | Mianya | Micaleah | Michalee | Michelys | Mickinzi | Migis |
| Mia-Angelina | Miar | Micalee | Michalena | | Mickinzy | Mignonette |
| Miabella (0.01) | Miara | | | | Mickita | Mignot |
| Mia-Carmella | Miari | | | | Mickiya | Migsuly |

| | | | | | | |
|---|---|---|---|---|---|---|
| Miguel | Mika-Eve | Mikaylan | Mikeshia | Mikole | Milarys | Milianne- |
| Miguelina | Mikah *(0.02)* | Mikaylee | Mikevia | Mikria | Milasha | Cristina |
| Miguelle | Mikahá | Mikayleigh | Mikeya | Mikya | Milasia | Miliany |
| Mih'asia | Mikahila | Mikayleighia | Mikeyah | Mikyah | Milaura | Milianys |
| Miha | Mikahla | Mikaylen | Mikeyia | Mikyia | Milaya | Milia-Rose |
| Mihaela | Mikahlya | Mikayli | Mikeyla | Mikyira | Milayah | Milica |
| Mihaly | Mikahlyn | Mikaylie | Mikhaela *(0.01)* | Mikyla *(0.02)* | Milayka | Milicia |
| Mihayanna | Mikahya | Mikaylin | Mikhaela Leiann | Mikylah | Milayla | Milie |
| Miher | Mikai | Mikaylyn | Paguia | Mikylee | Milayna | Mili-Jade |
| Miheshia | Mikaia | Mikaylynn | Mikhaelah | Mikyleigh | Milayshka | Milijana |
| Mihiaroha | Mikaiah | Mikayna | Mikhaila *(0.01)* | Mikyna | Milaysia | Milila |
| Mihika | Mikaiella | Mike | Mikhala | Mikynzie | Milayzia | Milin |
| Mihira | Mikaila *(0.02)* | Mike'ayla | Mikhalia | Mikyra | Milbrey | Milina |
| Mihjae | Mikailah | Mikea | Mikhaya | Mil'dasia | Milca | Milissa |
| Mihkayla | Mikaili | Mikeala | Mikhayla | Mil'dreioniá | Milcah | Militza |
| Mihonga | Mikaily | Mikeale | Mikhelya | Raymia | Milda | Miliya |
| Mihret | Mikailya | Mikeay'la | Mikhia | Mil'khia | Mildred *(0.02)* | Milka |
| Mihsne | Mikailynn | Mikeayla | Mikhiya | Mil'lanni | Milea | Milla *(0.03)* |
| Mihyana | Mikaitlyn | Mikehla | Mikhiyah | Mila *(0.10)* | Mileadrionna | Millahcent |
| Mihyia | Mikaiya | Mikeia | Mikhya | Mila Chai | Mileah | Millan |
| Mii'angil | Mikaiyah | Mikeiah | Mikhyia | Mila Jane | Milecia | Millani |
| Miia | Mikajalita | Mikeila | Miki *(0.01)* | Mila'n | Milee | Millee |
| Miicolaahrae | Mikal | Mikeiley | Mikia *(0.01)* | Milaan | Mileena *(0.01)* | Millena |
| Miikka | Mikala *(0.04)* | Mikeira | Mikiah *(0.01)* | Mila-Christine | Milei | Milleni |
| Miina | Mikalah *(0.09)* | Mikel | Mikiai | Milady | Mileidis | Millennia |
| Miiranda | Mikalaida | Mikela | Mikiara | Milady Isabella | Mileidy | Milleonne |
| Mija | Mikale | Mikeldra | Mikiaya | Milaena | Mileigh | Miller |
| Mijah | Mikalea | Mikelee | Mikihya | Milaey | Mileika | Milli |
| Mijal | Mikalen | Mikell | Mikiko | Milagro *(0.01)* | Milen | Milli'anna |
| Mijay | Mikaley | Mikella | Mikila | Milagros *(0.04)* | Milena *(0.03)* | William |
| Mije | Mikalie | Mikelle | Mikilah | Milah | Milene | Millian |
| Mijeanne | Mikalin | Mikellyn | Mikinley | Milai | Milenka | Milliann |
| Mijernae | Mikalle | Mikelyn | Mikinli | Milaina | Mileny | Milliannah |
| Mijia | Mikaly | Mikelyne | Mikinzi | Milaine | Miles | Millicent *(0.01)* |
| Mijoi | Mikalya | Miken | Mikinzie | Milaka | Miletsa | Millie *(0.03)* |
| Mijoo | Mikalyn *(0.01)* | Mikena | Mikinzy | Milam | Milette | Millieann |
| Mik'ah | Mikalynn | Mikenah | Mikira | Mi-Lan | Milexandrie | Millionna |
| Mik'eayla | Mikanna | Mikenlee | Mikisha | Milan *(0.05)* | Miley *(0.02)* | Millisen |
| Mik'quall | Mikara | Mikenley | Mikita | Milana *(0.04)* | Mileya | Milly *(0.01)* |
| Mika *(0.05)* | Mikari | Mikenna *(0.02)* | Mikiya *(0.01)* | Milanda | Mileyda | Millyanie |
| Mika Agatha | Mikarose | Mikennah | Mikiyah | Milandra | Mileydi | Milly-Anne |
| Mikaala | Mikasia | Mikenzi | Mikiyia | Milane | Mileydy | Milo-Ivelisse |
| Mikaeh | Mikay | Mikenzie *(0.02)* | Mikka *(0.01)* | Milaní | Mileyna | Milon |
| Mikaeja | Mikaya *(0.01)* | Mikeonna | Mikkailah | Milani *(0.02)* | Mileyne | Miloury |
| Mikael | Mikayah | Mikera | Mikkayla | Milania | Mileyshka | Milre |
| Mikaela *(0.16)* | Mikayala | Mikerah | Mik-Keizcha | Milaniya | Milgo | Milsy |
| Mikaelah | Mikayela | Mikerda | Mikkel | Milanna | Mili | Miltiyanna |
| Mikaele | Mikayia | Mikeria | Mikkeya | Milanni | Milia | Miluska |
| Mikaeli | Mikayla *(0.97)* | Mikeriha | Mikki | Milannia | Miliah | Milvia |
| Mikaella | Mikayla Angel | Mikeriya | Miklyn | Milannie | Miliana | Mily |
| Mikaella Oceane | Mikayla Suns | Mikerly | Miknia | Milanova | Miliani | Milyann |
| Mikaelle *(0.01)* | Mikaylah *(0.05)* | Mikerria | Miko | Milanpreet | Milianie | Milyna |
| Mikaelynn | Mikayla-Lynn | Mikesha | Mikoal | Milanyé | Milianne | Milynn |

The Baby Name Countdown

| | | | | | | |
|---|---|---|---|---|---|---|
| Mima | Minhthu | Miracle Alliyah | Mirelsi | Miry | Miss Felixcah | Miyae |
| Mimas | Miniah | Miracle La | Mirelys | Mirya | Miss'saniya | Miyah *(0.04)* |
| Mimi *(0.01)* | Miniroath | Miracle Mystic | Mirembe | Miryah | Missaouda | Miyahna |
| Mimika | Miniya *(0.01)* | Miradith | Mirenna | Miryam | Missiah | Miyahta |
| Mimiq | Miniyah | Mirage | Mireya *(0.05)* | Miryan | Missiely | Miyako |
| Mimiracle | Minjee | Mirah | Mireyah | Miryana | Missouri | Miyala |
| Mimmi | Min-Ji | Mirahcle | Mireyda | Miryha | Missy | Miyana |
| Mimoza | Minjoon | Mirahkhal | Mireyli | Miryssa | Mistajia | Miyanah |
| Min Yi | Minju | Mirai | Mirhan | Miryuah | Mistee | Miyanna |
| Mi-Na | Minka | Mirainda | Mirhonda | Mirzeta | Misten | Miyanni |
| Mina *(0.09)* | Minky | Miraix | Miri | Mis'sheoni | Misti | Miyashia |
| Mina Debra Sue | Minna *(0.01)* | Miraje | Miriah *(0.01)* | Misa *(0.01)* | Mistiann | Miyasia |
| Minadora | Minnah | Mirakle | Mirial | Misaki | Mistidawn | Miyawâta |
| Minah | Minnie *(0.01)* | Miralda | Mirialys | Misam | Mistieriyah | Miyea |
| Minahil | Minnivere | Miralica | Mirialyz | Misaray | Mistijah | Miyel |
| Minako | Minnoli | Miralie | Miriam *(0.39)* | Misarin | Mistique | Miyell |
| Minal | Minran | Miraliese | Miriam | Misato | Mistura | Miyer |
| Minalea | Minta | Miramaya | Hadassah | Mischa *(0.02)* | Misty *(0.04)* | Miyera |
| Minami | Mintah | Miran | Miriama | Mischa Nastassj | Misty-Jade | Miyette |
| Minatagbe | Mintra | Miranda *(1.06)* | Miriamdeliz | Mischelle | Misty-Lee | Miyianna |
| Minaya | Minuette | Miranda K | Miriamme | Miseli | Misty-Lucille | Miyima |
| Minayah | Minwella | Mirandah | Miriam-Ros | Misgana | Miszenna | Miykayah |
| Minayla | Minxie | Mirandi | Mirian *(0.02)* | Misha *(0.02)* | Mitali | Miykennie |
| Mincie | Minyah | Mirane Kayssy | Miriana | Mishaa | Mitari | Miyo |
| Mincy | Minyanah | Mirannda | Mirianna | Mishaal | Mitchel | Miyoko |
| Minda | Minyla | Miranova | Mirianne | Mishae | Mitchell | Miyona |
| Mindi | Minyoung | Mirany | Mirical | Mishael | Mitchella | Miyonna *(0.01)* |
| Mindie | Mio | Miranyda | Miricle | Mishaila | Mitchelle | Miyonne |
| Mindy *(0.05)* | Mioftu | Mirapia | Mirielle | Mishal | Mitha | Miyonni |
| Mindy Destiny | Mioh | Mirari | Miriem | Mishandra | Mithea | Miyosiwin |
| Mindye | Miona | Mirary | Mirissa | Mishanliz | Mithila | Miyoso |
| Mineasha | Mionn | Mirasol | Mirium | Misharra | Mithni | Miyra |
| Minelly | Mionna | Mirax | Miriya | Mishayla | Mithra | Miyranda |
| Minen | Miosha | Miraya | Miriyah | Mishca | Mitilda | Miyu |
| Minerva *(0.01)* | Miozotis | Mirayah | Mirka | Mishe | Mitra | Miyuka |
| Minesha | Miquazia | Mircal | Mirkaelle | Misheel | Mitsselle | Miyuki |
| Minette | Miquela | Mircale | Mirkani | Mishel | Mitsu | Mizaelle |
| Miney-Saray | Miquelina | Mircea | Mirla | Mishell | Mitsuika | Mizar |
| Ming | Miquella | Mircle | Mirlanda | Mishelle | Mitsuko | Mizhalee |
| Minga | Miquita | Mirea | Mirlande | Misheya | Mitzana | Mizki |
| Mingjia | Mir'acle | Mireia | Mirloca | Mishiella | Mitzi | Mizuki |
| Minglu | Mira *(0.10)* | Mireilla | Mirna *(0.01)* | Mishka | Mitzy | Mizzaray |
| Mingni | Mira'je | Mireille *(0.01)* | Miroshlava | Mishline | Miu | Mizziyha |
| Mingzhu | Mirabel | Mireily | Miroslava | Mishoniya | Miucci | Mk'ala |
| Minh | Mirabella | Mireja | Mirra *(0.01)* | Mishti | Miumi | Mkayla |
| Minh Thuong | Mirabellah | Mirel *(0.01)* | Mirrah | Mishyia | Mivan | Mkenna |
| Minhal | Mirabelle *(0.01)* | Mirela | Mirranda | Mishyra | Miwa | Mkenzie |
| Minhanh | Mirabhai | Mirelia | Mirriam | Misionare-Lei | Mixel | Mkenzy |
| Minhat | Mirac'lle | Mirelis | Mirryn | Miske | Mixtli | Mkii |
| Minhtam | Miracale | Mirell | Mirta | Miski | Mixtly | Mkyia |
| Minhthi | Miracel | Mirella *(0.02)* | Miruna | Misky | Miya *(0.09)* | Mkyla |
| Minhtho | Mirachle | Mirelle | Mirunalini | Misleidy | Miya'nah | Mlaieka |
| Minh-Thu | Miracle *(0.22)* | Mirellis | Mirvette | Misqa | Miyabi | Mlak |

| | | | | | |
|---|---|---|---|---|---|
| Mlia | Mohuwa | Mon'tarah | Moniqa | Monteniece | Mora | Morley |
| Mlila | Moia | Mona *(0.03)* | Monique *(0.10)* | Monter'rai | Moraes | Morning |
| Mlliyah | Moika | Mona Rae | Monique Gloria | Monterria | Morag | Morning Star |
| Mma | Moira *(0.03)* | Monaé | Monique-Aly | Monterriana | Moraiya | Morningstar |
| Mme | Moira Grace | Monae *(0.01)* | Monirsha | Monterrosa | Mora-Lee | Morningstarr |
| Mnito | Moira-Grace | Monai | Monisha | Montesia | Morales Sorrell | Morouge |
| Mo'kniyyah | Moire | Monaisa | Monishka | Montez | Morane | Morounfolu |
| Mo'lasia | Moisha | Monaja | Monisse | Montgomery | Morasha | Morraea |
| Mo'naesia | Mojadesola | Monalisa | Monita | Monthida | Moraya | Morrajah |
| Mo'naisa | Mojave | Monaque | Moniya | Montia | Morea | Morraya |
| Mo'naisia | Mojhgan | Monashia | Moniyah | Montianá | Moreen | Morria |
| Mo'nasia | Moka | Monasia | Monnay | Montiasia | Morela | Morriah |
| Mo'nasjha | Mokera | Monay | Monne | Montiera | Morelia | Morrigan *(0.01)* |
| Mo'nay | Moksha | Monaye | Monnyahla | Montierra | Morellianne- | Morrisa |
| Mo'nayzah | Mokshada | Monazhia | Monroe *(0.01)* | Montika | Lenna | Morrison |
| Mo'nek | Molasia | Monce | Monse | Montisha | Morena | Morrissa |
| Mo'ney | Molca | Moncerad | Monserá | Montonasia | Morenike | Morsal |
| Mo'nieha | Moleigh | Moncerrat | Monserad | Montorria | Morgaine | Morwenn |
| Mo'nique | Molie | Moncerrath | Monserat | Montrea | Morgan *(3.39)* | Mory-Elizabeth |
| Mo'riah | Molina | Monci | Monserath | Montrecia | Morgan Ann | Morysa |
| Moa | Molinda | Moncia | Monseratt | Montrice | Morgan Faith | Moselle |
| Moana | Molisha | Mondeisha | Monserradt | Montriona | Morgana | Mosha |
| Moani | Molitahisi | Mondinisha | Monserrat | Montserrat | Morgance | Moshea |
| Mobina | Mollee *(0.01)* | Mone | *(0.06)* | *(0.02)* | Morgandee | Mosunmola |
| Mobokoli | Molleigh | Moné | Monserrate | Montserrath | Morgandy | Motaysia |
| Modesta | Molley *(0.01)* | Mone't | Monserrath | Montsserrate | Morgane *(0.02)* | Motolani |
| Modesté | Molli *(0.01)* | Monea | Monserray | Montzerrat | Morgan- | Motria |
| Modesty | Mollie *(0.14)* | Monecia | Monsetrrat | Montzerrath | Marcella | Motunrayo |
| Modhi | Molly *(1.79)* | Monee | Monsoon | Monuay | Morgan-Mary | Moukonjae |
| Modupe | Molly Cooper | Moneera | Monsserat | Monunique | Morgann *(0.01)* | Mouktika |
| Moe | Molly Elissa | Moneet | Monsserath | Monya | Morganna | Mouly |
| Moeaqic | Molly Kate | Moneisha | Monsserrat | Monyae | Morganne *(0.01)* | Moumita |
| Moeay | Molly-Alice | Monera | Monsserrath | Monyale | Morganryan | Mouna |
| Moeih | Molly-Ann | Moneray | Mont'asia | Monyeah | Morgen *(0.03)* | Mounia |
| Moeka | Mollyann | Monesha | Montaisa | Monyrah | Morgenn | Mouram |
| Moekah | Molly-Anne | Monet *(0.02)* | Montaisia | Monysohn | Morghan *(0.02)* | Mouryha |
| Moeniahya | Mollybelle | Monet Maria | Montajah | Monzerat | Morghyn | Mousli |
| Moesha | Mollycia | Monete | Montana *(0.11)* | Monzerat | Morgin | Mousselyne |
| Mofe'yisará | Mollyclarie | Monetta | Montana-Rae | Grabriela | Morgyn *(0.01)* | Mowenda |
| Mofiyinfol | Mollye | Moneyka | Montane | Monzerath | Moria | Mowha |
| Mofopefolu | Mollyemma | Moni | Montanique | Monzerrat | Moriah *(0.09)* | Mowzar |
| Mogan | Molly-Hunter | Moni'jah | Montanna *(0.01)* | Monzerrath | Morica | Moxxi |
| Mohagani | Mollyka | Monia | Montasia | Monzyria | Morigan | Moya |
| Mohaiman | Molly-Kate | Moniah | Montavia | Mookopaw | Morigane | Moyin-Oluwa |
| Mohama | Molly-Rose | Monia-Junelie | Montaya | Moonhee | Morillea | Moyinoluwa |
| Mohammad | Mololu | Monica *(0.39)* | Montayja | Moonjade | Morina | Moyosore |
| Mohana | Momena | Monica Leonie | Montayna | Moonya | Morissa | Moyra |
| Mohazatou | Momina | Monicia | Montea | Moonyoung | Morissey | Moyra Christina |
| Moheema | Momo | Monick | Montea'jah | Moore | Moriya | Bridgid |
| Mohga | Momoko | Monieque | Monteasha | Moorea | Moriyah | Mozea |
| Mohijaha | Mon'alissa | Monija | Monteisha | Mopelola | Morjan | Mozel |
| Mohini | Mon'naja | Monika *(0.03)* | Montejha | Mor | Morjane | Mozella |
| Mohogany | Mon'taja | Monina | Montelaijah | Mor'dasha | Morkaya | Mridhula |

| | | | | | | |
|---|---|---|---|---|---|---|
| Mridula | Muni | Mutsumi | My'keylia | Myaah | Myari | Myela |
| Mridulaa | Muniba | Muwaahidah | My'keyshia | Mya-Alexandra | Myaruot | Myell |
| Mrinalini | Munira (0.01) | Muyassar | My'khia | Mya-Alicia | Myasha | Myella |
| Mrinmayee | Munirah | Muzan | My'kia | Myadoar | Myasia (0.01) | Myelle |
| Mrinmayi | Munisa | Muzette | My'kiah | Myae | Myasia Star | Myellie |
| Mriseis | Muniya | Muzique | My'kiya | Mya-Elise | Mya-Sky | Myerr |
| Mrunal | Munjot | Muziwethu | My'kiyerah | Myah (0.17) | Myat | Myersha |
| Ms Acosha | Munroe | Muzn | My'kiyia | Myah-Lynn | Myatta | Myesa |
| Ms'jada | Munsha | Muzon | My'la | Myahlynn | Myauna | Myesah |
| Msemewa | Muntaha (0.01) | Muzyk | My'lady | Myahn | Myaunna | Myesha (0.01) |
| Elisabeth | Muntara | Mwamba | My'lah | Myahna | Myauria | Myeshia |
| Msizi | Muntas | Mwangaza | My'lan | Myah-Neikole | Myazah | Myfanwy |
| Mtab | Muram | Mwynen | My'lashia | Myai | Myazihia | Myha |
| Muah | Muranatu | My | My'lasia | Myaijha | Myca | Myhaa |
| Mubariah | Murayo | My 'Jaya | My'layah | Myainna | Myca Alexandria | Myi |
| Mubassira | Murceyiss | My Hien | My'lazia | Myair | Mycaela | Myi'asia |
| Mubina | Muriah | My Lady Dianna | My'leah | Myaisa | Mycah | Myi'asiah |
| Mudiaga | Muriel (0.01) | My Linh | My'lena | Myaisha | Mycaiah | Myia (0.02) |
| Mudiwa | Murielle | My Tien | My'linda | Myaja | Mycaiden | Myiah (0.01) |
| Muen | Murissa | My Triniti | My'liondi | Myakalia | Mycal | Myianna |
| Muerella | Muriya | My'ah | My'liyah | Myakayla | Mycalya | Myiera |
| Muhayya | Murly | My'airra | My'love | Myakel | Mycedes | Myiesha |
| Muhiba | Murphey | My'aisha | My'najsha | Myakka | My-Ceonia | Myigenia |
| Muhkayah | Murphy (0.01) | My'ajah | My'naya | Myala | Mycha | Myika |
| Muireall | Murray | My'ana | My'-Niya | Myalajah | Mychael | Myikayla |
| Muirinn | Murrin | My'anna | My'niysha | Mya-Lashaw | Mychaya | Myima |
| Muizza | Murron | My'arere | My'onna | Myale | Mychayla | Myint |
| Mujda | Murryn | My'arose | My'onnia | Mya-Lee | Mychealle | Myisha |
| Muji | Mursadie | My'asia | My'ra | Myaleez | Mychell | Myivana |
| Mukia | Mursal | My'asiah | My'racle | Myalicia | Mychelle | Myjaé |
| Mukiya | Muryam | My'auna | My'riah | Myalin | Mychiah | Myjanei |
| Mukta | Musandi | My'azia | My'rical | Mya-Lisa | Mychol-Mishell | Myjena |
| Mulan | Musarah | My'azzia | My'rie | Myalissa | Mycka | Myjoré |
| Mulawnya | Musarat | My'calasha | My'sarah | Myalyn | Myckala | Myk'ayla-Rose |
| Mulki | Musasia | My'caline | My'shalaka | Myalynn | Myckayla | Myk'jah |
| Mullin | Musbah | My'che | My'shauna | Mya-Lynne | Myckenzye | My-K'la |
| Mumba | Musenga | My'eisha | My'shaunta | Mya-Marie | Mycole | Myka (0.02) |
| Mumbi | Musfirah | My'erra | My'shawnna | Myamee | Mydasia | Myka Angela |
| Mume | Mushka | My'esha | My'shayla | Myamie-Rae | Mydejah | Mykael |
| Mumina | Mushkah | My'fredriana | My'tariah | Myan | Mydelis | Mykaela (0.01) |
| Muminah | Mushtaq | My'ionna | My'yasjha | Myana (0.01) | Mydiah | Mykaela |
| Mumlu | Mush-Teh | My'isha | My'yon | Myanah | Mydinaisa | Kaylene |
| Nanngaaq | Musizetta | My'jahna | My'yonna | Myangel (0.01) | Mye'resa | Mykaella |
| Mumtaza | Muskaan (0.01) | My'jaila | Myá | Myani | Myea | Mykaelle |
| Muna (0.01) | Muskan (0.01) | My'jaiona | Mya (1.88) | Myanicole | Myeanjell | Mykaeya |
| Munaya | Muskuda | My'jaya | Mya Amelia | Myann | Myeasha | Mykah (0.01) |
| Munazza | Musqaan | My'kail | Mya Darlene | Myanna (0.01) | Myeciah | Mykah Amerie |
| Mundi | Mussia | My'kala | Mya Elizabeth | Myannah | Myegedra | Mykah Janelle |
| Muneeba | Mustaham | My'kalynn | Mya Johanne | Myannia | Myeisha (0.01) | Mykaia |
| Muneera | Musu | My'kayla | Mya Kelsee | Myaona | Myejah | Mykaila |
| Muneerah | Musulyne | My'kaylah | Mya Maria | Mya-Pamela | Myeka | Mykailah |
| Munera | Muteeba | My'keria | Mya Nancy | Myara | Myekera | Mykailin |
| Munford | Mutima | My'keyia | Mya Rayne | Mya-Rhyann | Myekeyya | Mykal |

| | | | | | | |
|---|---|---|---|---|---|---|
| Mykala (0.02) | Mykieriah | Mylène | Myonnia | Myrrakale | Myvonjayla | Na Shyra |
| Mykalah (0.01) | Mykila | Mylene (0.01) | Myonta | Myrrh | Myya | Na Tavia |
| Mykalai | Mykilee | Myles | Myquaella | Myrsha | Myyah | Na Val |
| Mykaleigh | Mykinsi | Mylese | Myra (0.07) | Myrtice | Myzhane | Na'ahnni |
| Mykali | Mykinzie | Mylessya | Myra O | Myrtille | Myzshia | Na'air |
| Mykalia | My-Kira | Myley | Myrabella | Myrtle | | Na'ama |
| Mykalin | Mykira | Myli | Myrabelle | Myrva | | Na'amah |
| Mykalina | Mykirah | Myli'lei | Myracle (0.01) | Myrzhanai | ~ N ~ | Na'arah |
| Mykalynn | Mykiria Su | Mylia (0.01) | Myracul | Mysaiah | | Na'ari |
| Mykashie | Mykiya | Myliah | Myrah | Mysha | N | Na'asia |
| Mykavia | Mykiyah | Myliane | Myraiha | Myshadi | N Blin | Na'asiah |
| Mykaya | Mykka | Myliaya | Myraj | Myshala | N Ia | Na'ava |
| Mykayah | Mykl | Mylicen | Myrakal | Myshanae | N Jayah | Na'bria |
| Mykayela | Mykle | Mylie (0.02) | Myrakle | Myshauya | N Zuria | Na'caira |
| Mykayla (0.04) | Mykol | Myliesha | Myralia | Myshawna | N'akyra | Na'chasity |
| Mykaylah | Mykya | Mylijah | Myralie | Myshaya | N'cohle | Na'cori'yi |
| Mykayla-Lynne | Mykylah | Mylika | Myranda (0.03) | Myshayla | N'coreyia | Na'coya |
| Myke'la | Mykynna | Mylin | Myrani | Myshca | N'dehya | Na'davia |
| Mykea | Myla (0.09) | Mylina | Myranie | Myshell | N'deya | Na'deja |
| Mykeal | Myladie | Mylinda | Myrcale | My-Shineak | N'deye Anna | Na'dia |
| Mykeara | Mylady | My-Linh | Myrdelle | Myshjua | N'dia | Na'diya |
| Mykeira | Mylah (0.02) | Mylinh | Myre | Myskina | N'dia | Na'drea |
| Myke-Kayla | Mylaine | Mylisa | Myreen | Mystarria | N'dira | Na'geria |
| Mykel (0.01) | Mylaisha | Mylisha | Myreille | Mystery | N'diya | Na'gies |
| Mykela | Mylaishia | Mylissa | Myrelle | Mysti | N'dya | Na'haley |
| Mykelia | Mylaiya | My-Lissa Rae | Myreonia | Mystic (0.01) | N'gila Dar | Na'hiya |
| Mykell | Mylakia | Mylitta | Myria | Mystica | N'jre | Michelle |
| Mykelle | My-Lan | Nekawbah | Myriah (0.01) | Mystical | N'kayla | Na'ila |
| Mykenli | Mylan | Myliyah | Myriam (0.10) | Mystie | N'kheyma | Na'ilah |
| Mykenna (0.01) | Mylana | Myllanie | Myriame | Mystik | N'kiya | Na'imah (0.01) |
| Mykensie | Mylani | Mylo | Myriam- | Mystika | N'kiyah | Na'iman |
| Mykenzee | Mylanna | Mylove | Yasmine | Mystin | N'kya | Na'ina |
| Mykenzey | Mylanne | Myluv | Myrianna | Mystina | N'kylah | Na'ira |
| Mykenzi (0.01) | Mylaree | Mylyn | Myrical | Mystique (0.01) | N'kyra | Na'iyma |
| Mykenzie (0.01) | Mylashia | Myna | Myricle | Mystrey | N'myah | Na'jada |
| Mykenzy | Mylasia | Myndee | Myridean | Mystri | N'nacynt | Na'jae |
| Mykenzye | Mylayaah | Mynevaeh | Myrie | Mysty | N'na-Mayi | Na'jah |
| Myker Lovely | Mylayaha | My-Ngan | Myriem | Mystykah | N's' | Na'jai |
| Mykeriah | Mylaysia | Mynia | Myrika | Mystyna | N'shay | Na'jayh |
| Mykeriyah | Mylazia | Myniah | Myrikah | Mystyque | N'siyah | Na'jayle |
| Mykerria | Mylea | Mynika | Myrikal | Mytae | N'talya | Na'jia |
| Mykeshia | Myleah | Mynilya | Myrikel | Mytashia | N'tashia | Na'jiyah |
| Mykeyan | Myleahia | Mynique | Myrissa (0.01) | Mytasia | N'ydia | Na'kale |
| Mykhala | Myleanna | Myniya | Myrista | Myté | N'zinga | Na'kari |
| Mykheal | Myleé | Mynk | Myrizjah | Mythili | Na | Na'kaya |
| Mykhi | Mylee (0.03) | Myo Thi Dar | Myrka (0.01) | Mythily | Na Allah | Na'kayla (0.01) |
| Mykhia | Myleena | Myoinna | Myrla | Mythri | Na Asiah | Na'kaylah |
| Mykhiara | Myleesha | Myona | Myrlayja | Mytia | Na Bri | Na'kayln |
| Mykhila | Mylei | Myonia | Myrna (0.01) | Mytrang | Na Kayla | Na'keeta |
| Mykhl | Myleigh (0.01) | My-Onna | Myrnangelis | Mytreyi | Na Kiyah | Na'kell |
| Mykia | Mylen | Myonna (0.01) | Myrneliss | Mytzelth | Na Laya | Na'kenya |
| Mykiah | Mylena | Myonnah | Myrra | Myuana | Na Mya | Na'kerria |
| Mykie | Mylenah | Myonni | Myrrah | Myuri | Na Ryah | Na'khia |

| | | | | | | |
|---|---|---|---|---|---|---|
| Na'khyla | Na'shya | Naadirah | Nachianna | Nadelynn | Nadrea | Nageli |
| Na'kia | Na'shyra | Naadiya | Nachly | Nadene | Nadria | Nagelys |
| Na'kiah | Na'sia | Naafiah | Nacia | Naderah | Nadriah | Nageska |
| Na'kiiya | Na'sigh | Naáilah | Naciamaj | Nadesh | Nadwah | Nagham |
| Na'kima | Na'sydia | Naairah | Nacie | Nadeysha | Nadxieli | Nagiaad |
| Na'kira | Na'syia | Naajah | Nacira-Salma | Nadezhda | Nadya (0.03) | Nagiah |
| Na'kiya | Na'tae | Naajay | Naciya | Nadhiezdha | Nadyah | Nagisa |
| Na'kiyah | Na'taejah | Naajé | Naciyah | Nadhri | Nadyne | Nagwa |
| Na'kya | Na'tahje | Naaliya | Nacole | Nadiá | Nadysen | Nah Drese |
| Na'kyah | Na'taiya | Naaliyah | Nacomi | Nadia (0.59) | Nae | Nah'jay |
| Na'kyaha | Na'taja | Naama | Nacona | Nadia Addison | Nae'la | Nah'lah |
| Na'kyia | Na'tajyia | Naana | Nacoria | Nadia Anay | Nae'mya | Nah'ree |
| Na'kyie | Na'talia | Naarah | Nacya | Nadia Jane | Naechal | Nah'shiya |
| Na'kyla | Na'taliyeh | Naárah | Nada (0.02) | Nadia Rose | Naéelah | Nah'zaie |
| Na'kyra | Na'tasha | Naara-Samai | Nadaia | Nadia Theres | Naeem | Nahaby |
| Na'laicia | Na'taysha | Naashar | Nadaija | Nadiah (0.01) | Naeema | Nahama |
| Na'laiyah | Na'tazia | Naasia | Nadaijah | Nadiajames | Naeemah | Nahanni |
| Na'layah | Na'teasha | Naasira | Nadaisha | Nadia-Jewel | Naeheva | Nahara |
| Na'leah | Na'theija | Naasirah | Nadaja | Nadializ | Naeimah | Naharai |
| Na'liah | Na'tica | Naatya | Nadalee (0.01) | Nadiay | Naeisha | Nahari |
| Na'lijah | Na'tihya | Naava | Nadaleigh | Nadiayvonn | Naej | Nahasia |
| Na'mani | Na'tiyah | Naavah | Nadalie (0.01) | Nadica | Naejah | Nahaviah |
| Na'miah | Na'torya | Naavya | Nadaline | Nadiea | Naekiah | Nahayla |
| Na'mya | Na'toshya | Naazilah | Nadalle | Nadielys | Naela | Nahayva |
| Na'myah | Na'trale | Naba | Nadalley | Nadifa | Naelle | Nahdia |
| Na'nisha | Na'tyah | Nabaa | Nadallie | Nadifo | Naelly | Nahe |
| Na'omi | Na'tyia | Nabaad | Nadaly | Nadiia | Naelou | Naheda |
| Na'omie | Na'vaeh | Nabah | Nadalyn | Nadija | Naely | Naheemah |
| Na'osha | Na'vaughna | Nabeeha | Nadar | Nadilee | Naema | Naheessah |
| Na'rah | Na'vayahia | Nabeel | Nadara | Nadilia | Naemy | Nahela |
| Na'reyona | Na'vayiah | Nabeela | Nadasar | Nadima | Naesah | Nahele |
| Na'riah | Na'veah | Nabeelah | Nadasyn | Nadin | Naesheré | Naheliah |
| Na'riya | Na'viah | Nabela | Nadavlyn | Nadina | Naestra | Naheliy |
| Na'riyah | Na'viya | Nabia | Nadaya | Nadine (0.07) | Naetasia | Nahellis |
| Na'rrie | Na'ya | Nabie-Anna | Nadayja | Nadine-Anne | Naetzy | Nahelou |
| Na'rya | Na'yania | Nabiha | Nadaysha | Nadira (0.02) | Naeva | Nahema |
| Na'ryah | Na'yla | Nabiile | Naddly | Nadirah (0.01) | Naeyka | Nahemy |
| Na'ryiah | Na'zaria | Nabila (0.01) | Nadea | Nadiver | Nafeesa | Nahia |
| Na'shae | Na'zayiah | Nabilah | Nadeah | Nadiya (0.02) | Nafeesah | Nahiah |
| Na'shai | Na'zharia | Nabirah | Nadean | Nadiya-Bhaktika | Nafeeza | Nahiara |
| Na'shanti | Na'zia | Nabiya | Nadeen | Nadiyah (0.01) | Nafi | Nahid |
| Na'shawni | Na'ziaha | Nabneet | Nadeera | Nadiyyah | Nafijah | Nahidalyn |
| Na'shay | Na'zion | Nabrea | Nadege | Nadja | Nafisa | Nahiemah |
| Na'shaya | Na'ziya | Nabria | Nadège | Nadjade | Nafisah | Nahika |
| Na'shayla | Na'ziyah | Nabriya | Nadegesha | Nadja-Leena | Nafisat | Nahila |
| Na'shaylyn | Na'zjaye | Nacalia | Nadeisha | Nadjat | Nafiso | Nahile |
| Na'shia | Na'zyia | Nacari | Nadeja | Nadjeen | Nafissa | Nahili |
| Na'shiaya | Naa | Nacaria | Nadeleine | Nadjeka-Theresa | Nafissah | Nahily |
| Na'shirah | Naa Bessa | Nacayla | Nadelia | Nadjie | Nafissatou | Nahima |
| Na'shiyah | Naa Shidaa | Nacayle | Nadelie | Nadly | Nafka | Nahimi |
| Na'shiyia | Naa-Adkwei | Naceli | Nadellie | Nadlynn | Naftalienne | Nahimma |
| Na'shoanti | Naa-Ameley | Nacelis | Nadelyn | Nadonna | Naftarie | Nahiomi |
| Key'erraha | Naadia | Nachenide | Nadelyne | Nadonya | Nagapujitha | Nahir |

| | | | | | | |
|---|---|---|---|---|---|---|
| Nahiriah | Naidelin Anahi | Naiome | Najeah | Nakauraq | Nakirah | Naleayh |
| Nahja | Naidelis | Naiomi *(0.01)* | Najee | Nakava | Nakirea | Naledi |
| Nahjae | Naidelyn | Naiomie | Najeé | Nakaya | Nakisha | Nalee |
| Nahjai | Naidelyne | Naiomy | Najee'ah | Nakayela | Nakita *(0.01)* | Naleen |
| Nah-Jay | Naiderin | Naionna | Najeejah | Nakayia | Nakitah | Naleesha |
| Nahjayiah | Naidine | Naiqusha | Najeera | Na-Kayla | Nakitta | Naleigha |
| Nahje | Naidirah | Naira | Najeli | Nakayla *(0.02)* | Nakiya *(0.02)* | Nalejah |
| Nahla | Naidzalis | Nairah | Najelyz | Nakaylyn | Nakiyah *(0.02)* | Nalena |
| Nahlani | Naieli | Nairi | Najgy | Nakea | Nakiyha | Nalexy |
| Nahlannah | Naiella | Nairobi | Najha | Nakedra | Nakiyia | Nalia |
| Nahleyha | Naielle | Nairy | Najhae | Nakeemah | Nakkia | Naliah |
| Nahlia | Naielys | Naish | Najhaia | Nakeera | Nakkyta | Naliandrah |
| Nahliyah | Naiema | Naisha *(0.01)* | Najhe | Nakeesha | Nakoda | Nalijah |
| Nahmiyyah | Naieya | Naishada | Najhé | Nakeia | Nakoiya | Nalin |
| Nahmya | Naiha | Naishalee | Najhea | Nakeisha | Nakoma | Naline |
| Nahmyah | Naiimah | Naishaly | Najia | Nakeisha Nicole | Nakota | Nalini |
| Nahomi *(0.01)* | Naija | Naisia | Najiba | Nakeishia | Nakotah | Nalisa |
| Nahomie | Naijae | Naisola | Najiea | Nakeita | Nakoura | Nalisha |
| Nahomy | Naijah | Naissa | Najila | Nakeiya | Nakoya | Nalitha |
| Nahrie | Naijah'lee | Naisy | Najirah | Nakelle | Nakria | Naliya |
| Nahsiah | Naijalin | Naitza | Najiyah | Nakendall | Nakshatra Pillai | Naliyah *(0.01)* |
| Nahsialis | Naijay | Naivy | Najiyyah | Nakera | Nakya *(0.01)* | Nalja |
| Nahsya | Naijeonna | Naiya *(0.02)* | Najla | Nakeria | Nakyah | Naljah |
| Nahumyra | Naijonae | Naiyah | Najlaa | Nakerria | Nakyia | Nalla |
| Nahvia | Naika *(0.01)* | Naiyali | Najli | Nakeshia | Nakyiah | Nallani |
| Nahviae | Naikay | Naiyana | Najm | Nakeviona | Nakyla *(0.01)* | Nalleli *(0.01)* |
| Nahvien | Naikesha | Naiyanna | Najma *(0.01)* | Nakeya | Nakylah | Nallely *(0.02)* |
| Nahyana | Naikia | Naiydelin | Najmo | Nakeyah | Nakyra *(0.01)* | Nallerli |
| Nahyelli | Naikyla | Naiyeni | Najonah | Nakeyda | Nakyrah | Nalliah |
| Nahyiah | Naila *(0.02)* | Naiyenne | Najoni | Nakeyla | Nala *(0.03)* | Nally |
| Nahyla | Naila Marie | Naiymia | Najua Marjai | Nakeysha | Nalaaya | Nalo |
| Nahzani | Nailah *(0.05)* | Naiyyira | Najwa | Nakeyshla | Nalae Ja | Nalon |
| Nai Jah | Naile | Naj'lisa | Najyia | Nakeytiah | Nalah | Nalonda |
| Nai'aja | Nailea | Naja *(0.01)* | Nak'ira | Nakhia *(0.01)* | Nalaha | Naloni |
| Nai'jae | Nailette | Najaad | Naka'ya | Nakhiya | Nalaiya | Nalonnie |
| Nai'la | Nailey | Najabi | Nakaelah | Nakhya | Nalaiyah | Nalouzha |
| Nai'lah | Naili | Najad | Nakahya | Nakhyia | Nalanah | Nalyce |
| Nai'taija | Nailla | Najaé | Nakai | Nakhyndra | Nalaney | Nalydia |
| Naia *(0.02)* | Nailyah | Najae *(0.01)* | Nakaila | Nakhyra | Nalani *(0.03)* | Nalynn |
| Naiaathena | Nailyn | Na-Jaee | Nakaiya | Naki | Nalanie | Nama |
| Naiah | Nailyne | Najaeia | Nakaizha | Naki'a | Nalanie Marinel | Namah |
| Naiaja | Naima *(0.10)* | Najah *(0.01)* | Nakaja | Nakia *(0.03)* | Nalanie-Bella | Namaine |
| Naianna | Naima Angelie | Najai | Naka-Kissya | Nakiah *(0.01)* | Nalanis | Namakaokalani |
| Naiara | Naimah *(0.01)* | Najaia | Nakalah | Nakiaya | Nalaniu | Naman |
| Naiaria | Naimah-Joyce | Najaira | Nakangela | Nakiera | Nalanna | Namani |
| Naibeth | Naimah-Shierah | Najaiyah | Nakareia | Nakiesha | Nalany | Namanjit |
| Naica | Naima-Marie | Najalah | Nakareya | Nakiha | Nalasia | Namarah |
| Naiccole | Naime | Najalese | Nakari | Nakiia | Nalaya | Namari |
| Naida *(0.01)* | Naimia | Najanae | Nakaria | Nakiiya | Nalayah | Namasvi |
| Naidalizeth | Naimo | Najat | Nakarri | Nakilah | Nalaysia | Namaya |
| Naideea | Naina | Najay | Nakaseyia | Nakilia | Nalea | Namayan |
| Naideli | Naiobi | Najayah | Nakasha | Nakioma | Naleah | Namayka |
| Naidelin | | Najda | Nakasia | Nakira | Naleanna | Nameera |

| | | | | | | |
|---|---|---|---|---|---|---|
| Nameerah | Nancer | Naomi-Gail | Naresha | Nascha | Nashla | Nastaho |
| Namgyal | Nancey | Naomih | Naressa | Nascheline | Nashley | Nastasha |
| Nami | Nanci *(0.01)* | Naomii | Narges | Nascia | Nashliane | Nastashea |
| Namia | Nancie | Naomi-Ife | Nargis | Nasdya | Nashly | Nastasia |
| Namiah | Nancy *(0.27)* | Naomi-Lynn | Narhia | Naseehah | Nashlyn | Nastasja |
| Namiaya | Nancy Ladaysha | Naomi-Merveille | Nari | Naseerah | Nashmia | Nastassia |
| Namibia | Nancy Nhu-Y | Naomis | Naria | Naseyah | Nashona | Nastassja |
| Namika | Nanda | Naomy *(0.03)* | Na-Riah | Nasha | Nashonda | Nastassjia |
| Namina | Nandana | Naoudgi | Nariah *(0.04)* | Nashad | Nashuana | Nastasya |
| Namine | Nandi | Naoussa | Nariah-Jade | Nashae | Nashunti | Nastatia |
| Namira-Dona | Nandika | Napat | Nariahsia | Nashaé | Nashwah | Nasteeho |
| Namissa | Nandini *(0.01)* | Napiera | Narialis | Nashai | Nashya | Nasteha |
| Namita | Nandita | Naputt | Nariangely | Nashaina | Nashyah | Nasteho |
| Namitha | Nanditha | Naquaija | Narianna | Nashalee | Nashyia | Nastexo |
| Namitra | Nandni | Naquaisha | Narica | Nashali *(0.01)* | Nashyla | Nastisija |
| Namiya | Nandy | Naquanna | Narie | Nashalie | Nashyrah | Nasya *(0.01)* |
| Namiyah | Nandyali | Naquerra | Narielleisha | Nashalle | Nasia | Nasyah |
| Namiyha | Nanea | Naquicha | Narihya | Nashaloni | Nasia Jessenia | Nasyah Chante |
| Namomee | Nanetta | Naquinda | Narimane | Nashaly *(0.01)* | Nasiah | Nasyia |
| Namonie | Nanette | Naquya | Narine | Nashalyn | Nasier | Nat'alia |
| Nam-Phuong | Nangelie | Nara *(0.01)* | Narisa | Nashalyt | Nasiha | Nat'Lea |
| Namrata | Nangelina | Narah | Narissa *(0.01)* | Nashandy | Nasim | Nata'ja |
| Namratha | Nangiba | Narahommy | Nariya | Nashanna | Nasimah | Natacha *(0.01)* |
| Namroz | Nani | Narajani | Nariyah *(0.01)* | Nashara | Nasir | Natacia |
| Namrta | Nanika | Naraliz | Nariyana | Nashari | Nasira | Natadria |
| Namununa | Naniki | Naraly | Nariyza | Nasharie | Nasirah | Nataeja |
| Namwene | Nanine | Naraly- | Narja | Nashay | Nasiriya | Nataejah |
| Namya | Nanissa |    Guadalupe | Narjis | Nashaya | Nasiriyah | Nataejai |
| Namyi | Nankya | Naramin | Narkeasha | Nashayla | Nasirra | Nataeya |
| Nan | Nannette | Narangelis | Narkissa | Nashaylin | Nasiya | Natahlia |
| Nana *(0.01)* | Nannibah | Narashaey | Narmin | Nashayra | Nasiyah | Nataija |
| Nana Afua | Nannie | Narasia | Narmine | Nashea | Nasiyona | Nataijah |
| Nana Akua | Nansi | Narassevone | Narnia | Nashee | Nasja | Nataijah-De'jai |
| Nana Ama | Nanyika | Naraya | Naroline | Nasheera | Nasjae | Nataile |
| Nana Amma | Nao | Narayana | Narrah | Nashel | Nasjah | Nataisha |
| Nana Saa | Naobi | Narayanni | Narreona | Nasheli | Nasjahnae | Natajah |
| Nana-Aborah | Naoko | Naraylea | Narriah | Nashelle | Naskyya | Natajha |
| Nanaakua | Naola | Narcell | Narrissa | Nashelly | Nasly | Natajia |
| Nanadwoa | Naolie | Narcesia | Narshay | Nashely | Nasoni | Natajly |
| Nanaea | Naoma | Narcisse | Narsie | Nashelys | Nasra *(0.01)* | Natakia |
| Nanahbah | Naome | Nardaja | Narura | Nashenna | Nasreen | Natale |
| Nanaho | Naomee | Nardia-Lynn | Narwuo | Nashetah | Nasri | Natalea *(0.01)* |
| Nanaka | Naomei | Nardjes | Naryah | Nashia | Nasrin | Nataleah |
| Nanaki Preet | Naomi *(1.07)* | Nardos | Naryaiha | Nashiana | Nasrine | Nataleann |
| Nanako | Naomi Ann | Nare | Naryia | Nashia-Zaman | Nasro | Natalee *(0.20)* |
| Nanaliyah | Naomi Edith | Narea | Naryssa | Nashila | Nassa | Natalee-Rose |
| Nanami *(0.01)* | Naomi Jewel | Naree | Nas'celia | Nashina | Nasshae | Nataleigh *(0.02)* |
| Nanatu | Naomi-Amita | Nareena | Nas'jay | Nashira | Nassiah | Nataleighann |
| Nanaya | Naomie *(0.09)* | Nareh | Nas'sir | Nashita | Nassim | Nataley *(0.01)* |
| Nanayaa | Naomie Deseray | Nareli | Nasai | Nashiya | Nassima | Natali *(0.04)* |
| Nanayah | Naomie Mia | Nareliss | Nasara | Nashiyah | Nassoma | Nataliá |
| Nancarrow | Naomie-Rachele | Narelle | Nasari | Nashka | Nasta'shia | Natália |
| Nanceé | Naomie-Rose | Narely | Nasaya | Nashkelly | Nastacia | Natalia *(1.69)* |

Natalia Isabel
Nataliah
Nataliby
Natalice
Natalie *(5.02)*
Natalie Lynn
Natalie Melinda
Natalie-Br
Nataliee
Natalie-Rae
Nataliese
Natalija
Natalijah
Natalin
Natalina
Natalirose
Natalisa
Natalise
Nataliya *(0.01)*
Nataliyah
Natallia
Natalliah
Natallie
Natally
Natallya
Nataly *(0.12)*
Natalya *(0.10)*
Natalyah
Natalye *(0.01)*
Natalyia
Natalyn
Natalynn
Natalyz
Natane
Natanee
Natani
Natania *(0.01)*
Nataniele
Natanii-
  Elizabeth
Natanya
Natanyah
Natara
Nataria
Natasa
Natascha
Natash
Natasha *(0.47)*
Natashah
Natasha-Marie
Natashauna
Natashca
Natashia

Natashiana
Natashjah
Natasia *(0.01)*
Natasja
Natassia
Natassja
Natavia *(0.01)*
Nataya *(0.01)*
Natayah
Natayezha
Natayia
Natayja
Natayjah
Natayla
Natayle
Nataysha
Nataysia
Natayvia
Natayzha
Natchaya
Nate'sia
Natea
Nateah
Nateesha
Nateiya
Nateja
Natelee
Nateleigh
Nateli
Natelia
Natelie
Natelle
Natellica
Nateria
Nateriyah
Natesa
Natesia
Nateya
Natgeene
Nathael
Nathaelle
Nathale
Nathalee
Nathali
Nathalia *(0.07)*
Nathalie *(0.15)*
Nathalie-
  Camille
Nathaliyah
Nathallie
Nathaly *(0.05)*
Nathalya
Nathalye

Nathan
Nathanael
Nathania
Nathaniel
Nathasha
Nathayeli
Nathea
Nathiona
Nathria
Nati
Nati'rah
Natia
Natiah
Natiasha
Natica
Natielee
Natielys
Natiesha
Natika
Natile
Natilea
Natilee *(0.01)*
Natileigh
Natiley
Natili
Natilie
Natillie
Nation
Natisha
Natishka
Nativa
Natividad
Nativya
Natiya
Natiyah
Natkida
Natla
Natlaie
Natlee
Natlie
Natlin
Natorey
Natori
Natoria
Natoryae
Natosha
Natoya
Natracha
Natran
Natrice
Natsha
Nattalee
Nattaly

Nattangelly
Nattania
Nattasia
Nattelie
Natti
Natulie
Naturaile
Naturale
Nature
Naturel
Naturell
Naturelle
Naturi
Natya
Natyah
Natycia
Natyiah
Natyla
Natylee
Natyma
Natyra
Natzeli
Nau'kenya
Naudea
Naudia *(0.02)*
Naudiya
Naudya
Naudyniah
Naugeria
Naughtya
Naujahze
Naunna
Naura
Naurah
Naureen
Nauria
Naurica
Nauricia
Naushawnna
Nausheen
Nausika
Nautaliah
Nautia
Nautica *(0.02)*
Nautical
Nautika
Nautikah
Nauvia
Nauz'jalee
Nava *(0.01)*
Navada
Navaé
Navaeh *(0.03)*

Navaeh Lee
Navaeleigh
Navaesous
Navah
Navaha
Navaih
Navala
Navalinn
Navana
Navanah
Navannah
Navanya
Navara
Navarah
Navaria
Navarra
Navarria
Navaya
Navayah
Navayshia
Navdeep
Navdip
Nave'yah
Navea
Naveá
Naveah *(0.01)*
Naveda
Navee
Naveen
Naveena
Naveera
Naveha
Navela
Navelinne
Naverah
Naveree
Naverina
Naveya
Naveyah
Navi
Navia *(0.01)*
Naviah *(0.01)*
Navidhi
Navie
Naviel
Navieus
Navika
Navina
Navinder
Navisha
Navissa
Naviyah
Naviyanna

Navjot
Navkeerat
Navla
Navleen
Navlin
Navneed
Navneet
Navona
Navonah
Navontanai
Navpreet
Navprince
Navreen
Navreet
Navrit
Navroop
Navtej
Navy
Navya *(0.01)*
Navyasri
Navyee
Nawaal
Nawal *(0.02)*
Nawar
Nawel
Nawranafsin
Nawras
Nawshin
Nay Asia
Nay'ana
Nay'jae
Nay'kiah
Nay'taisha
Nay'vey
Naya *(0.02)*
Naya Dyvana
Nayah
Nayahjah
Nayala
Nayalece
Nayali
Nayalie
Nayaliz
Nayaly
Nayamari
Nayami
Nayana *(0.01)*
Nayanika
Nayanka
Nayann
Nayanna
Nayara
Nayarett

Nayaris
Nayarit
Naycia
Nayda
Naydalin
Naydamar
Naydeli
Naydelin *(0.02)*
Naydelis
Naydia
Naydrian
Nayeema
Nayeema-
  Hamaelle
Nayehli
Nayelee
Nayeli *(0.16)*
Nayelie
Nayelis *(0.01)*
Nayelle
Nayelli *(0.01)*
Nayellie
Nayelly *(0.01)*
Nayely *(0.03)*
Nayely-Britney
Nayely-Sundia
Nayeska
Nayeva
Nayha
Nayheli
Nayia
Nayika
Nayilah
Nayima
Nayimah
Nayimmi
Nayisel
Nayja
Nayjeli
Nayka
Nayla *(0.02)*
Naylah
Naylana
Naylani
Naylea
Nayleen
Naylene
Naylenid
Nayley
Nayli
Naylia
Naylianni
Naylin

| | | | | | | |
|---|---|---|---|---|---|---|
| Nayliz | Nazeeya | Ne'jyia | Nechama (0.03) | Neeya | Neidi | Nekerryia |
| Naylley | Nazek | Ne'kenley | Nechamah | Neeyah | Neidily | Nekesha |
| Nayma | Nazerene | Ne'kia | Nechanté | Neeysa | Neidy | Nekhail |
| Naymejwak | Nazerin | Ne'kyah | Nechell | Nefertare Hotep | Neiel | Nekhamah |
| Nayna | Nazgol | Ne'liyah | Nechoma | Ivory | Neige | Nekhia |
| Nayome | Nazhaya | Ne'mecia | Necia | Nefertari | Neigh'keisha | Nekhya |
| Nayomee | Nazhiya | Ne'rya | Necora Serenity | Neferti | Neighujah | Nekia |
| Nayomi (0.01) | Nazhoni | Ne'ryah | Nectaria | Nefertiti (0.01) | Neika | Nekiah |
| Nayomie | Nazia | Ne'shayla | Neda | Nefertitilli | Neil | Nekichwey |
| Nayomy | Naziah | Ne'shell | Neda'a | Nefretari | Neila (0.01) | Nekila |
| Nayon | Nazifa | Ne'shya | Nedaa | Neftali | Neila Dani | Nekima |
| Nayona | Nazighah | Ne'siah | Nedaijah | Neftaly | Neila-Lorelai | Nekira |
| Nayoni | Nazira | Ne'vaeh (0.02) | Nedda | Nefthali | Neilani | Nékirah |
| Nayonna | Nazirah | Ne'vaeha | Nedely | Nefthari | Neilanie | Nekisha |
| Nayoung | Naziray | Ne'vaehjah | Nedjy | Negasi | Neili | Nekiya |
| Nayovi | Naziya | Ne'veah | Nedra | Negesti | Neilie | Nekoda |
| Naysa (0.01) | Naziyah | Ne'veyah | Nedryana | Negie | Neilka | Nekolo |
| Naysah | Naziyah' | Nea | Neeah | Negina | Neillani | Nel |
| Naysha | Nazleea | Nea'ja | Neean | Neglan | Neilsia | Nel'lasia |
| Nayshalinez | Nazli | Nea'jah | Neeca | Neha (0.08) | Neily | Nela |
| Nayshaly | Nazmim | Neaderia | Neecya | Neha'viya | Neilyana | Néla |
| Nayshannalee | Nazneen | Neah | Neeharika | Nehaa | Neily-Anne | Neladia |
| Nayshe'll | Nazo | Neaira | Neeia | Nehal | Neima | Nelah |
| Nayshera | Nazohni | Ne-Airia | Neeka | Nehama | Neiman | Nelajia |
| Naysia | Nazri | Neala (0.01) | Neeki | Nehanda | Neina | Nelanee |
| Naysira | Nazya | Nealey | Neekie | Neharica | Neirah | Nelani |
| Nayssa | Nazyah | Nealie | Neekya | Neharika | Neisah | Nelasiah |
| Nayu | Nazyaih | Neally | Neela (0.02) | Nehavai | Neisha | Nelaya |
| Nayya | Nazyia | Nealy | Neelah | Nehaya | Neishaley | Nelca |
| Nayyirah | Nazyiah | Neamah | Neelakshi | Nehema | Neishaliz | Nelci |
| Nayzeth | Nbf | Neamani | Neelam | Nehemiah | Neishaly | Nelda |
| Naz | Nciya | Neamari | Neelayadhakshi | (0.01) | Neishalys | Neldy |
| Naz'satha | Nclonca | Neamiah | Neelee | Nehemie | Neishawnti | Nele |
| Nazaeha | Ndele | Neamiyah | Neeley | Nehemiya | Neishly | Neleah |
| Nazaha | Ndeye (0.01) | Neamyah | Neelia | Nehemoni | Neissa | Neleh |
| Nazahyla | Ndeye Binette | Neariah | Neelie | Nehemya | Neissah | Neleigh |
| Nazaiyah | Ndeye Fatou | Nearra | Neeliya | Nehir | Neissia | Neleigha |
| Nazalia | Ndeye- | Neasha | Neelofur | Nehkiyah | Neito | Nelesse'a |
| Nazaliyah | Ramatoulaye | Neashia | Neely (0.02) | Nehmat | Nejai | Nelhia |
| Nazanin | Ndiate | Neasia | Neelyah | Nehme | Nejiey | Neli |
| Nazara | Ndukwe | Neaujee | Neema | Nehmia | Nejla | Nelia |
| Nazarae | Ndyah | Neava | Neena (0.01) | Nehmiah | Nejla Rachida | Neliah |
| Nazarene | Ne Kiah | Neave | Neenah | Nehpertarry | Nejmee | Nelianne |
| Nazaret | Ne Kya | Neaven | Neera | Nehtal | Nejoud | Neliany |
| Nazareth | Ne Taeja | Nebahat | Neeraja | Nehya | Nejra | Nelia-Rose |
| Nazari | Ne Veah | Nebeela | Neeramy | Nehyla | Nekaelah | Nelices |
| Nazaria | Ne'ahra | Nebhtalie | Neesa | Nehziya | Nekai | Nelida |
| Nazariah | Ne'ali | Nebiyah | Neesan | Nei | Nekaybah | Nelie |
| Nazariyah | Ne'amoneé | Nebraska | Neese | Neia | Nekea | Nelis |
| Nazaryah | Ne'ariah | Nebula | Neesha | Neiana | Nekeiara | Nelisa |
| Nazbah | Ne'asia | Neccia | Neeva | Ncicha | Nekeisha | Nelisha |
| Nazdhia | Ne'ja | Necely | Neevah | Neida (0.02) | Nekendra | Nelissa |
| Nazeerah | Ne'jai | Necha | Neeve | Neidelin | Nekeria | Nelisse |

| | | | | | | |
|---|---|---|---|---|---|---|
| Nelitza | Nemeira | Nerland | Nether | Nevanna | Neyling | Nhyla |
| Neliya | Nemesis | Nerlande | Nethra | Nevaya | Neylinne | Nhyziera |
| Nelizbeth | Nemi | Nerle | Neththela | Nevayah | Neylizvette | Ni Jasia |
| Nelizeh | Nemiah | Nerlie | Netia | Nevayeh | Neyllin | Ni Mah |
| Nelka | Némiah | Nerlsyah- | Netra | Nevé | Neyllynn | Ni'a |
| Nell *(0.01)* | Nemos | Jarryka | Netsanet | Nève | Neymi | Ni'aira |
| Nella *(0.01)* | Nena *(0.01)* | Nerlyne | Netta | Neve *(0.02)* | Neyomi | Ni'aisia |
| Nellani | Nenani | Nerman | Nettie *(0.01)* | Nevea | Neyrin | Ni'aja |
| Nelle | Nene | Nermeen | Nettle | Neveaeh | Neysa | Ni'ajah |
| Nelleke | Nenet | Nermina | Neuaeh | Neveah *(0.07)* | Neysha | Ni'angela |
| Nelleke | Nenika | Nermine | Nev | Nevear | Neysha- | Ni'arie |
|   Anneliese | Neojam | Nerosh | Nev'aeh | Neveen |   Carmesley | Ni'asia *(0.01)* |
| Nellena | Neola | Nerry | Nev'aeh Martina | Neveene | Neytani | Ni'asiah |
| Nelli | Neolani | Nerutha | Nevá | Neveiahah | Neyunna | Ni'aysa |
| Nelliane | Neolanie | Nervijaeh | Neva *(0.02)* | Nevella | Neza | Ni'azhia |
| Nellianne | Neomarie | Nerys | Neva'eh | Nevellie | Nezae | Ni'azia |
| Nellianni | Neomi | Nesara | Nevach | Nevena | Nezarya | Ni'caria |
| Nellicia | Neona | Neshaan | Nevada *(0.03)* | Nevenah | Neziah | Ni'cayla |
| Nellida | Neoneilla | Neshae | Nevae | Neveyah | Neziyah | Ni'dashya |
| Nellie *(0.03)* | Neoni | Neshawna | Nevaeah | Nevi | Nezly | Ni'dijah |
| Nellie Rose | Neonilla | Neshiah | Ne-Vaeh | Nevia | Nezma | Ni'diria |
| Nellie-Ann | Neonjanae | Neshmia | Névaeh | Neviah *(0.01)* | Nezyha | Ni'ema |
| Nellieza | Neosha | Neshmy | Nevaeh *(2.46)* | Nevillia | Nga | Ni'jael |
| Nelliezeth | Nephateria | Nesiah | Nevaeh Antione | Nevin | Ngaio | Ni'jah |
| Nellika | Nephatyeria | Nesibe | Nevaeh C'lee | Nevina | Ngaire | Ni'jai |
| Nelliyah | Nephitetti | Nesiyah | Nevaeh Charity | Nevohshea | Ngan | Ni'jayah |
| Nelly *(0.05)* | Nephtalie | Neslihan | Nevaeh July | Nevona | Ngao | Ni'jera |
| Nelly Anne | Nephthally | Nesma | Nevaeh Jv' | Nevontay | Nghi | Ni'ka |
| Nelly-Ann | Neptune | Nesmah | Nevaeh Lee | Nevraj | Ngoc My | Ni'kayla |
| Nellyanne | Nepty | Nesmarie | Nevaeh Lyn | Nevya | Ngoc-Nhu | Ni'kaysha |
| Nellybeth | Neqita | Nesreen | Nevaeh Niechia | Nevyah | Ngonda-Rebecca | Ni'kereyah |
| Nellye | Nequeshia | Nesrine | Nevaeh Rae | Nevyn | Ngoni | Ni'khara |
| Nellyha | Neray | Nessa *(0.01)* | Nevaeh Rain | Newborn | Ngoyera | Ni'kia |
| Nelly-Kim | Nerayjha | Nessah | Nevaeh' | Newilda | Ngozi | Ni'kima |
| Nellymaris | Nereida *(0.01)* | Nesshea | Nevaeha *(0.03)* | Nexdy | Ngozichukwu | Ni'kiyah |
| Nellyris | Nereido | Nessia | Nevaeh-Jade | Neya | Ngum | Ni'kya |
| Nelly-Rose | Nereimar | Nessiah | Nevaehlee | Neyah | Nguyen | Ni'kylah |
| Nelmarie | Nerelyn | Nessie | Nevaehly | Neyamiah | Nha | Ni'kyrah |
| Nelofare | Nereyda | Nessya | Nevaeh-Raye | Neyana | Nhezija | Ni'laja |
| Nelsi | Nergis | Nesta | Nevaeh-Skhy | Neyani | Nhi *(0.01)* | Ni'laysha |
| Nelsie | Nergiz | Nesthalee | Nevaeh-Sky | Neyari | Nhia | Ni'lijah |
| Nelusigwe | Nerhia | Nestrin | Nevaen | Neyarii | Nhiache | Ni'querya |
| Nely | Neri | Nesy | Nevaett | Neyat | Nhialyn | Ni'ryah |
| Nelya | Neria | Netalia | Nevah | Neyawynn | Nhtaya | Ni'shai |
| Nelyann | Neriah *(0.01)* | Netalya | Nevaha | Neycha | Nhu | Ni'shaya |
| Nelyaris | Nerica | Netania | Nevaiah | Neyda | Nhu Quynh | Ni'taesha |
| Nelyda | Nerida | Netanya | Nevaie | Neydean | Nhu Y | Ni'tiana |
| Nely-Feliza | Neriman | Netavia | Nevaiya | Neydi | Nhu-Han | Ni'treasur |
| Nelymar | Nerina | Netaya | Nevajah | Neyeli | Nhu-Kim | Ni'ya |
| Nelyssa | Nerissa *(0.01)* | Neteara | Nevajra | Neyiah | Nhy'teaisia | Ni'yah |
| Nema | Neriya | Neter | Nevaleah | Neyla | Nhya | Ni'yaire |
| Nemah | Neriza | Nethania- | Nevan | Neylah | Nhyariah | Ni'yana |
| Nemeh | Nerjes |   Medgie | Nevanmee | Neylan | Nhyel | Ni'yanah |

| | | | | | | |
|---|---|---|---|---|---|---|
| Ni'yanna | Nianni | Nicheé | Nicola (0.02) | Nienke | Nikacie | Niki-Lynn |
| Ni'yanni | Niansha | Nichele | Nicolai | Nierica | Nikaela | Nikinla |
| Ni'yasha | Niany | Nichella | Nicolane | Nierra | Nikahia | Nikiquoia |
| Ni'yauna | Niaomi | Nichelle (0.01) | Nicolas | Niesha (0.01) | Nikaida | Nikira |
| Ni'yona | Nia-Pascale | Nicheyla | Nicolasa | Nieshia | Nikaila | Nikiria |
| Ni'yonna | Niara (0.01) | Nichol | Nicole (2.46) | Niessa | Nikailyn | Nikita (0.04) |
| Ni'youna | Niarah | Nichola | Nicole Ivy | Nieva | Nikaiya | Nikitaa |
| Ni'zaia | Niari | Nicholas | Nicole Madeline | Nieve | Nikaiyah | Nikitha |
| Ni'zayveonna | Niarobe | Nichole (0.08) | Nicole Maria | Nievea | Nikala | Nikitia |
| Ni'zeria | Niarra | Nichole Foster | Nicole Roz | Nieves | Nikallynn | Nikitko |
| Ni'zuria | Nia-Shahida | Nicholee | Nicole-Abiola | Nieya | Nikalya | Nikitta |
| Nia (0.25) | Niasia (0.01) | Nicholett | Nicole-Danae | Nieyah | Nikara | Nikiya (0.01) |
| Nia'asia | Niasiai | Nicholette | Nicole-La'ree | Nigá | Nikari | Nikiyah (0.01) |
| Nia'ja | Niasijah | Nicholle | Nicolena | Nigabedria | Nikasha | Nikiyra |
| Nia'jahaya | Niaujah | Nichollett | Nicolet | Nigeela | Nikashana | Nikka |
| Nia'nyiah | Niaulani | Nichollette | Nicolett | Nigella | Nikaya | Nikkayla |
| Nia'sya | Niauna | Nicka | Nicoletta (0.01) | Nigel-Lyn | Nikayia | Nikkea |
| Niaann | Niaunna | Nickacia | Nicolette (0.06) | Nigeria (0.01) | Nikayla (0.01) | Nikkei |
| Niachie | Niavah | Nickay | Nicolianna | Nigeria Jiliana | Nike | Nikkeya |
| Niagé | Niavani | Nickayla | Nicolina | Nighye | Nikea | Nikki (0.07) |
| Niah (0.01) | Niaya | Nickcolette | Nicolita | Nigira | Nikeda | Nikkia |
| Niahna | Niayah | Nickée | Nicolle (0.02) | Nigirey | Nikeesha | Nikkie |
| Niaijah | Niayea | Nickell | Nicolle Sophia | Nih'keria | Nikel | Nikkielyn |
| Niaimah | Niayla | Nickey | Nicollette (0.01) | Nihal | Nikeleia | Nikkilecia |
| Niaimy | Niaysia | Nickeya | Nicolly (0.01) | Niharika (0.01) | Nikema | Nikkilee |
| Niaira | Niazalia | Nickhya | Nicoly | Niheir | Nikendre'a | Nikki-Lynn |
| Niaisha | Niazaya | Nicki | Nicora | Nihita | Nikerah | Nikkindra |
| Niaishia | Nibel | Nickia | Nicoy | Nihla | Nikeria | Nikkita |
| Niaja | Nic'kirra | Nickiah | Nicquet | Nihya | Nikeria Iyana | Nikkiya |
| Niajah (0.01) | Nic'kyah | Nickie | Nicquiara | Niiah | Nikeriah | Nikky |
| Niajha | Nica | Nickindra | Nida | Niibin-Niibeesh | Nikerria | Nikky-Jade |
| Niakasha | Nicacia | Nickira | Nidaya | Niicole | Nikese | Niko |
| Niala | Nicah | Nickita | Nidea | Niina | Nikesha | Nikol |
| Nialha | Nicah'el | Nickiya | Nidhal | Niinimoshe | Niketa | Nikola |
| Nialise | Nicala | Nickla | Nidhi (0.01) | Niirene | Nikeva | Nikolai |
| Nialonie | Nicaleigh | Nicknise | Nidia | Nija | Nikeya | Nikolas |
| Nialys | Nicaria | Nickol | Nidian | Nijae | Nikeyla | Nikole (0.03) |
| Niam | Nicaulineda | Nickolas | Nidon | Nijah (0.01) | Nikeyma | Nikolena |
| Niama | Nicaury | Nickole (0.01) | Nidyene | Nijahne | Nikeyra | Nikoletta |
| Niamah | Nicaya | Nickolette | Niecee | Nijahria | Nikeyria | Nikolette |
| Niamani | Nicayia | Nickolia | Nieka | Ni-Jane | Nikhita (0.01) | Nikoli |
| Niamh (0.02) | Nicayla | Nickshala | Niela | Nijasritha | Nikhole | Nikolina (0.01) |
| Niamia | Nicca | Nickurah | Nieleah | Nijay | Niki (0.01) | Nikolle |
| Nia-Michel | Nicci | Nicky | Nielina | Nijaya | Niki'yah | Nikollette |
| Niamora | Nicciah | Nickya | Nielka | Nijayah | Nikia (0.01) | Nikosha |
| Niamya | Niccole | Nickyah | Niella | Nijenska | Nikiah | Nikowa |
| Nian | Niccolette | Nickyra | Nielle | Nijeria | Nikiara | Nikoya |
| Niana | Niceia | Nickza | Nielsen | Nijhay | Nikie | Nikxy |
| Nianah | Nicella | Nico | Niema | Nijialyn | Nikiela | Nikya |
| Niani | Nicena | Nicoah | Niemah | Nijmah | Nikiesha | Nikyah |
| Niania | Nichawn | Nicoe | Niemmeiah | Nijueria | Nikija | Nikyale |
| Nia-Nijah | Nichayla | Nicol (0.01) | Nien Nyree | Niká | Nikiji | Nikyia |
| Nianna | Nichea | Nicolá | Niena | Nika (0.01) | Nikila | Nikyla |

| | | | | | |
|---|---|---|---|---|---|
| Nikylah | Nimerah | Niquela | Nishoni | Nityasiri | Niyarah | Noahkym |
| Nikyra | Nimerpreet | Niquia | Nishtha | Nitza | Niyasia | Noahlani |
| Nikyrah | Nimisha | Nira | Nishuta | Nitzia Victoria | Niyat | Noahlynn |
| Nikyta | Nimitha | Nirah | Nishyah | Nitzy | Niyathi | Noahmy |
| Nil | Nimiyah | Nirai | Nishylla | Niugaali | Niyati | Noala |
| Nila *(0.02)* | Nimo | Nirali | Nishyya | Caroline | Niyawnah | Noalani |
| Nilah *(0.01)* | Nimoni | Nirayana | Nisi | Niurkalin | Niyazha | Noa-Leianne |
| Nilaja | Nimra | Niree | Nisiyah | Niushka | Niyema | Noam |
| Nilajah | Nimrah | Nireese | Nislande | Niuvis | Niyer | Noami |
| Nilaniha | Nimrat | Nirel | Nisma | Niva | Niyesha | Noamy |
| Nilay | Nimrit | Nirelym | Nisme | Nivaah | Niyet | Noa-Zoe |
| Nilayah | Nimsi | Nirenee | Nisreen *(0.01)* | Nivaeh | Niyhairra | Nobalean |
| Nilaysia | Nimue | Niriah | Nisrin | Nivai | Niyia | Nobalee |
| Nilce | Nimya | Niriel | Nisrine | Nivea *(0.02)* | Niyiab | Nobie |
| Nilda | Nimyia | Nirja | Nissa *(0.01)* | Niveah | Niyla | Noble |
| Nile | Nina *(0.48)* | Nirjal | Nissa Alexanne | Niveah Sky | Niylah | Noche |
| Niles | Nina | Nirmal | Enen | Niveahna | Niyma | Noddia |
| Nilexy | Francheska | Nirro | Nissara | Niveda | Niyoacxyn | Nodesha |
| Niley | Nina Loren | Nirubie | Nissi | Nivedha | Niyol | Noe |
| Nilha | Nina-Amel | Niruelli | Nissiah | Nivedita | Niyona | Noee |
| Nili | Nina-Giselle | Nirushana | Nissi-Jired | Niveditha | Niyonna | Noehmi |
| Niliah | Ninah *(0.01)* | Nirvaa | Nisso | Niveen | Niyrah | Noeiani |
| Nilien | Ninalyn-Kaheal | Nirvana *(0.01)* | Nissrine | Niveka | Niyu | Noeily |
| Nilim | Nina-Maria | Nirvani | Nissy | Nivelka | Niyya | Noeka |
| Nilima | Ninamarie | Niryah | Nistaisa | Niven | Nizaria | Noël |
| Niliyaah | Ninamay | Nirzia | Nistasia | Niveshitha | Nizeria | Noel *(0.06)* |
| Niliyah | Nina-Taye | Nisa *(0.01)* | Nisya | Nivet | Nizerria | Noela |
| Nilka | Nindaanis | Nisaa | Nita | Nivia | Nizeth | Noelani *(0.03)* |
| Nill | Niné | Nisai | Nitaamigabawii | Nivri | Nizhoni *(0.01)* | Noelanni |
| Nilleia | Ninea | Nisaiah | kwe | Niwa Kerakeha | Nizhoni | Noelany |
| Nilly | Ninel *(0.01)* | Niscelly | Nitai | Tie | Sunshine | Noelda |
| Nilofar | Nineliez | Nischala | Nitaijha | Niwre | Njeri | Noeli |
| Niloufar | Ninet | Niseaa | Nitaliya | Nixa | Njideka | Noelia *(0.05)* |
| Nilsa | Ninett | Nisefora | Nitara | Nixea | Nkauj | Noelie |
| Nilufer | Ninette | Nisel | Nitasha | Nixie | Nkauj Xw | Noelis |
| Nilukshana | Ninfa | Niseli | Nitaya | Nixon | Nkaujlis | Noelisa |
| Nilvia | Ninga | Nisha *(0.01)* | Nitda | Nixxie | Nkechi | Noelise |
| Nily | Nini | Nishalys | Nithali | Nixy | Nkechinyere | Noeliz |
| Nilyia | Ninive | Nishan | Nithi | Niy'aisha | Nkem | Noell |
| Nilyn | Ninon | Nishanti | Nithini | Niy'asia | Nkennanyerem | Noëlla |
| Nilyne | Ninoshka | Nishara | Nithiya | Niyá | Nkoya | Noella *(0.01)* |
| Nilynn | Ninoska | Nishat | Nithusini | Niya *(0.06)* | Nmonjay | Noelle *(0.22)* |
| Nilyssa | Ninti | Nishaunna | Nithya *(0.01)* | Niyah *(0.03)* | Nnediuto | Noelle-Rainne |
| Nilzari | Ninya | Nishaye | Nithyasri | Niyahna | Nneka | Noelli |
| Nima | Niobe | Nishea | Niti | Niyai | Nnenna | Noellia |
| Nimah | Niomee | Nishelle | Nitika | Niyala | Nneoma | Noellie |
| Nimar | Niomi *(0.01)* | Nishiime | Nitiya | Niyale | Nnonye | Noelly |
| Nimarah | Niomy | Nishika | Nitorian | Niyamiya | No | Noellyn |
| Nimaway | Niona | Nishita | Nitquita | Niyana *(0.01)* | No'el | Noely |
| Nimco | Nionnia | Nishithasri | Nittaya | Niyanah | Noa *(0.06)* | Noelys |
| Nime | Niosha | Nishka | Nittidda | Niyani | Noa Angelica | Noema |
| Nimeera | Nique'la | Nishley | Nittilai | Niyanna | Noah *(0.01)* | Noémi |
| Nimeesha | Niquel | Nishna | Nitya *(0.02)* | Niyanza | Noaha | Noemi *(0.10)* |

| | | | | | | |
|---|---|---|---|---|---|---|
| Noemi-Belen | Nomalanga | Noraiya | Nory | Novell | Nuóer | Ny' Kasia |
| Noémie | Nomaris | Nora-Jane | Nory'm | Novella | Nupoor | Ny'aira |
| Noemie *(0.25)* | Nomble | Noralee | Nosaj | Novelle | Nupur | Ny'airah |
| Noemie Alicia | Nomin | Noraly | Nosirrah | Novelly | Nur *(0.01)* | Ny'aire |
| Noemie-Anne | Nominzul | Norane | Not | Novely | Nur Aisha | Ny'aisa |
| Noemie-Rose | Nomrota | Noraneli | Nouchee | Novelynne | Nur Shaheera | Ny'aisha |
| Noemi-Loriana | Nomy | Nora-Raisa | Nouchi | November | Nura | Ny'aisyha |
| Noémy | Non | Norayma | Nouela | *(0.01)* | Nurah | Ny'aizjah |
| Noemy *(0.04)* | Nona *(0.01)* | Nore | Nouha | Novena | Nuralayn | Ny'aja |
| Noemye | Nonah | Norea | Nouha Anassi | Novenda | Nuran | Ny'ajah |
| Noga | Nonasya | Noreah | Nouhad | Novera | Nure | Ny'akira |
| Nogol | Noni | Noreen | Nouhaila | Novia | Nureen | Ny'ana |
| Nogoye | Nonie | Norehyona | Nouhayla | Noviante | Nurelayn | Ny'areia |
| Noha *(0.01)* | Noniyah | Norell | Nouk | Novie | Nurgul | Ny'arie |
| Noha-Ambre | Nonnah | Norelle | Nounejie | Novieanna | Nurhy | Ny'ariel |
| Nohaila | Nonoka | Norelly | Nour *(0.06)* | Novy | Nuri | Ny'asha |
| Nohamin | Noon | Norely | Nour Al Hoda | Nowah | Nuria *(0.01)* | Ny'ashia |
| Nohea | Noongy | Norelys | Nour Elhouda | Nowell | Nuriel | Ny'asia *(0.03)* |
| Nohelani | Noor *(0.08)* | Norene | Noura *(0.01)* | Noya | Nurit | Ny'asiah |
| Nohelia | Noor Naji | Norey | Nourah | Noylahna | Nuriyah | Ny'asya |
| Nohely | Noorah | Nori | Nouralhuda | Noyonika | Nurlika | Ny'aunah |
| Nohema | Noor-Deeyanah | Nori'yauna | Nouran | Nryah | Nursery | Ny'auri |
| Nohemi *(0.01)* | Noore | Noria | Nour-Deya | Nseya | Nurto | Ny'avean |
| Nohemi Mar | Noor-E-Fatma | Noriah | Nour-El Houda | Nsikan | Nurul | Ny'avia |
| Nohemy | Noorkiran | Norializ | Nour-Khadija | Ntanga | Nury | Ny'azia |
| Noi | Noor-Ul-Ain | Noriane | Nourrou | Nteina | Nusaybah | Ny'bree |
| Noina | Noorun | Noriann | Nousheen | Ntela | Nushin | Ny'chae |
| Noire | Noorvir | Norianna | Noussaiba | Ntshiab Si | Nushrat | Ny'chelle |
| Noki | Nooshon | Norico | Nouvelle | Ntshiabsi | Nusrat | Ny'ciunna |
| Nokiesha | Nor | Noriece | Nouye | Ntsiab Liaj | Nusratadia | Ny'daijah |
| Nokomi | Nor'lona | Noriko | Nova *(0.04)* | Ntxhais | Nutan | Ny'darrea |
| Nola *(0.05)* | Nor'ree | Norimar | Nova Collette | Nu | Nuthara | Ny'dra |
| Nolah | Nora *(0.51)* | Norine | Novah | Nu'caila | Nuthi | Ny'eah |
| Nolan | Nora Ann | Norissa | Novahlee | Nuala | Nuurta | Ny'earie |
| Nolancia | Dorthy | Norivette | Novahlie | Nubah | Nuvara | Ny'eema |
| Nolande | Nora Cruz | Norly | Novaj | Nube | Nuvia *(0.01)* | Ny'eisha |
| Nolani | Nora Delaney | Norma *(0.04)* | Novajean | Nubi | Nuzhat | Ny'ema |
| Nolania | Nora Eve | Norma Yithzel | Nova-Katarina | Nubia *(0.01)* | Nuziyah | Ny'emah |
| Nolé | Nora Grace | Normah | Novalea | Nubian | Nvaya | Ny'era |
| Nolee | Nora Rae | Normaines | Novalee *(0.02)* | Nubya | Nvea | Ny'esha |
| Noley | Noraa | Normandy | Novaleen | Nuckea | Nvy | Ny'geria |
| Nolhvia | Nora-Ann | Normarie | Novaleia | Nuckyra | Nwal | Ny'gia |
| Nolie | Norah *(0.27)* | Normaris | Novaleigh | Nuechi | Nwasinachi | Ny'ierre |
| Nolleigh | Norah Celeste | Normia | Novalena | Nuemi | Ny | Ny'ila |
| Nollie | Norah Lena | Normiyah | Novaley | Nuha *(0.01)* | Ny Asha | Ny'ima |
| Nolwen | Norah Symone | Norra | Novali | Nuhamin | Ny Ashia | Ny'imah |
| Nolwenn | Norah | Norriah | Novalie *(0.01)* | Nuhr | Ny Asia | Ny'ja |
| Noly | Washteshkun | Norriea | Novalley | Nukemah | Ny Awna | Ny'jaea |
| Nolya | Norah-Jane | Norritta | Novaly | Numa | Ny Elle | Ny'jah |
| Nolyn | Norah-Katrina | Norshaya | Novarah | Nuna | Ny Erica | Ny'jai |
| Nolynn | Nora-Indiana | Norshelys | Novea | Nung | Ny Isabelle | Ny'jay |
| Noma | Noraini | Norsyah | Noveen | Nunga | Ny Kieria | Ny'jaya |
| Nomah | Nora-Isabella | Norwai | Noveleen | Nunnaya | Ny Yonna | Ny'jayah |

| | | | | | | |
|---|---|---|---|---|---|---|
| Ny'jeria | Ny'rionna | Nyale | Nyayul | Nyemma | Nyjai | Nylah-Simone |
| Ny'jia | Ny'shafon | Nyalee | Ny-Aza | Nyenyezi | Ny-Jariah | Nylaisha |
| Ny'jyah | Ny'shanti | Nyalei | Nyazha | Nyeobie | Nyjayah | Nyla-Janae |
| Ny'jyahi | Ny'shayl | Nyali Vanesa | Nyazia | Nyera | Nyjayé | Nyla-Jean |
| Ny'kaela | Ny'sheria | Nyalie | Nybella | Nyeria | Nyjerria | Nylajshia |
| Ny'kasia | Ny'sherica | Nyalin | Nybria | Nyerie | Nyjhia | Nyla-Lee |
| Ny'kayla | Ny'shiya | Nyalis | Nychelle | Nyesha *(0.01)* | Nyjia | Nylan |
| Ny'keara | Arbianna | Nyalisse | Nychole | Nyeshia | Nyka | Nyla-Shemonia |
| Ny'kedra | Ny'stacia | Nyalite | Nycia | Nyethok | Nykae'sha | Nyla-Teana |
| Ny'keera | Ny'tasha | Nyalizé | Nycie | Nyethong | Nykai | Nylaya |
| Ny'keira | Ny'tasia | Nyaluak | Nyciella | Nyeve | Nykaiha | Nylaysia |
| Ny'keirah | Ny'te'asia | Nyalual | Nycole | Nyewal | Nykala | Nyle |
| Ny'keiriah | Ny'teriah | Nyamad | Nycolle | Nygeria | Nykarah | Nyleah |
| Ny'keiya | Ny'trayla | Nyamal | Nydashia | Nyha | Nykarsha | Nyleiah |
| Ny'kela | Ny'via | Nyamirin | Nydasia | Nyhaja | Nykavia | Nyleigh |
| Ny'kenianna | Ny'yana | Nyamouch | Nydea | Nyhanni | Nykaya | Nyleighia |
| Ny'kenya | Ny'zeriah | Nyamuoc | Nydeara | Nyhema | Nykayla | Nyleiyah |
| Ny'kera | Ny'zirea | Nyana *(0.01)* | Nydeja | Nyhia | Nyke | Nylejhia |
| Ny'keren | Ny'zyria | Nyanachom | Nydera | Nyhira | Nykeeria | Nylen |
| Ny'keria *(0.01)* | Nya *(0.10)* | Nyanasir | Nyderah | Nyhkia | Nykeira | Nylene |
| Ny'keriah | Nyabel | Nyanen | Nyderia | Nyi'asia | Nykell | Nylesha |
| Ny'keriana | Nyabol | Nyangel | Nydia *(0.01)* | Nyi'azsia | Nykella | Nyleshia |
| Ny'kerria | Nyacia | Nyanhail | Nydiah | Nyi'ema | Nykelle | Nyleve |
| Ny'kerriyauna | Nyadar | Nyanhial | Nydira | Nyi'lah | Nykenya | Nylia |
| Ny'kevia | Nyadeng | Nyanjah | Nydirah | Nyi'llah | Nykera | Nyliah |
| Ny'kia | Nyadheal | Nyanjok | Nye Nyi | Nyia *(0.01)* | Nykerah | Nylie |
| Ny'kiere | Nyadiel | Nyanna *(0.01)* | Nye'asia | Nyiah | Nykeria *(0.01)* | Nylijah |
| Ny'kieria | Nyadieng | Nyannah | Nye'kese | Nyiah-Rose | Nykeriah | Nylin |
| Ny'kira | Ny-Aela | Nyanpal | Nye'mah | Nyianna | Nykerria | Nylina |
| Ny'kivia | Nyagach | Nyanpu | Nyebol | Nyianza | Nykeva | Nylisha |
| Ny'kuria | Nyagoa | Nyanuer | Nyeda | Nyiara | Nykevia | Nylissa |
| Ny'la | Nyah *(0.06)* | Nyanyiek | Nyeece | Nyiashia | Nykeyba | Nyliyah |
| Ny'lah | Nyai | Nyanza | Nyeela | Nyiazia | Nykhia | Nylla |
| Ny'laree | Nyaijah | Nyara | Nyeelah | Nyiema | Nykia *(0.01)* | Nylla-Marianne |
| Ny'lasia | Nyaila | Nyari | Nyeema | Nyiera | Nykiah | Nyllia |
| Ny'layah | Nyair | Nyaria | Nyeemah | Nyiesha | Nykiera | Nylwiz |
| Ny'leah | Nyaira | Nyariak | Nyeesha | Nyiessa | Nykila | Nymali |
| Ny'leema | Nyaire | Nyaruaac | Nyeil | Nyija | Nykinya Camya | Nymaree |
| Ny'lexius | Nyairra | Nyaruot | Nyeine | Nyila | Nykira | Nymaria |
| Ny'mari | Nyaisa | Nyasha | Nyeisha | Nyima *(0.01)* | Nykirah | Nymbe |
| Ny'miracle | Nyaisha | Nyashia | Nyeja | Nyimah | Nykisha | Nymbia |
| Ny'quajha | Nyaja | Nyasia *(0.08)* | Nyekeila | Nyiona | Nykita | Nymera |
| Ny'quariona | Nyajá | Nyasiah | Nyekeira | Nyir | Ny-Kiyah | Nymeria |
| Ny'quashia | Nyajah | Nyasija | Nyela | Nyira | Nykiyah | Nymesha |
| Ny'quavia | Nyajia | Nyasisa | Nyelah | Nyirah | Nykol | Nymira |
| Ny'rae | Nyakan | Nyassia | Nyeli | Nyiria | Nykole | Nymirah |
| Ny'raya | Nyakiir | Nyasunday | Nyelie | Nyisa | Nykole Dav | Nyna |
| Ny'ree | Nyakir | Nyasya | Nyell | Nyisha | Nykosha | Nynaia |
| Ny'reisha | Nyakoach | Nyau | Nyelle | Nyja | Nykyera | Nyneeshia |
| Ny'rena | Nyakuei | Nyauna | Nyellie | Nyjada | Nyla *(0.30)* | Nyoakla |
| Ny'reonna | Nyala | Nyaveia | Nyema *(0.02)* | Nyjae | Nylaeya | Nyobee |
| Ny'rice | Nyalah | Nyawargak | Nyemah | Nyjah *(0.01)* | Nylah *(0.06)* | Nyobi |
| Ny'rie | Nyalam | Nyayla | Nyemia | Nyjaha | Nylah-Roas | Nyoka |

Nyome
Nyomee
Nyomi *(0.02)*
Nyona
N-Yonna
Nyonna
Nyoshi
Nyquada
Nyquaia
Nyquasia
Nyquerra
Nyquiel
Nyra *(0.01)*
Nyrah
Nyrai
Nyrania
Nyrdia
Nyre
Nyreasia
Nyree *(0.01)*
Nyrell
Nyriah
Nyrie
Nyrisa
Nyrobee
Nyrobi
Nyrome
Nyruby
Nysa *(0.01)*
Nysahna
Nysalee
Nysania
Nysaria
Nysha
Nyshaela
Nyshalee
Nyshanti
Nyshawna
Nyshay Kalise
Nyshaye
Nyshea
Nysheal
Nysheria
Nyshiah
Nyshira
Nysia
Nysiah
Nyssa *(0.02)*
Nystasia
Nytaiya
Nytalia
Nytasha

Nytashia
Nytasia
Nytawni
Nyteria
Nythashia
Nytil
Nytionna
Nytreana
Nytyia
Nyura
Nyvaeh
Nyvah
Nyvea
Nyveah
Nyviah
Nyvorii
Nyx
Nyyah
Nyyanna
Nyzae
Nyzai
Nyzaila
Nyzarah
Nyzarea
Nyzavia
Nyzaya
Nyzeria
Nyzeth
Nyzhae
Nyzhazia
Nyziar
Nyzirah
Nyzjah
Nyzza-Keyaira
Nzinga
Nzingah
Nzubechi

~ O ~

O'anesia
O'brianna
O'ciana
O'dasia
O'deja
O'desia
O'donesty
O'hara
O'hona
O'kera
O'lani

O'lisia
O'llaysia
O'mari
O'marionya
O'melia
O'meria
O'mugoli
O'mya
O'nareah
O'neilya
O'nijah
O'nivea
O'noreen
O'repha
O'rieanna
O'rienne
O'rya
O'shara
O'sharia
O'sheauna
O'sheay
O'shonna
O'tesha
O'thea
Oahlani
Oaklei
Oakleigh
Oakley *(0.01)*
Oakli
Oaklie
Oaklyn
Oaklynn
Oanh
Oasa
Oasis
Obaashiikwe
Obdulin
Obeishka
Obelyn
Obianuju
Obinechi
Obinnamdi
Obna
Obsee
Obsiee
Ocea
Ocean *(0.03)*
Oceana *(0.01)*
Oceananna
Oceanasea
Océane
Oceane *(0.20)*

Oceane Lina
Océane-Marie
Oceania
Oceanika
Ocean-Joy
Oce-Ann
Oceann
Oceanna *(0.01)*
Océanne
Oceanne *(0.12)*
Oceannie
Oceanny
Oceaonna
Oceashanna
Ocenya
Ocheda
Ocianna
Ocie
Ociee
Ocires
Oct'avia
Octariah
Octave
Octavia *(0.05)*
Octavia Jamyra
Octaviah
Octavie
Octay'jah
Octayvia
October
Odali
Odalis *(0.02)*
Odaliss
Odaliz
Odaly
Odalys *(0.01)*
Odalyz
Odanelis
Odaru
Oddyssey
Ode
Odelia *(0.01)*
Odelie
Odell
Odesa
Odessa *(0.02)*
Odesses
Odessey
Odeth
Odette *(0.01)*
Odhyll
Odia

Odile
Odilia
Odilis
Odille
Odina
Odinakachukwu
Odisitty
Odline
Odneesha
Odreanna
Odura
Ody
Odyessy
Odyssey
Oe
Oed
Oeruia
Ofelia *(0.01)*
Ofir
Ofnide
Ogechukwu
Ogenna
Oghenefejiro
Oghenetega
Ogheneyoma
Oghmwen
Ogiemaakwe
Ogochukwu
Ohahnna
Ohakara
Ohana
Ohanna
Ohenewah
Ohndrela
Ohneiyah
Ohnicah
Ohnika
Ohona
Ohriyana
Oi
Oishee
Oita
Ojal
Ojetta
Okedia
Okilani
Oklahoma
Okoye
Okoyea
Oksana *(0.01)*
Oksanah
Oksanna

Oktavia
Okwo-Serena
Ola
Olaleye
Olamide
Olandria
Olani
Olanma
Olathe
Olathia
Olaumi
Olaundra
Olawunmi
Olearna
Olee
Oleisia
Olena
Olesia
Olesya
Oleta
Oletha
Olevia
Olexa
Olexis
Olexzondra
Oley
Oleyse
Olga *(0.02)*
Olga Ana
Olia
Oliana Andrea
Olianne
Oliba
Olicia
Olidy
Olieá
Olievea
Olihvia
Oliia
Olilvia
Olin
Olina
Olinda
Olinka
Olisa
Olisia
Oliva
Olive *(0.02)*
Olivea *(0.01)*
Oliveah
Oliver
Olivera

Olivet
Olivett
Olivia *(7.45)*
Olivia Ale
Olivia Claire
Olivia Delsie
Olivia Grace
Olivia Luisa
Olivia Marisa
Olivia Tranise
Oliviaa
Olivia-Gra
Olivia-Grace
Oliviah *(0.01)*
Oliviah-Maree
Olivia-Ly
Oliviana
Olivianne
Olivia-Paige
Olivia-Rose
Oliviya
Oliviyha
Olivya *(0.01)*
Olivyah
Olleke
Olley
Ollie
Ollieah
Ollieshiah
Ollinca
Olliviah
Olliyiah
Ollwyn
Ololade
Ololade Grace
Olubusola
Oluchukwu
Oludamilola
Olufayola
Olufimi
Olufunke
Olukemi
Olusewa
Olutoyosi
Oluwabusayo
Oluwadamilola
Oluwadara
Oluwademilad
Oluwafemi
Oluwafikayomi
Oluwafisayo
Oluwafunmilayo

| | | | | | | |
|---|---|---|---|---|---|---|
| Oluwakemi | Omarys | Onamae | Onnesty | O-Ren | Orrianna | Ossiliyah |
| Oluwalayomi | Omaya | Onaraya | Onnickajo | Orenda | Ortadra | Ossilyn |
| Oluwamayowa | Omayma | Onasia | Onnika | Oreofeoluwa | Ortavia | Ot'tyanna |
| Oluwasegun | Omayra | Onazia | Onnisty | Oreoluwa | Oryana | Otelia |
| Oluwasemire | Ome'da | Ondai | Onolea | Orezimena | Oryanna | Oteria |
| Oluwaseyi | Omea | Ondi | Onome | Orga | Oryon | Othelia |
| Oluwashayo | Omega | Ondraia | Ontaria | Oria | Oryona | Othny |
| Oluwashemilore | Omena | Ondre'ne | Ontariona | Oriah | Oryonne | Otilia |
| Oluwatimil | Omenukoh | Ondrea | Ontranee | Oriana (0.03) | Orysya | Otisa |
| Oluwatobil | Omer | One | Onya | Oriane | Orzanna | Otisha |
| Oluwatofunmi | Omera | Oneasha | Onyai | Orianna (0.02) | Osa | Otoria |
| Oluwatomisin | Omi | Oneida | Onyca | Oriannah | Osahenoma | Otteona |
| Oluwatoni | Omia | Oneissia | Onycha | Orianne | Osaka | Ottilie |
| Oluwatunmise | Omiah | Oneissy | Onyinye | Oriel | Osaly | Otyanna |
| Oluyemisi | Omijah | One-One | Onyinyechukwu | Orielle | Osanna | Ouiame |
| Olvia | Omini | Onesha | Onyja | Orienne | Osaro | Oujanae |
| Olwenn | Ominiki | Onesti | Onyx | Oriette | Osasere | Oujhier |
| Olya | Omisa | Onestie | Onyxia | Oriname | Osaviona | Oulimata |
| Olympe | Omiyah | Onesty | Onyza | Oriole | Osayawe-Erica | Oumaima |
| Olympia (0.01) | Omneet | Oneyba | Oona (0.01) | Orion | Oscar | Oumayma |
| Olympyia | Omni | Oneyda | Oonah | Oriona | Osciel | Oumeyma |
| Olyssa | Omnia | Oni | Opal (0.02) | Orionna | Oshan | Oumie |
| Olysta | Omni-Janaye | Onia | Opale | Orisa | Oshawnna | Oumkaithoum |
| Olyvea | Omnisity | Oniaca | Ophania | Orissa | Osheana | Oumou (0.01) |
| Olyvia (0.03) | Omobola | Oniara | Opheelie | Orit | Oshene | Oumousalama |
| Olyvia Sarah Joy | Omobolanle | Onicah | Ophelia (0.02) | Oriya | Osheona | Oumquone |
| Olyviah | Omolabake | Onicka | Ophelie (0.04) | Oriyan | Osheydi | Oumy |
| Olyvija | Omolola | Onickah | Ophelie J | Orjeta | Oshiana | Oun |
| Om | Omorinsola | Onieda | Ophelie Minh | Orkerria | Oshianna | Ounej'a |
| Oma | Omotara | Onielis | Thu | Orla | Oshien | Ourania |
| Omaia | Omotolani | Onika | Ophely | Orla'sia | Oshione | Ouro Adei |
| Omaima | Omsi | Onikah | Ophilie | Orlaith | Oshira | Ousmane |
| Omaira | Omunique | Onipa'a | Ophir | Orlandra | Oshiry | Ovia |
| Omairys | Omya | Oniris | Ophira-Lei | Orlandria | Oshshey | Oviya |
| Omalara | Omynee | Onisha | Opichi | Orlanne | Oshun | Owahee |
| Omani | Omyra | Onisty | Oqoia | Orli | Oshyan | Owan |
| Omanie | Omyzhanae | Onita | Oquin | Orlie | Oshyn | Owen (0.01) |
| Omar'a | On'dreia | Onixsha | Or'landria | Orlonda | Osiana | Owennesha |
| Omara | On'yae | Oniya | Or'teasha | Orlonshay | Osion | Owere |
| Omaralyz | Ona | Oniyá | Ora | Orly | Osiris (0.01) | Owika |
| Omare | Ona Marie | Oniza | Orah | Orlyanka | Osjanai | Own |
| Omari | Onada | Onizia | Oralee | Ormana | Osleidy | Owyn |
| Omarí | Onadee | Onjaniah | Oralia | Ormoni | Oslyn | Oyafunke |
| Omaria | Onae | Onjolie | Oralis | Orna | Oslynn | Oyindamola |
| Omariah | Onaisha | Onjuli | Orchid | Ornella | Osmarie | Oyinkansola |
| Omariana | Onaje | Onna (0.01) | Oreana | Ornina | Osmary | Oyiyechukwu |
| Omarie | Onajevwe | Onnah | Oreanna | Orpha | Osmel | Oyonola |
| Omaries | Onalea | Onnaka | Oreiana | Orphee | Osriana | Oyuky |
| Omarisse | Onalee | Onnaleaya | Orelie | Orquidea | Osrina | Ozaine |
| Omariya | Onalisa | Onnaliece | Orelle | Orquidia | Ossai | Ozalee |
| Omariyah | Onaly | Onnasia | Orelly | Orr | Ossian | Ozane |
| Omarria | Onalysse | Onnastie | Orema | Orreonah | Ossiana | Ozannae |

| | | | | | | |
|---|---|---|---|---|---|---|
| Ozareia | Paden | Paislee (0.01) | Panagiota (0.01) | Parineeta | Parveen | Patricia (0.24) |
| Ozareya | Pader | Paisleigh | Panagoula | Parinita | Parwinder | Patricia Lynn |
| Ozaria | Padmini | Paisley (0.08) | Panchami | Parionna | Parys | Patricia-Elea |
| Ozeisha | Paedra | Paisley-Maria | Pandora (0.01) | Paris (0.61) | Pascale (0.01) | Patrick |
| Ozge | Paedyn | Paislie | Pandora Paris | Paris Maria | Pascalie | Patrika |
| Oziomachi | Paegan | Paisly | Paneet | Paris Talay | Pascaline | Patrina |
| Ozjoahnaé | Paeghton | Paisynce | Panella | Paris'angel | Pascalle | Patrisha |
| Ozlynde | Paeshents | Paitan | Pang | Parisa (0.01) | Pascalou | Patrishia |
| Ozlynne | Paeslee | Paiten (0.01) | Pangxeng | Parisal | Paschan | Patrishka |
| Ozora | Paesli Jo | Paiton (0.02) | Panhia | Parisana | Pasha | Patrisia |
| Ozzlyn | Paeton | Paityn (0.03) | Pankti | Paris-Dion | Pashalia | Patrisiana |
| Ozzlynn | Paetyn | Paityn-Ann | Pannell | Parise | Pashan | Patriz |
| | Paetynn | Paitynn | Pansy | Parish | Pashance | Patrycja |
| | Paeyton | Paiyton | Pantera | Parisha | Pashanti | Patsha |
| | Page (0.01) | Paizlee | Panya | Parishay | Pashence | Patsy |
| ~ P ~ | Pagelyn | Paizleigh | Panzi | Parisia | Pashion | Patterson |
| P Kylah | Pagie | Paizley | Panzie | Paris-Mari | Pashmal-Bukhat | Patti |
| P Mia | Pagoda | Paizley-Nicole | Paol | Pariss | Pashun | Patti-Ann |
| P. Kennedy | Pahniaku | Paj | Paola (0.20) | Parissa | Pashunce | Pattielee |
| Pa (0.01) | Pahwa | Paja | Paolaitzel | Paristy | Pasia | Patty |
| Pa Da | Paicey | Pajai | Paolan | Parita | Pasidee | Pattyjo |
| Pa Hou | Paiden | Pajdib | Paole | Pariyachut | Paskale | Pau |
| Pa Joua | Paidin | Pajhuab | Paolina | Pariz | Paskimina | Paul |
| Pa Ntshai | Paidyn | Pajnplaimdej | Paolo | Park | Pasley | Paula (0.09) |
| Pa Yeng Ja | Paig | Pajurí | Paonia | Parker (0.13) | Pason | Paula Anaelle |
| Pa Ying | Paige (2.83) | Pakanli | Papatya | Parkker | Passion (0.03) | Paula Andrea |
| Pa'leriah | Paige Ann | Pakeeza | Papion | Parleen | Passion'al | Paula Scar |
| Pa'niyah | Paige Liliane | Pakou | Paquie-Grace | Parmdeep | Passionate | Paula-Julianna |
| Pa'ris | Paige Ponciano | Pakyla | Paradise (0.01) | Parmeet | Passionett | Paulayzsa |
| Pa'shea | Paigelyn | Palace | Paradyce | Parmind | Passions | Paule |
| Paacarah | Paige-Mackenzie | Palak (0.01) | Parah | Parmis | Pastions | Paule Eva |
| Paajlaim | | Palar | Paralee | Parmpreet | Patelyn | Pauleasha |
| Paarngoak | Paige-Marie | Palavi | Paramitha | Parneet (0.01) | Paten | Paulecia |
| Pablina | Paigena | Palia | Parananda | Parnia | Paterchee | Pauleena |
| Pablo | Paigeronna | Palina | Paras | Parniece | Patiance (0.01) | Paulene |
| Pabola | Paighten | Palkpreet | Paraskeva | Parnika | Patiecents' | Pauleshia |
| Paccana | Paighton | Pallas | Paraskevi | Parnikaa | Patience (0.17) | Pauleth |
| Pace | Paightyn | Pallavi | Parbhnoor | Paroma | Patiencee | Paulette (0.01) |
| Pacee | Paijah | Palma | Pardis | Parramoijon | Patienz | Paulina (0.13) |
| Pacelyn | Paije | Palmer | Pardise | Parri | Patil | Pauline (0.03) |
| Pacey (0.01) | Paijha | Palmina | Paree | Parris (0.02) | Patling | Pauline Jazmin |
| Pacharapon | Pailei | Palmpreet | Pareena | Parrish | Paton | Pauline Mae |
| Pachee | Pailey | Paloma (0.07) | Pareer | Parry | Patool | Paulsafira |
| Pachi | Paili | Paluk | Pari (0.01) | Parrys | Patra | Paulshyni |
| Pachia | Pailin | Palvasha | Parice | Parteek | Patrece | Paulynn |
| Pachium | Pairess | Pamba | Paridhi | Parthenia | Patrecia | Paulynna |
| Pachiun | Pairique | Pamela (0.12) | Paridice | Parthvi | Patrena | Paungayuk |
| Paci | Pairtip | Pamela Marie | Paridise | Partik | Patrene | Pavan |
| Pacie | Paisely | Pamella | Paridyse | Parus | Patria | Pavana |
| Pacience | Paishance | Pamila | Pariis | Parvaan | Patriana | Pavanjit |
| Paciyess | Paishence | Pamula | Pari-K | Parvaneh | Patrianna | Pavanjot |
| Padden | Paishynce | Pamyla Chelbie | Parina | Parvathy | Patrica | Pavanpreet |
| Paddy | Paislea | Pana | Parinamika | Parvati | Patrice (0.02) | Paveena |

| | | | | | | |
|---|---|---|---|---|---|---|
| Pavika | Payyton | Peniel | Perrin | Peyton-Destany | Phelicia | Phoebie |
| Pavitar | Paz | Penina | Perrine | Peytton | Phelicitie | Phoeby |
| Pavithira | Pazao | Peninah | Perris | Peytyn | Phelisia | Phoena |
| Pavithra | Pazee | Pennelope | Perriyona | Peytynn | Pheniox | Phoenix (0.10) |
| Pavitra | Pazeng | Pennie | Perry (0.01) | Peyvin | Phenix | Phoenix Aniya |
| Pavitt | Pazia | Pennilopi | Perryn | Pfeiffer | Phenix-Dezaree | Phoenix Xiahra |
| Pavleen | Pazlee | Penny (0.01) | Persadijah | Pfifer | Phenyx | Phoenyx |
| Pavlina | Pe'asia | Penny-Lou | Persaeus | Pgianna | Pheobe (0.01) | Phonsirie |
| Pavneet | Pe'yton | Penosway | Persafres | Pha Dae | Pheobey | Phontiet |
| Pawanjot | Pea | Peony | Persaia | Pha'lesydih | Pheona | Phontricia |
| Pawanreet | Pea'nyiha | Pepa | Persais | Pha'rae | Pheonia | Phrona |
| Paxson | Peace | Pepin | Persaua | Pha'tiah | Pheonix (0.01) | Phtasia |
| Paxten | Peaches | Pepper | Persaya | Phadashia | Pheonyx | Phull |
| Paxton (0.01) | Pearcenten | Per | Persayiss | Phaedra (0.01) | Phetdala | Phung |
| Paxtyn | Pearl (0.07) | Per'jah | Persayous | Phailine | Phetlany | Phuong |
| Paxyn | Pearl Ann | Per'shay | Perseis | Phaith | Phetsara | Phuong Mai |
| Payal | Pearla | Perah | Persephanie | Phaizan | Phiasia | Phuongvi |
| Paycen | Pearleen | Perasia | Persephany | Phakrista | Phierce | Phylena |
| Paychun | Pearlie | Perceaiz | Persephone | Phalan | Phierra | Phylicia |
| Payci | Pearlprabhleen | Percephany | (0.01) | Phalanda | Phil'nasia | Phyliece |
| Paycience | Pearl-Susan | Perci | Persephoni | Phallyn | Philana | Phylisia |
| Paycin | Pearl-Taylor | Percilla | Perseus | Phamarya | Philasia | Phyllis (0.01) |
| Payden (0.01) | Pearson | Percy | Perseya | Phancie | Philene | Phyllisha |
| Paydge | Pearsyn | Perel (0.01) | Pershae | Phaniya | Philicia | Phyllisity |
| Paydn | Pebbles | Peres | Pershais | Phantasia | Philiesa | Phyllissa |
| Payeng | Pecola | Peresa | Persia (0.01) | Phantasy | Philine | Phyniah |
| Payge (0.02) | Pedro | Perfecta | Pertania | Phar'ever | Philippa | Phynioux |
| Paying | Peer | Peri (0.01) | Pervaysia | Phara | Philippine | Phynix |
| Payje | Peggy (0.01) | Peri'onna | Perveen | Pharadiah | Philisa | Phyona |
| Payne | Peggy Ellen | Perignon | Peshalini | Pharoah | Philles | Phyrra |
| Payola | Peggyrose | Perignsn | Pesly | Pharrah | Philleshay | Phyusen |
| Paysen | Peggy-Sue | Peris | Pessi | Phasia | Phillicia | Pia (0.01) |
| Payshence | Peighton | Perisa | Pessie | Phatasia | Phillip | Piara |
| Payshense | (0.02) | Perissia | Pessy (0.01) | Phateama | Phillydia | Pia-Tamara |
| Payshintz | Peightyn | Perl (0.01) | Peta | Phathum | Philnia | Piath |
| Payshonce | Peinda | Perla (0.13) | Petal | Phatima | Philomena | Pie |
| Payslee | Peiqi | Perla Taina | Peter | Phauline | (0.01) | Piedad |
| Paysli | Peityn | Perlanish | Petra (0.05) | Phaviny | Philomene | Pieper |
| Payslie | Peja | Perla-Ruby | Petrea | Phawn | Philomise- | Pier |
| Payson | Pelaija | Perle | Petrena | Phayth | Shelda | Piera |
| Paytan | Pele | Perle Hermine | Petrona | Phearia | Phina | Pierce |
| Payten (0.05) | Pele-Olam | Perle Maude | Petronia | Pheasay | Phinees | Pierina |
| Paytence | Pelin | Perle Merode | Petros | Pheaudra | Phinell | Pierlynne |
| Payten-Raye | Pema | Perle-Merode | Petty-Tien | Phebe (0.01) | Phiona | Pierra |
| Paytin (0.01) | Penda | Perlita | Pewahpun | Phebee | Phiya | Pierre-Louis |
| Paytlyn | Pendili | Perlle | Peydan | Phebe-Elaine | Phlicia | Pierria |
| Paytn | Peneloope | Perlmaeson | Peyge | Phebie | Phloann | Pierson |
| Payton (0.95) | Pénélope | Perlynnia | Peyris | Phedre | Phlorizell | Piersten |
| Payton-Piper | Penelope (0.22) | Pernika | Peytan | Pheebie | Phobe | Pierzi |
| Payttin | Penelope-Ly | Perri (0.01) | Peyten (0.01) | Pheenyx | Phoebe (0.29) | Pieta |
| Paytun | Peneloppe | Perrianna | Peytience | Pheera | Phoebe Laurie | Pigehmah |
| Paytyn (0.01) | Penelopy | Perrie | Peytin | Pheibe | Lise | Piia |
| Payveen | Penie | Perrier | Peyton (1.23) | Phelan | Phoebe-Desiree | Pikea |

Pikiea
Pilar (0.02)
Pilar-Jeanae
Pilate
Pillar
Pilly
Pimprenelle
Pimtawan
Pinelope
Pinilope
Pinkal
Piper (0.50)
Piper-Jolie
Piper-Rain
Pipier
Pippa (0.01)
Pipper
Piquard
Piquette
Piragadi
Pirnaaz
Pisimpiyesis
Piteo
Piujuq
Piumi
Pixie
Pixie Anne
Pixley
Pixxi
Piya
Piyamard
Plaisha
Plantasia
Pleiades
Plyfah
Pneet
Poe
Poem
Poeme
Poet
Poetry
Poinsettia
Pola
Polet
Polete
Poliana
Polianna
Polina (0.01)
Pollianna
Polly (0.01)
Pollyanna
Polly-Faye
Poloma

Polymnia
Polyna
Poma
Pomari
Pomee
Ponette
Poni
Pooja (0.01)
Poojita
Poor
Poorvanjali
Poorvi
Pootnavi
Pope
Popham
Poppy (0.02)
Porcha
Porche
Porchea
Porcilynn
Porscha
Porsche
Porsché
Porschea
Porschia
Por-Sha
Porsha
Porshay
Porshe
Porshia
Porter
Portia (0.03)
Portia-Rose
Portland
Portugal
Posey
Posseh
Posy
Poupisey
Powell
Powers
Poy
Pra'lisha
Praachi
Prabh Preet
Prabha
Prabhakum
Prabhdeep
Prabhgun
Prabhjot
Prabhjyot
Prabhkia
Prabhkiran

Prabhkirat
Prabhleen
Prabhnoor
Prabhpreet
Prabhsharon
Prabhsimran
Prabhvir
Prableen
Prabpreet
Prachi
Pracilla
Prada
Pradasjai
Pradhja
Pradniya
Pragati
Pragna
Pragnya
Pragya
Praiar
Prailynn
Prairie
Praise (0.01)
Praises
Praize
Prajna
Prakaythip
Pramati
Pramila
Pramiti
Pramodani
Prana
Pranathi
Pranati
Pranavi (0.01)
Praneesha
Praneeta
Pranika
Pranita
Pranithi
Pranjal
Pranya
Prapti
Prarthana
Prasaes
Prasamsa
Praskovya
Prateeka
Pratishtha
Pravalika
Pravleen
Praxton
Pray

Prayanshi
Praydeanah
Prayer
Prayleigh
Pre'ahsha
Pre'neise
Pre'niya
Preanna
Preceious
Preci'onna
Precia
Precilla
Preciosa
Precious (0.18)
Precious
  Miracle
Precious Tre
Preciouse
Precioushope
Precious-
  Raphaela
Preere
Preet (0.01)
Preethi
Preeti
Preeyom
Preksha
Premier
Prenaaz
Prenneka
Prentisha
Prentyce
Prerna
Prescilla
Prescious
Presence
Presha
Preshai
Preshas
Preshious
Preshious
  Angel
Preshus
Presilee
Presily
Presilya
Presiosa
Presious
Preslea
Preslee (0.02)
Preslei
Presleigh (0.01)
Presleisav

Presley (0.22)
Presli
Preslie (0.01)
Preslielyn
Presly
Preslye
Presslee
Pressley
Pressly
Prestageah
Prestigious
Prestina
Prestiona
Prestley
Preston (0.01)
Prestyn
Pretira
Pretty
Prettydeer
Preya
Preyia
Preysaya
Prezennia
Prezlee
Prezley
Prezlie
Pri'ya
Pria
Prianka
Priasha
Priceless
Priceliss
Priciela
Pricila (0.01)
Pricilla (0.01)
Pricilla Maria
Prilynn
Prima
Primrose
Prina
Princelia
Princella
Princes
Princesa (0.01)
Princess (0.11)
Princess Branae
  Kolby
Princess H
Princess Hipes
Princess Jalaya
Princess Julan
Princess Megan
Princess Nisa

Princess
  Niseemah
Princess
  Patricia
Princess Skylar
Princess Willow
Princess Zakiya
Princess Zaria
Princess Zyaria
Princess'heavenly
Princessa
Princess-Aldaria
Princess-Anck-
  Su
Princesse
Princesse Janise
Princess-
  Israelah
Princess-
  Modupeoluwa
Princess-
  Salemah
Princezz-Aniyah
Princisca
Princy
Prinnie
Prinsaya
Prinscilla
Prisaeis
Prisca
Prisca Emilie
Prisceis
Priscella
Priscila (0.05)
Priscilia
Priscilla (0.17)
Priscilla Iris
Priscilla-Marie
Priscille
Priscille
  Wroedoove
Priscillia
Priscyla
Priscylla
Priseis
Prisha (0.02)
Prishtina
Prisila (0.01)
Prisilla
Priska
Prissila
Prisslie
Prissy

Pristyne
Pritam Jot
Prithee
Prithika
Priti
Prittie
Priya (0.06)
Priyah
Priyal
Priyana
Priyanka (0.01)
Priyanshi
Prom'miss
Promesse
Promice
Promis
Promise (0.04)
Promisee
Promiss
Promiss-Darryll
Prommiss
Promyse
Promyse Dkayla
  Asia
Promyss-Grace
Prona
Prophecy
Prorineity
Protina
Providence
Providence-
  Eugenelle
Providence-
  Lafleche
Prscilla
Prudence (0.01)
Pruedence
Pruitt
Pryce
Pryelle
Pryia
Pryncess
Prysaud
Pryscilla
Pryshae
Psalm
Psalmn
Psalms
Pueylanie
Puja
Pulelehua
Pulin
Punarvi

Puneet *(0.01)*
Punjjapoa
Pura
Purbita
Purdee
Pureza
Purity
Purpose
Purshia
Purva
Pushpita
Pushti
Puspasara
Puwatida
Pyeper
Pylair Alanyss
Pyper *(0.02)*
Pyper-Scout
Pypre

~ Q ~

Q'lexis
Q'nique
Q'urious
Qa Dia
Qa'dazia
Qa'niya
Qadira
Qadirah
Qahira
Qai'ri
Qaijaet
Qakie
Qali
Qalkidan
Qamar
Qamara
Qamarah
Qattalik
Qavia
Qawyyah
Qearyahana
Qemora
Qeriyah
Qetsia
Qeyanni
Qhaliyah
Qheun
Qi'ashia
Qiah
Qian

Qiana *(0.01)*
Qiana-Arazara
Qianisha
Qianna
Qianni
Qiara
Qiarra
Qiary
Qierrah
Qilonni
Qimora
Qing
Q-Ionnie
Qipitak
Qira
Qiuming
Qiyanni
Qiyawni
Qonte'via
Qorrie
Qristal
Qrystil
Qtiahna
Qu'ryia
Qu'tanna
Qua Dirah
Qua'deara
   Seyerrai
Qua'jané
Qua'mirah
Qua'myiah
Qua'nesha
Qua'niyah
Qua'shima
Qua'-Terri
Qua'tina
Quadaja
Quadasia
Quaddirah
Quadeara
Quadent
Quadir
Quadira
Quadirah
Quadraniya
Quaeria
Quaja
Quajhane
Qualayah
Qualazia
Qualyn Emma
Quamaya
Quameisha

Quamiye
Quamya
Quan
Quan'dasia
Quana'dra
Qua-Naesha
Quanaisha
Quanasia
Quandesha
Quane
Quaneksha
Quanetta
Quaniah
Quanika
Quanise
Quanita
Quaniya
Quanne
Quanniya
Quantasia
Quantavia
Quantayvia
Quantazia
Quante
Quanteria
Quanterria
Quanterric
Quantica
Quantrese
Quanya
Quanyah
Quanyia
Quarin
Quarnayza
Quar-Niah
Quartilla
Quartnee
Quartney
Quasaia
Quashauna
Quashaunte
Quasheerah
Quashyla
Quataisha
Quataja
Quatasha
Quatehya
Quaterria
Quatonia
Quatrell
Quay'ahnis
Quaya'na
Quayla

Que'janna
Que'la
Queanh
Queanya
Queara
Quederiah
Queen *(0.02)*
Queen Elizabeth
Queen Maatkara
Queen Roszia
Queen Ta'm
Queen Teja
Queen
   Yaasantewa
Queena
Queenasia
Queencyana
Queene
Queeneice
Queenie *(0.01)*
Queennet
Queijah
Queintasia
Quelcy
Queli
Quelsey
Quelyn
Quen'niya
Quenahia
Quenasia
Quenayah
Quenburly
Quenby
Quencey
Queni
Quenia
Quenie
Quenniya
Quentasia
Quentaya
Quenterria
Quentin
Quentoriel
Quenya
Quenyshia
Queonia
Queontirri
Queren
Querene
Queria
Querida
Querrah
Ques.La

Quesence
Queshala
Quest
Questa
Quetajia
Quetzal
Quetzali
Quetzalli
Quetzally
Quetzaly
Quí Naysha
Qui'ana
Qui'nae
Qui'niyah
Quiana *(0.01)*
Quianna
Quiara
Quieeny
Quielssy
Quiera
Quierra
Quilecia
Quilianys
Quilla
Quimauria
Quimayah
Quimbirli
Quimora
Quimorah
Quimzilyn
Quin
Quin T'aisha
Quin'asia
Quin'nesha
Quin'niah
Quin'nya
Quin'tay'sia
Quina
Quinaby
Quinaria
Quinasia
Quinavea
Quinaya
Quinazia
Quincee
Quincey *(0.01)*
Quinceyonna
Quinci
Quincie
Quincy *(0.03)*
Quincyana
Quindasia
Quindlan

Quindrea
Quineasha
Quineesha
Quinel
Quinelle
Quinesha
Quinia
Quinice
Quiniece
Quinisiah
Quiniya
Quiniyah
Quinlan *(0.01)*
Quinley
Quinlin
Quinlon
Quinlyn *(0.01)*
Quinlynne
Quinn *(0.20)*
Quinna
Quinnasian
Quinnayah
Quinndalynn
Quinne
Quinnesha
Quinnisha
Quinnlan
Quinnlin
Quinnlyn
Quinnyra
Quinnyria
Quinshe
Quinshell
Quinsye
Quintaijah
Quintaira
Quintana
Quintanna
Quintasia
Quintavia
Quintaviah
Quintavious
Quintazya
Quinteasha
Quintejah
Quintella
Quinteria
Quinterica
Quinterria
Quintesha
Quintessa
Quintessence
Quintina

Quintoniesha
Quintoria
Quintoriua
Quinyah
Quinyana
Quinyce
Quinyonna
Quira
Quiree Mahko
Quishani
Quishea
Quisiana
Quitayvi'a
Quiyaina
Quiyana
Quizzy
Qumia
Qumyra
Quneisha
Qunique
Qunisha
Qunya
Quonet
Quontasia
Quoreen
Quriah
Qurionna
Qurria
Qusiema
Qusondra
Qutan
Qutiara
Quyda
Quyen
Quyncee
Quynh
Quynh Lan
Quynh-Anh
Quynh-Tran
Quynlen
Quynn
Quynne
Quysha
Qw'nerria
   Takeia
Qwanaya
Qwanea
Qwanisha
Qwen
Qwinn
Qwinnya
Qwynn
Qwyntayvea

Qy
Qyara
Qyerrah
Qyiara
Qynne
Qyrah
Qyshaya
Qytara
Qzora

~ R ~

R'breyhanna
R'dashia
R'el
R'emy
R'iell
R'ielle
R'ionne
R'jewels
R'kayla
R'kira
R'love
R'lunyae
R'mani
R'manii
R'mauni
R'meyeni
R'naya
R'niyah
R'reanna
R'reyanna
R'reyanti
R'riana
R'riel
R'riyana
R'riyanna
R'shuntia
R'toriya
R'veioné
R'yanha
R'yianna
R'zjona
Ra Niah
Ra Shonda
Ra'chelle
Ra'gyn
Ra'jenai
Ra'jhay
Ra'jona
Ra'kai
Ra'kayla

Ra'kell
Ra'keria
Ra'keyah
Ra'khia
Ra'kiyah
Ra'knyia
Ra'kyah
Ra'kyaha
Ra'kyiah
Ra'kyla
Ra'laysia
Ra'lea
Ra'leeceya
Ra'lia
Ra'liah
Ra'liya
Ra'londa
Ra'mairyea
Ra'maya
Ra'mayia
Ra'miah
Ra'miya
Ra'miyah
Ra'mya
Ra'myah
Ra'naja
Ra'nardra
Ra'nasia
Ra'nayahi
Ra'nayzia
Ra'neah
Ra'neka
Ra'nelle
Ra'nesha
Ra'neshia
Ra'ni
Ra'niah
Ra'nijah
Ra'nijha
Ra'niya (0.01)
Ra'niyah
Ra'niyrah
Ra'nya
Ra'nyah
Ra'nyia
Ra'ozhana
Ra'quia
Ra'shaa
Ra'shaun
Ra'shaunda
Ra'shawnda
Ra'sheeda
Ra'sheena

Ra'shelle
Ra'shonda
Ra'shyla
Ra'shyra
Ra'ven
Ra'yona
Ra'yonna
Ra'zaria
Raadhika
Raaf'i
Raamalaxmi
Raan
Raashi
Raasia
Raavi
Raavin
Raawiya
Rabab
Rabah
Rabecca
Rabeka
Rabekah
Rabi
Rabia
Rabina
Rabiyya
Rabraya
Racara
Race
Racealene
Racelynn
Racha (0.01)
Racha Ghalia
Rachada
Rachael (0.33)
Rachaell
Rachaely
Rachal
Rachall
Rachana
Rachaunda
Rache
Racheal (0.04)
Rachel (2.91)
Rachel Aal
Rachel Ann
Rachel Annalise Hall
Rachel Joyce
Rachel Katrina
Rachel Maegan
Rachel Marie
Rachel Sukeena

Rachel-Ann
Rachel-Anne
Rachel-Buanda
Rachele
Rachel-Esther
Rachell (0.01)
Rachella
Rachelle (0.07)
Rachelle-Annie
Rachel-Madison
Racheln
Rachel-Sarah
Rachely
Rachey
Rachida
Rachna
Rachney
Rachyl
Racía
Racine
Racquaiya
Racquel (0.01)
Racquell
Racynne
Radaisha
Raddany
Rade'ja
Radella
Radena
Radet
Radha
Radhika (0.01)
Radhiya
Radia
Radiajah
Radiance
Radiant
Radieha
Radiya
Radiyah
Radmila
Radwa
Radyant
Rae (0.01)
Rae Ane
Rae Ann
Rae Leigh
Rae Lynn
Rae Real
Rae'ana
Rae'anna
Rae'ellen

Rae'jean
Rae'jianna
Rae'kim
Rae'leigh
Rae'lynn
Rae'nesha
Rae'nya
Rae'shawn
Rae'unna
Rae'vyn
Rae'yhona
Raea
Rae-Ahna
Raeana
Raeania
Raeann (0.02)
Rae-Anna
Raeanna (0.02)
Raeannah
Rae-Anne
Raeanne (0.01)
Raearnen
Raeaunna
Raechel (0.01)
Raechell
Raechelle
Raecko
Raedawn
Raedell
Raeden
Raedonna
Raedyn
Raeeba
Raeesah
Raegan (0.22)
Raegann
Raegen (0.01)
Raegene
Raeghan (0.01)
Raeghyn
Raegin
Raegon
Raegyn
Raeha
Raeina
Raeionna
Raejanae
Raejen
Raejon
Raejuanae
Rael
Raela
Raelan

Raelana
Raelani
Raelawn
Raele
Raeleane
Raelee (0.01)
Raelei
Raeleigh (0.01)
Raelen
Raelene (0.01)
Raeli
Raelianah
Raelie
Raeliegh
Raelin (0.01)
Raelinn
Raelissa
Raella
Raelle
Raelon
Raely
Raelyn (0.08)
Rae-Lynn
Raelynn (0.05)
Raelynne
Raelyon
Rae-Marie
Raemesha
Raemiah
Raemichel
Raemya
Raen
Raena (0.02)
Raeneen
Raeni
Rae-Niyah
Raenna
Raenya
Raeon
Raesa
Raeshell
Raeshon
Raeshun
Raetina
Raevaughn
Raeven (0.01)
Raevien
Raevin
Raevon
Raevyn (0.01)
Raevynn
Raewyn
Raeya

Raeyah
Raeyanna
Raeyi
Raeyna
Rafaela
Rafaele
Rafaella
Rafaella Claire Curva
Rafaelle (0.02)
Rafaelle-Ann
Rafef
Raffaela
Raffaele
Rafferty
Rafia
Rafiah
Rafiekha
Rafiya
Rafka
Ragad
Ragan (0.01)
Ragean
Ragen
Raghad
Raghd
Raghid
Ragin
Rah'esha
Rah'jae
Rah'layzhaa
Rah'mere
Rah'miya
Rah'nasia
Rah'niah
Rah'niya
Raha
Rahadra
Rahaf
Rahamanpreet
Rahana
Rahasia
Rahat
Rahazia
Rahbraijah
Raheeg
Raheel
Raheema
Raheemah
Raheena
Rahel
Rahenatu
Rahi

| | | | | | | |
|---|---|---|---|---|---|---|
| Rahiel | Raicha | Rainie | Rajneet | Ralivia | Ramsay | Randline |
| Rahil | Raichel | Rainlynn | Rajpreet | Rally | Ramsey (0.02) | Randy |
| Rahilo | Raichelle | Rainn | Rajshai | Ralna | Ramsha | Rane |
| Rahima | Raida | Rainna | Rajuona | Ralnekia | Ramy'a | Rané |
| Rahitha | Raiden | Rainne | Rajvi | Ralonda | Ramya (0.01) | Ranea |
| Rahjae | Raieli | Rainny | Rajvinder | Ralyia | Ramya Shree | Ranecya |
| Rahjah | Raigan (0.01) | Rainy (0.01) | Rajvir | Ralyn | Ramyaa | Ranee |
| Rahjanae | Raigen | Rainyan | Rajwinder | Ralynn | Ramyah | Raneem (0.01) |
| Rahkayla | Raighan | Raionna | Rakaihla | Rama (0.01) | Ramyaka | Raneen |
| Rahkeema | Raighen | Raisa (0.01) | Rakaiya | Ramaiyah | Ramya-Nicole | Raneetria |
| Rahkel | Raighlyn | Raisah | Rakasia | Ramanda | Ramylah | Raneka |
| Rahkeria | Raighnaid | Raisel | Rakaya | Ramandeep | Ramzee | Ranem |
| Rahkina | Raign | Raisha | Rakayla (0.01) | Ramani | Ramzi | Ranesha |
| Rahkyjah | Raiha | Raisina | Rakeb | Ramanprit | Ramzia | Raness |
| Rahkyla | Raihana | Raissa (0.01) | Rakeiah | Ramanya | Ramzie | Raney |
| Rahma (0.01) | Raihanna | Raissa-Danielle | Rakeirra | Ramarea | Ran'eiá | Raneya |
| Rahmah | Raijé | Raiva | Rakel | Ramaree | Ran'nashai | Rani (0.01) |
| Rahmara | Raijene | Raiven | Rakeleigh | Ramari | Ran'nya | Rania (0.04) |
| Rahmia | Raikeria | Raiya (0.01) | Rakell | Ramata | Rana (0.02) | Rania Noor |
| Rahmiah | Raile | Raiyah | Rakelle | Ramatou | Ranaa | Raniah |
| Rahmika | Railé | Raiyanah | Rakeria | Ramatoulay | Ranada | Rania-Renée |
| Rahmirah | Railea | Raiyn | Rakeya | Ramatu | Ranae | Rania-Yasmine |
| Rahmo | Railee | Raiyna | Rakhia | Ramaya | Ranai'yah | Ranie |
| Rahmya | Railei | Raiyne | Rakhira | Ramayah | Ranaiya | Raniesha |
| Rahna | Raileigh | Raiza | Rakhiyah | Ramayani | Ranaiyah | Raniha |
| Rahnaya | Railey (0.01) | Raizel (0.01) | Rakia | Rameen | Ranajha | Ranija |
| Rahne | Raili | Raizelle | Rakiah | Rameena | Ranasia | Ranijah |
| Rahnee | Railin | Raizy (0.04) | Rakiaya | Rameesha | Ranavy | Ranijia |
| Rahnesha | Railycia | Raj Begum | Rakibe | Ramella | Ranay | Ranijiah |
| Rahni | Railyn | Raja | Rakiera | Rameria | Ranaya | Ranim |
| Rahnique | Railynn | Rajae | Rakieria | Ramey | Ranayah | Ranime |
| Rahniya | Railynn Lisette | Rajah | Rakindra | Rami | Rand | Raniqua |
| Rahniyah | Raime | Rajah Lee | Rakira | Ramia | Randa | Ranique |
| Rahnney | Raimey | Rajaha | Rakiya (0.01) | Ramiah (0.01) | Randah | Ranisha |
| Rahwa | Raimi | Rajahnae | Rakiyah | Ramih | Randaisha | Ranit |
| Rahya | Raimoni Lee | Rajai | Rakiyiah | Ramija | Randall | Raniya (0.02) |
| Rahzlynde | Rain (0.02) | Rajaiha | Raksha | Ramirah | Randalyn | Raniyah (0.02) |
| Rai | Rain Divine | Rajanae | Rakshambika | Ramiro | Randalynn | Ranjana |
| Raí | Raina (0.11) | Rajané | Rakya | Ramirrah | Randarriya | Ranjini |
| Rai Moni | Raina Carmelie | Rajanee | Rakyah | Ramisa | Randasia | Rankeyvian |
| Rai'el | Rainah | Rajanique | Rakyia | Ramises | Rande | Ranna |
| Rai'janay | Rainbow | Rajasi | Rakyla | Ramisha | Randee | Ransome |
| Rai'nell | Rain-E | Rajasree | Ralaine | Ramitha | Randelaysia | Rantaisha |
| Rai'niyah | Raine (0.02) | Rajee | Ralanadae | Ramiya (0.01) | Randelle | Ranvir |
| Rai'nya | Rainee | Rajeshwari | Ralane | Ramiyah (0.02) | Randi (0.06) | Ranya (0.01) |
| Rai'seania | Rainell | Rajessa | Ralatris | Ramiyahsuitofi | Randie | Ranyah |
| Rai'ven | Rainelsi | Rajhenae | Raleea | Ramiza | Randié | Ranyel |
| Raia | Rainetta | Rajiana | Raleigh (0.01) | Ramla (0.01) | Randii | Ranyia |
| Raiah | Rainey (0.01) | Rajina | Ralen | Ramlah | Randijah | Ranyla |
| Raiana | Raini | Rajinder | Raley | Ramneek | Randilyn | Ranym |
| Raiana Nowelle | Rainfeather | Rajit | Ralia | Ramneet | Randi-Lynn | Raouaa-Nasrine |
| Raianna | Raini | Rajman | Ralin | Ramona (0.03) | Randilynn | Raphaela |
| Raicelyn | Rainia | Rajmeet | Ralina | Ramoni | Randisha | Raphaelanne |

| | | | | | | |
|---|---|---|---|---|---|---|
| Raphaele | Rashiya | Ravpreet | Rayca | Raylinda | Raysammona | Re'ginis |
| Raphaella | Rashjana | Ravreet | Raychel *(0.02)* | Rayline | Raysanna | Re'jané |
| Raphaella-Rassem | Rashon | Ravyn *(0.03)* | Raychelle | Raylon | Rayshanaye | Re'ka |
| | Rashonda | Ravyyn | Raycie | Raylyn *(0.01)* | Rayshanda | Re'khasia |
| Raphaelle *(0.09)* | Rashonna | Rawaa | Raycine | Raylynn *(0.02)* | Rayshauna | Re'mya |
| Raphaelle Emily | Rashvaira | Rawan *(0.02)* | Raydah | Raylynne | Rayshell | Re'najsa |
| Raphaelle Grace | Rashya | Rawane | Rayden | Rayma | Rayshunda | Re'nieyah |
| Rapinder | Rashyia | Rawan-Mofid | Raye | Raymah | Rayssa *(0.01)* | Re'nisha |
| Raqeh | Rashynda | Rawda | Rayea | Raymanecc | Rayuana | Re'niy |
| Raqiya | Rasia | Rawnag | Rayeanne | Raymari | Rayvan | Re'niya |
| Raquana | Rasika | Ray | Rayegon | Raymecia | Rayven *(0.03)* | Re'niyah |
| Raqueal | Rasima | Ray Celi | Rayel | Raymee | Rayvend | Re'nya |
| Raquel *(0.16)* | Rasleen | Ray'ah | Rayelee | Raymeleen | Rayvenn | Re'nyah |
| Raquelina | Rasmey | Ray'ahna | Rayelin | Raymesha | Rayvin | Re'nyia |
| Raquell | Rasmi | Ray'ana | Rayelle | Raymia | Rayviona | Re'nyjah |
| Raquelle | Rasmia | Ray'ani | Rayelynn | Raymiah | Rayvn | Re'shia |
| Rasa | Rasna | Ray'chel | Rayene | Raymie | Rayvon | Re'zaria |
| Rasaesha | Rasnoor | Ray'jon | Raygan *(0.02)* | Raymieliz | Rayya | Rea *(0.01)* |
| Rasalin | Rassun | Ray'la | Raygann | Raymisha | Rayyan | Rea'gan |
| Rasaun | Rasyah | Ray'lynn | Raygen *(0.01)* | Raymona | Rayyana | Reachel |
| Ra-Sean | Ratalia | Ray'mesha | Rayghen | Raymond | Rayza | Reagan *(1.22)* |
| Rasey | Ratanjot | Ray'miya | Rayhanah | Rayn *(0.01)* | Raza | Reagan Giang-Tien |
| Rasha | Rathsathida | Ray'nah | Rayhanatou-Soraya | Rayná | Razafy | |
| Rashada | Ratiba | Ray'nesha | | Rayna *(0.13)* | Razahria | Reagann |
| Rashaddra | Ratna | Ray'nesiah | Rayhanna | Raynae | Razan *(0.01)* | Reaganne |
| Rashae | Ratoia | Ray'nya | Rayiona | Raynah | Razberrie | Reagan-Skye |
| Rashaé | Ratza | Ray'nyja | Rayionna | Raynalie | Razeail | Reagen *(0.01)* |
| Rashae Dawn | Ratzzath | Ray'shari | Rayiyyah | Rayné | Razene | Reaghan *(0.02)* |
| Rashana | Raujia | Ray'zanel | Rayja | Rayne *(0.09)* | Razhané | Reaghen |
| Rashanda | Raul | Raya *(0.04)* | Rayjohnna | Raynecia | Razhonae | Reagin |
| Rashanti | Raulista | Raya Izet | Raykale | Raynee | Razi | Reagon |
| Rashara | Rauni | Rayah *(0.01)* | Raykira | Rayneisha | Razia | Reagyn |
| Rasharda | Rauscher | Rayan *(0.02)* | Raykiya | Raynell | Raziah *(0.01)* | Reah |
| Rasharia | Rauyn | Ray-Ana | Raykya | Raynelle | Razielle | Reahanna |
| Rashauna | Rav'eana | Rayana *(0.01)* | Rayla *(0.01)* | Rayneshia | Razina | Reahman |
| Rashauni | Ravan | Rayanah | Raylan | Rayney | Raziya | Reahnee |
| Rashawn | Raveaya | Rayane | Raylawnce | Rayni | Raziyah | Realitie |
| Rashawna | Raveen | Rayani | Rayle | Raynia | Raziye-Reyhan | Reality |
| Rashawnda | Raveena | Ray-Ann | Raylea | Rayniah | Razjahnae | Reality-Constancs |
| Rashay | Raven *(0.30)* | Rayann *(0.02)* | Rayleah | Raynie | Razmia | |
| Rashaye | Raven Nathania | Rayanna *(0.02)* | Raylean | Rayniely | Rclynn | Realyn |
| Rasheeda | Ravena | Rayanna Michelle | Raylee *(0.03)* | Raynique | Ré | Ream |
| Rasheema | Raven-Jade | | Rayleen | Rayniya | Re Naiga | Reama |
| Rasheena | Ravenna | Rayanne *(0.01)* | Raylei | Rayniyah | Re'ale | Reana *(0.01)* |
| Rashel *(0.01)* | Raven-Star | Rayannua | Rayleigh *(0.02)* | Rayn-Juel | Re'ana | Reanah |
| Rashell | Raven-Winter | Rayara | Raylen | Raynn | Re'anna | Reane |
| Rashelle | Ravia | Rayaria | Raylena | Rayona | Re'asia | Reann |
| Rashelyn | Raviana | Raya-Sun | Raylene *(0.01)* | Rayonia | Re'asija | Reanna *(0.07)* |
| Rasheta | Ravin *(0.01)* | Rayauna | Rayleta | Rayonie Charlese | Re'auna | Reanna Marie |
| Rashida | Ravleen | Rayawna | Rayley | | Re'cya | Reannah *(0.01)* |
| Rashide | Ravneet *(0.01)* | Rayayna | Rayli | Rayonna *(0.02)* | Re'gan | Reannan |
| Rashione | Ravon | Raybekah | Raylie | Rayouna | Re'gia | Reanne *(0.01)* |
| Rashiy'ah | Ravona | Raybeliz | Raylin *(0.01)* | Rayquel | Re'ginae | Reannen |

Rease
Reauna
Reaves
Reayleigh
Reaynne
Reaza
Reazil
Reba *(0.01)*
Rebacka
Rebaeka
Rebbeca
Rebbecah
Rebbecca
Rebbeka
Rebeca *(0.09)*
Rebecca *(2.11)*
Rebecca Amber
Rebecca Ann
Rebecca Lynn
Rebecca-Alexandra
Rebecca-Eleonore
Rebeccah
Rebeccakay
Rebecca-Lynn
Rebecca-Raquel
Rebecka *(0.02)*
Rebeckah
Rebeka *(0.03)*
Rebeka G
Rebekah *(0.48)*
Rebekeh
Rebekha
Rebekka *(0.01)*
Rebekkah *(0.01)*
Rebekkeh
Rebel
Rece
Recetta
Rechelle
Recky
Reda
Redding
Reddy
Redeait
Redeat
Rediate
Reeah
Reeann
Reeanna
Reeba
Reece *(0.08)*

Reecey
Reed *(0.01)*
Reeder
Reef
Reegan *(0.02)*
Reeghan
Reeham
Reel
Reem *(0.03)*
Reema *(0.01)*
Reena *(0.01)*
Reene
Rees
Reesa *(0.01)*
Reese *(0.81)*
Reese Joyce
Reeselin
Reeslyn
Reet
Reetaj
Reetal
Reethee
Reethusri
Reeti
Reetu
Reeva
Reeve
Reeves
Reevise
Reeya
Reeyah
Reeyhannah
Refah
Refentse
Refoncia
Refugia
Reg'iauna
Regan *(0.26)*
Reganell
Regann
Reganne *(0.01)*
Regeana
Regen
Regena
Regenae
Regenia
Reggan
Reggi
Reggie
Reghan *(0.02)*
Reghyn
Regi
Regi'nae

Regia
Regie
Regiena
Regin
Regina *(0.15)*
Reginae
Reginahh
Reginalda
Regina-Marie
Regina-Shayna
Regine
Reginee
Regine-Odelia
Reginiyah
Reginna
Regirah
Regon
Regyn
Reham
Rehana
Rehani
Rehanna
Rehannah
Rehap-Allislame
Rehat
Rehea
Rehet
Reheth
Rehgan
Rehgyn
Rehmin
Rehtaeh
Rehwa
Rehyn
Rei
Reia
Reial
Reiana
Reianna
Reianne
Reiara
Reiayanami
Reice
Reichelle
Reichelys
Reid *(0.01)*
Reidun
Reigan
Reigann
Reigen
Reigh
Reigha-Lynn
Reighanna

Reighn
Reighney
Reign *(0.01)*
Reigna
Reignah
Reigne
Reigny
Reihgyn
Reika
Reilani
Reilee
Reiley *(0.01)*
Reiliyah
Reilleigh
Reilley
Reilly *(0.08)*
Reily *(0.01)*
Reily-Kalyn
Reilyn
Rein
Reina *(0.09)*
Reina Kasey
Reinajen Mareli
Reinaly
Reinarosa
Reine
Reinika
Reinna
Reinya
Reirdon
Reis
Reisa
Reise
Reitta
Reiyako
Reiyi
Rej'na
Reja
Rejah
Rejana
Rejanique
Rejean
Rejenai
Rejhan
Rejhonae
Rejina
Rejoice
Reka
Rekaye
Rekayla
Rekenya
Rekeura
Rekeya

Rekha
Rekhai
Rekhayla
Rekia
Rekio
Relaneve
Relani
Relannah
Releena
Releigh
Reliegh
Relindria
Relisa
Relissa
Relyne
Rem
Rema
Remani
Remasha
Remda
Reme
Remedy
Remee
Remeece
Remember
Remeny
Remethia
Remey
Remhy
Remi *(0.02)*
Remia
Remiah
Remie
Remijia
Remilea
Remington *(0.02)*
Remingtyn
Reminisce
Reminise
Remith
Remiya
Remmie
Remonii
Remy *(0.02)*
Remzi
Ren
Ren E
Rená
Rena *(0.02)*
Rena Marie
Rena'jyah
Renad

Renadja
Renae *(0.03)*
Renaeshia
Renah
Renai
Renaissance
Renaja
Renajah
Renalda
Renanshia
Renarda
Renasia
Renat
Renata *(0.02)*
Renate
Renatica
Renatta
Renaude
Renay
Renaya
Renayah
Renayjah
Renda
Rendayshá
Rendi
Rendy
René
Rene *(0.01)*
Renea
Reneah
Renecie'a
Renée
Reneé *(0.01)*
Renée *(0.01)*
Renee *(0.21)*
Renee Marlene
Renee Ning
Renee'la
Renee'sha
Renee-Jewels
Renee-Laure
Renee-Leah
Renee-Lou
Renée-Lynn
Reneese
Reneesha
Renehja
Reneijah
Renejah
Reneka
Renell
Renelle
Renesha

Reneshia
Reness
Renessa
Renet
Renethia
Renette
Reneva
Renhya
Renia
Reniayh
Renick
Renie
Reniecia
Renieya
Renija
Renijah
Renika
Renil
Renique
Renise
Renisha
Renissa
Renita
Reniya
Reniyah
Reniyaha
Reniyiah
Renlee
Renley
Renna
Rennah
Renne
Rennie
Renny
Renotta
Reny
Renya
Renyah
Reny-Rose
Renza
Renzi
Reoandra
Reola
Reona
Reonin
Reonna
Repinder
Requilla
Resah
Rese
Reseana
Resha
Reshanna

| | | | | | | |
|---|---|---|---|---|---|---|
| Reshawna | Reyli | Rhayne | Rhianna-Lee | Rhyanne | Rianna *(0.06)* | Richland |
| Reshiya | Reyly | Rhazae | Rhiannan | Rhyann-Elise | Riannabelle | Richleigh |
| Reshma | Reyna *(0.08)* | Rhea *(0.08)* | Rhianne | Rhyannon | Riannah | Richlyn |
| Reshunna | Reynae | Rhea Katerina | Rhiannion | Rhyelle | Riannan | Richmayla |
| Reshyah | Reynahliz | Rhea Rosalina | Rhiannon *(0.14)* | Rhyen | Rianne *(0.01)* | Richona |
| Resi | Reynaldo | Rheagan *(0.01)* | Rhianon | Rhyera | Riannon | Richthard |
| Ressa | Reynalis | Rhéah | Rhiauna | Rhyianna | Rianon | Richylin |
| Ressey | Reynalise | Rhea-Lee | Rhiely | Rhyin | Riara | Richyra |
| Ressie | Reynasia | Rhealee | Rhihanna | Rhylan | Riashna | Rickaya |
| Reta | Reynesha | Rhealeigh | Rhiiaunna | Rhyland | Riasia | Rickayala |
| Retal | Reyniah | Rhealyn | Rhikya | Rhylanna | Riata | Rickayh |
| Retha | Reynid | Rhealynn | Rhilee | Rhylea | Riauna | Rickayla |
| Rethi | Reyonna | Rheana *(0.01)* | Rhiley *(0.01)* | Rhylee *(0.02)* | Riayn | Rickee |
| Rethida | Reyse | Rheann | Rhilyn | Rhyleigh | Ribka | Rickeicia |
| Rethola | Reysha | Rheanna *(0.02)* | Rhilynn | Rhyley | Ric'cyia | Rickell |
| Retisha | Reyshun | Rheanne | Rhima | Rhyli | Ric'kevia | Rickelle |
| Retta | Reyvin | Rheannon | Rhina | Rhylie | Ric'kiyah | Rickendra |
| Reubensa | Reyvon | Rheannyn | Rhionna | Rhyli-Rose | Ric'kya | Rickesha |
| Reva *(0.01)* | Reza | Rheanon | Rhita | Rhyonnan | Ric'kyia | Rickey |
| Reva Leah | Rha'necia | Rhedyn | Rhiver | Rhys | Ric'shariah | Rickhia |
| Reva Sagar | Rha'nyai | Rheece | Rhiya | Rhysa | Rica | Ricki |
| Revan | Rhaashana | Rheema | Rhiyan | Rhythm | Ricaiya | Rickia |
| Revati | Rhadenelle | Rheena Pearl | Rhmyia | Rhythm'irie | Ricaline | Rickiah |
| Revecca | Rhaea | Rheese | Rhoan | Ri'ann | Ricara | Rickie |
| Reveena | Rhaegan | Rhegan *(0.01)* | Rhoane | Ri'aunna | Ricarda | Rickisha |
| Revelation | Rhaelynn | Rheganne | Rhoda *(0.02)* | Ri'brazsha | Ricasha | Rickiya |
| Revelle | Rhagan | Rheia | Rhoda Rachel | Ri'chele | Ricayah | Rickiyah |
| Revin | Rhagen | Rheianna | Rhodas | Ri'chyia | Ricayla | Rickkia |
| Rewa | Rhaili-Em | Rheilly | Rhode Shana | Ri'en | Ricci | Rickkya |
| Rexanna | Rhaine | Rhema *(0.01)* | Rhoderra | Ri'khia | Ricciah | Ricky |
| Reya *(0.01)* | Rhaissa | Rhen | Rhodes | Ri'kiya | Riccy | Ricky Lu |
| Reyah | Rhaiza | Rhena | Rhomely | Ri'kiyah | Richá | Rickya |
| Reyan | Rhakyhia | Rhenn | Rhona | Ri'nai | Richa *(0.01)* | Rickyah |
| Reyana | Rhamani | Rhenna | Rhona Nicole | Ri'naja | Richael | Rickyra |
| Reyann | Rhamya-Luv | Rheo | Rhonda *(0.02)* | Ri'niya | Richaelyn | Ricnisha |
| Reyanna | Rhanaija | Rheonna | Rhone | Ri'yonna | Richana | Ricocia |
| Reyanne | Rhanchys | Rhesa | Rhoneisha | Ria *(0.07)* | Richanna | Ricoria |
| Reyannie | Rhand | Rheya | Rhonesty | Ria'yanni | Richara | Ricoya |
| Reya-Noir | Rhanda | Rheyanna | Rhonni | Riah *(0.01)* | Richaranna | Ricquazia |
| Reyce | Rhandi | Rheyea | Rhonnie | Riahanna | Richard | Ricquelle |
| Reychael | Rhandie | Rheyna | Rhori | Riahleigh | Richarda | Ricyonna |
| Reydimar | Rhandy | Rhi'anna | Rhoslyn | Riahna | Richardline | Rida *(0.01)* |
| Reydon | Rhane | Rhi'kasia | Rhoyalti | Riahnna | Richaria | Riddah |
| Reyenne | Rhania | Rhia | Rhumani | Rialeigh | Richarianna | Riddhi |
| Reyettea | Rhanija | Rhian *(0.02)* | Rhy'azia | Rialey | Richca | Ridejah |
| Reygan *(0.01)* | Rhaniya | Rhiana *(0.02)* | Rhy'zhane | Rialissa | Riché | Ridgely |
| Reygann Clarke | Rhaniyah | Rhianah | Rhya | Rian *(0.04)* | Richeé | Ridgina |
| Reyhan | Rhannon | Rhianen | Rhyan *(0.03)* | Riana *(0.02)* | Richell | Ridham |
| Reyhaneh | Rhanora | Rhiann | Rhyana | Riane | Richelle *(0.02)* | Ridhi |
| Reyjona | Rhaquell | Rhianna *(0.09)* | Rhyane | Riane-Noellie | Richelsea | Ridhwana |
| Reykicha | Rhashya | Rhianna Jayden | Rhyann *(0.01)* | Riania | Richena | Ridley |
| Reylana | Rhaya | Rhianna Lei | Rhyanna | Rianka | Richerine | Ridwaan |
| Reylene | Rhaylisha | Rhiannah | Rhyannah | Riann *(0.01)* | Richie | Rieane |

| | | | | | | |
|---|---|---|---|---|---|---|
| Rieann | Rikka | Rinah | Ritchina | Ro Nellia | Robrihanna | Rodnaye |
| Rieanna | Rikki (0.02) | Rinaz | Rith | Ro'ison | Robyen- | Rodnayzia |
| Riece | Rikkia | Rindha | Rithi | Ro'keria | Menyeah | Rodne'y |
| Riedwan | Rikkie | Rindi | Rithika | Ro'keya | Robyin | Rodnea |
| Riehle | Rikkilyn | Rinesa | Rithika Reddy | Ro'maya | Robyn (0.09) | Rodneesha |
| Rieisha | Riko | Rini | Rithu | Ro'myah | Robyn Elizabeth | Rodneisa |
| Riel | Riky'a | Riniya | Riti | Ro'nayiah | Robynette | Rodneisha |
| Rielee | Rikya | Rinlada | Ritika (0.01) | Ro'necia | Robynn | Rodneshia |
| Rieleigh | Rikyah | Rinn | Ritisha | Ro'nijha | Robyr'iona | Rodneta |
| Rieley | Rikyiara | Rinnah | Ritoja | Ro'niyah | Rocco | Rodneve |
| Rieli | Rikyla | Rinoa (0.01) | Ritricia | Ro'nyah | Rocelyn | Rodneya |
| Rielie | Rikza | Rinora | Ritsika | Ro'shaia | Rocha Aguinaga | Rodneyah |
| Rielley | Rile | Rinrada | Ritsu | Ro'siya | Rochel (0.03) | Rodneyka |
| Riellie | Rilea | Rinthy | Ritter | Ro'veasia | Rochell | Rodnia |
| Rielly | Rileah | Rinyia | Ritzy | Ro'ya | Rochelle (0.04) | Rodnique |
| Riely | Rilee (0.05) | Rio (0.01) | Riva | Roaa | Rochellys | Rodnisha |
| Rielyn | Rileeann | Rio-Bella | Riven | Roadha | Rochely | Rodnysha |
| Rien | Rileen | Rion | River (0.04) | Roah | Rochnica | Rodre'cia |
| Riena | Rilei | Riona | Riverah | Roan | Rocibel | Rodrenique |
| Rienna | Rileigh (0.08) | Rionagh | Riveranne | Roane | Rocio (0.04) | Rodrianna |
| Ries | Rilen | Rionn | Riverine | Roann | Rockayla | Rodricka |
| Riese | Riley (2.50) | Rionna (0.01) | Rivers (0.01) | Roarie | Rockcelle | Rodrickah |
| Rieslynn | Riley Breanna | Riordan | Riviera | Roaryie | Rockel | Rodrigo |
| Rifky | Riley Jo | Ripan | Rivka (0.08) | Robbaniquea | Rockell | Rodriguez |
| Rigel | Riley Katharine | Ripleigh | Rivkah (0.01) | Robbeona | Rockelle | Rodriguez- |
| Rigin | Riley Lauren | Ripley (0.01) | Rivky (0.03) | Robbeonna | Rockeriauna | Forero |
| Rigina | Riley Lise | Riquell | Rivver | Robbi | Rockette | Rodrika |
| Riglie | Riley Mont | Riquetta | Rixy | Robbianna | Rocki | Rodrineka |
| Rihaana | Rileyann | Risa (0.01) | Riya (0.10) | Robbie | Rocklyn | Rodrionna |
| Riham | Riley-Grace | Riselle | Riyaan | Robbie Jane | Rocksann | Rodshaé |
| Rihana (0.01) | Riley-Nicole | Risha | Riyad | Robbilynn | Rocquel | Rod-Zjae |
| Rihanique | Riley-Rose | Rishae | Riyah | Robbin | Rocyera | Roeishah |
| Rihanna (0.07) | Rili | Rishana | Riyahna | Robbirana | Rod Nia | Roen |
| Rihannon | Rilie | Rishanna | Riyan | Robbriasia | Rod Nya | Roena |
| Rihauna | Riliegh | Rishawna | Riyana | Robbyah | Rod'lynn | Roenaysia |
| Rihonna | Rilla | Rishayla | Riyanna | Robbye | Rod'neyshia | Roensia |
| Rihonnalyn | Rily | Rishelda | Riyasha | Robenekia | Rod'nisha | Rofyda |
| Rihuna | Rilye | Rishelle | Riye'l | Roberline | Roda | Rogan |
| Rija | Rilyn (0.02) | Rishika | Riyo | Robernique | Rodaijah | Roge |
| Rijja | Rilyne | Rishita | Riza | Roberta (0.02) | Rodalles | Rogellia |
| Rijka | Rilynn (0.01) | Rishitha | Rizael | Robey | Rodas | Rogette |
| Rika | Rim | Rishma | Rizaria | Robi | Rodasha | Rogina |
| Rikay | Rim Titrite | Rishyah | Rizelle | Robianna | Rodasia | Rogue |
| Rikaycia | Rima | Rishyla | Riziki | Robin (0.08) | Rod-Dreikia | Roha |
| Rikee | Rimalie | Riskita | Rizyah | Robina | Rodelle | Rohan |
| Rikeisha | Riman | Rissa | Rizzie | Robinette | Rodenza | Rohana |
| Rikelle | Rime | Rissviny | Rjavia | Robinson | Roderica | Rohanda |
| Rikeriya | Rimel | Rista | Rjhanise | Robion | Rodericka | Rohanni |
| Riki | Rimi | Rita (0.08) | Rmani | Robiona | Rodhermine | Rohen |
| Rikia | Rimsha | Ritaj | Rmidjie | Robiyonne | Rodhnika | Rohiatou |
| Rikiana | Rin | Ritaje | Rmoni | Robmarie | Rodia | Rohini |
| Rikinya | Rin'niya | Rita-Maria | Rneem | Robreya | Rodina | Rohinii |
| Rikiyah | Rina (0.02) | Ritch | Ro | Robrianna | Rodmya | Rohma |

| | | | | | | |
|---|---|---|---|---|---|---|
| Rohmane | Romelia | Roneli | Ronniesha | Rosabelle | Rosanna (0.03) | Roseguintz |
| Rohwan | Romeo | Ronella | Ronnika | Rosaisela | Rosanne (0.01) | Rose-Helene |
| Roisin | Romey | Ronelle | Ronnisha | Rosajulia | Rosanne | Roseily |
| Roisyn | Romi | Ronesha | Ronnisia | Rosalba (0.01) |   Katherine | Roselande |
| Roiya | Romiah | Roneshia | Ron-Niyah | Rosa-Leah | Rosany | Roselandee |
| Rojae | Romie | Ronette | Ronny | Rosa-Lee | Rosaria | Roselany |
| Rojaya | Romina (0.02) | Roní | Ronny'ah | Rosalee (0.02) | Rosariah | Roselea |
| Rojda | Romisha | Roni (0.01) | Ronnyah | Rosaleen | Rosario (0.02) | Roseleen |
| Rojeen | Rommie | Roni'ya | Ronnyie | Rosaleena | Rosario | Roselena |
| Rojera | Rommiea | Ronia | Ronshay | Rosaleigh |   Guadalupe | Roselene |
| Rojevahn | Rommya | Roniah | Ronshea | Rosalen | Rosario- | Roselia |
| Rojoan | Romona | Roniayah | Rontashia | Rosalena |   Carmelo | Roselie |
| Rokaia | Romoni | Ronica | Rontayvia | Rosalene | Rosaura (0.01) | Rose-Lilas |
| Rokale | Romy (0.02) | Ronicha | Rontazia | Rosali | Rosavia | Roselilliam |
| Rokayia | Romya | Ronicia | Rontina | Rosalia (0.03) | Rose (0.50) | Roselin (0.01) |
| Rokhaya | Romyah | Ronie | Ron-Torrieah | Rosalianyelis | Rose Aimee | Roselina |
| Rokhsana | Romyia | Roniea | Rony | Rosalidia | Rose Alyana | Roselind |
| Rokia | Ron Nique | Roniesha | Ronya | Rosalie (0.29) | Rose Barbara | Roselinda |
| Rokiya | Ron'kyla | Ronijah | Ronyae | Rosalie Marie- | Rose Cosette | Roseline (0.01) |
| Rokiyra | Ron'nae | Ronika | Ronyahlee |   Jeanne | Rose D | Roselith |
| Rokkyn | Ron'naysha | Ronilyn | Ronyé | Rosalie Megane | Rose Elyse | Rosella (0.01) |
| Rola | Ron'necia | Ronin | Ronyea | Rosalin | Rose Emie | Roselle |
| Rolanda | Ron'niece | Ronique | Rooaa | Rosalina (0.01) | Rose Mala | Rosely |
| Rolandria | Ron'niya | Ronise | Roobielle | Rosalina Grace | Rose Marie | Roselyn (0.10) |
| Rolda | Ron'terrak | Ronisha | Rood | Rosalind (0.01) | Rose Mary | Roselynda |
| Roldnise | Ron'yale | Ronit | Rookia | Rosalinda (0.03) | Rose'zina | Roselyne |
| Rolemide | Rona | Ronita | Roop | Rosalindah | Rose-Aimee | Roselynn (0.01) |
| Rolena | Ronae | Roniya | Roopa | Rosalinde | Rosealee | Rosemany |
| Rolesha | Ronahy | Roniyah | Roopkotha | Rosaline | Rosealexis | Rose-Maria |
| Rolincia | Ronaijau | Roniyia | Roos Marie | Rosalita | Rose-Alice | Rose-Marie |
| Roline | Ronald | Ronja | Roosetta | Rosaliz | Rose-Ally |   (0.01) |
| Rollins | Ronalda | Ronjanique | Roossiana | Rosallina | Rosealyiha | Rosemarie |
| Roma (0.01) | Ronalene | Ronkaylia | Roper | Rosalva | Rosealyn |   (0.04) |
| Roma Lynn | Ronalya | Ronkeria | Rora | Rosa-Ly | Rosealynne | Rose-Marilou |
| Romaine | Ronan | Ronna | Roree | Rosaly (0.02) | Roseana | Rose-Mary |
| Romaira | Ronashia | Ronnae | Rorey | Rosalya | Roseane | Rosemary (0.11) |
| Romaissa | Ronasia | Ronnasha | Rori (0.02) | Rosalye | Rose-Angelique | Rosemary- |
| Roman | Ronasiá | Ronnasya | Rorie (0.01) | Rosalyha | Roseann |   Chioma |
| Romana | Ronaya | Ronnayja | Rorieann | Rosalyn (0.03) | Rose-Anna | Rosemaryjane |
| Romance | Ronaysia |   Shadria | Rorrey | Rosalyne | Roseanna (0.01) | Rose-Maxim |
| Romane (0.02) | Ronayza | Ronnda | Rorri | Rosalynn (0.01) | Rose-Anne | Rose-Medalion |
| Romaneisha | Ronda | Ron-Neah | Rorrie | Rosamaria | Roseanne | Rosemekah |
| Romani | Rondasha | Ronnee | Rory (0.08) | Rosamarina | Rosebeline | Rosemery |
| Romanie | Rondasia | Ronneé Lyn | Ros | Rosamond | Roseberlin | Rosemie |
| Romantica | Rondesha | Ronneria | Ros'cyanah | Rosamund | Rosedeep | Rosemond |
| Romany | Rondine | Ronnesha | Rosa (0.18) | Rosan | Rosee | Rosenaiely |
| Romanza | Rondrell | Ronnetta | Rosa Eliza | Rosana | Rose-Eliane | Rosenally |
| Romarie | Ronecca | Ronni (0.01) | Rosa Laura | Rosane | Rose-Emilie | Rosene |
| Romayssaa | Ronecia | Ronnice | Rosa Linda | Rosangel | Rose-Emy | Rosenel |
| Rome | Ronee | Ronnicia | Rosa Lucia | Rosangela | Rose-Esther | Rose-Neley |
| Romea | Roneelyn | Ronnicka | Rosa Luz | Rosangely | Rose-Evariste | Roseny |
| Romee | Roneisha | Ronnie (0.01) | Rosa Maria | Rosangly | Rose-Gabrielle | Rosepetal |
| Romeka | Roneka | Ronnieann | Rosabella | Rosann | Rosegladiniah | Rosesherlynda |

Rosett
Rosetta *(0.01)*
Rosette
Rosevanie
Rosevitte
Rosey
Roseymy
Roshaadea
Ro-Shae
Roshan
Roshana
Roshanee
Roshar'zanae
Roshauna
Roshawna
Roshay
Roshaye
Roshell
Roshelle
Roshia
Roshna
Roshnda
Roshni *(0.01)*
Roshonda
Rosi
Rosiana
Rosiane
Rosianna
Rosianne
Rosibel
Ros-I-Carmen
Rosie *(0.04)*
Rosie Eve
Rosie Mary Ann
Rosie-Ann
Rosie-Anne
Rosiebel
Rosielea
Rosiely
Rosiland
Rosiliana
Rosilyn
Rosime
Rosina
Rosine
Rosio
Rosita *(0.01)*
Rosivel
Rosizela
Roslin
Roslin Marie
Roslyn *(0.02)*
Roslynn

Rosmery
Ross
Rossa
Rossalyn
Rossamiah
Rossana
Rossandra
Rossangelie
Rosse
Rosselin
Rossella
Rosselle
Rosselyn
Rossemary
Rosshely
Rossi
Rossie
Rosslan
Rossly
Rosslyn
Rosslynn
Rossmary
Rossolin
Rossy
Rossymar
Rostan
Roswen
Rosy *(0.01)*
Rosyane
Rosy-Ann
Rosyvette
Rotchana
Rotem
Roth-Canyca
Roua
Roughiatou
Rougui
Rouguiatou
Roui
Rouneka
Rouqaya
Roury
Rous
Roushanai
Rousmary
Routh
Rowa
Rowan *(0.17)*
Rowana
Rowanne
Ro-Way
Rowda
Rowdy

Rowe
Rowen *(0.01)*
Rowena *(0.01)*
Rowyn *(0.01)*
Rowynn
Roxalyn
Roxan
Roxana *(0.04)*
Roxane *(0.02)*
Roxane-Emilie
Roxann
Roxanna *(0.02)*
Rox-Anne
Roxanne *(0.09)*
Roxanne Aline
Roxel
Roxella
Roxely
Roxianne
Roxie *(0.01)*
Roxiyuridia
Roxonna
Roxsana
Roxxann
Roxxi
Roxxie
Roxxymar
Roxy *(0.01)*
Roy'esha
Roy'neesha
Roya
Royal
Royale
Royalti
Royalty
Royce
Royeisha
Royette
Roylynn
Royniya
Royniyia
Royonna
Royonnah
Roystani
Royton
Royuni
Roz
Roza
Roza Batya
Rozalena
Rozalett
Rozalia
Rozalin

Rozalyn *(0.01)*
Rozalynd
Rozalynn
Rozalynne
Rozanna
Rozariah
Rozatinna
Roze
Rozelle
Rozellyn
Rozelyn
Roze-Mary
Rozemary
Rozene
Rozenn
Rozerin
Rozetta
Rozina
Rozlyn *(0.01)*
Rozlynn
Rozlynne
Rozmeen
Rozyna
Rozzlynn
Rraevan
Rriauna
Rrutu
Rryana
Rselah
R-Shenae
Ru'nyia
Ruaa
Ruaaqah
Ruane
Ruari
Ruba
Rubbenae
Rubeana
Rubee
Rubeen
Rubelinda
Rubí
Rubi *(0.09)*
Rubi Guada
Rubi Yamileth
Rubiana
Rubiangel
Rubianna
Rubichisel
Rubie *(0.01)*
Rubiela
Rubil
Rubina

Rubisela
Rubjot
Rubrina
Rubus
Ruby *(1.26)*
Rubyana
Rubydee
Rubye
Ruby-Jane
Rubyjane
Rubylou
Ruby-Louise
Ruby-Marie
Rubyrain
Ruchi
Ruchika
Ruchita
Rudelle
Rudi
Rudianelly
Rudra
Rudy
Rudyasiá
Rue
Ruey
Rufina
Rufo
Rugiatu
Ruhama
Ruhana
Ruhani
Ruhayma
Ruhee
Ruhi
Ruhri
Ruihuang
Ruiwen
Rujul
Rujula
Rukaiya
Rukaya
Rukeme
Rukevwe
Rukia
Ruksha
Rukundo
Rukya
Rula
Rulena
Rulillia
Rumaisa
Rumalia
Ruman

Rumanda
Rumaysa
Rumeisha
Rumina
Rumor
Rumsha
Rumya
Runa
Runarea
Rune
Runet
Runnee
Runqi
Runyssa
Ruo
Ruoming
Ruoqin
Ruoxuan
Rupan
Rupashree
Rupinder
Ruqaia
Ruqaiyah
Ruqaya
Ruqayya
Ruqayyah *(0.01)*
Ruqaiya
Ruqio
Ruqiya
Ruriko
Rus'shawna
Rusham
Rushauna
Rushel
Rushella
Rushelle
Rushika
Rushya
Ruslana
Rusna
Russetta
Russia
Rustie
Rut *(0.01)*
Ruta
Rutendo
Ruth *(0.30)*
Ruth Angel
Ruth Ann
Ruth June
Ruth Meredith
Ruth-Abigail
Ruth-Ann

Ruthann *(0.01)*
Ruthanna
Ruthanne
Ruthashley
Ruthdaliz
Ruthe
Ruthee
Ruthellen
Ruthemma
Ruthie *(0.03)*
Ruthinna
Ruth-Irona
Ruthlyne
Ruthnika
Ruthsha
Ruthvika
Ruupala
Ruusa
Ruveyda
Ruvianna
Ruvimbo
Ruvy
Ruwa
Ruwaa
Ruwaida
Ruwayda
Ruwaydo
Ruweidha
Ruweyda
Ruzica
Rwan
Ry'ann
Ry'anna
Ry'anne
Ry'aun
Ry'chelle
Ry'keiria
Ry'keria
Ry'lee
Ry'najah
Ry'naya
Ry'neisha
Ry'neisseya
Ry'nesha
Ry'nyria
Ry'quel
Ry'shira
Rya *(0.01)*
Ryaan
Ryah *(0.01)*
Ryairia
Ryalah
Ryale

Ryalea
Ryall
Ryalynn
Ryan *(0.20)*
Ryana
Ryanah
Ryandi
Ryane *(0.01)*
Ryann *(0.13)*
Ryanna *(0.02)*
Ryannah
Ryanne *(0.03)*
Ryann-Elizabeth
Ryannen
Ryaquel
Ryatt
Rybin
Rycah
Rychanna
Rydasjha Alkeira
Ryder
Rydia
Ryeann
Ryeanna
Ryece
Rye-Elle
Ryek
Ryeleagh
Ryelee
Ryeleigh
Ryeley
Ryeli
Ryeliegh
Ryelin
Ryelle
Ryelly
Ryely
Ryelynn
Ryen *(0.01)*
Ryen Elizabeth
Ryeniah
Ryenn
Ryenne
Ryen-November
Ryeona
Ryese
Ryesha
Ryeya
Ryha
Ryhana
Ryhanna
Ryia
Ryiana

Ryien
Ryilee
Ryin
Ryka
Rykelle
Ryker
Rykia
Rykierra
Rykiria
Rykky
Ryla
Rylah
Rylaijha
Rylan *(0.06)*
Ryland *(0.01)*
Rylann
Ryle
Rylea *(0.02)*
Ryleah
Rylee *(1.45)*
Rylee-Ann
Ryleegh
Ryleeh
Rylee-Jade
Rylee-Nicole
Rylei *(0.01)*
Ryleigh *(0.35)*
Ryleigh Ann
Ryleigh-Lynn
Ryleigh-Sh
Rylen *(0.01)*
Ryley *(0.08)*
Ryli *(0.01)*
Rylianna
Rylianne
Rylicia
Rylie *(0.34)*
Ryliegh
Rylien
Rylin *(0.01)*
Rylinn
Rylli
Ryllie
Rylye
Rylyn *(0.01)*
Rylynn *(0.01)*
Rylynne
Rym *(0.01)*
Ryma
Ryme
Rymia
Rymirah
Ryna

Rynasia
Rynasiah
Ryneah
Rynecia
Ryneisha
Ryniah
Ry-Nier
Rynyae
Ryo
Ryoko
Ryona
Ryonna
Ryqual
Rysh'anna
Rysha
Ryshena
Ryssa
Ryta
Rytisha
Ryun
Ryver
Ryyan

## ~ S ~

S
S Myiah
S Myriah
S'aliah
S'aravia
S'heaven
S'jariel
S'linedee
S'liyah
S'mariya
S'monya
S'moriyah
S'mya
S'nahya
S'nayá
S'niyah
S'pria
Sa Nija
Sa Nye
Sa Riah
Sa'ada
Sa'bana
Sa'bria
Sa'bria
Sa'brina
Sa'briyah
Sa'de

Sa'diyah
Sa'jada
Sa'jae
Sa'jah
Sa'jocye
Sa'keena
Sa'keira
Sa'kerah
Sa'khira
Sa'kniya
Sa'leema
Sa'liyah
Sa'mahri
Sa'maiya
Sa'maiyah
Sa'mani
Sa'mara
Sa'marah
Sa'mari
Sa'marian
Sa'mariea
Sa'marria
Sa'marya
Sa'maya
Sa'meara
Sa'mearia
Sa'meia
Sa'merya
Sa'miah
Sa'mira
Sa'miriya
Sa'mitra
Sa'miya
Sa'mone
Sa'monie
Sa'mya *(0.01)*
Sa'myah
Sa'myai
Sa'myia
Sa'myiah
Sa'myra
Sa'na'ria
Sa'naa
Sa'nah
Sa'nahia
Sa'nai
Sa'nareia
Sa'naudiya
Sa'nay
Sa'naya
Sa'nayia
Sa'ni
Sa'niah

Sa'nie
Sa'niece
Sa'nijah
Sa'nina
Sa'niya *(0.02)*
Sa'niyah *(0.01)*
Sa'niyeah
Sa'niyya
Sa'nja
Sa'nya *(0.01)*
Sa'nyah
Sa'nyai
Sa'nyia
Sa'nyiah
Sa'nyya
Sa'onna
Sa'peara
Sa'phia
Sa'quora
Sa'rae
Sa'rai
Sa'rayhia
Sa'renity
Sa'riah
Sa'rieya
Sa'riya
Sa'riyah
Sa'ron
Sa'rye
Sa'tara
Sa'tiah
Sa'toriah
Sa'von
Sa'yanna
Saabaya
Saabirah
Saabiriin
Saachi
Saada
Saadah
Saade
Saadet
Saadia
Saadiqa
Saadiya
Saady
Saafiyah
Saahithi
Saahiti
Saaiyanka
Saajidah
Saakshi
Saalexiss

Saalihah
Saaliyah
Saamia
Saamira
Saamiya
Saamya
Saána
Saa-Ni
Saaniyah
Saanti
Saanvi *(0.02)*
Saanya
Saanyá
Saara
Saarah
Saari
Saarika
Saatchi
Saaya
Saayeh
Saayona
Saba *(0.01)*
Sabaa
Sabaata
Sabah
Sabal
Sabarin
Sabastiana
Sabbath
Sabdrine
Sabdy
Sabeeha
Sabeeka
Sabeen
Sabeina
Sabel
Sabella *(0.02)*
Sabelle
Saber
Sabia
Sabian
Sabiha
Sabila
Sabina *(0.04)*
Sabina Miel
Sabine *(0.03)*
Sabir
Sabirah
Sabireen
Sabirin
Sable
Sabra *(0.01)*
Sabrah

Sabre
Sabrea
Sabreanna
Sabreé
Sabreea
Sabreen
Sabreena *(0.01)*
Sabregan
Sabrena
Sabri
Sabria *(0.01)*
Sabriah
Sabrial
Sabrianne
Sabrie
Sabriell
Sabriella
Sabrin
Sabrina *(0.86)*
Sabrina Daniela
Sabrina
    Elizabeth
Sabrina Marisol
Sabrina Rose
Sabrina
    U'niephe
Sabrina
    Uashtessiu
Sabrina-Anissia
Sabrina-
    Arocha
Sabrinah
Sabrina-Ines
Sabrina-Ma
Sabrine *(0.01)*
Sabrinha
Sabrinna
Sabriya
Sabriyah
Sabriye
Sabriyya
Sabriyyah
Sabruna
Sabrya
Sabryn
Sabryna *(0.01)*
Sabrynna
Sabrynnah
Saby
Sabyhaelle
Sacadi
Sacaiah
Sacaria

| | | | | | | |
|---|---|---|---|---|---|---|
| Sacario | Sadie Marie | Saffiyah | Sahale | Sahnii-A'lyn | Sailee | Sajani |
| Sacha (0.01) | Sadie Susanna | Saffrehn | Sahali | Sahnija | Sailer | Sajara |
| Sachary | Sadieann | Saffrin | Sahalie (0.01) | Sahniya | Sailia | Sajayah |
| Sachelin | Sadielynn | Saffron (0.01) | Saham | Sahnya | Sailor (0.01) | Sajda |
| Sachelle | Sadies | Safha | Sahana (0.02) | Sahnyia | Saily | Sajdah |
| Sachelly | Sadiey | Safhia | Sahanah | Sahori | Sailyn | Saje |
| Sachenca | Sadija | Safi | Sahanna | Sahra (0.01) | Saima (0.01) | Sajeah |
| Sachi (0.01) | Sadini | Safia (0.01) | Sahar (0.01) | Sahrah | Saimanasaa | Sajeda |
| Sachleen | Sadiqah | Safiah | Sahara (0.07) | Sahrena | Saimara | Sajeena |
| Sachneez | Sadira | Safian | Saharah | Sahrinity | Saina | Sajel |
| Sachsen | Sadita | Safiatou | Saharai | Sahrobbi | Sainabou | Saji |
| Sacia | Sadíya | Safiena | Sahara-Rhy | Sahvana | Saindy | Sajiah |
| Sacora | Sadiyah | Safina | Saharra | Sahvanna | Saini | Sajida |
| Sacoreya | Sadiyyah | Safire | Saharrah | Sahvannah | Sainny | Sajidah |
| Sacoria | Sadlynn | Safiya (0.03) | Sahary | Sahvyn | Saintya | Sajine |
| Sacoriah | Sadona | Safiyah | Sahasra (0.01) | Sahyra | Saiona | Sajiyah |
| Sacorra | Sadonah | Safiyan | Sahaudiya | Sai | Saionna | Sajiyy'a |
| Sacorria | Sadoria | Safiye | Sahayla | Saí | Saiphunya | Sajol |
| Sacoya | Sadra | Safiyo | Sahayra | Sai Shriya | Saipriya | Sakaá |
| Sacred | Sadri | Safiyyah (0.01) | Sahdahya | Sai'ann | Saira (0.03) | Sakah Amina |
| Sadá | Sadriah | Safkth Reese | Saheira | Saia | Sairah | Sakahtay |
| Sada (0.01) | Sadrina | Safoorahbibi | Sahej | Saiah | Sairahbenedicte | Sakai |
| Sadaa | Saduri | Safrina | Saheli | Saiarrah | Sairdee | Sakaia |
| Sadae | Sadusha | Safwa | Sahena | Saiauna | Sairish | Sakaií |
| Sadaé | Sady | Safya | Saher | Saibra | Sairy | Sakaiya |
| Sadaf | Sadya | Sagal | Saherah | Saida (0.01) | Sairyn | Sakara |
| Sadaí | Sadyah | Sagan | Sahhara | Saidah | Saisha | Sakari (0.01) |
| Sadarah | Sadye (0.01) | Sagara | Sahia | Saidah Sultanah | Saishree | Sakariya |
| Sadaya | Sae | Sagarika | Sahib | Saide | Saishreya | Sakauri |
| Saddler | Saeda | Sage (0.33) | Sahiba | Saide Allaynah | Saishruthi | Sakayhia |
| Saddy | Saedi | Sage Ilona | Sahibnoor | Saidee | Saisri | Sakeena |
| Sadé | Saee | Marie | Sahidatu | Saidelle | Saisruthi | Sakeenah |
| Sade (0.07) | Saeeda | Sagebelize | Sahij | Saidey | Saitar | Sakenah |
| Sade'a | Saejun | Sagel | Sahijdeep | Saidi | Saityiana | Sakeydra |
| Sade'jah | Saelah | Sagellyn | Sahilly | Saidie | Saiva-Simran | Sakhara |
| Sadearia | Saelina | Sagely | Sahira (0.01) | Saidlynn | Saivibha | Sakhi |
| Sadeclaire | Saelyr | Sage-Marie | Sahirah | Saidsha | Saivionne | Sakhia |
| Sadee (0.01) | Saeryn | Sagemarie | Sahithi | Saidy | Saiya | Saki |
| Sadeel | Saesha | Sagette | Sahiti | Saiesha | Saiyaina | Saki'yah |
| Sadeen | Safa (0.02) | Sagine | Sahiyyah | Saige (0.12) | Saiyaka | Sakia |
| Saden | Safaa (0.01) | Sagnolah | Sahki | Saigen | Saiyan | Sakianna-Ntanis |
| Sadey | Safana | Sagrario | Sahkiya | Saihaj | Saiyannah | Sakihikan |
| Sadeya | Safara | Sah Mya | Sahkoka | Saihithi | Saiyara | Sakile |
| Sadhana | Safari | Sah'drina | Sahleen | Saihrah | Saiyarah | Sakin |
| Sadhna | Safe | Sah'nui | Sahlera | Saihriah | Saiyette | Sakina |
| Sadi | Safeeah | Sah'ria | Sahmara | Saij | Saiyge | Sakina-Fatima |
| Sadia (0.01) | Safeeya | Sah'ryia | Sahmia | Saija | Saiyonna | Sakinah |
| Sadiana | Saffa | Sahaara | Sahmira | Saijal | Saj'a | Sakira |
| Sadianne | Saffad | Sahadya | Sahmiya | Saije | Saja (0.01) | Sakiya |
| Sadie (0.93) | Saffet | Sahai | Sahmiyah | Saijel | Sajaah | Sakiyah |
| Sadie Cynthia | Saffi | Sahaina | Sahmya | Saila | Sajadah | Sakkara |
| Sadie Li | Saffia | Sahaira | Sahnaii | Sailajalakshmi | Sajaila | Sakkarra |
| Sadie Mae | Saffire | Sahajpreet | Sahni | Saile | Sajana | Sakora |

| | | | | | | |
|---|---|---|---|---|---|---|
| Sakorah | Saleste | Saloni | Samanhtha | Samarrí | Sameyah | Sammiah |
| Sakoya | Salestial | Saloua | Samani | Samarria | Samhia | Sammie |
| Sakoyia | Saley | Salsabeel | Samanie | Samarrie | Samhita | Sammi-Jo |
| Sakshi | Saleya | Salsabila | Samanta (0.02) | Samartha | Samhitha | Sammita |
| Sakthi | Saleyia | Saltina | Samantha (6.01) | Samary | Sami (0.01) | Sammy |
| Sakthi Priya | Salia | Salvadora | Samantha | Samarya | Sami'ya | Sammya |
| Sakura (0.02) | Saliah | Salvanna | Angela | Samaryi'a | Samia (0.05) | Sammy-Jo |
| Sakurah | Salianez | Salwa (0.01) | Samantha | Samatha (0.01) | Samia-Ann | Samoira |
| Sakweya | Saliauna | Saly | Delorse | Samatha Joe | Samiah (0.02) | Samone (0.01) |
| Sakyiea | Salicia | Salyce | Samantha | Samathea | Samiaya | Samoni |
| Sakyla | Saliena | Salymatou | Grace | Samathie | Samie | Samonie |
| Sakyra | Saliha | Salyna | Samantha J | Samatra | Samientha | Samonika |
| Sakyrah | Salihah | Salysabil | Samantha Jo | Samaura | Samiera-Imeen | Samonna |
| Sakyré | Salim'ah | Salyse | Samantha- | Samauree | Samiha (0.01) | Samony |
| Sal'leah | Salima | Sam (0.01) | Ashley David | Samauri | Samihah | Samonyia |
| Sala | Salimah | Sam'iah | Samanthafayte | Samauria | Samiia | Samora |
| Salaam | Salima- | Sama (0.01) | Samantha-Jane | Samauriaye | Samiira | Samorae |
| Salah | Johannese | Sama'ara | Samantha-Jo | Samavia | Samiiya | Samorah |
| Salali | Salimata | Samaa | Samantha-Lynn | Samaya (0.04) | Samiiyah | Samoria |
| Salam | Salimatou | Samaah | Samanthan | Samayah | Samijah | Samorica |
| Salamah | Salina (0.02) | Samaara | Samantha-Rae | Samayia | Samika | Samorra |
| Salamasina | Saline-Sherly | Samaarie | Samantha-Rhe | Samayra | Samiksha | Samorrah |
| Salamata | Salisea | Samadhi | Samantha-Rose | Samayya | Samina (0.01) | Samorriah |
| Salamatu | Saliya | Samadi | Samantha-Sue | Sambria | Saminah | Samoryia |
| Salameva | Saliyah | Samady | Samanthi | Sameah | Samindhi | Samoya |
| Salana | Saliyha | Samaele | Samanthia | Samechi | Samir | Samra |
| Salanah | Salla | Samaelle | Samantta | Sameck | Samira (0.10) | Samrah |
| Salandra | Sallee | Samah (0.01) | Samanvi | Samee'ah | Samirah (0.02) | Samrawit |
| Salara | Sallee Mae | Samaha | Samanvitha | Sameeha | Samirea | Samreen-Joy |
| Salaria | Sallesmith | Samahela | Samar (0.01) | Sameen | Samiria | Samreet |
| Salay'na-Sincere | Salley | Samai | Samara (0.30) | Sameena | Samirr | Samria |
| Salaya | Salli | Samaiah | Samara Joy | Sameenah | Samirrah | Samriddhi |
| Salayandrina | Sallie (0.01) | Samair | Samara-Grace | Sameer | Samisha | Samruthi |
| Salayeh | Salliha | Samaira (0.01) | Samarah (0.04) | Sameera (0.01) | Samit | Samsam |
| Salayha | Sallissia | Samairaa | Samaraha | Sameerah | Samitha | Samsara |
| Salaysia | Sally (0.09) | Samairah | Samarahjade | Sameeya | Samiya (0.05) | Samshrita |
| Salea | Sally Ann | Samaire | Samaree | Sameia | Samiyah (0.05) | Samuel (0.01) |
| Saleah | Sallyann | Samairé | Samareya | Sameira | Samiyah Nasir | Samuela |
| Saleasa | Sallye | Samairia | Samarha | Sameitra | Samiyra | Samuela Sky |
| Saleeah | Sallymata | Samaiya (0.01) | Samari (0.01) | Samej | Samiyyah | Samuella |
| Saleema | Salma (0.14) | Samaiyah | Samaria (0.08) | Samelly | Samla | Samuelle (0.01) |
| Saleemah | Salmaa | Samaj | Samaria Ty'sha | Samelyn | Samma | Samvida |
| Saleen (0.01) | Salmah | Samaj'nia | Samariae | Samenah | Sammantha | Samy |
| Saleena (0.01) | Salmahi | Samajae | Samariah | Samentha | (0.01) | Samya (0.04) |
| Saleh | Salma-Lou | Sama- | Samariaye | Samer | Sammara | Samyah (0.01) |
| Saleisha | Saloma | Mardochee | Samarie | Samera (0.01) | Sammarah | Samyerah |
| Salem (0.01) | Salomae | Samamtha | Samaris | Samerawite | Sammari | Samyi |
| Salema | Salomé | Saman | Samariya | Sameria | Sammarra | Samyia |
| Salena (0.02) | Salome (0.03) | Samana | Samariyah | Sameriah | Sammatha | Samyiah |
| Salencia | Salon | Samanatha | Samarra | Samerra | Sam-Meiya | Samy-Jade |
| Salene | Salondria | Samandeep | Samarrae | Samerria | Sammeria | Samyjah |
| Salenia | Salone | Samandha | Samarrah | Sameshley | Sammi (0.01) | Samyjoe |
| Salenna | Salonee | Samandi | Samarri | Sameya | Sammia | Samyla |

Samylle
Samyra *(0.01)*
Samyrah
Samyrrah
Samyukta
Samyuktha
Samyya
San
San Antasya
San Cho
San'brya
San'cori
San'drea
San'garyia
San'keya
San'quenella
San'terika
San'yah
Sana *(0.04)*
Sana'a
Sanaá
Sanaa *(0.13)*
Sanaah
Sanaaiya
Sanaaya
Sanaayah
Sanaaz
Sanadia
Sanae
Sanaé
Sanaee
Sanaeja
Sanah
Sanaí
Sanai *(0.07)*
Sanaia *(0.01)*
Sanaiah
Sanaiha
Sanaii
Sanaiia
Sanairious
Sanaisa
Sanaiya *(0.01)*
Sanaiyah
Sanaja
Sanam
Sananna
Sanari
Sanarria
Sanatani
Sanau
Sanay
Sanaya *(0.01)*

Sanayah
Sanayjah
Sanayyia
Sancia
Sanda
Sandasia
Sandee
Sandeep
Sandeline
Sander
Sanderella
Sanderia
Sanders
Sandhana
Sandhya
Sandi
Sandia
Sandianar
Sandiarely
Sandie
Sandieliz
Sandifer
Sandivel
Sandra *(0.27)*
Sandra Lynn
Sandran
Sandrasia
Sandrea *(0.01)*
Sandreah
Sandria
Sandrianna
Sandrica
Sandrina
Sandrine *(0.07)*
Sandrine
  Hermala
Sandriona
Sandryne
Sandwin
Sandy *(0.08)*
Sandylynn
Sandy-Rose
Sanea
Saneé
Sanee'a
Saneea
Saneeyah
Sanei
Saneia
Saneiah
Saneice
Saneisha
Sanem

Sanesha
Sanette
Sangeeta
Sangeetha
Sango-Aza
Sanhi
Sani
Saní
Sani'a
Sania *(0.04)*
Saniaa
Saniah *(0.02)*
Saniaya
Saniayah
Sanieah
Sanieya
Sanihya
Sanii
Saniiya
Sanija
Sanijah
Sanijua
Sanika
Sanika/Sania
Saniriya
Sanirra
Sanita
Sanitra
Sanittha
Saniya *(0.16)*
Saniyah *(0.13)*
Saniyah
  Christine
Saniyah-Marie
Saniye
Saniyha
Saniyia
Saniyya
Saniyyah *(0.01)*
Saniyyih
Sanja
Sanjali
Sanjam
Sanjana *(0.04)*
Sanjaya
Sanjh
Sanji
Sanjida
Sanjimah
Sanjita
Sanjot
Sanjuana
Sanjuanita

Sanjula
Sanjvi
Sanjyot
Sankeria
Sankruti
Sanmeet
Sanna *(0.01)*
Sannah
Sannaya
Sanne
Sannearry
Sannera
Sanni
Sannidhi
Sannie
Sanniyah
Sannyah
Sannyiah
Sanoa
Sanoe
Sanon
Sanora
Sanoria
Sanquese
Sansana
Sansita
Sanskriti
Santa
Santa Olivia
Santaisa
Santaizia
Santaja
Santajah
Santalena
Santana *(0.04)*
Santana-Danae
Santanah
Santanita
Santanna *(0.01)*
Santaria
Santasha
Santasia
Santau
Santavia
Santaysha
Santaz
Santazia
Santee
Santhija
Santhiya
Santi
Santia
Santianna

Santiea
Santina *(0.01)*
Santonia
Santoria
Santoria-Marie
Santorya
Santrell
Santrice
Santyana
Sanura
Sanuye
Sanvanah
Sanvi
Sanvika
Sanviti
Sanya *(0.02)*
Sanyaa
Sanyadeep
Sanyah
Sanyaha
Sanyam
Sanye
Sanyé
Sanyha
Sanyia
Sanyiah
Sanyla
Sanyrah
Sanyukta
Sanyya
Saoirse *(0.01)*
Saomie
Saorla
Saphaija
Saphara
Saphera
Saphia
Saphiah
Saphina
Saphira
Saphire *(0.01)*
Saphrin
Saphryn
Saphyre
Saphyrra
Sapir
Sapna
Sapphaire-Pasha
Sapphira
Sapphire *(0.02)*
Sapphyre
Saprena
Saprina

Sapthavy
Saqa
Saqqara
Saquarriah
Saquin
Saquoia
Saquoin
Saquora
Sara *(2.10)*
Sara Ann
Sara Beatriz
Sara Beth
Sara Cassidy
Sara Dawn
Sara Hana
Sara Hiba
Sara Jade
Sara Jessi
Sara Kate
Sara Kay
Sara Larielle
Sara Maude
Sara Mckenzie
Sara Nicole
Sara Paige
Sara Rose
Sara Sofia
Sara'ah
Sara-Allison
Sara-Anais
Sara-Ann
Saraann
Sara-Anna
Sara-Anne
Sara-Ashlee
Sara-Aude
Sarabel
Sarabella
Sarabelle
Sara-Beth
Sarabeth *(0.01)*
Sara-Claude
Sarae *(0.01)*
Saraee
Sara-Eliza
Sara-Emanuelle
Sara-Eve *(0.01)*
Sarafay
Sarafaye
Sarafena
Sarafina
Sara-Frederique
Sara-Grace

Saragrace
Sarah *(5.76)*
Sarah Alicia
Sarah Allison
Sarah Amy
Sarah Ann
Sarah Anne
Sarah Beth
Sarah Celina
Sarah Elizabeth
Sarah Ellen
Sarah Eve
Sarah Grac
Sarah Grace
Sarah Jade
Sarah Jane
Sarah Jeanne
Sarah Jo
Sarah Kathryn
Sarah Kathy
Sarah Kim
Sarah Lee
Sarah Lloy
Sarah Luna
Sarah Malka
Sarah Mia
Sarah Morgan
Sarah Noel
Sarah Rose
Sarah Ruth
Sarah Sophia
Sarahah
Sarah-Amali
Sarah-Amelie
Sarah-Andreea
Sarah-Ann
Sarahann
Sarah-Anna
Sarah-Anne
Sarahanne
Sarahashley
Sarah-Aya
Sarahbeth
Sarah-Chevalier
Sarah-Elisabeth
Sarah-Elizabeth
Sarah-Elizabeth
  Koshie
Sarah-Ellen
Sarah-Elyse
Sarah-Emily
Sarah-
  Emmanuelle

Sarah-Eve (0.02)
Sarah-Grace
Sarahgrace
Sarahi (0.05)
Sarah-Isa
Sarah-Isabelle
Sarahit
Sarah-Jade (0.01)
Sarah-Jane
Sarahjane
Sarah-Jean
Sarah-Jeanne (0.01)
Sarah-Jen
Sarah-Jessica
Sarahjune
Sarah-Katharine
Sarahkeisha
Sarah-Kent
Sarah-Kim (0.01)
Sarah-Laurence
Sarah-Lea
Sarah-Louisa
Sarah-Luce
Sarah-Lucia
Sarah-Lynn
Sarahlynn
Sarah-Mae
Sarah-Maeva
Sarah-Mai
Sarah-Maude (0.05)
Sarah-May
Sarah-Maylody
Sarah-Meggan
Sarah-Michelle
Sarah-Myriam
Sarah-Nadedje
Sarah-Naomi
Sarah-Nicole
Sarahnicole
Sarah-Rose
Sarah-Wilt
Sarahy (0.01)
Saraí
Sarai (0.15)
Sarai Francine
Sarai'lee
Saraia
Saraiah

Saraih
Saraily
Saraina
Sara-Ines
Sarainiah
Sarais
Saraiya
Sara-Jade
Sarajade
Sarajah
Sara-James
Sara-Jane
Sarajane
Sara-Jeanne (0.01)
Sarajee
Sarajo
Sara-Kim (0.01)
Sara-Klaude
Sarala
Saralane
Sara-Laurence
Sara-Lee
Saralee
Saraleen
Saraleidy
Saralie
Sarallyn
Sara-Lou
Saralucia
Saraly
Sara-Lyn
Saralyn
Sara-Lynn
Saralynn
Saramae
Sara-Marie
Sara-Maud
Sara-Maude (0.02)
Saramaude
Saramelia
Saramiah
Sara-Michèle
Sara-Michelle
Saramonni
Saran
Sarana
Saranae
Saranayé
Sarandon
Sarangdeep
Sarann

Saranna
Saranne
Sarantha
Saranya
Sara-Nycole
Saraphiah
Saraphina
Saraphina-Gaoxue
Sararae
Sara-Renee
Sararose
Sarashea
Saraswati
Sarathena
Saratou
Sarauswathy
Saravady
Sara-Virginia
Saray (0.02)
Saraya (0.02)
Sarayah (0.01)
Saraye
Sarayi
Sarayia
Sarayna
Sarayne
Sarayu (0.01)
Sara-Zakia
Sardasia
Sare
Sarea
Sareah
Sareana
Saredo
Saree
Sareece
Sareen
Sareena
Sareenah
Sareh
Sarei
Sarekah
Sarela
Sareli
Sarely
Sarelys
Sarena (0.01)
Sarenitee
Sarenity (0.01)
Sarenna
Sareth
Saretta

Sareya
Sareyna
Sargam
Sargun
Sarh
Sarha
Sarhaii
Sarhya
Sarí
Sari (0.02)
Saria (0.01)
Sariaa
Sariah (0.09)
Sariaha
Sariahna
Sariana
Saribel
Saribeth
Sarie
Sarik
Sarika
Sarikarmen
Sarila
Sarin
Sarina (0.06)
Sarina Therese
Sarine
Sarine-Annie
Sarinity
Sarionah
Sarira
Sarisa
Sarisati
Sarisha
Sarissa
Sarita (0.01)
Sarita-Dora
Sariya (0.01)
Sariyah (0.02)
Sariyan
Sariyha
Sariyyah
Sarleen
Sarlentia
Saroja
Soukeyna Dior
Saron
Sarra (0.01)
Sarrah (0.01)
Sarray
Sarrena
Sarrieann
Sarrinah

Sarriyah
Sarryah
Sarryn
Sartu
Sarunya
Saruul
Sarvani
Sarvat
Sary
Sa-Ryah
Saryah (0.01)
Saryana
Sarycarmen
Saryela
Saryha
Sa-Ryiah
Saryiah
Saryn
Saryna
Sarynity
Sarynna
Sasa
Sasamat
Sascha (0.01)
Sasha (0.33)
Sasha'rhea
Sashaco
Sashaly
Sashana
Sashani
Sashelle
Sashenka
Sashenkalee
Sashi
Sashia
Sashirekha
Sashka
Sashley
Sasilya
Sasjarae
Saskha
Saskia (0.02)
Saskya
Sasmitha
Sassa
Sassha
Sassie
Sasuena
Sata'jha
Satang
Satanh
Satara
Satarah

Satasha
Sataya
Sataylor
Satene
Saterra
Sathusa
Sathvika
Sathya
Sati
Satia
Satin
Satina
Satine
Satinka
Satish
Sativa (0.01)
Satkirat
Satonia
Satori
Satorian
Satsie
Satsuki
Sattah
Sattyrn
Satu
Saturn
Saturna
Saturnina
Satvika
Satvir
Satwat
Satya (0.01)
Satynne
Sauceray
Sauda
Saudah
Saudia
Sauiyah
Saul
Saule-Alexia
Sauliha
Saumara
Saumarra
Saumya (0.01)
Saumyaa
Saundra
Saunesy
Sauni
Saunja
Saunte
Saur
Saure
Saurina

Sausha
Savada
Savae
Savaeh
Savaelyn
Savaha
Savahanna
Savahna
Savaiah
Savaira
Savana (0.10)
Savanaa
Savanah (0.15)
Savanah-N
Savanan
Savanarose
Savanh
Savanha
Savania
Savanna (0.50)
Savannah (3.09)
Savannah Bro
Savannah Jasminel
Savannah Sue
Savannaha
Savannah-Belle
Savannah-Joyce
Savannah-Lee
Savannahlee
Savannah-Rae
Savannah-Rose
Savanna-Lynn
Savannamarie
Savannha
Savanny
Savany
Savara
Savaria
Savarra
Savasia
Savaughn
Savauna
Savayah
Saveah
Saveea
Saveen
Saveena
Savega
Saveia
Saveka
Saverah
Saveria

| | | | | | | |
|---|---|---|---|---|---|---|
| Saveya | Saydi | Sceonela | Scylar | Seantrease | Sedeal | Seirah |
| Savhana | Saydie (0.01) | Schade | Sdyney | Seara | Sedelle | Seirena |
| Savhanna | Saydra | Schala | Se | Searah | Sedia | Seirra (0.01) |
| Savhannah | Saye | Schalen | Se Laniyah | Searat | Sedina | Seirsha |
| Savhaunna | Sayeeda | Schaley | Se'aunna | Searenitie | Sedney | Seiya |
| Savher | Sayeh | Schammie | Se'driunna | Searia | Sedona (0.02) | Seja |
| Savia | Sayeli | Schaylee | Se'kayla | Searra (0.01) | Sedra | Sejal |
| Saviah | Sayen | Schealthia | Se'maj | Searrah | Sedrianna | Sejaljeet |
| Saviana | Sayer | Scheherazade | Se'majia | Searri | Sedricia | Sejalpreet |
| Savilla | Sayge (0.01) | Schehl | Se'mari | Seasa | Seedra | Sejeira |
| Savin | Sayje | Schelby | Se'miyah | Seasha | Seefen | Sejin |
| Savina | Sayla (0.01) | Schelene | Se'mya | Season | Seela | Sejla |
| Savita | Saylah | Schemea | Se'niya | Seath | Seema | Sejmora |
| Saviya | Saylar | Schenley | Se'nya | Seaton | Seena | Sekai |
| Savoi | Saylee | Scherea | Se'quoia | Seatra | Seeranie | Sekaiyah |
| Savoiya | Sayleese | Scherlyn | Se'raya | Seayany | Seerat | Sekayi Asha |
| Savon | Sayleigh | Schidny | Se'riyah | Seayarah | Seerit | Sekeenia |
| Savona | Saylem | Schmiley | Se'ryah | Seayra | Seevahn | Sekoi |
| Savonda | Sayler | Schnaida | Se'yonee | Seba | Seeya | Sekoija |
| Savonna | Sayli-Lynn | Schoene | Sea | Sebaga | Sefanet | Sekret |
| Savonnah | Saylor (0.04) | Schuler | Seaaira | Sebanna | Seferina | Sela (0.02) |
| Savonya | Saynab | Schuylar | Seaana | Sebastian | Sefia | Selaam |
| Savory | Saynareia | Schuyler (0.01) | Seaanna | Sebastiana | Sefika | Selafina |
| Savoy | Sayniel | Schuyler-Mae | Seadra | Sebastien | Sehaam | Selah (0.08) |
| Savreen | Sayona | Schvonie | Seaenna | Sebella | Sehairase | Selahnna |
| Savriel | Sayone | Schwanica | Seaera | Sebenet | Sehaj | Selaina |
| Savskia | Sayonsai | Schylar | Seainna | Sebria | Seham | Selana |
| Savvanah | Sayra (0.01) | Schyler | Seaira (0.01) | Sebrin | Sehana | Selassia |
| Savvy | Sayrah | Schylia | Seairra | Sebrina | Sehar | Selbie |
| Sawa | Sayran | Sciana | Seajay | Sebryn | Seharra | Selby |
| Sawab | Sayress | Sckarlett | Sealey | Sebstian | Seher | Selden |
| Sawarani | Sayrha | Scky | Sealiah | Secelia | Sehila | Sele'ya |
| Sawarine | Saysha | Scot Lynn | Sealy | Secenia | Sehja | Seleana |
| Sawatha | Saysia | Scotia (0.01) | Sean | Secia | Sehraaj | Selebriti |
| Sawda | Sayth | Scotland | Sean' Tae | Secili | Sehrish | Selecia |
| Sawdiatou | Saytun | Scotlyn (0.01) | Sean'ia | Secilia | Seianna | Seleen |
| Sawera | Sayumi | Scotlynn | Sean'tarrah | Secily | Seiara | Seleena |
| Sawood | Sayuri (0.01) | Scott | Seana | Secinda | Seidi | Seleidy |
| Sawsan | Sayury | Scotta'sia | Seanae | Secora | Seidiah | Seleighna |
| Sawyer (0.05) | Sayvia | Scottaisa | Seanctanae | Secoya | Seidl | Seleima |
| Sawyier | Sazel | Scottdraicus | Seandeniece | Secquoia | Seidy | Selen |
| Saxon | Sazleen | Scotti | Seanie | Secret (0.01) | Seige | Selena (0.47) |
| Saxten | Sazna | Scotti Jo | Seaniece | Secrett | Seigna | Selena Isabelle |
| Saya (0.01) | Sazz | Scottia | Seanise | Seda | Seija | Fontillas |
| Sayahat | Scarlet (0.09) | Scottie | Seanita | Seda'ja | Seijah | Selena Maria |
| Sayaka | Scarleth | Scottlyn | Seankiria | Sedaeh | Seikaya | Selena Sav |
| Sayana | Scarlett (0.30) | Scott-Lynn | Seanna (0.04) | Sedaeha | Seila | Selenah |
| Saybah | Scarlett-Arianne | Scottlynn | Seanna Marie | Sedajah | Seina | Selene (0.03) |
| Sayda | Scarlette (0.01) | Scotyana | Seannan | Sedanur | Seinata | Selenee |
| Sayde (0.01) | Scarllett | Scout (0.02) | Seannecia | Sedara | Seinna | Selenia |
| Saydee (0.01) | Scarlott | Scuhlyer | Seannetta | Sedaria | Seionni | Selenne |
| Saydes | Scayla | Scushe | Seantavia | Seddiqa | Seiquoya | Selest |
| Saydey | Scemorrea | Scyan | Seantia | Seddrina | Seira | Seleste |

| | | | | | | |
|---|---|---|---|---|---|---|
| Selestine | Semhar | Sennae | Serae | Serenitii | Serwah | Seychelle |
| Seleta | Semia | Sennen | Serafima | Serenity (0.86) | Seryna | Seydi |
| Selexa | Semiah | Sennett | Serafina (0.01) | Serenity Ricarda | Serynadee | Seydie |
| Seli | Semiha | Sennia | Serah | Serenity | Sesalie | Seyedeh |
| Selia | Semija | Senoa | Serahline | Serenity-Dai | Sesen | Seyenna |
| Seliah | Semilli | Senoah | Serai | Serenity-Hanifah | Sesilia | Seyerra |
| Selica | Semilola | Senoja | Seraiah | Serenityi | Sesily | Seyi |
| Seliena | Semini | Senon | Serajum | Serenity-Lynn | Seskia | Seyla |
| Selika | Semira (0.01) | Senora | Seralyn | Serenity-Sue | Sessy | Seylin |
| Selima | Semiya | Senovia | Serana | Seren-Mohamad | Setara | Seymone |
| Selin (0.01) | Semiyah | Senria | Seranity | Serenna | Setareh | Seynab |
| Selina (0.12) | Semma | Senseitvity | Seraph | Serennie | Setasia | Seynabou |
| Selina-Cung | Semmoli | Sentaya | Seraphia | Seretta | Setdrea | Seyona |
| Selinam | Semoay' | Senterion | Seraphim | Sereya Rayne | Setel | Seyonna |
| Selinda | Semoney | Sentha | Seraphin | Sereyla | Seth | Seyoung |
| Seline | Semra | Sentiya | Seraphina (0.01) | Sereyna | Sethumi | Seyria |
| Selinette | Semya | Sentra | Seraphine | Sergyana | Setina | Seysha |
| Selise | Sena | Sentrezury | Serat | Seri | Setoria | Sezja |
| Seliz | Senada | Sentri | Serax | Seriah | Setta | Sfeva |
| Sellena | Senae | Sentrila | Seray | Seriaha | Settaira | Sgarneth |
| Sellers | Senah | Senya | Seraya | Seriann | Seva | Sh Dymond |
| Sellome | Senai | Senyah | Serayah | Serianna | Seva Lakeysha | Sh'anora |
| Selma (0.04) | Senaida | Senyce | Serayna | Serigne | Sevan | Sh'kira |
| Selphie | Senaii | Seo | Serdenity | Serilda | Sevana | Sh'kiya |
| Selsabela | Senait | Seo Hyun | Serea | Serima | Sevanna (0.01) | Sh'marah |
| Selsabila | Senay | Seol | Sereen | Serin | Seveah | Sh'mareona |
| Selsobeil | Senaya | Seon | Sereena | Serina (0.03) | Seven | Sh'myah |
| Seluvaia | Sendy | Seona | Sereene | Serine (0.01) | Sevena Lyn | Sh'niya |
| Selver | Senea | Seongeun | Sereiba | Serinitee | Sevene | Sh'niyah |
| Selvia | Seneca (0.02) | Seonghoo | Seren (0.01) | Seriniti | Seveness | Sh'nya |
| Selvira | Senecca | Seoni | Serena (0.39) | Serinity (0.03) | Severeign | Sh'ray |
| Selwa | Senecia | Sephina | Serena Brianna | Serinne | Severiana | Sha |
| Selyane | Senee | Sephira | Serena Emily | Seris | Severina | Sha Diamond |
| Selyn | Seneka | Sephora | Serena Mika | Serissa | Severine | Sha Kieyah |
| Selyna (0.01) | Senekah | Sephora-Agathe | Serenade | Serita-Soledad | Severn | Sha Leon |
| Sema'j | Seneria | Sephorah | Serenady | Seriya | Seveyah | Shá Niya |
| Sema'ja | Seney | Sephra | Serenah | Seriyah | Sevginaz | Sha On |
| Semadgirlah | Seneye-Anajah | Sepriana | Serenanfa | Sermarjay | Sevika | Shá Yanna |
| Semahj | Sengmany | September (0.01) | Serena-Nour | Sermonnie | Sevim | Sha'alyah |
| Semaj (0.02) | Sengton | Seqiyah | Serena-Penelope | Sernea | Sevin | Sha'bria |
| Semaj' | Senia | Seqouia | Serenaty | Sernity | Sevita | Sha'cala |
| Semaj'a | Seniah | Sequioa | Serendipity | Seromome | Seviyah | Sha'cara |
| Semaja | Senijah | Sequira | Serene (0.02) | Serra (0.01) | Sevoí | Sha'coreya |
| Semajah | Senika-Jean | Sequoia (0.03) | Serenea | Serrah | Sevonei | Sha'dae |
| Semajia | Senille | Sequolia | Sereneti | Serrai | Sevrina | Sha'daesha |
| Semajiah | Seniqwa | Sequora | Serenety | Serrayia | Sevyn | Sha'dajiah |
| Semara | Senita | Sequoria | Serenidi | Serrena | Sewa | Sha'darriy |
| Semariah | Seniya | Sequoya | Serenidy (0.01) | Serrenah | Seya | Sha'day |
| Semaury | Seniyah | Sequoyah (0.01) | Serenitee | Serria | Seyairra | Sha'deja |
| Semay | Seniye | Ser'rya | Serenitey | Serrica | Seyan | Sha'diamon |
| Semeeka | Senja | Sera (0.02) | Sereniti (0.01) | Serrina | Seyanh | Sha'diamond |
| Semera | Senjaka | Sera Janelle | Serenitie | Sersnity | Seyanna | Sha'dimon |
| Semerah | Senna | | | | Seyara | Sha'diya |

| | | | | | | |
|---|---|---|---|---|---|---|
| Sha'dymond | Sha'montae | Sha'vaughn | Shadarrah | Shaeana | Shahanaj | Shailee |
| Sha'jiyah | Sha'mya *(0.01)* | Sha'vonna | Shadavia | Shae-Ann | Cedrikah | Shailey |
| Sha'kara | Sha'myah | Sha'zariah | Shadavya | Shaeann | Shahara | Shaili |
| Sha'karee | Sha'myia | Sha'zariyah | Shadawn | Shaedyn | Shaharazon | Shailia |
| Sha'karia | Sha'myiah | Sha'zion | Shaday | Shaela *(0.02)* | Shahayla | Shailie |
| Sha'kayla | Sha'myra | Shaakhini | Shadaya | Shaelagh | Shahaylee | Shailin |
| Sha'kaylen | Sha'myron | Shaam | Shadayjah | Shaelah | Shahaylie | Shailyn *(0.01)* |
| Sha'kedra | Sha'nari | Shaan | Shadaysia | Shaelan | Shahd *(0.01)* | Shailynn *(0.01)* |
| Sha'kei | Sha'nay | Shaana | Shadazia | Shaelaun | Shahdi | Shailynne |
| Sha'keia | Sha'naya | Sha-Annah | Shaddai | Shae-Lee | Shahed | Shailyon |
| Sha'keira | Sha'naydria | Shaanvi | Shadday | Shaelee *(0.01)* | Shaheema | Shaima |
| Sha'kela | Sha'naysha | Shaari | Shadden | Shaeleigh | Shaheera | Shaimaa |
| Sha'kenya | Sha'neece | Shabana | Shaddia | Shaelen | Shaherra | Shaimara |
| Sha'kera | Sha'nia | Shabina | Shade | Shaelene | Shahid | Shaimari |
| Sha'kevia | Sha'niah | Shabnam | Shadé | Shaeli | Shahidah | Shaimeer |
| Sha'keya | Sha'nickqueya | Shabrayla | Shadea | Shaelie | Shahiddah | Shaimma |
| Sha'khia | Sha'nieyah | Shabrea | Shadeana | Shaeliegh | Shahina | Shaimonica |
| Sha'kia | Sha'nijah | Shabree | Shadee | Shaelin *(0.01)* | Shahira | Shaina *(0.05)* |
| Sha'kiah | Sha'niya *(0.02)* | Shabrei | Shadeea | Shaelind | Shahjanesi | Shaina Marie |
| Sha'kiara | Sha'niyah *(0.01)* | Shabreia | Shadei | Shaeliyah | Shahmeen | Shainah |
| Sha'kimeha | Sha'niyha | Shabrela | Shadeidra | Shaellyn | Shahna | Shaina-Ivana |
| Sha'kira | Sha'niyla | Shabrell | Shadelyn | Shaely | Shahnaz | Shainay |
| Sha'kiyah | Sha'nizah | Shabreona | Shaden | Shae-Lyn | Shahrayaar | Shaindy *(0.03)* |
| Sha'kya | Sha'nya *(0.01)* | Shabreonna | Shaderia | Shaelyn *(0.06)* | Shahyd | Shaine |
| Sha'kyah | Sha'nyah | Shabria | Shadette | Shaelyne | Shahydaa | Shainna |
| Sha'kyah | Sha'nyia | Shabriel | Shadey | Shae-Lynn | Shahydah | Shainyce |
| Unique | Sha'nyiah | Shabriya | Shadi | Shaelynn *(0.02)* | Shahyra | Shai-Quann |
| Sha'kyla | Sha'nyla | Shabryah | Shadia | Shae-Lynne | Shahzia | Shaire |
| Sha'kylah | Sha'nyra | Shacara | Shadiah | Shaelynne | Shai *(0.01)* | Shaireen |
| Sha'kyra | Sha'nyria | Shacari | Shadiamon | Shae-Marie | Shai Anne | Shairenne |
| Sha'lamar | Sha'quanna | Shacarra | Sha-Diamond | Shaemia | Shai'ana | Shairy |
| Sha'laura | Sha'quayveona | Shachristian | Shadiamond | Shaemya | Shai'ann | Shaitimal |
| Sha'leah | Sha'railyn | Shacia | Shadie | Shaen | Shai'auna | Shaivi |
| Sha'lice | Sha'rell | Shacora | Shadin | Shaena | Shai'mari | Shaivona |
| Sha'lon | Sha'riya | Shacoreyia | Shadire | Shaenah | Shai'yannah | Shaiyan |
| Sha'lyria | Sha'riyah | Shacori | Shadiya | Shaenin | Shaia | Shaiyana |
| Sha'maiya | Sha'riyah JC | Shacoria | Shadiyah | Shaeniya | Shaiane | Shaiyenne |
| Sha'maiyah | Sha'sariah | Shacoriah | Shad-Len | Shaer | Shaiann | Shajaih |
| Sha'mari | Sha'tara | Shacorra | Shadnaz | Shaeronna | Shaianna | Shajanthini |
| Sha'maria | Sha'tavia | Shacoya | Shadow | Shaetiel | Shai-Anne | Shajia |
| Sha'mariah | Sha'tayah | Shacura | Shadowlynn | Shaeyna | Shaianne | Shakada |
| Sha'marionna | Sha'tayvia | Shada | Shadrea | Shafa | Shai-Asia | Shakai |
| Sha'mauri | Sha'teciya | Shadaé | Shadrei | Shafarrah | Shaiasia | Shakaila |
| Sha'maya | Sha'teja | Shadae *(0.01)* | Shady C | Shafirah | Shaica | Shakair |
| Sha'mee | Sha'tejah | Shadai | Shadya | Shafiria | Shaida | Shakaira |
| Sha'meiah | Sha'tiah | Shadaia | Shadyamond | Shagarika | Shaidalys | Shakairah |
| Sha'mera | Sha'tiyah | Shadaiah | Sha-Dymon | Shagnika | Shaiday | Shakala |
| Sha'mere | Sha'tonna | Shadaijah | Shaé | Shagun | Shaidya | Shakalya |
| Sha'miaya | Sha'toria | Shadainea | Shae *(0.06)* | Shahad | Shaiel | Sha-Kara |
| Sha'mira | Sha'torria | Shadaja | Shae Leigh | Shahada | Shaienne | Shakara *(0.01)* |
| Sha'miracl | Sha'toya | Shadan | Shae'lonn | Shahadah | Shaila *(0.02)* | Shakara Charde |
| Sha'miya | Sha'tyia | Shadana | Shae'meir | Shahaley | Shailah | Shakari |
| Sha'monie | Sha'tyiah | Shadany | Shae'ron | Shahalie | Shailayha | Shakaria |

| | | | | | | |
|---|---|---|---|---|---|---|
| Shakaya | Shakira (0.09) | Shalayia | Shally | Shamaria (0.01) | Shamikia | Shan'naise |
| Shakayla (0.02) | Shakirah | Shalayla | Shallyn | Shamariah | Shamil | Shan'toryonna |
| Shakaylia | Shakirat | Shalayna | Shaloh | Shamariana | Shamin Akhter | Shan'tyona |
| Shakaylin | Shakire | Shalaysha | Shalohm | Shamaria-Renée | Shamine | Shana (0.05) |
| Shakearra | Shakiro | Shalaysia | Shalom (0.01) | Shamariauna | Shamira (0.01) | Shana Rain |
| Shakeathia | Shakirra | Shalazí | Shalome | Shamarie | Shamiracle | Shanacea |
| Shaked | Shakiya (0.01) | Shale | Shalon | Shamarié | Shamirah | Shanae (0.01) |
| Shakedra | Shakiyah | Shalea | Shalonda | Shamariea | Shamiri | Shanae Larae |
| Shakeela | Shakiyna | Shaleah (0.01) | Shalondra | Shamarija | Shamiria | Ro |
| Shakeema | Shaknea | Shaleah Shanay | Shalonn | Shamariyona | Shamiriah | Shanae'la |
| Shakeena | Shaknowa | Shalece | Shalontae | Shamarra | Shamirica | Naima |
| Shakeerah | Shakoorah | Shalecia | Shalonté | Shamarreana | Shamiriya | Shanaea |
| Shakeila | Shakora | Shaleda | Shalva | Shamarri | Shamirra | Shanaesia |
| Sha-Keira | Shakori | Shalee (0.01) | Shaly | Shamarria | Shamirria | Shanah |
| Shakeira (0.01) | Shakoria | Shaleedra | Shalya | Shamary | Shamiryah | Shanai (0.01) |
| Shakeiria | Shakota | Shaleen | Shalyah | Shamaryah | Shamiso | Shanaia |
| Shakela | Shakoyiah | Shaleena | Shalyla | Shamasha | Shamiya (0.03) | Shanaiah |
| Shakell | Shakria | Shalei | Shalyn (0.02) | Shamaunie | Shamiyah (0.01) | Shanaica |
| Shakena | Shakrya | Shaleigh (0.01) | Shalyna | Shamaya (0.02) | Shamiyjné | Shanaii |
| Shakenaah | Shakthi | Shaleisha | Shalynda | Shamayah | Shamiyla | Shanail |
| Shakendall | Shakundala | Shaleita | Shalyne | Shamaye | Shammah | Shana-India |
| Shakendra | Shakura | Shalena | Shalynn (0.01) | Shambhavi | Shammara | Shanaira |
| Shakequila | Shakya | Shalene | Shalynne | Shambreal | Shammi | Shanaiya |
| Shakera | Shakyah | Shalese | Shalyric | Shamea | Shammy | Shanajah |
| Shakeria (0.01) | Shakyia | Shalev | Shalysia | Shamecka | Shamoeri | Shanaldriah |
| Shakeriana | Shakyla | Shaley (0.01) | Shalyz | Shameelah | Shamonae | Shanale |
| Shakerriun | Shakylah | Shaleya | Shalyza | Shameema | Shamonta | Shanalee |
| Shakesmara | Shakyna | Shaleyah | Sham | Shameerah | Shamora | Shanali |
| Shakevia | Shakynah | Shaleyska | Sham'ya | Shameia | Shamoria | Shanaliea |
| Shakevionna | Shakyra (0.01) | Shali | Shama | Shameka | Shamorrah | Shanalise |
| Shakeya | Shakyrah | Shalia (0.01) | Shamaa | Shamekia | Shamour | Shanalla |
| Shakeyia | Shakyria | Shaliah | Shamacus | Shamel | Shamoya | Shanan |
| Shakeyicia | Shakyriah | Shaliaya | Shamada | Shamela | Shams | Shanann-Stenia |
| Shakeyra | Shakyrra | Shalice | Shamaiah | Shamelodia | Shamsa | Shanara |
| Shakhia | Shakyya | Shalicia | Shamaila | Shameona | Shamsah | Shanarah |
| Shakhiaya | Shala (0.01) | Shalie | Shamaim | Shamer | Shamsey | Shanari |
| Shakhirah | Sha-Lacia | Shalila | Shamaine | Shamera | Shamsie | Shanaria |
| Shakherah | Shalae | Shalima | Shamaira | Shamere | Shamso | Shanariah |
| Shakia (0.01) | Shalah | Shalimar | Shamaire | Shameria | Shamurii | Shanarii |
| Shakiah (0.01) | Shalahjia | Shalin | Shamaiya | Shames | Shamya (0.04) | Shanariyh |
| Shakiara | Shalaia | Shalini (0.01) | Shamaiyah | Shameya | Shamyaa Jezzier | Shanarri |
| Shakiene | Shalaine | Shalisa | Sha-Mani | Shameyre | Shamyah | Shanasey |
| Shakiera | Shalaiyah | Shalise | Shamani | Shamia (0.01) | Shamyai | Shanashia |
| Shakierra | Shalalai | Shalisha | Shamaniq | Shamiah (0.01) | Shamyea | Shanasia |
| Shakiiya | Shalamar | Shalishah | Shamanthi | Shamiaha | Shamyia (0.01) | Shanatanadrea |
| Shakijah | Shalancya | Shalisheia | Shamar | Shamiarah | Shamyiah | Shanatavia |
| Shakila | Shalanda | Shalissa | Shamar'ya | Shamiaya | Shamyila | Shanavia |
| Shakilla | Shalante | Shaliya | Shamara (0.01) | Shamica | Shamyla | Shanay |
| Shakilra | Shalat-Megan | Shaliyah (0.01) | Shamarah | Shamieka | Shamyra (0.01) | Shanay Denise |
| Shakina | Shalay | Shaliyaha | Shamare | Shamier | Shamyra'h | Shanaya (0.01) |
| Shakinah | Shalaya (0.01) | Shalla | Shamaree | Shamiera | Shamyrica | Shanayah |
| Shakinayah | Shalayaa | Shalleah | Shamareon | Shamiere | Shan | Shanaye |
| Shakir | Shalayah | Shallen | Shamari (0.02) | Shamika | Shan'daria | Shanayi |

| | | | | | | |
|---|---|---|---|---|---|---|
| Shanayja | Shanesa | Shaniyah K | Shantalaya | Shanya-Michelle | Shaqutia | Sharenda |
| Shanayla | Shanese | Shaniyha | Shantale | Shany-Ann | Shaqwana | Sharen-Daniela |
| Shanaz | Shanesha | Shaniyla | Shantara | Shanyce | Shar'dajai | Shareny |
| Shanazah | Shanessa | Shaniyra | Shantasa | Shanye | Shar'dasha | Sharese |
| Shanazz | Shanette | Shaniyyah | Shantasia | Shanyea | Shar'kandi | Sharesse |
| Shanda | Shaney | Shanjida | Shantaveiy | Shanyese | Shar'niya | Sharey |
| Shandalin | Shaneya | Shankeria | Shantavia | Shanyha | Shara | Shareyla |
| Shandalyn | Shaneydi | Shankevia | Shantavya | Sha-Nyia | Sharachina | Sharfa |
| Shandell | Shanez | Shan-Kyria | Shantay | Shanyia (0.01) | Sharada | Sharhonda |
| Shanden | Shangri-La | Shanley | Shantaya | Shanyiah | Sharadha | Shari (0.01) |
| Shanderia | Shanhia | Shanley Nicole | Shante (0.01) | Shanyjah | Sharae | Sharia |
| Shandette | Shani (0.02) | Shanlie | Shante Shania | Shanyka | Sharaé | Shariah (0.01) |
| Shandi (0.01) | Shani'ja | Shanlynn | Shantea | Shany-Kim | Sharah | Sharianel |
| Shandiin | Shani'ya | Shanna (0.04) | Shantee | Shanyla | Sharai | Sharianne |
| Shandin | Shania (0.34) | Shanna Faye | Shantel (0.02) | Shanylah | Sharaliz | Sharibel |
| Shandra | Shania Zykia | Shannae | Shantell (0.01) | Shanyna | Sharan | Sharica |
| Shandre'a | Shania-Ann | Shannah | Shantelle (0.01) | Shanyra | Sharandeep | Sharice |
| Shandrea | Shaniah (0.03) | Shannai-Catherine | Shanteria | Shanyria | Sharanetta | Sharice Zynaiá |
| Shandreaka | Shanialynn | Shannan (0.01) | Shanterica | Shanyssa | Sharanjit-Kaur | Sharick |
| Shandreya | Shanica | Shannara | Shanterika | Shanyyia | Sharann | Sharicka |
| Shanduray | Shanice (0.04) | Shannays | Shanterra | Shanzay | Sharanya | Sharie |
| Shandy | Shanico | Shanneal | Shanterrika | Shanzeh | Sharar | Sharieli |
| Shané | Shanie (0.01) | Shanneil | Shanteryl | Shanzia | Sharay | Sharielle |
| Shane (0.01) | Shaniece (0.01) | Shannel | Shantesha | Shanziya | Sharaya | Sharielys |
| Shane'nise | Shaniecee | Shannell | Shanthi | Shao Yang | Sharayah | Shariff |
| Shanea | Shaniel | Shannelle | Shanti (0.02) | Shaojia | Sharaylynn | Sharifo |
| Shaneal | Shanielle | Shannen (0.01) | Shantia | Shaolin | Sharayu | Sharik |
| Shanece | Shaniese | Shannia | Shantiah | Sha-Oná | Shardae (0.01) | Sharika |
| Shanee | Shanieyah | Shannie | Shantiana | Shapierria | Shardaesha | Sharilyn |
| Shaneek | Shanih | Shannise | Shantie | Shapna | Shardaius | Sharim |
| Shaneekqua | Shanija | Shanniyah | Shantierra | Shapreea | Sharday | Sharin |
| Shaneese | Shanijah | Shannon (0.40) | Shantin | Shapreia | Shardayiah | Sharina |
| Shaneil | Shanik | Shannty | Shantiona | Shaprice | Shardayzah | Sharini |
| Shaneira | Shanika (0.01) | Shanny (0.01) | Shantisé | Shaqaysia | Shardé | Sharis |
| Shaneisha | Shanikwa | Shannyn (0.01) | Shantisha | Shaqiangeliz | Shardei | Sharisa |
| Shaneka | Shanila | Shanoah | Shantonai | Shaqkayla | Shardenay | Sharise |
| Shanel (0.01) | Shanilah | Shanon | Shantora | Shaquala | Shardina | Sharisma |
| Shanela | Shanilene | Shanonia | Shantorá | Shaquan | Shardly | Shariss |
| Shanele | Shanilia | Shanoria | Shantoria | Shaquana | Shardynae | Sharissa |
| Shaneli | Shanina | Shanpreal | Shantorria | Shaquanna | Sharea | Sharisse |
| Shanell (0.01) | Shanine | Shanquella | Shantoya | Shaquashia | Shareatha | Sharita |
| Shanella | Shaniqua | Shanquisha | Shantrel | Shaquasia | Sharecé | Shariya |
| Shanelle (0.03) | Shanique | Shansa | Shantrell | Shaquavia | Sharee | Shariyah (0.01) |
| Shanelle Angelina | Shanira | Shanse | Shantreonna | Shaquayla | Shareece | Shariyha |
| Shanellea | Shanise | Shanta | Shantrese | Shaquena | Shareema | Shariyia |
| Shanen | Shanisha | Shanta Ja'cole | Shantrice | Shaquetta | Shareen | Shariza |
| Shanequa | Shanissa | Shantae | Shantriece | Shaquia | Shareena | Sharkeshia |
| Shanerah | Shanita | Shantaesia | Shanty | Shaquila | Shareese | Sharkita |
| Shaneria | Shanivia | Shantah | Shantyana | Shaquira | Shareida | Sharla (0.01) |
| Shaneriah | Shaniyá | Shantaisa | Shany (0.01) | Shaquiria | Sharell (0.01) | Sharlea |
| Shanerrah | Shaniya (0.18) | Shantaja | Shany'ia | Shaquita | Sharelle | Sharleah |
| Shanery | Shaniyah (0.06) | Shantal | Shanya (0.04) | Shaquoia | Sharely | Sharlee |
| | Shaniyah Jaliah | | Shanyah (0.01) | | Sharelyn | Sharleen |

| | | | | | | |
|---|---|---|---|---|---|---|
| Sharlena | Sharon (0.18) | Shatayah | Shaunesty | Shavonne | Shawnta | Shayela |
| Sharlene (0.01) | Sharon Emi | Shatayla | Shauni | Shavonta | Shawntae | Shayelah |
| Sharlett | Sharona | Shataysia | Shaunice | Shavonte | Shawntasia | Shayeleigh |
| Sharley | Sharonda | Shatera | Shaunie | Shavvonda | Shawntavia | Shayelyn |
| Sharlie | Sharoon | Shateria | Shauniyah | Shavy | Shawntavius | Shayelynne |
| Sharlie-Anne | Sthephanie | Shaterica | Shaunna | Shaw | Shawntay | Shayenne |
| Sharlimar | Sharquia | Shaterra | Shaunnell | Shaw'neice | Shawnte | Shayiana |
| Sharlin | Sharrell | Shaterria | Shaunnessy | Shawanda | Shawnté | Shayiona |
| Sharlinda | Sharrene | Shatha | Shaunquila | Shawanna | Shawnteanna | Shayka |
| Sharlise | Sharria | Shatiana | Shaunta | Shawaunna | Shawntee | Shaykendra |
| Sharlisse | Sharriah | Shatiara | Shauntae | Shawdae | Shawntel | Shayla (0.37) |
| Sharliyah | Sharrion | Shatirrica | Shauntasia | Shawina | Shawntele | Shayla Marie |
| Sharlize | Sharron | Shativa | Shauntay | Shawlynn | Shawn-Thomas | Shaylah (0.01) |
| Sharllese | Sharryce | Shatiyaa | Shauntaya | Shawn (0.01) | Shawnti | Shaylan |
| Sharlon | Sharukesei | Shatona | Shaunte | Shawn Iya | Shawntí | Shaylan Chloe |
| Sharlotta | Sharunda | Shatora | Shaunté | Shawn'ae | Shawntia | Shaylana |
| Sharlotte | Sharvani | Shatoria | Shauntel | Shawn'tay | Shawntiana | Shaylanise |
| Sharly | Sharvaree | Shatorria | Shaunteria | Shawn'terykah | Shawntiel | Shayla-Rae |
| Sharlyn | Sharvari | Shatorya | Shaunti | Shawna (0.08) | Shawntiere | Shayle |
| Sharlyne | Sharvi | Shatoya | Shauntia | Shawnae | Shawntya | Shaylea |
| Sharlyne Mathilda | Sharviona | Shatoya Samira | Shauntoya | Shawnajah | Shawntyona | Shayleah |
| Shar-Lynn | Sharvon | Shatta | Shauntrell | Shawnala | Shawny | Shaylean |
| Sharlynn | Shary | Shattle | Shauntrey | Shawnaly | Shawnyae | Shay-Lee |
| Sharlys | Shary'a | Shatya | Shauntya | Shawnalynn | Shawnyel | Shayleé |
| Sharmain | Sharya | Shatyler | Shauntyana | Shawnay | Shawqi | Shaylee (0.10) |
| Sharmaine | Sharyah | Shatyra | Shauntyl | Shawnda | Shawsha | Shayleece |
| Sharman | Sharyce | Shau'naria | Shauny | Shawndale | Shawtaya | Shayleemar |
| Sharmane | Sharyhia | Shauda | Shaunyce | Shawndell | Shawunkeia | Shayleen |
| Sharmara | Sharyn | Shaudae | Shaurice | Shawndrayu | Shay (0.04) | Shayleese |
| Sharmariah | Sharyse | Shaudia | Shautaye | Shawnece | Shay Lynn | Shaylei |
| Sharmaya | Sharyssa | Shaughnessy | Shavadea | Shawnee | Shay'ann | Shayleigh (0.01) |
| Sharmayne | Shasety | Shaulin | Shavae | Shawnell | Shay'la | Shayleigha |
| Sharmeia | Shasha | Shaum | Shavaha | Shawnelle | Shay'nija | Shaylen (0.01) |
| Sharmella | Shashawna | Shaun (0.01) | Shavani | Shawn-Epiphany | Shaya (0.01) | Shaylena |
| Sharmelle | Shashaylah | Shaun'tia | Shavanna | Shawnessy | Shayah | Shaylene (0.01) |
| Sharmia | Shashi | Shauna (0.05) | Shavara | Shawnesy | Shayahn | Shaylese |
| Sharmila | Shashonna | Shaunae | Shavari | Shawnetta | Shayamae | Shayley |
| Sharmiline | Shaskia | Shaunah | Shavaria | Shawney | Shayan | Shayli (0.01) |
| Sharmitha | Shasmeen | Shaunassey | Shavarieon | Shawnia | Shayana | Shaylia |
| Sharna | Shasmita | Shaunassi | Shavell | Shawnice | Shayann (0.01) | Shaylie (0.01) |
| Sharnae | Shasta (0.01) | Shaunay | Shaveriya | Shawnie | Shayanna | Shaylieze |
| Sharna-Kay | Shastina | Shauncey | Shavez | Shawniece | Shayanne (0.01) | Shaylin (0.03) |
| Sharndeep | Shat'errica | Shaunciajah | Shavia | Shawniel | Shayanti | Shayline |
| Sharnease | Shataha | Shaunda | Shavida | Shawnika | Shayauna | Shaylinn |
| Sharnee | Shatanna | Shaundejah | Shavila | Shawnique | Shay-D | Shaylinnette |
| Sharnell | Shatara | Shaundel | Shavis | Shawnise | Shayd | Shaylisha |
| Sharnice | Shataria | Shaundi | Shaviyah | Shawniyah | Shayda | Shaylla |
| Sharnise | Shatarian | Shaundria | Shavon (0.01) | Shawniza | Shaydan | Shayln |
| Sharntae | Shatarra | Shaunee | Shavonah | Shawnmynek | Shaydc | Shaylon |
| Sharole-Lynn | Shatavia | Shaunée | Shavonda | Shawnna (0.01) | Shayden (0.01) | Shaylona |
| Sharolyn | Shatawn | Shaunel | Shavondria | Shawnnessy | Shaye (0.03) | Shayluan |
| Sharome | Shatawni | Shaunese | Shavonie | Shawnquana | Shaye Lynn | Shaylyn (0.03) |
| | Shataya | Shaunessy | Shavonna | | | Shay-Lynn |

| | | | | | |
|---|---|---|---|---|---|
| Shaylynn *(0.02)* | She'mya | Sheelah | Shelbee *(0.01)* | Shelly-Ann | Sheneariah | Sherdrina |
| Shaylynne | She'nice | Sheena *(0.02)* | Shelbey | Shellyce | Sheneil | Sherea |
| Shayma | She'niya | Sheenangel | Shelbi *(0.02)* | Shellycea | Shenell | Sherece |
| Shaymaa | She'nyah | Sheerly | Shelbie *(0.04)* | Shellyn | Shenelle | Sheree |
| Shaymar | She'ree | Sheery | Shelbi-Rae | Shelna | Shenese | Shereece |
| Shaymarie | She'shauna | Shefaa | Shelby *(1.44)* | Shelniya | Sheneva | Shereen |
| Shaymel | She'shawn | Shefaali | Shelby Anne | Shelona | Sheney | Shereena |
| Shaymi | She'von | Shefali | Shelby Dawn | Shelonda | Sheng | Shereene |
| Shayn | Shea *(0.10)* | Shehrazad | Shelby Grace | Shelse | Shengkhi | Sherell |
| Shayna *(0.13)* | Shea'on | Shehreen | Shelby Liane | Shelsea *(0.01)* | Shengyeng | Sherelle |
| Shaynah | Shea-Anna | Shehreena | Shelby Rae | Shelsey | Shenia | Sheren |
| Shayndel | Sheaanna | Sheida | Shelbyanna | Shelsi | Sheniah | Sherene |
| Shayne *(0.02)* | Sheaden | Sheidelly | Shelby-Lee | Shelsie | Sheniajah | Sherette |
| Shayneiya | Sheadiamond | Sheikh | Shelby-Lynn | Shelsy | Shenica | Sheri *(0.01)* |
| Shaynenya | Sheah | Sheila *(0.08)* | Shelbylynn | Shelsye | Shenika | Sheriah |
| Shaynia | Shealan | Sheilana | Shelcy | Shelton | Shenille | Sherice |
| Shayniah | Shealand | Sheilat | Sheldae | Shelvie | Shenise | Shericka |
| Shaynna | Shealaney | Sheiley | Sheldene | Shelya | Sheniya | Sheridan *(0.05)* |
| Shayomi | Shealee *(0.01)* | Sheili | Sheldon | Shelyn | Sheniyha | Sheriden |
| Shayon | Shea-Lei | Sheilian | Sheldyne | Shelyse | Shenna | Sheridtton |
| Shayona | Shealeigh | Sheilina | Shelea | Shelzza | Shennelly | Sheridyn |
| Shayonia | Shealen | Sheilnonnda | Sheleah | Shemaiah | Shenneya | Sherie |
| Shayonn | Shealene | Sheily | Sheleea | Shemanda | Shennielle | Sherifa |
| Shayonna *(0.01)* | Shealey | Sheilymar | Shelekeia | Shemani | Shennoa | Sherika |
| Shayqavia | Shealie | Sheilyn | Shelena | Shemara | Shenny | Sherikah |
| Shayquanna | Shealiegh | Sheilynn | Shelia | Shemari | Shenoah | Sherilee |
| Shayra | Shealin | Sheima | Shelia-Ann | Shemarí | Shentae | Sherill |
| Shayraliz | Shealinn | Sheina | Shelijah | Shemariah | Sheny | Sherily |
| Shayreighana | Shealisa | Sheinayah | Shelilah | Shemarshia | Shenya | Sherilyn |
| Shayria | Shealla | Sheiny | Shelina | Shemaya | Shenyah | Sherilynn |
| Shayuana | Shealor | Sheira | Shelis | Shemayah | Shenyiah | Sherin |
| Shayunna | Shealy | Shekeela | Shelissa | Shemeiah | Shenylah | Sherina |
| Shayveona | Shealyn *(0.01)* | Shekeira | Sheliya | Shemeka | Shenyvia | Sherine |
| Shaywanda | Shea-Lynn | Shekena | Shella | Shemera | Sheona | Sherionna |
| Shaza | Shealynn *(0.01)* | Shekera | Shellary | Shemetria | Sheonna | Sherise |
| Shazaiyh | Shealynne | Shekhinah | Shellbi | Shemia | Sheppard | Sheriss |
| Shazanie | Shean | Shekina | Shellby | Shemiah | Sher'maine | Sherissa |
| Shazanna | Sheana | Shekinah *(0.02)* | Shelleah | Shemira | Sher'ron | Sherisse |
| Shazaria | Sheanne | Shekylah | Shellee | Shemiya | Sheradan | Sherita |
| Shazia | Sheanny-Grace | Shekyra | Shelleiney | Shemiyah | Sheradin | Sheriyah |
| Shazimya | Sheanrica | Shela | Shellene | Shemoya | Sheradon | Sheriza |
| Shazorrhia | Sheashauna | Shelagh | Shellenid | Shemya | Sherae | Sherlanda |
| Shazz'mere | Sheba | Shelah | Shelley *(0.01)* | Shemyah | Sherah | Sherlayne |
| Shckeria | Sheccid | Shelaja | Shelley An | Shemyria | Sheraia | Sherleen |
| Shdeja | Shechinah | Shelal | Shelli | Shemyriah | Sheraina- | Sherlen |
| She'daleon | Sheckina | Shelan | Shellie *(0.01)* | Shena | Sharon | Sherley |
| She'dymond | Shecyd | Shelandria | Shellina | Shenai | Sherany | Sherleyn |
| She'kara | Shedda | Shelara | Shelliyah | Shenaksa | Sheraton | Sherleyna |
| She'kinah | Shedelanne | Shelaya | Shellsea | Shenandoa | Sheray | Sherlhyn |
| She'kira | Shedkayla | Shelayne | Shellsey | Shenaugh | Sheraya | Sherli |
| She'layah | Shedra | Shelba | Shellsy | Shendli | Sheraz | Sherlian |
| She'mia | Shedre-Ann | Shelbe | Shelly *(0.04)* | Shendra | Sherdian | Sherlie |
| She'miya | Sheekyna | Shelbea | Shellyan | Shenea | Sherdora | Sherlime |

| | | | | | | |
|---|---|---|---|---|---|---|
| Sherlin *(0.01)* | Sherylyn | Shi'terra | Shikeria | Shiniya | Shirnel | Shnia |
| Sherline | Sheryn | Shi'tyanna | Shikerra | Shiniyah | Shironaka | Shniyah |
| Sherlly | Shesh | Shi'wandra | Shikerria | Shinningstar | Shiryna | Shnya |
| Sherly *(0.01)* | Sheterriah | Shia *(0.01)* | Shikha | Shinoda | Shisa | Shnyah |
| Sherly'n | Sheuna | Shiah | Shikhara | Shinta | Shish | Shoba |
| Sherlyin | Sheva | Shialyia | Shikia | Shinya | Shitager | Shoghla |
| Sherlyn *(0.10)* | Shevaun | Shiaman | Shikiar | Shin-Yi | Shi-Teuna | Shoiney |
| Sherlyna | Shevell | Ardiana | Shikira | Shinyla | Shiva | Shoko |
| Sherlyne | Shevelle | Shian *(0.01)* | Shikoda | Shiomara | Shivali | Shokri |
| Sherlynn | Sheviann | Shiana *(0.01)* | Shikyna | Shion | Shivana | Shola |
| Shermaine | Shevon | Shiane *(0.01)* | Shila *(0.01)* | Shionna | Shivani *(0.02)* | Sholanda |
| Shermarria | Shey | Shiangela | Shilah | Shionnah | Shivanni | Sholay |
| Shermeen | Sheyann | Shiani | Shilat | Shioré | Shivanya | Shomoya |
| Shermiá | Sheyanne *(0.01)* | Shianjah | Shilayna | Shiori | Shivette | Shon'drea |
| Shermiah | Sheyda | Shiann *(0.02)* | Shilee | Shiphrah | Shivika | Shon'ti |
| Shermiyah | Sheydilimar | Shianna *(0.01)* | Shileene | Shiprah | Shivley | Shona |
| Shermorri | Sheyenna | Shi-Anne | Shilei | Shiquita | Shiwangini | Shonal |
| Shermya | Sheyenne *(0.02)* | Shianne *(0.03)* | Shileigh | Shira *(0.04)* | Shiwaye | Shonara |
| Shernaz | Sheyiana | Shianne-Nicole | Shiley | Shirah | Shiya | Shonasha |
| Sherniyah | Sheyla *(0.04)* | Shianti | Shilin | Shira-Lee | Shiyah | Shonda |
| Shernya | Sheylee | Shiara | Shiliya | Shiran | Shiyan | Shondale |
| Sherre | Sheyleen | Shiarah | Shiliyah | Shiranui | Shiyana | Shondeasha |
| Sherreen-Astride | Sheyli | Shiatious | Shillae | Shiraya | Shiyann | Shondell |
| Sherrell | Sheylin | Shiaunna | Shilo *(0.01)* | Shiraz | Shiyanna | Shondra |
| Sherri *(0.01)* | Sheylli | Shiayel | Shiloah | Shiré | Shiyannah | Shondrea |
| Sherri'yonna | Sheylo | Shiayzhia | Shiloh *(0.04)* | Shirea | Shiyanne | Shondreal |
| Sherria | Sheyly | Shidaé | Shilon | Shiree | Shiyawna | Shonedra |
| Sherriann | Shey-Lynn | Shidaisha | Shilpi | Shireen | Shiyla | Shoneisha |
| Sherrice | Sheylynn | Shiderlyn | Shilyah | Shirel | Shiyoncé | Shonesty |
| Sherridan | Sheyna | Shidrea | Shilyce | Shirelle | Shiyonna | Shonetta |
| Sherrill | Sheynna | Shiea | Shilyn | Shiren | Shiza | Shoney |
| Sherrilyn | Sheyris | Shiela | Shilyndrai | Shiri | Shizeria | Shonice |
| Sherrod | Sheza | Shiema | Shilyne | Shiria | Shjael | Shonise |
| Sherry *(0.03)* | Shi | Shiempoo | Shilynn | Shirian | Shjuan | Shonjaysha |
| Sherryah | Shi Air | Shienise | Shima | Shirika | Shkeela | Shonna |
| Sherryana | Shi Ann | Shienne | Shimear | Shirin | Shkeelah | Shonnda |
| Sherwana | Shi Yan | Shiera | Shimmer | Shirine | Shkira | Shonneah |
| Sherwin | Shi Yonna | Shierina | Shimrith | Shiriya | Shkurte | Shonnia |
| Sherwine | Shi'aire | Shierra | Shimya | Shirkiah | Shkyia | Shonquaishia |
| Shery | Shi'ann | Shifa | Shimyria | Shirkyla | Shkyra | Shontae |
| Sheryanna | Shi'asia | Shifaa | Shin Ang | Shirleen | Shlania | Shontaria |
| Sheryce | Shi'aujanea | Shiffa-Aabru | Shina | Shirleen Nayla | Shlayah | Shontasia |
| Sherydane | Shi'daviyah | Shifra *(0.02)* | Shinae | Shirlene | Shlema | Shontatvia |
| Sheryia | Shi'keria | Shifrah | Shinaia | Shirley *(0.09)* | Shmaryon | Shontavia |
| Sheryka | Shi'kira | Shigire | Shinaiyaa | Shirley Ann | Shmikka | Shontaya |
| Sheryl *(0.01)* | Shi'kyria | Shihla | Shinary | Shirley Shanel | Shmya | Shontaysha |
| Sheryl Lynn | Shi'leeya | Shijia | Shinaya | Shirleya | Shmyra | Shonte |
| Sherylane-Wapikon | Shi'maya | Shijuan | Shine | Shirley-Ann | Shmyriana | Shonteau |
| Sherylann | Shi'myra | Shikai | Shinequa | Shirlina | Shn'tyrria | Shontereya |
| Sheryln | Shi'nara | Shikara | Shinese | Shirlisa | Shnaya | Shontiana |
| Sheryl-Oriane | Shi'naziah | Shikelah | Shing | Shirly | Shnaya-Cheyenne | Shontiaza |
| | Shi'nya | Shikena | Shingisai | Shirlyn | Shnell | Shontice |
| | Shi'nyaha | Shikenya | Shinia | Shirmica | | Shontiona |

| | | | | | | |
|---|---|---|---|---|---|---|
| Shontya | Shrumika | Shundria | Shyaa | Shykarah | Shyne | Si'nya |
| Shontyla | Shruta | Shuni | Shyah | Shyke'asia | Shynea | Si'onna |
| Shoodlyne | Shruthi | Shunique | Shyaira | Shykedra | Shynecé | Si'renity |
| Shooter | Shruthika | Shunmei | Shyairah | Shykeria | Shynel | Si'rya |
| Shophia | Shruthilaya | Shunnie | Shyaire | Shykeyria | Shynemei | Si'yanda |
| Shorine | Shruti *(0.01)* | Shuntasia | Shyama | Shy-La | Shyneria | Sia *(0.01)* |
| Shortia | Shterna | Shunteon | Shyan *(0.01)* | Shyla *(0.09)* | Shyni | Siadilee |
| Shosannah | Shu | Shuntia | Shyana | Shylah *(0.02)* | Shynia | Siah |
| Shoshana *(0.04)* | Shu Yue | Shuntiauna | Shyanah | Shylah Ann | Shyniah | Siahna |
| Shoshanah | Shu'twauna | Shuntoia | Shyanda | Shylan | Shynicee | Siaira |
| Shoshanna | Shua | Shuntrese | Shyane *(0.01)* | Shylanah | Shyniece | Siaisia |
| Shoshannah | Shuachua | Shurease | Shyane | Shylar | Shynika | Siam |
| Shoshauna | Shubarry | Shurlynn | Elizabeth | Shyla-Ruth | Shynique | Siamara |
| Shoshona | Shubeeb | Shushan | Shy-Ann | Shylasia | Shynise | Siân |
| Shoua | Shubh | Shuteen | Shyann *(0.11)* | Shylayla | Shyniyah | Sian *(0.01)* |
| Shouana | Shubha | Shu-Tong | Shyann Marie | Shyleah | Shyona | Siána |
| Shouna | Shubhee | Shuttera | Shyanna *(0.03)* | Shy-Lee | Shyonesty | Siana *(0.01)* |
| Shoval | Shubhreet | Shviti | Shyannah | Shylee *(0.01)* | Shyonna | Sianah |
| Showdamini | Shuborno | Shwana | Shy-Anne | Shyleen | Shyra *(0.01)* | Siandra |
| Shqavianna | Shuchi | Shwati | Shyanne *(0.14)* | Shylei | Shyrah | Siane |
| Shraddha | Shuhadah | Shwaw | Shyanne-Teliyah | Shyleigh | Shyreanna | Siani *(0.02)* |
| Shravani | Shuixin | Shy | Shyanniah | Shyler | Shyree | Siann |
| Shravni | Shuka | Shy Anna | Shyara | Shyli | Shyreka | Sianna *(0.02)* |
| Shravya | Samhitha | Shy'aira | Shyarya | Shylia | Shyreni | Siannah |
| Shrayder | Shukara | Shy'anna | Shyasia | Shyliah | Shyrese | Siannali |
| Shrea | Shukri | Shy'anne | Shyayne | Shyliece | Shyri | Siannan |
| Shree | Shukria | Shy'asia | Shyaysha | Shyliena | Shyrie | Sianne |
| Shreeakshara | Shukriya | Shy'bre | Shycaria | Shylila | Shyrielle | Sianni *(0.01)* |
| Shreeja | Shukura | Shy'bria | Shyda | Shylin | Shyrique | Siany |
| Shreelekha | Shukya | Shy'daisa | Shydá | Shylina | Shysie | Siany-Adalis |
| Shreena | Shukyra | Shy'dasia | Shydaya | Shylisia | Shy-Tasia | Siao |
| Shreepriya | Shulamis | Shy'diamond | Shydé | Shylit-Rae | Shytasia | Siara *(0.03)* |
| Shreevarshinee | Shulammite | Shy'era | Shydea | Shyliyah | Shytera | Siarah |
| Shreeya *(0.01)* | Shulazia | Shy'erra | Shydoria | Shylla | Shyteria | Siarah-Lynne |
| Shrell | Shumaya | Shy'esha | Shye | Shyllia | Shyterria | Siara-Marie |
| Shreshta | Shumayaha | Shy'ira | Shye'ann | Shylo | Shyterrica | Siarha |
| Shresta | Shumayela | Shy'kendra | Shyeen | Shyloe | Shytheoria | Siarra *(0.01)* |
| Shrestha | Shu-Min | Shy'keria | Shyeena | Shyloh | Shytiera | Siasie |
| Shreya *(0.07)* | Shun Huang | Shy'kira | Shyeesha | Shylyn | Shyvah | Siava |
| Shri | Phenix | Shy'kirea | Shyela | Shylynn | Shyyanna | Siayla |
| Shria | Shun'derri | Shy'la | Shyen | Shymara | Shyza | Siba |
| Shriddha | Shun'keriael | Shy'lia | Shyenah | Shymaria | Shyzie | Sibdi |
| Shridula | Shun'teeuna | Shy'lyria | Shyene | Shymeir | Shyzlyn | Sibel |
| Shrihitha | Shunashi | Shy'mariah | Shyenne *(0.01)* | Shymera | Si'asia | Sibella |
| Shrika | Shunasti | Shy'modiest | Shyera | Shymerra | Si'aungii | Siberia |
| Shrimayi | Shunbaah | Shy'myra | Shyerize | Shymia | Si'era | Sibil |
| Shrinidhi | Shunbervia | Shy'nerria | Shyi'ajjah | Shymira | Si'haria | Sibna |
| Shrinithaa | Shundeen | Shy'nise | Shyia | Shymirra | Si'iaé | Siboney |
| Shristi | Shunderric | Shy'niya | Shyiah | Shymiya | Si'mear | Sibongile |
| Shritha | Shundiin | Shy'tearial | Shyian | Shymiyah | Si'miya | Sibreya |
| Shriya *(0.01)* | Shundini | Shy'tyra | Shyiann | Shymonte | Si'mya | Sibrina |
| Shriyadita | Shundra | Shy'won | Shyionna | Shynaejah | Si'myah | Sibyl |
| Shrock | Shundrea | Shya | Shyira | Shynaisha | Si'nivea | Sicile |

| | | | | | | |
|---|---|---|---|---|---|---|
| Sicilee | Sienna *(0.52)* | Silali | Simmone | Sincerely | Sir Toura | Sita |
| Sicilia | Siennah | Silan | Simmons | Sincerity | Sira | Sitana |
| Sicily *(0.02)* | Sienna-Lee | Silas | Simms | Sinclair | Siraha | Sitara |
| Sicilya | Siera *(0.03)* | Sile | Simoana | Sinclaire | Sirai | Sitayla |
| Siclali | Sierah | Silea | Simon | Sinda | Sirandou | Sitelle |
| Siclaly | Siera-Madison | Silena | Simona *(0.02)* | Sindhu | Sirat | Siteye |
| Sid'nieazah | Sierea | Silenay | Simond | Sindhuja | Siraye | Sitharah |
| Sida | Sierha | Silence | Simone *(0.19)* | Sindhura | Sirayiaa | Sitialy |
| Sidali | Sieriah | Silia | Simoneta | Sindi | Sireel | Sitina-Kethya |
| Sidda | Sierra *(1.35)* | Silja | Simonetta | Sindia | Sireen | Sitinha |
| Siddalee | Sierra Emily | Silje | Simoni | Sindy *(0.01)* | Siren | Sitka |
| Siddaly | Sierra Evalina | Silkia | Simonne | Sinéad | Sirena *(0.01)* | Sitladi |
| Siddeeqah | Sierra Vanessa | Sillouette | Simons | Sinead *(0.01)* | Sirene | Sitlali |
| Siddha | Sierrah *(0.01)* | Silmarie | Simoria | Sinella | Sirenitee | Sitlalli |
| Siddhi | Sierralynn | Silmayg | Simotu | Sinem | Sirenity *(0.01)* | Sitlaly |
| Siddissie | Sierra-Rose | Silmee | Simoyah | Sinemarie | Sirenne | Sittiy |
| Siddra | Sierria | Siloah | Simplicitie | Sing | Sirenytie | Sittre |
| Sideria | Sierrra | Siloam | Simra | Sinia | Siri *(0.03)* | Siu |
| Sidlali | Sierry | Silva | Simrah | Siniah | Siria | Siubhan |
| Sidley | Siesta | Silvana *(0.01)* | Simran *(0.05)* | Siniaya | Siriah | Siulianny |
| Sidne | Sieyoon | Silvanna | Simranjit | Sinijah | Siriana | Siv Yeing |
| Sidnea | Sifa | Silvee | Simranpreet | Siniya | Sirikanya | Siva |
| Sidnee *(0.02)* | Sifairey | Silver | Simrat | Siniyah | Sirinda | Sivan |
| Sidnei | Sifan | Silveria | Simreet | Sinna | Sirine *(0.01)* | Sivani |
| Sidney *(0.32)* | Sifene | Silvia *(0.05)* | Simret | Sinnai | Siriphone | Sivanna |
| Sidney Jill | Sigal | Silvia Carolina | Simri | Sinsation | Sirisone | Sivapriya |
| Sidney-Ann | Sigalia | Silvie | Simrin | Sinsear | Sirita | Sivayah |
| Sidneyanne | Sigalit | Silvita | Simrit *(0.01)* | Sinseve | Sirius | Sives |
| Sidney-Lynn | Signe | Sim'fanee | Simrith | Sinthia | Si-Riyah | Siwar |
| Sidni | Sigourney | Sima *(0.02)* | Simron | Sinthya | Siriyha | Six |
| Sidnie *(0.01)* | Sigrid *(0.01)* | Simaiya | Simrun | Sintia | Sirkiaia | Sixtilin |
| Sidny | Sigryn | Siman | Simryn | Sintoshia | Sirrayah | Siy'asia |
| Sidnye | Sihaam *(0.01)* | Simany | Simya *(0.01)* | Sinuo | Sirree | Siya *(0.01)* |
| Sidonia | Siham *(0.01)* | Simar | Simyah | Sinya | Sirrenadi | Siyade |
| Sidonie | Sihan | Simara | Simyia | Sinyada | Sirrenidy | Siyah |
| Sidor | Sihana | Simarah | Simyra | Sinyae | Sirrenna | Siyan |
| Sidra *(0.01)* | Sihani | Simarkae | Sin | Sinyaha | Sirriah | Siyanah |
| Sidrah | Sihaya | Simarpreet | Sina | Sinzeal | Sirui | Siyani |
| Sidra-Kazma | Sihera | Simaya | Sinaa | Siobain | Sisaleigh | Siyanna |
| Sidratul | Sihieda | Simcha | Sinaai | Siobhan *(0.03)* | Sisely | Siyé |
| Sie | Sihira | Simea | Sinae | Siobhann | Siselya | Siyha |
| Sieana | Sihyun | Simer | Sinahi | Siomara | Sisi | Siyona |
| Sieanna | Siigwin | Simeran | Sinai *(0.01)* | Siomariz | Sisley | Siyonni |
| Sieanne | Siiri | Simerdeep | Sinaii | Sion | Sisly | Sjhamar |
| Siearra | Sijya | Simes | Sinaja | Siona | Sisnie | Skai |
| Siearrah | Sikiu | Simi | Sinalei | Sione | Sissi | Skaila |
| Sieasia | Siklaly | Simia | Sinalyn | Sionie | Sissiley | Skaiste |
| Sieayla | Sikoi | Similoluwa | Sinam | Sionna | Sissy | Skarlet |
| Sieeda | Sikoia | Simina | Sinaya | Sionné | Sistina | Skarlett |
| Sielo | Sikora | Simiya | Sinayae | Sionnie | Sistine | Skarlette |
| Siena *(0.10)* | Sikwanowey | Simiyah | Sincer | Siouxanne | Sistine Marie | Skatlynn |
| Sienah | Sikya | Simmei | Sincera | Sipo | Rab | Skaya |
| Sienie | Sila | Simmona | Sincere *(0.02)* | Sipriana | Sisy | Skayla |

| | | | | | | |
|---|---|---|---|---|---|---|
| Skhye | Skyelin | Skyly | Sneha (0.02) | Sofia Andrea | Solah | Solida |
| Ski | Skyelinn | Skylyhn | Snehi | Sofia Geraldine | Solaira | Solidad |
| Ski'lan | Skyelur | Skylyn (0.01) | Sneirluze | Sofia Paola | Solana (0.03) | Solie |
| Ski'lynn | Skye-Lynn | Sky-Lynn | Sneyla | Sofia-Anabelle | Solane | Soliel |
| Ski'monee | Skyelynn | Skylynn (0.02) | Snezhana | Sofia- | Solange (0.01) | Solielle |
| Skie | Skye-Michelle | Skylynne | Snigdha | Gabriella | Solangel | Solimar (0.01) |
| Skielah | Skye-Terria | Skylyr | Snit | Sofiah | Solangie | Solina |
| Skieler | Skyi | Skylyte | Snizhana | Sofia-Isella | Solanje | Soline |
| Skielinn | Skyira | Skyonna | Snough | Sofia-Lucia | Solany | Solis |
| Ski-Jah | Skykerria | Skyra | Snow | Sofía-Maria | Solara | Solita |
| Skila | Skyklar | Skyri | Snowda | Sofiana | Solaris | Soliyana |
| Skilahr | Skyla (0.20) | Skysha | Snowden | Sofiane | Solarys | Soljhan |
| Skilar | Skyla Angel | Skyta'ja | Snowdon | Sofia-Nikoleta | Solas | Sollay |
| Skileigh | Skylaa | Skyy (0.02) | Snyiah | Sofianne | Solash | Sollina |
| Skiler (0.01) | Skylaar | Skyy Michelle | So'lae | Sofia-Rose | Solay | Solly |
| Skilynn | Skylah (0.02) | Skyye | So'mara | Sofie (0.05) | Solaya | Solmari |
| Skitasia | Skylair | Skyylar | So'myrah | Sofija | Solbjorg | Sol-Marie |
| Skiya | Skylan | Skyzia | So'ren | Sofina | Solciries | Solo |
| Skky | Skylar (1.13) | Sladjana | Soa | Sofina Marcelle | Solcristal | Soloma |
| Skkyla | Skylar Jo | Slana | Soad | Sofiya (0.01) | Solcy | Solomecia |
| Skler | Skylar-D'angel | Slanda | Soaiba | Sofoni | Sole | Solomiya |
| Sklyer | Skylar- | Slater | Soana | Sofya | Solé | Solomon |
| Sky (0.10) | Mackenzie | Slava | Sobat | Soha | Soleah | Solongo |
| Sky Lynn | Skylar-Rayne | Slavena | Sobeya | Sohailah | Soleane | Solonia |
| Sky'isha | Skylar-Rose | Sleka | Sobhita | Sohana | Solece | Soloures |
| Sky'la | Skylea | Sloan (0.02) | Sobia | Sohani | Soleda | Solstice |
| Sky'lar | Skyleah | Sloane (0.04) | Sobiyah | Sohar | Soledad (0.01) | Solstice-Rose |
| Sky'yanah | Sky-Lee | Sloka | Sobiye | Sohayla | Solee | Soluchi |
| Skya | Skylee (0.01) | Slwa | Sobreen | Sohayla-Zeba | Soleha | Soluchukwu |
| Skyace | Skylee-Marie | Slynn | Society | Sohee | Soleí | Solveig (0.01) |
| Skyah | Skyleen | Sma | Socorro | Soheiry | Solei (0.01) | Solveigh |
| Skyann | Skyleigh (0.01) | Smairey | Soda | Sohema | Soleia | Solveil |
| Skyanna | Skylen | Smantha | Sodaly | Soheyla | Soléil | Solveille |
| Skyanne | Skyler (0.36) | Smaraki | Sodarany | Sohni | Soleil (0.04) | Solyana |
| Skyasha | Skyler Isabel | Smaria | Sodi | Sohpia | Soleil Alize | Solycia |
| Skybrasia | Skyler-Jo | Smarlinne | Soegia | Soibon Elise | Soleil Anne | Solymar |
| Skybree | Skyler-Sage | Smeera | Soel | Soigne | Soleilnea | Soma |
| Skydancer | Skylette | Smera | Soelie | Sojood | Soleina | Somai |
| Skyé | Skyley | Smita | Soelys | Sokhna Aicha | Soleiyah | Somaia |
| Skye (0.29) | Skyli | Smith | Soemy | Sokhonthia | Solenda | Somaira |
| Skye Elizabeth | Skylia | Smood | Soeni | Sokhuntida | Solene | Somalia |
| Skye Lynn | Skyliana | Smreet | Soephia | Sokmavattey- | Solène | Somara (0.01) |
| Skye Marie | Skylie | Smret | Sofaea | Rachel | Solenne | Somarah |
| Skye Phung | Skylier | Smrithi | Sofeea | Sokona | Solerika | Somaria |
| Tien | Skylin (0.01) | Smriti | Sofeeya | Soksotoun | Soless | Somarra |
| Skyeann | Skylinia | Smrti | Sofeya | Sol (0.01) | Soley | Somaya |
| Skyeanna | Skylinn | Smruti | Soffia | Sol Liliana | Solgiana | Somayah |
| Skyel | Skylla | Smya | Soffy | Sol Yenith | Solia | Somayeh |
| Skyela | Skyllar | Smyah | Sofhia | Sola | Soliana | Sombole |
| Skyelar (0.01) | Skylne | Smyra | Sofi (0.01) | Solace | Soliane | Somea |
| Skye-Lashay | Skylor | Smyrna | Sofi'a | Soladileny | Solianys | Somer (0.01) |
| Skye-Leigh | Skylre | Snayah | Sofía | Solae | Solicia | Somerset |
| Skyeler | Skylur | Sneet | Sofia (2.67) | Solaf | Solicity | Somfechukwu |

| | | | | | | |
|---|---|---|---|---|---|---|
| Somia | Sonita | Sophia Eve | Soraida | Soukaina | Spoorthi | Srivaishnavi |
| Somiya | Soniya | Sophia Faith | Soraida | Souky-Leila | Spree | Srivani |
| Somma | Soniyah | Sophia Isabella | Biririana | Soula | Sprihaa | Srivarsha |
| Sommah Ale | Sonja *(0.06)* | Llanos | Soralie | Soulé | Spring *(0.01)* | Srivarshika |
| Sommar | Sonja-Jocelyn | Sophia Isabelle | Soralla | Soulia | Spring-Anne | Srivatasa |
| Sommer *(0.04)* | Sonja-Sade | Sophia | Sorany | Soulriah | Spruha | Sriya *(0.01)* |
| Sommer-Anne | Sonje | Lizavetta | Soraya *(0.05)* | Soumaya | Spshita | Srujana |
| Sommur | Sonjia | Sophia Lysette | Sorayah | Soumaya- | Spurthi | Sruthi |
| Somore | Sonna | Sophia Maria | Sorayda | Assitou | Spyrit | Sruthy |
| Sompous | Sonnet | Sophia Nichole | Sorcha | Soumeya | Sraddha | Sruti |
| Somya | Sonni | Sophia- | Sorell | Soumia | Sragvi | Sryah |
| Somyiai | Sonni Rae | Alejandra | Sorelle | Soumya | Sravika | Sta Niya |
| Somyria | Sonnia | Sophia-Belle | Sorely | Sounali | Sravya | Sta'naya |
| Sona | Sonniah | Sophiah | Soren | Soundous | Sravyaanushka | Stacee |
| Sonae | Sonnie | Sophia-Lauren | Sorenity | Sounisha | Sree | Stacey *(0.09)* |
| Sonai | Sonniya | Sophiamarie | Sorenja | Souparnika | Sreeja *(0.01)* | Staceyjo |
| Sonaí | Sonny | Sophiana | Sorgul | Souraiya | Sreejasuhaila | Stachys |
| Sonaiya | Sonoma | Sophiane | Soriah | Souraya | Sreenidhi | Staci *(0.01)* |
| Sonaj | Sonora *(0.01)* | Sophianna | Sorida | Souri | Sreesha | Stacia *(0.01)* |
| Sonal | Sonté | Sophianne | Sorim | Soury | Sreeveda | Stacie *(0.03)* |
| Sonali *(0.01)* | Sontiera | Sophia-Noel | Sorine | Sovannatey | Sreeyuktha | Stacy *(0.11)* |
| Sonam | Sonum | Sophia-Rae | Soriya | Sovanny | Sreeyutha | Stacy-Erika |
| Sonara | Sonya *(0.08)* | Sophia-Ray | Sori-Yah | Soveida | Sreshtha | Stacy-Lee |
| Sonassa | Sonya Marie | Sophia-Rose | Soriyah | Sovelor | Sreya *(0.01)* | Stacyona |
| Sonatra | Sonyae | Sophia-Victoria | Soriyanie | Sovely | Sri | Staelle |
| Sonaya | Sonyael | Sophia-Zoe | Soroya | Sovilla | Sri Jaya | Staicy |
| Sonayah | Sonyah | Sophie *(1.55)* | Sorraya | Sowda | Sri Supraja | Stalaysia |
| Sonda | Sonyia | Sophie Celestin | Sorrayah | Sowillay | Srigouri | Stalesha |
| Sondess | Soo | Sophie Sara | Sorreia | Sowjanya | Sriharika | Stamatia |
| Sondos | Soo Youn | Sophie Sayen | Sorrel | Sowmya | Sriharshitha | Stancy |
| Sondra | Soo-Jin | Sophie-Ann | Sorrell | Sowndarya | Srihita | Standia |
| Sondra Marie | Soonae | Sophie-Anne | Sorriah | Sowndharya | Srija | Stanford |
| Sondrine | Sooner | Sophie-Baohan | Sorrosh | Sowona | Srijani | Staniya |
| Sone | Soora | Sophie-Jade | Sorsha | Soyaida | Srilakshmi | Stanterria |
| Sonee | Sooru | Sophiella | Sortia | Soyala | Srilasya | Stanya |
| Soneé | Sooyin | Sophie-Marie | Soryn | Soyla | Srilekha | Stanzi |
| Sonessa | Sophaiberta | Sophie-Rose | Sosan | Spain | Srimala | Staphanie |
| Soneya | Sophair | Sophie-Satu | Sosaya | Spandana | Srimayi | Star *(0.06)* |
| Songre | Sophanie | Sophina | Sosepatra | Sparkle | Srimedha | Star'asia |
| Songui | Sophary | Sophira | Sosha | Sparrow | Srina | Star's |
| Songwe | Sophaya | Sophiya | Sosi | Sparsha | Srinidhi | Star'tesha |
| Soni | Sophea *(0.01)* | Sophonie | Sosie | Special | Srinika | Staranna |
| Soni'yah | Sopheaktra | Sophonise | Soss | Special-Amira | Srinithya | Starchauna |
| Sonia *(0.15)* | Sopheara | Sophorn | Sotera | Spencer *(0.01)* | Srinitya | Starcia |
| Soniah | Sophee | Sophrona | Soteria | Spenciana | Sriprada | Starciana |
| Sonialee | Sophey | Sophy | Sotheara | Spenser | Sriranjani | Stardasia |
| Sonibel | Sophi *(0.01)* | Sophya | Sotiria | Spera | Srisha | Staresa |
| Sonie | Sophia *(6.10)* | Sopia | Soua | Spire | Srishti *(0.01)* | Staretta |
| Sonija | Sophia | Soquanie | Souad | Spiridoula | Srishty | Starialee |
| Sonika | Ambrine | Sora *(0.01)* | Souanoo | Spirit *(0.02)* | Sristhi | Starielle |
| Sonika-Silver | Sophia Berg | Soraeya | Souha | Spiritual | Sriteesha | Starienne |
| Soni-Kay | Sophia Camille | Soraia | Souhaila | Spirt | Sritha | Stariona |
| Sonila | Sophia Chloe | Soraiah | Souhana | Spohia | Sriti | Starionna |

| | | | | | | |
|---|---|---|---|---|---|---|
| Starita | Stazy | Stephaine | Stevi Lynn | Styler | Suecia Nathalia | Suhela |
| Star-Jasmine | Ste Vee | Stephaná | Stevia | Styliani | Sueda | Suhera |
| Star-Kayla | Ste'vion | Stephane (0.01) | Steviana | Stylize | Suede | Suhey |
| Starkeria | Ste'vonna | Stephanesha | Stevie (0.05) | Styrling | Suedy | Suheyda |
| Starkesha | Stecoya | Stephaney | Steviee | Su | Sueelynn | Suhina |
| Starkwaysia | Stecy | Stephani | Stevielee | Su'ad | Sueha | Suhita |
| Starlá | Stedasia | Stephania (0.01) | Stevilyn | Su'kiyia | Suehaile | Suhur |
| Starla (0.02) | Steeley | Stephanida | Stevinah | Su'priya | Sueheili | Suhuur |
| Starlaya | Steelie | Stephanie (2.28) | Steviona | Su'raya | Suehyun | Suhyon |
| Starlena | Stefahni | Stephanie Anne | Stevona | Su'riah | Sueie | Sui |
| Starlene | Stefani (0.02) | Stephanie-Catalina | Stevonna | Sua | Suein | Suilcuea |
| Starlet | Stefani Eva | | Stevy | Suaad | Suejeanna | Suili |
| Starlette | Stefani Melissa | Stephanie-Michelle | Stewart | Suabnaag | Suekaina | Suilma |
| Starlexus | Stefani Rose | | Sthefani | Suabnag | Sue-Lang | Suipha |
| Starley | Stefania (0.01) | Stephanie-Rebekah | Sthefania | Suacua | Suelin | Sujana |
| Starlight | Stefanida | | Sthefanney | Suad (0.01) | Suella | Sujata |
| Starline | Stefanie (0.04) | Stephani-Veraly | Sthefany | Suada | Suellen | Sujely |
| Starlit | Stefannie | Stephannie | Sthephany | Sualanna | Suelynn | Sujey |
| Starlline | Stefanny | Stephanny | Sthuthi | Suangel | Suemina | Sujitha |
| Starly | Stefany (0.03) | Stephany (0.07) | Stiehl | Suani | Suemy | Sujood |
| Starlyn | Stefanya | Stephanye | Stivana | Suanne | Suendy | Sujvalita |
| Star-Lynn | Stefawna | Stephashia | Stoan | Suanshi | Suene | Sukaina |
| Starlynn (0.01) | Stefen | Stephayne | Stokely | Suany | Suenyia | Sukannya |
| Starneisha | Stefeny | Stephen | Stokley | Suban | Suesanne | Sukanya |
| Starnesha | Steffang | Stephene | Stonay | Subashini | Sufferann | Sukara |
| Starr (0.04) | Steffani (0.01) | Stephenie (0.01) | Stone | Su-Been | Sugar | Sukarai |
| Starria | Steffany | Stephens | Stoney | Subeyda | Sugey | Sukari |
| Starriana | Steffi | Stepheny | Storey | Subha | Sugeydy | Sukayla |
| Starriy | Steffie | Stephfany | Stori | Subika | Sughey | Sukayna |
| Starrkiah | Steffy | Stephiane | Storie | Subin | Sugur | Sukaynah |
| Starrleau | Stefhanie | Stephianna | Storm (0.02) | Subrina | Suguy | Sukhdeep |
| Starrletta | Steinunn | Stephine | Stormee | Sucdi | Suha (0.01) | Sukhjit |
| Starrlynn | Stela | Stephnie-Jo | Stormey | Sucheta | Suhaana | Sukhleen |
| Starsha | Stella (0.56) | Stephónique | Stormi (0.01) | Suchin | Suhaani | Sukhman (0.01) |
| Startaisha | Stella Blue | Stephonny | Stormie (0.02) | Sucora | Suhail | Sukhmandeep |
| Staryonna | Stella Marie | Stephy | Stormie Anne | Sudan | Suhailah | Sukhmani |
| Stasha | Stella Rose | Stephy-Lourdes | Stormy (0.03) | Sudatreia | Suhailee | Sukhneet |
| Sta-Sharia | Stella'anne | Sterkeria | Storm | Sude | Suhailey | Sukhpreet |
| Stasia | Stella-Blue | Sterlene | Storry | Sudeeksha | Suhaily | Suki |
| Stasja | Stellaisha | Sterling (0.01) | Story (0.01) | Sudeepthi | Suhair | Sukie |
| Staton | Stellalou | Sterlingfaith | Stosha | Sudeepti | Suhaley | Sukinah |
| Stauroula | Stella-Mae | Stetsyahna | Strawberrie | Sudenaz | Suhali | Sukirat |
| Stav | Stella-Maria | Stevana | Strawberry | Sudhiksha | Suhaliyah | Sukiyah |
| Stavroula | Stella-Marie | Stevane | Streda-Sybel | Sudie | Suhaly | Sukleen |
| Stavroula Era | Stellanie | Stevani | Streesa | Sudiksha | Suhani (0.01) | Suknya |
| Stavya | Stella-Rose (0.01) | Stevanna | Streya | Sue | Suhawani | Sukrithi |
| Stayce | | Stevaria | Sttarletta | Sue Ellen | Suhay Pa | Sukriti |
| Staycee | Stellie | Stevee | Sttephanie | Sue Maya | Suhayla | Sukura |
| Staylie | Stelly | Steveena | Stutee | Sueana | Suhaylah | Sukyria |
| Staysha | Stena | Steven | Stuthi | Sue-Ann | Suheidi | Sula |
| Stayson | Stenajah | Stevena | Sty'aisha | Sueann | Suheidy | Sulaal |
| Staytlen | Stenasia | Stevey | Sty'lasia | Sueanna | Suheily | Sulai |
| Stazia | Stepahnie | Stevi | Styjah | Suebee | Suheiry | Sulakshika |

| | | | | | | |
|---|---|---|---|---|---|---|
| Sulakshiya | Sumayyah | Sunai | Sunseurhe | Surtaj | Suzanna (0.03) | Sy'kiah |
| Sulame | (0.01) | Sunaina | Sunshine (0.02) | Sury (0.01) | Suzannah (0.01) | Sy'lah |
| Sulamita | Sumedha | Sunalei | Sunshyne | Surya | Suzanne (0.04) | Sy'lavian |
| Sulanee | Sumeet | Sunaly | Sunshynne | Suryia | Suzed | Sy'maya |
| Sulani | Sumehi | Sunamy | Suntavia | Susa | Suzely | Sy'mirrah |
| Sulav | Sumer (0.01) | Sunara | Sunvir | Susan (0.18) | Suzetta | Sy'mone |
| Sulayka | Sumerha | Sunashi | Sun-Ya | Susana (0.05) | Suzette (0.01) | Sy'monique |
| Sulaymana | Sumerlyn | Sunayana | Sunya | Susana Danae | Suzie | Sy'moree |
| Suleen | Sumeya (0.01) | Sunayna | Sunyca | Susanah | Suzonna | Sy'mya |
| Suleika | Sumeyah | Sunayra | Sunydrian | Susangeline | Suzu | Sy'nai |
| Suleima | Sumi | Suncherea | Supanpreet | Susanna (0.07) | Suzuki | Sy'naijah |
| Suleiqa | Sumii | Suncheska | Suparna | Susannah (0.04) | Suzulan | Sy'ra |
| Sulekha | Sumiko | Sunchyna | Superia | Susanne (0.01) | Suzy (0.01) | Sy'rai |
| Suleko | Sumire | Sundae | Supini | Suse Wanny | Suzyn | Sy'ria |
| Sulema | Sumiya | Sundance | Supneet | Susel | Suzzanna | Sy'riah |
| Suleni | Sumiya-Troi | Sundara | Supreet | Susely | Suzzet | Sy'ryla |
| Suley | Summar | Sunday | Suprener | Suset | Suzzett | Sy'vonna |
| Suleyma | Summari | Sundie | Supreya | Suseth | Suzzette | Sya |
| Suleymi | Summaya | Sundra | Supria | Susette | Svanja | Syah |
| Suli | Summayah | Sundus (0.01) | Supriya | Susi | Svannah | Syaira |
| Suliajar | Summayyah | Sunee | Sur'leizeoniaa | Susida | Svarneet | Syairra |
| Suliana | Summer (1.06) | Suneeya | Surabhi | Susie (0.03) | Svea (0.01) | Syan |
| Sulianna | Summer Marie | Suneha | Surai | Susleni | Svea-Liv | Syana |
| Suliem | Summer | Sunelane | Suraiya | Susmita | Svenja | Syanah |
| Suling | Wahienhawe | Sunem | Suraly | Sussan | Svetlana (0.01) | Syani |
| Sulis | Summer-Ann | Sunera Rochelle | Surata | Sussel | Svetlana Lezia | Syann |
| Sullivan (0.01) | Summer-Lee | Sunflower | Suray | Sussie | Svoni | Syanna |
| Sully | Summerlee | Sungeet | Suraya (0.01) | Susthynn | Swabra | Syanne |
| Sullyannie | Summerly | Sungi | Surayha | Susy | Swaisie | Syara |
| Sulmi | Summerlyn | Sunhawk | Surayya | Sutherland | Swamini | Syarah |
| Sultaana | Summerlyne | Sunidhi | Sureena | Sutherlyn | Swanetta | Syarrah |
| Sultaanah | Summerlynn | Sunijha | Sureet | Suttida | Swar | Syasia |
| Sulvia | Summernique | Sunisa | Sureidi | Suttiphonne | Swar'niya | Syauna |
| Suly | Summerose | Sunita | Sureima | Sutton (0.01) | Swara | Sybaris |
| Suma | Summer-Paige | Suniya | Sureli | Suttun | Swathi | Sybel |
| Sumaita | Summer-Rain | Sunjana | Surely | Suvannah | Swati | Sybela |
| Sumaiya (0.01) | Summerrain | Sunjhna | Surer | Suvi | Sway | Sybella |
| Sumaiyah | Summer-Rayne | Sunlejah | Sureya | Suvilla | Swaylan | Sybelle |
| Sumaiyyah | Summit | Sunlight | Surhi | Suwani | Swaylashaure | Syberia |
| Sumajane | Summitt | Sunmarie | Suri (0.01) | Suwannee | Sweeta | Sybia |
| Suman | Summoira | Sunna | Suriah | Suwayda | Sweetcharlotte | Sybil (0.01) |
| Sumana | Summonie | Sunnah | Suriayah | Suweida | Swendy | Sybille-Adurey |
| Sumana | Summyr | Sunni (0.01) | Surin | Suweyda | Swenvina | Syble |
| Chowdary | Sumner | Sunnie (0.01) | Surina | Suya | Sweta | Sybrina |
| Sumar | Sumona | Sunniva | Suriyah | Suyai Naemi | Swetha | Sycely |
| Sumara | Sumr | Sunniya | Surona | Suyasha | Swuendy- | Sycora |
| Sumarah | Sumsaar | Sunnova | Surpreet | Suyma | Rosario | Syd'nia |
| Sumat | Sumyah | Sunny (0.03) | Surraane | Su-Young | Sxiomi | Sydalee |
| Sumay'ya | Sumyaree | Sunny Dae | Surraya | Suz | Sy Anne | Sydalia |
| Sumaya (0.03) | Sumyyah | Sunsara | Surrendin | Suza | Sy'ajia | Sydalie |
| Sumayah (0.01) | Sun | Sunsarrah | Surreya | Suzan | Sy'asia | Sydel |
| Sumayo | Sun'niya | Sunserae | Surrie | Suzana | Sy'coriah | Sydell |
| Sumayya | Suna | Sunset | Surrya | Suzann | Sy'khora | Sydella |

| | | | | | | |
|---|---|---|---|---|---|---|
| Sydelle | Syleena | Symphanie | Synthya | Szaddiah | T'kaiah | T'ona |
| Sydeon | Sylena | Symphany | Syntoria | Szajko | T'kaila | T'rayah |
| Syderah | Sylenah | Symphoni | Syntyche | Szi | T'kaiya | T'shantae |
| Sydey | Sylence | Symphonie | Syntyna | | T'kaiyah | T'shanti |
| Sydhalie | Sylenna | Symphony | Synya | | T'kara | T'shara |
| Sydiya | Sylenni | *(0.01)* | Syon | ~ T ~ | T'kari | T'shauna |
| Sydjie | Syler | Symya | Syona | | T'kayla-Crystal | T'shay |
| Sydknee | Sylese | Syn'cere | Syoniee | T | T'kerior | T'sheira |
| Sydly | Syleste | Syna | Syonni | T Aja | T'keyah | T'sheylah |
| Sydne *(0.01)* | Sylia | Syná | Sypartice | T Kaiya | T'khirah | T'shyra |
| Sydneé | Sylina | Synahsti | Sypharia | T Keyah | T'khyia | T'vatia |
| Sydnee *(0.12)* | Sylinn | Synai *(0.01)* | Syprus | T Yanna | T'kia | T'yahnna |
| Sydnei *(0.01)* | Syllah | Synaira | Syra | T.J. | T'kiza | T'yana |
| Sydney *(3.37)* | Sylmaris | Synaizjah | Syrae | T'aerra | T'knijha | T'yanná |
| Sydney Marie | Sylmya | Synaka | Syrah | T'airah | T'kya | T'yanni |
| Sydney Oze | Sylnya | Synakah | Syrai | T'aisjha | T'kyah | T'yerra |
| Sydney-Ann | Syltayvia | Synammin | Syraih | T'ajah | T'kyejah | T'yonia |
| Sydney-Anne | Sylvana | Synanthia | Syrdera | T'aliyah | T'kylah | T'yonna |
| Sydney-Ellen | Sylvania | Synavia | Syre'ine | T'ana | T'kyra | T'yuanna |
| Sydneyn | Sylvanna | Synayah | Syree | T'andra | T'laya | T'yunna |
| Sydni *(0.05)* | Sylvena | Syncere | Syreena | T'andria | T'leah | T'zaria |
| Sydnie *(0.06)* | Sylvesteasia | Syncerytiti | Syreeta | T'angeline | T'leisha | Ta |
| Sydny | Sylvette | Qualitys | Syren | T'anna | T'leiyah | Ta Aliah |
| Sydonia | Sylvi | Synciere | Syrena *(0.01)* | T'antionet | T'liya | Ta Karra |
| Sydonnie | Sylvia *(0.23)* | Syndahl | Syrenity | T'araji | T'liyah | Ta Kayla |
| Sydra | Sylvian | Syndal | Syri | T'ari | T'lyhia | Ta Kylah |
| Syeanna | Sylvie *(0.03)* | Syndee | Syria | T'arie | T'mayla | Ta Liyah |
| Syecret | Sylvie-Ann | Syndel | Syriah *(0.01)* | T'asia *(0.01)* | T'mia | Ta Mya |
| Syed | Sylvie-Anne | Syndelle | Syriahh | T'awna | T'miyah | Ta Myia |
| Syeda *(0.01)* | Sylvina | Syndey *(0.01)* | Syriahna-Lorre | T'ayja | T'mya | Ta Nazha |
| Syeda Afrah | Sylwia | Syndia | Syriana *(0.01)* | T'ayna | T'myah | Ta Niah |
| Syeena | Symantha | Syndl | Syrianna | T'azjah | T'myrah | Ta Niya |
| Syena | Symara | Syndney | Syrie | T'bria | T'nahj | Tá Niya |
| Syenna | Symarea | Syndra | Syrihia | T'brya | T'naijha | Ta Niyah |
| Syennah-Saige | Symari | Synekwah | Syrina | T'challa | T'naiyah | Ta Nyia |
| Syera | Symarria | Syneria | Syrine | T'chyane | T'najah | Ta Nyjia |
| Syeria | Symeah | Synia *(0.01)* | Syringa | T'daria | T'nasia | Ta Shanti |
| Syerra | Symeara | Syniah | Syriona | T'ea | T'nasiah | Ta Shun |
| Syesha | Symeria | Syniah' | Syris | T'emimimo | T'nayah | Tá Sonya |
| Syheaven | Symerrian | Synica | Syrit | T'eniya | T'neil | Ta Tianna |
| Syhx | Symfini | Synihia | Syrra | T'erah | T'nerica | Tá Zia |
| Syian | Symia | Synii | Syrriah | T'erica | T'nesa | Ta'aliyah |
| Syianna | Symiah | Synique | Syrus | T'ericka | T'nesha | Ta'arah |
| Syion-Dorothy | Symintha | Syniyah | Syska Sequoia | T'errica | T'nia | Ta'asia |
| Syjayah | Symira | Synkyia | Sytasia | T'hana | T'niaya | Ta'asiah |
| Sykora | Symirra | Synnamon | Sytieia | T'iara | T'nidzha | Ta'chandlo |
| Syl'ajaha | Symmantha | Synneva | Syvainnah | T'ionna | T'niya | Ta'ciana |
| Syla | Symona | Synnove | Syvannah | T'Ja | T'niyah | Ta'cireyha |
| Sylah | Symoné | Synomi | Syvannarae | T'jada | T'noi | Ta'cora |
| Sylaris | Symone *(0.04)* | Synovia | Syvawn | T'jai | T'nya | Ta'cori |
| Sylderria | Symone-Arie | Synoya | Syve | T'jasiah | T'nyah | Ta'corie |
| Sylea | Symonne | Synteria | Syxx | T'kaelyn | T'nye | Ta'correyha |
| Sylee-Ann | Symphané | Synthia *(0.01)* | Syylar | T'kai | T'nyia | Ta'corya |

| | | | | | | |
|---|---|---|---|---|---|---|
| Ta'daejaah | Ta'koya | Ta'metriya | Ta'nivea | Ta'tiana | Tabor | Tae'yahna |
| Ta'dajah | Ta'kya | Ta'mia | Ta'niya (0.02) | Ta'tianna | Taborionna | Tae'yanni |
| Ta'dashia | Ta'kyah | Ta'miah | Ta'niyah (0.02) | Ta'tiannha | Tabreah | Taea |
| Ta'day | Ta'kyaih | Ta'miia | Ta'niyh | Ta'tiannia | Tabria | Taebor |
| Ta'dazya | Ta'kyi | Ta'mircle | Ta'nya | Ta'tiyana | Tabriah | Taedem |
| Ta'hadeia | Ta'kyia | Ta'miria | Ta'nya Malyah | Ta'tiyiana | Tabrizia | Taeden |
| Ta'honesty | Ta'kyiah | Ta'miya | Ta'nyah (0.01) | Ta'tiyuanna | Tabytha | Taedyn |
| Ta'imah | Ta'kyjah | Ta'miyah | Ta'nyaha | Ta'tyana | Tacaiya | Taeeun |
| Ta'ja | Ta'kyla | Ta'mya (0.02) | Ta'nyce | Ta'tyanna | Tacalah | Taegan (0.02) |
| Ta'jae | Ta'kylee | Ta'myaha | Ta'nyha | Ta'varejha | Tacambia | Taegen |
| Ta'jah | Ta'kymra | Ta'myiah | Ta'nyia | Ta'vazia | Tacara | Taehee |
| Ta'jaha | Ta'kyra | Ta'myla | Ta'nyiah | Ta'vee | Tacaria | Taeiona |
| Ta'jai | Ta'kyrah | Ta'naeja | Ta'nyjah | Ta'veonna | Tacarra | Taeja |
| Ta'jakieri | Ta'lasia | Ta'naesia | Ta'nyla | Ta'verah | Tacarrie | Taejah |
| Ta'jara | Ta'lasih | Ta'nahiah | Ta'nyll | Ta'vianna | Tace | Taejhuan |
| Ta'jayla | Ta'laya | Ta'nahzi | Ta'nyshia | Ta'vinae | Tacey | Taejia |
| Ta'jaylen | Ta'layah | Ta'naija | Ta'nyzia | Ta'yana | Tachana | Taela |
| Ta'jazmyn | Ta'laycia | Ta'naijah | Ta'prell | Ta'ylorria | Tachara | Taelar |
| Ta'jeiana | Ta'layha | Ta'naisa | Ta'qiera | Ta'yona | Tachelle | Taeler |
| Ta'jeria | Ta'layla | Ta'naja | Ta'queria | Ta'yonce | Taci | Taeley |
| Ta'jha | Ta'lazsha | Ta'najha | Ta'quira | Ta'zharia | Taciah | Taelin |
| Ta'jihya | Ta'leah | Ta'naji | Ta'quisha | Ta'zhiyah | Tacie | Taelor (0.02) |
| Ta'jiri | Ta'leia | Ta'najshia | Ta'rae | Ta'zier | Tacoma | Taelyn (0.01) |
| Ta'jiyanah | Ta'leigha | Ta'nashia | Ta'raven | Ta'zyia | Tacora | Taelynn (0.01) |
| Ta'jzaya | Ta'leya | Ta'nashjia | Ta'riah | Taahirah | Tacora-Ann | Taelyr |
| Ta'kai | Ta'leyah | Ta'nasia | Ta'rrie | Taáibah | Tacoreya | Taem |
| Ta'kali | Ta'leyha | Ta'nassia | Ta'ryah | Taaijah | Tacori | Taenea |
| Ta'kara | Ta'lia | Ta'nay | Ta'sha | Taaira | Tacoria | Taeniya |
| Ta'karah | Ta'liah | Ta'naya | Ta'shae | Taala | Tacorvee | Taer |
| Ta'karie | Ta'ligah | Ta'nayasia | Ta'shana | Taaliya | Tacourtney | Taerion |
| Ta'karii | Ta'lir | Ta'naycia | Ta'shanda | Taaliyah | Tacoya | Taeriyl |
| Ta'kaya | Ta'lisa | Ta'nayjah | Ta'shaniqu | Taanika | Tacoyia | Taeryn |
| Ta'kayiah | Ta'lise | Ta'naysha | Ta'shanti | Taaron | Tacueira | Taesha |
| Ta'kayla | Ta'lisha | Ta'nayziah | Ta'shara | Tabandeh | Tacy | Taeshaundra |
| Ta'kaylor | Ta'liyah (0.01) | Ta'nazia | Ta'sharia | Tabarak | Tadaisa | Taetum |
| Ta'keira | Ta'love | Ta'nazja | Ta'shaun | Tabark | Tadan | Taevfia |
| Ta'kenya | Ta'lur | Ta'nea | Ta'shauna | Tabasm | Tadasia | Taevyn |
| Ta'kera | Ta'lyshia | Ta'neal | Ta'shawna | Tabassum | Tadea | Taeya |
| Ta'keriaun | Ta'maira | Ta'neema | Ta'shawni | Tabatha (0.02) | Tadeane | Taeyanaeh |
| Ta'keviya | Ta'maiyah | Ta'neisseya | Ta'shayla | Tabaya | Tadeja | Taeylor |
| Ta'keyrah | Ta'majah | Ta'nescia | Ta'shaylyn | Tabbatha | Taden | Taeyona |
| Ta'khiya | Ta'maria | Ta'nesha | Ta'shee | Tabbitha | Tadia | Taeyonna |
| Ta'khya | Ta'mariyah | Ta'nevaeh | Ta'sheona | Tabea | Tadyn | Taeyoung |
| Ta'khyla | Ta'marria | Ta'neya | Ta'shiria | Taber | Tae | Tafale |
| Ta'kia | Ta'mauriana | Ta'ni | Ta'shiya | Tabetha (0.01) | Taé | Tafara |
| Ta'kiara | Ta'maurya | Ta'nia (0.01) | Ta'shoni | Tabethia | Tae Vianna | Tafaul |
| Ta'kierra | Ta'maya | Ta'niah | Ta'shonna | Tabiana | Tae'awn | Tagan |
| Ta'kila | Ta'mecia | Ta'niesseya | Ta'shya | Tabish | Tae'driana | Tagen |
| Ta'kira | Ta'meia | Ta'nijah | Ta'shyla | Tabita | Tae'jah | Tageyonah |
| Ta'kiya | Ta'meka | Ta'nijha | Ta'shylia | Tabith | Tae'lei | Tagianna |
| Ta'kiyah | Ta'merah | Ta'ninah | Ta'staria | Tabitha (0.21) | Tae'ona | Tagora |
| Ta'kiziana | Ta'meria | Ta'niqua | Ta't'yannah | Tabithah | Tae'onna | Tah'jae |
| Ta'koriya | Ta'metris | Ta'nisha | Ta'taha | Tabiyah | Tae'viona | Tah'jai |

| | | | | | | |
|---|---|---|---|---|---|---|
| Tah'jay | Tahjé | Tahyanna | Taileen | Taityn | Tajlor | Takenzie |
| Tah'jinae | Tahjeanna | Tahylor | Taileisha | Taiva | Tajmara | Takera |
| Tah'maurah | Tahjeé | Tahzalia | Tailema | Taiwnie | Tajmonae | Takeria |
| Tah'mya | Tahjelani | Tai (0.01) | Tailer | Taiya (0.01) | Tajnae | Takerra |
| Tah'myah | Tahji | Tai'ahna | Tailey | Taiyah | Tajohna | Takerria |
| Tah'naya | Tahjiana | Tai'aisha | Taili | Taiyana | Tajohnique | Takerya Ke |
| Tah'nez | Tahjianna | Tai'driana | Tailing | Taiyanah | Tajonae'a | Takesha |
| Tah'niyah | Tahjlyn | Tai'jae | Taillynn | Taiyler | Tajryan | Takeshia |
| Tah'nyah | Tahjzané | Tai'lee | Tailor (0.01) | Taiylor | Tajsa | Takeya |
| Tah'siah | Tahkeria | Tai'ler | Tailyn | Taizah | Tajshae | Takeyah |
| Tah'taina | Tahkia | Tai'lon | Tailynn (0.01) | Taizja | Tajuana | Takeyna |
| Tahael | Tahleah | Tai'lynn | Tailynn-Amirrah | Taj | Tajza | Takhadja |
| Tahaira | Tahleea | Tai'na | Tailyr | Taj'rionna | Tajzah | Takhara |
| Tahaliah | Tah-Leigha | Tai'nasia | Taima | Taja (0.01) | Tajzaí | Takharee |
| Tahana | Tahleigha | Tai'rayah | Taimane | Tajaa | Takahla | Takhia (0.01) |
| Tahanee | Tahlequah | Tai'shawnna | Taimara | Tajae | Takai | Takhira |
| Tahani | Tahler | Tai'tyana | Taimaris | Tajah | Takaia | Takhyra |
| Tahanni | Tahleya | Tai'yahna | Taïna | Tajaha | Takaila | Takia |
| Tahany | Tahlia (0.03) | Tai'yana | Taina (0.05) | Tajahlynn | Takaile | Taki-Ah |
| Tahara | Tahlissia | Taia (0.01) | Taïna-Maïka | Tajahnay | Takairah | Takiah |
| Taharah | Tahliya | Taiah | Tainayris | Tajai | Takaiya | Takiea |
| Tahayla | Tahliyah | Taiana | Taini | Taj-Aliah | Takaiyah | Takiera |
| Tahaylee | Tahlor | Taianna | Tainia | Tajana | Takajiah | Takiesha |
| Tahdiana | Tahlya | Taiara | Tainya | Tajanae (0.01) | Takala | Takija |
| Taheerah | Tahmea | Taiavna | Tainyziah | Tajanah | Takalah | Takijah |
| Tahel | Tahmeara | Taibah | Taira | Tajanai | Takara (0.01) | Takila |
| Tahela | Tahmei | Taichelle | Tairah | Tajanay | Takarea | Takiona |
| Taheshia | Tahmya | Taidom | Tairicha | Tajanaye | Takarehia | Takira (0.01) |
| Tahia | Tahmyah | Taiesha | Tairrah | Tajané | Takari | Takirah |
| Tahia-Lee | Tahnauj | Taifa | Tairy | Tajanea | Takarra | Takiria |
| Tahila | Tahnaya | Taiga | Tairyn | Tajanee | Takarria | Takirra |
| Tahina | Tahnayshia | Taigan | Tais | Tajania | Takaryia | Takisha |
| Tahina Nita | Tahnegsa | Taigen | Taisashia | Tajashia | Takaya | Takiya (0.01) |
| Tahina | Tahneja | Taighen | Taisen | Tajaune | Takayah | Takiyah (0.02) |
|   Phylomene | Tahnia | Taigon | Taisey | Tajay | Takaydra | Takiyha |
| Tahira | Tahnissa | Taiha | Taisha (0.01) | Tajayla | Takayia | Takiyla |
| Tahirah (0.01) | Tahniya | Taihja | Taishan | Taje |   Shaijasmine | Takiyrah |
| Tahiran | Tahniyah | Taija (0.01) | Taishawna | Tajenay | Takayla (0.02) | Tako |
| Tahirih | Tahnya | Taijah | Taishay | Tajeneque | Takayrolen | Takoda |
| Tahiry | Tahoora | Taijanae | Taisia | Tajera | Takdeer | Takora |
| Tahiyah | Tah-Quierah | Taije | Taisim | Tajeyah | Takdir | Takorei |
| Tahj | Tahra | Taijiona | Taisjanae | Tajha | Takeara | Takoria |
| Tahja | Tahrea'ah | Taika | Taissa | Tajhami | Takedi-Myriam | Takoya |
| Tahjae | Tahreem | Taikaila | Tait | Tajhay | Takeena | Takoyia |
| Tahjaé | Tahryah | Taikayla | Taite | Taji | Takeera | Takudzwa |
| Tahjah | Tahshaye | Taikoreya | Tai-Teona | Tajia | Takeeyah | Takurani |
| Tahjahne | Tahsjae | Taila | Taitiana | Tajiah | Takeija | Takwa |
| Tahjai | Tahsya | Tailah | Taitianna | Tajiana | Takeila | Takwana |
| Tahjaila | Tahtiana | Tailaiya | Taitlyn | Tajinae | Takeima | Takya |
| Tahjanae | Tahtianna | Tailar | Taitlynn | Tajinea | Takeira | Takyah |
| Tahjanay | Tahtyanna | Tai-Laya | Taitum | Tajira | Takeiyah | Takyia |
| Tahjania | Tahya | Taileaha | Taityana | Tajirah | Takena | Takyinaa |
| Tahje | Tahyana | Tailee | Taitym | Tajiya | Takenya | Takyla (0.01) |

| | | | | | | |
|---|---|---|---|---|---|---|
| Takyra (0.01) | Talee | Talijah | Talulah | Tamarae | Tameika | Tamire |
| Takyrah | Taleea | Talika | Talulla | Tamarah | Tameina | Tamirea |
| Takyya | Taleeia | Talim | Talus | Tamara-Lynn | Tameira | Tamiria |
| Tal | Taleen | Talina (0.01) | Talvinder | Tamaran | Tameisa | Tamiris |
| Tal'iya | Taleena | Talina Krystal | Taly | Tamare | Tameisha | Tamirrah |
| Tala (0.03) | Taleesha | Taline | Talya (0.03) | Tamarea | Tameka (0.01) | Tamisa |
| Talacia | Taleeya | Talisa (0.01) | Talyah | Tamareya | Tamel | Tamisha |
| Talahya | Taleeyah | Talisaya | Talyann | Tamarha | Tamela | Tamitha |
| Talaija | Taleia | Talise (0.01) | Talyanna | Tamari (0.01) | Tamelia | Tamiya (0.03) |
| Talainy | Taleigh | Talisea | Talyanne | Tamaria (0.01) | Tamelie | Tamiyah (0.01) |
| Talaisia | Taleigha (0.01) | Taliseia | Talyha | Tamariah | Tamella | Tamiyra |
| Talaiyah | Taleijah | Talisha (0.01) | Talyia | Tamarian | Tamera (0.02) | Tamiza |
| Talajah | Taleise | Talishae | Talyiah | Tamariana | Tamerah | Tammalee |
| Talajiah | Taleisha | Talisia | Tályn | Tamarin | Tamerehia | Tammanie |
| Talan (0.01) | Talel | Talissa (0.01) | Talyn (0.02) | Tamariona | Tameria (0.01) | Tammara |
| Talana | Talen | Talita | Talyna | Tamaris | Tameriah | Tam-Meeya |
| Talanda | Talena | Talitha (0.01) | Talynn | Tamariunna | Tameron | Tammi |
| Talane | Talene | Talithea | Talyr | Tamarlei | Tamerra | Tammiah |
| Talanoa | Taler | Taliya (0.02) | Talyra | Tamarra | Tamerria | Tammial |
| Talar | Talesa | Taliya Tal | Talysa | Tamarrah- | Tamery | Tammiane |
| Talara | Talese | Taliyah (0.11) | Talyse |   Neycole | Tamesha | Tammie |
| Talariyah | Talesha | Taliyaha | Talyson | Tamarria | Tameshia | Tammisha |
| Talasha | Talesia | Taliyuah | Talyssa | Tamarya | Tametrius | Tammra |
| Talashia | Taletta | Taliza | Talysta | Tamasha | Tameya (0.01) | Tammy (0.05) |
| Talasia | Taleya | Talla | Tam | Tamasin | Tameyah | Tammy Lynette |
| Talasya | Taleyah | Tallah | Tam Nguyen | Tamatha | Tameyia | Tammyka |
| Talaun | Taleygenai | Tallan | Tam're-Marie | Tamauria | Tameyria | Tamonie |
| Talauny | Talhya | Tallee | Tama | Tamaya (0.02) | Tameysha | Tamonika |
| Talawna | Tali (0.01) | Tallena | Tamahine | Tamayah | Tami | Tamore |
| Talaya (0.01) | Talia (0.36) | Tallera | Tamai | Tamayia | Ta-Mia | Tamoryia |
| Talayah (0.01) | Taliah (0.04) | Talletta | Tamaia | Tamayra | Tamia (0.18) | Tamra (0.01) |
| Talayasia | Taliaha | Talley | Tamaija Lemara | Tamayshia | Tamia Octa | Tamrah |
| Talayeh | Taliamalefiafia | Talli | Tamaijah | Tamber | Tamiah (0.01) | Tamralie |
| Talayia | Taliana | Tallia | Tamaira | Tamberly | Tamiara | Tamron |
| Talayiah | Taliana-Alicia | Talliah | Tamaiya | Tamberlynn | Ta-Micheal | Tamryn |
| Talayja | Tali-Ann | Tallie (0.01) | Tamaiyah | Tamborah | Tamicka | Tamrynn |
| Talayla | Talianna | Tallis | Tamajae | Tambra | Tamie | Tamsen |
| Talayna | Tali-Anne | Talliyah | Tamajah | Tambrah | Tamieka | Tamsin |
| Talaynee | Talianys | Tallon | Tamajai | Tambrea | Tamiera | Tamsin Mel |
| Talaysha | Taliasen | Tallula | Tamajha | Tambria | Tamiia | Tamsyn |
| Talayshia | Taliayah | Tallulah (0.02) | Tamala | Tame'ria | Tamijah | Tamy |
| Talaysia | Taliayh | Tallulah-Belle | Tamaleana | Tamea (0.01) | Tamika (0.01) | Tamy'a |
| Talayza | Talibra | Tally | Tamana | Tameah | Tamikka | Tamyá |
| Talberlyn | Talica | Tallyah | Tamanna (0.01) | Tameaka | Tamiko | Tamya (0.06) |
| Tale'a | Talicia | Tallyn | Tamantha | Tameca | Tamilia | Tamya Kadija |
| Taleá | Talie (0.01) | Talnige | Tamar (0.04) | Tamecio | Tamilie | Tamyah (0.01) |
| Talea (0.01) | Taliea | Taloa | Tamar Aurora | Tamecka | Tamima | Tamy-Eve |
| Taleah (0.04) | Talieciah | Talon (0.01) | Tamara (0.19) | Tameea | Tamina | Tamyia (0.01) |
| Taleah' | Taliejia | Talor | Tamara Abygael | Tameeka | Taminique | Tamyiah |
| Taleaha | Taliese | Talora | Tamara Azina | Tameenna | Tamir | Tamyka |
| Taleana | Taliesin | Taloy | Tamara-Adeline | Tameera | Tamira (0.01) | Tamyra (0.04) |
| Taleayha | Taliha | Talton | Tamarac | Tameeya | Tamiraa | Tamyse |
| Talecia | Talija | Talula | Tamaradobra | Tameia | Tamirah | Tamysha |

| | | | | | |
|---|---|---|---|---|---|
| Tamzen | Tanaye | Tangaraya | Tanishka | Tantan | Taquiria | Taria |
| Tan'asha | Tanayia | Tangela | Tanishmarie | Tantania | Taquita | Tariah |
| Tan'mesha | Tanayja | Tangelia | Tanisi | Tantiyana | Taquiyah | Tariana |
| Tan'zya | Tanayjah | Tangerlynn | Tanissa | Tantyana | Taquoia | Tarianna |
| Tana *(0.01)* | Tanayla | Tangi | Tanita | Tanuja | Taquondra | Taricese |
| Tana'jah | Tanayri | Tangier | Tanith | Tanureet | Tara *(0.31)* | Tarie |
| Tanaaya | Tanaysha | Tang-Jia Deniz | Tanitoluwa | Tanushaa | Tara'naija | Tariell |
| Tanacious | Tanaysia | Tanher | Tanitra | Tanushree | Tarae | Tarika |
| Tanaé | Tanayzia | Tani | Tanivea | Tanvee | Tarae'ah | Tarima |
| Tanae *(0.01)* | Tanazah | Tani'jah | Taniyá | Tanveen | Tarael | Tarin |
| Tanaejah | Tanazia | Taniá | Taniya *(0.11)* | Tanveer | Tarah *(0.01)* | Tarina |
| Tanaeya | Tanazja | Tania *(0.18)* | Taniyah *(0.08)* | Tanvi *(0.03)* | Tarah Leana | Tarini |
| Tanah | Tandee | Tania Ginette | Taniyan | Tanvir | Tarai | Tarinikka |
| Tanahiri | Tandi | Tania Nies | Taniyh | Tanya *(0.11)* | Tarailah-Elishan | Tariq |
| Tanai | Tandice | Taniah *(0.02)* | Taniyha | Tanya Jade | Taraiona | Tariqua Jasmine |
| Tanaia | Tandra | Taniah | Taniyiah | Tanyah | Taraja | Taris |
| Tanaiah | Tandranika | Christine | Taniyjuh | Tanyaradzwa | Tarajai | Tarisa |
| Tanaih | Tane | Taniaya | Taniyyah | Tanyce | Taraji | Tarisha |
| Tanaija | Tanea *(0.01)* | Taniayah | Tanizia | Tanye'ua | Tarajii | Tarissa |
| Tanaijah | Taneah | Tanica | Tanizja | Tanyi | Taraka | Tariunna |
| Tanaijha | Taneal | Tanichia | Tanjaliar | Tanyia | Taraline | Tariya |
| Tanairi | Tanearah | Taniea | Tanjalina | Tanyiah | Taralyn | Tariyah *(0.01)* |
| Tanairis | Taneeja | Taniek | Tanjanée | Tanyjah | Tara-Lyne | Tarketa |
| Tanairy | Taneeka | Taniell | Tanjila | Tanyla | Taralynn | Tarlasia |
| Tanaisa | Taneekia | Tanielle | Tankeu Eunice | Tanyon | Taran | Tarlea |
| Tanaisha | Taneel | Taniesha | Tanleigh | Tanyr | Tarandeep | Tarlisha |
| Tanaiya | Taneen | Ta-Niessya | Tanley | Tanyra | Taranee | Tarman |
| Tanaiyah | Taneese | Tanieya | Tanlynn | Tanyrah | Taraneekia | Tarmar |
| Tanaja | Taneesha | Taniirah | Tanmayi | Tanysha | Taraneh | Tarmara |
| Tanajah | Taneia | Tanija *(0.01)* | Tanmeet | Tanysia | Taranique | Tarmarie |
| Tanaje'a | Taneiah | Tanijae | Tanna *(0.01)* | Tanyyah | Tarannumjit | Tarmine |
| Tanajha | Taneijah | Tanijah *(0.01)* | Tannah | Tanzania | Taranpreet | Tarn |
| Tanaji | Taneil | Tanijha | Tannar | Tanzeela | Taraoluwa | Tarnjot Kaur |
| Tanajia | Taneille | Tanijia | Tanneh | Tao | Tarasia | Tarnpreet |
| Tanajsha | Taneisha *(0.01)* | Tanijuh | Tannei | Taojanique | Taraya | Taronda |
| Tanaka | Taneiysha | Tanika *(0.01)* | Tannell | Taomy | Taraye | Taronica |
| Tanara | Taneizah | Tanika-Lynn | Tanner *(0.02)* | Taonga | Taraysha | Tarquin |
| Tanareyé | Taneja | Tanikia | Tanneria | Taonia | Tarazja | Tarquinn |
| Tanaria | Taneka | Tanila | Tanneya | Taormina | Tarbrisha | Tarra |
| Tanaryi | Tanelis | Tanima | Tannia | Tapaingia | Tareah | Tarrah |
| Tanasha | Taneria | Tanin | Tannile | Tapanga *(0.01)* | Tareana | Tarrah Anne |
| Tanashaé | Tanerria | Tanina | Tannis | Tapange | Tareeae | Tarraja |
| Tanashei | Tanesa | Taningja | Tannith | Tapasiya | Tareesa | Tarralyn |
| Tanashia | Tanesha *(0.01)* | Taniqua | Tannon | Tapley | Tareka | Tarranum |
| Tanashua | Taneshia | Tanique | Tannya | Taqilla | Taren | Tarren |
| Tanasia *(0.02)* | Tanessa | Tanis | Tannyn | Taqiya Abdulahi | Tarena | Tarrence |
| Tanasya | Tanessa-Norah | Tanisan | Tanor | Taqiyyah | Taress | Tarresah |
| Tanasyah | Taney | Tanise | Tanora | Taqua | Taressa | Tarria |
| Tanatswa | Taneyá | Tanish | Tanoria | Taquanna | Tareya | Tarrin |
| Tanavia | Taneya *(0.01)* | Tanisha *(0.05)* | Tanreet | Taquari | Tareyn | Tarrina |
| Tanay | Taneyja | Tanisha Singh | Tansen | Taquasia | Targen | Tarriyah |
| Tanaya *(0.03)* | Tang | Tanishi | Tansley | Taquay'za | Tarhaka | Tarryn *(0.01)* |
| Tanayah | Tangaray | Tanishiana | Tansy | Taquila | Tari | Tarshai |

| | | | | | | |
|---|---|---|---|---|---|---|
| Taruna | Tasheik | Tasmine | Tatiannamarie | Tauren | Tawiana | Tayer |
| Tarunika | Tashena | Tasmiya | Tatianya | Taurence | Tawina | Tayera |
| Tarya | Tasheona | Tasneem (0.01) | Tatiara | Tauri | Tawna | Taygan |
| Taryah | Tasheonia | Tasnem | Tatiauna | Tauriae | Tawne | Taygen |
| Taryjae | Tashera | Tasnema | Tatiayana | Taurisha | Tawnea | Tayhler |
| Taryn (0.27) | Tasherah | Tasnia | Tatiayanna | Tauryn | Tawney | Tayhlore |
| Tarynn | Tasheria | Tasniim | Tatiaynea | Tausha | Tawni | Tayia (0.01) |
| Tarynne | Tasherree | Tasnim (0.02) | Taticha | Tausie | Tawn-Nay | Tayiah |
| Tarynpreet | Tashi | Tasnimah | Tatihana | Tautiana | Tawnneylin | Tayiana |
| Taryssa | Tashia | Tasnime | Tatineshia | Tautianna | Tawny (0.01) | Tayin |
| Tasadie | Tashiana | Tasnuba | Tatinna | Tautyonna | Tawnya | Tayina |
| Tasaiyah | Tashifa | Tasnuva | Tationa | Tauvia | Tawtiana | Tayja |
| Tasanee | Tashika | Tassa | Tationna | Tauvie | Tay'ler | Tayjah |
| Tasani | Tashina | Tassara | Tationnya | Tava | Tay'lor | Tayjen |
| Tasara | Tashiona | Tassha | Tatium | Tavae | Tay'onia | Tayjha |
| Tasaundra | Tashionna | Tassi | Tatiwanna | Tavaé | Tay'quanna | Tayl'rlee |
| Tasavor | Tashira | Tassija | Tatiyana (0.02) | Tavanna | Tay'shaun | Tayla (0.07) |
| Tascha | Tashiya | Tassneem | Tatiyanah | Tavareya | Tay'sia | Tayla Rai |
| Tascheena | Tashiyah | Tassnim | Tatiyanna (0.01) | Tavaria | Tay'zhana | Tayla-Fay |
| Tasciana | Tashiyana | Tastasia | Tatiyna | Tavariah | Taya (0.11) | Taylah |
| Taseana | Tashiyanna | Tastiya | Tatiyon | Tavariona | Tayaag-Kaur | Taylalea |
| Tasha (0.04) | Tashline | Tasya | Tatiyona | Tavarria | Tayah (0.03) | Tayla-Maria |
| Tasha Pakita | Tashlynn | Tat'auna | Tatiyonna | Tavashia | Tayana (0.01) | Tayla-Marie |
| Tashae | Tashni | Tata | Tatjana | Tavelyn | Tayanayh | Taylan |
| Tashaeyah | Tashnova | Tatania | Tatlana | Taven | Tayandrea | Taylar (0.03) |
| Tashah | Tashona | Tatanya | Tattiana | Tavena | Tayanita | Taylaur |
| Tashailya | Tashonda | Tatayana | Tattianna | Tavera | Tayanna | Taylea |
| Tashala | Tashondaly | Tate (0.01) | Tattiaunna | Tavi | Tayannah | Tayleah |
| Tashana | Tashondria | Tateanna | Tatum (0.35) | Tavia (0.02) | Tayara | Taylee (0.01) |
| Tashani | Tashonee | Tateeana | Tatumn | Taviah | Taya-Renee | Tayleesha |
| Tashanna | Tashonna | Tatei'onna | Tatum-Star | Taviana | Tayasir | Tayleigh |
| Tashannah | Tashrai | Ta-Teianna | Tatyahna | Tavianily | Tayauna | Taylen |
| Ta-Shanuna | Tashreale | Tateiona | Tatyana (0.10) | Tavianna | Tayayra | Taylena |
| Tashara (0.01) | Tashubi | Tatelynn | Tatyana Iteka | Tavie | Tayba | Taylene |
| Tashareeh | Tashya | Tatem (0.01) | Tatyanah | Tavielle | Tayber | Tayler (0.10) |
| Tashari | Tashyah | Taten | Tatyania | Tavifa | Taybianna | Tayler-Rae |
| Tasharieé | Tashyana | Tatenda | Tatyanie | Tavin | Taybreea | Tayleur |
| Tasharra | Tashyanna | Tateona | Tatyanna (0.03) | Taviona | Taybri | Taylia |
| Tasharria | Tashyia | Tateonna | Tatyianna | Tavionna | Tayce | Taylin (0.02) |
| Tashauna | Tashyla | Tateum | Tatym | Tavish | Taycee | Taylince |
| Tashaunie | Tashyra | Tate-Win | Tatyona | Tavishi | Taycha | Taylinn |
| Tashawn | T-Asia | Tateyana | Tatyonna | Tavjot | Taydem | Taylir |
| Tashawna | Tasia (0.02) | Tathena | Tau'jaiya | Tavneet | Tayden | Tayllor |
| Tashawnna | Tasiah | Tathyana | Tauheedah | Tavoneshia | Taydence | Tayllore |
| Tashay | Tasiana | Tati'yana | Taujala | Tavrie | Taydin | Tayloe |
| Tashaya | Tasih | Tatiana (0.45) | Tauley | Taw'yia | Taydria | Taylon |
| Tashayda | Tasina | Tatiana Anaelle | Taulmaril | Tawakalitu | Taye | Taylor (4.20) |
| Tashaye | Tasira | Tatiana | Taumi | Tawan | Tayea | Taylor Ann |
| Tashayia | Tasiya | Ni'quaua | Tauni | Tawana | Tayeko | Taylor Jade |
| Tashayla | Taskia | Tatianah | Taunnaa | Tawananyasha | Tayelor | Taylor Von |
| Tashearia | Taslime | Tatiana-Thais | Taura | Tawanda | Tayem | Taylor-Ann |
| Tashee | Tasmia | Tatianna (0.09) | Taurance | Tawanna | Tayen | Taylor-Anne |
| Tasheena | Tasmin | Tatiannah | Taurean | Tawheedah | Tayena | Taylore |

| | | | | | | |
|---|---|---|---|---|---|---|
| Taylor-Elisabeth | Tayton | Te'ana | Te'onni | Tealaisha | Teeale | Teilani |
| Taylor-Grace | Taytriona | Te'anah | Te'ora | Teamaira | Teeanna | Teilor |
| Taylorh | Taytum *(0.01)* | Te'anna | Te'raiya | Tea-Marie | Teedra | Teinya |
| Taylor-Jean | Taytumn | Te'anna Marie | Te'ren | Teana | Teegan *(0.01)* | Teion |
| Taylor-Jo | Tayubah | Te'ara | Te'ryah | Teanasia | Teegin | Teiona |
| Taylor-Judith-Lynn | Tayva | Te'arah | Te'shawanda | Teandra | Teegyn | Teionerahtathe |
| Taylor-May | Tayven | Te'aree | Te'shawna | Teania | Teeia | Teionna |
| Taylor-Mckenzie Denise | Tayveonna | Te'arika | Te'shayla | Teanna *(0.01)* | Teeira | Teira |
| Taylor-Nicole | Tayvia | Te'arra | Te'tasha | Teannah | Teeiyah | Teirini |
| Taylor-Paige | Tayviana | Te'asia *(0.01)* | Te'ya | Teanya | Teela | Teirnan |
| Taylor-Reece | Tayyaba | Te'asjah | Te'yahna | Teaona | Teelah | Teirra |
| Taylor-Simone | Tayyabah | Te'aurie | Te'yana | Tear | Teena | Teirsa |
| Taylor-Symone | Tayyana | Te'coria | Te'yanna | Teara | Teeryauna | Teisha |
| Taylour | Tayyiba | Te'elle | Te'yonna | Tearagan | Teesa | Teiya |
| Taylre | Tayyibah | Te'errah | Te'yuauna | Tearanie | Teeta | Teiyana |
| Taylur | Tayzah | Te'ijah | Te'zjir | Tearesa | Teeya | Teiyonna |
| Taylyn *(0.01)* | Tayzha | Te'kaijah | Teá | Tearia | Teeyliah | Teizya Alexis |
| Taylyne | Tayzja | Te'kara | Téa *(0.01)* | Tearney | Teeyonna | Tej'ashia |
| Taylynn *(0.01)* | Tayzsha | Te'karia | Tea *(0.02)* | Tearra *(0.01)* | Teeyono | Teja |
| Taylyr | Taz Marie | Te'kayla | Tea'asia | Tearrance | Teeziona | Tejá |
| Tayma | Taz'ekiah | Te'kaylah | Tea'ijai | Tearraney | Tefarriyah | Teja'hnae |
| Taymiyyah | Tazaira | Te'khia | Teadja | Tearria | Teffany | Tejah |
| Taymra | Tazanna | Te'kia | Teadrea | Tearsa | Teffrie | Tejal |
| Tayna | Tazaria | Te'kiahe | Teagan *(0.28)* | Tearstyn | Tegan *(0.06)* | Tejana |
| Taynaiyh | Tazariah | Te'kira | Teagan Sarai | Tearsyn | Tegbir | Tejanae |
| Tayneiha | Tazarria | Te'kiya | Teagan-Ann | Tearteauna | Teghan *(0.01)* | Tejasha |
| Taynesha | Tazhanae | Te'kyia | Teagann | Tearuh | Tegwen | Tejasvi |
| Taynia | Tazhia | Te'kylah | Teagan-Ruth | Tearyn | Tegwin | Tejaswini |
| Tayoleen | Tazia | Te'layia | Teagan-Shauna | Tearza | Tegyan | Tejay |
| Tayona *(0.01)* | Taziarayia | Te'laysha | Teagen *(0.01)* | Tearzyn | Teha | Tejh |
| Tayonna | Tazin | Te'leah | Teaghan *(0.01)* | Teasa | Tehanay | Tejhuana |
| Tayonni | Taziyah | Te'lia | Teaghan-Pearl | Teasha | Tehani *(0.01)* | Tejiana |
| Tayra | Tazleonia | Te'liyah | Teaghen | Teashani | Tehila | Tejinder |
| Tayraya | Tazlynn | Te'lor | Teagon Dior | Teasia *(0.01)* | Tehilla | Tejini |
| Tays | Tazlynne | Te'mia | Teague | Teauna | Tehillah | Tekai'jah |
| Taysen | Tazsyah | Te'misha | Téah | Teaundreh | Tehreem | Tekail |
| Taysha *(0.01)* | Tazy Jay | Te'mya | Teah *(0.01)* | Teawrie | Tehreen | Tekaira |
| Tayshara | Tazyiah | Te'myaia | Teahana | Teaya | Te-Huei | Tekala |
| Tayshauna | Tazyla | Te'nahya | Teahauna | Teaysa | Tehya *(0.04)* | Tekayla |
| Tayshaunda | Tazzeonia | Te'nasia | Teahni | Teaysha | Tehyen | Tekeira |
| Tayshaunna | Tchisa Madalene | Te'naya | Teaira *(0.01)* | Techell | Tei'eonne | Tekera |
| Tayshee | Te | Te'nazja | Teairee | Tecoreia | Teia *(0.01)* | Tekeria |
| Tayshia | Te Asia | Te'nelle | Teairra *(0.02)* | Tecoria | Teiana | Tekerria |
| Tayshonna | Te Ki'rah | Te'nija | Teairra-Marie | Ted'naysia | Teiarra | Tekeya |
| Taysia *(0.01)* | Te Naria | Te'nijah | Teairria | Teda | Teigan *(0.01)* | Tekiah |
| Taysia-Keera | Te Nasia | Te'niya | Teaisha | Tedaisa | Teige | Tekilha |
| Taytan | Te'a | Te'niyah | Teaja | Teddi | Teigen | Tekira |
| Taytanna | Te'aera | Te'nya | Teajah | Teddrianna | Teighan | Tekira Adeonne |
| Tayte | Te'ahnah | Te'nyia | Teajuana | Teddy | Teighn | Tekiyah |
| Taytem | Te'airra | Te'ojanae | Teakin | Tedia | Teigyn | Tekla |
| Tayten | Te'aja | Te'ona | Teakowa | Tedjanae | Teiha | Tekoa |
| | Te'ajha | Te'onia | Teal | Tedre'a | Teija | Tekoah |
| | | Te'onna | Teala | Tedriona | Teila | Tekoya |

Tekoyia
Tekyhia
Tekyra
Tekze
Tel'nesha
Tela (0.01)
Telaciya
Telah
Telaja
Telajha
Telaya
Telayjah
Telayjia
Teleah
Teleia
Telena
Telena Martha
Teley'a
Teleya
Teli
Telia
Teliah
Teliana
Telicia
Teliesha
Telijah
Telilah
Telina
Telise
Telisha
Telissa
Teliyah
Telleigh
Teller
Tellise
Tellissa
Tellita
Teloris
Telsa
Telsey
Telucia
Telyric
Telysa
Telysia
Telyssa
Temaleti
Temar
Temara
Temaria
Temarie
Temarra
Tember
Tembra

Tembreanna
Tembur
Temeisha
Temera
Temia
Temiah
Temidoluwa
Temika
Temilola
Temiloluwa
Temima
Temira
Temitope
Temitopeoluwa
Temiyah
Temneat
Temoni
Temonnie
Tempal
Temperance
Temperence
Tempest (0.01)
Temple
Temprance
Temuulen
Temya
Temyah
Temyia
Temyrian
Ten Sumyah
Tena
Tenae
Tenaeya
Tenaisha
Te-Naizha
Tenaj
Tenalya
Tenashia
Tenasia
Tenay
Tenaya
Tenaye
Tenayia
Tenayja
Tené
Tenea
Teneah
Teneal
Tenealle
Tenearia
Tenedja
Tenee
Teneiah

Teneice
Teneil
Tenenke
Tenerika
Tenese
Tenesha
Teneya
Tenger
Tenhiya
Tenia
Teniah
Tenicka
Tenieh
Tenijah
Tenille
Teniola
Tenise
Tenisha (0.01)
Tenitta
Teniya
Te-Niya
Teniyah
Teniyia
Tenizee
Tenjah
Tenlee
Tenleigh
Tenley (0.02)
Tenly
Tennaya
Tennessa
Tennessee
Tennessen
Tennessy
Tennia
Tennie
Tennille
Tennison
Tennleigh
Tennley
Tennya
Tennyson
Tensaye
Tenslee
Tensoelhamo
Tenya
Tenzin (0.02)
Teo
Teobane
Teo-Djiamal
Teodora
Teodora-
  Cristina

Te-Ona
Teona (0.01)
Teondria
Teonia
Teonie
Teonika
Teonna (0.01)
Teonnie
Teonté
Teonti
Teonya
Tep-Krishna
Tequa'yah
Tequila (0.01)
Tequirra
Tequoia
Ter'dejah
Ter'kiraon
Ter'koiyah
Ter'mya
Ter'quyanna
Ter'vonna
Tera (0.02)
Terache
Terae
Terah
Terai
Teraii
Teralyn
Teralynn
Teranika
Terannikia
Teras
Terasa
Tercora
Terece
Tereedra
Tereeq
Tereia Janea
Terel
Tereliz
Terena
Terenity Ja'vonii
Terensha
Tererra
Teresa (0.20)
Teresa Jesus
  Guadalupe
Terese
Teresha
Teresita (0.01)
Teressa (0.01)
Teresse

Tereyn
Tereza
Terezia
Terezsa
Teri (0.01)
Teri'ya
Teria
Teriah
Teriana (0.01)
Terianna
Teriasia
Terica
Tericka
Terikah
Terikka
Terilyn
Teri-Lynn
Terilynn
Terin
Terina
Terinn
Terionné
Terisa
Terissa
Teriyah
Teriyana
Terkira
Terlynn
Termari
Termarion
Terme
Termira
Ternayja
Ternika
Terniya
Teron
Teronna
Terr'esha
Terra (0.04)
Terra Jo
Terrace
Terracina
Terrah
Terralisia
Terralyn
Terralynn
Terrameka
Terran
Terrance
Terranesha
Terranique
Terraniya
Terrasia

Terraya
Terrayah
Terre
Terreka
Terrell
Terren
Terren T'yna
Terrena
Terresa
Terrhyon
Terrí
Terri (0.03)
Terri Ann
Terri Anne
Terri'elle
Terri'onna
Terria
Terriah
Terriali
Terrian
Terriana (0.01)
Terri-Ann
Terrianna (0.01)
Terri-Anne
Terriauna
Terriaunna
Terrica
Terricka
Terrie
Terriea
Terriel
Terrietta
Terrika
Terrille
Terrilyn
Terri-Lynn
Terrilynne
Terrin
Terrina
Terrinesha
Terrinisha
Terriny
Terrion
Terriona
Terrionna
Terris
Terrisha
Terrisonah
Terrissa
Terriuana
Terriya
Terriyah
Terriyah-Renee

Terriyana
Terry (0.01)
Terry'ona
Terryana
Terry-Ann
Terryanna
Terrycinia
Terryl
Terry-Lyne
Terryn
Terrynaia
Terryne
Terrynn
Teruni
Tervanna
Tervian
Teryana
Terykah
Teryn (0.01)
Teryoná
Terzah
Tes
Tes'cionna
Tesa (0.01)
Tesalynn
Tescia
Teshaiya
Teshara
Teshauna
Teshawn
Teshio
Teshirah
Tesia
Tesiah
Tesla (0.01)
Tesla Ann Mary
Tesla Aurora
Teslea
Teslin
Teslyn
Tesneem
Tesnem
Tesnim
Tesnime-Farah
Tess (0.17)
Tessa (0.52)
Tessa Maria
Tessa Marie
Tessa-Gene
Tessah (0.01)
Tessalee
Tessalonica
Tessalyn

| | | | | | | |
|---|---|---|---|---|---|---|
| Tessa-Maika | Teynan | Thaiyanna | Thaomy | Theodora *(0.01)* | Thiowa | Thuytien |
| Tessa-Rae | Teyona | Thajmara | Thaqueena | Theolyn | Thireytaa | Thuy-Tien |
| Tesse | Teyoncé | Thalassa | Thara | Theona | Thirshikka | Thy |
| Tessi | Teyondria | Thalaya | Thara Naisha | Theoni | Thirza | Thy Thy |
| Tessia | Teyoni | Thaleia | Thara-Gaelle | Theonie | Thisbe | Thy'nasha |
| Tessica | Teyonna | Thalene | Tharah-Alexia | Theonna | Thishan | Tionna |
| Tessie | Teyrissa | Thalia *(0.16)* | Tharuna | Theory | Thishana | Thyara |
| Tessla | Teyss | Thalia Marie | Tharyn | Theresa *(0.15)* | Thivya | Thyatira |
| Tesslee | Teyuon | Thalia Rose | Tharza | Theresalynn | Thiwara | Thyfani |
| Tesslin | Teyva | Thalia-Lynn | Thasmita | Theresa-Marie | Thiyana | Thyla |
| Tesslina | Tezakiyah | Thaliana | That | Thérèse | Thiyanna | Thyme |
| Tessly | Jasminj | Thalianna | Thathiayanne | Therese *(0.03)* | Tho | Thyonna |
| Tesslyn | Tezelli | Thalicia | Thatiana | Theresia | Tho'mya | Thyra |
| Tesslynn | Teziah | Thalie *(0.01)* | Thatiyana | Thereza | Tho'mysha | Thyrza |
| Testiny | Tezla | Thalie-Anne | Thavie | Theria | Thomaria | Thythy |
| Tesudia | Tezoyia | Thalina | Thavita | Therian | Thomas | Thyziri |
| Tetchong | Tezzie | Thalissa | Thavy | Therin | Thomasin | Ti |
| Tetiana | Th'nasia | Thalissia | Thayana | Thermya | Thomasina | Ti Aisia |
| Tetlee | Tha'lesha | Thalita | Thayden | Theron | Thomasine | Ti Asia |
| Tettra | Tha'savia | Thaliya | Thayina | Therry | Thomasja | Ti Jayla |
| Tettrina | Thaana | Thaliyah | Thayna | Theryn | Thomassina | Ti Marilyn |
| Teula | Thabisile | Thallia | Thays | Theryza | Thomawney | Tí Yana |
| Teva | Thabiso | Thaly *(0.01)* | Thaysha | Thesha | Thomeisha | Ti'aira |
| Tevan | Thaddaeus | Thalya | Thayshaly | Theshyra | Thomesha | Ti'ana |
| Tevelyn | Thadea | Thalyanne | Thaysse | Thessaly | Thomeshia | Ti'andrea |
| Tevin | Thadia | Tha-Lye | Thayvin | Theta | Thomia | Ti'anna |
| Tevini | Thadjina | Thalyiah | Théa | Thevy | Thomika | Ti'anye |
| Tevy | Thaé | Thalyssa | Thea *(0.05)* | Theynuga | Thomisia | Ti'arah |
| Tevyn | Thaelen | Thamara | Thea Angela | Theysha | Thomnia | Ti'arra |
| Tewana | Thai | Thamia | Thea Gladys | Thi | Thomora | Ti'asia |
| Texanie | Thai Dra | Thamin | Theadora | Thi Huynh Mai | Thomya | Ti'aundria |
| Texus | Thaianna | Thammy | Theadosia | Thi Phuong Anh | Thora | Ti'ausha |
| Teya *(0.02)* | Thaicianna | Thamy | Theadra | Thi Quynh Ann | Thracie | Ti'azia |
| Teya Bea-Y | Thaidyn | Thanaa | Theama | Thi Thi | Thraya | Ti'chara |
| Teyadora | Thai-Kennedy | Thanachcha | Theandra | Thia | Thressa | Ti'chianna |
| Teyah *(0.01)* | Thaila | Thanae | Theano | Thiana | Thrisha | Ti'erra |
| Teyana | Thailand | Thanai | Theanujaah | Thianna | Thrynna | Ti'imbra |
| Teyanah | Thaileah | Thanairy | Theany | Thianyka Paris | Thu *(0.01)* | Ti'jah |
| Teyanna *(0.01)* | Thailee | Thandi | Theary | Thida | Thuc Doan | Ti'jai |
| Teyara | Thailey | Thandie | Theasijah | Thien | Annie | Ti'jay |
| Teygan | Thai-Li | Thanh | Theerthaa | Thien Tam | Thuc Vy | Ti'keirah |
| Teyhlor | Thailia | Thanh-Lan | Theia | Thien-Huong | Thu-Hang | Ti'kereah |
| Teyina | Thailih | Thanhthanh | Thelea | Thien-Kim | Thulani | Ti'kiyah |
| Teyjah | Thailin | Thanh-Thuy | Thelesie | Thien-Nhi | Thunder | Ti'kya |
| Teyla | Thaily | Thania *(0.01)* | Thelia | Thiennhu | Thundra | Ti'kyah |
| Teylar | Thailyk | Thanisha | Thelma *(0.01)* | Thieny | Thung | Ti'kyia |
| Teyleisa | Thailyn | Thankful | Thelorm | Thien-Y-Allison | Thuraya | Ti'layah |
| Teylent | Thailynn | Thanmai | Thema | Thierry | Thurman | Ti'layzha |
| Teyler | Thaina | Thanna | Thembeka | Thiffany | Thursday | Ti'lee |
| Teylin | Thairyn | Thanya | Thembi | Thillaiampalan | Thutop | Ti'leria |
| Teylor | Thais | Thao | Themily | Thillainayaki | Thuy | Ti'liyah |
| Teylyn | Thaisha | Thao Vy | Thenneh | Thimas | Thuy Vy | Ti'maria |
| Teylynn | Thaislyn | Thao-Hien | Theo | Thi-Nhung | Thuya | Ti'meriya |

| | | | | | | |
|---|---|---|---|---|---|---|
| Ti'miya | Tia-Marie | Tiayanna | Tiersen | Tikah | Timajá | Tim-Nija |
| Ti'miyah | Tiameh | Tiayna | Tierstyn | Tikal | Timara (0.01) | Timnit |
| Ti'monica | Tiamorah | Tiazanna | Tieryn | Tikara | Timarah | Timniya |
| Ti'myah | Tian | Tiazee | Tierza | Tikari | Timaress | Timnyiah |
| Ti'myia | Tian Yu | Tibyan | Tiesha | Tikayla | Timaura | Timone |
| Ti'myra | Tiana (0.26) | Tica | Tieu-Quynh-My | Tikeria | Timauri | Timoni |
| Ti'nasia | Tianah | Ticcora | Tieya | Tikeriah | Timaya (0.01) | Timonnie |
| Ti'neeke | Tiana-Jade | Tice | Tieyanna | Tikerra | Timayae | Timor |
| Ti'nija | Tianan | Tichael | Tifa | Tikerria | Timayah | Timora |
| Ti'niyah | Tianda | Tichelle | Tifanasia | Tikia | Timber (0.01) | Timotha |
| Ti'nya | Tiandra | Ticia | Tifani | Tikierah | Timberland | Timothea |
| Ti'nyia | Tiandrea | Ticora | Tifanie | Tikierra | Timberlee | Timothy |
| Ti'ona | Tiani | Ticyannah | Tifanny | Tikiya | Timberleigh | Timothyean |
| Ti'onah | Tiann | Tida | Tifany | Tikoah | Timberley | Timouri |
| Ti'ondra | Tianna (0.17) | Tidence | Tifara | Tikya | Timberlie | Timya (0.01) |
| Ti'onni | Tianna Ali | Tie Layvia | Tifaya | Tikyla | Timberly | Timyah |
| Ti'quasha | Tiannah | Tie'meria | Tiffane | Tikyra | Timberlyn | Timyia |
| Ti'shaunna | Tianne | Tieanna | Tiffaney | Tikyriah | Timberlynn | Timyra |
| Ti'syiah | Tianni | Tieara | Tiffani (0.03) | Tila | Timea | Timyrah |
| Ti'teonna | Tiannia | Tiearney | Tiffanie (0.01) | Tilajah | Ti-Mecia | Timyrriah |
| Ti'tiana | Tiannie | Tiearra | Tiffani-Paige | Tilaya | Timeeka | Tin |
| Ti'tyonna | Tianti | Tiegan | Tiffanni | Tilda | Timeidra | Tina (0.12) |
| Ti'yana | Tianya | Tiegen | Tiffanny | Tilda-Jane | Timeka | Tina Marie |
| Ti'yanna | Tianyi | Tiegra | Tiffany (0.62) | Tilden | Timera | Tinaisha |
| Ti'yannah | Tianza | Tieler | Tiffany-Dawnmarie | Tilea | Timeria | Tinaja |
| Ti'yonna | Tiaolla | Tieleshia | | Tileciá | Timerra | Tinajah |
| Tia (0.20) | Tiara (0.17) | Tielyr | Tiffany-Lynn | Tilena | Timeya | Tina-Lise |
| Tia Asia | Tiara Laura | Tiembra | Tiffini | Tiler | Timi'ya | Tina-Marie |
| Tia Ayedon | Tiara Marie | Tien | Tiffiny | Tilethea | Timia (0.02) | Tinamarie |
| Tia Lee | Tiarah | Tiena | Tiffylane | Tiley | Timiah | Tinan |
| Tia Lynn | Tiaralynn | Tienery | Tifiantea | Tilia | Timiaya | Tinarah |
| Tia Rosalee | Tiaramari | Tienesha | Tifini | Tiliyah | Timie | Tinaria |
| Tia'miyah | Tiare | Tienna | Tigen | Tillana | Timijiana | Tinasha |
| Tia'wanna | Tiareanna | Tiensa | Tiger | Tillanea | Timilyn | Tinashe |
| Tia-Devona | Tiareht | Tiera (0.01) | Tiger Lily | Tillarah | Timirah | Tinasica |
| Tiaerria | Tiaret | Tierah | Tigerlilli | Tilli | Timita | Tinay |
| Tiah | Tiareyana | Tierani | Tigerlilly | Tillia | Timiya | Tinaya |
| Tiahjia | Tiari | Tierany | Tigerlily | Tillie (0.01) | Timiyah | Tinazjha |
| Tiahma | Tiarra (0.03) | Tiergan | Tigidankay | Tilliyah | Timiyha | Tindell |
| Tiahna | Tiarrah | Tieriney | Tigis | Tillmon'ie | Timlasia | Tindra |
| Tiahona | Tiarri | Tierna | Tigst | Tilly | Timlony | Tinera |
| Tiahra | Tiasha | Tiernan | Tiguida | Tilsley | Timmari | Tinesha |
| Tiaira | Tiasia | Tiernee | Tihanna | Tilyana | Timmariah | Tineya |
| Tiajah | Tiasiah | Tiernen | Tihona Elizbeth | Tilynn | Latoya | Ting |
| Tiajha | Tiasjah | Tierney (0.02) | Tiinesha | Tim'era | Timmea | Ting Xue |
| Tiaka | Tiatyana | Tierni | Tiirnyn-Brynn | Tim'irra | Timmerian | Ting-Ting |
| Tiala | Tiauna (0.01) | Tierny | Tijah | Tim'mia | Timmi | Tinia |
| Tialeah | Tiaunna | Tieronay | Tijana | Tim'mya | Timmia | Tinijah |
| Tialia | Tiaunta | Tierra (0.07) | Tijarah | Tim'taeshaj | Timmie | Tinila |
| Tialya | Tiaurá | Tierrah | Tijerria | Timagaha | Timmya | Tinisha |
| Tiamani | Tiawna | Tierralynn | Tijina | Timaiah | Timna | Tinisia |
| Tiamara | Tiawnna | Tierrany | Tijona | Timairah | Timnah | Tinity |
| Tiamarie | Tiaya | Tierre | Tika | Timaiya | Timnaisa | Tiniya |

| | | | | | | |
|---|---|---|---|---|---|---|
| Tiniyah | Tirzah (0.02) | Tiyarnnah-Kylie | Tocarra | Tomarrow | Tondalaya | Tore |
| Tinizee | Tirzariah | Tiyauna | Toccara (0.01) | Tomasa | Toné | Toree |
| Tinlee | Tish'jhaya | Tiye | Toccarra | Tomasia | Toneé | Torekca |
| Tinleigh | Tisha | Tiyiah | Tochi | Tomasue | Toneeyah | Torella |
| Tinley | Tishairie | Tiyjah | Tocrara | Tomaura | Toneija | Torence |
| Tinnley | Tishan | Tiylee | Todaisa | Tomeah | Tonejah | Toreona |
| Tinslee | Tishana | Tiyler | Toddá | Tomee | Tonesha | Torey |
| Tinsley (0.01) | Tishantris | Tiylisha | Toddai | Tomeecia | Tonetta | Tori (0.31) |
| Tinslie | Tishaun | Tiyona | Toddionya | Tomeira | Toni (0.09) | Tori Ann |
| Tinyjah | Tishawna | Tiyoni | Ashtynn | Tomeka | Tonia | Toria |
| Tinzlee | Tisheanna | Tiyonia | Toddkayla | Tomeris | Toniá | Toriah |
| Tinzley | Tishell | Tiyonna | Todja'nae | Tometria | Toniah | Torian |
| Tiodocia | Tishika | Tiyonni | Todjanae | Tomeya | Toniana | Toriana (0.01) |
| Tioga | Tishina | Tiyonnie | Todjiera | Tomeyka | Toni-Ann | Torianna (0.01) |
| Tiojjia | Tishnya | Tiyra | Todleauna | Tomi (0.01) | Tonice | Torianna- |
| Tiombe | Tishshara | Ti-Yuna | Togiva | Tomi'ona | Tonie | Georgia |
| Tion | Tishunti | Tizariah | Tohvia | Tomia (0.01) | Toniesha | Torianne |
| Tiona (0.01) | Tishyah | Tizeta | Tohy'ree | Tomiah | Toni-Foladele | Toribia |
| Tionah | Tishyla | Tizhaunna | Toi | Tomie | Tonihya | Torica |
| Tiondra | Tisjea Adell | Tiziana | Toi'yuan | Tomiko | Tonija | Torie (0.01) |
| Tione | Tisya | Tizibet | Toiree | Tomiwa | Tonika | Toriell |
| Tionesha | Tita | Tizjae | Tojeria | Tomiya | Toni-Marie | Torielle |
| Tioni | Titera | Tj'ana | Toka | Tomiyah | Tonimay | Torielynn |
| Tionie | Titiana | Tjoet | Tokala | Tomjai | Tonique | Torii |
| Tionis | Titianna | Tkala | Tokarah | Tomka | Tonisha (0.01) | Torika |
| Tionna (0.03) | Titiaunia | T-Keria | Tokeria | Tommí | Toniya | Toril |
| Tionne (0.01) | Titilayo | Tkeyah | Toko | Tommi (0.01) | Toniyah | Tori-Lee |
| Tionni | Titiyanna | Tkyhia | Tola | Tommie (0.01) | Tonja | Torin |
| Tionnia | Titrit | Tlalnantzin | Tolani | Tommiea | Tonna | Torina |
| Tionnie | Tityanna | Tlaly | Tolby | Tommiesha | Tonnetta | Torince |
| Tionta | Tiuana | Tlitha | Toleen | Tommiko | Tonnie | Torionna |
| Tipatipa | Tiuanna | Tliya | Toleesia | Tommilynn | Tonniea | Torlisa |
| Tiphaine | Tiuni | Tmador | Tolina | Tommiya | Tonniesha | Tornash |
| Tiphani | Tivara | Tmarryannha | Tolis | Tommiyah | Tonnique | Torneshia |
| Tiphanie | Tivia | Tmiyah | Tolleigh | Tommy | Tonsaieronhiast | Torr'aijah |
| Tiphany | Tivian | Tneen | Tolor | Tommyah | arath | Torra |
| Tiquasia | Tivona | Tniyah | Toluca | Tommyra | Tony | Torrae |
| Tiqueria | Tivonne | To Nay | Tolulope | Tomnesha | Tonya (0.03) | Torrance (0.01) |
| Ti-Quetta | Tivonnie | To Nguyen | Toluwalayo | Tomoko | Tonyae | Torre |
| Tiquori | Tivorcia | To'ney | Toluwalayomi | Tomorah | Tonyanisha | Torrea |
| Tiqurria | Tiy'uana | To'niyah | Toluwani | Tomorrow | Tonyiah | Torrecia |
| Tira | Tiya (0.01) | To'riah | Toluwanimi | Tomunisha | Tonyla | Torree |
| Tirah | Tiyaben | Toakase | Toly-Anne | Tomya | Tonynae | Torren |
| Tiranie | Tiyah | Toba | Tolyn | Tomysha | Tonyzha | Torrence (0.01) |
| Tirhaya | Tiyaja | Tobeigh | Tom'esha | Ton'nasia | Tooba | Torrencia |
| Tirina | Tiyajané | Tobey | Tomaaliyah | Tonae | Topanga (0.01) | Torres |
| Tirion | Tiyana (0.01) | Tobi (0.01) | Tomacina | Tonahja | Topaz | Torrey |
| Tirna | Tiyanah | Tobiah | Tomaira | Tonajah | Topenga | Torri (0.02) |
| Tirneai | Tiyandra | Tobie | Tomara | Tonajaha | Tor'lanedria | Torriana |
| Tirnity | Tiyanea | Tobilola | Tomara-Fawn | Tonasha | Tora | Torrianna |
| Tirrany | Tiyanetkw | Tobin | Tomari | Tonayah | Tora'nisha | Torrié |
| Tirsa | Tiyanna (0.01) | Toby (0.04) | Tomaria | Tonayja | Torah | Torrie (0.02) |
| Tirza | Tiyara | Tocarayna | Tomariia | Tonazia | Torance | Torrin |

| | | | | | | |
|---|---|---|---|---|---|---|
| Torrion | Tra'laeziah | Tralexia | Trashaly | Tre'zaryia | Trenajah | Trevalynn |
| Torrionna | Tra'miah | Tralia | Trasie | Tre'zure | Trenasia | Trevani |
| Torriyah | Tra'miya | Tralie | Traunda | Trea | Trenay | Treveia |
| Torriyanna | Tra'mya | Traliya | Travanique | Trea'zur | Trenecia | Treviana |
| Torry | Tra'nae | Tram | Travanna | Treajir | Trenee | Trevinna |
| Torryn | Tra'nasia | Tram-Anh | Travasia | Trealynne | Trenekia | Trevoiana |
| Torsha | Tra'naya | Tramani | Trave'ona | Treamell | Trenel | Trevor |
| Tory *(0.02)* | Tra'nhai | Tramari | Travena | Treana | Trenese | Trew |
| Torye | Tra'nia | Trameeka | Traveonna | Treann | Trenia | Trey |
| Toryn | Tra'niya | Trameisha | Travia | Treanna | Trenice | Trey'vianna |
| Toryse | Tra'niyah | Tramell | Travielle | Treanya | Trenidy | Treya |
| Toscane | Tra'nyah | Tramia | Traviona | Treaona | Treniece | Treyahna |
| Tosha | Tra'onna | Tramiya | Travis | Treasa | Trenika | Treyana |
| Toshera | Tra'shona | Tramiyah | Travisha | Treassa | Trenisha | Treyanna |
| Toshinia | Tra'shyah | Tramya | Traviyana | Treassare | Trenitee | Treyannah |
| Toshiya | Tra'taeje | Tran *(0.01)* | Traviyanna | Treasure *(0.06)* | Treniti | Treyhauna |
| Tosia | Tra'taevia | Trana'ya | Travonna | Treasuri | Trenitiy | Treylynn |
| Tosiana | Tra'vaisia | Tranae | Travonnah | Treasury | Trenitty | Treyonna |
| Tosja'nay | Tra'ziyah | Tranaé | Travonya | Treau | Trenity *(0.01)* | Treysi |
| Totiana | Trace | Tra-Naija | Tray | Treavonia | Treniya | Trezanque |
| Toti-Anna | Tracee | Tranaiya | Tray'nya | Treawna | Treniyah | Trezaria |
| Totsianna | Tracey *(0.02)* | Tranajia | Trayce | Treazure | Trenna | Trezure |
| Tottianna | Trachelle | Tranay | Trayianna | Trecarichi | Trennedy | Trezureé |
| Tottionna | Traci *(0.01)* | Tranayé | Traykhemis | Trecy | Trentity | Tri'niya |
| Totyona | Traciana | Tranaysha | Traylise | Tredena | Trenton | Tria |
| Tou Tou | Tracie *(0.01)* | Trance | Traynell | Tredia | Trenya | Triana *(0.01)* |
| Touleen | Tracie-Lynn | Tranea | Traynyce | Treena | Trenyah | Trianah |
| Touqa | Tracilyn | Tranece | Trayona | Treesa | Trenyce | Trianna *(0.01)* |
| Touriya | Tracsette | Tranecia | Trayonna | Trefena | Trenyia | Triany |
| Touty | Tracy *(0.06)* | Traneer | Trayronda | Trehonestie | Trenyla | Trianya |
| Tova *(0.01)* | Tracy Lee | Traneise | Trazahria | Treiona | Trereyonna | Trichelle |
| Tovah | Tracy-Lee | Tranell | Trazaria | Trejanae | Tresa | Tricia *(0.02)* |
| Tove | Tracylia | Tranese | Trazarrieya | Trejanai | Tresana | Tricia-Elza |
| Tovi | Tracy-Melanie | Trang | Trazidie | Trekaiya | Trescelle | Tricianne |
| Tovia | Tracyonna | Tranh | Trazydie | Trelana | Treseanna | Tricity |
| Towanda | Tradijah | Traniah | Tré Vonna | Trelani | Treselle | Tricyanah |
| Townley | Trae'anna | Tranice | Tre'auna | Trelawny | Tresha | Trikia |
| Townsend | Trae'shona | Tra-Niece | Tre'dreona | Trelaya | Treshanae | Trillian |
| Toy | Traeh | Traniha | Tre'johnna | Trellasia | Treshelle | Trillion |
| Toy Aii | Traelyn | Tranika | Tre'jor | Trellis | Tresher | Trillium |
| Toy Ann | Traelynn | Tranira | Tre'jour | Tremaya | Treshonna | Trimya |
| Toya | Traeva | Tranisha | Tre'kasia | Tremayia | Treshure | Trina *(0.03)* |
| Toylin | Trai'lisha | Tranity | Tre'laya | Tremia | Tressa *(0.02)* | Trinadee |
| Tpanga | Trail-Dancer | Traniya | Tre'lyn | Tremiah | Tressen | Trinadi |
| Tra Shauna | Trailee | Traniyah | Tre'meshia | Tremieah | Tressia | Trinady |
| Tra'daysha | Trajan | Trannon | Tre'miaya | Tremoni | Tressica | Trinae |
| Tra'dezmia | Trakhia | Tranya | Tre'miryah | Tremya | Tressie | Trinajah |
| Tra'kayla | Trakyia | Tranyah | Tre'mya | Tren | Tresta | Trinatee |
| Tra'keera | Tralaka | Tranyia | Tre'myia | Trena | Trestan | Trinati |
| Tra'keira | Tralana | Tranyla | Tre'nace | Trenadi | Tresuar | Trinatie |
| Tra'keyah | Tralayah | Traqira | Tre'naisha | Trenady | Tresur | Trinaty |
| Tra'kia | Tralee | Trasairya | Tre'ness | Trenae | Treutlen | Trinaya |
| Tra'kyrrah | Traleigh | Traschelle | Tre'sur | Trenaisa | Treva | Trinayah |

| | | | | | | |
|---|---|---|---|---|---|---|
| Trinayaraye | Trish *(0.01)* | Trixie | Trynytie | Tucker-Anne | Tvl | Ty'asya |
| Trinda | Trisha *(0.07)* | Triyasree | Tryp | Tucson | Twa'naja | Ty'auna |
| Trineice | Trisha Camille | Trnyhia | Tryphena | Tudora | Twainneshia | Ty'aune |
| Trinell | Trishala | Troanna | Tryphosa | Tue | Twalijah | Ty'aziah |
| Trinette | Trishathi | Troi | Tryreeonna | Tuesday *(0.01)* | Twan'nae | Ty'azijah |
| Trinety | Trishauna | Troi'yana | Trysha | Tuga | Twan'niyah | Ty'breonna |
| Trineyah | Trishaunna | Tronaé | Tryska | Tukirqi | Twanaeja | Ty'cara |
| Trinh | Trishcelle | Troniece | Trysta *(0.01)* | Tukiya | Twanajah | Ty'cennaya |
| Trini | Trishell | Tronique | Trystan *(0.01)* | Tula *(0.01)* | Twanasha | Ty'chelle |
| Trinia | Trishelle *(0.01)* | Troniya | Trystanne | Tulani | Twanda | Ty'cianna |
| Triniaté | Trishena | Trónyah | Trysten *(0.01)* | Tulasi | Twaney | Ty'ciara |
| Trinicie | Trishia | Troy | Trystian | Tuleen | Twanisha | Ty'cinta |
| Trinidad | Trishiana | Troya | Trystin *(0.01)* | Tuley | Twienshai | Ty'cionna |
| Trinide | Trishita | Troyanna | Trystin Nicole | Tuline | Twila *(0.01)* | Ty'coria |
| Trinidea | Trishitha | Troyell | Trystyn | Tullia | Twilla | Ty'daisha |
| Trinidee | Trishma | Troyonah | Tsaday | Tullian | Twinkle | Ty'drianna |
| Trinidi | Trishna | Troyonna | Tsafira | Tully | Twinyja | Ty'eisha |
| Trinidy *(0.01)* | Trishten | Tru *(0.03)* | Tsai | Tulsi | Twolla | Ty'enna |
| Triniece | Trishtin | Truc | Tsalie | Tumaris | Twonaisha | Ty'era |
| Trinika | Trishtyn | Truce | Tsarah | Tumberlynn | Twybreia | Ty'eria |
| Trinita | Trisitty | Trucilla | Tsavo | Tumi | Twyla *(0.01)* | Ty'ese |
| Trinité | Trisity | Trudi | Tschuashua- | Tumra | Twylah | Ty'esha |
| Trinitee *(0.02)* | Trissa | Trudie | Yiikou | Tunalaaq | Twylla | Ty'hara |
| Trinitey | Trissharra | Trudy *(0.01)* | Tseday | Tu-Nhi | Ty *(0.01)* | Ty'ilor |
| Triniti *(0.05)* | Trissta | True | Tsedenia | Tuni | Ty Anna | Ty'iona |
| Triniti Lee | Trista *(0.16)* | Trué | Tselmuun | Tunita | Ty Keria | Ty'ionne |
| Trinitie *(0.01)* | Tristah | Trueth | Tsengyang | Tuniza | Ty Kia | Ty'jada |
| Trinitii | Tristan *(0.05)* | Truett | Tshari | Tunu | Ty Lasia | Ty'jae |
| Trinitiy | Tristania | Truey | Tshelsea-Anna | Tuong | Ty Lynn | Ty'jahnae |
| Trinitty | Tristann | Truitt | Tsheng | Tuonganh | Ty Rhwanda | Ty'janae |
| Trinity *(2.60)* | Tristanni | Trulee | Tshia | Tuong-Van | Ty' Zeria | Ty'janay |
| Trinity Carmen | Tristany | Truley | Tshiabsi | Tuong-Vi | Ty'aanna | Ty'janique |
| Trinity-Ann | Tristen *(0.05)* | Trulie | Tshiya | Tupou | Ty'airh | Ty'jarvia |
| Trinity-Lynn | Tristenne | Truly *(0.01)* | Tsion | Turan | Ty'airie | Ty'jeahna |
| Trinity-Raven | Tristeonna | Trulyn | Tsithembile | Turina | Ty'aisa | Ty'jha |
| Trinity-Star | Tristian *(0.01)* | Trusha | Tsiyon | Turner | Ty'aisha | Ty'jira |
| Triniyah | Tristiana | Trushai | Tsneem | Turquoise | Ty'aivian | Ty'junae |
| Trinka | Tristianne | Trusten | Tsoni | Tursantini | Ty'aizjah | Ty'junay |
| Trinnie | Tristien | Trustess | Tsophie | Tuscany | Ty'aja | Ty'kala |
| Trinnity | Tristin *(0.03)* | Truth | Tsotewe | Tusekire | Ty'ajah | Ty'kara |
| Trinnum | Tristina *(0.01)* | Truus | Tstarria | Tushawn | Ty'ana | Ty'keasha |
| Trinny | Tristine | Trycia Annabelle | Tsukuru | Tushiyah | Ty'anah | Ty'keeya |
| Trintity | Tristiny | Trynadee | Tsunai | Tussanawaluck | Ty'ann | Ty'keia |
| Trintiy | Tristiona | Trynatee | Tsunami | Tussy | Ty'anna | Ty'keila |
| Trinty | Triston | Trynaty | Tsyonne | Tuttapon | Ty'annah | Ty'kera |
| Trinya | Tristonna | Trynda | Tu Anh Alicia | Tuyet | Ty'ara | Ty'keria |
| Triona | Tristun | Trynde | Tu'niya | Tuyet Nhi | Ty'asea | Ty'kerionn |
| Trionna | Tristy | Trynica | Tu'shay | Stacey | Ty'asha | Ty'kerria |
| Tripata | Tristyn *(0.03)* | Trynitee | Tuara | Tuyet-Trang | Ty'asia *(0.01)* | Ty'kerriah |
| Triphene | Tristyne | Tryniti | Tuba | Tuzdae | Ty'asia Na'riah | Ty'keya |
| Triphinia | Tristynn | Trynity *(0.01)* | Tubrina | Tuzhiuh | Monique | Ty'ki |
| Tripta | Trivia | Trynnity | Tucara | Tvisha | Ty'asiah | Ty'kia |
| Tripti | Trivina | Trynyn | Tucker | Tvishi | Ty'asja | Ty'kiara |

| | | | | | | |
|---|---|---|---|---|---|---|
| Ty'kiera | Ty'quincyia | Ty'zeria | Tyciara | Tyhlar | Tykeaja | Tyleaha |
| Ty'kierra | Ty'quisha | Ty'ziana | Tycie | Tyhleyah | Tykeema | Tyleasha |
| Ty'kierria | Ty'qwasia | Tyá | Tycorria | Tyhrena | Tykeira | Tylecia |
| Ty'kira | Ty'ra | Tya (0.01) | Tydasza | Tyi Dae | Tykendra | Tylee (0.01) |
| Ty'kirah | Ty'reana | Tya'na | Tydericka | Tyi'tianna | Tykendrion | Tyleeah |
| Ty'kiria | Ty'reasure | Tyaaliyah | Tydia | Tyia | Tykenya | Tyleecia |
| Ty'kiyra | Ty'reaunna | Tyah | Tydrianna | Tyiana | Tykera | Tyleena |
| Ty'kyla | Ty'ree | Tyahja | Tye | Tyianna | Tykeraj | Tyleese |
| Ty'laijha | Ty'rejuana | Tyahna | Tye'juanay | Tyierra | Tykeria (0.01) | Tyleeyah |
| Ty'laila | Ty'reona | Tyaina | Tye'kyirah | Tyiesha | Tykerra | Tylei |
| Ty'laisha | Ty'reyaunna | Tyaira | Tye'meshia | Tyijhia | Ty-Kerria | Tyleia |
| Ty'lasia | Ty'reyonna | Tyairah | Tye'ya | Tyikerria | Tykerria | Tyleigh |
| Ty'lee | Ty'riah | Tyaisha | Tyeecia | Tyiler | Tykevia | Tyleigha |
| Ty'leeria | Ty'rianna | Tyajah | Tyeela | Tyina | Tykeyah | Tyleisha |
| Ty'leia | Ty'riona | Tyalia | Tyeena | Tyinah | Tykeydria | Tyleisheya |
| Ty'leiah | Ty'rone | Tyana (0.02) | Tyeesha | Tyinna | Tykhia | Tyleiya |
| Ty'leyah | Ty'shae | Tyanah | Tyeisha | Tyion | Tykia | Tylen |
| Ty'lia | Ty'shai | Tyanaja | Tyeishia | Tyiona | Tykiara | Tylena |
| Ty'liah | Ty'shanay | Tyandra | Tyelee | Tyionna | Tykiera | Tylene |
| Ty'lisha | Ty'shann | Tyani | Tyeleigh | Tyira | Tykierea | Tyler (0.13) |
| Ty'liyah | Ty'shawn | Tyania | Tyeler | Tyisai | Tykierria | Tyleriah |
| Ty'lyn | Ty'shawna | Tyann | Tyelia | Tyisha | Tykimah | Tylermarie |
| Ty'maria | Ty'shdrea | Tyanna (0.04) | Tyemeria | Tyja | Tykionna | Tyler-Rose |
| Ty'merriah | Ty'shea | Tyanne | Tyenisha | Ty-Jae | Tykira | Tyleshia |
| Ty'mya | Ty'shelle | Tyar | Tyenna | Tyjah | Tykirra | Tyley |
| Ty'nae | Ty'shema | Tyara (0.01) | Tyeon | Tyjah'a | Tykiya | Tyleya |
| Ty'naija | Ty'sheria | Tyarah | Tyerah | Tyjahnae | Tykota | Tylia (0.01) |
| Ty'naisa | Ty'she-Una | Tyarra | Tyerena | Tyjairria | Tykyra | Tyliah (0.01) |
| Ty'nasha | Ty'shia | Tyashia | Tyerin | Tyjamira | Tyla (0.04) | Tyliana |
| Ty'nasia | Ty'shiyanna | Tyashia | Tyerney | Tyjanae | Tyla Abeni | Tylicia |
| Ty'nasjia | Ty'shonda | Diamond | Tyesa | Tyjanay | Tylagrace | Tylie (0.01) |
| Ty'nausha | Ty'shunti | Ty-Asia | Tyese | Tyjaniah | Tylah | Tyliea |
| Ty'nayia | Ty'tasia | Tyasia (0.02) | Tyesha (0.01) | Tyjanna | Tylaisha | Tylihya |
| Ty'naysha | Ty'teanna | Tyasiah | Tyeshia | Ty-Jay | Tylaja | Tylin |
| Ty'neatris | Ty'teonna | Tyasija | Tyetta | Tyjaya | Tyla-Marie | Tylindia |
| Ty'neice | Ty'teyaina | Tyasya | Tyeyonna | Tyjeerah | Tylan | Tylir |
| Ty'neise | Ty'tiana (0.01) | Tyaudra | Tyfanie | Tyjenae | Tylan Dwayne | Tylis |
| Ty'neshia | Ty'tianna | Tyauna | Tyfanny | Tyjenya | Tylana | Tylisa |
| Ty'nesia | Ty'tiara | Tyaunia | Tyffani | Tyjerrica | Tylandra | Tyliscia |
| Ty'nia | Ty'tienna | Ty-Aunna | Tygen | Tyjha | Tylandria | Tylise |
| Ty'niah | Ty'tiuana | Tyaunna | Tyger | Tyjhanae | Tylandriyah | Tylisha |
| Ty'nic | Ty'tyanna | Tyaveon | Tygina | Tyjharionna | Tylar (0.01) | Tylishaun |
| Ty'nique | Ty'uanna | Tyazia | Tygir-Lillia | Tyjiah | Tylashia | Tylisia |
| Ty'niya | Ty'unique | Tybia | Tyha | Tyjiauna | Tylasia | Tylissa |
| Ty'ona | Ty'unna | Tybreon | Tyhaiyrah | Tyjiri | Tylauna | Tyliviya |
| Ty'onah | Ty'yari | Tycambrice | Tyhanda | Tyjouna | Tylaya | Tyliyah (0.01) |
| Ty'onna | Ty'yawna | Tycee | Tyhara | Tyjuan | Tylayah | Tylor |
| Ty'qavia | Ty'yona | Tychandreana | Tyheerah | Tyjzae | Tylayla | Tylor-Marie |
| Ty'quashia | Ty'yonna | Tyché | Tyheira | Tykara | Tylazia | Tylydia |
| Ty'quasia | Ty'yonnah | Tychelle | Tyhesia | Tykaria | Tylea | Tylyn |
| Ty'quazhia | Ty'yunna | Tyciana | Tyhira | Tykaya | Tyleá | Tylynn (0.01) |
| Ty'queria | Ty'zaria | Tyciannaa | Tyhiya | Tykaydra | Tyleah (0.01) | Tylyr |

| | | | | | | |
|---|---|---|---|---|---|---|
| Tylyrhia | Tynequa | Tyramarie | Tysania | Tywanda | Ujala | Uniah |
| Tymaia | Tyner | Tyramorgn | Tysha | Tywreanna | Ukiah | Unica |
| Tymani | Tyneria | Tyranae | Tyshae | Tyy'shell | Uknique | Uniecia |
| Tymara | Tynese | Tyranique | Tyshai | Tyyana | Ul'azia | Unijah |
| Ty-Mare | Tynesh | Tyrannette | Tyshala | Tyyonna | Ula | Unikki |
| Tymari | Tynesha | Ty-Rayah | Tyshana | Tyza | Ulaina | Uniq'ueek |
| Tymarra | Tynesia | Tyraye | Tyshani | Tyzaiyah | Ulainna | Uniqke |
| Tymaya | Tynessa | Tyre'a | Tyshanna | Tyzay | Ulalume | Uniqua |
| Tymayi | Tynia *(0.01)* | Tyre'sha | Tyshanta | Tyzhane | Ulani | Uniquah Sa |
| Tymber | Tyniah | Tyrea | Tyshanti | Tyzhe | Ulanny | Uniqué |
| Tymberlee | Tynija | Tyreanna | Tyshaona | Tyzi | Ularia | Unique *(0.07)* |
| Tymberlyn | Tynijah | Tyreanu | Tyshara | Tzara | Ulethia | Unique Keynew |
| Tyme | Tynique | Tyreca | Tysharii | Tzarina | Ulita | Unity *(0.01)* |
| Tymeara | Tynisa | Tyree | Tyshauna | Tzeitl | Uliyana | Universe |
| Tymearis | Tynise | Tyreeana | Tyshauna | Tzeitty | Ulrieyah | Uniyah |
| Tymeka | Tynisha *(0.01)* | Tyreemah | Latonya | Tze-Jing | Ulrike | Unnathi |
| Tymera | Tynishia | Tyreeona | Tyshawanna | Tzipora *(0.01)* | Ulynis | Unnimaya |
| Tymerah | Tynlee | Tyreesha | Tyshawna | Tziporah | Ulyssa | Unycia |
| Tymeria | Tynley | Tyreeyah | Tyshawnda | Tzipporah | Ulyssia | Unyea |
| Tymesha | Tynli | Tyreeyonna | Ty-Shawnna | Tzirel *(0.01)* | Uma *(0.01)* | Unyqué |
| Tymeshia | Tynnise | Tyreka | Tyshay | Tziril | Umaema | Upala |
| Tymesia | Tynsley | Tyreke | Tyshelle | Tzirl | Umahiya | Upma |
| Tymia | Tynyah | Tyrekia | Tyshera | Tzivia | Umaima | Uptasia |
| Tymiah | Tyoaka | Tyren | Tyshia | Tzortel | Umaiza | Ura |
| Tymika | Tyoannia | Tyrené | Tyshianna | Tzvia | Umalkhar | Uranus |
| Tymikeyiona | Tyona | Tyrenee | Tyshiea | | Umamah | Urasia |
| Tymira | Tyondra | Tyreni | Tyshiera | | Umani | Urdia |
| Tymirrah | Tyoni | Tyreonna | Tyshine | | Umayma | Uri |
| Tymone | Tyonia | Tyreonna | Tyshona | ~ U ~ | Umayna | Uriah *(0.01)* |
| Tymothea | Tyonna *(0.01)* | Tyresa | Tyshonia | U'kari | Umayrah | Urias |
| Tyna | Tyonne | Tyresha | Tyson | U'kiyah | Umayyah | Uriel |
| Tynaesha | Tyori | Tyreshia | Tysoni | U'llyriah | Umeara | Uriele |
| Tynaiha | Tyornia | Tyressa | Tytania | U'nica Chna | Umi | Uririnoghene |
| Tynaija | Typhanie | Tyreyanna | Tytannia | U'nique | Umika | Urja |
| Tynairi | Tyqaisha | Tyreyonna | Tyteanna | U'nitee | Umilbeneen | Urjasree |
| Tynaisha | Tyqasia | Tyrez | Tyteanne | U'niyah | Um-Khathum | Urjita |
| Tynaja | Tyqeria | Tyria | Tyteeuna | U'nya | Ummayyah | Urmi |
| Tynajah | Tyquasha | Tyriah | Tyteonia | U'todrianna | Umme | Urmoni |
| Tynajiah | Tyquasia | Tyriana *(0.01)* | Tytiahnya | Uashia | Umna | Urrassia |
| Tynari | Tyquasiya | Tyrianna | Tytiana *(0.01)* | Uashtushkueu | Umneya | Urriya |
| Tynasha | Tyquasya | Tyrica | Tytianha | Uchechi | Umran | Ursula *(0.01)* |
| Tynashia | Tyquesha | Tyrina | Tytianna *(0.01)* | Udochadaé | Umunique | Urtina |
| Tynasia | Tyquiahna | Tyrionna | Tytiaona | Udochukwu | Un'dreana | Urtorria |
| Tynaya | Tyquira | Tyrisha | Tytiara | Udval | Una *(0.01)* | Urvi |
| Tyne | Tyquisha | Tyrissa | Tytiauna | Uelina | Unarya | Usha |
| Tynecia | Tyra *(0.16)* | Tyriyonna | Tytiona | Ugbad | Unaswi | Ushananthini |
| Tyneesha | Tyra'kel | Tyrne | Ty-Tionna | Ugenia | Undrea | Usher |
| Tyneeuh | Tyraah | Tyroneshia | Tytionna | Ugne | Undreanna | Ushna |
| Tyneisha | Tyrah *(0.01)* | Tyronica | Tyuna | Ugochi | Undreya | Usra |
| Tyneishia | Tyrai | Tyronique | Tyuonna | Ugochinyere | Undriya | Ustat |
| Tynel | Tyraiana | Tyronna | Tyveria | Uhlaya | Une | Ustina |
| Tynell | Tyra-Kai | Tyrra | Tywahna | Uhnasté | Unia | Uswah |

| | | | | | | |
|---|---|---|---|---|---|---|
| Utah | Vailyn | Valeriana | Valtagrace- | Vanetta | Vany | Vayla |
| Uy'niah | Vaimoana | Valérie |   Annie | Vanette | Vanya (0.01) | Vaylah |
| Uyen | Vaina Anais | Valerie (1.40) | Valyah | Vaneza | Vanyesa | Vayle |
| Uyen Tranh | Vairah | Valerie Faith | Valyn | Vanezjah | Vanysha | Vayley |
| Uyen Vy | Vaishaali | Valerie-Anne | Valyncia | Vanezza | Var'asia | Vaylyn |
| Uyenthy | Vaishali | Valerissa | Valynn | Vangelina | Var'niyah | Vayolete |
| Uyiosa | Vaishnavi (0.01) | Valerius | Valyntina | Vangelis | Varajaz-Marie | Vazaria |
| Uzmaan | Vaishnavy | Valeriya | Vamia | Vangie | Varayla | Vazquez |
| Uzoma | Vaishvi | Valery (0.06) | Vamika | Vani | Varbah | Ve'era |
| Uzziah | Vajra | Valerya | Van | Vania (0.01) | Varda | Ve'yonna |
| Uzziya | Vakeisha | Valerye | Van Anh Vanna | Vania | Vardhini | Veandra |
| | Vakeya | Valeryn | Vanae |   Alessandra | Varenya | Veanna |
| | Vakiah | Valeshia | Vanajaih | Vanicia | Varianne | Veannie |
| ~ V ~ | Vala | Valeska (0.01) | Vanamarie | Vaniea | Varikira | Vechny Jouly |
| | Valacha | Valexi | Vanashia | Vaniece | Varinder | Veda (0.03) |
| V'asja | Valamarie | Valexis | Vanasia | Vaniessa | Varinia | Vedette |
| V'miyah | Valancia | Valezka | Vanaya | Vanijia | Varnavi | Vedha |
| V'nina | Valanda | Valhala | Vancella | Vanika | Varniga | Vedika |
| V'niya | Valandra | Valhallah | Vanchesca | Vanilla | Varnika | Veditha |
| V'rajah | Valange | Valia | Vanda | Vanina | Varonda | Veeionee |
| V'shae | Valantina | Valiant | Vandaijiah | Vanique | Varsha (0.01) | Veena |
| V'yon | Valaree | Valicita | Vandaja | Vanisha | Varshini | Vega |
| Va | Valarie (0.02) | Valicity | Vanda-Jolye | Vanishia | Vartika | Vegas |
| Vá Niyah | Valasha | Validia | Vandalee | Vanita | Varvara | Veida |
| Va'lilliya | Valashia | Valieria | Vandana | Vaniti Jayda | Varzidy | Veil |
| Va'nayzia | Valasia | Valilah | Vandessa | Vanitta | Vasana | Veiola |
| Va'nesa | Valaurie | Valinci | Vandy | Vanity | Vasantha | Veisha |
| Va'niya | Valaysa | Valinia | Vanecsha | Vaniya | Vascity | Vekaama |
| Va'shell | Valdar | Valissa | Vaned | Vaniyah | Vash | Vela |
| Va'yanna | Valdreidy | Valkyrie | Vaneese | Van-Khanh | Vash'ti | Velada |
| Vaani | Vale'lla | Vallanda | Vaneet | Vankira | Vashanti | Velaina |
| Vaanika | Valecia | Vallati | Vaneisha | Vann | Vashara | Velan |
| Vaanya | Valecianna | Vallee-Rae | Vaneja | Vanna | Vashay | Velandria |
| Vaari | Valedia | Valleri | Vanellie | Vannalei | Vashti (0.01) | Velane |
| Vaché | Valeina | Vallerie | Vanelly | Vannary | Vashun | Velanise |
| Vada (0.02) | Valeishka | Vallery | Vanelys | Vannesa (0.01) | Vasiah | Velaria |
| Vadaisha | Valen | Valleyciea | Vanerry | Vannessa (0.01) | Vasiliki (0.01) | Veleicia |
| Vadania | Valence | Valli | Vanesa (0.03) | Vannetta | Vasilisa | Velena |
| Vaeda | Valencia (0.04) | Valli Manaswini | Vanesha | Vannette | Vason | Velencia |
| Vaeila | Valencia-Lyd | Vallon | Vanesia | Vanneza | Vassilena | Velendi |
| Vaeja | Valenda | Vallori | Vanessa (2.18) | Vanohra | Vassiliki | Veleria |
| Vaelyn | Valenjudie | Vally | Vanessa Camille | Vanora | Vasty | Velexius |
| Vaelynn | Valentin | Vallyn | Vanessa Candy | Vanquinty | Vasundhara | Velicity |
| Vaera | Valentina (0.24) | Valmesha | Vanessa | Vanshell | Vata | Velina |
| Vahini | Valentina Sofia | Valora |   Gabriella | Vanshi | Vatia | Velita |
| Vahsti | Valentine | Valore | Vanessa Marie | Vanshika | Vatica | Velkin |
| Vahyna | Valeny | Valori | Vanessa-Bebe | Vantashia | Vaude | Vellani |
| Vai | Valenza | Valoria | Vanessah | Vantasia | Vaughn | Vellenia |
| Vaibhavi | Valera | Valorie (0.01) | Vanessa-Jade | Vantazma | Vaughn'nasia | Velma |
| Vaida | Valeree | Valory | Vanessa-Lee | Vante'sia | Vaughn'nesha | Veloria |
| Vaidehi | Valerey | Valoure | Vanessea | Vanterria | Vava | Velouria |
| Vail | Valeri | Valquiria | Vanessia | Vantora | Vayda (0.01) | Velsie |
| Vaïla | Valeria (1.90) | Valree | Vanessyah | Vantrease | Vayden | Velvie |

Velzy
Ven'lencia
Vena
Vendela
Vendetta
Venecia (0.01)
Veneeta
Venerina
Venesa
Venesia
Venessa (0.01)
Venetta
Venezeula
Venezuela
Venianna
Venice (0.01)
Veniel
Venis
Venisa
Venise
Venisha
Venissa-Lyn
Venita
Venius
Venize
Venja
Venjazia
Venkata
Venkata Naga
Venkayya
Venla
Venna
Vennaysha
Venus (0.01)
Venus-Itzel
Venya
Venyce
Veona
Ver'kayla
Ver'million
Ver'naisa
Ver'shiyah
Vera (0.05)
Vera Xue Rou
Vera-An
Verah
Veralyn
Verana
Veranda
Verania
Veranika
Verannika
Verataylor

Verba
Vercina
Verda
Verdell
Verdondalena
Vered
Verena (0.01)
Verenice
Verenis
Verenise
Verenisse
Vergie
Verity (0.01)
Verkeisha
Verlinda
Verline
Vermarie
Vermarro
Verna (0.02)
Verna Lindsey
Vernae
Vernandra
Verndaja
Vernecia
Vernecya
Vernée
Vernesia
Vernessa
Vernetta
Vernette
Vernice
Vernicia
Vernija
Vernisha
Vernishia
Vernitrious
Verniya
Verniyah
Vernyah
Vero Oddel
Veroinca
Verona
Veroni
Veronica (0.56)
Veronica Clare
Veronica Jenny
Veronica Kelly
Veronica-Jayne
Veronicka
Veronik
Véronik
Veronika (0.03)
Véronique

Veronique (0.01)
Veronique-Maya
Véronyke
Verrah
Verriah
Versailles
Versavia
Verser
Vershay
Vershell
Versia
Versinda
Vertrecia
Veruca
Veruke
Veruza
Vesakhone
Vesna
Vesper
Vesscilia
Vesslei
Vessy
Vesta
Vestine
Vetta
Vetzaira
Vetzaveth
Veva
Veverlin
Veyandra
Veyanna
Veyara
Veyda
Veyonte
Veyounce
Vheda
Vhisia
Vi
Vi Anh
Vi'asia
Vi'dona
Via
Vialsy Lisseth
Vian
Viana
Vianay
Vianca (0.01)
Vianeith
Vianelis
Vianeth
Vianey (0.02)
Viangela

Vianice
Vianka
Vianna (0.01)
Vi-Anne
Vianne (0.01)
Viannee
Vianney (0.01)
Vianni
Vianny
Vibha
Vic'torya
Vicabeth
Viceiry
Vicenta
Vicenta Mae
Vicente
Viché
Vichelle
Vicidria
Vicitoria
Vickaina
Vickayla
Vickeisha
Vickey
Vicki (0.01)
Vickie (0.01)
Vicktoria
Vicky (0.09)
Vickylian
Vicky-Rose
Victasha
Victavia
Victocia
Victoire
Victoire Divine
Victor
Victorea
Victori
Victoria (3.77)
Victoria Anna
Victoria Anne
Victoria Faith
Victoria Kerry
Victoria Leigh
Victoria Nhu
Victoria Phuong-Tram
Victoria Ray
Victoria Rose
Victoria Sidney
Victoria Sum-Yee
Victoria W

Victoria-Alysee
Victoriah
Victoria-Lee
Victoria-Lissette
Victoria-Lynn
Victorian
Victoriana
Victoriane
Victorianna
Victoria-Rose
Victoria-Sandra
Victoria-Yesenia
Victorie
Victorinia
Victorionnah
Victoriya
Victory (0.01)
Victorya (0.01)
Victoryia
Victoya
Victyoria
Vida (0.01)
Vida Nathania
Vida Zian
Vidahlia
Vidal Angel
Vidalia
Videhi
Videl
Vidhi (0.01)
Vidhya
Vidlynn
Vidmahi
Vidula
Vidushi
Vidya
Vieira
Vien
Vieng Savanh
Vienna (0.04)
Vienne
Viera
Viergena
Vietta
Viet-Thy
Vigeline
Viha
Vihenna
Vijay
Vijaya Lakshmi
Vika
Vikayla
Vikesia

Viki
Vikki
Vikky
Viktoria (0.03)
Viktorianikol
Viktorie
Viktoriea
Viktorija
Viktoriya
Viktoriyah
Viktorya
Viky
Vilandrya
Vilayvanh
Vildan
Vilea
Vilen
Vilencia
Vilenda
Vileyka
Vilma
Vimala
Vimanna
Vimaris
Vina
Vinae
Vinay
Vincé
Vincee
Vincena
Vincent
Vincenza
Vincenzo
Vinchenza
Vinci
Vinciona
Vincy
Vindhya
Vinesa
Vinessa
Vinetta
Vinh
Vinia
Vinique
Vinisa
Vinisha
Viniyah
Vinkitta
Vinna
Vinny
Vinya
Vinyl
Vinzetta

Viod
Viola (0.02)
Violaine
Violena
Violet (0.33)
Violeta (0.02)
Violet-Harmony
Violet-Joy
Violett
Violetta (0.01)
Violette (0.02)
Viollette
Viona
Vionna
Vionney
Vionya
Viosa
Viquinah
Vir'nesha
Virada
Virag
Virankha
Virann
Virengia
Virge
Virgelina
Virgina
Virginia (0.23)
Virginia Louise
Virginia Lynn
Virginie (0.03)
Virginy
Viridiana (0.02)
Viridiana Adela
Viridianna
Virnesha
Vironika
Virpal
Virtue
Virvena Giallanza
Virydiana
Vishanti
Vishme
Vishva
Vishwadha
Vision
Viskya
Vismaad
Vismaya
Vista
Vistella Gaju
Vita

| | | | | | | |
|---|---|---|---|---|---|---|
| Vitalia | Void (0.01) | Vyolet | Waleah | Wasuk | Wesenline | Wiktoria |
| Vitalina | Volette | Vyolett | Walena | Water | Weslee | Wil'leah |
| Vitality | Von Noel | Vyolette | Walesca | Watson | Wesleigh | Wil'lena |
| Vitaliya | Von'tashia | Vyshali | Waleshka | Waurica | Wesley | Wil'miracle |
| Vitania | Vonaija | Vyshnavi | Waletsy | Wausena | Weslyn | Wil'naeja |
| Vitanya | Vonda | Vyteiha | Walker | Waverly (0.01) | Wesmilka | Wil'neryia |
| Vithao | Vondrea | Vyveanna | Walkiria | Way'neek | Wessie | Wil'niyyah |
| Vithusha | Vongai | Vyvi | Walkiry | Waya | Westania | Wilamina |
| Vitoria (0.01) | Vonia | Vyvianne | Walla | Wayleen | Westiny | Wilanda |
| Vitrina | Voniqua | Vyvyen | Wallace | Waylon | Weston | Wilandine |
| Vittoria (0.01) | Vonmarie | | Wallis | Waynecia | Whanaijah | Wilandy |
| Viva | Vonmeishia | | Walt'tayja | Wayonna | Wheatley | Wilane |
| Vivacia | Vonnia | ~ W ~ | Waltasia | Wayra | Wheimelly | Wilannie |
| Vivan | Vonria | | Waltavia | Weam | Whelan | Wilayna |
| Viveca | Vonshaia | W | Walteria | Weather | Whiddon | Wilaysia |
| Vivegha | Vonshay | Wa'nayja | Wamia | Weatherly | Whipkey | Wilazia |
| Viveka | Vontae'sha | Wa'teria | Wamikka | Webb | Whislese | Wilbianta |
| Vivekka | Vontaja | Waabigwan | Wan | Wedjina | Whisper (0.01) | Wilda |
| Vivenne | Vontasia | Waad | Wan'hi Lorena | Wednesday | Whisper-Marie | Wildalys |
| Vivi | Vontavia | Wabami Tariana | Wanbdi | (0.01) | Whiteney | Wildalyz |
| Vivia | Vontea | Wacey | Wanda (0.02) | Wedny | Whitlee | Wilder |
| Vivian (0.42) | Vontrela | Wad'zahria | Wandaira | Wedoel | Whitleigh | Wildiane |
| Viviana (0.12) | Vontricia | Wadie | Wandalis | Weedor | Whitley (0.03) | Wilena Rabel |
| Viviana'naya | Vonyah | Wadnesia | Wandisile | Weeja | Whitly | Wilenda |
| Viviane (0.02) | Vorya | Wadnie | Waneta | Weibing | Whitnee | Wiley |
| Vivian-James | Vowal | Wae Man | Wanetra | Weidy | Whitney (0.22) | Wilghinah |
| Viviann | Vpridiana | Wafa | Wanetta | Weijia | Whitney Rose | Wilhelmina |
| Vivianna (0.02) | Vrai | Wafaa | Wangui | Weiran | Whitnie | (0.01) |
| Vivianne (0.02) | Vraja | Wafeeqa | Wania | Weiya | Whitny | Wilhemina |
| Vivianni | Vrajpriya | Wahi | Wanida | Weline | Whitnye | Wiliana |
| Vivian-Ros | Vrayelle | Wahiba | Wanita | Wells | Whittany | Wilinda |
| Vivica (0.01) | Vrinda | Wahl | Waniya | Wellslee | Whitten | Wiline |
| Vividiana | Vrindavani | Wai | Waniyah | Wenda | Whittney | Willa (0.05) |
| Vivie | Vritika | Wailea | Waniyetu | Wendalyn | Whittnie | Willadawn |
| Vivien (0.03) | Vrndavana | Waim | Wanjiru | Wendi (0.01) | Whitton | Willaena |
| Vivienne | Vrunda | Wairimu | Wanya | Wendkuni | Whiwhikiterangi | Willa-Kate |
| (0.03) | Vrusha | Rhiannon | Wanying | Wendlassida | Whodejah | Willaneisha |
| Vivienne- | Vtalya | Wajeeha | Warda | Wendoly | Whodiana | Wil-Lasha |
| Tamtinh | Vung | Wajia | Wardah | Wendolyn | Whytney | Willena |
| Vivika | Vy (0.01) | Wajiha | Wared | Wendolyne | Whytt | Willene |
| Vivikka | Vy Ai | Waka | Warishah | Wendooly | Wi'yanna | Willesha |
| Vivina | Vyan | Wakan-Heja | Warniyah | Wendy (0.20) | Wiaame | Willette |
| Vivionna | Vyana | Tokapa | Warren | Wendyam | Wiam | Willia |
| Vivvan | Vyanh | Wake | Warreniya | Wendy- | Wiame | William (0.01) |
| Vivvy | Vycktoria-Jean | Wako | Warud | Elizabeth | Wichan | Williana |
| Vivyan | Vyctoria | Wala | Wasamo-Jii- | Weniah | Wida | Willianny |
| Vivyann | Vyktoria | Walaa | Gash-Kosiw | Weniyah | Widad | Willie |
| Viya | Vyky | Walae | Wasanodaé | Wenke | Widline | Willie Morgan |
| Viyana | Vyla | Walaesha | Waselah | Wenonah | Widlyne | Williemina |
| Viza | Vylet | Walden | Waseya | Wensly | Widney | Williette |
| Vjosana | Vyllyn | Waldina | Wasia | Weris | Widnie-Rose | Willimiah |
| Vlada | Vyniah | Waldriana | Waskone To | Weronika | Wiem | Willimina |
| Vlora | Vyochana | Walea | Wassima | Wescarla | Wignar | Willisha |

| | | | | | | |
|---|---|---|---|---|---|---|
| Willmya | Winnyia | Wraylisha | Wyona | Xaniah | Xelyna | Ximena Yaretzi |
| Will-Niyah | Winola | Wreigna | Wysha | Xaniya | Xelynn | Ximorra |
| Willo | Winona *(0.01)* | Wren *(0.03)* | Wyvonne | Xaniyah | Xena *(0.01)* | Xin *(0.01)* |
| Willoh | Winslet | Wrenna | | Xannah | Xenah | Xin Yi |
| Willora | Winslow | Wright | | Xansibella | Xenia *(0.01)* | Xin Yu |
| Willow *(0.25)* | Winsome | Wrigley | ~ X ~ | Xantara | Xeniah | Xincere |
| Willow Rose | Winsor | Wrya | | Xantha | Xenobia | Xindi |
| Willowbi | Winta | Wryan | X | Xanthe | Xenora | Xindia |
| Willow-Marie | Winter *(0.06)* | Wryn | X'aviana | Xanthea | Xenoshha | Xinity |
| Willowrose | Winter Aal | Wuendi | X'kari | Xanthi | Xeoie | Xintong |
| Wilma *(0.01)* | Winter Angifak | Wuendy | X'zareia | Xara | Xeona | Xinyan |
| Wilmarie | Winter-Rose | Wuliya | X'zariah | Xaramia | Xerena | Xinyi |
| Wilmary | Winty | Wvrynn | X'zaveyona | Xareiah | Xerenah | Xinyu |
| Wilmecha | Wisal | Wy'anna | X'zia | Xaria *(0.01)* | Xery | Xiola |
| Wilnada | Wisam | Wy'naja | X'zirria | Xariah | Xevlynn | Xiolymarie |
| Wilnaiya | Wisbel | Wy'nerria | X'zona | Xariana | Xhairaj | Xiomara *(0.07)* |
| Wilneliz | Wisdom *(0.01)* | Wya | X'zyria | Xarianna | Xharia | Xiomara |
| Wilnesha | Wisenide | Wyanette | Xa'niah | Xarielle | Xhyla | Elizabeth |
| Wilnica | Wislande | Wyatt | Xa'riah | Xariona | Xi | Xiomari |
| Wilniyha | Wisper | Wyaunee | Xa'yani | Xaritzy | Xi Zhi | Xiomarie |
| Wilnya | Wissal | Wydlynn | Xackarriyah | Xariyanna | Xi'keria | Xiomarra |
| Wilnye | Wissale | Wyesha | Xadia | Xarra | Xi'yannah | Xiomary |
| Wilnyia | Wissam | Wyeth | Xaee | Xaryah | Xia | Xiomayra |
| Wilshir | Wissem | Wyidada | Xaeleah | Xatia | Xiah | Xiomi |
| Wilson | Wisser | Wykeena | Xafsa | Xaura | Xia-Li | Xion |
| Wilson-Lauren | Witchenie | Wykia | Xah'myiah | Xavia | Xiamara | Xiona |
| Wiltina | Withchelie | Wylee | Xai | Xaviah | Xiamarie | Xiora |
| Wilyana | Withney | Wyleigh | Xaia | Xaviana | Xiamora | Xiovon |
| Wilythza | Withnise | Wyler | Xaiana | Xavianna | Xian | Xipatly |
| Wilyuana | Witley | Wyli | Xaime | Xaviannia | Xiana | Xithlaly |
| Wimberly | Witt | Wylicia | Xainab | Xaviara | Xianali | Xitlali *(0.02)* |
| Winacia B | Wittlee | Wylie *(0.01)* | Xaira | Xavien | Xianan | Xitlali Montserr |
| Winaya | Witty | Wyllo | Xairya | Xavier | Xiandra | Xitlalic |
| Winbush | Wiyanna | Wyn'niya | Xaiyana | Xaviera | Xiang | Xitlalik |
| Windia | Wllow | Wyndi | Xaiyna | Xaviona | Xianghua | Xitlalit |
| Windie | Wod | Wyndrea | Xajah | Xavionna | Xiani | Xitlalli |
| Windsor-Rose | Wohalea | Wyneesea | Xalia | Xaviyonce | Xiann | Xitlally |
| Windy | Woldina | Wynette | Xalin | Xaviyonna | Xianni | Xitlaly *(0.01)* |
| Winehya | Woldine | Wyniah | Xamara | Xaybelith | Xiao | Xitlalyt |
| Wing | Wolfframmina | Wynn *(0.01)* | Xamira | Xayeltzy | Xiao Jun | Xiu Xiu |
| Wing Yan | Womack | Wynn Grace | Xamirah | Xayla | Xiao Wen | Xiya |
| Wing-Yen | Won | Wynne | Xamyra | Xaylah-Grace | Xiaolan | Xiyan |
| Winifred | Wondyana | Wynnlee | Xan | Xaymara | Xiara | Xiyanna |
| Winita | Wongelawit | Wynona | Xana-Claire | Xayre | Xiarh | Xkaila |
| Winiya | Wordna | Wynonna | Xanaya | Xeana | Xiayana | Xo'lani |
| Winky | Worship | Wynowa | Xander | Xebriela | Xiaye | Xoana |
| Winner | Wouline | Wynsday | Xandra *(0.01)* | Xee | Xica | Xochi |
| Winnette | Wo-Wi-Ca-La- | Wynston | Xandrea | Xeina | Xiclaly | Xochial |
| Winney | Win | Wyntar | Xandreah | Xela | Xictlaly | Xochil *(0.01)* |
| Winni *(0.01)* | Wraith | Wynter *(0.04)* | Xandreaya | Xelee | Xiloj | Xochilt *(0.02)* |
| Winnie *(0.03)* | Wramsey | Wynter Aunesty | Xandria *(0.01)* | Xelha | Xilone | Xochilt Lizeth |
| Winnifred | Wrangler | Wynter Grace | Xandrianna | Xelyam | Ximariya | Xochitl *(0.02)* |
| Winny | Wraye | Wyntre | Xania | Xelymar | Ximena *(0.12)* | Xodus |

| | | | | | | |
|---|---|---|---|---|---|---|
| Xoe | Xzandria | Ya'nya | Yaelin | Yahnique | Yajayra | Yamaris |
| Xoee | Xzanna | Ya'nyla | Yaelis | Yahnise | Yajhayra | Yamary |
| Xoey | Xzaria | Ya'nyrah | Yaelit Sunamy | Yahniya | Yakalayah | Yamaya |
| Xoie | Xzaryia | Ya'quija | Yaelle | Yahreli | Yakarya | Yamdra |
| Xola | Xzav'ianna | Ya'riyah | Yaemi | Yahrysha | Yakeisha | Yameily |
| Xolani | Xzaveiona | Ya'shevia | Yaemy | Yahshae | Yakelim | Yamekia |
| Xolanie | Xzaveria | Ya'tae | Yaena | Yahsirahn | Yakelin | Yamel |
| Xona | Xzavia | Ya'tonnie | Yafa-Reem | Yahtney | Yakeline | Yamelay |
| Xondra | Xzavieona | Yaa | Yagmur | Yahveli | Yakelyn | Yamelet |
| Xorah | X-Zavionna | Yaaasantewa | Yagyata | Yahzra | Yakiah | Yameli |
| Xoria | Xzavona | Yaannet | Yah Naesha | Yahzya | Yakima | Yamelly |
| Xorriyah | Xzeria | Yaashira | Yahadia | Yai'janeh | Yakine | Yamely |
| Xotchilth | Xzila | Yaasmeen | Yahaidee | Yaide | Yakira (0.01) | Yamelyn |
| Xqwayvia | Xziyah | Yaasmin | Yahaira (0.04) | Yaidelin | Yakiya | Yamese |
| Xstaria | Xzoriona | Yaassmeen | Yahaitta | Yaiden | Yakzahira | Yami |
| Xuan Hoang | Xzya | Yabdelisse | Yahalice | Yaigri | Yalainet | Yamiah |
| Yen | Xzyia | Yabriah | Yahancy | Yaila | Yalana | Yamiaha |
| Xuan Mai | Xzyla | Yabsera | Yahani | Yailana | Yalanie | Yamielys |
| Xuan Nhi | | Yabsira | Yahara | Yaileen | Yalaya | Yamiguelis |
| Xuanmai | | Yabsra | Yaharia | Yailen | Yaleeha | Yamija |
| Xuanxi | ~ Y ~ | Yacaranday | Yaharie | Yailene | Yaleia | Yamil |
| Xue | | Yachanon | Yaharmony | Yaileny | Yaleisa | Yamila (0.01) |
| Xuine | Y | Yachet (0.01) | Yahayra (0.01) | Yailer | Yaleissa | Yamilah |
| Xunaxich | Y'gypt | Yacine | Yahdah | Yailin | Yalena | Yamile (0.01) |
| Xutmara | Y'necia | Yacinth | Yahdira | Yailine | Yaleska | Yamilec |
| Xuyin | Y'nubia | Yackelin | Yahdirah | Yailiz | Yalesky | Yamiled |
| Xx | Y'shun | Yacquelin | Yahel | Yailyn | Yalette | Yamilee |
| Xxyah | Y'xavyiah | Yacqueline | Yaheli | Yailynn | Yalexa | Yamileph |
| Xy'kera | Ya Mi | Yacqui | Yahely | Yaimary | Yalimar | Yamilet (0.04) |
| Xy'kerria | Ya Shiuan | Yacsy | Yahida | Yaineese | Yalin | Yamileth (0.02) |
| Xyana | Ya Yu | Yacyra | Yahienesse | Yainet | Yalina | Yamilethl |
| Xyaniya | Yá Zariah | Yada | Yahilin | Yaira (0.01) | Yalisa | Yamiletsy |
| Xyanna | Ya'brill | Yadalis | Yahilyn | Yairaliz | Yalise | Yamilett |
| Xyara | Ya'cari | Yadani | Yahinet | Yaire | Yalissa | Yamilette (0.01) |
| Xyiairiah | Ya'derrell | Yadelis | Yahir | Yairelis | Yalitza (0.01) | Yamilex (0.01) |
| Xykaysha | Ya'driayana | Yadeliz | Yahira | Yaireliz | Yaliveth | Yamilexi |
| Xykeela | Ya'hara | Yadelyn | Yahire | Yaireth | Yalivia | Yamilexs |
| Xyla | Ya'haria | Yaden | Yahkini | Yairi | Yalixa | Yamiley |
| Xylee | Ya'hiarra | Yadhira (0.03) | Yahla | Yairiany | Yalixza | Yamilia |
| Xylia | Ya'keira | Yadieliz | Yahleeyah | Yairin | Yaliyah | Yamilka |
| Xylianne | Ya'keisha | Yadielys | Yahleia | Yaisa | Yaliza | Yamilla |
| Xylie | Ya'kira | Yadimar | Yahlisa | Yaisel | Yalley | Yamille |
| Xylina | Ya'kirasky | Yadira (0.11) | Yahliyah | Yaisleen | Yalona | Yamillet |
| Xylis | Ya'lan | Yadirah | Yahlonnie | Yaislin | Yalorie | Yamilly |
| Xymia | Ya'najah | Yadislay | Yahm | Yaisman | Yalussa | Yamily |
| Xynia | Ya'neia | Yaditza | Yahmarri | Yaismely | Yaly | Yamina |
| Xynovia | Ya'nequa | Yadmarie | Yahmira | Yaisy | Yamaara | Yaminah |
| Xyoi | Ya'nia | Yadmil | Yahmoni | Yaitzel | Yamaira | Yamini |
| Xyomara | Ya'niah | Yae | Yahna | Yaiza | Yamama | Yamins |
| Xyon | Ya'nireah | Yaedy | Yahnari | Yajahira | Yaman | Yamir |
| Xzadia | Ya'nis | Yael (0.03) | Yahneisha | Yajaira (0.03) | Yamani | Yamira |
| Xzalyah | Ya'niya | Yael Chaya | Yahnel | Yajairah | Yamari | Yamirah |
| Xzandra | Ya'niyah | Yaeli | Yahney-Marie | Yajana | Yamariah | Yamirka |

| | | | | | | |
|---|---|---|---|---|---|---|
| Yamisel | Yandhi | Yangelis | Yanne | Yareisi | Yaribeth | Yarizel |
| Yamiska | Yandi | Yangzee | Yanneisy | Yareisy | Yaricelis | Yarizmar |
| Yamisleydi | Yandri | Yang-Zhi | Yannelie- | Yareli (0.07) | Yaricza | Yarkara |
| Yamiya | Yaneah | Yangzijiao | Alejandra | Yarelie | Yarid | Yarleen |
| Yammile | Yanebel | Yani | Yannely | Yarelih | Yaridsa | Yarlenys |
| Yamna | Yanecia | Yania | Yannet | Yarelin | Yarie | Yarleth |
| Yamtyah | Yaned | Ya-Niah | Yanni | Yareline | Yariela | Yarlin |
| Yamya | Yaneetche | Yaniaya | Yannick | Yarelis (0.01) | Yarielis | Yarly |
| Yamyira | Yaneht | Yanibah | Yannicka | Yareliz (0.01) | Yarielise | Yarmani |
| Yamyled | Yaneidy | Yanibel | Yannie | Yarelli | Yarieliz | Yarneese |
| Yan | Yaneiliz | Yanica | Yannie-Jade | Yarelly | Yariely | Yarnesha |
| Yan Yan | Yaneily | Yanice | Yannika | Yarely (0.02) | Yarielys | Yarrisa |
| Yana (0.02) | Yaneiry | Yanicel | Yannis | Yarelys | Yarilexy | Yartiza |
| Yanabah | Yaneishly | Yanicet | Yannitze | Yarelyz | Yariliz | Yarymar |
| Yanae | Yaneisi | Yanick | Yannys | Yaremi | Yarilynn | Yas |
| Yanah | Yaneisy | Yanie | Yanouela-Avigail | Yarency | Yarilysol | Yas'mear |
| Yanai | Yaneiza | Yaniece | Yansi | Yareni | Yarilyz | Yas'meen |
| Yanaia | Yanel | Yaniela | Yansia | Yarenis | Yarimar | Yas'myne |
| Yanaijah | Yanela | Yanieli | Yante | Yarennis | Yarin | Yasa |
| Yanailiz | Yanelee | Yanieliz | Yantis | Yaresdi | Yarina | Yasamin |
| Yanaily | Yaneli (0.02) | Yaniella | Yanya | Yaresli | Yarinel | Yasamine |
| Yanaira | Yanelia | Yaniely | Yanydria | Yaresly | Yarineliz | Yasary |
| Yanairaliz | Yanelie | Yanielys | Yanyla | Yaressi | Yarinell | Yasbel |
| Yanairis | Yanelis | Yanien | Yaquecline | Yaret | Yarines | Yaselin |
| Yanais | Yaneliss | Yaniera | Yaquelin (0.02) | Yaretci | Yarinet | Yaselinn |
| Yanaisis | Yaneliz (0.01) | Yaniia | Yaqueline | Yaretcy | Yarineth | Yaselly |
| Yanaisy | Yanell | Yanil | Yaquelinne | Yareth (0.01) | Yarinette | Yaselyn |
| Yanaiza | Yanella | Yanilou | Yaquieline | Yarethsy | Yarinex | Yasemin |
| Yanaja | Yanelle | Yanilsa | Yaqute | Yarethzi | Yaris | Yasemina |
| Yanalet | Yanelli | Yanina | Yar | Yarethzy | Yarisa | Yasemina |
| Yanali | Yanellie | Yanique | Yar'quetea | Yaretshi | Yarisbel | Bianca |
| Yanalis | Yanelly | Yanira (0.01) | Yara (0.03) | Yaretsi | Yarisbeli | Yasenia |
| Yanalise | Yanellys | Yaniris | Yara-Chiraze | Yaretsy | Yarisel | Yasha |
| Yanamarie | Yanelsis | Yanis | Yaradin | Yarett | Yarisell | Yashaé |
| Yanamilegh | Yanely (0.01) | Yanisa | Yaraeli | Yaretzi (0.01) | Yarisely | Yashaira |
| Yanancy | Yanelys | Yanise | Yarah | Yaretzie | Yarisleidy | Yashall |
| Yanara | Yanem | Yanisel | Yarahi | Yaretzy (0.01) | Yarisma | Yashana |
| Yanari | Yaneri | Yanishka | Yarai | Yarexi | Yarismar | Yashasvini |
| Yanariel | Yaneris | Yanisleidi | Yaraime | Yarexsa | Yarismarie | Yashauna |
| Yanaris | Yanesa | Yanisleidys | Yaraith | Yarexy | Yarissa | Yashawini |
| Yanasey | Yanesia | Yanissa | Yaralis | Yarezhit | Yaristza | Yashi |
| Yanate | Yaneska | Yanisse | Yaraliz | Yarha | Yarit | Yashibell |
| Yanay | Yanessa | Yanit | Yarandy | Yari | Yarithza | Yashica |
| Yanaya | Yanet (0.01) | Yanitza (0.01) | Yaranelly | Yariah | Yarithzy | Yashika |
| Yanayri | Yaneth | Yanitzi | Yarayvah- | Yarializ | Yaritsa | Yashila |
| Yanci | Yanett | Yanivea | Elianah | Yariam | Yaritza (0.05) | Yashili |
| Yancy | Yanette | Yanixa | Yarden | Yarian | Yaritzel | Yashimary |
| Yancy Daniela | Yaneyri | Yaniya | Yareccy | Yariana | Yaritzi | Yashira |
| Yandel | Yaneysa | Yaniyhia | Yarecsia | Yariani | Yaritzy | Yashmi |
| Yandelina | Yaneyshka | Yankho | Yarecy | Yarianis | Yarivette | Yashoda |
| Yandeliz | Yaneysis | Yanna (0.01) | Yaredi | Yarianny | Yarixa | Yashra |
| Yanderi | Yanfang | Yannaeve | Yareina | Yaribel | Yarixia | Yashvi |
| Yandery | Yangchen | Yannah | Yareisee | Yaribet | Yariya | Yasiana |

| | | | | | | |
|---|---|---|---|---|---|---|
| Yasir | Yassli | Yaziara | Yecenia (0.01) | Yelixa | Yenriqua | Yesinia |
| Yasira | Yasslin | Yaziby | Yedani | Yelixsa | Yensis | Yesley |
| Yasirah | Yassmin | Yazira | Yedanix | Yelizavett | Yenty | Yesli (0.01) |
| Yasirie | Yassmine (0.01) | Yazlen | Yeddis | Yelizsa | Yeny | Yesliy |
| Yasje | Yasumi | Yazli | Yede | Yellenia | Yenyfeer | Yesly |
| Yasleidi | Yasury | Yazlin | Yedibah | Yelly | Yenyzia | Yesly Hiromi |
| Yaslin | Yatana | Yazline | Yedid | Yelyna | Yenzi | Yeslyn |
| Yaslind | Yatanha | Yazlyn | Yee | Yelysavet | Yeon Woo | Yesmeen |
| Yaslyn | Yathira | Yazlynn | Yeem | Yemara | Yeona | Yesmene |
| Yasmaine | Yathzari | Yazman | Yeesmin | Yemayá | Yeonhwa | Yesmin |
| Yasmalinda-Rosa | Yathziri | Yazmariah | Yehelena | Yemeka | Yer | Yesmina |
| Yasmara | Yatia | Yazmarian | Yehileen | Yemeli | Yeraimie | Yesminde |
| Yasmari | Yatirrah | Yazmarie | Yehudis (0.02) | Yemile | Yeraisi | Yesmine |
| Yasmarie | Yatna | Yazmary | Yei | Yemilet | Yeraldeen | Yessenia (0.04) |
| Yasme'ana | Yatniellys | Yazmean | Yeida | Yemiliz | Yeraldi | Yessenya |
| Yasmean | Yatri | Yazmeen | Yeidi | Yemin | Yeraldin | Yesserelys |
| Yasmeen (0.06) | Yatsiri | Yazméen | Yeidy | Yemiya | Yeraldine | Yessi |
| Yasmeena | Yatzari | Yazmen | Yeila | Yemya | Yeraldy | Yessica (0.02) |
| Yasmeen-Rania | Yatzary | Yazmenda | Yeilani | Yen | Yerani | Yessiel |
| Yasmein | Yatzel | Yazmene | Yeilee | Yen Nhi | Yerania | Yessly |
| Yasmeli | Yatziri | Yazmera | Yeileeana | Yena | Yeray | Yessnia |
| Yasmely | Yatziry | Yazmia | Yeilen | Yenci | Yerelyn | Yesverendy |
| Yasmen | Yaumara | Yazmien | Yeili | Yency | Yeressys | Yethara |
| Yasmena | Yauncie | Yazmiin | Yeilianis | Yendi | Yeretsia | Yethlanezi |
| Yasmene | Yaurice | Yazmin (0.08) | Yeily | Yeneisi | Yerialis | Yetsamin |
| Yasmeri | Yauvani | Yazmina | Yeilyn | Yenelis | Yerielia | Yetta |
| Yasmi | Yavaughn | Yazminda | Yeimi (0.01) | Yenelyn | Yerin | Yetzabeth |
| Yasmiere | Yavianca | Yazmine (0.02) | Yeimilen | Yenesis | Yeritza | Yetzaira |
| Yasmiin | Yavidia | Yazmineá | Yeimy | Yenevi | Yerlenne | Yetzel |
| Yásmin | Yavielis | Yazmyn | Yein | Yeni (0.01) | Yerli | Yeva |
| Yasmin (0.27) | Yavilka | Yazmyne | Yeira (0.01) | Yenializ | Yerliza | Yevett |
| Yasmina (0.03) | Yavne'el | Yazna | Yeiribeth | Yeniar | Yerly | Yevette |
| Yasmine (0.22) | Yavonn-Elise | Yaznely | Yeiry | Yenifer (0.01) | Yeron | Yewande |
| Yasmine Iyas | Yavonty | Yazreal | Yeisly | Yeniffer | Yerrell | Yewon |
| Yasmine Maya | Yawa | Yaztmarie | Yeismin | Yenilca | Yes | Yexenia |
| Yasmine-Bambi | Yawen | Yazully | Yeismy | Yenilen | Yesabel | Yeylin |
| Yasmine-Hidaya | Yawnie | Yazurie | Yejee | Yeniliz | Yesalyn | Yeymi |
| Yasming | Yaxelis | Yazury | Yekaterina | Yenille | Yescenia | Yezabel |
| Yasmini | Yaxeni | Yazzmean | Ye-Kyung | Yenis | Yesehida | Yezenia |
| Yasminka | Yaxeny | Yazzmen | Yelady | Yenisei | Yeseina Analicia | Yezmine |
| Yasminne | Yaxminellie | Yazzmine | Yelayna | Yenisel | Yesel | Yhadira |
| Yasmique | Yaxslin | Yazzmyn | Yelci | Yeniset | Yeselin | Yhamiyla |
| Yasmire | Yaya | Ydaliz | Yelda | Yenisett | Yeselisse | Yhana |
| Yasmith | Yayda | Ydelisa | Yeldis | Yenisis | Yesely | Yhan-Arnella |
| Yasmyn (0.01) | Yayla | Ydelsie | Yelena (0.01) | Yenisleysi | Yesenia (0.14) | Yhara |
| Yasmyne | Yaynel | Ydiana | Yelen-Fanta | Yenisse | Yeseniah | Yharlm |
| Yasra | Yayra | Ye | Yelenna | Yenitza | Yesennia | Yhasmine |
| Yassée | Yayren | Ye Na | Yeliana | Yenly | Yesenra | Yhatzubely |
| Yasser | Yaz'min | Yeabsera | Yeliaris | Yenna | Yesenya | Yhoalibeth |
| Yassin | Yazaarely | Yeali | Yelina | Yenni | Yeshaila | Yhoana |
| Yassine | Yazahira | Yeardley | Yelissa | Yennifer | Yeshayah | Yhozuany |
| | Yazarehia | Yeausmeanea | Yelitza (0.01) | Yenny (0.01) | Yesica (0.02) | Yhuliza |
| | Yazen | Yeccenia | Yelitzabet | Yeno | Yesika | Yi |

| | | | | | | |
|---|---|---|---|---|---|---|
| Yi Ding | Yiping | Ymani | Yojannis | Yomaris | Yoshigey | Ysabella |
| Yi Ping | Yiqian | Ymayá | Yojari | Yomaritza | Yoshighet |   Catherine |
| Yi Ran | Yiraliz | Ymira | Yojeved | Yomayra | Yoshime | Ysabella Quelsly |
| Yi'la | Yiran | Ymorgan | Yo-Jia | Yon'cea | Yoshita | Ysabelle |
| Yian | Yireth | Yna | Yokheved | Yon'tira | Yosielys | Ysamar |
| Yiana | Yiriana | Ynajihea | Yoko | Yona | Yosiris | Ysane |
| Yiandra | Yisari | Ynanna | Yokotani | Yonaely | Yosis | Ysani |
| Yianna | Yiscarly | Ynes | Yola | Yoneli | Yoslene | Ysanna |
| Yianney | Yiscenya | Yness | Yolanda (0.04) | Yong | Yoslin | Ysariah |
| Yianni | Yiseiri | Ynnjade | Yolandaelena | Yong-Yi | Yosline | Ysatis |
| Yianys | Yisel | Ynobe | Yolande | Yongzhu | Yosmery | Ysderlene |
| Yiara | Yisel Marisol | Ynue'l | Yolandria | Yoni | Yosr | Ysee |
| Yicel | Yisela | Yoakaire | Yolandy | Yonika | Yosra | Ysela |
| Yicette | Yiseli | Yoali | Yolani | Yonna | Yossaria | Ysenia |
| Yiddisha | Yisell | Yoalis | Yolanihe | Yonnyli | Yosselin (0.01) | Yseult |
| Yides (0.02) | Yiselle | Yoana (0.01) | Yolanne | Yoon | Yosseline | Ysha |
| Yidida | Yishmaya | Yoana Claire | Yolannie | Yoona | Yosselyn | Ysidra |
| Yididiya | Yisleidi | Yoandra | Yolany | Yoonah | Yosselyne | Yssabelle |
| Yihnae | Yisrael | Yoandry | Yolawnda | Yophi | Yossi | Yssaidra |
| Yijia | Yissa | Yoani | Yoldine | Yoraldin | Yossra | Yterniti |
| Yikeshia | Yissel | Yoann | Yoleena-Skyy | Yoranny | Yossy | Ytzabel |
| Yilailah | Yissell | Yoanna | Yoleinis | Yorbeline | Yostena | Ytzayana |
| Yileivis | Yiszel | Yoannie | Yoleiny | Yordalys | Yotzin | Ytzel |
| Yileydi | Yitcel | Yobana | Yolene | Yordana | You Na | Ytzell |
| Yilian | Yiting | Yocelin (0.01) | Yolenny | Yordanos | Youmna | Yu |
| Yilin | Yitta | Yocelyn (0.01) | Yolet | Yorel | Youna | Yu Qing |
| Yillian | Yitty (0.01) | Yocelynn | Yoleth | Yorelix | Youneek | Yu Ying |
| Yilmari | Yitxia | Yocheved (0.02) | Yolett | Yori | Younesse | Yu'mya |
| Yimary | Yitzel | Yodira | Yolette | Yorielis | Young | Yu'nijah |
| Yimierah | Yitzirah | Yodit | Yoleyana | Yorleni | Youni | Yu'nique |
| Yin | Yiwei | Yoeli | Yoliana | Yorleny | Younique | Yualani |
| Yina | Yixian | Yoelin | Yolianys | Yorlie | Yousif | Yuan |
| Yinairi | Yixuan | Yoely | Yolibel | Yoryet | Yousra (0.01) | Yuany |
| Yinarie | Yiyang | Yoemy | Yolibet | Yoryina | Youssaira | Yubilee |
| Yineira | Yizhi | Yohadria | Yolibeth | Yorysmar | Youssra | Yubin |
| Yineiris | Yja | Yohaira | Yolidia | Yosalin | Youstina | Yucara |
| Yinel | Yladia | Yohali | Yolimar | Yosan | Youvika | Yucari |
| Yineliz | Ylaina | Yohaly | Yolisia | Yosara | Youzada | Yucca |
| Yinellix | Ylana | Yohana (0.01) | Yolissa | Yosaris | Yovana | Yuceli |
| Yinelly | Ylanca | Yohanah | Yolissett | Yoselim | Yovani | Yucuhita |
| Yinette | Ylani | Yohanca | Yollaine | Yoselin (0.07) | Yovanna | Yudaesia |
| Ying | Yleana | Yohane | Yolonda | Yoselinda | Yovela | Yudelkis |
| Ying Lei | Ylena | Yohanis | Yolothzin | Yoseline | Yoxana | Yudelkiss |
| Ying Ting | Yliana | Yohanna (0.01) | Yolotzin | Yoseliz | Yozelin | Yudi |
| Ying-Chu | Ylianna | Yohannah Mae | Yoly | Yosellin | Ypasia | Yudira |
| Yingkou | Ylianni | Yohelly | Yomah | Yosely | Yram | Yudit |
| Yinglay | Yliany | Yohisy | Yomaina | Yoselyn (0.01) | Yris | Yudith |
| Yingmei | Ylieniece | Yohley | Yomaira | Yoshalay | Yrneh | Yudithcel |
| Yingying | Yllana | Yohlik | Yomairalyz | Yoshie | Yrsa | Yudy |
| Yingyue | Ylleana | Yohnyah | Yomairis | Yoshiegey | Ysabel (0.01) | Yue |
| Yinica | Yllka | Yoineris | Yomara | Yoshiena | Ysabela | Yue Han |
| Yiomari | Ylsa-Jayne | Yois | Yomari | Yoshier | Ysabell | Yue Huan |
| Yionnah | Ylucia | Yojana | Yomaries | Yoshigei | Ysabella (0.01) | Yuen |

Yuen Yi
Yuetong
Yufu
Yuhani
Yuheli
Yuhki
Yuhong
Yuhridia
Yuiidia
Yuika
Yuiko
Yuilianna
Yuisa
Yu-Jin
Yujin
Yuka
Yukary
Yuki *(0.02)*
Yukie
Yukiko
Yukiko-Anne
Yukina
Yukino
Yuktha
Yulaine
Yulanda
Yulandria
Yulduz
Yuleana
Yuleanna
Yulee
Yuleesa
Yuleidi
Yuleidy
Yuleimy
Yuleisy
Yuleithy
Yuleivi
Yuleni
Yulesmy
Yuleyci
Yuli
Yulia
Yulian
Yuliana *(0.03)*
Yulianie
Yulianna *(0.01)*
Yulibel
Yuliebeth
Yuliet
Yulilsi
Yulimar
Yu-Ling

Yulisa *(0.02)*
Yulisa Lisbet
Yulisd
Yulissa *(0.02)*
Yulitza
Yuliz
Yuliza *(0.01)*
Yulvení
Yulvia
Yumaca
Yumara
Yume
Yumeko
Yumeng
Yumi
Yumiki
Yumiko
Yumin
Yumna
Yumnah
Yuna *(0.02)*
Yunah
Yunalesca
Yunaliska
Yunasis
Yundi
Yune
Yuneli
Yunenci
Y-Unesti
Yuni
Yunica
Yuniett
Yunika
Yunique
Yuniya
Yunjoo
Yunna
Yunnelsy
Yunny
Yunuen
Yunying
Yura
Yurae
Yuraida
Yuraima
Yuralitz
Yuramis
Yurayma
Yureidi
Yureidy
Yureima
Yureli

Yurely
Yureymi
Yuri *(0.01)*
Yuria
Yuriah
Yuriana
Yuri-Ann
Yurianna
Yurianni
Yuriannis
Yuricza
Yuridia *(0.04)*
Yuridiana
Yuriely
Yuriko
Yurin
Yurina
Yurisi
Yurisleidy
Yurithza
Yuritxy
Yuritza
Yuritzi *(0.01)*
Yuritzia
Yuritzy
Yurixi
Yuriza
Yurizzy
Yurope
Yuruhem
Yuruhen
Yury
Yury Lizbe
Yuryanna
Yuryko
Yuryn
Yusairah
Yusalet
Yusbeiri
Yuselin
Yuselly
Yusha
Yushigee
Yusra *(0.01)*
Yusrah
Yusselin
Yussra
Yussra Halima
Yustyna
Yusur
Yuthi
Yuthziry
Yuti

Yu-Ting
Yutong
Yutzely
Yutzi
Yuuko
Yuumi
Yuval
Yuvia
Yuviana
Yuvie
Yuvika
Yuxin
Yuyeng
Yuying
Yuzmily
Yuzori
Yva
Yvah
Yvan
Yvanna
Yve
Yveana
Yvelis
Yvemarthe
Yvena
Yvett
Yvette *(0.04)*
Yvettelyna
Yvonna
Yvonne *(0.06)*
Yvonnia
Yvonnie
Yvontaysia
Yxzi
Yyana
Yyetta
Yza
Yzabela
Yzabella
Yzabelle
Yzette
Yzhanae

## ~ Z ~

Z Niyah
Z' Aria
Z'amiya
Z'ani
Z'anobia
Z'arija
Z'asia

Z'corya
Z'etta
Z'hane
Z'hreamier
Z'iara
Z'ionna
Z'kara
Z'kiiya
Z'kiyah
Z'kyah
Z'kyha
Z'marea
Z'mareya
Z'mari
Z'mharie
Z'miya
Z'mora
Z'mya
Z'naria
Z'nasia
Z'naya
Z'nei
Z'nirya
Z'niya
Z'niyah
Z'nya
Z'nyree
Z'onia
Z'quoia
Z'riah
Z'yra
Za Asia
Za Kierra
Za Moni
Za Mya
  Leighandria
Zá Nyah
Za Nyra
Za Riya
Za'ajzsa
Za'breya
Za'cariya
Za'carria
Za'coria
Za'hara
Za'hariah
Za'hiah
Za'hnnae
Za'hyra
Za'kai
Za'kaiyah
Za'kala
Za'karah

Za'kariah
Za'kavia
Za'kayla
Za'kenya
Za'keria
Za'keriah
Za'kerya
Za'kevia
Za'kharrea
Za'khia
Za'khiya
Za'khya
Za'khyla
Za'kia
Za'kiah
Za'kira
Za'kiya
Za'kiyah
Za'kya
Za'kyah
Za'kyhia
Za'kyia
Za'kyla
Za'kyra
Za'laia
Za'lanna
Za'lea
Za'leah
Za'liyah
Za'mahj
Za'mani
Za'maria
Za'mariah
Za'mariasia
Za'mariya
Za'mariyah
Za'marreya
Za'marria
Za'merah
Za'meria
Za'mia
Za'miaya
Za'miayh
Za'mirah
Za'mirrah
Za'miya
Za'miyah
Za'mora
Za'moria
Za'morrow
Za'mya
Za'myah
Za'myia

Za'myra
Za'myriah
Za'naiya
Za'naja
Za'nara
Za'naree
Za'nariah
Za'nariayah
Za'navia
Za'naya
Za'nayshia
Za'nia
Za'niah
Za'nija
Za'nijah
Za'nirea
Za'niya *(0.01)*
Za'niyah *(0.01)*
Za'nobia
Za'nya *(0.01)*
Za'nya Aaliyah
Za'nyah
Za'nyhia
Za'nyia
Za'nyiah
Za'nyla
Za'nylah
Za'nyri
Za'nyza
Za'quasja
Za'quia
Za'quoia
Za'raiviah
Za'reyana
Za'rhia
Za'ria
Za'riah
Za'riel
Za'riya
Za'riyah
Za'rya
Za'ryiaha
Za'shaiya
Za'torria
Za'veonna
Za'vionna
Zaah
Zaairah
Zaakirah
Zaambriya
Zaaminah
Zaara *(0.01)*
Zaaria

| | | | | | |
|---|---|---|---|---|---|
| Zabana | Zaddie | Zahayra | Zaida-Malicka | Zakara | Zakkiyya | Zalinea |
| Zabdi | Zade | Zahdya | Zaidea | Zakareya | Zakkyyiah | Zalira Yé |
| Zabella | Zaden | Zahee | Zaidelliz | Zakari | Zaklin | Zalise |
| Zabhelye | Zadia | Zaheeda | Zaidmyra | Zakaria | Zakora | Zaliya |
| Zabre | Zadie *(0.01)* | Zaheedah | Zaidy | Zakariya | Zakoria | Zaliyah |
| Zabreyuna | Zadina | Zaheen | Zaige | Zakariyah | Zakoya Shavon | Zalla |
| Zabria | Zadrea | Zahera | Zaihra | Zakary | Zakrya | Zalma |
| Zabriel | Zadria | Zahia | Zaija | Zakashi | Za-Kya | Zalora |
| Zabrina | Zadrianna | Zahida | Zaijah | Zakat | Zakya | Zaloren |
| Zabrinaleigh | Zady | Zahidah | Zaikiah | Zakaya | Zakyah | Zaltana |
| Zabriya | Zae'sha | Zahina | Zaila | Zakayiah | Zakyaria | Zalya |
| Zac'keria | Zaeda | Zahira | Zailei | Zakayla | Zakyia | Zalyah |
| Zacara | Zaedra | Zahirah | Zailey | Zakaylan | Zakyiah | Zamairys |
| Zacari | Zaedyn-Chase | Zahira-Nour | Zaily | Zakaylen | Zakyila | Zamaiya |
| Zacaria | Zaéerah | Zahiyah | Zailyn | Zakeah | Zakyla | Zamantha |
| Zacariah | Zaela | Zahiyyah | Zailynn Rachel | Zakearah | Zakylah | Zamar'ya |
| Zacariyah | Zaelah | Zahkyrah |   Minah | Zakeelah | Zakyra *(0.01)* | Zamara |
| Zacarria | Zaele | Zahlee | Zaima | Zakeina | Zakyrha | Zamare |
| Zacauree'a | Zaeleigh | Zahmerriel | Zaimah | Zakeira | Zakyria | Zamareya |
| Zacchea | Zaeli | Zahmiya | Zaimahia | Zakeldra | Zala | Zamarhia |
| Zacchia | Zaelie | Zahmya | Zain | Zakena | Zalae | Zamari |
| Zaceria | Zaelin | Zahn | Zaina *(0.03)* | Zakenzie | Zalaeh | Zamaria *(0.01)* |
| Zach'riah | Zaely | Zahniya | Zaina Aali | Zakera | Zalah | Zamariah |
| Zachaire | Zaelyn | Zahnyah | Zainab *(0.07)* | Zakerria | Zalaia Anne | Zamariana |
| Zachaiyah | Zaelys | Zah-Nye | Zainabe | Zakeyia | Zalauria | Zamariya |
| Zachanna | Zaemia | Zahra *(0.06)* | Zainabou | Zakhai | Zalay | Zamariyah |
| Zachara | Zaeminio | Zahra'a | Zainabu | Zakharia | Zalaya | Zamariyona |
| Zacharah | Zaeona | Zahraa *(0.02)* | Zainah | Zakhi | Zalayah |   Denise |
| Zacharee | Zaeriona | Zahrah *(0.01)* | Zainatun-Nur | Zakhia | Zalayna | Zamarona |
| Zacharia | Zafa | Zahrea | Zaine | Zakhialya | Zale | Zamarra |
| Zachary *(0.01)* | Zafeerah | Zahria *(0.02)* | Zaineb | Zakhiya | Zalea | Zamarria |
| Zachel | Zafina | Zahriah | Zainub | Zakhya | Zaleah | Zamary |
| Zachenka | Zafirah | Zahrion | Zaionna | Zakhyriah | Zaleea | Zamaya |
| Zachiera | Zafiro | Zahriya | Zair | Zakia *(0.01)* | Zaleeah | Zamayah |
| Zachikeyra | Zafreen | Zahriyah | Zaira *(0.02)* | Zakiah | Zaleeyah | Zambia |
| Zachkia | Zagiri | Zahrryona | Zairah | Zakiaha | Zalei | Zambrano |
| Zackary | Zah'kiyah | Zahrya | Zaira-Sophia | Zakiaih | Zaleiah | Zameah |
| Zackayla | Zah'nyah | Zahur | Zairayeah | Zakiara | Zaleigh | Zamera |
| Zackia | Zah'quandra | Zahuur | Zaire *(0.01)* | Zakiayah | Zalena | Zameria |
| Zackiera | Zahairah | Zahyra | Zairy | Zakiera | Zalesha | Zamia |
| Zackiyah | Zaham | Zahyrah | Zairya | Zakila | Zalexus | Zamiah |
| Zackura | Zahara *(0.03)* | Zai'aria | Zaisha | Zakilya | Zalexyia | Zamiayah |
| Zackya | Zaharah | Zai'kia | Zaiveonna | Zakir | Zaley | Zamiere |
| Zackyia | Zahari | Zai'veionna | Zaiya | Zakira *(0.01)* | Zali | Zamilya |
| Zacobia | Zaharí | Zai'yanna | Zaiyah | Zakirah | Zalia | Zamina |
| Zacoria | Zaharia | Zaiah | Zaiyannah | Zakiria | Zaliah | Zamira *(0.01)* |
| Zacoriah | Zahariah | Zaiba | Zajah | Zakiya *(0.03)* | Zaliana | Zamirah *(0.01)* |
| Zacoyia | Zaharie | Zaibin | Zajahniem | Zakiyaa | Zaliayah | Zamiraha |
| Zacuria | Zahariea | Zaibra | Zaji | Zakiyah *(0.02)* | Zalicia | Zamireua |
| Zada *(0.03)* | Zaharria | Zaicia | Zakada | Zakiyya | Zalidya | Zamiriyah |
| Zada-Kay | Zahava | Zaida *(0.02)* | Zakailah | Zakiyyah *(0.01)* | Zalie | Za-Mirra |
| Zadaria | Zahavah | Zaidah | Zakailey | Zakiyyia | Zalieiah | Zamiya *(0.01)* |
| Zadayah | Zahavon | Zaidali | Zakajun | Zakkiah | Zalika | Zamiyah *(0.01)* |

| | | | | | | |
|---|---|---|---|---|---|---|
| Zamiza | Zandrea | Za-Nyhia | Zareta | Zaryah *(0.01)* | Zaydrian | Ze'nya |
| Zamon | Zandreah | Zanyhia | Zareth | Zaryanah | Zayia | Ze'ryah |
| Zamoni | Zandri | Zanyia | Zareya | Zaryelle | Zayiah | Zea |
| Zamonie | Zandria | Zanyiah | Zareyah | Zaryha | Zayiana | Zéabelle |
| Zamonié | Zandrina | Zanyjha | Zarha | Zaryia | Zayla *(0.01)* | Zeada |
| Zamora *(0.01)* | Zandryale | Zanyla | Zari | Zaryuah | Zaylah | Zealand |
| Zamorah | Zandy | Zanylah | Zari'auna | Zasha | Zayle | Zealie |
| Zamorelle | Zane | Zanyri | Zari'ya | Zasheli | Zayleah | Zeanb |
| Zamoria | Zaneb | Zao | Zari'yah | Zashenka | Zaylee *(0.01)* | Zeanee |
| Zamoriah | Zanecia | Zaory | Zariá | Zaslea | Zayleigh | Zeani |
| Zamorra | Zaneria | Zapatista | Zaria *(0.13)* | Zaterria | Zaylexis | Zeannaleaha |
| Zamorriah | Zaneya | Zaphen | Zariae | Zatiyia | Zayley | Zeanne |
| Zamsam | Zanhiya | Zaphia | Zariah *(0.10)* | Zatori | Zayli | Zeariah |
| Zamyá | Zanhya | Zaphire | Zariaha | Zaubreail | Zaylie | Zeba |
| Zamya *(0.01)* | Zani | Zaporah | Zaria-Milan | Zaukira | Zaylin | Zebbi'niqu |
| Zamyah | Zania *(0.01)* | Zaqiuah | Zariana | Zaundria | Zaylisha | Zebee |
| Zamyia | Zaniah *(0.02)* | Zaqorya | Zarianna | Zauria | Zayly | Zebrayia |
| Zamyra | Zaniah Tina | Zaquala | Zariay'en | Zava | Zaylyn | Zebria |
| Zam-Zam | Zaniaya | Zaquira | Zarie | Zavannah | Zaymarie | Zebrina |
| Zamzam *(0.01)* | Zanib | Zar Riah | Zariea | Zaverie | Zayna *(0.01)* | Zechariah |
| Zan | Zanidah | Zar'nasia | Zariefa | Zavia | Zaynab *(0.02)* | Zecharier |
| Zan Niah | Zanieah | Zar'niria | Zariel | Zavianna | Zaynabo | Zechaya |
| Zana *(0.01)* | Zanihia | Zara *(0.12)* | Zariela | Zavie | Zaynah | Zed'dra |
| Zanadia | Zanihya | Zarael | Zarielle | Zavieiona | Zaynalyc | Zeddesha |
| Zanae | Zanii'yah | Zaraeyah | Zarieya | Zaviena | Zayne | Zee |
| Zanaeya | Zanijah | Zarah *(0.02)* | Zariha | Zavion | Zayneb | Zee'naya |
| Zanah | Zanijeonna | Zarahi | Zariiyah | Zavismary | Zaynia | Zeejah |
| Zanai | Zanika | Zarahyha | Zarijah | Zavley | Zaynna | Zeelan |
| Zanaia | Zaninqua | Zarah-Yseult | Zarilyn | Zavry | Zaynne | Zeelia |
| Zanaide-Rose | Zanique | Zarai | Zarina | Zavyer | Zayonah | Zeena |
| Zanaijah | Zanirah | Zaraih | Zarionna | Zawadi | Zayra *(0.01)* | Zeenat |
| Zanaiya | Zanita | Zara-Inez | Zariria | Zaxlee | Zayre | Zeenat-Ul-Nisa |
| Zanaiyah | Zaniya *(0.05)* | Zaraiya | Zarisleidy | Zay'dah | Zayree | Zeesa |
| Zanajea | Zaniyah *(0.05)* | Zarajah | Zariya *(0.01)* | Zay'driana | Zayret | Zeesy |
| Zanaka | Zaniyaha | Zaraly | Zariyah *(0.02)* | Zay'keyria | Zayria | Zeeyah |
| Zanarea | Zanna *(0.01)* | Zaramia | Zariyaha | Zay'veaire | Zayrreah | Zeeza |
| Zanaria | Zannah | Zaraphina | Zariyonna | Zaya *(0.01)* | Zaysha | Zefrione |
| Zanasia | Zannika | Zaravia | Zarmina | Zayah | Zayshia | Zeham |
| Zanaudia | Zanobi | Zaray | Zarnayesha | Zayaini | Zaythel | Zehda |
| Zanaurya | Zanobia | Zaraya | Zarra | Zayan | Zayveanna | Zehra |
| Zanaviya | Zanolie | Zardaija | Zarrea | Zayana | Zayvia | Zehra Khan |
| Zanay | Zanovia | Zardiah | Zarreah | Zayani | Zazil | Zehraa |
| Zanaya *(0.01)* | Zantaja | Zare'onna | Zarreyanah | Zayanna | Zazzmiyanna | Zei'nabou |
| Zanayah | Zantaria | Zarea | Zarrhea | Zayanoria | Zcheta | Zeibre |
| Zanayia | Zantasia | Zareaha | Zarria *(0.01)* | Zayara | Zdenka | Zeidie |
| Zanayiah | Zantia | Zareaunna | Zarriah *(0.01)* | Zayaria | Ze | Zeillin |
| Zanayzia | Zantoria | Zareena | Zarriana | Zayda *(0.03)* | Ze'breona | Zein'g |
| Zanaza | Zantranique | Zareenah | Zarriel | Zaydah | Ze'kayla | Zeina *(0.01)* |
| Zandae'jiah | Zany'ah | Zarefa | Zarrin | Zayde | Ze'kyah | Zeinab *(0.02)* |
| Zandra *(0.01)* | Zanya *(0.01)* | Zareiyah | Zarriya | Zaydee | Ze'maria | Zeinalsharaf |
| Zandralee | Zanyah | Zarela | Zarvione | Zayden | Ze'mira | Zekeah |
| Zandraya | Zanyane | Zareonna | Zarya *(0.01)* | Zaydha | Ze'niya | Zekeia |
| Zandre | Zanyelle | Zaret | Za-Ryah | Zaydi | Ze'niyah | Zeketa |

| | | | | | | |
|---|---|---|---|---|---|---|
| Zekia | Zenarah | Zerenity | Zhane *(0.01)* | Zhyariah | Ziada | Zikira |
| Zekiah | Zenath | Zeriah | Zhanell | Zhyion | Ziah *(0.01)* | Zikiya |
| Zekira | Zenaya | Zerika | Zhanelle | Zhykia | Ziahra | Zikoora |
| Zekiyah | Zenayda | Zerina | Zhania | Zhyla | Ziahyn | Zikya |
| Zelaina | Zendmeni | Zeriyah | Zhaniá | Zhylah | Ziaira | Zikyria |
| Zelaynia | Zendora | Zeruiah | Zhaniah | Zhyon | Ziaire | Zilah |
| Zelda *(0.01)* | Zendra | Zeryia | Zhaniya | Zhyona | Zialynn | Zilan |
| Zelea | Zendzi | Zesarus | Zhaniyah | Zhyonna | Zia-May | Zilana |
| Zeleah | Zene'a | Zestrianna | Zhanya | Zhyria | Ziambra | Zilaya |
| Zelena | Zenecianna | Zeta *(0.01)* | Zhanye | Zhyron | Zian | Zilea |
| Zelene | Zenei | Zeta-Marie | Zhara | Zi | Ziana | Zi-Li |
| Zelenna | Zeneida | Zetta | Zharah | Zi Aire | Zianah | Zilmarie |
| Zelia | Zeneryia | Zetti | Zharahy | Zi Qing | Ziandra | Zilya |
| Zeliana | Zeneta | Zev | Zhare'ya | Zi'adrian | Ziane | Zimara |
| Zelica Kristine | Zeni | Zeva | Zharea | Zi'ah | Ziangel | Zimaria |
| Zelie | Zenia *(0.01)* | Zeven | Zhareya | Zi'aire | Zianna | Zimiel |
| Zeliha | Zenia Ruby | Zevene | Zhareylis | Zi'aja | Zianne | Zimmari |
| Zelina | Zeniada | Zevonie | Zhari | Zi'asia | Ziannie | Zimree |
| Zelira | Zeniah | Zevonyah | Zharia *(0.01)* | Zi'auna | Zianobu | Zimri |
| Zeliscia | Zeniy'ah | Zeyah | Zhariah | Zi'azya | Ziany | Zimya |
| Zelize | Zeniya | Zeyda | Zharianne | Zi'kea | Zianya | Zina |
| Zella *(0.01)* | Zeniyah | Zeyhnaia | Zharick | Zi'keiah | Ziara | Zinab |
| Zelle | Zenna | Zeyiah | Zharielle | Zi'kendra | Ziarah | Zinadia |
| Zellie | Zennia | Zeyla | Zhasia | Zi'keria | Ziare | Zinae |
| Zelly | Zenobia *(0.01)* | Zey-Lee | Zhatalia | Zi'keya | Ziari | Zinai |
| Zelma | Zenobya | Zeynab | Zhaylinn | Zi'khia | Ziaria | Zinara |
| Zelphia | Zenoria | Zeynabu | Zhe Wai | Zi'kierah | Ziarra | Zinasia |
| Zelthcin | Zentavia | Zeynep | Zhen | Zi'kirya | Ziarre | Zinay |
| Zeltzin | Zeny | Zh | Zhenasia | Zi'kiya | Ziasia | Zinaya |
| Zelyn | Zenya | Zh'ariea | Zheniah | Zi'kyah | Ziatera | Zind Zhi |
| Zemannie | Zenyana | Zha Kariah | Zhenya | Zi'laziah | Ziayrah | Zindzi |
| Zemaria | Zenye | Zha'mari | Zheriia | Zi'niah | Ziba | Zinearia |
| Zeme | Zephania | Zha'niyah | Zheta | Zi'nya | Zibiyah | Zineb |
| Zemi | Zephaniah | Zha'nya | Zhi'auni | Zi'onna | Zicely | Zingtin |
| Zemia | Zephanie | Zhadia | Zhi'nae | Zi'onyah | Ziearia | Zinhle- |
| Zemiah | Zephara | Zhakera | Zhian | Zi'ora | Zielia |    Ntombikayise |
| Zemir | Zephraniah | Zhakerria | Zhiarae | Zi'priya | Zienab | Zinia |
| Zemira | Zephyr | Zhakiyah | Zhiarah | Zi'quiria | Zienna | Ziniaha |
| Zemirah | Zephyre |    Nyiana | Zhijia | Zi'ree | Ziera | Ziniyah |
| Zemyria | Zephyrin | Zhakyiah | Zhi-Mei | Zi'riyah | Zierra | Zinneth |
| Zemzem | Zeporia | Zhalandrea | Zhireana | Zi'tavia | Zierrah | Zinnia *(0.01)* |
| Zen | Zeppora | Zhaliyah | Zhkarrela | Zi'torria | Ziham | Zinobia |
| Zen'tasia | Zer'riya | Zhamaria | Zhniya | Zi'yahna | Ziharha | Zintkala Luta Wi |
| Zena *(0.02)* | Zera | Zhamariah | Zhniyah | Zi'yalah | Zihya | Zinya |
| Zena'ja | Zerada | Zhamirah | Zhoe | Zi'yana | Ziigwan | Zinygeá |
| Zenab | Zerae | Zhan'a | Zhoey | Zi'yaunah | Zijah | Zinyia |
| Zenaeh | Zerahiah | Zhana | Zhoi | Zi'yier | Zijri | Zinyon |
| Zenah | Zeraiah | Zhanae | Zhonae | Zi'yonah | Zikeria | Zion *(0.09)* |
| Zenahida | Zerakiya | Zhanaé | Zhonteria | Zi'yonna | Zikerra | Zion Josephaine |
|   Zenaida | Zeraline | Zhanay | Zhor-Ines | Zi'yonneia | Zi-Kerriah | Zion'ae |
| Zenai | Zeray | Zhanaysia | Zhuoyi | Zia *(0.02)* | Zikeya | Zion'ashae |
| Zenaida | Zereda | Zhanazha | Zhy'teria | Zia'kayla | Zikiah | Zion'na |
| Zena-Marie | Zerelda | Zhané | Zhyan | Ziaakiya | Zikiaha | Ziona *(0.01)* |

Zionah
Zionanah
Zioni
Zioninique
Zionna (0.01)
Zionnah
Zionne
Zionya
Zipa
Ziporah
Zipporah (0.02)
Zipporrah
Ziqi
Ziqing
Zira
Zirah
Ziraili
Ziraily
Ziranda
Zirayha
Ziri
Zirrae
Zirrell
Zisherrie
Zissy (0.01)
Zita
Zitesha
Zitlali
Zitlalic
Zitlalin
Zitlallic
Zitlally
Zitlaly
Zitounia
Ziva
Zivia
Ziwei
Zixygany
Ziy'mayla
Ziyá
Ziya (0.01)
Ziyah (0.01)
Ziyan
Ziyana
Ziyanna
Ziyaunna
Ziye'ra
Ziyel
Ziyha
Ziyi
Ziyiah Bre
Ziyian
Ziyodulla

Ziyon
Ziyona
Ziyonna
Ziyonnah
Ziyuanna
Ziza
Zizalitza
Zizhen
Zja Zjané
Zja'via
Zjah'riaah
Zjara
Zjhona
Zjonwheu
Zkiah
Zkirah
Zkiyah
Zkyah
Zmariona
Zmya
Znae
Znaia
Znieya
Zniya
Znya
Znyiah
Zo'el
Zo'myah
Zo'myria
Zo'rhiyah
Zoa
Zoah
Zobaida
Zodia
Zoé
Zöe
Zoé (0.01)
Zoë (0.03)
Zoe (2.51)
Zoe Anna
Zoe Jane
Zoe Lee
Zoe Maria
Zoeana
Zoe-Caralie
Zoedaisha
Zoee (0.03)
Zoeey
Zoefia
Zoé-Gabrielle
Zoehy
Zoei (0.01)
Zoeie

Zoe-Jane
Zoe-Jo
Zoel
Zoël
Zoeladia
Zoelia
Zoelie
Zoell
Zoelle
Zoë-Lyn
Zoe-Lynn
Zoe-Mara
Zoenique
Zoequria
Zoeria
Zoeryah
Zoey (1.35)
Zoey Angel
Zoey Ashyah
Zoey Karen
Zoey Wai Kwan
Zoeya
Zoeyana
Zoeyann
Zoey-Anne
Zoey-Lee
Zoeylyn
Zofia (0.01)
Zoha (0.01)
Zohaa
Zoha-Azeem
Zohal
Zohar
Zohée
Zohely
Zohha
Zohmaree
Zohni
Zohra
Zohrah
Zohreh
Zohwea
Zoí
Zoi (0.01)
Zoie (0.17)
Zoiee
Zoie-Jaine
Zoiey
Zoila
Zoilynda
Zoin
Zoina
Zoish

Zok
Zoke
Zokhia
Zokia
Zola (0.01)
Zola May
Zolah
Zolangie
Zola-Rain
Zolaria
Zolayshia
Zoleena
Zolie
Zolimarie
Zolivia
Zoliyah
Zolynn
Zomara
Zomba
Zona
Zonaiah
Zonaira
Zondra
Zonghao
Zongsee
Zonia
Zoniah
Zonkece
Zonkya
Zonyell
Zooey
Zoomba
Zophia
Zophie
Zophyah
Zoquayla
Zora (0.02)
Zorah
Zorah-Helena
Zoraida
Zoraly
Zorana
Zorane
Zoraya
Zorbari
Zoreanna
Zoreenah
Zorenau
Zorene
Zoret
Zori
Zoria
Zoriah (0.01)

Zoriana
Zoriane
Zorianna
Zorica
Zorie
Zorin
Zorisbel
Zoriya
Zormaris
Zorrah
Zorrana
Zorri
Zorria
Zorryunna
Zoryana
Zoryelle
Zoryn
Zosha
Zosia (0.01)
Zoua
Zougaida
Zouri
Zovianna
Zowey
Zowie (0.01)
Zoya (0.03)
Zoyah
Zoyee
Zoyia
Zoyl
Zoyla
Zozee
Zriyah
Zsa Zsa
Zsanae
Zsane
Zsaraiiyah
Zsazsa
Zshonna
Zsofia
Zu'maya
Zubaida
Zubayda
Zubi
Zubieda
Zucette
Zucy
Zueheily
Zuenny
Zuezsanna
Zugeily
Zuha
Zuhailee

Zuham
Zuheidi
Zuhein
Zuhnyda
Zuhoor
Zuhra
Zujailee
Zujeidi
Zujeily
Zujey
Zukeriah
Zula
Zulai
Zulaika
Zulaikha
Zulaine
Zulal
Zulana
Zulaykha
Zulaynna
Zulehimy
Zulei
Zuleica
Zuleidy
Zuleika
Zuleima
Zuleimi
Zuleimy
Zulekha
Zulema (0.01)
Zulexia
Zuley
Zuleydy
Zuleyka (0.01)
Zuleyma
Zuleymi
Zuleyska
Zulfah
Zuliana
Zulianah
Zuliany
Zulli
Zully
Zullybel
Zulma
Zulmalyz
Zuly
Zulyana
Zulyene
Zulymar
Zumara
Zumyli
Zunairah

Zundus
Zuneida
Zunzeiry
Zurai
Zurayah
Zurenity
Zuri (0.03)
Zuria
Zurianna
Zurie
Zuriel
Zurisadai
Zuriya
Zurnaisa
Zury
Zusana
Zuya
Zuzanna
Zuzu
Zuzzette
Zxochitl
Zy'
Zy'adria
Zy'ahna
Zy'air
Zy'aira
Zy'aire
Zy'airea
Zy'aja
Zy'anne
Zy'area
Zy'aria
Zy'asia
Zy'daria
Zy'dasia
Zy'daysia
Zy'dayzia
Zy'diair
Zy'eir
Zy'eria
Zy'eriah
Zy'erica
Zy'hierra
Zy'ian
Zy'karia
Zy'kayzia
Zy'keera
Zy'keia
Zy'keira
Zy'kena
Zy'kenya
Zy'kera
Zy'keri

| | | | | | | |
|---|---|---|---|---|---|---|
| Zy'keria (0.01) | Zy'nia | Zyaira | Zyeiar | Zy-Keria | Zymaria | Zyon (0.01) |
| Zy'keriah | Zy'niah | Zyairah | Zyekia | Zykeria (0.01) | Zymarie | Zyona |
| Zy'kerria | Zy'niajah | Zyaire (0.01) | Zyemoria | Zykerianna | Zymekia | Zyonah |
| Zy'kerrianna | Zy'niya | Zyaisha | Zyen-Isis | Zykeriya | Zymereria | Zyonn |
| Zy'keyria | Zy'niyiah | Zyaiysha | Zyerah | Zykerra | Zy-Mia | Zyonna (0.01) |
| Zy'kheria | Zy'on | Zyalexisiyah | Zyeri | Zykerria | Zymia | Zyonne |
| Zy'kiah | Zy'onah | Zyalyce | Zyeria | Zykerriua | Zymira | Zyra |
| Zy'kiara | Zy'onna | Zyamari | Zygia | Zykerriyah | Zymirra | Zyrae |
| Zy'kiera | Zy'onni | Zyan | Zyhanni | Zykevia | Zymoni | Zyrelisse |
| Zy'kieria | Zy'qeria | Zyanah | Zyhnique | Zykeyka | Zyna | Zyria |
| Zy'kierra | Zy'quariah | Zyandra | Zyhrina | Zykia (0.01) | Zynab | Zyriah |
| Zy'kierria | Zy'quavia | Zyani | Zyi'kerria | Zykiah | Zynae | Zyrianna |
| Zy'kira | Zy'quia | Zyann | Zyia | Zykiera | Zynaejha | Zyrie-Ana |
| Zy'kiria | Zy'rasia | Zy-Anna | Zyiah | Zykira | Zynaja | Zyrinn |
| Zy'kiya | Zy'reyana | Zyanna | Zyian | Zykirah | Zynajah | Zyrion |
| Zy'koyiah | Zy'ria | Zyannah | Zyianna | Zykirea | Zynara | Zyriyahnua |
| Zy'learya | Zy'rianna | Zyanne | Zyiara | Zykiria | Zynaria | Zyrre |
| Zy'lelia | Zy'swaya | Zyanya | Zyier | Zykirria | Zynasia | Zyryll |
| Zy'mani | Zy'tashia | Zyara | Zyilah | Zykria | Zynasiah | Zysean |
| Zy'mara | Zy'teliyah | Zyaria | Zyion | Zykyria | Zynayah | Zyshaun |
| Zy'meirah | Zy'terria | Zyariah | Zyionna | Zyla (0.01) | Zynazia | Zytanique |
| Zy'merriah | Zy'yana | Zyariel | Zyire | Zylah | Zynesha | Zytasia |
| Zy'mirrea | Zy'yhea | Zyasia | Zyjana | Zylasia | Zynia (0.01) | Zytavia |
| Zy'miya | Zya | Zyasiah | Zykara | Zylayah | Zyniah | Zyteria |
| Zy'myiah | Zyaan | Zyberia | Zykariah | Zylbeeia | Zynialee | Zyterria |
| Zy'naijha | Zyah | Zycia | Zykeara | Zyleen | Zynique | Zytlaly |
| Zy'naisha | Zyahna | Zydani | Zykeeah | Zylia | Zynita | Zyun |
| Zy'naizha | Zyaih | Zyderia | Zykeiah | Zylina-Jonmari | Zyniyah | Zy-Unnia |
| Zy'nasia | Zyailah | Zy-Derricka | Zykeliyah | Zylinn | Zynleigh | Zyviairah |
| Zy'neasia | Zyair | Zyeaire | Zykera | Zymaiha | Zyny | Zywona |

# Boys' Names—The Complete List

*Popularity ratings indicate usage per thousand baby boys.*
*Rare names with usage lower than one in 100,000 have no popularity rating numbers.*

### ~ A ~

A
A B
A Bricklin
A G
A J
A Mauri
A Myson
A Shawn
A V
A.B.
A.Hannan
A.J.
A.K.I.L.
A'aimauree
A'briyahn
A'coreyon
A'darion
A'darius
A'den
A'deriyon
A'detrick
A'dien
A'din
A'donis
A'donus
A'jalyon
A'jani
A'jarion
A'javeon
A'javion

A'jaye
A'jaylan
A'jee
A'jious
A'kari
A'keem
A'kese
A'khai
A'khari
A'ki
A'kilieze
A'kirien
A'kirrion
A'kiyo
A'kobi
A'lante
A'lexis
A'lontae
A'lyus
A'ma'rie
A'mahd
A'mahn
A'majah
A'mar
A'marcus
A'mare
A'mari *(0.01)*
A'marion *(0.01)*
A'marius
A'mariyan
A'markus
A'marrion

A'marrius
A'maurey
A'mauri
A'maurion-
    Maurice
A'maury
A'mear
A'meer
A'mere
A'million
A'mir
A'mirion
A'monté
A'murie
A'myron
A'quavius
A'quiwe
A'quori
A'qwaun
A'rick
A'rieon
A'ron
A'sa
A'sad
A'sahi
A'santé
A'santee
A'sean
A'shawn
A'sijah
A'tavion
A'tayvion

A'timere
A'toinje
A'treal
A'vantae
A'vari
A'veion
A'veyion
A'veyon
A'viane
A'vonntae
A'vont
A'zarion
A'zarius
A'zavian
A'zayvier
A'zayvion
A'zhani
A'zirean
A'zsan
Aá Von
Aaban
Aabid
Aadam
Aadarsh
Aaden *(0.01)*
Aadesh
Aadhidhya
Aadhith
Aadhithia
Aadhithya
Aadhitiya
Aadi *(0.01)*

Aadil
Aadin
Aadinadh
Aadit
Aadithya
Aaditya
Aadivion
Aadyn *(0.01)*
Aaen
Aagneya
Aahan
Aahil
Aahmaad
Aahmad
Aahren
Aahzier
Aai
Aaidan
Aaiden
Aaiyaun
Aakarsh
Aakash
Aakyrie
Aala
Aalan
Aalap
Aaleen Abbas
Aali
Aalias
Aalijah
Aaliyah
Aaliyo

Aalok
Aaloke
Aamad
Aamahod
Aamar
Aamareé
Aamari
Aámaris
Aamarr
Aameen
Aamere
Aamil'ion
Aamir *(0.01)*
Aamogh
Aamond
Aamori
Aanav
Aanden
Aandre
Aanek
Aanen
Aaniydras
Aanjay
Aanna
Aannin
Aans Zakria
Aanyi
Aaorn
Aaqil
Aaquil
Aaran
Aarav *(0.01)*

Aaren *(0.01)*
Aarenamon
Aarenton
Aareon
Aarez
Aari
Aarib
Aaric
Aarik
Aarin
Aarinton
Aarion
Aarionn
Aariyan
Aariz
Aarjav
Aarmaan
Aarman
Aarnav
Aarnell
Aaron *(3.57)*
Aaron Alexander
Aaron Ariel
Aaron Danilo
Aaron James
Aaron Jared
Aaron Josiah
Aaron Julian
Aaron
    Longtruongp
Aaron Matthew
Aaron Miguel

| | | | | | | |
|---|---|---|---|---|---|---|
| Aaron Trenton | Ab. | Abdel-Hamid | Abdifath | Abdoulaye | Abdulbari | Abdul-Rahman |
| Aaron' | Abacuc | Abdelhamid | Abdifitaah | *(0.01)* | Abdulfatah | Abdulrahman |
| Aaron-Afful | Abad | Abdelhamid- | Abdifitah | Abdoulie | Abdul-Fattah | *(0.01)* |
| Aarondeep | Abala | Najmeddin | Abdihakim | Abdoullah | Abdulfattah | Abdulraman |
| Aaron-Gaspar | Abaldo | Abdeljalil | Abdihkeem | Abdoullaye | Abdulgalim | Abdulraqeeb |
| Aaron-Jahmil | Aban | Abdelkarim | Abdijabar | Abdoulsamad | Abdulghaffar | Abdulraqib |
| Aaronn | Abanezer | Abdellah | Abdijibaar | Abdoul-Wadoud | Abdul-Hakeem | Abdul-Rashad |
| Aaronontae | Abarr | Abdel-Latif | Abdikadir | Abdourahman | Abdulhakiim | Abdul-Rehman |
| Aaronson | Abas | Abdellatif | Abdikani | Abdourahmane | Abdul-Halim | Abdulrehman |
| Aarreon | Abasi | Abdelmalak | Abdikhadar | Abdouramane | Abdul-Hameed | Abdulvorith |
| Aarron | Abass | Abdelmalek- | Abdikhadir | Abdourrahmane | Abdulhameed | Abdulwadud |
| Aarush *(0.01)* | Abayomi | Amine | Abdikhaliq | Abdrahman | Abdul-Hamid | Abdul-Wahaab |
| Aarv | Abbad | Abdelmoez | Abdilahi | Abdramane | Abdulhamid | Abdulwahab |
| Aarya | Abbas *(0.01)* | Abdelnour | Abdillahi | Abdrhman | Abdulhohaimen | Abdul-Wali |
| Aaryan *(0.01)* | Abbass | Abdelqader | Abdimajid | Abdu | Abdul-Jaleel | Abdulwali |
| Aaryash | Abbdulahi | Abdel-Rahman | Abdimalik *(0.01)* | Abdualmajid | Abduljaleel | Abdul-Wasai |
| Aaryes | Abbie | Abdelrahman | Abdinacm | Abduaziz | Abdul-Jalil | Abdul-Zahir |
| Aaryh | Abbiezer | *(0.01)* | Abdinafi | Abdu-Errahman | Abdulkadir | Abdunasir |
| Aaryn | Abbigail | Abdelraoof | Abdinajib | Abduhu | Abdulkaliq | Abdun-Nur |
| Aasa | Abbner | Abdelraouf | Abdinasir *(0.01)* | Abdukhadr | Abdul-Kareem | Abdur |
| Aasah | Abbott | Abdelrazeq | Abdiqadar | Abdul *(0.05)* | Abdul-Karim | Abdur Rahman |
| Aasem | Abbott Cobain | Abdelrehman | Abdiqadir | Abdul Ahad | Abdulkarim | Abdur Rakib |
| Aasen | Abby | Abdelrhman | Abdiqalib | Abdul Fattah | Abdulkhani | Abduraham |
| Aashir | Abd | Abdeltareek | Abdiqani | Abdul Hadi | Abdulla | Abdu-Rahman |
| Aashish | Abd Alrahman | Abdelwahab | Abdirahim | Abdul Kader | Abdullaah | Abdurahman |
| Aashrut | Abd El Hadi | Abdelwahhab | Abdirahman | Abdul Karim | Abdullaahi | *(0.01)* |
| Aashton | Abd El Malik | Abdelwally | *(0.04)* | Abdul Malik | Abdul-Lah | Abdurazak |
| Aasi | Abd El-Rahman | Abdenour | Abdirahmen | Abdul Mannan | Abdullah *(0.08)* | Abdurraafe |
| Aasim | Abd Elrahman | Abderahman | Abdiraouf | Abdul Massud | Abdullah | Abdur-Rabbi |
| Aasin | Abd Ur Rahman | Abderahmane | Abdirashid | Abdul Muqit | Almahdi | Abdur-Raheem |
| Aásir | Abdal | Abderaouf | Abdiraxmaan | Abdul Qadir | Abdullah-Hatam | Abdurrahim |
| Aasiya | Abdala | Abderhamane | Abdirazaq | Abdul Raheem | Abdullahi *(0.02)* | Abdurrahmaan |
| Aathavan | Abdale | Abderrahim | Abdiresaq | Abdul Rahman | Abdul-Latif | Abdur-Rahman |
| Aathman | Abdalkareem | Abderrahman | Abdirisak | Abdul Razzaqq | Abdull- | Abdurrahman |
| Aathmanathan | Abdalla | Abderrahmane | Abdisa | Abdul Shahid | Rahmaan | Abdur-Rahman |
| Aatish | Abdallah *(0.02)* | Abderraouf | Abdisalaam | Abdul Wahab | Abdulmajed | Ibn Sul |
| Aatlas | Abdalmalek | Abdes | Abdisalan | Abdula | Abdulmajeed | Abdurrohim |
| Aatman | Abdalrahim | Abdhul | Abdisamad | Abdulaahi | Abdul-Malik | Abdus |
| Aaven | Abd-Alrahman | Abdi | Abdisamed | Abduladif | Abdulmalik | Abdusalom |
| Aávian | Abdalrahman | Abdi Kani | Abdishakur | Abdulah | Abdulmoez | Abdusamad |
| Aavin | Abd-Alrhaman | Abdi Mumini | Abdiwahab | Abdulahad | Abdul- | Abdushakur |
| Aavir | Abdeali | Abdi Rahman | Abdiwali | Abdulahi *(0.01)* | Muhaimin | Abdus-Saboor |
| Aavonté | Abdeel | Abdi Rizak | Abdou | Abdulai | Abdulmujeeb | Abdussalam |
| Aayaan | Abdel *(0.01)* | Abdiaiziz | Abdou | Abdul-Akir | Abdul-Nasir | Abdussamad |
| Aayan *(0.01)* | Abdel Karim | Abdias *(0.01)* | Arahmane | Abdul-Alim | Abdulqaadir | Abduz Zahir |
| Aayden | Abdel Malik | Abdiasis | Abdou Azize | Abdulallaam | Abdulqadir | Abe *(0.01)* |
| Aayush *(0.01)* | Abdel Wahab | Abdi-Aziz | Abdou-Alhakin | Abdulazeez | Abdul-Quadri | Abebram |
| Aazan | Abdelah | Abdiaziz | Abdouallah | Abdulaziz | Abdulrafay | Abed |
| Aazavier | Abdel-Azim | Abdicasiis | Abdou-Aziz | Abdul-Aziz | Abdul-Rahaman | Abed-Aljabbar |
| Ab | Abdelaziz | Abdidahir | Abdoul | Abdul-Azizz | Abdul-Raheem | Abedallah |
| Ab Air | Abdelghani | Abdiel *(0.02)* | Abdoul Wahab | Abdul-Badi | Abdulraheem | Abedalrahman |
| Ab Christopher | Abdelhakim | Abdieser | Abdoula | Abdulbaki | Abdulrahim | Abedelrahman |
| Ab Gotti | Abdel-Halim | Abdifatah | Abdoulay | Abdulbaki | Abdul-Rahma | Abederrahmen |

| | | | | | | |
|---|---|---|---|---|---|---|
| Abednego | Abi | Abrahm (0.01) | Acea | Adalverto | Adbe | Adelon |
| Abeesh | Abiam | Abraj | Acéa | Adam (3.40) | Adbell | Adelrione |
| Abeezar | Abid | Abram (0.10) | Aceland | Adam Arnold | Addain | Adem (0.01) |
| Abel (0.12) | Abidail | Abran (0.01) | Acelin | Adam Bradle | Addam | Ademar |
| Abelard | Abidany | Abrar | Acelyn | Adam Le | Addan | Ademilola |
| Abelardo (0.01) | Abidullah | Abraum | Acen | Adam | Addason | Ademir |
| Abeldain | Abie | Abraxas | Aceson | Minhnhan | Addeash | Ademola |
| Abele | Abiel (0.01) | Abraxin | Achal | Adam Robert | Addem | Ademole |
| Abel-Gerard | Abiel-Aa | Abreaham | Achaz-Azor | Adam Samuel | Adden | Ademore |
| Abelicio | Abiemalecks | Abrehm | Achee | Adam Ul Haque | Adderly | Aden (0.39) |
| Abelino | Abigael | Abren | Achelous | Adam Zachary | Addiel | Adeniyi |
| Aben | Abigail (0.01) | Abreon | Achely | Adam's Laurin | Addin | Adeon |
| Abenezer | Abigayle | Abreun | Acheton | Adambradley | Addington | Aderian |
| Aberum | Abijah | Abrey | Achilies | Adam-Hamza | Addis | Aderion |
| Abey | Abimael (0.01) | Abreyun | Achille | Adamiah | Addison (0.13) | Aderius |
| Abeyarno | Abimbola | Abrham | Achilleas | Adamie | Addison James | Aderlyn |
| Abgul-Qadir | Abimelec | Abrhan | Achilles (0.03) | Adam-Li | Addison John | Aderris |
| Abhai | Abinav | Abrhm | Achilles Amor | Adam- | Addisson | Adesh |
| Abhan | Abiodun | Abrian | Achilles Daniel | Mohamed | Addler | Adeshpratap |
| Abhav | Abir | Abriel | Achillies | Adamo (0.01) | Addly | Adesoji |
| Abhay | Abisahim | Abron | Achillius | Adamo- | Addonez | Adess |
| Abhaya | Abisai (0.01) | Abrum | Achim | Gabrielle | Addonis | Adetola |
| Abhayjeet | Abisan | Abryan | Achimelec | Adam-Olivier | Addrienne- | Adeyn |
| Abhayjit | Abishai | Abryon | Achintya | Adams | Santos | Adgie |
| Abhaypartap | Abishek | Abshir | Achit | Adam-Saeed | Addy | Adham |
| Abhayroop | Abiye Antoine | Abtin | Achor | Adam-Trung | Addys | Adhan |
| Abheek | Abizai | Abu | Achraf (0.01) | Adan (0.16) | Addyson | Adharsh |
| Abhel | Able | Abu Bakar | Achtin | Adan Chalio | Ade | Adhbuth |
| Abhey | Abm | Abu Bakarr | Achuil | Adanaz | Adeb | Adheem |
| Abhi | Abnaas | Abu'bakr | Achyut | Adandé | Adebayo | Adheesh |
| Abhi Vasisht | Abner (0.03) | Abu-Bakar | Acie | Adante | Adebe | Adhem |
| Abhibir | Abnian | Abubakar (0.01) | Ackiem | Adanté | Adebola | Adhemar |
| Abhigya | Abo-Bakr | Abubakarr | Acner | Adao | Adedeji | Adhik |
| Abhiiraam | Abou | Abubakary | Acorion | Adaon | Adedoyin | Adhisht |
| Abhijay | Abou Bakr | Abubakr | Acoya | Adar | Adeeb | Adhithya |
| Abhijaya | Abouakar | Abudllahi | Acxel | Adareon | Adeel | Adhm |
| Abhijeet | Aboubacar | Abuhamdeh | Acy | Adareus | Adeesson | Adhvaith |
| Abhik | Aboudoulaye | Abuhurairah | Acyon | Adari | Adeethyia | Adi (0.01) |
| Abhimaan | Aboulay | Abukar | Ada | Adarian | Adefemi | Adian (0.03) |
| Abhimanyu | Aboulaziz | Abukhalil | Adadrian | Adarien | Adeim | Adian-Oscar |
| Abhinav (0.03) | Abraam | Abuubakar | Adael | Adarin | Adein | Adiath |
| Abhinay | Abraao | Abuzar | Adahel | Adarion | Adekunle | Adib |
| Abhineet | Abraar | Aby | Adahir | Adarious | Adel (0.01) | Adiel (0.01) |
| Abhinu | Abraham (0.40) | Abyan | Adain (0.01) | Adaris | Adelaido | Adien (0.01) |
| Abhiram (0.01) | Abraham | Abymael | Adair (0.01) | Adarius (0.01) | Adelaja | Adil (0.01) |
| Abhisar | Marlon | AC | Adaira | Adarrius | Adelan | Adilali |
| Abhishek (0.01) | Abraham | Aca | Adairius | Adarsh (0.01) | Adelard | Adili |
| Abhishka | Romario | Acacio | Adajion | Adauto Juan | Adelfo | Adilson |
| Abhiuday | Abraham-Akiva | Acardea | Adal | Adaveion | Adelio | Adim |
| Abhiyash | Abrahan | Acardo | Adalai | Adavian | Adeliz | Adin (0.04) |
| Abhram | Abraheem | Acarrius | Adalberto (0.01) | Adavieon | Adell | Adin Matthew |
| Abhrum | Abrahem | Acasson | Adalid | Adavion | Adelle | Adionyse |
| Abhyas | Abrahim | Ace (0.03) | Adalith | Adayr | Adelmo | Adir |

Adis
Adisa
Adison (0.01)
Adisson
Adisun
Adit
Adith
Adithan
Adithya (0.01)
Aditya (0.07)
Adityabh
Adityan
Adityye
Adiv
Adiya
Adje
Adjulika
Adlai
Adlay
Adlee
Adleigh
Adlene-El Hadj
Adler (0.02)
Adley
Admieré
Admin
Admir
Admire
Admiryan
Admyre
Adnaan
Adnan (0.02)
Adnane
Adnash
Adner
Adniel
Adofo
Adolfo (0.07)
Adolfo Cecilio
Adolph
Adolphus
Adom
Adon (0.01)
Adonael
Adonai
Adonais
Adonay
Adoneus
Adoni
Adonia
Adonias
A-Don-I-Be'-Zek
Adonijah

Adonijah
　Anthony
Adoniram
Adonis (0.08)
Adonit
Adoniyahu
Adonizio
Adonnis
Adonniss
Adonte
Adonté
Adontre
Adonus
Adonys
Adonyss
Ador
Adorian
Adorion
Adragus James
Adrahaxxen
Adrain
Adran
Adre
Adre'ion-Shon
Adrean
Adreane
Adreean
Adreece
Adreion
Adrel
Adren
Adrese
Adrevius
Adrew
Adreyan
Adreyce
Adreyon
Adriaan
Adrial
Adriam
Adrián
Adrian (3.40)
Adrian Amerigo
Adrian Jay
Adrian Jr
Adrian Paris
Adrian Sky
Adriana
Adriane
Adrian-Jesus
Adrian-Kevin
Adrianne
Adrian-Nicholas

Adrianno
Adriano (0.03)
Adriano Ang
Adrian-Sorin
Adric
Adrick
Adriean
Adriel (0.06)
Adriel Cesar
Adriel Jephte
Adrien (0.10)
Adrien David
Adrien Romain
　Gaston
Adriene
Adrienn
Adrienne
Adrientimothy
Adrieon
Adrik
Adrin
Adrine
Adrion
Adrionne
Adris
Adron
Adryan (0.01)
Adryc
Adryel
Adryen
Adryian
Adryiana
Adryon
Adu
Adul
Adulfo
Advait
Advaith
Advan
Advay
Advian
Advik
Advin
Advit
Advith
Adwaith
Adyan (0.01)
Adyen
Adyn (0.03)
Adyne
Adyn-Michael
Adynn
Adyson

Aebad
Aedan (0.06)
Aeddon
Aeden (0.02)
Aedhan
Aedian
Aedin
Aedon
Aedraen
Aedrian
Aedric
Aedyn
Aegis
Aeidan
Aeiron
Aejai
Aekadan
Aeknoor
Aekum
Aelfred
Aemon
Aen
Aendi
Aeneas (0.01)
Aengus
Aeon
Aer
Aeran
Aereon
Aerhan
Aerian
Aeric
Aeric-Denzel
Aerick
Aeriel
Aerik
Aerik Jakob
Aero
Aeron
Aeros
Aerren
Aerrian
Aerrion
Aeryk
Aeryn
Aeshan
Aesir
Aeson
Aethan
Aethelwulf
Aether
Aévaun
Aevin

Aevyn
Aeyden
Aezron
Afasik
Afdhal
Afeef
Affan
Affeon
Afhan
Afid
Afif
Afnaan
Afnan
Afolabi
Afonso
Afraz
Afrim
Aftaab
Aftab
Afton
Afzal
Aga
Agam
Agamjot
Agan
Agar
Agassi
Agastya
Agdren
Agee
Agel
Agentry
Agereon
Aghilas
Agimanna
Agnaldo
Agnew
Agok
Agostino
Agrim
Agripino
Aguibou
Aguolu
Agustas
Agusten
Agustin (0.05)
Agustine
Agusto
Agustus
Agyei
Agyeman
Ah'darius
Ah'daryall

Ah'daveion
Ah'daviyon
Ah'jah
Ah'jamari
Ah'jymon
Ah'kari
Ah'kie
Ah'king
Ah'maj
Ah'mani
Ah'marion
Ah'mir
Ah'monté
Ahaban
Ahad
Ahadu
Ahamed
Ahan
Ahanu
Ahanyu
Aharon (0.01)
Aharron
Ahdi
Ahdir
Ahearn
Ahern
Ahijah
Ahilten
Ahimelec
Ahjaden
Ahjay
Ahjere
Ahjmeir
Ahkeem
Ahkeen
Ahkerio
Ahki
Ahkim
Ahkym
Ahlan
Ahlijah
Ahlixander
Ahmaad
Ahmad (0.16)
Ahmad Ashraf
Ahmad Moussa
Ahmad Noah
　Uqail
Ahmade
Ahmadeus
Ahmad-Kayden
Ahmadou
Ahmadrick

Ahmadyasin
Ahmahd
Ahmahn
Ahmahz
Ahmair
Ahmaliki
Ahman (0.01)
Ahmand
Ahmane
Ahmani
Ahmanté
Ahmar
Ahmard
Ahmardré
Ahmare
Ahmaré
Ahmaree
Ahmari (0.01)
Ahmarien
Ahmarion
Ahmarraé
Ahmarri
Ahmarrion
Ahmaud
Ahmd
Ahme're
Ahmed (0.18)
Ahmed Rayan
Ahmed Rida
Ahmed Yacine
Ahmed Yassine
Ahmed Youcef
Ahmed-Ali
Ahmed-Bille
Ahmedeaus
Ahmed-Mounir
Ahmednur
Ahmed-Rayane
Ahmed-Reda
Ahmed-Salim
Ahmedullah
Ahmed-Walid
Ahmed-Yacine
Ahmeen
Ahmer
Ahmere
Ahmet
Ahmetcan
Ahmet-Yesevi
Ahmi
Ahmias
Ahmid
Ahmijah

| | | | | | | |
|---|---|---|---|---|---|---|
| Ahmik | Aicen | Aikan | Aisa'lin | Ajavien | Akashpreet | Akileus |
| Ahmilleon | Aid | Aikee | Aisah | Ajavious | Akaye | Akilez |
| Ahmir (0.01) | Aida | Aiken | Aisara | Ajax | Akaylam | Akili |
| Ahmire | Aidan (4.45) | Aikhem | Aishmayel | Ajaxion | Akayle | Akilis |
| Ahmiyan | Aidan Alexandre | Aiki | Aishveer | De'andre | Akaylis | Akilles |
| Ahmnad | Aidan Francesco | Aikim | Aislee | A-Jay | Akbar | Akillian |
| Ahmod | Aidan Hilarion | Aikimie | Aislin | Ajay (0.03) | Ake | Akillius |
| Ahmon | Aidan Joao | Aiklie | Aison | Ajaydeep | Akea | Akim (0.01) |
| Ahmond | Aidan Manuel | Aikman | Aisosa | Ajayln | Akeam | Akimak |
| Ahmoni | Aidan Phillip | Ailan | Aiston | Ajaylon | Akee | Akin |
| Ahmoyre | Aidan Rufino | Aili | Aitan | Ajaypal | Akeeb | Akinle |
| Ahmyr | Aidan-James | Ailie | Aitaro | Ajayveer | Akeel | Akintade |
| Ahn | Aidan-Jay | Ailim | Aitch | Ajazion | Akeelah | Akinwumi |
| Ahnab | Aidann | Aimal | Aithan | Ajdin | Akeem (0.02) | Akio |
| Ahnaf | Aidanon | Aiman | Aito | Ajeer | Akeen | Akir |
| Ahneef | Aidan-Ray | Aimane | Aitor | Ajeet | Akeena | Akira (0.01) |
| Ahnias | Aidarus | Aimar | Aiven | Ajenavi | Akeeontae | Akira Franco |
| Ahnrei | Aiddan | Aimen | Aiveon | Ajene | Akeli | Akire |
| Ahnye | Aidden | Aimer | Aivery | Ajeya | Akelle | Akireon |
| Ahnyus | Aidden-Joseph | Aimeric | Aivian | Ajhari | Akello | Akiro |
| Ahoora | Aiddin | Aimerick | Aivin | Ajibola | Akelo | Akis |
| Ahrash | Aidean | Aimery | Aiwen | Ajilon | Akemi | Akito |
| Ahren (0.01) | Aiden (4.74) | Aimin | Aixel | Ajime | Akene | Akiva (0.02) |
| Ahriel | Aiden James | Aimis | Aiyana | Ajinkya | Akerreon | Akiva-Hillel |
| Ahrod | Aiden Jesus | Aimon | Aiydan | Ajion | Akeveyahn | Akiyle |
| Ahron | Aiden Maderick | Aimory Quevon | Aiyden | Ajit | Akevi'an | Akiyon |
| Ahrwel Harry | Aiden-Jeffrey | Ainiu | Aiyidiyien | Ajitesh | Akhari | Akksayan |
| Ahsaan-Ahmad | Aiden-Joseph | Ainnelhyethum | Aiyon | Ajith | Akheel | Akmal |
| Ahsan | Aiden-Lee | Ainsley | Aizaaz | Ajmal | Akheem | Aknupheap |
| Ahssan | Aidenn | Ainsworth | Aizak | Ajohntae | Akheim | Ako |
| Ahtesham | Aiden-Noah | Airacus | Aizek | Ajon | Akhil (0.01) | Akobie |
| Ahtryhlue | Aidian | Airasen | Aizeyah | Ajourius | Akhilann | Akol |
| Ahundraye | Aidin (0.01) | Airean | Aizhon | Ajpreet | Akhil-Anthony | Akongnwi |
| Ahustin | Aidlen | Airech | Aizic | Ajuel | Akhile | Akorede |
| Ahvaanish | Aidn | Airees | Aizik (0.01) | Ajulius | Akhilesh | Akori |
| Ahvant | Aidon (0.01) | Airen | Aj (0.01) | Ajustice | Akhir | Akos |
| Ahviel | Aidrean | Aireyon | Aj Aden | Ajwad | Akhyrie | Àkos |
| Ahvion | Aidric | Airic | Aja | Akaash | Aki | Akosh |
| Ahvri | Aidrik | Airik | Ajaden | Akachi | Aki're | Akot |
| Ahyaan | Aidurus | Airious | Ajae | Akachukwu | Akia | Akram (0.01) |
| Ahyan | Aidyn (0.03) | Airiss | Ajaelen | Akadian | Akiam | Akrama |
| Ahyende | Aiedan | Airixs | Ajah'tuborri | Akadin | Akian | Akrem |
| Ahzayvion | Aieden | Airon | Ajahni | Akai | Akiann | Aksel (0.01) |
| Ahzeem | Aiedon | Airon Aniston | Ajahnni | Akaidin | Akiba | Akshaj |
| Ahzeil | Aiesha | Airren | Ajai | Akally | Akie | Akshar |
| Ahziah | Aiham | Airryn | Ajalon | Akam | Akiel | Akshat |
| Ahzir | Aihem- | Airton | Ajamu- | Akan | Akiem | Akshay (0.01) |
| Ahzise Sultan | Abderrahmen | Airus | Osbourne | Akanyanka | Akif | Akshay Varma |
| Ahzjai | Aiijion | Airvoy | Ajani (0.02) | Akar | Akil (0.01) | Akshayan |
| Ahzstin | Aijah | Airy | Ajani-Karif | Akarius | Akilees | Akshaye |
| Ai | Aijalon | Airyen | Ajani-Rahman | Akarsh | Akiles | Akshdeep |
| Ai'kiyren | Aijaylon | Aisa | Ajarius | Akash (0.02) | Akilesh | Akshraj |
| Aian | Aijon | Aisa Eddy Aitu | Ajavie | Akashdeep | Akileshwar | Akua |

Akul
Akurai
Akwasi
Akye
Akyl
Akyle
Akylie
Al *(0.01)*
Al Harith
Al' Hudsone
Al'amin
Al'azuwan
Al'darrian
Al'hassane
Al'javeon
Al'maud
Al'mon
Al'tavion
Al'tavious
Al'zaire
Alá
Ala Yahya
Alaa
Alaae
Alaan
Aladen
Aladine
Aladj
Alae
Alah
Alain *(0.02)*
Alain Jose
Alain Junior
Alain Mathieu
Alair
Alaire
Alajandro
Alakai
Alakhai
Alaku
Alaku Jimmy
Al-Amin
Alamin
Alán
Alan *(1.60)*
Alan Jesus
Alan M
Alan Ray
Alana
Aland
Aland Jackson
Alanda
Alandan

Alander
Alandis
Alando
Alandos
Alandrae
Alandro
Alani
Alanic
Alan-Michael
Alano
Alans
Alantae
Alantay
Alante
Al-Anwar
Alanzé
Alanzo
Alaqmar
Alare
Alareon
Alaric *(0.01)*
Alarik
Alarious
Alarric
Alasdair
Alashawn
Alassandro
Alassane
Alastair *(0.01)*
Alastor
Alataua
Alava
Alavin
Alawnzo
Alayn
Alayna
Alayus
Alazaeh
Alazar
Alazare
Alaze
Alban
Albara
Albaro
Alben Raul
Alber
Alberico
Albert *(0.20)*
Albert Kyle
Alberth
Albertini
Alberto *(0.14)*
Alberto David

Alberto Manuel
Alberto-Jose
Albertt
Albertuni
Albi
Albie
Albierto
Albin
Albino
Albion
Alborz
Albrecht
Albrino
Albritton
Alcee
Alceo
Alchristopher
Alcibiades
Alcide
Alcides
Alcidez
Alclaine
Alcon
Alcus
Aldahir
Aldair *(0.01)*
Aldan
Aldane
Aldante
Aldar
Aldarrianté
Aldayr
Aldayshein
Alde
Aldem
Aldemar
Alden *(0.08)*
Alden Nicuis
Alder
Alderic
Alderick
Alderson
Aldin *(0.01)*
Aldion
Aldo *(0.05)*
Aldo-Alberto
Aldolfo
Aldon *(0.01)*
Aldotfus
Aldouriel
Aldous
Aldre
Aldred

Aldrei Tristan
Aldriano
Aldric
Aldrich
Aldrick
Aldridge
Aldrik
Aldrin
Aldryn
Aldwin
Aldy
Alé
Ale Jandro
Ale'andro
Aleah
Aleb
Alec *(0.34)*
Alec Benjamin
Alec Jaden
Alec'zander
Alecei
Aleck
Aleckzander
Alecs
Alecsander
Alecxander
Alecxandre
Alecxis
Alec-Zander
Aleczander *(0.01)*
Aleczandr
Aleczavior
Aledjin
Aledxi
Alee
Aleem
Alef
Aleff
Alegandro
Alegario
Alehandro
Aleil
Aleister
Alejandra
Alejandro *(2.25)*
Alejo
Alek *(0.04)*
Alek Olivier
Alekh
Alekisanita
Aleks
Aleksa

Aleksandar *(0.02)*
Aleksander *(0.02)*
Aleksandr
Aleksei
Aleksey
Aleksi
Aleksy
Alekxy
Alekz
Alekzandar
Alekzander *(0.01)*
Alekzandr
Alelis
Alem
Alen *(0.01)*
Alend
Alens
Alensky
Alenxander
Aleqzander
Aleric
Alerik
Alert
Ales
Alesaga
Alesander
Alesandro
Alesiram
Alesky
Alessadro
Alessander
Alessandra
Alessandre
Alessandro *(0.09)*
Alessi
Alessio *(0.01)*
Aleto
Alex *(2.99)*
Alex Irwin
Alex Jayqwan
Alex Jordan
Alex Khai
Alex Long
Alex Mihail
Alex Romeo
Alex Wenwei
Alex William
Alexai
Alexaiver

Alexandar *(0.01)*
Alexanded
Alexandel
Alexander *(8.01)*
Alexander Jael
Alexander Jordanq
Alexander Joseph
Alexander Krasimir
Alexander Kyle
Alexander Maurice
Alexander Zevie
Alexander-Elie
Alexander-Lucas
Alexandern
Alexander-Paul
Alexander-Radu
Alexandir
Alexando
Alexandor
Alexandr
Alexandra
Alexandré
Alexandre *(0.35)*
Alexandre Leo
Alexandre Lucas Andres
Alexandre Noah
Alexandre Quang Minh
Alexandre Sacha
Alexandre Sebastien
Alexandre-Anthony
Alexandre-Benoit
Alexandre-Edward
Alexandre-Harout
Alexandre-Olivier
Alexandre-Phillippe
Alexandrez
Alexandria
Alexandro *(0.03)*

Alexandro Ronald
Alexandro-Dali
Alexandros *(0.01)*
Alexandru
Alexandrus
Alexaner
Alexanter
Alex-Antoine
Alexavian
Alexavier *(0.04)*
Alexavier L
Alexavior
Alexaviour
Alexazender
Alexci
Alexciano
Alexei *(0.01)*
Alexender
Alexendre
Alexer
Alexey
Alexeyé
Alexhaidyn
Alexi *(0.03)*
Alexi Charles
Alexia
Alexie
Alexim
Alexio
Alexion
Alexios
Alexiou
Alexis *(1.90)*
Alexis Khiem
Alexis Lucas
Alexis Mart
Alexis Raphael
Alexis Shushep
Alexis-Jacob
Alexis-Lou
Alexis-Mathias
Alexiss
Alexis-William
Alexius
Alexix
Alexiyahn
Alexiz
Alexksandar
Alexnader
Alexnder

Alexrodney
Alexsander
  *(0.01)*
Alexsandor
Alexsandr
Alexsandre
Alexsandro
Alexsandry
Alex-Sea
Alexsi
Alexsis
Alexsnder
Alexus
Alexx
Alexxander
Alexxis
Alexy *(0.04)*
Alexy Heinrich
Alexy Nathan
Alexy-Eryx
Alex-Yohannes
Alexys *(0.01)*
Alexzandar
Alexzander
  *(0.10)*
Alexzandore
Alexzandres
Alexzandro
Alexzavier
Alexzavior
Alexzay
Alezander
Alezandro
Alfie
Alfonanzo
Alfondzo
Alfonso *(0.05)*
Alfonson
Alfonza
Alfonzo *(0.01)*
Alford
Alfrado
Alfre
Alfred *(0.07)*
Alfred Antonio
Alfred-James
Alfredo *(0.12)*
Alfredrick
Algenis
Algeren
Algernon
Alghassimou
Algis

Algizouli
Alhaji
Alhali
Alhamza
Alhan-Gabriel
Alharith
Al-Hassan
Alhussein
Alhux
Ali *(0.39)*
Ali Al Hadi
Ali Arman
Ali Ataellah
Ali El-Hadi
Ali Imran
Ali Khaldoun
Ali Khan
Ali Kumale
Ali Rahmaan
Ali Wahiz
Ali'jah
Aliabshir
Aliajah
Ali-Alkbar
Ali-Alreda
Alian
Aliano
Alias *(0.01)*
Alic
Alice
Ali-Cem
Alicia
Alicio
Alick
Alide Mickael
Alidean
Aliel
Ali-Emir
Aliere
Alies
Alieu
Ali-Francis
Alighieri
Alihan
Alihas
Alija
Alijah *(0.10)*
Alijaih
Alijandro
Alijea
Alijiah
Alijuah
Alijuandro

Alik
Alika
Alikeem
Alikhan
Aliko
Alikzander
Alim
Ali-Mahdi
Alimamy
Alimanuel
Alimmajid
Alin
Alind
Alinson
Aliou
Alioune
Alique
Alireza
Alirio
Alis
Ali-Sahin
Alisha
Alishan
Alisjah
Alisjhah
Alistair *(0.01)*
Alistair-Asher
Alistair-
  Nathanael
Alistar
Alister
Aliune
Alius
Aliva
Alivia
Ali-Waheed
Alix *(0.01)*
Alixander
Alix-Ange
Alix-Bigwi
Alixon
Alixx
Alixzandar
Aliyah
Aliyahon
Aliyan
Aliyas
Aliyoow
Aliyus
Alizae
Alizah
Alizander
Alizay

Alizayvion
Alize
Alizedrik
Alizer
Aliziah
Aljavonnie
Aljawuan
Aljermaine
Aljernod
Aljon
Alkeon
Alkevious
Alkin
Alkra
All'wahid
Allah
Allahjah
Allahkin
Allal
Allan *(0.14)*
Allan Jahir
Allan Joseph
Allan Jr
Allan-Alexis
Allan-Joseph
Allantae
Allante
Allanté
Allassan
Allazander
Allden
Alldrey
Alleck
Allen *(0.33)*
Allen Ray
Allend
Allen-Keith
Allen-Michael
Allen-Mychael
Allens
Allester
Allex
Allexander
Allexandor
Allexy
Alley
Allheim
Allick
Allie
Alliester
Allik
Allikai
Allin

Allique
Allison
Allistair
Allister
Alliuq
Allix
Allon
Allston
Allton
Allye
Allyn
Allysen
Allyson M J
Allyus
Alma
Almain
Al-Mallah
Al-Mamun
Almand
Almando
Almani
Almanzo
Almari
Almarious
Al-Marri
Almas
Al-Matini
Almedin
Almehdi
Almeir
Almer
Almicar
Almin
Almir
Almon
Almontasser
Almonte
Almonté
Almonzo
Alofi
Alohi
Alois
Aloje
Alok
Alomanz
Alon *(0.01)*
Alondo
Alondra
Alondre
Alonso *(0.05)*
Alonso Ignacio
Alonta
Alontae

Alontay
Alonte
Alonté
Alonza
Alonzo *(0.09)*
Aloshia
Aloupa
Alousious
Aloysius *(0.01)*
Aloysius-Xavier
Alozie
Alp
Alpay-Nazim
Alperen
Alpha *(0.02)*
Alpha-Lamine
Alphanso
Alpheaus
Alpheus
Alphonse
Alphonso *(0.02)*
Alphonze
Alphonzo
Alpoim
Alqsie
Alquan
Alqueven
Alquez
Alqussam
Alred
Alreginald
Alric
Alrick
Alrico
Alrik
Alsadig
Al-Sadiq
Al-Shamar
Alson
Alston *(0.01)*
Altaf
Altair
Al-Tariq
Altaryque
Altayeb
Altayr
Alten
Alteriek
Althony
Altillio
Altin
Altion
Alton *(0.03)*

Altonard
Altonio
Altravian
Altre
Altwon
Alu-Ci-Ic
Alukka
Alusaine
Aluse
Alusine
Alux
Alva
Alvah
Alvan
Alvanny
Alvante
Alvardo
Alvarez Cabrera
Alvaro *(0.05)*
Alvarojose
Alvash
Alvee
Alveion
Alveno
Alveontae
Alverto
Alvettle
Alvey
Alvi
Alvin *(0.16)*
Alvino
Alvion
Alvis Felip
Alvondre
Alvonta
Alvoye
Alvyn
Alwaleed
Alwan
Alwin
Alxander
Aly *(0.01)*
Alyais
Alyan
Alyas
Alyazan
Alycia
Alyis
Alyja
Alyjah *(0.01)*
Alyk
Alykhan
Alym

| | | | | | | |
|---|---|---|---|---|---|---|
| Alyn | Amalio | Amarian (0.01) | Amaziye | Amgad | Amish | Amory |
| Alyosha | Aman (0.02) | Amarian | Amberson | Amgalan | Amit (0.01) | Amoryan |
| Alyric | Amana |   Tyshon | Ambert | Ami | Amitaj | Amos (0.06) |
| Alysa | Amancio | Amarie | Ambiorix | Amiagg | Amitesh | Amos Gabriel |
| Alyshawaughn | Amanda | Amarien | Ambiquous | Amias | Amitoj | Amos-David |
| Alyssa | Amandley | Amarieon | Ambroise | Amicah | Amitva | Amosjohn |
| Alyus | Amando | Amariez | Ambrose (0.01) | Amico | Amius | Amoszeah |
| Alyx | Amandrae | Amarii | Ambrosio | Amid | Amjad | Amou |
| Alyxander | Amani (0.03) | Amario | Amburgey | Amie | Amking | Amparo |
| Alyxandros | Amani-Gregory | Amario-James | Ambuskah | Amiel (0.01) | Amley | Amr (0.01) |
| Alyzen | Amanii | A-Marion | Amby | Amier | Ammaar | Amrad |
| Al-Zahiere | Amani-Jordan | Amarion (0.08) | Amdi | Amierre | Amman | Amram |
| Alzair | Amanjot | Amarione | Amdi | Amiid | Ammanuel | Amran |
| Alzavion | Amann | Amarionté |   Moustapha | Amiin | Ammar (0.03) | Amrese |
| Alzeah | Amanpreet | Amarious | Ame | Amijah | Ammar-Ul- | Amri |
| Alzerene | Amantay | Amaris | Amear | Amiko |   Haque | Amrik |
| Ama're | Amante | Amarius | Amechi | Amil | Ammen | Amrin |
| Amaad | Amanté | Amariyé | Amed | Amil'yon | Ammiel | Amrinder |
| Amaahd | Amanti | Amarjae | Amede | Amilcar (0.01) | Ammon (0.01) | Amrit (0.01) |
| Amaan (0.01) | Amanu | Amarjay | Amedeo | Amileon | Ammond | Amritesh |
| Amaar | Amanuale | Amarjot | Ameem | Amiliano | Ammr | Amrith |
| Amad | Amanuel | Amarli | Ameen (0.01) | Amilie | Amner | Amrit-Mantar |
| Amadayus | Amanvir | Amaro | Ameer (0.04) | Amilio | Amnon | Amritpal |
| Amadeo (0.01) | Amar (0.04) | Amarque | Ameesio | Amill | Amogh (0.01) | Amritveer |
| Amadeus (0.01) | Amara | Amarr | Amehweh | Amilleon | Amogh Reddy | Amro (0.01) |
| Amadeus- | Amarachukwu | Amarre | Ameil | Amillia | Amol | Amron |
|   Saavat | Amarai | Amarren | Ameir | Amín | Amon (0.01) | Amru |
| Amadian | Amaran | Amarri | Ameko | Amin (0.01) | Amonchai | Amruthsai |
| Amadin | Amarante | Amarrion | Amel | Amina | Amond | Amry |
| Amado | Amaratunga | Amartazis | Amelia | Aminadab | Amondrae | Amsden |
| Amado Rey | Arac | Amartrell | Amelio | Amine (0.02) | Amondre | Amsel |
| Amador | Amaray | Amartya | Amén | Amine Sodek | Amondré | Amsher |
| Amadou (0.02) | Amarayon | Amaru | Amen (0.01) | Amin-Wael | Amoni | Amsi |
| Amadrick | Amard | Amarus | Amen Ra | Amione | Amonie | Amsini |
| Amadu | Amardeep | Amaryan | Amer (0.01) | Amir (0.28) | Amonn | Amston |
| Amaeel | Amaré (0.01) | Amaryon | Ameran | Amir Antonio | Amonta | Amuary |
| Amahd | Amare (0.08) | Amashi | Ameré | Amir | Amontae | Amuel |
| Amahni | Amare | Amaud | Amere (0.01) |   Christopher | Amontaye | Amurabi |
| Amahzeon |   Tayshaun | Amaun | Ameri | Amira | Amonté | Amuyjae |
| Amai | Amarea | Amaunti | Ameriah | Amirah | Amonte (0.01) | Amy |
| Amaia | Amareé | Amaurae | Americ | Amiré | Amontez | Amya |
| Amaige'jon | Amaree (0.01) | Amauré | America | Amire (0.01) | Amonti | Amyis |
| Amair | Amareen | Amauree | Americo | Amireddean | Amontraé | Amyr |
| Amaj'aeon | Amare-Joseph | Amauri (0.01) | Americus | Amir-Georges | Amontrea | Amyre |
| Amajai | Amaren | Amaurian | Ameriess | Amiri (0.01) | Amony | Amyrion |
| Amaje | Amareon | Amaurie | Amerikus | Amir-Ibnkhalil | Amor | Amzie |
| Amajh | Amareón | Amauriyen | Amerion | Amirr | Amore | An (0.01) |
| Amajhah | Amareyá | Amaury (0.01) | Ameriyon | Amirre | Amoree | An'dea |
| Amajuoritse | Amareyin | Amauryon | Ameron | Amirré | Amori | An'derrius |
| Amal | Amarí | Amaurys | Amery | Amir-Reshard | Amoriaus | An'dreas |
| Amalaki | Amari (0.18) | Amavion | Ames | Amirri | Amorion | An'jay |
| Amalie | Amari'a | Amay | Ametrez' | Amisadai | Amorionne | An'qwyon |
| Amalik | Amari-Amani | Amaye | Ameya | | Amorris | An'tavius |

An'teus
An'ton
An'tonio
An'twan
Ana
Ana'je
Anaan
Anad
Anael
Anah Okemah
Anahad
Anahat
Anahita
Anaia
Anailah
Anairan
Anajae
Anak
Anakin (0.04)
Anakym
Anakyn
Anan
Ananaius
Anand (0.01)
Anandjot
Anandsai
Ananias (0.01)
Ananious
Ananiyas
Anant
Ananth
Anantha
Anantvir
Ananya
Anar
Anardis
Anari
Anas (0.02)
Anas-Abdelkader
Anasjah
Anass
Anasse
Anastacio
Anastasio
Anastasios
Anatay
Anatoly
Anavrin
Anavut
Anay
Anazanin
Ancelmo

Anchor
Anciel
Ancient
Ancinio
And'terrieo
Andal
Andaleeb
Andan
Andani
Andargachew
Andarious
Andarius
Andarrien
Anddrew
Anddy
Andelesio
Anden (0.01)
Ander
Anderious
Anders (0.04)
Andersen (0.01)
Anderson (0.16)
Andersson
Anderw
Anderzon
Andherzo
Andhy
Andi (0.01)
Andie
Andin
Andino
Andis
Andito
Andlin
Andolin
Andon (0.02)
Andoni
Andonis
Andonny
Andony
Andra
Andraé
Andrae (0.01)
Andrai
Andran
Andras
András
Andray
André (0.05)
Andre (0.48)
Andre Felix
Andre'as

Andre'az
Andre's
Andre'z
Andreá
Andrea (0.01)
Andréas
Andreas (0.05)
Andree (0.01)
Andree-Pierre
Andreese
Andreesheree
Andre-Genaro
Andrei (0.03)
Andrei David
Andreidi
Andrein
Andrei-Pierre
Andreis
Andreiz
Andrej
Andrejs
Andrel
Andrell
Andre-Martin
Andreo
Andre-Philippe
André-Phillippe
Andre-Pierre
Andre-Rus
Andrés
Andres (1.28)
Andres Daniel
Andres Felipe
Andres'
Andresen
Andretti
Andreu
Andreus (0.01)
Andrevious
Andrevius
Andrew (8.68)
Andrew Adrian
Andrew Alexander
Andrew Amadeu
Andrew Emile
Andrew John
Andrew Johnne
Andrew Martin
Andrew Nikofor
Andrew Timothy
Andrew Tri
Andrew-Derek

Andrew-Jason
Andrewn
Andrews
Andrewus
Andrey (0.02)
Andreyv
Andrez (0.01)
Andri
Andrian
Andrias
Andric
Andrick
Andrick Eduardo
Andricus
Andries
Andrieu
Andrik (0.01)
Andris
Andriu
Andrius
Andriy
Andro
Andros
Androth
Andru (0.01)
Andrue (0.01)
Andruw (0.01)
Andruw-Longin
Andry
Andry Ryan
Andryd
Andryv
Andrzej
Anduei
Anduen
Anduin
Andwane
Andwell
Andy (0.48)
Andy Joey
Andy-Dowell
Andyjames
Andy-Marlone
Andyn
Andyphuoc
Andys
Aneas
Anecio
Aneeb
Aneesh (0.01)
Aneil

Aneirin
Aneisaac
Anel
Aneldy
Anell
Anelson
Aneres
Anes
Anesi
Anes-Mehdi
Aness
Anesu
Anesushe
Aneto
Anetrí
Aneudi
Aneudy
Aneurin
Aneurys
Anfarnee
Anfernee
Anfim
Angad (0.01)
Angadroop
Angadveer
Angat
Angatdeep
Ange Audran
Ange-Aime
Angel (5.38)
Angel Alberto
Angel Emilio
Angel Gabriel
Angel Jahir
Angel Jarrett
Angel Kevin
Angel Louis
Angel Manuel
Angel Martin
Angel Nathaniel
Angel Samuel
Angel Uziel
Angela
Angel-Alexander
Angelbert
Angel-David
Angelde
Angel-Gabriel
Angelgabriel
Angelgael
Angelino
Angelio

Angelique
Angelis
Angelitio
Angelito
Angell
Angello (0.01)
Angel-Luis
Angellus
Angelo (0.35)
Angelo Fabrizio
Angelo Gerry Matthew
Angelo Joseph
Angelo Sai
Angelo Symeon Oliver
Angelond
Angelo-Owen
Angelos
Angelous
Angelrey
Angelus (0.01)
Angeny
Anghel
Anghello
Angianiel
Angier
Angiras
Angle
Anglin
Anglino
Angok
Anguel
Angus (0.05)
Angut
Angy
Anh
Anh Huy
Anhad
Anhadpreet
Anhtri
Anhuar
Anhvinh
Anias
Anibal
Anibal-Daniel
Anickin
Anickoli
Aniel
Aniguel
Anihith
Anijah
Anik

Anikan
Anikashan
Aniken
Aniket
Aniketh (0.01)
Anikin
Anil
Anila
Anilan
Anilton
Anim
Animesh
Aniq
Anir
Aniruddh
Aniruddha
Anirudh (0.02)
Anirudhh
Anirvin
Anirvinya
Anis
Anis-Bilal
Anise
Anish (0.03)
Anisley
Anisse
Aniston
Anis-Yacoub
Anitema
Anius
Anival
Aniyas
Anja
Anjan
Anjaun
Anjay
Anjel (0.01)
Anjelito
Anjelo
Anjelouse
Anjer
Anjoel
Anjuan
Anker
Ankhe'lo
Ankit (0.01)
Ankith
Ankoma
Ankur
Ankush
Anmario
Anmol
Anmoldeep

| | | | | | | |
|---|---|---|---|---|---|---|
| Ann'uurh Ishmael | Anson (0.04) | Anthen | Anthony-Thomas | Antonio (2.11) | Anttwon | Anvith |
| Anna | Anson-Gia | Antheney | Anthony-Vesna | Antonio Curtis | Antuan (0.01) | Anwaar |
| Annabella | Anspatry | Antheny | Anthony-William | Antonio Gilbert | Antuan Darcel | Anwar (0.02) |
| Annabelle | Anstin | Antheon | Anthown | Antonio Jesus | Antuane | Anwarkhon |
| Annafi | Ansu | Anther | Anthoyne | Antonio Jose | Antuann | Anyah |
| Annaliese | Ansulay | Anthian | Anthren | Antonio Jr | Antulio | Anyang |
| Annas | Ansuman | Anthnoy | Anthwone | Antonio Miguel | Antun | Anyas |
| Anndy | Ansumana | Anthny | Anticius | Antonio-Eliseo | Antvan | Anyedeka |
| Annel | Ansun | Anthon | Antime | Antonio-Jose | Antwaan | Anykel |
| Annelsonne | Ant'juan | Anthone | Antin | Antonio-Kikinunu | Antwain (0.01) | Anyr |
| Annias | Ant'tonyo | Anthonee | Antione (0.02) | Antoniomanuel | Antwaine | Anzavion |
| Annie | Antae'viaun | Anthoney (0.01) | Antione Gavin | Antonios | Antwan (0.07) | Anzony |
| Annika | Antaeus | Anthoney-Alan | Antionia | Antonious | Antwan James | Aodan |
| Annis | Antaeyo | Anthoni (0.01) | Antionio | Antonitto | Antwand | Aodh |
| Annisana | Antaiveon | Anthonie (0.01) | Antionne | Antonius | Antwane | Aodhan |
| Anno | Antajuan | Anthonin | Antiono | Antónné | Antwann | Aodnis |
| Annuar | Antal | Anthonio | Antjuan | Antonni | Antwanne | Aohdan |
| Anojan | Antar | Anthonny | Antjuane | Antonny | Antwan-Shemar | Aoiden |
| Anoke | Antareo | Anthony (8.52) | Antle | Antony (0.09) | Antwaun (0.01) | Aola |
| Anoki | Antario | Anthony Alirico | Antoin | Antony Kevin | Antwayn | Aon |
| Anon | Antarious | Anthony Andres | Antoine (0.46) | Antonyeo | Antwayune | Aonghus |
| Anonhkwaienton | Antaun | Anthony Anh Tuan | Antoine Christopher | Antonyio | Antwhan | Aoun |
| Anoop | Antaveon | Anthony Dat | Antoine Jacques | Antonyn | Antwhane | Aous |
| Anoosh | Antavion | Anthony Etienne | Antoine-Dominic | Antonyo (0.01) | Antwhuan | Aowyn |
| Anosh | Antavione | Anthony Greg | Antoine-Olivier | Antoon | Antwine | Apallo |
| Anothai | Antavious | Anthony Hugo | Antoinne | Antorie | Antwione | Apar |
| Anothony | Antawan | Anthony Izack | Antoino | Antorio | Antwoin | Aphirack |
| Anothy | Antawn | Anthony James | Antojuan | Antorion | Antwoine (0.01) | Apiram |
| Anotonio | Antayvious | Anthony Junior | An-Ton | Antorn | Antwon (0.04) | Apolinar |
| Anquan | Antayvius | Anthony Marques | Anton (0.08) | Antorrio | Antwone (0.02) | Apolinario |
| Anquon | Antbony | Anthony Patrick Alexander | Anton Mikael | Antoun | Antwonne | Apollo (0.01) |
| Anquonn | Ante | Anthony Rogerio | Antone | Antowine | Antwoyne | Apollo Emmanuel |
| Anri | Antelmo | Anthony Tuan | Antoné | Antowon | Antwuan (0.01) | Apollo Jared |
| Anric | Anteneh | Anthony Tyree | Antonearnold | Antowyne | Antwuean | Apolonio |
| Anrico | Antenio | Anthony Vincent | Antonello | Antoyne | Antwyne | Apoorv |
| Anrik | Anteo | Anthony-Angel | Antoneo | Antquavion | Anuart | Apor |
| Anriku | Antereyun | Anthony-Birane | Antoney | Antrace | Anubhav | Apostoli |
| Ansar | Anteriel | Anthony-Braxon | Antoni (0.02) | Antravion | Anubis | Apostolos |
| Ansa-Wondai | Anterio | Anthony-Gabriel | Antonia | Antravious | Anudveg | Apple |
| Ansch | Anterion | Anthony-Glicerio | Antoniao | Antrel | Anuj (0.01) | Appomattox |
| Ansel (0.01) | Anterious | Anthony-James | Antonie | Antrell (0.01) | Anukam | Apprentice |
| Anselm | Anterius | Anthony-Luca | Antonieco Digno | Antrelle | Anukrit | Aptickasic |
| Anselmo | Antero | Anthonyn | Antoniel | Antreveus | Anurag | Apton |
| Ansen (0.01) | Anterrio | Anthony-Robert | Antonieo | Antrevus | Anureet | Apurva |
| Ansgar | Anterrion | | Antoni-Joseph | Antreyvion | Anurodh | Aqeel |
| Ansh (0.01) | Anterrione | | Antonin (0.03) | Antrez | Anury | Aqib |
| Anshul (0.01) | Anterrious | | Antonine | Antrion | Anusan | Aqil |
| Anshuman | Anterriyo | | Antonino (0.01) | Antroine | Anush | Aqilleus |
| Anshveer | Anterson | | | Antron (0.01) | Anushal | Aquan |
| Ansil | Antez | | | Antrone | Anutye | Aquanis |
| Ansis | Anth Ony | | | Antti | Anuv | Aquarian |
| Ansley | Anthanasios | | | Antton | Anvay | Aquarius |
| | Anthany | | | | Anveer | |

Aquaryus
Aquavian
Aquavion
Aquavious
Aquavis
Aquavius
Aquayo
Aqueel
Aquemini
Aquiba
Aquila
Aquilen
Aquiles
Aquilies
Aquilino
Aquill
Aquilla
Aquille
Aquillia
Aquinetice
Ar
Ar'darius
Ar'demerious
Ar'juan
Ar'kasidy
Ar'kobie
Ar'marion
Ar'mon
Ar'mone
Ar'quan
Ar'rion
Ar'ron
Ar'shaun
Ar'shawn
Ar'tavious
Ar'tavis
Ar'terrian
Ar'zion
Ara
Araam
Arabel
Arabian
Arad
Araf
Arafat
Arago
Aragon
Aragorn
Arahkwaneken
Araht
Arai
Aralius
Aram *(0.01)*

Arameus
Aramis *(0.02)*
Aramist
Aramus
Aran *(0.01)*
Arandeep
Arash
Arashdeep
Arashi
Arason
Arata
Arath *(0.01)*
Arav
Aravat
Aravind
Arayus
Arayven
Araz
Arbaz
Arbel
Arbel Yonuel
Arber
Arbey
Arbi
Arbid
Arbies
Arbor
Arbuns
Arcadi
Arcadio
Arcardio
Arcenio
Archellies
Archer *(0.03)*
Archi
Archibald
Archie *(0.01)*
Archill
Archillies
Archimedes
Archith
Arcilous
Ard
Arda
Ardan
Ardany
Ardarien
Ardarion
Ardarius
Ardel
Ardell
Arden *(0.02)*
Ardens

Ardi
Ardi Bafandjo
Ardian
Ardie
Ardilars
Ardin
Ardit
Ardo
Ardon
Ardonit
Ardreck
Ardu
Are's
Are'uan
Arean
Areaon
Arec
Arecko
Aree
Areeb
Arees
Areese
Aref
Arek
Arel
Arelious
Arell
Arellano
Arem-Efrem
Aren *(0.01)*
Aren Thane
Arend
Areness
Arenthious
Arenza
Areon
Areonte
Arerion
Ares *(0.01)*
Ares'
Areston
Aretanegbe
Areyeh
Areyel
Arfain
Arfin
Argel
Argelys
Argenis
Argenyz
Argi
Argjend
Argjent

Argustus
Argyle
Argyrios
Argyris
Arhab
Arham *(0.01)*
Arhan
Arhant
Arhit
Ari *(0.08)*
Aria
Ariah
Ari-Alexandre
Arian *(0.02)*
Ariana
Ariandy
Ariane
Arianna
Ariano
Arias
Ariav
Arib
Ariben
Aric *(0.02)*
Aricceo
Ariceo
Aricin
Arick
Arico
Aridai
Arie *(0.01)*
Ariea
Arieh
Ariel *(0.13)*
Ariel Bryan
Ariel-Joseph
Ariemere
Arien
Arieon
Arieonta
Aries *(0.02)*
Aries-Zion
Ariez
Arif
Arifinal
Arihan
Arii
Arijit
Arik *(0.01)*
Ariken
Ariles
Arimas
Arimonei

Arin *(0.01)*
Arindom
Arinzechukwu
Ario
Ariol
Arion *(0.02)*
Arione
Arionn
Ariq
Aris *(0.01)*
Arish
Arismendy
Arisniel
Arison
Aristedes
Aristeo
Aristhene
Aristide
Aristides
Aristobal
Ariston
Aristotelis
Aristotle *(0.01)*
Aritra
Ariuise
Arius
Arixon-Isael
Ariya
Ariyan
Ariyaun
Ariyeh
Ariyen
Ariyo
Ariyon
Ariz
Arizona
Arjae
Arjaie
Arjan *(0.01)*
Arjay
Arjen
Arjewus
Arjin
Arjohn
Arjuan
Arjun *(0.10)*
Arjuna
Arjunbir
Arjundeep
Arka
Arkadi
Arkadiy
Arkady

Arkangel
Arkavion
Arkayden
Arkayvion
Arkée
Arkel
Arkell
Arkemon
Arkenn
Alexandre
Arkevius
Arkeyel
Arko
Arlan *(0.01)*
Arlanden
Arleigh
Arlejandro
Arlemaro
Arlen *(0.01)*
Arleon
Arles
Arlet
Arlex
Arlexis
Arley
Arlice
Arlie
Arlin *(0.01)*
Arlind
Arlington
Arlis
Arliss
Arlo *(0.02)*
Arlon
Arlondo
Arlonte
Arlonzo
Arlus
Arly
Arlyn
Arlyss
Armaan *(0.07)*
Armaandeep
Armaanjit
Armadi
Armahd
Armahn
Armajaé
Arman *(0.04)*
Armand *(0.02)*
Armand Kader
Armandas
Armandeep

Armando *(0.19)*
Armando Jose
Armando-
    Martin
Armanei
Armani *(0.09)*
Armanie
Armanii
Armanilavon
Armanjeet
Armanjit
Arman-John
Armann
Armanndeep
Armanni
Armannjit
Armannveer
Armanté
Armanti
Armanvir
Armardo
Armaree
Armareon
Armari
Armaria
Armarion
Armary
Armaun
Armaund
Armeen
Armel
Armello
Armem
Armen
Armend
Armendiz
Armer
Armias
Armin *(0.01)*
Arminder
Arminius
Armistead
Armmon
Armod
Armon *(0.02)*
Armon'te
Armond *(0.01)*
Armondo
Armondoluis
Armone
Armoni *(0.01)*
Armonie
Armonn

| | | | | | | |
|---|---|---|---|---|---|---|
| Armonni | Arodis | Arrow | Arterius | Arvin Xander | Asah | Ashbee |
| Armonnie | Arodys | Arryan | Arterrio | Arvind (0.01) | Asahel | Ashbey |
| Armont | Arohan | Arsai | Artez | Arvion | Asahiah | Ashby (0.01) |
| Armonta | Aroldo | Arsal | Artezz | Arvon | Asahn | Ashden (0.01) |
| Armontae | Aron (0.09) | Arsalan | Arth | Arvontay | Asaiah | Ashdon |
| Armontaé | Aronde | Arsaneose | Arthem | Arwen | Asair | Ashdyn |
| Armonte | Arondé | Arsean | Arthis | Arwold | Asajay | Ashe |
| Armonté | Aroonnan | Arsen | Arthor | Arwood | Asam | Asher (0.39) |
| Armonty | Arosco | Arsene | Arthur (0.24) | Arwyn | Asamanu | Asher River |
| Armoud | Aroun | Arsenio | Arthur Robert | Arwynn | Asan | Asheton |
| Armstead | Arpad | Arseny | Arthur Takhini | Ary | Asaneet | Ashgen |
| Armstead | Arpan | Arsh (0.01) | Arthur- | Arya (0.02) | Asani | Ashgin-Raines |
|   Houston | Arpit | Arshaan |   Emmanuel | Aryaan | Asantae | Ashian |
| Armstrong | Arpith | Arshad | Arthurian | Aryaman | Asante | Ashier |
| Armundo | Arqam | Arsham | Arthur-Tae- | Aryan (0.07) | Asanté | Ashik |
| Army | Arquarius | Arshan | Artice | Aryana | Asaph | Ashim |
| Armyius | Arque Bufor | Arshdeep | Artie | Aryanul | Asar | Ashir |
| Arnaldo (0.01) | Arquelious | Arshel | Artigues | Aryaun | Asariel | Ashish |
| Arnando | Arquez | Arshia | Artimus | Aryavardhan | Asarius | Ashkan |
| Arnar | Arquimedes | Arshjot | Artin | Aryavir | Asavir | Ashkii |
| Arnaud (0.05) | Arquimides | Arshkabir | Artis | Aryc | Asbial | Ashkir |
| Arnav (0.05) | Arquimidis | Arshmeet | Artiss | Arycin | Ascalyn | Ashkon |
| Arnavh | Arquis | Arshom | Arto | Arye | Ascencion | Ashlai |
| Arnaz | Arquise | Arshraj | Arton | Aryeh (0.02) | Ascher | Ashlan |
| Arne | Arquisto | Arshun | Artorious | Aryel | Aschlyn | Ashland |
| Arné | Arrak | Arshveer | Artorius | Aryen | Aschton | Ashlar |
| Arneeke | Arran | Arshvinder | Artrell | Aryian | Asean | Ashlee |
| Arnek | Arreion | Arshvir | Artrevian- | Aryis | Ased | Ashlein |
| Arnel | Arrell | Arslan |   Amani | Aryk | Aseel | Ashlen |
| Arnelius | Arren | Arslane-Salim | Artrevion | Ary-Marc | Aseem | Ashley (0.02) |
| Arnell | Arren Kayle | Arson | Artur | Aryn | Aseemveer | Ashley-Reuben |
| Arnes |   Brana | Art | Arturo (0.13) | Aryon | Aser | Ashlin |
| Arness | Arreno | Artago | Arturojovani | Aryton | Asfandyar | Ashlon |
| Arnesto | Arreon | Artan | Artwain | Arzad | Ash (0.01) | Ashlyr |
| Arnett | Arreyton | Artance | Artyom | Arzahn | Ashá | Ashmaan |
| Arney | Arri | Artarian | Aruj | Arzale | Ashaad | Ashmen |
| Arnez (0.01) | Arri Philliposie | Artaven | Arul | Arzaviah | Ashaan | Ashmit |
| Arnfinn Erik | Arric | Artaveous | Arul Br Kubera | Arzavian | Ashaaz | Ashmith |
| Arnick | Arrick | Artavion | Arun (0.01) | Arzayveon | Ashab | Ashmitsingh |
| Arnie | Arrid | Artavious | Arunan | Arzell | Ashad | Ashmon |
| Arnieus | Arrie | Artavis | Arunan Barathi | Arzeyvian | Ashada | Ashna |
| Arnio | Arriel | Artavius | Arunav | Arzie | Ashair | Ashneet |
| Arnize | Arrieton | Artayvion | Arush | Arzjon | Ashak | Ashod |
| Arno (0.01) | Arrik | Arteen | Arusha | Arzorius | Ashalon | Ashok |
| Arnob | Arrington | Artell | Arushigan | As'ahel | Ashan | Asholan |
| Arnold (0.04) | Arrio | Artem | Aruv | As'on | Ashantaé | Ashon |
| Arnold Junior | Arrion | Artemio (0.01) | Arvan | Asa (0.09) | Ashantez | Ashondré |
| Arnoldo (0.01) | Arris | Artemis | Arveen | Asa Joe | Asharaun | Ashraf |
| Arnon | Arrison | Artemus | Arvell | Asaad | Ashaun | Ashraff |
| Arnot | Arrius | Artemus Ren | Arven | Asad (0.01) | Ashaundae | Ashrafi |
| Arnuel | Arrmon |   Kai | Arvey | Asadi | Ashawn | Ashraful |
| Arnulfo (0.01) | Arron (0.02) | Artemy | Arvid | Asael (0.01) | Ashaz | Ashrif |
| Arnuwat | Arron-Sharp | Arterion | Arvin (0.02) | Asaf | Ash-Batomene | Ashrith |

Ash-Shahied
Ashtan
Ashteen
Ashten *(0.02)*
Ashti
Ashtin *(0.02)*
Ashton *(1.83)*
Ashton
  Kendrich
Ashton Louis
Ashton-Alexis
Ashton-Michael
Ashtun
Ashtyn *(0.02)*
Ashu
Ashuna
Ashur *(0.01)*
Ashura
Ashutosh
Ashvin *(0.01)*
Ashvinder
Ashvith
Ashvyn
Ashwat
Ashwath
Ashwin *(0.01)*
Ashwynn
Ashytn
Asia
Asiah
Asiel
Asier
Asif
Asil
Asim *(0.01)*
Asinceon
Asini
Asir
Asjad
Askar
Askari
Askia
Aslam
Aslan
Asman
Asmar
Asmin
Asmir
Ason
Asonte
Aspen *(0.01)*
Aspen James
Aspil

Asraf
Asriel
Asrith
Assane
Assante
Assi
Assim-Ayman
Assyl
Asthen Kheaven
Asthon
Astin
Aston *(0.01)*
Asuka
Asvin
Asvinth
Aswad
Aswan
Aswat
Aswin
Asya
Aszeem
Aszeir
Aszon
Ata
Ataa
Ataa-Adjetey
Ataas
Atabong
Ataevius
Atahan
Atajae
Atalay
Atanas
Atarius
Atash
Ata-Ur-Rehman
Atavian
Atavion
Atayis
Atayzion
Ateeq Ur
Atelea
Atemnkeng
Aten
Ateon
Aterio
Aterries
Aterrion
Aterrious
Ates
Atevien
Athaloskan
Athan *(0.01)*

Athan Jin
Athanael
Athanaius
Athanase
Athanasios
  *(0.01)*
Athanasios
  Tommyb
Athanasius
Athanel
Athar
Atharv
Atharva *(0.01)*
Athavan
Atheddeaus
Atheer
Athen
Athena
Athens
Atheus
Athey
Athish
Athmiken
Athon
Athony
Athor
Athrin
Athul
Athur
Athusan
Athyin
Ati
Atiba
Atif
Atilano
Atilla
Atinderpal
Atiqullah
Atish
Atitus
Atiyyah
Atlahi
Atlai
Atlan
Atlas
Atlee *(0.01)*
Atley *(0.01)*
Atli
Atly
Atnateos
Atnuntra
Atohi
Atom

Atomm
Atoumane
Atouri
Atraeo
Atravius
Atrayius
Atrayl
Atredes
Atreju
Atreyeu
Atreyu *(0.02)*
Atreyu-Vonn
Atris
Atrius
Atron
Atrus
Atryk
Atsani
Attar
Attari
Attash
Atte
Attean
Attics
Atticus *(0.06)*
Attikus
Attila
Attilio
Atul
Atumre
Atwiine
Atya
Atyallian
Atzel
Au'joni
Au'shaun
Au'vontae
Auaris
Aubal
Auben
Aubert
Aubie
Aubin
Aubre
Aubrey *(0.04)*
Aubreyon
Aubri
Aubrie
Aubry
Aubyn
Auctavian
Audam
Audecel

Auden *(0.01)*
Audie
Audiel
Audley
Audon
Audreanne
Audrey
Audric
Audrice
Audrick
Audrik
Audrion
Audryck
Audy
Auggustus
Augus
August *(0.10)*
Augusta
Auguste
Augusten
Augustice
Augustin *(0.01)*
Augustine *(0.03)*
Augustiniano
Augustino
Augustis
Augusto
Augusts
Augustus *(0.07)*
Auhmyhis
Auhner
Auhsten
Aujori
Aukan
Aukeim
Auku
Aulden
Auldin
Auleon
Auliesha
Aulii
Aultin
Aulton
Aum
Aumaluk
Aumani
Aumari
Aumarii
Aumarion
Aumarrius
Aun
Aundrá
Aundray

Aundré
Aundre *(0.01)*
Aundrees
Aundrel
Aundrey
Aundreyas
Auneeb
Auner
Aung
Aunner
Aunterrius
Auquistus
Auralius
Aurel
Aurele
Aurel-Guershon
Aurelien
Aurelio *(0.01)*
Aurelius
Aurey
Auri
Auric James
Aurick
Aurie
Auriel
Aurilus
Aurion
Aurjoun
Aurkheem
Aurmoni
Aurnab
Auron *(0.01)*
Aurshawn
Aurther
Aurthur
Aurum
Ausar
Ausen
Ausencio
Aushin
Aussam-
  Youssef
Aussy
Austale
Austan *(0.01)*
Austen *(0.06)*
Austin *(4.68)*
Austin Elliott
Austin John
Austine
Austin-Jacob
Austin-Lane
Austin-Mich

Austin-Reid
Auston *(0.03)*
Austyn *(0.06)*
Austynn
Autavious
Auther
Authniel
Authur
Auto
Autrevion
Autreyl
Autry
Autumn
Auvont
Auyan
Auztin
Auzuum
Ava
Avaan
Avaiss
Avalon
Avan
Avand
Avander
Avaneesh
Avanni
Avant *(0.01)*
Avanta
Avantaé
Avantae *(0.01)*
Avantay
Avanté
Avante *(0.01)*
Avantre
Avar
Avari
Avarie
Avarius
Avarrion
Avaruhom
Avary
Avash
Avatar
Avaughn
Avaughnte
Avaugn
Avaun
Avauntay
Avauntre
Avayon
Avazbek
Avdirrahman
Avdo

| | | | | | | |
|---|---|---|---|---|---|---|
| Avedis | Avinadad | Avrohom *(0.02)* | Axten | Ayers | Ayrion | Azara |
| Aveeon | Avinas | Avrom | Axton | Ayesan | Ayron | Azarel |
| Aveer | Avinash *(0.01)* | Avron | Axxel | Ayesh | Ayrreon | Azarel Alfredo |
| Aveion | Avion *(0.02)* | Avrre | Axzamein | Ayeyondre | Ayrton | Azareon |
| Avel | Avione | Avruhum | Ay'asia | Ayham | Ayryan | Azari |
| Avelino | Avir | Avrum | Aya | Ayhem | Ayryon | Azari'el |
| Aven *(0.01)* | Aviral | Avry *(0.01)* | Ayaad | Ayhm | Aysa | Azaria |
| Avencyon | Aviram | Avyan | Ayaan *(0.02)* | Ayiden | Aysander | Azariah *(0.02)* |
| Avenicio | Avirey | Avyay | Ayaan Butt | Ayidon | Ayshaun | Azarian |
| Avenir | Avis | Avyeris | Ayal | Ayin | Ayshton | Azarias |
| Aveon *(0.01)* | Aviscenne | Avyione | Ayan *(0.01)* | Aykam | Ayson | Azarion |
| Aver | Avishai | Avyn | Ayan'dante | Aykeith | Aysun | Azarion'tae |
| Averee | Avishka | Avyon | Ayanda | Aykum | Aytae | Azarious |
| Averell | Avisoa Fredrick | Avyukt | Ayanfeoluwa | Ayla | Ayub *(0.02)* | Azarius |
| Averett | Aviv | Avyukta | Ayanle | Ayler | Ayul | Azarni |
| Averey | Aviya | Awab | Ayanze | Aylin | Ayuob | Azarrey |
| Averi | Aviyon | Awais | Ayat | Aylmer | Ayur | Azarya |
| Averian | Avjeet | Awal | Ayax | Aylor | Ayush *(0.02)* | Azaul |
| Averic | Avneet | Awale | Ayaz | Aymaan | Ayushman | Azaurien |
| Averick | Avner | Awaleh | Aybee | Ayman *(0.02)* | Ayushvir | Azavian |
| Averie | Avni | Awan | Ayce | Aymane | Ayuub | Azavier |
| Averill | Avniiel | Awar | Aycen | Aymar | Ayvan | Azavion |
| Averille | Avnil | Awed | Aydain | Aymen *(0.01)* | Ayven | Azayle |
| Averin | Avnish | Awen | Aydam | Aymen- | Ayvin | Azazel |
| Averius | Avnoor | Aweso | Aydan *(0.10)* | Abdelbasset | Ayyaan | Azdan |
| Averup | Avny | Awesome | Ayddan | Aymeric *(0.01)* | Ayyan | Azden |
| Avery *(0.58)* | Avo | Awestun | Aydden | Aymerick | Ayyoub | Aze'on |
| Avery Lewis | Avon | Awet | Aydeen | Aymerik | Ayyub | Azea |
| Averyion | Avon'tea | Awin | Aydehn | Aymir | Az | Azeem |
| Averyn | Avondale | Awindolba | Ayden *(1.28)* | Aymon | Aza Zelio | Azeen |
| Averyon | Avondre | Awman | Ayden James | Aymric | Azaad | Azeez |
| Averytt | Avone | Awnaur | Ayden Trist | Aymrick | Azaan | Azeglo |
| Avesh | Avontá | Awni | Aydence | Aymrik | Azaani | Azekel |
| Aveyon | Avontae | Awston | Aydenn | Aynté | Azabien | Azel |
| Avi *(0.03)* | Avontaé | Awtimos | Ayden-Quincy | Ayo | Azabren | Azem |
| Avi'ale | Avontai | Awwab | Aydens | Ayobanji | Azack | Azen |
| Aviad | Avontay | Awwad | Ayder | Ayodeji | Azad | Azfar |
| Avian *(0.01)* | Avontaye | Axan | Aydian | Ayodele | Azadar | Azhaan |
| Avianton | Avonte | Axander | Aydin *(0.06)* | Ayoki | Azael *(0.01)* | Azhael |
| Aviaun | Avonté | Axcel | Aydinn | Ayokunle | Azahel | Az-Hakim |
| Avidan | Avontre | Axcell | Aydn | Ayom | Azahn | Azhan |
| Avie | Avorey | Axeel | Aydon *(0.01)* | Ayomide | Azai | Azhar |
| Aviel *(0.01)* | Avory | Axel *(0.18)* | Aydoon | Ayomikun | Azaia | Azhariah |
| Avien | Avraham *(0.03)* | Axel David | Aydrean | Ayoola | Azaiah | Azi |
| Avieon | Avram | Axel Karol | Aydren | Ayooluwa | Azairius | Azi'yah |
| Avier | Avree | Axell | Aydrian | Ayoub *(0.02)* | Azajuan | Azia |
| Avigdor | Avren | Axel-Prince | Aydric | Ayouba | Azal | Aziah |
| Avijay | Avrey *(0.01)* | Axes | Aydrik | Ayoube | Azalie | Azian |
| Avijeet | Avrhee | Axill | Aydun | Ayran | Azaın | Aziel |
| Avijit | Avri | Axis | Aydyn | Ayren | Azan | Azier |
| Avik | Avrian | Axl | Ayemvi | Ayres | Azanor | Azijon |
| Avin *(0.01)* | Avriel | Axle | Ayen | Ayrian | Azanté | Azim |
| Avinaash | Avrion | Axmed | Ayer | Ayrington | Azar | Azion |

| | | | | | |
|---|---|---|---|---|---|
| Azir | B'carii | Baha-Furkan | Balen | Bannen | Barik | Basam |
| Azire | B'hjone | Bahajj | Balentin | Banner | Barinedum | Bascom |
| Azir-Shahid | B'lovied | Bahar | Baler | Bannon | Barjam | Baseer |
| Aziun | Ba'ith | Bahe | Baley | Banroop | Barkale | Basel |
| Azius | Ba'ron | Bahez | Baleyon | Banshjot | Barker | Basem |
| Aziya | Baadhon | Bahir | Balfre | Bantam | Barkley | Basen |
| Aziyah | Baajkaran | Bahiyud-Deen | Balian | Banujen | Barley | Basey |
| Aziyon | Baasil | Bahodir | Balihar | Banyan | Barnabas | Bashaer |
| Aziz *(0.01)* | Baasit | Bahraam | Balin *(0.01)* | Banyon | Barnaby | Bashair |
| Aziz Junior | Bab | Bahram | Balint | Banywesize | Barnard | Bashar |
| Azlan | Baba | Bahsil | Baljot | Bao | Barnes | Bashea |
| Azlee | Babacar | Bahzad | Balkaran | Bao Duc | Barnett | Basheer |
| Azlif | Babafemi | Bai'lee | Balkarn | Johnathan | Barney | Basher |
| Azmain | Babak | Baiden | Balke | Bao Dylan An | Barnnon | Bashiir |
| Azmar | Babasola | Baila | Balkirat | Quoc | Barohn | Bashir *(0.01)* |
| Azmedaeus | Babatunde | Bailee | Ballan | Baptist | Barok | Bashir Ahmad |
| Azmi Walid | Baboucar | Bailen | Ballin | Baptiste *(0.01)* | Baron *(0.02)* | Bashkim |
| Azmir | Babrak | Bailey *(0.16)* | Balmore | Baqir | Barran | Bashon |
| Azonte | Babsi | Bailian | Balmori Alonso | Baraa | Barranquilla | Bashshar |
| Azor | Babucar | Bailin | Balpreet | Barabbas | Barre | Basie |
| Azra | Babucarr | Bailon | Balraj *(0.01)* | Baracca | Barrec | Basil *(0.01)* |
| Azra Kellan | Bacari | Bailor | Balshaan | Barach | Barreece | Basile |
| Azrae | Bach | Baily | Baltaj | Barachiel | Barret *(0.01)* | Basilio |
| Azrael | Bachar | Bailynd | Baltaran | Baracus | Barrett *(0.08)* | Basim |
| Azrel | Bachelere | Bain | Baltasar | Barak *(0.01)* | Barrick | Basir |
| Azrick | Bachir | Baine | Baltaza | Baraka | Barrie | Basirh |
| Azrie | Baci | Baion | Baltazar | Barak-Rawchaa | Barrin | Basit |
| Azriel *(0.01)* | Bacil | Baird | Baltazay | Baran | Barrington | Bassam |
| Azro | Bacilio | Bairoh | Baltej | Barauch | Barris | Bassel |
| Azsean | Bacorian | Bairon | Balter | Barauh | Barritt | Bassem |
| Azurah | Badden | Bajim | Balthazar | Barbaro | Barron *(0.01)* | Bassil |
| Azure | Bade | Bajmeir | Balthus | Barchelet | Barry *(0.06)* | Bassm |
| Azuriah | Baden *(0.01)* | Bakal | Balton | Barchie | Barryford | Bastian *(0.01)* |
| Azuryn | Bader | Bakar | Bam | Barclay | Bart | Bastien *(0.02)* |
| Azyiah | Badge | Bakari *(0.01)* | Bamon | Bard | Barthalow | Bates |
| Azyiaheze | Badger | Bakary | Bamone | Bardaan | Barthelemy | Bathushan |
| Azyir | Badir | Bakeé | Banajamin | Bardeep | Bartholamew | Batista |
| Azyz | Badou | Baker *(0.01)* | Banan | Barden | Bartholomew | Batiste |
| Az-Zahir | Badr | Bakhari | Bandar | Bardiya | *(0.01)* | Batrikus |
| Azzahir | Badra | Bakima | Banderas | Bardley | Bartlett | Battle |
| Azzam | Badreddine | Baksheesh | Bane *(0.01)* | Bardo | Bartolo | Battulga |
| Azzeddine | Badri | Baktash | Banebridge | Bardomiano | Barton | Batuhan |
| Azziz | Badru | Balaji | Baneet | Bardya | Bartosz | Batula |
| Azzizz | Bae | Balal | Bangaley | Bare | Bartti | Baubakar |
| Azzo | Baeden | Balazs | Bangaly | Barek | Baruc | Baudilio |
| Azzurey | Baehlor | Balázs | Bani | Barel | Baruch *(0.01)* | Bauer *(0.01)* |
| Azzyah | Baela | Baldemar | Banjamin | Barend | Baruch Shlomo | Bauly |
| | Baelie | Baldo | Banjo | Barento | Sh | Bautista |
| | Baggio | Baldomero | Bank | Bares | Barun | Bavanjot |
| ~ B ~ | Baha | Baldwin | Banker | Baret | Barzan | Baver |
| | Bahaa | Bale | Banks *(0.01)* | Barfuo | Barzin | Bavian |
| B | Bahadur | Baleighan | Bankston | Barggio | Bas | Bavneet |
| B. | Bahaeldein | Balem | Banllery | Barhett | Basabose | Bawan |

| | | | | | | |
|---|---|---|---|---|---|---|
| Bawathuxzan | Beauden | Belder | Beneti | Benjemon | Benyamin | Bernardo (0.02) |
| Bawikung | Beaudon | Beleif | Benett (0.01) | Benjemyn | Benyomin | Bernave |
| Bawilian | Beaudy | Belen | Benge | Benjeremiah | Benyto | Bernd |
| Bawithathawng | Beauen | Beleniel | Bengerman | Benjerman | Benzel | Bernell |
| Bawkhee | Beaufort | Belford | Bengi | Benjermen | Benzic | Bernett |
| Baxley | Beauman | Belisario | Bengie | Benjermin | Benzino | Bernhard |
| Baxter (0.01) | Beaumont | Belkhatni | Bengimin | Benjhmen | Benzion (0.01) | Bernie (0.01) |
| Bay | Beauregard | Belki | Benginho | Benji (0.01) | Beonco | Berniel |
| Bayan | Beaux | Bellen | Benhard | Benjie | Beondre | Bernis |
| Bayard | Bebe | Bellin | Beni | Benjiman (0.01) | Bepeh | Bernstein |
| Bayardo | Becan | Belly | Beniah | Benjimen | Bephnoti | Berny |
| Bayd | Bechir | Belmin | Beniamin | Benjimin | Bequer | Berrek |
| Bayden (0.01) | Beck (0.04) | Beloved | Benicio (0.01) | Benjirman | Berardino | Berrisford |
| Baydon | Beckam | Belquin | Benie | Benjmain | Berdandino | Berry |
| Baye | Beckem | Belssen | Benigno | Benjoeysen | Berdyasky | Bersan |
| Bayete | Becken | Belton | Benin | Benjun | Berechiah | Bershadd |
| Baylan | Beckenbauer | Beluchi | Beniphontae | Benjuno | Berek | Bershard |
| Baylee (0.01) | Becker (0.01) | Belyn | Benito (0.02) | Benjy | Bereket | Bershon |
| Baylen (0.01) | Becket | Belzar | Benjadiel | Benjyman | Bereketeab | Bersimanuel |
| Bayler | Beckett (0.05) | Bemshima | Benjahmin | Benley | Berekte | Bert |
| Bayley | Beckham (0.02) | Ben (0.15) | Benjaimen | Benn | Beren | Berthancourt |
| Baylian | Beckhan | Ben Aaron | Benjaman | Bennane | Berend | Berthier |
| Baylin | Beckhem | Ben Bangaly | Benjamein | Benndy | Berg | Bertholy |
| Baylis | Beckler | Ben Jaylin | Benjamen (0.02) | Benner | Bergan | Berthony |
| Bayllon | Beckley | Benaiah (0.01) | Benjamin (6.39) | Bennet | Bergen (0.01) | Berthum |
| Baylon | Beckman | Benaise | Benjamin Bruno | Bennett (0.23) | Bergin | Bertin |
| Baylor (0.03) | Bedford | Benajah | Benjamin Eric | Bennie (0.01) | Berhanie | Bertine |
| Bayne (0.01) | Bedirhan | Ben-Alexis | Benjamin Frankl | Benning | Berhaun | Bertini |
| Bayon | Bedrick | Benamici | Benjamin Franklin | Bennington | Beric | Bertley |
| Bayr | Bee | Benancio | Benjamin Jacab | Bennito | Bering | Bertoldo |
| Bayram | Beecher | Benard | Benjamin Jaykob | Bennjamin | Berish | Bertony |
| Bayro | Beekan | Benat | Benjamin Nils | Benno | Berit | Bertram |
| Bayron | Beenadd | Benayah | Benjamin Rafik | Benny (0.04) | Berji | Bervensky |
| Bayu | Beethoven | Bence | Benjamin Takashi | Benoit (0.02) | Berk | Bervin |
| Bayze | Beguah | Bency | Benjamin Viet Hun | Benoit Joseph | Berkan | Berwyn |
| Bazen | Behnam | Bendarus | Benjamine (0.01) | Benoit-Hubert | Berkay | Beryl |
| Bazi | Behrod | Bendeguz | Benjamin-Ian | Benoni | Berke | Besarb |
| Bazil | Behruz | Bender | Benjammin | Bensalih | Berkeley | Besart |
| Bazon | Beijon | Benditto | Benjamyn (0.01) | Bensen | Berkley (0.01) | Beshoy |
| BB | Beilian | Bene | Benjamyn-Mathew | Bens-Harley | Berlange | Besim |
| Be'andre | Beion | Benecio | Benjavis | Benson (0.05) | Berlin | Besir |
| Be'kel | Bejamin | Benedek | Benjavontea | Benson Clarck | Berlly | Besmir |
| Be'la | Bejoy | Benedict (0.04) | Ben-Jefferson | Benten | Berman | Besnik |
| Beaman | Bek | Benedicto | Benjemin | Bentlee | Bermane | Best |
| Beamon | Beker | Benedikt | | Bentley (0.04) | Bernabe | Betanya |
| Bear | Bekim | Beneditto | | Bentlie | Bernabet | Bethany |
| Bearett | Bekzod | Benedykt | | Bently | Bernal | Bethel |
| Bearon | Bela | Beneiam | | Benton (0.03) | Bernan | Bethuel |
| Beary | Belafonte | Benel | | Bentton | Bernandino | Betuel |
| Beatrice | Belafonté | Benelli | | Bentzion | Bernard (0.07) | Betzalel |
| Beattie | Belal (0.01) | Benelson | | Benuel (0.01) | Bernarde | Bevan |
| Beatty | Belcher | Benen | | Beny | Bernardi | Bevandeep |
| Beau (0.18) | Belden | Benet | | Benyam | Bernardino | Bevin |

| | | | | | | |
|---|---|---|---|---|---|---|
| Bex | Bije | Biran | Blaize Edward | Blestin | Bogdan *(0.01)* | Bora |
| Bexlee | Bikram | Birch | James | Bleu | Bohan | Borden |
| Bexson | Bikrampal | Birekam | Blaizz | Bliss | Bohanin | Borders |
| Beyan | Bil'zavier | Birgen | Blake *(2.10)* | Blitz | Bohcan | Bordy |
| Beyla | Bilaal | Birkeland | Blakelee | Blong | Bohdan *(0.01)* | Borel |
| Bhagat | Bilal *(0.05)* | Birman | Blakeley | Blonzell | Bohdi | Boris *(0.02)* |
| Bhagwan | Bilal Naeem | Biro | Blakely *(0.01)* | Bloua | Bohdistava | Boriz |
| Bhanu | Bilal-Sa'id | Birraa | Blake-Mcclain | Blu | Bohdon | Borja |
| Bharat | Bilbil | Biruk | Blakemon | Blue | Boimah | Borna |
| Bharathkumar | Bile | Bisesh | Blakley | Blue Horse | Bojia | Boropa |
| Bhargav | Bilel | Biship | Blaklyn | Bluebear | Bokarik | Borribo |
| Bhargava | Bilguun | Bishop *(0.05)* | Blanding | Bluford | Bokee | Boruch |
| Bharmen | Bili | Bishoy | Blandon | Bluntarian | Bokolo | Bo-Ruei |
| Bhaskar | Biliam | Bisire | Blane *(0.01)* | Bly | Bokuma- | Bosco |
| Bhav | Bilind | Bismar | Blanton | Blyth | Joseph-Martin | Boscoe |
| Bhavan | Bill *(0.02)* | Bismarck | Blare | Blythe | Bol | Bosic |
| Bhavandeep | Billal | Bismark | Blas | Blythen | Bola | Bosland |
| Bhavdeep | Billel | Bismeet | Blasco-Antonio | Bo *(0.09)* | Boland | Boss |
| Bhavish | Billie *(0.01)* | Bitan | Blase | Bo'kyte | Bolefa-Jean- | Bossant |
| Bhavnish | Billind | Biyamin | Blaten | Boadie | Pierre | Bossy |
| Bhavpreet | Billion | BJ | Blaton | Boaz *(0.01)* | Bolling | Bosten |
| Bhavraj | Billkui | Bjarki | Blay | Bob *(0.01)* | Bolong | Bostin |
| Bhavsahil | Billoh | B-Jay | Blayd | Boban | Bolten | Boston *(0.12)* |
| Bhavshan | Billy *(0.19)* | Bjoern | Blayde | Bobbe | Bolton | Botan |
| Bhavtaran | Billy Boy | Björn *(0.02)* | Blayden *(0.01)* | Bobby *(0.16)* | Boluwatife | Botond |
| Bhavya | Billy David | Blace | Blaydon | Bobby Bernard | Bo-Magnus | Bottra |
| Bhima | Billy Jack | Blackwell | Blayk | Bobby-Ray | Boman | Bouba |
| Bhodram | Billy Joe | Bladden | Blayke *(0.01)* | Bobbyrey | Bomani | Boubacar |
| Bhrayan | Billy Wayne | Blade *(0.02)* | Blayn | Bobvi | Bon | Boubakar |
| Bhrugu | Billy-Andrew | Blade Alexander | Blayne *(0.03)* | Bocar | Bona | Boubker |
| Bhumit | Billyjo | Joshua | Blays | Bocephus | Bonard | Boudey |
| Bhuvan | Billyjoe | Bladein | Blayse | Bodan | Bonaventure | Boulder |
| Bhuvanesh | Billy-Rey | Blademir | Blayson | Bode *(0.03)* | Bond | Bounthala |
| Bhuvas | Bilson | Bladen *(0.01)* | Blaytin | Bo-Dean | Boni | Bouraima |
| Bhuvnoor | Bima | Bladimil | Blayton *(0.01)* | Bo-Dee | Boniface | Bourne |
| Bi | Bin | Bladimir *(0.01)* | Blayz | Bodee | Bonifacio | Bourque |
| Biaggio | Binar | Bladimiro | Blayze *(0.01)* | Bodei | Bonix | Boustyn |
| Biagio | Binay | Bladyn | Blayze Frederic | Boden *(0.03)* | Bonjayzhiey | Boux |
| Bianco | Bindon | Blaec | Blaz | Bodey *(0.01)* | Bonn | Bouyagui |
| Bianey | Bingham | Blaeytten | Blaze *(0.07)* | Bodhi *(0.02)* | Bonner | Bovent |
| Biantre | Bingrui | Blaez | Blaze Raymond | Bodi | Bonnie | Bovon |
| Biar | Binh | Blaiden | Blazen | Bodie *(0.03)* | Bonsa | Bow |
| Bibek | Biniam | Blaike | Blazer | Bodiezepha | Bonsan | Bowan |
| Bibentz | Binjamin | Blain *(0.01)* | Bleart | Bodin | Bonshavior | Bowden *(0.01)* |
| Bickram | Binney | Blainde | Bleeze | Bodine | Bonya | Bowdie |
| Bienvenido | Binni | Blaine *(0.11)* | Bleon | Bodyn | Bonyad | Bowdoin |
| Biftu | Bintzen | Blair *(0.03)* | Blerton | Boe | Bonyeka | Bowdy |
| Big | Binyam | Blaire | Bless | Boede | Booker *(0.01)* | Bowe |
| Big William | Binyamin | Blais | Blessen | Boeden | Bookie | Bowen *(0.05)* |
| Bighnaraj | Binyomin | Bláise | Blessin | Boedey | Boomer | Bowie |
| Bihjan | Biong | Blaise *(0.05)* | Blessing | Boedy | Boone *(0.01)* | Bowman |
| Biidaash | Bior | Blaiss | Blesson | Boen | Boots | Bowte |
| Bijan | Biously | Blaize *(0.02)* | Blest | Bogart | Boping | Boy Of Shantay |

| | | | | | | |
|---|---|---|---|---|---|---|
| Boyan | Bradley-Joseph | Braidyn | Brandi | Branon | Bravis | Braylinn |
| Boyce | Bradli | Braige | Brandin (0.02) | Branquez | Bravlio | Brayln |
| Boyd (0.01) | Bradly (0.04) | Braij'sion | Brandious | Bransan | Brawton | Braylon (0.26) |
| Boyer | Bradney | Brailand | Brando (0.02) | Bransen (0.01) | Brax | Braylon Terrell |
| Boysie | Brado | Braileigh | Brandol | Branshaun | Braxden | Braylyn |
| Bra'cari | Bradon (0.03) | Brailen | Brandom | Branskey | Braxin | Brayn |
| Bra'ezhaun | Bradrik | Brailin | Brandon (5.63) | Branson (0.06) | Braxon | Brayni |
| Bra'juan | Bradson | Brailon | Brandon Adam | Branston | Braxsten | Brayon |
| Bra'kye | Brady (1.56) | Brailun | Brandon Alberto | Bransun | Braxston | Brayriver |
| Bra'shawn | Bradyden | Braily | Brandon Alexis | Bransyn | Braxten (0.01) | Braysen |
| Brabiel | Bradyen | Brailyn | Brandon | Brant (0.04) | Braxtin | Brayshawn |
| Brac | Bradyn (0.12) | Brailynn | Christian | Brantavious | Braxtinn | Brayson (0.02) |
| Brace | Bradynn | Brain | Brandon Lee | Brantez | Braxton (0.60) | Braytan |
| Bracen | Brae | Brainerd | Brandon Mauro | Branthon | Braxton | Brayten |
| Bracey | Brae'lyn | Braison | Brandon Ron | Brantin | Azaybien | Brayton (0.02) |
| Brach | Braecen | Braiten | Brandon Zack | Brantley (0.03) | Braxtyn | Braz |
| Bracken | Braed'n | Braith | Brandon-Aaron | Brantly | Bray | Brazdon |
| Brackin | Braedan (0.02) | Braizlee | Brandon- | Branton | Brayah | Brazen |
| Brackley | Braede | Brajden | Anthony | Brantrell | Brayam (0.01) | Braziel |
| Brackston | Braéden | Brajsuan | Brandon- | Brantson | Brayan (0.18) | Brazous |
| Brackton | Braeden (0.32) | Braken | Damian | Brantt | Brayand | Bre |
| Bracy | Braedenn | Brakyren | Brandoneil | Brantz | Brayant | Bre'dyn |
| Bracyn | Braedey | Bralaen | Brandon-Lee | Brantzen | Brayben | Bre'lan |
| Brad (0.05) | Braedin | Braldy | Brandon- | Branum | Braycen | Bre'land |
| Brad Jason | Braedon (0.09) | Bralen | Maurice | Branyan | Braycon | Bre'lyn |
| Brad William | Braedy | Braley | Brandonn | Branyi | Braydale | Bre'shawn |
| Bradach | Braedyn (0.03) | Bralin | Brandonn- | Branyon | Braydan (0.03) | Bre'yon |
| Bradan (0.01) | Braejon | Bralla | Wayne | Branzin | Brayde | Bre'zhaun |
| Bradd | Braelan | Brallam | Brandon-Tiago | Brasden | Braydehn | Brea'on |
| Bradden | Braelee | Brallan (0.01) | Brandon-Yves | Brasean | Brayden (3.05) | Breadon |
| Braddlee | Braelen | Bralon | Brandrius | Brasen (0.01) | Brayden Just | Breadon Lee |
| Braddley | Braeley | Braluhn | Brandt (0.03) | Brashad | Brayden | Breadyn |
| Braddock | Braelin (0.01) | Braly | Brandton | Brashaun | Michael | Breagan |
| Braddon | Braelon (0.01) | Bralyn (0.01) | Brandun | Brasil | Brayden Sidney | Breagin |
| Bradee | Braelyn (0.01) | Bralynn | Brandus | Brason | Brayden- | Brean Stevens |
| Bradely | Braeson | Bramley | Brandy | Braston | Alexander | Breandan |
| Braden (1.14) | Braeton | Bran | Brandyn (0.03) | Brat | Braydence | Breandán |
| Braden | Brahden | Branaviyun | Brandyn Bruce | Brath | Braydenn | Breandon |
| Christopher | Braheem | Brance | Braniel | Brathan | Braydie | Breaven |
| Bradey (0.01) | Brahiam | Branch | Branigan | Bratton | Braydin (0.01) | Brec |
| Bradford (0.03) | Brahim | Brand | Branimir | Braublio | Braydn (0.01) | Breccan |
| Bradick | Brahlie | Brandal | Branko | Brauch | Braydon (0.27) | Brechan |
| Bradie | Brahm | Brandan (0.03) | Branlee | Brauk | Braydun | Breche |
| Bradien | Brahman | Brandarious | Branly | Braulio (0.03) | Braydyn | Breck (0.01) |
| Bradin (0.01) | Braian | Brandavion | Brannan | Braun | Brayeden | Breckan |
| Bradison | Braid | Branddon | Branndon | Brauner | Brayen | Brecken (0.02) |
| Bradlan | Braidan | Branddon | Branndonn | Braunson | Brayion | Breckin (0.01) |
| Bradle | Braidee | Drayshawn | Brannel | Brauntae | Braylan (0.01) | Breckin Skylar |
| Bradlee (0.03) | Braiden (0.13) | Brandell | Brannen | Brava | Brayland | Bredan |
| Bradlee-Pierce | Braidey | Branden (0.19) | Brannigan | Bravaun | Braylen (0.06) | Bredon |
| Bradley (0.84) | Braidin | Brandenlee | Brannoc | Brave | Brayley | Bredyan |
| Bradley | Braidon (0.01) | Brander | Brannon (0.02) | Braven | Braylhan | Bredyn |
| Connolly | Braidy | | Brannum | Braverick | Braylin (0.02) | Breeden |

| | | | | | | |
|---|---|---|---|---|---|---|
| Breelin | Brendun | Breton | Briant | Brinen | Broaden | Brom |
| Breeon | Brendyn (0.02) | Brett (0.43) | Briantay | Brink | Broadie | Bron |
| Brehdyn | Brendynn | Brett Willliam | Briar (0.04) | Brinkley | Broady | Bronc |
| Brehon | Brene | Brettan | Briawn | Brinlee | Broc (0.01) | Bronce |
| Breidon | Brenen | Bretton (0.01) | Brice (0.09) | Brinley | Brocc | Bronco |
| Breighden | Brenenn | Brev | Bricen (0.01) | Brinly | Broche | Brondy |
| Breighton | Brenin | Brevan | Briceson | Brinston | Brock (0.41) | Bronko |
| Breilys | Brenley | Breven | Briceton | Brinton | Brockden | Bronsen |
| Breimen | Brennan (0.39) | Brevin (0.02) | Bricey | Brio | Brockett | Bronson (0.05) |
| Brein | Brenndan | Brevon | Bricio | Brion (0.01) | Brockington | Bronston |
| Breion | Brennden | Brevyn | Brick | Brione | Brockman | Brontavious |
| Breishaun | Brennen (0.11) | Brewer | Brick Shon | Briquon | Brockton | Bronte |
| Breixo | Brenner (0.01) | Brexley | Bricken | Brisait | Brockway | Bronx |
| Breiyon | Brennigan | Brexton | Bricker | Brisan | Brocton | Bronz |
| Brek | Brennin | Brey | Brickey | Brise | Brodan | Brook |
| Brekel | Brennir | Breyan | Bricson | Brisen | Brodde | Brooke |
| Brekien | Brennnan | Breydan | Briden | Brishawn | Brodderyk | Brookes |
| Brekk | Brennon (0.03) | Breyden (0.01) | Bridger (0.08) | Brishon | Broddie | Brooklen |
| Brekken | Brenny | Breydon (0.01) | Bridget | Brison (0.01) | Broddrick | Brooklyn (0.02) |
| Brekkin | Brennyn | Breydyn | Bridon | Bristen | Brode | Brooks (0.09) |
| Brekyn | Breno | Breyen | Brien (0.01) | Bristol | Brodee (0.01) | Brose |
| Brelan | Brenon | Breyer | Brienan | Briston | Broden (0.03) | Brosnan |
| Breland | Brensan | Breylan | Briendel | Bristyn | Broder | Brostrie |
| Brelen | Brensen | Breylin | Brier (0.01) | Brisyn | Broderic | Broty |
| Brelend | Brenson | Breylind | Briere | Britain (0.01) | Broderick (0.06) | Broughton |
| Brelin | Brent (0.17) | Breylon | Briesen | Britan | Broderik | Brouke |
| Brelyn | Brentan | Breyon (0.01) | Brigg | Briten | Broderyck | Broward |
| Brelynn | Brentavious | Breyson | Briggs (0.01) | Britian | Brodes | Browden |
| Bremen | Brentell | Breyton | Brigham (0.01) | Britley | Brodey (0.02) | Browdy |
| Bremere | Brenten | Breyuan | Bright | Briton | Brodi (0.01) | Browin |
| Bremmen | Brenterius | Brezlan | Brighten | Britt (0.01) | Brodick | Brown |
| Bren | Brentez | Bri'rell | Brightin | Brittain | Brodie (0.18) | Browning |
| Bren Kerby | Brenthon | Briac | Brighton (0.02) | Brittan | Brodiey | Broxton |
| Brenan (0.01) | Brentin | Briace | Brightyn | Brittaney | Brodik | Broxyn |
| Brenann | Brentlea | Brial | Brigidi | Brittany | Brodin | Broz |
| Brenard | Brentlee | Briam | Brigz | Britten | Brodon | Brshnauder |
| Brenda | Brentley (0.01) | Brian (2.97) | Brihad | Brittian | Brodric | Bru'shawn |
| Brendal | Brently | Brian Aydan | Brij | Brittin | Brodrich | Bruce (0.16) |
| Brendan (0.86) | Brent-Michael | Brian Boyuan | Brijian | Brittney | Brodrick (0.01) | Bruce K |
| Brendan-John | Brenton (0.07) | Brian Christoph | Brijwon | Britton (0.04) | Brodryck | Bruce Lee |
| Brendann | Brentton | Brian Lawrence | Brik | Brivic | Brody (0.95) | Bruce Leroy |
| Brendaun | Brentyn | Brian Marcel | Brilee | Brix | Brody Don' | Bruce Rain |
| Brenden (0.31) | Brenyn | Briana | Briley (0.03) | Brixen | Brodye | Bruce Vinh |
| Brenden Mich | Breon (0.01) | Brian-Alejandro | Brill | Brixten | Brodyn (0.01) | Brucely |
| Brenderious | Breondice | Briand | Brillig | Brixter | Broedy | Brucio |
| Brendhan | Bresaus | Brianjohnson | Brimokani | Brixton | Brogain | Bruck |
| Brendin (0.01) | Bresean | Brian-Lee | Brin | Briyam | Brogan (0.07) | Brues |
| Brendle | Breshaun | Briann | Brince | Briyan | Brogen | Bruin |
| Brendon (0.17) | Breshawn | Brianna | Brinden | Briycen | Broghan | Bruk |
| Brendon- | Breshon | Briann- | Brinder | Briylee | Brohden | Bruke |
|   Delaroche | Breslin |   Cameron | Brindin | Briyon | Brohn | Brukzer |
| Brendston | Bret (0.04) | Briano | Brindon | Briyson | Brok | Brunner |
| Brendt | Bretlynn | Brianson | Brindyn | Brizen | Broly | Bruno (0.05) |

| | | | | | | |
|---|---|---|---|---|---|---|
| Bruno-Nicolas | Bryen | Brysten | Burklan | C'zar | Caden *(2.28)* | Cahetano |
| Bruno-Pierre | Bryennt | Brystin | Burkley | Ca Lique | Cadence *(0.02)* | Cahke |
| Brunson | Bryent | Bryston *(0.01)* | Burl | Ca Mareius | Caden-Ray | Cahleb |
| Bruook | Bryer *(0.01)* | Brysyn | Burnell | Ca Monne | Cadet | Cahlil |
| Bruse | Bryere | Brytan | Burnett | Ca'darius | Cadge | Cahmani |
| Brushawn | Bryeson | Bryten | Burney | Ca'darrius | Cadian | Cahmrin |
| Brushon | Bryeton | Brytin | Burton *(0.01)* | Ca'leb | Cadience | Cahner |
| Bry | Bryhan | Bryton *(0.03)* | Buryle | Ca'lloydric | Cadigio | Cahse |
| Bryam | Bryheem | Bryun | Bush | Ca'mar | Cadillac | Cai *(0.01)* |
| Bryan *(3.04)* | Bryheen | Bryzon | Buster | Ca'mareon | Cadillion | Caibhan |
| Bryan Josue | Bryheim | Bshar | Butch | Ca'mari | Cadin *(0.02)* | Caid |
| Bryan Nathaniel | Bryhiem | Bubba | Butler | Ca'marion | Cadis | Caidan *(0.01)* |
| Xavier | Bryin | Buchanan | Buynum | Ca'myren | Cadmiel | Caide |
| Bryan Thomas | Bryison | Buchannon | Buzz | Ca'naree | Cadon | Caiden *(0.30)* |
| Bryan Vu | Bryjen | Buchi | By'drez | Ca'ron | Cadonnie | Caiden Austin |
| Bryance | Brykel | Buck *(0.01)* | By'key | Ca'rron | Cadren | Caidence |
| Bryandriquez | Brylan *(0.01)* | Buckley | By'ris | Ca'sanova | Cadyn *(0.02)* | Caidin |
| Bryann | Bryland | Buckminster | By'ryen | Ca'shon | Cadyne | Caidn |
| Bryanna | Brylar | Buckner | By'shir | Ca'vontae | Cae'sar | Caidon |
| Bryan-Oscar | Bryle | Buckston | Byeese | Caaden | Caedan | Caidonn |
| Bryan-Oti | Brylee | Bucky | Byer | Caanan | Caeden *(0.03)* | Caidrian |
| Bryan-Renald | Brylen | Bud | Byishimo | Cabbet | Caeden-Michael | Caidyn *(0.01)* |
| Bryant *(0.22)* | Bryler | Budd | Byliah | Cabe | Caedin | Caige |
| Bryant-Curtis | Bryley | Buddy *(0.01)* | Bynton | Cabel | Caedmon *(0.01)* | Caihlem |
| Bryanty | Bryli | Buel | Byounghoon | Cabell | Caedon *(0.01)* | Cail |
| Bryar *(0.01)* | Brylin *(0.01)* | Buell | Byram | Cabett | Caedyn | Cailan |
| Bryar Lee | Bryln | Buerk | Byran | Cable | Caehdryc | Cailean |
| Bryars | Brylon | Buffalo | Byrd | Cabo | Cael *(0.04)* | Caileb |
| Brycan | Brylond | Bufford | Byren | Cabor | Caelan *(0.02)* | Caileito |
| Bryce *(1.66)* | Bryn | Buford | Byriane | Cabot *(0.01)* | Caeleb *(0.01)* | Cailen |
| Bryce Steven | Brynavious | Bujar | Byrin | Cabrae | Caelen | Cailer |
| Bryce William | Bryndan | Bukari | Byron *(0.13)* | Cabram | Caelib | Cailin |
| Bryceden | Brynden *(0.01)* | Bullet | Byron-Enrique | Cabran | Caelin | Caillen |
| Brycedon | Brynin | Bulmaro | Byryn | Cabraun | Caellum | Caillou |
| Bryce-Kerri | Brynn | Bulo | Bysil | Cabri | Caelum | Caillum |
| Brycen *(0.11)* | Brynnan | Bultum | Bysir | Cabrick | Caelyb | Cailo |
| Bryceon | Brynnen | Bulut | Byson | Cacel | Caelyn | Cailon |
| Bryceson | Brynton | Bundit | Byulha | Cache | Caelynn | Cailou |
| Bryceston | Bryon *(0.02)* | Bunker | Byung Jae | Cacheton | Caeman | Cailyb |
| Brycetin | Bryquell | Bunny | | Cacne | Caene | Cailyn |
| Bryceton *(0.01)* | Bryron | Buntereth | | Cactus | Caesar *(0.01)* | Caiman |
| Brychan | Brysan | Burak | ~ C ~ | Cadan *(0.01)* | Caescaré | Caimen |
| Brychen | Bryse | Burech | | Cadance | Caeser | Caimin |
| Brycien | Brysen *(0.02)* | Buren | C L | Cadarius | Caewood | Caimon |
| Brycin | Bryshawn | Burg | C Magnus | Caddell | Caezar | Cain *(0.03)* |
| Brycn | Bryshon | Burgan | C.J. | Cadden | Cagan | Cainan *(0.01)* |
| Brycon | Brysin | Burgess | C'andré | Cadderick | Cage *(0.01)* | Caine *(0.01)* |
| Brycton | Bryslan | Burgwyn | C'ante | Caddin | Cagen | Cainen *(0.01)* |
| Brydan | Bryson *(0.96)* | Burhan | C'aureon | Cade *(0.29)* | Cager | Caine-Robert |
| Brydell | Bryson | Burhanuddin | C'drick | Cadeem | Cager-Denzel | Cainin |
| Bryden *(0.02)* | Alexander | Burim | C'ewaldo | Cadel | Cagney | Cainnon |
| Brydon *(0.01)* | Bryson O'mar | Burke *(0.02)* | C'mauri | Cadell | Cah'dyn | Cainon |
| Brydun | Bryson-Eze | Burkeley | C'quan | Cademan | Cahel | Cainwyn |

| | | | | | | |
|---|---|---|---|---|---|---|
| Caio *(0.01)* | Caleel | Callom | Camareon | Cameron-Lee | Can'trelle | Caprio |
| Caio Victor | Caleem | Callon | Camareus | Cameronlee | Cana | Captain |
| Caiomyn | Calef | Callowae | Camari *(0.01)* | Cameronn | Canaan *(0.03)* | Captian |
| Caiou | Caleigh | Calloway | Camarie | Cameroun | Canada | Car Shawn |
| Cairell | Caleik | Callum *(0.06)* | Camarien | Camerron | Canai | Car'lito |
| Cairo *(0.01)* | Calel | Callun | Camario | Cameryn *(0.01)* | Canaji | Carac |
| Caisar | Calem | Calman | Camarion *(0.01)* | Cameryne | Canan | Carbari |
| Caise | Calen *(0.01)* | Calnesto | Camarius | Camet | Canarie | Carbe |
| Caisen | Caleob | Calo | Camariyon | Cameya | Canathan | Carben |
| Caison | Caleon | Calob *(0.01)* | Camaro | Camian | Candelario | Carcello |
| Caisson | Calepp | Calobe | Camaron *(0.01)* | Camicee | Canden | Carcin |
| Caiten | Caleste | Calogero | Camarreus | Camiel | Candido | Cardale |
| Caitlin | Calet | Caloway | Camaureon | Camil | Candilario | Cardar |
| Caitlyn | Calex | Calton | Camauri | Camille | Candin | Cardarius |
| Caius *(0.01)* | Calhenry | Calub | Cambden | Camillo | Candler | Cardavise |
| Caivan | Cali | Calum *(0.02)* | Cambel | Camillo Luis | Candon | Cardeinian |
| Caiwo | Calib *(0.01)* | Calup | Cambell | Camillus | Cane | Cardel |
| Caj | Caliban | Calvain | Cambren | Camilo *(0.04)* | Canie | Cardell |
| Cajani | Calibb | Calve'on | Cambreon | Camir | Canin | Carden |
| Cajen | Calibe | Calveal | Cambreyon | Camiren | Caniyis | Carder |
| Caji | Caliber | Calven | Cambrian | Camiron | Cannah | Cardezz |
| Cajun | Calid | Calveon | Cambridge | Camirye | Cannan | Cardier |
| Cal *(0.02)* | Calieb | Calvert | Cambrien | Cammer | Cannen | Cardiff |
| Cal'el | Caliel | Calvin *(0.52)* | Cambron | Cammeron | Cannin | Cardin |
| Cal'lel | Calif | Calvin Laras | Cambryn | Cammeyun | Cannizzaro | Cardiss |
| Calab | Calil | Calvin Noa | Camby | Cammron | Cannon *(0.05)* | Cardius |
| Calaeb | Calill | Calvineon | Camdan | Camo | Canoa | Cardoso Herrera |
| Calaghan | Calin *(0.01)* | Calvino | Camdem | Camoci | Canon *(0.01)* | Cardyairé |
| Calahan | Calintz | Calvinson | Camden *(0.46)* | Camon | Canorris | Careb |
| Calais | Calios | Calvyn | Camdien | Camoni | Cansin | Caree |
| Calan *(0.01)* | Caliph | Calwin | Camdin | Camontae | Canson | Careef |
| Calaway | Calir | Calyb | Camdon *(0.01)* | Camorian | Canton | Carel |
| Calbert | Calis | Calyn | Camdyn *(0.02)* | Camorrie | Cantrell | Carel-Ange |
| Calder *(0.01)* | Calison | Calynn | Camdyne | Camp | Canvas | Carey *(0.01)* |
| Cale *(0.10)* | Calisto | Calyton | Came'ren | Campbell *(0.06)* | Canyan | Caribe |
| Calea | Calistro | Calyx | Came'ron | Campden | Canye | Cariel |
| Caleab | Calix *(0.01)* | Calzvier | Cameise | Camper | Canyen | Carim |
| Caleb *(5.02)* | Calixte | Cam *(0.01)* | Camelle | Campsey | Canyon *(0.03)* | Carin |
| Caleb | Calixto | Cam Ron | Camellien | Camran *(0.01)* | Cao Thien | Carinna |
|   Christopher | Caliyahl | Cam'erion | Camen | Camrein | Caolan | Carintyn |
| Caleb Joseph | Caliyph | Cam'ren | Cameo | Camren *(0.10)* | Cao-Tri | Cario |
| Caleb Jude | Call | Cam'rhen | Cameran *(0.01)* | Camrenn | Cape | Carion |
| Caleb Kamra | Callaghan | Cam'ron *(0.03)* | Cameren *(0.01)* | Camrick | Caper | Carios |
| Caleb Nelson | Callahan *(0.01)* | Cam'ryn | Camereon | Camrin *(0.02)* | Capers | Carius |
| Caleb Zebediah | Callan *(0.01)* | Camajae | Camerian | Camron *(0.22)* | Caphias | Car-Jhae |
| Caleb-Alexander | Callanan | Camani | Camerien | Camronn | Caplan | Carl *(0.23)* |
| Caleb-Andre | Callaway | Camanni | Camerin *(0.01)* | Camrun | Capon | Carl Adam |
| Calebe | Calleb | Camar | Camerion | Camry | Capone | Carl Anderson |
| Caleb-Jordan | Callen *(0.02)* | Camaran | Camern | Camryn *(0.05)* | Cappi | Carl Benjam |
| Caleb-Rey | Calleon | Camardre | Camerohn | Camrynn | Cappreon | Carl Borg |
| Caleby | Callief | Camaré | Camerom | Camyren | Capree | Carl Francis |
| Caleeb | Callin | Camaree | Cameron *(4.29)* | Camyron | Capri | Carl Jermaine |
| Caleed | Callister | Camaren | Cameron' Jaleel | Can | Caprice | Carl Jonathan |

| | | | | | | |
|---|---|---|---|---|---|---|
| Carl Marquell | Carlos Brian | Carmoni | Carther | Cashton *(0.01)* | Cate | Cayan |
| Carl'von | Carlos Daniel | Carmyne | Carthik | Cashun | Catelyn | Cayce |
| Carl-Alain | Carlos Esteban | Carndyn | Cartier | Cashus | Cates | Caycen |
| Carl-Alex | Carlos Gabriel | Carnelius | Cartinez | Casi | Cathal | Caydan |
| Carl-Alexander | Carlos Javier | Carnell *(0.01)* | Cartrail | Casie | Cathan | Cayddan |
| Carl-Alexandre | Carlos Juan | Carnez | Cartravine | Casimir | Catherine | Cayde |
| Carl-Andre | Carlos Manuel | Carneze | Cartrell | Casin | Catlin | Cayden *(0.51)* |
| Carl-Antoine | Carlos Miguel | Carnike | Carvell | Casino | Cato | Cayden Sir' |
| Carl-Charbel | Carlos Octavio | Carob | Carvelle | Casious | Caton | Caydence |
| Carl-Daniel | Carlos Uriel | Carol | Carver *(0.02)* | Casius | Catrae | Caydene |
| Carldayle | Carlos-Andres | Caroline | Carvin | Cason *(0.06)* | Catrayis | Cayden-Noble |
| Carlder | Carlos-Daniel | Carolyn | Carviontray | Casonick | Catrell | Caydin |
| Carldreyko | Carlos-Emanuel | Carolyntz | Cary *(0.01)* | Caspar | Catron | Caydn |
| Carle | Carlos-Luis | Ca-Ron | Caryon | Caspen | Cat-Tuong | Caydon *(0.01)* |
| Carledo | Carlos-Manuel | Caron *(0.01)* | Carzelle | Casper *(0.01)* | Caua | Caydyn |
| Carlee | Carlos-Miguel | Carr | Cas | Caspian | Caughlin | Cayel |
| Carleeto | Carlos-Raul | Carre | Casanova | Cass | Cauillou | Cayen |
| Carl-Ely | Carlostadeo | Carrell | Casaun | Cassady | Caulden | Cayeshaun |
| Carlen | Carlou's | Carreon | Cascey | Cassanova | Caulder | Cayetano |
| Carlen's | Carlous | Carreyon | Cascious | Cassaun | Caulee | Cayin |
| Carlens | Carlsen | Carrice | Cascius | Cassean | Caulek | Caylan |
| Carleous | Carlson | Carrick *(0.01)* | Casdell | Cassell | Caulin | Cayle |
| Carless | Carlton *(0.04)* | Carrington | Case *(0.03)* | Cassen | Caullan | Cayleb *(0.01)* |
| Carl-Etienne | Carltún | *(0.01)* | Casean | Cassey | Caullin | Caylee |
| Carleton | Carlven | Carrio | Casee | Casshus | Caulyn | Caylem |
| Carley | Carlwin | Carrion | Caseem | Cassian | Caundre | Caylen |
| Carliff | Carly | Carriss | Casek | Cassidy *(0.01)* | Caunnor | Cayler |
| Carlile | Carly-Henry | Carroll | Casel | Cassin | Caupert | Caylib |
| Carlin *(0.01)* | Carlyieon | Carron | Casen *(0.02)* | Cassini | Caurie | Caylin |
| Carlione | Carlyle | Carrson | Casey *(0.35)* | Cassious | Cauryae | Caylob |
| Carlique | Carlyon | Carsen *(0.04)* | Casey John | Cassium | Caution | Caylon |
| Carlis | Carlysia | Carshun | Casey-Christon | Cassius *(0.02)* | Cauy | Caylub |
| Carlisle | Carm | Carslie | Caseys | Casson | Cavalli | Caylum |
| Carlito *(0.02)* | Carman | Carson *(2.41)* | Cash *(0.11)* | Cassteel | Cavan *(0.01)* | Cayman *(0.01)* |
| Carlitos *(0.01)* | Carmane | Carson Reed | Cashan | Cast | Cavanaugh | Caymen |
| Carlitto | Carmani | Carson W | Cashaun | Castan | Cavaran | Caynan |
| Carlix | Carmarion | Carstan | Cashaus | Castely | Cavari | Cayne |
| Carl-James | Carmel | Carsten *(0.02)* | Cashawn | Casten | Cavarian | Caynen |
| Carl-Jonathan | Carmell | Carsteyn | Cashel | Caster | Cavarius | Caynnithe |
| Carl-Laurent | Carmell'o | Carston *(0.01)* | Cashen | Castle | Cavarro | Cayron |
| Carlmarion | Carmello *(0.03)* | Carstyn | Cashis | Caston | Cavel | Caysen *(0.01)* |
| Carlmelo | Carmelo *(0.06)* | Carsyn *(0.01)* | Cashius | Castor | Caven | Caysen-Jeffery |
| Carl-Michael | Carmelos | Cartaivion | Cashlin | Casuál | Cavendish | Caysey |
| Carlnel | Carmen *(0.01)* | Cartan | Cashmere | Casuan | Caveona | Caysn |
| Carlnell | Carmeron | Cartavion | Cashmerrick | Caswell | Caveryn | Cayson *(0.01)* |
| Carlo *(0.04)* | Carmi | Cartavious | Cashmier | Casy | Cavett | Caythen |
| Carlofranco | Carmichael | Cartel | Cashmiere | Casyn | Cavin *(0.01)* | Cayton |
| Carl-Olivier | Carmie | Carter *(3.35)* | Cashmir | Caszel | Cavion | Cazh |
| Carlo-Moises | Carmik | Carter Ezek | Cashon | Caszhmere | Cavit | Cazian |
| Carlon | Carmillo | Carter-Reed | Cashous | Caszir | Cavon | Cazic |
| Carlo-Rami | Carmilo | Cartes | Cashtan | Catalino | Cavontaé | Cazimire |
| Carlos *(3.01)* | Carmine *(0.04)* | Cartez | Cashtien | Catarino | Cawon | Cazma'n |
| Carlos Alberto | Carmon | Cartezz | Cashtin | Catcher *(0.01)* | Cawthorn | Cazmere |

| | | | | | | |
|---|---|---|---|---|---|---|
| Ce Vion | Cedrico | Cengizhan | Chaca'rta | Chaise *(0.01)* | Chanceller | Chanpreet |
| Ce'aundreis | Cédrik | Censear | Chacanslee | Chaisyn | Chancellor | Chanrence |
| Ce'chawn | Cedrik *(0.03)* | Centana | Chacavee | Chaitanya | (0.01) | Chanse *(0.01)* |
| Ce'dreon | Cedrix | Centauri | Chace *(0.03)* | Chaithanya | Chancelor | Chanthalaporn |
| Ce'montez | Cedrych | Centeon | Chacellor | Chaithen | Chancelyn | Chantit |
| Ce'quille | Cedryck | Centrell | Chachimeng | Chakaadan | Chancery | Chantrell |
| Ce'sar | Cedryk | Ceon | Chad *(0.27)* | Chakah | Chancey | Chantry |
| Ceabon | Cedsick | Cephas | Chad Evan | Chakaron | Chanchiz | Chants |
| Ceabriel | Cedtron | Cephus | Chad Yoan | Chake | Chancie | Chantz *(0.01)* |
| Ceaphus | Cee | Cerdrac | Chadai | Chaker | Chancler | Chantze |
| Ceasar *(0.01)* | Cee Jay | Cerek | Chadaiden | Chakong | Chancollor | Chanvir |
| Ceaser | Ceeb Tsheej | Cergio | Chadd | Chakonie | Chancy | Chanvisothir |
| Ceazar | Ceegan | Ceriffe | Chaddlee | Chakotay | Chand | Chanwoo |
| Cebastian | Ceejay | Cerin | Chaddrick | Chakwang | Chandan | Chanz |
| Cebran | Ceferino | Cerreyon | Chade | Chalan | Chandell | Chanza |
| Cebron | Cegan | Cerry | Chaden | Chaldin | Chanden | Chanzavion |
| Cecedric | Ceidan | Cervante | Chad-Evan | Chaldrez | Chander | Chanze |
| Ceceric | Ceigon | Cervantes | Chad-Felix | Chalee | Chandlar | Chanzell |
| Cecero | Ceion | Cervier | Chadi | Chalen | Chandler *(0.25)* | Chao |
| Cechario | Ceiran | Cesai | Chadlee | Chalier | Chandlerr | Chaos |
| Ceciel | Cejae | César | Chadley | Chalil | Chandlor | Chapel |
| Cecil *(0.03)* | Cejay | Cesar *(1.24)* | Chad-Pidaben | Chalino | Chandly | Chapell |
| Cecilia | Celbin | Cesar David | Chadric | Chalis | Chandon | Chapin |
| Cecilio | Celedonio | Cesar-Antonio | Chadrick | Chalker | Chandra | Chapman *(0.01)* |
| Ced | Celerino | Cesare | Chad-Rowen | Challan | Chandrae | Chappel |
| Ced'tron | Celeste | Cesareo | Chad-Samuel | Challen | Chandrasekhar | Chaquan |
| Cedar *(0.01)* | Celestin | Cesario | Chadsen | Challis | Chandric | Chaquarious |
| Cedarious | Celestino | Cesar-Nicolas | Chadwic | Chalmer | Chandrick | Chaquez' |
| Cedaris | Celestino | Cesil | Chadwich | Chalmers | Chandry | Char'kel |
| Cedarius | Matthew | Cesilio | Chadwick *(0.01)* | Chamaar | Chanduh | Char'marion |
| Ceddrick | Celian | Cesko | Chadwin | Chamar | Chane | Charalambos |
| Cederian | Celio | Cesnae | Chadzjuan | Chamarae | Chanel | Charan |
| Cederic | Celister | Cessar | Chae | Chamari | Chaney | Charan Sai |
| Cederick | Celli | Cessna | Chae'mere | Chamarion | Chang | Charard |
| Cederik | Cellou | Cetan Hota | Chaedon | Chamber | Chang Feng | Charbel *(0.01)* |
| Cederique | Celmikewood | Cetan Wakiyan | Chael | Chamberlain | Changkuoth | Charbel-Fred |
| Cederyck | Celso *(0.01)* | Ceveion | Chaellis | Chameetut | Chanh | Charcari |
| Cédéryk | Celtin | Cevetius | Chaem | Chameng | Chanhee Joshua | Chardarius |
| Cedimo | Celton | Cevin | Chahat | Champ | Chaniel | Jamir |
| Cedquedrick | Celvin Nycier | Cevion | Chahine | Champeon | Chaning | Chardell |
| Cédric *(0.01)* | Cem | Ceylon | Chahire | Champion | Chanlan | Charderian |
| Cedric *(0.18)* | Cemarion | Ceylub | Chahta | Chamren | Chanler | Chardier |
| Cedric A | Cemetrius | Ceyón | Chai | Chamylle | Chanlyn | Chardon |
| Cedric Bernard | Cemijai | Cezanne | Chaibou | Chan | Chanmackara | Chardson |
| Cedric Lam | Cemonte | Cezar | Chaiden | Chanakya | Chann | Chareion |
| Cedric Lok-Hine | Cemuel | Ch'mar | Chailen | Chanan | Channel | Charels |
| Cedric- | Cen | Cha | Chaim *(0.09)* | Chanara | Channen | Charez |
| Alexandre | Cena | Cha'marious | Chaimongkon | Chanard | Channie | Chari'on |
| Cedric-Brandon | Cenard | Chaabane | Chaince | Chancé | Channing *(0.01)* | Charis |
| Cédrick | Cencere | Chaas | Chaine | Chance *(0.36)* | Channler | Charity |
| Cedrick *(0.06)* | Cendi | Chabari | Chainey | Chancee | Channon | Charity Elijah |
| Cedrick-Jones | Cendrick | Chaben | Chairo | Chanceler | Chano | Charking |
| Cedrickus | Cendrix | Chable | Chais | Chancellar | Chanoch | Charl |

| | | | | | | |
|---|---|---|---|---|---|---|
| Charldre | Charles-David | Charmarion | Chasz | Chayme | Cheltz | Chevalier |
| Charle | Charles- | Charmarlin | Chasze | Chaynce | Chelzhiyen | Chevanon-Verin |
| Charle Antoine | Edouard | Charmeer | Chatavis | Chayne | Chemai | Chevar |
| Charlee | (0.01) | Charmer | Chattum | Chayse (0.03) | Chemar | Chevares |
| Charle-Edward | Charles-Edward | Charming | Chatur | Chaysen | Chemeng | Chevei |
| Charle-Eugene | Charles-Edwin | Charmous | Chau | Chaysin | Chen | Chevel |
| Charleigh | Charles-Elie | Charnaz | Chaucer | Chayson | Chenard | Chevelle |
| Charlemagne | Charles-Elliot | Charnez | Chaud | Chaysten | Chen-Chi | Cheveyo |
| Charlen | Charles-Eloi | Charnocus | Chaudhry | Chayston | Chencho | Chevez |
| Charles (3.79) | Charles-Emile | Charnold | Chaumar | Chayten | Cheng | Chevie |
| Charles Aiden | (0.01) | Charnpreet | Chaun | Chayton (0.03) | Cheng Guang | Chevin |
| Charles | Charles-Eric | Charod | Chaunce | Chaz (0.06) | Cheng Kong | Chevintha |
| Alexandre | Charles-Erik | Charone | Chauncely | Chazaiah | Cheng Sing | Chevis |
| Charles Allen | Charles-Etienne | Charquez | Chauncey | Chazden | Chengjun | Chevonna |
| Charles | (0.01) | Charrick | (0.03) | Chazdon | Chengleng | Chevron |
| Anthony | Charles-Felix | Charrod | Chauncey To | Chaze | Chenney | Chevry |
| Charles Antoine | Charles-Henri | Chartavion | Chaunci | Chaziah | Cheny | Chevy (0.02) |
| Charles - | Charles-Henry | Chartchai | Chauncy | Chazir | Chenya | Chevyon |
| Antoine | Charles-Hugo | Charum | Chaunte | Chazon | Cheo | Cheyanne |
| Charles Ashby | Charles- | Charvel | Chauntez | Chazton | Cheparney | Cheycin |
| Charles Dean | Jonathan | Charven | Chauntice | Chazwon | Cher Der | Cheyenne |
| Charles | Charles-Joseph | Charveze | Chaunzey | Chazyn | Cherif | Cheyne |
| Edouard | Charles-Kieffer | Charvin | Chavan | Chazz (0.01) | Cherin | Cheyon |
| Charles Edw | Charles-Lee | Charvis | Chavanne | Ché | Cherjay | Cheyten |
| Charles Edward | Charles-Levy | Charvon | Chavarous | Che (0.01) | Chermak | Cheyton |
| Charles | Charles-Mathieu | Charvorious | Chavarro | Che'nijohn | Cherokee | Chez Micah |
| Emmanuel | Charles-Olivier | Charzell | Chavelo | Che'vion | Cherokee-Mua | Chezdon |
| Charles Etienne | (0.03) | Chas (0.01) | Chavez | Chea | Cherstopher | Chezerae |
| Charles Henri | Charles-Olyvier | Chas Nicolas | Chavi | Cheabunthon | Cherubim | Chhavaddy |
| Charles Hugo | Charles-Philippe | Chase (2.67) | Chavias | Cheang Phu | Cheryee | Chhenrety |
| Charles Junior | Charles-Thomas | Chased | Chavin | Chebon | Ches | Chi |
| Charles Olivier | Charleston | Chasedon | Chavis | Checkna | Chesed | Chi Nou |
| Charles Rob | (0.01) | Chaseir | Chavon | Checotah | Cheskel (0.01) | Chi Tai |
| Charles St. | Charlesvester | Chaseley | Chavosky | Chedson | Chesky | Chia |
| George | Charles-William | Chasemon | Chavous | Chee | Chesley | Chiagozie |
| Charles Thomas | Charles-Xavier | Chasen (0.01) | Chawakorn | Chee Meng | Cheslor | Chiali |
| Charles | Charleton | Chaseston | Chawki | Cheemeng | Chesnay | Chiante |
| Williams | Charley (0.02) | Chasetin | Chawn | Cheenue | Chesnel | Chianti |
| Charles-Albert | Charli | Chaseton | Chaxton | Cheequah | Chesney | Chibuike |
| Charles- | Charlie (0.29) | Chasetyn | Chay | Chefor | Chesron | Chibuikem |
| Alexandre | Charlie John | Chashaun | Chayahn | Chefren | Chesserray | Chibundum |
| Charles-Alexis | Charlie Mil | Chashe | Chayanne | Cheick Zackael | Chesten | Chibuzo |
| Charles-Alexy | Charlie-Etienne | Chasin | Chayapol | Cheick-Moussa | Chester (0.03) | Chicago |
| Charlesallen | Charlij | Chasiti | Chayce (0.01) | Cheik | Chestian | Chico |
| Charles-Andre | Charlis | Chaska | Chayce-Aaron | Cheik Tidiane | Chestley | Chicory |
| Charles- | Charlisha | Chaske | Chaydan | Cheikh | Cheston | Chidanand |
| Anthony | Charlize | Chason (0.01) | Chayde | Cheikh Bay | Chet (0.01) | Chideraa |
| Charles-Antoine | Charlotte | Chastan | Chayden | Cheikh Tidiane | Chetan | Chidi |
| (0.03) | Charlton (0.01) | Chasten | Chaydon | Cheikhou | Chetan-Bikram | Chidike |
| Charlesbury | Charly (0.02) | Chastin | Chayeng | Cheikhou Omar | Chetanya | Chidler |
| Charles- | Charlystiv | Chaston | Chayil | Cheikhouna | Chethan | Chidube |
| Christophe | Charlz | Chasval | Chaylon | Chelik | Chett | Chidubem |
| Charles-Connor | Charmarcus | Chasyn | Chaym | Chelsea | Chevaier | Chidumeje |

Chief
Chiemela
Chiemelie
Chiemeziem
Chien
Chigozie
Chihean
Chihuu
Chika
Chikara
Chikosi
Chilenson
Chilokim
Chilton
Chim
Chima
Chimaobi
Chimaobim
Chimarion
Chimeng
Chimeremeze
Chimezirim
Chimier
Chimnedum
Chimoe
Chimong
China
Chinakrid
Chindo
Chinedu
Chinelo
Chinemelum
Chinezi
Chinmay
Chino
Chinonso
Chinowso
Chinu
Chinue
Chioke
Chip
Chipman
Chipper
Chira
Chirag
Chiranjoesh
Chiron
Chirstian
Chisamalo
Chise
Chisom
Chistopher
Chitarrius

Chitau
Chitto
Chivari
Chivas
Chiyou
Chiyoung
Chi-Yuet Nathan
Chizaram
Chloe
Choctaw
Choey
Choice
Choirtzerre
Chois
Choj
Chol
Chon
Chon Nhu
Chondru
Chone
Chonsey
Chontez
Chordarius
Chordie
Chosen
Chosten
Chou Young
Choua
Chouaib
Choudhary Ahmad
Choue
Chouneng
Choyce
Chozen
Chrey
Chri'shun
Chridarious
Chriestopher
Chris (0.17)
Chris De-Lei
Chris'shaun
Chris'shawn
Chris'shon
Chris-Allen
Chris-Angel
Chrisangel
Chrisangelo
Chris-Anthony
Chrisaun
Chrisaune
Chrischon

Chrisdionta
Chrisdon
Chrisean
Chrishad
Chrisharivs
Chrishaun
Chrishauntae
Chrishawn (0.01)
Chrishion
Chrishnald
Chrishon
Chrishoun
Chrishtan
Chrishtian
Chrishtin
Chrishun
Chris-Isaac
Chrisitian
Chrisjan
Chrisjavion
Chrisjen
Chrisjon
Chris-Kelly
Chrisler
Chrislin
Chrisly
Chrismael
Chrismark
Chrismarvel
Chrismen
Chrismond
Chrisneeder
Chrispin
Chriss
Chrissean
Chrisshawn
Chrissie
Christ (0.01)
Christ'on
Christaffer
Christain (0.01)
Chri-Stan
Christan (0.01)
Christan John
Christanley
Christapher
Christavier
Christavious
Christayvio
Christdon
Christeen
Christeferson

Christ-Elie
Christen (0.01)
Christenden
Christepher
Christeropher
Christ-Erwane
Christhian
Christhoffer
Christhopher
Christi'en
Christiaan
Christiam
Christian (6.23)
Christian Angel
Christian Charles
Christian Dexter
Christian Isaie
Christian Jacob
Christian Joshua
Christian Jr
Christian Kyle
Christian Lydon
Christian Paul
Christianant
Christian-Anthonv
Christian-C
Christiandior
Christian-John
Christian-Lee
Christian-Michel
Christiann
Christiano
Christian-Octavian
Christian-Raphael
Christians
Christian-T
Christian-Th
Christian-Xavier
Christie
Christien (0.01)
Christin
Christina
Christine
Christino
Christio
Christion (0.01)
Christiopher

Christipher
Christison
Christiveon
Christjon
Christlyn
Christmas
Christo
Christobal
Christof
Christofer (0.01)
Christoffer
Christofher
Christofinn
Christohper
Christon
Christon Is
Christoper
Christoph (0.01)
Christophe (0.05)
Christophe Manh-Kha
Christophe-Antoine
Christopher-Christopher (8.11)
Christopher Anthony
Christopher Arm
Christopher De'troy
Christopher Dylan
Christopher Jam
Christopher Jason
Christopher John
Christopher Justin
Christopher Kensy
Christopher Lewis
Christopher Micha
Christopher Michael
Christopher-Alexande

Christopherandr
Christopher-Daniel
Christopher-Derek
Christopher-Gabriel
Christopher-Henok Es
Christopher-Long
Christopher-Mateo
Christopher-Robeg
Christopher-Scotd
Christopherson
Christophert
Christopher-Troy
Christophor
Christophr
Christophye
Christopkher
Christopkher Jagger
Christorpher
Christos (0.01)
Christoval
Christpher
Christphor
Christrian
Christ-Stephen
Christvimean
Christy
Christyan
Christyler
Chritopher
Chritrell
Chriztian
Chrome
Chronis
Chrsitopher
Chrysander
Chrysanthus
Chryshaun
Chrystiam Aldair
Chrystian (0.01)
Chrystion
Chrystophe
Chrystopher
Chrystyan

Chu Ye
Chuakun
Chuancey
Chuan-En
Chuasue
Chuba
Chuck
Chucka
Chuckie
Chuckquel
Chucky
Chucquan
Chue Nou
Chue Seng
Chue Yee
Chuexeng
Chufeng
Chuka
Chuks
Chukwudera
Chukwudumaga
Chukwuebuka
Chukwuemeka
Chukwuka
Chukwuma
Chukwunyere
Chukwuzitelum
Chuma
Chunetu
Chung
Chung Sing
Chuntay
Chuntemaza
Chunxunphon
Chun-Yin
Chuong
Church
Churchill
Chur-Yong
Chuxiong
Chuye
Chuyi
Chy
Chy'quine
Chyckwudiogo
Chylan
Chyle
Chylen
Chyler
Chylunn
Chyne
Chyon
Chyree

Chyrin
Chyvonn
Chyyon
Ci Rece
Ci Yante
Ciah
Cian (0.04)
Ciano
Ciaran (0.01)
Cibian
Ciciyak
Cid
Cid Fernando
Cid Xaivzeeg
Cidney
Cidronio
Cielo
Cier
Cieran
Cierra
Cikhure
Cillian
Cimeon
Cimmaron
Cimmeron
Cimmy
Cincade
Cincere (0.01)
Cincero
Cinder
Cindy
Cinncere
Cinquain
Cinque
Cinseir
Cion
Cion'te
Ciondae
Cip-Jr
Cipriano
Cirdan
Cire
Cirilo
Cirino Daniel
Cirius
Ciro
Cirrus
Cirstan
Cirus
Cisar
Cisco
Ciser-Camilo
Ciserrn

Citlali
Civin
Ciwan
Ciyllis
Ciyon
Ciyus
CJ
C-Jay
Ckai
Ckaiden
Ckris-Ryan
Ckwen
Cky
Clae
Claeb
Claes
Claiborne
Clair
Claire
Claityn
Clamorari
Clance
Clancey
Clancy
Clarance
Clare
Clare'shon
Claren
Clarence (0.08)
Clarens
Clarissa
Clark (0.08)
Clark Xander
Clarke (0.01)
Clartavion
Clarventz
Clary
Claton
Clatus
Claud
Claudae
Claudarius
Clauddavid
Claude (0.02)
Claude-
    Emmanuel
Claude-Eric
Claude-Francois
Claudel
Claudell
Claudel-Paul
Claude-Olivier
Claudio (0.01)

Claudious
Claudius
Claven
Clavensti
Clavonne
Clavorn
Claxton
Clay (0.10)
Claybourne
Clayden
Claydin
Claydon
Clayland
Claymon
Clayobrian
Clayon
Clayson
Clayten
Claytin
Clayton (0.54)
Clayton Dale
Clayton Lewis
Claytor
Clayvens
Clayvin
Cleason
Cleaster
Cleaver
Cleaverson
Cleavon
Clebson
Clede
Clee
Clefton
Clem
Clemens
Clement (0.03)
Clemente
Clemeth
Clemmons
Clemson
Cleo
Cleofas
Cleon
Cleonde
Cleonte
Cleophis
Cleophus
Clerow
Clervenshon
Cleshandy
Clesio
Clesney

Cleston
Clete
Cletus
Cleve
Cleveland (0.01)
Clevelle
Clevens
Cleveon
Clever
Clevis
Clevon
Clevonte
Cleyton
Cleyver
Clezio
Cli Vone
Cliff
Clifford (0.05)
Cliff-Paul
Cliffton
Clifton (0.03)
Cline
Clint (0.03)
Clinten
Clintez
Clinton (0.08)
Clinton Charles
Clinton Wesley
Clio
Cliptson
Clisby
Clisean
Clive (0.01)
Clivin
Clochard
Cloe
Cloison
Cloud
Clouden
Clovia
Clovis (0.02)
Clovis Ludovic
Cluverius
Cly'tavious
Clyce
Clyde (0.04)
Clyde Helmer
Clydell
Co
Co'hiem
Co'ron
Coady
Coal (0.01)

Coale
Coalton
Coastas
Coastlon
Cob
Cobain
Coban
Cobane
Cobe (0.01)
Cobee
Coben
Cobey (0.01)
Cobi
Cobie
Cobin
Coble
Cobra
Cobran
Cobun
Coburn
Coby (0.07)
Cobyn
Cocami
Cochese
Cochise
Coda (0.02)
Codah
Coda-Lee
Coddy
Codee
Coden
Codey (0.01)
Codi (0.01)
Codie (0.02)
Cody (1.87)
Cody Bill
Cody Johnat
Codyack
Codyjames
Codylee
Codyn
Codyus
Coe
Coehen
Coehyn
Coen (0.06)
Coeur
Cocy
Coffey
Cofy
Cogan
Coggins
Cohan

Cohbey
Cohean
Cohen (0.22)
Cohl
Cohlton
Cohnar
Cohven
Cohwen
Cohyn
Coii
Coilin
Coit
Cojuan
Coker
Cola
Cola'jero
Colagero
Colan
Colban
Colbe
Colbee
Colben
Colbert
Colbey (0.01)
Colbi
Colbie
Colbin
Colburn
Colby (0.47)
Colbyn
Colby-Ray
Colden (0.01)
Coldin
Coldren
Cole (2.97)
Cole Gabriel
Cole-Anthony
Coleby
Coledan
Coleder
Coledon
Coledrine
Coleman (0.11)
Colemann
Colemin
Colen
Colentae-Anirr
Coleon
Coleraine
Coleridge
Colerion
Coleson (0.01)
Coleston

Coletan
Coleten
Coletin
Coleton (0.04)
Coletrane
Coletyn
Coley
Colgan
Colie
Colima
Colin (1.90)
Colin David
Colin Joseph
Colin Michael
Colin Ray
Colin Vincent
Coll
Collan
Collby
Collen (0.01)
Colliege
Collier (0.01)
Colliin
Collin (0.80)
Collin Jr
Collins (0.01)
Collis
Collon
Collton
Collum
Collyn (0.01)
Colm (0.01)
Colma
Colman
Colmcille
Colodius
Colon
Colorado
Colour
Colsen
Colson (0.03)
Colston (0.01)
Colt (0.05)
Coltan (0.01)
Colten (0.15)
Colter (0.02)
Coltin (0.03)
Coltlon
Colton (1.25)
Colton Ashton
Colton Weston
Coltrane
Coltt

| | | | | | | |
|---|---|---|---|---|---|---|
| Coltton | Connelly | Copper | Corderious | Coriyon | Corsoni | Cosme |
| Coltyn *(0.01)* | Conner *(1.28)* | Cor'byrian | Corderis | Corleone | Cort *(0.01)* | Cosmen |
| Coltyr | Conner Russell | Cor'dae | Cordero | Corliss | Cortareon | Cosmo |
| Columbus | Connery | Cor'dai | Corderries' | Cormac *(0.02)* | Cortavion | Cosmos |
| Colvado | Connie | Cor'javeon | Corderrius | Cormani | Cortavious | Costa |
| Colvin | Conniedevon | Cor'marei | Corderro | Cormaree | Cortayv'ion | Costantino |
| Colwen | Connir | Cor'nyis | Cordia | Cormarious | Cortayveos | Costanzo |
| Colwyn | Connley | Cor'tavion | Cordilus | Cormick | Corte'z | Costas |
| Colyer | Connolly | Cor'tez | Cordius | Cormilus | Corterius | Costavius |
| Colyn *(0.01)* | Connor *(4.49)* | Cor'vontae | Cordrice | Cormontez | Cortes | Costell |
| Colynn | Connor Jacob | Cor'zon | Cordy | Corneal | Cortex | Costin |
| Comari | Connor Timo | Cora | Cordyell | Cornealivs | Cortez *(0.07)* | Coston |
| Comarion | Connor-Douglas | Corad | Coreal | Corneilius | Corteze | Cota |
| Come | Connor-Riley | Corahn | Corean | Corneille | Cortezz | Cote |
| Comenzo | Connor-Wryn | Coran | Coreas | Corneilus | Cortilius | Coti |
| Cominic | Conoley | Corban *(0.04)* | Coredell | Cornel | Cortiz | Cotter |
| Commer | Conor *(0.17)* | Corben *(0.02)* | Coree | Cornelio | Cortlan | Cotton |
| Common | Conor Seamus | Corbet | Corei | Cornelion | Cortland *(0.01)* | Coty *(0.01)* |
| Compie | Conrad *(0.06)* | Corbett | Corel | Cornelious | Cortlen | Cougar |
| Compton | Conrad-Cheddi | Corbin *(0.34)* | Corell | Cornelis | Cortlin | Coulee |
| Cona | Conrade | Corbitt | Coren | Cornelius *(0.05)* | Cortlyn | Coulgan |
| Conagher | Conrado | Corbley | Corentin | Cornell *(0.02)* | Cortlynd | Coulson |
| Conah | Conri | Corbon | Coreon | Cornellius | Cortney *(0.01)* | Coulter |
| Conal | Conric | Corby | Coreonte | Cornellus | Corton | Coulton |
| Conald | Conroy | Corbyn *(0.02)* | Coretease | Cornelrion | Cortrayvion | Countrez |
| Conall *(0.01)* | Constant | Corcon | Coretevious | Cornez | Cortrell | Couper |
| Conan *(0.01)* | Constantin | Cord | Corey *(0.53)* | Cornilios | Cortt | Courage |
| Conar | Constantine *(0.02)* | Corda | Corey Allen | Cornilious | Cortve | Cournelious |
| Conard | Constantine Randall | Cordae | Corey Tyler | Cornilius | Cortzuruna | Couron |
| Condai | Constantino | Cordai | Corey' | Cornilous | Corvagn | Courtavious |
| Condarius | Constantinos | Cordail | Corey'l | Corniulis | Corval | Courtavius |
| Coneil | Constantio | Cordale | Coreyan | Corny | Corvarie | Courterreon |
| Conelius | Conswello | Cordalyn | Coreyaunte | Corohn | Corvaughn | Courtland *(0.01)* |
| Conell | Contastino | Cordareon | Corey-James | Coron | Corvell | Courtline |
| Conellius | Contavious | Cordarion | Coreyon | Coronardo | Corven | Courtlyn |
| Conen | Conterio | Cordarious | Corey-Thomas | Corr | Corvin *(0.01)* | Courtney *(0.04)* |
| Coner | Contorius | Cordarius *(0.01)* | Coreyun | Corrado | Corvon | Courtyus |
| Cong-Huy | Contrell | Cordaro | Corgan | Corran | Corvus | Courvoseay |
| Congson | Contrelus | Cordarow | Cori | Corrdi | Corwin *(0.01)* | Couy |
| Coniah | Contrial | Cordarrel | Cori'awntae | Corre | Corwren | Covache |
| Conlan *(0.01)* | Conville | Cordarrius | Corian | Correll | Corwyn | Covae |
| Conlee | Conway | Cordarryl | Coriden | Correon | Corwynn | Coven |
| Conley *(0.01)* | Conya | Cordavious | Corie | Correy | Cory *(0.24)* | Covenant |
| Conlin | Conye | Corday | Corien | Corrian | Cory Mitchell | Coveno |
| Conlon | Conyer | Corde | Corieon | Corriander | Corydon | Covey |
| Conlucy | Cook | Cordé | Corin *(0.01)* | Corrick | Coryell | Covie |
| Connall | Coo-Nah | Cordel | Corinthian *(0.01)* | Corrie | Coryion | Covieon |
| Connan | Cooper *(1.50)* | Cordele | Corinthians | Corrigan | Corylee | Covington |
| Connar *(0.01)* | Copeland *(0.01)* | Cordell *(0.04)* | Corion | Corrin | Coryn | Covon |
| Connard | Copelin | Cordell Darrnya | Corione | Corrion | Coryon | Covy |
| Connel | Copelyn | Cordelle | Coriontae | Corry | Cosby | Cowan |
| Connell *(0.01)* | | Cordellian | Corithian | Corsen | Cosimo | Cowen *(0.01)* |
| Connell Lee | | Corden | | Corson | Cosmas | Coy *(0.04)* |

| | | | | | | |
|---|---|---|---|---|---|---|
| Coydarius | Creston | Cristian | Cruze | Curtlyn | Cymrin | D Avion |
| Coye | Cresus | Alessandro | Cruziano | Cynan | Cynan | D Kyah |
| Coyle | Creswell | Cristiane | Cruzito | Curtrell | Cynceir | D Marcus |
| Coylin | Crete | Cristiano (0.01) | Crystal | Curtron | Cyn-Cere | D Quai |
| Coyote | Crevan | Cristien | Crystian | Curvin | Cyncere (0.01) | D R Levi |
| Coyt | Crew (0.01) | Cristinel | Crystien | Curvitch | Cyngen | D Sean |
| Coyte | Crewz | Cristino | Crystihan | Cury | Cyntell | D.J. |
| Cr | Crhistian | Cristion | Crystofer | Curzandre | Cynthia | D' Marco |
| Cra'don | Criag | Cristo (0.01) | Crystopher | Cush | Cypher | D'aaron |
| Craddock | Cricsir | Cristoangel | Csaba | Cushan | Cypress | D'acquel |
| Crae | Criel | Cristobal (0.02) | Csongor | Cushi | Cyprian | D'adyn |
| Craft | Crighton | Cristobel | Cuahuizo | Cusieque | Cyprien | D'allo |
| Craig (0.16) | Crimson | Cristof | Cuahutemoc | Cusman | Cypriss | D'alton |
| Craig Trevon | Crimston | Cristofer (0.03) | Cuatellis | Custer | Cyprus | D'amarion |
| Craige | Crintas | Cristoff Jorel | Cuatemoc | Custodio | Cyr | D'amery |
| Craigin | Criostoir | Cristoffer | Cuauhtemoc | Custom | Cyrane | D'ames |
| Craigory | Cris | Cristofori | Cuchulain | Cutberto | Cyrano | D'andra |
| Craigtavious | Cris Donnel | Cristopher | Cuda | Cutino | Cyree | D'andrae |
| Crain | Cris'zhier | (0.08) | Cuinn | Cutler | Cyrek | D'andray |
| Cramer | Crisanto | Cristopor | Culann | Cutter (0.01) | Cyrel | D'andré |
| Crash | Crisantos | Cristoval | Cullan | Cuyler (0.01) | Cyrell | D'andre (0.05) |
| Craven | Crisean | Cristy | Cullen (0.09) | Cuylor | Cyrene | D'andrea |
| Craven Wade | Crish | Cristyan | Culley | Cuzaar | Cyrian | D'andrei |
| Cravon | Crishaun | Critian | Cullin | Cvavtemoc | Cyric | D'angelo (0.05) |
| Cravyn | Crishon | Criton | Culliyon | Cy (0.03) | Cyril (0.02) | D'anglo |
| Crawford | Crishton | Critzpaul | Cullom | Cy'von | Cyril-Elias | D'antae |
| Cray | Crisjen | Criz Dari | Culver | Cyair | Cyrill | D'anté |
| Crayton | Crisjin | Crocifisso | Culvin | Cyan | Cyrille | D'anthonie |
| Creadon | Crisjon | Crofford | Cumari | Cyaseer | Cyris | D'anthony |
| Creagen | Crislitzangel | Croft | Cuong | Cyde | Cyrisia | (0.01) |
| Creagh | Crisnel | Croix (0.01) | Curbrian | Cyden | Cyriss | D'antonio |
| Credence | Crisolo | Crompton | Cure | Cydnee | Cyron | D'antrell |
| Cree | Crisologo | Croni | Cureton | Cye | Cyrone | D'antwan |
| Creed (0.01) | Crisop | Crosby | Curien | Cyeran | Cyrrus | D'aree |
| Creed R | Crispen | Crosley | Curk | Cyheed | Cyruis | D'ari |
| Creedance | Crispin (0.01) | Cross (0.01) | Curmarion | Cyheem | Cyrus (0.14) | D'aria |
| Creeden | Crispyn | Crossett | Curnelius | Cyilus | Cyrus Samuel | D'arick |
| Creedence | Criss | Crossifisso | Curran (0.01) | Cyire | Cyruss | D'ario |
| Creedon | Crissna | Crosslan | Curren | Cykeer | Cyton | D'arius |
| Creegan | Crisstopher | Crow | Currie | Cylan | Cyyeed | D'ariyah |
| Creeghan | Crist | Croy | Curry | Cylas | Czar | D'arrae |
| Creek | Cristain | Cru | Curt (0.01) | Cyle (0.01) | Czaron | D'arrious |
| Cregan | Cristan | Cruise | Curtavion | Cylen | | D'artagan |
| Cregg | Cristaniel | Cruiz | Curtavious | Cyler (0.01) | | D'artagnan |
| Creighton (0.01) | Cristhiam | Cruize | Curtaz | Cylias | ~ D ~ | D'artagnon |
| Creighty | Cristhian (0.01) | Crumpton | Curtez | Cylis | | D'artagyan |
| Crenshaw | Cristhian-Xavier | Crus | Curtis (0.41) | Cyliss | D | D'ashley |
| Creole | Cristho | Cruse | Curtis Alfred | Cyllel | D Aaron | D'asian |
| Creon | Cristhofer | Crusen | Curtis Lee | Cylon | D Alessandro | D'august |
| Cresencio | Cristhyan | Crusoe | Curtis-Even | Cylor | D Angelo | D'aundra |
| Creshaun | Cristiam | Cruz (0.09) | Curtis-Locas | Cylus | D Anthony | D'aundre |
| Creshawn | Cristian (1.30) | Cruz Marin | Curtiss | Cymian | D Ari | D'auntea |
| Crespin | Cristian Adrian | Cruzcito | Curtland | Cymon | D Artagnan | D'avee |

D'aveion
D'avery
D'avion
D'azjon
D'bronx
D'cari
D'corian
D'edrick
D'el
D'elio
D'eran
D'eric
D'evion
D'garious
D'geon
D'hani
D'iego
D'ira
D'ivion
D'jains-Lee
D'jamesy
D'javion
D'john
D'jour
D'juan
D'kardi
D'karr
D'kary
D'kaui
D'kerrion
D'kharion
D'khouri
D'korie
D'kota
D'kwan
D'kwon
D'landos
D'lawrence
D'lijah
D'liyah
D'lon
D'maceo
D'majae
D'majah'
D'mani
D'mar
D'marcianos
D'marco
D'marcus
D'mareon
D'mari
D'mario
D'marion *(0.01)*

D'maris
D'marius
D'marko
D'marquez
D'marrein
D'marreion
D'mauri
D'mawuko
D'mayan
D'metrius
D'metry
D'michael
D'mikal
D'mitri
D'moie
D'mon
D'mon'te
D'mondrious
D'moni
D'monta
D'montay
D'monte
D'monté
D'montre
D'montriel
D'morion
D'mottrio
D'nard
D'narius
D'naruis
D'nary
D'navion
D'nerriyo
D'nico
D'niko
D'noz
D'nyem
D'on
D'ondre
D'ontai
D'onte
D'ospon
D'qorian
D'quan
D'quann
D'quarion
D'quintonio
D'qwell
D'robertin
D'ron
D'ron'te
D'sani
D'saun

D'sean
D'shaun
D'shaune
D'shawn
D'shawn
Alexander
D'shawntae
D'shay
D'shellis
D'shun
D'tonio
D'treyvion
D'undraé
D'van
D'vantae
D'vante
D'vari
D'varian
D'varie
D'vincent
D'von
D'vonte
D'vonté
D'vontre
D'waivon
D'wan
D'wayne
D'won
D'ylan
D'ymier
D'ysious
D'zareaun
Da
Da Jaun
Dá Jhan
Da Khari
Da Marion
Da Mere
Da Mirone
Da Narius
Da Quan
Dá Quean
Da Ron
Da Ronn
Da Shawn
Dá Shawn
Dá Tavion
Da Von
Da Vonte
Dá Vyon
Da'amari
Da'andre
Da'brian

Da'bronne
Da'cion
Da'codis
Da'coreyon
Da'corian
Da'don
Da'garious
Da'gean
Da'hmaij
Da'jae
Da'jaius
Da'jaun
Da'jian
Da'jin
Da'john
Da'jon
Da'juan *(0.01)*
Da'juante
Da'jun
Da'kaari
Da'karai
Da'karee
Da'kari
Da'kese
Da'koryeon
Da'kwan
Da'kyis
Da'kyri
Da'lanron
Da'leon
Da'lin
Da'lose
Da'lynn
Da'mahj
Da'mai
Da'majh
Da'mani
Da'mantez
Da'mar
Da'marcus
   *(0.01)*
Da'mare
Da'marea
Da'mareion
Da'mareon
Da'mari *(0.01)*
Da'marian
Da'marien
Da'marieon
Da'mario
Da'marion
   *(0.02)*
Da'mariuan

Da'marius
Da'marko's
Da'markus
Da'marques
Da'marquise
Da'marrion
Da'marrius
Da'martez
Da'marvion
Da'mauri
Da'maury
Da'meir
Da'mericaul
Da'michael
Da'micheal
Da'mien
Da'mikal
Da'mir
Da'mon
Da'mond
Da'mone
Da'mont
Da'monta
Da'monte
Da'montez
Da'montré
Da'montrell
Da'morae
Da'morie
Da'mory
Da'myon
Da'myren
Da'myrin
Da'myron
Da'nan
Da'narie
Da'nario
Da'narious
Da'nas
Da'niel
Da'niko
Da'nurí
Da'nyis
Da'nyjus
Da'ombrien
Da'ondre
Da'perio
Da'prince
Da'qarius
Da'qavious
Da'quan *(0.02)*
Da'quantay
Da'quanté

Da'quarius
Da'quavius
Da'quaylon
Da'quez
Da'quincy
Da'quine
Da'quise
Da'quon
Da'qurryon
Da'qwan
Da'qwaun
Da'qwaylin
Da'qwon
Da'ray
Da'realist
Da'rel
Da'rell
Da'rellis
Da'ren
Da'rico
Da'rion
Da'rius
Da'rod
Da'ron
Da'ronte
Da'rrell
Da'sean
Da'shaad
Da'shaun
Da'shaun *(0.01)*
Da'shawn *(0.02)*
Da'shjuan
Da'shon
Da'shonquez
Da'shouan
Da'shuan
Da'shun
Da'shyne
Da'sir
Da'sjon
Da'son
Da'tarius
Da'taruis
Da'tavas
Da'tavian
Da'tavious
Da'teyun
Da'toine
Da'traylin
Da'treavious
Da'tron
Da'twon
Da'vahn

Da'vante
Da'various
Da'varrius
Da'vaughn
Da'vean
Da'veeon
Da'veion
Da'velle
Da'veon *(0.01)*
Da'vey
Da'veyon
Da'veyun
Da'viea
Da'vien
Da'vion *(0.01)*
Da'vione
Da'von *(0.01)*
Da'vone
Da'vonta
Da'vontae
Da'vontaé
Da'vontay
Da'vonte
Da'vontz
Da'wan
Da'waun
Da'won
Da'yante
Da'zarius
Da'zaylan
Da'zone
Daahiy
Daan
Daane
Daani
Daanish
Daanyaal
Daariyous
Daaron
Daa-Von
Dabari
Dabaris
Dabdy
Daberechi
Dabid
Dable
Daborieon
Dabryan
Dabyus
Dac
Dacari
Dacarion
Dacarree

| | | | | | | |
|---|---|---|---|---|---|---|
| Dacarreon | Dae'quarious | Daemiane | Daevyon | Dahsir | Dailynn | Daitravehon |
| Dacarri | Dae'quon | Daemien | Daeyeshawn | Dahsun | Daimar | Daitrel |
| Dacarris | Dae'ron | Daemion | Daeymen | Da-Hua | Daimeer | Daityn |
| Dace | Dae'sean | Daemir | Dafydd | Dahvee | Daimein | Daivari |
| Dacen | Dae'shaun | Daemiyn | Dag | Dahvi | Daimen | Daivarus |
| Dachajae | Dae'shawn | Daemon (0.01) | Dagan (0.02) | Dahvious | Daimeon | Daivd |
| Dacharvrick | Dae'shean | Dae-Mond | Dagemawe | Dahvon | Daimeyon | Daivel |
| Dacian | Dae'shoine | Daemonte | Dagen | Dai | Daimian | Daiveon |
| Dacien | Dae'shuan | Daemon-Xavier | Dager | Dai Shawn | Daimien | Daiveonn |
| Dacieyion | Dae'toine | Daemorion | Dagger | Dai Vion | Daimiir | Daivieon |
| Dacion | Dae'twan | Daemyn | Dagim | Dai'brion | Daimion | Daivik |
| Dacoby | Dae'veon | Daen | Dagin | Dai'dieon | Daimir | Daivion |
| Dacoda (0.01) | Dae'vion | Daenar | Dagla | Dai'jon | Dai-Mon | Daiviri |
| Dacodah | Dae'von | Daenen | Dagm | Dai'lon | Daimon (0.01) | Daivon (0.01) |
| Dacoreyn | Dae'vonne | Daenin | Dagmawi | Dai'marion | Daimond | Daivone |
| Dacoreyon | Dae'wan | Daeqoun | Dagnny | Dai'mauraei | Daimyan | Daivonta |
| Dacorion | Dae'zhun | Daequan | Dago | Dai'nahjae | Daimyo | Daivontae |
| Dacota | Dae'zjon | Daequante | Dagoberto | Dai'quan | Dain (0.01) | Daiyaan |
| Dacotah | Dae'zohyn | Daequon | Dagon | Dai'quane | Daina | Daiylan |
| Dacoyta | Daedalus | Daeqwan | Dagotheson | Dai'saun | Daine | Daizehr |
| Dacquari | Daeden | Daeren | Dah'kari | Dai'sean | Dainen | Daizharie |
| Dacray | Daedrian | Daerion | Dah'mair | Dai'shawn | Daineóntez | Daizon |
| Dacre | Daeem Ibrahim | Daeron | Dah'mir | Dai'shun | Dainian | Daj'amel |
| Dacy | Daegan (0.01) | Daeryon | Dahab | Dai'veion | Dainien | Daja |
| Daddy | Daegen | Daesan | Dahani | Dai'von | Dainin | Dajaeh |
| Dade (0.01) | Daejahn | Daesean | Daheim | Dai'vontay | Dainjerous | Dajahaqutumi |
| Dadeey | Daejeon | Daeshan | Dahenson | Dai'wan | Daion | Dajameous |
| Daden | Daejhaun | Daeshaun (0.01) | Dahgan | Dai'zheim | Daione | Dajan |
| Dadisi | Daejion | Daeshawn (0.01) | Dahir | Daichawn | Daiquan (0.01) | Dajaughn |
| Dadon | Daejohn | Daeshon | Dahiry | Daichen | Daiquarious | Dajaun |
| Dadrian | Daejon | Daeshonnie | Dahjvar | Daichi | Dairbhre | Dajavon |
| Dadrien | Daejore | Daesjonte | Dahleal | Daiden | Dairek | Dajhaun |
| Dadson | Daejuan | Daeson | Dahlen | Daidon | Daireon | Dajhon |
| Dadyen | Daejung | Daeten | Dahlton | Daidrick | Dairian | Dajhuan |
| Dae | Daekwon | Daethan | Dahlyn | Daieem | Dairin | Dajion |
| Dae Hyun | Dael | Daethon | Dahmal | Daigan | Dairius | Dajohn |
| Dae Jaun | Daelan | Daeton (0.01) | Dahmere | Daijah | Dairo | Dajon (0.01) |
| Dae Jon | Daelano | Daetraun | Dahmier | Daijan | Dairon | Dajour |
| Dae Kobe | Daelen | Daetrinn | Dahminick | Daiji | Dairyon | Dajuan (0.02) |
| Dae Lyn | Daelend | Daetuane | Dah-Mir | Daijier | Daisaun | Dajun |
| Dae Sean | Daelin | Daetyn | Dahmir (0.01) | Daijon | Daisean | Dajus |
| Dae Shaun | Daellon | Daevaughn | Dahmon | Daijour | Daishaun (0.01) | Dak |
| Dae'jhun | Daelmontae | Daeveion | Dahmonni | Daijuan | Daishawn (0.01) | Dakaiyah |
| Dae'john | Daelon | Daeven | Dahneel | Daikail | Daishen | Samuel |
| Dae'jon | Daelontae | Daeveon | Dahnelle | Daiki | Daishon | Dakajion |
| Dae'kwom | Daelyn | Dae-Vie-On | Dahnir | Dailand | Daishun | Dakalin |
| Dae'marion | Daeman | Daevion | Dahntay | Dailen | Daisjaun | Dakanai |
| Dae'merick- | Daemar | Daevione | Dahnte | Dailey | Daitan | Dakarai (0.01) |
| Dae'sean | Daemarco | Daevon (0.01) | Dahol | Dailiqon | Daiten | Dakaré |
| Dae'mohn | Daemauni | Daevone | Dahosan | Daillen | Daithan | Dakarí |
| Dac'quan | Daemen | Daevonte | Dahreed | Dailon | Daithen | Dakari (0.02) |
| Dae'quann | Daemeon | Daevvone | Dahryl | Dailton | Daito | Dakarius |
| Dae'quantae | Daemian | Daevyn | Dahseir | Dailyn | Daiton | Dakarree |

Dakarri
Dakaydan
Dakelin
Daken
Dakendall
Dakeri
Daketrious
Dakevian
Dakhai
Dakhari
Dakhori
Dakhylin
Dakia
Dakin
Dakkotah
Daklen
Dako Ta
Dakoa
Dakoata
Dakobe
Dakobi
Dakóda
Dakoda (0.05)
Dakodah
Dakoetah
Dakohta
Dakolby
Dakori
Dakoriye
Dakota (1.02)
Dakota Charl
Dakotah (0.03)
Dakotta
Dakouta
Dakovan
Dakri
Daksh
Dakshin
Dakurtis
Dakwon
Dakyel
Dakyria
Dakyz
Dal
Dalan
Dalandon
Dalas
Dalason
Dalbert
Dalcin
Daldien
Dale (0.09)
Dale-Curtis

Daleep
Dalefino
Dalen (0.02)
Dalen-Bryce
Dalequan
Dalerion
Daleshawn
Dalgere
Dalha
Dali
Dalil
Dalin
Dalio
Dalion
Dalitso
Daljit
Dallace
Dallan
Dallan'tae
Dallas (0.25)
Dallas-Christian
Dallen (0.01)
Dallien
Dallin (0.03)
Dallion
Dallis
Dallon
Dallos
Dallus
Dally
Dallyn
Dalmacio
Dalmesio
Dalon
Dalonja
Dalontae
Dalonte
Dalos
Dalraj
Dalron
Dalson
Dalston
Daltan
Dalten (0.01)
Daltharin
Daltin
Dalton (0.88)
Dalton Levi
Daltry
Daltyn
Daltyne
Dalvany
Dalvin

Dalvon
Dalvonté
Daly
Daly-Mike
Dalyn (0.01)
Dalys
Dalziel
Dam
Damacio
Damacious
Damaein
Damahntae
Damai
Damain
Damaine
Damair
Damajah
Damajay
Damajea
Damajh
Daman
Damani (0.02)
Damanjeet
Damanjot
Damann
Damanveer
Damany
Damaon
Damar
Damarco
Damarcus (0.02)
Damare
Damarea
Damareay
Damaree
Damarein
Damareon (0.01)
Damareyon
Damarí
Damari (0.04)
Damarian (0.01)
Damarie
Damarieion
Damarien
Damarieon
Damariez
Damarii
Damario
Damarion (0.09)
Damarious (0.01)

Damaris
Damarius (0.02)
Damariviauz
Damariyon
Damarkues
Damarley
Damarlon
Damarous
Damarquez
Damarquis
Damarqus
Damarreyon
Damarri
Damarrian
Damarrio
Damarrion
Damarrius
Damarro
Damarsheaun
Damarsja
Damarus
Damarveon
Damarvieon
Damarye
Damarzah
Damas
Damascus
Damasio
Damaso
Damaunte
Damauri
Damauriyae
Damauriyon
Damaury
Damaya
Damazjion
Damean
Dameare
Damecko
Dameer
Dameian
Dameil
Damein (0.01)
Dameion (0.01)
Da-Meir
Dameir
Dameire
Dameiun
Damek
Dameko
Damell
Dame-N
Damen (0.02)

Dameon (0.03)
Damera
Damere
Damerian
Damerieon
Damerion
Damerious
Damerrius
Dameshon
Dametreous
Dametrese
Dametri
Dametric
Dametrious
Dametrius
Dameyn
Dameyon
Dami
Damian (1.45)
Damian-Ayden
Damiano (0.01)
Damianos
Damiaus
Damica
Damie
Damiean
Damiek
Damiel
Damiell
Damielle
Damien (0.61)
Damien Chad
Damien Vont
Damien-Coel
Damien-Lucas
Damieon
Damier
Damiere
Damietrius
Damieyon
Damiin
Damikah
Damillion
Damin
Damine
Da-Ming
Daming
Damingo
Daminick
Daminik
Damion (0.14)
Damioni
Damir (0.01)

Damiracle
Damiran
Damircle
Damirien
Damishé
Damitree
Damitrias
Damitrius
Damiun
Damius
Damiyan
Damiyon
Damiyone
Damiyr
Damjan
Dammein
Damniohn
Damodreon
Damon (0.32)
Damon Kenzie
Damon'te
Damon-Allan
Damond (0.01)
Damondre
Damone
Damoni
Damonick
Damonn
Damonpreet
Damont
Damonta
Damontae
Damontaé
Damontay
Damonté
Damonte (0.01)
Damontena
Damontez
Damonti
Damonton
Damontra
Damontray
Damontre
Damontriel
Damonz
Damorian
Damorier
Damorion
Damoron
Damorris
Damriyon
Damurquis
Damy'on

Damyan (0.01)
Damyanti
Damydre
Damyean
Damyen
Damyien
Damyn (0.01)
Damyn-Joe
Damyon
Damyr
Damyrin
Damyris
Damyron
Damyus
Dan (0.03)
Dan Tam
Dan'nachai
Dan'quariahz
Dan'travien
Dan'uel
Dana (0.02)
Danael
Danah
Dana-Jahziah
Danali
Danalle
Danameo
Danan
Danari
Danarian
Danarie
Danarii
Danarius
Danat
Danaven
Danavin
Danavion
Danavir
Danavyon
Danayee
Danaz
Danazha
Dancan
Dancing Spirit
Dancon
Dandapoojith
Dandrae
Dandre
Dandrea
Dandrell
Dandy
Dane (0.18)
Daneal

| | | | | | | |
|---|---|---|---|---|---|---|
| Danee | Daniel-Edgardo | Dannvel | Danukollie | Da-Quan | Darell (0.01) | Dariuse |
| Daneiro | Daniel-Felipe | Danny (0.27) | Danumon | Daquan (0.03) | Darelle | Dariush |
| Danek | Danielito | Danny Bang | Danush | Daquane | Daren (0.02) | Dariyan |
| Danel | Daniel-John | Danny Joseph | Danveer | Daquantae | Darence | Dariyn |
| Danell | Daniel-John- | Samy | Danvir | Daquantay | Darens | Dariyon |
| Danen | Joseph | Danny Junior | Danwonye | Daquarius | Dareon | Dariyun |
| Danere | Daniell | Danny Kriss | Dany (0.02) | Daquavius | Dareonta | Dariyus |
| Danerrian | Daniel-Lafoi | Danny-Ian | Dany Jr | Daquevion | Darerick | Darjen |
| Danesh | Daniellane | Danny-Ray | Danyael | Daquil | Darest | Darkari |
| Danford | Danielle | Dano | Danyai | Daquin | Dareus | Darken-Isiah |
| Dang (0.01) | Daniellie Tony | Danovan | Danyal | Daquintus | Dargan | Darki |
| Dang Huy | Daniels | Danoven | Danyale | Daquis | Darh'ious | Darko |
| Dangel'o | Danielsen | Danovic | Danyck | Daqun | Dari'us | Darla |
| D-Angelo | Danielson | Danquereiou | Danye | Daquna | Darian (0.13) | Darlene |
| Dangelo | Daniil | Danrick | Danyeal | Daquon | Darianel | Darly |
| Danger | Danijel | Danseh | Danyeil | Daquone | Darianne | Darman |
| Dangkhoa | Danik (0.01) | Danson | Danyel (0.01) | Daqureon | Dariante | Darmar |
| Dang-Quang | Danik- | Dant | Danyell | Daqwan | Darias | Darmas |
| Pascal | Nasomana | Danta | Danyiel | Daqwerian | Dariaun | Darmel |
| Danh | Danil | Dantabreil | Danyk | Dar | Daric | Darmir |
| Dani | Danila | Dantae (0.01) | Danyk Albert | Dar Tayvious | Darick (0.01) | Darmon |
| Dania | Danilah | Dantauius | Danyl | Dar'ian | Darico | Darnail |
| Danial (0.01) | Danilé | Dantavious | Danylen | Dar'ius | Darie | Darnal |
| Danick (0.02) | Danilo (0.01) | Dantavius | Danylo | Dara | Dariel (0.03) | Darne'z |
| Danick Ian | Danily | Dantay | Danymanuel | Daragh | Darien (0.08) | Darneil |
| Danie | Danion | Dantaye | Danyon | Daragh Louis | Darieon | Darnel |
| Daniel (8.86) | Danique | Danté (0.03) | Danyrius | Darain | Darieous | Darnell (0.09) |
| Daniel Albert | Danirion | Dante (0.32) | Dany-Ryan | Daral | Daries | Darnerian |
| Daniel | Danish | Dante'vian | Danys | Daram | Darik (0.01) | Darnez |
| Alexander | Danissia | Dantee | Danza | Daran | Darikson | Darnile |
| Daniel Andres | Danito | Dante-Leo | Danzeer | Daray | Darin (0.05) | Darny |
| Daniel Anto | Daniyaal | Dante-Lorenzo | Danzel | Darayus | Darin Dong- | Darnzell |
| Daniel Bruno | Daniyal | Danterious | Danzell | Darbin | Quan Phuong | Daro |
| Daniel | Daniyel | Dante- | Danzhel Gabriel | Darby (0.01) | Darin Reece | Darold |
| Christopher | Daniyl | Thomasn | Danzig | Darcae | Darine | Daron (0.02) |
| Daniel Ernesto | Danl | Danteveon | Dao | Darcel | Darinel | Daronde |
| Daniel Felipe | Danley | Dantevious | Daokham- | Darci | Daring | Darontae |
| Daniel Georges | Dannan | Danthony | Billy | Darcy (0.01) | Dario (0.05) | Daronte |
| Daniel John | Danneal | Danti | Daomiron | Dardan | Dario Kelvin | Darquahn |
| Daniel Jr | Dannel | Dantie | Daoo | Darden | Darion (0.05) | Darquavion |
| Daniel Kade | Dannen | Dantino | Daoud | Dare | Darion Hunter | Darques |
| Daniel Lawr | Danner | Danton | Daouda | Darean | Darionta | Darqureous |
| Daniel Logan | Dannevin | Dantonio | Daoude | Dareck | Darionte | Darrail |
| Daniel Loic | Danney | Dantrel | Dapaul | Dareen | Darionté | Darrain |
| Daniel Mich | Danni | Dantrell | Daperrion | Dareeque | Dariontez | Darral |
| Daniel P | Dannial | Dantu | Dapre | Daregán | Darios | Darrale |
| Daniel Phillip | Dannick | Dantus | Dapree | Dareginald | Darious (0.01) | Darrall |
| Daniel Vincent | Dannie (0.01) | Dantwan | Daqay | Dareian | Dariq | Darran |
| Daniel William | Danniel (0.01) | Danu | Daqhawn | Dareion | Darique | Darrazzio |
| Daniela | Danniel's | Danual | Daqua | Dareios | Daris | Darreck |
| Daniel-Dang | Danniela | Danube | Daquaivian | Darejon | Dariuce | Darreion |
| Daniel-Davíd | Danniell | Danuel | Daqualin | Darek (0.01) | Darium | Darreiou |
| Daniele | Dannon | Danuga | Daqualyn | Darel | Darius (0.34) | Darrek |

Darrel *(0.01)*
Darrell *(0.11)*
Darrelle
Darrellvon
Darren *(0.26)*
Darreon
Darreston
Darret
Darreyl
Darreyn
Darria
Darrian *(0.03)*
Darrian James
Darrias
Darric
Darrick *(0.01)*
Darriel
Darrien *(0.03)*
Darrin *(0.05)*
Darrington
Darrio
Darrión
Darrion *(0.05)*
Darriontay
Darrious
Darriouzz
Darriq
Darriron
Darris
Darrison
Darriun
Darrius *(0.05)*
Darrius Leevon
Darriyon
Darrly
Darrnell
Darrol
Darrole
Darron *(0.01)*
Darronne
Darrow
Darroyl
Darruis
Darry
Darryan
Darryck
Darryen
Darryl *(0.07)*
Darryll
Darryn *(0.01)*
Darrynmarc
Darryon
Darryus

Darsen
Darsh
Darshan
Darshann
Darshay
Darshbir
Darshil
Darshveer
Darson
Darst
Dart
Dartagnan
Dartaine
Dartalian
Dartamian
Dartanian
Dartaniel
Dartanine
Dartanion
Dartanius
Dartanyan
Dartanyen
Dartanyin
Dartanyon
Dartavian
Dartavious
Dartavius
Dartel
Dartes
Dartyn
Daruis
Darvell
Darventz
Darvesh
Darveysh
Darvin *(0.01)*
Darvion
Darvon
Darvonne
Darvonni
Darvyn
Darvyon
Darwin *(0.07)*
Darwinsky
Darwlyn
Darwson
Darwyn
Dary
Daryan *(0.01)*
Daryce
Daryel
Daryel-Alonso
Daryen

Daryis
Daryise
Daryk
Daryl *(0.05)*
Daryle
Darylregus
Daryn *(0.01)*
Daryn Dayne
Daryon
Daryonel
Daryonte
Daryus
Darzelle
Das
Das' Nakeem
Das'juan
Dasaan
Dasan *(0.01)*
Dasanee
Dasani
Dasarathi
Dasario
Dasaun
Dasaundre
Daschall
Daschel
Dascher
Dasean *(0.01)*
Dasenica
Daseven
Dash *(0.01)*
Dasha
Dashaad
Dashahn
Dashane
Dashaquelle
Dashare
Dashaud
Dashaun *(0.02)*
Dashawd
Dashawn
  *(0.07)*
Dashay
Dashean
Dasheir
Dashel
Dashene
Dasheon
Dashiel
Dashiell *(0.02)*
Dashir
Dashod
Dashon *(0.01)*

Dashone
Dashonn
Dashont
Dashun
Dasiel
Dasin
Dasionn
Dasir
Dasjaun
Dasjohn
Dasjon
Dasmen
Dasmon
Dason *(0.01)*
Dassan
Dassel
Dastun
Dat
Dat Luan
Data
Datari
Datarion
Datarrious
Datavian
Datavion
Datayveon
Daterrius
Dathan *(0.01)*
Dathen
Dathyn
Datin
Datiyus
Datjuan
Daton
Datonion
Datravious
Datrist
Datrius
Datron
Datryl
Datus
Datwaun
Daud
Daudi
Dauhvondrio
Daulten
Daultin
Daulton *(0.01)*
Daun'tre
Daundre
Daune
Daunique
Daunjae

Daunovan
Dauntae
Dauntah
Dauntay
Dauntaye
Daunté *(0.01)*
Daunte *(0.02)*
Dauntez
Dauor
Dauron
Dauson
Dauwlin
Dav'aughn
Dav'eion
Dav'oer
Dav'on
Dav'von
Davad
Davades
Davaen
Davahn
Davain
Davaion
Davairius
Davais
Davalon
Davan
Davanand
Davani
Davanta
Davantá
Davanté
Davante *(0.01)*
Davanye
Davar
Davardo
Davaree
Davareis
Davarest
Davarez
Davari
Davarick
Davarion
Davarious
Davaris
Davarius
Davartrious
Davaughn *(0.01)*
Davaugn
Davaun
Davaun'te
Davauris

Davaveon
Davayon
Davd-William
Dave *(0.03)*
Dave Junior
Daveantae
Dave-Anthony
Daveaoun
Daved
Davee
Daveed
Daveeun
Dave-Hardens
Daveion *(0.01)*
Davel
Davell
Davelle
Daven *(0.04)*
Davens
Daventa
Daventino
Daventon
Daveon *(0.02)*
Daveonie
Daveonta
Daveontae
Daverian
Daverick
Daverion
Daverton
Daveuntae
Davey *(0.01)*
Daveyon
Davez
Davhan
Davi *(0.01)*
Davi'on
Davi'yon
Davia
Daviad
Davian *(0.08)*
Davian Joel
Daviano
Daviar
Daviaun
David *(7.67)*
David
  Alexander
David Alexandre
David Anthony
David Arthur
David Benoit
David Christian

David Christian
  Wesley
David Eduardo
David Jesse
David Jonah
David Jordan
David Joseph
David Junior
David Khiem
David Lee
David Michael
David Olivier
David Patrick
David Paul
David Rambom
David Samuel
David Ulises
David William
David-Alejandro
David-Alexander
David-Alexandre
David-Alexis
David-Anthony
David-Benjamin
David-Charles
Davidde
Davide *(0.01)*
Davidee
Davidiyou
David-Jonathan
David-Joseph
David-Keawe
David-Meir
Davidmichael
David-Ray
Davidson *(0.01)*
David-Sun
David-Thom
Davidwarren
David-Wayne
Davie
Davieaun
Daviegh
Daviel
Davielle
Davien *(0.01)*
Daviene
Davieon
Davier
Davierre
Daviion
Davil
Daville

| | | | | | | | |
|---|---|---|---|---|---|---|---|
| Davin (0.12) | Davorsrick | Dax (0.04) | Dayle | Dayshaun (0.01) | Dchaun | De'anta |
| Davin Joseph | Davriel | Daxavier | Daylen (0.03) | Dayshawn (0.01) | Ddonavon | De'antae |
| Davinci | Davrin | Daxen | Dayli | Dayshine | Ddwayne | De'antay |
| Davin-David | Davron | Daxian | Daylin (0.01) | Dayshon | De | De'anthani |
| Davinder | Davu | Daxon | Dayln | Dayshun | Dé | De'anthoni |
| Davine | Davud | Daxsen | Daylon (0.02) | Dayso | De Airus | De'anthony |
| Davinn | Davun | Daxson | Daylyn | Daysohn | De Andre | De'antonie |
| Davinus | Davven | Daxston | Daylynd | Dayson | De André | De'areon |
| Davio | Davvon | Daxten | Daylynn | Dayten | De Andrew | De'arikk |
| Davion (0.17) | Davy (0.01) | Daxter | Daymare | Dayten Kakage | De Angelo | De'aris |
| Davione | Davyan | Daxton (0.03) | Daymaree | Dayteon | De Aurdre | De'arius |
| Daviontay | Davyd | Daxtyn | Daymarion | Daythen | De Jesus | De'arize |
| Davionte | Davyen | Daxwell | Daymarious | Daython | De Lonte | De'armonie |
| Davis (0.21) | Davyn (0.01) | Day | Daymauri | Daytin | De Marceano | De'arron |
| Davis-Antoine | Davyon | Day'cion | Dayme | Dayton (0.16) | De Marcus | De'asa |
| Davish | Dawa | Day'len | Dayme'un | Daytona | De Mari | De'aundraye |
| Davis-James | Dawan (0.01) | Day'quan | Daymeian | Daytraess | De Mario | De'aundre |
| Davison | Dawann | Day'Quan | Daymein | Daytrell | De Marion | De'aunte |
| Davisson | Dawarren | Day'sean | Daymeir | Daytrin | De Marques | De'auntray |
| Davit | Dawaun | Day'shawn | Daymen | Daytron | De Micah | De'aveon |
| Davius | Dawawn | Day'shon | Daymeon (0.01) | Daytwon | De Michael | De'avien |
| Daviyon | Dawayne | Day'son | Daymian (0.01) | Dayvahj | De Ondraé | De'avion |
| Davlet | Dawcen | Day'vion | Daymien (0.01) | Dayve | De Ondre | De'avis |
| Davocci | Daweed | Day'von | Daymion | Dayveion | De Santi | De'avon |
| Davohn | Dawens | Day'yon | Daymn | Dayveiontay | De Sean | De'avontae |
| Davon (0.09) | Dawhii | Daya | Daymon (0.01) | Dayven | Dé Shan | De'ayshawn |
| Davon'te | Dawian | Dayan | Daymond | Dayveon (0.01) | De Shawn | De'boris |
| Davondrey | Dawin | Dayandan | Daymontray | Dayveone | De Shon | De'brince |
| Davone | Dawine | Dayant | Dayn | Dayvian | De Shun | De'carlo |
| Davoné | Dawit | Daycen | Dayne (0.03) | Dayviaun | De Torian | De'carlos |
| Davoni | Dawlton | Daycota | Daynel | Dayvin | De Van | De'coreon |
| Davonn | Dawn | Dayde | Daynin | Dayvion | De Vonn | De'corey |
| Davonne | Dawntrell | Daydon | Daynon | Dayvionne | De Wayne | De'corian |
| Davontá | Dawnyai | Daydrien | Dayo | Dayvis | De Wet | De'coriyeon |
| Davonta (0.01) | Dawnye | Dayelin | Dayon | Day-Von | De'adrian | De'cree |
| Davontaé | Dawnyeah | Dayen | Dayon'dre | Dayvon (0.01) | De'aigo | De'curtis |
| Davontae (0.01) | Dawon | Dayeon | Dayone | Dayvonn | De'aire | De'darius |
| Davontai | Dawood | Dayevon | Da-Yong | Dayvonne | De'airis | De'earis |
| Davontay | Dawoud | Dayfon | Dayonn | Dayvontae | De'airus | De'emory |
| Davonté | Dawsan | Daygan | Dayontae | Dayvontay | De'ajanee | De'erick |
| Davonte (0.02) | Dawsen | Daygen | Dayonte | Dayzhon | De'albert | De'errick |
| Davontey | Dawsin | Dayin | Dayontice | Daz | De'alvion | De'faith |
| Davontez | Dawson (0.58) | Dayious | Day-Quan | Daza'vion | De'amarray | De'garrian |
| Davontrae | Dawson Danial | Dayjaun | Dayquan | Dazani | De'ampherney | De'idrien |
| Davontré | Dawson Daniel | Dayjha | Dayquin | Dazarion | De'amthyst | De'jan |
| Davontye | Dawson Noah | Day-Jour | Dayquon | Dazaun | De'an | De'jarius |
| Davonye | John | Daykeice | Dayrel | Dazhon | De'andra | De'jaun |
| Davonyi | Dawsyn | Daykenson | Dayrian | Dazley | De'andrae | De'jaundre |
| Davorion | Dawton | Daykwon | Dayrion | Dazmane | De'andré | De'jaylen |
| Davoris | Dawuan | Daylan (0.02) | Dayron | Dazshawn | De'andre (0.04) | De'jean |
| Davorius | Dawud | Dayland | Dayse | Dazuan | De'andte | De'jion |
| Davorris | Dawuh | Daylann | Daysean | Dcamreon | De'angelao | De'john |
| | Dawyne | Daylanta | Daysen | Dcarri | De'angelo (0.02) | De'jon (0.01) |

De'jour
De'juan
De'kamron
De'karee
De'karion
De'kontee
De'korion
De'kyln
De'lamarr
De'lamondre
De'lance
De'lavaunte
De'leon
De'lonta
De'majae
De'mane
De'mar
De'marco
De'marcus (0.01)
De'mare
De'marea
De'marean
De'mareion
De'mareo
De'mareyon
De'mari
De'marian
De'marie
De'mario (0.01)
De'marion (0.02)
De'marion
  De'vontay
De'marious
De'marius
De'markis
De'markus
De'marlo
De'marlon
De'marqueis
De'marques
De'marquez
De'marquis
De'marrio
De'marrion
De'marrius
De'martez
De'materion
De'maurean
De'mauri
De'maurian

De'maurion
De'meier
De'metree
De'metrion
De'metrione
De'mhir
De'mikal
De'mir
De'mondré
De'mont
De'monta
De'montae
De'montay
De'monte
De'moris
De'muntra
De'nai'ro
De'nali
De'nerick
De'nero
De'niro
De'nivea
De'oavionne
De'ondera
De'ondre
De'ontae
De'ontay
De'onte
De'onteay
De'ontrea
De'ovion
De'paul
De'pierreon
De'qavion
De'quan (0.01)
De'quandre
De'quarius
De'quavieon
De'quavion
De'quawn
De'quese
De'quinya
De'quirien
De'quon
De'qwuan
De'reion
De'reyous
De'rhon
De'rico
De'rome
De'ryon
De'saun
De'sean (0.01)

De'sekou
De'shannan
De'shannon
De'shard
De'sharion
De'shaun (0.01)
De'shaveon
De'shawn (0.02)
De'shawrion
De'shon
De'shuan
De'shun
De'smond
De'son
De'tarion
De'tavious
De'tavius
De'tayvious
De'terrion
De'terron
De'tonio
De'travion
De'trayrouis
De'trell
De'trick
De'troyreion
De'uan
De'unni
De'untez
De'untrae
De'vandre
De'vante
De'varrius
De'vaughn
De'vaughnté
De'veon
De'veron
De'vian
De'vion
De'von (0.01)
De'vonta
De'vontae
De'vonte
De'Vonté
De'vyon
De'wann
De'wayne
De'wight
De'xien
De'yuan
De'ywan
De'zane
De'zaun

De'zavie'on
De'zhaun
De'Zhawn
De'zhon
De'zorain
De'zure
Dea Jay
Dea'shuwn
Dea'taveon
Deaaron
Deacan
Deackon
Deacon (0.10)
Deadrian
Deadrick
Deagan (0.02)
Deagen
Deaghan
Deaglan (0.01)
Deago
Deagon
Deaire
Deairious
Deairius
Deairriko
Deajae
Deajon
Deakan
Deaken
Deakin
Deakon (0.01)
Deakyn
Dealhn
Dealvon
Deamarr
Deambra
Deamian
Deamontae
Deamonte
Deamonti
Deamontray
Deamonyae
Dean (0.22)
Dean Berkley
Deananthony
Deandr'a
De-Andre
Deandré
Deandré (0.01)
Deandre (0.12)
Deandrea
Deandrew
Deandrey

Deandrez
Deane
Deangalo
Deangela
Deangelas
Deangeló
Deangelo (0.05)
Deangelon
Deangi
Deangleo
Deanglo
Deanjalo
Deanna
Deanrd
Deantaé
Deantai
Deante
Deanté
Deanthony (0.01)
Deantione
Deanton
Deantonio
Deantre
Deantuan
Deantwone
Deanwar
Deaquan
Deareo
Deari
Dearic
Dearioh
Dearion
Dearis
Dearius
Dearl
Dearmonie
Dearndre
Dearonton
Dearrell
Dearrion
Dearron
Dearte
Dearyon
Deasean
Deashawn
Deashton
Deasis
Deathony
Deaton
Deaundra
Deaundre
Deaundré

Deaundrea
Deauntay
Deaunte
Deauri
Deavante
Deavanti
Deaven (0.01)
Deaveon
Deavery
Deavian
Deavin
Deavion
Deavious
Deavis
Deavon
Deavyonte
Deayris
Deaze
Deazel
Debanjon
Debarber
Debareon
Debaughn
Deben
Debin
Debjoti
Deblyn
Deboris
Debrandon
Debren
Debron
Decalun
Decambre
Decameren
Decameron
Decamron
Decan
Decar
Decari
Decario
Decarious
Decaris
Decarius
Decarlis
Decarlo
Decarlon'tae
Decarlos
Decarvion
Decasey
Decater
Decatur
Decaun
Deccan

Deccaro
Decerrick
Decha
Dechlan
Decimus
Deckard
Decker
Decklin
Declan (0.30)
Declen
Declin
Declyn
Deco
Decode
Decon
Decordia
Decorelle
Decorey
Decori
Decorian
Decoriun
Decorreion
Decorrion
Decortnee
Decory
Decosta
Decota
Dectrick
Dedar
Deddrick
Dedrey
Dedric (0.01)
Dedrich
Dedrick (0.01)
Dedrick Karl
  Ludvig
Dedrien
Dedris
Dee
Dee'eric
Deed
Deedric
Deegan (0.03)
Deegen
Deejay
Dee-John
Deekin
Deelan
Deemarck
Deemarco
Deen
Deendayaal
Deeondrae

| | | | | | | |
|---|---|---|---|---|---|---|
| Deep | Deionte | Dekavious | Delali | Delmarco | Delupa | Demariay |
| Deepak | Deiontrae | Dekaylan | Delamar | Delmarieon | Delusan | Demarice |
| Deepan | Deiontré | Dekaylen | Delan | Delmarion | Delvan | Demariel |
| Deepit | Deiontreay | Dekayne | Delance | Delmarius | Delvarious | Demarien |
| Deeric | Deion-Ya | Deke | Delancey | Delmas | Delvarius | Demario (0.03) |
| Deerlyn | Deiquan | Dekedric | Delandis | Del-May | Delven | Demarion |
| Deeshawn | Deireon | Dekeeyvious | Delando | Delmekko | Delvin (0.01) | (0.04) |
| Deeshawon | Deisel | Dekel | Delandon | Delmer | Delvin Ladr | Demarioun |
| Deeson | Deison | Dekell | Delandré | Delmetrius | Delvion | De-Marious |
| Deevani | Deiten | Deken | Delandrous | Delmond | Delvis | Demarious |
| Deevian | Deiton | Dekendrick | Delaney | Delmond- | Delvohn | Demaris |
| Deevya | Deitrec | Dekentrek | Delaney- |   Rudolph | Delvon | Demariun |
| Deeyar | Deitric | Dekerian |   Jermanie | Delmonie | Delvonta | Demarius (0.02) |
| Defferson | Deitrich | Dekevious | Delanio | Delmont | Delvontae | Demariyae |
| Defynes | Deitrick | Dekhari | Delano (0.01) | Delmonté | Delvontaé | Demarjae |
| Dega | Deitrik | Dekin | Delante | Delmontee | Delvonte | Demarkas |
| Degan (0.01) | Deivarsi | Dekkam | Delarentia | Delmontinez | Delvonté | Demarkes |
| Degarris | Deivi | Dekken | Delarian | Delo | Delwin | Demarko |
| Degeryan | Deivin | Dekker | Delarric | Delon | Delwyn | Demarkus |
| Deh'veah | Deivy | Dekklan | Delasio | Delondre | Delynn | Demarlon |
| Dehmar | Deivys | Deklan (0.01) | Delawrence | Delone | Dem'monte | Demarlow |
| Dehmir | Deizel | Deklen | Delay | Delonn | Dema | Demaron |
| Dehnial | Deizy | Deklin | Delazarus | Delonte | Demacio | Demarquay |
| Dehrick | Dejai | Deklun | Delbert (0.01) | Delonté | Demadrick | Demarque |
| Dehven | Dejan | Deklyan | Delbys | Delorean | Demairus | Demarques |
| Dehvin | Dejarrius | Deklyn | Delcour | Delorian | Demajia | Demarquez |
| Dehvon | Dejaun | Dekoda | Deldrick | Delos | Demani | Demarqus |
| Dehvyn | Dejaune | Dekon | Delemetris | Delosh | Demante | Demarr |
| Dei'marion | Dejavion | Dekoriaé | Deleon | Delpasso | Demanuel | Demarre |
| Dei'shaun | Dejavious | Dekorian | Delet | Delphis | Demar | Demarreon |
| Dei'zhaun | Dejavon | Dekoryian | Delfin | Delphus | Demar | Demarri |
| Deiago | Dejavonny | Dekota (0.01) | Delfino | Delquan |   Alessandro | Demarrion |
| Deibrion | Dejay | Dekotah | Delford | Delrico | Demar'ae | Demartavion |
| Deidre | Dejean | Dekova | Delhot Ewame | Delrius | Demarai | Demartrius |
| Deidrich | Dejeremy | Dekovan | Delice | Delroy | Demaray | Demarus |
| Deidrick | Dejerrian | Dekwada | Delicio | Delroye | Demaraye | Demarviay |
| Deietrick | Dejesus | Dekwone | Delijah | Delshaun | Demarc | Demarxé |
| Deigan | Dejohn | Dekyi | Delin | Delshawn | Demarcio | Demaryl |
| Deighton | Dejohnny | Dekyler | Delin Joseph | Delshon | Demarco (0.02) | Demaryon |
| Deigo | Dejon (0.01) | Dekyus | Delio | Delshun | Demarcos | Demau'ray |
| Deijah | Dejonte | Del | Deljaun | Delsin | Demarcus (0.04) | Demaur |
| Deijin | Dejour | Del Ray | Delkedric | Delsyn | Demardre | Demauray |
| Deil'malik | Dejuan (0.03) | Del'kesean | Dell | Deltaveon | Demare | Demauri |
| Deilan | Dejuane | Del'lante | Dell Jontae | Delterio | Demarea | Demaurie |
| Deili | Dejuanta | Del'marrieo | Dell'sean | Delton (0.01) | Demaree | Demaurien |
| Deillin | Dejuantae | Del'shon | Dellante | Deltorrio | Demarein | Demaurin |
| Deimos | Dejuante | Del'tarri | Dellavon | Deltric | Demareion | Demaurion |
| Dein | Dejuantez | Del'vontae | Dellen | Deltron | Demareon | Demauris |
| Deinner | Dekai | Del'vontay | Dellestric | Deltroy | Demareues | Demaury |
| Deion (0.02) | Dekan | Delacruz | Delleven | Deltwan | Demari (0.02) | Demauze |
| Deiondra | Dekari | Delaino | Dellkwan | Deluca | Demari'a | Demba |
| Deiondre (0.01) | Dekauri | Delair | Dellwin | Deluka | Demariah | Demeatrice |
| Deiontae | Dekaveon | Delairius | Delmar (0.01) | Delun | Demarian | Demeatrick |

| | | | | | | |
|---|---|---|---|---|---|---|
| Demeatrise | Demian *(0.01)* | Demorion | Deni | Deny | Deontra | Deray |
| Demeatrius | Demichael | Demoris | Denicco | Denys | Deontrae | Dere'ontae |
| Demecia | Demien | Demorius | Denico | Denza | Deontraé | Derea'on |
| Demede | Demiere | Demorre | Denicolaus | Denzel *(0.06)* | Deontray | Derec |
| Demeir | Demierio | Demorrieus | Deniel | Denzell | Deontre | Dereck *(0.04)* |
| Demeko | Demietre | Demorrio | Deniem | Denzial | Deontré | Dereck-Anthony |
| Demel | Demijah | Demorris | Denilson *(0.01)* | Denzil *(0.01)* | Deontrell | Derecke |
| Demenia | Demikyo | Demorrius | Denilzon | Deo | Deontrez | Derek *(0.82)* |
| Dementrius | De-Mil | Demos | Denim *(0.02)* | Deodatus | Deonzae | Derek James |
| Demere | Demil | Demosthenes | Denio | Deolo | Deorderick | Derek-Anthony |
| Demerious | Demilleo | Demountré | Denireo | Deombre | Deoree | Dereke |
| Demeriss | Demir *(0.01)* | Demoyne | Deniro | Deon *(0.07)* | Deorion | Derekio |
| Demerius | Demirre | Demparion | Denis *(0.05)* | Deon Trai | Deotis | Derek-Mauricio |
| Demerize | Demis | Dempsey | Denish | Deon'dre | Deovanny | Derell |
| Demerrial | Demitrea | Demrick | Denislav | Deon'ko | Deovione | Derelle |
| Demerrick | Demitreaun | Demris | Denis-Luccian | Deon'ta | Depaul | Deren |
| Demerrion | Demitreus | Demrquis | Denison | Deon'tae | Depedro | Dereon |
| Demeterius | Demitri *(0.01)* | Demusico | Denium | Deon'te | Deppner | Derex |
| Demetirus | Demitrias | Demyan | Denivo | Deonate | Depravion | Dereze |
| Demetre | Demitrick | Demylon | Deniz | Deonce | Dequ'aiseon | Derian *(0.01)* |
| Demetré | Demitrie | Demyran | Denmar | Deondrae | Dequae | Deric *(0.01)* |
| Demetrea | Demitrios | Demytri | Denney | Deondray | Dequan *(0.01)* | Dericco |
| Demetrek | Demitrious | Demytris | Dennie | Deondraze | Dequane | Derice |
| Demetres | Demitris | Den | Dennier | Deondré *(0.01)* | Dequarion | Dérick |
| Demetreus | Demitrius *(0.01)* | Denahi | Dennis *(0.32)* | Deondre *(0.02)* | Dequarious | Derick *(0.10)* |
| Demetri *(0.02)* | Demitriy | Denairius | Dennis James | Deondre Nashaun | Dequarius | Derick Ventura |
| Demetric *(0.01)* | Demitry | Denali *(0.01)* | Dennison | Deondrea | Dequatez | Derick-Dat |
| Demetrice *(0.01)* | Demmanuel | Denan | Dennis-Pavel | Deondrey | Dequavian | Derico |
| Demetrick | Demola | Denard *(0.01)* | Dennisson | Deondrez | Dequavine | Derief |
| Demetricus | Demoley | Denardo | Dennon | Deondrick | Dequavion | Derieon |
| Demetrie | Demond *(0.01)* | Denaree | Denny *(0.01)* | Deondrius | Dequavious | Derieonte |
| Demetrik | Demondré | Denari | Dennys | Deone | Dequavius | Derik *(0.02)* |
| Demetrio *(0.01)* | De-Mone | Denarii | Deno | Deonetaye | Dequawn | Derikson |
| Demetrion | Demone | Denario | Denoah | Deonete | Dequay | Derimiah |
| Demetrios *(0.01)* | Demoné | Denarious | Denohj | Deongelo | Dequez | Derin |
| Demetrious *(0.01)* | Demoni | Denarius | Denon | Deongjaquaon | Dequincey | Derio |
| Demetriq | Demont | Denaro | Denorris | Deonis | Dequinn | Derion |
| Demetris *(0.01)* | Demonta | Denarrius | Denry | Deonje | Dequion | Derious |
| Demetrist | Demontaé | Denathean | Dens Pacheco | Deonquentin | Dequndray | Deriq |
| Demetrius *(0.16)* | Demontae *(0.01)* | Denavion | Densel | Deonsae | Dequne | Derius |
| Demetriuse | Demontay | Denby | Densley | Deont'ae | Dequon | Deriyon |
| Demetrous | Demonté | Dencil | Denson | Deontá | Der Mante | Derk |
| Demetruis | Demonte *(0.01)* | Deneco | Densyl | Deonta *(0.01)* | Der Ren Thomas | Derkkentz |
| Demetrus | Demontez | Deneen | Dent | Deontaé | Der'rell | Derlin |
| Demetry | Demontra | Deneiro | Dentan | Deontae *(0.03)* | Der'reon | Derlyn |
| Demetryl | Demontrae | Den-El | Dentavious | Deontavis | Der'riointez | Dermane |
| Demeytrian | Demontray | Denel | Dente | Deontay *(0.01)* | Derail | Dermit |
| Demi | Demontre | Denell | Dentin | Deontaye | Deraile | Dermond |
| Demiah | Demontrez | Denem | Denton *(0.01)* | Deonté *(0.01)* | Deraj | Dermot |
| | Demonye | Denerian | Dentrayives | Deonte *(0.03)* | Derak | Dermott |
| | | Denes | Dentry | Deonthe | Derald | Dernard |
| | | Deng *(0.01)* | Denum | Deonti | Deraun | Dernell |
| | | Denham | Denver *(0.05)* | | | |

| | | | | | | |
|---|---|---|---|---|---|---|
| Derodick | Deryc | Desrearo | Deurym | Devdon | Devlon | Devry |
| Deron (0.01) | Deryck (0.01) | Desric | Deus | Devean | Devlun | Devryn |
| Derond | Deryell | Desrick | Dev (0.02) | Deveion | Devlyn (0.01) | Devryon |
| Derone | Deryk | Dessiah | Dev Srikar | Devell | Devlynn | Devun |
| Deronta | Deryl | Destan | Dev'n | Develle | Devn | Devuntae |
| Deronte | Deryn | Desten | Dev'yonne | Develyn | Devohn | Devunte |
| Deronté | Deryon | Destin (0.05) | Devaal | Deven (0.13) | Devon (0.71) | Devvin |
| Deroy | Deryus | Destine | Devaan | Deven David | Devon | Devvon |
| Derquan | Des'mon | Destined | Devaen | Devendra | Neekolas | Devyn (0.08) |
| Derr'ion | Des'ziis | Destiny | Devajae | Devenn | Devon Vion | Devyne |
| Derrall | Desale | Deston | Devak | Deveon | Devon'ta | Devynn |
| Derran | Desaussure | Destry | Devale | Dever | Devon'te | Devynn Frank |
| Derrean | Desdan | Destyn | Devalin | Devereau | Devonaire | Devyn-Tyler |
| Derreck | De-Sean | Destynd | Devalius | Deverell | Devond | Devyon |
| Derrek (0.01) | Desean (0.02) | Deswaylo | Devam | Deveren | Devonde | Dewain |
| Derrel | Deseon | Deswyuan | Devan (0.12) | Deverin | Devondre | Dewaine |
| Derrell (0.01) | Deshae | Deszion | Devandre | Deverious | Devone | Dewan (0.01) |
| Derren | Deshaine | Deszmund | Devane | Devery | Devoné | Dewane |
| Derrence | Deshan | Detarion | Devani | Devesh | Devonn | Dewanye |
| Derreq | Deshance | Detarius | Devann | Deveyn | Devonne (0.01) | Deward |
| Derri'on | Deshane | Detaveon | Devano | Deveyon | Devonsha | Dewarren |
| Derrian | Deshari | Detavious | Devansh | Deveyone | Devonta (0.01) | Dewaun |
| Derric (0.01) | Deshaun (0.04) | Deterion | Devanson | Deveyonté | Devontaé | Dewaune |
| Derrick (0.38) | Deshaw | Deterrior | Devantae | Devezeon | Devontae | Dewayne (0.05) |
| Derrico | Deshawn (0.11) | Detmer | Devantay | Devhan | (0.01) | Dewei |
| Derriell | Deshawntae | Detoine | Devanté | Devian | Devontal | Dewell |
| Derrien | Deshay | Detorious | Devante (0.02) | Devid | Devontariou | Dewey (0.01) |
| Derrik (0.01) | Deshea | Detorris | Devantre | Devien | Devontaviou | Dewhite |
| Derrin | Deshon (0.01) | Detrail | Devaon | Deviin | Devontay | Dewight |
| Derrion (0.01) | Deshone | Detraill | Devareous | Devik | Devontaye | Dewitt |
| Derrione | Deshoun | Detravion | Devari | Devilin | Devonté (0.01) | Dewley |
| Derrious | Deshuan | Detrevion | Devarian | Devin (1.91) | Devonte (0.04) | Dewon |
| Derriq | Deshun (0.01) | Detrevyon | Devarin | Devin Alexa | Devontea | Dewonn |
| Derris | Deshune | Detrez | Devario | Devin Austin | Devonti | Dex |
| Derrius (0.01) | Desi (0.01) | Detric | Devarion | Devin Roy | Devontia | Dex'shon |
| Derriyon | Desiderio | Detrick | Devarious | Devinchi | Devontra | Dexiel |
| Derron (0.01) | Desiell | Detriel | Devariq | Devinder | Devontravion | Dexion |
| Derrontay | Desion | Detrik | Zemoine | Devine (0.01) | Devon-Tray | Dexter (0.06) |
| Der-Ronte | Desiree | Detrion | Devarius | Devin-John | Devon-Tre | Dexton |
| Derrus | Desjean | Detroit | Devarjae | Devinn | Devontré | Deyaa |
| Derry | Desman | Detrone | Devaron | Devinne | Devontte | Deyan |
| Derry Donta | Desmand | Detroy | Devarus | Devins | Devonzia | Deyarian |
| Derryck | Desmen | Detryick | Deva-Shay | Devinyair | Devou | Deybi |
| Derryk | Desmend | Detryon | Devaugh | Devion (0.01) | Devoures | Deybyn |
| Derryl | Desmere | Deu'ron | Devaughn | Devionta | Devoyne | Deycon |
| Derryon | Desmick | Deuce | (0.02) | Devito | Devran | Deyde |
| Dershawn | Desmin | Deundray | Devaughnte | Deviyon | Devrey | Deyian |
| Derven | Desmon (0.01) | Deundre | Devaujeh | Deviyuone | Devrick | Deyiran |
| Dervin | Desmond (0.16) | Deundré | Devaun | Devjon | Devrie | Deyishon |
| Dervins | Desmond Ami | Deunta | De-Vaunte | Devlan | Dcvries | Deyken |
| Dervontae | Desmond | Deunte | Devaurius | Devlen | Devrim | Deykin |
| Derward | Termell | Deuntray | Devdas | Devlin (0.04) | Devrin | Deylan |
| Derwin (0.01) | Desperado | Deuntre | Devdeyin | Devlinn | Devron | Deylen |

| | | | | | | |
|---|---|---|---|---|---|---|
| Deylin | Dezrick | Dhillan | Diamantae | Diea | Dilbert | Dimari |
| Deylon | Dezrion | Dhimani | Diamante | Dieago | Diler | Dimario |
| Deymari | Dezron | Dhimas | Diamanté | Diedrich | Dileyta | Dimarka |
| Deymian | Dezroy | Dhimitri | Diamantis | Diedrick | Dili | Dimarkis |
| Deymon | Dezshawn | Dhir | Diamel | Diègo | Dilian | Dimarriea |
| Deymor | Dezso | Dhiran | Diamo | Diego (3.79) | Dilin | Dimas |
| Deyon | Dezton | Dhiren | Diamon | Diego Alberto | Diljeevan | Dimetreas |
| Deyondré | Dezzmen | Dhiya Eddine | Diamond | Diego Alexis | Diljot | Dimetry |
| Deyonn | Dezzmon | Dho'mari | Diamond- | Diego Dario | Diljyot | Dimi |
| Deyonna | Dha'zyrin | Dhonavanh | Angelo | Diego Jose | Dilkaran | Dimico |
| Deyonta | Dhairyon | Dhonte | Diamonte | Diego Manuel | Dillan (0.09) | Dimitar |
| Deyontá | Dhaki | Dhron | Diamonté | Diego Zachary | Dillan Tyler | Dimitrei |
| Deyontae | Dhakir | Dhruba | Diamonz | Diego-Alejandro | Dilland | Dimitri (0.07) |
| Deyonte | Dhamani | Dhrumil | Dian | Diego-Enrique | Dilland John | Dimitric |
| Deyonté | Dhameer | Dhruv (0.02) | Dian'te | Diego-Jesus | Dillanger | Dimitrii Alvaro |
| Deyoung | Dhamir | Dhruva | Diana | Diego-Matheo | Dillard | Lucien |
| Deyrek | Dhamon | Dhruve | Diandre | Diehl | Dillen (0.01) | Dimitrije |
| Deyrin | Dhamyus | Dhruvil | Diangelo | Dieh-Mario | Dillenger | Dimitrios (0.01) |
| Deyring | Dhane | Dhul Qarnain | Dianni | Diell | Dillian (0.01) | Dimitrique |
| Deysaud | Dhangaa | Dhyan | Dianotae | Diemar | Dillian Lee | Dimitrius |
| Deyshaun | Dhani | Dhyeya | Diantay | Dieneji | Dillin (0.01) | Dimitrix |
| Deyshon | Dhanin | Di | Diante | Dieon | Dillinger | Dimitriy |
| Deysin | Dhanjay | Di Nari | Dianté | Dierk | Dillion (0.02) | Dimitry (0.01) |
| Deyton | Dhante | Di Shon | Dianthony | Dierks | Dillon (0.53) | Dimmy |
| Deyvi | Dhantei | Di Vaughn | Diarius | Dierre | Dillon Aidara | Dimon |
| Deyvis | Dhany | Di'andrae | Diarra | Dierrick | Dillon | Dimorian |
| Deyvon | Dhanya | Di'angelo | Diasani | Dierrious | Christopha | Din |
| Deyvonté | Dhanyaal | Di'anthony | Diashauede | Diesel (0.01) | Dillon Francis | Dinard |
| Deyvy | Dharam | Di'chad | Diashon | Diesil | Dillyn (0.01) | Dinari |
| Dez | Dharamvir | Di'eondre | Diaun | Dieter | Dilmar | Dinasio |
| Dez'mond | Dharek | Di'marion | Diauntae | Dietrich (0.01) | Dilmer | Dinero |
| Dezaveon | Dharmik | Di'moni | Diaviyun | Dieubesen | Dilneet | Dinesh |
| Dezekiah | Dharnel | Di'nijai | Diaz | Dieudonne | Dilon | Dinesha |
| Dezhon | Dharon | Di'quarious | Dib | Dieukemson | Dilpreet | Ding Ming |
| Dezi | Dhartanion | Di'quarius | Dibyajyoti | Dieuly | Dilraj | Dingzhi |
| Dezi'mon | Dhaval | Di'vad | Dicari | Diezel | Dilrob | Dinh |
| Dezjuan | Dhavan | Di'venchie | Dicarlo | Diezel-Blaze | Dilshaan | Dinh Quang |
| Dezlan | Dhavin | Di'yon | Dice | Digby | Dilshad | Khai |
| Dezleon | Dhavlen | Dia'mond | Dicen | Dignan | Dilshan | Dinisio |
| Dezlynd | Dheaven | Diab | Dick | Diher | Dilshawn | Dino (0.01) |
| Dezman | Dhecent | Diabe | Dickens Jr | Dihon | Dilsher | Dinura |
| Dezmand | Dhedrick | Diabre | Dickson | Dijant | Dilshod | Diogenes |
| Dezmen (0.01) | Dheeman | Diadie | Dicky | Dijohn | Dilveer | Diogenis |
| Dezmend | Dheeraj | Diago | Didane | Dijon (0.01) | Dilyan | Diogo (0.01) |
| Dezmin | Dheeran | Diakan | Didar | Dijuan | Dilyn | Diohnny |
| Dezmine | Dhemari | Diakavanté | Diddel | Dijwar | Dilyn Andrew | Diomonti |
| Dezmir | Dhemian | Diako | Diddier | Dikran | Dilynn | Dion (0.05) |
| Dezmon (0.01) | Dheo | Diallo (0.01) | Diderot | Dikwez | Dilyon | Dion'dre |
| Dezmond (0.03) | Dhevan | Dialo | Didier (0.01) | Dil | Dima | Dionandre |
| Dezmone | Dhevin | Dialyn | Didier Duy-An | Dilan (0.03) | Dimaggio | Dionardo |
| Dezmun | Dhia | Diamani | Didier-Andre | Dilano | Dimarco | Diondre (0.01) |
| Dezmyn | Dhiego | Diamanis | Didimo | Dilaver | Dimarcus | Dione |
| Dezren | Dhilan | Diamantá | Didlaire | Dilbaag | Dimarh | Dioneesis |

| | | | | | | |
|---|---|---|---|---|---|---|
| Dionel | Dishon | Djanhoiy | Doby | Domario | Dominque | Donald Tripp |
| Diongelo | Disma | Djani | Doc | Domarion | Dominus | Donaldo |
| Dionicio | Dison | Djasahn | Dock | Domariyea | Dominyck | Donaldson |
| Dionisio | Ditameon | Djavan | Dodge | Domarko | Dominyk | Donale |
| Dionisios | Ditan | Djay | Dodong | Dome'nic | Dominykas | Donalson |
| Dionissio | Diterrius | Djeferson | Dodson | Domenek | Dominyke | Donaly |
| Dionne | Ditravious | Djefeson | Dodylove- | Domenic (0.07) | Domirac | Donaphin |
| Dionni | Ditter | Djehi | Kabalo | Domenick | Dommenik | Donaterius |
| Dionnie | Diundre | Djelimory | Doel | (0.01) | Dommenyk | Donathan |
| Dionta | Divad | Djerry | Doffis | Domenico | Domminick | Donathon |
| Diontae | Divakar | Djerven | Dogen | (0.02) | Domminnicke | Donato (0.01) |
| Diontaé | Divan | Djeven | Doggale | Domenik | Dommonic | Donatus |
| Diontay | Divantay | Djibril | Dohn | Domennic | Domnick (0.01) | Donavain |
| Diontaye | Divante | Djibrilou | Dohnavan | Domenyck | Domoni | Donavan (0.06) |
| Diontayye | Divari | Djibrine | Dohnavin | Dometrice | Domonic (0.02) | Donavan-Aiden |
| Dionté | Divaris | Djimé | Dohnovan | Domicick | Domonick | Donavaughn |
| Dionte (0.01) | Divas | Djimon | Dohonna | Domicnic | Domonicke | Donaven (0.02) |
| Diontey | Divaud | Djordje | Dohren | Domico | Domonik | Donaven Zane |
| Diontre | Divenson | Djosh | Dohryen- | Domiko | Domoniq | Donavin (0.05) |
| Dionus | Divij | Djovanie | Rinaldi | Domimic | Domonique | Donavinn |
| Dionys | Divin | Djuan | Dokata | Dominac | Domontay | Donavon (0.03) |
| Dionysios | Divine (0.02) | Djulyo | Dokota | Dominec | Domunic | Donavonalexander |
| Dionysius | Divine Jahzmil | Djuvens | Dolan (0.01) | Domineek | Domynic | Donavyn (0.01) |
| Dior (0.01) | Divion | Dkari | Dolin | Dominek | Domynick | Donavynn |
| Diore | Divjot | Dmarcius | Dollarian | Domineq | Domynik | Dondi |
| Dioris | Divon | Dmareon | Dolon | Domingo (0.02) | Don (0.03) | Dondoza |
| Diorre | Divonni | Dmari | Dolorian | Dominguez | Don Anthony | Dondrae |
| Diosbel | Divonta | D-Mariean | Dolph | Dominic (2.59) | Don Ibrahima | Dondre |
| Dioshua | Divonte | Dmarion | Dolrich | Dominic Jospeh | Don Jakaree | Dondrell |
| Diovanni | Divy | Dmariontae | Dolson | Dominic Munn | Don Samy | Dondric |
| Diovion | Divya | Dmarques | Doltan | Dominic-Xavier | Don Torez | Dondrick |
| Dioz | Divyansh | Dmarquis | Doltn | Patrick | Don'arion | Doneau |
| Dipak | Divyesh | Dmarrion | Dolton | Dominica | Don'avyn | Donel |
| Dipesh | Divyye | Dmarue | Dom'nic | Dominicc | Don'quaviio | Donell (0.02) |
| Dipjoy | Diwan | Dmetrian | Doman | Dominice | Don'ta | Donelle |
| Diquan | Diwud | Dmetrius | Domani | Dominick (0.49) | Don'tavious | Donellrious |
| Diquann | Dixan | Dmistry | Domanic (0.02) | Dominick Lee | Don'tay | Doneta |
| Diquarious | Dixon (0.01) | Dmitri (0.01) | Domanick | Dominic-Nasir | Don'te | Doneto |
| Diquavious | Dixson | Dmitrii | (0.02) | Dominico | Don'terrius | Donevan |
| Diramaj | Diyaa Eddine | Dmitrius | Domanicq | Dominic- | Don'tez | Donevin |
| Dirck | Diyaael Hak | Dmitriy | Domaniel | Vincent | Don'tre | Donevon |
| Direll | Diyaan | Dmitro | Domanik | Dominie | Don'vielle | Dong Hyun |
| Dirick | Diyar | Dmitry (0.01) | Domanikk | Dominik (0.11) | Don'ya | Dongjin |
| Dirir | Diyor | Dmontaé | Domaniq | Dominike | Donae | Doni |
| Dirk (0.02) | Diyorbek | Dmonte | Domanique | Dominiko | Donagh | Donial |
| Dirul | Dizario | Dmytro | Domantas | Dominikos | Donahann | Donicio |
| Dirwin | Dizel | Dnekko | Domante | Dominiq | Donahven | Donick |
| Disaiah | Dizzy | Dnilson | Domanyc | Dominiqu | Donahven | Doniell |
| Disani | DJ | Dnison | Domanyk | Dominique | Cedric | Donielle |
| Disciple | Djake | Do | Domarco | (0.09) | Donal | Donif |
| Disean | Djamal | Doan | Domareyan | Dominique- | Donald (0.37) | Donile |
| Dishan | Djamolodine | Doasha | Domari | Wilson | Donald Jr | Donilee |
| Dishawn | Django | Dobson | Domarien | Dominiquo | Donald Ross | Donineek |

| | | | | | | |
|---|---|---|---|---|---|---|
| Doninique | Donquarius | Dontez *(0.02)* | Dorian *(0.19)* | Dourell | Draigen | Drayten |
| Donis | Donquaveon | Dontrael | Dorian Esteban | Douryun | Draigon | Drayton *(0.02)* |
| Donivan *(0.01)* | Donquavious | Dontral | Dorian' | Dousheet | Draike | Drayven |
| Doniven | Donque | Dontravious | Doriane | Dov *(0.02)* | Draimon | Drayvin |
| Donivin | Donquel | Dontravis | Dorians Edu | Dovan | Draion | Drayzen |
| Donjae | Donquerio | Dontray | Dorick | Dovante | Drakayne | Drazel |
| Donjarey | Donquez | Dontre | Doriean | Dovavyn | Drake *(0.42)* | Drazen |
| Donjay | Donqwa | Dontré | Doriel | Dovber | Draken *(0.01)* | Drazic |
| Donje | Donray | Dontrell | Dorien *(0.02)* | Dove | Drakeo | Drazic Edmond |
| Donjoel | Donrelle | *(0.02)* | Dorin | Dovid *(0.02)* | Draki | Drazik |
| Donkayle | Donshay | Dontrelle | Dorino | Dovion | Drakious | Dre |
| Donlon | Dont'a | Dontrey | Dorion | Dovon | Drakko | Dre 'Vonne |
| Donlontae | Dontá | Dontrez | Doriono | Dovonte | Drako | Dre'dan |
| Donmerick | Donta *(0.01)* | Dontril | Dorisel | Dovydas | Drakonus | Dre'ion |
| Donmetrius | Donta'i | Dontrille | Dorius' | Dow | Dramaiya | Dre'kevan |
| Donmonick | Dontaé | Donuia | Doriyan | Dowan | Dramayne | Dre'men |
| Donmonique | Dontae *(0.04)* | Donvin | Dorjan | Dowayne | Dramell | Dre'mond |
| Donn *(0.01)* | Dontaee | Donwan | Dorji Chogdup | Dowjang | Drammel | Dre'neal |
| Donnavan | Dontaeus | Donya | Dormonta | Downe | Dramon | Dre'on |
| Donnaven | Dontaevian | Donyae | Dorne | Dowon | Drannon | Dre'quan |
| Donnavin | Dontai | Donyaé | Dornell | Doy | Draper | Dre'shawn |
| Donnavon | Dontaivies | Donyai | Dornigan | Doyl | Draquan | Dre'tyus |
| Donnel | Dontarieous | Donye | Doron | Doyle *(0.01)* | Drasen | Dre'vehion |
| Donnell *(0.02)* | Dontarious | Donyé | Dorr | Doyral | Drason | Dre'veon |
| Donnelle | Dontarius | Dony'e | Dorrell | Dozer | Dravan | Dre'vin |
| Donnevin | Dontarrious | Donyea | Dorren | Dozick | Dravanté | Dre'vion |
| Donnez | Dontarrius | Donyeal | Dorrian | Dra'gan | Drave | Dre'von |
| Donnie *(0.04)* | Dontate | Donyel | Dorrien | Dra'kal | Draven *(0.11)* | Dre'vontae |
| Donnie Ray | Dontave'on | Donyell | Dorrion | Dra'quez | Draven Martin | Dre'vyon |
| Donnivan | Dontaveon | Donzarius | Dorris | Dra'tavious | Draveyn | Dreaden |
| Donnivyn | Dontavion | Donzay | Dorron | Drace | Dravid | Dreagan |
| Donnley | Dontavious | Donzeek | Dorson | Drache | Dravien | Dreagon |
| Donnovan | *(0.02)* | Donzell | Dortell | Draco *(0.01)* | Dravin *(0.01)* | Drean |
| *(0.01)* | Dontavis | Donziar | Dorthanius | Dracon | Dravis | Dreas |
| Donnovin | Dontavius | Doodly | Doruk | Draden | Dravon | Dreaun |
| Donnovon | Dontay *(0.01)* | Doogan | Dorvil | Dradon | Dravyn | Dreaven |
| Donny *(0.01)* | Dontaye | Doohyun | Dory | Drady | Draxtyn | Dreaw |
| Donnyae | Dontayvis | Doorol | Doryan | Dradyn | Dray | Drecar |
| Donnylee | Donté *(0.01)* | Dophie | Doryen | Drae | Dray'auntae | Dred |
| Donotta | Donte *(0.05)* | Dor'rius | Doryun | Draeden | Drayan | Dredan |
| Donovahn | Donte Antonio | Doran *(0.01)* | Doson | Draegen | Drayden *(0.02)* | Dreden |
| Donovan | Donte Latrell | Dorant | Dossie | Draegon | Drayder | Dredon |
| *(0.63)* | Donte'vis | Dorcely | Dosswayé | Draeke | Draydon | Dredyn |
| Donovann | Dontea | Dorean | Dotayne- | Draeon | Draygen | Dreiden |
| Donovan- | Dontel | Doreen | Tebekew- | Dragan | Draygon | Dreidy |
| Thomas | Dontell | Dorein | Belachew | Dragomir | Drayk | Dreikken |
| Donoven | Donterious | Dorell | Dothan | Dragon | Drayke | Dreim |
| Donovin | Donterius | Doremy | Doug | Dragos | Draylen | Dreissen |
| *(0.01)* | Donterrell | Doren | Douglas *(0.27)* | Drah'cir | Draylin | Dreivayn |
| Donovon | Donterrias | Doreon | Douglass | Drahcir | Draylon | Drekho |
| Donovyn | Donterrious | Doreye | Douglun | Drahken | Draysen | Drelen |
| Donovynn | Donterrius | Doreyen | Doulgas | Draiden | Draysin | Drelick |
| Donquaill | Donteveis | Doriam | Doumic | Draidyn | Drayson | Drelon |

Drelyn
Drelynn
Dremani
Dremar
Dremon
Dren
Drennan
Drennen
Drenon
Drent
Dreon
Dreontez
Drequahn
Drequan
Dresden
Dresean
Dreseann
Dreshan
Dreshaun
Dreshawn
Dreshone
Dreson
Dreton
Dreux
Dreux-Akira
Drevan
Drevaughn
Dreveon
Drevin
Drevion
Drevon (0.01)
Drevoun
Drevyn
Drew (0.63)
Drewett
Drewey
Drewry
Drex
Drexden
Drexel
Drey
Dreydan
Dreyden
Dreydin
Dreydon
Drey-Ellis
Dreyfus
Dreylan
Dreylee
Dreylin
Dreylon
Dreyon
Dreyshaun

Dreyshon
Dreyson
Dreyton
Dreyven
Dreyvin
Drez
Drezden
Drezdin
Drezyon
Dri'ques
Dricen
Drifus
Drightan
Drikeston
Drin
Drini
Drinnen
Drión
Driquavious
Drique
Driss
Dristan
Dristen
Dristian
Dristin
Driton
Drizz
Drizztan
Drizzten
Dru (0.01)
Dru Ryen
Druce
Drucel
Drudan
Drue
Druhan
Drune
Drunta
Drushuan
Drwesh
Dryan
Dryden (0.01)
Drygen
Drystan
Drysten
Drystyn
Dsean
Dshaun
Dshawn
Dshon
Dtavion
Du Whon
Du'hmon

Du'juan
Du'pri
Du'varius
Duain
Duale
Duale-Zachary
Dually
Duane (0.05)
Duang
Duanne
Duanta
Duarick
Duarl
Duban
Dubber
Duberry
Dublin
Dubose
Dubray
Duc
Duc Duy
Duc Tai
Duc Tam
Ducainson
Duce
Duc-Huy
Duckens
Dudley
Duelio
Dueshonta
Duey
Duff
Duffie
Duffy
Dugan (0.01)
Dugarry
Duggan
Duglaz
Dugrei
Duilio
Dujuan
Duke (0.02)
Duke Daniel
Duke-Aia S
Dukens
Dulajan
Dulani
Dulcé
Dulcenea
Dulton
Duly
Dumakatochukwu
Dumarqus

Dumel
Dumir
Dumitru
Dumonnie
Dumont
Dunavan
Dunaway
Duncan (0.13)
Dunchesze
Dune
Dung
Dunkan
Dunmatti
Dunnie
Duntay
Duntaye
Dunyea
Duojaun
Duong
Duong Quy
Dupablo
Dupree
Duqe
Duran
Durand
Duranté
Durbin
Durden
Duree
Durell (0.01)
Durelle
Dureon
Duressa
Durgkaran
Durham
Durian
Durias
Duric
Duriel
Durin
Durobb
Duron
Durrah
Durran
Durrel
Durrell
Durrett
Durst
Durstan
Duruv
Durval
Durvesh
Durvish

Durwin
Durwood
Dushan
Dusharpreet
Dushawn
Duskin
Dustan
Dustano
Dustee
Dusten (0.01)
Dustey
Dustin (0.48)
Dustin Ian
Dustin-Thomas
Dustion
Duston
Dusty (0.03)
Dustyn (0.02)
Duszynski
Dutch (0.01)
Dutt
Duuna
Duval
Duvan
Duvaun
Duvens
Duvid
Duviel
Duvon
Duvyontarius
Duwan
Duwayne
Duwon
Duwyne
Duy (0.01)
Duy An
Duythinh
Dvan
Dvij
Dvir
Dvon
Dwain
Dwaine
Dwajuan
Dwan
Dwane
Dwane Ali
Dwanell
Dwann
Dwante
Dwardensky
Dwaun
Dwayne (0.10)

Dwayne
Valentino
Dwight (0.04)
Dwij
Dwith
Dwjuan
Dwone
Dwren
Dwyane
Dy Heim
Dy' Qarius
Dy'ghell
Dy'kendrick
Dy'lahn
Dy'lan
Dy'lon
Dy'lond
Dy'on
Dy'quawn
Dy'qwuan
Dy'shaun
Dya'ron
Dyaire
Dyaln
Dyami
Dyango
Dyantae
Dyantre
Dyaren
Dyban
Dyearrius
Dyemir
Dyer
Dyeton
Dyhron
Dyian
Dyilan
Dyiriun
Dy-Jhauné
Dykes
Dykwon
Dylahn
Dylan (5.94)
Dylan Aina
Dylan Alexa
Dylan Alexander
Weng
Dylan Bradley
Dylan Byron
Dylan Chase
Dylan Cyrisse
Dylan Dean
Dylan Hoang

Dylan Joseph
Dylan Phillip
Dylan Raven
Dylan Steeve
Dylan-Alexis
Dyland
Dylane
Dylan-Fabien
Dylanie
Dylan-Jacob
Dylan-John
Dylan-Lukas
Dylann
Dylan-Steve
Dylan-Xavier
Dylen (0.01)
Dyles
Dylhann
Dylian
Dylin (0.01)
Dyllan (0.03)
Dyllen
Dyllian
Dyllin
Dyllion
Dyllon (0.01)
Dyllynne
Dyln
Dylon (0.05)
Dylun
Dylyn
Dylynn
Dymare
Dymeer
Dymeir
Dymek
Dymen
Dymer
Dymere
Dymetrious
Dymieré
Dymir
Dymire
Dymitri
Dymond
Dymontae
Dymonté
Dynarian
Dynasty
Dynero
Dyniro
Dyon
Dyondrea

Dyone
Dyonté
Dyordan
Dyquan
Dyral
Dyree
Dyrell
Dyricus
Dyrin
Dyron
Dyrone
Dysen
Dyshaun
Dyshawn
Dyshjuan
Dyshon
Dysjuan
Dyson *(0.02)*
Dytaan
Dytadius
Dytavius
Dytwand
Dyvonne
Dywane
Dyward
Dywon
Dyzaac
Dyzairean
Dyzavian
Dzan
Dzevad
Dzevat
Dzinh

## ~ E ~

E
E N
E'averi
E'darius
E'davione
E'derian
E'derrionte
E'jayvion
E'juan
E'kamion
E'lazruse
E'lias
E'lijah
E'mari
E'marion
E'maseo

E'mecha
E'monjae
E'montae
E'monte
E'monti
E'montre
E'morej
E'mory
E'mydray
E'nahsalem
E'on
E'reekay
E'ronnie
E'saundre
E'shaun
E'shon
E'shone
E'shun
E'syious
E'tienne
E'torian
E'vante
E'xavier
E'zaiah
E'zekeon
E'zell
E'ziyah
Eaamon
Eaden
Eadric
Eaen
Eagan *(0.01)*
Eagle
Eagle-Rayne
Eagletalon
Eagon
Eagyn
Eakmbir
Eaman
Eammon
Eamon *(0.04)*
Eamonn *(0.01)*
Ean *(0.07)*
Eanjay
Eann
Earick
Earl *(0.06)*
Earle
Earlen
Earlie
Earlmoni
Earlsworth
Early Jonas

Earnest *(0.01)*
Earnie
Earns
Earrious
Earron
Earth
Earvin
Easa
Eashan
Easi
Easie
Eason *(0.01)*
Eastan
Easten
Easter
Eastin
Eastlin
Eastlynn
Easton *(0.29)*
Eastyn
Eastynn
Eath
Eathan *(0.02)*
Eathen *(0.01)*
Eathin
Eathn
Eathon
Eathyn
Eaton
Eaunest
Eavan
Eaven
Eavin
Eazy
Eb
Eba
Eba'isa
Ebad
Eban
Ebb
Ebben
Eben *(0.02)*
Ebene
Ebeneezer
Ebenezer
Eber *(0.01)*
Eberardo
Eberth
Ebin
Ebisaa
Ebisso
Ebner
Ebon

Ebony
Ebraheem
Ebrahim
Ebrain
Ebrien
Ebrima
Ebubekir
Ecerwv
Ecire
Ector
Ed
Ed'gerrin
Edace
Edaevion
Edam
Edan *(0.01)*
Edarius
Edasso
Edber
Edbin
Edd
Eddee
Edder
Eddi
Eddie *(0.17)*
Eddie Carlos
Eddie Eriberto
Eddie Manuel
Eddie Morris
Eddiel
Eddie-Tomas
Eddie-William
Eddin
Eddison
Eddrice
Eddrick
Eddriyon
Edduan
Eddy *(0.05)*
Eddy Antonio
Eddye
Eddy-Edmont
Ede
Edekin
Edel *(0.01)*
Edell
Edelmiro
Edelweiss
Eden *(0.03)*
Edenilson
Edenir
Edens
Edeogheheseri

Eder *(0.01)*
Eder-Issai
Ederlix
Edga
Edgar *(1.10)*
Edgar Alan
Edgar Joel
Edgar-Josue
Edgar-Alexander
Edgard *(0.01)*
Edgardo *(0.02)*
Edgariel
Edgar-Leon
Edgarmanuel
Edgar-Maurysio
Edge
Edger
Edgerinn
Edgerrin
Edgran
Edguar Yano
Edhel
Edher
Edhil
Edi
Ediberto
Edicio-Nicolas
Edie
Ediel
Edien
Edier
Edik
Edil
Edilberto
Edilgardo
Edilsar
Edilson
Edilson De
  Jesus
Edilsson
Edilvier
Edilzar
Edilzer
Edin *(0.01)*
Edinam
Edinson
Edinson-Samuel
Ediriz
Edis
Edison *(0.06)*
Edisson
Edith
Edjahir

Edjvon
Edleoned
Edler
Edlin
Edlner
Edman
Edmanuel
Edmar
Edmari
Edmer
Edmeyer
Edmi
Edmilson
Edmon
Edmond *(0.02)*
Edmund *(0.03)*
Edmundo *(0.01)*
Edmyer
Ednel
Ednilson
Edo
Edoardo
Edoardo-Diego
Edon
Edonnez
Edorian
Edouard *(0.11)*
Edouard
  Barthelemy
Edouard Jr
Edouard
  Samuel
Edouard-
  Laurent
Edouardo
Edouelledo
Edraniel
Edred
Edrees
Edreese
Edreick
Edrek
Edrekius
Edren
Edrey
Edreyk
Edrian
Edric
Edrice
Edrick *(0.01)*
Edrick-James
Edricks

Edriece
Edriel
Edrik
Edris
Edrise
Edrith
Edrjel
Edryk
Edsal
Edsel
Edson *(0.02)*
Edson Cleay
  Junior
Edtavious
Eduado
Eduar
Eduard *(0.01)*
Eduard
  Maverick
  Holland
Eduardo *(1.64)*
Eduardo Jesus
Eduin
Eduordo
Edurie
Edvaldo
Edvar
Edvard
Edvardo
Edvin *(0.01)*
Edwar
Edward *(0.97)*
Edward Jame
Edward Ramiro
Edward-Joseph
Edwardo *(0.01)*
Edward-William
Edwarz
Edwens
Edwidge-
  Dandee
Edwin *(0.58)*
Edwin Alexa
Edwin Alvaro
Edwin Antonio
Edwin Govan
Edwin Gregorio
Edwin Timoteo
Edwin-
  Christopher
Edwinel
Edwing
Edwuanis

| | | | | | | |
|---|---|---|---|---|---|---|
| Edwuin | Ege | Eisryell | Elaj | Eleyeh | Eli-Charles | Elijawah |
| Edwyn | Eghan | Eissa | Elam *(0.01)* | Elgar | Elida | Elijeh |
| Edwynn | Eghosa | Eiston | Elan *(0.02)* | Elgen | Eli-Daniel | Elijel |
| Edxon | Egide | Eistyn | Elan Kai | Elgeron | Elidav | Elijha *(0.01)* |
| Edy *(0.01)* | Egidio | Eitan *(0.02)* | Elanore | Elgin *(0.01)* | Elidio | Elijiah *(0.01)* |
| Edyangel | Egledi | Eithan *(0.01)* | Elanté | Elgis | Elidyn | Elijin |
| Edylson | Eguew | Eithel | Elaunté | Elgron | Élie | Elijous |
| Edyn | Egunn | Eithen | Elay | Elguin | Elie *(0.04)* | Elijuah |
| Edzar | Ehab | Eittan | Elbasan | Elhadj | Elie Daniel | Elijuan |
| Edzavier | Ehab Taha | Eivi | Elbert *(0.01)* | Elhadj-Alimou | Elie Hamissou | Elijuwon |
| Eeamon | Ehan | Eivin | Elberth | Elhadj-Amadou | Elie Junior | Elijz'ah |
| Eedyn | Ehibrajam | Eivy | Elbin | Elhadj-Oury | Elieb | Elik |
| Eelan | Ehidiamen | Eizayah | Elbis | Elhajie | Elie-Bryan | Elikana |
| Eeland | Ehijie | Eizele | Elbon | El-Hajj | Eliecer | Elilan |
| Eemaan | Ehman | EJ | Elcarlos | Elhan | Elie-Charles | Elim |
| Eeowyn | Ehren | Ejay | Eldalang | Elhanan | Elie-Joe | Elim Bob |
| Eero | Ehrick | Ejlin | Eldar | Elhannen | Eliel *(0.04)* | Elimane |
| Eerol | Ehronn | Ekain | Elden *(0.01)* | Elhassan | Elier *(0.01)* | Eli-Manuel |
| Eeron | Ehsaan | Ekam | Elder *(0.01)* | Elhody | Elie-Raphael | Elimelach |
| Eesa | Ehsan | Ekambir | Eldin *(0.01)* | Eli *(1.06)* | Elies | Elimelech *(0.01)* |
| Eesaa | Ehsanullah | Ekamjot | Eldis | Eli Adrian | Elieser | Eli-Michael |
| Eesher | Ehssan | Ekampreet | Eldon *(0.01)* | Eli Chad | Eliezel | Elin |
| Eeshwar | Ehtan | Ekamveer | Eldred | Eli Charles | Eliezer *(0.04)* | Eline |
| Eeson | Ehukai | Ekansh | Eldreen | Eli Faithlord | Eligah | Elinneaus |
| Efaobasi | Ehzriel | Ekbir | Eldrerion | Eli Jah | Eligh | Elio *(0.01)* |
| Efe | Eialand | Eke | Eldric | Eli Yan | Eligha | Eliodoro |
| Efeosa | Eian *(0.02)* | Ekem | Eldrich | Eli'jah | Eligia | Elioe |
| Eferem | Eibi | Ekemdeep | Eldrick | Elia | Eligiah | Elioenai |
| Eferli | Eibrahan | Ekenedilichukwu | Eldridge | Eliab | Eligio | Elio-Joe |
| Eferson | Eicca | Ekenna | Eldrin | Eliad | Elihu | Elioke |
| Effah | Eid | Ekhayo | Eldwin | Eliada | Eliiah | Eliomar |
| Effrem | Eidan | Ekiel | Ele'sia | Eliades | Eliijah | Elionaid |
| Effrom | Eidyn | Ekin | Eleazar *(0.01)* | Eliah *(0.01)* | Elija *(0.01)* | Elionair |
| Efim | Eighan | Ekjot | Eleazer | Eliahs | Elijael | Elior |
| Efoniction | Eihab | Ekkuluk | Elec | Eliajah | Elijah Israel | Eliot *(0.07)* |
| Efrahin | Eihadi | Eknoor | Eleftherios | Eliakim | Elijah *(5.15)* | Elioth |
| Efraim *(0.01)* | Eiji | Eknoor Singh | Eleftheris | Eliam | Elijah Gabriel | Eliott *(0.05)* |
| Efrain *(0.04)* | Eila | Ekow | Elek *(0.01)* | Elian *(0.04)* | Elijah Sammy | Eliott-Raphael |
| Efrain Jesus | Eilan | Ekraj | Elena | Eliana | Elijah'bleu | Eliphaz |
| Efram | Eiljah | Ekrem | Elenilson | Elianthony | Elijaha | Elique |
| Efrayim | Eimmij | Ekundayo | Eleno | Eliar | Elijah-Blue | Eliroy |
| Efrem | Ein | El Emanuel | Eleodoro | Elias *(0.55)* | Elijah-Ishan | Elis |
| Efren *(0.02)* | Einar | El Habib | Eleonel | Eliasar | Elijahjohn | Elisabeth |
| Efrum | Eion *(0.01)* | El Haji | Eleonor | Eliasha | Elijahjose | Elisah |
| Efrym | Eiraj | El Jachin | Eleric | Eliasib | Elijahjuan | Elisaih |
| Efstathios | Eirik | El Ninode | Elesay | Eliason | Elijahjuon | Elisandro |
| Efstratios | Eirnin | El Roy | Eleseo | Eliasz | Elijah-Kyle | Elise |
| Efthimios | Eisa | El'cindor | Eleucterio | Eliav | Elijah-Lee | Elisee |
| Egal | Eisenhower | El'shawn | Eleuterio | Eliaz | Elijah-Mbuyi | Eliseo *(0.02)* |
| Egan *(0.01)* | Eishawn | Elaa | Elex | Eliaza | Elijahmel | Eli-Sha |
| Egbaroghene | Eishi | Elad | Elexender | Eliazar *(0.01)* | Elijah-Paul | Elisha *(0.10)* |
| Egbert | Eisley | Eladio | Elexier | Eliazim | Elijahrieon | Elisha Antonio |
| Egdestiny | Eison | Elai | Eley | Elibrham | Elijahwon | Elishah |

| | | | | | |
|---|---|---|---|---|---|
| Elishai | Elizjha | Elmamy | Elson | Elyias | Emauel | Emile Jacques |
| Elisha-Ishmael | Elizur | Elman | Elston | Elyijah | Emaun | Emile Lucas |
| Elishia | Elizy | Elmar | Elsworth | Elyize | Emauri | Emile-Antoine |
| Elishja | Eljae | Elmer *(0.05)* | Eltaf | Elyjah *(0.02)* | Emaurien | Emile-Joseph |
| Elishjon | Eljah | Elmer Josue | Eltahir | Elyjaih | Emaz | Emilian |
| Elishua | Eljahrah | Elmerl | Eltarro | Elyjiah | Ember | Emilian Ioan |
| Elishuah | Eljai | Elmerson | Elton *(0.01)* | Elyjuelle | Emberlyn | Emiliano *(0.10)* |
| Elisiah | Eljan | Elmerton | Eltoria | Elyle | Embery | Emilianomiguel |
| Elisio | Eljavontay | Elmi | Elucio | Elyo | Embree | Emilie |
| Elision | Eljay | Elmino | Eluiner | Elyo Noel | Embry | Emilien *(0.01)* |
| Elisjsha | Eljay Marco | Elmir | Eluis Angel | Elyot | Emden | Emilio *(0.21)* |
| Elison | Elkan | Elmo | Elum | Elyott | Eme'yrr | Emilio Darenz |
| Elisseo | Elkan Zayden | Elmore | Eluzai | Elyse | Emecheion | Emiliyan |
| Elisson | Elkens | Elmursy | Elvan | Elysha | Emediong | Emille |
| Eliu | Elkin | Elmus | Elvar | Elysia | Emeillio | Emilliano |
| Eliuah | Elko | Elnad | Elvarie | Elysiah | Emeka | Emillien |
| Eliud | Elkon | El-Nasr | Elvashio | Elysium | Emelio | Emillio |
| Elius | Ella | Elne | Elve | Elyssa | Emely | Emilo |
| Eliut | Ellajah | Elo | Elvedin | Elyzah | Emeory | Emilson |
| Eliute | Elleon | Eloa | Elven | Elzie | Emerald | Emily *(0.01)* |
| Elix | Eller | Éloah | Elver | Emaaj | Emeree | Emilyan |
| Elixander | Ellery | Elodien | Elverne | Emaan | Émeric | Emilyano |
| Elixavier | Ellesay | Eloge | Elvernon | Emad | Emeric *(0.02)* | Emin |
| Eliy | Ellessar | Elohan | Elvick | Emadd | Emerick *(0.03)* | Emir *(0.02)* |
| Eliyaan | Ellezer | Éloi | Elvie | Emadeldin | Emerick Yuutin | Emisael |
| Eliyab | Elli | Eloi *(0.04)* | Elvin *(0.05)* | Emahd | Emerik *(0.01)* | Emit |
| Eliyah | El-Liam | Eloic | Elvir | Emahjé | Emerio | Emitt |
| Eliyahs | Ellian | Eloick | Elvis *(0.06)* | Emajae | Emerito | Emiyare |
| Eliyahu *(0.03)* | Ellias | Eloik | Elviyon | Emajah | Emerlin | Emjay |
| Eliyamou Chaz | Ellie | Eloique | Elviz | Emajé | Emersen | Emky |
| Eliyan | Elliegerman | Eloiso | Elvy | Emale | Emerson *(0.12)* | Emma *(0.01)* |
| Eliyas | Ellies | Elolo | Elvyn | Emam | Emersyn | Emmad |
| Eliyiah | Elligaherie | Elom | Elway | Emani | Emery *(0.06)* | Emmalee |
| Eliyjah | Ellijah *(0.01)* | Elon | Elwin | Emanial | Emeryck | Emman |
| Eliyon | Elling | Elonas | Elwiss | Emaniel | Emeryk | Emmanel |
| Eliz | Ellington | Elonzo | Elwood | Emanni | Emerzon | Emmanoel |
| Eliza | Ellio | Eloui | Elwyn | Emannuel | Emet | Emmanual |
| Elizabeth | Ellion | Elouyk | Ely *(0.04)* | Emano | Emethelus | *(0.01)* |
| Elizah | Elliot *(0.32)* | Eloy *(0.02)* | Elya | Emanual | Emett | Emmanueal |
| Elizai | Elliot-Piraux | Elque | Elyace | Emanuèl | Emhile | Emmanuel |
| Elizandro | Elliott *(0.22)* | Elrades | Elyaer | Emanuel *(0.30)* | Emi Jwan | *(0.57)* |
| Elizar | Elliott Reid | Elray | Elyah | Emanuel Eli | Emiaz | Emmanuel- |
| Elizardo | Ellis *(0.07)* | Elrey | Elyan | Emanuel Jos | Emida | Arthur |
| Elizavier | Ellison | Elric | Elyaqim | Emanuele | Emidio | Emmanuele |
| Elizen | Elliston | Elric Nicholas | Elyas *(0.01)* | Emanuell | Emidson | Emmanuel- |
| Elizeo | Elliyass | Elricko | Elyas Zain | Emanull | Emiel | James |
| Elizer | Ellmar | Elrie | Elyass | Emare | Emigdio | Emmanuell |
| Elizeu | Elloney | Elrik | Elyaz | Emaree | Emijah | Emmanuel-La |
| Eliziah | Ellsworth | Elroy | Elycio | Emari *(0.01)* | Emil *(0.03)* | Fleche |
| Eliziar | Elly | Elsen | Elydel | Emarian | Emil Mircea | Emmanuelle |
| Elizijah | Ellyas | El-Shaddai | Elye | Emarie | Emildar | Emmanuel- |
| Elizijuh | Ellyot | Elshadey | Elyes | Emarion | Émile | Lorenz |
| Elizjah | Elly-Raphael | Elshod | Elyhas | Emariono | Emile *(0.24)* | Emmanuel-Paul |

Emmanuel-Wesley
Emmanule
Emmaous
Emmarion
Emmaus
Emmeka
Emmeraud
Emmerick
Emmerson
Emmery
Emmet (0.03)
Emmett (0.12)
Emmette
Emmit (0.01)
Emmitt (0.02)
Emmon
Emmoni
Emmory
Emmrey
Emo
Emon
Emon'da
Emondre
Emoni
Emonni
Emonnie
Emonte
Emoree
Emorej
Emorio
Emory (0.03)
Emounty
Emperior
Emperous
Emrah
Emran
Emray
Emre (0.01)
Emrecan
Emrek
Emrel
Emrey
Emrhe
Emri
Emric (0.01)
Emrick (0.03)
Emrie
Emrik (0.01)
Emril
Emron
Emrri
Emry

Emryck
Emryk
Emrys Michael
Emseh
Emsud
Emuhn
Emy
Emyl
Emyrick
Enam
Enan
Enbo
Ender
Enderson
Endesha
Endgi
Endi
Endjy
Endre
Endri
Endrick
Endrit
Endurance
Endy
Endymion
Eneas
Enediel
Enegil
Eneko
Enemias
Ener
Enereo
Enerildo
Enerson
Enes
Engel
Engel John
Engelo
Engels
Engjel
England
Engli
Enias
Enie
Enigk
Enijah
Enijal
Enijuel
Enik
Enio
Enique
Enirique
Enis

Enkang
Enki
Enmanuel (0.01)
En-Ming
Enner
Ennery
Ennio
Ennis
Enno
Enobong Jeremiah
Enoc
Enoch (0.03)
Enock
Enoeht
Enorck
Enos (0.02)
Enosh
Enri
Enrice
Enrick (0.01)
Enrico (0.01)
Enrigue
Enrike
Enrique (0.20)
Enrique Alexander
Enrique-Ivan
Enriquejovani
Enrique-Manuel
Enriquez
Enris
Enrrigue
Enrrique
Enrry
Enshaal
Ensizziyo
Ensley
Enson
Enten
Enting
Enver
Envy
Enyang
Enyce
Enyze
Enzo (0.09)
Eoann
Eogan
Eoghain
Eoghan (0.01)
Eoin (0.01)

Eomer
Eon
Eonte
Eoseff
Eoys
Ephesians
Ephn
Ephraim (0.04)
Ephraim Tzvi
Ephram (0.01)
Ephrem
Ephriam
Ephrim
Ephrym
Epifanio
Epoo
Eppie
Epson
Equadzanere
Equan
Equaz
Equon
Er'marion
Er'mon
Era
Eracleo
Eragon
Eragorn
Erale
Erami
Eran
Erardo
Erasley
Erasmo (0.01)
Erasmus
Eraviano
Eraycheo
Erbey
Erbie
Erbin
Erblin
Erby
Erdenedalai
Erech
Eredin
Ereiron
Erek
Erem
Eren (0.01)
Ereon
Erez
Erfan
Erfaun

Ergar
Erges
Ergi
Eri
Eri K
Eri'on
Erias
Eriberto
Eric (3.03)
Eric Junior
Eric Michae
Eric Scott
Eric Trung
Eric Tyquonte
Eric'ki
Erica
Ericason
Ericberto
Ericc
Ericelle
Erich (0.02)
Erick (0.41)
Erick Junior
Erick Nathan
Erick-Alejandro
Erickana
Erick-Armando
Ericksen
Erickson
Eric-Martin
Ericnael
Ericpaul
Ericq
Eric-Simon
Ericson
Ericu
Eric-Vincent
Erie
Erieberto
Eriel
Erielle
Erieon
Eries
Erif
Erijae
Erik (0.43)
Erik Anthony
Erikami
Erikberto
Erik-Christian
Eriks
Erikson
Eriksyn

Erilinyth
Erimi
Erimola-Alfredo
Esara
Erin (0.01)
Erind
Erinson
Erinto Bulito
Erion (0.01)
Erionte
Eriq
Erique (0.01)
Eriren
Eris
Erius
Eriyen
Erjon
Erlan
Erlensky
Erlin
Erlind
Erlyn
Erlyns
Ermaan
Ermario
Ermarion
Ermel
Ermenegildo
Ermias
Ermin
Ermon
Ermuun
Ermyn
Ernad
Ernando
Ernanii
Ernell
Ernesly
Ernest (0.08)
Ernestly
Ernesto (0.11)
Ernie
Ernmanion
Ernsito
Ernst
Ernts
Erny
Ero
Erodney
Erodson
Erol
Eron
Eros (0.01)

Eros Neto
Eross
Erran
Errick
Errik
Errington
Errion
Errol (0.01)
Errol-Julio
Erroll
Erron
Ersham
Erskine
Erson
Ersonder
Erton
Ertugrul
Erubiel
Eruckson
Erustus
Ervan
Ervans
Erven
Ervens
Erviel
Ervieonta
Ervin (0.03)
Ervine
Ervins
Ervyn
Erwann
Erwin (0.01)
Erwing
Erwuin
Eryberto
Eryc
Eryck
Eryis
Eryk
Eryk Kamil
Eryn
Eryon
Eryx
Erza
Erzan
Esa
Esaam
Esaeyas
Esai (0.01)
Esaiah
Esaiahs
Esaias
Esaie

| | | | | | | |
|---|---|---|---|---|---|---|
| Esaiel | Esmic | Estevaun | Ethan-Charlie | Eudell | Evaristo | Evodio |
| Esaih | Esmin | Esteve | Ethaneal | Eudes | Evary | Evol |
| Esam | Esmir | Estevens | Ethanial | Eudyis | Evel | Evon *(0.01)* |
| Esar | Esmon | Estevin | Ethaniel *(0.01)* | Euel | Evelin | Evons |
| Esau *(0.01)* | Esmond | Estheban | Ethanielle | Eugene *(0.09)* | Evelio | Evren |
| Esaube | Esmrel | Estheben | Ethan-Isaac | Eugene David | Evelyn | Evrest |
| Esaul | Esnaider | Esthuardo | Ethan-James | Eugene-Gabriel | Evelyo | Evrett |
| Esaum | Esner | Estif | Ethann | Eugene-Olivier | Even *(0.01)* | Evrick |
| Esay | Esosa | Estin | Ethan-Patric | Eugenio *(0.01)* | Evence | Evrin |
| Esban | Espedito | Estive | Ethanson | Eugeniy | Evenn | Evrol |
| Esben | Espen *(0.01)* | Estiven | Ethanuel | Eujah | Evens *(0.01)* | Evsevio |
| Esber | Esperance | Estivin | Ethean | Eujay | Evensky | Evsey |
| Esbin | Espin | Estle | Ethen *(0.05)* | Eujene Joseph | Evenuel | Evyn *(0.01)* |
| Eschelon | Espn | Estlin | Ethen-Andrew | Eulises | Ever *(0.03)* | Evyn-Isaak |
| Escher | Espy | Eston *(0.01)* | Ether | Eulisis | Everade | Evynn |
| Escolastico | Espyn | Estuardo | Ethian | Eulisses | Everardo *(0.01)* | Ewald |
| Esdcas | Esra | Estyben | Ethien | Eulius | Everest | Ewan *(0.05)* |
| Esden | Esron | Estyn | Ethin *(0.01)* | Euloge | Everet | Ewardo |
| Esdram | Essac | Esvi | Ethinn | Eulogio | Everett *(0.15)* | Ewen |
| Esdras *(0.01)* | Essam | Esvin | Ethiur | Eun | Everett James | Ewing |
| Esdraz | Essamuel | Eswin | Ethon | Eunchelle | Everette | Ewonyé |
| Eseavian | Essay | Esyn | Ethren | Euoel | Everhett | Ex'ziriaun |
| Eseckiel | Essense | Etagio | Ethun | Eurie | Evering | Exaiver |
| Esequiel | Essex | Etai | Ethyan | Euriel | Everitt | Exander |
| Eset | Essey | Etan | Ethyenn | Euris | Everly | Exavier *(0.01)* |
| Esfren | Essiah | Etavian | Ethyn *(0.02)* | Euron | Everol | Exavion |
| Esgar | Essien | Etawn | Ethyne | Eusebio *(0.01)* | Everon | Excel |
| Esha | Esslin | Etay | Eti | Eustace | Everpaul | Excell |
| Eshaan *(0.01)* | Estaban | Etelberto | Etiene | Eusvin | Everret | Excelsius |
| Eshad | Estaben | Eternal | Étienne | Eutimio | Everrett | Exile |
| Eshai | Estafany | Eternity | Etienne *(0.16)* | Eutrevian | Everrstien | Exiquio |
| Eshan *(0.01)* | Estan | Ethaen | Etienne Bao | Euwin | Evers | Exivan |
| Eshander | Estarlyn | Ethan *(9.71)* | Etienne | Eva | Everson | Exodus |
| Eshaninder | Estavan | Ethan Alexander | Maximilian | Evain | Evert | Exon |
| Eshant | Estavon | Ethan Allan | Gabriel | Evan *(4.49)* | Everth | Expliss |
| Eshanth | Estavyon | Kippy | Etione | Evan Bryce | Everton | Exson |
| Eshaun | Esteaven | Ethan Andrew | Etka | Evan Kumar | Evertt | Exzard |
| Esher | Esteban *(0.16)* | Ethan Anthony | Etniel | Evander *(0.01)* | Evett | Exzarion |
| Eshton | Esteban Alexi | Ethan Carter | Eton | Evandro | Evette | Exzavian |
| Eshvar | Esteban Dario | Ethan | Etornam | Evangelion | Evgenia | Exzavier |
| Eshwar | Esteban Haby | Christophet | Etornam-Bright | Evangelo | Evhan | Exzavior |
| Eshwary | Estebane | Ethan Ella | Etoryan | Evangelos | Evi | Exzavious |
| Esiah | Estefano | Maxime | Etsahel | Evangolas | Evian | Exzavius |
| Esiquiel | Esteffano | Ethan Ezequiel | Ettore | Evan-Guy | Evin *(0.03)* | Exzayvia |
| Esius | Esteffon | Ethan Hayden | Etuk | Evan-Jace | Evincarel | Exzayvier |
| Eslin | Estela | Ethan Josh | Etuoku | Evan-Lee | Evinh | Ey'rie |
| Esly | Esten | Ethan Julian | Etzahel | Evan-Michael | Evion | Eyad |
| Esmael | Estephan | Ethan Kyle | Etzel | Evann *(0.01)* | Evioss | Eyal |
| Esmail | Estephanie | Ethan Luke | Eu'riqkus | Evanray | Evit | Eyan *(0.02)* |
| Esman | Estephe | Ethan Neftali | Euan | Evans *(0.01)* | Evitan | Eyas |
| Esme | Estephon | Ethan Zion | Eubene | Evanson | Eviyn | Eyasu |
| Esmeralda | Estevan *(0.04)* | Ethanael *(0.01)* | Eucar | Evanston | Evnel | Eybbie |
| Esmeraldo | Estevao | Ethan-Andre | Eucevio | Evantay | Evo | Eybi |

Eydon
Eyen
Eyevan
Eyhad
Eyiram
Eykker
Eymard
Eymeric
Eyn
Eyner
Eyoale
Eyob
Eyobell
Eyoel
Eyon
Eyosias
Eyosyas
Eyouel
Eyrah
Eysaia
Eysan
Eysaw
Eytan
Eythan (0.01)
Eythen
Eythin
Eythor
Eyual
Eyvin
Eyvind
Eyzaiah
Eyziah
Eyzic
Ezael
Ezai
Ezana (0.01)
Ezariah
Ezavier
Ezavious
Ezayah
Ezayvor
Ezbin
Ezechael-Synai
Ezechiel (0.01)
Ezeckhyel
Ezeckiel
Ezedrick
Ezeikeal
Ezeikiel
Ezekeal
Ezekeil
Ezekeul
Ezekhiel

Ezekial (0.01)
Ezekias
Ezekiel (0.31)
Ezekiel Joross
Ezekiel Wil
Ezekiel Xavier
Ezekiell
Ezekil
Ezekyel
Ezel
Ezell
Ezelle
Ezequeil
Ezequias
Ezequiel (0.08)
Ezera
Ezerarein
Ezeriah
Eziah
Eziekiell
Eziequel
Ezikiel
Ezinna
Ezio
Ezion
Eziquel
Eziquiel
Ezkiel
Ezman
Ezra (0.26)
Ezrael
Ezrah
Ezri
Ezriah
Ezriel (0.01)
Ezrith
Ezry
Ezykiel
Ezzadeen
Ezzard
Ezzat
Ezzykiel

~ F ~

F
F Wilson
Fa'bioan
Fa'keem
Fa'shawn
Faaiq

Faarid
Faaris
Faaruuf
Fabain
Fabbian Christyl
Faber
Fabian (0.18)
Fabiana
Fabian-Arturo
Fabian-Eduardo
Fabiano
Fabien (0.01)
Fabien-Zachary
Fabinio
Fabio (0.02)
Fabion
Fabiyan
Fable
Fabolous
Fabriano
Fabrice (0.02)
Fabrice-Gabriel
Fabricio (0.01)
Fabris
Fabrisio
Fabrisse
Fabrizio (0.01)
Fabrizzio
Fabrizzio
   Enrique
Fabron
Fabyan
Fabyian
Facundo (0.01)
Faddy
Fadel
Faden
Fadi
Fadi Rachid
Fadil
Fadl
Fadrelle
Fadul
Fady
Faebian
Faegan
Faelin
Faelong
Faez
Fahad (0.01)
Fahardo
Fahd
Fahed

Faheem (0.01)
Faheiim-Nafis
Fahim (0.01)
Fahmi
Fahrear
Faiben
Faien
Faimafili
Faine
Fainet
Faiq
Fairless
Fairley
Fairres
Faisal (0.01)
Faissal
Fait
Faith
Faiyaz
Faiz
Faizaan
Faizalikhan
Faizan
Faizhon
Faizon
Fakeem
Fakhir
Fakhri
Falco
Falcon
Falconer
Falkin
Fallando
Fallon
Fallou
Falmata
Falon
Falonte
Falyte
Famayne
Famer
Famere
Famous
Fan
Fanek
Fanes
Fannings
Fannon
Fanon
Fansico
Fanyang
Faolan
Faolino

Faouk
Faraan
Faraaz
Faraban
Farah
Farai
Faraj
Farajudin
Farako
Faraz
Farbod
Fardaad
Fardeen
Fardin
Fardy
Fareed
Farel
Farell
Faren
Fares (0.01)
Farezdq
Farhaan
Farhad
Farhan (0.01)
Farhat
Farheem
Farhuck
Farid (0.01)
Faridh
Faris (0.02)
Faris Munir
Fariss
Farjan
Farley
Farmaan
Farmanullah
Farnaam
Farnsisco
Faron
Farouk
Farouto
Farrakhan
Farrel
Farrell
Farrellton
Farrel-Noah
Farren
Farrior
Farris (0.01)
Farron
Faruk
Faruq
Faruz

Faryn
Farzaan
Farzad
Farzan
Faseeh
Fasial
Fassa
Fatbardh
Fate
Fateh
Fatehpal
Faten
Fathee
Fathi
Fathom
Fatlum
Faustin
Faustina
Faustino (0.01)
Fausto (0.01)
Fautino
Faven
Favian (0.01)
Favio
Favor
Favour
Fawaz
Fawwaz
Fawzi
Faxon
Fay
Fayad
Fayadh
Fayeon
Fayera
Fayez
Fayiz
Fay-J
Faysal
Fayt
Fayyaz
Fayzaan
Fayzan
Fayzon
Fazeel
Fazil
Fazillath
Fazine-Benaissa
Fazion
Fazl
Fearless
Fede
Fedel

Fedele
Federer
Federico (0.01)
Federrico
Fedhassa
Fedhi
Fedir
Fedjy
Fedno
Fedor
Fedrick
Fedy
Feedele
Feenix
Feguener
Fehoko
Fei
Fei Hong
Feisal
Fejzo
Fela
Felder
Felein
Feleite
Felice
Feliciano
Felicien
Felicity
Feliks
Felip
Felipe (0.11)
Felipe De Jesus
Felipe Nahem
Felippe
Félix (0.01)
Felix (0.54)
Felix Antoine
Felix Arvin
Felix III
Felix Jose
Felix Jose
   Huertas
Felix Liu Rene
Felix Mica
Felix Nicolas
Felix Olivier
Felix Samuel
Felix-Andre
Felix-Anthony
Felix-Antoine
   (0.04)
Felix-Antoyne
Felix-David

| | | | | | | |
|---|---|---|---|---|---|---|
| Felix-Gabriel | Fernardo | Finess | Flekjunior | Forest *(0.02)* | Franco *(0.04)* | Franqui |
| Felix-Luis | Ferozudin | Finesse | Fleming | Forrest *(0.04)* | Franco-Dimitri | Fransado |
| Felix-Olivier | Ferrell | Finest | Flen | Forrest Junior | François | Fransico |
| Felixs | Ferrill | Fineus | Fletcher *(0.05)* | Forrest Luke | Francois *(0.03)* | Fransisco *(0.01)* |
| Felix-Xavier | Ferris | Finian *(0.01)* | Flex-Sammy | Forrest Rainbow | Francois III | Franskelly |
| Feliz | Ferro | Finias | Flin | Forrester | Francois Jr | Fransley |
| Feliziano | Ferrous | Finland | Flinn | Fortino | Francois Nicolas | Fransz |
| Fellipe | Ferzulis | Finlay *(0.02)* | Flint | Fortner | Francois | Frantisek |
| Felong | Fesshayé | Finley *(0.06)* | Flip | Fortress | Someth | Frantz *(0.01)* |
| Felton | Fethi | Finn *(0.16)* | Flomo | Fortunato | Francois Xavier | Frantzci |
| Felton James | Fetthi | Finnbar | Flomy | Fortunatus | Francois-Emile | Frantzley |
| Felty | Feuter | Finnbarr | Floran | Foster *(0.03)* | Francois-Xavier | Franyariel |
| Felyx | Fewcell | Finnean | Florence | Foti | *(0.01)* | Franz *(0.01)* |
| Femi | Feyisayo | Finneas | Florencio | Fotis | Franddy | Fraquan |
| Fen | Feysal | Finnegan *(0.07)* | Florent *(0.01)* | Fouad | Franden | Fraser *(0.01)* |
| Fender | Fhabian | Finneghan | Florentino | Foussenyni | Frandon | Frashawn |
| Fenel | Fhenyx | Finnen | Florenz | Fox *(0.02)* | Frandray | Frashod |
| Feng | Fibian | Finnén | Florian | Foxtyn | Frandy | Frashon |
| Fenick | Fida | Finneus | Floriano | Foxx | Frandys | Frashua |
| Fenix | Fidel *(0.02)* | Finnian *(0.02)* | Angelino | Foy | Franek | Frasier |
| Fenjy | Fidelio | Finnias | Floriberto | Fozi | Franey | Fraysson |
| Fenley | Fidencio | Finnigan *(0.01)* | Florin | Fra'juan | Frangel | Frazer |
| Fenn | Fielding | Finnlee | Floryan | Frale | Frangisko | Frazier |
| Fennton | Fields | Finnleigh | Flotarco | Fran | Franisco | Fre'darious |
| Fenris | Fige | Finnley *(0.01)* | Floyd *(0.03)* | Fran'quez | Franjo | Fre'tavion |
| Fentin | Figueroa | Fintan | Floyderria | Franc-David | Frank *(0.36)* | Fred *(0.04)* |
| Fenton *(0.01)* | Fiifi | Fionn *(0.01)* | Flynn *(0.02)* | France | Frank Allan | Fredarious |
| Fenwick | Fikret | Fionnian | Flynt | Frances | Frank Asa | Fred- |
| Feodor | Fila | Fionntan | Focus | Francesco *(0.06)* | Frank Mickey | Christopher |
| Fephilipe | Filaberto | Fiorente | Foday | Francesco David | Frank William | Fredd |
| Fequer | Filadelfo | Firas | Fode | Franchescko | Franka | Fred-David |
| Feran | Filbert | Firdavs | Fodie | Franchez | Frank-Anderson | Freddell |
| Feras | Filberto | Firman | Fodil | Francis *(0.19)* | Frankay | Fredderic |
| Ferd | Fildreg | Firoz | Fofana | Francis Enrique | Franke | Fredderick |
| Ferdinand | Filiberto | Fischer *(0.02)* | Folger | Francis Gerard | Frankey | Fredderius |
| Feree | Filimon | Fisher *(0.05)* | Foli | Francis Martin | Franki | Fredderyle |
| Ferencz | Filionel | Fisk | Folis | Francis Patrick | Frankie *(0.06)* | Freddi |
| Fergus | Filip *(0.02)* | Fitchpatrick | Folson | Castillo | Frank-Johnson | Freddie *(0.03)* |
| Ferguson | Filipe | Fitta | Fomo-Beri | Francis- | Franklee | Freddis |
| Ferhat | Filippe | Fitz | Foncedric | Alexandre | Frankli | Freddrick |
| Ferlin | Filippo | Fitzroy | Fontaine | Francisco *(1.36)* | Franklin *(0.17)* | Freddricka |
| Ferlundo | Filiverto | Fitzwilliam | Fontane | Francis-James | Franklin-Brian | Freddrion |
| Ferman | Fillip | Fixin | Fontané | Franciso | Frankly | Freddy *(0.06)* |
| Fermando | Fillipp | Fiyinfolu | Fontious | Franck | Franklyn *(0.01)* | Freddy |
| Fermin *(0.01)* | Filogonio | Fiyinfoluwa | Fontroy | Franckenson | Franklynn | Alessandro |
| Fernado | Finan | FJ | Fonz | Franck-Hali | Frankneal | Freddy- |
| Fernado Jose | Finbar | Flabi | Fonzo | Franck-Herman | Franko | Alejandro |
| Fernand | Finbarr | Fladimyr | Fopefoluwa | Franck-Hubert | Franktavious | Freddy-David |
| Fernandes | Findlay *(0.01)* | Flamur | Ford *(0.01)* | Franck-Oliver | Franky *(0.01)* | Freddys |
| Fernandez | Findley | Flatron | Forde | Franck-Olyvier | Frankye | Fredell |
| Fernandito | Fineas | Flavie | Fordham | Franck-Sinclair | Franoll | Frédéric |
| Fernando *(1.33)* | Finegan | Flavien | Foreman | Francky | Franpaul | Frederic *(0.07)* |
| Fernando-Jesus | Finely | Flavio *(0.01)* | Fores | Franclyn | Franqiz | |

| | | | | | | |
|---|---|---|---|---|---|---|
| Frederic | Frenando | Fysher | Gabriel Anthony | Gady | Galaad M | Gardner |
| Antoine | Frenchie | | Gabriel Antonio | Gaebrial | Galan | Gardon |
| Frederic- | Fresean | | Gabriel Bennett | Gaebriel | Galantae | Gared |
| Alexandre | Fretrez | ~ G ~ | Gabriel Chanel | Gaege | Galdino | Garek |
| Frédérick | Freud | | Gabriel Eduardo | Gaël | Gale | Garen (0.01) |
| Frederick (0.23) | Freud-Williams | G Shan | Gabriel Emilio | Gael (0.12) | Galed | Garet (0.01) |
| Frederick | Freycer | G'avani | Gabriel Jacques | Gaelan | Galen (0.02) | Gareth (0.02) |
| Fernando | Freyer | G'iana | Gabriel Jaw | Gael-Darbens | Galiel | Garett (0.04) |
| Frederick- | Freyser | G'iovanni | Gabriel Manuel | Gaelen | Galilei | Garette |
| Nicolas | Friederich | G'isaiah | Gabriel Michael | Gael-Francisco | Galipu | Garfield |
| Frederico | Friedrich | G'mari | Gabriel Nathan | Gaerick | Gallant | Garhet |
| Frederic-Olivier | Frierson | G'marion | Gabriel | Gaetan | Gallau | Garhett |
| Frédérik | Frindly | G'onni | Normand | Gaetano (0.01) | Gallen | Garhyson |
| Frederik (0.01) | Frisco | G'raius | Gabriel Oliver | Gaethan | Galliher | Gari |
| Frederik- | Frisli | G'ron | Gabriel Simon- | Gaevin | Galo | Garian |
| Alexandre | Fritz (0.01) | G'shon | Pierre | Gagan | Galveston | Garick |
| Frederique | Fritzgerald | G'von | Gabriel Sylvain | Gagandeep | Galvin | Garid |
| Frederyk | Froilan | G'zareon | Gabriel Zion | Gaganjit | Galy | Garik |
| Fredginald | Frost | Ga | Gabriela | Gaganpreet | Galyn | Garikoitz |
| Fredi (0.01) | Froylan | Ga'darius | Gabriel-Alou | Gage (1.15) | Gamada | Garin (0.01) |
| Fredic | Fruma | Ga'khy | Gabriel-Cedric | Gage Allan | Gamael | Garion |
| Fredico | Fu'ad | Ga'kyah | Gabriele (0.01) | Gage | Gamal | Garionte |
| Fredie | Fuad | Ga'varion | Gabriel-Evan | Christophe | Gamaliel (0.01) | Garis |
| Fredis | Fuamai | Ga'vontae | Gabriel-Isioma | Gage Kehlii | Gamari | Garison |
| Fredler | Fudayl | Gaard | Gabriell | Gage Reily | Gamarion | Garit |
| Fredley | Fudil | Gaas | Gabriella | Gage-Allen | Gambit | Garitt |
| Fred-Louis | Fue | Gabariel | Gabrielle (0.01) | Gagge | Gamble | Garjuwan |
| Fredly | Fue Chee | Gabby | Gabriel-Michael | Gagou | Gamier | Garland (0.01) |
| Fredmurphy | Fuechee | Gabe (0.03) | Gabriel-Ngoma | Gahannon | Gamylo | Garlen |
| Fredner | Fuechi | Gabeiel | Gabriel-Prince | Gahel | Ganard | Garlon |
| Fredric | Fulbert | Gaberael | Gabriel-Roi | Gah-Ho | Ganasham | Garlyam |
| Fredrich | Fuller | Gaberal | Gabrien | Gahqui | Gandan | Garnar |
| Fredrick (0.05) | Fulton | Gaberial (0.01) | Gabril | Gahvin | Ganden | Garnell |
| Fredrico | Fundador | Gaberiel (0.01) | Gabriyel | Gaibral | Gandhi | Garner (0.01) |
| Fredrik | Funtain | Gaberiele | Gabriyel Imad | Gaibrial | Ganen | Garnet |
| Fredrion | Furii | Gaberil | Gabryal | Gaige (0.07) | Ganesh | Garnett |
| Fredryck | Furious | Gaberille | Gabryeal | Gaije | Gangriel | Garnier |
| Fred-Shema | Furkan | Gabin | Gabryel (0.01) | Gaijin | Ganmarcos | Garo |
| Fredshondra | Furnanza | Gabino (0.01) | Gaby (0.01) | Gailen | Gannan | Garold |
| Fredson | Furnell | Gable | Gacien | Gailyn | Gannon (0.06) | Garon |
| Fredy (0.04) | Furqan | Gaborik | Gacin | Gaines | Gannyn | Garrad |
| Fredy | Furquan | Gabreal | Gacolby | Gairen | Ganon | Garran |
| Emmanuel | Furrell | Gabreil (0.01) | Gad | Gairie | Gantre | Garreion |
| Fredys | Further | Gabrel | Gadan | Gais | Gantt | Garren (0.01) |
| Free | Future | Gabreyll | Gaddiel | Gaitlin | Ganyn | Garret (0.10) |
| Freedom | Fuya | Gabrial (0.02) | Gade | Gaiton | Gaoussou | Garrete |
| Freelin | Fwm | Gabrian | Gaden | Gaius | Garardo | Garreth |
| Freelyn | Fyheem | Gabrieal | Gadge | Gaje | Garbriel | Garretson |
| Freeman (0.01) | Fynn (0.01) | Gabriel (5.73) | Gadi | Gajé | Garcia | Garrett (1.09) |
| Freeston | Fynneus | Gabriel A | Gadiahwan | Gajen | Garcia | Garrett Logan |
| Freiman | Fynnian | Gabriel Adolfo | Gadiel (0.01) | Gakuto | Hernandez | Garrette |
| Fremarion | Fynnley | Gabriel Aime | Gadon | Gal | Gardener | Garrey |
| Fremont | Fyodor | Gabriel Alex | Gadriel | Galaad | Gardiah | Garric |

| | | | | | | |
|---|---|---|---|---|---|---|
| Garrick (0.01) | Gatlyn | Gayvion | Gemarkus | Geoni | Gerald-Gunder | Germey |
| Garrien | Gator | Gazi | Gemarri | Geor'rion | Gerald-Michael | Germill |
| Garrik | Gattin | Gbemileke-T | Gemini | Geordan | Geraldo (0.01) | Germin |
| Garrin (0.01) | Gattlin | Ge Ho | Gemmanuel | Geordanny | Gerald-Oliver | Germitch |
| Garrionn | Gatwech | Ge'land | Gemoi | Geordany | Geramiah | Germont |
| Garris | Gaudencio | Ge'quais | Genari | Geordi | Gérard | Germontae |
| Garrison (0.06) | Gaudensio | Ge'shaun | Genariyon | Geordin | Gerard (0.02) | Germonte |
| Garrit | Gauge (0.06) | Gean | Genaro (0.01) | Geordon | Gerard Jr | Germycah |
| Garritt | Gaurav | Geancarlos | Genarro | Geordy | Gerardo (0.15) | Gerold |
| Garrity | Gaurinandan | Gearald-Matt | Genavi | Georffrey | Gerardo Trae | Gerome |
| Garron | Gautam (0.01) | Gearldo | Genc | George (0.92) | Gerardo-Emmanuel | Geron |
| Garry (0.02) | Gautham | Gearóid | Gendri | George Irvin | Gerasimos | Geronimo (0.01) |
| Garryn | Gautom | Geary | Gendry | George Mark | Geraud | Gerquon |
| Garryt | Gavan (0.02) | Geatano | Gene (0.01) | George Scott | Gerber | Gerran |
| Garson | Gavann | Geavoni | Gene'vion | George W | Ger-Briyantt | Gerrard |
| Garth (0.01) | Gaved | Geavonie | Genenoe | George Washington | Gere | Gerraud |
| Garv | Gaven (0.08) | Geavonni | Geneo | George William | Gereco | Gerred |
| Garva | Gavens | Gebari | General | George-Adams | Gerek | Gerrel |
| Garvan | Gavenson | Ged | Genesis (0.02) | George-Emile | Gerell | Gerrell |
| Garvani | Gaveriel | Gedalias | Genevieve | George-Etienne | Gerelle | Gerremy |
| Garvens | Gavian | Gedalye | Genin | Georges (0.01) | Geremi | Gerren |
| Garver | Gavianni | Geddwin | Genini | Georges Michael | Geremiah | Gerret |
| Garvey | Gavien | Geddy | Genis | Georgi | Geremias | Gerrick |
| Garvin | Gavin (4.42) | Gede | Genisis | Georgie | Geremie | Gerrie |
| Gary (0.27) | Gavin Keshean | Gedeon | Genji | Georging | Geremy (0.01) | Gerrik |
| Garyan | Gavin Seth | Gedmon | Genki | Georgio | Geret | Gerrion |
| Garyel | Gavin Thomas | Gedolya | Gennaro (0.01) | Georgios (0.01) | Gergo | Gerrious |
| Garyn (0.01) | Gavindeep | Gedontae | Genner | Georgy | Gerhard | Gerrit (0.01) |
| Garyoun | Gavinjit | Gee | Genneth | Georkiereon | Gerhart | Gerrod |
| Garyse | Gavin-Krishan | Gee'zon | Geno (0.01) | Georrell | Gerias | Gerrode |
| Garytt | Gavinmarc | Gee-Hun | Geno-Amare | Georshun | Geric | Gerrold |
| Garyus | Gavin-Micheal | Geeno | Genowa | Georvon | Gerick | Gerron |
| Gary-Wayne | Gavinn | Geeovanny | Genri | Geoterio | Gerico | Gerry (0.01) |
| Gasahn | Gavino (0.01) | Geepein | Genry | Geovani (0.01) | Geriel | Gerryiki |
| Gasim | Gavins | Geepure | Genser | Geovanie | Gerik | Gerryl |
| Gasnell | Gavinsky | Geetan | Gensi | Geovanni (0.02) | Gerimyah | Gerrymia |
| Gaspar (0.01) | Gavinveer | Geethan | Gensing | Geovannie | Gerius | Gersh |
| Gaspard | Gavire | Geevon | Gent | Geovanny (0.01) | Gerjan | Gershawn |
| Gasper | Gavlin | Geffrey | Genti | Geovany | Gerkees | Gershon |
| Gassan | Gavon (0.01) | Gehad | Gentrit | Geovon | Gerlen | Gerslen |
| Gast | Gavrie | Gehrig (0.01) | Gentry (0.01) | Geovoni | Germahad | Gerson (0.02) |
| Gastero | Gavriel (0.02) | Gehu | Geo | Geovonie | Germain | Gerval |
| Gaston (0.01) | Gavril | Geianni | Geodano | Geovonni | Germaine (0.01) | Gervaris |
| Gaston Gabriel | Gavrilo | Geion | Geoff | Geovonnie | Germainn | Gervens |
| Gastoné | Gavyn (0.10) | Geir | Geoffery | Geovontae | German (0.04) | Gervensky |
| Gasvin | Gavynn | Gekai | Geoffrey (0.04) | Ger | Germane | Gerver |
| Gatari | Gawain | Gelacio | Geoffroy | Ger'monte | Germani | Gerveyl |
| Gates | Gawen | Gelardz | Geoffroy Leon | Geraboni | Germany | Gervis |
| Gatewood | Gaydens | Geleio | Geoffry | Geral | Germari | Gervon |
| Gatian | Gaylen | Gelson | Geogory | Gerald (0.13) | Germarion | Gervonté |
| Gatlen | Gaylon | Gelvin | Geohany | Gerald Jr | Germaun | Gerwin |
| Gatlin (0.02) | Gaylord | Gemain | Geomar | Geraldarius | Germel | Gery |
| Gatlun | Gaynor | Gemari | Geonas | | | Gerysayn |

| | | | | | | |
|---|---|---|---|---|---|---|
| Gerzon | Gian Franco | Giavonne | Gilmoe Frankie | Giovanny (0.04) | Glace | Goku |
| Gesean | Gian Luca | Giavonni | Gilmore | Giovans | Gladimir | Golden |
| Geshawn | Gian Maria | Gibb's | Gilmoure | Giovantae | Gladwin | Goldskey |
| Gesser | Gian Markus | Gibbon | Gilson | Giovany (0.01) | Glady | Goldtooth |
| Gessy | Gian-Carlo | Gibbs | Gilyard | Giovauni | Glarry | Gomez |
| Gesu | Giancarlo (0.08) | Gibran | Gimeryo | Giovi | Glavin | Gomin |
| Getty | Gian-Carlos | Gibril | Ginno | Giovoni | Glayton | Gonsalez |
| Getzemani | Giancarlos | Gibron | Gino (0.04) | Giovonie | Gleb | Gonsalo |
| Gevari | (0.01) | Gibsen | Ginovanni | Giovonii | Gleen | Gontae |
| Gevarion | Gianco | Gibson (0.04) | Gintautas | Giovonni (0.02) | Glela | Gontran |
| Gevin | Gianfelix | Gicobbe | Gio | Giovonnie | Glen (0.04) | Gonzaleus |
| Gevino | Gianfranco | Giddeon | Gioacchino | Giovonny | Glen Alan | Gonzalo (0.02) |
| Gevon | (0.01) | Gidean | Gioachimo | Giovonte | Glen Cordell | Goodston |
| Gevongio | Giang | Gideon (0.09) | Gioani | Giovony | Glenallen | Goodwin |
| Gevonie | Giangelo | Gideon-Ephr | Gioanni | Giovvani | Glenard | Gopesh |
| Gevonni | Giani | Gidion | Gioantonio | Giovvanni | Glendal | Gopinath |
| Geyhssel | Gianie | Gielle | Giobert | Girard | Glendall | Goran |
| Gezer | Giankarlo | Gieroe | Gioivani | Girdhar | Glendan | Gordan |
| Ghabriel | Gian-Luca | Giesis | Giomar | Giresun | Glendarius | Gordei |
| Ghadi | Gianluca (0.04) | Giezi | Gion | Giridhari | Glendon (0.01) | Gordey |
| Ghage | Gianlucas | Gifford | Gione | Girigovardhana | Glene | Gordie |
| Gha-Is | Gianlucca | Giftson | Gionell | Girish | Glenford | Gordon (0.07) |
| Ghaleb | Gianluigi | Gihon | Gioney | Girmy | Glenmore | Gorge |
| Ghalib | Gianluka | Gihovani | Gionner | Girum | Glenn (0.08) | Gorgies |
| Ghamal | Gianmarco | Gikeelyn | Gionni (0.01) | Girvin Ellis | Glenn Adrian | Gorje |
| Ghammald | (0.01) | Gil | Gionnie | Gisaiah | Glennie | Gorman- |
| Ghanim | Gianmark | Gilad | Gionté | Gisel | Glenwood | Gonzalez |
| Gharrel | Gian-Marko | Gïlan | Giordan | Giselle | Glit | Gorvin |
| Ghassan | Gianmatteo | Gilani | Giordanio | Gislain | Glodensky | Gosiah |
| Ghaven | Giann | Gilbert (0.05) | Giordanni | Gissel | Glonder | Gotti |
| Ghazi | Giann Carlo | Gilbert Devin | Giordanny | Gitais | Glyn | Gourav |
| Ghe-Hori | Gianna | Gilbert Isaac | Giordano (0.01) | Giulian | Glynn | Govani |
| Gherin | Gianncarlo | Gilberto (0.04) | Giordin | Giuliani | Glynne | Govanni |
| Gherry | Gianncarlos | Gilby | Giorgi | Giuliano (0.02) | Glysandy | Govanny |
| Ghilas | Gianne | Gilcyane | Giorgio (0.01) | Giulio | Gmarion | Governor |
| Ghiles | Gianni (0.10) | Gildardo | Giorgios | Giuseppe (0.04) | Go | Govind |
| Ghiovani | Gianni Arnel | Giles (0.01) | Giorgos | Giusseppe | Goal | Govinda |
| Ghislain | Giannii | Gilford | Giorgyo | Antonil | Goap | Govindan |
| Ghivon | Giannluca | Gili | Giosepp | Giustino | Gobind | Gowain |
| Ghufran | Gianno | Gill | Gioser | Givanni | Goblaije | Gowan |
| Ghulam | Gianny | Gillam | Giouanni | Givari | Godefroy | Gowesh |
| Muhammad | Gianpaolo | Gillan | Giovan | Given | Godfrey | Goy |
| Abdurrahman | Gian-Paul | Gillean | Giovane | Givenson | Godric | Grabiei |
| Ghulam- | Gianpier | Gillermo | Giovaney | Giveson | Godsend | Grabiel |
| Mustafa | Gianpiero | Gilles | Giovangel | Givoanny | Godson | Grabriele |
| Gi Chan | Gianpierre | Gilles III | Giovani (0.04) | Givon | Godspower | Grace |
| Gi'nye | Gian-Pietro | Gillespie | Giovanne | Givonn | Godswill | Gracen (0.01) |
| Giacomo (0.01) | Gianthomas | Gillian | Giovanni (1.28) | Givonni | Godwin (0.01) | Graceson |
| Giage | Giarley | Gillien | Giovanni | Givonnie | Goerge | Gracian |
| Giampaolo | Gia-Thien Jetli | Gillispie | Eleazar | Gizelle | Gogo | Gracie |
| Gian (0.03) | Giauluca | Gilman | Giovanni Jesus | Gjin | Gohan | Gracin (0.01) |
| Gian Angelo | Giavanni | Gilmen | Giovanni Kiou | Gjorn | Goi | Gracin Abel |
| Gian Carlo | Giavon | Gilmer | Giovannie (0.01) | Gjuro | Goin | Liam |

| | | | | | | |
|---|---|---|---|---|---|---|
| Gracyn | Graston | Gresham | Guang Yu | Guiseppe | Gurion | Gurshawn |
| Graden (0.01) | Grasyn | Greshaun | Guanin | Guiseppi | Guritman | Gursimar |
| Gradey | Grath | Gresi | Guardian | Guitano | Guriva | Gurtaj |
| Gradi | Gratton | Gretchen | Gudiel | Guitherme | Gurjaap | Gurtej |
| Gradin | Gray (0.01) | Grevon | Gudmundur | Guivard | Gurjap | Guruttam |
| Gradon | Gray Alan | Grevy | Guedel | Guivens | Gurjeet | Guruyugan |
| Grady (0.16) | Grayam | Grey (0.02) | Guener | Gulamhusain | Gurjeevan | Gurv |
| Gradyn | Graycen | Greycen | Guerbens | Guled | Gurjot | Gurvansh |
| Grae | Graycin | Greyden | Guerdy | Guleid | Gurjovan | Gurveer (0.01) |
| Graecen | Graydan | Greydin | Guerian | Gulfaam | Gurkamal | Gurveet |
| Graeden | Grayden (0.02) | Greydon | Guerin | Guliano | Gurkaman | Gurvir (0.01) |
| Graedon | Graydon (0.02) | Greylan | Guering | Gulius | Gurkaran (0.01) | Gurwin |
| Graem | Grayer | Greylin | Guerin-Junior | Gullian | Gurkarn | Guryash |
| Graeme (0.02) | Grayford | Greyling | Guerley | Gullick | Gurkirat | Gus (0.04) |
| Graesen | Graylan | Greysen (0.01) | Guerlin | Gulraj | Gurkirit | Gussan |
| Graeson | Graylin | Greysn | Guerra | Gulyano | Gurlagan | Gusset |
| Grafton | Grayling | Greyson (0.11) | Guerrby | Guma | Gurlal | Gust Tyler |
| Graham (0.23) | Graysen (0.01) | Greysun | Guerreros | Gumaro | Gurmaan | Gustabo |
| Graham- | Graysin | Grier | Guerric | Gume | Gurman (0.01) | Gustaf |
| Michael | Grayson (0.40) | Griffen (0.02) | Guershon | Gunar | Gurmandeep | Gustav (0.01) |
| Grahm | Graysun | Griffey | Guersley | Gunder | Gurmat | Gustave (0.01) |
| Grahme | Graython | Griffin (0.47) | Guerson | Guneet | Gurmohit | Gustavius |
| Grahmm | Grayton | Griffinn | Guevany | Guner | Gurmoney | Gustavo (0.17) |
| Graicely | Graziel | Griffith | Guevinton | Gungor | Gurmukh | Gustavus |
| Graicen | Gre'shawn | Griffon | Guhan | Gunjan | Gurmun | Gustie |
| Graiden | Greby | Griffyn | Guian | Gunnar (0.12) | Gurn | Gustin |
| Graidey | Greco | Grifon | Guidado | Gunnarr | Gurnaib | Guston |
| Graidyn | Gredis | Griggs | Guidman | Gunner (0.11) | Gurnaj | Gustovo |
| Grainger | Greeir | Grigore | Guido | Gunnor | Gurnawab | Guthrie |
| Graisen | Green | Grimaldi | Guidry | Guntas | Gurneel | Guutu |
| Graison | Greenwood | Grimm | Guifferson | Guntash | Gurnell | Guy (0.04) |
| Gralen | Greer | Griphon | Guignarldo | Gunter | Gurnie | Guy-Akim |
| Gralyn | Greffin | Grissom | Guile | Gunther | Gurnoor | Guyaume |
| Gram | Greg (0.01) | Gron | Guilfort | Gun-Woo | Gurpartap | Guyaume- |
| Gramenos | Gregary | Grosvin | Guilherm | Gunwoo | Gurparwesh | Philippe |
| Gramm | Gregg (0.01) | Grover | Guilherme | Guos | Gurpinder | Guyford |
| Gran | Greggory (0.01) | Gruffydd | (0.01) | Guquory | Gurpreet | Guy-Leocardy |
| Grandell | Greglin | Gryffin | Guiliano | Curami | Gurprit | Guyllaume |
| Grandin | Grego | Gryffon | Guillaum | Gurarman | Gurraj | Guy-Marie |
| Grandt | Gregoire (0.01) | Gryffyn | Guillaume | Gurbaksh | Gurrajan | Guyn |
| Granger | Gregor | Gryphen | (0.11) | Gurbaz | Gurroop | Guyo |
| Granison | Gregori | Gryphin | Guillaume- | Gurcharan | Gursagar | Guyon |
| Granite | Gregorie | Gryphon (0.01) | Antoine | Gurcharankama | Gursahib | Guyton |
| Grant (1.05) | Gregorio (0.01) | Gryphyn | Guillermo | lpreet | Gursaje | Guyvan |
| Grant Alexander | Gregory (0.57) | Guachi | (0.07) | Gurchetan | Gursevak | Guywini |
| Grant Frederick | Gregory James | Guadalupe | Guillermo | Gurdarshan | Gursevek | Gvon |
| Sazon | Gregory Troy | (0.02) | Abraham | Gurdas | Gursewak | Gvonny |
| Grantham | Gregoryontay | Guage | Guilmer | Gurdeep | Gurshaan (0.01) | Gwakisa |
| Grantland | Gregory-Rolfe | Gualberto | Guiness | Gurdeya | Gurshabd | Gwaloan |
| Grantley | Gregshaun | Gualterio | Guinov | Gurdhian | Gurshan (0.02) | Gwendolyn |
| Granton | Gregson | Guan | Guion | Gurek | Gursharan | Gwillym |
| Granville | Greimen | Guanar | Guiosmar | Gurik | Gursharn | Gwilym |
| Grason | Greiner | Guang | Guiseann | Gurinder | Gurshaun | Gwon Woo |

Gwyn
Gwynyth
Gy'ayire
Gyanlucca
Gyann
Gyanni
Gyasi
Gybram
Gybran
Gye'eontai
Gylind
Gym
Gynner
Gyon
Gyslain
Gyson
Gyu

~ H ~

H
H Caston
Ha
Ha'sauni
Ha'seem
Ha'sson
Haadi
Haakan
Haaken
Haakon
Haamir
Haani
Haaris
Haaroon
Haashir
Haba
Hababi
Habacuc
Habakkuk
Haben
Habib
Habib Allah
Habib Junior
Habib-Allah
Habiballah
Habibllah
Habibullah
Habishai
Hachel
Hachem
Hachim
Haci-Omer

Hack
Hackeem
Hadan
Hadara
Haddan
Hadden (0.01)
Hadder
Haddin
Haddis
Haddix
Haddon
Hadee
Haden (0.06)
Haden-Zander
Hadeon
Hadey
Hadi (0.03)
Hadi Jaheim
Hadif
Hadin
Hadirudeen
Hadler
Hadley (0.01)
Hadly
Hadon
Hadrian (0.01)
Hadrien
Hadryan
Hady
Hadyen
Hadyn (0.01)
Haeden (0.01)
Haedin
Haedon
Haedrian
Haedyn
Hael
Haelix
Haelow
Haeyoung
Hafeez
Hafese
Hafi
Hafid
Hafiz
Hagan (0.01)
Hagen (0.03)
Haggard
Haggen
Hagin
Hah
Hai
Haidan

Haidar
Haiden (0.06)
Haiden-
   Alexander
Haider (0.01)
Haidin
Haidon
Haidy
Haidyn (0.01)
Haig
Haik
Haikiem
Hail
Hailey
Hailu Kidane
Haina
Hainan
Haipeng
Hairo
Haisten
Haiston
Haitam
Haitham
Haj Mohamed
Hajari
Haji
Hakam
Hakan
Hakar
Hakara
Hakeem (0.02)
Hakeim
Hakiem
Hakim (0.02)
Hakimuddin
Hakyhm
Hakym
Hal
Halas
Halayn
Halbert
Halbest
Halcon
Haldeine
Halden
Hale (0.01)
Haleem
Halen (0.01)
Halet
Haley
Halian
Halikson
Halim

Halimou
Halis
Hall
Halle
Hallie
Hallston
Halsey
Halston
Haluk
Halvor
Hamaali
Hamad
Hamada
Hamadi
Hamady
Hamam
Hamas
Hamath
Hamaz
Hamdael
Hamdan
Hamdi
Hamdia
Hamdija
Hamed
Hamed Noreyni
Hameda
Hameed
Hameem
Hamelton
Hamid
Hamidou
Hamidu
Hamiltom
Hamilton (0.01)
Hamim
Hamir
Hamish
Hammad
Hammam
Hammed
Hammond
Hammza
Hamo
Hamodd
Hamond
Hamood
Hamp
Hamptom
Hampton (0.02)
Hamraj
Hamsa (0.01)
Hamse

Hamza (0.11)
Hamzah (0.01)
Hamze
Hamzeh
Hamzh
Han
Hanad (0.01)
Hanae
Hananeel
Hanani
Hananiah
Hancsy
Handel
Hander
Handley
Handsome
Handson
Handy
Hane
Haneef (0.01)
Haneif
Haner
Hani
Hanief
Haniel
Hanif (0.01)
Hanish
Hank (0.03)
Hankama
Hanley
Hanlon
Hannael
Hannah
Hannan
Hanner
Hannes
Hannibal
Hanniel
Hannigan
Hanns
Hanoi
Hanon
Hanrik
Hans (0.03)
Hans Alexandre
Hans-Benjamin
Hansel
Hansen (0.01)
Hansley
Hansol
Hansom
Hanson
Hanssel

Hantoni
Hantouli
Hantz
Hanuel
Hanul
Hanwen
Hanyao
Hanyer
Hanyu
Hanz
Hanzalah
Hanzla
Hao
Haoran
Haotian
Haowei
Haoxiang
Happy
Har
Harace
Harah
Harald
Haralmbos
Haran
Harandesh
Hararjun
Haratio
Haraum
Harbanjot
Harbin
Harbir
Harbor
Harbson
Harchetan
Harcourt
Hardeep
Harden
Hardhik
Hardil
Hardin
Harding
Hardley
Hardy
Hareet
Harein
Harekam
Harel
Haren
Haresh
Hargun
Hari
Harikrishna
Harilaos

Harim
Harin
Harinder
Hariram
Haris (0.01)
Harisaran
Harish
Harishan
Harishanth
Harison
Harit
Harith
Harjaap
Harjan
Harjap
Harjas
Harjasjit
Harjeevan
Harjinder
Harjit
Harjivan
Harjoban
Harjobanjit
Harjodh
Har-Jordan
Harjot (0.01)
Harjoth
Harjyn
Harkabir
Harkamal
Harkaran
Harkarn
Harkavin
Harkeerat
Harkeet
Harkirat
Harkirt
Harl Jabez
Harlam
Harlan (0.02)
Harland
Harlee (0.01)
Harleem
Harlem (0.01)
Harlen (0.01)
Harley (0.16)
Harley Sherman
Harlie
Harlin
Harlis
Harlon
Harlos
Harlow

Harlowe
Harlyn
Harm
Harman *(0.02)*
Harmanav
Harmandeep
Harmanjeet
Harmanjot
Harmanpreeet
Harmeet
Harmen
Harmilan
Harmn
Harmohit
Harmon *(0.01)*
Harnishan
Harnoor
Harol
Harold *(0.10)*
Harold Huan
Haron
Haronkar
Haroon *(0.01)*
Haroun
Harpartaap
Harparvann
Harper *(0.04)*
Harper-Gene
Harpratap
Harpreet
Harqua
Harrattanbir
Harrel
Harrell
Harrendiran
Harrie
Harrigan
Harrin
Harris *(0.03)*
Harrison *(0.51)*
Harrisson
Harristan
Harron
Harry *(0.15)*
Harryson
Harsahib
Harsajjan
Harsarwan
Harsehaj
Harsh *(0.01)*
Harsha
Harshaan
Harshad

Harshal
Harshan
Harshavardhan
Harshawn
Harshdeep
Harshil
Harshit
Harshith
Harshiv
Harshpreet
Harshvir
Harsimrat
Harsith
Harsujal
Harsukh
Hart
Hartaj
Harte
Hartej
Hartford
Hartley
Hartwell
Hartwick
Haru
Haruhi
Haruki
Harun
Haruto
Haruyuki
Harveen
Harveer
Harvell
Harvery
Harvest
Harvey *(0.05)*
Harviell
Harvier
Harvin
Harvir
Harvon
Harvrinder
Harvy
Harvyn
Hasaan
Hasadiah
Hasan *(0.02)*
Hasani
Hasanpreet
Hasauhn
Hasber
Haseeb
Haseem
Haseer

Haseib
Haseim
Haseir
Hasel
Hashaam
Hashaan
Hasham Saeed
Hashan
Hashaun
Hasheem
Hashem
Hashi
Hashiem
Hashim *(0.01)*
Hashir
Hashitomi
Hashley
Hashond
Hasib
Hasim
Hasin
Hasir
Haskel
Haskell
Haskell Russell
Hasko
Hasnain
Hasnpreet
Hason
Haspard
Haspin
Hassaan
Hassahn
Hassan *(0.10)*
Hassan Al-
    Rayyan
Hassanain
Hassan-Ali
Hassell
Hassem
Hassen
Hassin
Hassineen
Hassn
Hassnain
Hasson
Hassoon
Hast
Hasten
Hastin
Hastings
Haston

Haszzeki
Hatan
Hatcher
Hatem
Hathen
Hatim
Hatimu
Hatmee
Hatton
Hatuey
Haugen
Hauk
Haukee
Haulten
Havan
Haven *(0.03)*
Havi
Havier
Havin
Havis
Havish
Havok
Havyn
Hawie
Hawk
Hawke
Hawken
Hawkens
Hawkin
Hawkins
Hawkiya
Hawksley
Hawley
Hawthorne
Haxcel
Haxel
Hayaat
Hayato
Haydan *(0.01)*
Hayde
Haydee
Haydell
Hayden *(3.12)*
Hayden
    Lawrence
Hayden Seth
Hayder
Haydin *(0.01)*
Haydn *(0.03)*
Haydon *(0.02)*
Haydyn *(0.01)*
Hayen
Hayes *(0.02)*

Haygen
Haylan
Haylee
Haylem
Haylen
Hayley
Haylix
Haylton
Haymant
Haymen
Haymerick
Hays
Hayston
Haytam
Haytham
Hayven
Hayward
Haywood
Hayyan
Hayyim
Hayzen
Hazael
Hazar
Haze
Hazeem
Hazem
Hazen *(0.01)*
Haziel *(0.01)*
Hazik
Hazim
Haziq
He
Headley
Healey
Heano
Heanok
Hearld
Heart
Heath *(0.08)*
Heath Ezkiela
Heathe
Heathley
Heathrow
Heaton
Heaven *(0.01)*
Hebeer
Heber *(0.01)*
Heberto
Hebertson
Hebron
Hecnuel
Hector *(1.21)*
Hector Ivan

Hector Jr
Hector-Rafael
Hedber
Hedely
Heder
Hedi
Hedjgardsky-
    Droulson
Hee
Hee Cheol
Hee Soo
Heeho
Heer
Hee-Won
Heeyoung
Heidar
Heighden
Heikkinen
Heiko
Heindy
Heiner
Heinrich
Heinrich-Alexy
Heinrick
Heinrik
Heinz
Heiron
Heisman
Heith
Heitor
Heivar
Hekash
Hektor
Heladio
Helal
Helber
Helden
Helder
Helen
Heleno
Heli
Helih
Helio
Hellington
Helmer
Helmut
Helton
Helwan
Hemanath
Hemang
Hemanth
Hemasilox
Hemat

Hemerson
Hemesh
Hemi
Hemii
Hemil
Hemme
Hemrik
Hemunta
Hemza
Henacious
Henari
Hency
Henderson
Hendric
Hendrick
Hendricks
Hendrik *(0.01)*
Hendrix *(0.01)*
Hendrix Marc
Hendry
Hendryck
Hendy
Heneri
Henesey
Heng
Hengest
Henjo
Henley
Hennary
Henner
Henning
Hennry
Henoc
Henoch
Henok
Henos
Henre
Henrey
Henri *(0.03)*
Henrich
Henrick
Henri-Dawson
Henrie
Henri-Joseph
Henrik *(0.01)*
Henri-Louis
Henrionta
Henrique *(0.01)*
Henrry
Henry *(2.08)*
Henry Alexi
Henry J
Henry James

| | | | | | | |
|---|---|---|---|---|---|---|
| Henry-Christos | Hernan (0.01) | Hezckiah | Hinad | Hobbs | Hongxiao | Howard (0.05) |
| Henry-Danniel Jr | Hernandez | Hezekai | Hineef | Hobby | Hongyi | Howe |
| Henry-Megold | Herny | Hezeki | Hines | Hober | Honor | Howei |
| Henry-Michel | Hero | Hezekiah (0.04) | Hinesley | Hobert | Honoray | Howen |
| Henry-Paul | Herold | Hezekiah Daniel | Hinhan | Hobie | Honore | Howie |
| Henschen | Heron | Heziakia | Hinmer | Hobson | Honore-Tshibindi | Howston |
| Henser | Herrington | Hezikah | Hinote | Hoby | Honovi | Hoyas |
| Hensley | Herrison | Hezikiah | Hinslee | Hocine | Honul | Hoyce |
| Henson | Herschel | Hezikiyah | Hinton | Hodari | Hoon | Hoyt (0.01) |
| Henton | Hersh (0.01) | Hezzakhi | Hiott | Hodarie | Hope | Hoyte |
| Hepburn | Hershel (0.01) | Hezzie | Hipolito | Hody | Horace (0.01) | Hoziel |
| Heraclio | Hershraj | Hiader | Hiraim | Hogan (0.01) | Horacio (0.01) | Hozierious |
| Heraj | Hershvardhan | Hiaxxou | Hiram (0.01) | Hogen | Horatio | Hrag |
| Heraldo | Hershy (0.01) | Hibaq | Hiran | Hoger | Horberth | HRH Prince Haythaima |
| Herasmo | Herson (0.01) | Hicham | Hiren | Hogin | Horico | Hridai |
| Herasto | Hersson | Hicsar | Hiro | Hoke | Horrace | Hriday |
| Herb | Herstill | Hidalgo | Hiroki | Hol | Horry | Hridhay |
| Herbert (0.03) | Heru | Hideaki | Hiroshi | Holandis | Hosain | Hrishi |
| Herbey | Hervin | Hidekel | Hiroto | Holbach | Hosbaldo | Hrishik |
| Herbie | Hervyn | Hideki | Hirotomi | Holcomb | Hosea (0.01) | Hrishikesan |
| Herbier | Herwen | Hideya | Hiruy | Holdan | Hosey | Hrishikesh |
| Herby | Hery | Hien | Hirving | Holden (0.22) | Hoshang | Hristijan |
| Herchel | Heryia | Hien-Minh | Hisan | Holder | Hosia | Hrithik |
| Hercules | Hesham | Hieu | Hisham (0.01) | Holdien | Hosiel | Hritik |
| Herder | Hesikiah | Higazi | Hishwaar | Holdin | Hosmann | Hronde |
| Herdwin | Hessel | Higor | Hismael | Holdon | Hosmay | Hrothgar |
| Heri | Hessom | Hikaru | Hisui | Holdyn (0.01) | Hoss | Hrudai |
| Herialberto | Hesteban | Hikeem | Hitalo | Holiber | Hossain | Hrushikesav |
| Heribert | Hesten | Hilaal | Hitam | Holland | Hossam | Hsiang-Chen |
| Heriberto (0.02) | Heston | Hilaire | Hitansh | Hollis (0.01) | Hosteen | Hstep |
| Heriberto Jr | Het | Hilal | Hiten | Hollister | Hostin | Hsu |
| Herie | Hetil | Hilario | Hitesh | Holly | Hothlepoyachabon | Htoo |
| Heritier-Joel | Hevan | Hilbert | Hitham | Holmes | Houd | Hu'ng |
| Heriverto | Hever (0.01) | Hilfred | Hiu | Holmeyen | Hou-Loen | Huan |
| Herlim | Hevert | Hillel | Hivin | Holston | Housam | Huandiego |
| Herling | Hevin | Hillis | Hiwa | Holt | Houssam | Huba |
| Herlis | Hewitt | Hilmer | Hiyab | Holten | Houssameddine | Hubble |
| Herlyn | Hewson | Hilmi | Hiyee | Holton | Houssein | Huber |
| Hermaan | Hewston | Hilton (0.01) | Hizia | Holvis | Houssem | Hubert (0.03) |
| Herman (0.02) | Heyab | Hilvin | Hmza | Holy | Houssen | Hubie |
| Herman Ben | Heyati | Himan | Ho | Homar | Housseynou | Huck |
| Herman Christof | Heydan | Himanish | Ho'ohanohano | Homas | Houssine | Hud |
| Hermann | Heyden | Himanol | Ho'oheno | Homer | Houstan | Hudaifa |
| Hermas | Heydin | Himanshu | Ho'okeleo'kekai | Homero | Housten | Hudayfah |
| Hermelindo | Heydon | Himat | Hoai Duong | Homoel | Houstin | Hudayfe |
| Hermena | Heylin | Himatsurjit | Hoai-Nam | Homran | Houston (0.07) | Hudayfi |
| Hermes | Heyner | Himel | Hoak | Honan | Houstyn | Huddson |
| Hermilo | Heysam | Himesh | Hoang | Honest | Houyar | Hudefa |
| Herminio | Heyward | Himmat | Hoang-Ryan | Hong | Hoven | Hudeyfa |
| Hernaldo | Heywood | Himmet | Hoaseng | Hongchan | Hovey | Hudeyfi |
| | Hezahkiah | Himmut | Hoban | Hong-Jun | Hovsep | Hudeyva |
| | Hezakiah | | Hobart | Hongli | | |

Hudhafah
Hudhaifa
Hudhaifah
Hudhayfah
Hudsen
Hudson (0.35)
Hudsyn
Hue
Hueche
Huekong
Huestyn
Huett
Huey
Hufton
Hugarlee
Hugenson
Hugh (0.05)
Hughdowns
Hughes
Hughey
Hughie
Hughston
Hugo (0.22)
Hugo Kafung
Hugo Magnus
Hugo-Asael
Hugoberto
Hugo-Loic
Hugomar
Hugo-Pier
Hugue
Huguens
Hugues
Hugueschinaydyi
Hui
Hukum
Hulian
Hulises
Hulon
Humayd
Humayl
Humbefto
Humbert
Humberto (0.03)
Humberto Gabriel
Hume
Hummza
Humza (0.01)
Humzah
Hunayfh

Hung
Hunner
Hunor
Hunten
Hunter (4.23)
Hunter Clark
Hunter Eugene
Hunter-Blake
Hunter-Joshua
Huntley
Huntor
Huntter
Huntur
Huntyr
Hur
Hurchel
Hure
Huri
Huriel
Hurlee
Hurley
Hursel
Hurshel
Hurst
Husain
Husam
Husayn
Husein
Husnain
Husni
Hussain (0.01)
Hussam
Hussan
Hussein (0.03)
Hussein Sam
Hussen
Hussien (0.01)
Hussin
Hustin
Huston
Hutao
Hutch
Hutchenson
Hutcheson
Hutchinson
Huthaifa
Huthayfah
Hutheifi
Hutreal
Hutson
Hutton

Hutu Owen Victor
Huu Thien
Huw
Huxley
Huy
Huy Kevin
Huzaifa
Huzaifah
Huzefa
Hwj
Hy
Hy Lik
Hy Saun
Hy'neif
Hy'nif
Hyadi
Hyajah
Hyan
Hyatt (0.01)
Hyban
Hyche
Hydar
Hyde
Hyden
Hydir
Hyeon
Hygor
Hykeem
Hykima
Hyland
Hylden
Hyllamour
Hylland
Hyllel
Hylon
Hylton
Hyman
Hymir
Hymmet
Hyneef
Hyneeph
Hyniff
Hyon
Hyovannie
Hyren
Hyrum (0.01)
Hysan
Hysheem
Hyun
Hyun Kyun
Hyung Joon

Hyungyu
Hyunjune
Hyun-Woo
Hyunwoo
Hyven
Hyzell

~ I ~

I
I Putu
I'divine
I'jaaz
I'jazz
I'jon
I'keile
I'leek
I'lek
I'marion
I'meen
I'mere
I'mir
I'sear
I'siah
I'terrious
I'vante
I'verryus
I'vion
I'yohn
I'zaiah
I'zaya
I'zayah
Iacob
Iaden
Iago
Iain (0.03)
Iakov
Iam
Iameer
Iamine
Ian (2.74)
Ian Alexander
Ian Augusto
Ian Benedict
Ian Domasang
Ian Hawk
Ian John
Ian Luis
Ian Luke
Ian Richard
Ian Shaun

Ian Sheng
Ian Timothy
Ian Yang
Iana
Ianakim
Ian-Alexis
Ian-Gabriel
Ianis
Iann
Iannick
Ian-Olivier
Iante
Iarley
Iarod
Iasiah
Iassac
Iaukwaa
Iavieon
Ibaad
Ibad
Ibai
Iban
Ibashim
Ibayn
Ibblem
Ibeyon
Ibn
Ibn Khary
Ibraahim
Ibraham
Ibraheem (0.01)
Ibrahem
Ibrahim (0.15)
Ibrahim Abduallah
Ibrahim Ahmed
Ibrahima (0.02)
Ibrahimakalil
Ibrahima-Khalil
Ibre Hiem
Ibrehem
Ibrion
Ibukunoluwa
Icabaud
Icaro
Icaros
Icarus
Iceon
Ices
Icesis
Icham
Ichiro

Icker
Ida
Ida Bagus Indra Manggala
Idae
Idair
Idal
Idaly
Idan
Idarius
Idassan
Iddo
Idel
Idell
Idelvis
Iden (0.01)
Idin
Idir
Idiris
Idowu
Idrees
Idres
Idress
Idrian
Idriis
Idris (0.01)
Idriss
Idrissa
Idrissa-Edenge
Idryss
Iean
Iebe
Iedian
Ien
Iesa
Iestin
Ievan
Ieyasu
Ifatoda
Ifdaias
Ifeanyi
Ifeanyi-Chukwu
Ifeanyichukwu
Ifeoluwakitan
Ifeoluwatomi
Ifrael
Ifriam
Iganaxi
Igancy
Igentry
Iggy
Igima

Igmel
Ignac
Ignacio (0.05)
Ignacius
Ignas
Ignashus
Ignasio
Ignatious
Ignatius
Ignazio
Ignesius
Igor (0.01)
Iguame
Iguel
Ihab
Ihan
Ihassan
Ihekwoaba
I-Hisiang Sebastien
Ihsaan
Ihsahn
Ihsan
Iisac
Ijahii
Ijtahad
Ikaele
Ikaia
Ikaika (0.01)
Ikamjot
Ike (0.01)
Ikeanyi Chukwu
Ikechi
Ikechukwu
Ikeem
Ikeim
Ikelle
Ikemba
Ikenga
Ikenna
Iker (0.01)
Iker-Elan
Ikes
Ikese
Ikiam
Ikie
Ikjot
Ikman
Ikon
Ikpal
Ikran
Ikume

| | | | | | | |
|---|---|---|---|---|---|---|
| Ikuna | Ilye | Imranullah | Innocente | Irby | Isaah | Isaiyah |
| Il'lijahjuan | Ilyes *(0.01)* | Imron | Inobemhe | Ireal | Isaaic | Isak *(0.01)* |
| Ila | Ilyess | In Hyuk | Inocencio | Iredele | Isaak *(0.06)* | Isakk |
| Iladio | Ilyich Esser | Inacio | Inocente | Ireland | Isaal | Isam |
| Ilai | Ilyjah | Inafis | Inouk | Irell | Isaaq | Isander |
| Ilaisha | Im | Inaj | Inri | Irelle | Isaaul | Isandro |
| Ilam-Paul | Imaad | Inaki | Inri Adonay | Iren | Isabel | Isaq |
| Ilan *(0.02)* | Imaadul | Inbaa | Insaaf | Ireneusz | Isabella | Isar |
| Ilario | Imaan | Indeep | Inshaal | Ireoluwa | Isabelle | Isarael |
| Ilas | Imaani | Inder | Insung | Irfaan | Isac *(0.03)* | Isau-De Jesus |
| Ilcorian | Imaan-Uzzafar | Inderbir | Intehas | Irfan | Isacc *(0.01)* | Isaviah |
| Ildi | Imad | Inderdeep | Intelligent | Irfawn | Isack | Isavier |
| Iler | Ima-Eddine | Inderjot | Inti | Iri | Isackoh | Isayah *(0.01)* |
| Ilerioluwa | Imael | Inderpal | Inti-Jesus | Iriah | Isadore | Isayd |
| Iles | Image | Inderpreet | Intisar | Irick | Isael *(0.01)* | Isayiah |
| Iles-Abdeslam | Imáge | Inderveer | Inuaraq | Iridian | Isaeya | Isazk |
| Ileyk | Imahad | Indervir | Inuk | Irie | Isah | Isbel |
| Ilg | Imaim | Indi | Inuyasha | Irieal | Isaha | Isbert |
| Ilhan | Iman | India | In-Woo | Iriel | Isahah | Isbon |
| Ilia | Iman-Aly | Indiana *(0.01)* | Inyas | Irijah | Isahak | Iseah |
| Ilian | Imani | Indie | Inzamam | Irim | Isahi | Isear |
| Ilias *(0.02)* | Imanol *(0.02)* | Indigo | Io | Irin | Isahia | Iseem |
| Iliass | Imanuel *(0.01)* | Indio | Ioan | Irinea | Isahias | Isen |
| Iliasse | Imar | Indraj | Ioannes | Irineo | Isai *(0.04)* | Isgiah |
| Ilias-Ziad | Imaran | Indrani | Ioannis | Iriney | Isai Eliel | Ishaan *(0.04)* |
| Ilie | Imari *(0.01)* | Indrashish | Ioannis-Yanni | Irion | Isai'as | Ishaanpreet |
| Iliesse | Imarian | Indu | Iokua | Iris | Isaia | Ishaaq |
| Ilija | Imarion | Induran | Iola | Irish | Isaiah *(4.42)* | Ishak |
| Ilijah | Imauari-Lasean | Indy | Iolaus | Irnel | Isaiah Christian | Isham |
| Ilisha | Imaurii | Indy-Nehemy | Ion | Iroquois | Isaiah Jordan | Ishamael |
| Iliya | Imaurion | Ineir | Ionnis-Christos | Iroshawn | Isaiah Thomas | Ishan *(0.02)* |
| Iliyaan | Imear | Ines | Ionut | Irtaza | Isaiah'thomas | Ishaq |
| Iliyas | Imeen | Inesh | Iorek | Irubel | Isaiah-Darrold | Ishar |
| Ilkehan Omer | Imen | Inez | Iori | Irus | Isaiahis | Ishatva |
| Ilkim | Imer | Infamous | Iory | Irven | Isaiah-Mikael- | Ishaun |
| Illan | Imere | Infinite | Iosea | Irvenson | Tafari | Ishayu |
| Illari | Imery | Ingozis | Ioshua | Irvin *(0.06)* | Isaiah-Ray | Ishhod |
| Illeana | Imevar | Ingrem | Iosu | Irvine | Isaiah-Seth | Ishileem |
| Illen | Imier | Inho | Iosua | Irving *(0.03)* | Isaiah-Taji | Ishkaran |
| Illes | Imilyo | Iniaki | Iovan | Irving-Yahir | Isaiah-Vaughn | Ishma |
| Illia | Imir | Iniko | Iqbal | Irvinn | Isaias *(0.08)* | Ishma'el |
| Illiam | Imire | Iniovosa Felix | Iqqali | Irwin | Isaias-Lecbardo | Ishmael *(0.03)* |
| Illias | Immanu'ul | Iniyavan | Ira *(0.02)* | Irwvin | Isaic | Ishmail |
| Illias'anthony | Immanual | In-Jae | Irad | Irwyn | Isaick | Ishmale |
| Illyes | Immanuel | Inkawat | Irael | Is'saun | Isaie *(0.01)* | Ishmeal |
| Ilmerk | *(0.05)* | Inman | Iraj | Isá | Isaih *(0.01)* | Ishmel |
| Ilstlo | Imon | Inmar | Irak | Isa *(0.01)* | Isaiha | Ishmiel |
| Ilya *(0.01)* | Imona | Innasio | Iraklis | Isa Sander | Isaik | Ishmil |
| Ilyaas | Imoree | Inner | Iram *(0.01)* | Isaaac | Isail | Ishmyel |
| Ilyan | Imraan | Innes | Iran | Isaac *(4.27)* | Isais | Ishpreet |
| Ilyas *(0.02)* | Imran *(0.02)* | Inness | Irany | Isaac Jeffery | Isaish | Ishrael |
| Ilyass | Imrane | Innis | Irauraq | Isaach | Isai-V | Ishrandeep |
| Ilyasse | Imran-Lmahdi | Innocent | Irbin | Isaack *(0.01)* | Isaiya | Ishtiyaq |

| | | | | | | |
|---|---|---|---|---|---|---|
| Ishua | Israal | Italo | Iyjier | Izayrius | Izyiis | J'ali |
| Ishwar | Israel *(0.32)* | Itamar | Iyon | Izayveion | Izyk | J'andrian |
| Isia | Israel Isaiah | Itching | Iyori | Izayveous | Izzaac | J'angelo |
| Isiaah | Israel Khai | Ithaan | Iysyn | Izea | Izzac | J'ante |
| Isiac | Israel-Meir | Itho | Iyush | Izeah | Izzach | J'anthony |
| Isiah *(0.23)* | Israt | Ittetsu | Iz'iah | Izeal | Izzak | J'anyas |
| Isiah Edward | Israth | Itzael | Izaac *(0.03)* | Izece | Izzear | J'avier |
| Isiaha | Israyel | Itzhak | Izaah | Izeck | Izzedine | J'avonni |
| Isiah-Thomas | Isreal *(0.02)* | Ivahn | Izaaih | Izeha | Izzet | J'bari |
| Isiaih | Isrrael | Iván | Izaak *(0.03)* | Izek | Izziah | J'breon |
| Isiais | Issa *(0.01)* | Ivan *(1.64)* | Izaan | Izeke | Izzic | J'brian |
| Isiana | Issaac | Ivan Dolin | Izac *(0.01)* | Izel | Izzy | J'caden |
| Isias | Issac *(0.13)* | Ivan-Damien | Izacc | Izell | Izzyah | J'cailon |
| Isic | Issach | Ivander | Izack *(0.01)* | Izera | | J'caius |
| Isidor | Issachar | Ivandy | Izae | Izese | | J'chaun |
| Isidore | Issack | Ivan-Mauricio | Izaeah | Izeyah | **~ J ~** | J'cier |
| Isidoro | Issah | Ivano | Izaeh | Izeyha | | J'cil |
| Isidro *(0.02)* | Issai | Ivans | Izael | Izhar | J-Fren | J'coby |
| Isimeme | Issaiah | Ivan-Strashimir | Izaell | Izia | J *(0.02)* | J'cory |
| Isiq | Issaic | Ivante | Izaem | Iziack | J Arvonte | J'dan |
| Isis | Issaih | Ivantrae | Izahaa | Iziah *(0.02)* | J B | J'daniel |
| Iskandar | Issain | Iven | Izahi | Iziak | J C | J'davion |
| Iskander | Issak *(0.01)* | Iveniej | Izahia | Izian | J Cruz | J'den |
| Islam | Issam | Iver | Izaia | Iziana | J D | J'dn |
| Islaman | Issanchor | Iverson *(0.01)* | Izaiah *(0.14)* | Iziaya | J Jesus | J'drian |
| Islam-Jalil | Issavior | Ivery | Izaiak | Iziayah | J Kai | J'drien |
| Island | Issay | Ives | Izaias | Izic | J Kye | J'dryk |
| Isley | Isschar | Ivey | Izaiayah | Izick | J Laez | J'dyn |
| Islwyn | Isse | Ivin | Izaiaz | Izidor | J Lin | J'dynn |
| Ismachiah | Isseah | Ivinn | Izaid | Izik *(0.01)* | J Marcus | J'emann |
| Ismael *(0.19)* | Issei | Ivo | Izaih | Izike | J On | J'hakeem |
| Ismael Francois | Issiac | Ivon | Izaiha *(0.01)* | Izlee | J P | J'hay'lyn |
| Ismael-Ahmet | Issiaeh | Ivor | Izairve | Izley | J Rocco | J'heim |
| Ismael-Amadou | Issiah *(0.02)* | Ivorice | Izait | Izmael | J Ron | J'iantanez |
| Ismai | Issiaih | Ivory *(0.01)* | Izaiya | Izo | J Stevie | J'kai |
| Ismaiil | Issic | Ivory Isaiah | Izaiyah | Izrael | J T | J'karri |
| Ismail *(0.03)* | Issifou | Ivoryon | Izajah | Izrahiah | J Travis | J'kenneth |
| Ismail Diaa | Issis | Ivron | Izak *(0.03)* | Izreal | J Vian | J'kerion |
| Elhak | Issyah | Ivryn | Izak-Liam | Izrel | J Vion | J'khari |
| Ismaila | Issyk | Ivvan | Izanuel | Izrhiel | J Voine | J'kharri |
| Ismaile | Istimir | Ivy *(0.01)* | Izarel | Izryal | J. | J'kien |
| Ismail-Jalal | Istvan | Ivyn | Izari | Izsak | J. Carmen | J'kobe |
| Isman | Isuan | Ivyon | Izarian | Izsák | J.R. | J'kobi |
| Ismar | Isum | Ixel | Izaugh | Izsiah | J.T | J'koby |
| Ismeal | Isyssl | Iyaas | Izavier | Izsik | J.Vincent | J'kwan |
| Ismiel | Iszac | Iyad | Izavion | Izson | J.Wesley | J'kwanye |
| Ismil | Iszack | Iyad Yahia | Izay | Izuchukwu | J' | J'kwez |
| Ismlael | Iszak | Djelloul | Izaya *(0.01)* | Izudiin | J'aaron | J'kwon |
| Ismmael | Iszayah | Iyahn | Izayah *(0.04)* | Izudin | J'ace | J'kyle |
| Isoke | Iszeya | Iyair | Izayaih | Izunna | J'adam | J'kyron |
| Isom | Iszic | Iyan | Izayha | Izyaiah | J'adore | J'lan |
| Ison | Iszmar | Iyassu | Izayiah | Izyan | J'ahni | J'len |
| Ispakhi | Itai | Iydris | Izayik | Izyek | J'alan | J'lhen |

| | | | | | | |
|---|---|---|---|---|---|---|
| J'lin | J'veontae | Ja'barri | Ja'davious | Ja'keh | Ja'leal | Ja'marri |
| J'lonn | J'veontay | Ja'boris | Ja'daylen | Ja'keice | Ja'lean | Ja'marrie |
| J'lyn | J'viaire | Ja'bre | Ja'deaun | Ja'keish | Ja'leayre Jamier | Ja'marriea |
| J'lynn | J'vion | Ja'bree | Ja'dell | Ja'keith | Ja'lein | Ja'marrien |
| J'male | J'vione | Ja'brelle | Ja'den *(0.01)* | Ja'kel | Ja'len | Ja'marrion |
| J'marcus | J'von | Ja'brey | Ja'derian | Ja'kelleus | Ja'leo | Ja'marrius |
| J'mari | J'vonn | Ja'brian | Ja'deric | Ja'kelton | Ja'leon | Ja'marriya |
| J'marion | J'vontae | Ja'bryant | Ja'derius | Ja'kelyn | Ja'liel | Ja'marryus |
| J'marion Devont | J'vor | Ja'bryl | Ja'derrick | Ja'kenean | Ja'lik | Ja'martae |
| J'marion-Kentravius | J'wuan | Ja'byron | Ja'dien | Ja'kerius | Ja'lil | Ja'martez |
| J'marrion | J'ylen | Ja'camreon | Ja'din | Ja'kerrian | Ja'lill | Ja'marvion |
| J'martino | J'ziah | Ja'caquel | Ja'dir | Ja'kevion | Ja'lin | Ja'masz |
| J'maurie | J'zyn | Ja'caree | Ja'don | Ja'kevious | Ja'lind | Ja'mauri |
| J'me | Ja | Ja'cari | Ja'dore | Ja'Khai | Ja'lon | Ja'maurie |
| J'meil | Já | Ja'caria | Ja'duan | Ja'khari | Ja'loni | Ja'mauriea |
| J'meire | Ja Darrius | Ja'carie | Ja'dyaiz | Ja'ki | Ja'lontae | Ja'maurin |
| J'mel | Ja Den | Ja'carion | Ja'dyn | Ja'kiarain | Ja'lyn | Ja'maury |
| J'mere | Ja Hid | Ja'carious | Ja'eriq | Ja'kiaus | Ja'lynn | Ja'maveon |
| J'mir | Já Hym | Ja'carreon | Ja'gotti | Ja'kiee | Ja'lyson | Ja'mearion |
| J'mori | Ja Ja | Ja'carri | Ja'had | Ja'kiem | Ja'mace | Ja'meer |
| J'nai | Já Jon | Ja'carrion | Ja'har | Ja'kivon | Ja'mahri | Ja'meir |
| J'nore | Ja Kesse | Ja'cere | Ja'hari | Ja'kiy | Ja'mair | Ja'meire |
| J'nyus | Ja Khiem | Ja'chym | Ja'hayveion | Ja'kobby | Ja'mais | Ja'mel |
| J'ontay | Ja Lonnie | Ja'clarence | Ja'heem | Ja'kobe *(0.01)* | Ja'malachi | Ja'mere |
| J'quan | Ja Marcus | Ja'cobe | Ja'heim | Ja'kobi | Ja'mani | Ja'merius |
| J'qwan | Ja Marion | Ja'cobi | Ja'heym | Ja'kobie | Ja'mar | Ja'mes |
| J'ren | Ja Markiss | Ja'cobie | Ja'hiem | Ja'koby | Ja'marcus *(0.01)* | Ja'mez |
| J'rias | Ja Marr | Ja'coby | Ja'imari | Ja'kodey | Ja'mare | Ja'miah |
| J'ron | Ja Maurone | Ja'colby | Ja'imer | Ja'koi | Ja'maree | Ja'micah |
| J'sai | Ja Meel | Ja'conn | Ja'ire | Ja'korey | Ja'mareion | Ja'michael |
| J'sean | Ja Mier | Ja'corey *(0.01)* | Ja'juan *(0.01)* | Ja'kori | Ja'mareon | *(0.01)* |
| J'shaun | Ja Ming | Ja'cori | Ja'juanas | Ja'korie | Ja'marey | Ja'micheal |
| J'shawn | Ja Myre | Ja'corian | Ja'kahis | Ja'kourian | Ja'mari *(0.01)* | Ja'miel |
| J'shon | Ja Nairi | Ja'corie | Ja'kahl | Ja'kovien | Ja'marian | Ja'mier |
| J'shun | Ja Nye | Ja'corieus | Ja'kahoury | Ja'kwan | Ja'marie | Ja'miere |
| J'siah | Ja Quan | Ja'coriyous | Ja'kai | Ja'kwaveous | Ja'marien | Ja'mierian |
| J'suan | Já Quan | Ja'corrie | Ja'kaiden | Ja'kwon | Ja'marieon | Ja'mir |
| J'sun | Ja Quise | Ja'cory | Ja'kaleb | Ja'kwondriu | Ja'mariion | Ja'Mir |
| J'tavious | Ja Shaun | Ja'coryn | Ja'kalen | Ja'kye | Ja'mario | Ja'mire |
| J'terien | Ja Shawn | Ja'coryon | Ja'karean | Ja'kyeri | Ja'marion *(0.02)* | Ja'mius |
| J'terrius | Ja Shon | Ja'coyrien | Ja'karee | Ja'kyii | Ja'mariun | Ja'mon |
| J'til | Ja Shuea Sky | Ja'cravious | Ja'kari *(0.01)* | Ja'kyle | Ja'marius | Ja'mondré |
| J'toris | Ja Shun | Ja'dan | Ja'karri | Ja'kyra | Ja'mariyon | Ja'moni |
| J'tory | Ja Shuyn | Ja'darian | Ja'karrion | Ja'kyri | Ja'marjhe | Ja'monie |
| J'tyler | Ja Twon | Ja'darious | Ja'karus | Ja'kyrian | Ja'markeon | Ja'monta |
| J'vaariez | Ja Von | Ja'darius *(0.01)* | Ja'kavion | Ja'kyrie | Ja'markis | Ja'monte |
| J'vari | Ja Vonn | Ja'darrell | Ja'kavius | Ja'laal | Ja'markus | Ja'montrea |
| J'varius | Já Vonte | Ja'darrian | Ja'kayrion | Ja'lan | Ja'marlon | Ja'morian |
| J'vaughn | Ja Yeon | Ja'darrin | Ja'kayven | Ja'Lan | Ja'marqius | Ja'morie |
| J'vaun | Ja'amir | Ja'darrion | Ja'keaun | Ja'landyn | Ja'marques | Ja'morien |
| J'veaune | Ja'aun | Ja'darrius | Ja'kee | Ja'larrious | Ja'marr | Ja'morris |
| J'veon | Ja'ayr | Ja'davian | Ja'keem | Ja'lawn | Ja'marree | Ja'mree |
| | Ja'bari | Ja'davion | Ja'keen | Ja'layvion | Ja'marren | Ja'mye |

| | | | | | | |
|---|---|---|---|---|---|---|
| Ja'mykle | Ja'quincy | Ja'tarius | Ja'vonce | Jaare | Jabier | Jacario |
| Ja'myle | Ja'quintis | Ja'taryin | Ja'vondre | Jaariq | Jabin | Jacarion |
| Ja'myrick | Ja'quirea | Ja'taveous | Ja'vone | Jaaron | Jabir | Jacarious |
| Ja'myrria | Ja'quis | Ja'tavion | Ja'vonne | Jaasai | Jabiyr | Jacaris |
| Ja'myuz | Ja'quise | Ja'tavious | Ja'vont | Jaasiel | Jabneel | Jacarius |
| Ja'narious | Ja'quon | Ja'tavis | Ja'vonta | Jaason | Jabon | Jacarré |
| Ja'naris | Ja'quorrie | Ja'tavius | Ja'vontae | Jaaundra | Jaboree | Jacarrey |
| Ja'narius | Ja'qwan | Ja'tayvious | Ja'vonte | Jaaven | Jabori *(0.01)* | Jacarri |
| Ja'nathan | Ja'qwon | Ja'tayvis | Ja'Vonte | Jaavin | Jabori Octa | Jacarrie |
| Ja'nile | Ja'qwone | Ja'teese | Ja'vonté | Jaaxeil | Jaborie | Jacarrious |
| Ja'nique | Ja'qyvoun | Ja'tell | Ja'vonterius | Jaaylan | Jaborris | Jacarrius |
| Ja'nius | Ja'rae | Ja'terious | Ja'vori | Jaay-R | Jabraé | Jacarter |
| Ja'niyah | Ja'rahn | Ja'terius | Ja'vorian | Jaazaniah | Jabraeus | Jacary |
| Ja'niyas | Ja'randall | Ja'terrian | Ja'voris | Jaaziah | Jabrahn | Jacc Mckenzie |
| Ja'norric | Ja'randis | Ja'thomas | Ja'vyon | Jaaziel | Jabrail | Jaccari |
| Ja'nyion | Ja'raylin | Ja'tione | Ja'vyonne | Jabaar | Jabralynn | Jaccob |
| Ja'ontae | Ja'ree | Ja'toin | Ja'warren | Jabaari | Jabraye | Jacdon |
| Ja'ontay | Ja'rell | Ja'toine | Ja'waun | Jabal | Jabrayln | Jacé |
| Ja'perrio | Ja'reon | Ja'tony | Ja'won | Jabar | Jabré | Jace *(0.76)* |
| Ja'peth | Ja'rese | Ja'torian | Ja'yan | Jabarai | Jabreail | Jace Colin |
| Ja'qazz | Ja'rian | Ja'torie | Ja'yon | Jabardre | Jabree | Jacearian |
| Ja'quahvis | Ja'rico | Ja'torione | Ja'zai | Jabare | Jabreel | Jaceb |
| Ja'quail | Ja'rod | Ja'torrian | Ja'zavier | Jabaree | Jabrei | Jaceb-Douglas |
| Ja'qualin | Ja'rome | Ja'twan | Ja'zayvon | Jabareé | Jabreice | Jace-Carter |
| Ja'qualyn | Ja'ron *(0.01)* | Ja'vae | Ja'zeay | Jabari *(0.10)* | Jabreil | Jacedon |
| Ja'quan *(0.03)* | Ja'royal | Ja'vahris | Ja'zeric | Jabarie *(0.01)* | Jabrell | Jaceion |
| Ja'quante | Ja'rrell | Ja'vaier | Ja'ziah | Jabarion | Jabrey | Jacek *(0.01)* |
| Ja'quari | Ja'run | Ja'van | Ja'zias | Jabaris | Jabri | Jacelin |
| Ja'quarion | Ja'sahn | Ja'vanti | Ja'zir | Jabarius | Jabrian | Jacen *(0.02)* |
| Ja'quarious | Ja'saiah | Ja'var | Ja'zon | Jabarri | Jabrie | Jaceon |
| Ja'quaris | Ja'saveion | Ja'vari | Jaaarion | Jabarrion | Jabriel *(0.01)* | Jacer |
| Ja'quarius | Ja'savion | Ja'varian | Jaabir | Jabarrious | Jabriil | Jacetin |
| Ja'quarrias | Ja'Sean | Ja'vario | Jaad | Jabarris | Jabril *(0.01)* | Jaceton |
| Ja'quarrie | Ja'sean *(0.01)* | Ja'varion | Jaad Gaetan | Jabarry | Jabrill | Jaceun |
| Ja'quavais | Ja'shaed | Ja'various | Jaadarion | Jabary | Jabrli | Jacey *(0.01)* |
| Ja'quavian | Ja'sharie | Ja'vaughn | Jaaden | Jabbaar | Jabron | Jaceyon |
| Ja'quavien | Ja'shaun *(0.01)* | Ja'vaun | Jaafan | Jabbar | Jabryan | Jachai |
| Ja'quavier | Ja'shawn *(0.01)* | Ja'veion | Jaahid | Jabbarie | Jabryiius | Jachan |
| Ja'quavion | Ja'sheed | Ja'vell | Jaahsir | Jabdiel | Jabryl | Jachaun |
| Ja'quavione | Ja'sheem | Ja'veon *(0.01)* | Jaaiden | Jabe | Jabrylan | Jachin *(0.01)* |
| Ja'quavious | Ja'shi | Ja'veontai | Jaaish | Jabe'auz | Jabulani | Jachob |
| Ja'quavius | Ja'shon | Ja'veus | Jaakir | Jabeez | Jac | Jaci |
| Ja'quavon | Ja'shuan | Ja'vi | Jaalah | Jabel | Jac'que | Jaciah |
| Ja'quavyon | Ja'shyiua | Ja'vian | Jaalin | Jaben | Jac'ques | Jacian |
| Ja'quay | Ja'shyne | Ja'vien | Jaalyn | Jaber | Jac'quez | Jacie |
| Ja'quazeon | Ja'siah | Ja'vier | Jaamayl | Jabere | Jacadyn | Jaciel |
| Ja'que | Ja'sid | Ja'viian | Jaamir | Jaberie | Jacan | Jacin |
| Ja'quell | Ja'sir | Ja'vin | Jaan | Jabes | Jacanden | Jacine |
| Ja'querious | Ja'son | Ja'vion *(0.01)* | Jaanbaz | Jabez *(0.01)* | Jacardo | Jacinto |
| Ja'quesse | Ja'sonee | Ja'vione | Jaancarlos | Jabez Meek | Jacaree | Jacir |
| Ja'quez *(0.01)* | Ja'ston | Ja'virgil | Jaani | Jabez Tailib | Jacari *(0.03)* | Jacire |
| Ja'quez Jer | Ja'syas | Ja'viyon | Jaap | Jabhari | Jacarie | Jaciyah |
| Ja'quil | Ja'tarias | Ja'von *(0.02)* | Jaaquon | Jabias | Jacarii | Jack *(4.85)* |

| | | | | | | |
|---|---|---|---|---|---|---|
| Jack C | Jacob Ryan | Jacorraun A | Jacyn | Jaderreck | Jae'lon | Jaemarion |
| Jack Michael | Jacob Timothy | Jacorrey | Jad (0.02) | Jaderrio | Jae'lynn | Jaemel |
| Jack Oliver | Jacob William | Jacorri | Jad Mehdi | Jaderrius | Jae'mere | Jaemin |
| Jackamo | Jacoba | Jacorrian | Jad'ean | Jadex | Jae'quan | Jaemon |
| Jackari | Jacob-Aidyn | Jacory (0.01) | Jada | Jadeyen | Jae'sean | Jaemos |
| Jack-Cody | Jacob-Angelo | Jacoté | Jadaan | Jadhon | Jae'shaun | Jaems |
| Jackee | Jacobb | Jacourious | Jadair | Jadiah | Jae'trell | Jaeon-Alfred |
| Jackey | Jacobbie | Jacoury | Jadan (0.02) | Jadian | Jae'veon | Jaeori |
| Jack-Hayden | Jacob-Daniel | Jacoven | Jadaniel | Jadie | Jae'vien | Jae-P |
| Jackie (0.04) | Jacob-Danny- | Jacovie | Jadar | Jadiel (0.02) | Jae'von | Jaep |
| Jackkeem | Micheal | Jacovy | Jadarain | Jadien | Jaebrion | Jaepriest |
| Jacklindy | Jacobdavid | Jacqarie | Jadareis | Jadier | Jaece | Jaequan |
| Jackman | Jacobe (0.01) | Jacqawn | Jadareus | Jadin (0.02) | Jaecob | Jaequin |
| Jackob | Jacobee | Jacqorios | Jadaria | Jadine | Jaecobey | Jaeran |
| Jackobie | Jacob-Eliezer | Jacquae | Jadarian | Jadinsingh | Jaecyn | Jaeris |
| Jackoy | Jacob-Ennio | Jacquai | Jadarius (0.01) | Jadir | Jaedan | Jaeron |
| Jackquan | Jacobey | Jacquail | Jadarren | Jadirius | Jaedan- | Jaerron |
| Jackron | Jacobi (0.02) | Jacquais | Jadarrian | Jadis | Alexandre | Jaesaun |
| Jack-Ryan | Jacobian | Jacquan | Jadarrien | Jadiss | Jaeded | Jaesean |
| Jacks | Jacobie (0.01) | Jacquarious | Jadarrius | Jadiyn | Jaedee | Jae-Seoung |
| Jacksel | Jacob-Joshua | Jacquary | Jadas | Jadlen | Jaeden (0.08) | Jaeshaun |
| Jacksen (0.01) | Jacob-Major | Jacquavius | Jadaveon | Jadlyn | Jaedin (0.01) | Jaeshon |
| Jackson (4.46) | Jacob-Marcus | Jacquaz | Jadavion | Jadon (0.19) | Jaedn | Jaeson |
| Jackson | Jacobo (0.01) | Jacque | Jadavon | Jadonte | Jaedon (0.04) | Jaeton |
| Christopher | Jacob-Olivier | Jacque Daniel | Jadd | Jadonté | Jaedrein | Jaevan |
| Jackson Claude | Jacob-Raphael | Jacquel | Jadden (0.01) | Jadore | Jaedrian | Jaeven |
| Alfre | Jacobson | Jacqueline | Jadden-Matt | Jadorrian | Jaedric | Jaeveon |
| Jackson David | Jacob-Tony | Jacquell | Jaddin | Jadrian | Jaedyan | Jaevic |
| Jackson Junior | Jacobus | Jacquelson | Jade (0.02) | Jadrick | Jaedyn (0.02) | Jaevien |
| Jackson Thomas | Jacoby (0.04) | Jacqueri | Jadean | Jadriel | Jaegar | Jaevin |
| Jackson-Daniel | Jacob-Zisis | Jacquerious | Jadeen | Jadrien | Jaeger (0.01) | Jaevion (0.01) |
| Jackson-Riley | Jacoden | Jacques (0.03) | Jadeith | Jadus | Jaegon | Jaevon |
| Jacksun | Jacodi | Jacques Zana | Jadel | Jady | Jaehecious | Jaevonte |
| Jacksyn | Jacody | Jacquese | Jadell | Jady'n | Jaehl | Jaevynlee |
| Jacky (0.03) | Jacoiry | Jacques-Michel | Jadem | Jadyce | Jaekwan | Jaevyon |
| Jackzin | Jacolbe | Jacqueson | Jaden (2.21) | Jadyel | Jaekwon | Jae-Won |
| Jacno | Jacolby (0.01) | Jacquess | Jaden Alexa | Jadyl | Jaël | Jaewon |
| Jaco | Jacon | Jacquette | Jaden Demitra | Jadyn (0.08) | Jael (0.03) | Jaewoos |
| Jacob (11.25) | Jacorbian | Jacquey | Jaden Dior | Jadyne | Jaeland | Jaeydon |
| Jacob Alan | Jacore | Jacquez (0.01) | Jaden Earl | Jadynn | Jae-Len | Jaeymisen |
| Jacob Antonio | Jacoreion | Jacquezs | Jaden Ian | Jae (0.01) | Jaelen (0.01) | Jaeyon |
| Jacob Benjamin | Jacorey (0.01) | Jacqui | Jaden Nicho | Jae Hee | Jaeleon | Jaezeon |
| Jacob Cole | Jacoreyon | Jacquil | Jaden Tomas | Jae Hwan | Jaeleous | Jaezon |
| Jacob Don't | Jacori (0.01) | Jacquior | Jaden Zander | Jae Min | Jaelik | Jafar |
| Jacob Edouard | Jacoria | Jacquis | Jadence | Jae Myre | Jaelin (0.02) | Jafaree |
| Jacob Henry | Jacorian | Jacquise | Jadenn | Jae Rim | Jaelind | Jafari |
| Jacob John | Jacorie | Jacsean | Jadent | Jae'anthony | Jaelinh | Jafarkhan |
| Edward | Jacoriean | Jacsen | Jadeon | Jae'dan | Jael-Kemiah | Jafarou |
| Jacob Kimbrell | Jacorieion | Jacson | Jader | Jae'den | Jaelon (0.01) | Jafaru |
| Jacob Lee | Jacorien | Jacub | Jaderian | Jae'kell | Jaelub | Jafeon |
| Jacob Luis | Jacorion | Jacxon | Jaderick | Jae'kori | Jaelyn (0.01) | Jafer |
| Jacob Michael | Jacorious | Jacy (0.01) | Jaderis | Jae'kwon | Jaelynd | Jafet |
| Jacob Patrick | Jacorrain | Jacylin | Jaderius | Jae'li | Jaelynn | Jafeth |

Jaffari
Jaffe
Jaffer
Jaffete
Jaffeth
Jaffret
Jafus
Jag
Jagan
Jagar
Jagdeep
Jagdev
Jagen
Jager
Jager-Sean
Jaggar
Jagger *(0.04)*
Jagjeet
Jagjit
Jagjot
Jagnoor
Jago
Jagoldy
Jagor
Jagr
Jagraj
Jagrav
Jagre
Jagroop
Jagruth
Jagtej
Jagur
Jagveer
Jagvir
Jah
Jah Bari
Jah Kiya
Jah Wei
Jah'air
Jah'bias
Jah'codi
Jah'cure
Jah'darius
Jah'heem
Jah'hem
Jah'keim
Jah'kelsen
Jah'khai
Jah'kourie
Jah'kye
Jah'kyi
Jah'kyle
Jah'kyree

Jah'leel
Jah'lijah
Jah'manii
Jah'mar
Jah'mari
Jah'marion
Jah'marrion
Jah'meir
Jah'mil
Jah'mir
Jah'morris
Jah'mun
Jah'nair
Jah'nhy
Jah'nij
Jah'quii
Jah'quinton
Jah'reon
Jah'rian
Jah'rie
Jah'seir
Jah'sere
Jah'siah
Jah'son
Jah'syed
Jah'torre
Jah'vadis
Jah'vauhnta
Jah'verious
Jah'viair
Jah'von
Jah'wan
Jah'zarrius
Jah'zeel Amor
Jah'zire
Jaha
Jahad
Jahai
Jahaiah
Jahaire
Jahaleel
Jahama-II
Jahan
Jahann
Jahaqez
Jahara
Jaharee
Jaharence
Jahari *(0.01)*
Jaharious
Jaharis
Jaharri
Jaharryon

Jahaud
Jahaven
Jahaviea
Jahavion
Jahavon
Jahazani
Jahaziel *(0.01)*
Jahbari
Jahbari Naasir
Jahbarie
Jahbori
Jahbree
Jahbriel
Jahbril
Jahcal
Jahcari
Jahcere
Jahcinth Exodus
Jahcobi
Jahcorey
Jahdarius
Jahdee
Jahden
Jahdiel
Jahdo
Jahdyn
Jaheed
Jaheem *(0.02)*
Jaheen
Jaheim *(0.06)*
Jaheim Azael
Jahein
Jahel
Jahem
Jahenry
Jahfari
Jahfarie
Jahfear
Jahhim
Jahi
Jahick
Jahid
Jahiem *(0.02)*
Jahiem Nathan
Jahil
Jahim
Jahin
Jahir *(0.01)*
Jahire
Jahiro
Jahkahi
Jahkai
Jahkaivious

Jahkaree
Jahkari
Jahkeame
Jahkeem *(0.01)*
Jahkeir
Jahkel
Jahkeleus
Jahkerris
Jahkese
Jahki
Jahkie
Jahkiem
Jahkim
Jahking
Jahkir
Jahkius
Jahkiy
Jahkobe
Jahkwel
Jahkwen
Jahky
Jahkye
Jahkyé
Jahlani
Jahlanie
Jah-Lanne
Jahlanni
Jahleal
Jahleel *(0.01)*
Jahlen
Jahlia
Jahliel
Jahlijah
Jahlil *(0.02)*
Jahlion
Jah-Lore
Jahlyl
Jahlyn
Jahlyte
Jahmaad
Jahmaal
Jahmad
Jahmae
Jahmai
Jahmaie
Jahmair
Jahmal
Jahmal-
  Cameron
Jahmali
Jahmalik
Jahmall
Jahmani

Jahmar
Jahmaraé
Jahmaree
Jahmari *(0.01)*
Jahmarian
Jahmarion
Jah-Marley
Jahmarley
Jahmarr
Jahmarye
Jahmaud
Jah-Mear
Jahmeek
Jahmeel
Jahmeer
Jahmeere
Jahmeir
Jahmeke
Jahmel
Jah-Mere
Jahmere
Jahmerion
Jahmet
Jahmeyir
Jahmi
Jahmiel
Jahmier
Jahmiere
Jahmik
Jahmil
Jahmir *(0.03)*
Jahmir'
Jah-Mire
Jahmire
Jahmiryus
Jahmiyr
Jahmoi
Jahmon
Jahmone
Jahmonie
Jahmonte
Jahmoy
Jahmy
Jahmye-
  Mandella
Jahmyl
Jahmyron
Jahn
Jahnai
Jahnarey
Jahnari
Jahnavi
Jahneer

Jah-Neil
Jahni
Jahnier
Jahnius
Jahniyus
Jah-Noah
Jahnoah
Jahntavious
Jahod
Jah-Oda
Jahóun
Jahqaé
Jahqarius
Jah-Qhuan
Jahquarius
Jahquavious
Jahquay
Jahquel
Jah-Quez
Jahquez
Jahquezz
Jahquis
Jahquise
Jahreal
Jahred
Jahree
Jahreil
Jahrel
Jahrell
Jahren
Jahrese
Jahrez
Jahrid
Jahrome
Jahron
Jahroy
Jahrrelle
Jahrreon
Jah-Ryah
Jahryn
Jahsaan
Jahsai
Jahse
Jahsean
Jahseem
Jahseer
Jahseir
Jahsharie
Jah-Shaun
Jahshua
Jahshun
Jahsi
Jahsia

Jahsiah
Jahsier
Jahsiere
Jahsil
Jahsim
Jahsir
Jahsire
Jahsius
Jahson
Jah-Sur
Jahsyah
Jahtarious
Jahtarius
Jahtavian
Jahtavious
Jahtay
Jahtayo
Jahtez
Jahtrez
Jah-Tye
Jahuan
Jahun
Jahuntae
Jahvair
Jahval
Jahvan
Jahvann
Jahvanté
Jahvar
Jahvari
Jahvaughn
Jahveale
Jah-Vez
Jahvez
Jahvian
Jahvir
Jahvodd
Jahvon *(0.01)*
Jahvonte
Jahvontea
Jah-Vyon
Jahwanzinni
Jahwaune
Jahwayne
Jahwin
Jahy'vion
Jahyd
Jahyea
Jahylan
Jahylin
Jahymari
Jahyn
Jahzair

| | | | | | | |
|---|---|---|---|---|---|---|
| Jahzayd | Jaicari | Jaikob Dhaniel | Jair *(0.05)* | Jaiven *(0.01)* | Jakardra | Jakez |
| Jahzeel | Jaice | Jaikub | Jairadan | Jaiveon | Jakare | Jakhai |
| Jahzeem | Jaiceon | Jaikwon | Jairah | Jaiver | Jakaree | Jakhari |
| Jahzekiel | Jaicere | Jailan | Jairaj | Jaivian | Jakari *(0.03)* | Jakharie |
| Jahzere | Jaicheon | Jaile | Jairam | Jaivien | Jakari Korleon | Ja-Khaydin |
| Jah-Ziah | Jaicie | Jailen *(0.01)* | Jairamir | Jaivieon | Jakarie | Jakhayre |
| Jahziel | Jaicin | Jailin | Ja-Iran | Jaivier | Jakarius | Jakhi *(0.01)* |
| Jahzier | Jaico | Jailon | Jairdan | Jai-Vion | Jakarre | Jakhyven |
| Jahzion | Jaico Charlie | Jailya | Jaire | Jaivion *(0.01)* | Jakarri | Jaki |
| Jahzir | Jaicob | Jailyn *(0.01)* | Jaired | Jaivionta | Ja-Karriyia | Jakiah |
| Jaí | Jaicy | Jailynn | Jairell | Jaivir | Jakarta | Jakias |
| Jai *(0.03)* | Jaicyee | Jailyric | Jairemyah | Jaivohn | Jakary | Jakidrien |
| Jai 'Zon | Jaid | Jai-Lyrick | Jairen | Jaivon *(0.01)* | Jakauri | Jakie |
| Jai Liam | Jaidaen | Jaimaine | Jairese | Jaivoné | Jakavan | Jakiem |
| Jai Lin | Jaidahn | Jaimaison | Jairesiah | Jaivyan | Jakaveous | Jakiire |
| Jai Shaun | Jaidai | Jaiman | Jairiel | Jaivyn | Jakavian | Jakin |
| Jai'ahn | Jaidamandeep | Jaimar | Jairien | Jaiwan | Ja-Kavion | Jaking |
| Jai'dall | Jaidan *(0.01)* | Jaimari | Jairius | Jaiy'sion | Jakavion | Jakir |
| Jai'den | Jaidas | Jaimarri | Jairmee | Jaiyden | Jakavious | Jakiri |
| Jai'dyn | Jaidden | Jaimaury | Jairo *(0.06)* | Jaiye | Jakawon | Jakirus |
| Jai'harri | Jaideep | Jaime *(0.16)* | Jairo Jose | Jaiylaun | Jakaylon | Jakivion |
| Jai'kob | Jai-Den | Jaime III | Jairo Mathias | Jaiylen | Jakcrus | Jakiyah |
| Jai'kwon | Jaïden | Jaime Naythan | Jairon | Jaiyson | Jake *(1.54)* | Jakiyous |
| Jai'len | Jaiden *(0.47)* | Jaime Xavier | Jairón | Jaizion | Jake David | Jakkai |
| Jai'lyn | Jaiden-Jermaine | Jaimeariel | Jairus *(0.02)* | Jaizon | Jake Scott | Jakkob |
| Jai'lynd | Jaidenn | Jaimeer | Jairzino | Jaizyn | Jake Thomas | Jakob *(0.47)* |
| Jai'meir | Jaiden-Thomas | Jaimeir | Jais | Jaja | Jakeb *(0.02)* | Jakob David |
| Jai'mere | Jaidev | Jaime-Jose | Jaisaiah | Jajaun | Jakeden | Jakob Riley |
| Jai'quan | Jaidhen | Jaimelias | Jaisaih | Jajuan *(0.01)* | Jakeel | Jakob-Claude |
| Jai'quareion | Jaidian | Jaimell | Jaisal | Jak | Jakeem *(0.01)* | Jakobé |
| Jai'quel | Jaidin | Jaimen | Jaise | Jakabreyon | Jakeim | Jakobe *(0.03)* |
| Jai'quinte | Jaidis | Jaimer | Jaisean | Jakadin | Jakeise | Jakobee |
| Jai'rion | Jaido | Jaimer' | Jaiseven | Jakael | Jake-Kenneth | Ja-Kobi |
| Jai'ron-Ramier | Jaidon *(0.02)* | Jaimeson | Jaishaun *(0.01)* | Jakah | Jakel | Jakobi *(0.01)* |
| Jai'rus | Jaidrean | Jaimes-Ross | Jaishawn | Jakahari | Jakeldrick | Jakobi Fran |
| Jai'sean | Jaidstyn | Jaimi | Jai-Shon | Jakahd | Jakelin | Ja-Kobie |
| Jai'shaun | Jaidus | Jaimie | Jaishon | Jakahi | Jakell | Jakobie |
| Jai'shawn | Jaidyn *(0.06)* | Jaimie-Aidan | Jaison *(0.01)* | Jakahran | Jakem | Jakoblee |
| Jai'shon | Jaieden | Jaimier | Jaissan | Jakahri | Jaken | Jakobus |
| Jai'siah | Jaienn | Jaimin | Jaisun | Jakahrie | Jakendrick | Jakob-Walter |
| Jai'than | Jaier | Jaimir | Jaitarius | Ja-Kai | Jakeob | Jakoby *(0.01)* |
| Jai'uan | Jaiger | Jaimoi | Jaitavius | Jakaí | Jakeon | Jakoda |
| Jai'veon | Jai-Haziel | Jaimon | Jaithan | Jakai *(0.01)* | Jakerion | Jakodié |
| Jai'viaun | Jaihden | Jaimyn | Jaithra | Jakaii | Jakeryon | Jakody |
| Jai'vion | Jaihdin | Jaineef | Jaitin | Jakaire | Jakesse | Jakoeb |
| Jai'von | Jaihki | Jainesh | Jaitoine | Jakaiwyn | Jakesteion | Jakofi |
| Jai'vyn | Jaihlen | Jaion | Jaitrel | Jakale | Jakeup | Jakolbe |
| Jai'vyon | Jaihon | Jaipal | Jaival | Jakaleb | Jakevion | Jakolby |
| Jai'won | Jaik | Jaipreet | Jaivan | Jakalen | Jakevious | Jakorei |
| Jai'zon | Jaikaran | Jaiquan | Jaivante | Jakalub | Jakey | Jakorey |
| Jaian | Jaike | Jaiquavious | Jaivaon | Jakalyn | Jakeyce | Jakori |
| Jaibren | Jaiken | Jaique'z | Jaivarae | Jakan | Jakeyl | Jakorian |
| Jaibrien | Jaikob | Jaiquon | Jaiveer | Jakar | Jakeylian | Jakorien |

| | | | | | | |
|---|---|---|---|---|---|---|
| Jakorion | Jalee | Jalyne | Jamareon | Jamarrion | Jameir | James-Anthony |
| Jakory | Jaleeh | Jalynn | Jamareun | Jamarrious | Jameire | James-Charles |
| Jakota | Jaleek | Jama | Jamarey | Jamarris | Jamel (0.06) | James-Dean |
| Jakovi | Jaleel (0.04) | Jamaa | Jamarez | Jamarrius | Jamell (0.01) | Jamesean |
| Jakovie | Jaleen | Jamaal (0.04) | Jamarhe | Jamarus | Jamen (0.01) | James-Edward |
| Jakovis | Jaleik | Jamaal-Amin | Jamarí | Jamarvion | Jamere (0.01) | Jameseins |
| Jakovo | Jalein | Jamaar | Jamari (0.17) | Jamaryan | Jamereous | James-Eli |
| Jakoy | Jaleir | Jamaari | Jamari'a | Jamaryon | Jamerian | Jamesen |
| Jakquir | Jalel | Jamael | Jamaria | Jamasen | Jameriaz | James-Gudiel |
| Jakri | Jalen (0.50) | Jamaeson | Jamarian (0.01) | Jamason | Jamerick | James-Haim |
| Jaks | Jalend | Jamahal | Jamarias | Jamaud | Jamerio | Jamesian |
| Jaksen | Jalene | Jamahl | Jamaric'o | Jamaul | Jamerion | Jamesie |
| Jaksin | Jalen-Latrell | Jamahr | Jamarice | Jamauni | Jamerious | James-Jeffrey |
| Jakson (0.01) | Jalenn | Jamahrae | Jamaricus | Jamaur | Jameriquae | James-Joshua |
| Jakstavious | Jalens | Jamahri | Jamarié | Jamaure | Jameris | Jamesky |
| Jaksyn | Jaleo | Jamai | Jamarie (0.01) | Jamauree | Jamerison | Jamesley |
| Jakub (0.04) | Jaleon | Jamái | Jamarien | Jamauren | Jamerius | Jamesly |
| Jakup | Jalevion | Jamaiel | Jamarii | Jamauri (0.01) | Jameriyon | James-Michael |
| Jakur | Jali | Jamail | Jamarin | Jamauric | Jamerrio | Jameson (0.17) |
| Jakurius | Jaliah | Jamaile | Jamario (0.01) | Jamaurien | Jamerson | James-Peter |
| Jakus | Jalian | Jamain | Ja-Marion | Jamaurion | James (7.12) | James-Richard |
| Jakwaiy | Jaliek | Jamaine (0.01) | Jamarión | Jamaurius | James Alixander | Jameston |
| Jakwan | Jaliel | Jamair | Jamarion (0.17) | Jamaurri | James Alvie | James-Travis |
| Jakwiil | Jalien | Jamaire | Jamarion Al | Jamaury | James Antoine | Jametave'z |
| Jakwon (0.01) | Jaligha | Jamais | Ja-Marious | Jamauryunn | James Ashby | Jametri |
| Jakye | Jalijah | Jamal (0.15) | Jamarious | Jamaya | James Calvin | Jamey (0.01) |
| Jakyi | Jalijiah | Jamale | (0.01) | Jamayca | James Dale | Jameyson |
| Jakyla | Jalik | Jamaliki | Jamaris | Jamayne | James Dinh | Jamez |
| Jakylin | Jalil (0.02) | Jamalin | Jamarise | Jame | James Edward | Jamez' |
| Jakyous | Jalile | Jamall (0.01) | Jamariuan | Jame're | James Elijah | Jamezen |
| Jakyran | Ja-Lin | Jamané | Ja-Marius | Jameake | James Finnbarr | Jamfert |
| Jakyre | Jalin (0.01) | Jamani | Jamarius (0.03) | Jameal | James Ian | Jami |
| Jakyree | Jalin-Alex | Jamanté | Jamariya | Jamear | James Jamic | Jamiach |
| Jakyri | Jaline | Jamanuel | Jamariyen | Jameare | James Jihwan | Jamiael |
| Jakyrin | Jalinn | Jamar (0.10) | Jamarkcus | Jamearl | James Joel | Jamiah |
| Jakyron | Jalino | Jamar Lee | Jamarkis | Jameas | James Jr | Jamiahis |
| Jakyus | Jalio | Jamar'reon | Jamarkous | Jameason | James L | Jamian |
| Jal | Jalique | Jamar'rion | Jamarkus | Jamecen | James Lawton | Jamiar |
| Jal'an | Jaliyah | Jamarae | Jamarl | Jamed | James Lorenzo | Jamias |
| Jal'en | Jaliyn | Jamarco | Jamarlon | Jamee | James Micha | Jamicael |
| Jalael | Jallah | Jamarcus | Jamarlyn | Jameeier | James Michael | Jamicah |
| Jalahn | Jallen | (0.03) | Jamaron | Jameek | James Monta | Jamical |
| Jalal (0.01) | Jalloub | Jamarcuse | Jamarqis | Jameel (0.02) | James Najhar | Jamichael (0.01) |
| Jalal Mathys | Jalmani | Jamard | Jamarques | Jameen | James Parker | Jamicheal |
| Jalan (0.01) | Jalmar | Jamaré | Jamarquez | Jameer (0.02) | James Patri | Jamico |
| Jalandis | Jalon (0.02) | Jamare (0.01) | Jamarquis | Jameere | James Patrick | Jamie (0.13) |
| Jalani (0.01) | Jaloni | Jamareá | Jamarqus | Jameh | James Philip | Jamie Thomas |
| Jalanso | Jalonnie | Jamarean | Jamarr (0.01) | Jamei | James Rober | Jamie'on |
| Jalany | Jalonntay | Jamareay | Jamarre | Jameial | James Robert | Jamie-Alan |
| Jalaun | Jaluan | Jamaree (0.01) | Jamarree | Jameice | James Sawyer | Jamiean |
| Jalawn | Jalue | Jamarei | Jamarri (0.01) | Jameil | James T | Jamiel (0.01) |
| Jaleal | Jalycis | Jamareion | Jamarrian | Jameilion | James Willi | Jamielamar |
| Jaleb | Jalyn (0.02) | Jamaren | Jamarrie | Jameion | James William | Jamien |

| | | | | | | |
|---|---|---|---|---|---|---|
| Jamieon | Jamon *(0.01)* | Jamyre | Janhi | Jany-Evrard | Jaquavis | Jaraius |
| Jamie-Paul | Jamon' | Jamyreon | Janhoy | Janzel | Jaquavius | Jaraiyah |
| Jamier *(0.01)* | Jamond | Jamyron | Jani | Jaomarion | Jaquavunta | Jarall |
| Jamier Dwight | Jamondre | Jamysen | Janichols | Jaon | Jaquawn | Jaramiah |
| Jamieson *(0.01)* | Jamone | Jamyson | Janiel *(0.01)* | Japdeep | Jaquay | Jarard |
| Jamiher | Jamoni | Jan *(0.04)* | Janiel Nestor | Japeth | Jaquaylon | Jaray |
| Jamiir | Jamonn | Jan Carlos | Janielle | Japgur | Jaquaz | Jarayne |
| Jamijay | Jamonque | Jan Denzel | Janier | Japhet | Jaque | Jarayveon |
| Jamik | Jamont | Jan Lil | Janigil | Japheth *(0.01)* | Jaqué | Jarcus |
| Jamikeia | Jamonta | Jan Luis | Janik | Japhirian | Jaque'z | Jardan |
| Jamikkol | Jamontae | Jan Zachary | Janilan | Japjot | Jaqueecé | Jardaruis |
| Jamiko | Jamontaé | Jan'esen | Janile | Japjyot | Jaquel | Jardon |
| Jamil *(0.04)* | Jamontay | Janado | Jani-Marik | Japnoor | Jaquell | Jare |
| Jamile | Jamonte | Janai | Janine | Japrice | Jaquen | Jarec |
| Jamilion | Jamonté | Janak | Janio | Japroj | Jaquenza | Jared *(0.91)* |
| Jamilius | Jamontes | Janar | Janiro | Japsen | Jaquerius | Jared Daniel |
| Jamill | Jamontez | Janard | Janiun | Japsimran | Jaques | Jared Denis |
| Jamillah | Jamontre | Janared | Janiyo | Jaqai | Jaquese | Jared Jason |
| Jamille | Jamonty | Janari | Jankel | Jaqari | Jaquest | Jared-Ian |
| Jamilton | Jamor | Janari'es | Jan-Michael | Jaqaun | Jaquevis | Jaredth |
| Jamin *(0.03)* | Jamore | Janarie | Janmichael | Jaqaveion | Jaquez *(0.01)* | Jaree |
| Jaminique | Jamori | Janarious | Jann | Jaqavis | Jaqui | Jareece |
| Jamion | Jamorian | Janaris | Janncarlos | Jaqavius | Jaquice | Jareeh |
| Jamir *(0.07)* | Jamoriaun | Janaro | Janne | Jaqkal | Jaquielle | Jareek |
| Jamir' | Jamorion | Janarri | Jannelier | Jaqori | Jaquil | Jarees |
| Jamire | Jamorri | Janathian | Janniel | Jaqson | Jaquille | Jareese |
| Jamiree | Jamorrious | Janbaaz | Janniell | Jaqu'i | Jaquin | Jareht |
| Jamireon | Jamorris | Jancarlo | Jano | Jaqua | Jaquine | Jareis |
| Jamireus | Jamos | Jancarlos *(0.01)* | Janoah | Jaquae | Jaquinn | Jarek *(0.01)* |
| Jamirh | Jamour | Jance | Janoah Thomas | Jaquail | Jaquirius | Jarel *(0.01)* |
| Jamiri | Jamourice | Jancef | Janpiere | Jaqual | Jaquis | Jarell *(0.03)* |
| Jamirion | Jampiero | Jancen | Janpierre | Jaqualen | Jaquise | Jarelle *(0.01)* |
| Jamiris | Jamree | Jancer | Janpol | Jaqualine | Jaquon | Jarem |
| Jamiro | Jamri | Janco | Janrey | Ja-Quan | Jaquorious | Jaremiah |
| Jamirson | Jamses | Jandel | Jansel | Jaquan *(0.06)* | Jaquorrion | Jaremy |
| Jamis | Jamshaid | Jandell | Jansen *(0.01)* | Jaquane | Jaqureyon | Jaren *(0.05)* |
| Jamisen *(0.01)* | Jamshed | Jander | Jansiel | Jaquann | Jaqurius | Jarend |
| Jamison *(0.15)* | Jamsheed | Janderi | Jansky | Jaquantae | Jaquro | Jaress |
| Jamiu | Jamshell | Jandoel | Janson *(0.01)* | Jaquante | Jaquwan | Jaret *(0.02)* |
| Jamiyen | Jamuanté | Jandon | Janssen | Jaquar | Jaqwan | Jareth *(0.01)* |
| Jamiz | Jamuel | Jandre | Janston | Jaquari | Jaqwaun | Jareth-Aiden |
| Jammal | Jamul | Jandy | Janten | Jaquarion | Jaqwavion | Jarett *(0.01)* |
| Jammel | Jamuori | Janei | Janthony | Jaquarious | Jaqwel | Jarez |
| Jammi | Jamus | Janeil | Jantuan | Jaquarius *(0.01)* | Jaqwon | Jari |
| Jammie | Jamy | Janeison | Jantzen | Jaquarri | Jaqx | Jarian |
| Jammil | Jamyang | Janek | Janu | Jaquarrius | Jar'navius | Jaric |
| Jammy | Jamychael | Janeko | Januario | Jaquarus | Jar'quez | Jaricho |
| Jammyl | Jamyias | Janel | January | Jaquavian | Jar'rone | Jarick |
| Jamod | Jamyica | Janer | Januel | Jaquavin | Jar'varian | Jarico |
| Jamoderick | Jamyius | Jan-Erik | Janus | Jaquavion | Jarad | Jarid |
| Jamoi | Jamykhal | Janero | Janwu | Jaquavionn | Jaraé | Jarieah |
| Jamol | Jamyle | Jang Koon | Jany | Jaquavious | Jarah | Jaried |
| | Jamyr | Jangel | Janye | *(0.01)* | Jarail | Jariel *(0.02)* |

| | | | | | | |
|---|---|---|---|---|---|---|
| Jariem | Jarquaze | Jarvier | Jashandip | Jaskirat | Jasseim | Jatias |
| Jarien | Jarqueise | Jarvinder | Jashanjot | Jaskirit | Jassel | Jatin |
| Jarieus | Jarquellis | Jarvis (0.05) | Jashanpal | Jasleon | Jassem | Jatinder |
| Jarik | Jarques | Jarvius | Jashanveer | Jaslok | Jassen | Jatniel |
| Jarim | Jarquez | Jarvon | Ja-Shaun | Jasman | Jasser | Jatoby |
| Jarin (0.01) | Jarquin | Jarvonté | Jashaun (0.02) | Jasmandeep | Jassiel | Jaton |
| Jarion | Jarquise | Jarvoris | Jashawan | Jasmanjot | Jassirit | Ja-Tonio |
| Jarious | Jarqurius | Jarvous | Jashawn (0.02) | Jasmany | Jassnoor | Jatonio |
| Jarique | Jarrad | Jaryd | Jashen | Jasmeet | Jasson | Jatorian |
| Jaris | Jarral | Jarye-Anthtony | Jasher | Jasmeher | Jastanley | Jatorrion |
| Jarison | Jarran | Jaryn (0.01) | Jashhon | Jasmin (0.02) | Jasten | Jatravious |
| Jaritt | Jarrard | Jaryoil | Jashia | Jasmine | Jastevio | Jatwan |
| Jarius (0.01) | Jarratt | Jaryon | Jashiem | Jasnam | Jastin | Jatym |
| Jariyan | Jarred (0.04) | Jaryus | Jashik | Jasneel | Jastinvir | Jatyren |
| Jarkarvion | Jarreius | Jarzinoh | Jashir | Jasnoor | Jaston | Jauden |
| Jarkavian | Jarrel | Jas | Jashon | Jason (3.77) | Jasuan | Jaudon |
| Jarkeese | Jarrell (0.02) | Jas Keerat | Jashone | Jason Brian | Jasun | Jaugar |
| Jarkel | Jarren (0.02) | Jasaan | Jashoua | James | Jasur | Jaukin |
| Jarkes | Jarret (0.02) | Jasai | Jashten | Jason James | Jasvir | Jaumal |
| Jarkevis | Jarreth | Jasaia | Jashton | Jason Jashon | Jaswanth | Jaume |
| Jarl | Jarrett (0.12) | Jasaiah | Jashua (0.01) | Jason Jesus | Jaswinder | Jaumell |
| Jarlath | Jarrette | Jasaic | Jashun | Jason Jr | Jaswon | Jaun |
| Jarlem | Jarrian | Jasair | Jashvant | Jason Justynn | Jasya | Jauncy |
| Jarmaine | Jarrick | Jasaire | Jashyne | Jason Minh | Jasyah | Jauntevion |
| Jarman | Jarrid | Jasan | Jasi | Jason Robert | Jasyn | Jauqkice |
| Jarmane | Jarrie | Jasandeep | Jasiah (0.04) | Jason Scott | Jaszon | Jauren |
| Jarmar | Jarrik | Jasani | Jasiaha | Jason Skyla | Jatai | Jaurian |
| Jarmard | Jarrin | Jasante | Jasiahs | Jason William | Jataivion | Jaurice |
| Jarmarion | Jarrington | Jasareth | Jasiel | Jason Xavier | Jataivious | Jauriesh |
| Jarmarius | Jarrious | Jasarin | Jasiel Sostenes | Jason-Daniel | Jatan | Jauseff |
| Jarmarkis | Jarris | Jasaun | Jasiem | Jasondeep | Jatari | Jauson |
| Jarme | Jarrison | Jasayvion | Jasier | Jason- | Jatarious | Jaustin |
| Jarmon | Jarrius | Jascea | Jasiiyah | Emmanuel | Jatarrious | Jauston |
| Jarmonia | Jarrod (0.04) | Jaschandan | Jasim | Jason-Jimmy | Jataureis | Jauvani |
| Jarmoris | Jarron (0.01) | Jasdeep | Jasin | Jason-John | Jatavian | Jauwan |
| Jarmyia | Jarrot | Jasdip | Jasinn | Jasonlee | Jatavion | Jav'ion |
| Jarnell | Jarrott | Jase (0.12) | Jasir (0.02) | Jason-Michael | Jatavious | Javaan |
| Jarnin | Jarryd | Jasean (0.01) | Jasire | Jason-Paul | Jatavis | Javae |
| Jarno | Jarryn | Jaseer | Jasiri | Jasonpreet | Jatavius | Javah |
| Jaro | Jartavious | Jasef | Jasiyah | Jason-Raynier | Jatayvien | Javahn |
| Jarod (0.03) | Jaru | Jasel | Jasiyous | Jason-Richard | Jate | Javahrien |
| Jarodd | Jarule | Jasem | Jasjeet | Jason-Thomas | Jaten | Javain |
| Jarol | Jarus | Jase-Michael | Jasjit | Jaspal | Jaterius | Javaire |
| Jarold | Jarvarie | Jasen (0.01) | Jasjot | Jasper (0.15) | Jaterreon | Javaius |
| Jarolt | Jarvaris | Jaseph | Jaskaram | Jasper Lloyd | Jaterrian | Javall |
| Jarom | Jarvarius | Jaser | Jaskaran (0.01) | Jasper Marco | Jaterrion | Javan (0.02) |
| Jarome | Jarvell | Jasere | Jaskaran Singh | Jaspreet | Ja-Terrious | Javan Lee |
| Jaromil | Jarvelle | Jaset | Jaskaranpreet | Jaspur | Jaterrius | Javani |
| Jaron (0.07) | Jarvelles | Jasey | Jaskaran-Singh | Jasraj | Jatezz | Javanie |
| Jaronn | Jarvez | Jasha | Jaskarn | Jasrajan | Jathan (0.02) | Javanni |
| Jaroslav | Jarví | Jashad | Jaskeerit | Jasrajpreet | Jathen | Javant |
| Jarquaveon | Jarvian | Jashan | Jaskeet | Jass | Jathon | Javantae |
| Jarquavious | Jarviel | Jashandeep | Jaski | Jassan | Jathyn | Javante |

Javaon
Javar
Javare
Javarea
Javareon
Javares
Javareta
Javari *(0.02)*
Javaria
Javarian
Javarias
Javarick
Javarie
Javarien
Javarion
Javarious
Javaris *(0.01)*
Javarius *(0.01)*
Javariy
Javariyoung
Javarous
Javarr
Javarre
Javarri
Javarrie
Javarus
Javary
Javaryn
Javaryonte
Javas
Javasay
Javasea
Javaughn
Javaun
Javay
Jave
Javé
Jave'ir
Jave'on
Javeale
Javed
Javee
Javeen
Javein
Javeion
Javeir
Javel
Javell
Javelle
Javelyn
Javen *(0.04)*
Javen Bruce
Javenson

Javeoin
Javeon *(0.02)*
Javeon Antonio
Javeon Jamaal
Javeontae
Javeoun
Javere
Javerius
Javerson
Javery
Javes
Javey
Javeyin
Javeyn
Javeyon
Javez
Javhon
Javi
Javi'on
Javia
Javian *(0.03)*
Javiane
Javiar
Javid
Javiel
Javien *(0.01)*
Javieon
Javier *(1.14)*
Javier-Abdon
Javier-Antonio
Javiere
Javier-Esteban
Javier-Omid
Javieyn
Javin *(0.03)*
Javinee
Javino
Javion *(0.08)*
Javion Mess
Javione
Javionne
Javiontae
Javior
Javious
Javir
Javire
Javis
Javit
Javius
Javiv
Javohn
Ja-Von
Javon *(0.21)*

Javon James
Javonate
Javondre
Javone
Javoni
Javon-Najee
Javonne
Javonni
Javonnie
Javonta *(0.01)*
Javon-Tae
Javontae *(0.02)*
Javontah
Javontavious
Javontay
Ja-Vonte
Javonté
Javonté
Javonte *(0.02)*
Javontees
Javontei
Javontez
Javontie
Javontious
Javontri
Javori
Javorick
Javorious
Javoris
Javoriyan
Javorous
Javory
Javoun
Javquez
Javuan
Javy
Javyion
Javyis
Javyn
Javyon
Javyun
Jawa
Jawaad
Jawad *(0.01)*
Jawadhasan
Jawahski La
Jawan
Jawand
Jawann
Jawantaé
Jawaski
Jawaun
Jawauntae

Jawed
Jawesley
Jawil
Jawlie
Jawon *(0.01)*
Jawuan
Jawwad
Jax *(0.04)*
Jaxall
Jaxcen
Jaxe
Jaxel
Jaxen *(0.02)*
Jaxiel
Jaxier
Jaxil
Jaxin
Jaxn
Jaxom
Jaxon *(0.57)*
Jaxon-Miles
Jaxs
Jaxsen *(0.01)*
Jaxson *(0.22)*
Jaxston
Jaxsun
Jaxsyah
Jaxsyn
Jaxten
Jaxton *(0.01)*
Jaxx
Jaxxen
Jaxxin
Jaxxon *(0.01)*
Jaxyn
Jaxzel
Jaxzen
Jaxzon
Jay *(0.24)*
Jay D'n
Jay Davinci
Jay Don
Jay Kwon
Jay Michael
Jay Saun
Jay Shawn
Jay Vion
Jay Wesley
Jay'
Jay'areon
Jay'cari
Jay'corian
Jay'dari

Jay'den *(0.01)*
Jay'don
Jay'donis
Jay'ki
Jay'korey
Jay'kwon
Jay'lee
Jay'leen
Jay'len
Jay'len Latrell
Jay'lenn
Jay'lin
Jay'lon
Jay'lyn
Jay'mar
Jay'mari
Jay'marion
Jay'meir
Jay'mere
Jay'mier
Jay'mon
Jay'on
Jay'quan
Jay'quaviou
Jay'quel
Jay'quon
Jay'relle
Jay'sean
Jay'shaun
Jay'shawn
Jay'shon
Jay'sincere
Jay'son
Jay'v'eon
Jay'vaughn
Jay'vaun
Jay'veair
Jay'veion
Jay'veon
Jay'vian
Jay'vien
Jay'vion
Jay'von
Jay'vonne
Jay'zaun
Jaya
Jayakrisna
Jay-Allen
Jayamonte
Jayamuni
Jayan
Jayana
Jayanna

Jayant
Jayanth
Jayapraveen
Jayaram
Jayare
Jay-Arza
Jayathins
Jayauntae
Jayawn
Jaybe
Jaybin
Jaybran
Jaybre
Jaybreon
Jaybriel
Jaybron
Jayby
Jaybyon
Jayce *(0.17)*
Jaycean
Jaycee *(0.01)*
Jaycek
Jaycel
Jaycen *(0.01)*
Jayceon *(0.01)*
Jaycer
Jayceton
Jaychaun
Jaycian
Jaycik
Jaycin
Jaycion
Jaycn
Jayco
Jaycob *(0.03)*
Jaycon
Jayd
Jaydaan
Jaydan *(0.04)*
Jaydarian
Jayddren
Jayde *(0.01)*
Jaydean
Jaydee
Jaydel
Jaydell
Jaydem
Jay-Den
Jayden *(3.95)*
Jayden Kiet
Jayden Leo
Jayden Mathew
Jayden Mekhi

Jayden R
Jayden Todd
Jayden Warren
Jaydence
Jaydenio
Jaydenn
Jayden-Pharell
Jayden-Ray
Jaydes
Jaydhyn
Jaydian
Jaydidiah
Jaydien
Jaydin *(0.06)*
Jaydis
Jaydiz
Jaydn *(0.01)*
Jaydohn
Jaydon *(0.17)*
Jaydon-Ray
Jaydouglas
Jaydrean
Jaydrese
Jaydric
Jaydrien
Jaydun
Jaydyn *(0.01)*
Jaye
Jayedon
Jayedyn
Jayelin
Jayelon
Jayen
Jayeren
Jayesh
Jayesiah
Jayeson
Jayexson
Jayfonz
Jayfric
Jaygan
Jayger
Jay-Gustavo
Jayhahn
Jayhdyn
Jayhlen
Jayhonb
Jayiah
Jayiln
Jayin
Jayion
Jayivon
Jay-J

| | | | | | | |
|---|---|---|---|---|---|---|
| Jayjouir | Jaylus | Jay-Pherson | Jaysin | Jayvier | Jazelle | Je'ontae |
| Jayk | Jaylyn *(0.03)* | Jayqoi | Jaysinh | Jayvin *(0.01)* | Jazen | Je'quan |
| Jaykab | Jaylynn | Jayqon | Jaysir | Jayvion *(0.02)* | Jazerin | Je'raymein |
| Jaykar | Jaymaina | Jay-Quan | Jayslen | Jayvione | Jazheer | Je're'mie |
| Jayke *(0.01)* | Jaymar | Jayquan *(0.01)* | Jaysn | Jayvionte | Jaziah *(0.01)* | Je'shaun |
| Jaykedric | Jaymareon | Jayquane | Jayson *(0.29)* | Jayvious | Jazid | Je'shawn |
| Jayken | Jaymarion | Jayquel | Jaysonn | Jayvis | Jaziel *(0.01)* | Je'shon |
| Jaykil | Jaymarious | Jayquez | Jayson-William | Jayvn | Jazier | Je'shuah |
| Jaykin | Jaymark | Jayquiese | Jaysson | Jayvne | Jaziher | Je'siah |
| Jayko | Jaymarr | Jayquion | Jaysten | Jay-Von | Jazil | Je'stevion |
| Jaykob *(0.01)* | Jaymason | Jayquis | Jaystin | Jayvon *(0.05)* | Jazimeth | Je'sus |
| Jaykobe | Jaymaurie | Jayquise | Jayston | Jayvone | Jazion | Je'tannue |
| Jaykoda | Jay-Me | Jayquon | Jaysun | Jayvonie | Jazious | Je'taurian |
| Jaykovis | Jayme *(0.01)* | Jayquwan | Jaysun-Darold | Jayvonne | Jazir | Je'vaughn |
| Jaykub | Jayme Jevon | Jay-Qwon | Jay-T | Jayvonni | Jaziyah | Je'vion |
| Jay-Kwan | Jaymee | Jayraj | Jaytaylor | Jayvonní | Jazmeer | Je'vyon |
| Jaykwan | Jaymeer | Jayram | Jayten | Jayvonta | Jazmund | Je'zer |
| Jaykwon | Jayme-Lee | Jayreal | Jaythan *(0.01)* | Jayvontae | Ja-Zon | Jeaden |
| Jaykwone | Jaymen *(0.01)* | Jayrees | Jaythaniel | Jayvonte | Jazon | Jeams |
| Jayla | Jaymere | Jayreese | Jaythel | Jayvon-Warrick | Jazsaib | Jean *(0.09)* |
| Jaylahn | Jaymes *(0.02)* | Jayrell | Jaythen | Jayvyn *(0.01)* | Jazsper | Jean Baptiste |
| Jaylain | Jaymeson *(0.01)* | Jayren | Jaythien | Jaywan | Jazuan | Jean Benoit |
| Jaylan *(0.07)* | Jaymhere | Jayreon | Jaython | Jaywin | Jazuel | Jean Carlos |
| Jayland | Jaymi | Jayrese | Jaytn | Jaywon | Jazyel | Jean Charle |
| Jay-Laquan | Jaymiah | Jay-Rion | Jayton | Jayx | Jazyren | Jean Christof |
| Jayleb | Jaymian | Jayrion | Jaytoriun | Jayzaiah | Jazz *(0.01)* | Jean Claude |
| Jaylee | Jaymie | Jayrius | Jaytton | Jayzanielle | Jazz'rion | Jean Colson |
| Jayleen | Jaymier | Jayro *(0.01)* | Jaytwan | Jayzee | Jazzmale | Jean Emilien |
| Jaylehn | Jaymin *(0.01)* | Jayron *(0.01)* | Jaytwon | Jayzel | Jazzmere | Jean Felix |
| Jaylein | Jaymir | Jayrone | Jayun | Jayzen | JB | Jean Fraancois |
| Jaylen *(0.82)* | Jaymire | Jayronni | Jayush | Jayzer | JC | Jean Francois |
| Jaylen Antonio | Jaymis | Jaysaan | Jayvaire | Jayzhoun | JD | Jean Gabriel |
| Jaylen Mikeal | Jaymison *(0.01)* | Jaysahn | Jayvan | Jayziah | Jden | Jean Luka |
| Jaylend | Jaymmes | Jaysaiah | Jayvani | Jayzik | Jdon | Jean Marino |
| Jaylens | Jaymon | Jaysal | Jayvante | Jayzin | Je Bron | Jean Michel |
| Jayleon | Jaymond | Jaysan | Jayvaughn | Jayzmael | Je Neil | Jean Mike |
| Jayler | Jaymone | Jaysarr | Jayvaun | Jayzn | Je Ronn | Jean Nardy |
| Jaylian | Jaymont | Jaysaul | Jayvee | Jayzohn | Je'andre | Jean Olivier |
| Jaylib | Jayms | Jaysay | Jayveer | Jayzon | Je'bari | Jean Paul |
| Jaylien | Jaymz *(0.01)* | Jayse *(0.02)* | Jayvein | Jaz | Je'calvin | Jean Philip |
| Jaylin *(0.16)* | Jaynald | Jaysean *(0.01)* | Jayveion | Jaz'ques | Je'cario | Jean Philippe |
| Jaylin Daiquan | Jaynard | Jaysen *(0.02)* | Jayven *(0.01)* | Jazae | Je'carious | Jean Robert |
| Jaylin Jontez | Jayneel | Jayshaun *(0.01)* | Jayven | Jazael | Je'caryous | Jean Samuel |
| Jaylin-Anthony | Jayneil | Jayshawan | Nathaniel | Jazariah | Je'dan | Jean Sebastien |
| Jaylind | Jaynel | Jayshawn *(0.02)* | Jayveon *(0.02)* | Jazarian | Je'dehl | Jean Thomas |
| Jaylinn | Jayniel | Jayshawnn | Jayveontay | Jazarion | Je'don | Jean Xavier |
| Jaylix | Jayohn | Jayshon *(0.01)* | Jayveonte | Jazavier | Je'dyn | Jean-Alexandre |
| Jayln *(0.01)* | Jay-Omarion | Jayshone | Jayvian *(0.01)* | Jazavion | Je'kysaun | Jean-Alexis |
| Jayln'd | Jayon *(0.01)* | Jayshua | Jayviant | Jazaya | Je'lani | Jeanathan |
| Jaylon *(0.14)* | Jayoni | Jay-Shun | Jayvias | Jazean | Je'marie | Jean-Baptiste |
| Jayluhn | Jayovine | Jayshun | Jayviaun | Jazeb | Je'marion | Jean-Baptiste |
| Jaylum | Jaypden | Jaysiah | Jayvien | Jazel | Je'mere | Lanza |
| Jaylun | Jaypen | Jaysilus | Jay-Vieon | Jazell | Je'noa | Jean-Bernadeau |

| | | | | | | |
|---|---|---|---|---|---|---|
| Jean-Carlo | Jean-Normand | Jebodiah | Jeevaa | Jehiel | Jele | Jenai |
| Jeancarlo | Jeano | Jebrell | Jeevan *(0.01)* | Jehjot | Jeleel | Jenaro |
| Jeancarlos *(0.01)* | Jean-Olivier | Jebron | Jeevanjit | Jehkai | Jelenik | Jency |
| Jean-Cedric | Jeanot | Jebzier | Jeevatjai | Jehki | Jeliel | Jenderzon |
| Jean-Cedrik | Jean-Pascal | Jec'queline | Jeeven | Jehlear | Jelijah | Jendri |
| Jean-Charles | Jean-Patrice | Jecamryn | Jeevin | Jehmal | Jelio | Jendrik |
| Jean-Christophe *(0.02)* | Jean-Patrick | Jecari | Jef'fon | Jehmeel | Jellil | Jenel |
| Jean-Claude | Jean-Paul | Jecarry | Jeferson | Jehmi | Jelmontae | Jenesis |
| Jean-Daniel | Jeanpaul | Jecht | Jeff *(0.03)* | Jehmir | Je-Lon | Jengiz |
| Jeandavid | Jean-Philip | Jechwa | Jeffa | Jehonathan | Jelon | Jeniel |
| Jean-Diego | Jean-Philippe *(0.01)* | Jeci | Jeffer | Jehova | Jelonie | Jeniesus |
| Jeaneel | Jean-Phillip | Jeciah | Jefferey | Jehovah | Jelonte | Jenina |
| Jean-Elie | Jean-Pierre | Jecis | Jeffereyson | Jehovanny | Jelonté | Jenkin |
| Jeanero | Jeanpierre | Jeckonia | Jefferson *(0.09)* | Jehri | Jelontré | Jenkins |
| Jean-Evens | Jean-Raphael | Jecob | Jefferson-Alexis | Jehu | Jelun | Jenner |
| Jean-Felix *(0.01)* | Jean-Remi | Jecon | Jeffery *(0.19)* | Jehziah | Jelyjah | Jennifer |
| Jean-François | Jean-Remy | Jeconiah | Jeffery Uri | Jei'el | Jelzon | Jen-Nikolas |
| Jean-Francois *(0.01)* | Jean-Samuel | Jecori | Jeffery-Lee | Jei'lyn | Jem | Jennings *(0.01)* |
| Jean-Francois III | Jean-Saurel | Jecory | Jeffin | Jeice | Jemain | Jeno |
| Jean-Frederic | Jeansea | Jecqael | Jefflee | Jeicod | Jemal | Jenoah |
| Jean-Frederick | Jean-Sébastien | Jed *(0.01)* | Jeffney | Jeicyn | Jemale | Jenoire |
| Jeanfredo | Jean-Sebastien *(0.01)* | Jed Enzo | Jeffory | Jeidez | Jemar | Jenri |
| Jean-Gabriel | Jean-Simon *(0.01)* | Jed Francis | Jeffrantz | Jeidyn | Jemarcus | Jenrique |
| Jean-Gilles | Jean-Steven | Jedadiah | Jeffred | Jeiel | Jemarean | Jenrre |
| Jean-Guy | Jeanté | Jedaiah | Jeffren | Jeighden | Jemaree | Jenrri |
| Jeanique | Jean-Thoams | Jedayus | Jeffrenson | Jeilen | Jemari | Jenrry |
| Jean-Jacques | Jean-Thomas *(0.01)* | Jedd | Jeffrey *(0.85)* | Jeilyn | Jemariaun | Jens *(0.01)* |
| Jean-Krystophe | Jeantiel | Jeddidiah | Jeffrey Peter | Jeimin | Jemarion | Jensel Allen |
| Jean-Lou | Jeanti-Samuel | Jedediah *(0.01)* | Jeffrey Roy | Jeinez | Jemarion Ulyesses | Jensen *(0.03)* |
| Jean-Louis | Jean-Troy | Jeden | Jeffreychufeng | Jeinner | Jemarqus | Jenser |
| Jeanlu | Jean-Vincent | Jedens | Jeffrey-Roni | Jeins | Jemeh | Jensi |
| Jean-Luc | Jean-Vital | Jederick | Jeffrey-Wayne | Jeiran | Jemel | Jenslie |
| Jean-Luke | Jeanyck | Jedes | Jeffrie | Jeiser | Jemell | Jenson *(0.01)* |
| Jean-Manuel | Jean-Yves | Jed-Ethan | Jeffries | Jeison | Jemelson | Jens-Peter |
| Jean-Marc | Jean-Yves Jr | Jedi | Jeffrin | Jeisser | Jemerical | Jenssy |
| Jean-Marie | Jeaquan | Jediael | Jeffriy | Jeissey | Jemerion | Jensun |
| Jean-Mathieu | Jearamy | Jediah | Jeffry *(0.01)* | Jeisson | Jemerius | Jensy |
| Jean-Maxim | Jearim | Jedidiah *(0.03)* | Jeffryn | Jeje | Jemiah | Jensyn |
| Jean-Maxime | Jearmiah | Jediel | Jeffsen | Jejuan | Jemiahs | Jentezen |
| Jean-Michael | Jearrold | Jedin | Jeffvence | Jekai | Jemier | Jentry |
| Jean-Michee | Jeavanni | Jednela | Jeff-Yvan | Jekala | Jemil | Jentzen |
| Jean-Michel *(0.01)* | Jeaven | Jedon | Jefrei | Jekaleb | Jemirrion | Jenuel |
| Jean-Mickael | Jeavion | Jedrek | Jefrey | Jekari | Jemiyus | Jenzel |
| Jean-Mikael | Jeavon | Jedrian | Jefrin | Jekhi | Jemmal | Jeo Marvin |
| Jean-Mischael | Jeb *(0.02)* | Jedric | Jefry | Jekhiel | Jemmy | Jeobanni |
| Jean-Nicolas *(0.01)* | Jebby | Jedrick | Jeg | Jekhy | Jemon | Jeoffry |
| Jeannin | Jebediah *(0.01)* | Jedrik | Jegir | Jekil | Jemone | Jeofrey |
| | Jebidiah | Jedsada | Jehad | Jekori | Jemorad | Jeon |
| | Jebidyah | Jedyn | Jehan | Jelahn | Jemore | Jeong |
| | | Jeef | Jehanzabe | Jelaini | Jemsly | Jeong Yoon |
| | | Jeeison | Jehaziel | Jelan | Jemuel | Jeordie |
| | | Jeep | Jeheiel | Jelani *(0.02)* | Jenae | Jeorge |
| | | Jeet | Jehezkiel | Jelani Malachi | | Jeos |

Jeovahny
Jeovan
Jeovane
Jeovani
Jeovanie
Jeovanni
Jeovanny
Jeovany
Jeovonnie
Jeovunté
Jeph
Jepheth
Jephson
Jephte
Jephthah
Jephthe
Jeptha
Je-Quan
Jequan
Jequavius
Jequelen
Jer'darrien
Jer'kereion
Jer'maree
Jer'marian
Jer'mauri
Jer'micah
Jer'michael
Jer'mound
Jer'myzio
Jer'quise
Jer'rel
Jer'rontae
Jer'ryan
Jer'shad
Jer'varieus
Jer'von
Jerachi
Jerad
Jeradiah
Jeradyn
Jerae
Jerahmel
Jeral
Jerald *(0.02)*
Jeraldo
Jerale
Jeralth
Jeramani
Jerame
Jeramey
Jerami
Jeramia

Jeramiah *(0.06)*
Jeramie *(0.01)*
Jeramie Andru
Jeramiel
Jeramiha
Jeramion
Jeramitrius
Jeramius
Jeramiyah
Jeramy *(0.01)*
Jeramya
Jeramyah
Jeran *(0.01)*
Jerard
Jerardo
Jerardy
Jeray
Jerayl
Jerbari
Jerbree
Jerbrelle
Jerbrye
Jercardo
Jercarvie
Jerciano
Jerdaine
Jerdarius
Jere
Jere'miah
Jere'micah
Jereamiah
Jered *(0.01)*
Jered-Daniel
Jereian
Jereimah
Jerein
Jereis
Jerek *(0.01)*
Jerekiel
Jerel
Jerell *(0.01)*
Jerelle
Jeremaí
Jeremaiah
Jeremaih
Jeremain
Jeremaine
Jeremayah
Jereme
Jeremee
Jeremey
Jérémi
Jeremi *(0.03)*

Jeremia
Jeremiaah
Jeremiah *(2.94)*
Jeremiah Des
Jeremiah Kasim
Jeremiah Kwasi
Jeremiah
   Leviticus
Jeremiah-James
Jeremiahuz
Jeremias *(0.02)*
Jérémie *(0.01)*
Jeremie *(0.10)*
Jeremie Lucas
Jeremie Xavier
Jeremie-
   Jambalo
Jeremiel
Jeremie-
   Lambert
Jeremiha
Jeremi-Joel
Jereminah
Jeremis
Jeremitrius
Jeremiya
Jeremiyah
Jeremmi
Jérémy
Jeremy *(1.61)*
Jeremy Daniel
Jeremy Jordan
Jeremy Roenick
Jeremya
Jeremyah *(0.01)*
Jeremy-David
Jeremy-Filipe
Jeremy-Frank
Jeremy-Gabriel
Jeremyiah
Jeremy-James
Jeremy-
   Jefferson
Jeremy-Matthew
Jeremyn
Jeremy-Ngoy
Jeremy-Nick
Jeremy-Noel
Jeremyon
Jeremy-Ryan
Jeren
Jereniah
Jerens

Jereson
Jeret
Jerett
Jerezz
Jerhyn
Jeri
Jeriah *(0.01)*
Jeriahes
Jerian
Jeric
Jericho *(0.02)*
Jericho Bryce
Jerick
Jerick Luke
Jerico
Jerid
Jeriden
Jeriel *(0.01)*
Jeries
Jerik
Jeriko
Jerilmy
Jerilyle
Jerimah
Jerimaih
Jerime
Jerimeiha
Jerimi
Jerimia
Jerimiah *(0.04)*
Jerimiaha
Jerimiyah
Jerimy
Jerimya
Jerin *(0.01)*
Jerion
Jerious
Jeris
Jerisiah
Jerius
Jerjis
Jerjuan
Jerkarion
Jerkell
Jerkelvon
Jerkens
Jerl
Jermaal
Jermahd
Jermahi
Jermahl
Jermaiah
Jermain *(0.01)*

Jermaine *(0.19)*
Jermaini
Jermaire
Jermal
Jermale
Jermall
Jerman
Jermane
Jermani
Jermanz
Jermar
Jermarcus
Jermarh
Jermari
Jermario
Jermarion
Jermarious
Jermarius
Jermarkest
Jermarris
Jermaurhiyun
Jermauri
Jermayne
Jermeer
Jermeil
Jermel *(0.01)*
Jermere
Jermereis
Jermeriah
Jermero
Jermey
Jermi
Jermiah *(0.03)*
Jermichael
Jermicheal
Jermico
Jermie
Jermiha
Jermihia
Jermikkos
Jermil
Jermin
Jermir
Jermire
Jermiya
Jermiyah
Jermiyan
Jermole
Jermon
Jermone
Jermont
Jermontaé
Jermonte

Jermonté
Jermori
Jermuni
Jermy
Jermyah
Jermyiah
Jermyius
Jermyn
Jermyren
Jernell
Jernie
Jernimus
Jerny
Jerod *(0.01)*
Jerode
Jeroen
Jeroham
Jerold
Jerollice
Jerom
Jérôme
Jerome *(0.19)*
Jerome
   Augustine
Jerome
   Ephnaim
Jerome Francis
Jerome Ramo
Jeromee
Jeromi
Jeromiah
Jeromy *(0.01)*
Jeron *(0.01)*
Jerone
Jeronimo
Jerontay
Jerosme-Henri
Jerovani
Jerquavious
Jerquavis
Jerquawn
Jerr'ion
Jerrad
Jerrado
Jerrald
Jerramy
Jerramyah
Jerran
Jerrard
Jerraylin
Jerrayllius
Jerrayus
Jerre

Jerreal
Jerred
Jerreil
Jerrel *(0.01)*
Jerrell *(0.02)*
Jerren
Jerreth
Jerrett *(0.01)*
Jerrhan
Jerrhyon
Jerri
Jerriah
Jerriamiah
Jerrian
Jerricho
Jerrick *(0.01)*
Jerrico
Jerrid
Jerrie
Jerriel
Jerrih
Jerrik
Jerriki
Jerril
Jerrill
Jerrimi
Jerrin
Jerrion
Jerrique
Jerris
Jerrish
Jerrison
Jerritt
Jerrius
Jerrob
Jerrod *(0.01)*
Jerrodd
Jerrol
Jerrold
Jerron *(0.01)*
Jerrus
Jerry *(0.29)*
Jerry Ryan
Jerryck
Jerryd
Jerrydel
Jerryion
Jerryl
Jerrylee
Jerrylin
Jerryll
Jerrymiah
Jerryon

| | | | | | | |
|---|---|---|---|---|---|---|
| Jersain | Jesiyah | Jesufewa | Jevaul | Jeyvon | Jhamarius | Jhigh |
| Jersey | Jeslie | Jesup | Jevaun | Jezayvion | Jhamere | Jhikevyn |
| Jershaun | Jesly | Jesurun | Jeve | Jezekial | Jhamier | Jhilil |
| Jerson *(0.01)* | Jesmy Alejandro | Jesús | Jeveion | Jezer | Jhamir | Jhirmack |
| Jertavien | Jesner | Jesus *(3.25)* | Jevenson | Jezhua | Jhamontae | Jhirosky |
| Jertavious | Jesny | Jesus Aiden | Jeverette | Jeziah | Jhamonte | Jhirvonté |
| Jertrell | Jesohn | Jesus Aleja | Jeverson | Jezic | Jhamore | Jhiveon |
| Jeruel Jude | Jesper | Jesus Jair | Jeveyon | Jeziel | Jhamorious | Jhleo |
| Jerusalem | Jesrel | Jesus Jr | Jevier | Jezniel | Jhan | Jhmar |
| Jerusalen | Jess *(0.02)* | Jesus-Antonio | Jevin *(0.01)* | Jezoar | Jhancarlos | Jhmear |
| Jervais | Jesse *(2.17)* | Jesxva | Jevion | Jezrael | Jhani | Jhmeire |
| Jervanti | Jesse James | Jet *(0.02)* | Jevis | Jezreel *(0.01)* | Jhanias | Jhmouri |
| Jervarie | Jesse Lee | Jetavion | Jevohn | Jezriel | Jhanik | Jhoan |
| Jervarion | Jesse Luis | Jeter | Jevon *(0.03)* | Jezyah | Jhansel | Jhojan |
| Jervaris | Jesse Michael | Jethro *(0.01)* | Jevonald | Jh'alyn | Jhansiddh | Jhomar |
| Jervarrest | Jessea | Jethursan | Jevone | Jh'couriyon | Jha-Quan | Jhon *(0.01)* |
| Jervay | Jesse-Amine | Jetlee | Jevonta | Jha'dar | Jhaquay | Jhonah |
| Jervis | Jessee *(0.01)* | Jetli | Jevontae | Jha'i | Jhared | Jhonas |
| Jervon | Jessef | Jetly | Jevonte | Jha'kavion | Jharell | Jhonatan *(0.01)* |
| Jervonte | Jesse-James | Jeton | Jevonté | Jha'mari | Jharen | Jhonatay |
| Jerwin | Jessejames | Jetro | Jevyn | Jha'meir | Jharet | Jhonathan |
| Jerwyt | Jesse-Jay | Jetry | Jewel | Jha'miere | Jharon | *(0.01)* |
| Jeryes | Jesselee | Jetsen | Jewell | Jha'myle | Jhase | Jhonathon |
| Jeryl | Jessen | Jetson | Jewellius | Jha'quavious | Jhashon | Jhonaven |
| Jeryle | Jessep | Jetsun | Jewelyn | Jhaad | Jhavard | Jhonen |
| Jerym | Jessey | Jett *(0.11)* | Jewen | Jhace | Jhavianne | Jhoner |
| Jerymiah | Jessi *(0.01)* | Jetta | Jewett | Jhadan | Jhavier | Jhones |
| Jeryn | Jessiah *(0.01)* | Jetthra | Jewish | Jhadbiel | Jhavon | Jhoni |
| Jerys | Jessica | Jettln | Jewlien | Jhaden | Jhavoni | Jhonjairo |
| Jerz | Jessie *(0.11)* | Jettrin | Jewon | Jhadin | Jhavonte | Jhonluis |
| Jerzee | Jessie-James | Jettsyn | Jewsaiah | Jhaeden-Tru | Jhay | Jhonnathan |
| Jerzey | Jessiel | Jet-Ty | Jexiel | Jhaedien | Jhayden | Jhonny |
| Jerzy | Jessikel | Jetwan | Jexon | Jhaedin-Jon | Jhaylen | Jhonny Fabricio |
| Jesael | Jessiyah | Jetzael | Jey | Jhael | Jhaylon | Jhonnyel |
| Jesaiah | Jessjuan | Jetzain | Jeyce | Jhaelyn | Jhayrolle | Jhonsi |
| Jescey | Jesson | Jetzeel | Jeyden | Jhaheim | Jhayvin | Jhontez |
| Jese | Jesstifur | Jetzibe | Jeydin | Jhahid | Jheldoff-Carlo | Jhony |
| Jesé | Jessua | Jetziel | Jeydn | Jhai Sean | Jhenspe | Jhordan |
| Jesean | Jessun | Jetzu | Jeydon | Jhai'ray | Jheric | Jhorden |
| Jesha'iah | Jessup | Jeube | Jeydrick | Jhailynd | Jherkeem | Jhordy |
| Jeshaud | Jessy *(0.05)* | Jeudin | Jeyffrin | Jhair | Jhermie | Jhordyn |
| Jeshaun | Jessy James | Jeulien | Jeylan | Jhakam | Jhermil | Jhoseen |
| Jeshawn | Jessy-James | Jeury | Jeylen | Jhakarie | Jhernadrik | Jhosep |
| Jeshiah | Jessy-Jaymes | Jevah | Jeyren | Jhakeem | Jhery | Jhoseth |
| Jeshua *(0.03)* | Jestan | Jevan | Jeyser | Jhakobi | Jhet | Jhoshua |
| Jeshuah | Jester | Jevani | Jeyshan | Jhalan | Jhett | Jhosimar |
| Jeshua-Jean- | Jesterson | Jevanni | Jeyshua | Jhalen | Jhevion | Jhosman |
| Philippe | Jestin | Jevante | Jeysin | Jhalil | Jhi'aire | Jhossiel |
| Jeshwa | Jeston | Jevany | Jeyson *(0.01)* | Jhamal | Jhi'mier | Jhostin |
| Jesiah *(0.02)* | Jestyn | Jevar | Jeysson | Jhamar | Jhi'sean | Jhosue |
| Jesiel | Jesu | Jevaris | Jeytoine | Jhamaree | Jhi'yiere | Jhotsan |
| Jesip | Jesua | Jevaughn | Jeyveon | Jhamari | Jhiaan | Jhovani |
| Jesire | Jesudson | Jevaughny | Jeyvinson | Jhamarian | Jhiale | Jhovanni |

| | | | | | | |
|---|---|---|---|---|---|---|
| Jhovanny | Jiawei | Jimarri | Jintré | Jizar | Jo'wan | Job (0.01) |
| Jhovany | Jiaxin | Jimbo | Jinu | JJ | Jo'ziah | Joban |
| Jhowalli | Jiayi | Jimeal | Jinup | Jjoseph | Joab | Jobani |
| Jhuehoua | Jiaylle | Jimego | Jinwon | Jjoshua | Joabb | Jobanpreet |
| Jhunior | Jibrael | Jimeir | Jinwoo | Jkhai | Joachim (0.01) | Jobanvir |
| Jhustice | Jibrail | Jimere | Jinx | Jkhari | Joachlen | Jobany |
| Jhy'kirious | Jibran | Jimi (0.01) | Jiomar | J-Kuwon | Joackim | Jobary |
| Jhydan | Jibreal | Jimin | Jionté | J-Kwon | Joah (0.01) | Jobe (0.01) |
| Jhylian | Jibreel (0.01) | Jiming | Jiovani | Jkwon | Joahan | Jobeh |
| Jhylil | Jibri | Jimir | Jiovanní | Jkyan | Joahem | Joben |
| Jhyman | Jibriel | Jimison | Jiovanni (0.02) | Jlamar | Joahimit | Jobert |
| Jhymarri | Jibril (0.01) | Jimiyah | Jiovanny | Jlani | Joahkim | Jobie |
| Jhyneik | Jibson | Jimm'tavis | Jiovany | Jlishawon | Joahn | Jobin |
| Jhynevious | Jicah' | Jimmar | Jiovhanny | Jlymyra | Joakim | Jobindeep Singh |
| Jhyree | Jice | Jimmell | Jiovionni | Jmari | Joakym | Job-Noe |
| Jhyzir | Jickenson | Jimmey | Jiquais | Jmarion | Joal | Jobson |
| Jhza'marion | Jicorian | Jimmi | Jiquavis | Jmarrcus | Joalain | Joby |
| Ji | Jidechukwu | Jimmie (0.03) | Jirah | Jmauri | Joaly | Jocbie |
| Jí Hler | Jie | Jimmie Charles | Jiramyha | Jmel | Joam | Jocelyn |
| Ji Kai | Jie'on | Jimmier | Jiree | J-Mika | Joame | Jocelynn |
| Ji Oh | Jieciere | Jimmill | Jireeh | Jmmy | Joan (0.03) | Jochi |
| Ji Sung | Jiequell | Jimmire | Jireh | Jmon | Joanasie | Jock |
| Ji'had | Jigar | Jimmy (0.28) | Jirehn | Jnai | Joanassie Juan | Jockir |
| Ji'kai | Jigme | Jimmy Ellie | Jiri | Jnana | Lucas | Jocob |
| Ji'kese | Jignesh | Jimmy William | Jirique | Jnson | Joancarlos | Jocqese |
| Ji'miere | Jihaad | Jimmy-Adrian | Jiro | Jo | Joandre | Jocques |
| Ji'montae | Jihad (0.01) | Jimmye | Jirrisen | Jo Anthany | Joandrew | Jocquet |
| Ji'myrian | Jihadd | Jimmy-Isaiah | Jis Chang | Jo Kaury | Joandri | Jocquez |
| Ji'quel | Jihan | Jimmynel | Jisan | Jo Seph | Joandry | Jocquin |
| Ji'quon | Jiheem | Jimothy | Jisaun | Jo'anthony | Joandy | Jocsan |
| Ji'rah | Jiheimance | Jimu | Jishun | Jo'cobe | Joanel | Jocsel |
| Jia (0.01) | Jihondreé | Jimy | Jismael | Jo'el | Joanfelipe | Jocum |
| Jia Ming | Jihoo | Jin (0.01) | Jissah | Jo'kanye | Joangel | Jod |
| Jia Qz | Jihoon | Jin Wei | Jitamanyu | Jo'karrian | Joani | Jodaiah |
| Jia Yao | Jii | Jin Yue | Jithin | Jo'kobi | Joanie | Jodan |
| Jiabao | Jijuan | Jinald | Jitsi | Jo'lontae | Joann | Jode |
| Jiah | Jilani | Jinde | Jiu | Jo'mariyon | Joanne | Jodeci |
| Jiakai | Jilber | Jindo | Jivan | Jo'nah | Joanpher | Jodee |
| Jiali | Jilbert | Jinesh | Jivander | Jo'norius | Joanthony | Jodel |
| Jialong | Jilberto | Jing-Ho | Jivari | Jo'quane | Joany | Jodell |
| Jiamar | Jiles | Jingyang | Jivario | Jo'ron | Joao (0.02) | Joden |
| Jiaming | Jillian | Jinh | Jivesh | Jo'saun | Joao Gabriel | Joderson |
| Jian (0.01) | Jillien | Jinhun | Jivone | Jo'savion | Joao Pedro | Jodey |
| Jian Wen | Jilmer | Jinijshua | Jivontay | Jo'seff | (0.01) | Jodey Jo |
| Jian-Carlos | Jim (0.03) | Jinit | Jiwanjot | Jo'shaun | Joao Roberto | Jodh |
| Jiancarlos | Jimae | Jinka | Jiy'king | Jo'siah | Joao Victor | Jodhbir |
| Jianni | Jimale | Jinkif | Jiy'son | Jo'van | Joaqin | Jodhin |
| Jianzhang | Jimar | Jinli | Jiyang | Jo'vannie | Joaquan | Jodhveer |
| Jiaqian | Jimarcus | Jino | Jiyan-Serwan | Jo'vantae | Joaquane | Jodhvir |
| Jiar | Jimaree | Jinoby | Jiyeon | Jo'von | Joaquim (0.01) | Jodian |
| Jiarrel | Jimareon | Jinping | Jiyon | Jo'vonnie | Joaquin (0.15) | Jodie |
| Jiasheng | Jimari | Jinsu | Ji-Young | Jo'vontay | Joas | Jodin |
| Jiavanni | Jimarien | Jinton | Jizaih | Jo'vonte | Joash | Jodnel |

| | | | | | | |
|---|---|---|---|---|---|---|
| Jodon | Joe-Natthan | Johancy | John Jack | Johnathan-Thanh | John-Luka | Johntavis |
| Jodonis | Joenell | Johaned | John Junior Serge | Johnathen (0.01) | John-Luke | Johntay |
| Jody (0.02) | Joeniel | Johanes | John Khristian | Johnathin | Johnly | Johntaye |
| Joe (0.13) | Joep | Johann (0.02) | John Mark | Johnathon (0.15) | John-Mark | Johnte |
| Joe Anthony | Joer | Johann Frederic | John Marvin | Johnathyn | Johnmark | Johnté |
| Joe Ayden | Joerg | Johann Samuel | John Matthew | Johnattan | John-Marshall | Johnteer |
| Joe Del | Joe-Rogelio | Johannes (0.01) | John Michae | John-Augusto | John-Martin | Johntell |
| Joe Joe | Joeron | Johanni | John Michael (0.01) | Johnavan | John-Michael | Johnteris |
| Joe Ray | Joeryia | Johanny | John Micheal | Johnaven | Johnmichael | Johnterrian |
| Joe'cory | Joeseff | Johansen | John Mikhael | Johnavin | John-Miller | Johnthan |
| Joe'l | Joeseph (0.01) | Johanssen | John Nicolas | Johnavon | Johnn | John-Thomas |
| Joe'leo | Joesephi | Johany | John Patric | Johnavun | Johnnari | Johnthon |
| Joe'mar | Joesey | Johari | John Patrick | John-Benedict | Johnnatan | Johnthun |
| Joe'marion | Joesf | Johariel | John Paul (0.03) | John-Brendon | Johnnaton | Johnti |
| Joe'quan | Joesh | Johary | John Quessy | Johncarlo | Johnnell | John-Timothy |
| Joean | Joeshua | Johathan | John Roger | John-Carlos | Johnney | Johntre |
| Joe-Anthony | Joesia | Joha-Zackary | John Ross | Johnce | Johnni | Johntrell |
| Joeavion | Joesiah | Johde | John Ryan | Johncherl | John-Nicholas | Johnvel |
| Joedan | Joesiph | Joheaven | John Sebastien | John-Connor | Johnnie (0.03) | Johnwayne |
| Joedavid | Joeson | Johen | John Taylor | Johndarrion | Johnniel | John-Wood |
| Joe-Derek | Joesph (0.02) | Johenny | John Thomas | John-David | Johnno | Johny (0.01) |
| Joedimarco | Joetaruis | Johenson | John Tyler | Johndel | Johnny (0.32) | Johny Joel |
| Joedy | Joevanni | Johjan | John Victor | Johndell | Johnny Glenn | Johquais |
| Joe-Evans | Joevany | Johmar | John Vinson | John-Denis | Johnny Ray | Johran |
| Joeffrey | Joevoneey | Johmarion | John Wayne | John-Denzel | Johnny-Lee | Johrel |
| Joeie | Joevonne | John (6.62) | John William | John-Douglas | Johnny-Rashaad | Johron |
| Joël | Joevontea | John (Jack) | John'tayvain | Johndvaris | Johnnyreign | Johsa |
| Joel (1.24) | Joevony | John Allen | John'traveo | Johned | Johnothan | Johsaun |
| Joel Lynn | Joewelle | John Angelo | Johna | Johnell | Johnothon | Johsua |
| Joel-Alahandro | Joexavier | John Anthony | John-Abraham | Johneric | Johnovan | Johsuan |
| Joel-Daniel | Joey (0.18) | John Blake | John-Adler | Johnes | John-Paul (0.01) | Johsue |
| Joele | Joey Jacob | John Brandon | Johnaireo | John-Ethan | Johnpaul (0.01) | Johtraveon |
| Joe-Lian | Joey John | John Buck | John-Alexander | Johnethan | John-Philip | Johvan |
| Joeliano | Joezer | John Carlo | John-Alvin | Johnethen | Johnqaue | Johvani |
| Joelier | Joffett | John Charley | Johnan | John-Evan | Johnquez | Johvanni |
| Joelijah | Joffre | John Christian | John-Anson | John-Henerick | John-Rafael | Johvon |
| Joelique | Joffrey | John Christopher | Johnanthan | John-Henry | Johnray | Johwaun |
| Joel-Kevin | Joffua | John Christopherr | John-Anthon | John-Hollis | John-Rhodes | Johwon |
| Joell | Jofrank | John David | John-Anthony | Johnical | John-Riley | Johziah |
| Joelle | Jofrey | John Dean | Johnarieus | Johnie | Johnrisha | Joiakim |
| Joel-Pascal | Joh'deonté | John Douglas | Johnas | Johnifer | John-Robert | Joiden |
| Joelree | Joh'tarik | John Ethan | Johnason | John-James | John-Rosaire | Joie |
| Joelton | Johabian | John Evan | Johnatan (0.01) | John-Jene | Johnsair | Joinel |
| Joel-Valentino | Johacim | John F | Johnatan-Ajenga | John-Jesus | Johnsey | Jojhan |
| Joelvie | Johah | John Felix | Johnathan (0.60) | John-John | Johnshay | Joji |
| Joelyn | Johaly | John Francis | Johnathan Bruce | Johnkell | Johnson (0.02) | Jojuan |
| Joelynus | Joham | John Frankl | Johnathann | John-Lewis | Johnston | Joj-Van |
| Joemari | Jo-Han | John Gabrie | | Johnley Bryan | Johnta | Jokota |
| Joemel | Johan (0.10) | John Grahame | | Johnluca | Johntae | Joktan |
| Joemy | Johan Harold | John Henry | | Johnluis | Johntaivis | Jolain |
| Joemyir | Johan Rafael | John Hunter | | | Johntarius | Jolan |
| Joenah | Johana | | | | Johntavin | Joldaniel |
| Joenathan | Johanan | | | | Johntavious | Jole |

| | | | | | | |
|---|---|---|---|---|---|---|
| Joleth | Jon'logan | Jonathan | Joneric | Jon-Raul | Joram | Jordit |
| Jolexis | Jon'mani | George | Jones (0.01) | Jon-Ryan | Joran (0.01) | Jordnel |
| Jolhan | Jon'mikael | Jonathan Hoang | Jonez | Jonta | Joran-Nate | Jordon (0.10) |
| Jolie | Jon'paul | Jonathan | Jon-Fayne | Jontaé | Joravar | Jordon-Lee |
| Jolin | Jon'quail | Michael | Jonh | Jontae (0.01) | Jorawer | Jordono |
| Jollan | Jon'quaviou | Jonathan | Jon-Henry | Jontaveis | Jorbin | Jordun |
| Jolliffe | Jon'te | Miguel | Jonhenry | Jontaviar | Jordache | Jordy (0.05) |
| Jolon | Jon'tez | Jonathan Shane | Jonhson | Jontavious | Jordae | Jordy-Eloyn |
| Jolson | Jon'travias | Jonathan- | Jon-Hunter | Jontavius | Jordain | Jordyin |
| Jolten | Jon'travious | Fabrice | Joni (0.01) | Jontay | Jordaine | Jordyn (0.05) |
| Jolvon | Jona | Jonathan-James | Jonico | Jon-Tayveus | Jor-Dan | Jordyne |
| Jolyn | Jonacy | Jonathanli | Jonie-Galton | Jonte | Jordan (4.37) | Jordyn-Kenta |
| Jolyon | Jonadab | Jonathann | Joniel (0.01) | Jonté | Jordan | Jordynn |
| Jomai | Jon-Aden | Jonathan- | Jonjay | Jontea | Alexander | Jordy-Thien |
| Jomal | Jonae | Thomas | Jonlei | Jonteau | Jordan Allen | Joreh |
| Jomall | Jonael | Jonathen (0.01) | Jonluca | Jonterrius | Jordan Anthony | Jor-El |
| Jomally | Jonaeya | Jonathin | Jon-Luke | Jontez | Jordan Cyle | Jorel |
| Jomanny | Jonah (0.72) | Jonathon (0.29) | Jonluke | Jonthan | Jordan Enzo | Jorell |
| Jomar (0.04) | Jonah Adrien | Jonathon | Jonmanuel | Jonthomas | Jordan Maurice | Joren |
| Jomari | Jonah Gabriel | Kayden | Jon-Marc | Jonthon | Jordan Tyler | Jorenh Gester |
| Jomarian | Jonah Michael | Jonathyn | Jon-Marcos | Jon-Torvic | Jordan-Adams | Jorenza |
| Jomarion | Jonah-James | Jonaton | Jonmark | Jontré | Jordane | Jorey |
| Jomarrion | Jonahs | Jonattan | Jonmauri | Jontreaz | Jordan-Eligh | Jorgé |
| Jomarzion | Jonahtan | Jonavan | Jon-Michael | Jontrell | Jordani | Jorge (1.75) |
| Jomaun | Jonahvick | Jonaven | Jonmichael | Jontu | Jordanie | Jorge Alexandre |
| Jomauri | Jonaith | Jonavin | Jonmichall | Jonus | Jordaniel | Jorge Amir |
| Jomel | Jonaldy | Jonavon | Jonmokee | Jonvion | Jordanis | Jorge Andre |
| Jomel Gabriel | Jon-Alexander | Jonaz | Jonn | Antonine | Jordan-Isaiah | Jorge Andres |
| Jomette | Jonalexander | Jonben | Jonnaetotn | Jonwesley | Jordan-Lee | Jorge Luis |
| Jomey | Jonan | Jonbradley | Jonnah | Jony | Jordan-Michael | Jorge- |
| Jomez | Jonangelo | Jon-Carlo | Jonnathan | Jonyale | Jordann | Alexandro |
| Jomi | Jonanthan | Joncarlo | (0.01) | Jonzel | Jordanny | Jorgeariel |
| Jomiah | Jon-Anthony | Joncarlos | Jonnathon | Joohanny | Jordano | Jorgegabriel |
| Jomil | Jonanthony | Jon-Carter | Jonnavon | Joohyung | Jordanson | Jorgeluis |
| Jomnote | Jonarei | Joncarver | Jonni | Joon | Jordan-Taylor | Jorgen |
| Jomny | Jonas (0.25) | Jon-Celo | Jonnie | Joon Soo | Jordantaylor | Jorgie |
| Jomo | Jonas Uriel | Jon-Colin | Jonny (0.01) | Joonas | Jordany | Jorhdyn |
| Jomyco | Jonasan | Joncy | Jonny Ray | Joonha | Jordany-Moise | Jori |
| Jon (0.16) | Jonasis | Jondarian | Jonoah | Joonie | Jordaun | Jorian |
| Jon Bryant | Jonatahn | Jondarious | Jonothan | Joon-Jay | Jordee | Joric |
| Jon Cade | Jonatán | Jon-David | Jonothin | Joonyoung | Jordell | Jorick |
| Jon Carlos | Jonatan (0.02) | Jondavid | Jonothon | Joose | Jorden (0.07) | Joriel |
| Jon Christopher | Jonatan- | Jondel | Jonovan | Joost | Jorden Trevor | Jorien |
| Jon Diego | Dominic | Jondell | Jonoven | Joplin | Jorden's | Jorik |
| Jon Matthew | Jonatha | Jondon | Jonpatrick | Joquam | Jorden- | Jorinjher |
| Jon Paul | Jonathan (6.32) | Jondre | Jon-Paul | Joquavious | Anthony | Jorion |
| Jon Richard | Jonathan | Jonee | Jonpaul | Joquelle | Jordens | Jorja |
| Jon Sevastian | Aboubacar | Joneil | Jon-Pierre | Joquez | Jordhen | Jorje |
| Jon Tavious | Jonathan Alan | Jon-El | Jonqavis | Jor'dan | Jordi (0.02) | Jorkaeff |
| Jon Tryll | Jonathan | Jonel | Jonqez | Jor'dyn | Jordian | Jorlen |
| Jon'darious | Andrew | Jonell | Jonquaye | Jora | Jordie | Jorluis |
| Jon'eil | Jonathan David | Jonelle | Jonquevious | Jorace | Jordin (0.02) | Jorn |
| Jon'kaus | Jonathan Erik | Joner | Jonquil | Jorai | Jordis | Jornal |

| | | | | | | |
|---|---|---|---|---|---|---|
| Jorod | Jose Jael | Joseph Alan | Josh (0.09) | Joshua-Braden | Josphau | Jouse |
| Jorran | Jose Jairo | Joseph Alexander | Josh Christophe | Joshua-Cyril | Josphe | Joush |
| Jorrdon | Jose Juan | Joseph Alexandre | Josh Matthew | Joshua-Daryel | Joss | Jousha |
| Jorrell | Jose Julian | Joseph Alfredo | Josh Vincent | Joshua-David | Jossemar | Joushua |
| Jorren | Jose L | Joseph Antonio | Josh'ali | Joshua-Dwayne | Jossemiere | Jouvence |
| Jorrian | Jose Luis | Joseph Austin | Josh'shaun | Joshuah (0.02) | Jossie | Jouvon'tae |
| Jorron | Jose Manuel | Joseph Benjamin | Josha | Joshuajaniel | Jossiel | Jova |
| Jorronay | Jose Marian | Joseph Bruce | Joshae | Joshual | Josson | Jová |
| Jorryn | Jose Martin | Joseph Camilo | Joshah | Joshua-Michael | Jossue | Jovahn |
| Jors | Jose Miguel | Joseph Christiana | Joshaies | Joshuan | Josswar | Jovahny |
| Jorshee | Jose Roberto | Joseph Christophp | Josh-Akim | Joshua-Nathan | Jostahn | Joval |
| Jorshua | Jose Rodrigo | Joseph David | Josh-Alann | Joshuant | Jostchyn | Jovall |
| Jorviel | Jose Rolando | Joseph Dominic | Josh-Ashley Lucas | Joshua-Robert | Josten | Jován |
| Jorvik | Jose Rosalino | Joseph Elan | Joshaun | Joshua-Skyler | Jostik | Jovan (0.08) |
| Jory (0.01) | Jose'angel | Joseph Elijah | Joshawa (0.01) | Joshua-Tanner | Jostin (0.01) | Jovan' |
| Joryn | Jose'antonio | Joseph Ernest | Joshawa-Brayden | Joshua-Teagan | Jostin David | Jovane |
| Joryton | Joseah | Joseph Gil | Joshdip | Joshue | Joston | Jovanhy |
| Jos' | Jose-Aljee | Joseph Gregoire | Josheb | Joshuel | Josua (0.01) | Jovani (0.05) |
| Josafat | Josean | Joseph James | Joshep | Joshuia | Josuan | Jovanie |
| Josaiah | Joseandres | Joseph Jere | Joshewa | Joshula | Josué (0.01) | Jovanjeet |
| Josaih | Joseangel | Joseph Jonathan | Joshia | Joshunn | Josue (0.31) | Jovanna |
| Josair | Joseanthony | Joseph Jr | Joshiah (0.01) | Joshuwa | Josue Angel | Jovanne |
| Josaiyah | Jose-Arnel | Joseph Karlos | Joshio | Joshwa (0.01) | Josue Gabri | Jovanni (0.04) |
| Josanuel | Joseba | Joseph Kyle | Joshit | Joshwah | Josue Nkushi | Jovannie |
| Josaphat | Jose-Cruz | Joseph Mathieu Ken | Joshiua | Joshwa-Michael | Josue-Alejandro | Jovanny (0.03) |
| Josaphett | Jose-De | Joseph Michael | Josh-Kristian | Josi | Josued | Jovanpreet |
| Josaphine | Joseef | Joseph Moise | Joshkun | Josi'ah | Josueh-Jacques | Jovans |
| Josaya | Joseemilio | Joseph Ryan | Josh-Michael | Josia | Josuel | Jovante |
| Josbriel | Jose-Enrique | Joseph Samuel | Joshnail | Josiah (1.09) | Josueth | Jované |
| Josca | Joseer | Joseph Troy | Joshoa | Josiah Hood | Josuhe | Jovany (0.03) |
| Joscar | Josef (0.07) | Joseph-Charbel | Joshod | Josiah Judah | Joswel | Jovar |
| Josceff | Josef-Antony | Josephchester | Joshshawn | Josiaha | Joswen | Jovares |
| Joscelyn | Josefat | Joseph-Dale | Joshshon | Josiah-John | Josyah | Jovarious |
| Josch | Joseff | Joseph-Emile | Joshswade | Josian | Josyan | Jovarius |
| Jos-Deven | Jose-Gabriel | Joseph-Emilio | Joshtaylor | Josias (0.01) | Josyas | Jovary |
| José (0.03) | Jose-Isidore | Joseph-Emir | Joshu | Josie | Josyhia | Jovas |
| Jose (5.30) | Jose-Javier | Joseph-Ephraim | Joshua (10.39) | Josiel | Josymar | Jovaughn |
| Jose Alfredo | Josel | Josephlee | Joshua Alfred | Josigah | Jotahvious | Jovaun |
| Jose Andres | Joseleonardo | Joseph-Louis | Joshua Allen | Josih | Jotham | Jove |
| Jose Angel | Joselino | Joseph-Marie Sitamze | Joshua Andrew | Josiha | Jothan | Jovell |
| Jose Anthony | Joselito | Joseph-Samuel | Joshua Connor | Josimar | Jotveer | Joven |
| Jose Antonio | Joselo | Josephus | Joshua Donald | Josip | Joud | Jovener |
| Jose Armando | Joseluis (0.01) | Joseph-William | Joshua Eli | Josi-Sam | Joude | Jovens |
| Jose Carlos | Joselyn | Joseth | Joshua Emanuel | Josiyah | Joul | Jovensky |
| Jose Damian | Jose-Manuel | Joseus | Joshua Israel | Joskar | Joulian | Jovi |
| Jose Daniel | Josemanuel | Josey | Joshua Jacob | Joslan | Jourdain | Jovian |
| Jose David | Josemaria | | Joshua Karim | Josman | Jourdan (0.01) | Jovick |
| Jose De Jesus | Jose-Mateo | | Joshua Lee | Josmar (0.01) | Jourden | Jovie |
| Jose Esteban | Jose-Miguel | | Joshua Tyler | Josmel | Jourdin | Joviel |
| Jose Franci | Josemiguel | | Joshuaa | Josner | Jourdyn | Jovin |
| Jose Francisco | Josemmanuel | | Joshua-Allan | Josniel | Journee | Jovohnsky |
| Jose Guadal | Josenrique | | | Joson | Journey (0.01) | Jovon (0.01) |
| Jose Guadalupe | Joseph (7.77) | | | Jospeh (0.01) | Jourvanni | Jovoni |

| | | | | | | |
|---|---|---|---|---|---|---|
| Jovonni | Jrell | Juan Jose | Juatin | Juelz (0.03) | Julian Zachary | Julyus |
| Jovonny | JS | Juan Jr | Juavarious | Juelz-Sameek | Julianiz | Julz |
| Jovontae | Jsaiah | Juan Junior | Juave | Juenp | Julian-James | Juma |
| Jovonte | Jsean | Juan Luis | Juawan | Juewan | Juliann | Jumari |
| Jovonté | Jseth | Juan Manuel | Juba | Juftin | Julianni | Jumarias |
| Jovonti | J-Shad | Juan Martin | Jubai | Jugaad | Julianno | Jumarion |
| Jovony | J-Shawn | Juan Miguel | Jubal | Jugar | Julianny | Jumarlin |
| Jovun | Jshawn | Juan Pablo | Jubari | Jugat | Juliano (0.01) | Jumaunti |
| Jovvani | Jshon | (0.01) | Jubarion | Jugens | Julian-Philippe | Jumel |
| Jovyn | Jsun | Juan Ramon | Jubay | Jugeshwaran | Julian-Tali | Jumeng |
| Jovyon | JT | Juan Ruben | Jubbar | Jugmohit | Juliany | Jumer |
| Jowad | Jtaiveon | Juan Sebastian | Jubel Romer | Jugraj | Julianye | Jumere |
| Jowan | Jtavon | Juan Tommy | Jubenal | Ju-Ha | Juliart | Jumiah |
| Jowany | Ju | Juan'taviou | Jubin | Juha | Julias | Jumiere |
| Jowdat | Ju Laron | Juan-Agustin | Jublain | Juhlyun | Julie | Jumondre |
| Jowel | Ju'darrian | Juanalberto | Jubraun | Juhrell | Julien (0.23) | Jun (0.01) |
| Jowell | Ju'donte | Juanale | Jud | Juian | Julien James | Jun Han |
| Jowick | Ju'elz | Juan-Angel | Juda | Juidah | Julien Min Soo | Jun Il |
| Joxari | Ju'leon | Juan-Antonio | Judaea | Juilie Qaunaq | Park | Jun One |
| Joy | Ju'lien | Juanantonio | Judah (0.15) | Juilin | Juliene | Jun Yin |
| Joy'dan | Ju'marcus | Juanasi Jashua | Judah Ben | Jujhar | Julienn | Jun'nyrin |
| Joyce Alberto | Ju'mario | Juancarlos | Judanis | Jujuan | Julienne | Junah |
| Joydan | Ju'maz | (0.01) | Judarius | Jukari | Julien-Nicolas | Junaid |
| Joydien | Ju'tario | Juandaniel | Judas | Juke | Julieta | Junayd |
| Joytirgamaya | Ju'tarious | Juan-David | Judd (0.01) | Jukhyr | Julieus | Jundell |
| Joyuanki | Ju'vante | Juandavid | Juddah | Jukil | Julill | June |
| Joza | Ju'vaughn | Juander | Juddixo | Jukolby | Julinho | Junealous |
| Jozaiah | Ju'von | Juandiego | Judd-Peter | Jul | Julio (0.27) | Juned |
| Jozef (0.01) | Jua | Juane | Juddson | Julain | Julio Alberto | Juneus |
| Jozel | Juain | Juanelias | Jude (0.30) | Julani | Julio Angel | Jung Hee |
| Jozell | Jual | Juanelo | Jude Renuel | Julante | Julioalberto | Jungshua |
| Jozemiguel | Juamine | Juanes | Judea | Jule | Julioangel | Jung-Soo |
| Jozeph | Juamonte | Juanfelipe | Judenson | Jule'z | Juliocesar | Junha |
| Jozi | Juan (3.72) | Juani | Jude-Thomas | Julean | Julion | Junias |
| Jozia | Juan Adolfo | Juanito (0.01) | Judge (0.01) | Jule-Char | Julious | Juniel |
| Joziah (0.02) | Juan Alberto | Juanjose | Judiah | Juleel | Julissa | Junier |
| Joziaha | Juan Alejandro | Juan-Lucas | Judian | Julein | Julisys | Juniho |
| Joziel | Juan Alex | Juanluis | Judidiah | Julen | Juliun | Junior (0.08) |
| Joziph | Juan Alexander | Juanlund | Judines | Juleon | Julius (0.24) | Junior Temaj |
| Jozo | Juan Andres | Juanmarco | Judon | Jules (0.04) | Julius Octavius | Junior-Steve |
| Jozsef | Juan Arthur | Juan-Marcos | Judson (0.04) | Jules Stephan | Jullian (0.02) | Junious |
| Jozshua | Juan Atonio | Juanmarcos | Judson Dallas | Jules-Baptiste | Jullian-Lou | Junito |
| Jozsiah | Juan Camilo | Juan-Pablo | Jueal | Jules-Thorton | Jullien | Junius |
| Jozua | Juan Carlos | Juanpablo | Juehl | Juleun | Jullious | Junjia |
| Jozy | (0.01) | Juanrey | Juel | Julia | Julliun | Junlin |
| JP | Juan David | Juansebastian | Juel | Juliahn | Jullius | Junmonte |
| Jr | Juan De Dios | Juantavious | Christopher | Julían | Julrus | Juno |
| Jr Dago | Juan Diego | Juantez | Jueli'en | Julian (3.09) | Juluan | Junsung |
| Jr. | Juan Esteban | Juanti | Juelius | Julian Armando | July | Junuh |
| Jrake | Juan Fidel | Juanya | Juell | Julian David | Julyah | Junus |
| Jrayden | Juan Francisco | Juaqin | Juelle | Julian Robert | Julyan | Junye |
| Jraydian | Juan Gilbert | Juaquin (0.01) | Juellez | Julian Victor | Julyen | Junyei |
| Jraydon | Juan Jesus | Juarez | Juelwel | Julian Yang | Julyon | Junyor |

Junyoung
Jupe
Jupinder
Jupitur
Jupsy-
  Mondonga
Juqua
Juquan
Juquis
Juquon
Juraé
Jurbin
Jurell
Jurgen
Jürgen
Juridia
Juris
Jurius
Jurmane
Jurnell
Jurode
Juron
Jurrien
Jurvarion
Jury-Adony
Jurzy
Jus'cian
Jus'tus
Jusaiah
Jusayn
Jusden
Jusdon
Jushane
Jushaun
Jushua
Jushua
  Miqualaaq
Jusle
Jusniel
Juso
Justah
Justahllyiase
Justan
Justas
Justavian
Juste
Justen (0.01)
Justes
Justhin
Justhyn
Justi
Justian
Justice (0.20)

Justice Car
Justice-Hope
Justin (4.86)
Justin Alexandre
Justin Anthony
Justin Blaze
Justin Darw
Justin Dat
Justin David
Justin Foisy
Justin Injun
Justin Jack
Justin Khang
Justin Luis
Justin Micheal
Justin Micho
Justin Nicholas
Justin Patrick
Justin Peter
Justin Philippe
Justin Pierre
Justin Youri
Justinas
Justin-Charles
Justine (0.01)
Justine Iris
Justinian
Justin-Isaiah
Justin-Jace
Justin-James
Justin-Kenneth
Justino
Justin-Patrick
Justin-Pierre
Justin-Ray
Justintaylor
Justin-Ulysse
Justion
Justis (0.01)
Justise
Justiss
Justiz
Justn
Justo
Juston (0.01)
Justten
Justus (0.07)
Justyce (0.01)
Justyn (0.03)
Justyne
Justynn
Jusuf
Jut

Juterrion
Juterrious
Jutice
Jutoriaus
Juvan
Juvar
Juvary'll
Juvé
Juvenal
Juvenaly
Juvencio
Juvens
Juvensly
Juvensny
Juventino
Juvey
Juvinson
Juviny
Juvon
Juvonta
Juvontae
Juvraj
Juvris
Juwaan
Juwan (0.01)
Juwan'
Juwann
Juwantay
Juwaun
Juwelz
Juwon
Juwuan
Juxton
Juystise
Juyun
Juzer
Juztyn
Jveion
Jven
Jveon
Jvion
Jviyan
Jvon
Jvontre
Jvyon
JW
Jwan
Jwann
Jwish
Jwokdoj
Jwyan
Jxsyn

Jy
Jy Air
Jy Aire
Jy'air
Jy'kerion
Jy'lan
Jy'lell
Jy'lin
Jy'mar
Jy'marion
Jy'mel
Jy'mire
Jy'onne
Jy'quan
Jy'quarius
Jy'quavious
Jy'querious
Jy'quez
Jy'rah
Jy'reke
Jy'rell
Jy'rese
Jy'ron
Jy'savion
Jy'sean
Jy'shaun
Jy'shawn
Jy'terius
Jya'lin
Jyahmeen
Jyair
Jyaire
Jyamir
Jyaron
Jyathniel
Jybree
Jybrie
Jyce
Jyceon
Jyceri
Jycerin
Jydin
Jye-Asean
Jyeer
Jyéer
Jy-Ell
Jyell
Jyere
Jyerrion
Jyheim
Jyier
Jyii
Jyiqualynn

Jyiree
Jykean
Jykese
Jykiah
Jylare
Jyle
Jylen
Jyler
Jyles
Jyles Jacob
Jylil
Jylin
Jymair
Jymani
Jymari
Jymel
Jymere
Jymmi
Jyni
Jynx
Jyon
Jyothi
Jyoti
Jyou
Jyovanni
Jyquan
Jyquawn
Jyquiez
Jyrah
Jyran
Jyreek
Jyreese
Jyren
Jyreon
Jyrese
Jyrez
Jyrin
Jyrine
Jyrome
Jy-Ron
Jyron
Jyrrell
Jysaiah
Jyshan
Jyshaun
Jyshawn
Jysiah
Jysire
Jysirius
Jyson
Jytez
Jyvion
Jyz'juan

Jyzaiah
Jyzere

~ K ~

K
K C
K Jon
K Leon
K Mari
K O G
K Wan
K.C.
K'amar
K'ayvion
K'dan
K'deldrick
K'den
K'dyn
K'eon
K'gene
K'hanajay
K'jahny-Kurl
K'joreus
K'leb
K'lijah
K'mareon
K'mari
K'marion
K'mauri
K'mydee
K'neill
K'oas
K'on
K'ron
K'rysiax
K'sean
K'shaun
K'shawn
K'shon
K'uan
K'veion
K'veon
K'von
K'vonn
K'vontarious
K'vyon
K'zhen
K'zjohn
Ka Hin
Ka Rai
Ka Von

Ka'daries
Ka'darion
Ka'darius
Ka'darvion
Ka'derius
Ka'doniss
Ka'dre
Ka'drick
Ka'eo
Ka'inoa
Ka'jaylon
Ka'jayvon
Ka'jon
Ka'laylan
Ka'le
Ka'lee
Ka'leel
Ka'lerrio
Ka'lih
Ka'lynn
Ka'ma'ron
Ka'mareon
Ka'mari
Ka'maries
Ka'marion
Ka'markus
Ka'marre
Ka'marri
Ka'mauri
Ka'mauryon
Ka'me're
Ka'mere
Ka'meron
Ka'mileon
Ka'myia
Ka'myrion
Ka'nard
Ka'nazion
Ka'neil
Ka'ory
Ka'ron
Ka'rron
Ka'ryn
Ka'savion
Ka'sean
Ka'sharrad
Ka'shawn
Ka'sona
Ka'sye
Ka'tari
Ka'terrion
Ka'ton
Ka'torrion

| | | | | | | |
|---|---|---|---|---|---|---|
| Ka'trevion | Kacper | Kadrein | Kaes | Kahlen | Kai'onn | Kailand |
| Ka'trieq | Kacy (0.01) | Kadreon | Kaesan | Kahli | Kai'ron | Kailani |
| Ka'vari | Kacyn | Kadrian | Kaesean | Kahlial | Kai'sar | Kailas |
| Ka'various | Kadaar Allen | Kadyl | Kaeshawn | Kahlid | Kai'yonn | Kailash |
| Ka'veaun | Kadafie | Kadyn (0.05) | Kaesi | Kahlieal | Kaiah | Kaile |
| Ka'veion | Kadam | Kadyne | Kaeson | Kahlief | Kaialani | Kaileb (0.01) |
| Ka'veon | Kadan (0.02) | Kadynn | Kaesyn | Kahliel | Kaian | Kailee |
| Ka'veone | Kadance | Kae | Kaevaun | Kahliem | Kaiariyian | Kailen |
| Ka'vion | Kadar | Kae Shawn | Kaeven | Kahlif | Kaiaz | Kailer (0.01) |
| Ka'von (0.01) | Kadarian | Kae'dan | Kaeveon | Kahlil (0.03) | Kaiba | Kailiam |
| Ka'vone | Kadarius (0.01) | Kae'lub | Kaevon | Kahlin | Kaiben | Kailib |
| Ka'vonta | Kadasé | Kae'shone | Kaeyden | Kahlon | Kaice | Kailin |
| Ka'wayne | Kadd | Kaebi | Kaeyus | Kahlor | Kaid (0.01) | Kaillum |
| Ka'zarion | Kadden | Kaed | Kaezon | Kahlyl | Kaidaeo | Kailob |
| Ka'ziya | Kaddin | Kaedan (0.01) | Kafil | Kahlyn | Kaidan (0.01) | Kailohb |
| Ka'zorrion | Kaddon | Kaeden (0.08) | Kafiyl | Kahmadre | Kaidden | Kailon |
| Kaaden | Kaddyn | Kaedin (0.01) | Kagan | Kahmani | Kaide | Kailor |
| Kaadim | Kade (0.19) | Kaedlyne | Kage (0.01) | Kahmari | Kaiden (0.43) | Kailyn |
| Kaal | Kadeam | Kaedmon | Kagen (0.01) | Kahmarii | Kaidence | Kailyr |
| Kaaleem | Kadeem | Kaedn | Kagie | Kahmauri | Kaiden-Lee | Kailyson |
| Kaalid | Kadeen | Kaedon (0.01) | Kagon | Kahmel | Kaidenn | Kaim |
| Kaaliyah | Kadeis | Kaedren | Kah Mari | Kahmeron | Kaidense | Kaima |
| Kaamil | Kadem | Kaedyn (0.01) | Kah Mauri | Kahmi | Kaiden-Xei | Kaimalino |
| Kaamil | Kademon | Kaedynn | Kah'lil | Kahmir | Kaidhyn | Kaimana |
| Jahromino | Kaden (2.11) | Kaeen | Kah'mari | Kahmlah | Kaidien | Kaimani |
| Kaan | Kaden Chase | Kaegan | Kah'marian | Kahn'ye | Kaidin (0.01) | Kaimbrian |
| Kaanan | Kadence (0.01) | Kaehler | Kah'suam | Kahnawi Io | Kaidiyn | Kaimbryn |
| Kaari | Kadenn | Kaehvine | Kahale | Kahne | Kaido | Kaimen |
| Kaawah | Kaden-Ray | Kael (0.05) | Kahari | Kahnen | Kaidon (0.01) | Kaimere |
| Kabarshenay | Kadenyce | Kaelan (0.02) | Kahavian | Kahner | Kaidryn | Kain (0.02) |
| Kabe | Kadeo | Kaelb | Kahceem | Kahnye | Kaidun | Kainaan |
| Kabeer | Kader | Kaeleb (0.01) | Kahden | Kahnyeh | Kaidyn (0.02) | Kainalu (0.02) |
| Kabeer Ali | Kaderious | Kaelem | Kahdir | Kahongo-David | Kaie | Kainan (0.01) |
| Kabell | Kaderius | Kaelen (0.01) | Kaheel | Kahpone | Kaiel | Kaine (0.02) |
| Kabey | Kaderrick | Kaelex | Kaheem | Kahree | Kaien | Kainekenechi |
| Kabien | Kadeyn | Kaelib | Kaheen | Kahreem | Kaienne | Kainen (0.01) |
| Kabilan | Kadian | Kaelin (0.01) | Kahentaienni | Kahrem | Kaientaronkwen | Kaing |
| Kabili | Kadifee | Kaelo | Kahgee | Kahriem | Kaif | Kainin |
| Kabine | Kadin (0.13) | Kaelob | Kahiem | Kahron | Kaifang | Kainn |
| Kabir (0.01) | Kadince | Kaelon | Kahil | Kahsaan | Kaigan | Kainoa (0.02) |
| Kabriel | Kadinz | Kaelub | Kahil Dravid | Kahseam | Kaige (0.01) | Kaio |
| Kabryel | Kadir | Kaelum | Kahim | Kahseem | Kaigh | Kaiolohia |
| Kabryn | Kadiri | Kaely | Kahin | Kahsim | Kaigh'den | Kaiori |
| Kabyn | Kadix | Kaeman | Kahion | Kahsir | Kaihdan | Kaipo |
| Kace (0.01) | Kadjay | Kaemell | Kahjeer | Kahssim | Kaihelae | Kaique |
| Kacee | Kadmiel | Kaemen | Kahjel | Kahvier | Kaii | Kairahn |
| Kacen | Kado | Kaemon | Kahl | Kahvon | Kaijon | Kairay |
| Kacey (0.01) | Kadon (0.01) | Kaen | Kahlan | Kahyan | Kaikane | Kaire |
| Kach | Kadran | Kaenan | Kahle | Kahyir | Kaike | Kairee |
| Kaci | Kadravion | Kaene | Kahleal | Kai (0.42) | Kaiki | Kairen |
| Kacie | Kadrean | Kaenen | Kahleb | Kai Anthony | Kaikoa | Kairi |
| Kacin | Kadree | Kaenon | Kahleel | Kai'den | Kail (0.01) | Kairo |
| Kacius | Kadreese | Kaeon | Kahlel | Kai'ire | Kailan | Kairoe |

| | | | | | | |
|---|---|---|---|---|---|---|
| Kairon | Kaj-Riis | Kaleis | Kaliub | Kam'ran | Kamaris | Kameryon |
| Kairos | Kajuan (0.01) | Kaleitri | Kaliup | Kam'raun | Kamarius | Kamey |
| Kairyn | Kajule | Kaleke | Kalius | Kam'ren | Kamariyon | Kamhil |
| Kaisan | Kajus | Kal-El (0.01) | Kaliv' | Kam'rin | Kamarjá | Kamican |
| Kaiseak | Kajyn | Kalel (0.01) | Kalix | Kam'ron (0.01) | Kamarjae | Kamii |
| Kaisei | Kakeru | Kalel Justin | Kalixto | Kam'ryn | Kamarlin | Kamijha |
| Kaisen | Kaktis | Kalell | Kallah | Kamaal | Kamaro | Kamil (0.02) |
| Kaiser (0.01) | Kal | Kalelle | Kallan | Kamaar | Kamarohn | Kamillo |
| Kaishan | Kal El | Kalem (0.01) | Kalle | Kamael | Kamaron | Kamin |
| Kaisho | Kal'el | Kalen (0.03) | Kalleb | Kamahl | Kamarr | Kamireon |
| Kaishon | Kalaan | Kaleo | Kal-Lee | Kamahrion | Kamarre | Kamiuian |
| Kaishyne | Kalab (0.01) | Kaleo Trystin | Kallee | Kamaj | Kamarri | Kamm |
| Kaison (0.01) | Kalael | Kaleolani | Kallen (0.01) | Kamajah | Kamarrion | Kammari |
| Kaisyn | Kalaeo | Kalep | Kallin | Kamaje | Kamartio | Kammarri |
| Kaitaro | Kalaimaran | Kaler | Kallob | Kamajé | Kamaryon | Kammaryn |
| Kaith | Kalam | Kalerei | Kallon | Kamal (0.02) | Kamasi | Kammeryn |
| Kaithen | Kalama | Kaleri | Kallum | Kamal Eldeen | Kamata | Kammrin |
| Kaitlyn | Kalan (0.02) | Kaletri | Kalman | Kamali | Kamathi | Kammryn |
| Kaito (0.01) | Kalandis | Kalev | Kalob (0.02) | Kamali'i | Kamau | Kammy |
| Kaiton | Kalani (0.01) | Kalex | Kalobe | Kamaljeeth | Kamauri (0.01) | Kamnden |
| Kaius | Kalar | Kalhleif | Kaloeb | Kamaljit | Kamaurie | Kamo |
| Kaivalya | Kalayaan | Kalhyb | Kalon (0.01) | Kamalpreet | Kamaurion | Kamon |
| Kaivan | Kalayvion | Kali | Kalond | Kaman | Kamaurn | Kamondre |
| Kaivarious | Kalden | Kaliah | Kalondre | Kamanda | Kamaury | Kamonie |
| Kaivell | Kale (0.09) | Kaliath | Kalonie | Kamani (0.01) | Kamazen | Kamonra |
| Kaiveon | Kalea | Kalib (0.02) | Kaloon | Kamanon | Kamber | Kamonte |
| Kaivon | Kaleab | Kalibe | Kalop | Kamante | Kambry'n | Kamonté |
| Kaivyone | Kaleabe | Kalibur | Kalor | Kamany | Kambryn | Kamony |
| Kaiwin | Kaleaf | Kalic | Kaloyan | Etienne | Kambryon | Kamoran |
| Kaiya | Kaleb (1.66) | Kalid | Kalp | Kamar (0.02) | Kamdan | Kamore |
| Kaiyang | Kaleb Daniel | Kalidas | Kalrius | Kamaran | Kamden (0.06) | Kamori |
| Kaiyden | Kaleb Erik | Kalidou | Kalsen | Kamarde | Kamdin | Kamorion |
| Kaiydon | Kalebb | Kalieal | Kalson | Kamardre | Kamdon | Kamorris |
| Kaiyon | Kalebh | Kalieb | Kalub (0.01) | Kamare (0.01) | Kamdun | Kamory |
| Kaiyu | Kalebi | Kalief | Kalum (0.01) | Kamarea | Kamdyn (0.01) | Kamoryn |
| Kaizan | Kaleb-Jay | Kaliel | Kalun | Kamarean | Kamebridge | Kampbeul |
| Kaizen | Kalec | Kaliem | Kalup | Kamaree | Kameen | Kamraj |
| Kaizer | Kaled | Kalier | Kaluza | Kamarein | Kameer | Kamran (0.02) |
| Kaizha | Kaleden | Kalif | Kalvan | Kamareion | Kameir | Kamranul |
| Kaizhan | Kaledrek | Kalife | Kalven | Kamaren | Kamel | Kamrean |
| Kaizon | Kalee | Kaliff | Kalvin (0.04) | Kamareon | Kamell | Kamrem |
| Kaj | Kaleel (0.01) | Kaliga | Kalvis | Kamarey | Kamelo | Kamren (0.04) |
| Kajae | Kaleem (0.01) | Kalijah | Kalvyn | Kamarhi | Kamen | Kamrey |
| Kajaé | Kaleen | Kalijin | Kalwyn | Kamarí | Kameon | Kamrin (0.01) |
| Kajanan | Kalef | Kalik | Kalyan | Kamari (0.09) | Kameran (0.01) | Kamrinn |
| Kajaun | Kalefe | Kaliko | Kalyari | Kamarian | Kameren (0.01) | Kamrion |
| Kajauntae | Kaleh | Kalil (0.01) | Kalyb | Kamarie | Kamereon | Kam-Ron |
| Kajavias | Kalehon | Kalill | Kalyb-Oz | Kamarien | Kameril | Kamron (0.08) |
| Kajay | Kalei | Kalim | Kalym | Kamarik | Kamerin | Kamry |
| Kajeon | Kalei Christian | Kalin (0.01) | Ka-Lyn | Kamarington | Kamerion | Kamryan |
| Kajerrius | Noynay | Kaliq | Kalyn | Kamario | Kameron (0.37) | Kamrym |
| Kajoly | Kaleigh | Kalique | Kalynn | Kamarioan | Kamerun | Kamryn (0.03) |
| Kajoure | Kaleio | Kalissa | Kam | Kamarion (0.02) | Kameryn (0.01) | Kamryne |

Kamuela
Kamuy
Kamya
Kamyar
Kamyian
Kamyn
Kamyne
Kamyren
Kamyri
Kamyrn
Kamyron
Kanaan
Kanada
Kanahaje
Kanai
Kanaí
Kanais
Kanaiveon
Kanalu
Kanan
Kananga
Kanara
Kanard
Kanari
Kanasa
Kanav
Kanaya
Kanaye
Kanayochukwu
Kanbren
Kancherla
Kandan
Kandarius
Kanden
Kandjoura
Kandler
Kandon
Kane *(0.08)*
Kane Thomas
Kanee
Kaneef
Kanel
Kanen
Kaneon
Kanewt
Kanez
Kangdrake
Kanglek
Kangmin
Kanha
Kan-Hong
Kaní
Kani *(0.01)*

Kanian
Kanib
Kanie
Kaniejice
Kaniel
Kanih
Kanijai
Kanil
Kanin
Kaninn
Kanion
Kanire
Kanish
Kanishk
Kanistan
Kanius
Kaniyen
Kanize
Kaniziá
Kannaa
Kannan
Kannathasan
Kannen
Kannon *(0.01)*
Kannyn
Kannyon
Kano
Kanoa
Kanon *(0.01)*
Kanorris
Kanroy
Kansai
Kansas
Kansen
Kansire
Kant
Kantaro
Kanten
Kantin
Kanton
Kantrell
Kantries
Kanunu
Kanussh
Kanutiss
Kanwar
Kanwardeep
Kanwarpal
Kanya
Kanyá
Kanyae
Kanyarith
Kanyé

Kanye *(0.06)*
Kanyechukwu
Kanyen
Kanyle
Kanyon *(0.01)*
Kanyun
Kao
Kaobimdi
Kaori
Kaorian
Kaos
Kapax
Kape
Kapil
Kapingiri
Kaplan
Kaplin
Kapone
Kaprie
Kaquan
Kar'monie
Karabo
Karac
Karacus
Karam *(0.01)*
Karamdip
   Singh
Karamoko
Karampal
Karamveer
Karan *(0.02)*
Karanbir
Karandip
Karanjodh
Karanjot
Karanpreet
Karanveer
Karanveer
   *(0.01)*
Karanveer-
   Singh
Karanvir
Karar
Kararius
Karata
Karaun
Karch
Kardae
Kardavian
Kardeair
Kardeashajon
Kardeé
Kardell
Karden

Karder
Kardia
Kardian
Kardin
Kardion
Kardracus
Kardyaire
Kaream
Karee
Kareece
Kareem *(0.10)*
Kareem Walied
   E
Kareim
Kareion
Karel *(0.01)*
Karel-Kandi
Karem
Karey
Kareyon
Karez
Karge
Karhaun
Karheem
Karhlyle
Kari
Karianna
Karic
Kariff
Karii
Kariim
Karik
Karim *(0.04)*
Karim Junior
Karime
Karin
Karion
Karish
Kariyah
Kariz
Karl *(0.11)*
Karl Andrew
Karl Antoine
Karl-Alexandre
Karlan
Karl-Antoine
Karl-Bradley
Karlcedric
Karl-Christian
Karlee
Karlendos
Karlens
Karlenski

Karlenz
Karl-Eric
Karl-Etienne
Karlin
Karlis
Karl-Loic
Karl-Matthew
Karlo
Karl-Olivier
Karlon
Karlos *(0.01)*
Karlos Tarv
Karlou
Karlsen
Karlton
Karlus
Karlvin Wesley
Karlvoseí
Karlyle
Karm
Karma
Karman
Karmanrni
Karmdeep
Karmel
Karmello
Karmellow
Karmelo
Karmese
Karmiel
Karmine
Karmiore
Karmon
Karmpreet
Karmveer
Karmvir
Karmyne
Karmyon
Karndeep
Karnez
Karnpreet
Karnveer
Karo
Karokus
Karol *(0.01)*
Karolis
Karoly
Karommo
Karomo Talibi
Ka-Ron
Karon *(0.02)*
Karone

Karonte
Karou
Karra
Karrar
Karrenton
Karrick
Karrie
Karriem
Karrington
Karron
Karsen *(0.02)*
Karson *(0.12)*
Karsor
Karstan
Karsten *(0.03)*
Karston *(0.01)*
Karstyn
Karsyn
Kartar
Kartavya
Kartayveion
Karter *(0.05)*
Kartez
Karthage
Karthan
Kartheek
Karthik *(0.01)*
Karthikeya
Kartik
Kartikeya
Karun
Karuna
Karvello
Karver
Karvez
Karvis
Karwan
Kary
Karym
Karyon
Karyus
Kas
Kasaan
Kasahn
Kasai
Kasan
Kasar
Kasaun
Kasavea
Kascine
Kascyl
Kasden
Kasdon

Kase *(0.01)*
Kasea
Kaseam
Kasean
Kasedré
Kasee
Kaseef
Kaseem *(0.01)*
Kasei
Kaseim
Kasel
Kasem
Kasen *(0.04)*
Kasenn
Kaseton
Kasey *(0.11)*
Kasey Alexander
Kaseyn
Kash *(0.03)*
Kashaad
Kashad
Kashan
Kashane
Kashaun
Kashawn *(0.01)*
Kashden
Kasheem Cahlil
Kashef
Kasheton
Kashia
Kashies
Kashiez
Ka-Shilo
Kashin
Kashius
Kashmier
Kashmir
Kashmyr
Ka-Shon
Kashon
Kashtin
Kashton
Kashtyn
Kashun
Kashus
Kashyss
Kasi
Kasiah
Kasian
Kasib
Kasiim
Kasil
Kasiley

| | | | | | | |
|---|---|---|---|---|---|---|
| Kasim *(0.01)* | Kateron | Kavaughn | Kaxwtikn | Kayke | Kayoree | Kazin |
| Kasim Daimyae | Katerrion | Kavaun | Kay | Kayl | Kayori | Kazio |
| Kasimir | Kateryn | Kaveer | Kay Shawn | Kayla | Kayque | Kaziya |
| Kasin | Kateyo | Kaveion | Kay'juan | Kaylab | Kayravy | Kaziyah |
| Kasion | Kathan | Kavel-Dil | Kay'leon | Kaylahn | Kayron | Kazjahn |
| Kasir | Katharice | Kavelle | Kay'meign | Kaylan *(0.01)* | Kaysan | Kazmin |
| Kasius | Kathen | Kaven *(0.01)* | Kay'sean | Kaylavin | Kaysar | Kazmir |
| Kasiyah | Katherine | Kaveon | Kay'shawn | Kaylb | Kaysaun | Kazra |
| Kaslo | Kathryn | Kavesh | Kay'veon | Kayle *(0.01)* | Kaysea | Kazu |
| Kason *(0.04)* | Kathyrn | Kaveyon | Kay'vion | Kayleb *(0.02)* | Kaysean | Kazuhiro |
| Kaspar | Katien | Kavi | Kaya | Kayleb Xavier | Kaysell | Kazuki |
| Kasper *(0.01)* | Katino | Kavi'on | Kayaan | Kayled | Kaysen *(0.01)* | Kazumasa |
| Kaspir | Katlyn | Kavier | Kayan | Kaylee | Kayshaun | Kazumi |
| Kaspirian | Katlynn | Kavin *(0.01)* | Kaybe | Kaylem | Kayshawn | Kazuo |
| Kaspur | Kato | Kavinn | Kaybrien | Kaylen *(0.01)* | Kayshen | Kazuto |
| Kasra | Kato Neve | Kavinvasan | Kayce | Kaylen Nasir | Kayshon | Kazuya |
| Kass | Katonio | Kavion *(0.01)* | Kaycee | Kaylen Wong | Kaysin | Kazuyoshi |
| Kassady | Katorrean | Kavious | Kaycey | Nicolas | Kayson *(0.01)* | Kazyi |
| Kassani | Katory | Kavis | Kayd | Kayles | Kaysun | Kazyne |
| Kassate | Katoryan | Kavish | Kaydan *(0.01)* | Kaylib | Kayt | Kazz |
| Kasseem | Katour | Kavisha | Kayde | Kaylie | Kayten | Kazzer |
| Kassell | Katravion | Kavith | Kaydee | Kaylijawon | Kayth | KC *(0.01)* |
| Kassem *(0.01)* | Katrell | Kavius | Kayden *(0.46)* | Kaylin | Kaythen | KC Joe |
| Kassey | Katron | Kaviyon | Kayden- | Kaylo | Kaytin | Kcarheem |
| Kassiah | Katsuhiro | Kavneer | Alexander | Kaylob | Kaytlen | Kcyten |
| Kassian | Katuba | Kavoendrea | Kaydence | Kaylon | Kayto | K-Den |
| Kassidy | Kauan *(0.01)* | Kavon *(0.02)* | Kaydenn | Kaylor | Kaytrez | Kdince |
| Kassim | Kaue | Kavon Deshawn | Kaydeon | Kaylub | Ka-Yunce | K-Dyn |
| Kassius | Kaujjakuluk | Kavone | Kaydien | Kaylum | Kayvan | Kdyn |
| Kasson | Kaulder | Kavonne | Kaydin *(0.01)* | Kaylup | Kayven | Ke |
| Kassra | Kaulen | Kavonta | Kaydince | Kaylus | Kayveon | Ke John |
| Kassten | Kauner | Kavontae | Kaydn | Kaylyn | Kayvion | Ke Juan |
| Kasta | Kauni | Kavori | Kaydon *(0.01)* | Kaylzeah | Kayviyan | Ke Marion |
| Kastan | Kauras | Kavrey | Kaydon Amadou | Kayman | Kayvon *(0.01)* | Ke Marr |
| Kastden | Kauryon | Kavronte | Kaydreon | Kaymani | Kayvonne | Ke Montae |
| Kasten | Kausar | Kavryon | Kaydrienne | Kaymann | Kayvonte Jasper | Ke Trelle |
| Kaster | Kaushal | Kavy | Kaydron | Kaymar | Kaywon | Ké Untay |
| Kasthuriraj | Kaushik | Kavyesh | Kaydyn | Kaymarian | Kaz | Ke Vonne |
| Kastin | Kaustubh | Kavyn | Kaydynn | Kaymen | Kaz'zus | Ke Vonte |
| Kastle | Kauvan | Kawa | Kaye | Kaymir | Kazan | Ke Yon |
| Kaston | Kavahn | Kawahn | Kaye'jon | Kaymon | Kazarius | Ke'ahjay |
| Kaswel | Kavahrice | Kawaiola | Kayeden | Kaymond | Kazden | Ke'an |
| Kasy | Kavajzhe | Kawan | Kayel | Kaymone | Kaze | Ke'andré |
| Kasyir | Kavan *(0.01)* | Kawasikatotc- | Kayeng | Kaynai | Kazem | Ke'andre *(0.01)* |
| Kasym | Kavanagh | Malcolm | Kaygan | Kaynan | Kazen | Ke'antae |
| Kasyn | Kavanaugh | Kawbemael | Kaygay | Kayné | Kazey | Ke'ante |
| Katavien | Kavante | Kawika | Kayhan | Kayne *(0.02)* | Kazeyn | Ke'anthony |
| Katavis | Kavares | Kawin | Kayin *(0.01)* | Kaynen | Kazhmere | Ke'anzae |
| Katch | Kavari | Kaw-Liga | Kayir | Kaynon | Kaziah | Ke'ari |
| Kate | Kavarie | Kawliga | Kayisaun | Kayo | Kazim | Ke'arian |
| Kateeon | Kavarion | Kawnlahn | Kay-J | Kayode | Kazimier | Ke'arieon |
| Katelyn | Kavarius | Kawon | Kayjon | Kayon | Kazimierz | Ke'aris |
| Katerina | Kavarrie | Kawone | Kayjuan | Kayonne | Kazimir | Ke'aundra |

| | | | | | | |
|---|---|---|---|---|---|---|
| Ke'aundre | Ke'onte | Kealead | Keatin | Keedan | Keese | Kei'on |
| Ke'avious | Ke'ontez | Kealey | Keaton *(0.25)* | Keeden | Keeshan | Kei'onte |
| Ke'aviyon | Ke'orland | Kealin | Keaton Andr | Keedon | Keeshaun | Kei'sean |
| Ke'ayrious | Ke'quavyeion | Keallach | Keatrell | Keedrick | Keeshawn | Kei'shon |
| Ke'daren | Ke'ron | Kealon | Keatrick | Keefe | Keeshon | Kei'shun |
| Ke'darius | Ke'sean *(0.01)* | Kealt | Keats | Keefer *(0.01)* | Keeshum | Keian |
| Ke'dariyan | Ke'shaun *(0.01)* | Kealyn | Keatyn | Keegan *(0.57)* | Keesiah | Keiaren |
| Ke'darrie | Ke'shawn *(0.02)* | Keaman | Keatz | Keegan-Joshua | Keeson | Keiaro |
| Ke'darrius | Ke'shon | Keamare | Keaudre | Keegan-Murphy | Keetan | Keiaunta |
| Ke'donte | Ke'shun | Keamari | Keaun | Keegann | Keethan | Keiber |
| Ke'dric | Ke'silias | Keamon | Keaundre | Keegen *(0.01)* | Keetin | Keidan |
| Ke'ele | Ke'tavion | Kean | Keaunté | Keeghan | Keeton *(0.01)* | Keidas |
| Ke'essen | Ke'tavis | Keanan *(0.01)* | Keave | Keegin | Keets | Keiden |
| Ke'ire | Ke'twan | Keanathun | Keaven | Keegon | Keetyn | Keidence |
| Ke'jaun | Ke'untae | Keanau | Keaveon | Keegun | Keevan | Keidene |
| Ke'jon | Ke'vannio | Keandale | Keavion | Keehan | Keevaris | Keidgiler |
| Ke'juan | Ke'varis | Ke-Andre | Keawe | Keehmon | Keeveen | Keidi |
| Ke'leil | Ke'varri | Keandré | Kebai | Keeian | Keeven | Keidis |
| Ke'leyon | Ke'veion | Keandre *(0.01)* | Kebbie | Keelan *(0.03)* | Keevin | Keidjerick |
| Ke'lin | Ke'velle | Keandrea | Kebin | Keeland | Keevon | Keidran |
| Ke'lon | Ke'vhanta | Keane *(0.01)* | Kebron | Keelen | Keeyir | Keidre |
| Ke'londraus | Ke'vion | Keanen | Kechan | Keeleon | Keeylan | Keidren |
| Ke'lyn | Ke'von | Keani | Keda | Keeler | Keeyon | Keidrich |
| Ke'mahr | Ke'vontae | Keanie | Kedaar | Keelin | Keeyoneyeah | Keidrien |
| Ke'maje | Ke'vonte | Keanius | Kedan | Keely | Keeze | Keidyn |
| Ke'mar | Ke'wan | Keanno | Kedar | Keelyn | Kefir | Keifer *(0.01)* |
| Ke'mari | Ke'won | Keano | Kedari | Keemen | Kefrain | Keiffer |
| Ke'marian | Ke'wun | Keanon | Kedarius | Keen | Kefren | Keigan *(0.01)* |
| Ke'marion | Ke'yanni | Keantae | Kedarrius | Keena | Kefryn | Keige |
| Ke'marious | Ke'yon | Keanté | Kedell | Keenan *(0.13)* | Kegan *(0.03)* | Keigen |
| Ke'marius | Ke'yontay | Keanthony | Keden | Keenay | Kegen | Keigh |
| Ke'mariyon | Ke'yonte | Keanu *(0.05)* | Kedens | Keene | Keghan | Keighan |
| Ke'marri | Ke'zavious | Keanue | Kederrius | Keenen *(0.01)* | Keghon | Keighden |
| Ke'marrion | Ke'zohn | Keardan | Kedesh | Keeneye | Kehareon | Keighlib |
| Ke'mauri | Kea'shawn | Keare | Kedimir | Keenian | Keharryon | Keighvan |
| Ke'maurion | Keaden | Kearieon | Kedin | Keenin | Kehdyn | Keigo |
| Ke'mauriya | Keadin | Kearin | Kedouglas | Keeno | Kehinde | Keigun |
| Ke'maury | Keadon | Kearion | Kedren | Keenom | Kehlan | Keihland |
| Ke'metrius | Keadrin | Kearlen | Kedric | Keenon | Kehler | Keiji |
| Ke'mon | Keagan *(0.11)* | Kearnan | Kedrick *(0.01)* | Keenroy | Kehndryck | Kei-Juan |
| Ke'monei | Keagen *(0.02)* | Kearnold | Kedrin | Keentae | Kehon | Keijuan |
| Ke'montae | Keaghan | Kearston | Kedron | Keen-Yean | Kehvon | Keil |
| Ke'montay | Keaghun | Kearyn | Kedus | Keenyn | Kehwent | Keila |
| Ke'montez | Keagin | Keas | Keduse | Keeonte | Kei | Keilahn |
| Ke'muri | Keagon | Keasear | Kee | Keeper | Kei 'Shaun | Keilan *(0.01)* |
| Ke'nai | Keagun | Keashaun | Kee Shawn | Keeran | Kei Ellis | Keilen |
| Ke'nais | Keagyn | Keashun | Kee'nan | Keerat | Kei Marion | Keiler |
| Ke'nardious | Keahi | Keasion | Keean *(0.01)* | Keeron | Kei'andre | Keilet |
| Ke'nigie | Keahnu | Keason | Keeanu | Keertan | Kei'deion | Keilijah |
| Ke'nile | Keaj | Keaston | Keeayatas | Keerthan | Kei'jhawn | Keilind |
| Ke'non | Keajuan | Keaten *(0.01)* | Keechaun | Keerthanan | Kei'marr | Keillan |
| Ke'omauri | Kealan | Keath | Keechen | Kees | Kei'mydré | Keillor |
| Ke'on | Kealand | Keathon | Keechi | Keesaan | Kei'norris | Keilon |

| | | | | | | |
|---|---|---|---|---|---|---|
| Keiltorian | Keisy | Kel'von | Kellondray | Kelvyn | Kemory | Kenchin |
| Keilyn *(0.01)* | Keita | Kelab | Kells | Kelvynn | Kemouri | Kencorya |
| Keimare | Keite | Kelaien | Kellsyn | Kely | Kemoy | Kendahl |
| Keimari | Keiten | Kelan *(0.02)* | Kellum | Kelyan | Kemp | Kendai |
| Keimarrion | Keith *(0.36)* | Keland | Kelly *(0.04)* | Kelyjah | Kemper *(0.01)* | Kendail |
| Keimaurie | Keith Allen | Kelando | Kelly-Mike | Kelyn | Kempter | Kendal *(0.02)* |
| Keimearleon | Keith Mark | Kelandré | Kellyn | Kelzon | Kempton | Kendale |
| Keimen | Keithan | Kelani | Kelmar | Kem | Kemris | Kendall *(0.10)* |
| Keimer | Keithan Frank | Kelbe | Kelmer | Kema | Kemu | Kendall |
| Keimir | Keithen | Kelbee | Kelmon | Kemahj | Kemua | Anthony |
| Keimoe | Keither | Kelbert | Keloe | Kemahz | Kemuel | Kendalle |
| Keimoni | Keithland | Kelbey | Kelon | Kemaine | Kemyah | Kendan *(0.01)* |
| Keimonte | Keithon | Kelby *(0.02)* | Keloni | Kemaj | Kemydré | Kendari |
| Keimore | Keithrick | Kelcey | Kelonni | Kemal | Kemyon | Kendariann |
| Keimorion | Keithstan | Keldan | Kelonte | Kemani | Ken *(0.03)* | Kendarion |
| Keimylo | Keito | Kelden | Kelonté | Kemar *(0.01)* | Ken Darius | Kendarious |
| Kein | Keitoin | Keldin | Kelron | Kemarcus | Ken Darrius | Kendarius |
| Keinan | Keiton | Keldon | Kelse | Kemare | Ken Guadalupe | *(0.01)* |
| Keino | Keitrayon | Keldric | Kelsean | Kemaree | Ken Mar | Kendarrion |
| Keio | Keitron | Keldrick | Kelsen | Kemareon | Ken'dahrius | Kendarrius |
| Keiojhae | Keitton | Keleante | Kelsey *(0.01)* | Kemareyae | Ken'dedric | Kendaruis |
| Keion *(0.02)* | Keitwon | Kelebrant | Kelsin | Kemari *(0.01)* | Ken'dell | Kendawn |
| Keion'dre | Keityn | Kelechi | Kelso | Kemarion *(0.01)* | Ken'montae | Kendeall |
| Keiondre | Keiun'dré | Kelechukwu | Kelson *(0.01)* | Kemariun | Ken'nard | Kendel |
| Keiondrea | Keivaun | Kelekolio | Kelsor | Kemarr | Ken'narrius | Kendell *(0.01)* |
| Keioni | Keiven | Kelen | Kelston | Kemarrious | Ken'shawn | Kenden |
| Keionn | Keiveon | Kelenna | Kelsyn | Kemarrius | Ken'tavis | Kenderick |
| Keionsa | Keiveri | Kelgin | Keltan | Kemaun | Ken'terrius | Kenderiez |
| Keiontae | Keividrick | Keli'i | Kelte'se | Kemauri *(0.01)* | Ken'treyz | Kenderius |
| Keiontay | Keivin | Kelian | Kelten | Kemaury | Ken'vontae | Kenderrian |
| Keiper | Keivon | Kelijah | Keltic | Kemcy | Ken'yon | Kenderrise |
| Keir *(0.01)* | Keivonta | Kelijiah | Keltie | Kemel | Kenaan | Kenderrius |
| Keira | Keivyn | Kelik | Keltin | Kemen | Kenaaz | Kendi |
| Keiran *(0.02)* | Keiwan | Kelin *(0.01)* | Kelton *(0.05)* | Kemet | Kenada | Kendin |
| Keirden | Keiwaun | Kell | Keltravious | Kemi | Kenadi | Kendion |
| Keiren | Keiwon | Kellan *(0.05)* | Keltyn | Kemieo | Kenaf | Kendirck |
| Keireth | Keiya | Kelland | Kelven | Kemjika | Kenai *(0.01)* | Kendis |
| Keirin | Keiyashawn | Kellaneo | Kelveonta | Kemmbree | Kenaji | Kendle |
| Keirnan | Keiyleer | Kellar | Kelverieyon | Kemoh | Kenami | Kendley |
| Keirnen | Keiyon | Kellee | Kelvin *(0.17)* | Ke-Mon | Kenan *(0.02)* | Kendon *(0.01)* |
| Keiron | Keizo | Kellen *(0.15)* | Kelvin Charlles | Kemon | Kenandré | Kendrale |
| Keiroy | Keizon | Keller *(0.04)* | Kelvin Junior | Kemond | Kenaniah | Kendrall |
| Keiryn | Kejaun | Kelley | Kelvin Mack | Kemondrae | Kenard | Kendre |
| Keisaunn | Kejion | Kelli | Kelvion | Kemondrea | Kenari | Kendreal |
| Keisean | Kejohn | Kellie | Kelvionte | Kemondrell | Kenaris | Kendree |
| Keisen | Ke-Juan | Kellieomark | Kelvis | Kemoney | Kenau | Kendrek |
| Keishan | Kejuan *(0.01)* | Kellin | Kelviyon | Kemoni | Kenauz | Kendrell *(0.01)* |
| Keishaun | Kekeli | Kellington | Kelvon | Kemonie | Kenay | Kendren |
| Keishawn *(0.01)* | Keko | Kellis | Kelvonta | Kemonta | Kenaz | Kendrew |
| Keishon | Kekoa *(0.01)* | Kelljoh | Kelvontae | Kemontae | Kencaid | Kendreyeus |
| Keistan | Kel | Kellmontae | Kelvontaé | Kemonte *(0.01)* | Kencere | Kendreyik |
| Keisten | Kel'bon | Kellmy | Kelvsha | Kemontez | Kenchaun | Kendrez |
| Keiston | Kel'v | Kellon | Kelvy | Kemonti | Kenchavious | Kendrial |

| | | | | | | |
|---|---|---|---|---|---|---|
| Kendrian | Kenjy | Kenntaevion | Kentaé | Keny | Keondré | Kermicheal |
| Kendric (0.01) | Kenjy-Melnick | Kenntairious | Kentaevon | Kenya | Keondre (0.01) | Kermit |
| Kendrick (0.11) | Kenlando | Kenny (0.16) | Kentarion | Kenyada | Keondrick | Kermiz'a |
| Kendrid | Kenley (0.01) | Kenny Jr | Kentarious | Kenyader | Keone | Kermond |
| Kendriel | Kenley-Omary | Kenny Kai | Kentaro | Kenyale | Keoni (0.02) | Kern |
| Kendrik | Kenlie | Kenny Khoa | Kentarou | Kenyan (0.01) | Keonn | Kernelius |
| Kendrious | Kenlorsen | Kenny Matthew | Kentashawu | Kenyan Dale | Keonta | Kerns |
| Kendrique | Kenly | Kennyatta | Kentaun | Kenyarta | Keontá | Kerolos |
| Kendrix | Kenmar | Kennyen | Kentavious (0.01) | Kenyata | Keontae (0.01) | Keron (0.01) |
| Kendry | Kenmari | Kenny-John | Kentavis | Kenyatta (0.01) | Keontay | Keronda |
| Kendryck | Kenmarius | Kennyn | Kentavius | Kenyatti | Keontaye | Keronte |
| Kendryk | Kenna | Kennyon | Kentawan | Kenyaun | Keonte (0.01) | Kerouan |
| Kendy | Kennado | Kenny-Roman | Kentcen | Kenyava | Keonté (0.01) | Keroy |
| Kendyl | Kennan (0.01) | Kennyth | Kente | Kenye | Keonte'a | Kerran |
| Kendyle | Kennard | Keno | Kentel | Kenyel | Keontea | Kerric |
| Kendyll | Kennaris | Kenobi | Kentell | Kenyen (0.01) | Keontez | Kerrick |
| Kendy-Love | Kennaya | Kenobii | Kenten | Kenyetta | Keontrail | Kerrigan |
| Kendyn | Kennedey | Kenon | Kenterion | Kenyez | Keontre | Kerrigen |
| Kene | Kennedy (0.03) | Kenorris | Kenterious | Kenyin | Keontrey | Kerrin |
| Kenean | Kenneeth | Kenoy | Kenterius | Kenyion | Keontrez | Kerrington |
| Kenechi | Kenneil | Kenreall | Kenterrious | Kenynè | Keopatrick | Kerrion |
| Kenechukwu | Kennen | Kenric | Kentin | Kenynn | Keori | Kerris |
| Kenedy | Kenner | Kenrich | Kentish | Ken-Yon | Keorion | Kerron |
| Keneen | Kenneth (1.33) | Kenrick | Kentius | Kenyon (0.08) | Keoshon | Kerrton |
| Keneke | Kenneth Gene | Kenroy | Kento | Kenyonnie | Keovin | Kerrvon |
| Kenen Ivan Dean | Kenneth Jacob | Kenry | Kenton (0.05) | Kenyonta | Keovonte | Kerry (0.02) |
| Keneolisa | Kenneth Kalen | Kensaac | Kentorrie | Kenyontay | Keown | Kerryon |
| Kener | Kenneth Macayah | Kensandrez | Kentrae | Kenyotta | Kepa | Kerryonte |
| Kenet | Kenneth Stuart | Kensei | Kentrail | Kenyun | Kepha | Kersean |
| Keneth | Kenneth'jr | Kenses | Kentraill | Kenzavian | Kepson | Kershunta |
| Keneun | Kenneth-Dale | Kenseth | Kentral | Kenzavion | Ker'rion | Kersten |
| Keng | Kenneth-Gregory | Kensey | Kentravious | Kenzel | Ker'ron | Kerstin |
| Ken-Gabriel | Kennethius | Ken-Shawn | Kentravis | Kenzell | Keramat | Kertus |
| Kengi | Kenneth-Shawn | Kenshawn | Kentravius | Kenzeryas | Kerby | Kerven |
| Kengo | Kennett | Kenshea | Kentrayveus | Kenzie (0.01) | Kerek | Kervens (0.01) |
| Kenguirho | Kennette | Kenshi | Kentreal | Kenzington | Kerel | Kervenshi |
| Keni | Kenney | Kenshin | Kentreaz | Kenzo | Kerell | Kervin |
| Kenian | Kenni'on | Kenshin Bailey | Kentrel | Kenzy | Kerem | Kervins |
| Kenice | Kennidy | Kenshin Louis | Kentrell (0.02) | Keo | Keremcan | Kervion |
| Kenichi | Kennie | Kenshing | Kentrevious | Keoben | Kerenden | Kervoceo |
| Keniel | Kennieth | Kenshiro | Kentrez | Keoghan | Kereon | Kervontae |
| Keniet | Kennijas | Kenshun | Kentstan | Keoke | Keri | Kerwens |
| Kenijah | Kennin | Kensington | Kentyn | Keola | Kerian | Kerwin (0.01) |
| Kenin | Kennion | Kenslee | Kentyree | Keón | Keric | Kerwins |
| Kenious | Kennis | Kensley | Kenuel | Keon (0.08) | Kerie | Kerzy |
| Kenith | Kennison | Kensly | Kenvar | Keon'jay | Kerin | Kes'john |
| Kenius | Kennith (0.01) | Kenson (0.01) | Kenvaris | Keona | Kerington | Kesaan |
| Keniver | Kennody | Kenston | Kenveer-Singh | Keonahae | Kerion | Kesan |
| Kenjchie | Kennon | Kensuke | Kenwa | Keonalokelagi | Kerjames | Kesang |
| Kenjgi | Kennotti | Kensun | Kenwin | Keondell | Kerlin | Kesaun |
| Kenji (0.02) | | Kent (0.04) | Kenwon | Keondravius | Kerlos | Keschan |
| Kenjuan | | Kentá | Kenwood | Keondray | Kerly | Kesean (0.01) |
| | | Kenta (0.01) | | | Kermari | Keshan |

| | | | | | | |
|---|---|---|---|---|---|---|
| Keshaun (0.02) | Keva | K-Evon | Key'vaurie | Keylyn | Keyshun | Khadan |
| Keshav (0.01) | Keval | Kevon (0.03) | Key'veuntav | Keymajah | Keyson | Khadar |
| Keshavan | Kevalin | Kevondae | Key'von | Keymani | Keystan | Khadari |
| Keshawn (0.05) | Kevan | Kevonne | Key'vonta | Keymari | Keyston | Khadarrion |
| Keshewn | Kevarion | Kevonnee | Key'vontay | Keymarion | Keytin | Khadeem |
| Keshin | Kevaris | Kevont'a | Key'vontaye | Keymaurii | Keyto | Khaden |
| Keshon (0.01) | Kevarius | Kevonta | Keya | Keymn | Keyton (0.01) | Khader |
| Keshua | Kevarris | Kevontae | Keyaan | Keymon | Keytravious | Khadim |
| Keshuan | Ke-Vaughn | Kevontaé | Keyadre | Keymond | Keyun | Khadin |
| Ke-Shun | Kevaughn | Kevontay | Keyan (0.01) | Keymonta | Keyundre Qu | Khadir |
| Keshun (0.01) | Kevaun | Kevonte | Keyandé | Keymontae | Keyuntea | Khadolphie |
| Keshunn | Keveion | Kevonté | Keyandre | Keymontie | Keyur | Khadorey |
| Keshwar | Kevell | Kevontez | Keyani | Keyn | Keyvan | Khadri-Jareé |
| Keshyon | Kevelle | Kevonti | Keyanne | Keynadrick | Keyvant | Khadyn |
| Keshzewn | Keven (0.05) | Kevontj | Keyanno | Keynan | Keyven | Khael |
| Kesiena | Kevens | Kevontre | Keyanta | Keynder | Keyveon | Khaelin |
| Kesin | Kevensley | Kevonyé | Keyantae | Keynen | Keyvin | Khafarrell |
| Kesler (0.01) | Keveon | Kevork | Keyante | Keyno | Keyvion | Khagee |
| Keslor | Keveontae | Kevoyah | Keyanté | Keynon | Keyvon | Khai (0.01) |
| Kesly | Keveun | Kevrayn | Keyanu | Keyo | Keywan | Khai'ree |
| Kesmir | Kevi | Kevron | Keyari | Keyoda | Keywaun | Khaiden |
| Kesner | Keviante | Kevvié | Keyatis | Keyohveon | Keywon | Khail |
| Kesny | Kevieon | Kevvon | Keyaun | Keyon (0.05) | Keyyun | Khailaun |
| Kessen | Kevin (4.82) | Kevwyon | Keyaundre | Keyonce | Keyzhawn | Khailik |
| Kessin | Kevin Andres | Kevy | Keyauntae | Keyondre | Kez'ron | Khaine |
| Kessle | Kevin Armando | Kevyn (0.01) | Keyave | Keyondrick | Kezaro | Khair |
| Kessler | Kevin Axel | Kevyn Anthony | Keyawn | Keyonne | Keziah | Khairi |
| Kessy-Fred | Kevin Cupertino | Kevyn-Christian | Keyci | Keyonta | Kezo | Khaiwyn |
| Kestian | Kevin Eduardo | Kevyon | Keydan | Keyontá | Kezon | Khalab |
| Kestin | Kevin Gabriel | Kevyunon | Keydarius | Keyontae | Kezten | Khalaf |
| Keston (0.01) | Kevin Gustavo | Kewaan | Keydel | Keyontay | Kezziah | Khalar |
| Kesus | Kevin Omar | Kewan | Keyden | Keyonte | Kh'moni | Khaldoon |
| Ketan | Kevin Roman | Kewarren | Keydon | Keyonté | Kh'montre | Khale |
| Ketanpreet | Kevin-Diacre | Kewaun | Keydrick | Keyontre | Kh'unzye | Khaleal |
| Ketch | Kevine | Kewayne | Keydrin | Keyony | Kha | Khaleb |
| Ketcher | Keving | Kewon | Keye | Keyoun | Kha Mari | Khaled (0.01) |
| Keterrious | Kevin-Gabriel | Kewonn | Keyel | Keyquan | Kha Seim | Khalee |
| Kether | Kevin-Georges | Kewuan | Keyen | Keyrahza | Kha'lani | Khaleeb |
| Keton | Kevin-Kauam | Key | Keyeon | Keyran | Kha'lee | Khaleed |
| Ketorus | Kevinley | Key Ki | Keygan (0.01) | Keyrell | Kha'lil | Khaleef |
| Ketrick | Michael | Key'arion | Keygin | Keyron | Kha'mari | Khaleel (0.01) |
| Ketriel | Kevinn | Key'darius | Keygon | Keysahd | Kha'marion | Khaleem |
| Ketron | Kevin-Rodolfo | Key'marion | Keyin | Keysan | Kha'mauri | Khalefala |
| Ketroy | Kevin-Russell | Key'marius | Keyion | Keysean | Kha'maurie | Khaleiam |
| Kettrick | Kevin-Shiyuan | Key'maury | Keyjuan | Keyshaad | Kha'maury | Khaleif |
| Ketyn | Kevinson | Key'morie | Keylan (0.01) | Keyshan | Kha'ri | Khaleil |
| Keuanta | Kevin-Tai | Key'nijdrick | Keyland | Keyshaun (0.01) | Kha'saun | Khaleim |
| Keun | Kevin-Yichen | Key'once | Keylen | Key-Shawn | Khaalid | Khalel |
| Keundra | Kevion (0.01) | Key'ontae | Keylhan | Keyshawn (0.05) | Khaaliq | Khalem |
| Keuntay | Kevis | Key'oun | Keylien | Keyshawn | Khabeer | Khalen |
| Keunté | Kevius | Key'shaun | Keylin | Alexander | Khabir | Khälen |
| Keuri | Kevlar | Key'shawn | Keyloh | Keyshon (0.01) | Khadafi | Khaleo |
| Kev'ion | Kevn | Key'un | Keylon | Keyshone | Khadair | Khalfani |

| | | | | | | |
|---|---|---|---|---|---|---|
| Khalfini | Khamauri | Khasen | Khemari | Khoda | Khyair | Ki'yontai |
| Khali *(0.01)* | Khamazii | Khaseym | Khemoni | Khoddy | Khyale | Ki'yontias |
| Khali'ed | Khamazja | Khashaun | Khemraj | Khoen | Khyden | Kia |
| Khalial | Khambrell | Khashirah | Khendell | Khoeny | Khydir | Kia Len |
| Khalib | Khamdee | Khasi | Khenley Inelson | Khoi | Khye | Kiadree |
| Khalid *(0.06)* | Khamden | Khasil | Khenoul | Khol | Khyeem | Kiah |
| Khalidí | Khamerin | Khasim | Khentrell | Khole | Khyel | Kiahji |
| Khalie | Khameron | Khasir | Khepera | Kholsyn | Khyerre | Kialyn |
| Khalief | Khammari | Khason | Kheperaen | Kholton | Khyheim | Kiame |
| Khaliel | Khamoni | Khassia | Kherl | Khoner | Khyier | Kian Grant |
| Khalif *(0.01)* | Khamonie | Khasyr | Khery | Khong Kou | Khyis | Kian *(0.09)* |
| Khalif Khamoge | Khamouri | Khatai | Khetan | Khongmong | Khyjaire | Kian Adriel |
| Khalifa | Khamphet | Khatchig | Khevin | Khongmung | Khylan | Kiandré |
| Khalifah | Khamrin | Khaterion | Kheye | Khonor | Khyle | Kiantaé |
| Khalife | Khamron | Khatravion | Khi | Khor | Khylee | Kiante |
| Khaliff | Khamrone | Khatron | Khi'lee | Khorason | Khylek | Kianthony |
| Khalih | Khamryn | Khavirlo | Khia're | Khorbin | Khyler | Kianyzia |
| Khaliif | Khamsing | Khavon | Khian | Khori | Khylin | Kiar |
| Khalik | Khamsy | Khavy | Khiari | Khorion | Khylle | Kiara |
| Khalil *(0.16)* | Khamyrahn | Khawaja | Khidhar | Khorteze | Khymari | Kiaran |
| Khalil Rodney | Khan | Khawara | Khidhr | Khotan | Khymel | Kiarash |
| Khalil-Kamal | Khanai | Khaya | Khiem | Khouri | Khyon | Kiari |
| Khalil- | Khang *(0.01)* | Khayade | Khieng | Khourian | Khyree *(0.01)* | Kiariyahn |
| Mohamed | Khang-Anh | Khayae | Khiheem | Khoury | Khyreek | Kiaron |
| Khalin | Khanh | Khayam | Khilan | Khove | Khyrez | Kiarsis |
| Khalio | Khani | Khayari | Khiland | Khovit | Khyri | Kias |
| Khaliq | Khanigan | Khayden | Khilen | Khr'mhle | Khyron | Kiasaun |
| Khalique | Khanlun | Khaydin | Khilon | Khris | Khyrue | Kiaus |
| Khalir | Khanrad | Khayeah | Khilyn | Khrisstofer | Khyrus | Kiaveon |
| Khalis | Khanye | Khayel | Khimanie | Khristen | Khyryn | Kibar |
| Khalius | Khanyé | Khayid | Khimauri | Khristgen | Khysim | Kibzaim |
| Khaliyl | Khapri | Khayree | Khine | Khristian *(0.02)* | Khyver | Kico |
| Khallan | Kharan | Khayri | Khire | Khristion | Khyzaiah- | Kidan |
| Khallel | Kharee | Khayrie | Khiree | Khristoffer | Kassadi | Kidd |
| Khallid | Khareem | Khazavion | Khiren | Khristopher | Ki | Kidder |
| Khalon *(0.01)* | Kharek | Khazeem | Khirron | *(0.01)* | Ki Shawn | Kidron |
| Khalongi | Kharentez | Khe'ron | Khiryck | Khriz | Kí Yon | Kidus |
| Khalum | Kharese | Kheam | Khisean | Khrouchtchev | Ki'ajalon | Kie |
| Khalvin | Khari *(0.01)* | Kheathan | Khit | Khrystian | Ki'ante | Kie'andre |
| Khalyel | Khari Amir | Khedit | Khiva | Khubaib | Ki'darius | Kie'shawn |
| Khalyias | Khariel | Khedyn | Khiyan | Khunais | Ki'eve | Kiean |
| Khalyl | Kharl | Kheelin | Khiye | Khup | Ki'mahre-Zion | Kieasha |
| Khamaari | Kharlill | Khegan | Khiyel | Khuran | Ki'marion | Kieem |
| Khamadie | Kharlos | Kheitler | Khiymeri | Khush | Ki'maris | Kieeme |
| Khamadré | Kharmel | Khejei | Khiyon | Khushkarn | Ki'maud | Kiefer *(0.02)* |
| Khamajee | Kharon | Khelan | Khizar | Khushman | Ki'monie | Kieffer |
| Khamani *(0.02)* | Kharonn | Khelben | Khizer Hayat | Khushpreet | Ki'sean | Kiegan |
| Khamar | Kharry | Khelden | Khizr | Khwai | Ki'shaun | Kiehl |
| Khamaré | Khary | Khelil | Khmani | Khwaja | Ki'shawn | Kieju'an |
| Khamaree | Khasan | Kheller | Khmorris | Khwarmi | Ki'sion | Kiel *(0.01)* |
| Khamari *(0.03)* | Khase | Khelyn | Khoa | Khy | Ki'vaughn | Kielan |
| Khamarri | Khaseem | Khemani | Khoa Anh | Khy'juan | Ki'von | Kielar |
| Khamarrie | Khaseen | Khemar | Khoan | Khy'on | Ki'yon | Kielarr |

| | | | | | | |
|---|---|---|---|---|---|---|
| Kiele | Kiiaji | Kimeko | Kinley | Kiril | Kittridge | Klayton *(0.01)* |
| Kielein | Kiichiro | Kimi | Kinmonte | Kirill | Kiun | Kleant |
| Kieler | Kiimire | Kimiah | Kinneth | Kirin | Kius | Kleavon |
| Kiell | Kijana | Kimkotnip | Kinnick | Kirion | Kiva | Kleber |
| Kielyn | Kijani | Kimmahd | Kinnith | Kirit | Kivan | Klebler |
| Kien | Kijon | Kimmaorian | Kino | Kirith | Kiven | Kledus |
| Kienan | Kijuan | Kimmorley | Kinsdly | Kirk *(0.03)* | Kiven Otou | Kleet |
| Kien-An-Nam | Kiko | Kimo | Kinser | Kirk | Kiveon | Kleighton |
| Kiene | Kilan | Kimon | Kinsey | Christopher | Kivion | Klejdi |
| Kienen | Kilby | Kimoni | Kinsleigh | Kirklan | Kiviyán | Klemen's |
| Kieon | Kile | Kimoy | Kinsley | Kirkland *(0.01)* | Kivon | Klement |
| Kieph | Kileigh | Kimper | Kinson | Kirklin | Kiwa | Klent |
| Kier | Kilek | Kimren | Kinsson | Kirklyn | Kiwan | Klenth |
| Kieran *(0.17)* | Kilen | Kim-Thien | Kinston | Kirolos | Kix | Kleomar |
| Kierce | Kiley | Kimyade | Kint | Kiron | Kiyah | Klever |
| Kiere | Kilian *(0.01)* | Kimyone | Kinta | Kirondré | Kiyan | Klevis |
| Kieren | Kilian Quentin | Kin | Kintaro | Kirril | Kiyanii | Kleyman |
| Kierian | Kiliann | Kinai | Kintavis | Kirshawn | Kiyanté | Klian |
| Kierin | Kilias | Kinal | Kintay | Kirsten | Kiyaunté | Kline |
| Kierk | Kiliel | Kincade | Kinter | Kirstian | Kiyedin | Klint |
| Kiernan *(0.02)* | Kilien | Kincaid | Kinti | Kirstofer | Kiyel | Klinten |
| Kiernen | Kiliq | Kincaide | Kinye | Kirstopher | Kiyem | Klinti |
| Kieron | Killean | Kincayde | Kinyn | Kirtan | Kiyeondre | Klinton |
| Kierran Trey | Killian *(0.05)* | Kindell | Kinyon | Kirthen | Kiyhan | Klisman |
| Kierre | Killian Ronan | Kinden | Kinzer | Kirtrell | Kiyle | Klo |
| Kierson Carter | Killyam | Kindle | Kinzie | Kirtveer | Kiylon'dre | Kloee |
| Kierstan | Kilmer | Kindo | Kio | Kirubel | Kiyo | Klye |
| Kiersten | Kilo | Kindred | Kion | Kirubell | Kiyon | Klyfenson |
| Kiervan | Kilough | Kindrel | Kiondre | Kirvin | Kiyoshi | Klyton |
| Kieryn | Kilver | Kindrick | Kioni | Kirzion | Kiyran | Kmaree |
| Kiesha | Kilyan | Kindyn | Kionne | Kisai | Kiyrese | Kmari |
| Kieshye | Kilyr | Kineo | Kiontae | Kiseem | Kiy-Ron | Kmarion |
| Kiesin | Kim | Kinfe | Kionte | Kiser | Kiyu | Kna'ledge |
| Kiestin | Ki-Mani | King *(0.05)* | Kiovanni | Kiserian | Kiyus | Knai |
| Kiet | Kimani *(0.01)* | King David | Kiowa | Kishan *(0.01)* | Kizele | Knakai |
| Kieth | Kimare | King Richard | Kip *(0.01)* | Kishande | Kizer | Knaré |
| Kiev | Kimareon | King Victor | Kipling | Kishaun | KJ | Knash |
| Kievian | Kimari | King Zion | Kipp | Kishawn | Kjeld | Knathum |
| Kievion'tai | Kimarin | King'semaj | Kir | Kishen | Kjeran | Knaulij |
| Kiewan | Kimarion | Kingavares | Kira | Kishon | Kjolby | Kneiva |
| Kiewon | Kimarius | Kingchen | Kirakis | Kîsik | Kjuan | Knell |
| Kieya | Kimarje | King-David | Kiran *(0.02)* | Kisimi | Klaas | Knicklus |
| Kieyon | Kimarly | Kingdom | Kirat | Kisler | Klae | Knight |
| Kiezer | Kimaro | Kinggolden | Kirby *(0.01)* | Kison | Klai | Knighten |
| Kifayeh | Kimathi | King-Isaiah | Kirby-Lucard | Kisor | Klamareon | Knighton |
| Kigel | Kimatni | Kingsley *(0.01)* | Kire | Kisuhs | Klancey | Knivek |
| Kiger | Kimauni | Kingsly | Kiree | Kisun | Klane | Knoa |
| Kigh | Kimaury | Kingson | Kireese | Kit | Klark | Knoah |
| Kighon | Kimball | Kingstin | Kirek | Kito | Klaus | Knoel |
| Kihan | Kimberly | Kingston *(0.03)* | Kirese | Kitson | Klavs-Dieter | Knolan |
| Kiheem | Kimbiel | King-William | Kirhy | Kitt | Klay | Knorlan |
| Kiheim | Kimble | Kinh | Kiri | Kittrel | Klayson | Knovell |
| Kihew | Kimdrick | Kinkade | Kiriakos | Kittrick | Klayten | Know |

| | | | | | | |
|---|---|---|---|---|---|---|
| Knowel | Kody Michael | Kolaiah | Komi | Korae | Korvyn | Koven |
| Knowlan | Koebin | Kolar | Komil | Koraejus | Kory *(0.04)* | Kovens |
| Knowledge | Koedyn | Kolawole | Kominiko | Koran | Kory Nathan | Koveyontez |
| *(0.01)* | Koehin | Kolbe *(0.01)* | Komiwon | Koray | Kory'on | Kovii |
| Knowlen | Koehler | Kolbet | Komontay | Korban | Koryon | Kowaii |
| Knowlind | Koehn | Kolbey | Komoyangi | Korben *(0.02)* | Koryonte | Kowan |
| Knowlton | Koein | Kolbi | Kon | Korbin *(0.06)* | Kosal | Kowen |
| Knox *(0.01)* | Koel | Kolbie | Kona | Korbyn *(0.02)* | Kosar | Kowin |
| Knut | Koen *(0.06)* | Kolbjorn | Konai | Kord | Kosay | Koy *(0.01)* |
| Knute | Koen-Phi | Kolby *(0.12)* | Konar | Kordae | Kose | Koye |
| Kny' | Koenraad | Kolbyn | Konayis | Kordail | Kosei | Koyer |
| Ko'dehreun | Koewan | Kolbyrne | Koner | Kordale | Kosey | Koyln |
| Ko're | Koeyn | Kolden | Kong *(0.01)* | Kordall | Koshown | Kozson |
| Ko'ron | Kofa | Kole *(0.11)* | Kong Meng | Kordé | Kosmas | Kquartazz |
| Koa | Koffi | Kolebe | Kong Pheng | Kordel | Kosmo | Kr'shawn |
| Koah | Kofi *(0.01)* | Kolebi | Kongchang | Kordell *(0.01)* | Koss | Kradyn |
| Koal | Kofie | Koleman | Kongcheng | Korden | Kosta | Krae |
| Koalyen | Kogen | Kolerain | Kongfeng | Korderrian | Kostadinos | Kraig *(0.01)* |
| Koan | Koger | Koleten | Kongmeng | Kordonte | Kostandino | Kraigory |
| Kobbi | Kohan | Koleton | Kongmong | Kore | Kostandinos | Kraigyn |
| Kobby | Kohbi | Koletrin | Kongpheng | Koree | Kostantinos | Kramer |
| Kobé | Koheen | Kolhbi | Kongseng | Korell | Kostas | Krar |
| Kobe *(0.14)* | Kohei | Koli | Kongsue | Koren | Kostin | Krash |
| Kobee | Kohen *(0.04)* | Kolin *(0.02)* | Kongyen | Korey *(0.06)* | Koston | Krason |
| Koben | Kohga | Kolleem | Kongying | Kori *(0.01)* | Kostya | Kraven |
| Kobey *(0.01)* | Kohl *(0.01)* | Kollen | Konhue | Korian | Kota | Kravion |
| Kobi *(0.01)* | Kohlbe | Kollin *(0.02)* | Konipher | Korie | Kotah | Kray |
| Kobie | Kohlden | Kollin-Micheal | Konje | Koriehn | Kotaro | Kraython |
| Kobin | Kohle | Kollyn | Konlan | Koriel | Koti | Kream |
| Kobina | Kohler | Kolo Jamison | Konley | Korion | Koty | Kreed |
| Kobishan | Kohlor | Kolos | Konnar | Korlan | Kou | Kreedence |
| Kobitee | Kohls | Kolsen | Konner *(0.07)* | Korliss | Kou Yeng | Kreegin |
| Kobrin | Kohlson | Kolson | Konnor *(0.06)* | Kormac | Koudi | Kreem |
| Kobryn | Kohlten | Kolston | Kono | Kormale | Koufan | Kreg |
| Koby *(0.04)* | Kohlton | Kolt *(0.01)* | Konor | Koron | Kouhei | Kregan |
| Kobylee | Kohn | Koltan | Konraad | Korren | Kouki | Kreid |
| Kobyn | Kohner | Kolten *(0.04)* | Konrad *(0.01)* | Korrey | Koul | Kreig |
| Kobyon | Kohre | Kolten Scott | Konstantin | Korri'dell | Koulten | Kreighton |
| Kod'di | Kohta | Kolter | Konstantine | Korrie | Kounew | Kreishaun |
| Koda *(0.03)* | Kohv | Koltin *(0.01)* | Konstantinos | Korrigan | Kouper | Krenar |
| Kodah | Kohvyn | Kolton *(0.12)* | *(0.01)* | Korry | Kourdai | Krenzel |
| Kodan | Kohwen | Koltun | Kontrell | Korsal | Kourion | Kres |
| Kode | Koi | Koltyn *(0.01)* | Konyae | Kort | Kourosh | Krescyn |
| Kodee *(0.01)* | Koichi | Kolven | Konyaé | Kortaevious | Kouroush | Kreshaad |
| Koden | Koien | Kolvin | Konye | Kortayzi'an | Kourtez | Kreshawn |
| Kodey *(0.01)* | Koiyer | Kolvyn | Konyé | Kortez | Kourtney | Kressley |
| Kodi *(0.02)* | Kojarvious | Kolya | Konyeh | Kortland | Koury | Krew |
| Kodiak | Koji | Kolyn | Koob | Kortlen | Kousha | Krichun |
| Kodice | Kojo | Komani | Koolanny | Kortnie | Kouvaris | Kriday |
| Kodie *(0.01)* | Koki | Komarion | Kooner | Kortny | Kova | Krieg |
| Kodilichi | Kokou | Komavi | Kooper *(0.02)* | Korto | Kovan | Krieger |
| Kodin | Kol | Kombe | Koplin | Korvin | Kovarick | Krillin |
| Kody *(0.17)* | Kol El | Komei | Kor | Korvion | Kove | Krimsonn |

| | | | | | | |
|---|---|---|---|---|---|---|
| Kris (0.01) | Kristiahn | Krymson | Kumaren | Kuvarie | Ky (0.01) | Kyan Jakob |
| Krisan | Kristian (0.17) | Kryndon | Kumari | Kuwasi | Ky Juan | Kyandre |
| Kris-Angel | Kristian Llo | Krys | Kumasi | Kuy | Ky Rell | Kyane |
| Krischan | Kristien | Kryslavon | Kumaya | Kuyper | Ky To | Kyaon |
| Krisean | Kristijan | Krystafer | Kumayl | Kvion | Ky'air | Kyare |
| Krish (0.04) | Kristin | Krystal | Kumber | K-Von | Ky'aire | Kyas |
| Krishal | Kristina | Krysthopher | Kunaal | Kwa'lik | Ky'anthony | Kyashawn |
| Krishan (0.01) | Kristion | Krystian (0.01) | Kunal | Kwa'mel | Ky'bir | Kyaujah |
| Krishang | Kristipher | Krystifer | Kunchok | Kwaali | Ky'eir | Ky-Aun |
| Krishaun | Kristján (0.01) | Krystofer | Kundar | Kwabena | Ky'ell | Kyaunn |
| Krishav | Kristo | Krystoffer | Kunga | Kwade | Ky'jeir | Kyaw |
| Krishawn | Kristof | Krystopher | Kunj | Kwadir | Ky'jhaun | Kyber |
| Krishay | Kristofer (0.03) | (0.01) | Kunta | Kwadjo | Ky'juan | Kybrion |
| Krishi | Kristoff | Krystyn | Kunyri | Kwadwo | Ky'leal | Kyce |
| Krishiv | Kristoffer (0.01) | Kryton | Kuol | Kwaku | Ky'lee | Kyd |
| Krishiva | Kristofor | Kryztopher | Kuothnyuer | Kwali | Ky'lin | Kydavien |
| Krishkaarthik | Kriston | Krztian | Kuper | Kwalik | Ky'lon | Kyden (0.01) |
| Krishna (0.02) | Kristoper | Krzystopher | Kupono | Kwamaye | Ky'mahri | Kydir |
| Krishna Kaushik | Kristoph | Kshaunish | Kur | Kwame (0.01) | Ky'mani | Ky-Dree |
| Krishnadev | Kristopher (0.21) | Kshitij | Kurby | Kwan | Ky'marion | Kydreece |
| Krishnam | Kristopher Michael | Ku'masi | Kuren | Kwaniel | Ky'meek | Kydric |
| Krishnan | Kristorfer | Ku'shauntis | Kurik | Kwanique | Ky'mer | Kye (0.04) |
| Krishnasanhi | Kristos | Kua Shawn | Kurmarius | Kwantrell | Ky'mir | Kye'on |
| Krishnashish | Kristpoher | Kuanen | Kuron | Kwanyoung | Ky'mon | Kye'ran |
| Krishnav | Kristrian | Kuba | Kurrin | Kwanzaa | Ky'moni | Kyedehl |
| Krishod | Kristyan | Kuberli | Kursat | Kwasi | Ky'montae | Kyéem |
| Krishon | Krisver | Kudakwashe | Kursten | Kwasie | Ky'ontae | Kyeir |
| Krishtan | Krithick | Kudzanayi | Kurt (0.05) | Kwayde | Ky'ree | Kyelan |
| Krishtyn | Krithik | Kue | Kurt Dwayne | Kwayell | Ky'rell | Kyele |
| Krishveer | Krithikk | Kue-Hwan | Kurtavius | Kwaymaine | Ky'ren | Kyelen |
| Krish-Vivek | Kriz | Kuert Dominicq | Kurtez | Kwaymon | Ky'riek | Kyeler |
| Krishwan | Krizler | Kueven | Kurtis (0.06) | Kwazay | Ky'rik | Kyell |
| Krisi | Krizt | Kuffin | Kurtis-Job | Kweku | Ky'rim | Kyelyn |
| Krisian | Kriztyan | Kuhaya | Kurtus | Kweli (0.01) | Ky'rique | Kyen |
| Krisire | Krome | Kuhl | Kurtyz | Kwentin | Ky'ris | Kyer |
| Krisjen | Kronos | Kuider-Yassine | Kuruk | Kwentrell | Ky'ron | Kyeran |
| Krisli | Krosby | Kukes | Kuryis | Kwentyn | Ky'rus | Kyere |
| Kriss | Kross | Kulancekee | Kuryon | Kwesi | Ky'shaun | Kyeree |
| Krisster | Kroy | Kularrius | Kush (0.01) | Kwestjen | Ky'shun | Kyeren |
| Krisstian | Kroywen | Kulee | Kusha | Kwinten | Ky'siem | Kyeron |
| Krist | Krrish | Kulen | Kushaan | Kwintez | Ky'wunski | Ky-Ese |
| Kristafer | Krue | Kull Japheth | Kushagra | Kwmaee | Ky'yonte | Kyeshon |
| Kristan | Kruise | Kullen | Kushal | Kwok-Qiang | Ky'zaiah | Kyestin |
| Kristana | Kruize | Kully | Kushan | Kwonbok | Ky'zir | Kyesyn |
| Kristaps | Krunal | Kulraj | Kushmir | Kwondrey | Kya | Kyeyon |
| Kristauff | Kruse | Kulshaan | Kushy | Kwowbeer | Kyah | Kyez |
| Kristchan | Krushn | Kulshan | Kustandy | Kwuan | Kyahron | Kygan |
| Kristein | Kruz | Kulue | Kustom | Kwuenton | Kyair | Kyh'nard |
| Kristen | Kruze | Kumail | Kutay | Kwydir | Ky-Aire | Kyhbr |
| Krister | Krymani | Kumani | Kutler | Kwynci | Kyaire | Kyheem |
| Kristi | | Kumar | Kutter | Kwynsie | Kyale | Kyhem |
| | | Kumaran | Kuvar | Kwynton | Kyan (0.10) | Kyian |

Kyien
Kyier
Kyierhanzá
Kyiese
Kyilan
Kyin
Kyindel
Kying
Kyion
Kyiron
Kyis
Kyjaun
Kyjhai
Kyjuan
Kyl
Kyla
Kylae
Kylan *(0.08)*
Kyland
Kylann
Kylar *(0.01)*
Kylas
Kyle *(3.22)*
Kyle Emmanuel
Kyle Issac
Kyle Jay
Kyle Nathan
Kyle Owen
Kyle Vincent
Kyle'rese
Kyleaf
Kyleak
Kylear
Kyle-Colin
Ky-Lee
Kylee
Kyleek
Kyle-El
Kyleel
Kyleem
Kyleigh
Kyleik
Kyle-Kwaku
Kylel
Kylelin
Kylellell
Kyle-Luis
Kylen *(0.02)*
Kyler *(0.35)*
Kyler James
Kyler Jo
Kyleshes

Kylian
Kylian Cele
Kylic
Kylie
Kylieb
Kylief
Kyliefe
Kyliek
Kylier
Kylif
Kylik
Kylil
Kylin *(0.01)*
Kylind
Kylion
Kyllen
Kyller
Kyllin
Kylmer
Kylon *(0.01)*
Kylor
Kylum
Kylun
Kylur
Kylyn
Kyma're
Ky-Mani
Kymani *(0.02)*
Kymari
Kymarri
Kymaury
Kymaz
Kymee
Kymeir
Kymere
Kymier
Kymin
Kymir *(0.01)*
Kymon
Kymondre
Kymoni
Kymontae
Kymree
Kynami
Kynan
Kyndal
Kyndall
Kyndarius
Kyndel
Kynden
Kyndle
Kyndreaviyu

Kyndrick
Kyndrik
Kyne
Kyng
Kynief
Kynjaveon
Kynkade
Kynyel
Kyo
Kyodi
Kyon *(0.01)*
Kyondre
Kyontae
Ky-Onte
Kyonté
Kyori
Kyota
Kyotte
Kyoung
Kyoungmoo
Kyperion
Kyprian
Ky-Rail
Kyran *(0.02)*
Kyre
Kyre Knox
Ky-Ream
Kyree *(0.03)*
Kyreece
Kyreem
Kyreese
Kyreik
Kyreion
Kyrek
Kyrel
Kyrell *(0.01)*
Kyrelle
Kyren *(0.02)*
Kyrese
Kyresse
Kyrez
Kyri
Kyrian
Kyric
Kyrie
Kyril
Kyrillos
Kyrillus
Kyrin *(0.01)*
Kyrion
Kyriq
Kyrique

Kyris
Kyrollos
Kyrollous
Kyrollus
Kyron *(0.03)*
Kyrus
Kysaiah
Kysair
Kysean
Kyseem
Kyseir
Kyser
Kyshad
Kyshaun
Kyshaunn
Kyshawn
Kyshawne
Kysheen
Kysheim
Kyshein
Kysheir
Kyshon
Kyshun
Kysiem
Kysir
Kyson *(0.01)*
Kyssac
Kyston
Kysyn
Kyten
Kytin
Kytis
Kyto
Kyton
Kyu
Kyuana
Kyundra
Kyung
Kyungseo
Kyuss
Kyvaughn
Kyveon
Ky-Vinh
Kyvon
Kywaun
Kywoan
Kywon
Kyzack
Kyzahn
Kyzair
Kyzaun
Kyzen

Kyzer *(0.01)*
Kyzhon
Kyzick
Kyzien
Kyzin
Kyzjaner
Kz

## ~ L ~

L
L Dene
L.C.
L.H.
L'darius
L'javion
L'juan
L'kendre
L'marian
L'nauhré
L'zoriyen
La
La Dainian
La Danion
La Darious
La Daruis
La Davian
La Fleche
La Juan
La Marion
La More
La Quinton
La Ray
La Ron
La Rue
La Stat
La Tayvion
La Von
La Vone
La'adrain
La'adreion
La'brandon
La'brian
La'bron
La'bryan
La'bryce
La'brysen
La'cameron
La'cliffton
La'corian
La'dailyon

La'dainian
La'damion
La'danian
La'danien
La'darian
La'darien
La'darius
La'darren
La'darrius
La'daunice
La'davion
La'deen
La'delvin
La'derion
La'derrick
La'don
La'dontae
La'donte
La'dorrein
La'drikious
La'dur
La'ernest
La'floyd
La'grand
La'harry
La'jaevien
La'jalyn
La'javen
La'javien
La'javius
La'juan
La'kayvion
La'kel
La'kell
La'kelvin
La'kendrick
La'kerioan
La'kwain
La'mar
La'marco
La'marcus
La'mario
La'marion
La'marious
La'marius
La'markus
La'maron
La'marrieon
La'marrion
La'maun
La'mikel
La'mirr

La'monte
La'na'jie
La'neir
La'nell
La'norris
La'nyan
La'nyzjah
La'pharoah
La'quan
La'quavion
La'quayvion
La'quez
La'quinton
La'quniton
La'quria
La'qwayvion
La'renzo
La'reo
La'reon
La'rez
La'rodrick
La'roi
La'ron
La'ronta
La'rontae
La'roy
La'royce
La'ryan
La'samuel
La'sean
La'shan
La'shawe
La'shawn
La'shayne
La'tavion
La'terius
La'terrance
La'terrence
La'tib
La'ticus
La'tolan
La'travion
La'tre
La'treal
La'trell
La'trevious
La'varis
La'vaunta
La'vette
La'von
La'vontae
La'vonte

| | | | | | | |
|---|---|---|---|---|---|---|
| La'wayne | Ladadrien | Lado | Laiken | Lakiem | Lamarkus | Lamyja |
| La'zan | Ladae | Ladoia | Laikiaz | Lakien | Lamarquis | Lan |
| La'zerion | Ladainian (0.01) | Ladon | Laile | Lakietric | Lamarr | Lanair |
| La'zerrick | Ladainion | Ladonnivin | Laim | Lakin (0.01) | Lamarri | Lanard |
| Laal | Ladale | Ladonta | Lain | Lakior | Lamarrion | Lanardo |
| Laangelo | Ladameon | Ladontis | Laindsay | Lakiy | Lamarrius | Lanardre |
| Laban | Ladamian | Ladorian | Laine (0.01) | Laklen | Lamarrn | Lanauveon |
| Labar | Ladamien | Ladorien | Lainy | Lakobe | Lamartra | Lanazares |
| Labaron | Ladamion | Ladrell | Laiquendi | Lakoda | Lamaunt | Lanbrent |
| Labarron | Ladanian | Ladrese | Laird (0.01) | Lakon | Lamaure | Lanc |
| Labeeb | Ladaniel | Ladrevion | Laish | Lakota (0.02) | Lamaurion | Lancaster |
| Labian | Ladanion | Ladrey | Laison | Lakotah | Lamauris | Lance (0.33) |
| Labinot | Ladareious | Lae'la | Laith (0.02) | Laksh | Lambert (0.01) | Lance Brandon |
| Labisan | Ladaren | Lae'shelle | Laithan | Lakshman | Lamberto | Lance Matthew |
| Labrae | Ladareon | Laeg | Laithon | Lakshmisaketh | Lameak | Lance Ranier |
| Labraé | Ladarian | Laek | Laivon | Lakshya | Lamech | Lancelot |
| Labrandon | Ladarien | Lael | Lajabron | Lakwon | Lameer | Lancer |
| Labrandus | Ladarin | Laemadon | Lajames | Lakyn | Lamel | Lancin |
| Labraun | Ladarion | Laene | Lajarvis | Laland | Lamell | Landan (0.05) |
| Labrawn | Ladarious | Laeon | Lajaun | Lalit | Lamere | Landavius |
| Labrentae | La-Daris | Laeton | Lajavious | Lall | Lamez | Landden |
| Labrice | Ladaris | Lafayette | Lajavius | Lalo | Lami | Landehn |
| Labroderick | Ladarius (0.02) | Lafe | Lajear | Lalruat | Lamichael | Landen (0.55) |
| Labrodrick | Ladariyon | Lafeyette | Lajereane | Lalu | Lamiché | Landen Connor |
| Labron | Ladarrein | Laffeatte | Lajerrett | Laly | Lamier | Landenn |
| Labronson | Ladarrian | Lafiere | Lajon | Lam | Lamikal | Lander |
| Labryant | Ladarrien | Lafleche | Lajos | Lamaar | Lamin | Landerius |
| Lac | Ladarrion | Lafleche- | Laju | Lamair | Lamine | Landerjoe |
| Lacardar | Ladarrious |   Eugene | Lajuan | Lamaj | Lamir | Landin (0.06) |
| Lacarious | Ladarrius | Lafranco | Lajuene | Lamanii | Lammon | Landion |
| Lacas | Ladarron | Lafredrick | Lakadoe | Lamar (0.10) | Lamon | Landiran |
| Lacavaler | Ladaverick | Lagarian | Lakai | Lamarco | Lamon'tez | Landis (0.01) |
| Lace | Ladavian | Lagarius | Lakan'ye | Lamarcus (0.01) | Lamoncho | Landiss |
| Lacedric | Ladavion | Lagarrian | Lakavius | Lamarcuse | Lamondre | Lando |
| Lacedron | Ladavius | Laghtine | Lake (0.01) | Lamare | Lamone | Landon (4.40) |
| Lacen | Ladaynian | Lagon | Lake Barrek | Lamarean | Lamonroe | Landon James |
| Lacey | Ladd | Lagoon | Lake Sene | Lamareon | Lamont (0.05) | Landon John |
| Lachance | Ladden | Lagrant | Lakeaih | Lamareontez | Lamont James |   Abel |
| Lachario | Ladedric | Lahaad | Lake-Charles | Lamareus | Lamonta | Landon Jordan |
| Lachase | Ladedrick | Lahad | Lakee | Lamareyone | Lamontae | Landon |
| Lachaunt | Ladell | Lahans | Lakeem | Lamari | Lamontaye |   Puamun |
| Lachey | Laden | Lahayi | Lakeis | Lamari'on | Lamonté | Landon Thanh |
| Lachian | Laderal | Lahiru | Lakeisha | Lamarian | Lamonte (0.01) | Landonignatius |
| Lachlan (0.03) | Laderek | Lahmi'r | Lakeith | Lamario | Lamontea | Landre |
| Lachon | Laderrian | Lahmyn | Lakeldrick | La-Marion | Lamontez | Landren |
| Lachoneus | Laderric | Lahne | Lakelen | Lamarion (0.02) | Lamontrae | Landrew |
| Lac-Leon | Laderrick | Lahorace | Lakell | Lamarione | Lamontray | Landrez |
| Lacoda | Laderrius | Lai | Laken (0.01) | Lamarious | Lamontré | Landri |
| Lacon | Ladigo | Lai'vian | Lakendrick | Lamariun | Lamontzrae | Landrick |
| Lacorey | Ladin | Laia | Lakentrye | Lamarius | Lamorris | Landrik |
| Lacoste | Ladino | Laid | Laker | Lamariyon | Lamount | Landris |
| Lacota | Ladjee | Laiden | Lakerion | Lamark | Lampton | Landro |
| Lacy | Ladji | Laik | Lakhan | Lamarkis | Lamuel | Landrum |

| | | | | | | |
|---|---|---|---|---|---|---|
| Landry *(0.01)* | Laprince | Larmarion | Lasha | Laterrance | Latrevian | Lavale |
| Landryn | Laqoda | Larmy | Lashad | Laterrence | Latrevion | Lavan |
| Landson | Laqreus | Larne | Lashai | Laterreon | Latreyvious | Lavance |
| Landunn | Laquaine | Larnel | Lashane | Laterrian | Latreyvius | Lavandern |
| Landy | Laqualle | Larnell | Lashaun *(0.01)* | Laterrious | Latrez | Lavandre |
| Landyan | Laquan *(0.01)* | Larnelle | Lashaunt | Laterrius | Latrielle | Lavant |
| Landyce | Laquandrae | La-Robb | Lashaurd | Laterry | Latrius | Lavanta |
| Landyn *(0.09)* | Laquantay | Laroce | Lashavion | Lateryeon | Latrodrick | Lavante |
| Landyne | Laquarius | Larod | Lashawn *(0.01)* | Latevien | Latron | Lavar *(0.01)* |
| Landynn | Laquavion | Laroger | Lashay | Latez | Latronzo | Lavaré |
| Lane *(0.31)* | Laquavius | Larome | Lashin | Latham | Latroy *(0.01)* | Lavarence |
| Lane Maverick | Laquay | Laron *(0.03)* | Lashod | Lathan *(0.02)* | Lattimer | Lavareon |
| Laneden | Laquayvius | Larond | La-Shon | Lathaniel | Lattreal | Lavares |
| Lanegan | Laquentin | Larone | Lashon | Lathari | Latwan | Lavarice |
| Lanell | Laquenton | Laronte | Lashondae | Lathem | Latwuan | Lavarion |
| Laney | Laquin | Laronus | Lashone | Lathen | Lauchlan | Lavarious |
| Lang | Laquincy | Laroy | Lashun | Lathereo | Lauchlin | Lavaris |
| Langden | Laquinta | Larr | Lashundez | Latherious | Lauchnor | Lavarius |
| Langdon *(0.01)* | Laquintan | Larrado | Lashune | Lathias | Laudie | Lavarriohn |
| Langh | Laquintin | Larrel | Lasighis | Lathom | Laudyn | Lavaruis |
| Langham | Laquist | Larrenz | Lasius | Lathomas | Lauer | Lavasko |
| Langholm | Laquon | Larreon | Lasner | Lathon | Laughlin | Lavaughn |
| Langhston | Laqwon | Larret | Lason | Lathria | Laughton | Lavel |
| Langley | Lar'rion | Larrian | Lasse | Lathum | Lauille | Lavell *(0.01)* |
| Langsten | Laraje | Larriano | Lassen | Latif | Laura | Lavelle *(0.01)* |
| Langston *(0.03)* | Laramic | Larrie | Lastant | Latimie | Laurel | Laven |
| Lanhai | Laramie | Larrion | Lastat | Latodric | Lauren *(0.01)* | Laventrey |
| Lani | Laramy | Larriyon | Laszlo | Latony | Laurence *(0.01)* | Laveon |
| Laniell | Larance | Larrmie | László | Latori | Laurence Ariane | Lavern *(0.01)* |
| Lanier | Laraun | Larron | Lat'ariek | Latorion | Laurencio | Laverne |
| Lanigan | Laray | Larry *(0.23)* | Latae | Latowan | Laurens | Lavertus |
| Laniirr | Larbi | Larrye | Lataevious | Kendric | Laurent *(0.06)* | Lavhon |
| Lanis | Laredo | Larryn | Lataj | Latrail | Laurent Xavier | Lavi |
| Lannen | Larell | Larryntae | Latarey | Latraivion | Laurent-Benoît | Laviathan |
| Lannon | Larentrio | Lars *(0.03)* | Latari | Latral | Laurent- | Lavin |
| Lanny | Larenz | Lars Oliver | Latariq | Latrale | Christoph | Lavindeep |
| Lanoris | Larenze | Larsen | Lataurus | Latraveus | Laurent- | Lavindu |
| Lanorris | Larenzen | Larson *(0.01)* | Lataveious | Latravian | Christophe | Lavir |
| Lansana | Larenzo | Lartavious | Lataveon | Latravion | Laurenzo | Lavneet |
| Lansen | Laret | La-Rue | Latavian | Latravious | Lauric | Lavoctris |
| Lansina | Lareu | Laruntray | Latavion | Latravis | Lauricko | Lavod |
| Lansing | Larhence | Larus | Latavious | Latravius | Laurie | Lavohn |
| Lanson | Lari | Laryan | Latavis | Latrayven | Laurier *(0.01)* | Lavon *(0.02)* |
| Lansper | Lariante | Laryc | Latavius | Latre | Lauris | Lavon'tae |
| Lanthier | Larico | Lasaan | Latayveon | Latreal | Laurnez | Lavon'te |
| Lantry | Larien | Lasale Lee | Latayvian | Latreaze | Lauro | Lavondre |
| Lantz | Larimie | Lasalle | Latchlon | Latrel | Lauron | Lavondré |
| Lantzer | Larinthian | Lasandchiez | Lateef | La-Trell | Lauryn | Lavonis |
| Lanujan | Lario | Lascelles | Laten | Latrell *(0.04)* | Lautaro | Lavonn |
| Laouenan | Lark | Lasdislao | Laterian | Latrell Dama | Lauwens-Gerald | Lavonne |
| Laprada | Larken | Lasean | Laterion | Latrelle | Lavaar | Lavonske |
| Laprea | Larkin *(0.01)* | Lasedric | Laterius | Latrellis | Lavadous | Lavont |
| Lapriest | Larkun | Laser | Laterl | Latreon | Lavalas | Lavonta |

Lavontae
Lavonte
Lavonté
Lavontis
Lavontrae
Lavontre
Lavor
Lavorian
Lavoris
Lavrell
Lavurice
Law
Lawan
Lawande
Lawann
Lawarren
Lawaune
Lawayne *(0.01)*
Laween
Lawerance
Lawerence
Lawin
Lawon
Lawrance
Lawren
Lawrence *(0.20)*
Lawrence
  Edward
Lawrenzo
Lawron
Lawsen
Lawson *(0.08)*
Lawton *(0.01)*
Lawuan
Lawvens
Lawyer
Laxaivyion
Laxya
Lay'quan
Laybbn
Laybreaun
Laydan
Layden *(0.01)*
Laydon
Layehmarn
Layfette
Layke
Layken
Layla
Layland
Laylyn
Laymon
Layn

Layndin
Layndon
Layne *(0.11)*
Layne Nolan
Layshon
Laytan
Layten
Layth
Laython
Laythyn
Laytin
Layton *(0.07)*
Layundray
Layvonne
Laywandre
Laywayain
Lazabion
Lazar
Lazariah
Lazarian
Lazario
Lazarion
Lazarius
Lazaro *(0.03)*
Lazaros
Lazarrius
Lazarus *(0.02)*
Lazarusie Tukai
Lazavier
Lazaviyer
Lazer *(0.01)*
Lazerik
Lazerius
Lazerus
Lazius
Lazo
Lazon
Lazura
Lazuriea
Lazz
Lazzare
Lcuas
Le
Le Aaron
Le Bron
Le Darian
Le Quentin
Le Tian
Le'aaron
Le'andre
Le'andrea
Le'anthony
Le'augustus

Le'ayr
Le'breil
Le'bron
Le'brontae
Le'bryon
Le'darius
Le'darrion
Le'davius
Le'derrius
Le'gregory
Le'jai
Le'jon
Le'joun
Le'keyon
Le'lon
Le'mar
Le'marcus
Le'marion
Le'maurion
Le'oni
Le'pedro
Le'quan
Le'quent
Le'raile
Le'ron
Le'roy
Le'shan
Le'shawn
Le'shuan
Le'torrian
Le'travius
Le'var
Le'vari
Le'varie
Le'varrius
Le'vel
Le'von
Le'vontae
Le'vontay
Le'vonte
Le'zavion
Lea
Leadell
Leaf
Leafar
Leah
Leahland
Leal
Lealan
Lealand
Leam
Leamon
Lean

Leande
Leander *(0.02)*
Leanders
Leandré
Leandre *(0.01)*
Leandrei
Leandres
Leandrew
Leandro *(0.06)*
Leandros
Leanne
Leanthony
Leantoine
Lear Arnaud
Leart
Leaston
Leathen
Leaton
Leavest
Leavy
Leban
Lebaron
Lebarron
Leboris
Lebran
Lebrandon
Lebrannon
Lebraun
Lebron *(0.03)*
Lebrunt
Lebryant
Lebryn
Lecarius
Lecedric
Lecester
Lecharles
Lechi
Lechristoph
Lecory
Lecosta
Ledaniel
Ledany
Ledarius
Ledarrius
Ledavion
Ledawel-Eval
Leday
Ledbin
Leddiel
Ledel
Lederris
Ledge
Ledgen

Ledger
Ledion
Ledius
Ledjun
Lee *(0.10)*
Lee Allen
Lee Andrew
Lee Billy
Lee Edward
Lee Hanief
Lee Roy
Lee'isaac
Lee'juan
Lee'marion
Lee'martay
Lee'modgeia
Lee'twon
Lee'vaughn
Leeallen
Leeam
Leeandrew
Leeandro
Leeann
Leeanthon
Leeanthony
Leedan
Leedor
Leeds
Lee-Eden
Leein
Lee-J
Leekoda
Leelan *(0.01)*
Leeland *(0.02)*
Leelean
Leelend
Leelin
Leenard
Leeodis
Leeondre
Leepang
Leephor
Lee-Quwann
Leeram
Leeric
Leeroy
Leerye
Leesander
Leesandro
Lee-Shaun
Leeshawn
Leeto
Leeton

Leevan
Lee-Van
  Sakianny
Leevanta
Leevi *(0.01)*
Lee-Von
Leevon
Leevonte
Leewell
Leezack
Lefmonscrapcu
Lefonso
Lefonzie
Lefrederick
Lefteri
Legacy
Legal
Legend *(0.01)*
Legend Adel
Legion
Lehi
Lehman
Lehman-David
Lehy
Lei'leon
Leiam
Leib *(0.01)*
Leiber
Leiby
Leid
Leidy
Leif *(0.05)*
Leife
Leifur
Leigh
Leigham
Leighlan
Leightin
Leighton *(0.04)*
Leiham
Leilan
Leiland
Leilani
Leilend
Leilund
Leini
Leirr
Leisker
Leitarion
Leith *(0.01)*
Leithen
Leivin
Lejaiden

Lejon
Lejuan
Lejuiles
Lekai
Lekedric
Lekeith
Lekeveyunat
Lekh
Lekhi
Lekiam
Lekian
Leks
Leksi
Leksvin
Lelan
Leland *(0.20)*
Lelane
Lele
Lelen
Lelena
Lelend
Lelin
Lelious
Lelon
Lelund
Lem
Leman
Lemanuel
Lemar *(0.01)*
Lemarcus
Lemareon
Le-Mari
Lemarion
Lemel
Lemenuel
Lemine
Lemir
Lemitrias
Lemmy
Lemont
Lemonte
Lemonté
Lemontrey
Lemorris
Lemoyne
Lemuel *(0.01)*
Lemuel-Jeffrey
Lemuel-Ken
Len
Len'darius
Lenai
Lenair
Lenan

| | | | | | | |
|---|---|---|---|---|---|---|
| Lenard | Lenville | Leonell | Leshane | Levare | Lex *(0.02)* | Liance |
| Lenardo | Lenwood | Leonelle | Leshaun | Levares | Lexadrian | Liandro |
| Lenarion | Leny | Leonicy | Leshauwn | Levarion | Lexander | Liandy |
| Lencorya | Lenz | Leonid | Leshawn | Levarious | Lexani | Liangtao |
| Lend | Lenz's | Leonidas *(0.01)* | Le-Shon | Levaris | Lexian | Liano |
| Lendale | Lenzie | Leonilson | Leslee | Levarus | Lexiel | Lias |
| Lendel | Leo *(0.48)* | Leonizio | Lesley | Levathian | Lexier | Libaan |
| Lendl | Leo Angelo | Leonni | Leslianna | Leve | Lexin | Liban |
| Lendol | Leo Anthony | Leonta | Leslie *(0.02)* | Levell | Lexington | Libane Leo |
| Lendon | Leo Atilla | Leonte | Lesly | Levelle | Lexiss | Liber |
| Lendric | Leo Cyrus | Leonty | Leslye | Leven | Lexter | Liborio |
| Lendy | Leo Pauldo | Leonzoe | Lesnel | Levente | Lextin | Librado |
| Lenele | Leo Stephen | Leo-Paul | Lesniel | Leventé | Lexton | Libronio |
| Lenell | Leo-Alexis | Leo-Pier | Lesra | Levern | Lexus | Lico |
| Lenexx | Leoant | Leo-Pierre | Lestadt | Levi *(1.29)* | Lexus Wesley | Liddel |
| Leng | Leobardo *(0.01)* | Leopino | Lestar | Levi Donovan | Lexx | Liden |
| Leni | Leocadio | Leopol | Lestat *(0.01)* | Levi Emerald | Lexxington | Lidia |
| Lenier | Leocarlo | Leopold *(0.01)* | Lestate | Levi Ryan | Leyandro | Lidwon |
| Lenila | Leo-Charles | Leopoldo | Lestaut | Levi Yehuda | Leyden | Lief |
| Lenin | Leodan | Leopoldo III | Lester *(0.04)* | Leviathan | Leyfer | Lieff |
| Lenix | Leodanis | Leor | Lesther | Leviathin | Leyin | Liel |
| Lenixx | Leodsky | Leorenzo | Leston | Levie | Leylan | Lieland |
| Lenmone | Leo-Eric | Leosmer | Letarion | Leviev | Leyland | Liell |
| Lennan | Leoj | Leotrim | Letarius | Levigaddy | Leymar | Liem |
| Lennard | Leolito | Leovani | Letarrian | Levi-Garrett | Leyner | Liet |
| Lennart | Leoloup | Leovardo | Letavion | Levi-James | Leyon | Liev |
| Lenneil | Leomar | Leovoni | Leterrance | Levin *(0.01)* | Leyten | Lieven |
| Lennell | Leo-Mathieu | Lepage | Leterrian | Levi-Paul | Leythan | Lievin |
| Lennert | Leo-Michel | Lequan | Leterrius | Levis | Leyton *(0.04)* | Lieyton |
| Lenni | Leon *(0.17)* | Lequandre | Letez | Levis-Jhon | Leyver | Life |
| Lenniek | Leon Austin | Lequarious | Lethanial | Levis-John | Lez'leon | Lightning |
| Lennin | Leon Marcel | Lequentin | Lethaniel | Levita | Lezan | Lihan |
| Lennix | Leon'tay | Lequincy | Leto | Leviticus *(0.01)* | Lezander | Liiban |
| Lennon *(0.02)* | Leonaldo | Lerandros | Letre'vian | Levn | Lezayn | Lija |
| Lennox *(0.02)* | Leonard *(0.12)* | Lerenzo | Letrel | Levon *(0.01)* | Lezerick | Lijah |
| Lennoxx | Leonardas | Lerin | Letrell | Levon Jeremiah | Lhayse | Likai |
| Lenny *(0.03)* | Leonardgi | Leroderick | Létrell | Levone | Lhor | Likenson |
| Lenny-Jeremy | Leonardo *(0.35)* | Leroi | Letrevon | Levonte | Li | Likhit |
| Lenon | Leonardo Anton | Leron | Letrez | Levontrez | Li'rodrick | Likith |
| Lenorris | Leonardo-Enrique | Leronn | Letroy | Levy *(0.01)* | Li'troy | Lil |
| Lenox | Leonardus | Leross | Lettwan | Levy Yitzchak | Liahm | Lil Bruis |
| Lenoxx | Leonare | Leroy *(0.06)* | Leuka | Levyn | Liam *(2.60)* | Lil Mario |
| Lenquez | Leonce | Leroy King | Leul | Lewa | Liam Anthony | Lil Patrick |
| Lenroy | Leoncio | Leroytana | Leumn | Lewan-Terry | Liam Gregory | Lil'darius |
| Lens | Leondardo | Lerrell | Leundre | Lewayne | Liam Harold | Lil'greg |
| Lens-Ashley | Leondo | Lerroy | Leuntae | Lewenki | Liam John | Lil'james |
| Lensky | Leondra | Lerry | Leuris | Lewin | Liam Oliver | Lilal |
| Lenso | Leondrae | Leryan | Leutrim | Lewis *(0.12)* | Liam-Isaac | Lilas |
| Lentavius | Leondray | Les | Lev *(0.01)* | Lewis Malachi | Liamm | Lilcourtney |
| Lenten | Leondre | Lesae | Levan | Lewison | Liam-Michael | Lile |
| Lenton | Leonel *(0.09)* | Lesday | Levant | Lewiste | Liam-Nathan | Liliana |
| Lentz | Leonelby | Lesean | Levantis | Lewkus | Liam-William | Liljessie |
| Lenuel | | Leshad | Levar | Lewton | Lian *(0.01)* | Lillian |

Lillianne
Lilly
Lilmarion
Lilton
Lily
Lim
Limber
Limbert
Liming
Limon
Lin
Linaire
Linald
Linber
Linci
Lincoln (0.25)
Lincon
Lindel
Lindell
Linden (0.02)
Lindino
Lindo
Lindon
Lindrick
Lindsay
Lindsey
Lindsley
Lindyn
Lindzell
Linford
Ling Jun
Linghan
Linius
Link
Linken
Linkin (0.01)
Linkoln
Linkon
Linkyn
Linley
Linmar
Lino (0.01)
Linor
Linse
Linton
Linus (0.01)
Linwood
Liomar
Lion
Lionardo
Lionel (0.02)
Lioneld
Lionell

Lionso
Lior
Lioshandry
Lioux
Lipa (0.01)
Lirijan
Lirim
Lirit
Liron
Lisa
Lisaad
Lisael
Lisander
Lisandro (0.01)
Lisjen
Lisle
Lismark
Lismel
Liston
Lisvan
Litermin
Lithasack
Litt
Little
Little Hail
Littlewayne
Litton
Liul
Liusbany
Liuvent
Liuvi
Livan
Liverio
Lives In The
	Clouds
Livingston
Livingstone
Liviu
Livjot
Lixadro
Lixandro
Liyang
Lizaldo
Lizandro
Lizeth
LJ
Lla'korr
Llair
Llaython
Llejend
Llesica
Llewellyn
Llewelyn

Lleydon
Lleyhan
Lleyton (0.02)
Lliam
Llilberto
Llivethan
Llonie
Llovani
Lloyd (0.04)
Lloyd Daniel
Lloyd Sidney
Lloyd-Olivier
Llyod
Lo
Loagen
Loagon
Loal
Lo-Ammi
Loan
Loann
Lobbe-Gilbert
Lobjot
Lobner
Lobo
Loc
Locagerian
Locario
Lochlainn
Lochlan (0.02)
Lochlann
Lochlin
Lochlund
Lochlyn
Locke
Lockin
Locklan
Locklear
Lodan
Loden
Loegan
Loek
Loewen
Loften
Loftin
Lofton
Logan (6.32)
Logan James
Logan Lew
Logan Ray
Logan Sky
Logan-Alberto
Logann
Logan-Trent

Logehn
Logen (0.02)
Loggen
Loghan (0.01)
Login
Logon
Logun (0.01)
Logunn
Logyn
Lohami
Lohan
Lohann
Lohann Doryan
Lohden
Lohgan
Lohgen
Lohitesh
Lohn
Lohnito
Lohr
Loïc
Loic (0.14)
Loic Anthony
Loic-Anthony
Loic-Antoine
Loic-Daiki
Loick (0.02)
Loïk
Loik (0.03)
Loik Aurele
Loik-Victor
Lois
Loises
Loishooki
Lok
Lok Hai-Kazif
Lokai
Lok-Chun
Loken
Lokesh
Loki (0.01)
Lokie
Lokosang
Lola
Lolin
Lomar
Lomarr
Lon
Lon'darren
Lon'nard
Lonaki
Lonald
Loncelle

Londarius
Londen
London (0.09)
London Bevyne
London Kyle
London-Ashley
Londun
Londyn
Lonell
Long
Long Ryan
Longino
Lonja
Lonndale
Lonnel
Lonnell
Lonnie (0.04)
Lonnie Tyler
Lonnie Zaman
Lonnit
Lonny
Lonray
Lonson
Lontac
Lontavious
Lonzel
Lonzell
Lonzo
Loocka
Lopez
Lopez-Mendez
Loqman
Lora
Loran
Lorcan
Lord
Lord Diacono
Lorden
Lordon
Lord-Tyrik
Loren (0.02)
Lorenje
Lorenso
Lorent
Lorentz
Lorenz
Lorenza
Lorenzo (0.27)
Lorenzo David
Lorenzo
	Enrique
Lorenzo
	Estefano

Lorenzo Joh
Lorenzo-
	Eduardo
Lorenzo-Gbagbo
Lorenzo-Katron
Loreto
Loreyntae
Lorgens
Loric
Lorick
Lorik
Lorimar
Lorin
Lorinc
Lorio
Loris
Lorne
Loron
Loronzo
Lorrenzo
Lorrin
Lorvic
Lorymer
Los
Loshyne
Lotabean
Loten
Lotfi
Lotka
Lott
Lottrell
Lotus
Loty
Lou (0.02)
Lou'anthony
Lou'cardi Air
Louai
Loubert
Louby
Louca
Loucas (0.01)
Loucious
Louciouse
Loudan
Loudarius
Louden (0.01)
Loudon
Loudovick
Lou-Felix
Lou-Gabriel
Lougaele
Loughan
Loughin

Loughlin
Louhan
Loui
Louian
Louick
Louie (0.01)
Louie Charles
Louije
Louik
Louin
Louis (0.35)
Louis Alex
Louis Alexandre
Louis Charles
Louis David
Louis Edouard
Louis Mathis
Louis Philip
Louis Philipe
Louis Philippe
Louis Thomas
Louis Victor
Louis-Adrien
Louis-Alex
Louis-Alexandre
Louis-Alexis
Louis-Andre
Louis-Antoine
Louis-Baptiste
Louis-Charles
	(0.01)
Louis-
	Christophe
Louis-Daniel
Louis-David
	(0.01)
Louis-Dominic
Louise
Louis-Eliott
Louis-Emile
Louis-Etienne
Louis-Félix
Louis-Felix
	(0.02)
Louis-Francois
Louis-Gabriel
Louis-Georges
Louis-Jacob
Louis-Joseph
Louis-Justin
Louis-Laurent
Louis-Martin
Louis-Mathis

| | | | | | |
|---|---|---|---|---|---|
| Louis-Maxime | Lovedeep | Lucan | Luckner | Luis Igacio | Luko | Lycan |
| Louis-Napoleon | Lovehandsome | Luc-Antoine | Luckny | Luis Javier | Lukus *(0.01)* | Lychau |
| Louis-Olivier | Lovell | Lucardo | Luckster | Luis Jesus | Lukyan | Lydall |
| Louison | Lovelle | Lucas *(3.94)* | Lucky *(0.01)* | Luis Miguel | Lumas | Lydell |
| Louis-Patrick | Lovemarionta | Lucas Bradl | Luc-Olivier | Luis Oscar | Lumin | Lyden |
| Louis-Paul | Lovenoor | Lucas Brady | Lucson | Luis Reynaldo | Lunan | Lydia |
| Louis-Philip | Lovens | Lucas Conno | Lucus *(0.01)* | Luis Roberto | Lunar | Lydon |
| Louis-Philipe | Lovensky | Lucas Gabriel | Luder | Luisalberto | Lunden *(0.01)* | Lyedric |
| Louis-Philippe *(0.04)* | Lovepreet | Lucas Istvan | Ludim | Luisangel | Lundon | Lyeke |
| Louis-Phillip | Loveveer | Lucas Jaedin | Ludivic | Luisao | Lundonn | Lyem |
| Louis-Phillip | Lovic | Lucas Mateus | Ludo | Luisariel | Lundy | Lyes |
| Louis-Phillipe | Lovick | Lucas-Alec | Ludovic *(0.07)* | Luis-Daniel | Lunyhe | Lyfe |
| Louis-Pierre | Loviel | Lucas-Alexandre | Ludovick *(0.02)* | Luis-Eduardo | Lunzy | Lyhour |
| Louis-Raphael | Lovik | Lucas-Esteban | Ludovic-Martin | Luisfernando | Luo | Lyja |
| Louis-Samuel | Lovins | Lucas-Frederic | Ludovico | Luisjordan | Luony | Lyjah |
| Louis-Simon *(0.01)* | Lovit | Lucas-Kane | Ludovik *(0.02)* | Luiss | Lupe | Lykaios |
| Louis-Thomas *(0.01)* | Lovon | Lucas-Patrick | Ludovyk | Luissaulo | Lupé | Lyla |
| Louis-Victor | Low | Lucatoni | Ludrik | Luitchen | Lupin | Lyle *(0.02)* |
| Louis-Vincent | Lowan | Lucaus | Ludvens | Luiyi | Luqmaan | Lylle |
| Louis-Xavier | Lowden | Lucavelli | Ludvik | Luiz *(0.01)* | Luqman *(0.01)* | Lyman |
| Louiyie | Lowell *(0.01)* | Lucavi | Ludwig | Luiz Augusto | Luriel | Lymont |
| Lou-K | Lowen | Lucaz | Ludwin | Luiz Felipe | Lusala | Lyn'navion |
| Louka *(0.04)* | Lowery | Lucca *(0.03)* | Ludwing | Luizandro | Luscian | Lyna |
| Loukas *(0.01)* | Lowis | Lucca-Michel | Luekaz | Luiz-Mario | Luscio | Lynail |
| Loukass | Lowrens | Luccas | Luemar | Lujuan | Lusvin | Lynch |
| Loukens | Lowyn | Lucciano | Luen | Luk | Lutalo | Lyncoln |
| Loukha | Loyal | Lucean | Lueranze | Luka *(0.10)* | Lute | Lyndale |
| Loukian | Loyd | Lucent | Lueshen | Luka Jozo | Luterian | Lyndean |
| Lou-Mael | Loyde | Lucero | Lugman Abdul | Lukacs | Luther *(0.03)* | Lyndel |
| Loumyr | Loydon | Luc-Etienne | Lugwyn | Lukah | Lutrell | Lyndell |
| Lounes | Loye | Luchas | Luhan | Lukaius | Lutula | Lynden *(0.01)* |
| Lou-Olivier | Lric | Luchian | Luiderek | Luk-Alexy | Luu Minh Tri | Lyndin |
| Loup | Lu'es | Luchiano | Luie | Luka-Pierre | Luukas | Lyndon *(0.03)* |
| Loup-Gabriel | Luaay | Lucian *(0.07)* | Luigi *(0.02)* | Lukas *(0.50)* | Luvens | Lynell |
| Lou-Philip | Lual | Lucianio | Luigino | Lukas-Gregg | Luvin | Lynk |
| Lou-Philippe | Luan | Lucianno | Luigy | Lukasz | Luvinson | Lynken |
| Lourenco | Luanglith | Luciano *(0.06)* | Luii | Luke *(4.42)* | Luvjot | Lynkin |
| Louric | Luave | Luciant | Luis *(3.63)* | Luke Aaron | Lux | Lynkon |
| Lourick | Lubens | Lucias | Luis Albert | Luke Elijah | Luxon | Lynkyn |
| Louroy | Luberto | Lucien *(0.03)* | Luis Alonso | Luke Isaac | Luxsan | Lynn *(0.01)* |
| Louscion | Lubin | Luciene | Luis Andres | Luke Michael | Luxurious | Lynnard |
| Louvens | Lubin-Victor | Lucille | Luis Angel | Luke Okeimute | Luygi | Lynndale |
| Louvens Chy-De | Luc *(0.07)* | Lucilo | Luis Antonio | Lukecus | Luzer | Lynnell |
| Louvik | Luc Chhanak | Lucio *(0.01)* | Luis Armando | Luken | Luziano | Lynnen |
| Louwashyouwa | Lucá | Lucion | Luis Arthuro | Lukes | Luzyus | Lynnwood |
| Louxenski | Luca *(0.39)* | Lucious *(0.01)* | Luis Arturo | Lukeson | Ly | Lynque |
| Louyk | Luca Anthony | Lucis | Luis Daniel | Lukez | Ly'quavious | Lyns |
| Lovalle | Luca Charles | Lucius *(0.04)* | Luis Eduard | Lukhman | Ly'torien | Lynson |
| Lovando | Lucadio | Lucjan | Luis Eliam | Lukian | Ly'vi'el | Lyntrell |
| Lovanskey | Lucael | Luck | Luis Enrique | Lukias | Lyad | Lynwood |
| Love | Lucah | Luckas | Luis Ernesto | Lukin | Lyam *(0.01)* | Lynx |
| | Lucain | Luckens | Luis Felipe | Lukis | Lyander | Lynzell |
| | Luca-Ioan | Luckey | Luis Fernando | Lukkas | Lyandon | Lyon |

Lyonel
Lyonel-Gonzalo
Lyontez
Lyran
Lyric (0.02)
Lyrick
Lyrickney
Lyriik
Lyrik (0.01)
Lysander
Lysandre
Lystad
Lyster
Lyston
Lyteif
Lyterrell
Lyth
Lythe
Lytreeon
Lyvan
Lyvarius
Lyzander

## ~ M ~

M
M Alimu
M Atthew
M Darren
M.
M'hand
M'kel
M'kell
M'khai
M'khori
M'kwala
M'rick
Ma
Ma'ad
Ma'az
Ma'cai
Ma'chir
Ma'chuzhingah
Ma'en
Ma'jya
Ma'kai
Ma'kale
Ma'kel
Ma'khai
Ma'khi
Ma'ki
Ma'kyi

Ma'kyrion
Ma'lic
Ma'lik
Ma'lique
Ma'quess
Ma'rico
Ma'siah
Ma'sirvion
Ma'tavious
Ma'taya
Ma'vion
Maada
Maahir
Maaliah
Maalik (0.01)
Maalik-Jacian
Maan
Maanas
Maanav
Maanbo
Maan-David
Maanza
Maaran
Maarouf
Maarten
Maaseiah
Maasi
Maasiu Matthew
Maasiyah Yhwh
Maasyn
Maataua
Maaz
Maazelov
Maazin
Mabel
Mabon
Mabro
Mabry
Mac (0.02)
Mac Anthony
Mac Henry
Macadam
Macade
Macaden
Macahi
Macahri
Macaire
Macaja
Macaleb
Macallan
Macallister
Macar're
Macareé

Macari
Macario (0.01)
Macarthur
Macartney
Macary
Macauley
Macauthur
Macayden
Maccaidin
Macclain
Macclem
Maccoy
Macdiel
Mace (0.01)
Macean
Macen (0.01)
Maceo
Maceon
Maceson
Macewan
Maceyn
Macfred
Macgowan
Macgregor
Macguire
Macgyver
Machai
Machaiah
Machale
Machannon
Machi (0.01)
Machia
Machijah
Machiyah
Macho
Maci
Maciah
Maciej
Maciel
Macin
Macintyre
Mack (0.03)
Mackade
Mackaden
Mackai
Mackaleb
Mackay
Mackayle
Mackeenan
Mackelaus
Mackell
Mackenan
Mackenlee

Mackenly
Mackennon
Mackens
Mackenson
Mackenzi
Mackenzie (0.03)
Mackenzy
Mackeon
Mackey-Paul
Mackiah
Mackian
Mackie
Mackighen
Mackinley
Mackinnley
Macklan
Mackley
Macklin (0.01)
Mack-Massie
Maclain
Maclaine
Maclaren
Maclean (0.01)
Maclin
Macly
Macmannus
Macodou
Macohen
Macolm
Macon (0.01)
Macord
Macoy
Macrae
Macrin
Macsen
Macshawn
Macson
Macswel
Mactar
Maculeigh
Macus
Macy
Macy-Brett
Macyn
Madai
Madalyn
Madan
Maddax
Madden (0.03)
Maddeux
Maddex (0.01)
Maddisen

Maddix (0.02)
Maddixx
Maddoc
Maddock
Maddon
Maddoux
Maddox (0.38)
Maddoxx
Maddux (0.03)
Maddyn
Maddyx
Madeline
Madelyn
Maden
Maderic
Madex
Madhav
Madhavan
Madhu
Madia
Madigan
Madinwaaskum-Jared
Madison (0.02)
Madison Van
Madix
Madjid
Madlyn
Madoc
Madovick
Madox (0.01)
Madoxx
Madric
Madrick
Madrid
Madrigal
Madrox
Madryk
Mads
Madux
Madyck
Madyn
Madysin
Madyx
Maeb
Maech
Maecyn
Maek
Maekon
Maël
Mael (0.02)
Maelan
Maelie

Maequin
Maerg
Maeshall
Maeson
Maestro
Maesyn
Maethum
Maevan
Maeven
Maewyn
Maezon
Mafcellis
Magarsa
Magaven
Magavin
Magazu
Magd
Magdaleno
Magdi
Magdiel (0.01)
Magdouvins
Maggie
Magic
Magid
Magilani
Magkdick
Magno
Magnum
Magnus (0.04)
Magnuss
Magnvs
Magon
Maguire (0.01)
Magyver
Mah'kai
Mah'khaiy
Mah'lik
Mahaan
Mahad (0.01)
Mahadev
Mahad-Ryan
Mahama
Mahamad
Mahamadou (0.01)
Mahamat
Mahamed (0.01)
Mahammed Redda
Mahamud
Mahan
Maharai
Mahari

Maharye
Mahat
Mahatma
Mahavir
Mahd
Mahdasson
Mahde
Mahdi (0.03)
Mahdi-Mughtada
Mahdiu
Mahdy
Mahe
Maheen
Maheep
Maheer
Mahekun
Mahel
Mahendra
Maher
Maherchames-Eddine
Mahesh
Mahetaj
Maheu
Mahfuzul
Mahib
Mahid
Mahidhar
Mahim
Mahin
Mahino
Mahinur
Mahip
Mahir (0.01)
Mahir Al Emon
Mahir-Ahmed
Mahish
Mahith
Mahkagulshan
Mahkai
Mahkeil
Mahki (0.01)
Mahkis
Mahkye
Mahleek
Mahleik
Mahli
Mahlik
Mahlon (0.02)
Mahlyk
Mahmad
Mahmed

Mahmond
Mahmood
Mahmoud (0.02)
Mahmud
Mahmut
Mahon
Mahonri
Mahonry
Mahpia Pejuta
Mahrell
Mahrem
Mahreon
Mahri
Mahrius
Mahson
Mahsood
Mahtab
Mahtahc
Mahtim
Mahto
Mahtub
Mahungu
Mahzae
Mahzi
Maic
Maican
Maichus
Maickol
Maico
Maicol
Maicom
Maier
Maik
Maika
Maike
Maikel
Maikell
Maiki
Maiko
Maikol
Mailen
Maina
Mainol
Mainor
Maio
Maion
Maiqua
Mairam
Mairi
Maisa
Maisel
Maisen
Maishaun

Maison (0.02)
Maitham
Maithreya
Maitreya
Maitri
Majaden
Majadi
Majarak
Majavius
Majd
Majde
Majdi
Majed
Majeed
Majell
Majeni
Majestic
Majesty
Majid
Majok
Major (0.01)
Majoric
Majorick
Majorique
Mak
Maka
Makade
Makaden
Makaeio
Makaheya
Makahi
Makahlon
Makahri
Makai (0.05)
Makaiel
Makaio (0.01)
Makal
Makala
Makale
Makan
Makana
Makandian
Makane
Makani
Makaniokeakua
Makari
Makarian
Makario
Makarios
Makariy
Makarri
Makaveli
Makayla

Makayle
Makaylynn
Makayo
Makaz-Yowm
Make
Makeal
Makeegan
Makeel
Makeem
Makeen
Makei
Makein
Makel (0.01)
Makele
Makell
Makelle
Makelton
Makelvin
Maken
Makendre
Makendy
Makenlay
Makenly
Makenzie
Makeo
Makes
Makeye
Makeyon
Ma-Khai
Makhai
Makhail
Makhari
Makhay Samir
Makhi (0.05)
Makhii
Makhiy
Makhtar
Makhtar Andre
Makí
Maki (0.01)
Makia
Makiah
Makian
Makiba
Makieh
Makienan
Makigh
Makih
Makii
Makile
Makimba
Makin
Makinlee

Makinnis
Makis
Makiy
Makiyus
Makkah
Makkhara
Makky
Maklain
Maklen
Maklin
Mako
Makoa
Makobi'ja
Makon
Makori
Makoto
Makovsky
  Alexandre
Makquiel
Makrem
Maks
Maksim (0.01)
Maksim Richard
Maksimilian
Maksimillian
Maksym
Maksymilian
Maksymus
Makszi
Makuac
Makur
Makya
Makyah
Makye (0.01)
Makyi
Makyis
Makyle
Makylin
Makylor
Makyrin
Mal'akhi
Mal'aki
Mal'quan
Mala'kye
Malacai
Malach
Malachai (0.01)
Malachí
Malachi (1.10)
Malachi Amaree
Malachi Azariah
Malachi
  Daviean

Malachi
  Shalaban
Malachia
Malachy (0.01)
Malacih
Malacki
Malaha
Malahkai
Malahkaih
Malahki
Malahn
Malaika
Malaiki
Malaina
Malak
Malak Jonah
Malakahi
Malakai (0.08)
Malakaii
Malakas
Malakei
Malakhi (0.02)
Malakhy
Malaki (0.08)
Malakia
Malakiah
Malakih
Malakii
Malaku-Seyon
Malaky
Malakye
Malakyi
Malan Didier
Malani
Malaqhi
Malathi
Malaun
Malayko
Malaysinh
Malcalm
Malchiah
Malchiel
Malchijah
Malcolm (0.17)
Malcolm-
  Ralshad Teba
Malcolm-
  Wendell
Malcom (0.02)
Malcom-William
Malculm
Maldini
Maleahki

Maleak
Maleakia
Malec
Malech
Malechai
Malechi
Maleck
Maleec
Maleeik
Maleek (0.02)
Maleeq
Maleik
Ma-Lek
Malek (0.03)
Malekai
Malekaih
Maleke
Malek-Gabriel
Malekhai
Malekhi
Maleki
Maleko
Maleky
Malex
Malhaar
Malhar
Malhki
Mali
Mali Kisis
Maliak
Malic
Malicah
Malicai
Malichai
Malichi (0.01)
Malick (0.01)
Maliec
Maliek (0.01)
Malijah
Malik (0.41)
Malik Aghiles
Malik
  Biamourou
Malik Dany
Malik Jahki
Malik Jamal
Malik James
Malik Mohamed
Malik Samuel
Malik'
Malik-Abbas
Malikah
Malikahi

Malikai (0.01)
Malikaih
Malike
Malikh
Malikhai
Malikhi
Malikhih
Maliki (0.02)
Malikia
Malikiah
Malikie
Malikigh
Malikih
Malikius
Malikk
Malik-Noor
Maliky
Malikyah
Malikye
Malikyi
Malin
Maliq
Malique (0.02)
Malishes
Malith
Maliu
Malkai
Malkam
Malkiah
Malking
Malkolm
Malkom
Malla-Ki
Mallaki
Malla-Ky
Mallekhi
Mallex
Mallicae
Malliek
Malliig
Malliki
Mallon
Malloy
Mally Lloyd
Maloey
Malon
Malone
Malonn
Malory
Malosi
Malte
Maltius
Malvin

| | | | | | |
|---|---|---|---|---|---|
| Malvyn | Mandell | Mannix | Manuel *(1.28)* | Mar'quazion | Marc-Andrei | Marchiano |
| Malyk | Manderson | Mannoah | Manuel Cedric | Mar'quel | Marcangele | Marchon |
| Malykai | Mandison | Mannraj | Manuel | Mar'quell | Marc-Anthony | Marchris |
| Malyk-Djaffar | Mandol | Manny *(0.01)* | Fernando | Mar'quezz | Marcanthony | Marc-Hugo |
| Malykhi | Mandon | Manoah | Manuel Kent | Mar'quis | Marc-Antoine | Marcia |
| Malyki | Mandrake | Manoe | Manuel Thomas | Mar'rell | *(0.09)* | Marcial |
| Malyki Xave | Mandrel | Manoel | Manuela | Mar'reon | Marc-Antoine | Marcianno |
| Malykiah | Mandrell | Manohar | Manuele | Mar'rico | Mael | Marciano |
| Malykie | Mandy | Manoj | Manuel-Fabien | Mar'sean | Marcantonio | Marciello |
| Mamadee | Manear | Manolin | Manuelito | Mar'shawn | Marc-Antony | Marciellos |
| Mamadou *(0.03)* | Maneek | Manolito | Manuel-Jose | Mar'tae-Otis | Marc-Anwart | Marcin |
| Mamadou | Manfred | Manolo *(0.01)* | Manuelle | Mar'terrius | Marcarious | Marcio |
| Diouma | Manfredo | Manolo Ernesto | Manuello | Mar'trell | Marcas | Marcis |
| Mamadouba- | Manhattan | Manomay | Manuel-Luis | Mar'tresz | Marcato | Marcius |
| Cheri | Manh-Tang | Manor Luis | Manuelo | Mar'twan | Marcavion | Marc-James |
| Mamady | Mani | Manov | Manuere | Mar'von | Marcavious | Marck |
| Mamdouh | Maniang | Manpinder | Manumalo | Mar'zarius | Marc-Bendy | Marckedly |
| Mamikon | Manic | Manprabhat | Manus | Mar'zhon | Marc-Berny | Marckenry |
| Mamo | Manidhar | Manpreet | Manveer | Maran | Marc-Claudel | Marckens |
| Mamoon | Maniel | Manquell | Manville | Maraquis | Marce'on | Marckerby |
| Mamoud | Manij | Manraj *(0.01)* | Manvir *(0.01)* | Marat | Marc-Edouard | Marckinson |
| Mamoun | Manik | Manroop | Manyl | Marauise | Marc-Edro | Marckly |
| Mamuach | Manikant | Manrose | Manyok | Maravice | Marceion | Marckus |
| Mamudou | Manikanta | Mansa | Manzili | Marawan | Marcel *(0.06)* | Marc-Laurin |
| Mamuse | Manin | Mansahib | Manzilli | Marbel | Marcel Jr | Marcle |
| Man | Manir | Mansell | Manziuos | Marbin | Marceli | Marcly |
| Man Bir | Manis | Mansha | Manzo | Marbyn | Marc-Elie | Marco *(0.36)* |
| Man'tavious | Manish | Manshaan | Mao | Marc *(0.16)* | Marcelino *(0.01)* | Marco Antonio |
| Manaal | Manis-Islam | Manshant | Maolenin | Marc Adler | Marcelius | Marco Antonio |
| Manaf | Manison | Manshaun | Maon | Marc Alen | Marcell *(0.02)* | Marco Aurelio |
| Mana-Kenichi | Manit | Manson | Maor | Marc Alexandre | Marcellas | Marco Cesare |
| Manakonaau | Manius | Mansoor | Maquell | Marc Alexis | Marcelle | Peter |
| Manan | Manix | Mansor | Maquinna | Marc An Toan | Marcelles | Marco-Alejandro |
| Manandeep | Maniye | Mansour | Mar | Marc Andre | Marcellino | Marcoantoino |
| Manaow | Manjap | Man-Steverson | Mar'darius | Marc Anthony | Marcellis | Marcoantoni |
| Manas *(0.01)* | Manjevan | Mansukh | Mar'jay | Marc Antoine | Marcello *(0.04)* | Marcoantonio |
| Manases | Manjot | Mansur | Mar'kabrien | *(0.01)* | Marcellous | Marco-Daniel |
| Manassah | Manjowan | Mantaj | Mar'kal | Marc Olivier | Marcellus *(0.03)* | Marcogiovanni |
| Manasse | Mankaran | Mantana | Mar'kaveon | Marc Samuel | Marcelo *(0.04)* | Marco-Jose |
| Manasseh | Mankavi'on | Mantej | Mar'kavius | Marc'queiln | Marcelo Gabriel | Marc-Olivier |
| Manav *(0.01)* | Mankeerat | Mantel | Mar'kel | Marc-Adler | Marcelus | *(0.03)* |
| Manavdeep | Mankeson | Manti | Mar'kelynne | Junior | Marc-Emile | Marconi |
| Manaveer | Mankirat | Mantice | Mar'keon | Marcal | Marc-Etienne | Marcorios |
| Manavjay | Manley | Manton | Mar'kese | Marc-Alan | Marc-Gabriel | Marcos *(0.23)* |
| Manavjit | Mann | Mantonio | Mar'keystio | Marc-Albern | Marc-Gaetan | Marcos Jesu |
| Manavjot | Mannajeh | Mantrell | Mar'khi | Marcale | Marc-Garvin | Marcos-Antonio |
| Manchan | Mannan | Mantrevis | Mar'khizé | Marc-Alex | Marchal | Marc-Philippe |
| Manda Jason | Mannanuddin | Mantriel | Mar'kiez | Marc-Alexandre | Marchall | Marc-Pierre |
| Mandaar | Mannases | Mantzer | Mar'kwon | *(0.01)* | Marchaun | Marcquell |
| Mandar | Mannaure | Manu *(0.01)* | Mar'quan | Marc-Alexis | Marchawn | Marcquette |
| Mandeep | Manni | Manuael | Mar'quann | Marc-André | Marchaz | Marcquez |
| Mandel | Mannie | Manual | Mar'quaviou | Marc-Andre | Marchello | Marcquice |
| Mandela | Manning *(0.01)* | Manuchim | Mar'quavious | *(0.01)* | Marchez | Marcquis |

| | | | | | | |
|---|---|---|---|---|---|---|
| Marcqus-Hans | Marez | Marisa | Markei | Markkus | Marnix | Marquees |
| Marc-Roland | Marful | Mariss | Markeias | Markle | Maroine | Marquel (0.02) |
| Marcuis | Margaret | Marissa | Markeil | Markley | Maron | Marquelis |
| Marcuise | Margarito | Marius (0.02) | Markeis | Marklin Jr | Marouane | Marquell (0.01) |
| Marcus (1.50) | Marggens | Mariusz | Markeise | Marklon | Maroun | Marquelle |
| Marcus Andre | Marguille | Mariyan | Markeit | Marknathan | Marq | Marquentin |
| Marcus Coy | Marguinn | Mariyawn | Markeith | Marko (0.03) | Marqarious | Marquerius |
| Marcus Jay | Marhari | Mariyé | Markeivious | Markos | Marqarius | Marques (0.06) |
| Marcus Joshua | Mari | Mariyon | Markeivis | Markquez | Marqavion | Marquese (0.01) |
| Marcus Nicolas | Mari'a | Mariyoni | Markel (0.04) | Markquis | Marqavious | Marquesio |
| Marcus-Anthony | Maria | Marjai | Markelis | Markqus | Marqavis | Marquess |
| Marcuse | Mariana | Marjohn | Markelius | Markqwell | Marqe'vious | Marquet |
| Marcuse Oril | Marianito | Marjon | Markell (0.05) | Mark-Robert | Marqee | Marquetis |
| Marcus-Kyri | Marianne | Marjuan | Markelle | Mark-Ron | Marqeis | Marquett |
| Marcuss | Mariano (0.04) | Mark (1.20) | Markendy | Markson | Marqel | Marquette |
| Marcus-Seth | Marianté | Mark Allen | Markenley | Marktavis | Marqese | Marquevius |
| Marcutio | Marice | Mark Anthony | Markens | Marktrail | Marqiest | Marquez (0.04) |
| Marcux | Marick | Mark Ariel | Markense | Markues | Marqiis | Marquezray |
| Marc-Xavier | Marickus | Mark Robert | Markenson | Markuis | Marqis | Marqui |
| Mardale | Marico | Mark Rondel | Marker | Markum | Marqise | Marquia |
| Mardan | Marie | Mark'quelle | Markes | Markus (0.12) | Marqkel | Marquial |
| Mardarian | Marie-Cyel | Mark'quice | Markese (0.01) | Markusie | Marqoun | Marquias |
| Mardarius | Mariee | Mark'quise | Markesian | Markuz | Marquaan | Marquibe |
| Mardav | Mariek | Markaden | Markess | Markwail | Marquaé | Marquice |
| Mardean | Mariel | Markael | Markevion | Markwon | Marquail | Marquicious |
|   Jaikwone | Mariela | Markai | Markevious | Marky | Marquain | Marquiel |
| Mardel | Marien | Markaidrian | Markevis | Markyce | Marqual | Marquies |
| Mardell | Marieo | Markail | Markevius | Marland | Marquale | Marquil |
| Mardo | Marii | Markailan | Mar-Key | Marlando | Marqualis | Marquiles |
| Mardoche | Marik | Markal | Markey | Marlaun | Marquan (0.02) | Marquin |
| Mardochee | Marikevies | Markale | Markeyez | Marle | Marquand | Marquis (0.14) |
| Mardre'co | Mariko | Mark-Alex | Markeyse | Marleak | Marquane | Marquise (0.06) |
| Mardre'kis | Marin | Mark-Anthony | Markeyus | Marlee | Marquarious | Marquisean |
| Mardrecus | Maringlen | Mark-Antoyne | Markeyvon | Marlei | Marquarius | Marquisee |
| Mardriquez | Marino | Markarious | Markez | Marlen | Marquaun | Marquisn |
| Mardy | Marinos | Markas | Markeze | Marley (0.02) | Marquavian | Marquist |
| Marec | Mario (0.40) | Markavion | Markham | Marlija | Marquavies | Marquit |
| Marece | Mario Alejandro | Markavious | Markhi | Marlin (0.04) | Marquavion | Marquitos |
| Mareck | Mario Antoine | Markavius | Markian | Marlion | Marquavios | Marquives |
| Mareco | Mario Giovanni | Markavon | Markie | Marliq'Amari | Marquavious | Marquiz |
| Marecus | Mario Jr | Markayle | Markiee | Marlique | Marquavis | Marquize |
| Maree | Mario Ricardo | Markayveyis | Markiem | Marlito | Marquavius | Marqun |
| Mareese | Mariol | Markayvion | Markievion | Marlo (0.01) | Marquavyon | Marquon |
| Mareion | Marion (0.04) | Markaz | Markiis | Marlon (0.10) | Marquaxius | Marquos |
| Marek (0.05) | Marionn | Markcion | Markili | Marlon Jr | Marquay | Marqus (0.01) |
| Marell | Mariono | Marké | Markir | Marlone | Marquaylon | Marquwes |
| Mareng | Marionte | Markeal | Markis | Marlos | Marquaze | Marquyn |
| Mareno | Marionzae | Markease | Markis' | Marlous | Marquce | Marquz |
| Mareo | Mario-Pierre | Markece | Markise | Marlow | Marquces | Marr |
| Mareon | Mariounte | Markedus | Markiss | Marlowe | Marque | Marrcole |
| Marese | Marious | Markee | Markivieon | Marlyn | Marque'll | Marreco |
| Mareus | Mariquez | Markeem | Markiz-Azay | Marnarien | Marquece | Marrek |
| Marevo | Maris | Markeese | Markjomel | Marneimus | Marquee | Marreon |

| | | | | | | |
|---|---|---|---|---|---|---|
| Marriano | Martayo | Martir | Marzavier | Masseo | Maten | Mathis |
| Marriceon | Martayvious | Martivn | Marzavious | Masseri | Matensky | Alexandre |
| Marrico | Marte | Martize | Marzavis | Massi | Matéo | Mathis Jordan |
| Marrik | Marté | Marton | Marzayvion | Massiah | Mateo (0.31) | Mathis Xavier |
| Marrio | Marte'on | Martravious | Marzdin | Massil | Mateos | Mathis-Antoine |
| Marrion | Marte'z | Martravius | Marzell | Massillon | Matero | Mathis-Olivier |
| Marrione | Martea | Martré | Marzhaun | Massimiliano | Materrance | Mathison |
| Marrison | Marteé | Martrel | Marzon | Massimo (0.06) | Materry | Mathis-Ronald |
| Marrius | Marteece | Martrell | Marzooq | Massimo | Mateu | Mathiss |
| Marrquis | Marteek | Martress | Mas'ud | Raffaele | Mateus (0.01) | Mathis-William |
| Mars | Martel (0.01) | Martrez | Masa | Massin | Mateusz (0.01) | Mathius |
| Marsai | Martell (0.01) | Martrial | Masab | Massinissa | Matewoss | Mathok |
| Marsalis | Martellise | Martti | Masadq | Masson | Matex | Mathu |
| Marsalous | Martellus | Marty (0.02) | Masaharu | Massy | Mateyo | Mathue |
| Marsaul | Marten | Martyn | Masai | Massyl | Mathaios | Mathurin |
| Marsavier | Martene | Maru | Masakela | Massyle | Mathais | Mathy |
| Marsden | Martenez | Maruice | Masaki | Masten | Mathan | Mathyas |
| Marsean | Marteno | Marv | Masan | Master | Mathandzima | Mathyis |
| Marseilles | Marteon | Marvale | Masanori | Master Noah | Mathaniel | Mathyou |
| Marselis | Marteria | Marvan | Masao | Master'chan | Mathatiahou- | Mathys (0.06) |
| Marselles | Marterio | Marvel | Masaryk | Mastien | David | Matiás |
| Marsellus | Marternez | Marvell (0.01) | Masato | Mastin | Mathays | Matias (0.08) |
| Marselo | Marterrion | Marvelle | Mascen | Maston | Mathayus | Matias Wen |
| Marshal (0.02) | Martes | Marvelous | Mascio | Masud | Matheiu | Yang |
| Marshal-James | Martese | Marvelt | Mascon | Masum | Matheo (0.02) | Matias-Gabriel |
| Marshall (0.20) | Martesse | Marven | Mascud | Masun | Matheos | Matias-Isaac |
| Marshaun (0.01) | Martevion | Marvens (0.01) | Mase | Masyn (0.01) | Mather | Matias-Miranda |
| Marshavin | Martevious | Marveon | Maseiah | Masynn | Matherkens | Matice |
| Marshawn | Marteyon | Marverson | Maseion | Mat | Matheson | Matie |
| (0.01) | Martez (0.03) | Marvez | Masen (0.03) | Mataeo | Matheu (0.01) | Matiel |
| Marshawndre | Marteze | Marvin (0.20) | Mashawn | Mataeus | Matheus (0.03) | Matieu |
| Marshaya | Martha | Marvins | Mashquanon | Mataher | Mathew (0.30) | Matijah |
| Marshel | Marthin | Marvion | Masiah | Matai (0.01) | Mathew James | Matin |
| Marshell | Marti | Marvis | Masico | Mataio | Mathews | Matio |
| Marsheon | Martial | Marviyon | Masih | Matais | Mathewson | Matis (0.09) |
| Marshon | Martiano | Marvon | Masil | Mataius | Mathia | Matis Dominic |
| Marshun | Martice | Marvonni | Masimo | Matamba | Mathias (0.16) | Matis-Alexis |
| Marshyl | Martimiano | Marvyn | Masin (0.01) | Matan | Mathias- | Matiss |
| Marshyne | Martin (0.41) | Marwan (0.01) | Masium | Matao | Alexander | Matiss Calvin |
| Marsilles | Martin Charles | Marwane | Masius | Matapew | Mathias-Assane | Matisse (0.01) |
| Marson | Martin De Jesus | Marwin | Maslin | Matar | Mathias-Ra | Matisse-Goo |
| Marston | Martin Jr | Marwin Joshua | Masnun | Matavani | Mathieu (0.21) | Matis-William |
| Mart | Martin Khalil | Marwin-Noah | Mason (4.46) | Matayis | Mathieu- | Matius |
| Martaevious | Martine | Marx | Mason Bailey | Matayo | Aghiles | Matix |
| Martaevyon | Martines | Mary | Mason Jeffrey | Mate | Mathieu-Aksil | Matorrence |
| Martarius | Martinez | Maryanne | Mason Musa | Mateao | Mathieu- | Matrez |
| Martavies | Martineze | Marye | Masoniek | Mateem | Anthony | Matrien |
| Martavion | Martinian | Maryk | Masoud | Mateen | Mathieus | Matrim |
| Martavios | Martiniano | Marylin | Masroor | Mateen Ahmad | Mathieux | Matrix |
| Martavious | Martin-John | Maryon | Mass | Matei | Mathiew | Mats |
| (0.02) | Martino | Maryun | Massai | Matej | Mathijs | Matshilonda |
| Martavis | Martinus | Marzane | Massamba | Mateja | Mathios | Matson |
| Martavius (0.01) | Martin-Yoann | Marzavian | Massawaa | Mateli | Mathis (0.32) | Matt (0.02) |

| | | | | | | |
|---|---|---|---|---|---|---|
| Matt Utshinapeu | Matthews *(0.01)* | Mauricio *(0.13)* | Max Samuel | Maxim-Luther | Mayatta | Mazzari |
| Mattaeus | Matthias *(0.08)* | Maurico | Maxam | Maximo *(0.04)* | Maycein | Mazzie |
| Mattais | Matthieu *(0.02)* | Maurikeon | Maxamilian | Maximo Arturo | Maycen | Mazzin- |
| Mattayus | Matthieu | Maurilio | Maxamilion | Maximo Samuel | Mayceo | Mohammed |
| Mattee | Santiago | Maurince | Maxamillian | Maxim-Olivier | Mayci | Mazzn |
| Matteo *(0.23)* | Matthiew | Maurino | Maxamillion | Maximos *(0.01)* | Maycio | Mbanwi |
| Matteo Andres | Matthis | Maurio | Maxamus | Maximum | Mayco | Mbarouk |
| Matteo Angelo | Matthue | Maurion | Maxance | Maximus *(0.20)* | Maycol | Mbayo- |
| Matteo | Matthw | Maurisio | Maxandre *(0.01)* | Maximus | Maycon | Alexandre |
| Wardhana | Matthy | Maurits | Maxaner | Baruch | Mayden | Mboriundo |
| Matterius | Matthys | Maurius | Maxangel | Maximus | Mayeem | Mc Alister |
| Mattern | Matti | Mauriyhon | Max-Antoine | Gabriel | Mayer *(0.02)* | Mc Andre |
| Matteson | Mattia | Maurizio | Max-Antoine D | Maxis | Mayes | Mc Jensen |
| Matteus | Mattiâce | Maurlo | Maxat | Maxium | Mayhem | Mc'kel |
| Mattew | Mattias *(0.02)* | Mauro *(0.01)* | Max-Elias | Maxkolbe | Mayi | Mcaaron |
| Mattews | Mattie | Maurquez | Maxell | Maxleon | Mayia | Mcade |
| Matthaeus | Mattieu | Maurquis | Maxem | Maxmar | Mayke | Mcalister |
| Matthaios | Mattieux | Maurshaun | Maxemil | Maxmilian | Maykel | Mcallister |
| Matthais | Mattingly | Maurvalas | Maxemiliano | Maxmillian | Maykol | Mcandrew |
| Matthan | Mattis *(0.01)* | Maury | Max-Emilien | Maxn | Mayky | Mcarthur |
| Matthaus | Mattison | Mauryce | Maxen | Maxo | Maylon | Mcashton |
| Mattheao | Mattityahu | Mauryio | Maxence *(0.03)* | Max-Olivier | Maynard | Mcavoy |
| Mattheas | Mattius | Maurynn | Maxey | Maxomus | Mayne | Mcayden |
| Mattheau | Mattix | Mauryon | Maxfield *(0.01)* | Maxon *(0.01)* | Maynhard | Mcbensky |
| Mattheew | Mattox *(0.01)* | Mauzeel | Maxgold | Maxsilio | Maynor *(0.01)* | Mccabe |
| Matther | Mattrell | Mavdeep | Maxi | Maxsim | Mayo | Mccadden |
| Mattherion | Mattson | Maven | Maxiamillio | Maxsimo | Mayom | Mccaden |
| Mattheu | Mattthew | Maven G | Maxie | Maxson | Mayra | Mccafrey |
| Mattheus | Mattus | Maveren | Maxim *(0.13)* | Maxsumus | Mays | Mccage |
| Matthew *(9.46)* | Matty | Maveric | Maxima | Max-Thony | Maysen | Mccager |
| Matthew | Mattyeu | Maverick *(0.11)* | Maxime *(0.22)* | Maxtin | Mayshaun | Mccain |
| Alexandre | Mattys | Maverick | Maxime Lou | Maxton *(0.01)* | Maysin | Mccajah |
| Matthew | Matus | Robert | Maxime Olivier | Maxum | Maysn | Mccalister |
| Anthony | Matvey | Maverick | Maxime Varel | Maxumis | Mayson *(0.03)* | Mccall |
| Gonzales | Matwone | Xander | Maxime-Antoine | Maxwel | Maysson | Mccallon |
| Matthew | Maty | Maverik | Maxime-Samy | Maxwell *(1.08)* | Maysun | Mccallum |
| Dominic | Matyas | Maverrick | Maximiano | Maxx *(0.02)* | Maythan | Mccants |
| Baniqued | Matys *(0.02)* | Mavic | Maximiliaan | Maxxan | Mayumu | Mccarson |
| Matthew James | Matyss | Mavik | Maximiliam | Maxxim | Mayur | Mccarter |
| Matthew Jay | Matys-Tony | Mavin | Maximilian | Maxximus | Mayven | Mccarthy |
| Matthew Lewis | Mauhlik | Mavric | *(0.14)* | Maxximus | Mayz | Mccartney |
| Matthew Luis | Mauikaiko-Evan | Mavrick *(0.02)* | Maximiliano | Jayms | Mazaa | Mccarty |
| Matthew Luke | Maulood | Mavricky | *(0.03)* | Maxxum | Mazcu | Mccauley |
| Matthew Robert | Maura | Mavrik | Maximilien | Maxxwell | Maze | Mccaulley |
| Matthew Wil | Maurece | Mawien | *(0.01)* | Maxym *(0.01)* | Mazel | Mccayden |
| Matthew Xavier | Maurecio | Mawny | Maximilion | Maxyme | Mazen *(0.01)* | Mccaydyn |
| Matthew- | Maureece | Mawuel | Maximillan | Maxymis | Mazeo | Mcclain |
| Charlie | Maurell | Mawutoh | Maximillian | May | Maziah | Mcclaine |
| Matthew-Jeffrey | Mauren | Max *(0.92)* | *(0.05)* | Maya | Maziin | Mcclaren |
| Matthew-Justin | Mauri Orlando | Max Antoine | Maximilliano | Mayan | Mazin | Mcclarren |
| Matthew- | Maurice *(0.19)* | Max Aurelius | Maximillion | Mayank | Maziyar | Mcclayton |
| Kousaku | Maurice Jr | Max Elliott | *(0.01)* | Mayard | Mazlyn | Mcconnell |
| Matthew-Paul | Mauriceo | Max Golden | Maximino *(0.01)* | Mayas | Mazon | Mccormick |

| | | | | | |
|---|---|---|---|---|---|
| Mccory | Mckenzy | Mechak-Ouiror | Mehkai | Mekhyi | Melfin | Menachem- |
| Mccoy *(0.01)* | Mckevan | Mechel | Mehkhi | Meki | Meliek | Mendel |
| Mccrae | Mckewan | Mechiy | Mehki *(0.02)* | Mekiah | Melies | Menaik |
| Mccray | Mckeyl | Medard | Mehkil | Mekial | Melih | Menas |
| Mcculley | Mckian | Medardo | Mehmet *(0.01)* | Mekias | Melik | Mendel *(0.02)* |
| Mccullough | Mckinlee | Medarian | Mehmet-Han | Mekiel | Melikai | Mendl |
| Mcdaniel | Mckinley *(0.03)* | Meddie | Mehrab | Mekih | Melila | Mendy *(0.01)* |
| Mcdevon | Mckinnen | Medeiros-Baba | Mehrab Jihan | Mekii | Melione | Menelek |
| Mcdillon | Mckinney | Meden | Mehrad | Mekil | Melique | Meneleus |
| Mcewan | Mckinnley | Mederic *(0.01)* | Mehrali | Mekkai | Melissa | Menelik |
| Mcgarrity | Mckinnlie | Mederic-Alexis | Mehrbaan | Mekki | Meliton | Meng |
| Mcgregor | Mckinnon | Mederick *(0.01)* | Mehrdad | Mekkie | Melka | Mengmo |
| Mcguire | Mckinsey | Mederik *(0.01)* | Mehrraj | Mekko | Melki | Mengsukchetra |
| Mcgwire | Mckly | Mederik-Jacob | Mehrzad | Meko | Melkiel | Meng-Tien |
| Mchael | Mckonroy | Mederiq | Mehsen | Mekos | Melkin | Menilek |
| Mchenry | Mckoye | Mederyc | Mehtab *(0.01)* | Mekose | Melkior | Menmphis |
| Mchugh | Mckye | Mederyck | Mehul | Mekusapv | Melku-Menelik | Menno *(0.01)* |
| Mcintyre | Mckyia | Mederyk | Mehyar | Mekyah | Mello | Mennon |
| Mckade | Mckyle | Medgar | Meier | Mekyal | Mellouk | Menny |
| Mckaden | Mclain | Medhansh | Meiguele | Mekyas | Melmoth | Menphis |
| Mckae | Mclaine | Medina | Meikay | Mekye | Melo | Mensah |
| Mckai | Mclane | Medley | Meikeilio | Mekyhl | Melodias | Mensur |
| Mckaide | Mclaren | Medrawt | Meikel | Mel *(0.01)* | Melody | Mentesnot |
| Mckaidin | Mclaurin | Medrick | Meikhi | Melachi | Melokei | Mentoa |
| Mckaileb | Mclean | Medrik | Meiki | Melakah | Melovin | Menyelek |
| Mckale | Mclee | Mee'ka | Meilin | Melakai | Melquan | Menzel |
| Mckaleb | Mclein | Meechai | Meinyard | Melake | Melquez | Meo |
| Mckane | Mclemore | Meek | Meir *(0.03)* | Melakhi | Melqui | Mequon |
| Mckari | Mcowens | Meeko | Meka | Melaki | Melquior | Meran |
| Mckavin | Mcquade | Meela | Mekaale | Melanchi | Melrick | Merash |
| Mckay *(0.01)* | Mcqurne | Meelad | Mekaheal | Melaney | Melryk | Mercardo |
| Mckayle | Mcrae | Meer | Mekahehska | Melano | Meltarraus | Mercator |
| Mckayne | Mcwill | Meeshaw | Mekahi | Melantony | Melton | Mercer |
| Mckean | Me Khi | Meet | Mekai *(0.01)* | Melaqai | Melvenic | Mercurio |
| Mckei | Me Ky El | Meeyobin | Mekaia | Melawi | Melvi | Mercy |
| Mckel | Me Shaud | Megale | Mekaih | Melbern | Melvin *(0.17)* | Merda |
| Mckell | Me'caiyon | Megan | Mekail | Melbin | Melvin Evera | Merdi |
| Mckellan | Me'er | Megh | Mekaviel | Melburn | Melvin-Ikaze | Mereck |
| Mckendric | Me'lik | Megrit | Mekaya | Melbyn | Melvis | Meredaniel |
| Mckendrick | Meade | Meguial | Mekeih | Melca | Melvon | Meredist |
| Mckendrie | Meakare | Meguire | Mekel | Melchi | Melvyn | Merek *(0.01)* |
| Mckenize | Means | Meh'ji | Mekell | Melchia | Melvynn | Merga |
| Mckenlee | Mearl Jacki | Mehar | Mekelle | Melchiah | Melyk | Merhawe |
| Mckenley | Mearlyn | Mehardeep | Mekendy | Melchior | Melziah | Meric |
| Mckenly | Mearrin | Mehari | Mekhai | Melchizedek | Memphis *(0.06)* | Merick |
| Mckenna | Meason | Mehariit | Mekhail-Angel | Melchoir | Memphis-Alij | Merick Ludger |
| Mckennan | Meaven Jeffrey | Meharjot | Mekhailangelo | Melchor | Memphis-Ryan | Merico |
| Mckennen | Mec | Mehdi *(0.01)* | Mekhei | Meldin | Memphys | Meriet |
| Mckennon | Mecaes | Mehdi Zakaria | Mekhi *(0.24)* | Meldrick | Mena | Merik *(0.01)* |
| Mckensey | Mecahl | Mehdi-Nassim | Mekhi Urmee | Meleek | Menachem | Merilorme |
| Mckenzee | Mecca | Meher | Mekhiron | Meleeke | *(0.07)* | Meris |
| Mckenzie | Mecco | Meherab | Mekhius | Melegerius | Menachem | Merit |
| *(0.01)* | Mechael | Meherzan | Mekhy | Melesio | Mendel | Meriwether |

| | | | | | | |
|---|---|---|---|---|---|---|
| Merl | Mevludin | Micah *(0.93)* | Michael | Micheel | Micyle | Mika *(0.02)* |
| Merle *(0.01)* | Mewael | Micah Alan | Petrovicp | Micheil | Middleton | Mikaal |
| Merlin *(0.01)* | Meyandez | Micah Jon | Michael Ray | Michel *(0.03)* | Middy | Mikaeel |
| Merouane | Meyassar | Micah Ryan | Michael Robert | Michel Jr | Midhun | Mikaël |
| Merrek | Meycio | Micah'el | Michael | Michel- | Midnight | Mikael *(0.10)* |
| Merren | Meyer | Micah-Akil | Rommel | Alexandre | Midson | Mikael Bruce |
| Merric | Meyson | Micahi | Michael Scott | Michel-Ange | Miel | Mikael Minh |
| Merrick *(0.04)* | Meysyn | Micahl | Michael | Michelangelo | Mies | Long |
| Merriett | Meyzhon | Micah-Rimon | Theodore | *(0.01)* | Migael | Mikael |
| Merrik *(0.01)* | Meza | Micaiah *(0.02)* | Michael Thomas | Michele | Migdoel | Sebastien |
| Merrill | Mezael | Micaih | Michael Trevion | Michele Ange | Migel *(0.01)* | Mikael-Achille |
| Merrin | Mezziah-Jezus | Micajah | Michael' | Micheleau | Migelanjel | Mikael- |
| Merritt *(0.01)* | Mgdie | Mical | Michaelangel | Michel-Olivier | Miggel | Alessandro |
| Mersad | Mged | Micale | Michaelangelo | Michelot | Might | Mikael- |
| Mert | Mhalique | Micaleb | Michael- | Michelsein | Migual | Alexander |
| Merthan | Mharel | Micalt | Anthony | Michelson | Miguël | Mikael- |
| Mertis | Mharkel | Mican | Michaelanthony | Michi | Miguel *(2.39)* | Benjamin |
| Merton | Mharlon | Micarion | Michael- | Michiah | Miguel Angel | Mikaele |
| Mervin *(0.03)* | Mharquis | Micavion | Christian | Michias | *(0.01)* | Mikaele Junior |
| Mervins | Mheki | Micaya | Michael-David | Michiel | Miguel Anjel | Mikaell |
| Mervyn | Mhelakii | Micca | Michaeldivano | Michion | Miguel Junior | Mikael-Wayne |
| Merwin | Mhmoud | Miccah | Michael-Felix | Michles | Miguel-Ange | Mikael-Wissem |
| Merzekerim | Mhyko | Micceal | Michael-Jacob | Miciah | Miguel-Angel | Mikah *(0.03)* |
| Mesac | Mi | Micco | Michael-James | Mick *(0.01)* | Miguelangel | Mikahi |
| Mesay | Mi'cha | Miceal | Michael-Landon | Micka | *(0.01)* | Mikai *(0.01)* |
| Mesean | Mi'drick | Micgeal | Michael-Lee | Mickaël | Miguel- | Mikaiah |
| Meshach | Mi'kael | Micgill | Michael-Mikáil | Mickael *(0.04)* | Benjamin | Mikaih |
| Mësha-Rio | Mi'kai | Mich'kel | Michael-Ray | Mickaël-Wayne | Miguele Hayden | Mikáil |
| Meshawn | Mi'kale | Micha | Michael-Rey | Mickai | Miguelito | Mikail *(0.01)* |
| Meshilem | Mi'kel *(0.01)* | Michaeal | Michaelson | Mickale | Miguell | Mikaili |
| Meshon | Mi'kenzie | Michaël | Michael-Xavier | Mickalen | Miguequan | Mikail-Mirandad |
| Meshulem | Mi'khal | Micháel | Michah | Mickayan | Miguiel | Mikal *(0.02)* |
| Mesiah | Mi'kiyel | Michael *(10.08)* | Michai | Mickeal | Migule | Mikale *(0.01)* |
| Mesijah | Mi'kye | Michael Aidan | Michaiah | Mickel | Mihael | Mikalister |
| Messai | Mi'kyll | Michael Alain | Michail | Mickel-Ange | Mihai | Mikalle |
| Messiah *(0.06)* | Mi'leik | Michael All | Michailo | Mickell | Mihail | Mikalo |
| Messiah Shy- | Mi'qual | Michael Andre | Michajlo | Mickellito | Mihailo | Mikaly |
| Bazz | Mi'quel | Michael Andrei | Michal *(0.01)* | Mickey *(0.02)* | Mihalov | Mikan |
| Messijah | Mi'wuan | Michael Angelo | Michale | Mickey Patrick | Miheel | Mikani |
| Messiyah | Mi'yon | Michael Anthony | Michalen | Mickhale | Mihir *(0.01)* | Mikanoa |
| Messsiah | Mi'zion | Michael David | Michalle | Mickhi | Mihret | Mikari |
| Mesy'ah | Rashawn | Michael Don | Michan | Mickler | Mihsael | Mikarí |
| Mete | Mia | Michael Edw | Michaud | Micko | Miikka | Mikayel |
| Methias | Miach | Michael Elijah | Michdiani | Mickolas | Miit | Mikayla |
| Methun | Mialin | Michael Ian | Miche'l | Micky | Miitchell | Mikaylan |
| Methuselah | Mian | Michael Isaac | Micheal *(0.20)* | Miclain | Miizell | Mikaylin |
| Metichai | Miard | Michael James | Micheal Alfred | Mico | Mijael | Mikco |
| Metin | Miason | Michael Joe | Micheal-Chri | Micoh Jaeden | Mijan | Mike *(0.08)* |
| Met-Miku | Miatias | Michael Keith | Micheal-Joe | Micoriyun | Mije | Mike Jr |
| Metus | Mic | Michael | Michealsen | Mic-Quan | Mijhay | Mike Nassim |
| Metz | Mica | Kwabena | Micheas | Micquan | Mijyan | Mike Oscar |
| Mevan | Micadian | Michael | Micheaux | Micquel | Mik'a | Mikeal *(0.01)* |
| Mevin | Micael | Myroslav | Michee | Micquell | Mik'quan | Mike-Antoine |

Mikedoine
Mikeel
Mikeem
Mikeen
Mikei
Mikeil
Mikeky
Mikél
Mikel (0.05)
Mikel Gedeon
Mikele
Mikelis
Mikell (0.01)
Mikella
Mikelle
Mikelo
Mikelson
Mikelyn
Miken
Mikendall
Mikendrae
Mikendric
Mike-Olivier
Mikequel
Mikequez
Mikerlange
Mikerson
Mike-Ryan
Mikeson
Mikevious
Mikeviyon
Mikey
Mikeya
Mikeylin
Mikeyon
Mikha
Mikhael (0.01)
Mikhael-
　Alexandre
Mikhai
Mikhail (0.02)
Mikhailo
Mikhal
Mikhayah
Mikhei
Mikhel
Mikhi
Mikia
Mikiah
Mikiail
Mikial
Mikias

Mikie
Mikiel
Mikilen
Mikilian
Mikilus
Mikinak
Mikir
Mikiss
Mikito
Mikiyas
Mikiyel
Mikka
Mikkel (0.01)
Mikkelsen F
Mikko
Mikkwon
Mikkyle
Mikle
Mikley
Miklo
Miklos
Miko (0.01)
Mikobe
Mikoda
Mikolaj
Mikolas
Mikole
Mikulas
Miky
Mikyh
Mikyle
Mikyus
Milad
Milak
Milan (0.04)
Milan
　Alessandro
Miland
Milann
Milano
Milap
Milas
Mild
Mildo
Mileek
Milek
Mileke
Milekias
Milen
Milendez
Milenko
Miler

Miles (0.49)
Miles-Averi
Miley
Milez
Milford
Milijah
Milind
Milique
Milkaya
Milkessa
Milkias
Milko
Millan
Millard
Millen
Miller (0.04)
Millikin
Mills
Milo (0.09)
Miloh
Milon
Milos
Milo-Tiana
Milow
Milsteyn
Milter
Milthon
Milton (0.05)
Milton Giovanni
Miltonio
Milyejah
Milyk
Milyn
Mims
Min (0.01)
Min Soo
Min Suh
Min Sung
Mina
Minehlskhy
Ming
Minguel
Mingy
Ming-Yuan
Mingyuan
Minh (0.01)
Minh Dat
Minh Duy
　Alexandre
Minh Khoa
Minh Luan
Minh Tien

Minhal
Minh-Khang
Minh-Nhat
Minhtai
Min-Htet
Minhtri
Minhtuan
Minisare
Minjae
Minjun
Minkwon
Minn
Minnie
Mino
Minocqwae
Minodée
Minor
Minsi
Minsoo
Min-Suh
Min-Suk
Minuet
Minul
Mio
Mion
Miqual
Miquan
Mi-Quane
Mique
Miqueas
Miquel
Miquez
Mir
Mir Nader
Miracle
Mirajudeen
Miralem
Mircea
Mirco
Mirkamol
Mirko (0.01)
Mirnes
Miro
Miron
Miroslav
Miroslaw
Mirsad
Mirus
Mirvens
Miryel
Mirza (0.01)
Misael (0.06)

Misahel
Misaiah
Misaiel
Misaiun
Mischa
Mi-Sean
Misha
Mishael
Mishal
Mishan
Miskir
Miskwakone
Mison
Missael
Mission
Mista Zacary
Mistah
Mister
Mister Leonard
Misun
Misunshara
Mit
Mitalo
Mitavius
Mitch (0.01)
Mitchael
Mitchai
Mitcheal
Mitchel (0.04)
Mitchell (0.61)
Mitchell
　William
Mitchelle
Mitchill
Mitchum
Miten
Mithil
Mithun
Mitjo
Mitrell
Mitreyou
Mitt
Mittraparb
Mitzael
Mivil
Mixalis
Miyaki
Miyari
Miyazaki
Miycah
Miykael
Miykáel

Miyo
Miyon
Miyquavious
Miyuh
Miywapin
Mizael
Mizell
Mizrahi
Mizrahim
Mizraim
M-Kenzie
Mlton
Mmynt
Mnasie
Mo'nere
Moad
Moaiad
Moamal
Moamen
Moana
Moataz
Moawia Hashim
Moayad
Moaz
Mobeen
Mobein
Moctezumac
Modecai
Modesto
Modi
Modiahn
Modou
Moe
Moeez
Moehkum
Moen
Mogga
Moha
Mohab
Mohamad (0.04)
Mohamad Ali
Mohamad
　Kazem
Mohamad Kheir
Mohamad-Ali
Mohamad-
　Hussein
Mohamad-
　Karim
Mohamad-
　Mahdi
Mohamadoul

Mohamad-Ridha
Mohamco
Mohamd
Mohamed (0.26)
Mohamed
　Abdelatif
Mohamed
　Abdelmalek
Mohamed Ali
Mohamed Amin
Mohamed
　Amine
Mohamed Amir
Mohamed Aniss
Mohamed
　Ayman
Mohamed
　Cherif
Mohamed El
　Mehdi
Mohamed El
　Seddik
Mohamed
　Lamine
Mohamed
　Nazim
Mohamed Ramy
Mohamed Rayan
Mohamed
　Ryadh
Mohamed
　Yassine
Mohamed
　Younes
Mohamed-
　Adams
Moha-Medali
Mohamedamiin
Mohamedamin
Mohamedamine
Mohamed-
　Amine
Mohamed-Dhia
Mohamed-
　Elamine
Mohamed-
　Emene
Mohamed-
　Lemine
Mohamed-Nabil
Mohamed-
　Nordine

Mohamed-Rayan
Mohamed-Rayane
Mohamed-Rayen
Mohamed-Reda
Mohamed-Said
Mohamedwali
Mohamed-Yassine
Mohamed-Yaya
Mohamed-Zachary
Mohamid Ash
Mohammad *(0.14)*
Mohammad Ali
Mohammad Armaan
Mohammad Mahdee
Mohammad Shaher
Mohammad Siddiq
Mohammad Wahib
Mohammad Yassine
Mohammad-Alassam
Mohammadali
Mohammad-Ali
Mohammad-Ali-Abdelrahman
Mohammad-Hassan
Mohammad-Samir
Mohammed *(0.14)*
Mohammed Al Baker
Mohammed Ali
Mohammed Amin
Mohammed Amine
Mohammed Aziz

Mohammed Cherif
Mohammed Ibrahim
Mohammed Imran
Mohammed Rabbi
Mohammed Rayane
Mohammed Sajid
Mohammed Sayum
Mohammed Takee
Mohammed-Ali
Mohammed-Amine
Mohammed-Aymen
Mohammed-Bushra
Mohammed-Farouq
Mohammed-Gabriel
Mohammed-Houssam
Mohammed-Khalil
Mohammed-Reda
Mohammed-Wael
Mohammed-Yassine
Mohamud
Mohan
Mohanad
Mohand
Mohandass
Mohaned
Mohanned
Mohayat-Din
Mohd Adawi Shukury Abrahim
Mohdeep
Mohebullah
Moheldin
Mohemmed

Mohib
Mohibullah
Mohid
Mohil
Mohit
Mohitpal
Mohkam
Mohmad
Mohmed
Mohmed Kamal
Mohmmad
Mohnish
Mohommed
Mohomud
Mohriz
Mohsin
Mohtdah
Mohummed
Mohyadin
Mohzin
Moiae
Moice
Moier
Moin
Moise
Moïse
Moise's
Moises *(0.12)*
Moises-Aaron
Moishe *(0.01)*
Moivee
Moiyé
Moiz
Moiz Muhammad
Moiz-Ur-Rahman
Mojave
Mojeeb
Mojerelouwa
Moko
Moktar
Mole
Molefi
Moleni
Molicki
Molique
Mollie
Molly
Molo
Molu
Momar

Momcilo
Momen
Momin
Momo
Momodou
Momoh
Momolu
Mon'dae
Mon'eayah
Mon'quavian
Mon'terrious
Mon'tez
Mon'treal
Mon'trell
Moncef
Moncerey
Monchy
Mondarius
Mondrae
Mondravious
Mondré
Mondreaz
Mondrell
Mondy
Moneeb
Monel
Monem
Moneray
Monet
Moneysako
Mong
Mongzong
Monib
Monie
Monier
Monish
Monjed
Monntaevion
Monqel
Monquarious
Monquavius
Monquez
Monquis
Monroe *(0.01)*
Monserrat
Monsieur
Monta
Montá
Montae
Montaé
Montaez
Montaine

Montan
Montana *(0.02)*
Montanaz
Montanna
Montarie
Montario
Montarious
Montarius
Montaro
Montavein
Montavin
Montavion
Montavious
Montavis
Montavius *(0.01)*
Montay
Montaz
Montazr
Montazz
Montclair
Monté
Monte *(0.02)*
Monte'yon
Montease
Montee
Monteen
Monteff
Montega
Monteino
Monteiz
Montel
Montel Daylon
Montelius
Montell
Montellias
Montellius
Monteral
Monterio
Monterious
Monterius
Monterrio
Monterrion
Monterrius
Montez *(0.02)*
Monteze
Montezz
Montgomery *(0.02)*
Montgomory
Montgomrey

Monti
Monticus
Montie
Montiel
Montinez
Montoiya
Montonio
Montoya
Montra
Montrace
Montrae
Montrael
Montraeljun
Montraeviou
Montraivis
Montral
Montravious
Montray
Montre
Montré
Montreal
Montreall
Montreavious
Montree
Montrel *(0.01)*
Montrell *(0.02)*
Montrelle
Montrellis
Montrell-Kevon
Montrello
Montrese
Montress
Montreveon
Montrevion
Montrevious
Montrey
Montrez *(0.01)*
Montreze
Montrice
Montriel
Montrivelle
Monty *(0.01)*
Mony
Monydhar
Monyeh
Monzay
Mookie
Moon
Moonie
Moore
Moore Cheng
Mooreze

Moosa
Mor
Mor'kel
Morad
Moraes
Morai
Morakot Tayvon
Moran
Morcel
Morcellous
Morchun
Mordacai
Mordacia
Mordecai
Mordechai *(0.05)*
Morelio
Moreno
Morens
Morey
Morgaan
Morgahn
Morgan *(0.29)*
Morgan Alan
Morgan Gabriel
Morgan Mathew
Morgan-Samuel
Morgein
Morgen *(0.01)*
Morghan
Morghen
Morgin
Morgon
Morgun
Moriah
Morias
Morice
Moriel
Morinvil
Morkhi
Morley
Morly
Morne
Morningsky
Mornue
Moro
Morod
Moroni
Morphious
Morrell
Morrion
Morris *(0.02)*

| | | | | | | |
|---|---|---|---|---|---|---|
| Morrison | Mouakong | Muaadbinu | Muhammad Ali | Mujahid | Muriithi | Mutazz |
| Morsley | Mouaz | Muáawiyah | Muhammad | Mujasi | Murillo | Muthias |
| Mortaza | Mouctar | Muaaz | Amiin | Mujat | Muriz | Mutombo |
| Morterrious | Mouein | Muacha | Muhammad | Mujtaheed | Murllin | Muttaqi |
| Mortez | Mouhad | Muad | Dayaan | Mujeeb | Murphey | Muttee |
| Mortimah | Mouhamad | Muadh | Muhammad | Mujtaba | Murphy (0.01) | Mutullan |
| Mortique | Mouhamadou | Muahmoo | Haris | Mukarb | Murphy Lee | Muurloo |
| Morton | Mouhamed | Muaj Tsuas | Muhammad-Ali | Mukarram | Murray (0.01) | Muwafaq |
| Morvin | Mouhammadou | Muajkong | Muhammadali | Mukasa | Murry | Muzamil |
| Morwan | Mouhammed | Muajtsitee | Muhammadaziz | Mukhtar | Mursal | Muzammel |
| Mory | Mouhaned | Muakong | Muhammad- | Mukhwaak | Mursalin | Muzammil |
| Morye | Mouktik | Muamba | Bilal | Muktar | Murtada | Mwaffag |
| Mosa | Moultrie | Muammar | Muhammad- | Mukul | Murtadha | Mwile |
| Mosby | Mounir | Muammer | Ghazi | Mulan | Murtatha | My Kale |
| Mose (0.01) | Mountaga | Muath | Muhammad- | Muliek | Murtavion | My'aire |
| Moseley | Mountain | Muawiye | Mahad | Muller | Murtaza | My'ami |
| Moselle | Mourad | Muawiyyah | Muhammad-Mu | Muloki | Murtessa | My'esh |
| Moses George | Mourtada | Muayad | Muhammadul- | Multani | Murteza | My'kah |
| Moses (0.13) | Mourtada Fillali | Muayid | Fatixm | Mulvey | Murtuza | My'kale |
| Moses' | Mouslim-Kamel | Muaz | Muhammao | Mumia | Murvan | My'kel |
| Mosgaadacé | Moussa (0.02) | Mubai | Muhammed | Mun | Musa (0.02) | My'kell |
| Moshe (0.12) | Moussa- | Mubarak | (0.01) | Mun'trey | Musa'ab | My'kevious |
| Mosheh | Harouna | Mubarek | Muhammed | Munachi | Musab | My'khi |
| Mosiah | Moussa-Kamana | Mubarik | Shaheer | Munassar | Musaf | My'kwan |
| Mosie | Moustafa | Mubashir | Muhammedabd | Munawar | Musah | My'liak |
| Mosley | Moustapha | Mubeen | ulrahman | Muncy | Musaiq | My'on |
| Moslim | Moustapha- | Mubein | Muhammed-Al- | Mattewsie | Musan | My'quann |
| Moss | Latyr | Mudassir | Ameen | Mundur | Musavir | My'rann |
| Mossad | Mousthapha | Mudathir | Muhammet- | Muneeb | Musawwir | My'rell |
| Mossai | Mowat | Muddassir | Hamit | Muneer | Muscaf | My'rion |
| Mossaver | Mowgli | Mudtaji | Muhammud | Munib | Musdaf | My'sean |
| Mossimo | Moxen | Mueed-Ahmad | Muhanad | Munir (0.01) | Muse | My'shaun |
| Moss-Williams | Moxon | Mueez | Muhannad | Munis | Musharraf | My'son |
| Mostafa (0.01) | Moye | Muffrey | Muhanned | Munkhsaikhan | Mushegh | My'trell |
| Mostakim | Moyinoluwa | Muftaah | Muhemmed | Munn | Mushfiqur | My'zhirik |
| Mostbin | Moyo | Muhad | Muhib | Munro | Mushir | Mya |
| Mostyn | Moyorek | Muhaidin | Muhib-Ur- | Munsur | Musial | Myaire |
| Mosusie | Moyosoreoluwa | Muhamad | Rahman | Muntasir | Musicab | Myais |
| Moszio | Moyse | Muhamad- | Muhiedin | Muntasser | Muskwasis | Myalanski |
| Mot | Moyseis | Husayn | Muhisani | Muntathar | Mussa | Myan |
| Motahri | Moyses | Muhamadu | Muhmmad | Muntazam | Musse | Myatt |
| Moti | Mozamill | Muhamed | Muhsin | Munther | Mussie | Myca |
| Mottel | Mozell | Muhamed | Muhsin | Munyaun | Mustaan | Mycah |
| Mottrel | Moziah | Murry | Abdulrahma | Munzir | Mustaf | Mycahi |
| Motty | Mozza | Muhamet | Muhsinin | Muoch | Mustafa (0.04) | Mycajah |
| Moty | Mr' King | Muhammad | Muhtasim | Muotdid | Mustafe | Mycalia |
| Mou | Mryk | (0.12) | Muhudin | Muqeet | Mustapha (0.01) | Mychael (0.01) |
| Moua | Msizi | Muhammad A. | Muhyadin | Murad | Mustaqim | Mychai |
| Mouachi | Mtende | Muhammad | Muimayn | Murado | Mustfa | Mychal (0.01) |
| Mouad | Mu'aad | Aayan | Muiz | Murali | Mustjab | Mycheal |
| Mouadh | Mu'adh | Muhammad | Muizz | Murat | Mutarie | Mychel |
| Mouahmong | Mu'tasim | Ahmad | Mujaddid | Murdoch | Mutasir | Myckael |

Myckaël
Myckal
Myckeal
Myckel
Myeehkun
Myelle
Myelz
Myer
Myers
Myheir
Myian
Myintmo
Myiron
Myj'avian
Myka
Mykael *(0.01)*
Mykah
Mykahel
Mykah-Today
Mykai
Mykail
Mykal *(0.01)*
My-Kale
Mykale
Mykarye
Mykas
Myke
Myke'l
Mykeal
Mykeem
Mykei
Mykeil
Mykeile
Mykeith
Mykel *(0.03)*
Mykell *(0.01)*
Mykenessey
Mykese
Mykhael
Mykhail
Mykhal
Mykhari
Mykhary
Mykian
Myking
Mykkol
Myko
Mykol
Mykola
Mylan *(0.01)*
Myle
Myleik

Mylek
Mylen
Myles *(0.33)*
Myles James
Myles Vincent
Mylez
Mylies
Mylik
Mylikah
Mylin
Mylique
Myliyn
Mylo *(0.01)*
Mylon
Mylove
Mylz
Mynahja
Mynor
Myon
Myq'uan
Myqjuan
Myquel
Myracle
Myrakahl
Myran
Myr-Elayas
Myreo
Myreon
Myrhon
Myric
Myrick
Myrin
Myron *(0.04)*
Myrrell
Myrsha
Mysaiah
Mysan
Mysean
Myshaun
My-Shawn
Myshawn
Myshka
Myson
Mysterious
Mytchal
Mytchell
Myte
Mythayus
Mythius
Mytravis
Myxael
Myyay

Myylz
Myzel
Myzell
Myzere
Myziah
Myzik
Mzachary
Mzingaye

**~ N ~**

N
N'gai
N'hmyah
N'kosi
N'namdi
N'rique
N'tence
N'yahn
N'yla
N'yudi Yohan
N'zaeh
N'zayah
Na Quan
Na'darrius
Na'davion
Na'haven
Na'im *(0.01)*
Na'ir
Na'jai
Na'jawn
Na'jee
Na'jere
Na'kean
Na'koma
Na'kori
Na'kur
Na'kyis
Na'laysya
Na'lik
Na'mhere
Na'mir
Na'quan
Na'quise
Na'quwan
Na'rickio
Na'sean
Na'seem
Na'shaun
Na'shawn *(0.01)*
Na'shon

Na'shonn
Na'shuan
Na'sir
Na'tavys
Na'thaniel
Na'thyus
Na'tion
Na'varion
Na'vir
Na'yair
Na'zair
Na'zavion
Na'zeem
Na'zeer
Na'zier
Na'zin
Na'zir
Na'zyre
Naadir
Naam
Naaman
Naamen
Naamir
Naaol
Naasair
Naasir
Naason
Naasson
Naawel
Naayel
Naazim
Naazir
Nabari
Nabeel
Nabeel-Aahmed
Nabhi
Nabieh
Nabieu
Nabigi
Nabiil
Nabil *(0.01)*
Nabiln
Nabisouleye
Nabit
Nablebo
Nabor
Nabridius
Nacale
Nacarci
Nacaro
Naccio
Nace

Nacea
Nacere
Nachapon
Nachawn
Nachiketh
Nachman
Nachshon
Nacim
Nácle
Nacoby
Nacoma
Nacona
Nacosh
Nacyjaí
Nacyus
Nadab
Nadaniel
Nadarion
Nadarrian
Nadarrien
Nadarrius
Nadav
Nade
Nadeed
Nadeem
Nadeer
Naden
Nader *(0.01)*
Nadezious
Nadhif
Nadhir
Nadhish
Nadi
Nadiel
Nadiir
Nadim
Nadir *(0.01)*
Nadirah
Nadjel
Nadji
Nadonis
Nadre
Nadri
Nadron
Nae'shaun
Nae'shawn
Naéem
Naeem *(0.01)*
Naeer
Naeir
Naeje Tymir
Nael

Naeshaun
Naeshawn
Naesir
Naethan
Naethaniel
Naethen
Naethyn
Nafeece
Nafees
Nafeese
Nafi
Nafice
Nafiese
Nafir
Nafis *(0.01)*
Nafiyas
Naftal
Naftali *(0.02)*
Naftuli *(0.02)*
Nag
Naga Rishabh
Nageb
Nageed
Nagei
Nagi
Nagib
Nagisa
Naguy
Nah'eem
Nah'jee
Nah'shon
Nah'zeir
Nah'zir
Naha
Nahar
Nahari
Nahayviaz
Naheam
Naheem
Naheem
   Meshack
Naheime
Nahem
Naheyan
Nahfir
Nahieem
Nahiem
Nahil
Nahim
Nahim Uriel
Nahin
Nahir

Nahium
Nahjair
Nahjee
Nahji
Nahjier
Nahjir
Nahjon
Nahkai
Nahkeem
Nahki
Nahledge
Nahleeq
Nahmere
Nahmi
Nahmir
Nahole
Nahom *(0.01)*
Nahom-
   Befekadu
Nahome
Nahpeez
Nahquan
Nahsaih
Nahshawn
Nahshon
Nahsim
Nah-Sir
Nahsir
Nahsirr
Nahtif
Nahu
Nahuel
Nahum *(0.01)*
Nahun
Nahyan
Nahyaun
Nahyir
Nahzair
Nahzay
Nahzeak
Nahzeer
Nahzeke
Nahzi
Nahzier
Nahzir
Nai'kwon
Nai'quan
Nai'ron
Nai'shaun
Naicere
Naidon
Naidris

| | | | | | | |
|---|---|---|---|---|---|---|
| Naieem | Naji Ameen | Nalsiem | Naqibullah | Naseem (0.01) | Nasire | Natas |
| Naiezire | Najib (0.01) | Nalu | Naquan | Naseer (0.01) | Naslre | Natavias |
| Naif | Najiek | Nam | Naquantre | Nasei | Naslund | Natavion |
| Naigel | Najih | Namair | Naquarius | Naseim | Nasmay | Natavious |
| Naiim | Najiib | Naman | Naquavious | Naseime | Nason (0.01) | Natavis |
| Naiim' | Najiir | Namarcus | Naquavius | Naseir | Nasontae | Natavius |
| Naiime | Najirre | Namari | Naquelyn | Nasel | Nasque | Natay |
| Naikaj | Najmudeen | Namarrien | Naquil | Naser | Nasr | Natayar |
| Naike | Najon | Namatasa | Naquon | Nasere | Nasrat | Natchee |
| Naím | Najor | Namdag | Naqwan | Naseria | Nasratullah | Nate (0.06) |
| Naim (0.01) | Nakai | Nameer | Nar'davion | Naseric | Nasri | Nateshawn |
| Naimatullah | Nakaii | Namhoon | Naraen | Nash (0.07) | Nasrudin | Nateterius |
| Naim-Khailf | Nakair | Namier | Narain | Nashar | Nassaven | Natethan |
| Nain | Nakaita | Namir (0.01) | Naran | Nashaun (0.01) | Nasseem | Nathaddius |
| Nainoa | Nakale | Namit | Narayan | Nashawn (0.01) | Nasser (0.01) | Nathael |
| Na-Ir | Nakarie | Namith | Narayana | Nashawne | Nassi | Nathaiel |
| Nairobi | Nakavion | Namkhai | Narciso | Nasheed | Nassiah | Nathain |
| Nairr | Nakayo | Namone | Narcisse | Nasheedy | Nassier | Nathainel |
| Naishaun | Nakeem | Namraj | Narden | Nasheem | Nassif | Nathan (6.78) |
| Naisheen | Nakeil | Namya | Nardo | Nashide | Nassim (0.01) | Nathan Adam |
| Naisheme | Nakeim | Nana (0.01) | Nardos | Nashier | Nassim | Nathan Aridi |
| Naissier | Nakenton | Nana Kofi | Naree | Nashim | Abdelhamid | Nathan Gabriel |
| Naith | Nakhai | Nana Kwabena | Nareg | Nashir | Nassim Mostefa | Nathan Karl |
| Naithan | Nakhi | Nanakobina | Narek | Nashj'on | Nassim- | Nathan Khoa |
| Naithen | Naki | Nanakwadwo | Narely | Nashoba | Abderrazzak | Nathan Nael |
| Naivion | Nakia | Nanbon | Naremey | Nashod | Nassime | Nathan Patrick |
| Naivon | Nakiah | Nand | Naren | Na-Shon | Nassim- | Nathan Peter |
| Nai-Yuan | Nakie | Nandan | Nariem | Nashon | Mohamed | Nathan Pui-Hon |
| Naj'jah | Nakima | Nanddraw | Narimasa | Nashua | Nassir (0.01) | Nathan Ramon |
| Naja | Nakir | Nandor | Narqueece | Nashushi | Nasueir | Nathan Remi |
| Najad | Nakiveon | Nangelo | Narquell | Nashville | Nasxavier | Nathanael (0.21) |
| Najaé | Nakiyah | Nanthaniel | Narsaire | Nasi | Nasya | Nathanael- |
| Najaeh | Nakoa | Nanugak | Narumi | Nasi'r | Nasyr | Benjamin |
| Najah | Nakobe | Nao | Narvel | Nasia | Naszaiah | Nathanael- |
| Najahn | Nakobie | Naoaki | Narvell | Nasiah | Naszaire | Moise |
| Najai | Nakoda | Naod | Narvon | Nasiar | Naszar | Nathanail |
| Najair | Nakoma | Naode | Naryan | Nasiashia | Naszir | Nathanal |
| Najamir | Nakota | Naoki | Naryk-Devondre | Nasie | Naszire | Nathan-Anthony |
| Najari | Nakotah | Naol | Nas'zair | Nasiem | Naszshiae | Nathane |
| Naje | Nakoyiss | Naolin | Nasaan | Nasier (0.01) | Natael | Nathaneal (0.01) |
| Najé | Naksh | Naomi | Nasai | Nasif | Natahn | Nathaneil |
| Najea | Nakul | Naor | Nasaih | Nasih | Natale-Marco | Nathanel |
| Najee (0.01) | Nakusts'althat | Naoshi | Nasair | Nasiir | Natalia | Nathan-Emilio |
| Najeeb | Nakye | Naoto | Nasan | Nasille | Natalie | Nathan-Fleury |
| Najeebullah | Nakylan | Naoufal-Elias | Nasario | Nasim | Natan (0.01) | Nathan-Gabriel |
| Najeem | Nakyze | Napat | Nasay | Nasim Qu | Natanael (0.01) | Nathanh |
| Najeer | Naldau | Napata | Nasceah | Taybah | Natanel | Nathaniael |
| Najee-Ullah | Naleaf | Naphtali | Nascere | Nasip | Nataniel (0.01) | Nathanial (0.10) |
| Najeh | Naledi | Napo | Nasciam | Nasir (0.25) | Natanine | Nathanial |
| Najei | Nalen | Napoleon (0.01) | Naseal | Nasir Andrez | Natanya | Christian |
| Najeih | Nalex-Scott | Napoleon Ariel | Naseam | Nasir Nehemiah | Natarian | Nathaniel (2.99) |
| Najeim | Nalij | Napriest | Nasean | Nasir-Aldeen | Natarius | Nathaniel |
| Naji | Nalin | Napthali | Naseef | Nasiraldin | Natarriuant | Christopher |

Nathaniel David
Nathaniel Denis
Nathaniel Finn
Nathaniel J
Nathaniel
  Jeshua
Nathaniel Jesse
  Blessed E
Nathaniel
  Juliani
Nathaniel Ray
Nathaniel Yossef
Nathaniel-
  Alejandro
Nathaniel-
  Andres
Nathaniel-James
Nathaniell
Nathaniel-Tyler
Nathanieo
Nathanio
Nathan-Lou
Nathann
Nathanual
Nathanuel
Nathanul
Nathanyal
Nathanyel *(0.01)*
Nathanyl
Nathanyle
Nathan-Yves
Nathapol
Nathavian
Nathawoochai
Nathayden
Natheal
Nathean
Nathen *(0.06)*
Nathen
  Christopher
Nathene
Nathenial
Natheniell
Nathiah
Nathian
Nathias
Nathin
Nathion
Nathius
Nathnael
Nathon *(0.01)*
Nathyis
Nathyn

Nathys
Nathyus
Nation
Native
Natividad
Natiyas
Natna
Natnael
Natorien
Natorius
Natosha
Natravious
Natravius
Natrell
Natreyvus
Natsuki
Nattan
Natthan
Nattrell
Natuan
Natwahn
Natwan
Naufil
Naulige
Naum
Naun
Naunihal
Naushad
Nausicaa
Nautica
Nautone
Nav
Navada
Navadn
Navai
Navajo
Navann
Navar
Navari
Navarien
Navario
Navarious
Navaris
Navarius
Navaro
Navarre
Navarrion
Navarro
Navay'on
Navdeep
Nave
Naveen *(0.01)*
Navell

Naven
Naveo
Naveon
Navi
Navian
Navid
Navié
Naviere
Navieyon
Naviier
Navin
Navion
Navir
Navis
Navjoot
Navjot
Navkaran
Navnazpreet
Navnit
Navnoor
Navon
Navonn
Navonté
Navoris
Navpal
Navpreet
Navraaj
Navraj
Navroop
Navtaj
Navtej
Navvin
Navvir
Navviro
Navy
Navyion
Navyn
Nawaz
Naweed
Nawfal
Nawidullah
Nawon
Nawras
Nay'tese
Nay'tron
Nayab
Nayan
Nayarr
Naydariell
Nayden
Nayel
Nayely
Nayemur

Nayib
Nayim
Nayland
Naylon
Naymetha
Nayquan
Nayron
Naysean
Nayshaun
Nayshawn
Nayshen
Nayshon
Naysir
Nayten
Naythan *(0.01)*
Naythan Gael
Naythaniel
Naythenrey
Naytion
Naytric
Nayvon
Nazahveyaire
Nazaiah
Nazair
Nazar
Nazardio
Nazareno
Nazaret
Nazareth *(0.01)*
Nazario
Nazarye
Nazavier
Nazear
Nazeeh
Nazeem
Nazeer
Nazeir
Nazel
Nazele
Nazem
Nazeon
Nazere
Nazereth
Nazerith
Nazheir
Nazhier
Nazhir
Nazhon
Naziah
Nazier *(0.01)*
Naziere
Nazih
Nazik

Nazir *(0.04)*
Nazir
  Christopher
Nazire
Naziru
Naziun
Nazjah
Nazjay
Nazman
Nazmul
Nazon
Nazsir
Nazuri
Nazyair
Nazzal
Nazzareno
Nazzario
Nazzir
NB
Nbm
Nchiminyih
Ndangbi
Nderim
Ndia
Ndozi
Ndubuisi
Ndungidi
Ne Qwell
Ne Shaun
Ne'jon
Ne'kalis
Ne'kylan
Ne'lyus
Ne'miah
Ne'seant
Ne'shawn
Neakuteleab
Neal *(0.03)*
Neale
Nealon
Neamen
Neamiah
Nea-Ron
Neath
Neav
Neave
Neaven
Nebahel
Nebil
Nebiyou
Nebojsa
Nebraska
Nebu

Nebuchadnezzar
Neckolas
Neco
Nectario
Ned *(0.01)*
Nedal
Nedas
Nedaviyah
Nediloic-
  Muamba
Nedim
Nedvin
Neechytra
Needham
Neekan
Neekon
Neel *(0.02)*
Neelai
Neelan
Neelanjan
Neelesh
Neely
Neemah
Neer
Neeraj
Neesin
Neev
Neftali *(0.01)*
Neftaly
Negasi
Neguse
Nehaan
Nehal
Nehamiaa
Nehamiah
Nehem Zuriel
Nehemi
Nehemia
Nehemiah
  *(0.17)*
Nehemiah
  Darwin
Nehemiaha
Nehemiaih
Nehemias *(0.01)*
Nehemy
Nehemyah
Nehevonté
Nehiamiah
Nehlen
Nehmiah
Nehru
Nehuen

Nehven
Nehyzer
Neicol
Neifferth
Neifi
Neigel
Neight
Neihemiah
Neiko
Neil *(0.12)*
Neil Joseph
Neil Thomas
Neil Xincheng
Neilan
Neilen
Neill
Neilmoni
Neilson
Neiltaj
Neimad
Neiman
Neioh
Neiqueo
Neiser
Neison
Neithan
Neithen
Nejby
Neji
Nejib
Nejii
Nek
Nekai
Nekale
Nekeal
Nekear
Nekemar
Nekhei
Nekhi
Nekki
Nekkiya
Neko *(0.01)*
Nekoda
Nekodah
Nekolas
Nekori
Nekos
Nekyi
Nelan
Nelbin
Nelcio
Nelith
Nell

Nell'vonne
Nelly
Nels
Nelsen-Manfred
Nelson (0.18)
Nelson Yeaka
Nelven
Nelvin
Nelzear
Nelzon
Nemarion
Nemat
Nemesio
Nemiah
Nemias
Neminia
Nemion
Nemo
Nemyah
Nene
Neng
Ne-O
Neo (0.02)
Neofit
Neomiah
Neon
Neoshi
Neovanni
Nephi
Nephtali
Nepoleon
Nepomoseno
Neporah
Neptaly
Nepteria
Nepthali
Nequeo
Neri
Neria
Nerik
Nerio
Nero
Neroy
Neru
Nerva Alincir
Nervilus
Nery (0.01)
Nesanel (0.01)
Neshaun
Neshawn
Nesilio
Nesim
Ness

Ness-Mordechai
Nesta
Nestor (0.03)
Nestor-Alessandro
Nestor-Joseph
Neta
Netace
Netanel
Neth
Nethanael
Nethaneal
Nethanel
Nethanial
Nethaniel
Nethias
Neto
Netra
Neture
Neuris
Nev'aehs
Nevada
Nevaeh (0.01)
Nevaeh'
Nevahn
Nevajé
Nevan (0.02)
Nevarious
Nevaro
Nevayle
Neve
Neveda
Neveh
Neveion
Nevek
Neven (0.01)
Neville
Neville-Paul
Nevin (0.05)
Nevin Chung
Nevine
Nevin-Ramon
Nevio
Nevion
Nevo
Nevohn
Nevon
Nevonn
Nevruz
Nevyn
Newborn Male
Newlin
Newman

Newt
Newton (0.01)
Nexon
Nexus
Neyamiah
Neycer
Neyder
Neydious
Neyemiah
Neyl Hadj
Neyl Noor
Neyland
Neyon
Neyssen
Neyzer
Nezar
Nezariah
Nfn
Ngan
Ngawang
Nghi
Nghia
Ngoc Phuoc
Ngoc Vinh-Elvis
Nguan
Nguyen-Kha
Nguyen-Long
Nha
Nhan
Nhat
Nhat Khang
Nhat Quang
Nhat-Quang
Nhia
Nhikilos
Nhofaj
Nhoj
Nhut
Nhy'aire
Nhymir
Ni Jion
Ni'coleyer
Ni'davion
Ni'eem
Ni'jadakiss
Ni'jah
Ni'jel
Ni'jere
Ni'juan
Ni'Juel
Ni'kai
Ni'kerston
Ni'lyerin

Ni'quan
Ni'quarius
Ni'quawn
Ni'seer
Ni'yaz
Ni'yel
Ni'zae
Niair
Niaji
Niall (0.01)
Nialls
Niam
Niame
Niam-Olivier
Niamyah
Nian
Niarobi
Niasia
Niaz
Nibir
Nibraj
Nibras
Nibron
Nic
Nic'kyre
Nicade
Nicah
Nicali
Nicalos
Nicandro
Nicanor
Nicardo
Nicari
Nicario
Nicasio
Nicavian
Nicavius
Nicc
Nicco
Niccolo (0.01)
Nichalas
Nichalaus
Nichalos
Nichalous
Nichalus
Nichloas
Nichlos
Nicho
Nichoals
Nichol
Nichola
Nicholae
Nicholai (0.01)

Nicholaos
Nicholas (7.06)
Nicholas Jaden
  Samuel
Nicholas Xavier
  Zosa
Nicholas'
Nicholasali
Nicholas-
  Dai'Quan
Nicholas-Emad
Nicholas-
  Gregory
Nicholas-Ian
Nicholas-James
Nicholaus
  (0.01)
Nicholay
Nicholei
Nicholes
Nicholi
Nicholia
Nicholis
Nichollie
Nichollus
Nicholos
Nichols
Nicholsky
Nicholson
Nicholus
Nicholye
Nichoulas
Nicisse
Nick (0.06)
Nickademus
Nickalas
Nickalaus
Nickalei
Nickales
Nickali
Nickalis
Nickalos
Nickalous
Nickalus
Nickan
Nickari
Nickcara
Nickcolin
Nickdeep
Nicke
Nickefala
Nickelas

Nickelei
Nickellus
Nickelson
Nickenson
Nicket
Nickey
Nickhil
Nickhill
Nickholas
Nickie
Nickigel
Nickilas
Nickius
Nick-Kerwin
Nicklas (0.02)
Nicklaus (0.02)
Nicklie
Nicklos
Nicklous
Nicko
Nickoby
Nickohlus
Nickolai (0.01)
Nickolas (0.28)
Nickolaus (0.01)
Nickolay
Nickoles
Nickoli
Nickolias
Nickolie
Nickolis
Nickollas
Nickolos
Nickolous
Nickolous-John
Nickolus
Nickolys
Nickson
Nickveer
Nicky (0.01)
Niclas
Niclaus
Nico (0.09)
Nico
  Christopher
Nico Long
Nicoah
Nicodemo
Nicodemos
Nicodemus
  (0.01)
Nico-Donato
Nicoia

Nicola (0.02)
Nicolaas
Nicolae
Nicolai (0.01)
Nicolaj
Nicolaos
Nícolas
Nicolas (1.24)
Nicolas Albert
Nicolas Alexei
Nicolas
  Cinquieme
Nicolas Junior
Nicolas Raphael
Nicolas Robert
Nicolas Rodrigo
Nicolas Wayve
Nicolas-Agustin
Nicolas-Andre
Nicolas-Charles
Nicolas-
  Emmanuel
Nicolas-Gabriel
Nicolas-Lucian
Nicolas-
  Maximiliano
Nicolas-Mickael
Nicolat
Nicolaus
Nicolby
Nicole
Nicolei
Nicoles
Nicoli
Nicolie
Nicolin
Nicolino
Nicolis
Nicollas
Nicolo
Nicolos
Nicolous
Nicolson
Nicolson
  Limage
Nicolus
Nicoma
Nicoran
Nicorion
Nicos
Nicquavious
Nicquavius
Nicthanial

| | | | | | | |
|---|---|---|---|---|---|---|
| Nicxon | Nije'l | Nikkel | Nils (0.01) | Nishadh | Nizamuddin | Noah-James |
| Nidal | Nijeal | Nikkhil | Nilson | Nishal | Nizamudin | Noah-Jeremiah |
| Nidarrious | Nijee | Nikki | Nilton | Nishan | Nizar (0.01) | Noah-Kai |
| Nidhal | Nijeek | Nikko (0.02) | Nilyn | Nishant | Nizay | Noah-Kim |
| Nidhin | Nijel | Nikko Allan | Nilyne | Nishanth | Nizayiah | Noahkrem |
| Nidhish | Nijere | Nikkolai | Nima | Ni-Shaun | Nizer | Noah-Matis |
| Nie'jier | Nijiel | Nikkolas | Nimai | Nishaun | Nizhoni | Noah-Samuel |
| Nieco | Nijier | Nikkoli | Nimal | Nishimee | Niziah | Noah-Xavier |
| Nieem | Nijo | Nikkos | Nimale | Nishkarsh | Niziar | Noam (0.02) |
| Niegeil | Nijoel | Nikkoshae | Nimari | Nishon | Nizq | Noam- |
| Niehhi | Nijul | Niklas (0.03) | Nimay | Nishun | Nizzel |   Mordechai |
| Niek | Nik | Niklaus | Nimerson | Nisiah | Njazi | Noan |
| Nieko | Nika | Nikles | Nimesh | Nisir | Nji-Beza | Noatea |
| Niel | Nikai | Niklo | Nimish | Nissim | Njoroge | Nobaldeep |
| Niels | Nikaiya | Niko (0.04) | Nimrat | Nitai | Nkemdirim | Nobel |
| Nielsen | Nikal | Niko Wyatt | Nimrod | Nitavion | Nkemjika | Nobile |
| Niels-Laurens | Nikalas | Nikoah | Ninad | Niten | Nkenge | Noble (0.02) |
| Nielsun | Nikalieth | Nikodem | Ningeosiak | Niterson | Nkosi | Nobuto |
| Nieves | Nikalis | Nikodemus | Ninjai | Nithan | Nkosilathi | Nobutomo |
| Nifrael | Nikalus | Nikodimos | Ninja-Maddox | Nitharsan | Nkrumah | Nockragone |
| Nigan | Nikan | Nikohlas | Nino (0.01) | Nithik | Nkyveon | Nodin (0.01) |
| Nigawan | Nîkânkâ | Nikola (0.02) | Nio | Nithin | Nnaetochukwu | Noé |
| Nigel (0.09) | Nikao | Nikolai (0.05) | Niquae | Nithish | Nnamdi | No-É |
| Nigel | Nikarion | Nikolaos (0.01) | Niquan | Nithusan | Nnanna | Noe (0.08) |
|   Christopher | Nikash | Nikolas (0.27) | Niquarius | Nitin | No'ah | Noe Jr. |
| Nigel Mauricio | Nikavious | Nikolaus (0.01) | Niquavious | Nitish | No'feir | Noel (0.13) |
| Nigel-Ginola | Nikayle | Nikolay (0.01) | Nique | Nitya | Noa (0.02) | Noelan |
| Nighser | Nikel | Nikoli (0.01) | Niquel | Nitzan | Noa Mattison | Noelani |
| Nighte | Nikeli | Nikolias | Niquerrius | Niubel | Noach | Noelia |
| Nigier | Nikenson | Nikolis | Niquiveir | Niutunu | Noah (7.05) | Noeliel |
| Nigil | Nikerson | Nikolius | Niraj | Niv | Noah Alexander | Noell |
| Nigiler | Niket | Nikolos | Niraj J | Nivaldo | Noah Alphonse | Noelle |
| Nigral | Niketh | Nikoloz | Niranjan | Nivar | Noah Andrew | Noelson |
| Niguel | Nikeyvian | Nikolus | Niranjan Jai | Nivarro | Noah Avi |   Etienne |
| Nihaal | Nikhail | Nikolyn | Nirav | Niveah | Noah Christ | Noelyn |
| Nihaalkhan | Nikheel | Nikorri | Nirawit | Nivek (0.01) | Noah Elias | Noen |
| Nihad | Nikhi | Nikos (0.01) | Nirayan | Niven | Noah Gilbert | Noh'darrien |
| Nihal (0.01) | Nikhil (0.04) | Nikoshio | Nirel | Nividh | Noah Griffin | Noha |
| Nihar | Nikhilesh | Nikovyan | Nirjyot | Nivir | Noah Hansen | Noha Manolo |
| Nihit | Nikhir | Nikunj | Nirmal | Nivre | Noah Jade | Nohem |
| Nihjal | Nikholas | Nikyren | Nirmay | Nixon (0.02) | Noah Joel | Noiel |
| Nii | Nikhom | Nil | Niru | Nixon Zion | Noah Liam | Noimikos |
| Niicholas | Niki | Nilan | Nirvaan | Nixson | Noah Nahoua | Noir |
| Niigel | Nikia | Niland | Nirvan | Niy'jawan | Noah Pierre | Noirik |
| Nij'ah | Nikil | Nilarnab | Nis | Niya | Noah Scott | Nojai |
| Nij'ual | Nikill | Nilay | Nisaiah | Niyaz | Noah Siupi | Nokose |
| Nija | Nikishan | Nildo | Nisal | Niyjerr | Noah Wesley | Nolam |
| Nijah | Nikit | Nile | Nisarg | Niymire | Noah Yan | Nolan (1.30) |
| Nijai | Nikita (0.02) | Nilen | Nischal | Niyoo | Noaha | Noland |
| Nijal | Nikitas | Niles (0.01) | Nischay | Niyzaya | Noah-Alexander | Nolan-Ely |
| Nijall | Nikitha | Nilesh | Nish | Nizaha | Noah-Arun | Nolan-Michael |
| Nijaveus | Nikka | Nilo | Nishaan | Nizaih | Noah-Chaheim | Nolann |
| Nijay | Nikkai | Niloy | Nishad | Nizamdean | Noah-David | Nolawe |

| | | | | | | |
|---|---|---|---|---|---|---|
| Nolberto | Norlyn | Ntare | Ny'juan | Nydrevious | Nykyldrian | Nytese |
| Noldy | Norman (0.06) | Ntujcawmsiavtu | Ny'kayvion | Nye | Nyl | Nythanial |
| Nole | Normand | bcawmseej | Ny'keira | Ny-Eem | Nyla | Nytrayveon |
| Nolen (0.02) | Gabriel | Nu | Ny'kevious | Nyeem | Nylah | Nytrel |
| Noli | Norqavion | Nu Teng | Ny'kias | Nyeff | Nylan | Nytrell |
| Nolin (0.01) | Norris (0.01) | Nu'gotti | Ny'lan | Nyel | Nyle (0.01) | Nytwain |
| Nollan | Nortavius | Nu'man | Ny'mauzhe | Nyell | Nyleian | Nyuol |
| Nolle | Norvan | Nue | Ny'mere | Nyemba | Nyles | Nyvontaye |
| Nollenn | Norvel | Nue Chi | Ny'mhir | Nyen | Nyleven | Nywaun |
| Nollin | Norvell | Nuer | Ny'mill | Nyere | Nylin | Nyxavier |
| Nologistn | Norvis | Nuh | Ny'quan | Nygee | Nyliq | Nyyon |
| Asiatic | Norwin | Nujsisloob | Ny'quarius | Nygel | Nyln | Nyzae |
| Nolte | Nosaj | Nujtxeeg | Ny'quavion | Nygere | Nylon | Nyzaiah |
| Nolten | Noseef | Nukavion | Ny'quez | Nyheem | Nylynn | Nyzavious |
| Nolyn (0.01) | Noslen | Nulat | Ny're | Nyheim | Nymier | Nyzay |
| Nom Lauj | Nosson (0.01) | Numa | Ny'rell | Nyhiem | Nymir | Nyzayvien |
| Nomar | Not | Numair | Ny'seer | Nyhsir | Nyok | Nyzear |
| Nominus | Notol | Numan | Ny'shawn | Nyi'key | Nyoman | Nyzeir |
| Nong | Notoryan | Numani | Ny'shon | Nyigel | Nyong | Nyzer |
| Nono | Notromous | Numayr | Ny'sir | Nyijeer | Nyori | Nyzeria |
| Nooa | Nou | Nunez | Ny'sire | Nyill | Ny-Quae | Nyziah |
| Noobneej | Nouman | Nuno | Ny'tarion | Nyim | Nyquajison | Nyzir |
| Nooh | Nour (0.01) | Nunzio | Ny'tavius | Nyimajah | Nyquan | Nzere |
| Nooma-Mark | Nourallah | Nupole | Ny'troy | Nyir | Nyquavies | Nzubechukwu |
| Noor (0.01) | Noureldin | Nur | Ny'zaire | Nyjah | Nyqueze | |
| Noor Al-Deen | Nouri | Nuradiin | Ny'zarien | Nyjahi | Nyqwan | |
| Noor-A- | Nour-Islam | Nuraz | Ny'zere | Nyjai | Nyre'l | ~ O ~ |
| Muhammad | Nourullah | Nurdin | Ny'zi | Nyjal | Nyree | |
| Noorkamal | Nousheelong | Nurfadil | Ny'ziah | Nyjawon | Nyreec | O |
| Nora | Noushoua | Nuri | Ny'zier | Nyje | Nyreece | O Brian |
| Norah | Nouteng | Nurru | Ny'zir | Nyjé | Nyreem | O Lee |
| Noraion | Nova | Nurudeen | Nya | Nyjhae | Nyreesh | O Ryant |
| Noraiz | Novactin | Nusair | Nyael | Nyjhee | Nyrell | O'bed |
| Norbert | Nova-Din | Nusen | Nyagiah | Nyjiar | Nyri | O'brian |
| Norberth | Novah | Nuur | Nyaim | Nyjil | Nyrike | O'brien |
| Norberto (0.01) | Novaj | Nuurdiin | Nyaire | Nyjon | Nyrobie | O'bryan |
| Norbierto | Novak | Nvuselelo | Nyal | Nyjuel | Nyron | O'byran |
| Norbu | Novander | Ny'aire | Nyan | Nykalaus | Nysadean | O'cien |
| Nordell | Novashay | Ny'bron | Nyandre | Nyke | Nysaiah | O'connor |
| Nore | Novatus | Ny'cere | Nyarko | Nykeem | Nysaun | O'dari |
| Norell | Noveir | Ny'dariun | Nyawelo | Nykel | Nysean | O'darious |
| Noren | Novi | Ny'dier | Nybree | Nykell | Nysear | O'donovah |
| Norey | Novorra | Ny'dion | Nycere | Nykevion | Nyseem | O'jarrion |
| Norge | Nowell | Ny'eme | Nycholas | Nykhai | Nyser | O'jerion |
| Norhot | Nowen | Ny'hier | Nyck | Nykhi | Nyshawn | O'keefe |
| Nori | Noxollys | Ny'jae | Nyckai | Nykhirie | Nyshun | O'keelin |
| Noriaun | Noxtavious | Ny'jaeé | Nyckiole | Nykí | Nysiah | O'keema |
| Noriel | Noyck | Ny'jai | Nyckolous | Nykiea | Nysier | O'keyvon |
| Noriel Pierre | Noyon | Ny'jamahl | Nycolas | Nykko | Nysiir | O'khari |
| Norieta | Nozzey | Ny'javier | Nydarius | Nyko | Nysir (0.01) | O'lontae |
| Norkong | Nraug | Ny'jeer | Nydeer | Nykolas | Nyson | O'mad |
| Norlan | Nser | Ny'jesstin | Nydir | Nykolas-E'an | Nysoun | O'mar |
| Norland | Nsisong | Ny'jir | Nydresz | Nykolaus | Nytavion | O'maree |

| | | | | | |
|---|---|---|---|---|---|
| O'mari *(0.01)* | Obededom | Odak | Ohri | Olaudah | Olson | Olyver |
| O'marian | Obediah | Odarius | Ohwen | Olav | Olt | Olyvier |
| O'mariano | Obehi | Odas | Ohyaji | Olavo | Oludamilare | Om *(0.03)* |
| O'mariez | Obeida | Oddessy | Oi | Olayide | Oludemilade | Omade |
| O'marion *(0.02)* | Oben | Odeh | Oilvier | Olayinka | Oluebubechukwu | Omael |
| O'marius | Obento | Odelfi | Oisa | Oldemar | Olufemi | Omael-Yeshua |
| O'marrion | Oberhiri | Odell *(0.01)* | Oiseomoje | Oldemar-Jacobo | Olufikayo | Omaet |
| O'maundre | Oberlyn | Oden *(0.01)* | Oisin | Oldin | Olugbala | Omaha |
| O'mauri | Oberon | Oderic | Ojani | Ole | Olumide | Om-Ahsi |
| O'merion | Obeth | Oderion | Ojanis | Oleg | Oluranti | Omaid |
| O'myireia | Obey | Odessa | Ojas *(0.01)* | Olegario | Olusegun | Omair |
| O'neal | Obeyd | Odie | Ojay | Olek | Olusolabomi | Omaiss |
| O'neil | Obichukwu | Odilon | Ojayvion | Oleksa | Olutayo | Omall |
| O'niel | Obida | Odin *(0.04)* | Oji | Oleksandr | Oluteniola | Oman |
| O'reilly | Obie | Odinakachukwu | Ojochide | Olen | Oluwabukunmi | Omar *(1.31)* |
| O'ren | Obiel | Odis | Ojore | Olex | Oluwadamilola | Omar Abimael |
| O'rion | Obiesia | Odola | Ojuola | Oley | Oluwadara | Omar El Mehdi |
| O'rius | Obilmer | Odvani | Ojus | Olgens | Oluwademilade | Omar Marcelo |
| O'riyan | Obinna | Ody | Okan | Olger | Oluwadurotimi | Omar Towa |
| O'ryan *(0.01)* | Obinne | Odyseous | Okeefe | Olice | Oluwafemi | Omarah |
| O'ryn | Obiora | Odysseas | Okel | Olices | Oluwaferanmi | Omaraje |
| O'saiyah | Oblain | Odysseus | Okello | Olicio | Oluwafikayomi | Omarde |
| O'sha | Obotey | Oel | Okenze | Olijah | Oluwafimidara | Omaree |
| O'shane | Obrian | Oesya | Okey | Olin *(0.01)* | Oluwagbenga | Omaren |
| O'shaun | Obssa | Ofek | Okeythann | Olindo | Oluwaji | Omareon |
| O'shawn | Oby | Ofelio | Okhaibeso | Oliver *(0.59)* | Oluwamuyiwa | Omar-Farouk |
| O'shay | Ocean *(0.02)* | Ofere | Okie | Oliver Loenzzo | Oluwanifemi | Omari *(0.10)* |
| O'shea | Oceanus | Ofir | Okino | Oliver Uriel | Jason | Omari Quintin |
| O'tavious | Oche | Ofri | Okyis | Oliverio | Oluwapelumi | Omarian *(0.01)* |
| O'zarion | Ochiel | Ofure | Olabisi | Olivia | Oluwaroju | Omarie |
| O'zion | Ocie | Ogden | Oladapo | Olivie | Oluwasegun | Omarien |
| O'zyious | Ociel | Oghemeochucko | Oladele | Olivier *(0.38)* | Oluwasenu | Omario |
| Oak | Ocir | Oghena-Tejiri | Oladimeji | Olivier Joel | Oluwaseun | Omarion *(0.13)* |
| Oakes | Ocsar | Oghenemaro | Oladipupo | Olivier John | Oluwaseyi | Omarion |
| Oakland | Octave | Oghenerukevwe | Olaf | Olivier Ke Chen | Oluwashinaayo | Tye'sheem |
| Oaklee | Octaver | Oghenete | Olajide | Olivier-Jean- | mi Emmanuel | Auguay-Vious |
| Oakley *(0.03)* | Octaveus | Oghenew8runo | Olajuwan | Paul | Oluwasijibomi | Omarionjahlil |
| Oaks | Octavian *(0.01)* | Ogie | Olajuwon | Olivio | Oluwatamilore | Omarionte |
| Oan | Octaviano | Ogler | Olamide | Olivir | Oluwatayo | Omarius |
| Oassi | Octavias | Ognee | Olan *(0.01)* | Oliz | Oluwatimilehin | Omariyon |
| Oba | Octaviaus | Ogulcan | Oland | Ollerijon | Oluwatise | Omar-Jose |
| Obada | Octavien | Ogurian | Olander | Olli | Oluwatishe | Omarr |
| Obadah | Octavin | Ohad | Olandis | Ollie *(0.01)* | Oluwatobi | Omarre |
| Obadiah *(0.01)* | Octavio *(0.03)* | Ohajei | Olando | Olliver | Oluwatofarati | Omarree |
| Obaidah | Octavion *(0.01)* | Ohani | Olandus | Ollivor | Oluwatoki | Omarrey |
| Obakeng | Octavious *(0.01)* | Ohanis | Olangston | Olma | Oluwatomisin | Omarri |
| Obaloluwa | Octavis | Ohany | Olani | Olman | Oluwatomiwa | Omarrion |
| Obang | Octavius *(0.01)* | Ohene | Olanjuwon | Olmer | Oluwole | Omarris |
| Obaro | Octaviyon | Ohim | Olanrewaju | Olof | Olvin | Omart |
| Obataye | October | Ohin | Olaoluwa | Oloka | Olwens | Omartae |
| Obdaniel | Octovio | Ohm *(0.01)* | Olaoluwarotimi | Olorire | Olympia | Omartez |
| Obdulio | Ocyrus | Ohn | Olarinde | Olrik | Olyn | Omarvion |
| Obed *(0.02)* | Odair | Ohnaree | Olatomiwa | Olsen | Olyssa | Omary |

| | | | | | | |
|---|---|---|---|---|---|---|
| Omaryan | Ondre | Ora | Orlan | Osbeli | Osmin | Ottie |
| Omaryen | Ondré | Oracio | Orlanden | Osbin | Osmond | Ottis |
| Omaryon | Ondrea | Oracle | Orlandito | Osborn | Osmund | Otto *(0.04)* |
| Omauri Ke's | Ondreka | Oral | Orlando *(0.17)* | Osborne | Osnel | Otto Roberto |
| Omaurie | Ondrey | Oran | Orlandus | Osbourne | Osneth | Ottoniel |
| Omavi | Ondrique | Orane | Orlanina | Oscar *(1.77)* | Ossian | Ottoway |
| Omayra | One | Oranye | Orlany | Oscar Aviel | Ossie | Oualid |
| Omead | Oneal | Oranzo | Orleans | Oscar Bryan | Ossonny | Ouassim |
| Omeaid | Oneber | Orbelin | Orlin | Oscar Daniel | Osteen | Oubry |
| Omeare | Onecimo | Orbin | Orlis | Oscar | Osten | Oudny |
| Omearr | Oneil | Orbrell | Orman | Maximilian | Ostia | Oumar *(0.01)* |
| Omed | Onel | Orden | Ormena | Oscar Thomas | Ostin | Oumar-Michael |
| Omeed | Onell | Orebe | Ormond | Oscarlos | Ostyn | Ousman |
| Omega | Onesi | Oree | Ornandius | Oscer | Osvaldo *(0.06)* | Ousmane *(0.01)* |
| Omegon | Onesino | Oreilly | Orobosa | Osciel | Osvel | Ousmane Ben |
| Omelech | Onex | Orel | Oronde | Oscoren | Osver | Sahid |
| Omer *(0.02)* | Ongshu | Orelle | Orpheus | Osdiel | Osviel | Ousoumane |
| Omero | Oniah | Oren *(0.02)* | Orr | Oseas | Osvin | Oussama |
| Omezi | Oniel | Orenthal | Orran | Oseghale | Oswalcenit | Ousseini |
| Omid | Onil | Orentheal | Orrayon | Oseph | Oswald | Outhai |
| Omid Suliman | Onix | Orentheo | Orren | Osgar | Oswaldo *(0.05)* | Ouvenaly |
| Omilleo | Onjé | Orenza | Orreon | Oshae | Oswen | Ovadia |
| Omilyo | Onjuan | Oreoluwa | Orrie | Oshai | Oswin | Ovais |
| Omir | Onkar | Oreoluwapo | Orrin *(0.01)* | Oshay | Oswyn | Ovando |
| Omiri | Onner | Orestis | Orry | Oshea | Osyas | Ovani |
| Omkar | Onnez | Orey | Orryn | Osher | Otaevion | Ovante |
| Ommar | Onni | Orfanel | Orson | Oshion | Otaris | Ovanté |
| Omni | Onniel | Orhan | Ortavious | Oshobugie | Otarius | Ovaury |
| Omobadejo | Onno | Ori | Ortayevon | Osi | Otasowie | Oved |
| Omogbolahan | Onofre | Oriah | Ortez | Osias | Otema | Ovell |
| Omonah | Onrae | Orian | Ortheis | Osied | Otero | Overstreet |
| Omorione | Ontario | Orice | Ortis | Osiel *(0.01)* | Oterreyon | Ovi |
| Omoro | Ontarious | Orick | Orval | Osiris *(0.01)* | Oterrian | Ovidio |
| Omoruyi | Ontarius | Orid | Orville | Osiris | Oterrion | Oviyomar |
| Omoruyl | Ontarrius | Orie | Ory | Christophe | Otevon | Owain |
| Omory | Ontavius | Orié | Oryan | Osirus | Otha | Owais |
| Omraan | Onterion | Oriel | Oryen | Osivette | Othar | Owaisuddin |
| Omrao | Onterriaz | Orien | Oryk | Oskar *(0.01)* | Othello | Owan |
| Omri | Onteyas | Orienthial | Oryn | Oskr | Othie | Oways |
| Omron | Ontonio | Origin | Os'eir | Osley | Othin | Owen *(4.00)* |
| Omry | Onur | Orin *(0.01)* | Osa | Oslian | Othman | Owen Curtis |
| Omy | Onyango | Orinn | Osacr | Oslo | Othmane | Owen Q |
| Omyo | Onyebuchi | Oriol | Osagumwenro | Osman *(0.02)* | Othniel | Owen Stefan |
| Omyry | Onyekachi | Orion *(0.12)* | Osagyefo | Osmand | Otilio | Owen-Douglas |
| Omyyad | Onyn | Orion Thomas | Osah | Osmani | Otis *(0.03)* | Owens |
| Onáj | Onyx *(0.01)* | Orione | Osaias | Osmanuel | Otis Junior | Owen-William |
| Onajay | Onz | Oritsejolomi | Osajie | Osmany | Otmane | Owen-Zachery |
| Onaje | Oorjit | Oritsetimieyin | Osamudiamen | Osmar *(0.01)* | Otniel | Owin |
| Onam | Opemipo | Oritzyon | Osaun | Osmardo Jr | Otoniel | Owing |
| Onan | Opious | Oriya | Osavanh | Osmaro | Otorrieous | Owjen |
| Onasis | Oqtevious | Oriyon | Osayuki | Osmart | Otsuki | Own |
| Onassis | Oqurah | Orkan | Osazuwa | Osmen | Ottabwa | Owyn *(0.01)* |
| Ondra | Or | Orkun | Osbaldo *(0.01)* | Osmer | Ottar | Owyne |

| | | | | | |
|---|---|---|---|---|---|
| Owynn | Pace | Pa-Mananga | Parish | Pascal-Rene | Paul F | Pawel |
| Oxiris | Pacen | Pamela | Parith | Pascual *(0.01)* | Paul George | Pawell |
| Oxley | Pacer | Pana | Paritosh | Pascual Mariano | Paul John | Pawit |
| Oyagbemi | Pacey *(0.01)* | Panagioti | Parjot | Pasha | Paul Vincent | Pawlose |
| Oyama | Pachino | Panagiotis | Parkar | Pashawn | Paul William | Pax |
| Oyesiku | Pacian | Panav | Parke | Pasidu | Paul Xavier | Paxon |
| Oz | Pacie | Panayiotis | Parkees | Pasiente | Paul-Alexandre | Paxten |
| Ozaer | Pacifico | Panayotis | Parker *(1.56)* | Pason | Paul-Antoine | Paxton *(0.06)* |
| Ozair | Pacino | Panayotti | Parker B | Pasqual | Paul-Antony | Paxtyn |
| Ozan | Paco | Pancho | Parker Kade | Pasquale | Paul-Auguste | Payden *(0.01)* |
| Ozarion | Paddy | Panell | Parkin | Pasqualino | Muhizi | Paydon |
| Ozarrien | Paden *(0.01)* | Pani | Parkor | Pastor | Paul-Edouard | Paylon |
| Ozborn | Padlayat | Panos | Parks *(0.01)* | Paswell | Paul-Emile | Payne *(0.01)* |
| Ozcar | Padon | Pantaleon | Parley | Pat | Paul-Eric | Payon |
| Ozell | Padraic | Pantelis | Parlon | Patani | Paul-Imani | Payson |
| Ozgur | Padraig *(0.01)* | Panvir | Parm | Patavion | Paulino | Payt |
| Oziah | Padrick | Panya | Parman | Patchawit | Paulissen | Payten *(0.01)* |
| Ozias | Padrig | Paola | Parmdeep | Pate | Paulix | Paytin |
| Ozieion | Padro | Paolino | Parmeet | Pateton | Paulo *(0.03)* | Payton *(0.38)* |
| Oziel | Padruig | Paolo *(0.04)* | Parmjit | Pathe | Paulonzeo | Payton Lee |
| Ozioma | Paeden | Paolo | Parmjot | Pathen | Pauloosie | Payton-Carmine |
| Ozjan | Paeton | Christophe | Parmveer | Pathon | Pauloosie Paul | Paz |
| Ozka | Pagan | Papa | Parmvir | Patien | Jr | Pazcual |
| Ozlo | Page | Papa Kofi | Parneal | Patience | Paulossie | Pe'ytein |
| Ozmani | Pagerick | Papa Mady | Parneet | Patient | Paul-Ryan | Peaire |
| Ozmen | Paham | Papa Nar | Parnell | Patirck | Paul-Samuel | Peanut |
| Ozmond | Pahris | Pape | Paron | Paton | Paul-Sebastian | Pearce *(0.01)* |
| Ozric | Nektariosg | Papigutuk | Parqer | Patric *(0.01)* | Paulson | Pearcy |
| Oztin | Pahyton | Paquez | Parrami | Patrice | Paulus | Pearon |
| Ozvaldo | Paiden | Parabhjovin | Parriaye | Patricio *(0.01)* | Paulusi | Pearse |
| Ozz | Paidin | Paradis | Parris | Patrick *(1.81)* | Paulusie | Pearson *(0.01)* |
| Ozzie | Paige | Param | Parrish *(0.01)* | Patrick Andrew | Paulvu | Peate |
| Ozzy *(0.01)* | Paine | Paramahansa | Parry | Patrick Henry | Paul-William | Pecola |
| | Painter | Paramente | Parsa *(0.01)* | Patrick James | Paurian | Pecos |
| | Paisley | Paraminder | Parshantveer | Patrick | Pausha | Peddleford |
| | Paisyn | Paramith | Parson | Jonathan | Paushtikuss | Peder Josef |
| **~ P ~** | Paiten | Paramon | Parteek | Patrick Jr | Pavan *(0.01)* | Pedralvo |
| P | Paithan | Parampreet | Partej | Patrick Junior | Pavanvir | Pedram |
| P'ayre | Paithian | Paramveer | Parth *(0.02)* | Patrick Kean | Pavel *(0.01)* | Pedrimy |
| P'ere | Paitin | Paramvir | Parthiv | Patrick Peter | Paven | Pedro *(0.27)* |
| Paarth | Paiton | Parani | Parto | Patrick- | Pavi | Pedro Alberto |
| Paavan | Paityn | Parantapa | Parv | Santiago | Pavin | Pedro Daniel |
| Paavo | Pak | Paras | Parva | Patrieon | Pavit | Pedro Eduardo |
| Pablito | Pake | Parav | Parveer | Patrik | Paviter | Pedro Henrique |
| Pablo *(0.18)* | Pako | Parbir | Parvelle | Patrize | Pavith | *(0.01)* |
| Pablo | Pal | Parees | Parveshbir | Patron | Pavithran | Pedro Jose |
| Alessandro | Palakiko | Pareth | Parwaan | Patryck | Pavitpal | Pedro-Henrique |
| Pablo Daniel | Palani | Parez | Parwan | Patryk *(0.01)* | Pavitra | Pedroluis |
| Pablo Gabriel | Palco | Parham | Parwiz | Patscal-Andy | Pavle | Pedro-Michael |
| Pablo Jesus | Palden | Pariis | Parys | Patterson | Pavlos | Pedrum |
| Pablo Toety | Palilo | Parion | Pasavell | Patton *(0.01)* | Pavly | Peers |
| Pablo-Nadim | Pallav | Paris *(0.02)* | Pascal *(0.02)* | Pau | Pawanveer | Peeter |
| Pablo-Tadeo | Palmer *(0.02)* | Parise | Pascal Raphael | Paul *(1.06)* | Pawat | Pefong |

Pehja
Pehong
Pehri
Pei
Peighton
Peil
Peirce
Peja
Pekan Franck.L
Pela
Pele
Pelham
Peli
Pelle
Pellumb
Pemetrius
Pendarrin
Pendleton
Peng
Pengfei
Pengsu
Pengxue
Pengyu
Peniel
Penn
Peosamnang
Pepeisidro
Peppe
Pepper
Peras
Percell
Percennie
Percie
Percival
Percy *(0.02)*
Percy Samuel
Peregrin
Peregrine
Perez
Perferio
Perichian
Periklis
Perion
Periyuan
Perkari
Perlino
Pernell *(0.01)*
Pero
Perre
Perrett
Perri
Perrie
Perrin *(0.01)*

Perrion
Perris
Perry *(0.05)*
Perryon
Perryone
Perryuntay
Pershia
Persio
Persiris
Person
Perteek
Perun
Pervis
Perwer
Pesaleli Jr
Peshraw
Petar *(0.01)*
Pete *(0.01)*
Peter *(0.99)*
Peter Bobby
Peter Daniel
Peter Hayder
Peter Hisup
Peter Hong
Phuc
Peter James
Peter Jr
Peter Michael
Peter-Jason
Peter-John
Peterson *(0.01)*
Peterson
   Steiner
Petion
Petr
Petrie
Petrit
Petro
Petroff
Petronilo
Petros
Petros-Chris
Petrus
Pettagon
Petter
Petties
Peydon
Peysen
Peyten
Peytin
Peytn
Peyton *(1.05)*
Peytor

Peytun
Pezuta Waste
   Hoksina
Phabian
Phadel
Phaeton
Phafinee
Phakorn
Phalen
Phalon
Phaly
Phan
Phane
Phani Kumar
Phanuel
Pharalan
Pharaoh
Pharell
Phares
Pharoah
Pharon
Pharondus
Pharrel
Pharrell
Pharrin
Pharris
Pharroh
Pharsit
Pharyn
Phasias
Phat
Phatee
Phathana
Phay
Phaylon
Phazon
Pheanis
Phedyral
Pheinyx
Phelan
Pheleni
Phelim
Phelix
Pheness
Pheng
Phenis
Phenix *(0.01)*
Phennix
Pheno
Phenon
Phenyx
Pheonix
Pherell

Pherin
Pheron
Pherreous
Phersen
Phi
Phi'sario
Phidalien
Phi-Dan
Phi-Kiet
Phil
Phil Hardy
Philander
Philandis
Philbert
Philemon
Philhippe
Philibert
Philijuan
Philip *(0.32)*
Philip Khoi
   Nguyen
Philip-Diosdado
   Jr
Philipe
Philip-Ivan
Philipos
Philipp
Philippe *(0.14)*
Philippe
   Antoine
Philippe
   Etienne
Philippe Yannis
Philippe-
   Alexandre
Philippe-
   Antoine
Philippe-Arnaud
Philippe-Jacob
Philippe-Junior
Philippe-Olivier
Philippe-Ruben
Philix
Phill
Phillibert
Phil-Lip
Phillip *(0.37)*
Phillip Andrew
Phillip Jr
Phillip Michel
Phillip Nicolai
Phillipe *(0.01)*
Phillipe David

Phillipp
Phillippe
Phillipph
Phillup
Philmon
Philo
Philong
Philopateer
Philopater
Philorius
Philp
Philppe
Philstaviou
Philup
Phineas *(0.01)*
Phineaus
Phinehas
Phinnaeus
Phinneaus
Phinnigan
Phisher
Phivu
Phllip
Phlobater
Phoebus
Phoenix *(0.17)*
Phoenix Sky
Phoenixx
Phoenyx
Phoeuk
Phoneix
Phong
Phonvanxai
Phophet
Phorest
Phousavan
Phouthavong
Phoutthasinh
Phouvieng
Phrede
Phuc
Phuoc
Phuong
Phurious
Phusana
Phyllip
Phyness
Phynix
Phynx
Pi'shon
Pi'son
Piajae

Picasso
Picheth
Pickens
Pie-Jack
Piel
Pier
Pier Alexandre
Pier Luc
Pier-Alex
Pier-Alexandre
Pierangelo
Pier-Antoine
Pierce *(0.13)*
Pierce Aaron
Pierce Richard
Pierce Wesley
Piercen
Pierceson
Pierceston
Pierceton
Piercten
Piercy
Pierden
Piere
Pier-Etienne
Pier-Hugo
Pier-Jules
Pier-Luc
Piero
Pier-Olivié
Pier-Olivier
   *(0.01)*
Pierré
Pierre *(0.05)*
Pierre Alexandre
Pierre Charles
Pierre Emrick
Pierre Louis
Pierre Olivier
Pierre-Alex
Pierre-
   Alexandre
   *(0.01)*
Pierre-Alexis
Pierre-Amany
Pierre-Andre
Pierre-Anthony
Pierre-Antoine
Pierre-Auguste
   Muhiz
Pierre-Carl
Pierre-Charles
Pierre-Emile

Pierre-
   Emmanuel
Pierre-Etienne
Pierre-Hugo
Pierre-Hugues
Pierre-Louis
Pierre-Luc
   *(0.01)*
Pierre-Marc
Pierre-Olivier
   *(0.01)*
Pierre-Raphael
Pierre-William
Pierre-Yves
Pierrick
Pierrie
Pierrot
Pierry
Piers
Pierson *(0.03)*
Pierston
Pieter
Pietro *(0.01)*
Pietro-Giorgio
Pilani
Pilar
Pilot
Pincas
Pinchas *(0.01)*
Pinchos
Pinchus *(0.01)*
Pinny
Pio
Pio Khoa
Piotr
Pious
Pipehgwance
Piper
Piranavann
Piraveen
Piraveenkumar
Piriyash
Pirooz
Pisa
Pishoy
Pistol
Pito
Pittiula
Piuisi
Piyush
PJ
Plamedi
Plamen

Plasway
Platini
Platinum
Plato
Platon-Nicholas
Plez
Pmossamek
  Nolka
Po'okela
Poasie
Po-Chiang
Pocjowk
Pokii
Pol
Pollard
Ponesavanh
Ponnell
Pontius
Poojan
Pooranjot
Porche
Porchoua
Porfirio
Porofili
Port
Porter *(0.14)*
Poseidon
Poston
Potter
Poul
Pouya
Powell
Power
Powers
Poyraz
Praameshmoorthy
Prabh
Prabhas
Prabhath
Prabhav
Prabhdeep
Prabhgun
Prabhjeet
Prabhjot *(0.01)*
Prabhkarn
Prabhkeerat
Prabhnoor
Prabhroop
Prabjot
Prabnoor
Prabsimran
Prabujot
Prader

Pradham
Pradyumn
Prahalad
Praharsh
Praise
Praiyze
Praizz
Praja
Prajedes
Prajeeth
Prajesh
Prajwal
Prakhar
Prakit
Pramad
Pramath
Pramit
Pramith
Pramod
Pran
Pranabh
Pranav *(0.05)*
Pranavan
Pranavsai
Pranay
Pranday
Praneel
Praneeth
Pranish
Pranit
Pranith
Pranjal
Pranshu
Pranvir
Prasanna
Prasanth
Praseed
Prashan
Prashath
Prasheel
Prasidda
Prateek
Pratham
Prathamesh
Pratheek
Pratik
Pratosh
Pratyaksh
Pratyush
Praval
Praveen
Praveen Andres
Praven

Pravin
Pravir
Pravith
Praydon
Prayer
Prayvion
Preacher
Precious
Preet
Preetam
Preeth
Preetish
Preetpaul
Prem *(0.01)*
Premal
Premier
Premin
Premro
Prennis
Prenquan
Prentice
Prentis
Prentiss
Presanna
Prescott
Presean
Presley *(0.02)*
Preson
Press
Pressley
Prestan
Prestann
Presten
Prestin *(0.01)*
Prestine
Preston *(1.41)*
Preston-Lee
Prestonn
Prestyn *(0.01)*
Preteasion
Pretham
Prevarian
Prexton
Prezton
Price *(0.01)*
Price Mars
Pricer
Pride
Pridicus
Priest
Priestly
Primael
Prime

Primitivo
Primo
Prince *(0.06)*
Prince Ahmad
Prince Alejandr
Prince Alvin
Prince Andrew
Prince Anterio
Prince Charles
Prince
  D'abraham
Prince Ishmael
Prince Jon'
Prince Pal
Prince Pravin
Prince Royale
Prince Shea
Prince's
Prince-
  Alshawnee
Prince-
  Bradshawn
Prince-Charles
Prince-Elijha
Prince-Espoir
Princelee
Princely
Princenton
Prince-O'zarion
Princeraj
Princestin
Princeton *(0.01)*
Princton
Printerious
Printice
Printiss
Prior
Priscille
Prisylla
Prit
Pritam
Pritchard
Prithiv
Prithvi
Pritish
Pritpal
Pritpaul
Pritschet
Priyam
Priyamit
Priyan
Priyansh
Prodeepta

Prodigy
Prodromos
Promesse
Prometheus
Promise
Prophet
Prosper
Prospero
Prottoy
Prubjot
Pruitt
Pruvell
Pryce
Pryncedell
Pryor
Pryson
Pshanc
Psymon
Ptolemy
Pueokahi
Pujeet
Pujjuut
Pukhraj
Pulak
Pulei'vai
Pulkit
Pull
Puneet
Purav
Purcell
Purefire
Purin
Purleigh
Purnell
Putnam
Putu
Puyi
Pwalxken
Pyman
Pyper
Pyrce
Pythagorus

**~ Q ~**

Q
Q'andre
Q'kshawn
Q'lindsey
Q'terrion
Q'uantavius
Q'uran

Q'vieun
Qa'shaud
Qa'veon
Qaadair
Qaadir
Qaasim
Qadan
Qadar
Qadeer
Qaden
Qadir
Qahyim
Qaid
Qaiden
Qais
Qaiyim
Qaiyyim
Qalid
Qaman
Qamar
Qamarion
Qapik
Qarim
Qaseem
Qasim
Qassam
Qaunaq
Qavavau
Qavi
Qavontis
Qawiee
Qayden
Qays
Qayvier
Qazi
Qeavon
Qeirea
Qelizio
Qendrim
Qeylis Rhade
Qhalil
Qi Zhan
Qi'andre
Qi'moni
Qi'yel
Qi'Zeer
Qian
Qieriyón
Qingyuan
Qinyon
Qion
Qionte
Qmani

Qorbyn
Qortez
Qourell
Qronivah
Qtez
Qu'darius
Qu'ran
Qu'ron
Qu'vion
Qu'vonte
Qua'baughn
Qua'dar
Qua'darius
Qua'darrius
Qua'dee
Qua'dire
Qua'drevion
Qua'lek
Qua'li
Qua'lique
Qua'maine
Qua'marentin
Qua'nore
Qua'rae
Qua'ron
Qua'sim
Qua'tarious
Qua'von
Quaadir
Quabian
Quacy
Quadae
Quadafi
Quadair
Quadarious
Quadarius
Quaddariontae
Quade *(0.01)*
Quadeer
Quadeir
Quaden
Quaderkis
Quadhir
Quadier
Quadir *(0.03)*
Quadray
Quadream
Quadree
Quadreé
Quadri
Quadrieunz
Quadry
Quadyr

| | | | | | | |
|---|---|---|---|---|---|---|
| Quae'shon | Quaneal | Quashon | Qudeem | Quenton *(0.02)* | Quince | Quinten *(0.06)* |
| Quaeshawn | Quang | Quashun | Qudire | Quentrell | Quincey *(0.01)* | Quintenn |
| Quahara | Quang Dzung | Quasim | Que | Quentyn | Quinci | Quinterian |
| Quaheim | Richard | Quasuan | Que John | Querian | Quincie | Quinterious |
| Quahir | Quang Hung | Quasy | Que Shawn | Ques | Quincy *(0.15)* | Quinterius |
| Quahli | Quang Lap | Quatave'us | Que'an | Queshaun | Quinda'tris | Quintero |
| Qua-Hmeer | Nicolas | Quatavious | Que'arus | Queshawn | Quindarious | Quinterrious |
| Quaid *(0.01)* | Quang Nhat | Quatavis | Que'dedrick | Queshonte | Quin-Darius | Quinterrius |
| Quailon | Quang Olivier | Quatavius | Que'shawn | Quest | Quindarius | Quinterrous |
| Quajir | Quanneil | Quaterrius | Que'von | Queston | Quindavius | Quinterrus |
| Quajohn | Quanshon | Quatez | Queance | Quetin | Quindel | Quintevis |
| Qualan | Quantae | Quatir | Queben | Quevin | Quindell | Quintez *(0.01)* |
| Qualen | Quantarious | Quaton | Quebin | Quexi | Quinderius | Quintin *(0.13)* |
| Qualeyque | Quantarius | Quatraouvis | Quedellis | Queyoun | Quinderrick | Quinton *(0.18)* |
| Quali | Quantaveous | Quatrell | Queinton | Quheim | Quinderrius | Quintonio |
| Qualik | Quantaveus | Quavan | Queintravion | Quhvarie | Quindexter | Quinton- |
| Qualin | Quantavin | Quavareon | Quel'ron | Qui | Quindin | Sinclair |
| Qualique | Quantavion | Quavaughn | Quelen | Quí Ante | Quinell | Quintrell |
| Quallin | Quantavión | Quavian | Quelynn | Qui'darius | Quinlan *(0.03)* | Quintus |
| Quallyc | Quantavious | Quavion | Quemaar | Qui'nyah | Quinlann | Quintyn *(0.01)* |
| Qualon | Quantavis | Quavionne | Quemari | Qui'on | Quinlen | Quinyan |
| Qualyn | Quantavius | Quavious | Quen'shawn | Qui'shawn | Quinlin | Quinzarius |
| Quam | Quantay | Quavius | Quen'terriu | Qui'veon | Quinlyn | Quinzell |
| Quamaine | Quantaz | Quavon | Quen'terrius | Quiayeem | Quinn *(0.40)* | Quinzye |
| Qua-Maire | Quante | Quavonn | Quenarious | Quicy | Quinn'dariu | Quionre |
| Quamar | Quanteaz | Quavyon | Quenci | Quidear | Quinnell | Quionte |
| Quamarey | Quantel | Quawan | Quency | Quidere | Quinnie | Quis |
| Quamari | Quantell | Quawi | Quenda | Quienson | Quinnlan | Quiseir |
| Quamarius | Quanterian | Quawn | Quendarius | Quientearis | Quinnn | Quishad |
| Quamarri | Quanterris | Quay | Quenderius | Quientin | Quinntai | Quishaun |
| Quamay Da'sean | Quanterrius | Quay'sai | Quendon | Quienton | Quinntaye | Quishawn |
| Quamee | Quantez | Quay'shawn | Quendyn | Quiintin | Quinnten | Quissan |
| Quameen | Quantis | Quay'tez | Queneau | Quijuan | Quinntin | Quitman |
| Quameer | Quantravis | Quay'von | Queni | Quilan | Quinnton | Quiton |
| Quamel | Quantray | Quaye'nurion | Quenn | Quilem | Quinones | Quixote |
| Quamere | Quantrell | Quayjohn | Quennell | Quilen | Quinsontro | Quizhon |
| Quamiere | Quantum | Quaylan | Quenny Junior | Quill | Quinston | Qujuan |
| Quamir *(0.01)* | Quanye | Quayon | Quenshawn | Quillan | Quint | Qumari |
| Quamire | Quanzelle | Quayonta | Quent | Quillen | Quinta | Qumourie |
| Quamontae | Quaran' | Quayshaun | Quentarek | Quimaine | Quintae | Qunicy |
| Quamonte | Quardarious | Quayshawn | Quentavis | Quimale | Quintan | Quniton |
| Quan | Quardarius | Quayton | Quentaze | Quimel | Quintaris | Qunize |
| Quan Darius | Quari | Quayvaun | Quentcy | Quin *(0.02)* | Quintarius | Quntelliaus |
| Quan Ye | Quarice | Quayveun | Quentel | Quin Sean | Quintavanh | Quo'vadis |
| Quan'darius | Quarmey | Quayvion | Quenten *(0.01)* | Quin Tarius | Quintave'on | Quoc |
| Quan'tez | Quarterrio | Quayvon | Quenterious | Quin'darius | Quintavian | Quoc Khang |
| Quanah | Quartez | Quazahn | Quenterrio | Quin'darriu | Quintavin | Quoc Khong |
| Quanahn | Quartterio | Qua-Zeir | Quenterrius | Quin'terriu | Quintavion | Johnny |
| Quanardo | Quarun | Quazi | Quentez | Quin'tez | Quintavious | Quoc Nam |
| Quandarius | Quaseem | Quazir | Quentice | Quin'travious | *(0.01)* | Quoc Thang |
| Quandell | Quashaun | Quazon | Quentin *(0.28)* | Quinarise | Quintavius | Quoc-Hoang |
| Quandriques | Quashawn | Qudavious | Quention | Quinault | Quintel | Quoc-Thinh |
| Quane | Quashiem | Quddus | Quentiyan | Quinaze | Quintell | Quolee |

| | | | | | | |
|---|---|---|---|---|---|---|
| Quon | Qwinson | Ra'mir | Rachon | Rae-Anthony | Rafiel | Rahkir |
| Quonari | Qwinten | Ra'mond | Rachun | Raeburn | Rafiell | Rahkwon |
| Quonmy | Qwintin | Ra'najia | Raciel | Raecyn | Rafik | Rahkym |
| Quonterious | Qwinton | Ra'qalil | Racim | Raed | Rafiki | Rahlik |
| Quorben | Qwonta'vion | Ra'quan | Racine | Raeden | Rafiki Tchedan | Rahmair |
| Quord'air | Qwynne | Ra'quise | Racobe | Raedon | Rafila | Rahmale |
| Quorde | Qy'des | Ra'saan | Racquez | Raeen | Rafiq | Rahman *(0.01)* |
| Quores | Qydair | Ra'sean | Racso | Raef | Rafuel | Rahmane |
| Quortavius | Qydarius | Ra'shaad | Radames | Raeff | Ragan | Rahmare |
| Quortavyon | Qyimel | Ra'shad | Radarius | Raegan | Ragav | Rahmarion |
| Quortez | Qylan | Ra'shandre | Raddix | Raegon | Rage | Rahmat |
| Quotayveon | Qymere | Ra'shaun | Rade | Raehezekeil | Rageeb-Luis | Rahmear |
| Quoteas | Qynten | Ra'shawn | Radek | Raei | Ragein | Rahmed |
| Qur'an | Qyntin | Ra'sheed | Radel | Raeid | Raggio | Rahmeek |
| Qur-An | Qynton | Ra'tavious | Raden | Raeion | Raghav *(0.01)* | Rahmeer |
| Qurán | Qyntyn | Ra'veair | Rader | Raejin | Raghu | Rahmeir |
| Quran *(0.01)* | Qyse | Ra'von | Radesh | Raejon | Ragul | Rahmel |
| Quranalim | | Raad | Radford | Raekow | Rah'kemiyon | Rahmell |
| Quraun | | Raade | Radhames | Raekwan | Rah'quez | Rahmerce |
| Quron | ~ R ~ | Raadhaye | Radhey | Raekwon *(0.01)* | Rah'shad | Rahmeses |
| Qusai | | Raafat | Radi | Rael | Rah'yeim | Rahmia |
| Qusavon | R | Raafay | Radian Jorel | Raemeir | Rahair | Rahmir *(0.01)* |
| Qushawn | R J | Raaheem | Radice | Raemere | Rahat | Rahmyr |
| Qusim | R Jameson | Raahem | Radien | Raemier | Rahath | Rahn |
| Qustion | R Mon | Raahil | Radih | Raemon | Rahav | Rah-Nard |
| Qutab | R'eonne | Raahsahn | Radin | Raenard | Rahderious | Rahnon |
| Qutelleon | R'landis | Raamir | Radison | Raenello | Rahdin | Rahom |
| Quvareon | R'vahn | Raamiz | Radisson | Raequan | Raheam | Rahquel |
| Quvontae | Ra Kwon | Raanan | Radivoje | Raeqwon | Rahean | Rahsaan *(0.01)* |
| Quwantae | Ra Shon | Raashid | Radja | Raesean | Raheed | Rahsan |
| Quwaun | Ra'chad | Raashon | Radlee | Raeshawn | Raheel | Rahsann |
| Quy | Ra'darian | Raaya | Radley | Raevon | Raheem *(0.03)* | Rahshaan |
| Quynhduy | Ra'dario | Rabbinio | Radmir | Raeyn | Raheem Garson | Rahshad |
| Quynn | Ra'darius | Rabee | Radnor | Raeyon | Raheian | Rahshaun |
| Quynntin | Ra'dean | Rabeet | Radomir | Rafael *(0.34)* | Raheim *(0.01)* | Rahshawn |
| Quyntell | Ra'dell | Rabia-Taher | Radrail | Rafael Christse | Rahfi'r | Rahsheed |
| Qwabana | Ra'derick | Rabira | Radregus | Rafael-Enrique | Rahid | Rahsheen |
| Qwacean | Ra'ees | Rabon | Radu | Rafaelo | Rahieeme | Rahsir |
| Qwalil | Ra'el | Ra-Broun | Radu Sebastian | Rafan | Rahiem *(0.01)* | Rahson |
| Qwalin | Ra'fiel | Racari | Radwain | Rafay | Rahil | Rahsonne |
| Qwamair | Ra'haad | Racash | Radwan | Rafe *(0.01)* | Rahim *(0.01)* | Rahul *(0.03)* |
| Qwasere | Ra'jah | Race *(0.01)* | Radyn | Rafeal | Rahim-Justin | Rahyeine |
| Qwashon | Ra'jon | Racen | Radzil | Rafee | Rahim-Yamine | Rahzir |
| Qwauhtez | Ra'kai | Racer | Rae | Rafeeq | Rahjai | Rahzmier |
| Qwayaciiq | Ra'keem | Rachad | Rae Jhaun | Rafeh | Rahjher | Rai |
| Qwayshaund | Ra'keim | Rachae | Rae Kwon | Raffael | Rah-John | Rai'jon |
| Qwayvon | Ra'kell | Rachael | Rae'dale | Raffaele | Rahjohn | Rai'shun |
| Qwentavious | Ra'kyree | Rachard | Rae'kwon | Raffaello | Rahjon | Raiaan |
| Qwentin | Ra'lon | Rachel | Rae'mire | Rafferty | Rahkeem | Raian |
| Qwentine | Ra'meer | Rachem | Rae'montae | Raffi | Rahkel | Raice |
| Qwentyn | Ra'meirre | Rachid | Rae'shawn | Raffy | Rahki | Raick |
| Qwillen | Ra'mel | Rachit | Rae'zharion | Rafi | Rahkiem | Raid |
| Qwincee | Ra'mel Davon | Rachmiel | Raeamere | Rafic | Rahkin | Raidan |

| | | | | | | |
|---|---|---|---|---|---|---|
| Raidel | Raizhon | Ralden | Rame | Ramontai | Random | Rapha |
| Raiden (0.04) | Raj (0.01) | Raleigh (0.01) | Rameau | Ramontay | Randon (0.01) | Raphaël |
| Raiden Amir | Raja | Raley | Ramee | Ramontez | Randriquis | Raphael (0.38) |
| Raider | Raja Asuaka | Ralfiel | Rameek | Ramorion | Randsen | Raphael Antonio |
| Raidon | Rajae | Rali | Rameen | Ramsay | Randy (0.26) |    Duran |
| Raif (0.01) | Rajah | Ralique | Rameer | Ramsee | Randy-Johnson | Raphael Gem |
| Raife | Rajahn | Raliyah | Rameez | Ramses (0.02) | Raneem | Raphael Lucien |
| Raigan | Rajai | Ralleigh | Rameez Zafar | Ramses | Raneil | Raphael- |
| Raige | Rajaii Arkeem | Ralph (0.08) | Rameir |    Christophh | Ranen |    Emmanuel |
| Raigen | Rajan (0.01) | Ralph Chauncey | Rameire | Ramsey (0.02) | Raney | Raphael-Luis |
| Raigin | Rajandeep | Ralph David | Rameko | Ramson | Ranferi | Raphael-Miel |
| Raigin Llamari | Rajaratnam | Ralphael | Ramel | Ramsses | Rangel | Rapheal (0.01) |
| Raigon | Rajat | Ralph-Bradley | Ramele | Ramsy | Ranger (0.01) | Raphel |
| Raihan | Rajdeep | Ralphell | Ramell | Ramus | Ranginui | Rapids |
| Raiid | Rajean | Ralphi | Ramello | Ramy (0.01) | Rangle | Rapolas |
| Raijaun | Rajeev | Ralphie | Ramen | Ramzey | Rani | Raptor |
| Raikkonen | Rajendra | Ralphiel | Ramendra | Ramzi (0.01) | Ranief | Raqeeb |
| Raikwon | Rajesh | Ralph-Julien | Ramere | Ramzie | Raniem | Raqib |
| Railen | Rajh | Ralph- | Rameris | Ramzy | Raniyan | Raquan (0.01) |
| Railly | Rajhi |    Schmakerson | Ramerse | Ran | Ranjiv | Raquarius |
| Raim | Rajhzon | Ralphy | Ramesh | Rana | Ranjodh | Raquavien |
| Raimel | Rajin | Ralston | Rameshwar | Ranai | Ranjot | Raquavis |
| Raimon | Rajiv | Ram (0.01) | Ramesses | Ranaldo | Ranjote | Raquel |
| Raimond | Rajiz | Ram Chandra | Ramey | Ranario | Ranko | Raquibul |
| Raimone | Rajkamaldeep | Ram Shreyas | Ramez | Ranbir | Ranne | Raquinn |
| Raimoundo | Rajon | Ramadan | Ramhir | Rance (0.01) | Rannon | Raquionne |
| Raimundo-Noe | Rajpal | Ramadani | Rami (0.03) | Rancel | Ranny | Raquise |
| Raimy | Rajshi | Ramadhani | Ramie | Rances | Ranon | Rarity |
| Rain | Rajul | Ramadon | Ramiel | Rand | Ranquavious | Rariwaiens |
| Rain Jeremy | Rajun | Ramael | Ramier | Randal (0.01) | Ranses | Rarlin |
| Raina | Rajvanshdeep | Ramail | Ramiere | Randale | Ransey | Ras Menaham |
| Raine (0.01) | Rajveer (0.01) | Ramaine | Rami-Moad | Randall (0.11) | Ransford | Rasaan |
| Raineil | Rajvir (0.01) | Ramair | Ramin | Randall-Dakota | Ransley | Rasaijah |
| Rainen | Rakai | Ramal | Raminder | Randan | Ransom (0.01) | Rasana |
| Rainer (0.01) | Rakan | Raman | Ramir | Randarious | Ranson | Rasanvir |
| Rainey | Ra-Keam | Ramana | Ramireon | Randarius | Rantaj | Rasaq |
| Raini | Rakeem (0.01) | Ramani | Ramiro (0.05) | Randazelle | Ranteg-Singh | Rasar |
| Rainie | Rakeen | Ramaniah | Ramiro Adrian | Randdin | Rantel | Rasaul |
| Rainier | Rakeim | Ramanjot | Ramit | Rande | Rantereon | Rasauun |
| Rainn | Rakem | Ramar | Ramiz | Randeep | Rantz | Rasbernell |
| Rainor | Rakendu | Ramarco | Rammel | Randel | Ranu | Raschau |
| Rainy | Rakerrius | Ramare | Rammer | Randell (0.01) | Ranuk | Raschaud |
| Raion | Rakesh | Ramaré | Ramneek | Randen | Ranveer | Raschied |
| Raisean | Rakheem | Ramari | Ramnique | Randhal | Ranvir (0.01) | Raschodd |
| Raishaun | Rakiem | Ramario | Ramogi | Randhall | Ranyé | Rasean (0.01) |
| Raishawn | Rakim (0.01) | Ramarion | Ramoi | Randholph | Ranze | Rasedin |
| Raishoud | Rakin | Ramasey | Ramon (0.14) | Randie | Ranzen | Rasee |
| Raisi | Rakinder | Ramayne | Ramonchan | Randiel | Ranzer | Rasesh |
| Raistlin (0.01) | Raking | Ramazan | Ramond | Randin | Ranzie | Rashaad (0.01) |
| Raith | Rakis | Rambang | Ramoné | Randle | Ranzy | Rashaan (0.01) |
| Raivo | Rakiye | Ramces | Ramone (0.01) | Randol | Raoof | Rashaaud |
| Raiyan | Rakon | Ramchand | Ramong | Randolf | Raouf | Rashad (0.06) |
| Raiyyan | Rakyi | Ramdan | Ramont | Randolph (0.02) | Raoul | Rashad-Bahaa |

Rashalee
Ra-Shamel
  Jakee'm
Rashan
Rashandy
Rashard (0.02)
Rashaud (0.01)
Rashaun (0.02)
Rashaune
Rashawd
Rashawn (0.04)
Rashdan
Rashea
Rasheam
Rashean
Rasheb
Rashed
Rashee
Rasheed (0.02)
Rasheem (0.01)
Rasheen (0.01)
Rasheesh
Rashen
Rashid (0.01)
Rashidi
Rashie
Rashied
Rashif
Rashim
Rashion
Rashiv
Rashod
Rashon (0.01)
Rashown
Rashun
Rasik
Rasikh
Rasir
Rasjah
Rasjiwan
Rasmin
Rasmond
Rasmus
Rasnoor
Rason
Rasool
Raspinder
Rassan
Rassembleur
Rassiah
Rastafare
Rastislav
Rastum

Rasul
Ratael
Ratankumar
Ratanvir
Ratavius
Rateb
Ratha
Rathanak
Rathees
Rathik
Rathishsai
Ratib
Ratnam-
  Chanyadson
Ratnesh
Ratravious
Rattan
Raudel
Raudelaire
Rauf
Raujah
Raul (0.18)
Raul Jr
Raulph
Raunak
Raunaq
Raundae
Rauri
Raushan
Ravane
Ravanell
Ravee
Raveend
Ravell
Raven (0.02)
Ravi (0.01)
Ravidu
Raviel
Ravijit
Ravin
Ravinder
Ravindra
Ravinesh
Ravinger
Ravis
Ravitej
Raviv
Ravjit
Ravjot
Ravkaran
Ravnoor
Ravon
Ravonta

Ravonte
Ravraj
Ravyn
Ravyrothanak
Rawad
Rawkeeb
Rawleigh
Rawley
Rawling
Rawlings
Rawmarial
Raxiel
Ray (0.11)
Ray Jiang
Ray Junior
Ray Karoll
Ray Tian
Ray Vaughn
Ray Von
Ray Vonn
Ray'daun
Ray'kwon
Ray'nard
Ray'quan
Ray'sean
Ray'shaun
Ray'shawn
Ray'shun
Ray'vion
Ray'zaun
Rayaan
Rayahyah
Rayal
Rayallan
Rayan (0.08)
Rayan
  Abdelkrim
Rayan Abed El
  Rahim
Rayando
Rayane (0.01)
Rayan-Redwan
Rayan-Yanis
Ray-Bryan
Rayburn
Rayce (0.01)
Raycer
Raychard
Raychun
Raydain
Raydale
Raydan
Raydel

Rayden (0.02)
Raydiel
Raydon
Raydyn
Raye
Rayehan
Rayen
Rayes
Rayfe
Rayford
Rayfus
Raygar
Raygen
Rayhaan
Rayhan (0.01)
Rayheim
Rayion
Rayiona
Rayj
Rayjon
Rayjuan
Rayjzion
Rayk
Rayken
Ray-Kenny
Raykise
Raykoai
Raykwon
Raykwuan
Raylan
Rayle
Rayle Rhode
Raylen
Rayli
Raylin
Raylon
Raylond
Raymaan
Raymal
Rayman
Raymani
Raymar
Raymari
Raymarion
Raymas
Rayme
Raymeir
Raymel
Raymell
Raymen
Raymer
Raymere
Raymerre

Raymie
Raymier
Raymillo
Raymir
Raymo
Ray-Mon
Raymon (0.01)
Raymond (0.53)
Raymond Paul
Raymond
  Tyrone
Raymondo
Raymone
Raymoné
Raymont
Raymound
Raymund
Raymundo
  (0.02)
Rayn
Raynal
Raynaldo
Raynan
Raynard (0.01)
Raynardo
Raynardz
Rayne (0.01)
Rayne Lee
Rayneal
Rayneil
Raynell
Rayner
Raynieri
Raynor
Rayon
Rayoneil
Rayontae
Rayontay
Ray-Quan
Rayquan (0.01)
Rayquavous
Rayquawn
Rayquon
Rayqwaun
Ray-Ray
Raysean
Rayseir
Raysen
Rayshaan
Rayshade
Rayshard
Raysharwn
Rayshaud

Rayshaun (0.01)
Rayshawd
Rayshawn (0.02)
Rayshean
Rayshod
Rayshon
Rayshun
Rayteb
Rayth
Raython
Raytwone
Rayu
Rayvaughn
Rayveon
Rayvion
Rayvionte
Rayvohn
Rayvon (0.01)
Rayvone
Rayvonn
Rayvontay
Rayyan (0.01)
Rayyan Ahmed
Rayyan Ashraf
Rayyen
Rayz
Raza
Razavier
Razay
Razeen
Razel
Razeon
Razhon
Razi
Raziel (0.01)
Razin
Raziq
Razmus
RC
Re'ghae
Re'heon
Re'mari
Re'nard
Re'shaun
Re'shawn
Re'shod
Rea
Rea'shawn
Read
Reade
Reagan (0.07)
Reagen

Reagens
Realiti
Reander
Reanud
Reaqsa
Rearden
Rease
Reason
Reath
Reavely
Reavin
Reavyn
Reaz
Rebaz
Rebecca
Rebel
Reben
Rebhi
Recardo
Recari
Recartez
Rece
Recham
Rechard
Rechardson
Reche
Recko
Reco
Red
Reda (0.01)
Redarrius
Redden
Reddick
Redding
Reddrick
Redeemed
Reden
Rederick
Redggy
Redginald
Redha
Redick
Redik
Redin
Redjy
Redmond
Redon
Ree
Reean
Reece (0.25)
Reecel
Reech
Reeco

| | | | | | | |
|---|---|---|---|---|---|---|
| Reed *(0.17)* | Reice | Rekiez | Renardo | Renzo *(0.01)* | Reyansh | Rhalean |
| Reeddho | Reichen | Reko | Renars | Renzy | Reybel | Rhali |
| Reedi | Reichert | Relan | Renas | Reo | Reyce | Rhamel |
| Reef *(0.01)* | Reid *(0.21)* | Relic | Renato *(0.01)* | Reon | Reyci | Rhamello |
| Reegan | Reid Martin | Rellyis | Renaud *(0.03)* | Reontae | Reyd | Rhamere |
| Reehan | Reidan | Relondo | Renauld | Reontay | Reydell | Rhamses |
| Reelan | Reidell | Rely | Renchie | Rephoel | Reyden | Rhamsez |
| Reen | Reider | Rem | Rendall | Requildo | Reydesel | Rhance |
| Rees *(0.01)* | Reidyn | Remani | Rendarius | Requin | Reydin | Rhandyn |
| Reese *(0.22)* | Reier | Remar | Rendell | Resael | Reyes *(0.01)* | Rhashawn |
| Reese-Amir | Reif | Remari | Renden | Resalat | Reygon | Rhayden |
| Reetak | Reigan | Remarion | Rendi | Resaun | Reyhan | Rhaykem |
| Reeve *(0.01)* | Reighdyn | Remarius | Rendon | Resean | Reyhn | Rhayver |
| Reeves | Reign *(0.01)* | Remarke | Rendtavius | Reshad | Reyis | Rheace |
| Reeves-A- | Reignah | Remco | Rendy | Reshard | Reyland | Rheaume |
| Reeves-B- | Reigon | Reme | René | Reshaun | Reyli *(0.02)* | Rheayna |
| Reezin | Reiken | Remeco | Rene *(0.05)* | Reshawn | Reylunde | Rhede |
| Refat | Reilan | Remedios | Renee | Resrael | Reyly | Rheece |
| Refik | Reiland | Remedy | Rene-Henri | Resul | Reymel | Rhees |
| Refugio | Reiley *(0.01)* | Remetrious | Renel | Retavion | Reymer | Rheese |
| Refujio | Reiley Patrick | Remetrius | Renell | Retish | Reymil | Rheimil |
| Regan *(0.03)* | Reilies | Remhi | Rene-Louwis | Reuben *(0.07)* | Reymon | Rhema |
| Regean | Reilley | Rémi *(0.01)* | Renemanuel | Reubyn | Reymond | Rhenton |
| Regen | Reilly *(0.05)* | Remi *(0.05)* | Rene-Nathaniel | Reuel | Reymundo | Rheo |
| Regent | Reilly Paul | Remigio | Rene-Nicolas | Reuven | (0.01) | Rhet |
| Reggi | Reilly-Jason | Remilekun | René-Pierre | Reuven-Yossef | Reynaldo *(0.04)* | Rhett *(0.08)* |
| Reggie *(0.02)* | Reily *(0.01)* | Remingtin | Renesh | Revan | Reynandis | Rhian |
| Reggie-James | Reilynd | Remington | Reney | Revanth | Reynard | Rhilee |
| Reggion | Reimsley | (0.07) | Renick | Revel | Reynardo | Rhileigh |
| Reggy | Reimundo | Remlee | Renielle | Reven | Reynel | Rhilen |
| Reghan | Reimy | Remmer | Reniery | Reventer | Reynell | Rhiley |
| Reghen | Rein | Remmie | Renn | Reverence | Reyniel | Rhine |
| Reginal *(0.01)* | Reinabel | Remmington | Rennald | Reverson | Reynier | Rhiodin |
| Reginald *(0.13)* | Reinaldo *(0.01)* | Remmy | Rennan | Reveyontez | Reynold | Rho |
| Reginald | Reindl | Remnant | Rennek | Revin | Reynolds | Rhoan |
|   Stoeffel | Reinel | Remo | Rennen | Revonno | Reynoso | Rhobie |
| Reginaldo | Reinhart | Remone | Renner | Revontre | Reyshaun | Rhoden |
| Reginold | Reinhold | Remoro | Rennie | Rewmone | Reyshawn | Rhoderick |
| Region | Reinier | Remus | Rennuel | Rex *(0.06)* | Reyson | Rhodes |
| Regis *(0.01)* | Reint | Rémy | Reno *(0.01)* | Rex Jr | Reyver | Rhodri |
| Regromilio | Reionn | Remy *(0.04)* | Renoa | Rexford | Reyvon | Rhoen |
| Regulo | Reis *(0.01)* | Remy Laboue | Renold | Rexton | Reza | Rhomane |
| Regulus | Reise | Remzi | Renoldo | Rexx | Rezah | Rhonan |
| Rehaan | Reise-Shawn | Ren | Renollie | Rey *(0.02)* | Rezk | Rhonde |
| Rehan | Reiss | Ren Amiel | Renton | Rey Donaldo | Rezner | Rhondon |
| Rehia | Reiyaan | Renaaron | Renty | Rey Jr | Rezvan | Rhondre |
| Rehiem | Reiyan | Renald | Renxuan | Rey Thaddeum | Rezwan | Rhone |
| Rehki | Reiyu | Renaldo | Renya | Rey William | R-Firstson | Rhory |
| Rehman | Rejay | Renaldy | Renz | Rey'shawn | Rha'zarii | Rhoudy |
| Rehmat | Rejean Jr | Renall | Renz Godfrey | Reyaan | Rhadames | Rhougan |
| Rei | Rejjie | Renalson | Renzel Jake | Reyad | Rhaily | Rhownen |
| Reiben | Rejonald | Renando | Renzel-Ron | Reyadan | Rhaimel | Rhudene |
| Reiby | Rekai | Renard | Renzlael | Reyan | Rhain | Rhune |

Rhushath
Rhyan *(0.01)*
Rhyas
Rhyatt
Rhyce
Rhyd
Rhyder
Rhye
Rhyelyn
Rhyen
Rhygl
Rhyine
Rhylan
Rhyland
Rhyle
Rhylee
Rhylen
Rhyley
Rhylie
Rhylyn
Rhymz
Rhyn
Rhyon
Rhyon Jalil
Rhys *(0.06)*
Rhyse
Rhyshine
Rhyshon
Rhyslyn
Rhythm
Ri
Ri Chard
Ri'cardo
Ri'chard
Ri'key
Ri'qwon
Ri'shawn
Riad
Riadh
Riak
Rialee
Rialy
Riam
Rian *(0.03)*
Rian David
Riandro
Riane
Riann
Rianvir
Riaz
Ribal
Ribaldo
Ribav

Ribhi
Ric
Rica
Ricah
Ricahrd
Ricardo *(1.32)*
Ricardo Gab
Ricardon
Ricario
Ricarious
Ricaro
Ricarson
Riccardi
Riccardo
Riccardo Lee
Ricci
Ricco
Ricdriquez
Rich *(0.01)*
Rich'lord
Richard *(2.06)*
Richard
    Anthony
Richard Reuel
Richarde
Richard-John
Richard-
    Matthew
Richardo
Richards
Richardson
Richaud
Richawn
Richcardee
Richel
Richené
Richepin
Richer
Richerdson
Richey
Richhat
Richie *(0.01)*
Richirick
Richkender
Richley
Richman
Richmar
Richmond
    *(0.01)*
Richmyer
Richner
Richon
Richter

Richy
Richy-Hans
Rick *(0.03)*
Rickale
Rickardo
Rickee
Rickevious
Rickey *(0.05)*
Rickey Nyrickio
Ricki
Rickie *(0.01)*
Ricko
Rickshun
Rickson
Ricksone
Ricktrel
Rickul
Rickwon
Ricky *(0.19)*
Ricky Joshua
Ricky-Angel
Rickylee
Rico *(0.03)*
Ricole
Ricóri
Ricuel
Ricus
Ricutberto
Riczan
Rida
Ridah
Riddeck
Riddhik
Riddic
Riddick *(0.01)*
Riddik
Riddock
Ridel
Riden
Rider *(0.01)*
Ridge *(0.03)*
Ridgely
Ridgeway
Ridge-Yvens
Ridgley
Ridglley
Ridham
Ridhamjit
Ridhey
Ridhu
Ridik
Ridley *(0.01)*
Ridwan *(0.01)*

Ridycc
Riece
Riechan
Riechen
Riegar
Rieken
Riel
Rielen
Rieley
Rielly *(0.01)*
Riely
Rien
Riery
Ries
Riese
Riess
Rifat
Rife
Rifess
Rifet
Riffordigno
Rigaud
Rigby
Rigdin
Rigel
Rigg
Riggin
Riggs *(0.01)*
Righin
Righley
Righteous
Righter
Rightous
Rigin
Rigley
Rigo *(0.01)*
Rigoberto *(0.02)*
Rigoverto
Rigsby
Riguelme
Rihan
Rihine
Rijal
Rijel
Rijken
Rijul
Rijvan
Rikalvin
Rikard
Rikaylen
Rikelmer
Riker
Rikesh

Rikhil
Riki
Rikin
Rikkayjaun
Rikko
Riko
Rikquan
Riktavious
Riku
Rikus
Riky
Rilan
Rilee
Rilen
Riles
Riley *(2.11)*
Riley Jo
Riley Phill
Riley William
Riley-Giabao
Riley-Jon
Riley-Thomas
Rilie
Riller
Rilley
Rilmar
Rilo
Rilwan
Rilye
Rilyn
Rilynd
Rimon
Rimwinder
Rin
Rinaldi
Rinaldo
Rinnur
Rinold
Rinor
Rinsky
Rint
Rintaro
Rinto
Rio *(0.01)*
Rio Del Sol
Rion
Rionel
Rionte
Riony
Riordan
Riordon
Riot
Rip

Ripandeep
Ripkan
Ripken
Ripley
Ripp
Riquan
Riquarri
Rique
Riquelme
Riquelmer
Riqui
Risean
Risen
Rish
Rishaad
Rishaan
Rishab *(0.01)*
Rishabh *(0.01)*
Rishabh Niketan
Rishad
Rishan
Rishaud
Rishaurd
Rishav
Rishawn
Rishay
Rishem
Rishen
Rishi *(0.04)*
Rishie
Rishiekaarthik
Rishii
Rishik
Rishikesh
Rishikeshan
Rishikrit
Rishil
Rishin
Rishindra
Rishit
Rishith
Rishiv
Rishon
Rishul
Rissvin
Riston
Ritan
Ritch
Ritchel Herkens
Ritchell
Ritcherd
Ritchie
Ritchnel

Ritchy
Ritesh
Rith O'domm
Rithik
Rithson
Rithvik *(0.01)*
Rithwik
Ritik
Ritish
Rito
Ritojyoti
Ritrez
Ritter
Ritveek
Ritvik
Ritwan
Rityson
Rivaldo
Rivas
Rivea
Rivelino
River *(0.15)*
Rivera
River-Jordan
Rivers *(0.01)*
Rixen
Rixie
Riyaad
Riyaan
Riyad
Riyadh
Riyan
Riyazuddin
Riyen
Riyon
Rizal
Rizan
Rizerian
Rizhon
Rizwan
RJ
Rjandro
Rjaylin
Rjaymond
Rjhay
Rkan
Ro'mance
Ro'marieyanta
Ro'mauni
Ro'mere
Ro'mir
Ro'montey
Ro'shaun

| | | | | | | |
|---|---|---|---|---|---|---|
| Ro'shawn | Roberto Jr | Rockman | Rodlin | Roehl | Roishod | Romald |
| Ro'thonio | Roberts | Rocko | Rodly | Roel | Ro-Ja | Romale |
| Roag | Robertson | Rocksveel | Rodmann | Roelof | Rojas | Roman (0.44) |
| Roald | Robert-Stefan | Rockwell | Rodnee | Roemello | Rojauhn | Roman Chana |
| Roalquin | Robi | Rockwon | Rodnel | Roemyn | Rojel | Romanas |
| Roan (0.03) | Robian | Rocky (0.04) | Rodnell | Roen | Rojelio | Romance |
| Roan Joseph | Robie | Roclen | Rodner | Roenen | Rojen | Romance |
| Roanin | Robiel | Roclin | Rodney (0.18) | Roenick | Rojilio | Anthony |
| Roark | Robierre | Rocny | Rodneyson | Roey | Rojman | Romand |
| Roarke | Robin (0.04) | Rocque | Rodnnyel | Rofino | Rokari | Romandeep |
| Roary-Lee | Robinho | Rocshon | Rodny | Rogan (0.02) | Rokes | Romando |
| Rob | Robinio | Rod | Rodobaldo | Rogdrico | Rokeyse | Romane |
| Rob'qayveeu | Robinnson | Rod'darius | Rodolfo (0.04) | Rogebert | Rokko | Romane Jr |
| Robaire | Robino | Rodarious | Rodolphe | Rogelio (0.07) | Rokland | Romanoph |
| Robb | Robinpreet | Rodarius | Rodonovan | Rogelito | Roko | Romanos |
| Robbey | Robins | Rodarrius | Rodorian | Rogeon | Rolan | Romans |
| Robbi | Robinson (0.01) | Rodas | Rodrecious | Roger (0.16) | Roland (0.06) | Romar |
| Robbie (0.02) | Roble | Rodaulph | Rodreckus | Rogerio | Rolandas | Romare |
| Robbie Jay | Robley | Rodd | Rodrecus | Roger-Kalubi | Rolando (0.06) | Romaré |
| Robbin | Robney | Rodd'ney | Rodreguez | Rogers | Rolando Yoshio | Romari |
| Robby (0.01) | Robret | Roddarius | Rodregus | Rogge | Rolandrick | Romario (0.01) |
| Robby Michael | Robsan | Rodden | Rodreicas | Roghan | Rolayno | Romarion |
| Robect | Robson | Rodderick | Rodreiq | Roghlio | Rolbin | Romaris |
| Robeert | Robvintae | Roddfo | Rodrekus | Rogier | Roldan | Romaro |
| Robel (0.01) | Roby | Roddick | Rodrell | Rogue | Roldens | Romarr |
| Robele | Robyn | Roddney | Rodreques | Roguens | Roldson | Romarris |
| Robens | Roc | Roddrick (0.01) | Rodrequious | Rohaan | Roldy | Romarro |
| Robenson | Roc'keem | Roddrikus | Rodrequis | Rohail | Rolen | Romarus |
| Robenstein | Rocc | Roddy | Rodric | Rohak | Roleson | Romas |
| Roberrt | Rocco (0.15) | Rode | Rodrice | Rohan (0.14) | Rolf | Romaso |
| Roberson | Rocco Jr | Rodel | Rodrick (0.02) | Rohan | Rolf-Aiden | Romaur |
| Robert (4.21) | Rocendo | Rodeli | Rodrickus | Dushyanth | Rolfy | Romawn |
| Robert Allen | Roch | Rodell | Rodricous | Rohan Kumar | Rolin | Rome (0.01) |
| Robert Charles | Rochan | Roderas | Rodricus | Rohan Pier | Rolis | Romearo |
| Robert David | Rochard | Rodercus | Rodrige | Rohanes | Rollan | Romeir |
| Robert Edward | Rochene | Roderic | Rodrigo (0.10) | Rohawn | Rolland | Romel (0.01) |
| Robert Jack | Rochester | Roderich | Rodrigo Angel | Rohdy | Rollandy | Romelio |
| Robert Joel | Rochny | Roderick (0.07) | Rodrigue | Rohen | Rollen | Romelioe |
| Robert Joseph | Rochsten | Roderiez | Rodriguez | Rohene | Rollens | Romell (0.01) |
| Robert Jr | Rock | Roderix | Rodriques | Rohil | Rollie | Romello (0.01) |
| Robert Kwadwo | Rockeem | Roderrick | Rodriquez | Rohin | Rollin | Romelo |
| Robert Michael | Rockenley | Roderson | (0.01) | Rohit (0.01) | Rollins | Romen (0.01) |
| Robert Noel | Rocket | Rodey | Rodshaun | Rohith | Rolly | Romendi |
| Robert Samuel | Rockett | Rodger | Rodtrez | Rohkim | Rolner | Romeo (0.10) |
| Robert Willard | Rockey | Rodger-Lee | Rodulfo | Rohland | Rolon | Romeo Raphael |
| Robert- | Rockford | Rodgers | Rodvin | Rohlando | Rolondo | Eli |
| Christian | Rockinson- | Rodgrick | Rody | Rohman | Rolshawn | Romeo- |
| Robert-Edouard | Christo | Rodgy | Rodyz | Rohn | Roly | Armando |
| Robert-Elias | Rockland | Rodhael | Rodzale | Rohnan | Rolyn | Romeon |
| Roberth | Rocklund | Rodham | Roebel | Rohnik | Roma | Romerio |
| Robert-John | Rockly | Rodin | Roeby | Rohon | Romad | Romero (0.01) |
| Robert-Mikal | Rocklyn | Rodjé | Roegen | Rohr | Romail | Romez |
| Roberto (0.28) | Rocklynn | Rodley | Roehan | Rohullah | Romain (0.01) | Romiah |

| | | | | | |
|---|---|---|---|---|---|
| Romie | Rondale | Rontavius | Rosh | Roushan | Rozmus | Rudyard |
| Romiere | Rondall | Ronté | Roshad | Roushdi | Rozzell | Rueben *(0.01)* |
| Romil | Rondarious | Ronterius | Roshan *(0.01)* | Rouslan | Rron | Ruel |
| Romilio | Rondarius | Ronterrius | Roshankumar | Rousseau | Rryon | Ruenar |
| Romillo | *(0.01)* | Rontrell | Roshanul | Roustein | Rtam | Ruendy |
| Romin | Ronde | Rony *(0.01)* | Ro-Shard | Roux | Rtyahn | Ruey |
| Romion | Rondeal | Ronya | Roshard | Rovarro | Ru Ki | Ruffin |
| Romir | Rondel | Ronyea | Roshaud | Roven | Ru'darius | Rufino |
| Romis | Rondell *(0.01)* | Ronyell | Roshaun | Rovenel | Ru'juhn | Rufus *(0.01)* |
| Romit | Rondez | Ronylson | Roshawn | Roverto | Ru'marriez | Rugael |
| Rommel | Rondo | Ronzell | Roshawnn | Rovin | Ruairi | Rugar |
| Rommel Simon | Rondre | Ronzelle | Roshell | Rovinio | Ruan | Ruger *(0.01)* |
| Louis | Rondré | Roobens | Roshin | Rovinson | Ruandale | Ruggere |
| Rommell | Rondrell | Roodjeffrey | Roshod | Rowan *(0.24)* | Ruarc | Ruggiero |
| Romoan | Rondrick | Roodley | Roshun | Rowan Pascal | Ruari | Ruhab |
| Romon | Rone | Roodnhav | Roskiel | Rowben | Ruarigh | Ruhan |
| Romond | Roneal | Roody | Rosko | Rowdy *(0.01)* | Ruayer | Rui |
| Romonda | Roneil | Rook | Rosman | Rowen *(0.02)* | Rubaiyet | Ruic |
| Romone | Ronel | Rooker | Rosmel | Rowland | Rubal | Ruiz |
| Romuald | Ronell *(0.01)* | Rookie | Rosny | Rownon | Rubayat | Ruize |
| Romualdo | Ronelo | Roolansky | Rosoel | Rowyn *(0.01)* | Rubbens | Rujison |
| Romulo | Ronelsky | Rooney | Ross *(0.10)* | Roxid | Ruben *(0.21)* | Rujohn |
| Romulus | Ronen | Roony | Rossharion | Roxon | Ruben Adrian | Rukanah |
| Romy | Roney | Roop | Rossi | Roxsshan | Ruben Edgardo | Rukeem |
| Romye | Ronez | Roopak | Ross-Lyns | Roxton | Rubens | Rukshan |
| Romyn | Roneze | Roopkirat | Rosson | Roy *(0.15)* | Rubensky | Rulan |
| Ron *(0.02)* | Ron-Hunter | Roosevelt *(0.01)* | Rosswel | Roy Christopher | Rubert Jr | Rulian |
| Ron'dale | Roni | Roosh | Rostin | Roy Wesley | Rubin | Rulon |
| Ron'darius | Ronie | Rooshawn | Roston | Roy'dez | Rubio | Rumaine |
| Ron'dyere | Roniel | Rope | Roston-Leigh | Royal *(0.02)* | Rubuen | Rumaldo |
| Ron'el | Ronier | Roper | Rosvin | Royale | Ruby | Rumen |
| Ron'gee | Ronik | Roqez | Roswaldo | Royalty | Rubydianson | Rumi |
| Ron'jay | Ronin *(0.03)* | Roquavion | Roswell | Royaun | Rubyn | Rumir |
| Ron'tavius | Ronit *(0.01)* | Roque *(0.01)* | Rotario | Royce *(0.05)* | Rucker | Rumman |
| Ron'tayveon | Ronith | Rordan | Rotaveon | Royce Prest | Rud | Rumoire |
| Ron'travious | Ronjodh | Rorey | Rotavion | Roycetin | Rudar | Rumsie |
| Ron'trell | Ronmehn | Roric | Rotciv | Roydarrius | Ruddy | Rumzi |
| Ronain | Ronnel | Rorion | Rotem | Royden | Rudee | Rumzy |
| Ronak *(0.01)* | Ronnell *(0.01)* | Rory *(0.10)* | Rothal | Royel | Ruden | Runako |
| Ronal | Ronney | Rosa | Rothanak | Royer | Rudens | Rune *(0.01)* |
| Ronald *(0.42)* | Ronni | Rosaire | Rothapol | Royle | Rudhra | Rungano |
| Ronaldinho | Ronnie *(0.12)* | Rosalyo | Rotolua | Roylee | Rudi | Ruojin |
| Ronaldino | Ronnie-James | Rosandel | Rotrell | Royse | Rudis | Ruoyu |
| Ronaldo *(0.03)* | Ronny *(0.02)* | Rosario *(0.01)* | Roual | Royshaun | Rudolf | Rupert *(0.01)* |
| Ronaldy | Ronny-James | Rosbel | Rouan | Royston | Rudolfo | Ruperto |
| Ronale | Ronold | Roschen | Roubens | Roytanak- | Rudolph *(0.01)* | Rupesh |
| Ronalson | Ronoldo | Rosco | Roudy | Veetou | Rudolpho | Rupin |
| Ronan *(0.13)* | Ronone | Roscoe *(0.01)* | Rouen | Roytavious | Rudone | Rupinder |
| Ronan Jarome | Ronqarius | Rose | Rouge | Roytavius | Rudra | Ruriel |
| Ronard | Ronrico | Rosell | Roulstine | Royzell | Rudraksh | Rusbel |
| Roncorius | Rontae | Roselveth | Rounak | Royzire | Rudro | Rusbersonn |
| Ronda | Rontaveis | Rosendo | Rourke | Rozaire | Rudwan | Ruschut |
| Rondal | Rontavis | Rosessone | Rousend | Rozario | Rudy *(0.07)* | Rusdy |

| | | | | ~ S ~ | | | |
|---|---|---|---|---|---|---|---|
| Ruselot | Ry'neal | Ryeler | Rylin (0.01) | | Saajhe | Sabur |
| Rush (0.01) | Rya'sir | Ryeley | Rylind | S | Saajid | Sabyn |
| Rushabh | Ryaan | Ryely | Rylley | S Nangba | Saaketh | Sac've'on |
| Rushad | Ryad | Ryelynn | Ryln | S. | Saaleh | Sacari |
| Rushang | Ryaen | Ryen (0.01) | Rylon | S'horri | Saali | Sa-Cario |
| Rushar | Ryan (7.67) | Ryer | Rylun | S'mario | Saalih | Sacha (0.03) |
| Rushaun | Ryan Allen | Ryersen | Rylund | S'vante | Saalim | Sacha-Elias |
| Rushdi | Ryan David | Ryeun | Ryly | Sa Vion | Saam | Sacha-Felyx |
| Rusheek | Ryan Leander | Ryfee | Rylyn | Sa'ad | Saamar | Sacha-Gabriel |
| Rusheel | Ryan Michael | Ryhan | Rylynd | Sa'adia | Saami | Sachairi |
| Rushen | Ryan Muk Hei | Ryheem | Rylynn | Sa'daris | Saamir | Sachal |
| Rusher | Ryan Patrick | Ryheim | Rymazea | Sa'derris | Saámir | Sacha-Louis |
| Rushi | Ryan Robert | Ryhiem | Rymell | Sa'diavion | Saaren | Sachalsultan |
| Rushik | Ryan Timothy | Ryhlan | Rymir | Sa'eed | Saarim | Sachel |
| Rushil (0.01) | Ryan Tyler | Ryian | Rynaldon | Sa'fee | Saarung | Sachetan |
| Rusho | Ryand | Ryic | Ryndon | Sa'heem | Saarym | Sachh |
| Rushon | Ryandy | Ryin | Ryne (0.02) | Sa'id | Saawan | Sachial |
| Rushton | Ryan-Ernest | Ryion | Rynon | Sa'ief | Saba | Sachin (0.01) |
| Ruskin | Ryan-Jon | Ryis | Ryo | Sa'maad | Sabal | Sachit |
| Ruslan | Ryan-Mathew | Ryjan | Ryogo | Sa'mari | Sabashtain | Sachith |
| Russ | Ryan-Michael | Rykan | Ryoma | Sa'marjae | Sabashtien | Sachkeerat |
| Russail | Ryann | Rykeam | Ryon | Sa'mere | Sabashtion | Sachpreet |
| Russel (0.01) | Ryan-Pasquale | Rykel | Ryon Robert | Sa'mir | Sabastain | Sachsin |
| Russell (0.22) | Ryas | Ryken (0.01) | Ryonne | Sa'moht | Sabastean | Sackiwa |
| Russell-Diego | Ryatt | Ryker (0.12) | Ryosei | Sa'morrious | Sabastian (0.03) | Sad |
| Russhaun | Ryburn | Rykerious | Ryosuke | Sa'quan | Sabastien | Sadak |
| Russia | Ryce | Rykesh | Ryot | Sa'quon | Sabastion | Sadali |
| Russulle | Rychen | Rykevieus | Ryota | Sa'veon | Sabastyen | Sadarious |
| Rustam | Rycheous | Rykhel | Ryotaro | Sa'veyon | Sabastyn | Sadarius |
| Rusten | Ryck | Ry-Kiel | Ryoya | Sa'vion | Sabato | Saddarius- |
| Rustgen | Rycker | Rykker | Ryquez | Sa'von | Sabdiel | Amadd |
| Rustin | Rydan | Ryko | Rysaun | Sa'vyon | Sabe | Saddiq |
| Ruston | Rydarius | Rykor | Rysean | Saa | Sabel | Sadeem |
| Rusty (0.01) | Rydder | Rykurt | Ryser | Saabir | Saben | Sadeeq |
| Rustyn | Ryde | Rykwon | Ryshaad | Saad (0.02) | Saber | Sadeq |
| Rutger | Rydeesha | Rylah | Ryshaun | Saadeddine | Sabhyr | Sader |
| Ruth | Rydell | Rylahn | Ryshawn | Saadeddine | Sabi Saudith | Sadi |
| Rutker | Ryden (0.01) | Rylan (0.42) | Rysheed | Saadi | Sabian (0.01) | Sadid |
| Rutledge | Ryder (0.38) | Rylan Ladley | Ryson | Saadik | Sabien (0.01) | Sadie |
| Rutshe | Ryder-James | Ryland (0.08) | Rystrom | Saadiq (0.01) | Sabier | Sadiel |
| Ruvaen | Rydge | Rylander | Rysuln | Saadullah | Sabih | Sadik |
| Ruvim | Rye (0.01) | Rylan-James | Rysz | Saadvik | Sabin (0.01) | Sadiki |
| Ruy | Ryean | Ryle | Ryu (0.01) | Saaer | Sabino | Sadin |
| Ruyan | Ryeden | Rylee (0.09) | Ryuji | Saafir | Sabiq | Sadio |
| Ru-Zarious | Ryedrekus | Rylee-Kris | Ryuki | Saagar | Sabir (0.01) | Sadion |
| RW | Ryeheem | Rylei | Ryus | Saahas | Sabis | Sadiq |
| Rwabiza | Ryeheen | Ryleigh (0.01) | Ryvan | Saahil | Saboor | Sadir |
| Rwade | Ryein | Ryleik | Ryven | Saahir | Sabre | Sadler |
| Ry | Ryel | Rylen (0.02) | Ryver | Saaid | Sabrean | Sadok |
| Ry'darious | Ryelan | Rylend | Ryyan | Saaif | Sabree | Sadonnie |
| Ry'gil Ja'i | Ryeland | Ryler | Ryzen | Saaim | Sabri | Sadoon |
| Ry'kelus | Ryelee | Ryley (0.05) | Ryzon | Saair | Sabriel | Sador |
| Ry'n | Ryeleigh | Rylie (0.02) | Rzeznik | Saajan | Sabrina | Sadqic |

| | | | | | |
|---|---|---|---|---|---|
| Sadrac | Sahardeed | Saichandan | Saisri | Sakson | Salko | Samariel |
| Sadrian | Saharsh | Saiche | Saiszim | Saku | Sallahadin | Samario |
| Sadrio | Saharut | Said *(0.02)* | Saith | Saky Wayans | Salm | Samarion |
| Sadtroy | Sahas | Said Amirhon | Sai-Travion | Sakyo | Salmaan | Samarius |
| Sae'quan | Sahasro | Said Waris | Saiveon | Sal | Salmahn | Samarn |
| Sae'vonn | Sahat | Saida | Saivion | Sala | Salman *(0.02)* | Samarth |
| Saed | Sahdiq | Saide | Saiviyon | Salaah | Salman Kari | Samarvion |
| Saeed *(0.01)* | Sahdique | Saiden | Saivon | Salaam | Salmane | Samaryn |
| Sael | Saheed | Saidge | Saivoughn | Salaam-Rahim | Salmeem | Samatar |
| Saelor | Saheen | Saidou | Saiyir | Salaar | Salo | Samaud |
| Saelun | Sahej | Saidy | Saiyonn | Saladin | Salome | Samauri |
| Saencer | Sahel | Saied | Saiyyed | Salah *(0.01)* | Salomon *(0.01)* | Samaurii |
| Saerion | Sahi | Saief | Saizon | Salah Al Dean | Salomonie | Samay *(0.01)* |
| Saevyon | Sahib *(0.01)* | Saif *(0.01)* | Saj | Salah Edeen | Salot | Samazian |
| Safa | Sahibdeep | Saifalam | Sajad | Salahaddin | Salthel | Samba |
| Safaa | Sahibheera | Saifaldeen | Sajal | Salahadeen | Saluador | Sambath |
| Safair | Sahibjot | Saifallah | Sajan | Salahaldeen | Salud | Sambe |
| Safan | Sahibpreet | Saifan | Sajanvir | Salahaldin | Salv'adore | Sambhav |
| Safari | Sahid | Saifeldeen | Saje | Salah-Al-Din | Salvador *(0.10)* | Sameair |
| Safe El-Deen | Sahid Omri | Saige *(0.01)* | Sajed | Salahdeen | Salvador Adrian | Samear |
| Safee | Sahij | Saihaan | Sajen | Salaheddeen | Salvadore | Samedin |
| Safeer | Sahijpreet | Saihaj | Sajid | Salaheddine | Salvator | Sameem |
| Safet | Sahil *(0.04)* | Saiham | Sajin | Salahoddine | Salvatore *(0.09)* | Sameen |
| Saffat | Sahilpreet | Saihan | Sajith | Salahuddin | Salvatore-Nicolo | Sameer *(0.04)* |
| Safi | Sahin | Saihil | Sajithan | Salakiaku | Salwan | Sameet |
| Safin | Sahir | Saiid | Sajjad | Salam | Salym | Sameir |
| Safiq | Sahishnu | Saije | Sajohn | Salama | Salyn | Samel |
| Safir | Sahit | Saikou-Yaya | Sajuili | Salamah | Sam *(0.18)* | Samer *(0.01)* |
| Safiy-Allah | Sahith | Saikrishna | Sajun | Salaman | Sam Charlie | Sameré |
| Safiyy | Sahiym | Saile | Sajz | Salamon | Samaad | Samet |
| Safrazh | Sahkai | Sailor | Sakada | Salathiel | Samaajh | Sameul |
| Safwan | Sahkur | Saim | Sakai | Salazar | Samaale | Samh |
| Safwon | Sahle | Saimir | Sakara | Saleem *(0.01)* | Samad | Samhad |
| Sagal | Sahmir | Sain | Sakariye | Saleh *(0.01)* | Samadhi | Samhith |
| Sagan | Sahtu | Sainiket | Sakeam | Saleh Mahamat | Samael *(0.01)* | Sami *(0.05)* |
| Sagar | Sahvon | Saint | Sakeric | Ahamat | Samael Andy | Sami-Adam |
| Sage *(0.10)* | Sahyanh | Saint Joseph | Saket | Salehe | Samahd | Samiah |
| Sageion | Sahymear | Saintonio | Saketh | Salem *(0.01)* | Samahr | Sami-Alexander |
| Sageon | Sai *(0.01)* | Sainty | Sakhi | Salheen | Samai | Samian |
| Sager | Sai Adarsh | Saiohn | Sakhile | Salib | Samair | Samien-Ahmed |
| Saghir | Reddy | Saion | Sakhnovshy | Salic | Samaj | Samier |
| Sagi | Sai Inesh | Saipranav | Saki | Salieu | Samajai | Samihan |
| Sagon | Sai Sahvir | Saiquan | Sakia | Salif | Samajh | Samik |
| Sagun | Sai Santosh | Sair | Sakiannik | Salih | Samajhay | Sami-Karol |
| Sahaad | Varm | Sairaj | Sakib | Salim *(0.01)* | Saman | Samil |
| Sahadeo | Sai Siddarth | Sairam | Sakieh | Salimin | Samandeep | Samim |
| Sahaib | Sai Soham | Sairana | Sakik | Salim-Omar | Samantha | Samin |
| Sahaj | Sai Vignesh | Saire | Sakima | Salin | Samanyu | Samineyen |
| Sahajah | Sai Vivek | Sairek | Sakiy | Saliou | Samar *(0.01)* | Samino |
| Sahajvir | Sai'on | Saisaketh | Sako | Saliou Dioulde | Samaree | Samip |
| Sahal | Saiaditya | Saisarath | Sakoianonhawi | Salis | Samareon | Samiq |
| Sahar | Saib | Saisathvik | Sakorii | Salix | Samari *(0.01)* | Samir *(0.07)* |
| Saharath | Saibharadwaj | Saishon | Saksham | Saliym | Samarian | Samir Ahmad |

| | | | | | | |
|---|---|---|---|---|---|---|
| Samir Eesaa | Samtez | Samya | Sangeet | Santez | Sarbjit | Sathvik (0.01) |
| Samiran | Samtito | Samy-Adel | Sangkeun | Santford | Sardool | Sathya |
| Sami-Rayan | Samúa | Samyak | Sangki | Santharithan | Sardor | Satin |
| Samire | Samuael | Samyar | Sangvat | Santhonax | Sareg | Saton |
| Samisa Tukalak | Samual (0.03) | Samyon | Sani | Santhosh | Sarel | Satori |
| Samit | Samueal | Samyr | Sanidh | Santiago (0.27) | Sarfraz | Satoru |
| Samiuel | Samuel (6.56) | Samywade | Sanija | Santigo | Sargent | Satoshi |
| Samiullah | Samuel Anh- | San | Sanin | Santino (0.07) | Sargun | Satsuki |
| Samiya |   Quan | San Lazarito | Saniru | Santious | Sarib | Sattam |
| Samiyah | Samuel | San Tonyo | Sanit | Santito | Sarid | Saturday |
| Samka Amaru |   Demarcos | San'antonio | Sanitago | Santo (0.01) | Sariel | Saturnino |
| Samkavion | Samuel | San'dre | Saniy | Santoine | Sarim | Satveer |
| Samkee |   Francois | San'tana | San-J | Santon | Sarith | Satvik |
| Samley | Samuel Gresyn | Sana | Sanjai | Santonio (0.01) | Sariyah | Satwik |
| Samlih | Samuel J | Sanad | Sanjam | Santonious | Sarja | Satya |
| Sam-Luca | Samuel Jase | Sanah | Sanjan | Santoosh | Sarkar | Satyaj |
| Samm | Samuel Jr | Sanandan | Sanjay (0.02) | Santorion | Sarkis | Satyam |
| Sammael | Samuel Ka Lo | Sanat | Sanjeev | Santory | Sarlos | Satyapaul |
| Samman | Samuel | Sanaullah | Sanjey | Santos (0.04) | Sarmolue | Satyavan |
| Sammi |   Kenneth | Sanbawi Lian | Sanjh | Santosh | Sarnel | Saud |
| Sammie (0.01) | Samuel | Sanchez | Sanjin | Santoy | Saro | Saudie |
| Sammit |   Kiryakos | Sanchit | Sanjit | Santrez | Sarod | Saudo |
| Sammuael | Samuel Lucas | Sanchrez | Sanjith | Santrez Jaze | Saroeut | Saugat |
| Sammual | Samuel Richard | Sancobi | Sanjitt | Santuan | Saron | Saul (0.14) |
| Sammuel (0.01) | Samuel Robert | Sandar | Sanjiv | Santwaun | Saronne | Saular |
| Sammuell | Samuel Stern | Sandarius | Sanju | Santwon | Saronzo | Sauliam |
| Sammy (0.07) | Samuel Walter | Sandavion | Sankalp | Santy | Saroyan | Saulier |
| Sammye | Samuel William | Sandeep | Sanket | Sanveer | Sarp | Saulius |
| Sammyle | Samuel- | Sandel | Sanketh | Sany | Sarper | Sauljah |
| Sammyr |   Alexandre | Sander (0.01) | Sanmeet | Sanyii | Sarpreet | Saul-Miguel |
| Samnang | Samuel-Alfredo | Sanders | Sanmi | Sanyon | Sartaj | Saulo |
| Samod | Samuel-Angel | Sanderson | Sannad | Sanzhar | Sartajpreet | Saum |
| Samoel | Samuel-Benoit | Sandesh | Sannidh | Saoudkhan | Sarthak | Sauman |
| Samojah | Samuel-Birhanu | Sandheep | Sanniel | Saphal | Sartin | Saumya |
| Samonte | Samuele | Sandi | Sanon | Sapthadeep | Saru | Saunderson |
| Samontre | Samuel-Elise | Sandier | Sanpreet | Saqib | Sarugan | Sauntez |
| Samora | Samuel-James | Sandile | Sanquez | Saqohn | Saruthan | Saurabh |
| Samory | Samuel-Josue | Sandilya | Sanquraius | Saquan | Sarvesh | Saurav |
| Sampsen | Samuell | Sandler | Sanshray | Saquarious | Sarvin | Saurin |
| Sampson (0.01) | Samuelle | Sandlin | Sant | Saquon | Sarzin | Saurya |
| Samraj | Samuellé | Sandon | Sant'erio | Saquone | Sasa | Sauvernson |
| Samrath | Samuelson | Sandor | Santa | Sara | Sasaglino | Sava |
| Samria | Samuel-William | Sandra | Santale | Saraansh | Sascha (0.01) | Savaghna |
| Samrit | Samuil | Sandriano | Santana (0.03) | Sarac | Sasha (0.03) | Savahya |
| Samron | Samul | Sandro (0.01) | Santanna | Sarah | Sashank | Savaian |
| Samrudh | Samule | Sandtana | Santario | Sarah-Maude | Sasheen | Savalas |
| Samsher | Samur | Sandy (0.01) | Santarione | Sarai | Sashy | Savan |
| Samson (0.05) | Samurai | Sandy-Cruz | Santawan | Saraj | Sasie | Savanah |
| Samson Scott | Samvijet | Saned | Santaze | Saran | Sasir | Savanh |
| Samson- | Samwillie | Sanehdeep | Sante | Sarang | Satchel (0.01) | Savanna |
|   Alexander | Samwillie Isa | Sanford | Santel | Saranz | Satchell | Savannah |
| Samsouly | Samy (0.02) | Sang (0.01) | Santell | Saraquiel | Sateki | Savar |
| Samsudeen | Samy Alexandre | Sangat | Santerious | Saraswat | Sathaya | Savarí |

| | | | | | | |
|---|---|---|---|---|---|---|
| Savarien | Saxvi | Schawn | Se'viyon | Seantel | Sedgerick | Sekyé |
| Savas | Say'vion | Schaya | Se'von | Seantell | Sedin | Selah |
| Savatei | Say'von | Schayle | Seaandre | Seantez | Sedny | Selajah |
| Savaughn | Sayaad | Scheder | Seabastien | Seanute | Sedric | Selasie |
| Saveaun | Sayaan | Scheffe-Dirac | Seabrook | Seany | Sédric | Selasse |
| Savek | Sayaér | Scheinerder | Sead | Seath | Sedrick (0.01) | Selassie |
| Savell | Sayah | Schelby-Dorjean | Seadon | Seaton | Sedriq | Selby |
| Savelli | Sayan | Jr | Seagar | Seattle | Sedryone | Seldin |
| Savens | Sayaun | Schey | Seager | Seaven | Sedtavian | Seldion |
| Saveon (0.01) | Saybeoh | Schmaiahn | Seals | Seay | Sedtravian | Seldon |
| Saverino | Saybien | Schmari | Sealtiel | Seban | See Woo | Seleem |
| Saverio | Saybion | Schmaya | Seamus (0.09) | Sebashtian | Seedee | Selemon |
| Savhan | Sayd | Schneider | Seán | Sebastain | Seegwin | Selena |
| Savian | Sayed | Schneur | Sean (2.90) | Sebasthian | Seena | Selenne |
| Savian Eman | Sayeed | Schnieder | Sean Aaron | Sebastia | Seerah | Selim |
| Savic | Sayer | Schnyder | Sean Anthony | Sebastiaan | Seeros | Selkey |
| Savich | Sayfitdin | Scholar | Sean Cedrick | Sebastian (2.98) | Sef | Sellars |
| Savien | Sayge | Schon | Sean Dale | Sebastian | Sefat | Sellers |
| Savier (0.01) | Sayheem | Schrodrik | Sean Derick | Enrique | Sefin | Sellorm |
| Saviere | Sayidel | Schumacher | Sean Dosha | Sebastian Minh | Sefoni | Selman |
| Savin | Sayid-Omar | Schuylar | Sean Evan | Sebastian- | Segan | Selmin |
| Savine | Sayiid | Schuyler (0.01) | Sean Isaiah | Andr'eas | Segend | Selmir |
| Savino | Sayion'tez | Schyer | Sean Kyle | Sebastian- | Seger | Selso |
| Savio | Sayla | Schylar | Sean Luc | Anthony | Segundo | Selton |
| Savion (0.07) | Saylee | Schyler | Sean Paul | Sebastian-Izaak | Sehaj (0.01) | Selvaganesh |
| Savione | Sayler | Scintone | Sean Robert | Sebastiann | Sehajdeep | Selvin (0.01) |
| Savionne | Saylon | Sckylar | Sean'darius | Sebastiano | Sehajpal | Selwanes |
| Savior | Saylor (0.01) | Scliven | Sean'trez | Sebastian-Paul | Sehan | Selwyn |
| Saviour | Saylur | Scobe | Sean-Allen | Sebastiao | Sehbaz | Sem |
| Savir | Saymer | Scooter | Sean-Anthony | Sébastien (0.01) | Sehtaj | Semahj |
| Savit | Sayr | Scorpio | Seanard | Sebastien (0.11) | Sei'quan | Semai |
| Savitoj | Sayra | Scot (0.01) | Sean-Ayite | Sebastien- | Seid | Semáj |
| Saviyon | Sayre | Scotch | Sean-Carson | Olivier | Seif | Semaj (0.06) |
| Savon (0.01) | Sayveon | Scotland | Sean-Charles | Sebastin | Seifried | Semaj' |
| Savon'lavell | Sayvien | Scott (0.52) | Sean-Christian | Sebastion (0.01) | Seiji | Semaj'a |
| Savoné | Sayvion | Scott'tariou | Sean-Curtis | Sebastyan | Seikou | Semaja |
| Savonn | Sayviyun | Scott-David | Seandelle | Sebastyen | Sein | Semajá |
| Savonte | Sayvon | Scottie (0.01) | Seandre | Sebatien | Seina | Semajae |
| Savontre | Sayyar | Scottland | Sean-Keley | Sebbastian | Seion | Semajai |
| Savorn | Sbonnie | Scottreon | Sean-Kerry | Sebelah | Seith | Semaj-Auku |
| Savoy | Scadrick | Scotty (0.01) | Sean-Michae | Seber | Seiya | Semaje |
| Savreion | Scarlett | Scout (0.01) | Sean-Michael | Seberiano | Sejad | Semajj |
| Savren-Nate | Scemore | Scoye | Seanmichael | Sebron | Sejfudin | Semazhay |
| Savvon | Schadliegh | Scuyler | Sean-Micheal | Sebstian | Sejiero | Sem-Elie |
| Savyen | Schadrac | Scy | Seann | Seby | Sejonnoor | Semeon |
| Savyor | Schae | Scyler | Sean-Nathan | Sechee | Sejy | Semih |
| Sawal | Schaefer | Scythe | Seanon | Sechourveon | Sekai | Semih Mert |
| Sawyar | Schaeffer | Se | Sean-Patrick | Sedarien | Sekan | Semion |
| Sawyer (0.39) | Schamir | Se'amus | Seanpatrick | Seddrick | Sekem | Semiona |
| Sawyrr | Schanson | Se'ma'j | Sean-Paul | Sedeke | Sekie | Semione |
| Saxe | Schantell | Se'maj | Seanpaul | Sedem | Sekodah | Semir |
| Saxon (0.01) | Schaune | Se'monte | Seantario | Sederic | Sekou (0.02) | Semon |
| Saxton | Schauntell | Se'quaden | Seantavius | Sederick | Seku | Semyel |

| | | | | | | |
|---|---|---|---|---|---|---|
| Sen'cere | Seraj | Seth Angelo | Seyla | Shachor | Shafiq | Shai *(0.01)* |
| Sena | Serandon | Seth Gabriel | Seylan | Shacoby | Shafter | Shai'ron |
| Senai | Seraph | Seth Lastat | Seyler | Shacore | Shagai | Shaia |
| Senan | Seraphim | Sethalius | Seylon | Shacorey | Shaggy | Shaian |
| Senard | Serapio | Sethan | Seynina Issa | Shacorian | Shagiree | Shaiannie |
| Senate | Serbando | Sethaniel | Seyoung | Shacory | Shah | Shaid |
| Sencedrick | Serbrayden | Sethaun | Seyram | Shad *(0.01)* | Shah'nir | Shaid Devon |
| Sencere | Sercey | Sethe | Seyvon | Shadan | Shahaad | Shaidale |
| Sendley | Seren | Sethen | Seyyed | Shadd | Shahaan | Shaide |
| Sendrick | Serena | Sethikounvong | Sh'meck | Shaddai | Shahab | Shaiden |
| Seneca *(0.01)* | Serge | Seti | Sh'rod | Shaddix | Shahad | Shaiderius |
| Senecca | Serge-Anthony | Seton | Sha Diamond | Shaddy | Shahaid | Shaiem |
| Sened | Sergei | Seumas | Sha Rone | Shade *(0.01)* | Shahan | Shaighn |
| Sengchan | Sergeion | Seunda | Sha'an | Shaden *(0.01)* | Shahani | Shaiheem |
| Senglee | Sergej | Seungwon | Sha'darrian | Shadi | Shaharyar | Shaijmon |
| Sengsanouck | Sergey | Seungwoo | Sha'drach | Shadir | Shahdad | Shaikeem |
| Sengsavang | Sergi | Seuz | Sha'fiq | Shadley | Shahe'de | Shaikh |
| Seni | Serginio | Sevag | Sha'heym | Shadman | Shaheam | Shailen |
| Senia | Sergio *(0.27)* | Sevan | Sha'keim | Shadon | Shahed | Shailin |
| Senkeo | Sergio Fabian | Sevarrian | Sha'keyo | Shadow | Shahee | Shaim |
| Senley | Sergy | Sevastián *(0.01)* | Sha'mall | Shadra | Sha-Heed | Shain |
| Senmaru | Serhat | Seve | Sha'mar | Shadrach *(0.01)* | Shaheed | Shainader |
| Senna | Serigne | Sevee | Sha'mari | Shadrack | Shaheem *(0.01)* | Shaine *(0.01)* |
| Sennay | Serigne Saliou | Seveion | Sha'marioun | Shadrak | Shaheen | Shain-Michael |
| Sennet | Serious | Seven *(0.01)* | Sha'marr | Shadream | Shaheene | Shaion |
| Sennett | Seriyon | Seven Alexander | Sha'marrion | Shadrick | Shaheer | Shaip |
| Senon | Serj | Severe | Sha'mere | Shady | Shaheerul | Shaiquese |
| Sentel | Serjio | Severian | Sha'mond | Shadyn | Shaheim | Shaiyaz |
| Senthooran | Serkan | Severiano | Sha'nya | Shae *(0.02)* | Shahen | Shajir |
| Sentrel | Serkewt | Severin | Sha'quan | Shaeden | Shaheryar | Shajuan |
| Sentrell | Sermad | Severino | Sha'quavius | Shaedon | Shahid | Shaka |
| Seo | Seron | Severo | John | Shaeed | Shahida | Shakai |
| Seoirse | Serquince | Severt | Sha'quesst | Shaeef | Shahide | Shakarri |
| Seon | Serrel | Seveyon | Sha'ray | Shaefer | Shahidul | Shakaryan |
| Seong | Serrell | Sevier | Sha'ron | Shaeffer | Shahiem | Shakeam |
| Seoyeon | Serres | Seville | Sha'veh | Shael | Shahiim | Shakeel |
| Sepehr | Servacio | Sevin | Sha'vion | Shaelen | Shahil | Shakeem |
| Seph | Servando *(0.01)* | Sevion | Sha'von | Shaelyn | Shahim | Shakei |
| Sephan | Servante | Seviyon | Sha'yne | Shaemar | Shahin | Shakeith |
| Sephire | Servario | Sev-Louie | Sha'zon | Shaemus | Shahir | Shakeveous |
| Sephiroth | Servin Gilmar | Sevon | Shaad | Shaen | Shahmarrion | Shakhai |
| Sepp | Seryantes | Sevont | Shaafi-Ullah | Shaethyn | Shahmeer | Shakhandre |
| Septimus | Sesamwavatan | Sevren | Shaakir | Shafay | Shahmir | Shakhari |
|Seption | Sesar | Sevrin | Shaan *(0.02)* | Shafayet | Shaho | Shaki |
| Sequouia | Sesedrick | Sevven | Shaanpreet | Shafee | Shahrear | Shakia |
| Sequan | Seshun | Sevy | Shaanvir | Shafeeq | Shahron | Shakib |
| Sequoia | Sesilio | Sevyn | Shaayan | Shafek | Shahroze | Shakiih |
| Sequoya | Sesshu | Sewar | Shaban | Shafer | Shahrukh | Shakil |
| Sequoyah | Sessions | Sewell | Shabbir | Shaffa | Shahrum | Shakim |
| Ser'maruies | Setep | Seydina | Shabnoor | Shafi | Shahryar | Shakir *(0.01)* |
| Serafeim | Seterin | Seydina Issa | Shaborne | Shafici | Shahvaiz | Shakked |
| Serafin | Seth *(2.05)* | Seyed | Shabse | Shafick | Shahzad | Shakoor |
| Serafin Wilmer | Seth Andrew | Seyhan | Shace | Shafik | Shahzan | Shakuar |

| | | | | | | |
|---|---|---|---|---|---|---|
| Shakur (0.01) | Shamaur | Shane-Anthony | Sharef | Shaunak | Shawnathan | Shaylan |
| Shakurey | Shamaury | Shane-Jose | Shareif | Shaunavon | Shawn-Davens | Shaylar |
| Shakye | Shambhava | Shane-Michael | Shareyph | Shaundez | Shawndre | Shaylen |
| Shakyran | Shameek | Shanen | Sharick | Shaundrick | Shawndy | Shayler |
| Shakyre | Shamel (0.01) | Shanga-Ali | Sharief | Shaune | Shawne | Shaylon |
| Shalamar | Shamel Malik | Shaniel | Shariek | Shaunecy | Shawnee | Shayman |
| Shale | Shamell | Shanjae | Sharif (0.01) | Shaun-Elie | Shawn-Ian | Shaymar |
| Shalee | Shamere | Shankar | Shariff | Shaunessy | Shawn-Jamal | Shaymus |
| Shaleese | Shamhan | Shanker | Shariq | Shaunff | Shawn-Keven | Shayn |
| Shalen | Shaminder | Shanlee | Sharique | Shaunisaac | Shawn-Lee | Shayndrick |
| Shaler | Shamir (0.01) | Shan-Malek | Sharjeel | Shaunke | Shawn-Mathioux | Shayne (0.06) |
| Shalief | Shamirr | Shann | Sharkey | Shaunkis | Shawn-Mederick | Shayne Elias |
| Shalik | Shamit | Shannen | Sharl | Shaun-Micha | Shawn-Michae | Shaynn |
| Shalim | Shammah | Shannon (0.06) | Sharlamijahi | Shaunn | Shawnmoe | Shayth |
| Shalin | Shammaine | Shanoine | Sharlton | Shaun-Paul | Shawnn | Shayton |
| Shaliq | Shammar | Shanon | Sharmaarke | Shaunrell | Shawn-Samuel | Shayvon |
| Shalligy | Shammond | Shan-Paul | Sharmake | Shaunrik | Shawnta | Shaz |
| Shalom (0.01) | Shammyr | Shanson | Sharmar | Shauntavious | Shawntae | Shazab |
| Shalon | Shamod | Shant | Sharmarke | Shauntavius | Shawntas | Shazaria |
| Shalor | Shamon | Shante | Shar-Marque | Shaunterrion | Shawnte | Shazavion |
| Shalym | Shamond | Shanti | Sharme | Shauntrell | Shawnterrio | Shazeem |
| Shama'tae | Sha-Mont | Shantwon | Sharmond | Shaury | Shawnterris | Shazib |
| Shamaad | Shamont | Shanty | Sharod (0.01) | Shaurya | Shawntey | Shazihen |
| Shamad | Shamonte | Shanxiang | Sharon | Shauwn | Shawntez | Shazil |
| Shamadi | Shamore | Shanyu | Sharone | Shavar | Shawnton | Shazmil |
| Shamadre | Shamoreion | Shao | Sharontaé | Shavaree | Shawntre | Shazon |
| Shama-Eli | Shamori | Shao-An | Sharray | Shavarion | Shawntrell | She'fon |
| Shamah | Shamoron | Shaoyang | Sharrill | Shavell | Shawntrez | Shea (0.06) |
| Shamahil Sani | Shamoure | Shappa | Sharrod | Shavez | Shawntryl | Shea-Anthony |
| Shamaine | Shamrock | Shaqier | Shartez | Shavine | Shawntu | Sheadon |
| Sha-Maire | Shams | Shaqille | Sharuyan | Shavoka | Shawn-Vinh | Sheadyn |
| Shamal | Shams Habib | Shaqir | Sharva | Shavokie | Shawn-William | Sheamus |
| Shamall | Shamseddine | Shaquan | Sharvar | Shavon | Shawon | Shean |
| Shaman | Shamun | Shaquel | Sharvil | Shavonn | Shawrick | Shearod |
| Shamanique | Shamuri | Shaquez | Sharyan | Shaw (0.01) | Shawron | Shebora |
| Shamar (0.07) | Shamus (0.02) | Shaquezius | Shash | Shawan | Shaw-Tamien | Shedk'l |
| Shamard | Shamya Alexanderia | Shaquil | Shashank | Shawar | Shawyan Alonzo | Shedley |
| Shamare Jeremiah | Shamyarion | Shaquill | Shashank Varma | Shawatis | Shay (0.02) | Shedric |
| Shamarean | Shan (0.01) | Shaquille | Shashankdhar | Shawaun | Shay'lee | Shedrick |
| Shamaree | Shanan | Shaquir | Shashidhar | Shawayne | Shaya (0.01) | Sheehan |
| Shamaren | Shanard | Shaquon | Shashwat | Shawen | Shayaan | Sheel |
| Shamarge | Shanay-Abbas | Shaquwaun | Shaterrion | Shawka | Shayan (0.01) | Sheen |
| Shamari | Shanaye | Sharad | Shathey | Shawkat | Shayd | Sheffield |
| Shamarion (0.01) | Shance | Sharan | Shaud | Shawn (0.89) | Shaydan | Shefton |
| Shamarious | Shandeep | Sharanyan | Shaudi | Shawn Darren | Shayde | Sheham |
| Shamarius | Shandell | Sharar | Shaughn | Shawn Earl | Shaydem | Shehzaad |
| Shamark | Shandez | Sharard | Shaukeer | Shawn Frank | Shayden (0.01) | Sheikh |
| Shamarkis | Shandon (0.01) | Sharath | Shaul | Shawn Jude | Shaydin | Sheil |
| Shamarlin | Shandro | Sharbel | Shaulei | Shawn Lee | Shaydon | Sheimys |
| Shamarr | Shandy | Shardly | Shaumik | Shawn Mathieu | Shaye | Sheireef |
| Shamauhn | Shane (0.84) | Shardyn | Shaun (0.25) | Shawn Nuen | Shayen | Shekevian |
| | Shane Micheal | Shareef (0.01) | Shaun Cor | Shawn William | | Shelby (0.02) |
| | | Shareek | | Shawnanthony | | Shelden (0.01) |

| | | | | | | |
|---|---|---|---|---|---|---|
| Shelden-Elijah | Sherif | Shiloh (0.02) | Shivashish | Shonme | Shrod | Shwaas |
| Sheldens | Sheriff | Shilohael | Shiven | Shon-Michael | Shrode | Shy |
| Sheldin | Sherjuan | Shilon | Shivniel | Shonn | Shrone | Shy'dir |
| Sheldon (0.10) | Sherlyn | Shimaar | Shivpal | Shonon | Shrrayash | Shy'dravious |
| Sheldon | Sherman (0.02) | Shimari | Shivraj | Shonriquez | Shr-Shiang | Shy'heem |
| Deondrae | Shermann | Shimba | Shiwayne | Shonté | Shrung | Shy'kail |
| Sheldon-Bradley | Shermar | Shi-Mer | Shiyaazh | Shontez | Shu'aib | Shy'kem |
| Sheldon-Robert | Shermarco | Shimmer | Shiyon | Shontre'vious | Shua | Shy'on |
| Mikun | Shermon | Shimon (0.04) | Shizuma | Shooter | Shuab | Shy'quan |
| Sheldrek | Shermond | Shimon-Amram | Shjon | Shooter Brian | Shuai | Shyaan |
| Sheldyn | Shernod | Menache | Shloime (0.01) | Shota | Shuayb | Shyam (0.01) |
| Shell | Sherod | Shimon-Reuven | Shloimy | Shou | Shubam | Shyanne |
| Shellie | Sheron | Shimshon | Shlok | Shoumik | Shubansai | Shybon |
| Shelly | Sherord | Shimyael | Shloma (0.01) | Shoun | Shubh | Shyden-Kenai |
| Shelong | Sherrard | Shin | Shlome (0.01) | Shoup | Shubham | Shye |
| Shelten | Sherraton | Shinaayo | Shlomie | Shoutaro | Shubhan | Shyeem |
| Shelton (0.02) | Sherrill | Shine | Shlomo (0.05) | Shovair | Shubisan | Shyeme |
| Sheltonray | Sherrod | Shingen | Shlomo Chaim | Shovan | Shubkaran | Shyenne |
| Shelven | Sherron | Shinin | Shmar | Shovawn | Shubrey | Shyh'eim |
| Shelvin | Shervey | Shinji | Shmarr | Showes | Shucayb | Shyhaire |
| Shem | Shervin | Shinkai | Shmaya | Shragie | Shuermain | Shyheed |
| Shemaar | Sherwin | Shinta | Shmiel (0.01) | Shragy | Shuford | Shyheem (0.01) |
| Shemaiah | Sherwood | Shintaro | Shmon | Shravan | Shujuan | Shy-Heer |
| Shemar (0.02) | Sherwyn | Shion | Shmuel (0.04) | Shrayassai | Shukar | Shyheim (0.01) |
| Shemare | Sheryar | Shipton | Shmy | Shreemuth | Shukri | Shyhem |
| Shemarion | Shevach | Shiquan | Shneider | Shreesh | Shulem (0.01) | Shyhemi |
| Shemarri | Shevaun | Shiraud | Shneur | Shreshth | Shullem | Shyhiem |
| Shemaury | Sheyk Mohadis | Shiraz | Shniedel | Shrey (0.01) | Shuma | Shykevious |
| Shemaya-Meir | Sheyne | Shirdon | Sho | Shreyaan | Shumaris | Shykwon |
| Shemiah | Shi Quon | Shiren | Sho'hawnie | Shreyak | Shumuel | Shylan |
| Shemqula | Shi Yan | Shirer | Sho'mar | Shreyan | Shun | Shylen |
| Shems | Shi'mire | Shirish | Sho'ndell | Shreyank | Shunard | Shyler |
| Shemssoudine | Shi'on | Shiro | Shoaib | Shreyans | Shundarius | Shylik |
| Shemuel | Shi'quel | Shirone | Shoanari | Shreyas (0.01) | Shunkeith | Shymarion |
| Shenard | Shi'res | Shirron | Shobhit | Shreyash | Shunkhris | Shymeir |
| Sheng | Shia (0.01) | Shiryu | Shoby | Shreyes | Shunki | Shymere |
| Shengru | Shiah | Shishir | Shofan | Shreyus | Shunkichi | Shymien |
| Shentonie | Shiair | Shisui | Shogun | Shri | Shunn | Shymik |
| Shep | Shiaman | Shitab | Shoham | Shri Keshav | Shunquarius | Shymir |
| Shepard (0.01) | Shianti | Shitij | Shohei | Shrihari | Shunsuke | Shymire |
| Shephard | Shib | Shiv (0.01) | Shohn | Shrihash | Shuntaro | Shyne (0.01) |
| Shepherd (0.01) | Shicobeion | Shiva | Shohum | Shrikar | Shuntavian | Shy-Qua |
| Sheppard | Shie | Shiva Shankar | Sholom (0.01) | Shriman | Shuntavious | Shyquail |
| Shepperd | Shiegh | Shivaan | Shoma | Shriniket | Shuntez | Shyquon |
| Sher | Shietu | Shivaji | Shomar | Shripad | Shunti | Shyree |
| Sheradin | Shifan | Shivam (0.01) | Shomari (0.01) | Shriraam | Shurek | Shyvonte |
| Sherard | Shigeru | Shivan | Shomik | Shrish | Shurjo | Shyzear |
| Sheraz | Shihab | Shivane | Shon (0.01) | Shrisuvas | Shurmack | Si |
| Sherby | Shiheem | Shivang | Shonathan | Shritan | Shushant | Si Ming |
| Sherchue | Shikeem | Shivank | Shondell | Shrivardhan | Shusuke | Si'ayr |
| Sherebiah | Shikhar | Shivanker | Shondre | Shrivarshan | Shuta | Si'ed |
| Shereif | Shikuan Achille | Shivansh | Shondré | Shrivats | Shuvan | Si'haad |
| Sheridan | Shilo | Shivashankar | Shondrick | Shrivishnu | Shvant | Si'mor |

| | | | | | |
|---|---|---|---|---|---|
| Si'nai | Sienqué | Simcha (0.02) | Singh | Sir'que | Sirvonte | Skyler (0.43) |
| Si'on | Sieon | Sime | Singing Bird | Sir'wise | Sir-Wayne | Skylerdale |
| Si'quan | Siere | Simei | Sinica | Siradio | Sisomphone | Skylier |
| Sia'dale | Siew | Simeon (0.07) | Sinjin | Sirageddine | Sisto | Skylin |
| Siaam | Sifan | Simeone | Sinjon | Siraj | Sitca | Skylir |
| Siafa | Sig | Simeonie | Sino | Siraje | Sithyvong | Skyllar |
| Siah | Sigid | Simere | Sinon | Sirangelliobolique | Sitka | Skyln |
| Siaka | Sigifredo | Simion | Sin-Que | Sirapat | Siuol | Skylor (0.01) |
| Sialeak | Sigmund | Simione | Sinsear | Sirasak | Siuqram | Skylur |
| Siamo | Sigo | Simire | Sinseer | Sirbenjamin | Siva | Skylure |
| Siangay | Sigurd | Simitrio | Sinsere | Sircharles | Sivad | Skyrece |
| Siavosh | Sigurdur | Simmai | Sinsier | Sirchoice | Sivan | Skyshun |
| Sibi | Sigvald | Simmon | Sintel | Sircory | Sivaraman | Skytus |
| Sibmah | Siifan | Simohamed | Sintonyo | Sircrease | Siven | Skyveon |
| Sibo | Siitupe | Simon (0.72) | Sin-Tresz | Sir-Donald | Sivon | Skyy |
| Sice | Sikai | Simon Pier | Sinuhe | Sire | Siwon | Skyylor |
| Sid | Sikaida | Simon Pierre | Sinyorice | Sirealus | Siwoo | Slade (0.03) |
| Sid Dare | Sikandar | Simon Yi Peng | Siomar | Sireco Sir- | Siwr | Slade Lee |
| Sid'jaden | Sikander | Simon-Alexis | Sion | Marvin | Sixto | Sladen |
| Siddanth | Silace | Simone | Sione | Sirelijah | Siyal | Slader |
| Siddardh | Silas (0.24) | Simon-Gabriel | Siosaia | Sirell | Siyan | Slaid |
| Siddarth (0.01) | Silas Francis | Simonis | Siovany | Sirfrankie | Siymon | Slaiden |
| Siddesh | Silas Jr | Simon-Louis | Sipeng | Sirharrison | Sizhe | Slaman |
| Siddh | Silas Timot | Simon-Olivier | Sipuhsis | Siris | Sizwe | Slate |
| Siddhaarth | Silasi | (0.01) | Sir (0.01) | Sirith | Sjon | Slaten |
| Siddhant | Silas-Xavier | Simon-Pier | Sir Anthoney | Sirius | Sjors | Slater (0.02) |
| Siddhanth | Silen | Simon-Pierre | Sir Anthony | Sirivory | Skai | Slatts |
| Siddhardh | Siler | Simon-Raphael | Sir Charles | Sirjames | Skanda | Slaven |
| Siddharth (0.02) | Silesimeh | Simon-Sayam | Sir Chester | Sirkayden | Skander | Slayde |
| Siddhartha | Sileth | Simon-Yehuda | Sir David | Sir-Kyran | Skeet | Slayden |
| Siddiq | Silève | Simran | Sir Deljuan | Sirleaf | Ski'lr | Slayten |
| Siddique | Silfendz | Simranjot | Sir Derrick | Sirmarion | Skieler | Slayter |
| Sidhant | Silias | Simrat | Sir Donald | Sir-Michael | Skilar | Slayton |
| Sidhanth | Silicia | Simrit | Sir Glenn | Sirmod | Skiler | Sleeman |
| Sidhart | Silije | Simuel | Sir Jacob | Sirnatas | Skilur | Sleven |
| Sidharth | Silipai | Sin Cere | Sir James | Sirnevin | Skipper | Slevensky |
| Sidhartha | Silis | Sin'cere | Sir Jayden | Sirod | Skirell | Slewis |
| Sidharth-Kabier | Silkiack | Sina | Sir Je'yson | Siron | Sklyer | Slim |
| Sidhveer | Siloh | Sinai | Sir Julian | Sirquan | Skuoe-Marcet | Sloan (0.01) |
| Sidi | Silus | Sinaj | Sir Khaliq | Sirqwon | Sky (0.02) | Slone |
| Sidiar | Silvan | Sinan | Sir Lexzander | Sirr | Sky Alexand | Sly |
| Sidiki | Silvano | Sinbad | Sir Matthew | Sirr Thomas | Sky Alexander | Slyler |
| Sidiq | Silvanus | Sincear | Sir Pariss | Sirrece | Sky Blu | Slyvester |
| Sidiri | Silvestre | Sinceare | Sir Robert | Sirreese | Skye (0.01) | Smaran |
| Sidiyq | Silvestre Alex | Sincer | Sir Semaj | Sirrell | Skyelar | Smarion |
| Sidney (0.07) | Silveyon | Sinceré | Sir Tanaz | Sirrico | Skyeler | Smell Of Rain |
| Sidney Lance | Silviano | Sincere (0.10) | Sir Vell | Sirron | Skye-Michael | Smerly |
| Sidorian | Silvinsson | Sincere | Sir Vincent | Sirrulean | Skylan | Smiley |
| Sidquan | Silvio (0.01) | Alimayu | Sir Walter | Sirrye | Skyland | Smit |
| Siegfried | Sim | Sinciere | Sir William | Sirtan | Skylar (0.18) | Smith (0.01) |
| Siejohn | Simar | Sincire | Sir. Malachi | Sirtivan | Skylarr | Smyan |
| Siem | Simardeep | Sinclair | Sir'charles | Sirtristen | Skylee | Snaider |
| Siemien | Simba | Sindid | Sir'mhad | Sirus | Skylen | Sneferu |

| | | | | | | |
|---|---|---|---|---|---|---|
| Sneh | Solaimon | Sontino | Soul | Spur | Sruly | Stasio |
| Sneider | Solam | Sontonio | Soulayman | Spurgeon | St | Staten |
| Snev | Solan | Sontos | Soulemane | Spyridon | St John | States |
| Sneyder | Soldier | Sonvail | Souleyman | Squire | Sta'quan | Stathis |
| Snoweagle | Sole | Sony | Souleymane | Srael | Sta'shawn | Statik |
| Snyder | Soleil | Sooner | Souljah | Sravan | Stabien | Statler |
| Soa | Solim | Soorya | Souljur | Sravan Krishna | Stacee | Staton |
| Soane | Solis | Sopanphgna | Soulmontee | Sredrick | Stacey *(0.01)* | Statten |
| Soarin | Solis Lumen | Sopaul | Soumil | Sreeanilaj | Stacy *(0.01)* | Staven |
| Sobaan-Ahmed | Soljah | Sopeaktrar | Soumyadeep | Sreeauditya | Staevon | Stavion |
| Soban | Sollance | Sopeap | Souradeep | Sreekar | Stafford | Stavon |
| Sobhan | Soloman *(0.01)* | Sopeaq | Souran | Sreemahesh | Staige | Stavros *(0.01)* |
| Sobheet | Solomin | Sopheak | Sourav | Sreenidhi | Stajan | Stavros Stefano |
| Sobhi | Solomon *(0.19)* | Sopher | Sourena | Sreeraag | Stakaiyoz | Steachy |
| Sobit | Solomona | Sophia | Sourish | Sreesh | Staley | Steaddmenn |
| Sobtain | Solon | Sophie | Sourisong | Sreeteja | Stalin | Steade |
| Sochima J | Solson | Sophoklis | Souriyane | Sreevamsee | Staling | Steadval |
| Socorro | Solstice | Sopuluchi | Sovann | Sreyas | Stallon | Steafan |
| Socrates | Solttan | Sora | Soveone | Sri | Stamatios | Steaven |
| Sodd | Soluna | Soran | Sovereign | Sri Harsha | Stamatis | Steben |
| Soel | Solund | Sorel | Soverson | Sri Ragav | Stan | Stecardo |
| Sofarro | Solyais | Sóren | Sovine | Sri Sai | Stan Stefan | Stedman |
| Sofia | Soma | Soren *(0.07)* | Sovitou | Sri Sruthi | Stan'juan | Steel |
| Sofian | Somak | Sorena | Sovon | Sri Vaibhav | Standard | Steele *(0.01)* |
| Sofiane | Somar | Soreyn | Sovonn | Sricharan | Standing | Steeler |
| Sofonias | Somenosuke | Soriba | Sowile | Sridhar | Standley | Steeve |
| Sohaan | Somil | Sorin | Sowmik | Srihan | Stanford *(0.01)* | Steeve-Eric |
| Sohaib | Somjit | Soriyan | Sowmith | Sriharsha | Stanford- | Steeve-Mattheu |
| Sohail | Sommee | Sorjen | Soyeb | Srihaun | Lamont | Steeven *(0.01)* |
| Soham *(0.01)* | Sompeth | Sorley | Spade | Srihith | Stani-Silas | Steevens |
| Sohan *(0.01)* | Somrett | Sornram | Spandan | Srijan | Stanislas | Stefahn |
| Sohayb | Somtochukwu | Soroiu | Sparsh | Srikar *(0.01)* | Stanislaus | Stefan *(0.08)* |
| Sohayeb | Son | Soromtochi | Spartacus | Srikiran | Stanislav | Stefane |
| Soheib | Sonaa | Soroosh | Spartico | Srikrishna | Stanislaw | Stefano *(0.03)* |
| Soheil N'ir | Sondy | Sorrel | Spawntainous | Srikumar | Stanlee | Stefano-Josef |
| Sohil | Soneal | Sorren | Spear | Srilalith | Stanley *(0.14)* | Stefanos |
| Sohl | Sonel | Sory | Spears | Sriman | Stanley Deyonte | Stefaun |
| Sohum | Song | Soryu | Speed | Srinandan | Jeremiah | Stefen |
| Soi | Song Qian Felix | Sosa | Spence *(0.01)* | Sriniketh | Stanley-Pete | Steffan |
| Sojai | Songtsen | Sosene | Spencer *(0.92)* | Srinivas | Stanly | Steffano |
| Sokai | Sonic | Sosiah | Spencer Joseph | Sriraghav | Stantavis | Steffen *(0.01)* |
| Soken | Sonimichael | Sosimo | Spener | Sriram | Stanten | Steffon |
| Sokhaine | Sonith | Sosman | Spenser *(0.01)* | Sriramamurty | Stanton | Steffone |
| Sokobi | Sonkei | Sosuke | Sphere | Srisankalp | Stanway | Steffyn |
| Sokol | Son-Nam | Sotero | Spicer | Srish | Stargell | Stefhon |
| Sokratis | Sonney | Sotheara | Spider | Srishyam | Starley | Stefon *(0.01)* |
| Soksavoeun | Sonni | Sothearak | Spincer | Sriteja | Starlin | Stefontine |
| Sol *(0.01)* | Sonnie | Sotirios | Spirit | Srithan | Starling | Steforn |
| Sola | Sonny *(0.05)* | Sotonye | Spiro | Srithvik | Starlit | Stefphon |
| Solabomi Gavril | Sonny Boy | Soudyce | Spiros | Srivant | Starney | Stehcey |
| Oluwasanmi If | Sonok | Soufiane | Spivey | Srivathsava | Starr | Stein |
| Solace | Sonterrius | Souhail | Sport | Srivats | Starwyn | Stekarlos |
| Solaiman | Sontin | Souheil | Spruce | Srivatsan | Stasha | Stelio |

| | | | | | | |
|---|---|---|---|---|---|---|
| Stelios | Steve Junior | Strader | Suchir | Sukhmandeep | Sundance | Sutter |
| Stellan | Steve'terri | Straet | Suchit | Sukhmane | Sunday | Sutton (0.02) |
| Stellar | Steven (2.36) | Strahinja | Sudais | Sukhmanpreet | Sundeep | Suttree |
| Stellen | Steven Adam | Stran | Sudan | Sukhmeet | Sundiata | Sutv |
| Stelo | Steven Johnell | Strandreley | Sudarsan | Sukhminder | Sundrik | Suvaaghesh |
| Stelten | Steven Kelyan | Stranton | Sudarshan | Sukhnoor | Sundy | Suvaan |
| Sten | Steve-Nicolas | Stratford | Sudays | Sukhpal | Sunee | Suvad |
| Stenddy Hewitt | Steven-Lee | Straton | Sudharshan | Sukhpreet | Suneet | Suvan |
| Stenley | Steven-Orlando | Stratten | Sudhir | Sukhraj (0.01) | Sunel | Suvir |
| Steon | Stevens | Stratton | Sudhish | Sukhsaj | Sungjie | Suvrath |
| Step | Stevenson | Strauder | Sudman | Sukhsimran | Sungjin | Suyaan |
| Stepan | Steven-Tyler | Straughan | Sudonté | Sukhtaj | Sungtao | Suyoag |
| Stepfon | Stevenzon | Strauss | Sue | Sukhveer | Sungyoon | Suyog |
| Stephan (0.06) | Stevey | Stravenky | Suede | Sukhvin | Sun-Ian | Suzdar |
| Stephan Antoine C | Stevie (0.01) | Stravinsky | Sueziai | Sukhvir | Sunie | Svatopluk |
| Stephane (0.01) | Stevieray | Stravious | Sufiyan | Sukhwant | Sunil | Svein |
| Stephane Jr | Stevin | Strawdey | Sufwaan | Sukie | Sunith | Sven (0.01) |
| Stephanie | Stevion | Strawdie | Sufyaan | Sukirat | Sunjay | Svend |
| Stephano (0.01) | Stevland | Strayth | Sufyan | Sukirth | Sunji | Svyatoslav |
| Stephan-Shayan | Stevlen | Strength | Sugan | Sukirthan | Sunny (0.01) | Swa'ye |
| Stephaun | Stevon | Stribor | Suhaas | Sulabh | Sunoo | Swade |
| Stephden | Stevonta | Striden | Suhaib (0.01) | Sulaimaan | Sunraj | Swain |
| Stephen (0.86) | Stewart (0.03) | Strider | Suhaibe | Sulaiman (0.01) | Sunveer | Swalihudini |
| Stephen Mar | Stewie | Striker | Suhail | Sulayman | Sunwoo | Swaminsky |
| Stephenandre | Stian | Strong | Suhair | Suleiman | Suny | Swaraj |
| Stephenns | Stihl | Stryder (0.01) | Suhan | Suleman | Supier | Swarit |
| Stepheno | Stihltin | Stryker (0.01) | Suhas | Suleyman | Supreet | Swayde |
| Stephen-Paul | Stiles | Stryker-Ed | Suhayb (0.01) | Suliman | Supreme | Swazey |
| Stephern | Stilez | Stuardo | Suhaybe | Sullay | Suprieme | Sweeney |
| Stephfon | Stillman | Stuart (0.05) | Suheb | Sullivan (0.06) | Suprith | Sweet |
| Stephon (0.05) | Stinnett | Stuart Uno | Suheyb | Sully (0.01) | Suprotim | Sweetgrassman |
| Stephone | Stinson | Stuart-Amara | Suhith | Sully-Van | Surafail | Swepson |
| Stephonne | Stirling (0.01) | Soumoho | Suhuan | Sulmon | Surafel | Sy |
| Stephon-Phaeton | Stiven | Stuen | Suidi | Sultan (0.01) | Suraj (0.01) | Sy'ire |
| Stephron | Stivers | Styer | Sujad | Sum | Surcharles | Sy'jahnee |
| Stephton | Stockton (0.01) | Styger | Sujan | Sumahltza | Surefale | Sy'mir |
| Stergios | Stoker | Styles (0.01) | Sujay | Sumair | Suren | Sy'nard |
| Sterlin | Stokes | Stylianos | Sujeevan | Sumant | Surfel | Sy'ree |
| Sterling (0.06) | Ston | Styrk | Sujivan | Sumanta | Suriel | Syai'r |
| Sterlyn | Stone (0.05) | Styvack | Sujoy | Sumanth | Suriya | Syair |
| Sterlyng | Stonewall | Styvens | Sukaran | Sumar | Suriyan | Syan |
| Stern | Stoney (0.01) | Styves | Sukeeran | Sumari | Surjun | Sybree |
| Stetler | Stonne | Su | Sukeerth | Sumay | Surmodd | Sycove |
| Steton | Stony | Su Chang | Sukhchain | Sumedh | Surya (0.01) | Syd |
| Stetson (0.02) | Stori | Sual | Sukhdave | Sumeet | Suryan | Sydek |
| Stevan (0.01) | Storm (0.02) | Suat | Sukhdeep | Sumin | Susana | Sydnee |
| Stevaughn | Stormy | Suavé | Sukhjeet | Sumir | Susano | Sydney (0.02) |
| Steve (0.09) | Story | Subashton | Sukhjeetpal | Summer | Susej | Sydney Sandor |
| Steve Darre | Stoughten | Subeg | Sukhjit | Summit | Sushaant | Sydny |
| Steve Evan | Stourm | Suber | Sukhjot | Sumner | Sushanth | Sye |
| Steve Jr | Stover | Subhaan | Sukhkaran | Sumrath | Suskin | Sye'quan |
| | Stoyan | Subhaditya | Sukhkarn | Sun | Sutherland | Syeare |
| | Strachan | Subhan | Sukhman (0.01) | Sunay | Sutherlin | Syed (0.04) |

| | | | | | | |
|---|---|---|---|---|---|---|
| Syed Ahmed | Sylvian Marco | Szandor | Ta'carey | Ta'ria | Tabyus | Tae'vian |
| Syed Aryan | Sylvio Marcello | Szilveszter | Ta'corey | Ta'riq | Tacari | Tae'vion |
| Syed Kamil | Symar | Szuriel | Ta'cyus | Ta'ron | Tacarien | Tae'von |
| Syed Mahlon | Symeir | Szymon | Ta'darian | Ta'sareun | Tacarious | Taeahveon |
| Syed Murtaza | Symeon | | Ta'darien | Ta'saun | Tacarius | Taeberias |
| Syed Nathaniel | Symer | | Ta'darius | Ta'sean | Tacha | Taebron |
| Syed Noah | Symere | ~ T ~ | Ta'darrius | Ta'shaun | Tache | Taecyn |
| Syed Ra'ed | Symian | | Ta'derrius | Ta'shawn | Tachine | Taedem |
| Syed Shabir | Symichus | T | Ta'dimus | Ta'shean | Taciano | Taeden |
| Syed-Zarmaan | Symier | T Amari | Ta'don | Ta'shon | Tacir | Taedon |
| Syeed | Symikel | T Quan | Ta'heed | Ta'shun | Tacoda | Taedrian |
| Syeem | Symir (0.01) | T. Henry | Ta'hori | Ta'suade | Tacoma | Taegan (0.01) |
| Syeim | Symire | T.I. | Ta'ja | Ta'varion | Tacorean | Taegen |
| Syelis | Symode | T.J. | Ta'jaun | Ta'vaughn | Tacoreyon | Taeghan |
| Syere | Symon (0.01) | T'andre | Ta'javion | Ta'veion | Tacorion | Taegin |
| Syhé | Syn'cer | T'anthony | Ta'jay | Ta'veon | Tacorius | Taegun |
| Syheed | Syn'cere | T'daireon | Ta'jon | Ta'veyon | Tacory | Taehlor |
| Syheem | Synai | T'eleazar | Ta'joun | Ta'vijay | Tacoy | Taejan |
| Syhir | Synaih | T'eliq | Ta'jzhawn | Ta'vion | Tad (0.01) | Taejin |
| Syhire | Synandiaha | T'flun | Ta'karis | Ta'vione | Tadan | Tae-John |
| Syiear | Synceire | T'ijae | Ta'kaye | Ta'von | Tadarien | Taejon |
| Syiem | Syncere (0.02) | T'kai | Ta'khyri | Ta'vyion | Tadarius | Taejshon |
| Syimeer | Syncir | T'kari | Ta'kirrious | Ta'yon | Tadarrius | Taejuan |
| Syjerien | Synclair | T'khi | Ta'kwon | Ta'zhawn | Tadas | Taek |
| Syketo | Synde | T'kyas | Ta'kyi | Ta'ziyah | Tadashi | Taekwavon |
| Sylance | Syndey | T'lique | Ta'lageon | Taafe | Tadd | Taekwon |
| Sylan-Shawny | Syniea | T'maree | Ta'lariyun | Taahir | Tade | Taelar |
| Sylar | Synjin | T'mari | Ta'lee | Taaj | Tadeh | Taelen |
| Sylas (0.02) | Synnei | T'marion | Ta'lon | Taajir | Tadem | Tae-Lim |
| Syleek | Synorice | T'marvin | Ta'lyn | Taalib | Taden | Taelin |
| Syleem | Synseer | T'mical | Ta'mar | Taalib-Said | Tadeo | Taelohn |
| Sylek | Synser | T'nayvon | Ta'marcus | Taamir | Tadeusz | Taelon |
| Syler | Synsere | T'nye | Ta'mari | Taariq | Tadhg | Taelonta |
| Sylias | Syntario | T'quan | Ta'marion | Taavion | Tadi | Taelyn |
| Sylice | Syon | T'real | Ta'marious | Tabaaha | Tadley | Taeman |
| Sylier | Syonn | T'rez | Ta'marr | Taban | Tadom | Taemir |
| Sylis | Syphax | T'rique | Ta'marrius | Tabari | Tadrian | Taemon |
| Syliss | Syphee | T'sayveon | Ta'mere | Tabaris | Tadrique | Taen |
| Sylius | Syquan-Rachard | T'sean | Ta'myrick | Tabarron | Tadyn | Taeni |
| Sylon | Syraj Ali | T'sharri | Ta'narie | Tabb | Tae | Taeo |
| Sylph | Syrak | T'shon | Ta'narine | Tabe | Taé | Taeon |
| Sylton | Syran | T'vine | Ta'qee | Taben | Tae Shon | Taequan |
| Sylus | Syre | T'von | Ta'quan | Taber | Tae Woong | Taesean |
| Sylvain | Syree | T'yon | Ta'quan Shamor | Tabian | Tae'anthony | Tae-Shaun |
| Sylvain-Carl | Syris | T'yson | Ta'quari | Tabias | Tae'lavon | Taeshaun |
| Sylvan (0.01) | Syrjieo | T'zaddi | Ta'quarius | Tabiaz | Tae'marion | Taeshawn |
| Sylvanus | Syr-Justin | Ta | Ta'quawn | Tabious | Tae'qjuan | Taeshon |
| Sylvario | Syro | Ta Kai | Ta'quinn | Tabit | Tae'quan | Taesin |
| Sylvastion | Syrr | Tá Mar'rius | Ta'quon | Tabius | Tae'sean | Tae-Soo |
| Sylven | Syrus (0.01) | Ta Marion | Ta'quwereus | Tabor (0.01) | Tae'shaun | Taetyn |
| Sylver | Syrys | Ta Sean | Ta'qwan | Tabraiz | Tae'shawn | Taeuan |
| Sylvester (0.02) | Sytrevion | Ta Shaun | Ta'ray | Tabyias | Tae'shon | Taevan |
| Sylvian | Szander | Ta'bias | Ta'raye | Tabyis | Tae'veon | Taeven |

| | | | | | | |
|---|---|---|---|---|---|---|
| Taeveon | Taha-Youssef | Tahreasse | Taileek | Taj *(0.04)* | Takevius | Talil |
| Taevian | Tahbyis | Tahreek | Tailekk | Taj Nawruz | Takeyon | Talill |
| Taevin | Tahcowa | Tahrell | Tailor | Taj'drick | Takhais | Talim |
| Taevion | Taheed | Tahroj | Taima | Tajae | Takhari | Talin *(0.01)* |
| Taevis | Ta-Heem | Tahseen | Taimar | Tajah | Takhi | Talinnian |
| Taeviyon | Taheem | Tah-Shawn | Taimarcus | Tajai | Taki | Taliq |
| Taevon *(0.01)* | Taher | Tahshawn | Taimere | Tajbir | Takias | Talis |
| Taevyn | Taheton | Tahsin | Taimoor | Tajdael | Takis | Talisen |
| Taeyahn | Tahgoddio | Tahsir | Taimoore | Tajdar | Tako | Talith |
| Taeyion | Tahi | Tahsjee | Tainada | Taje | Takobe | Tallan |
| Taeyon | Tahid | Tahvir | Tainan | Tajee | Takoda *(0.02)* | Tallen *(0.01)* |
| Taezen | Tahiem | Tahvone | Taine | Tajen | Takodah | Tallon *(0.01)* |
| Tafara | Tahim | Tahylif | Taio | Tajeyon | Takoma | Tally |
| Tafari *(0.01)* | Tahír | Tai *(0.03)* | Taiquan | Tajh | Takomborerwa | Talmadge *(0.01)* |
| Tafarie | Tahir *(0.01)* | Tai John | Tairae | Tajh Amir | Takoreion | Talmage |
| Tafavi | Tahirou | Tai Kadin | Taire | Tajhawn | Takota *(0.01)* | Talmus |
| Tafim | Tahj *(0.02)* | Tai Shauyn | Tairee | Tajhay | Takuhiro | Talon *(0.13)* |
| Tafirenyika | Tahj'ameen | Tai'don | Tairi | Tajhe | Takumi | Talor |
| Tafsir | Tahjae | Tai'jeour | Tairjiv | Tajhja | Takumu | Talowja |
| Taft | Tahjay | Tai'quan | Tair-Rence | Taj-I | Takurian | Talshawn |
| Tafton | Tahjee | Tai'rell | Taisei | Taji | Takuru | Talton |
| Tag | Tahjeem | Tai'sean | Taisen | Tajier | Takuto | Talus |
| Tagaloa | Tahjeer | Tai'shan | Taishaun | Tajir | Takwon | Talyn *(0.02)* |
| Tagan | Tahjere | Tai'shawn | Tai-Shawn | Tajiri | Takyé | Talynn |
| Tage *(0.01)* | Tahji | Tai'shon | Taishawn | Tajkaunver | Takyi | Tam |
| Tagen | Tahjier | Tai'vell | Taishon | Tajma | Tal | Tama |
| Tager | Tahjir | Taichi | Taisir | Tajmeet | Tala | Tamairi |
| Tagert | Tahjmere | Taiden | Taison | Tajmir | Talaan | Tamais |
| Tagg | Tahjrick | Taidhgin | Taisuke | Tajon *(0.01)* | Talaelasi | Tamaja |
| Taggart | Tahkale | Taidou | Tait *(0.01)* | Tajon' | Talal *(0.01)* | Tamajae |
| Taggert | Tahkari | Taidron | Taite | Tajshay | Talalelei | Tamajah |
| Tagi | Tahkwel | Taiga | Taiten | Tajuan | Talan *(0.17)* | Tamajh |
| Tagish | Tahlee | Taigan | Taiton | Tajuddin | Talandrick | Tamal |
| Tagon | Tahleel | Taige | Taitsen | Tajveer | Talas | Tamaljé |
| Tagui | Tahleke | Taigen | Taitt | Tajzmique | Talat | Tamam |
| Tagun | Tahlif | Taigh | Taitum | Takahi | Talbert | Taman |
| Tah | Tahlon | Taighe | Taivan | Takai | Talbot | Tamani |
| Tah Mir | Tahmair | Taih | Taive | Takari | Taleb | Tamanjeet |
| Tah'ir | Tahmaj | Taihei | Taiven | Takarius | Taleem | Tamanta |
| Tah'ja | Tahmar | Taihrel | Taiveon | Takarreon | Taleil | Tamar |
| Tah'jir | Tahmari | Taij | Taiveyon | Takarrye | Talel | Tamara |
| Tah'keem | Tahmeed | Taijaan | Taivier | Takaya | Talen *(0.03)* | Tamaralria |
| Tah'leem | Tahmeer | Taijae | Taivion | Takayoshi | Talent | Tamarcus |
| Taha *(0.03)* | Tahmid | Taijahn | Taivon | Takayveon | Taler | Tamare |
| Taha Hashim | Tahmin | Taijay | Taivyn | Takeem | Talha *(0.01)* | Tamareon |
| Tahaj | Tahmir | Taije | Taiwan | Takehi | Talhah | Tamari *(0.01)* |
| Taha-Momain | Tahmyan | Taijhun | Taiwo | Takeithala | Tali | Tamariae |
| Tahar | Tahn | Taijion | Taiyan | Takel | Taliaferro | Tamarian |
| Tahar Amine | Tahniyad | Taijon | Taiyo | Takeo | Talib *(0.01)* | Tamarick |
| Tahara | Tahnyi | Taijuan | Taiyon | Takerry | Taliek | Tamarien |
| Tahari | Tahnyus | Taijvey | Taiyton | Takeru | Taliesin | Tamario |
| Taharien | Tahoma | Taiki | Taizer | Takeshi | Taliferrio | Tamarion *(0.01)* |
| Taha-Yasine | Tahoor-Ul | Tailan | Taizhon | Takevious | Talik | Tamarious |

| | | | | | |
|---|---|---|---|---|---|
| Tamaris | Tamoj | Tanish | Tapio | Tarelle | Tarrant | Tashrick |
| Tamarius | Tamon | Tanisha | Taqavion | Taren *(0.01)* | Tarrell *(0.01)* | Tashun |
| Tamarkis | Tamony | Tanishk | Taqi | Tarence | Tarren | Tashyne |
| Tamarlon | Tamoor | Tanishq | Taqi'ud-Din | Tareq | Tarrence | Tasi |
| Tamaro | Tamorion | Taniya | Taqiy | Tarey | Tarreon | Tasin |
| Tamarques | Tamorrest | Tanjot | Taqqee | Tareyon | Tarrik | Tasir |
| Tamarr | Tampa | Tank | Taqrim | Tarez | Tarrill | Tasman |
| Tamarrian | Tamren | Tan-Khoa | Taquae | Tarfariemanta | Tarrin | Tasmin |
| Tamarrion | Tamrin | Tanly | Taquan *(0.01)* | Targ | Tarris | Tasnim |
| Tamarris | Tamron | Tanmai | Taquarius | Tari'un | Tarrius | Tason |
| Tamarrius | Tamryn | Tanmay | Taquary | Taria | Tarrod | Tass |
| Tamaru | Tamsir | Tannar | Taquavion | Tarian | Tarron | Tat |
| Tamarvion | Tamunosiki | Tannen | Taquavis | Taric | Tarrus | Tatchi |
| Tamaryen | Tamyrion | Tanner *(1.27)* | Taquawn | Tarick | Tarryl | Taté |
| Tamas | Tan | Tannere | Taquerious | Taricus | Tarsh | Tate *(0.21)* |
| Tamasjai | Tan Thong Alex | Tanner-James | Taquerious | Tariek | Taru | Tate Oswald |
| Tamaso | Tanae | Tanner-Toan | Taquez | Tarif | Tarue | Nickolau |
| Tamaul | Tanai | Tannes | Taquie | Tarig | Tarues | Tatem |
| Tamaull | Tanaj | Tannin | Taquorean | Tarik *(0.02)* | Tarun *(0.01)* | Taten |
| Tamaurice | Tanaka | Tannon | Taquorion | Tarik Ali | Tarus | Tatenda |
| Tamaurse | Tanar | Tannor | Taqwa | Tarikh | Tarvan | Tateum |
| Tamaury | Tanarion | Tannraj | Taqwon | Tariko | Tarvares | Tatevon |
| Tamba | Tanarus | Tanny | Tara | Tarin | Tarvarious | Tathan |
| Tambwe | Tanas | Tannyn | Tarae | Tarion | Tarvaris | Tatian |
| Tameem | Tanavion | Tano | Tarahji | Tariq *(0.05)* | Tarvarus | Tatiana |
| Tameer | Tanawat | Tanoah | Taraia | Tarique | Tarvell | Tatianna |
| Tamel | Tanay | Tanor | Taraj | Taris | Tarvi | Tatin |
| Tamene | Tanbirul | Tanoris | Taraja | Tarius | Tarvion' | Tatiyana |
| Tamer *(0.01)* | Tancred | Tanorris | Taraji | Tarkan | Tarvis | Tatrevion |
| Tamere | Tan-Danny | Tanraj | Taran *(0.01)* | Tarkesh | Tarvos | Tatum *(0.03)* |
| Tameren | Tanden | Tanreon | Tarance | Tarl | Taryan | Tauhseem |
| Tamerious | Tandom | Tanri | Tarandeep | Tarlarico | Taryk | Taukedrik |
| Tameron | Tandrick | Tanrick | Tarandin | Tarlehseh | Taryl | Taumori |
| Tamesh | Tandyn | Tansley | Taranjit | Tarmarion | Taryll | Tauno |
| Tametrius | Tane | Tanthalas | Taranveer | Tarmenpreet | Taryn | Tauqeer |
| Tamez | Taneel | Tanton | Taranvir | Tarnveer | Tarynvir | Taurai |
| Tamian | Taneesh | Tantyn | Taras | Tarnvir | Tasa | Taurance |
| Tamicah | Taneil | Tanurag | Taravious | Taro | Tasean *(0.01)* | Taurean *(0.02)* |
| Tamichael | Taneko | Tanush | Taray | Tarod | Tasean-Malik | Taureen |
| Tamicheal | Tanen | Tanveer | Tarayvien | Tarok | Taseen | Tauren |
| Tamiek | Taner *(0.01)* | Tanvir | Tarbaree | Tarome | Tashad | Taureon |
| Tamier | Tanerio | Tanween | Tarcicio | Ta-Ron | Tashard | Taures |
| Tamij | Tanga | Tany | Tared | Taron *(0.01)* | Tashaud | Taurian |
| Tamijai | Tang-An Jacob | Tanyan | Taree | Taronald | Tashaun *(0.01)* | Tauric |
| Tamik | Tango | Tanyon *(0.01)* | Tareef | Taronté | Tashawn *(0.02)* | Taurie |
| Tamim | Tania | Tanzil-Hossain | Tareek | Tarpley | Tasheed | Taurin |
| Tamious | Tanidan | Tanzy | Tareem | Tarquez | Tasheem | Taurino |
| Tamir *(0.01)* | Tanie | Tao | Tareeq | Tarquin | Tashen | Taurique |
| Tamirat | Taniel | Tao D'juan | Tareik | Tarquinn | Tashi | Taurus *(0.01)* |
| Tamisq | Tanim | Taofiq | Tarek *(0.01)* | Tarran | Tashin | Tauryn |
| Tamjid | Tanin | Taona | Tareke | Tarrance | Tashir | Tausaruapik |
| Tammer | Tanir | Taos | Tarel | Tarrance | Tashon | Tausif |
| Tamoczun | Tanis | Tapan | Tarell *(0.01)* | Miracle | Tashown | Tausiq |

| | | | | | | |
|---|---|---|---|---|---|---|
| Taustin | Tavon *(0.02)* | Tayahndre | Taymonte | Tayvius | Te'mond | Tecumseh |
| Tauston | Tavone | Tayammun Al- | Taymour | Tayvn | Te'narius | Ted *(0.02)* |
| Tavaaris | Tavontae | Kharib | Taymur | Tayvon *(0.02)* | Te'on | Ted Patrick |
| Tavaile | Tavontay | Tayari | Taynon | Tayvone | Te'ondre | Ted'quarius |
| Tavairs | Tavonte | Taybren | Tayo | Tayvonn | Te'qawan | Tedarrel |
| Tavaj | Tavonté | Taybrim | Tayon | Tayyib | Te'quan | Tedarriyn |
| Taval | Tavontrius | Taychaun | Tayonne | Tayzhan | Te'quin | Tedd |
| Tavali | Tavor | Taydan | Tayoung | Taz | Te'ron | Teddi |
| Tavan | Tavoras | Tayde | Tay-Quan | Tazaran | Te'sean | Teddie |
| Tavaras | Tavorian | Taydem | Tayquan *(0.01)* | Tazaris | Te'shaun | Teddrick |
| Tavarence | Tavorious | Tayden *(0.02)* | Tayqwuin | Tazarr'ion | Te'shawn | Teddy *(0.02)* |
| Tavareon | Tavoris | Taydom | Tayrell | Tazarri | Te'shjohn | Tederian |
| Tavares *(0.02)* | Tavoy | Taydon | Tayren | Tazayvien | Te'shon | Tederick |
| Tavaress | Tavus | Taydyn | Tayriq | Taze | Te'von | Tedi |
| Tavarez | Tavy | Taye *(0.01)* | Tayro | Tazhaun | Te'vontaye | Tedo |
| Tavari | Tavyon | Taye Shawn | Tayron | Ta-Zi | Tea'von | Tedric |
| Tavarian | Tavyss | Tayeb-Amir | Taysean *(0.01)* | Tazion | Teacher | Tedrick |
| Tavarieun | Tawaan | Tayehari | Taysen | Taziyah | Teacon | Tedruhn |
| Tavarion | Tawab | Tayell | Tayshann | Tazlee | Teaden | Ted-Schindler |
| Tavarious *(0.01)* | Tawadi | Tayemar | Tayshaun *(0.05)* | Tazmin | Teag | Tedvon |
| Tavaris *(0.01)* | Tawain | Tayen | Tayshaune | Tazyr | Teagan *(0.08)* | Tee |
| Tavarish | Tawan | Tayeshawn | Tayshaunn | Tazz | Teage | Teearyan |
| Tavarius *(0.01)* | Tawanchai | Tayevion | Tayshaurn | Tazzden | Teagen *(0.01)* | Tee-Dee-Nae |
| Tavarous | Tawara | Tayewon | Tay-Shawn | Tazziem | Teaghan | Teegan *(0.02)* |
| Tavarren | Tawaski | Tayferrian | Tayshawn *(0.03)* | Tchad | Teagin | Teeghan |
| Tavarri | Tawban | Taygan | Tayshon | Tchiegam | Teagon | Tee-Jay |
| Tavarris | Tawd | Taygen | Tayshun *(0.01)* | Tcion | Teague *(0.02)* | Teenann |
| Tavarse | Tawfiq | Tayion | Tayshyne | Tdohasan | Teaguen | Teeray |
| Tavarus *(0.01)* | Tawon | Tayiujwan | Taysian | Te | Teagun | Teernan |
| Tavaughn | Tawson | Tayjhawn | Taysin | Té Von | Teaion | Teerth |
| Tavean | Tawun | Tayjhon | Taysir | Te Zhan | Teajawon | Teethlac |
| Taven *(0.02)* | Tay | Tayjohn | Tayson | Te'amos | Teak | Teferra |
| Taveon *(0.01)* | Tay Kevious | Tayjon | Taysuen | Te'andre | Teal | Teflonn |
| Taveous | Tay Shaun | Tayjuan | Tayt | Te'andré | Teamon | Teg |
| Tavern | Tay'jan | Taylan *(0.01)* | Tayte *(0.01)* | Te'aon | Teancum | Tega |
| Taveyon | Tay'jon | Taylar | Tayten *(0.01)* | Te'aundré | Teander | Tegan *(0.05)* |
| Tavi | Tay'jour | Tayleel | Tayton *(0.01)* | Te'bias | Te-Andre | Tegar |
| Tavian *(0.02)* | Tay'juan | Taylehn | Taytum | Te'darius | Teandre | Tegbir |
| Tavianxce | Tay'marious | Taylen *(0.01)* | Taytyn | Te'elijah | Teandré | Tegen |
| Taviaun | Tay'quan | Tayler *(0.02)* | Tayunta | Te'gan | Teao | Tegfateh |
| Taviaus | Tay'qwon | Taylier | Tayv'on | Te'Jahn | Tearell | Tegh |
| Tavien *(0.01)* | Tay'sean | Taylin | Tayvaughn | Te'jon | Teari | Tegh Fateh |
| Tavier | Tay'shaun | Taylon *(0.01)* | Tayve | Te'juan | Tearial | Teghan |
| Taviere | Tay'shawn | Taylor *(0.50)* | Tayveion | Te'kari | Tearin | Teghpal |
| Tavin *(0.02)* | Tay'shon | Taylor Joseph | Tayven *(0.01)* | Te'kavious | Tearon | Teghveer |
| Tavio | Tay'shun | Taylor-Andr | Tayveon *(0.01)* | Te'kel | Tearyn | Tegiri |
| Tavion *(0.04)* | Tay'veion | Taylor-Vonn | Tayvian | Te'kevious | Teashun | Tegler |
| Tavionne | Tay'veon | Taylos | Tayvien | Te'kii | Teavon | Tegran |
| Tavious | Tay'vion | Taylyn | Tayvieon | Te'kle | Teayon | Tegvir |
| Tavis *(0.01)* | Tay'von | Taymar | Tayvin *(0.01)* | Te'lijah | Tebarrion | Teh'rhon |
| Tavish *(0.01)* | Tay'vonne | Taymarion | Tayvion *(0.01)* | Te'mar | Tebiarous | Tehahente |
| Tavita | Tay'waun | Taymon | Tayvione | Te'marion | Techeltoech | Tehi |
| Tavius | Tay'zjonn | Taymont | Tayvis | Te'metreon | Tecondrey | Tehmari |

| | | | | | | |
|---|---|---|---|---|---|---|
| Tehmin | Tel | Tenneessee | Terell *(0.02)* | Terren | Teryck | Teydon |
| Tehorah | Telacy | Tennel | Terelle | Terrence *(0.12)* | Teryn | Teygan |
| Kwaneken | Telek | Tennell | Teren | Terrence James | Tesaih | Teygen |
| Tehrick | Telemachus | Tenneson | Terence *(0.03)* | Terrence-Len | Tesean | Teylan |
| Tehyen | Teleon | Tennessee | Terence Herbert | Terrentino | Tesfaalem | Teymarr |
| Teich | Telesforo | Tennesy | Terence Junior | Terreon | Teshan | Teymor |
| Teig | Teli | Tennison | Terence Za'bron | Terrex | Teshaun | Te-Yon |
| Teigan | Telijah | Tennyson | Terenzo | Terrez | Teshawn | Teyon |
| Teige | Telik | Teno | Terez | Terrian | Tesher | Teyreon |
| Teigen | Tell | Tenoch | Teriah | Terrick | Teshon | Teyric |
| Teighan | Telleus | Tenoli | Teric | Terrickos | Teshone | Teyrnen |
| Teigin | Telly | Tenson | Terick | Terrico | Teshwan | Teysean |
| Teihan | Telmen | Tentche | Terico | Terrill | Teson | Teyshaun |
| Teinge | Telmo | Tenwosa | Teriek | Terrin *(0.01)* | Tesoro | Teyton |
| Teion | Telmuun | Tenyson | Terik | Terrion *(0.02)* | Tessa | Teyvah |
| Teionte | Telson | Tenzin *(0.02)* | Terin | Terrious | Tessiah | Teyvian |
| Teiowerahtase | Telvin | Tenzing | Terio | Terrique | Tetas | Teyvonne |
| Teiren | Temaine | Téo | Terion | Terris | Tethion | Tezlim |
| Teisina | Temarcus | Teo *(0.01)* | Terioune | Terrison | Teton | Tgen |
| Teiviontey | Temarion | Teodor | Terius | Terrius | Tetric | Tgn |
| Teiwaz | Temarionté | Teodore | Teriyon | Terrix | Tetsuro | Th'darius |
| Tej | Temeko | Teodoro | Terje | Terriyon | Tev | Thaabit |
| Teja | Temell | Teodulo | Termaine | Terron *(0.01)* | Tev'ion | Thabisan |
| Tejacion | Temesgen | Teofilo | Termarcus | Terrtric | Teva | Thabit |
| Tejan | Temesghen | Teofisto | Termel | Terrvarious | Tevahn | Thabith |
| Tejas *(0.01)* | Temetriuse | Teo-Gael | Termontaye | Terry *(0.22)* | Tevan | Thabo |
| Tejaswi | Temidayo | Teon *(0.01)* | Ternage | Terry Glenn | Tevarion | Thackery |
| Tejay | Temiko | Teondre | Ternando | Terry Hien | Tevaris | Thad *(0.01)* |
| Tejbhai | Temilolu | Teondré | Terold | Terry Lane | Tevas | Thadd |
| Tejes | Temio | Teondrick | Teron *(0.01)* | Terry Lee | Tevaugn | Thaddaeus |
| Tejesh | Temir | Teontae | Terone | Terry Vasha | Teven | *(0.01)* |
| Tejinder | Temitayo | Teophilus | Teronn | Terryante | Tevens | Thaddaus |
| Tejpal | Temitope | Tequan | Teroz | Terryion | Teveon | Thadden |
| Tejuan | Temmrick | Tequez | Terquez | Terryjadis | Tevernicus | Thaddeous |
| Tejus | Temoáz | Tequirius | Terrace | Terryl | Teveyon | Thaddeus *(0.05)* |
| Tejveer | Temontae | Tequoi | Terrae | Terryn | Tevian | Thaddias |
| Tejvir | Temontez | Ter' Lajiah | Terran *(0.01)* | Terryohn | Tevin *(0.03)* | Thaddiaz |
| Tekai | Temple | Ter'dreón | Terrance *(0.19)* | Terryon | Tevion | Thaddieus |
| Tekana'tsahen | Temur | Ter'marqus | Terrance- | Terryontae | Tevita | Thaddius |
| Tekayen | Temuulen | Ter'monte | Tyshawn | Terryous | Tevlin | Thadeaus |
| Teke | Temzel | Ter'rell | Terrancey | Terry-Ray | Tevon | Thaden |
| Tekenyon | Tenaje | Ter'ron | Terrande | Terryun | Tevor | Thadeous |
| Tekerian | Tenarius | Terae | Terranton | Terschner | Tevye | Thades |
| Tekhi | Tenauri | Terak | Terrayon | Tershawn | Tevyn | Thadeus |
| Tekie | Tenear | Teramondis | Terreal | Tersoo | Texal | Thadiun |
| Tekierionne | Tener | Teran | Terrean | Tertian | Texas | Thadius |
| Tekius | Tenereo | Terance | Terreance | Teruaki | Texloi | Thaedan |
| Tekivious | Teng | Terayvion | Terrece | Terun | Texroy | Thaeden |
| Tekle | Tenger | Teree | Terrecus | Teruomi | Tey Vion | Thaedyn |
| Teko | Tengis | Tereek | Terreion | Tervaris | Tey'sean | Thaevanh |
| Tekoa | Tengtong | Tereeke | Terrel *(0.01)* | Tervon | Tey'shan | Thafari |
| Tekolve | Tenir | Terefe | Terrell *(0.16)* | Tervoris | Tey'veion | Thahue |
| Tekwan | Tenisee | Terek | Terrelle *(0.01)* | Tery | Teyachta | Thai *(0.01)* |

Thai Hao
Thai-Hoa
Thaijuan
Thailan
Thailand
Thailent
Thailin
Thailor
Thailyn
Thaine
Thairenn
Thairique
Thairy
Thai-Son
Thaison
Thaj
Thalin
Thallen
Thalles
Thallys
Thamario
Thambithurai
Thames
Thamian
Thamos
Thamphis
Thamyus
Than
Thanasi
Thandizo
Thandolwami
Thane (0.01)
Thane-Carter
Thanh
Thanh Nam
Thanh-Dat
Thanh-Vinh
Thanickson
Thaniel
Thaniel Reese
Thano
Thanon
Thanos
Thanushan
Thanuwat
Thanypiny
Thao
Thapelo
Tharang
Tharen
Tharon
Tharron
Tharun

Tharuun
Tharyn
Thashan
Thaswayne
Thatcher (0.04)
Thaufin
Thavixay
Thaweexab
Thawun
Thaxston
Thaxton
Thay
Thayaharan
Thayde
Thayden
Thayen
Thayeng
Thayer
Thaylon
Thayne (0.01)
Thazard
The
The Anh
   William
Theador
Theadore
Thean
Theandre
Theangelo
The-Anh
   Andrew
Theartis
Thebe
Theiden
Theirry
Theis
Theising
Theissen
Thejas
Thelio
Thelonious
Thelonius
Themaré
Themistocles
Thenic
Théo
Theo (0.07)
Theo Gerard
Theo James
Theo Raphael
Theoantony
Theoden
Theodhori

Theodis
Theodor
Théodore
Theodore (0.40)
Theodore Lee
Theodorek
Theodoric
Theodoros
Theodorre
Theodorus
Theodosious
Theodosis
Theodossi
Theodric
Theodrick
Theofanis
Theofilos
Theogene
Theonize
Theontae
Theo-Paul
Theophan
Theophers
Theophile
Theophilus
Theophulus
Theoppluis
Theordrick
Theoren (0.01)
Theorious
Theo-Russell
Theo-Salaam
Theotim
Theotis
Theotym
Theran
Theren
Therese
Therin
Therion
Theris
Theriyoun
Theron (0.03)
Therone
Therrance
Therray
Therrick
Therron
Therry
Therry-
   Alexandre
Theryn
Theunte

Theus
Theuwis
Thevenson
Theyaa
Thiago (0.02)
Thian
Thiaren
Thibault
Thiele
Thien (0.01)
Thien An
Thien Phuoc
Thien-An
Thienan
Thien-Phat
Thien-Theodore
Thien-Vu
Thierno
Thierno
   Boubacar
Thieron
Thierry (0.04)
Thierry Malcom
Thierry Thomas
Thierry-Kyle
Thiery
Thievang
Thiha
Thijis
Thijs
Thiland
Thimothe
Thimothee
Thinh
Thinura
Thiotis
Thisara
Thishook
Thith
Thivisan
Thobyas
Thom
Thomas (4.45)
Thomas
   Alexander
Thomas
   Alexandre
Thomas Alexis
Thomas Billy
Thomas Henry
Thomas Hugh
Thomas J
Thomas Jacques

Thomas James
Thomas John
Thomas Josep
Thomas
   Marshall
Thomas Maxime
Thomas Patr
Thomas Warren
Thomas William
Thomas-Andy
Thomas-Charles
Thomas-
   Edouard
Thomas-Elliot
Thomasie
Thomasj
Thomas-Jahson
Thomas-James
Thomas-
   Jameson
Thomas-Jay
Thomas-John
Thomas-Jules
Thomas-Lee
Thomas-Loic
Thomas-Louis
Thomas-Olivier
Thomas-
   Raphael
Thomas-Rares
Thomas-Samuel
Thomas-
   Thymothe
Thomastien
Thomas-Xavier
Thomax
Thomel
Thomias
Thommy
Thomoris
Thompson
   (0.01)
Thomsen
Thomson
Thomus
Thomussie
Thomy
Thong
Thongchai
Thony
Thoojavan
Thor (0.02)
Thorald

Thoralf
Thoran
Thorance
Thorbien
Thoren
Thorger
Thorihwaieri
Thorin (0.01)
Thorn
Thorne
Thornon
Thornton
Thorpe
Thorsan
Thorsen
Thorson
Thorsten
Thorton
Thorvaldur
Thoth
Thrasher
Thristen
Thristian
Thristone
Throck
Thron
Thryn
Thuan
Thuja
Thulasitharan
Thulisani
Thunder
Thundercloud
Thur-Kheem
Thurlow
Thurman (0.01)
Thurmari
Thurmin
Thurmond
Thurston (0.01)
Thuruna
Thushan
Thushanth
Thusmitha
Thy
Thyheous
Thyiem
Thyme
Thyrell
Ti
Ti Yer
Ti'avion
Ti'hme

Ti'jia
Ti'john
Ti'keem
Ti'-Lon
Ti'metrius
   Benard
Ti'mikel
Ti'quan
Ti'quon
Ti'ron
Ti'sean
Ti'shaun
Ti'shawn
Ti'yahn
Ti'yon
Tia
Tiaego
Tiago (0.02)
Tiam
Tian
Tian Kang
Tianna
Tiano
Tianshuo
Tiante
Tian-Wang
Tianxin
Tianyi
Tiarnan
Tiason
Tiaun
Tiawan
Tiberius
Tibor
Tibulo
Tibyas
Ticalvin
Ticeon
Tichaun
Tichone
Tico
Ti-Daryus
Tiden
Tidhar
Tidiani
Tidus
Tidwell
Tie'cognon
Tie'reese
Tiee
Tieg
Tiegan
Tiegen

| | | | | | | |
|---|---|---|---|---|---|---|
| Tiego | Tijuana | Timiko | Ting | Titian | Tobenna | Tolbert |
| Tiejaun | Tikai | Timir | Ting-Sheng | Tito *(0.01)* | Tobey *(0.01)* | Tolen |
| Tieko | Tikee | Timisye | Ting-Yung | Titobiloluwa | Tobi | Tolga |
| Tieler | Tiki | Timithey | Tinius | Titobioluwa | Tobi Ray | Tolkien |
| Tielor | Tikoyo | Timithy | Tino | Titouan | Tobiah | Tolson |
| Tielyn | Tikwon | Timm | Tinofili | Titus *(0.14)* | Tobian | Toluwalase |
| Tien | Til | Timmari | Tinotenda | Tiunda | Tobias *(0.17)* | Toluwaloju |
| Tiên | Tilak | Timmarik | Tinsley | Tiuntay | Tobiason | Toluwani |
| Tiepeng | Tilakkshan | Timmey | Tiny | Tius | Tobiaz | Tom *(0.04)* |
| Tierail | Tilar | Timmi | Tio | Tives | Tobie | Tom'quariou |
| Tieran | Tilden | Timmie | Tioluwalase | Tivis | Tobieus | Toma |
| Tiere | Tildon | Timmond | Tion *(0.01)* | Tivoli | Tobijah | Tomago |
| Tierell | Tileek | Timmothey | Tiondrea | Tivon | Tóbin | Tomah |
| Tiergan | Tileem | Timmothy | Tionne | Tivonte | Tobin *(0.03)* | Tomar |
| Tierin | Tiliyan | (0.01) | Tiontae | Tiwan | Tobit | Tomarcus |
| Tierler | Tilley | Timmy *(0.02)* | Tip | Tiwirek | Tobiyah | Tomare |
| Tiernan *(0.02)* | Tillman *(0.01)* | Timo | Tipoh | Tiwon | Tobler | Tomari |
| Tiernen | Tilly | Timoe | Tipton | Tiy | Toboris | Tomarie |
| Tierney | Tilman | Timofey | Tiquan | Tiy'shon | Tobryn | Tomarion |
| Tierno | Tilmon | Timohty | Tiquencie | Tiyae | Toby *(0.17)* | Tomarius |
| Tierre | Tilo | Timon | Tiqueze | Tiyam | Tobyas | Tomarrio |
| Tierren | Tilon | Timon'tae | Tiquon | Tiyarre | Tobyjay | Tomás |
| Tiersen | Tilor | Timoni | Tiquré | Tiyé | Toby-Joe | Tomàs |
| Tieryn | Tilton | Timonthy | Tiqwan | Tiyler | Tobyn | Tomas *(0.13)* |
| Tieveyeh | Tiltton | Timorion | Tiraj | Tiyon | Toby-Nicholas | Tomas Jr |
| Tiewan | Tilvin | Timote | Tiras | Tiyrell | Toccarian | Tomas' |
| Tiffani | Tim *(0.02)* | Timoteo | Tirawn | Tiyus | Tochi | Tomas-Esteban |
| Tiffany | Timaeus | Timotey | Tiray | Tizaeveon | Tocory | Tomasz |
| Tifften | Timain | Timothe *(0.01)* | Tirell | Tiziano | Tod | Tomauri |
| Tiger | Timajaé | Timothe Jr | Tireyk | Tizon | Tod'jai | Tomaviona |
| Tighe *(0.01)* | Timangiak | Timothee | Tirian | Tj *(0.01)* | Todd *(0.12)* | Tombe |
| Tigo | Timarcus | Timothei | Tirin | Tjayda | Toddarius | Tombeck |
| Tigran | Timareis | Timotheus | Tirion | Tjayden | Todd-Elvin | Tombis |
| Tigue | Timari | Timothy *(2.33)* | Tirmdi | Tjuandell | Toddheim | Tomei |
| Tihee | Timarion | Timothy Alvis | Tiron | TK | Toddre | Tomer |
| Tiice | Timarius | Timothy Eli | Tirone | Tkaii | Toddrick | Tomi |
| Tiicon | Timariyon | Timothy Lewis | Tirrell | T-Kwon | Toderick | Tomias |
| Tiivi Siquaq | Timarjiell | Timothy Ray | Tirsten | Tlaloc | Toderrick | Tomico |
| Tija | Timauri | Timouris | Tirth | Tmar | Todiah | Tomieko |
| Tijae | Timaury | Tim-Robert | Tirtho | Tmarion | Todrick | Tomily |
| Tijah | Timayahs | Timson | Tiryn | To Laydn | Toe | Tomisin |
| Ti-Jai | Timber *(0.01)* | Timu | Tirzah | To'mareon | Toeupu | Tomislav |
| Tijane | Timberland | Timur | Tisaiah | To'morrion | Tofi | Tomlinson |
| Tijani | Timberlyn | Timyan | Tishaun | To'san | Togan | Tomma |
| Tijay | Timbete | Tin | Tishawn | To'zavin | Togrul | Tommas |
| Tijean | Timeius | Tin Yik | Tisho | Toai | Tohrion | Tommaso |
| Tijere | Timere | Tinahj | Tishod | Toan | Toii | Tomme |
| Tijhay | Timerio | Tinashe | Tishon | Tobachia | Tokaji | Tommel |
| Tijii | Timerrick | Tinaye | Tislam | Tobbe | Token | Tommere |
| Tijion | Timethy | Tindell | Tison | Tobe | Tokobi | Tommey |
| Tijo | Timichael | Tine | Titan *(0.01)* | Tobechi | Tola | Tommi |
| Tijon | Timier | Tinei | Titato | Tobechukwu | Tolan | Tommie *(0.02)* |
| Tijuan | Timiere | Tinell | Tithing | Toben | Toland | Tommie-John |

| | | | | | | |
|---|---|---|---|---|---|---|
| Tommorion | Topher | Torrence *(0.01)* | Touzong | Tra'von *(0.01)* | Traevyn | Traquainn |
| Tommy *(0.28)* | Toprak | Torreon | Tovariyo | Tra'vone | Traften | Traquan |
| Tommy James | Tor *(0.01)* | Torres | Tovi | Tra'vonte | Trafton | Traquil |
| Tommy Josie | Torac | Torrey *(0.01)* | Tovian | Tra'vonté | Tragedy Aamour | Traron |
| Tommye | Torain | Torrey-Alle | Toviel | Tra'vonti | Tragen | Trase |
| Tommy-Frank | Toral | Torreyhon | Tovin | Tra'voughn | Trai | Trasean |
| Tommy-Lee | Toran | Torrez | Towa | Traa | Traian | Trashad |
| Tommyon | Torance | Torrian *(0.01)* | Towan | Traben | Traice | Trashaud |
| Tommy-Sean | Torben | Torrick | Towayne | Trabis | Traiden | Trashaun |
| Tomoharu | Torbjorn | Torrie | Townes | Tracary | Trailon | Trashawn |
| Tomoni | Tore | Torriean | Townsend | Traccie | Traiman | Trashoan |
| Tomontae | Torec | Torriek | Toxie | Trace *(0.13)* | Traisean | Trashon |
| Tomonte | Torei | Torrien | Toy'rodney | Tracell | Traishawn | Trashun |
| Tomorion | Torell | Torrin *(0.01)* | Toye | Tracen | Traister | Trask |
| Tomorreio | Toren *(0.01)* | Torrion | Toyin | Tracetin | Traiten | Trason |
| Tomorrious | Torence | Torris | Toyquarius | Traceton | Traiton | Tratavious |
| Tomoya | Torenzo | Torriyon | Toyrion | Tracey *(0.01)* | Traiveon | Tratavis |
| Tomquavious | Torey *(0.01)* | Torrose | Tr'edale | Tracie | Traivion | Trav'varius |
| Toms | Toreyon | Torry | Tr'emire | Tracien | Traivon | Trava'un |
| Tomson | Torez | Torryee | Tr'vonta | Tracin | Traivone | Travae |
| Tomungi | Torger | Torsten | Tra | Tracker | Traizen | Travain |
| Tomy *(0.01)* | Tori *(0.01)* | Torston | Tra Shawn | Tracstein | Trajan *(0.01)* | Travaira |
| Tomy Alexander | Tori'ahn | Torwin | Tra'cian | Tracy *(0.03)* | Trajen | Travale |
| Ton'varus | Torian *(0.01)* | Tory *(0.01)* | Tra'darius | Tracyn | Trakker | Travallion |
| Tonaijah | Torianno | Toryion | Tra'derious | Tradarion | Tralen | Travanti |
| Tonas | Toriano | Toryn | Tra'jon | Tradarious | Tralyn | Travares |
| Tonathiu | Toriaun | Toryon | Tra'juan | Tradarius | Tramahn | Travarese |
| Tonatiuh | Toribio | Tosh *(0.01)* | Tra'maine | Tradarrius | Tramaine *(0.01)* | Travarious |
| Tonazj | Toricious | Toshaun | Tra'mayne | Tradd | Tramari | Travaris |
| Tondrey | Torico | Toshio | Tra'mell | Traddin | Tramarice | Travarius |
| Tone | Torie | Toshwaun | Tra'melle | Trae *(0.04)* | Tramayne | Travarrius |
| Tonei | Toriean | Tosin | Tra'mun | Trae Shaun | Tramel | Travars |
| Toney *(0.01)* | Torin *(0.03)* | Tosner | Tra'mychael | Trae'von | Tramell | Travarus |
| Tong | Torion | Toson | Tra'nard | Traeger | Tramello | Travaughn |
| Tongon | Toriono | Totakeo | Tra'quan | Traelon | Tramil | Travayle |
| Toni *(0.01)* | Toris | Totch | Tra'quann | Traelyn | Tramine | Traveer |
| Tonickson | Toriyan | Tou | Tra'quon | Traeon | Tramir | Travele |
| Tonie | Toriyon | Tou Pao | Tra'sean | Traeqoine | Tramire'us | Travell *(0.01)* |
| Toniko | Tormon | Tou're | Tra'shaun | Traequan | Trammelle | Travelle |
| Tonio | Torna | Touger | Tra'shaune | Traeshaun | Tramon | Traven |
| Tonk | Torommia | Tougo | Tra'shawn | Traeshon | Tramonie | Travenno |
| Tonneey | Toronn | Toukee | Tra'shown | Traeshun | Tramontay | Travens |
| Tonnie | Torrae | Toukeng | Tra'shun | Traeten | Tramonte | Traveon *(0.01)* |
| Tonny | Torrance *(0.01)* | Touly | Tra'shunn | Traetin | Tran | Traveonn |
| Tony *(0.26)* | Torrando | Toumany | Tra'varis | Traeton | Tranard | Traveonne |
| Tony Daniel | Torray | Toumong | Tra'varria | Traetyn | Trance | Traver |
| Tony Li Cheng | Torre | Toure | Tra'vaugn | Traevaughn | Tranden | Traves |
| Tony Sebastien | Torre'a | Tourean | Tra'vay | Traeveon | Trandon | Travey |
|   Keyla | Torre'on | Tourell | Tra'vel | Traevian | Tranel | Traveyone |
| Tonyai | Torrean | Tourie | Tra'veonte | Traevion | Tranell | Travez |
| Tonye Daneeko | Tor-Rell | Tousao | Tra'vijuan | Traevios | Tranyle | Travian |
| Tonys | Torrell | Toussaint | Tra'vion | Traevon *(0.01)* | Trapper | Travier |
| Tonythanh | Torren *(0.01)* | Touyengkong | Tra'viyon | Traevun | Traqarius | Travierre |

| | | | | | | |
|---|---|---|---|---|---|---|
| Travin | Traylan | Tre'jawn | Tre'vonn | Trejean | Trennis | Trevaiss |
| Travinn | Traylin | Tre'jen | Tre'vonne | Trejhuan Iymari | Trennon | Trevan (0.01) |
| Travion (0.02) | Traylon | Tre'jion Frankie | Tre'vontay | Trejon | Trenquarius | Trevante |
| Travion Kahlil | Traylyn | Tre'john | Tre'vonte | Trejour | Trenston | Trevanti |
| Travione | Trayn | Tre'jon | Tre'yon | Trejun | Trent (0.37) | Trevar |
| Travionis | Trayniton | Tre'kwon | Tre'yvon | Trek | Trentan | Trevari |
| Travionne | Trayon | Tre'lijah | Trea | Trekista | Trenté | Trevarious |
| Traviontaye | Trayonne | Tre'lyn | Treá | Trekker | Trenten (0.05) | Trevaris |
| Travious | Trayontez | Tre'maine | Treabyron | Trelan | Trenter | Trevarris |
| Travis (0.76) | Traysean | Tre'mar | Tread | Trelane | Trentez | Trevas |
| Travis Jahmaad | Trayshaun | Tre'mari | Treadan | Trelanne | Trentice | Trevaughn |
| Travis-Maurice | Trayshawn | Tre'mel | Treamail | Trelen | Trentin (0.02) | (0.01) |
| Travis-Ray | Trayson | Tre'mell | Treamel | Trelin | Trently | Trevaun |
| Travius | Traysten | Tre'mon | Treandos | Trell | Trent-Michael | Trevear |
| Travois | Trayston | Tre'mont | Treaquane | Trelon | Trentn | Treveis |
| Tra-Von | Traytan | Tre'on | Treashawn | Trelvis | Trentny | Trevel |
| Travon (0.04) | Trayten | Tre'on-Luwayne | Treaston | Trelyn | Trenton (0.74) | Trevell |
| Travone | Traytien | Tre'quan (0.01) | Treasure | Tremain (0.01) | Trenton Joseph | Trevelle |
| Travonn | Traytin | Tre'quann | Treavion | Tremaine (0.02) | Trenton-Lee | Trevelyn |
| Travonne | Trayton (0.02) | Tre'quel | Treavon | Tremane | Trentt | Treven (0.01) |
| Travonta | Trayvaughn | Tre'quese | Treavonce | Tremar | Trentton | Trevenen |
| Travontae | Trayven | Tre'quez | Treavor | Tremari | Trentyn (0.01) | Treveno |
| Travonté | Trayveon | Tre'qwan | Treavos | Tremarion | Treonté | Tre-Veon |
| Travonteze | Trayvin | Tre'ron | Trebor (0.01) | Tremauryon | Trephaine | Treveon (0.01) |
| Travonty | Trayvion | Tre'saun | Trebreh | Tremayn | Treqaun | Treveontae |
| Travoris | Trayvionne | Tre'sean | Trebron | Tremayne (0.02) | Trequan (0.01) | Treveontay |
| Travos | Trayvis | Tre'shard | Trece | Tremeir | Trequez | Trever (0.05) |
| Travoughn | Tray-Von | Tre'shaun (0.01) | Tred | Tremel | Treron | Treverious |
| Travoy | Trayvon (0.03) | Tre'shawn (0.01) | Tredarious | Tremell | Treronn | Treves |
| Travun | Trayvon Jah | Tre'shir | Tredarius | Tremetrius | Tres | Trevett |
| Travuntae | Trayvonce | Tre'shon | Treddie | Tremil | Tresahn | Trevian |
| Travys | Trayvone | Tre'shone | Tredell | Trémir | Tresdon | Trevic |
| Trawick | Trayvonn | Tre'shun | Trederick | Tremirus | Tresean (0.01) | Trevier |
| Traxton | Trayvonne | Tre'vareiez | Trederious | Tremmel | Treshaun (0.01) | Trevierre |
| Tray (0.01) | Traz | Tre'varez | Tredon | Tremon | Tre-Shawn | Trevin (0.04) |
| Tray'christ | Trazavia | Tre'varis | Tree | Tremond | Treshawn (0.01) | Trevio |
| Tray'quan | Trazom | Tre'vaughn | Treedon | Tremont | Treshon | Trevion (0.02) |
| Tray'shawn | Tré (0.01) | Tre'vaun | Trefor | Trenadad | Treshun | Trevionté |
| Tray'vion | Tre (0.03) | Tre'vauris | Treg | Trenan | Treson | Trevious |
| Tray'von | Tre James | Tre'vawn | Tregan | Trenard | Tressel | Trevis |
| Tray'vone | Tre Quann | Tre'vell | Tregary | Trenauris | Trestan | Trevius |
| Trayandré | Tre Sean | Tre'veon | Trehvaun | Trendale | Tresten | Treviyis |
| Trayari | Tre Shaun | Tre'veonce | Trehy-David | Trendan | Trestin | Trevlyn |
| Trayc | Tre Shawn | Tre'veone | Trei'-Roan | Trendarious | Treston (0.01) | Trevoiyé |
| Trayce | Tré Vaughn | Tre'veyon | Trei'shaun | Trendell | Trestyn | Tre-Von |
| Traycer | Tre Vion | Tre'vian | Treiden | Trendon | Tret | Trevon (0.10) |
| Traydee | Tre'aire | Tre'viar | Treigh | Trendyn | Trete | Trevon' |
| Traydell | Tre'darius | Tre'vien | Treightn | Trenedy | Treton | Trevond |
| Trayden | Tre'darrius | Tre'vin | Treighton | Trenell | Trett | Tre-Vone |
| Traydinse | Tre'del | Tre'vion (0.01) | Treinton | Trenen | Trev | Trevone |
| Traydon | Tre'dell | Tre'vionne | Treishaune | Trenice | Trev'yon | Trevonn |
| Traye | Tre'don | Tre'viyon | Treivan | Trenity | Treva'on | Trevonne |
| Trayer | Tre'ion | Tre'von (0.02) | Treja'un | Trennan | Trevahn | Trevonné |

Trevontae
Trevonte
Trevonté
Trevonteah
Trevor *(1.27)*
Trevor Logan
Trevore
Trevor-John
Trevoughn
Trevour
Trevur
Trevyn *(0.01)*
Trevyon
Trevyonne
Trevyor
Trexler
Trexton
Trey *(0.48)*
Trey Michael
Trey Shaun
Trey Von
Trey'mon
Trey'on
Trey'shon
Trey'vion
Trey'von
Treyanosky
Trey-Anthony
Treyce *(0.01)*
Treycen
Treycin
Treydan
Treyden *(0.01)*
Treydn
Treydon
Treye
Treygen
Treygon
Treykwon
Treylan
Treylen
Treylen Don
Treylin
Treylon
Treymaine
Treymar
Treymel
Treymon
Treymont
Treynius
Treyon
Treyor
Treyquan

Treyron
Treysaan
Treyse
Treysean
Treysen
Treyshaun
Treyshawn
Treyshon
Treyshun
Treyson *(0.01)*
Treyten
Treytin
Treytn
Treyton *(0.05)*
Treyu
Treyun
Treyvahn
Treyvan
Treyvaris
Treyvaughn
Treyvaun
Treyven
Treyveon
Treyveontez
Treyvian
Treyvin
Treyvion *(0.01)*
Treyvionne
Treyvious
Treyvon *(0.03)*
Treyvone
Treyvonne
Treyvontae
Treyvontay
Treyvonté
Treyvor
Treyzen
Treyzhon
Trezden
Trezdon
Trezjon
Trez-Mynn
Trezon
Trezz
Trhisten
Tri
Tri Nhan
Tri'dell
Triallen
Tri-An
Trian
Triandous

Triany
Trias
Trice
Trico
Tridell
Triderius
Tridib
Tridyn
Triem
Triet
Trieu Quan
Trievon
Trigg
Trigyal
Trihas
Trilane
Trillion
Trillveyon
Trillyon
Trimaine
Trimund
Trin
Trine
Trinell
Trinety
Trinida
Trinidad *(0.01)*
Trinitee
Trinity *(0.01)*
Trinnity
Trinodad
Trinstin
Trinten
Trintin
Trintn
Trinton *(0.01)*
Trintyn
Trinyell
Trinzel
Trip
Tripen
Tripp *(0.02)*
Tripten
Tripton
Trisden
Trisdon
Trisen
Trishan
Trishaun
Trishon
Trishstyle
Trishtian
Trishtin

Trishton
Trisjin
Trisoan
Trison
Tristain
Tristam
Tristan *(2.47)*
Tristan
  Christopher
Tristan Michael
Tristan
  Thimotee
Tristan Tyler
Tristan-Andrew
Tristan-Costello
Tristan-
  Matthieu
Tristano
Tristdan
Tristden
Tristen *(0.27)*
Tristen Aiden
Tristen James
Tristen-Blake
Tristian *(0.07)*
Tristian Odee
Tristien
Tristin *(0.13)*
Tristin Jon
Tristine
Tristion
Tristn
Triston *(0.13)*
Triston Levi
Triston Quinn
Triston-Jason
Tristram
Tristun
Tristyn *(0.03)*
Trisztan
Tritan
Triten
Triton *(0.01)*
Trivain
Trivaries
Trivaun
Triveon
Trivett
Trivion
Trivitt
Trivon
Triztian
Triztin

Troah
Trocon
Troi
Troivon
Trokon
Trolando
Tromari
Tron
Trond
Trondariane
Trone
Trong
Trong Minh
  Justin
Trontavious
Trory
Trot
Trotter
Trovon
Troy *(0.47)*
Troy Leon
Troy Michael
Troyal
Troy-Carl
Troyce
Troydarius
Troy-Edward
Troyer
Troynesha
Troyvale
Troyvon
Tru
Trucker
True
Trueman
Truen
Truett *(0.01)*
Truex
Truit
Truitt
Trumain
Trumaine
Truman *(0.05)*
Truman-
  Alexander
Trumandray
Trumoni
Trung
Truong Dylan
Truong Manaho
Truong Phat
Truongvy
Trushaun

Truson
Truss
Trustan
Trusten
Trustin *(0.01)*
Trustyn
Truth *(0.01)*
Truves
Trux
Truxton
Try'von
Tryan
Tryce
Trycten
Trye'yone
Tryes
Tryg
Trygg
Trygve
Trymetrious
Trynston
Trynt
Trynten
Tryntin
Tryntun
Trynus
Trynyty
Tryp
Tryshien
Tryson
Trystan *(0.05)*
Trysten *(0.02)*
Trystian
Trystin *(0.01)*
Trystn
Trystne
Tryston *(0.02)*
Trystyan
Trystyn *(0.01)*
Tryten
Tryton
Tryun
Tsakai
Tsali
Tsaosha
Tsaykehden
Tscheng Xeng
Tse
Tseeb
Tsegabe
Tsering
Tshaj
Tshajkoob

Tshajlij
Tshajyeej
T-Shan
Tshayeng
Tshering
Tshombe
Tsi Muaj
Tsim Nou
Tsimnuj
Tsion
Tsiory
Tsjaad
Tsua
Tsubasa
Tsuefeng
Tsujzoo
Tu
Tuakimoana
Tuan
Tuan Kiet James
Tuan Kiet
  William
Tuan Luong
Tuari
Tubxyooj
Tuchili
Tuck
Tucker *(0.39)*
Tucker-Griffin
Tuckerman
Tuckor
Tucson
Tud
Tudor
Tuff *(0.01)*
Tug
Tugger
Tuhqwacea
Tukai
Tukaree
Tuker
Tukker
Tulee
Tulio
Tulisi Toia
Tulley
Tully *(0.01)*
Tumarye
Tunjaa
Tunner
Tunny
Tupac
Tupak

| | | | | | | |
|---|---|---|---|---|---|---|
| Tuquais | Ty'anthony | Ty'lik | Ty'san | Tydan | Tyeran | Tyjair |
| Turall | Ty'aris | Ty'linc | Ty'sean | Tydarian | Tyere | Ty-James |
| Turan | Ty'carius | Ty'liqe | Ty'shaun *(0.01)* | Tydarien | Tyerek | Tyjaun |
| Ture | Ty'caurean | Ty'lique | Ty'shawn *(0.02)* | Tydarious | Tyerese | Tyjawan |
| Turing | Ty'corey | Ty'malique | Ty'shawnta | Tydarius | Tyerick | Tyjawn |
| Turiq | Ty'coryion | Ty'marion | Ty'shon | Tyde | Tyes | Tyjay |
| Turk | Ty'darious | Ty'meek | Ty'shyne | Tydell | Tyesean | Tyjaylin |
| Turki | Ty'darius | Ty'meer | Ty'son | Tydeman | Tyeshown | Tyjear |
| Turner *(0.04)* | Ty'darrian | Ty'meir | Ty'trez | Tyden | Tyesn | Tyjeid |
| Turo | Ty'darrius | Ty'mirr | Ty'vanta | Tydere | Tyeson | Tyjeir |
| Turon | Ty'derek | Ty'nayis | Ty'veon | Tyderrick | Tyessence | Tyjen |
| Turone | Ty'derrius | Ty'nez | Ty'vi | Tyderrius | Tyeus | Tyjer |
| Turquandré | Ty'dravious | Ty'on | Ty'von | Tydeus | Tyezhé | Tyjere |
| Turrel | Ty'drez | Ty'one | Ty'vonn | Tydin | Tygan | Tyjerome |
| Turrell | Ty'dus | Ty'preest | Ty'vonte | Tydon | Tygár | Tyjhawn |
| Turron | Ty'eir | Ty'qarrius | Ty'wan | Tydralen | Tyge | Tyjhorn |
| Tuscan | Ty'eon | Ty'qorius | Ty'waun | Tydrea | Tygen | Tyji're |
| Tushaan | Ty'ere | Ty'quan *(0.01)* | Ty'won | Tydrecus | Tyger *(0.01)* | Tyjiere |
| Tushan | Ty'heem | Ty'quarius | Ty'wone | Tydrecuz | Tygh | Tyjin |
| Tushar | Ty'ion | Ty'quauion | Ty'wun | Tydreic | Tygir | Tyjion |
| Tushka | Ty'jae | Ty'quavious | Ty'yon | Tydrekis | Tygren | Tyjon |
| Tustin | Ty'jai | Ty'quawn | Ty'zaveous | Tydrick | Ty-Guan | Tyjuan *(0.01)* |
| Tut | Ty'jari | Ty'quell | Ty'zavionne | Tydriez | Anthony | Tyjuane |
| Tut-Kuoth | Ty'jaun | Ty'querrius | Tyaeirus | Tydus | Tygue | Tyjuné |
| Tuukak | Ty'jay | Ty'quez | Tyaharri | Tye *(0.06)* | Tyh'mir | Ty-Kari |
| Tuukka | Ty'jaylen | Ty'quiez | Tyair | Tye'kevion | Tyheed | Tykarri |
| Tuvia | Ty'jeir | Ty'quire | Tyaire | Tye'kwon | Tyheem | Tykarris |
| Tuwan | Ty'jeon | Ty'quize | Tyairon | Tye'ler | Tyheim | Tykarrius |
| Tuyen | Ty'jerius | Ty'ray | Tyairre | Tye'shaun | Tyheme | Tyke |
| Tuza | Ty'jhasun | Ty'reak | Tyairz | Tyeé | Tyhier | Tykee |
| Tvareyon | Ty'jhawn | Ty'rece | Tyan | Tyée | Tyhir | Tykeem |
| Tvonte | Ty'jhon | Ty'ree *(0.01)* | Tyanah | Tyee *(0.01)* | Tyhire | Tykeese |
| Twain | Ty'john | Ty'reek | Tyangelo | Tyeese | Tyhler | Tykeilin |
| Twan | Ty'jon | Ty'reese | Tyareik | Tyehimba | Tyhlin | Tykeir |
| Twanyishe- | Ty'juan | Ty'reik | Tyari | Tyehun | Tyhrnan | Tykeise |
| Daniel | Ty'kalo | Ty'rek | Tyariq | Tyeion | Tyi'juan | Tykel |
| Twayne | Ty'kavious | Ty'reke | Tyaris | Tyeir | Tyianah | Tykell |
| Twonyé | Ty'kedrian | Ty'rel | Tyarreis | Tyeis | Tyier | Tykem |
| Twuan | Ty'keem | Ty'rell | Tyarri | Tyejae | Tyiion | Tykenvion |
| Txujci | Ty'kei | Ty'ren | Tyaun | Tyekwon | Tyiland | Tykerion |
| Ty *(0.74)* | Ty'kell | Ty'reon | Tyaurice | Tyelan | Tyilee | Tykese |
| Ty 'Juan | Ty'kemeon | Ty'req | Tyavon | Tyelar | Tyiler | Tyketric |
| Ty Juan | Ty'kerrian | Ty'rese | Tybee | Tyele | Tyion | Tykeus |
| Ty Keydreian | Ty'keveon | Ty'rhez | Tyberius | Tyeleak | Tyiquis | Tykeveis |
| Ty Lee | Ty'kevion | Ty'riis | Tybree | Tyeleale | Tyir | Tykevion |
| Ty Lei | Ty'kevious | Ty'rik | Tybreion | Tyelek | Tyirek | Tykey |
| Ty Mari | Ty'kevius | Ty'rin | Tycamren | Tyeler | Tyis | Tykeyth |
| Ty Mykael | Ty'keyvius | Ty'riq | Tyce *(0.01)* | Tyelin | Tyiwion | Tykheem |
| Ty Oinne | Ty'lain | Ty'rique | Tycen | Tyell | Tyiwon | Tykie |
| Ty Vion | Ty'lan | Ty'ron | Tychaun | Tyemere | Tyjae | Tykieem |
| Ty. | Ty'lasia | Ty'rone | Tychicus | Tye-Michael | Tyjah | Tykies |
| Ty' Keem | Ty'lee | Ty'ronn | Tychique-Jurom | Tyen | Tyjai | Tykirian |
| Ty' Reece | Ty'leek | Ty'ryn | Tychon | Tyenjureke | Tyjailan | Tyko |

Tykorrian
Tykwan
Tykwon
Tylace
Tylair
Tylan (0.03)
Tyland
Tylar (0.01)
Tyleck
Ty-Lee
Tylee
Tylee Q
Tyleek
Tyleeke
Tyleem
Tyleen
Tyleeq
Tylef
Tylei
Tyleigh
Tylek
Tyleke
Tylen (0.01)
Tylen-Isaiah
Tyleon
Tyler (6.96)
Tyler James
Tyler Jason
Tyler Jean
Tyler Jemar
Tyler Jenson
Tyler Ray
Tyler Robenson
Tyler Robert
Tylere
Tyler-James
Tyler-John
Tyler-Michael
Tyler-Niko
Tyler-William
Tylete
Tyli
Tylib
Tylieek
Tyliek
Tyliest
Tylik (0.01)
Tylin
Tylind
Tylique
Tylir
Tylirius
Tyller

Tylo
Tylon (0.01)
Tylor (0.05)
Tylr
Tylun
Tylund
Tylyn
Tylynn
Tymair
Tymarco
Tymari
Tymarian
Tymarion
Tymarre
Tymason
Tymaun
Tymauri
Tyme
Tyme're
Tymeek
Tymeer
Tymein
Tymeire
Tymelle
Tymere (0.01)
Tymerias
Tymetrius
Tymhariaun
Tymier
Tymiir
Tymik
Tymir (0.02)
Tymire
Ty-Mon
Tymon
Tymon Gabri
Tymond
Tymondre
Tymondrick
Tymont
Tymoreon
Tymorrion
Tymothe
Tymothei
Tymothy
Tymun
Tynan (0.01)
Tynarian
Tynavi
Tyndale
Tyne
Tyneif
Tynell

Tyner
Tynez Robert
Tyohn
Tyon
Tyone
Tyonne
Tyont
Typhony
Typriest
Tyqavious
Tyqavis
Tyquan (0.02)
Tyquan'marion
Ty-Quantis
Tyquarius
Tyquavion
Tyquavious
Tyquavius
Tyquawn
Tyquawoné
Tyquell
Tyquez
Tyquil
Tyquin
Tyquis
Tyquise
Tyqune
Tyquon
Tyqurius
Tyquwon
Tyqwon
Tyr
Tyrae
Tyrahn
Tyrai
Tyrail
Tyraious
Tyrale
Tyran (0.01)
Tyrance
Tyrane
Tyranny
Tyrant
Tyras
Tyray
Tyrayé
Tyrayn
Tyré
Tyre (0.01)
Tyre'ale
Tyre'ke
Tyreak
Tyreák

Tyrease
Tyrec
Tyrece
Tyreck
Tyreé
Tyrée
Tyree (0.08)
Tyreece
Tyreef
Tyreek (0.02)
Tyreeké
Tyreem
Tyreen
Tyreeon
Tyreese (0.02)
Tyrees-Lee
Tyrees-Victor
Tyreeze
Tyreice
Tyreik
Tyreike
Tyreil
Tyrein
Tyreion
Tyreiq
Tyrek (0.01)
Tyreke (0.01)
Tyrel (0.01)
Tyrell (0.10)
Tyrelle
Tyren (0.01)
Tyrence
Tyreon
Tyreq
Tyreque
Tyres
Tyresé
Tyrese (0.09)
Tyress
Tyresse
Tyrey
Tyrez
Tyri
Tyrian
Tyric
Tyrice
Tyrick
Tyrico
Tyrie
Tyrieck
Tyriek
Tyrik (0.01)
Tyrike

Tyril
Tyrin (0.01)
Tyrion
Tyrione
Tyriq (0.02)
Tyriqué
Tyrique (0.01)
Tyris
Tyrise
Tyrius
Tyrohn
Tyrol
Tyrome
Tyron (0.03)
Tyrone (0.14)
Tyrone Charles
Tyrone III
Tyroni
Tyronn
Tyronne
Tyroy
Tyroyce
Tyrrell
Tyrrick
Tyrriel
Tyruan
Tyrum
Tyrus (0.02)
Tyruss
Tyryn
Tysaan
Tysahon
Tysan
Tysaughn
Tysaun
Tyse
Tyseam
Tysean (0.01)
Tyseem
Tyseer
Tysei
Tysen (0.02)
Tyshan
Tyshaun (0.01)
Tyshawan
Tyshawd
Ty-Shawn
Tyshawn (0.05)
Tysheed
Tysheem
Tysheim
Tyshiem
Tyshine

Tyshir
Tysho
Tyshombe
Tyshon (0.01)
Tyshop
Tyshun
Tyshyne
Tysiah
Tysin
Tysir
Tysjon
Ty-Son
Tyson (0.57)
Tyson Kayden
Tyson Richard
Tyson-Joseph
Tyssen
Tysson
Tysyn
Tytace
Tytain
Tytan
Tytarious
Tytavion
Tytis
Tyton
Tytravin
Tytrell
Tytrez
Tytus (0.01)
Tyus
Tyuss
Tyvaghn
Tyvan
Tyvarius
Tyvarres
Tyvaughn
Tyve'oun
Tyvek
Tyvel
Tyvell
Tyveon
Tyvin
Tyvion
Tyvon (0.01)
Tyvonna
Tyvonne
Tyvonta
Tyvor
Tyvori
Tyvyn
Tywan (0.01)
Ty-Waun

Tywaun
Tywayne
Tywin
Tywoine
Tywon
Tywone
Tywuan
Tyyon
Tyz'hon
Tyz'juan
Tyz'uan
Tyzae
Tyzaireus
Tyzarious
Tyzavion
Tyzel
Tyzhan
Tyzher
Tyzik
Tyzjai
Tyzzeon
Tzadkiya
Tzen-Wei
Tzion
Tzur
Tzuriel
Tzvi (0.03)

## ~ U ~

U'darrion
U'neek
Ua Shayne
Uatahouse
Uatesoni
Ubald-Murad
Ubaldo (0.01)
Ubayda
Uber
Ubertino
Uberto
Uche
Uchechukwu
Uchenna
Udaipal
Udaiveer
Uday
Udaymit
Udayveer
Udayvir
Uddam
Udechukwu

| | | | | | |
|---|---|---|---|---|---|
| Udhaibir | Umar-Ibn | Useth-Ali | Vahram | Valon | Vann-Mikael | Vasilios *(0.01)* |
| Udham | Umarpreet | Usher *(0.02)* | Vahtavio | Valor | Vannon | Vasilis |
| Udhay | Umarr | Ushon | Vai | Valorien | Van-Quang | Vasiliy |
| Udit | Umay | Usiel | Vaibhav | Valos | Vanrico | Vasily |
| Udo | Umayr | Usif | Vaibhav Narayan | Valsco | Vansh | Vasishta |
| Udomsack | Umed | Usmaan | Vaidan | Valyn | Vanshdeep | Vasjan |
| Udon'nis | Umer | Usman *(0.01)* | Vaiden | Vameng | Vanson | Vaso |
| Udonis | Umi | Utah | Vaigintas | Vamouyen | Vantavious | Vason |
| Uepi Pulupaki | Umjairell | Utchas | Vairon | Vamsee | Vantonio | Vasper |
| Ugnius | Umka | Uther | Vaishnav | Vamsi | Vantreaon | Vasquez |
| Ugo | Umut | Uthmaan | Vaishnavi | Van *(0.05)* | Vantrell | Vassagio |
| Ugochi | Unais | Uthman | Vaitua | Van Kiet Kelvin | Vanyel | Vassar |
| Ugochukwu | Unari | Utkarsh | Vakyus | Van Nam | Vanyn | Vassili |
| Ugonna | Unberto | Utwuan | Val | Van'treyvious | Vanzale | Vassilios |
| Uileam | Undra | Uwais | Valahmeire | Vana | Vaquwon | Vastiany |
| Uinniq | Undre | Uzair | Valanchie | Vanacel | Varad | Vasu |
| Ujo | Ungray | Uzarrian | Valdemar | Vanboower | Varaschi | Vasudev |
| Ujoma | Uni | Uziah | Valdez | Vance *(0.08)* | Vardaan | Vasudevan |
| Ukasha | Unique | Uzias | Valdhe | Vandalai | Vardaanpreet | Vasyl |
| Ukiah | Uniqueez | Uzico | Valdis | Vandan | Vareck | Vatallion |
| Uku | Unitas | Uziel *(0.01)* | Valdjy | Vanden | Varesh | Vatenjchumay |
| Ulan | Uno | Uzoma | Valdy | Vander | Vargas | Vaughan *(0.01)* |
| Ulando | Unray | Uzozie | Vale | Vanderlae | Varian | Vaughn *(0.09)* |
| Uldarico | Uohans | Uzzia | Valearno | Vandersen | Varick | Vaugn |
| Ulette | Updesh | Uzziah | Valedeo | Vandis | Varik | Vaun |
| Ulian | Upkaran | Uzziel | Valek | Vandon | Varnell | Vay'shun |
| Ulices *(0.01)* | Upraj | Uzziyah | Valen | Vandree | Varney | Vayden |
| Ulisban | Ura | | Valencio | Vandriel | Varra | Vayk |
| Ulise | Urbaine | | Valensky | Vandrious | Varrion | Vaylin |
| Ulises *(0.05)* | Urban | ~ V ~ | Valentae | Vandyke | Vartavious | Vayun |
| Ulisses | Urben | | Valente | Vandyn | Vartrell | Vazquez Phillips |
| Ulix | Urbin | V C | Valentin *(0.03)* | Vane | Varun *(0.03)* | Vcake |
| Ulizes | Uremyah | Va'akalasini | Valentine *(0.01)* | Vanek | Varunson | Vean |
| Ulli | Uri | Va'darius | Valentino *(0.04)* | Vanelly | Varyck | Veasna |
| Ullrich | Uri Nahir | Va'kariyh | Valeria | Vanes | Varyk | Ved |
| Ulric | Uria | Va'quwyen | Valerian | Vanessa | Vasan | Ved Karan |
| Ulrich | Uriah *(0.04)* | Va'shaun | Valeriano | Vangah Kakou | Vasanth | Reddy |
| Ulrick *(0.01)* | Urias | Vaali | Valerien | Christ | Vasco | Vedaant |
| Ulrico | Uribel | Vacariez | Valerio | Vangelis | Vascon | Vedan |
| Ulrik | Urie | Vacheng | Valeriy | Vangely | Vasean | Vedanga |
| Ulver | Uriel *(0.10)* | Vachon | Valery | Vanhelsen | Vash | Vedansh |
| Ulyces | Uriel-Kaider | Vada | Valerys | Vania | Vashan | Vedant *(0.01)* |
| Ulys | Uriy | Vaddant | Valhandal | Vaniel | Vashaun | Vedanth |
| Ulyses | Uriyus | Vadden | Vali | Vanier | Vashawn | Vedder |
| Ulysess | Ursher | Vaden *(0.01)* | Valiant | Vanik | Vasher | Vedh |
| Ulysis | Uruk | Vadim | Valin | Van-Khoi | Vashion | Vedik |
| Ulysse *(0.01)* | Ury | Vadin | Vallem | Vann *(0.01)* | Vashon | Veejay |
| Ulysses *(0.02)* | Uryah | Vadym | Vallen | Vannara | Vashton | Veer *(0.01)* |
| Umaar | Uryel | Vafee | Vallin | Vannarith | Vashun | Veer Arvin |
| Umair | Usaamah | Vagel | Vallo | Vannath | Vasil | Veeraj |
| Umajasty | Usalas | Vagellis | Valmiki | Vanndemier | Vasile | Veeran |
| Umar *(0.01)* | Usamah | Vagiba | Valmore | Vanner | Vasileios | Veeraraju |
| Umar Khan | Usayd | Vahn | Valo | Vanness | Vasili *(0.01)* | Veerinder |

| | | | | | | |
|---|---|---|---|---|---|---|
| Vega | Verlan | Vic | Viejo | Vincent Brodie | Viny | Viswa |
| Vegas | Verland | Vic' | Vielman | Vincent D | Vinzant | Viswas |
| Veguer | Verlin | Vicangelo | Vien | Vincent Daron | Violeta | Vitale |
| Vehbe | Verlyn | Vicari | Vieny | Vincent Emile | Vion'te | Vitali |
| Vehbija | Vermareon | Vicent | Vieri | Vincent Justin | Vionté | Vitaliano |
| Veictor | Vern | Vicenté | Viet *(0.01)* | Vincent Lee | Viontre | Vitalik |
| Veikko | Vernal | Vicente *(0.07)* | Viet Minh Quan | Vincent R | Viorel | Vitaliy |
| Velan | Vernan | Vicente Leoncio | Danny | Vincent- | Viplav | Vitaly |
| Velav | Vernando | Vicenzo | Viete | Anthony | Vipransh | Viterman |
| Velavan | Vernard | Vichael | Vietro | Vincente | Vishesh | Vithana |
| Velbin | Vernardino | Vichai | Viggo *(0.01)* | Vincenté | Vipul | Vithuran |
| Velcan | Vernell | Vichaud | Vighnesh | Vincentini | Vipulan | Vito *(0.02)* |
| Velez | Verner | Vickens | Vignesh | Vincent-Nicolas | Vir | Vito Antonio |
| Velintae | Vernie | Vickensley | Vigo | Vincent-Olivier | Viraaj | Vitor |
| Velix | Vernon *(0.04)* | Vickram | Vihaan | Vincent-Xavier | Viraat | Vitto |
| Veljko | Vernon Antho | Vickramjeet | Vihaari | Vincenzio | Viraj *(0.01)* | Vittorio *(0.01)* |
| Velko | Verntavious | Vicktor | Vihan | Vincenzo *(0.05)* | Virath-Alex | Vitus |
| Vellis | Verntrell | Vicler | Vijay *(0.01)* | Vincero | Virdaruis | Vivaan |
| Velmar | Verntron | Vico | Vijayaram | Vincesid | Virgil *(0.02)* | Vivam-Raaj |
| Veloglome | Veron | Victavion | Vikai | Vinchenzo | Virgile | Vivan |
| Veltrez | Veronica | Victoir | Vikas | Vinci | Virgilio | Vivek *(0.01)* |
| Vemana | Verontae | Victor *(2.10)* | Vikash | Vincin | Virgle | Vivenio |
| Ven | Verrazano | Victor A | Vikraanth | Vincinzo | Virickson | Viviana |
| Vencent | Verrick | Victor Anthony | Vikram *(0.01)* | Vineet | Virlinsky | Viviano |
| Vencenzo | Versel | Victor Bjorn | Vikramjit | Vineeth | Virlius | Vivin |
| Vences | Vershad | Victor Hugo | Vikrampal | Vinesh | Virsean | Vivon |
| Vencint | Vershard | Victor M | Vikrant | Vinet | Virshawn | VJ |
| Venedikt | Vershaun | Victor Remi | Vikranth | Vineth | Visai | Vlad *(0.01)* |
| Venedito | Vershawn | Victor-Alexandre | Viktor *(0.02)* | Vinh *(0.01)* | Visal | Vladamir |
| Venerche | Vershoud | Victor-Alexis | Vilai Souk | Vinhcent | Visar | Vladden |
| Venesee | Versipius | Victor-Andre | Vilas | Vinh-Khang | Visaya | Vlade |
| Veniamin | Vertavious | Victordean | Viler | Vinh-San | Vishaal | Vlademir |
| Venka | Vertone | Victore | Vilhelm | Vinicio | Vishael | Vladi |
| Venkat | Veshaun | Victor-Eliot | Viliami | Vinicius *(0.01)* | Vishal *(0.01)* | Vladik |
| Venkata | Veshod | Victoria | Vilma | Vinit | Vishal Sai | Vladimer |
| Venkatesh | Veshon | Victoriano | Vilnis | Vinith | Vishan | Vladimir *(0.04)* |
| Venmar | Vester | Victorino | Vilnius | Vinn | Vishar | Vladimir-Ramon |
| Vennis | Veston | Victorio | Vilson | Vinnee | Vishav | Vladislav *(0.01)* |
| Venom | Veto | Victorion | Vimal | Vinnicius | Vishavjeet | Vlad-Matei |
| Venoy | Vetol | Victorious | Vimbai Princess | Vinnieius | Vishawn | Vladmir |
| Venrry | Veton | Victor-Manuel | Vimel | Vinnsentt | Vishnoy | Vladyslav |
| Venson | Veydh | Victormanuel | Vin | Vinny | Vishnu | Vnokeckv |
| Ventrel | Vhaldimir | Victor-Nabiel | Vin Rilee | Vino | Vishnugupt | Voaz |
| Ventura | Vhamari | Victor-Radu | Vin'cere | Vinodh | Vishresh | Voghel |
| Venuk | Vi'cente | Victor-Xavier | Vinancio | Vinsent | Vishrut | Vohn |
| Venzo | Vi'jay | Victory | Vinay *(0.01)* | Vinson *(0.01)* | Vishruth | Void |
| Veondre | Vian | Victourius | Vinay Singh | Vinston | Vishu | Volkan |
| Verayn | Viandre | Vidal *(0.01)* | Vinayak | Vinten | Vishvak | Volomon |
| Verdell | Vianex | Vidath | Vinaydeep | Vinton | Vishwa | Voltaire |
| Verell | Viangelo | Vidipt | Vince *(0.03)* | Vintorion | Vishwajit | Von *(0.01)* |
| Verimayian | Viassna | Vidur | Vince Robert | Vintrell | Vishwavel | Von'diago |
| Verit | Vibhath | Viduram | Vincein | Vintriel | Visna | Vondarrial |
| Verkell | Vibhav | Vidvath | Vincent *(2.06)* | Vintwon | Visvajit | Vondran |

| | | | | | |
|---|---|---|---|---|---|
| Vondre | Vykai | Wagner | Walkens | Waris | Wayden | Wenceslao |
| Vonelle | Vyn | Wagosh | Walker (0.22) | Warner (0.01) | Waydon | Wenceslas |
| Vonellis | Vynce | Wah'keem | Walkins | Warnick | Waylan (0.01) | Wendal |
| Vong | Vyncent | Wahab | Wallace (0.03) | Warren (0.13) | Wayland (0.01) | Wendall |
| Vongeric | Vynn | Wahariwakeron | Waller | Warren Spencer | Wayle | Wendarius |
| Vonik | Vynt | Wahdatali | Wallie | Warren | Waylen (0.01) | Wendel |
| Vonjai | Vyom | Wahib | Wally | Waseskon | Waylin | Wendeldrick |
| Vonn | Vyon | Wahid | Walner | Warren-Allen | Wayling | Wendell (0.03) |
| Vonnie | Vyron | Wahinkpe | Walnic | Warrener | Waylon (0.11) | Wendley |
| Vonscott | Vyshawn | Wahkan | Walph | Warren-Robert | Waylund | Wendoll |
| Vonta | Vyshonne | Wahkeenyah | Walsh | Warrez | Waylyn | Wendon |
| Vontae | Vysiasavon | Waideko | Walson | Warrick | Waylynd | Wendy |
| Vontaj | Vytas | Wailin | Walt | Warrik | Waymon | Wendyam |
| Vontavious | Vyze | Wain | Waltarion | Warrin | Waymond | Weng |
| Vontavis | | Wais | Waltaveus | Warrior | Wayne (0.11) | Wenge-Hero |
| Vontazis | | Waiz Ali | Waltclaire | Warsame | Wayo | Wengel |
| Vonté | ~ W ~ | Wajah | Walter (0.22) | Warwick | Waytron | Weniu |
| Vontel | | Wajdaan | Walterione | Waryk | Wayvon | Wensderley |
| Vonterrius | W | Wajdi | Walter-Isaias | Wasan | Wazen | Wense |
| Vontez | W Ryan | Wajeeh | Walterjay | Wasay | Wazim | Wensky |
| Vontice | Wa Meng | Wajih | Walter-Jos | Wasckar | Wazir | Wenslee |
| Vontrayle | Wa'eem | Wakean | Walterking | Waseem (0.01) | Weah | Wensley |
| Vontraz | Wa'il | Wakee | Waltfredo | Wasef | Wealth | Wentao |
| Vontre'vious | Waaiz | Wakeem | Walton (0.01) | Waseskun | Wealthy | Wenther |
| Vontrel | Wa-Aizahmad | Wakeen | Waltrez | Wâseskwan | Webb | Wenyu |
| Vontrell | Waaris | Waki | Walvin | Washington | Weber | Werner |
| Vontrez | Waasay | Wakinson | Walynn | Washun | Webly | Wernher |
| Vophcy | Wacante | Wal | Wamah | Wasif | Webster | Wernick |
| Vory | Wacey | Walat | Wambdi | Wasil | Wedly | Wes (0.01) |
| Vosa | Wacim | Walber | Wambli | Wasim | Wedrell | Wesam |
| Voshon | Wacim-Walid | Walberto | Wameng | Wassim (0.01) | Wei | Wesdon |
| Voss | Wade (0.15) | Waldeck | Wamiq-Ali | Wassime | Wei-Bin | Weslee (0.01) |
| Voven | Wadedel | Waldemar | Wamorena | Wassim-Eddine | Weichin | Wesler |
| Vraj | Wadée | Walden | Wan | Wassim-Noufel | Weikai | Wesley (0.71) |
| Vrajnandak | Wadellow | Waldir | Wanderlay | Wataru | Weiler | Wesley-Bryan |
| Vrien | Waden | Waldo | Wanding | Wathel | Weili | Weslie |
| Vrisan | Wadi | Waldon | Wandy | Wathen | Weis | Wesly (0.01) |
| Vriseyda | Wadiea | Waldron | Wangavu | Watis | Weison | Wesly-Allen |
| Vrishank | Wadikonda | Walead | Wani | Watrell | Weiss | Weslyn |
| Vu | Wadleigh | Waled | Wanis-Fernando | Watson | Weizhi | Wesner |
| Vu Anh-Tuan | Wadley | Waleed (0.01) | Wanke | Watt | Welden | Wess |
| Vu-Dang | Wadnel | Waleed Ahmed | Jomarion | Wattana | Weldon (0.01) | Wessel |
| Vuk | Wadney | Waleem | Waposohseh | Watts | Welinton | Wessen |
| Vullas | Wadny | Walford | Warachi | Wattson | Wellan | Wessley |
| Vunty | Wadsen | Walfred | Ward (0.01) | Watzel | Welles | Wesson |
| Vuong | Wadson | Walfrido | Warda | Waun | Wellington | West (0.01) |
| Vutsanah | Waeal | Wali | Wardeer | Waveland | Wells (0.01) | Westan |
| Vuvu-Jude | Waeil | Wali Uddin | Wardell | Waverly | Welmer | Westdyn |
| Vwj | Wael | Walian | Ware | Waya | Welsh | Westel |
| Vy | Waeys | Walid (0.01) | Waric | Waydan | Welton | Westen |
| Vycere | Wafeed | Walid-Abdoullah | Warik | Wayde | Wen | Westher |
| Vyctor | Wafi | Walkeen | Waring | Waydell | Wenceslado | Westin (0.04) |

Westland
Westlee
Westley *(0.02)*
Westlie
Westly
Westlyn
Weston *(0.21)*
Weston Lee
Westyn *(0.01)*
Wexler
Weyland
Weylen
Weyman
Weyner
Wezlee
Wezley
Whalen
Whaley
Wharran
Whaylon
Whayne
Wheeler
Wheinholzky
Whenley
Wheylan
Wheylin
Whidley
Whip
Whispern
Whit
Whitaker
White
Whiteelk
Whitefield
Whitestar
Whitfield
Whitley
Whitman
Whitneon
Whitner
Whitney
Whitson
Whittaker
Whitten
Whittier
Whitton
Whyatt *(0.01)*
Whydmayer
Whyett
Wiatt
Wichensky
Wick

Wicleff
Widberg
Widinson
Widj
Widley
Widman
Widmarck
Wiilliam
Wikus
Wil *(0.01)*
Wil'kevious
Wil'travius
Wil'vontae
Wilbens
Wilber *(0.01)*
Wilber Enrique
Wilberson
Wilbert *(0.01)*
Wilberto
Wilborn
Wilbrod
Wilbur *(0.01)*
Wilburn
Wild
Wildbill
Wildelson
Wilden
Wilder *(0.01)*
Wilderson
Wildin
Wildon
Wildy
Wilem
Wilens
Wilert
Wiley *(0.02)*
Wilfedo
Wilfido
Wilfnier
Wilfny
Wilford
Wilfred *(0.01)*
Wilfred Jr
Wilfredo *(0.02)*
Wilfredy
Wilfrid
Wilfrido
Wilgains
Wilhel
Wilhelm
Wilhelmus
Wilhem-Darlin

Wili
Wiliam
William-Philyp
Wilian
Wilibaldo
Wilifrank
Wilik
Wililam
Wilinsky
Wilique
Wilken
Wilkens
Wilkenson
Wilkerson
Wilkes
Wilkievious
Wilkin
Wilkins
Wilkinson
Wilks
Wilky
Will *(0.15)*
Will Smith
Willaim
Willam
Willan
Willard *(0.02)*
Willaton
Willden
Willdrick
Willem *(0.05)*
Willer
Willetta
Willex
Willey
Willi
Willi'zhuan
William-
William *(8.77)*
William Alberto
William Alexis
William Conrad
William David
William Davis
William
   Emerson
William Eric
William
   Franklin
William Hoang
William James

William Jayson
   Cliff
William Jeff
William Joseph
William Jr.
William Marc
William Mason
William Preston
   Lee
William Real
William Rory
William Ryan
William Samuel
William
   Thacher
William Thomas
William Vaughn
William Wyatt
William'neil
William-
   Alexandre
William-Alexis
William-Andrew
William-Ash
William-Bofei
William-Cedrik
William-Dennis
William-Duy
William-
   Francisco
William-Jude
Williamn
William-Nicolas
William-Olivier
William-Patrick
William-
   Philippe
Williams *(0.01)*
Williams-
   Duchaine
Williamson
Williamsons
William-Wallace
William-Xavier
Willian
Willianh
Willians
Willie *(0.14)*
Willie B
Williem
Willier
Willijah

Willims
Willin
Willinton
Willis *(0.01)*
Willliam
Willmax
Willmer
   Alejandr
Willmon
Willmor
Willoughby
Willow
Wills
Willshawn
Willsiton
Willson
Willtin
Willum
Willy *(0.01)*
Will-Yam
Willyam *(0.01)*
Wilm
Wilman
Wilmar
Wilmark
Wilmer *(0.04)*
Wilmour
Wilmy
Wilnerson
Wilnick
Wilsane
Wilshawn
Wilshon
Wilson *(0.17)*
Wilson-Junior
Wilthin
Wilton *(0.01)*
Wiltreion
Wilvard
Wilvens
Wilver
Wilverson
Wily
Wilzon
Win
Winandus
Wincer
Wind
Windale
Windell
Windezz
Windham

Windy
Winfield
Winfred
Wing
Wingi
Wingrove
Winliam
Winnie
Winrich
Winsin
Winslett
Winslow
Winson
Winsor
Winsten
Winsthon
Winston *(0.07)*
Winston
   Mingzhe
Winter
Winthrop
Winton
Winzer
Wipusit
Wiremu
Wisaac
Wisdom
Wiseman
Wish
Wisiandel
Wisin
Wisnel
Wisnick
Wisny
Wispender
Wissam
Wissem
Wissin
Wisson
Wister
Wiston
Witchner
Witt
Witten
Wizdom
Wladimir
Wleed
Wofa Yaw
Wol
Wolf
Wolfe
Wolffe

Wolfgang *(0.01)*
Wollie
Wolney
Won'ye
Wonder
Wong
Wontea
Wontraious
Woo
Wood
Woodarius
Woodens
Woodford
Woodie
Woodley
Woodlinsky
Woodmyer
Woodnel
Woodrow *(0.01)*
Woodshell
Woodson
Woodwin
Woody *(0.01)*
Wooju
Wooley
Woordchel
Woosbend
Woran
Worlson
Worrick
Worthey
Wouance
Woudeson
Woudy
Wragneers
Wraith
Wraithe
Wrangler
Wraymond
Wren *(0.01)*
Wrenshel
Wrex
Wrian
Wriddhi
Wright
Wrigley
Wryder
Wryley
Wuences
Wuilberth
Wuiliam
Wuilmer

| | | | | | |
|---|---|---|---|---|---|
| Wuilver | Wyndom | Xai | Xaviebren | Xedrik | Xuefei | Xzhayvier |
| Wulian | Wyndsor | Xaidan | Xavien *(0.01)* | Xeebxaanti | Xuefeng | Xzheyvion |
| Wuma | Wynn | Xaiden | Xavieon | Xen | Xufeng | Xziah |
| Wuzhou | Wyns | Xain | Xavier *(2.81)* | Xeng | Xuriah | Xzierean |
| Wy'cameron | Wynstan | Xaine | Xavier Etienne | Xenny | Xxavier | Xzorion |
| Wy'kien | Wynston | Xairo | Xavier Isaiah | Xenophon | Xxyair | Xzvian |
| Wy'lee | Wynter | Xaisanna | Xavier Joshua | Xeo | Xy | Xzvonymir |
| Wyaitt | Wynton | Xaiver *(0.01)* | Xavier Yu Hin | Xerien | Xy'reus | Xzylaman |
| Wyat | Wyntr | Xaivier | Xavier- | Xerxees | Xybian | Xzyler |
| Wyatt *(2.83)* | Wytavious | Xaivyon |   Alexandre | Xerxes | Xyhlo | |
| Wyatte *(0.01)* | Wythe | Xak | Xavier-Carol | Xeth | Xykair | |
| Wyatt-Joseph | Wyzin | Xakery | Xaviere | Xever | Xylan | ~ Y ~ |
| Wyatt- | | Xameir | Xavier-James | Xevier | Xylenn | |
|   Kristopher | | Xamuel | Xavierjhon | Xhaiden | Xylus | Y'eshua |
| Wyatt-Tucker | ~ X ~ | Xamuell | Xavier-Martin | Xhakary | Xymir | Y'nnad |
| Wyck | | Xan | Xavier-Raphael | Xhovani | Xyomar | Y'quavces |
| Wydell | X Zayveion | Xanaly | Xavierre | Xialin | Xyon | Ya |
| Wyel | X' Zavyon | Xandar | Xavier-Samuel | Xian | Xyon-Garreth | Ya'brii |
| Wyeth | X'aveaur | Xander *(0.39)* | Xavierx | Xiang | Xzabian | Ya'darrius |
| Wyett | X'avier | Xander James | Xavin | Xiangbo | Xzabior | Ya'karie |
| Wyette | X'avin | Xanderlin | Xavion *(0.04)* | Xiao | Xzadrien | Ya'kub |
| Wyhitt | X'aviyon | Xandes | Xavion Prophet | Xiaoshan | Xzaevion | Ya'majeztie |
| Wyiaht | X'xavion | Xandier | Xavione | Xiathe | Xzaiver | Ya'morion |
| Wyiatt | X'zaevian | Xandor | Xaviont | Xin Lei | Xzaivion | Ya'nique |
| Wyielle | X'zalyn | Xandre | Xaviontay | Xincere | Xzander *(0.01)* | Ya'qoub |
| Wyit | X'zaveion | Xandrio | Xavior *(0.01)* | Xinen | Xzareon | Ya'seer |
| Wykel | X'zavian | Xandur | Xaviour | Xing | Xzarion | Ya'sin |
| Wykial | X'zaviaun | Xandynn | Xavious | Xingyu | Xzave'r | Ya'veon |
| Wykle | X'zavier *(0.01)* | Xandyr | Xavius | Xinh | Xzaveeon | Yaacov |
| Wyl | X'zavin | Xane | Xaviya | Xiomar | Xzaveion | Yaakov *(0.03)* |
| Wylah | X'zavion *(0.01)* | Xanhtier | Xaviyer | Xion | Xzaveon | Yaaseem |
| Wylan | X'zavior | Xannon | Xavyar | Xiong | Xzaver | Yaasiin |
| Wyland | X'zavon | Xanthine | Xavyer | Xionn | Xzavian | Yaasir |
| Wylde | X'zayvier | Xanthius | Xavyion | Xiovanni | Xzaviar | Yaaska |
| Wylder | X'zayvion | Xanthus | Xayasinh | Xipher | Xzavien | Yaazir |
| Wyle | X'zevian | Xa-Quan | Xayasone | Xishan | X-Zavier | Yabsera |
| Wylee *(0.01)* | X'zorion | Xarek | Xaydan | Xitlalli | Xzavier *(0.09)* | Yachua |
| Wylen | Xá Kari | Xarian | Xayden | Xivenwayne | Xzavion *(0.01)* | Yaciel |
| Wyler | Xa'kee | Xariel | Xaylan | Xoan | Xzavion' | Yacim Ibrahim |
| Wyles | Xa'kurious | Xarrick | Xayland | Xoaquin | Xzavior | Yacine *(0.01)* |
| Wyley | Xabiel | Xaryk | Xaylian | Xodus | Xzavir | Yackov |
| Wylhem | Xabier | Xarziver | Xaylon | Xol | Xzavius | Yacnael |
| Wyliam | Xaccaeus | Xathan | Xayvian | Xolani | Xzavyer | Yacob |
| Wylie *(0.02)* | Xaccai | Xaunder | Xayvion | Xomxah | Xzavyler | Yacoub |
| Wylik | Xachary | Xavaire | Xazavier | Xon | Xzavyur | Yacouba |
| Wylliam *(0.01)* | Xacry | Xaven | Xazavior | Xose | Xzaydrian | Yacouba |
| Wylliam Jules | Xadarius | Xaveon | Xazier | Xsabier | Xzayveer |   Sulayman |
| Wylliam- | Xade | Xaver | Xaziver | Xsavian | Xzayvier | Yacov |
|   Thomas | Xaden | Xavery | Xazvier | Xsavier | Xzayvion | Yacoyia |
| Wylson | Xadrian *(0.01)* | Xaveur | Xchyler | Xu | Xzedhen | Yacqub |
| Wyman | Xadyn | Xavian *(0.02)* | Xciden | Xuan | Xzekiel | Yacub |
| Wynaé | Xaeden | Xaviar *(0.01)* | Xearon | Xuanming | Xzharion | Yad |
| Wyndell | Xage | Xavie | Xedarion | Xuchee | Xzhavier | Yadan |

Yadani
Yaddiel
Yaddriel
Yader
Yadid
Yadiel *(0.03)*
Yadiell
Yadier
Yadikar
Yadir
Yadisson
Yadniel
Yadon
Yadrian
Yadriel
Yadukrishna
Yadyel
Yaed
Yaedam
Yaegel
Yael *(0.02)*
Yaemanuel
Yae-Sun
Yafet
Yafiet
Yagazie
Yago
Yah Sunn
Yah'mier
Yah'sehir
Yah'shua
Yaha Reh
Yahan
Yahance
Yahaya
Yahayra
Yahbet
Yahdel
Yahdiel
Yaheim
Yahel
Yahfet
Yahia *(0.01)*
Yahimmanuel
Yahir *(0.10)*
Yahiya
Yahkeem
Yahken
Yahlyl
Yahmier
Yahmil
Yahmir
Yahoathan

Yahonde
Yahseem
Yahseir
Yahshua
Yahshuah
Yah-Shuiah
Yahsir
Yahvé
Yahweh
Yahya *(0.02)*
Yahye
Yahyness
Yahzell
Yaidan
Yaihr
Yaimere
Yaimonie
Yair *(0.03)*
Yajaret
Yak
Yakee
Yakeen
Yakhez
Yakie
Yakim
Yakin
Yaknell
Yakov *(0.03)*
Yakson
Yakub
Yakup
Yal'resse
Yale
Yalen
Yalid
Yaliel
Yalith
Yam
Yama
Yamaan
Yamael
Yamahn
Yamair
Yamarcus
Yamari
Yamato
Yameen
Yamez
Yami
Yamicel
Yamil *(0.01)*
Yamille
Yamin

Yamir
Yamisadai
Yamiyn
Yamluck
Yan *(0.02)*
Yanakim
Yanal
Yan-Alexis
Yancarlo
Yancarlos
Yancey
Yancho
Yanci
Yancy
Yandel *(0.05)*
Yandell *(0.01)*
Yandi
Yandiel
Yandier
Yandres
Yandrew
Yandrick
Yandy
Yanek
Yanel
Yanell
Yan-Eric
Yaneric
Yan-Even
Yang
Yangel
Yango
Yanheng
Yanh-Michel
Yani
Yanic
Yanick *(0.01)*
Yanick Michel
Yaniel *(0.01)*
Yanik
Yanil
Yanis *(0.01)*
Yaniv
Yanive
Yankagi
Yan-Kazimir
Yankee
Yanko
Yanmanuel
Yann *(0.01)*
Yann Michael
Yanni *(0.01)*
Yannick *(0.02)*

Yannick Tranhy
Yannik
Yannis *(0.01)*
Yann-Michel
Yann-Peter
Yannsi
Yann-Xavier
Yanny Anhkhoi
Yanorie
Yan-Philip
Yanrick
Yanrik
Yansel
Yansey
Yansiel
Yansy
Yantrel
Yanuel
Yany
Yanzay
Yao
Yao Masoud
    Dian
Yaoki
Yaoman
Yaphet
Yaqoub
Yaquan
Yaqub
Yaquub
Yarade
Yarbough
Yared
Yarek
Yarel
Yareli
Yaret
Yarfee
Yari
Yaribeth
Yaried
Yariel *(0.02)*
Yarin
Yarion
Yarnell
Yaro
Yaron
Yaroslav
Yarrick
Yarsellay
Yarsi
Yarvin
Yasan

Yasdiel
Yasean
Yaseem
Yaseen *(0.02)*
Yasell
Yasen
Yaser
Yash *(0.04)*
Yasha
Yashar
Yashas
Yashaswi
Yashaun
Yashir
Yashman
Yashua
Yashvardhan
Yashveer
Yashwant
Yashwanth
Yasiel
Yasier
Yasin *(0.01)*
Ya-Sin-Siraj
Yasir *(0.02)*
Yasire
Yasirr
Yasmani
Yasmin
Yasniel
Yasseen
Yassen
Yasser *(0.02)*
Yasset
Yassin *(0.01)*
Yassine *(0.01)*
Yassin-Hirwa
Yassin-Yaqub
Yassir
Yassir Alejandro
Yastene
Yatau
Yatee
Yates
Yaunsene
Yava
Yavah
Yave Ben
Yaved
Yavens
Yavian
Yavianni
Yaviel

Yavier
Yavon
Yaw
Yawar
Yaweh
Yawen
Yaxiel
Yaxye
Yaya
Yaylon
Yayr
Yazal
Yazan *(0.01)*
Yazdan
Yazeed
Yazeek
Yazen
Yazene
Yazheed
Yazheem
Yazid
Yaziel
Yazier
Yazim
Yazin
Yazir
Yazmin
Yazon
Yban
Ybrahim
Ydan
Ydell
Ydger
Yeab
Yeabkal
Yeabsera
Yeabsira
Yeabssira
Yeah
Yeandry
Yeanwoo
Yechan
Yechezkel *(0.01)*
Yechiel *(0.01)*
Yedam
Yedidyan
Yee
Yeejhuam
Yeeleng
Yeepheng
Yefaeng
Yeffry
Yefri

Yegan
Yegor
Yehcob
Yehezkel
Yehia
Yehiel
Yehonatan
Yehoshua *(0.01)*
Yehuda *(0.06)*
Yehudah
Yehudah Leib
Yehya
Yeiben
Yeicab
Yeidon
Yeir
Yeisi
Yeisnel
Yeison
Yeisson
Yejezkel
Yejia
Yejoshua
Yejune
Yekan
Yeliazar
Yelisey
Yelrick
Yelsim
Yelsyn
Yemcel
Yemeng
Yemi'sone
Yemie
Yemil
Yemon
Yemuda
Yen
Yen Dan
Yen Hang
Yenchi
Yendrys
Yeng
Yenghoua
Yenghuam
Yengkhong
Yengkong
Yengtsim
Yengzong
Yenhua
Yenkazia
Yenkou
Yenri

Yerachmiel
Yerandy
Yeray
Yerdley
Yeremy
Yeriel
Yerik
Yerim
Yerin
Yerly
Yero
Yesaie
Yesaike
Yesenia
Yesh
Yesha'yahu
Yeshas
Yeshaya
Yeshe
Yesher
Yeshoua
Yeshua *(0.01)*
Yeshuva
Yesi
Yesiel
Yesir
Yesith
Yesniel
Yessiel
Yessine
Yessir
Yeta
Yethdriel
Yetkin
Yetli
Yeu-Chiang
Yeudiel
Yeudis
Yeupeng
Yeuriz
Yevgeny
Yewoo
Yexon
Yeyden
Yeye
Yeyms
Yeyson
Yezan
Yezrael
Ygnacio
Yhair
Yhan
Yhaquelyn

Yhaseer
Yhessi
Yhoan
Yhoel
Yhozimar
Yi
Yi Xin
Yi Ze
Yian
Yiandell
Yiandi
Yianni
Yianniko
Yiannis
Yibran
Yichen
Yicheng
Yieby
Yifan
Yi-Fei
Yifei
Yi-Hsin
Yikealo
Yilbert
Yilikal
Yilmer
Yilvin
Yim Leej
Yimier
Yiming
Yimis
Yimleej
Yimmi
Yimo
Yimzoo
Yin Bo
Yinchi
Ying
Yingkong
Yingqi
Yingsoon
Yingsum
Yiomar
Yiorgos
Yiovani
Yiovanni
Yisaac
Yisak
Yishai
Yishama
Yisrael *(0.01)*
Yisreal
Yisroel *(0.05)*

Yisruel
Yita
Yitao
Yitzchak *(0.01)*
Yitzchok *(0.04)*
Yitzhak
Yi-Van
Yixander
Yixin
Ykevion
Yksan
Ylai-Simon
Ylan
Ylann
Yleas
Ylisha
Ylli
Ylloyd
Yman
Ymanol
Ymanuel
Ymir
Ynglun
Yo'nell
Yo'son
Yoah-Elonga
Yoan *(0.04)*
Yoana
Yoan-Anthony
Yoan-Brandon
Yoandel
Yoander
Yoandi
Yoandry
Yoandy
Yoann *(0.01)*
Yoann Nik
Yoanni
Yoany
Yoaquin
Yoar
Yoary
Yoasin
Yoav
Yobachi
Yobani *(0.01)*
Yobany
Yobel
Yoceny
Yoch
Yod
Yoder
Yoel *(0.03)*

Yoesel
Yofrani
Yogesh
Yogi
Yogman
Yohab
Yohan *(0.03)*
Yohan Jonathan
Yohan Messod
Yohanan
Yohance
Yohander
Yohan-Emerick
Yohanes
Yohaness
Yohani
Yohan-Li
Yohann *(0.01)*
Yohannan
Yohannes
Yohann-Luboya
Yohanzy
Yohary
Yohas
Yohvonta
Yoichi
Yoiset
Yoj Dazyl
Yojam
Yojan
Yojanan
Yojann Gabriel
Yojany
Yoji
Yok
Yokoyama
Yolanda
Yolandria
Yolersy
Yolman
Yoltic
Yolver
Yolvin
Yolvinneill
Yolymiler
Yoma
Yomal
Yomar *(0.01)*
Yomir
Yon
Yona
Yonah
Yonas

Yonason
Yonata
Yonatan *(0.02)*
Yonathan *(0.01)*
Yonaton
Yonden
Yonder
Yonel
Yonel-Anthony
Yones
Yong
Yong-Joon
Yongsu
Yongyee
Yoni
Yoniel
Yonis
Yonny
Yonontan
Yonovan
Yontay
Yonus
Yony
Yoofi
Yoojin
Yoon
Yoon Hyun
Yoon-Ho
Yoonis
Yoonus
Yoosuf
Yophnia
Yoqsan
Yor
Yorbelys
Yorbi
Yordan
Yordany
Yordel
Yordenys
Yordi *(0.01)*
Yordiel
Yordin
Yordy
Yorel
Yorge
Yoric
Yorick
Yoriesky
Yoriko
Yoriko-Keren
York
York-Omama

Yorkwin
Yorneh
Yorney
Yoruba
Yorvin
Yosaira
Yosbani
Yosbel
Yosduane
Yosdy
Yosef *(0.07)*
Yoseh
Yosei
Yosel
Yosell
Yosem
Yoseph
Yosessh
Yosette
Yosh
Yoshet
Yoshi
Yoshiah
Yoshiaki
Yoshiharu
Yoshihiko
Yoshiki
Yoshio
Yoshtin
Yoshua
Yoshua-
    Benyamin T
Yosiah
Yosian
Yosias
Yosiel
Yosimar
Yosiyah
Yoskar
Yoslan
Yosmichael
Yosniel
Yossef
Yossel
Yossiel
Yossy
Yost
Yosteen
Yosten
Yostin
Yostyn
Yosual
Yosue

Yosuke
Yosvani
Yosvanni
Yosvany
Yosvel
Yosyas
Yotzer
You Jing
You Ming
    Alexandre
Youani
Youantis
Youcef
Youcef-Anis
Youchun
Youel
Youhdy
Youl
Younes *(0.01)*
Younes-
    Abdelhafid
Younes-Fawzi
Youness
Young
Young Shuh
Youngbuck
Youngin
Younis
Younkerri
Younous
Younus
Youpeng
Yourhinest
Yourhynis
Youri *(0.01)*
Youri-Ferhat
Yourik
Youry
Yousaf
Yousdan
Youseef
Yousef *(0.05)*
Youseph
Youshay
Yousif *(0.01)*
Yousof
Yousouf
Yousri
Youssef *(0.05)*
Youssef Amin
Youssef Nomer
Youssef-
    Philippe

| | | | | | |
|---|---|---|---|---|---|
| Youssel | Yuheng | Yusef (0.01) | ~ Z ~ | Za'ravion | Zacarius | Zachary Franz |
| Youssoaf | Yuilu | Yusha | | Za'rie | Zacarri | Zachary Imad |
| Youssouf | Yujay | Yushawn | Z | Za'shaun | Zacary (0.01) | Zachary James |
| Youssuf | Yujel | Yushay | Z'ani | Za'shawn | Zacarye | Zachary Ken |
| Yousuf | Yuji | Yushou | Z'kai | Za'tavien | Zacc | Zachary Ric |
| Yousuke | Yujie | Yusif | Z'karye | Za'tayveon | Zaccai | Zachary Ryan |
| Youtin | Yuki | Yusouf | Z'keyus | Za'terrion | Zaccardo | Zachary Tyler |
| Youvenson | Yukio | Yussef | Z'kharyah | Za'toyrien | Zaccari | Zacharyah |
| Yovan | Yukon | Yussele | Z'marius | Za'veon | Zaccaria | Zachary-Daniel |
| Yovani (0.02) | Yul | Yussuf | Z'mori | Za'vieon | Zaccariah | Zacharyeah |
| Yovanne | Yulee | Yusuf (0.06) | Z'morren | Za'vier | Zaccarion | Zachary-Junior |
| Yovanni | Yulian | Yusufu | Z'orey | Za'vinci | Zaccary | Zachary-Mitchell |
| Yovanny | Yuliano | Yusupha | Za Kai | Za'vion | Zaccery | |
| Yovany | Yuliy | Yuta (0.01) | Za Mareyon | Za'vreon | Zac-Chae'us | Zacharyus |
| Yovelix | Yulkeavyn | Yutaka | Zá Marion | Za'yan | Zacchaeus (0.01) | Zache |
| Yoviel | Yulkhari | Yutaro | Za'aire | Zaac | Zacchaeus-Leon | Zacheri |
| Yovy | Yulkhyis | Yuto | Za'cavian | Zaack | Zacchary | Zacheriah (0.01) |
| Yowan | Yulong | Yuuj | Za'cyus | Zaáfique | Zacchaus | Zacherie |
| Yoxer | Yulrick | Yuuki | Za'darius | Zaafir | Zaccheaus | Zacherié |
| Yozuet | Yuma | Yu-Un | Za'dreion | Zaahid | Zaccheo | Zachery (0.18) |
| Ysaac | Yumil | Yuunis | Za'dyn | Zaahir | Zaccheus | Zacheus |
| Ysaak | Yumin | Yuva | Za'hir | Zaahyr | Zaccihus | Zachi |
| Ysaivion | Yu-Ming | Yuval | Za'kaileon | Zaakir | Zach (0.03) | Zachia |
| Ysener | Yun | Yuvan | Za'karee | Zaamir | Zachael | Zachiel |
| Yslay | Yuna | Yuvany | Za'kari | Zaaven | Zachai | Zachieus |
| Ysmael | Yunal | Yuveer | Za'karri | Zab | Zachairah | Zachii |
| Ysrael | Yunam | Yuvinny | Za'karrius | Zabari | Zacharaiah | Zachilles |
| Yu | Yunell | Yuvraj (0.01) | Za'kaury | Zabdiel | Zacharee | Zachirious |
| Yu Qi | Yuniel | Yuvraj-Singh | Za'kee | Zabdy | Zacharey | Zachory |
| Yuan (0.01) | Yunier | Yuwei | Za'keem | Zabe | Zacharhia | Zachrey |
| Yuan Da | Yunior (0.01) | Yuxi | Za'khari | Zabeian | Zachari (0.01) | Zachry |
| Yuanfeng | Yunior | Yuyang | Za'kiim | Zaben | Zacharia (0.01) | Zachy |
| Yuania | Francisco | Yuzin | Za'kir | Zabeon | Zachariah (0.19) | Zack (0.08) |
| Yuan-Kai | Yunis | Yuzuki | Za'kobi | Zabian | Zachariaha | Zackahria |
| Yuankun | Yunny | Yvan | Za'kwan | Zabiela | Zacharias (0.01) | Zackaiyo |
| Yuanny | Yun-Song | Yvel | Za'kwez | Zabrey | Zachariasz | Zack-Anthony |
| Yuanyang | Yunus | Yvelt | Za'malik | Zabrian | Zacharie (0.04) | Zack-Antoine |
| Yuanze | Yun-Zhi | Yvemy | Za'marion | Zabriel | Zacharie Alexandre | Zackara |
| Yuari | Yuosuf | Yvenly | Za'marrian | Zabrien | Zacharie-Thomas | Zackaray |
| Yuba-Alex | Yupeng | Yvenslee | Za'marrion | Zabyan | Zacharii | Zackare |
| Yubin | Yupheng | Yves | Za'maurione | Zac (0.01) | Zacharis | Zackaree |
| Yubini | Yurel | Yveson | Za'maurius | Zac Zenos | Zacharius | Zackarey |
| Yudel | Yuri (0.01) | Yvon | Za'mear | Zac'chaeus | Zachariya | Zackari |
| Yue | Yuriana | Ywellv | Za'mi | Zac'queryon | Zachariyah | Zackaria |
| Yue Pheng | Yuriel | Ywj | Za'mikal | Zacaery | Zacharriyah | Zackariah (0.01) |
| Yuepheng | Yuri-Eloi | Yzaack | Za'mir | Zacahary | Zacharrias | Zackarias |
| Yueran | Yurien | Yzael | Za'mori | Zacara | Zacharue | Zackarie |
| Yufeng | Yuriy | Yzaia | Za'morie | Zacarayah | Zachary (5.35) | Zackariha |
| Yug | Yurman | Yzak | Za'myzic | Zacari | Zachary Alexande | Zackarius |
| Yugath | Yuro | Yzell | Za'phyr | Zacaria | Zachary Anton | Zackariya |
| Yugi | Yury | Yzjak | Za'quan | Zacariah | Zachary Eli | Zackariyah |
| Yugraj | Yusaf | Yzrael | Za'quez | Zacarias (0.01) | | Zackariye |
| Yuhan | Yuscani | Yzun | Za'qwon | Zacarious | | Zackarrey |

Zackary (0.36)
Zackarya
Zackaryah
Zackary-Benoit
Zackary-Robert
Zackawy
Zackerey
Zackeria
Zackeriah
Zackerie
Zackery (0.17)
Zackhari
Zack-Harry
Zackhery
Zacki
Zackiel
Zackiryah
Zack-Olivier
Zackory (0.01)
Zackqwon
Zackrey
Zackry
Zack-Yohan
Zacorian
Zacory
Zacquavius
Zacque
Zacquiel
Zacrey
Zacry
Zacrye
Zacurry
Zad
Zadarious
Zadarreon
Zadarrious
Zadarris
Zadayne
Zade (0.01)
Zadek
Zaden (0.02)
Zadian
Zadiel
Zadien
Zadin
Zadkiel
Zadock
Zadok
Zadrian
Zadyn
Zae
Zae'quon
Zae'vion

Zae'von
Zaedan
Zaeden
Zaedyn
Zaeem
Zaehon
Zaeim
Zael
Zaeland
Zaelijah
Zaelyn
Zaequone
Zaeshon
Zaevian
Zaevion
Zaevyon
Zafahr
Zafar
Zafir
Zagan
Zah'mir
Zah'qua
Zah'quan
Zah'ron
Zah'un
Zah'yon
Zahaire
Zaharias
Zaharius
Zahcary
Zahdi
Zaheem
Zaheer
Zaheim
Zahid (0.01)
Zahiem
Zahiir
Zahim
Zahin
Zahir (0.02)
Zahir Aki
Zahir'
Zahiym
Zahkee
Zahkeem
Zahki
Zahkiem
Zahlir
Zahmare
Zahmari
Zahmeir
Zahmir
Zahmyr

Zahnder
Zahr
Zahran
Zahrion
Zahveon
Zahvier
Zahvion
Zahyeer
Zai
Zai'dairrious
Zai'kyus
Zai'sharwn
Ziairé
Zai'vion
Zaiah
Zaibren
Zaic-Jet
Zaid (0.05)
Zaida
Zaidah
Zaidan
Zaidden
Zaide
Zaiden (0.02)
Zaidthavi
Zaidyn
Zaied
Zaieed
Zaier
Zaige
Zaigne
Zaihyon
Zaijohn
Zaik
Zaikee
Zailen
Zailin
Zailor
Zailyn
Zaim
Zaimauk
Zaimeer
Zain (0.06)
Zainabdin
Zainadeen
Zaine (0.01)
Zainildean
Zain-Ul
Zain-Ul-Abdin
Zaiquan
Zaiquawn
Zaiquis
Zair

Zaire (0.07)
Zairee
Zaireem
Zairein
Zairenis
Zaireth
Zaivean
Zaiveon
Zaivey
Zaivion
Zaiviyon
Zaivyon
Zaiyin
Zaiyln
Zajamin
Zajshad
Zak (0.02)
Zakael
Zakael Amoury
Zakah
Zakahri
Zakai (0.01)
Zakalious
Zakar
Zakarai
Zakaraih
Zakarea
Zakaree
Za-Karey
Zakarey
Zakareya
Zakari (0.01)
Zakaria (0.04)
Zakaria-Farouk
Zakariah (0.01)
Zakaria-Mohamed
Zakariaou
Zakarie
Zakariya (0.02)
Zakariya Boucata
Zakariyaa
Zakariye
Zakariyya
Zakarriya
Zakary (0.10)
Zakarya
Zakary-Alexandre
Zakaryus
Zakcariah
Zakee

Zakeen
Zakei
Zakel
Zakeria
Zakeriya
Zakery (0.01)
Zakeystun
Zakhai-Nasir
Zakhary
Zakhee
Zakhi
Zakhian
Zakhiir
Zakhilen
Zaki (0.01)
Zaki Arkell
Zakiah
Zakiel
Zakijah
Zakil
Zakir
Zakiry
Zakiya
Zakiyah
Zakk (0.01)
Zakkai
Zakkar
Zakkary (0.02)
Zakke
Zakkery
Zakki
Zako
Zakory
Zakoye
Zakry
Zaktorio
Zakwae
Zakwavis
Zaky
Zakyhya
Zakyi
Zakyius
Zaland
Zalarrious
Zale
Zalen
Zalman
Zalmay
Zalmen (0.01)
Zalmen Yoel
Zalmon
Zalon
Zalor Datreyon

Zalyn
Zamaine
Zamaire
Zaman
Zamani
Zamanta
Zamanuel
Zamar
Zamaree
Zamari
Zamarie
Zamarien
Zamarion (0.01)
Zamarius
Zamaron
Zamarrion
Zamarrious
Zamarvian
Zamaryion
Zamaryon
Zamauri
Zameer
Zamel
Zamere
Zamiel
Zamien
Zamier
Zamier Yaakov
Zamil
Zamir (0.02)
Zamiran
Zamire
Zamirr
Zamiyes
Zamone
Zamoreion
Zamorian
Zamorie
Zamuary
Zan
Zan'meyon
Zan'tonio
Zana
Zanayvion
Zandar
Zandarius
Zande
Zanden
Zander (0.30)
Zandon
Zandor
Zandrail
Zandrick

Zandyr
Zane (0.44)
Zanealexander
Zanedine
Zanekoda
Zang
Zaniel
Zann
Zanquan
Zant
Zantae
Zante
Zantrell
Zanu
Zan-Ul-Abdeen
Zanver
Zanye
Zanzie
Zao
Zaoul
Zaphenath-Paneah
Zappa
Zaquan
Zaquarias
Zaquarion
Zaquarius
Zaquavian
Zaqueo
Zaquiel
Zaquise
Zaquwan
Zarahan
Zarahiah
Zarak
Zaravion
Zared
Zareef
Zarein
Zareion
Zarek (0.01)
Zarell
Zareus
Zari
Zarian
Zaric
Zarick
Zarid
Zarif
Zarik
Zarin
Zarin-Afsan
Zario

| | | | | | | |
|---|---|---|---|---|---|---|
| Zarion | Zaviarre | Zaylyn | Zebulun | Zeke (0.03) | Zentarrius | Zethro |
| Zarius | Zavie | Zaymann | Zebulyn | Zekeria | Zentrail | Zeus |
| Zarkavyon | Zavien (0.01) | Zaymarion | Zechari | Zekerial | Zentrel | Zeuz |
| Zarmaan | Zavier (0.07) | Zayn (0.01) | Zechariah (0.08) | Zekeriya | Zenuf | Zev (0.02) |
| Zarnell | Zavier-Jwaun | Zayne (0.06) | Zecharius | Zekeriye | Zenun | Zevakiah |
| Zaro | Zavin | Zaynn | Zechary | Zekeual | Zenzo | Zevan |
| Zaron | Zavion (0.03) | Zayo | Zecheriah | Zekhary | Zeolahn | Zevanier |
| Zarquez | Zavior | Zayohn | Zechiriah | Zekharyah | Zeon | Zevariah |
| Zarrak | Zavious | Zayon | Zeckariah | Zekhi | Zeontre | Zevash |
| Zarren | Zaviyon | Zayquan | Zed | Zekhyi | Zephan (0.01) | Zevastian |
| Zarry | Zavon | Zayshawn | Zedaiyah | Zeki | Zephania | Zeven |
| Zarvan | Zavondre | Zaythen | Zedakiah | Zekiah | Zephaniah | Zeveran |
| Zarvell | Zavones | Zayveier | Zedan | Zekias | (0.02) | Zeviah |
| Zarvyair | Zavontaye | Zayveon | Zedaniel | Zekie | Zephaniah | Zevin |
| Zaryah | Zavorion | Zayvian | Zedarien | Zekiel | Barnabb | Zevon |
| Zaryian | Zavri | Zayvien | Zedarion | Zekieyh | Zephaniahn | Zevy |
| Zaryn | Zavyn | Zayvier | Zedarius | Zekke | Zephen | Zeyad (0.01) |
| Zaryon | Zavyone | Zayviion | Zedediah | Zeko | Zephil | Zeyade |
| Zarzck | Zavyous | Zayvin | Zedekiah (0.01) | Zekori | Zephniah | Zeyd |
| Zasha | Zawad | Zayvion (0.01) | Zedikyah | Zeland | Zephon | Zeydin |
| Zashaun | Zaxxon | Zayvious | Zednik | Zelby | Zephram | Zeydon |
| Za-Shawn | Zay | Zayvon | Zedquiel | Zeldon | Zéphyr | Zeyhan |
| Zashawn | Zay'quan | Zayvone | Zedric | Zelek | Zephyr (0.01) | Zeylaznd |
| Zashon | Zay'veon | Zayya | Zedrich | Zelin | Zeppelin | Zeylein |
| Zasir | Zay'veun | Zayyan | Zedrick | Zeljko | Zereian | Zeyn |
| Zaswan | Zay'vion | Zcobe | Zedtric | Zell | Zereke | Zha Teon |
| Zatara | Zayaan | Ze Lin | Zedueh | Zellal | Zeren | Zha'velle |
| Zatavius | Zayah | Ze Wei | Zee | Zelldin | Zeria | Zhaavion |
| Zatch | Zayan | Ze'ante | Zeek | Zeller | Zeriah | Zhaire Lynell |
| Zathan | Zayani | Ze'ev | Zeelan | Zelye | Zeric | Zhakeem |
| Zathaneze | Zayaun | Ze'karie | Zeelin | Zemeron | Zerick | Zhakeis |
| Zathen | Zaybien | Ze'marion | Zeem | Zemir | Zerik | Zhaki |
| Za-Tyun | Zaybron | Ze'monta | Zeeon | Zemitri | Zerin | Zhakir |
| Zaul | Zayd (0.03) | Ze'veuro | Zeerak | Zemmari | Zerion | Zhakirullah |
| Zavai | Zaydan | Zeaad | Zeeshan | Zemont | Zermarion | Zhakrin |
| Zavant | Zaydel | Zeagan | Zef | Zemora | Zeroun | Zhalin |
| Zavarion | Zayden (0.04) | Zealand | Zefer | Zen (0.01) | Zerrell | Zhamar |
| Zavarius | Zaydin | Zeamarea | Zeff | Zen Axl | Zerrick | Zha-Mare |
| Zave'ion | Zaydn | Zean | Zefram | Zen Earnest | Zerry | Zhamari |
| Zaveaire | Zaydoc | Zearian | Zehavi | Zen'tavius | Zerryl | Zhamen |
| Zavean | Zaydon | Zeb (0.01) | Zehn | Zenas | Zerubabbel | Zhamir |
| Zavein | Zaydynn | Zebablan | Zehner | Zeneck | Zerubbabel | Zhammyl |
| Zaveion | Zayed | Zebadia | Zeidaan | Zengseng | Zeryan | Zhamory |
| Zaven | Zayen | Zebadiah (0.01) | Zeidan | Zeni | Zeshan | Zhane |
| Zaveon | Zayin | Zebastian | Zeighvier | Zeniff | Zeshaun | Zhao |
| Zavery | Zaykwon | Zebb | Zeikel | Zenin | Zeshawn | Zhareé |
| Zaveyion | Zaykyle | Zebbidiah | Zein | Zenith | Zeshon | Zharin |
| Zavhier | Zaylan | Zebede | Zein Eldin | Zenki | Zesian | Zharquise |
| Zavi'an | Zaylavon | Zebedee | Zeion- | Zennie | Zeta | Zhatavious |
| Zaviaire | Zaylen (0.01) | Zebediah | Lafrederick | Zennon | Zeth (0.01) | Zhavier |
| Zavian (0.02) | Zaylin | Zebulan | Zeith | Zeno | Zethan | Zhavori |
| Zaviante | Zaylon | Zebulin | Zek | Zenobe | Zethaniel | Zhawn |
| Zaviar | Zaylor | Zebulon | Zekarias | Zenon (0.01) | Zethen | Zhaylon |

| | | | | | | |
|---|---|---|---|---|---|---|
| Zhayne | Ziaire | Zimmeree | Ziyhire | Zorain | Zy | Zy'quirious |
| Zhekai | Ziam | Zimon | Ziyindae | Zoran | Zy Aire | Zy'ryan |
| Zhelden | Zian | Zimor | Ziyon | Zorawar | Zy Quan | Zy'scenio |
| Zhen | Ziar | Zimorion | Ziyontrae | Zoren | Zy' Quan | Zy'sean |
| Zheng | Ziare | Zimraan | Ziyquan | Zorey | Zy'aaron | Zy'shaun |
| Zhi | Ziayan | Zimri | Ziyreeh | Zoriah | Zy'air | Zy'shawn |
| Zhi Peng | Zibi | Zinadean | Ziyun | Zorian | Zy'aire | Zy'shonne |
| Zhian | Zibo | Zinadine | Ziza | Zorien | Zy'airius | Zy'tavius |
| Zhijing | Zid | Zinan | Zjevon | Zorion | Zy'arvin | Zy'tayrion |
| Zhilin | Zidan | Zindine | Zjhan | Zorious | Zy'brion | Zy'terrious |
| Zhivago | Zidane (0.01) | Zineare | Zjhylique | Zorre | Zy'corian | Zy'travion |
| Zhivan | Zidaurius | Zinedine- | Zlampea | Zorro | Zy'derrious | Zy'trevious |
| Zhixuan | Zidon | Mohamed | Zlatan | Zorryn | Zy'dharion | Zy'trez |
| Zhong | Ziear | Zine-Eddine | Zmari | Zoryen | Zy'el | Zya're |
| Zhong-Han | Ziego | Zinko | Zmarrion | Zoser | Zy'ere | Zyaad |
| Zhongyu | Zieler | Zinos | Zmauri | Zosh | Zy'favion | Zyack |
| Zhonte | Zielle | Zion (0.35) | Zmontae | Zosser | Zy'guan | Zyad |
| Zhorah | Zien | Zion Aedan | Zmonté | Zouheir | Zy'heir | Zyaiah |
| Zhuojun | Ziens | Zion Damarri | Zn'aire | Zoushua | Zy'hiem | Zyaier |
| Zhy'maar | Zieon | Zion Isaiah | Zoan | Zovco | Zy'ierre | Zyair |
| Zhyaré | Ziere | Zion'khair | Zodyac | Zoysh | Zy'ion | Zyairé |
| Zhyiare | Zierre | Zionjah | Zoe | Zsa'mere | Zy'karious | Zyaire (0.01) |
| Zhyon | Zifan | Zionn | Zoemar | Zsacari | Zy'kavious | Zyairh |
| Zi | Ziger | Ziontaé | Zoenell | Zshojn | Zy'kei | Zyairre |
| Zi Ho | Ziggy | Zionte | Zoey | Zsolt | Zy'keil | Zyakki |
| Zi Liang | Zihaire | Ziovanni | Zohaib (0.01) | Zsombor | Zy'keith | Zyan |
| Zi Yang | Ziheem | Ziquan | Zohair | Zu'darian | Zy'keivious | Zyare |
| Zi'air | Ziheen | Ziquaryon | Zohar | Zubair | Zy'kemeon | Zyarous |
| Zi'aire | Zihire | Ziquio- | Zohayb | Zubari | Zy'kerion | Zyaughn |
| Zi'ale | Zihon | Sevastian | Zoheir | Zubayr | Zy'kerious | Zyaun |
| Zi'meer | Zihyon | Ziqwan | Zohran | Zuber | Zy'kerrian | Zycarius |
| Zi'mera | Zii | Ziran | Zoilo | Zuberi | Zy'kevis | Zydarius |
| Zi'mezmen | Zijad | Ziren | Zoin | Zubeyr | Zy'keye | Zyden |
| Da'quan | Zijie | Zireon | Zol | Zubin | Zy'keyvious | Zydir |
| R'trayvious | Zijuan | Ziron | Zolan | Zuhair | Zy'kharie | Zye |
| Zi'mir | Zikang | Zirus | Zoland | Zuhayb | Zy'kire | Zye'ied |
| Zi'ontay | Zikee | Ziryan | Zolen | Zuhayr | Zy'kyee | Zye'quez |
| Zi'quan | Zikein | Zishaan | Zoli | Zuheib | Zy'lan | Zyeair |
| Zi'quavious | Zikeith | Zishawn | Zolian | Zulfikar | Zy'maire | Zyee |
| Zi'reon | Zikell | Zitarreious | Zolis | Zulfqar-Ali | Zy'marcus | Zyeed |
| Zi'tarious | Zikem | Zitwaun | Zoltan | Zuliangelie | Zy'marri | Zyel |
| Zi'travion | Zikiah | Ziv | Zolten | Zuo-Wei | Zy'mere | Zyen |
| Zi'yan | Zikien | Zivan | Zomari | Zuri (0.01) | Zy'miir | Zyeon |
| Zi'year | Ziland | Ziven | Zomariyon | Zuriah | Zy'mir | Zyer |
| Zi'yon | Ziletai | Ziv-Or | Zoncheus | Zurich | Zy'mire | Zyere |
| Zi'yun | Zilfi | Ziya | Zong | Zuriel (0.01) | Zy'monie | Zyfeer |
| Zia | Zilong | Ziyaad | Zoniel | Zurin | Zy'on | Zygmunt |
| Zia'meir | Zilvano | Ziyaad-Na'jee | Zontae | Zuriod | Zy'quan | Zyhair |
| Ziad (0.01) | Zim | Ziyad (0.01) | Zontaelo | Zury-Shaday | Zy'quarius | Zyheem |
| Ziaera | Zimare | Ziyah | Zontavious | Zuya | Zy'quary | Zyhier |
| Ziah | Zimarion | Ziyan | Zonte | Zvi | Zy'quavian | Zyhir |
| Ziahn | Zimir | Ziyang | Zontrel | Zvonte | Zy'queil | Zyhmar |
| Ziair | Zimmer | Ziyen | Zorackus | Zxavier | Zy'quez | Zyhmir |

| | | | | | | |
|---|---|---|---|---|---|---|
| Zyhon | Zykeere | Zykir | Zymia | Zyquan *(0.01)* | Zyrian | Zyson |
| Zyhra | Zykei | Zykohr | Zymier | Zyquarious | Zyricus | Zytavieion |
| Zyhre | Zykeil | Zylan | Zymiere | Zyquarius | Zyrien | Zytavion |
| Zyia | Zykeis | Zyleek | Zymill | Zyquaun | Zyrig | Zytavious |
| Zyiad | Zykeise | Zyler *(0.01)* | Zymir *(0.01)* | Zyquon | Zyrin | Zytavis |
| Zyikerr'y | Zykell | Zylin | Zymire | Zyqwae | Zyrion | Zytavius |
| Zyion *(0.01)* | Zykerion | Zymarian | Zymon | Zyrael | Zyrome | Zyteries |
| Zyionna | Zykerius | Zymarione | Zyne | Zyran | Zyron | Zytez |
| Zyir | Zykese | Zymarius | Zyniccio | Zyrane | Zyrse | Zytrell |
| Zyire | Zyki | Zy-Marrian | Zyntreacs | Zyre | Zysean | Zyuan |
| Zy-Jon | Zyki'se | Zymeen | Zyon *(0.03)* | Zyreion | Zyshaun | Zyvair De'i |
| Zykarrion | Zykias | Zymeer | Zyonne | Zyrell | Zyshawn | Zyveon |
| Zykee | Zykie | Zymer | Zyphyr | Zyren | Zyshon | Zyvonta |
| Zykeem | Zykier | Zymere | Zyquaivius | Zyreon | Zyshonne | Zy-Yon |

# Acknowledgments

Sincere thanks to the following agencies, among others, for generously providing data for this book: Alabama Department of Public Health, Center for Health Statistics, Alaska Bureau of Vital Statistics Publications, Alberta Registries Vital Statistics, British Columbia Vital Statistics Agency, Colorado Vital Statistics Unit, Connecticut Vital Records Office, Florida Vital Statistics, Indiana State Department of Health vital records files, Kentucky Office of Vital Statistics, Louisiana Center for Health Statistics, Maine Office of Vital Records, Massachusetts Registry of Vital Records and Statistics, Michigan Vital Records Office, Minnesota Center for Health Statistics, New Brunswick Vital Statistics Office, New Mexico Vital Records, New York City Department of Health and Mental Hygiene, North Dakota Division of Vital Records, Northwest Territories Vital Statistics, Nova Scotia Vital Statistics, Nunavut Vital Statistics, Ohio State Vital Records Office, Ontario Vital Statistics, Oregon Center for Health Statistics, Pennsylvania Bureau of Health Statistics and Research, Québec Directeur de l'état civil, South Carolina Division of Vital Records, Tennessee Vital Records, Vermont Department of Health Vital Records System, Virginia Office of Vital Records, West Virginia Vital Research Records, Yukon Vital Statistics.

# Bibliography

Ames, Winthrop. *What shall we name the baby?* New York: Pocket Books, 1963.

Arthur, William, M.A. *An etymological dictionary of family and Christian names.* New York: Sheldon, Blakeman & Co., 1857.

Baby Name Network. www.babynamenetwork.com. June 2007.

Bains, Mohinder Singh. Punjabi Language School, Edmonton, Alberta, Canada. Personal correspondence, 1989.

Brar, Sandeep S. Sikh names and meanings. www.sikhs.org/names.htm.

Browder, Sue. *The new age baby name book.* New York: Workman, 1974.

Chuks-orji, Ogonna. *Names from Africa: their origin, meaning, and pronunciation.* Chicago: Johnson, 1972.

Dinwiddie-Boyd, Elza. *Proud heritage: 11,001 names for your African-American baby.* New York: Avon, 1994.

Discover Baby Names. www.discoverbabynames.com. June 2007.

Dunkling, Leslie Alan. *The Guinness book of names.* Guinness, 1986.

Dunkling, Leslie and William Gosling. *The facts on file dictionary of first names.* New York: Facts on file, 1983.

Ellefson, Connie Lockhart. *The melting pot book of baby names,* 3rd edition. Cincinnatti, Ohio: Betterway Books, 1995.

Fields, Maxine. *Baby names from around the world.* New York: Pocket Books, 1985.

Hanks, Patrick and Flavia Hodges. *A dictionary of first names.* Oxford: Oxford University Press, 1990.

Kolatch, Alfred J. *The complete dictionary of English and Hebrew first names.* New York: Jonathan David, 1984.

Kolatch, Alfred J. *The Jonathan David dictionary of first names.* New York: Penguin Books, 1980.

Kolatch, Alfred J. *Today's best baby names.* New York: Putnam, 1986.

Lansky, Bruce. *The best baby name book in the whole wide world.* Deephaven, Minnesota: Meadowbrook, 1984.

Lawson, Dr. Edwin D. Professor of Psychology, College at Fredonia, State University of New York. Board of Editors, *NAMES: A Journal of Onomastics.* Personal correspondence, 1989.

Le, Rev. Thanh Trung. President, Nguon Sang Heritage Language School Association, Edmonton, Alberta, Canada. Personal correspondence, 1989.

McCue, Marion J. *How to pick the right name for your baby.* New York: Grosset & Dunlap, 1977.

Sanduga, Dean. Arab Link, Edmonton, Alberta, Canada. Personal correspondence, 1989.

Stewart, George R. *American given names.* New York: Oxford, 1979.

Think Baby Names. www.thinkbabynames.com. June 2007.

Woods, Richard D. *Hispanic first names: a comprehensive dictionary of 250 years of Mexican-American usage.* Connecticut: Greenwood Press, 1984.

Zelo.com. First Names and What They Mean. www.zelo.com. June 2007.

# THE
# KINGDOM
*of*
# LITTLE WOUNDS

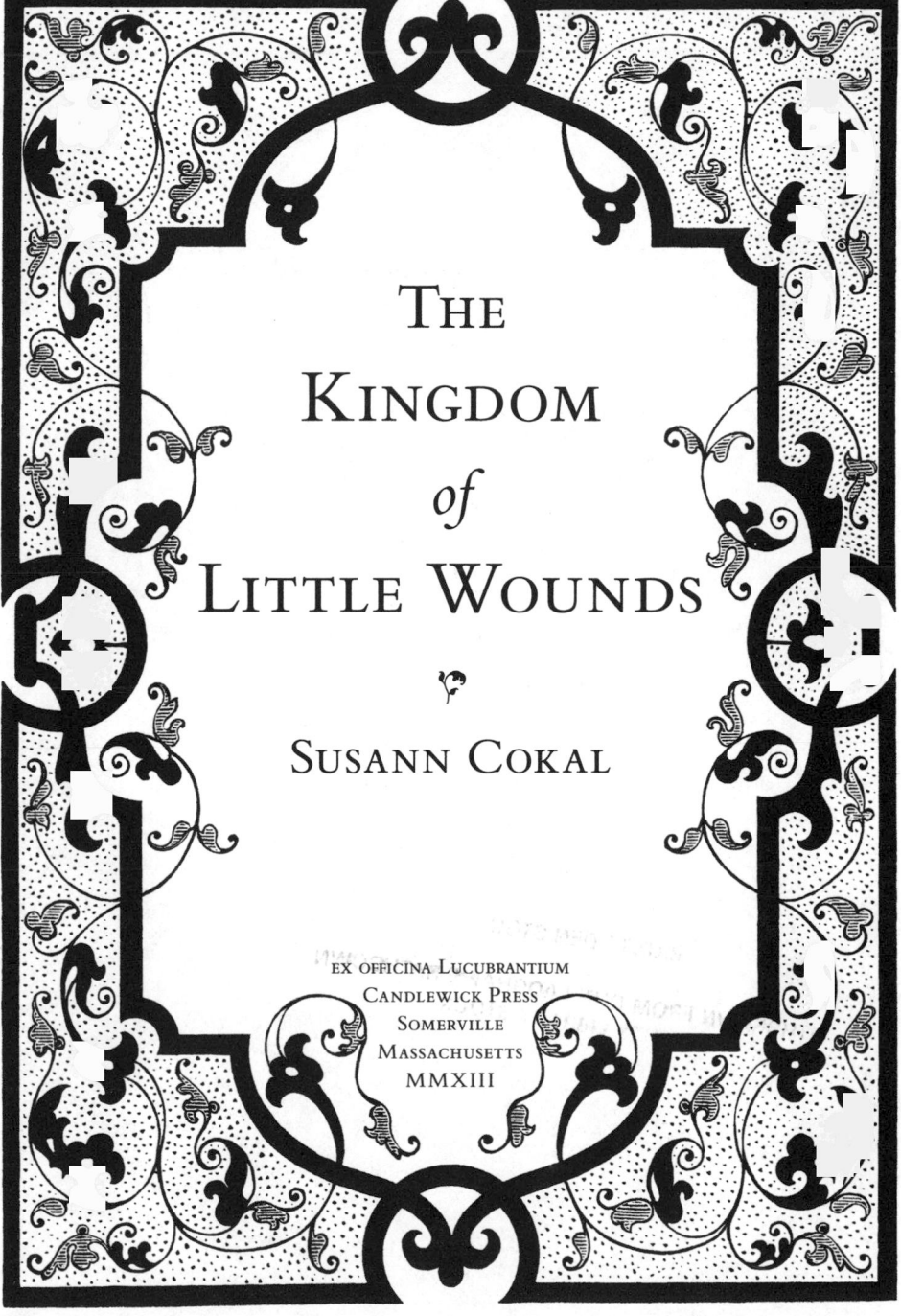

# THE
# KINGDOM
## *of*
# LITTLE WOUNDS

SUSANN COKAL

EX OFFICINA LUCUBRANTIUM
CANDLEWICK PRESS
SOMERVILLE
MASSACHUSETTS
MMXIII

This is a work of fiction. Names, characters, places, and incidents are either products of the author's imagination or, if real, are used fictitiously.

Copyright © 2013 by Susann Cokal

Coat of arms illustration copyright © 2013 by Pier Gustafson

First edition 2013

Library of Congress Catalog Card Number 2013933162
ISBN 978-0-7636-6694-1

14 15 16 17 18 BVG 10 9 8 7 6 5 4 3 2

Printed in Berryville, VA, U.S.A.

This book was typeset in Bembo.

Candlewick Press
99 Dover Street
Somerville, Massachusetts 02144

visit us at www.candlewick.com

*Nothing has value till it is given away or stolen;*
*therefore, I present this story to Gregory Osina Weatherford.*

In tenebris lumen metue meum

There is no substance which is not a poison; all are poisonous. Only the dose determines.

—Philippus Aureolus Theophrastus Bombastus von Hohenheim (Paracelsus), 1493–1541

# The Chronicles

# THE FOUR TRUTHFUL PRINCESSES

*There was once a family of princesses who were locked in a castle. By all reckonings this was for their own good, and indeed they had so rarely been outside that they would not have known what to do if they had been granted their freedom. As a consequence of their confinement, they took much pleasure in tales of distant lands as told by their nurses, some of whom came from quite far away.*

*The more estranged the tales' settings were from their own, the better the princesses liked them. Each night they demanded a new story, a longer one, with ever-greater invention on the part of the nurses and more of what the eldest girl (who by some law of the country was practically a queen) called Truth. By this she meant violence and heroic deeds and also details of how common people lived their lives from one day to the next. "To help me rule my subjects," she explained.*

*In the darkness of the curtained bed, her sisters made faces at one another. It would have been unnatural for them not to feel envy at the good fortune of her birth.*

*"But it must have magic as well," said the next-eldest princess.*

*"Magic is Truth," insisted the next-next-eldest. She was a scholar, interested in art and alchemy. She especially liked recipes for complicated poisons. "Or Truth is Magic."*

*"Never mind," said the youngest, who was sucking her thumb behind a gently blowing drape. "Shut up and let it begin."*

*The others pummeled her severely for her language. And then the story did begin.*

I.

LIGHT

# AVA BINGEN

It is while I stitch together the Queen's gown, on the night her eldest daughter is to die, that I first sense an uneasy power.

The feeling begins as I stand with hands humbly folded beneath my apron, a seamstress watching a queen unravel.

"To think this is what comes of the years," Queen Isabel laments as she picks at a rip in her blue-velvet bodice. "Such a night! Such calamities! We have been thoroughly cursed."

Every thread at the royal waist and armpit is straining, even the linen under-chemise (my work) and the stays laced beneath. The tear snakes beneath the sag of her bosom, sideways across the belly that has thickened with so many births.

My hands itch to stop her. But she is in a fit, and I have no right but to let her continue.

Queen Isabel is our kingdom's treasure, once a legendary beauty and now a devoted mother and dull background figure to the King's glittering majesty. Even so commonplace a matter as a ripped gown requires a retreat to the red draped damask and candles of her formal apartments, where she is attended by a historian as well as a host of ladies and aprons and dwarfs whose task is to amuse. A simple accident becomes a *Once there was a queen whose gown burst as she danced for her daughter's wedding . . .*

I have always loved a fairy tale.

If I were a keeper of histories (scratching busily at a wax tablet, bony fingers covered in the sticky stuff), this is what I would record:

With backs held straight by their corsets, ladies clad in rainbows lounge before gilded fireplace and blood-curtained bed. They fidget with their jewelry and shuffle their slippers on the floor tiles as music climbs through the shutters, a jangly old tune that Isabelle des Rayaux, this Isabel, brought from the Loire when she came to marry King Christian Lunedie V. It is a wedding song for a dance of hops and kisses; musicians play it floating in flat-bottomed boats on Skyggehavn's bay and canals. It hangs in the air with the sweetness of imported sugar out of which every possible morsel at the wedding feast has been made.

For this one night, there are sugar plates, sugar fruits, sugar goblets melting under spiced wine. And everyone has tasted it somehow, from King Christian on down to the little girl who sits in a nook and counts the dishes as they're washed. Lords and ladies flit from treat to treat in the airy banquet houses built in the courtyards, clad in their finest satin and brocade and cloth of tinsel, glowing with jewels, rippling at slashed breeches and sleeves, trickling ribbons from swollen hats. They are tended by servants in yellow livery or in made-over versions of the nobles' castoffs, and dwarfs run from spot to spot, enacting comic scenes of courtship. At every fragile little house, the gentles gorge themselves, and those who follow clean up after them, licking and nibbling what they can, blending that sweetness with the tang of sweat.

On such a fantastical evening, we aprons imagine that someday we, too, might wed, and it could be for love. Such is the privilege of servants; the nobles may have their money and their political alliances, but we have our feelings. I once did.

While the ladies think of dancing, my sister needlewomen and I stay tense and russet-gowned at the ready, anxious lest the work of so many hands and hours go flying to bits. To the nobility, we look like faded versions of humanity, being of the kingdom's original stock rather than the French who conquered it a century ago. Yellow-haired and white-complected, without powder or paint. Anxious to satisfy our conquerors so we might spend a few days longer among our dreams.

Our dreams are our riches; our hopes are our wealth. Our fears keep us working and thus let us live.

I truly would like to think I'm in the middle of a fairy tale, facing the period of hardship that precedes a triumph. But I am not a likely heroine. To the courtiers, I'm just another native of the city; in my father's home district, I'm the lovelorn object of gossip and shame. His neighbors among the glassmakers believe that, on a winter's day in front of Holy Spirit Church, I lost my one chance at marriage and happiness, and I did it in a way that forced me to disappear.

They are not wrong.

But, nonetheless, I brood over a nest of hope. I am only seventeen, after all, and still given to daydreams. Some of which have included a scene such as this, myself honored to be included in the seamstresses on hand, so close to noble ladies that I might touch them by moving an elbow. And breathing the same sweet air as the Queen. But as a simple seamstress, I can do nothing until given permission. Except invent stories to soothe myself into patience.

I have cause for fear now. Pink flesh is about to burst through Queen Isabel's gown, and that would be a wicked outcome, indeed: her body must be protected like a relic shut in a box. She seems eager to dwell in a coffin of misery, though, as she picks at the silver embroidery and costly white pearls with which the gown is adorned. Thus far she hasn't let anyone approach—not even Countess Elinor, who is her chief lady and confidante, and who makes another attempt now.

"Your Highness." Countess Elinor takes a cautious step forward. She is unusually pale for a noblewoman but wears silver brocade to complement the Queen's costume, even though it washes out what little color she might have. "*Most beloved* Highness, it may be true that we've lived through an age of misfortune, but this is a happy evening. Perhaps a happy end to our trials. Think of your daughter—"

"Sophia!" Isabel sobs, and the turquoise velvet gives another inch. "Twelve years old and *married*! To a *Swede*!"

"She might be Queen of Sweden one day, if Duke Magnus's older brothers die without issue." Countess Elinor makes her voice soft as she takes another step. "You raised her well." Another subtle step. "The entire kingdom sings praises of you both."

Queen Isabel wards her off with a clawing hand that flashes sapphire from a ring. She is behaving like a child. Hardship has done that to her.

The last eleven years have been cruel to the royal city of Skyggehavn — cruel to the whole kingdom, in fact. First came the Great Sickness of 1561, which took my mother and four brothers, then seven years of war throughout Scandinavia, and when that ended, a mysterious illness that invaded the royal nursery and holds all the children, including Princess Sophia, in its canker-some grasp: *Morbus Lunediernus,* sent by God to scourge the royal innocents and test the nation.

Now Countess Elinor has an idea. At a discreet signal, her maid and one of the in-waitings flap their skirts and shoo Queen toward Countess like a chicken.

"Your Highness." Triumphant, Countess Elinor finally manages to catch Queen Isabel's hands in her own fishy white ones. Her maid dabs at the Queen's cheeks as Elinor says, "Think of grandchildren. Isn't that happiness?"

Isabel's dripping dark eyes wander to an Annunciation that hangs over the desk where she writes her letters and does her accounts. In the picture, the Virgin sits with a book open on her lap, head tilted to let the golden banner of an angel's words tickle her right ear: she is going to birth a Savior.

"Oh." Queen Isabel sighs like a sail that the wind has forgotten. "Happiness."

Everyone — Queen, Countess, chronicler, assorted attendants and maids, dwarfs who are here to amuse — all are silent for a moment. We wonder when happiness, real happiness, will come to us. We breathe in and taste that tempting sweetness on the air. Maybe I, more than any, fill my lungs to the bottom.

My movement draws Countess Elinor's attention. She points a long white finger at me. "You. Fix this."

At first I'm astonished—I am the youngest and humblest of the needlewomen, responsible for linen undergarments and never chosen for the silks and velvets—so I'm unable to budge.

"Get to it," Countess Elinor snaps, as if this is my usual duty. But she would be the first with a slap if anyone approached the Queen without being ordered to do so.

Gudrun Tovasdatter, the ruddy Mistress of the Needle, hands me a basket of velvet scraps. She whispers, "Be careful, Ava. Pay attention. This could make your future."

Excited, nervous, clutching that basket as if it holds my dead mother's soul, I fall to my knees and make my way forward like a penitent in church. It has been thrilling enough before this day to think that my needle has stitched seams that would lie over royal skin; now it is to be my own fingers that feel for the Queen's flesh, just a few thin layers of fabric between me and her belly. I am to touch royalty. I have been chosen.

I crawl into the soft blue skirts until I'm close enough to smell Isabel's sweat—meaty overlaid with musk, some sort of whale-oil perfume—and feel the heat coming off her body. Suddenly she becomes real to me, an actual person rather than an idea. I am as afraid to touch her as I am eager to do it. I fumble in the pocket pouch at my waist for a pair of spectacles made by my father.

*"Hurtigt, hurtigt."* The Countess pushes at my shoulder. She has the high-sprung breasts of a virgin (indeed, she has given her crippled husband no children); they shake like milk jellies as she scolds, and in a gesture of annoyance she hoists them even higher. To the other ladies, she remarks, in the French that they use among themselves, "If this cow doesn't move quickly, the men will see to the Princess's *couchement* alone."

The Queen moans at this thought, her daughter put to bed without her blessing. "The Duke," she mourns, "is so much *hairier* than the men of this place . . ."

For speed, I abandon the search for my lenses and dig through the basket, trying to find a patch for the odd-shaped rip. I fold a piece into the shape of an eye, anchor one point to the top of the Queen's tear, and begin. Counting out the stitches to the rhythm of my breath: *One, two, three, pause. Adjust the loose thread end. One, two, three, pause.* The ancient rhythm known to every woman.

I am like the girl in the story who stitches up a lady cut to bits by thieves, to be rewarded afterward with a purse of gold . . . a purse that more thieves will steal from her before she can spend it, but perhaps we may stop before that happens.

With my hand on the Queen's side, I feel her breathing: in and out, slow, as if she's trying to calm herself too, though she unravels further with each inhalation.

Suddenly Isabel frees her hand to scratch around her wig. At this, of course, the rip in her bodice grows wider. She's stopped crying but not lamenting. "My daughter's new husband is mad. How can she find *happiness* with him? I have heard that he once jumped from a window because—"

Countess Elinor catches the hand again and pulls it down.

"—because he saw a mermaid in the moat below," Queen Isabel finishes miserably. She struggles, but Countess Elinor holds her fast.

I keep stitching.

"The mermaid . . . incident . . . was nine years ago," says the Countess. "And it is just gossip, told by Duke Magnus's enemies."

(Here is the full story: Magnus, Duke of Östergötland, was inspecting a castle in progress when from the fourth-level window he thought he saw a mermaid swimming in the moat. He jumped instantly from the window to the water, hoping to catch her. What he caught was a bad cold and a worse reputation; he's been known as Mad Magnus ever since.)

Countess Elinor continues smoothly, "Everyone loves a mermaid. Think of the charming legend about the land's first settlers . . ."

"Heathens," Queen Isabel says. "Witches! Servants of the devil!" She sobs again.

Countess Elinor loses patience. "Bring the Queen a sweet," she snaps, and her maid produces a sugar fig, expertly spun and painted. The Countess pops it into the Queen's mouth, and Isabel stops weeping and begins to suck.

In the sudden hush, the ladies stand as if they're at Mass. Only one of them murmurs a stream of flattery for the Queen, complimenting her on every silly thing, from her silvering hair to the sapphire ring that never leaves her hand. The others, including the dwarfs, mumble a litanous assent. *Our Queen is the greatest queen. The banquet she's planned is the greatest banquet. There is no love like the love of our Queen for her children.*

Underneath those voices run the whispers of the ladies' maids, who can speak without moving their lips.

". . . likes his fingers suckled while he's inside," one of them says. "I've seen it myself."

Still sewing (*one, two, three, pause*), I allow myself to glance up and recognize the green of Baroness Reventlow's made-over gown, now worn by her personal servant. So the speckly, chinless baroness (her husband blind from the war) is having an affair, and she doesn't make her maid leave the bedroom to conduct it.

Queen Isabel crunches up the last of the fig in her teeth. I feel the vibrations in her waist.

"'Swounds," breathes another maid. "That's a bit of nasty."

Absentmindedly, the Queen pulls a pearl from her gown and rolls it in her fingers. She puts it into her mouth like another confection, but when Elinor holds out her hand, Isabel spits the pearl into it. She looks ashamed, as if only just realizing what she's done. Elinor calls for another fig and pops it into Isabel's mouth.

*Poor Queen,* I think, with a compassion that surprises me; usually I consider her the luckiest woman in the world. Poor

Queen, whose beloved daughter is about to sail away to a part of Sweden called Östergötland. Poor Queen, who must always play a part scripted by others. Held in Elinor's steel grasp, Isabel is no more free to act than the rest of us.

She slumps against my hand, and the rip widens yet again. I stop caring about neat work and stitch madly against time.

*Our princesses are the loveliest princesses. Our prince is the handsomest prince . . .*

". . . handsome legs, and those white teeth," comes another whisper — clearly not about the Crown Prince, who is as comely as a stick insect. "Hair black as a Southerner's. But what I heard about him —"

"Gave his girl the Fire, he did," whispers Reventlow's maid, as the lady-in-waiting whose task it is to flatter declaims, *The most fortunate kingdom in all creation!*

The whisper gets even softer, the bare stirring of a breath: "And she killed herself for the pain. Mandrake and antimony. Stole them from the physicians' stores."

I try to blink a blurriness away from my eyes. That horrid illness, Italian Fire, strikes nobles and prostitutes more often than their servants — there's a famous wiggle in the court ladies' hips, as they give a subtle scratch to its itch — but no one is immune. Half the sellers of simples and unguents outside the palace gates are touting cures for that burning white ooze and the ache in the bladder, but the cures are as bad as the symptoms and, often as not, even deadlier.

However much we crave love, love brings danger. As I've found out too well — though not with the Fire.

And now, the very worst happens: dim-sighted with grief for my own lost happiness, I let my needle slip. Of its own will, it plunges through layers of velvet and lawn and stiff linen, between whalebones and into royal flesh. *One, two, disaster.* A tiny bud of red appears around the slim shaft, then blooms to the size of my fingernail.

I have just wounded the Queen.

For a moment, time is frozen. I hold my breath; the voices murmur on. I think, *Maybe I imagined it, the stab. Maybe I'm imagining the stain.*

Then Queen Isabel shrieks, tearing into the recitation of her praises. A piercing sound that seems forced from her very middle, as if her flesh has never been pricked before.

The women turn to look at me, all hidden as I am in the turquoise. I'm cold to the toes.

The Queen takes a step away, exposing me. She keeps her arms stiff and spread as if she's afraid they'll be splashed with blood.

"This seamstress," she says, staring forward, "is a clumsy troll."

Countess Elinor presses her lily-pale lips together. Her breasts are blue with fury. "What is your name?" she asks, one moment before she slaps my face.

So there is my power, to stab the Queen. And there is her power, nurtured by the drone bees who tend her.

# SOPHIA LUNEDIE

WELVE and one-third years ago, in the twilit morning of a dark December day, Princess Sophia Lunedie slipped out between her mother's legs and into a crown. Not her own crown but her father's, or her future husband's—it has never mattered whose. Invisible but no less insistent, a crown swaddled her through a childhood in which she was promised to a series of foreign princes that changed according to her father's need for alliances. With each year the crown grew tighter, until, this spring, her woman's courses stained its tines with blood. The rubies of a virtuous woman, more precious to her father's kingdom than a real gem would be.

*But these are the thoughts of a child,* Sophia tells herself. She will not always be a child. She has left the nursery for good and is standing in a bedroom, *her* bedroom for this week, and her husband's. She is to sleep (if she sleeps) far from her one brother's and five sisters' chaste sickbeds, where they doze or moan according to their dispositions, dreaming doses of antimony and ground gold, prayers to thank God for the affliction that tests their souls and refines them in holy fire as He refined His son on the holy Cross. Dear, sweet siblings, all still children who listen to nurses' stories and imagine themselves merely enchanted by the curse of some fairy jealous of their mother's beauty.

Maman is *not* beautiful, and her teeth are gray. She is fat and split her dress while dancing with a lord; it has been mended clumsily and is tearing further. But in this moment, Sophia loves her fiercely.

It is Sophia's last week at her parents' court, and she must spend it with the stranger she just married, in a palace that skates on the thin skin of land between bay and canals. From this night forward, she is a Swede and a Protestant. And a duchess. What little girl has not dreamed of being a duchess? Or someday (if Magnus's two older brothers die childless) a queen?

Candle flames shudder in the puddles of her jewels; the great diamond on what will someday be her bosom reflects the bed's draping of red damask.

Maman (Mother, Sophia must call her now) unties the lacing at the neck of the girl's stiff rose-and-gold gown. "Dear child," she whispers, "you must be brave."

Within this very hour, there will be blood again. The Princess already tastes it, there in the back of her throat, where her heart is trying to choke her.

Hands scrape Sophia like pincers, removing her jewelry, the pins in her scratchy ruff, the false curls in her thin hair. The ladies are ants, fat busy ants, seizing her sleeves and collar and overskirt. They strip her down to a frame of reedy limbs and hips.

"Begging pardon, Highness." One of her borrowed ladies,

Countess Ditlevnavn, tugs a wad of fabric down over Sophia's head. Sophia pulls her shoulders in to make this easier. Lunedie princesses go to bed in long white linen gowns; this one whistles down her body and pools at her feet with a spill of lace. It is too hot, and the starch prickles. Sophia wants to scratch herself, but of course she cannot. There is a bony white callus on her leg that itches hard, and it will make her howl with pain if she touches it.

Maman gestures at a maid who has been waiting with a tray (there are so many of these girls, all invisible till they move close).

"Spiced wine," says the Queen, picking up a glass goblet that glows with the heat of the drink, "for fertility and for restful sleep. Doctor Candenzius and I devised the recipe."

She holds the cup while Sophia swallows. Drinks in one long gulp, holding her breath, staring at the tapestries that weave the history of her homeland into wavering tableaux. Black-clad witches cast out of Norway in rowboats, green mermaids towing them to their new home. Priests in long robes, an astrologer in blue, under a great white burst of a moon that looks like a headache. A shipwrecked man living in the carcass of a whale, discovering the oils that make lamps and perfumes. The battle in which the first Count Lunedie of France, lured by access to whale oil and valuable amber, claimed the kingdom's throne. The marriage of Maman and Papa, by the golden altar of the cathedral where the bones of Saint Ruta—patron of fishers and fishnet knotters, rope twisters and lace makers—had miraculously manifested and then been interred. The drab, narrow panel depicting the signing of the Treaty of Stettin, the document that ended seven years of war with no benefit to anyone, except those who make their living by selling provisions and arranging marriages to smooth over hostility. Sophia and Magnus were part of that treaty. They will reconcile mighty Sweden to the rest of Scandinavia (Denmark, Norway, Poland, and Papa's land), all represented by her twiggish body.

As of tonight, Sophia is part of history. She will be woven into a tapestry herself. In Sweden.

This has been one of Sophia's good days, but she feels the curseful *Morbus Lunediernus* crouching in her anyway, like a wild cat that waits to pounce. There's the burn in her stomach and a rash around her mouth and on her palms that no unguent and powder cosmetic can conceal. Every one of her limbs aches, and patches of her skin itch. The wine helps, makes things duller. Her throat goes numb, and she can no longer feel her heart.

"Your mouth, Princess." Countess Elinor Parfis, her mother's chief lady, dabs at Sophia with a feathery puff. It leaves a bitter powder; Sophia's new husband, Duke Magnus of Östergötland, with his earthworm lips in a nest of dark beard, will not want to kiss her. But he will do it anyway, because that's his duty.

Maman makes a sound that is half sigh, half clearing of the throat. A signal to her ladies.

They sink to the floor to pray.

One last moment together, and it is on their knees before the man in the whale. Then it's time for Sophia's husband.

After Magnus's men have deposited him—also in nightdress, boisterous with drink—in the bed where Sophia's body is too slight to make either ridge or ravine; after they have all prayed together again; and after Magnus has ceremoniously touched Sophia's naked white stick of a leg with his own scratchy one (scarred from the war against her countrymen, for which the two of them are making peace now), the last thing Sophia sees is her mother's face. Drawn, yellow, its expression the same that Maman wears when visiting the nursery where the clutchy odor of *Morbus* fugs the air. This homely face peers around the edge of the dark oak door for a long, sad look, and Sophia blinks. She is very sleepy; it must be the spices in the wine. (Maman is so clever with medicines, quite as knowledgeable as the physicians she employs.) Sophia is grateful for the drowse that blunts her fear. Maybe she can sleep through what comes next . . . like the princess in the enslumbered castle . . . with thorns . . .

The tapestry priests fix her with a cold reproach. Of course she must be wakeful during what comes next; otherwise she cannot truly say she's given herself to her husband. She must be as attentive as she is faithful. She will be like her own parents in this. Her father doesn't even have a single bastard and has never been caught with a mistress; their marriage is the marvel of Europe.

The door closes, and the voices and shuffling feet retreat, to wait in the outer room until one of them (Sophia, Magnus) cries out. Then the lords and ladies and priests can look at each other with satisfaction, and the maids and in-waitings can try to guess if the new couple might need something or are simply expressing their pleasure in each other.

(Where is Östergötland? Someone once showed her on a map, but she can't for the life of her think of it now.)

So here she lies, in bed, next to her husband. Magnus. Who is large and hot and shaggy, his breath whistling, wind breaking from both ends. The banquet was rich. Sugar cheese, sugar cakes, a smell of rot. He is gazing at the mermaid tapestry. Sophia has heard it said that he once spotted a mermaid swimming in his castle moat and jumped from a window to catch her. He had to be dragged out half drowned and was delirious with fever for days. It is the kind of love that every girl wishes to inspire in a man.

Sophia waits for Magnus to speak. To excuse himself, to address her. Instead he scratches his crotch. The mermaids on the tapestry waver, as if they really are swimming through green threads of ocean. She grabs at her nightdress, feeling it dampen and crumple. Her hands are uncommonly pink.

"I'd like a sip of that wine," she says, trying to sound brave. Maman has left a jug by the bed, and Magnus heaves himself up to pour a whole cup of it for her. He has a belly and a wide behind; he makes the bed shake. As a wedding gift, he gave her an emerald parure cut in the new glittering style and closed in a glowy amber box. Now he just sits there while she drinks, scratching beneath his arms and yawning. She sips and sips, and soon the wine is gone.

"My lord," she says, with lids so heavy that her future children might be sitting on them. "If you would like — if I, *mmm* — I am yours to command," she concludes, conscious that she is mumbling. "And I am in perfect health today." She stifles an air bubble that ticks in her throat. She hears herself speak as if across an enormous room. "I am eager to please." And she concludes with what is actually a greeting: "Health to your soul."

He groans and takes the cup from her, strokes his beard, and sighs. He is clearly not so eager for any pleasure she might provide.

"Onward into the continent, then," he says, and reaches for her.

# AVA BINGEN

The jail floor is a surprise, warm in a land heated by the waters underground. It aches at my ankles, feet, buttocks, the progress of that burn and the swelling of my fear being the only way to mark time in the bright dead of a spring night, when I sit cross-legged and lean against a wall, roll a pilfered sugar cherry between my fingers, and wait for Fate.

Fate refuses to stop at the pretty part of the tale; Fate insists on more tests of courage and wit, a terrible end, even if the heroine's heart be pure and her crime accidental.

I remember to be grateful for small bounties. I have a window, in perhaps the last moments of my life. It seeps blue-gray light and the same jangle of far-off music, the faint savor of sweetness mixing with the tang of jail as I breathe in. The wedding banquet has continued, presumably with the Queen in fully restored turquoise stitched by someone else's needle, as Princess Sophia meets her husband in bed and the nobles celebrate the fact that tonight more royal blood will spill.

I remember that red droplet leaking around the tip of my needle, flowering onto white linen. Even in my fear, I feel a thrill. To have pierced royal flesh! How many can say they've done that? Let alone lived for more than a heartbeat afterward. My father tells of a tournament at which a stray splinter from the former Duke of Marsvin's lance accidentally rammed right through the old King's nose; the Duke was missing his head before the King had a chance to breathe his last. And then we had a new King, and a new Duke.

Perhaps I must also resign myself to death—at barely seventeen, unmarried if not untried, with only my father and stepmother to mourn me. A story passed around by gossips and then forgotten.

It is in fact a rare soul that's never felt the possibility of ready death—from falling mortar, hungry canals, waves of disease that sweep over the water and into city. When I faced mortality ten years ago, with the Great Sickness that took nearly half the souls in Skyggehavn, I shook it off—even though it claimed my mother and brothers. At the time, people called me lucky, as if I had visited the realm of trolls and fought my way back into the light, dragging their king by the beard.

"You alone have been saved," my father told me, "in order to accomplish some great good in this world." He mourned my mother and brothers very much and cursed himself for unluck.

"But you *are* lucky," I insisted to him, patting at his tears with my skinny child hands. I couldn't bear to see him weep, even though every other living soul around us wept. "God wants greatness from you too."

I believe it was then that he began his experiments with lens grinding, shaping his bits of glass to see not five feet away or even ten, as with the spectacles he normally fashioned, framed, and sold, but thousands of miles into the heavens—to find God or the spirits of our family. And I know it was then

22

that he recognized my talent for sewing and sent me to a special school for girls good with the needle, all in training to open their own shops or follow the courts of grand ladies, one of few honorable professions for women.

But here I am, underground and guilty. As afraid as if I were already facing a torturer, as hopeless as if I'd never had an education or a lover. As still as if already laid in the grave.

We are all on the brink of death anyway, all of us suffering some disease, though some may hide it better than others. The nobles have their Italian Fire, the King his constant stomach pains, which sometimes make him bleed into his breeches; the Queen is remote, as if a part of her is missing. And consider the royal children: all of them (except now Sophia) confined to their silver-paneled nursery, innocents suffering with *Morbus Lunediernus,* with boils and sores and rashes, aches in the bones, and fingernails eaten away. They have been deemed too ill to travel, even to one of the country castles where the Lunedies normally spend summer months gulping down clean air.

But it is far worse for us who are not noble. We cough and limp; we lose our hair, lose our teeth, catch fevers and chills; we grow cancers that split our bones and worms that gnaw through our bowels. We work till we drop dead from a sudden pain in the chest or side.

Illness makes us strangers in our own lives, and then it becomes our closest relation. Is it any wonder that we grab for what little bit of pleasure might come to us before death?

I mentioned I once had a lover. We loved each other fiercely; it might be said my life has already been full enough.

But I thought to have him longer and to have more with him: a family, a shop, a life. Yes, I've wanted what everyone wants, from sovereign to scullery maid. Love and home, happiness; a sense that I am living my own life, not that I've fallen into some other, a confused changeling who can't learn the rules before she's doomed.

By now the Queen's pinprick will have crusted over. I imagine her in a nightdress (one that I have sewn for her and embroidered with flowers I've never seen except in pictures and patterns). She rakes her nails over the spot, having forgotten why she itches, forgotten how that grain of scab arrived on her side. Perhaps there will be a scar—far smaller than the cherry between my fingers, even less than the bite of a louse . . .

I have an itch myself, on my neck, just beneath my left earlobe. When I scratch, a shred of skin comes away under my nail and a brittle black body no bigger than a pin's head. When I squash it between my nails, the insides burst in a minuscule stain.

There were bugs in Jacob's bed that first night, seething from the straw and through the mattress's seams to bite into flesh raw with autumn cold. We didn't care; we laughed and tossed handfuls of spiders at each other, plucked lice from each other's hair and smashed them on the wall. We kissed and were happy, drunk on having made our choice.

I was fifteen and a half (young for an apron bride but not impossibly so) and Jacob Lille just eight years older. He was a journeyman in the amber trade, and he always smelled giddily of the stuff. He was finishing his masterpiece, a finely wrought puzzle-globe clarified and hardened and carved to elaborate perfection; a nested series of lacy golden spheres fashioned from a single piece, one inside the other, growing smaller and smaller in succession until the eye could no longer see. He was about to become not only a master but quite likely famous. He was halfway to the tiniest of the lace spheres, which was to be smaller even than the pinprick in the Queen, when we first laid eyes on each other.

It was in the glassworkers' district, at Holy Spirit Church, which would site the beginning and the end of our story. His parish church had crumbled into a mud puddle, and his parents needed a new place for Mass. On the Feast of the Assumption, Jacob came with them to our Helligánds Kirke.

I saw him first as the ring of bronze bells marked a wooden Virgin's ascension into Heaven and drowned out the howls of the madmen locked in the nearby hospital. His eyes were very blue—no bluer than the eyes of a typical Skyggehavner, it is true, but they caught the last light of summer and smiled into mine, which I knew in that moment were just as blue as his, and that I was as lovely as a man could ever imagine.

Our families took Communion that day. When it was my turn for the cup, I took care to place my lips where he'd put his. I saw him notice my boldness, and we both flushed so red that our fathers laid wrists to foreheads to check us for fever. We stared forward at the wooden Christ with his five wounds; in a strange way, I found the sculpture exciting.

I learned only later that Jacob was actually a Protestant.

He believed in direct communication with the heavens; he belonged to a secret sect that met to pray and discuss the word of God, at least as much as was recognizable in our tongue, for the priests kept a stranglehold on Latinate verses and forbade translation. On that Assumption Day, he had brushed his lips on the cup only, refusing to take Communion through a priest.

Yes, the blue eyes burned for God as for me. But, in my presence, mostly for me. I was *his jewel, his treasure, his heart, his heart's desire.* He said he loved me to madness, and he joked that one day he'd be confined to the Holy Spirit Hospital for love of me. I laughed away his compliments, but a secret part of me hoped they were real, not simply poetry.

And soon came October. Officially betrothed, with our wedding just a week away, we took my father's little boat onto the canals to gaze at the green lights that blur the night sky in that season. We rowed bedazzled with light and love, ignoring the trash that struck the oars and the rats that paddled after us, toward the room he shared with another journeyman at his master's studio. While everyone else was out marveling at the skies, we tied up our boat and went inside and marveled at each other, tossed the spiders, and made them part of our love nest.

"The wedding is only a week away," I said in the teasing manner I had back then. His eyes sparkled and he grabbed at me.

By candlelight, Jacob unfastened my clothes and kissed every spot where I could dream of receiving a kiss. When

I was dizzy with pleasure, he rubbed himself against me—rubbed only, for he declared he still wanted to marry a virgin; he owed me that much. "It would be disrespectful to treat my wife otherwise," he said with a note of indignation, and I couldn't help grinning with delicious anticipation. I had a new red dress waiting for our wedding, embroidered and trimmed with lace of my own needles.

Jacob kissed me again, and again, and again. And again he rubbed himself on me until he couldn't rub anymore—with an exultant groan, he spent himself over my belly and thighs, and I felt the tickle of it dripping down the curves of me, and believed this was the first of many times together.

Jacob made me happy this way, happy with myself and with him. We parted as lovers, with more of his flowery declarations and a perfect kiss, as I returned to my father's house.

But Jacob also made me mistrust vows and songs and stories and their conceits ever after, as well as love itself. Because in the end, we did not marry.

All I know is what I heard from Jacob's father, who wouldn't look at me as he delivered the news. *Our boy's gone to sea,* he said, gazing into the throng that was filing into Helligánds Kirke that Sunday. He walked away before I could open my mouth.

I had to conclude the rest. Just that morning, our servant had reported that a forbidden vernacular translation of Holy Scripture had been discovered nearby. So I imagined soldiers tapping at the Lutheran sect-house door. I imagined a list of names with Jacob's prominent among them. I imagined Jacob imprisoned—and then, because I couldn't bear the thought, and because I was sure gossip would have named any who were arrested—I convinced myself that he had fled in time to protect himself.

In church I caught sight of the wounded Christ. I could not bear it.

Running home, I wept through the time of Mass, through bells ringing and madmen shouting, the plash of oars as some burgher or other traveled along the canal below my window.

Danger of death: this was the only reason I could think that Jacob would have abandoned me. It was the only reason I could accept. I was sure he'd gone to some country full of Lutherans—Denmark, Iceland, one of the Germanies. I was left to imagine him leaning from the deck of some great ship, casting a net to catch the amber with which he'd make his fortune in the new land. Or perhaps a mermaid to take as bride.

*Our boy's gone to sea.* Why did love come to me as a Protestant?

"We'll find you a husband," Father promised when he came home, through the door by the stone head that advertised his trade. "Your stepmother and I will take care of it."

Sabine added, "A better husband. A richer one. A good Catholic." So she, too, had added and made the same deduction; this made it all true in my mind, and I wept again. Abandoned for a different version of God—it felt worse, I sobbed, than if I were jilted for another girl.

"Nonsense," Father said; he meant well. "Nonsense," gently, over and over.

He and Sabine had just married that week themselves, also for love. Sabine was twice widowed, now prosperous. Both she and Father felt sorry for me, and generous, and eager to share their happiness. They even offered to increase my dowry.

I begged them to wait. I thought Jacob might change his mind and come back. Maybe he'd hear somehow that the names denounced in church did not include his, and he'd know it was safe to return. Or if he stayed gone, I pleaded to go after him.

Father and Sabine were shocked.

"Not by yourself," Sabine said.

"Not without knowing your destination," said Father.

I proposed going first to Copenhagen (somehow my bones told me he'd be there), then Iceland and elsewhere, but Father and Sabine held firm. They would not give me money to travel, to pay for myself and a companion to try our luck, and they would not go with me themselves unless I learned for certain where Jacob had gone.

"It would be better to marry someone else immediately," said Sabine. I heard the two of them talking in their bed at night, worrying that *I* had made myself mad with heartbreak.

I visited Jacob's parents in the fragrant amber-handlers' quarter, to find out what they knew.

"He's gone," said Jacob's mother.

"To sea," said his gaunt father.

My lover was their only son. His four unmarried sisters stared, and so did the neighbors who saw me at their door. The coincidence of Jacob's disappearance and the raid on the

Lutherans had made everyone draw that one conclusion, and there was a taint about the family now.

"If you have news from him before I do," I said boldly, "let him know that I don't give a pin for religion."

The whole family recoiled, crossing themselves, and I was never welcome there again.

I was desperate. I wondered if we were all wrong. I even thought that maybe—and this was madness itself—he had indeed lost his senses out of love and needed me to save him. I brought a basket of cakes to Helligånds Hospital and walked among the madmen, breaking off bits of sweetness for the poor souls inside (some meek, some fighting in chains), searching each grimy face for my beloved. I asked the monks about a tall blond, sweet-smelling man, and they (having taken vows of silence) sadly shook their heads.

So I forced myself to return home and wait, stitch collars and cuffs for the fine ladies of Sabine's acquaintance, and at last learn the virtue of patience. Like many a fool before me, I congratulated myself on having remained a virgin in deed if not intention (and though it was not *my* restraint that preserved my maidenhead).

Thereby I made everything worse, because for all our cleverness, Jacob and I had been careless. In time I discovered that as his seed dripped between my thighs, my greedy womb had reached down to grab a drop for itself. Though to any eyes a virgin, I began to grow a child. Not without some happiness; I had a notion, a tiny seed of hope, that the drop within me would call its father homeward. But when another month passed and then a third, the slow break of my heart scraped the seed away.

That it took riddance in a public place—in front of the church, no less—was my downfall. It was the Saturday before Epiphany, so there was a market on the *plads,* lit by torches on a dark winter midday. Father and Sabine and I put on our finest for it. Father had just sold a pair of spectacles to the court astrologer, who had also commissioned a perspective glass for looking at the heavens and a hat embroidered by me. Despite the embarrassment of my jilting, our family fortune looked full of promise, and Father and Sabine wanted to savor it, to bask in the neighbors' envy. They planned to buy little things at the stalls and to enjoy the antics of an acrobat troupe the guild master had praised.

I walked dully behind the two of them, trying to put a brave face on grief and fear. Many a girl has been rejected; many a love has been uprooted from the marsh of a wounded heart. But what was I to *do?* I pulled my stomach tighter and tighter, and pressed my fists into the hollow that would soon swell to become a baby, under cover of cinching my shawl.

I remember Father grumbling that he could not get one of the lenses on the perspective glass right, and with the clouds over the city, he would not be able to spot the stars all night. It was the sort of grumbling that's really a boast, for of course everyone thought it wonderful that the work of his hands would be mounted on the palace's flat west tower, perhaps even to be examined by the King's keen eye. This device was an innovation of my father's, the fulfillment of the promises we'd made to each other after the Great Sickness. It was much more sophisticated, with its system of glass wafers and tubes and candles, than the water-filled orbs used at most courts. It brought the stars halfway to the ground; it allowed the viewer to see the surface of the moon.

As Father bragged, I blew my nose into my sleeve, pretending to have a rheum. I wished he could grind me a glass that would show the way to my lost suitor. Looking around at the chilblained crowd, I wasted some small hope for following Sabine's advice, finding a new husband who would rescue me and accept my baby.

Sabine was in the full spirit of the day, walking broad and proud as a ship under sail. Her eyes sparkled through a pair of Father's lenses as, one after another, masters and their wives came to greet her and to congratulate Father on his success.

Eventually we found the acrobats, their breath pluming in the cold. We stopped to look as a man swallowed fire, then blew it before him like a dragon. A boy threw himself flat on his belly and planted his chin on the paving stones, then ran circles around his own head. I watched drearily, rubbing the beads of my mother's amber bracelet between my fingers and wishing the old wives' tales might be true: that amber brings happiness, fidelity, and a banishing of evil spirits.

As part of our wooing, Jacob had given me a needle case he'd made himself out of amber and brass. It was full of the best needles and pins, with a tiny scissor for snipping threads. A gift, he said, to sew our hearts together.

I hated amber in that moment. I tore the bracelet from

my wrist, but it was all I had of my mother. I shoved it into the pocket at my waist. I told myself, *I must try again, I must try not to mind, I must at least look as if all is well,* and forced a smile at a glassblower who had always blushed in my presence. He blushed now, too, and bowed at me.

My father bought Sabine some ribbons; she hinted flirtatiously that they were for a petticoat. A neighbor teased about the stone head on our house, which had recently come loose and was beginning to list to the right. The man in motley opened his mouth and slid a sword into his throat. And then I screamed.

It was as if the sword had entered my body. I felt myself tearing apart; I felt blood splashing my thighs. I knelt on the square, and the blood puddled under my skirts. It left a stain that remains on the stones to this day, if only to my eyes.

Back then, all entertainments stopped as fairgoers gathered 'round me, clucking with what seemed to be concern but was, naturally, speculation. Madmen bore witness in the hospital nearby. The glassblower vanished.

"She's always had spells at her monthlies," my stepmother said, fast and so loud I would have flamed red under any other conditions. Instead I clutched my stomach and groaned. "Poor thing!" Sabine fairly shouted, gesturing to my father. Naturally she'd already guessed what was happening to me.

"There, there, my dear," Father said stagily. He was as shrewd as his wife and caught her clue neatly. "This time will be fine, as it always is." He wrapped me in his cloak, and the two of them bore me home, my head a lolling broken daisy.

33

I took to my bed. I was fevered and sick, though the blood didn't last long. Our servant, Gerda, stayed with me day and night; Father and Sabine brought me soups and poultices of herbs. They campaigned in the neighborhood to insist that this was just an episode of terrible courses.

"Some virgins have a time, you know." I heard Sabine say it over and over, down by the canal below my window. "She'll be up and about soon."

Every soul has its secrets, and it is no secret that there are some who make it their business to ferret these out and spread them through town. I myself had been guilty of gossiping, telling stories to the girls at needle school or to my lover. Harmless secrets, I thought them; but I've since concluded there is no such thing. Not since I was the subject.

When my stepmother came upstairs, she repeated the rumors about me angrily. Not just that I'd fallen pregnant and Jacob had discarded me for it, not just that I miscarried from the shame of being abandoned. But even more: that the bloody squall was of my choosing too, and that I had defied holy law by bringing it on in front of a church. The kindest of the neighbors believed it was God or the Spirit Himself who purged me, enraged at a sinning presence on holy ground. The least kind thought me an abortioness and said I should be pilloried for the crime. Some—and these made Sabine angriest of all—said my new stepmother had given me the poison, as one of her previous husbands had been an apothecary.

Under Queen Isabel, who is so modest that she won't wear garments a man's hand has touched, Skyggehavn has

34

been a city of churchly virtue, the glassmakers' district particularly so. When a community develops aspirations toward gentility, suddenly the bastards disappear and all the women must be virgins.

I'm sure that among these *good people* there were women who had drunk bryony wine or chewed an oniony autumn crocus, thrust rocks or sticks inside themselves to expel unwanted occupants—I've heard of a glass master who specializes in a bauble that will do this—but at the whisper that I had done it too, they turned against me. I took on the guilt of every woman who had broken the law this way, and no one thought to make sure I had sinned in fact as well as in rumor.

And how can I be certain it was *not* my own wishes that caused my miscarriage? Sometimes wishes are granted, and I am not the first to observe that this is rarely for the best.

Father and Sabine worried that at any moment the city guardsmen might appear and haul me off to prison. But to their credit, they did not (so far as I know) consider tossing me out among the streets and canals; they kept me upstairs, kept nursing me, kept hoping for some fix to the situation. And I, who had been so impatient to push forward with my life—now I could not move, couldn't sleep or eat, paralyzed with shame and terror. I thereby made the speculation worse, for some say a natural miscarriage heals within a day, while a poisonous one takes weeks.

They also say a child conceived in love holds firm, no matter how a woman tries to dislodge it. This rumor I now know to be false.

It is true that the pain of that child did something to my bones, which have not been right since. They ache with the cold and throb with the heat; they no longer bend in the right places. I still have my maidenhead, but it is an awkward thing, especially here on the floor of the palace prison, as I listen to the last sounds of celebration and know I never had the pleasure of a full *couchement* myself.

But Father and his new wife saved me. They told me I had a different destiny, that I hadn't survived so long in order to languish in a bed of shame. They hauled me out and propped me up. Sabine laced me into a corset from the days when she had a waist, and the two of them took me to church.

The Latin gave me a headache. The incense made me sick. The statues and paintings were a dizzying array of figures that swam before me. But I stood for all three hours and managed not to vomit or fall down, and this slowed the wagging tongues, even if I could never dismiss suspicion completely.

I was ruined for the glassmakers' guild, certainly, and for the amber-handlers'. I might as well have died, for all they thought of me for marriage afterward. Even if it were just Eve's curse, no man wants a woman with such a violent cycle.

This was my life. Already I was a changeling in it.

Luckily, or else dreadfully—as I believe in this moment sitting in the doomful casemates—Sabine had a friend among the palace housekeepers, and she passed my name along with the chief astrologer's endorsement (he was very pleased with the hat I'd made him) to the needle mistress for the Queen. Mistress

Gudrun was impressed with my closed seams and cut lace; she offered a wage that might win me honor. A dowry someday. Or — sometimes I thought it, though I told myself sternly not to — a passage to Denmark, where I might find Jacob Lille among the Luther-loving amber handlers and take my rightful place beside him, saddened about our first baby but glad again for the poetry he would spill into our lives.

At other times, of course, I thought to slap his face, for sailing into such an easy life and leaving me a hard one. Nonetheless, I found I had to believe his life was easy; to think otherwise was to give up all hope.

So, in the house with the stone head, we convinced ourselves: Here was a triumph for the Bingens! A father with a commission for a splendid perspective glass, a daughter employed in the Queen's own household! Father and Sabine kissed me soundly on both cheeks, gave me their blessings, and, I suspect, leaned on the door with a sigh of relief when I left.

When I first stepped through the palace gates with my spare clothes bundled into a sack, I felt a sort of fizzy excitement, a hope that my life and heart were making themselves over. Now, I resolved, my tale would best end in becoming Mistress of the Needle myself, with a dozen women stitching my commands, the royal family developing a personal fondness for me; an independence that would not keep me bound to a man's affections. I would be queen of my own life and take pride in my loneliness.

So endings change. I fashioned a new fortune from the

rags of the old, and I smiled at all within the gates, in a bubble of good intentions that led to the honor of needle waiting at the banquet tonight.

And to prison after all.

I smash beetle after beetle, wondering if I should enjoy my sugar cherry now or wait to bite down and let it be the last taste in my mortal life.

The cell floor shakes with the force of the life beneath it . . . or, no, with a jailer's footsteps. The bugs go scuttling deep down for cover. I drop the sugar cherry back into my bosom, to be some comfort as I'm sent off to execution.

My prison master is a ruddy man in blue livery. His neck pouches like a hog seller's purse on market day, for he has grown fat from swallowed terror. Keys tinkle cheerfully from his belt.

"There you are, then," he says, holding the door open.

I feel foolish when I realize that he didn't have to unlock it. Though of course I never needed to be locked up; if the Queen's guard says to stay in a place, there is certain death for leaving it. Eleven months at the palace have taught me that much, and to spring to my feet when I'm summoned.

Blood rushes back to my ankles, and I wobble, smoothing my apron by reflex. *I am,* I think, *as cold as a star in the sky.* I rub my hands together and adjust my cap.

"God's wounds, *fröken,* you look well enough for where you're going," says the guard.

## MIDI SORTE

First she were a baby, then a girl, then a sick girl, then come her throes.

The first scream not so bad, just any woman's scream; the ladies and the maids look down their laps and nod, to say we all have this pain before and that some time it lead to pleasure.

For me, that pleasure came just recent, though I am in this cold land full seven years. The first man of this place who buy me from the boat take me in such a way as to savor me, though it not seem so nice at age eleven and tired from a long sail with many other men. He were the one who name me Black Midday, to make wit for his wife when he bring me home as her gift.

We do n't look to the men, though they sit here for listening too.

The girl scream again, and this time her nurses know. We have hear every kind of scream from Lunedie babies, and this the terror kind, from a girl grown too old for screams but told just press the hands together like saints in church, and moan if you must but not too loud.

We the nurses, we start to pull our skirts up ready to run inside that room, but the ladies do n't say to go. Countess Elinor, that once was my lady, make a back ward sigh in her skinny nose, and she do n't need to look around to make us keep our places. She push her bosom up.

"Duke Magnus is the King of Sweden's brother."

We wait.

But Magnus him self throw open the door, so hard it hit old Duchess Margrethe in the shoulder where she sitting. "Help!" he shout, as a woman in a fire. "Help in here!"

Then Countess Elinor will not stop us any more, we all go in. The Countesses and Duchess Margrethe and Lady Drin and Baroness Reventlow and Bridget Belskat, then all we nurses from pale Annas and Marias to including me. We know this Duke's story, we know he fall in love with some thing in the water and jumped him self fifty feets to meet her. We fear for our Sophia, what a mad man might do to her.

Fears ever justify.

Our girl is lying half off the bed, stiff like a board, with eyes staring at the bed drape. One side curtain come pulled down and puddling on the floor. All the candles blowing wild, like there been a wind, and some gone out.

We gape a minute. This be some thing never seen before.

Then she not stiff any more, she curling on her self like a snail, and her mouth foam like a snail too, once it poison with salt. This when she scream again and again, till she straighten out once more with that glass-eye look above her.

"She was asleep," say this Duke Magnus of Östergötland. His beard is neat and greasy, so I do n't know to trust him. He must fixed it before calling us. Madness may be on him again.

We pull back the sheets, and there am some blood but not

much. A little girl can 't sleep just after That, I know this to be true here as any where else.

"Too much wine," say that Magnus. He rubbing his arm in his night shirt, he have an itch like may be she scratch him. "She kept drinking till she went to sleep, and then this. I had some too," he adds, as if he worry for it now.

The Countess Elinor send some boy to fetch the Queen and King. She step her self to the bed and try to put a hand to Sophia's forehead, but the girl curl up again. Countess Elinor snatch her hand away like it be burned.

"Something's wrong," she say, and it is so obvious I want to laugh. Not for meanness but from what a lady call her nerves. But I press my hands like saints, and I put on that face of sorrow that every one wear for the *Morbus,* and I watch the ladies watching Sophia and waiting for the Queen.

Ladies think a Queen know best all ways, better than her three doctors and all they powders. Even this incomplete Queen. May be they are correct, not for me to say.

The Princess curl and straighten, curl and straighten, making messy in the bedclothes and pulling down the other curtains. She do n't fall from bed, though, stay just on the edge and some time pokering off it as if she going to float up to heaven with all the fire in her body. Her whole face flaming red now and her night dress wet in sweat, with the skirt rode up to show some shadow on her leg that might be blood, might be vanished all ready.

She scream again. And there come a thumping at the door.

Ladies wave apart, and three doctors walk in, black robes

41

and flat hats and assisters with bowls and things in jars. They all gape too, while the Princess throw back and forth and scatter foam from her mouth.

"Do you see those sores?" ask Doctor Candenzius, the chief of them. He come close and poke the Princess neck with a stick. "A plague necklace" he call the wounds, though I never seen a necklace from the Lunedie *Morbus.*

The second doctor, Venslov, the old one, say, "That is not the typical presentation." The third doctor agree, it is not what they expect. They gape some more.

No body say *poison* out loud. But ladies look at the floor and maids look at each other, all communicate in that perfect-quiet way of this place.

"Do something," Countess Elinor say to those doctors.

"We must wait for Queen Isabel," say a young lady.

The Countess cross arms below her bosoms, push them high as they will go, and look down her nose with one eye. This what she do when she most vexed with some body. She say sharp to the doctors, "Don't wait."

More screaming from that bed. I want to slide up and pat the Princess on her brow, but she all ready too far gone. Her necklace (so they call it) bursts, and the blood go shining out like the fountain of wine at her wedding feast. The ladies scream and Countess Elinor breathe in again. Even the doctors pale now, and they can 't but watch.

After Sophia spray her bed with blood, she fall back to her pillow with eyes wide. Not screaming any more.

There come howling, though, from rooms around, those

42

where the other princesses and their brother sleep with some maids and grooms and nurses. The children heard they sister and know they have the same *Morbus* she do. They howl so loud, it seem seven going to die instead of just one.

"See to them," the Countess say, still more sharp, with bosoms at her chin, and some ladies leave for that.

I do n't. I hold a shiny bowl, though I do n't know how I come to got it. The youngest doctor unpack little knifes and glass bubbles from a wooden box. His hands tremble and one glass thing break. A drop of mercury fall to the floor and divide in to a thousand little mirror-balls, they roll about and bounce off shoes and reflect what sit inside each lady's skirt. No matter, he want theriac instead. It be what they think best against a poison, though it be made with poison it self. Vipers.

I do n't see Duke Magnus any more, but he is not so tall and there be many around the bed now. And I am one of them. The young doctor push me to it so I hold my bowl under Sophia's elbow, where the blood flows now from a new cut.

"It 's black," say Candenzius, but then old Venslov bring his candle close and the blood look like ordinary blood.

"Ah," say Candenzius. He make another cut below the first, then tug my basin to make sure it catch Sophia's stream. I all most laugh again, though the moment be most awful. The bed so soaked in blood now I taste it in my throat, like a child that linger round a market on butcher day and lick the blocks. But he want to be sure none of it from *his* cutting go to waste.

"Something's wrong with that Negresse," say one lady, but every body ignore me be cause no body want to look away from Sophia. I bite my lip hard so no laughing come out. And true, no thing funny for Princess Sophia, but what nurse can watch doctors with out a laugh?

Now come the sound of leaves that fall in autumn. This be silk and gold, rubbing it self as the ladies and men go to they knees.

The Queen and the King walk in. Their gray hair down they half-dressed backs, their feet in velvet shoes.

King Christian stand like a bullock stunned, that girl were his treasure.

Queen Isabel rush to the bed. She lose one shoe. "My baby!" she shout, and then she hold her breath. There be no more sound than the *drip-drip-driiiip* of Sophia in the basin, slowing down be cause the Princess all most gone.

# AVA BINGEN

The thick-necked guard leads the way. We pass through a series of rooms like my cell, rectangles empty but for drifts of whitewash that have flaked to their floors. White dust clings to my shoes, my skirts, my nostrils; I cough. Filtered through that dust, the air smells sour, and I think these must be the palace grain bins, depleted for the celebration that perhaps only now is quieting in the great hall and courtyards. I imagine lords and ladies tottering drunkenly off to bed, Swedish knights sleeping where they fall, hordes of the poor outside the gates gone ecstatic over the scraps and sauce-sloppy bread saved as what the nobles call their charity.

The guard pulls open a heavy door and lifts a tapestry flap behind it. I think, *Here is my fate.* I step inside, feeling each little jostle of movement in my bones.

Fate wears a handsome face, being a dark man with light eyes and white teeth, a neat beard, black curls, black velvet clothes, an elaborate sword hilt, and an enormous red ruby on his first finger. I know him. I have gazed after him before, across courtyards and corridors; all the palace girls have. He is the finest fellow at court, murky and brooding and as unapproachable as a prince. Handsome, that is, in his own way;

on another man, his face might be too narrow, his nose too long, his eyes too hooded. But on him, perfection.

He is Nicolas Bullen af Bon. Steward of the Queen's household for the last year or so, appointed as a favor (I believe) to someone in the ranks of the King's household (it being tradition that each half of the royal couple keeps a separate staff); lord of lands on one of the western green islands and owner of a castle called Aftenslund; a great man known for his ambition to be greater.

He sits now at a table heaped with papers in the dim light of an oil candle. His teeth look as long and sharp as a wolf's, and they gleam like the pearl in his ear.

I have never trusted anyone with bright white teeth.

"So," he says, "here is a surprising turn of events. Who likes a surprise?"

I cannot speak. I keep my eyes down and make a curtsy. It is all I can think to do.

"I," says Lord Nicolas, crumpling a page with one elbow, "never have favored surprises myself. I prefer a good plan."

He dismisses the pouch-necked guard and the door latch *thonk*s as it falls in place. I imagine the guard waiting just beyond, ready to drag me off to some worse dungeon where I might be tortured. Lord Nicolas has only to raise his voice to make it so. He gestures toward me, *Come here,* and adds, "Look at me."

There is some relief in receiving an order, as now I know what to do. I use the servants' trick of focusing on his chin, so

46

it seems I'm attentive but still properly deferential. I notice a single gleam of silver among the dark hairs there.

"I must admit that surprises create opportunities," Lord Nicolas comments, as if continuing a conversation. His mouth has already settled back into the more smoothly pleasant expression it wears around the court. "But they also disturb the best-laid arrangements."

He lights another candle from the first; its spreading glow makes the room both smaller and larger, a storehouse of riches. What is not gilded is made of finest amber or glass, and the walls are hung with bright pictures and tapestries. He has an entire bowl of sugar cherries and lemons to himself. My own sugar cherry is growing sticky, melting between my breasts.

In the light, I feel him gazing at me a long time, know he's seeing the same things in my face that the nobles see in all of my station when they bother to look: pale, tall, with big strong bones for working and a wide brow for . . . not thinking, exactly, but remembering. Remembering their commands and our conquest, for while their blood bears the dark stamp of France, ours is said to belong to witches expelled from Norway in a long-ago time of pagans. We have a natural inclination to labor and a feel for the sea, since we lived long in those boats and (some say) mated with the mermaids who guided us to these islands of warm-water springs and floating yellow stone.

I may be a scrawny example now, but I carry the history as well as anyone else can manage.

All of this Lord Nicolas sees in me, and the pricked fingers and strained eyes that are a seamstress's badges of office. I think he guesses everything about me, down to the smell of the lanolin I rub into my hands and the flavor of parts I keep hidden.

Lord Nicolas is handsome and powerful and knowing and rich. He could make a woman feel pleasured and safe. And that woman would be a fool.

"Ava Mariasdatter Bingen," he says, and so he knows my name. "You have served in the Queen's household for how long?"

"Almost a year, my lord. Health to your soul." I keep my eyes on that single gray hair on his chin. "I sew her personal linens," I add unnecessarily, for of course he already knows what matters. I can't stop myself from chattering: "I've never worked on a dress before. I don't know why the Countess chose me to repair the Queen's bodice." (The Countess, far paler even than the sturdy descendants of Norway.) "And such a thing as tonight has never happened with me. I haven't even stuck a lady with a pin when attaching her ruff; I cannot explain it"—can't blame Isabel for moving, can't give any excuse but my own awkwardness—"but I assure you the injury was unintended . . ."

I don't mention the missing spectacles, which would make me look careless.

He lifts a hand to stop me. "Women have been dismissed from royal service for less."

I let my eyes flick upward again. Are we talking only of dismissal? But then, losing my position might be worse than being put to death; my family would be shamed once again, and I would lose my hope of independence. Who would hire a seamstress who's stabbed the Queen? Only the same non-existent person who would marry a virgin who miscarried on the church *plads*.

I hear a ticking somewhere in the room; Nicolas Bullen must have a clock.

"My lord." I squeeze the words around the lump in my throat. "I promise you—I meant no betrayal. That is, I have always worked to the Queen's trust. I have never—" I almost wish he would torture me; I think my body might take the assault better than my emotions.

Nicolas Bullen's hand silences me again. Long fingers for a man his size, I notice; they'd look even longer if he wore a smaller ring. I imagine that hand closing around my throat, squeezing the words back into my belly. I realize I am stretching my neck as if inviting him to do this. As if I deserve punishment.

Lord Nicolas smiles. His sharp teeth shine. He, too, sees an invitation in my gesture; he thinks I'm trying to tempt him. In this age of ruffs and high collars, bare necks are tempting spots. Anyway, I would never refuse—it would be unwise . . . He has such *power*.

And so it is not surprising that I find myself on the floor of that little room, with Lord Nicolas's courtly cloak spread around him to a pool of black velvet just beyond my russet skirts. Me on my knees, he on his haunches, and his fingers wormed in beneath my cap to my hair. The tines of his ring

49

yank out a strand. We are kissing, after a fashion. His tongue licks at my tongue, and mine tries to respond without choking. Does he think this is pleasurable? Does he think I'll melt at these brutal kisses? It feels as if he's exploring me, trying to find the secret nooks inside my head. His perfume is so strong my nose burns. His fingertips plug my ears, so I hear nothing but the rush of my own heart, and I clench my ribs to make that tattling organ slow.

Meanwhile his breath—both sulfurous and sweet, he's been chewing something like coriander—passes down into my lungs and out again through my nose, my mouth, into his nose and mouth. We are breathing together. I close my eyes, and for a moment I tell myself that it is the embrace of which young girls dream. With a nobleman. Perhaps this is all he wants from me; perhaps I can give myself to save myself. Perhaps it is only the memory of Jacob that prevents me from succumbing willingly . . .

Because I am myself and have learned fear from experience, the thought of salvation quickly turns to anxiety. Surely he expects more than a kiss. He is exacting a penance, after all; I am here because I pricked the Queen and made her bleed. No punishment stops with a kiss.

Yes, I am right. He takes my hand. I think I know what he wants, and I touch his chest, the slick prickles of gold embroidery. He shifts, and the chest is out of reach.

He stops the clumsy kissing to wrestle my hand inside his codpiece.

For a moment I recoil at the heat, the coarse hair. But

Lord Nicolas shifts, deftly trapping my hand before it can leave his breeches. He clears his throat and licks his wicked white teeth and stares at me with expectation.

What I must do now is unmistakable. I will be lucky if this is all.

I hold my breath to trap all my courage inside. Then I work my way deeper into the codpiece.

I find that Lord Nicolas is considerably smaller than Jacob Lille, which seems strange; a lord should be grander in all things. He is also limp within all that stiff cloth—like a bird fallen from its nest into a patch of brambles, lost and in need of solace; or a dead herring on a bed of dried eel weed, waiting for salt.

I curl my fingers against it, then around.

Thus I commit a sin. A worse sin, the priests would say, than the ordinary conversation between man and woman, because the goal of this act is pleasure only, not procreation, and it wastes the seed. But in this age of Italian Fire, the nobility is known for substituting new actions for the eternal one. And I know the apron class prefers this, as it does not lead to a baby that will mean a life in the streets and, most likely, a speedy death.

I can't help it, I am disgusted. Where once I thrilled to touch linens that would touch royal flesh, or reached out surreptitiously to brush a passing noble, now I want to scrub myself rather than continue what I'm doing. A gesture that echoes my night with Jacob—and that is why it upsets me. It is a betrayal of love. It is a duty of court. It is the act of a whore.

I try to imagine myself caught up in a fairy spell, with this another trial before a grand reward. I describe Lord Nicolas's little bird to myself: *yeasty, sticky, soft,* like nothing else on this night of spun-sugar treats. I try to make it harmless.

As if responding to my unspoken words, the little bird flutters. It grows firmer.

And then I stop. I wrench my wrist from his clothes and pull vehemently away, though this might mean a blow across the face for me. I am much more afraid of what I've already felt.

I felt the softness of skin, yes. The sponginess of flesh not yet fully erect. And some lumps wiggling beneath that skin, like eggs, or insects burrowed deep.

My palms scrub at my skirt, trying to wipe all trace of him onto my clothes.

Lord Nicolas grabs both of my hands.

"Don't be a goose," he says. "There's nothing for you to fear *there.*" When I shudder, he unlaces his codpiece, pushes himself into the light, and makes me watch while he counts off: "Emerald," flicking one of those lumps. "Turquoise. Ruby." Flick, flick. "Pearl, and another turquoise, and another . . ." Under his own fingers, naming jewels, he grows harder than my touch managed to make him.

Am I to believe that Lord Nicolas uses his manhood as a purse? The nobility are always doing mysterious things, but this defies any kind of sense. "Sir — why?"

He takes his hands away, gazes down as if he can see jewels on the outside, as if they adorn a gorgeous golden scepter. He thinks himself very fine, indeed. "A courtier should carry wealth on his person as a sign of his position. And in case called upon to, say, ransom a captured king or save a fair lady from ravishment."

He sounds so pleased that I think he might be telling the truth, that this is his logic and these are the contents of his manhood. Why not believe?

I put my fingers there again. I am a practical girl, after all, and a curious one; my father is a scholar in his way. I feel what I think must be the scars of stitches, tiny darts in skin that had to stretch to accommodate these foreign lumps. I bend close and think I see them, these scars.

It's dizzying to contemplate. A king's ransom in jewels, hidden in the same organ with which he piddles out an evening's worth of water and wine. And I am holding all that wealth in my hand.

Nicolas nudges himself into my fist. I have a task to complete, and I begin again.

As I give Lord Nicolas this dutiful caress, I think of my impossible task, to coax a transformation out of this reluctant little bird stuffed with precious eggs, to give the best pleasure if I am to save myself. Even if these lumps were the buboes of disease, I would have to do what I am doing now. And I'd have to do it better—Lord Nicolas grunts to signal that I've caused him pain.

*Pleasure,* I think, trying to inspire myself (and him) by mulling the word. *Pleasure.* I make my mind blank of anything else.

In a few minutes, it is finished. Lord Nicolas has grunted

53

again and sighed, and what he pours into my palms is not jeweled, just a pungent soup of what any man might produce.

He lets me sit up and passes me a handkerchief to wipe with, then takes it back—as if afraid I will play some trick with his juices if he leaves them with me.

"So, Ava Bingen," he says in a pleasant-enough tone, lacing his breeches together as if this is any ordinary discussion (as perhaps it is for him), "now we must face the question of atonement."

*There's more?* I think.

Lord Nicolas tosses the soiled handkerchief into the fire. I take off my cap and wipe my tongue and teeth with it, scrubbing away his kiss, then rub at hands that are already dry but will probably feel dirty forever.

I think again of Jacob Lille. I'm grateful that there is no possibility of pregnancy coming from tonight.

Lord Nicolas is watching me, almost as if he can read my thoughts. I push Jacob out of my mind—he doesn't belong here with us.

Lord Nicolas says, with a surprising sort of gentleness, "Ava Mariasdatter, I trusted you for a moment, just now. I trusted your hand and your discretion, to prove you aren't some mad woman running around with needles out and the intent to do harm. You must compensate one trust with another." When my confusion is obvious, he explains: "You must make yourself into someone I trust *forever.*"

Not gentleness, then—wiliness, setting a trap.

"Certainly, my lord." It is the only answer I can make. I

smell his breath on mine as the vow leaves my lips. I wonder for a wild moment if he plans to keep me as a mistress, and if a mutual trust and dependence might somehow develop between us. If I am to succeed at court, I shall need not only hard work and good luck but also a sponsor. A lord with influence and wealth.

And if some of that wealth were distributed to me, I would in time buy passage and a companion to look for Jacob abroad. Copenhagen, Stockholm, Aarhus . . .

Lord Nicolas acts as if he does not notice my thinking, only my assent. He tugs at his shirt, then his doublet, arranging himself to perfection. He lays out some terms of our agreement. "First," he says, "you must keep my secrets."

"Of course."

"This hidden wealth is not for others to know about."

I think of the ladies I have seen preening as he walks by, but I can keep a secret better than any lady, if I choose to. "Of course not."

"It isn't just wealth," he says incidentally, "but a guard against disease. Recommended by Eastern doctors. So I don't need to worry about contracting a poisonous Fire from you, nor you from me — each jewel has a special property that makes falling ill impossible."

"I was never worried. We didn't —"

He laughs. "Haven't you heard? The Fire burns best in warm, moist places, but there are those who've got it on their hands, their ears, their noses. No spot is safe. Except on *my* person, thanks to these medical advances."

"I'm not worried," I repeat, lying this time. Having survived the Great Sickness, I am a worrier by nature; I will worry about this evening as I lie in bed, and it will give me many sleepless nights. What I have seen of medical practices does not inspire trust.

"*Ah, bon.*" His white teeth show. He returns to his table, with the ghostly papers—none of them written on, I see now in the increased light—ruffling as he stirs the air. "And so," he says, thumbing from one blank page to the next, "on to our official contract. You are no longer a seamstress."

He makes a few marks with a pen on a white sheet, and my heart sinks to my knees. I have no sense of what he's writing; I can't read.

"You are not leaving the palace," he adds, as if presenting me with another treat. "From tomorrow onward, you will be an attendant in the royal nursery. You will be trusted with the King's—and Queen's—children; or rather, you will be trusted with waiting on their nurses, to begin with. And in your new position, you will have new duties. You will be eyes and ears, a trusted observer. For me."

I struggle to stand, though he hasn't told me to do so. My bones ache more deeply, even, than at any other time this past year. Shame has made me weak—first the pregnancy, then the miscarriage, now this: servicing a lord's casual lust has turned me into both whore and spy.

Nicolas clarifies, as if I didn't already understand, as if I'm as doltish as I feel: "You'll join what I call an army of angels who work in the Queen's household—to protect her and the children, of course."

Nicolas smiles as if expecting some reverence. Commander of an angel army, master of me. "What do you think, Ava?"

This is what I think: *Make one mistake and you find your life utterly changed. Your good graces gone, yourself in thrall to some dark lord.* But there's no sense lamenting it.

I curtsy on unsteady legs. "Thank you for your leniency."

Lord Nicolas seats himself in a chair carved and painted impressively enough to rival the King's throne. He reaches for a pen. "I assume you cannot write?"

I admit that it's true, though I've learned letters enough to make monograms on noble linens and to spell my name if necessary. Unless the family is very rich, an artisan's daughters do not learn the skill of making sense with ink.

"Then your promise will have to be enough."

"I promise."

"And your name."

This I do show him I can write, though in somewhat shaky letters; I am better with the needle than the pen. *AVA.* That's all I can spell of my name. I recall, with a new wave of revulsion, that it means "of the bird."

He studies my signature and takes back the pen, apparently satisfied. "There will, of course, be penalties if you disobey. Swift and unpleasant ones." He bares his wolfish teeth. "So, then. I will see you when summoned."

It seems I'm dismissed, and in a way that leaves me more

shamed than ever. Done with, disposed of, sent away. Property. Still bowing, and backing up as I would do in the King's or Queen's presence, I reach the door and lift the damask flap over it.

"One more thing"—he stops me, scratching at the paper that will reorder my life; making my skin crawl with fear— "you will move to a new dorter, one for servants of lower rank, not the needlewomen. And I would prefer that in the nursery you be known as Ava Mariasdatter, not Ava Bingen."

Of course. He wants me to use my peasant name, which emphasizes my relation to my mother, rather than following the merchants' and artisans' custom of maintaining a family surname through the father's line.

I curtsy again, accepting this degradation too. Why not? Being Mariasdatter will bring less shame on the father and stepmother who have treated me well.

A struggle with the latch, during which Lord Nicolas rattles his papers, and I get the door open. There I find the thick-necked guard managing to doze while he stands. And the sudden sound of bells ringing, so loud it nearly knocks me to my knees.

"Sainted lice and blowflies"—Lord Nicolas leaps behind me, scattering papers all around—"whatever could have happened?"

And so another trial is complete.

# The Scholar

LONE in his chamber, the King's archivist carefully transcribes his notes into an elegant account of the day's many events. Big, bony fingers stain black, as if they are already in mourning. They match his black garments; he always dresses this way, so he will disappear into the shadows of a room and overhear the secrets whispered when there seems to be nothing said. In this way, he is able to write a second chronicle, one best kept to himself, that records the hidden lives of both courtiers and their servants.

He is tall and has to hunch, writing both public record and secret history. He has never thought to ask for a taller table.

When he has finished, he sands the last page to dry the ink, then blows the sand away. His whole chamber is covered in sand at the end of a day, but there is no shortage of sand in this city. He rolls up the official chronicle, ready for his apprentices to copy several times over tomorrow. The private history of overheard rumors and confessions he keeps flat, so he may slide it into its place inside the tester over his bed. Once the curtain is hanging over the slit cloth, his secret history is truly secret. No one cleans in here but he himself, and in that he is as tidy as a monk. He sweeps away dunes of sand every morning.

The night is still dark, the candlewicks sputtering in their pools of fish oil. His mind is restless. The wedding, the wee incidents of torn gowns, stolen kisses, a dwarf breaking an ankle; and then the terrible death of the Princess, a fragile girl in the arms of a beastly husband. His thoughts race. He decides to use the light as long as he has it. Light: to him it means knowledge, to others justice, to most simply itself—light by which to work a little longer.

Idly, he writes King Christian's motto at the top of a page: *In tenebris lumen meum metue.* In the darkness, fear my light.

It is one of those royal mottoes that can mean anything— anything that inspires awe.

The scholar begins to play with the words, rearranging them in Latin and in the common tongue of this place. He is from one of the faraway green islands and grew up speaking the people's language more often than courtly French, though life at university beat that out of him. Sometimes it amuses him to write or think or even speak in the common tongue. Privately.

*Metue lumen meum in tenebris.* Fear my light in the darkness.

*Lumen meum in tenebris metue.* My light in darkness you must fear.

*Lumen meum metue in tenebris.* My light you must fear in the dark.

No, none of these versions is right; all are awkward. Light, fear, darkness—they come jumbled together, they come all at once, but there is an order in which they work best.

*In tenebris lumen meum metue.* A beautiful package of a

motto. But does it ever trouble anyone that King Christian's words are about terror? He orders his people to fear—not trust, not savor—his power. That sad, sheeplike King.

The scholar twists this page into a stick and, wastefully, puts it to a dying candlewick. For a second it smokes, and then with a *whoosh* it is in flames. Burning so brightly and so fast in the darkness at the end of a spring night.

He uses the twist to light another candle and sits down to contemplate the court in a new way, using a tale from the green island where he spent his boyhood coddled by a mother who told stories to chase away his fear of the dark.

## THE PRINCESS WHO CONSENTED

There was once a princess who agreed to be married, as her father wished, to a foreign king. She bade a brave farewell to her people, chiding her mother not to weep; for this was her fate, and a blessed one.

When she arrived at her new husband's court, the princess was shocked to discover that her father had betrothed her to a monkey. The little thing danced around her gleefully, clapping his leathery monkey hands and chittering his yellow monkey teeth. The crown teetered on his narrow monkey pate, held in place by his long monkey tail. He was so excited to meet his bride that he soiled the floor of his own great hall.

The princess was disgusted, but the courtiers—all of them human men and women, handsome if silent—treated their king and his bride with the utmost deference. So she endured the ceremony, put on the ring the monkey gave her, and climbed dutifully into bed with him that night.

In all this time, the monkey said not one word to her. Nor did she expect him to speak, for she guessed that if he were to become human, it could happen only after love's first kiss. And so she let him kiss her with his wet monkey lips, and she felt his coarse monkey body pressing against hers, and at every gesture she expected that he would transform into a husband as pleasing as his courtiers. In the morning, the king hung the bloodied sheets out the chamber window; a barbaric custom. And barbaric, too, was the transformation—for the princess discovered that while her husband had remained the same, all his courtiers had reverted into monkeys, which was their true shape.

Thenceforth she was the queen of a wild, speechless monkey-land. Her children had long hairy fingers and curling tails, with slobbering lips that the king insisted must suckle on no breasts but her own.

In time, the queen began to pray that she, too, would turn into a monkey, if only to make these circumstances easier to bear. But the angels of the monkey-land did not heed her prayers, for in all the years she lived among them, she never managed once to give her husband a loving kiss.

# History

O, writes the chronicler, *it always is for royal brides;* though Princess Sophia never had the chance to suffer among the apish Swedes. Perhaps this would be considered a sort of blessing. The chronicler has witnessed the sorrows of Queen Isabel and her gradual decline these past ten years; she might be glad to know her daughter has been spared those same trials.

But he is a historian, not a moralist. He does not interpret facts; nor does he make judgments. That is for others to do as time passes.

He slips this paper into his bed canopy to mingle with his other private observations.

HE Lunedie chapel, the great cathedral, the parish towers all over town: every church bell clucks its tongue over Sophia's death. They scour away sleep.

*In the midst of life,* shout the bells, *we are in death.* The householders of Skyggehavn rouse themselves, blinking, and hang black cloths from their windows. The canals reflect wavering black; the bakers char the bread.

The story of Sophia's death spreads with the waves of noise, till it is well established that the Devil himself (in the guise of a Swede) tried to pluck the girl from her bed, then fought an angel for her soul. The angel, it is said, carried the princess bodily to Heaven so that Satan couldn't ravish her.

"Nonsense," say the priests. "A fantasy," say the scholars. But there are many who believe, and who carve Sophia's portrait into their walls with knives and nails, praying that she might protect them from Devil, trolls, and Protestants.

At the palace, Sophia Lunedie has left a very real and material corpse. Before the bells ring the sun overhead, that corpse has begun to rot. It fills the rooms with the reek of an overripe strawberry, an odor that makes mouths water and stomachs churn at the same time. The green flies of May buzz around it, and black ants nibble from below. Blood and serum from her necklace of wounds have hardened into dark jewels around which the princess's flesh is starting to melt.

In the speed of its corruption, the girl's body presents several questions. Perhaps least among these is the *how* of her death; whether from *Morbus Lunediernus* or some other cause, it almost doesn't matter. More important: Is she Princess of the realm or Duchess of Östergötland—that is, did the Duke complete the union before his bride's demise? An answer must be found immediately. So much blood streaks the sheets that no one can be sure; even the Duke himself might not know, given the uproar in their marriage bed. No one would dream of breaching etiquette by posing him the question directly, and no one would trust Mad Magnus with an honest reply. Yet everything depends on the answer. If the marriage was not consummated, the treaty with Sweden hasn't been ratified, and the new peace may unravel. Then all of Scandinavia might very well be back at war.

To some of the nobles, Sophia's death is good news: the marriage was not universally popular. Several lords favored a connection with Denmark; but Denmark's Frederick chose a different Sophia, of the obscure Mecklenburg-Güstrow, whom he will marry this July. (And what a hurry to be sure that Magnus's wedding took place before Frederick's! There is no affair that does not become competition between Denmark and Sweden.) Others in the privy council loathe Protestants of any sort and insist that a Lunedie should marry only with Poland or France. Any of these men might have resolved to undo the treaty with a death, though without the greater offense of killing Duke Magnus himself.

In his grandly paneled Presence Chamber, King Christian charges the three physicians with finding an answer. "Dissection is not usual," he bleats, sounding something like the sheep to which his subjects often compare him. He has a long, sad face and graying curls; a long body clumping in the middle. Princess Sophia was the treasure of his heart, and he hates to think of her nude body inspected, much less sliced open—but better this than his land sliced apart in another war. "It is not usual, but in this instance it is essential. Investigate . . . by the necessary means . . . and determine whether she's my daughter or Magnus's wife."

His principal advisers and favorites—the aged Duke of Marsvin, sly Willem Braj, Lord Rafael af Hvas, and the handsome Lord Nicolas Bullen (this one having wandered over from Queen Isabel's household)—give nods of support. Their King is never alone in his decisions, never alone at all, in fact, even when he steps into his more private inner chamber and the cabinet of the stool. A few other favorites are draped about the room, toying with their jewels or snuffling pomanders to combat the stench of daily life and extraordinary death. Everyone's head aches, and no one wants to touch the remains of last night's feast.

"And try to see if Sophia was poisoned," says King Christian, deliberately but as if in afterthought. It is his secret hope that his darling has died from some such outside cause—

that it was not her marriage that brought on death. He would have kept her at court years longer if she hadn't been needed in this endless game of diplomacy. Of course, the poison might have resulted from the marriage act — or some unthinkable source close to home ... He feels the usual pain in his belly, so familiar, flare into intense cramping. Also increasingly familiar. He can hardly bear to sit, and a tear hovers at his eyelid.

Under their loose black hats, the three physicians dart looks at one another, seeing if any can guess the King's preference in this matter. Does he *want* his daughter to have been murdered? The general if unspoken conclusion is that he does; poison must be more desirable than a fatal disease of the Lunedie bloodline, as it speaks less to the other children's future. Those six children — five of them girls — are all that stand between an orderly succession and chaos. There isn't even a well-trained by-blow, for example, to take inheritance if King Christian dies suddenly, only some distant cousins who will squabble over the crown. It is somewhat to be lamented that this king has never made a bastard; he is so faithful to his wife that the favorites have often speculated as to his conscience, as if a small virtue must conceal a great secret sin.

"Yes, Your Majesty," murmur Candenzius, Venslov, and Dé, and they give a practiced bow as one. Both King and Queen like to see them in unison.

Perhaps there actually is a poison plot afoot. Perhaps the physicians really will detect it.

Two tears now roll down Christian's white-powdered face. "My poor pretty girl," he laments, almost inaudibly.

Nicolas Bullen appears at Christian's side without seeming to move. He offers the King a pomander in the shape of a skull, and his dark fingers brush against Christian's damp ones. When Nicolas touches a spring at the pomander's top, the skull breaks apart into eight sections, each with a different-smelling spice inside.

"Take solace," says Nicolas. His light blue-green eyes are wide and kind. "Health to your soul."

Christian likes Lord Nicolas very much. The Bullens are a clever family; they have curried favor and married well, though Nicolas is the last of them. His father was a minor officer in Christian's father's household, his grandfather little more than a craftsman who had something to do with building the palace but who managed to wed a baroness. Christian considers having Nicolas (who is not yet married) leave the Queen's household and take a position in his own. He could use a man like this, one who is quietly reliable.

Thinking, the King lifts the pomander to his face. He sniffs each of the eight spices in turn, then wipes his nose and eyes with a handkerchief also provided by Lord Nicolas. A ruby ring winks on Nicolas's forefinger and fills all Christian's vision.

Christian feels dizzy, dazed, light-headed. The figures in the room waver.

Lord Nicolas takes back the soiled handkerchief and tucks it into his sleeve.

"Very well," Christian says to the doctors, around a bubble of nausea. He waves limply, overcome by a falling sensation caused, he thinks, by grief. "Very well, you may begin on Sophia." His darling child, about to be sliced open as even a husband never would have done.

Head swimming, he looks up and there is Lord Nicolas again, nodding encouragement, lips parted and showing handsome white teeth inside.

The dissection takes place in a room near the nursery, a room with a good window, a high table, and a plentiful supply of beakers and basins, plus candles for places the window doesn't light.

Candenzius has been trusted with a key; he turns it in the lock. He will be the main operator. The most modern of the physicians, a student of the revolutionary Paracelsus rather than the ancient Galen, he made his reputation in Dresden by curing a baron's gout with a daring dose of caustic antimony. *Any substance can be either cure or poison,* he is fond of quoting. *It is only a matter of determining the dose.*

There's no question of curing Princess Sophia, unless it is to be in the manner of leather, preserving her long enough for the funeral. The cadaver has changed yet again since Candenzius last saw it. The skin is mottled yellow and blue where it is not marked with the dried crusts of Sophia's ulcerous wounds. That skin is peeling away in thick flakes. Her eyes, not yet sewn shut, stare cloudily toward Heaven, and her blue hands sit clenched in knots by her ribs, where her arms contracted in her final throes. Excepting that detail, she has been arranged quite prettily on the table by her former nursemaids and by Countess Elinor Parfis, Mistress of the Nursery. Sunlight caresses Sophia lovingly. The fine linen shift in which she died is spread in a swoop, its delicate embroideries stiff with blood and other fluids.

It falls to Doctor Candenzius to lift that skirt and pass judgment — first, on the state of what lies beneath it. The other two — hunched old Venslov and big-eared young Dé (whose youth makes him no less a believer in old Galen; he has yet to come down on one side or the other) — stand with basins and styluses at the ready, poised to collect viscera or take notes as needed.

What Candenzius sees under Sophia's skirt must interest him a great deal, for he spends some minutes staring at it, gathering an initial impression. Then, holding the shift in his left hand, he uses his right to nudge her legs farther apart. He asks for a candle and a sponge.

The other physicians don't dare gaze on the princess in this way. Venslov lights the candle and holds it at Sophia's feet, but he doesn't look. Dé averts his eyes, moistens a cloth in vinegar, and passes it to Candenzius, who seems satisfied, although this is not precisely what he asked for. He scrubs at the shadows on the Princess's thighs and then orders Venslov (who was chief physician before Candenzius's arrival last year) to hold the candle closer.

"And closer still," he barks, leading the other two to speculate that he is using this opportunity to remind Venslov once again of their relative positions in court hierarchy.

The flame flickers in air currents stirred by the physicians' robes. The space between Sophia's legs is getting crowded; her nightdress blooms with light. Candenzius bends so deep, his face disappears beneath the tent of cloth.

While her body is inspected, the departed Princess continues to stare upward. Her corneas have gone white as milk, so it is impossible to see that at one time her eyes were brown. Dé wonders if he should note this, as the other two are so intimately engaged. It may have some bearing on the cause of her death. He imagines the favors that King Christian would bestow on the man who could name the poison that felled her . . . Dé would very much like a room of his own in which to live and work, rather than sharing with Venslov, and perhaps one of the minor honorific orders that the King bestows on those who've pleased him. An enameled giraffe on a gold chain would mean the world to Dé.

Candenzius, still peering at the Princess's secret, stops short of probing it with his finger. He mutters to himself, wondering how the land and his own reputation are best served in this situation. Again, a question: Is there advantage to declaring the Princess *virgo intacta*? Might that finding anger Sweden — perhaps enough to inspire a murderous plot against a lowly court physician? Or the King: Is he likely to punish Candenzius for breaking the treaty, or would he be relieved to be released from a contract that will now yield limited advantages, given that there shall be no grandchildren, no commingling of royal seed?

He thinks of the Queen, his patroness and friend, who plucked him from Dresden on the basis of one long letter of application and an egg-size portrait enclosed with it. (Candenzius would not accuse himself of vanity, precisely, but he has been told he has fine eyes.) Isabel thought Sophia too young for marriage, too narrow for childbirth, her womanly courses a mere trickle. All this to be married off to Magnus's madness. *Don't we have more than reason for delay?* she asked Candenzius that winter, in one of the quiet conversations in which the two sat snug in the firelight of her chamber, attended only by a dozy lady-in-waiting whose ale Candenzius had treated with valerian. *Can't you convince my husband to wait?*

The King could not be persuaded, declaring that sacrifices must be made for the good of the land; and, in fact, he gave Candenzius a gold coin in exchange for a prescription of lamb's blood and coltsfoot that helped shake those courses free from Sophia's womb. So the marriage went forth, with Isabel so distraught, she needed soothing tinctures of poppy.

Out of sentiment for Isabel, and because some hunch tells him it is the desired answer, Candenzius makes a decision.

"The Princess is a virgin," he pronounces, withdrawing and dropping the nightdress over Sophia's legs so quickly that it nearly catches the candle.

Mercifully the gust of skirt wind blows the flame out. For good measure, Venslov licks his knobby fingertips and snuffs the wick. Fire in the palace would be a mortal calamity; his own books and papers, records of his private experiments, would surely burn.

So the Princess is declared intact, a daughter rather than a wife. But there still remains the matter of the poison.

73

"We must open her belly," Candenzius decides.

While Venslov helps push the girl's legs back together, Dé finds a pair of scissors so that Candenzius can slit the night-dress where needed—shielding that pleat between her thighs from the other men's gaze.

So they make their cuts into yellowed flesh and jellied veins, till they reach the Princess's entrails. Venslov fetches basins to accommodate her organs and the seventeen separate courses of last night's feast. Taking turns, the physicians bend to the yawning wound and sniff, trying to sort rich viands from rank poison.

As he dissects, Candenzius dictates observations, and Dé writes them down. *A sharp odor, a sweet odor, a lesion in the belly; watery intestinal matter, a leathery texture to the liver.*

Dé imagines horrible, thrilling possibilities: mandrake, wolfsbane, death cap mushrooms, belladonna. When he was at his French university, he made a special study of toxicity. Paracelsus wrote that disease comes from poisons emitted by unfavorable stars, but there are just as many lethal substances here on earth as there are pricks of light in the heavens.

Light pours thick through the window, angling down to fill the cavity in the center of Sophia. No candles are necessary here. The Princess is a split fig, with the claws of a dead bird, eyes gone to white marbles. She is animal, vegetable, mineral, and she reeks of an army's worth of injury.

"Shall you say it was murder?" old Venslov asks Candenzius, at last, as they run out of organs to unpack and have still failed to name a specific substance. "Shall you identify a cause?"

Candenzius draws a last breath, savoring the complicated odors around the corpse. Weighing the advantages of a spectrum of answers. Folding his sticky hands together.

"This is what I will tell the King," he says: "Although the Princess died a virgin, her body has been violated. The man — or woman — who killed her is extremely cunning, as sophisticated in skill as in evil, for the means used is still indeterminate. We shall dedicate ourselves to breaking down the poison into its components. We must begin by a meticulous distillation of the fluids in her liver, which we will ask the King to save from burial."

The three physicians nod solemnly, relieved to have found a direction. Dé admires Candenzius's artful turn of a speech, no less than his mastery of anatomy. He does not speak this admiration aloud, lest Candenzius's fall from favor — which seems inevitable, given his very particular views — come quickly, and Venslov resume the chief position. Fawning is an art even subtler than medicine.

"Well done, Doctor," Venslov flatters first, and Dé is relieved at the chance to echo him. Candenzius smiles modestly, blinking those fine eyes, and thanks the other two for their assistance.

Then the three of them look at the brimming basins, asking themselves how to put the Princess together again for her funeral, or if they should even try.

# QUICK

YING almost weightless in the simple bed of her inner chamber, Queen Isabel mourns her daughter. The first child to live after a series of miscarriages, the child who saved her from a shameful divorce, after which she would have returned to France forever disgraced and known for her inability to breed. Sophia, whose name means "wisdom" and whose character was forever pleasing, until the foul *Morbus Lunediernus* seized her and her siblings.

Princess (Duchess?) Sophia, twelve years old and now deceased.

Crown Prince Christian, eleven.

Princess Beatte, nearly ten.

Princess Hendrika, nearly nine.

Princess Amalia, seven.

Princess Margrethe (named after Christian's ancient cousin, the Duchess of Marsvin), six years old.

Princess Gorma, at five years of age the likely last child of the Lunedies.

Another series of miscarriages followed Gorma's birth, and Isabel is now thirty-nine, an age at which the womb turns rotten and bears bad fruit if any at all.

To distract herself from this grief and shame, Isabel remembers a journey she took as a child, before she'd even heard of this northern land and its capital city, when she was still young Isabelle des Rayaux, a daughter of the Loire Valley. As part of her education in the ways of the world, she traveled by barge to the palace of her extravagant Uncle Henri, Duke of Pau d'Impors, who was wealthier than any duke had the right to be and just a little bit (she heard her father say it) mad.

For pleasure, Uncle Henri had filled a pool at his summer castle with quicksilver. It was a beautiful, trembling thing, reflecting each face with a giddy accuracy, but at such an angle that one had to lean over farther and farther to see beyond one's chin and nose, to get a glimpse of one's own eyes. Visiting ladies used to incline so far—Isabel did this herself—that their scarlet lips very nearly touched the surface that quivered under their breath. It made their faces ever more beautiful, their minds ever more dreamy. It was the marvel of the Loire.

Until, that is, one dizzy baroness leaned so far that she tipped in and drowned. Her hat and hair tangled just under the fountain's spray, her tawny dress floating on the surface.

The spell, then, was broken. Uncle Henri's advisers (fearing war with the baroness's husband) forced him to pull the plug. A gardener waded in knee-deep and dug blindly through until he found the drain. With a deep shiver, all that beauty began to seep away.

The child Isabelle watched as quicksilver slinked down the smooth rock walls; she listened to the drain as it slurped, guiding the precious mercury to the waters of the river. Saw the silver beads on the corpse of that silly baroness, glistening on her skin, puddling in the cups of her ears.

Isabel mourns now as she did then.

Exquisite memory, beauty lost.

Sophia.

## MIDI SORTE

Fear make the Earth's worst odor, whether in bottom of a ship or some silvered palace room. The nursery smell sour and dark with sweat of one prince, five princess, all so afraid, though we wipe bodies with perfume and put them in new linen twice today all ready.

Six children cough like a family of dogs, but they sit in bed-thrones of fancier animal shapes, one yellow lion, five white swan. Every hair, every feather painted in, and each bed have a crown of crescent moon. Six moons under a ceiling of golden tree branch and leaves of colored glass. This be a poem-place for children, a set of extra chores for nurses. It be not easy to reach over wings to feed the Princess Gorma, but this is my task.

Countess Elinor have come for children's supper, and she likes all order to be held. All faces to be clean, all spoons a-moving like hands that feed time to a clock. Gorma try to spit out gruel, I scrape back in her mouth. She be five year old all ready but some time act a baby. She know full well that every prince and princess must empty one bowl before sleep.

That new maid with the face of a rat pass me linens to dab the Princess' face. Gorma's fever gone high since Sophia died, and she whimper, though she know words well enough. She say them some times, like *Maman* and *thirsty* and *no*. And *Midi,* be cause that be my name. *Midi Midi Midi.*

Another task is keep her quiet, so I put my finger to her mouth, hiss, *"Shhh, shh, sh,"* hope she stop her noise before the Countess hear.

Elinor sit now by Christian, the Crown Prince all most twelve. She feed him her self, for he favorite with her and she with him. He will be the King some day. He some time say he be much too old for feeding, but when *she* spoon the gruel, he relax. He is the most afraid just now, being all most so old as Sophia he think he must be next to die. Elinor murmur words to him, wave her sleeves, soothe his fears or try to. She act like a coquette who seek a husband, though she be married all ready to her wounded Count and also twelve years old times one-two-three.

Gorma moan. I take another cloth to wipe her mouth.

"I made that," say the ratty maid.

My eyes narrow. Some nurses gossip, but I do not.

"That towel." The maid point at my hand. She think I do n't under stand. "I cut and hemmed and embroidered it. That particular carnation pattern is always mine. Until this week, I was one of the Queen's needlewomen."

This girl is like a reed that scream a note each time the wind pass by. My eyes so slitty now I hardly see her stupid face. Far behind it is the Countess' black dress of grieving, and if this girl think it care to me that once she sew with a needle what now I fold up wet with Gorma spit, she be wrong as a frog in a cream pot.

When I were little, I lived with fifty aunts in a house made of turquoise. I had an arm of gold bracelet and four black cats I name my self. That make no differents now.

*"Shh,"* I tell her. *"Shhh, shh, sh."*

The Princess fret to hear me sound at some one else. *"No!"* she say, loud enough that Countess Elinor cock her ear, though she keep spooning to Crown Prince Christian and trying coax his smile.

*"Shh,"* I hiss to Princess again. I say it different to her, though, and stroke my hand downside her face — soft, wet pink skin. I tuck a curl in to her cap.

Gorma open her mouth like a baby bird. I spoon.

That maid come so close, I smell her woolly smell. She think she and I be friends now. I think this shall change with nursey-work. We all reek like bottoms of a moat, so our lovers hold their breath when we embrace. We none of us are friends.

Her voice lower to a whisper, and she talk in the way of those girls who do with out their lips. "Were you there when *it* happened? Princess Sophia?"

I do n't look, just shake my head. I knew what she mean before she spoke.

She go on: "Do you know what took her? Have you heard? Some sort of seizure, I heard. Or else a poison. But what kind?"

I ignore the maid, wipe Princess Gorma's face, do as I am supposed. After so many year, I can feel when the Countess my mistress coming close. If she leave the Prince, this mean he all ready asleep, and she wonder why the other children are n't.

After they all fall off, nurses and grooms will pick them up and put them in the little night rooms, where some body sit and watch each one till dawn.

I murmur in my throat, water on a stone, and see Gorma lids go droop. Soon she sleep.

That girl still have n't seen the Countess coming. "What do you *think*?" she ask. "What can you tell me?"

I turn to this stupid girl and open my eyes all they way. She believe this a kindly thing; she blink, smile, then part her mouth to speak again.

I open my mouth first and show her my tongue.

She scream.

# AVA BINGEN

They are no uncommon sights these days, the wounds of men who've been to war and the scars of disease at home. But there is something worse, something evil, in the tongue that Midi Sorte shows me.

The thing is forked. Split from the tip to the root and scarred thickly down the way. The two halves of it move, waving like snakes till they wind back into her throat and disappear.

Of course I scream.

My scream rouses Princess Gorma. She screams too, thinking Satan's wraiths have come to drag her to her sister's fate. The other children take up Gorma's cry, and there's such a general wail and clamor that the glass leaves tremble on their branches overhead.

Countess Elinor's face is a knot of fury when she descends upon Midi and me. She sees the twist of Midi Sorte's lips, now pressed tight together, and guesses what I've been looking at. She gives Midi a cuff across the jaw that wipes the lingering smirk clean away.

This is some small vindication for me, but not enough. I feel sorry for having brought Elinor Parfis's wrath on Midi Sorte, even though she did provoke me. Sorry, too, that it seems Midi cannot speak; she could have been my best source for what Lord Nicolas wants of me.

Later, while I sit among the deserted fanciful beds, waiting to be needed in one of the night chambers, that tongue troubles my mind. Midi Sorte has gone to her own cot in the nurses' dorter; but in the shadows I see her tongue licking the walls, splitting itself into a thousand parts, opening holes and passageways within the bricks; then knitting up again in a long, fat muscle that could make toothpicks even of Prince Christian's massive lion bed. It is a demon, a dragon, worse than the monster of any story I've ever heard.

I surmise this forking of the tongue must be some custom of the place Midi came from—I've heard she arrived from the south as a present for Countess Elinor, who in turn gave her to the Queen—but I can't figurate why the King and Queen allow her among their children.

I imagine Midi Sorte wagging her tongue, scaring Princess Sophia to death on her wedding night. But is it worth reporting to Lord Nicolas—as evidence of evil, witchcraft, something? Would a split tongue satisfy him?

That demon tongue is my only company in the long night hours. It divides and twists, gobbling up the room in which I sit.

# WAITING

T is long past midnight, a deep blue hour. Countess Elinor Parfis is waiting.

She waits not in the small chamber where the door must remain open so that she can hear if the Queen snores or hiccups in her sleep—that chamber where she is virtually a prisoner—but in another room deep in the bowels of the casemates. It is scarcely more than a nook, a pocket filled to bursting with objects of richness pilfered from here and there around the palace: a gilded chair, a rock-crystal swan, a clever silver pitcher that never empties. A clock sent to the Queen by some minor foreign prince, *tick-tick*ing away on a worktable piled with more rich stuff, measuring out the seconds and the minutes almost to an hour.

Elinor is not by nature a patient woman, though she has bided her time the last six years, traveling back and forth to court until she made herself indispensable. The Queen is now unable to act without the advice of her one true friend. Chief lady-in-waiting, Mistress of the Nursery, favorite of Crown Prince Christian. Not a woman who should wait any longer.

Elinor is just on the point of leaving—swiveling on the balls of her feet, swooping up a golden toothpick in the shape of a cruel Eastern scimitar, for she feels her time should be compensated—when she hears a key scraping into the other side of the door. She slips the toothpick into her high-sprung bodice as the complicated lock clicks into place, the latch rattles, the door opens.

And there he is, her partner. Standing framed in the doorway with a whale-oil candle, light dancing over the shadows of his doublet, cloak, and breeches. There never was a man so vain as this.

"You're late," she snaps. Then is annoyed with herself for letting her temper show. She hoists her bosoms even higher, never mind if the golden scimitar peeks out (it doesn't) or pricks her (it does).

She softens her voice to the purr she uses for the royal Lunedies. "You're late, and I must return to my post," almost as if she regrets it. Her eyes linger on him as if she is in love.

He plays the same game, looking at her tenderly and speaking in a voice that rolls over her like velvet. "Don't you know I would rather have been with you?" That voice gives the impression of size and substance, even though he is not a large man; it makes her tingle as she imagines she would if she were actually in love. She almost relents.

But the glint in his green-blue eyes keeps her purpose firm. She resists the impulse to ask where he was—let him have his secret; she has hers too.

"The Queen thinks I never leave her side."

He smirks. "Because you drug her before you disappear."

She shrugs; it's true. "What is the sense of having access to so many poisons if I don't put them to use?"

"Let me put *you* to use," he growls, stepping close enough for her to smell his perfume. He always uses too much of it; it's hard to trust a man who covers his own scent like a wolf.

"Not tonight," she says curtly. "I'm going back."

"Any news first?" He doesn't seem to care about keeping her anymore. She suspects he has no real interest in fleshly conversation, only uses it as a spider uses a web, to trap his prey, because he is so vain as to think himself universally desired. But she is not prey.

She could report that *Morbus Lunediernus* is moving swiftly through the other children, weakening their bones such that Princess Amalia's wrist snapped when she was shifted in bed. But he doesn't deserve to know, not after making her wait.

"No news," she says. Her purr has become the rasp of ice scraping against the hull of a ship.

He passes her and sets his candle down on the table, begins examining the papers lying there. (Nothing of interest; she already read through them.) "You still haven't made progress?"

"The Princess died, didn't she? No babies to come from Sweden." That was due more to luck than skill, but she won't tell *him* so. "And how about you—have you managed the King yet? Is the old sheep likely to name you an officer in his will?"

Her maddening conspirator apes her gesture and shrugs. The clock ticks loudly in the quiet between them.

These two are uneasy allies at best. Each suspects the other of keeping too many secrets, of being careless with the ones they do exchange. But for now they want the same thing: *power;*

and when they have it, Elinor fully intends to rid herself of her crippled old husband and marry this man. Who might be easily dispatched as well, once he's served her purpose; she really has learned an astonishing amount about poisons. Secrets she will keep to herself.

"Till next week, then," she says, looking over her shoulder as she lifts the damask door flap. "And don't keep me waiting again, or I'll find someone who *is* ready to plot."

He puckers his beautiful mouth (yes, Elinor is still susceptible to beauty, especially with such a husband as she has) and blows a kiss through the still air. He says, "Enjoy your new toothpick. Use it in good health."

"I shall." Her voice is as cold as the air in a long, dark winter.

She steps into the corridor, taking half the light in the room with her.

# THE KING'S HEART

ING Christian V is not in the habit of contemplating unpleasantness. But sometimes truth is undeniable, and here is a terrible truth: *He is in love.* At last, and for the first time in his life. He loves; it is pleasure and it is agony.

Who could capture the heart of a king who, perhaps alone out of all Christendom, and in forty-two years of life, has broken not a single marriage vow? For Christian V has been a model of that particular virtue: conjugal fidelity. The common people celebrate him for it, even as (he knows, has always known) the nobles speculate about his failure to take a mistress. His wife has been pleased to think him a Catholic like herself, decorous and loyal and nearly monklike.

But now Christian wants, needs, something different.

Of course, taking a mistress would be less terrible than a . . . something for which there is no word, or none that Christian will let himself think. There are priests, generous priests, who say that love makes a sin less serious. But that love is customarily one between man and woman.

Christian V is not in love with a woman. He loves Lord Nicolas Bullen af Bon.

This love came on suddenly; it came to him strong. He cannot believe now that he was dimly aware of Lord Nicolas without realizing the power of those light eyes, black hair, musky sweet perfume . . .

It is worse than unwise. It is impossible. He should send Lord Nicolas away, perhaps as ambassador to an important court. The man himself would be the first to say so . . . And yet it is in Nicolas's arms that Christian yearns to seek comfort for the loss of his daughter; Nicolas in whom Christian dreams of confiding his fears about a weakness of the Lunedie blood, the nightmarish sense that dark-winged doom is swooping swiftly toward him. Always, now, Nicolas—the only councillor whose opinion seems to matter. After a mere whiff from that eight-celled pomander, so thoughtfully provided at just the right moment, some kind of sorcery has enchanted Christian.

He barely knows the man, has only just asked him to leave the Queen's household and join Christian's own. But at last— and for the first time, yes—Christian knows what poets mean when they write of longing, burning, mingled joy and sadness. He experiences the sweet grief of the unattainable all day long. Nicolas finds a thousand subtle ways to praise Christian's kingly form, his just decisions. There is no king so judicious, no king so generous, so handsome. Each compliment is like a pearl cast before him. Nicolas hints that even if Christian were not king, there would be an endless string of willing suitors for his heart. He flatters so deftly that Christian might almost think Nicolas himself would be such a candidate.

This much is joy.

But there is despair in knowing that Nicolas—loved as he is—conducts his life in a different way, the way that involves women. Christian has heard rumors about Nicolas's traffic with apron wearers, even one or two of the court ladies. A Countess Ditlevnavn or Engberg, or some other . . .

Never mind.

So Christian frets, and resolves to love no one but his children, again, and become a better king. A better husband, a better father. He will give his daughter a glorious funeral, and her murderer (she must have been murdered, it is the only allowable possibility) a terrible punishment.

At the same time, he knows his resolution is in vain. Whether Nicolas is aware or not, he will keep the King's heart, for Christian is nothing if not faithful.

# Silence

UCH a splendor! Such riches that generous King Christian lavishes on his eldest daughter, even after her death! Every household and workroom and warehouse in each corner of the city prepares for her funeral. There will be a catafalque of gold cloth, a girdle of sapphires, a tower of the season's last white lilies, a feast of delicacies as fine as those at the wedding, for the Swedes must be shown, one final time, that this land is every bit as prosperous and refined as theirs. And Sophia, of course, must be mourned as befits the place she has held in her parents' hearts and hopes.

While she is on view in the cathedral, the restored Princess wears the emerald parure that Duke Magnus gave her for the wedding, as well as that sapphire girdle. Incense from Lebanon burns sweetly around the body, obscuring any hint of rot. Her rosy wedding costume has been expertly stuffed to give the illusion of more fullness than poor Sophia showed in life; her face, carefully painted. She is, for the first time, beautiful.

Sophia has become a figure of legend, like the original witches and mermaids and the secret stairways inside the palace walls that have never been found. She is the Virgin Bride, the Perished Lily, the land's greatest treasure. The chroniclers speculate that she will bring the land more honor and renown in death than she did in life.

During this time, Magnus of Östergötland mourns in a way traditional for males. Guided by one of Christian's trusted friends, he and his men go north to one of the green islands to hunt meat and birds for next week's feast. They plan to return in time for the grand ceremony, when Magnus will present his dead bride's parents with a drinking horn he has ordered inlaid with gold. The horn is from one of the oxen killed for the wedding feast. Christian, Isabel, and Magnus will drink to Sophia from it, then set it aside forever.

The people of Skyggehavn imagine these treasures will be used just once, then vanish into eternity when they are rowed out to Sophia's grave at the monastery of Saint-Peter's-on-the-Isle. But apart from the incense, everything has been put to service before, and after the funeral it will all return to the palace vaults along with the new drinking horn. Except the emeralds — they will sail back to Östergötland with Magnus. Such is the cycle of royal wealth and public fantasy.

As the monks of Saint Peter's rehearse the funeral songs, the limners paint their last dainty portraits of the dead Princess, and the goldsmiths fashion frames for them. The palace bakers roll out yet another pie crust; the butchers slaughter more cows, sheep, and pigs. Sophia's tragedy deepens all their souls. Poor Perished Lily. They contemplate her as they work; she has brought coins to pockets twice, first for her wedding and now for this.

When their work is done, the people visit her in the

glowing cathedral and leave little tokens of affection: a ribbon, a flower, a roasted nut. When she is to be entombed, they stand on the broad *plads* and watch while black-clad nobles pile into barges at the palace dock, then row out to the floating monastery of Saint-Peter's-on-the-Isle. They wait through the funeral ceremony, while their feet swell and ache, hoping to taste some scraps from the grieving feast.

The courtiers have much more to do. Through the long afternoon—the prayers, the songs, the interminable lecture in Latin—they maintain a rigid silence. They are silent in the boats; they are silent as they find their places at table in the great hall, and as they bow for the entrance of their King and Queen.

King Christian's ornamental sword sways in its hilt like a duck's tail, slapping him on the calf. No one laughs or even whispers. It would be the worst breach of etiquette to let go any sound during the funereal feast; lips must smack quietly, belches and farts be stifled no matter the agony they cause. The musicians in the gallery hold their instruments in their laps, staring dumbly forward. They are there as reminders of the absence of sound, the quiet of the grave.

King Christian sits, then Queen Isabel, then Duke Magnus and all the others. The dwarfs (Le Fariné, Wantonesse, Champignon, and all the other grotesques) sit at their tiny table without cutting a single caper.

At Isabel's right, Duke Magnus's eyes droop. He has had enough of life at this dull northern court. Even the whores have been in mourning this week, and the hunting was terrible.

Then comes the quiet padding of pageboys' feet as they carry out the first pie of the evening, so big that four of them must bear it together on a sturdy board. Eel and cod's roe in thick buttered gravy, with a flaky lard crust. Delicious in aroma; the diners' mouths water.

The pages kneel down and rest the corners of the board on their heads, which one day will wear the diadems of rank, for all are good boys from noble families.

King Christian stands, with mouth downturned, and unsheathes his sword. His wife's pale lips already tremble. Duke Magnus looks up with interest at last. Christian imagines that, somewhere down-table (as appropriate to his rank as a plain lord), Nicolas Bullen watches too.

The ceremonial sword plunges into the pie, releasing a spill of gray-and-brown innards. It is a clean cut; Christian has done well.

Nonetheless, the diners burst into tears. Such is the custom; at last it is time for noise. The trumpets play an ugly note. The Queen falls into a faint, to dream that it is she who has died, in a bubble of silver joy, instead of her daughter.

Once more, Christian brushes away the sense of dark-winged doom. Looking afar for the glow of Nicolas's ruby ring, he sits so his servants may distribute the pie. He is rewarded, or so he believes, with a red pulse down-table, heartbeat quick, heartlike in hue.

Christian's tears flow the more richly.

## Just Counsel

ATE at night, the King calls his councillors and favorites to his inner chamber, with its plainer furnishings and more intimate setting, its nook inside the fireplace for hiding in case of invasion. Nicolas Bullen is among these men.

*Nicolas.* He dares to speak although new to the gathering.

"Your Majesty, it was a magnificent ceremony," he says, a black feather bobbing in his hat. "Your daughter has twice united the kingdom—first with her marriage, then with this day."

Christian smiles, weak with pleasure, as he is each time he hears that voice.

The others wish they had Nicolas's gift of tongue. They embroider the pretty idea: *The Perished Lily will forever bloom . . . The Virgin Wife will bear much fruit . . . The flower will become the seed . . . The seed will . . . will . . .*

Nicolas listens with an amused smile on his red lips, but he does not contribute again. The black feather blows softly in the current of the others' speech.

Christian stops the words with a sudden gesture. "Enough! Are you trying to bury the girl again?"

The favorites lower their eyes and bow. Their words have tangled them up in one another. Now they resolve both to hate Nicolas and to curry his favor, since he clearly has the King's.

Christian secretly wishes for silence but wonders aloud what has become of the search for Sophia's poisoner. He reminds himself to be severe and awe inspiring; he turns to Sir Georg Oline, his State Secretary and commander of an army of spies. "Have you found any . . . any culprits?"

Sir Georg hesitates, and the favorites tense. Who will be blamed? A Lutheran? One of the country's few Jews? Or perhaps some cousin with a tenuous but plausible claim to succession—someone who should be removed for the health of the court anyway?

Sir Georg attempts to be sly and to show his erudition and industry at the same time. "There may be more than one assassin at work, Your Majesty. If there is one poisoner, there must also be conspirators. A hive of bees with fatal honey, as it were. We will smoke out them all."

The others nod (Nicolas's feather!), although several suspect the Secretary is merely trying to make himself important. He may have his eye on a lordship; he may want to become a baron or a count.

Now every individual's activities come in for examination: failure to sink all the way to the floor in a curtsy, presentation of a bill for what should have been a gift, unaccountable minutes spent traveling between banquet table and privy stool. Names are put forth, blown on, rubbed up, tossed into the air. Some are among the most prominent at court, others so obscure that the King has to be reminded who they are. "Your second cousin, now in Lithuania," "A count of Norway," or "The third wife of your great-uncle, just returned from the green islands."

Christian mulls the possibilities, bats them back at his advisers, lets them fall. He is a cat bored with an everlasting tangle of yarn, exhausted with suppressing his true emotions. Grief, longing, grief again. He would like nothing so much as to sleep, though sleep comes hard in the growing season of light, and the clock that Lord Nicolas just gave him (with the newly innovated second hand that cuts time into ever-smaller portions) shows two in the morning. He thinks of mad Duke Magnus, his onetime son-in-law, galloping through the forest with an arrow aimed at a wide-eyed stag. Christian's belly and bowels ache with his old sickness.

*Tick-tick-tick-tick-tick.* Talk, talk, talk.

"Enough!" he cries at last.

Pushing all his energy into limbs that have cramped from too much sitting, Christian stands. "Arrest all of them," he says. "All within reach. We'll sort out guilt later."

Sir Georg's jaw sags. Not even the wildest ambition could have foreseen such a command or would want truly to follow it. He looks around the chamber as if to beg for help, but no one will look up from the floor—no one except Lord Nicolas, who gazes at a dark window, and the ever-present historian, whose only purpose at court is to record, never to act, and who usually isn't seen at all. This tall, bony person meets

Sir Georg's eyes for just a moment, notes the anxious wrinkles around them and the contracted pupils at center, and returns to his tablet.

"Your Majesty," Sir Georg begins, "would some not find it prudent—"

But Christian is done with discussion; he stands. His attention is caught once again by that black feather. "Nicolas," he says haphazardly, "have my barge prepared. I will go out to Saint Peter's to pray among the tombs."

That island monastery floating in the bay is one of few places a king might find true peace. "And, Nicolas, you will accompany me." This much, surely, Christian can allow himself. They will pray together on their knees.

Lord Nicolas smiles. "As you command, Your Majesty."

## AVA BINGEN

I have been disappointed to discover that the life of a court—
dazzling as it is with jewels, soft with velvet, gleaming with
gold wires—is so often ugly. Among the apron wearers, especially, there is a hunger that cannot be satisfied in the kitchens
and dining halls.

The palace teaches us all to want more than we can ever
have. A little wealth, a bit of luxury, some measure of happiness such as the poets describe in their sonnets or the actors
in their plays. We do foolish things to satisfy a fraction of our
desire: We pilfer a sweetmeat here, a scrap of silk there—I
once took a piece as big as my hand, to stroke at night while
trying to fall asleep; it in turn was stolen from me the next
night. We have relations with nobles who offer little more than
the fleeting feel of a jewel beneath the hand or a case of Italian
Fire. We labor till we lose our eyesight in fine work, our fingers in rough.

When my father told me, "You must do your best," all of
these facts were contained in his simple words.

My next interview with Lord Nicolas takes place in the
afternoon. I give him my obedience in the same manner as
before, kneeling by the desk in the casemates where food and
miscreants are stored and marveling again at how much wealth

I can hold in my hand: a lord and his jewels, a king's ransom. Enough to buy a house and shop in some nice district or to start a new life in a foreign land.

I force my mind to focus on the order in which he identified his jewels: emerald, turquoise, ruby, pearl, turquoise . . . thrilling to me, and some compensation for the act I reluctantly perform; but to him, guardians against disease and poison. I know that amber is believed to cure almost every illness, from a cold to the pains of teething; rubies are for strength and help the wearer avoid resentment when caring for others. Emeralds attract love. Pearls bring good luck or bad, depending on how willing the oyster was to give up his treasure.

I count the bumps with my fingers, trying to think what good each one might bring me—that emerald might draw Jacob back or grant me some other love; that pearl might forgive and bestow something wonderful . . . But if we all make our own luck, as my mother used to insist, I will need to please Nicolas in some other way. My wrist is growing tired.

I do wish that, like a story's noble seducer, he might think to offer me some wine, or perhaps a lump of cake to remove the bitter taste that being with him leaves in my mouth. A little coin to add to my future. Of course, such a thing would make me a true whore rather than a member of the angel army.

So I keep at my task. Imagining what wonders lie beneath his thready scars and how they might make the refrain to a melancholy song (*O! for she was a dutiful girl . . . Ruby, turquoise, emerald, and pearl . . .*), I use my fingertips to tickle each jewel in the order that my mind rehearses it.

But Nicolas stops me, slapping my hand away. "Enough. Your skills are not up to the task tonight."

I draw back as if he's stung me. The little bird pecks hard.

"*Alors.*" Nicolas tucks himself into his breeches. He is in a poor temper. "On to our true business. Ava Mariasdatter, what news do you have for me today?"

"I . . ." Hesitate. I can't tell him that the one rumor I have uncovered is about Nicolas himself, or rather his family. He once had a father and mother, as we all have done, and an older brother as well; but they died suddenly (some say waylaid by bandits, others a hunting accident) when Nicolas was sixteen. It was one of those surprises of which Nicolas says he is not fond — though there are a few who hint that these deaths were no surprise to him.

"You have nothing?" he barks.

"I have planted seeds," I say humbly. "But it is difficult in my new position. The needlewomen are no longer my friends, and the nursemaids haven't accepted me yet."

"Excuses."

"Yes, my lord, but—"

"But nothing. Come back here. I will show you what use a woman is if she can't accomplish a subtle task."

Dutifully I reach out my hand, thinking I am sure of what he wants now.

But I am wrong. He puts his fingers inside my cap and wraps them in my braids; he pulls my head into his lap and orders me to untie his breeches again. He wants my mouth.

He tells me what to do; it is humiliating. Which may be

why he finds it exciting—my mouth on him, my tongue swirling around each jeweled boss as he tells me how to do it. I think even a prostitute would be reluctant. And he is harsh: not content with my hesitant movements, he begins to thrust himself at me, toward my throat, where he might choke me.

I am hot with the shame of corruption. I sweat, and I taste salt on him as well. Breath comes difficult.

Jacob Lille, Jacob Lille. Who smelled so sweetly of piney amber. For whom my heart still pines, the only man I ever kissed because I chose to, not because it was forced on me.

It is as if Lord Nicolas reads my thoughts and revels in them. He holds my hair tighter, thrusts himself deeper, faster. And then he grunts. He pulls himself out and spends over my fingers, ropes of seed that could sew up my future if he decided to loop them between my legs and give me a baby. At last I understand that he's avoiding any chance I would manage this; once again, he gives me his handkerchief to wipe with, then throws it behind him to be burned. He won't risk a bastard, not by me.

My whole body trembles; all of me would weep if I wasn't sure it would get me further punishment.

"Good," he says, adjusting himself so all fits as it should. "Now you know. Next time you will have information for me." To prove he hasn't forgotten my real purpose. And that he'll use me this way again if I need bringing into line.

My knees crack as I struggle to my feet. "I promise."

"Good girl," he says, "or at least, going to be good."

# Marriage

HRISTIAN V has established himself as a dutiful husband, yes. He has always treated conversation with his wife as the grave and vital matter that it is—but relations with Isabel cannot always be foremost in Christian's mind (no more than the idea of relations with Nicolas, which creep into his thoughts unbidden).

Affairs of state are particularly thick just now: peace so recently achieved but an alliance broken with Sophia's death, negotiations for a new whaling treaty with Scotland (now dominated by Calvinists, of whom Isabel disapproves), and a poisoner still to identify . . . if there even was a poisoner; Sir Georg has been vague on the matter, saying that the usual forms of questioning have yielded dubious results.

Privately, mulling it over in bed and at prayer and most of all upon his close-stool—where he relieves those crippling gastric pains while attended by the State Secretary, Sir Georg—Christian has come to the conviction that his daughter died of mere *Morbus*. In the wake of her death, all the children are suffering even more intensely than before. But he will not set the prisoners free, not yet, for it is good for the people to see the gestures of justice. All of his advisers agree.

And so on to think of other things kingly. More pleasant. The new observatorium, for example, which will offer an exciting prospect on the moon and stars . . . Abed, Christian lies in the darkness and imagines the sky. He imagines it so much and so hard that he almost drives away the unbidden picture of Nicolas's face, his fingers, the pomander and the handkerchief and the feather and the ring . . . Nicolas, with white teeth shining—like stars, Christian reminds himself to think. *Like stars.* He launches himself upward into a fantastical night sky while around him the attendants snore on their pallets.

On Monday in the palace chapel, Christian is so lost in dreams of the heavens as to be taken aback when Isabel leans toward him, touches his ring finger with her own, and murmurs, "The time is propitious."

Immediately Christian feels the prickles of sweat that precede a conjugal encounter. He makes a noncommittal murmur and crosses himself with particular ardor.

"I will take it under advisement," he says, staring forward at the amber statue of Saint Ruta, patron of fishermen and ropemakers.

That afternoon, leaving his councillors in the Presence Chamber, he consults with the physicians and with Stellarius, his astrologer. Is the time in fact well chosen? Is it likely to result in a healthy, well-formed prince? Or would he be wiser to wait till grief no longer assails the Queen, when tranquillity—if such can be attained in these days—makes her womb fertile for the planting?

"The stars *are* in favor," says Stellarius, who reads nuances of the heavens better than those of royal expression. He has spread out charts that Christian cannot understand. "It can happen this week, perhaps Thursday."

"But we are still in mourning!" Christian cries petulantly.

Candenzius speaks up: "Her Highness is ripe this very day." He says this on authority of regular study of her monthly cloths; he will also have Isabel disrobe and open her legs to his probing hand, if Christian wants this additional confirmation.

The King shudders at the thought. But it is even more upsetting to think he has only one son. Just one slender, puking princely life lies between him and the chaos of unclear succession.

"Then if it please the King," Doctor Venslov suggests with an old man's attempt at delicacy, "he might remember Galen's advice about marital intercourse, that it take place when the body is in a medial state: not empty nor too full, neither very hot nor very cold, too dry nor too moist. That is, perhaps only a light meal and a moderate draught of wine, maybe some comic entertainment by the dwarfs to lighten the spirits . . ."

Christian holds his features regally stern. Outnumbered by earnest goodwillers, he agrees to visit the Queen.

Christian himself was a third son (the older two died of the smallpox), and he surrendered his own name, Ludvig, to take the throne. He tries out the old name now, to see if he can remember how he was in those days. *So, Ludvig my man, it's time to prime your sword for the battle.*

He feels no difference. Only the injustice of being the most powerful man in the land and yet the one man above all who must not act on his true desires — or antipathies.

The large state bed where Isabel will receive her husband is draped in cloth of gold, not unlike Sophia's catafalque; but in this case the gold is woven with red, giving the effect of a shimmering curtain of blood. The color itself is a wish for fertility, that the blood of Isabel and Christian might congeal to form a new prince. Each great event in a woman's life is marked by it, from her birth to her wedding, her own childbeds, most probably her death.

Blue, in contrast, is the color of comfort: the Virgin's mantle, the sky, the ring that Isabel's grandmother gave her when her parents signed her marriage contract. It would remind her, said Grand-mère, that the same sky arches over both lands.

Knobby arthritic fingers slipped the ring onto a young slender one. "Nothing has value," said the old lady, "till it is given away or stolen." The blue stone glowed with a deep serenity. In all her weight gains and losses, Isabel has never let it leave her hand. She wears it now on her right pinky, where the flesh bulges above and below the golden band and bezel.

Twisting the ring, urging herself to gain serenity, Isabel orders the state bed scattered with cushions of blue satin and velvet, and her seamstresses rush to sew them. There are other preparations, too: the spiced wine that Christian likes to drink, candles greased with roses and violets, a phalanx of maids and ladies-in-waiting to fetch whatever last things are needed. Her dear Elinor, Mistress of the Nursery, arrives as if already to care for the child Isabel hopes she is about to conceive.

Even sweet Countess Elinor cannot distract Isabel today, as the slender white hands plump up the cushions and straighten Isabel's favorite painting of the Virgin Annunciate.

Isabel stands before the bed with hands clasped as if she is about to pray; but all she can think are the words to an old bawdy song from the Loire:

> *God, for I am such a young thing!*
> *I feel the first sweet pangs beneath my little belt . . .*

"Your Highness," hints Elinor. She is speaking loudly into the hollow of Isabel's ear.

Of course, Isabel is not young or sweet, and the pangs she feels are not the happy ones in the song. But she is brave; she allows her women to remove her robe.

Somehow Isabel and Christian are put to bed. Somehow the heavy door swings behind their grooms and ladies-in-waiting, and the tapestry panel swishes shut over it. Isabel stares at her own hands, chapped with the work of the nursery, that blue ring from Grand-mère their only ornament. Now is her time to act. She licks her lips and scratches at her palms, getting ready to do as Christian likes.

But as soon as the latch's tongue clicks into place, Christian is out of bed. He fills his goblet, swilling the wine as if it is the medicine that Isabel spoons down their children's throats. He refills the goblet and drinks again, and a third time. Only then, wobbling on his thin legs, with his long face softened and sillier than usual — she's heard it said that he looks like a sheep, and this is not inaccurate — does he grab a thick handful of counterpane to pull himself back up the mountain of mattresses and lie next to his wife. He does not kiss her. He burps.

She remembers her youth along the Loire, when King François went on progress and stayed at the Château des Rayaux for a fortnight of hunting, feasting, and dancing that nearly put her father in the poorhouse. Beautiful days of splendid frocks, fresh rushes on the floors, ribbons flying as courtiers rowed the girls in pleasure boats among the swans upon the river. Isabelle, she still was then, thirteen years old. And she had her first kiss. It was with a member of the King's privy council, out behind the ancient tithe barn that had been the very beginning of the family's château.

After that, young Isabelle became unbiddable, longing uncontrollably for the gay life of a court so that pleasure might continue forever ... and pleasure led her here.

There is a billow of cool air as the counterpane settles around her husband, and the smell of fowl from feathered pillows.

Christian sighs. He is still wearing his favorite pearl earring, given him last Christmas by Georg Oline. *"Ma chair,"* he says, and she knows just how it is spelled; he's calling to his flesh, not his dear. And then, obediently, her hand is on his flesh, rubbing him, with his long thin eyes shut and his lips pressed together in concentration.

She knows that at such a time Christian has to focus his thoughts very sharply, and the worst thing she can do is make a sound or change her rhythm before he is ready. So Isabel tries to keep her mind blank, while she is aware that Christian is doing just the opposite. He is filling it with images that come from someplace far from this bedchamber.

Isabel counts to 117. Not ready yet. She slows for just a moment, and Christian loses ground. She changes hands.

She tries to enter his mind and see where he has taken his thoughts. She knows he is not thinking about her great loose childbirthing canal. Rather, he must be imagining (a cruel cousin hinted this long ago, and somehow Isabel knew it to be true) much tighter spaces and bodies not so soft as hers. *Dirty places, dirty bodies,* she thinks; this is what excites Christian and allows him to manage his few minutes' firmness of purpose with her. She imagines him touching someone — she cannot imagine who, or won't imagine it — in that place which she knows to be expressly forbidden to persons of virtue.

For some reason, this thought of unholy places has begun to excite Isabel as well as (she imagines) Christian. She feels herself growing moist from her palms to her toes. Her hand moves more quickly, more confidently, on him. This is when Christian does achieve that firmness, and she flings herself down with her chemise up, so he can take the position sanctioned by the Church.

What Christian does now, too, is a mystery. Isabel can't quite picture the transaction, though she knows some of her ladies—perhaps even Elinor—have trained their hand mirrors on that spot or have stood open-legged over still water. (The baroness at Uncle Henri's castle, leaning over the quicksilver pond?) Isabel has seen what her husband carries between his legs, and she knows that what's inside her is a mirror image of his hot, dry generative equipment, only kept inside because of a woman's cold and moist nature. When they converse, they must fit together like links in a chain. But that is not pretty to contemplate.

Isabel thinks instead of the Annunciation painting, hanging somewhere beyond Christian's bobbing form and the bed curtains. She would like to consider it a reflection of a life more real than the one she is living. On the wooden panel, Mary's head bends gently, tickled by the ray of gilded light that bears Gabriel's words. The blue robe pools around her feet, the halo wisps around her as-yet-uncrowned head; the potted lily blooms, the white dove hovers. Mary's lips part gently. Surprised. Pleased, certainly, but also surprised. She is going to birth a Savior.

For some time in her youth, Isabel had thought she would conceive a child through the ear, just where the light of Gabriel's words slides into the Virgin; perhaps this was the purpose of each new couple's prayers for fertility, that the words, not the bodies, would produce a child. After the wedding night, she realized it was not a beam but a staff that would impregnate her—still, given all the actions, all the places, that

Christian attempted that night in his effort to please his country with a full consummation, she imagined it might be better accomplished if he put himself into her ear.

She does not know when this thought, too, became exciting to her. Her ears are sensitive, and there are holes in the lobes that her mother made with a hot steel needle; from these holes she can hang golden hoops or glowing sapphires or drops of clarified amber that hold tiny insects inside. All those things adorned her in the frivolous days before motherhood, when her ears were considered things of beauty and a poet composed a villanelle to praise them. (He is dead now, gone in the Great Sickness of 1561.) A baby will snatch at any object that dangles, and might pull the bauble straight out with some pain to the mother. So ear bobs became something for ceremonial occasions only, and Isabel's ears have gone neglected.

She remembers the day her mother pricked her lobes — the pain of it, but also the satisfaction when the tiny point made full puncture. There is excitement in that too, in the memory of pain — all pain of being with Christian long gone now, only to return in childbed — and before she is well aware, Isabel is imagining the King as a needle piercing her (as a needle pierced her recently — didn't it?). It brings small doses of pain as it opens one tiny wound after another in her.

It is thus, unexpectedly, that Isabel is surprised by an enormous, soul-shaking joy. Even down in the courtyard, people seem to feel her pleasure and cry out for it.

# MIDI SORTE

I do not like to hold a pen. Too thin for hands to cramp around, and delicate, as if I hold a grasshopper and try to make it walk like a cat. It feel a silly thing to me, to tell a story through the fingers.

But he say I must learn to put every thing on to paper. To be one more keeper of histories as if he do not keep enough, with histories both for king and for him self. He says this will be *my* secrets, but what secrets can I keep while he be reading each word as it come from the pen?

His room be hot, or hot for this place, and all those books and pages sweat smells of leather, ink, and dust that be worse to me than nursery smells. Those are just from people, but these be animal skins soaked full of poisons to make they last. My nose hurt more now than my hand.

He say keep writing and when I will be done, he shows how to fix the words for correct time and number and all the rest. Future, past, present time. He say I hear speech said right all day, why can I not use it right my self through the pen? But I choose not.

I write my own way, I write *my* language. Others speak so as they will.

Now he say I wasting time by writing nothingnesses, when I should express my thoughts. About what I see at court. About the Princess. About my life. And the hole that open in the great courtyard and frighten all the lords and ladies so.

How much more must be write about Sophia? She is dead and we all know she have the family complaint. Some believe a poison tale, but there be no poison we know to make a girl scream so, and lie straight, and raise through the curtain of her bed. This be not the land to invent new poisons.

Where I were small, in a land much more hot, I have one aunt who know all poisons well. She grow flowers and leaves; some smell of perfume, some of rotted meat. Some the size my thumb with thorns all over, so if you take one in the hand, your skin were full of needles to hurt for a week.

She were the favorite for most other aunts, who like to make each other sick, or make they husband slow or fast to love them. This poison-auntie live away from others, in a little house back of a garden, where the rain rise from the floor instead of through the roof, and even the guards afraid to go.

*Why did your father allow this woman on his grounds?* ask the history-keeper. He have interest now for my own story.

For this question there be no answer, only she was there and the others fear and love and hate her. At last some one kill her with her own plants, a stew of thorn and leaf and flower that may be she swallow be cause she were grown tired of so careful tending of the garden and no man to visit her.

It was from her funeral that I run away, between the horses' hooves when they pass the gate, and so in to the town. To walk just a little in the market and chase a spotted cat and then be caught and sold and shipped to this land.

At first it feel like some dream brought on by poison-auntie's tea. For a long time I be sick in the bottom of the boat, heaving up and down and fevered. Then my body come back to me, when the ship cut through a puzzle of ice and fish that spit ocean in to air, and I see my breath in clouds around me and frosting over the sail-captain who churn above and drip sweat in to my face. And then the man who buy me in a different market, in a great house with candles made of brass, where men come round to see they first Negresse and hear the sailors' tales of countries sleeping under sand.

Afric, China, Lebanon, Persia: all lands of sand and sun and dusky skin, might so well call them Greece, which be the farthest place from what the usual people here have imagine. I can 't say which land would be mine, which language I would speak if I had my tongue. Just that my tongue be not my own.

When that man give me to his Countess wife, I feel I come home to poison-auntie again. Her cold hand, her white eye, her skinny smile all new to me, but the bitter air around her make me feel like in the house at garden's end. I become her maid and learn the new clothes of this place and the way of keeping long white hair. Her husband like our differents, call her the moon and me the night. He like to sleep under us both, though this she pretend not to know.

Bad things happen in that place. I will not write them now.

It were the middle of the war. The man go away with a sword and the riches from his trip, and the wife keep me close.

We live in they castle on a green island; we visit the palace in the royal city, for the Countess make friend to the Queen. We go back to the castle, we are called to the palace, and here we stay, even when the Count return from war. His arm be gone and also his leg, may be his mind as well. He cry and cry for Elinor, but the Queen cry harder.

Elinor give me to her at war's end as gift and as promise, all naked but for sugar-sparks and holding a plum in my mouth that I were not allowed to eat. All the court clap when I step front to represent Peace and kiss the plum over to one lord who represent Justice, though I have heard Elinor tease him private that he be among the least just in her acquainting.

I do not like the taste of sweet. The men lick and lick and lick to get they sweetness off of me. The dwarfs make fun and the ladies clamor.

Today there been clamors, too, in the innerst courtyard, by where all they nobles sleep. A hole have opened right where ladies like to walk from they grand door to the portal where boats row them to the flower islands.

When we look in to this hole, we see the earth's inside. It is warm and wet and turning mud, and it suck at bricks and any thing we throw, swallow them and pull in to it stomach. Some apron tell a story and call this a witch's bed; such places be where the Devil lay his wives. One other girl say it be called a hollow and in no way part of Satan. Some say it is a new grave, that Princess Sophia be not resting on Saint Peter Isle but come to lie here, so she can call the man who gave her death and pull him down to Earth's hot heart. If she do n't find him, she will take her brother and her sisters so she have a playmate in the swampy land of souls.

These be stories, just as poison be one story for the Lunedies and a plum be one for me.

The historian say this is just a hole where earth give way to sand and water. It happen all the time be cause this city were built on islands made of trees and clay and not on land it self. Some time houses fall, or bridges, or once the market place for fish. Then a canal rush in to feed the bay, so the waves go silver from the scales and dead fish float away to feed bigger fish at sea. Now there is just a dock at that place, for little boats to use.

Here what Countess Elinor say about the witch's bed: *There will always be a clever man to invent a story, and a pack of silly women to repeat it.* She say this to the Queen by way of comfort. The Queen do not like that a smelly ditch be open by her window.

The Countess never tell a story her self, just explain and store up ideas of others.

The scholar tell me that some time in this place there be dark people (from Greece, China, Afric, Persia) who live by they selves, or dark people who have coins enough to sail away back to the sunshine. These sound like pretty stories to make a Greek work the harder.

Now I finish. Fix time and numbers if you like, Arthur Grammar. Be fore you kiss me.

## AVA BINGEN

Every half year, Christmas and Midsummer, I earn four silver shield coins and a new set of clothes. My wages have not
diminished with my new position, so this June I have a fresh
russet serge dress and a linen shirt that I plan to embroider to
display my skill, plus five shields to count (having spent two
on necessities as the months have gone by, then one on sweet
cakes and wine to wash away the feel that Nicolas Bullen left
on me).

In the narrow dorter that reeks of nurses, where I am
meant to sleep through daylight, I stir my coins against each
other and count one through five, again and again, as the
Queen would pray half the rosary. The noise chinks off the
whited bricks and fills my heart with gladness and yet with
wanting, for five are not enough to pay a ship for passage and
a friend for protection on the way to Copenhagen. I count
again. I am angry with myself for spending on frivolities, when
poverty just keeps me in Nicolas's clutches.

The nurses' dorter is long and narrow, crowded with cots
and pallets where we sleep two or three to a mattress; our
clothes hang from pegs on the walls, and the lone window has
no glass. We all get our monthlies at once (except Midi Sorte,

who never acts with any of us). I am not alone. Midi Sorte herself seems asleep on her cot—but she hears my sound. One brown eye opens wide and stares, not even wavering at the bright flash of silver.

I shape a brittle smile. Not quite daring Midi to covet my riches, but wanting to be recognized. Or even to win a friend—though I could never tell that split-tongued demon about my trials with Nicolas.

The brown eye closes again. I put the coins into the purse at my waist, settle back down for sleep.

In my imagination, I keep counting my coins, one through five.

Until the night I pricked the Queen, my palace friends were other needlewomen: Anna and Nidia, close to the age of blindness; Maria, Soria, Ente. Since that night, I have seen them only at meals in the kitchens or crossing the courtyards. They are either too embarrassed to address my change in fortune or too proud to acknowledge one who's fallen.

Gudrun, Mistress of the Needle, must acknowledge me— so I tell myself. When my position changed, Gudrun bundled up my sewing things, my amber needle case (the gift from Jacob Lille) and a book of embroidery patterns I brought with me, and tied them with twine to wait on my new cot. Nonetheless, the day after Midsummer, I go to the seamstresses' dorter to beg on my knees for her help.

"I stitch a good seam, you know that," I plead, even though the girls with whom I used to sew are looking on, either giggling or with pity. Some may giggle for pity itself.

"And you've praised my embroidery—can't you vouch for my return here?" For my escape from Nicolas Bullen.

Gudrun will not meet my eyes, uses an apron's trick of staring at my earlobe. "Ava, I can't," she says abruptly. "It has been decided already. And I must ask you not to come again."

"But you are my stepmother's friend!" My eyes well up. "Don't you want me to honor her? And the Queen?"

Gudrun stares beyond my ear, into the cracks in the wall. She says, "Even the lowliest turnspit boy or goose girl serves the Crown. Now stand up and go back to your place."

What can I do but obey?

I try to plot for a better life. My new position comes with new connections, and I count them up. During the physicians' nursery visits, I have smiled at short young Doctor Dé, and he at me; his position, too, must be a lonely one. I fetch basins and beakers for the great Candenzius and for the nurses who do most of the work there, and they speak kindly enough to me now. I fold linens sharply and starch the children's laces just before the daily opening of the doors for the Queen's visitations. I imagine myself like the miller's daughter in the fairy tale, working hard until one night, quite by chance, spinning straw into gold. Not as a member of a dark angel army.

One-two-three-four-five silver shields so far.


In this time, I miss my father and his new wife; it's been several months since I saw them. So on a Sunday I get permission to leave the palace and visit the house with the stone head.

After so much time, the city seems dull and ugly, but alive.

Walkers clog the footpaths by Skön Kanal, the "beautiful water," lined with fine houses where the mossy fundaments beckon with a promise of splendor and the kitchens push out smells of cinnamon and mace. Peasants sniff the air so the memory will make their brown bread richer at night. My feet clatter over wooden bridges and knock against stone ones under which trolls fight over animal bones; one of them has built himself a house of old fins and scales. My new russet skirts swing past canals and coppery churches, big houses with water gates that hiccup in the tide, humble ones that squat in between. Stray dogs, skinny cats, a furtive rat or two; children playing at some hop-dance among ropes stretched out to cure in the long yard that runs down Reb Kanal. In front of one magnificent house, a scattering of white petals curls along the water's surface, the remnant of some courtship or funeral.

Several times I must double back because a bridge has collapsed or an alley I once knew well has been filled in with a kitchen garden or privy. But soon enough, I am crossing the longest, sturdiest bridge in town and entering the district where I became myself, where the air sings with glass shivering against glass.

Glasvand Kanal. The glassworkers' waterway.

I *clack-clack* past Helligánds Kirke and see (or believe I see) that my blood still stains the square; then Helligánds Hospital, with madmen screeching out the torments of imagination. It's just a quarter mile farther to the wind-scrubbed stone head beside my father's door. Today the glass lenses on its nose shine like moons and the head has increased its lean to the right, like a scholar squinting to recognize a once-familiar face.

Gerda, our servant, lets me in. She curtsies to me, and I nearly topple her over with a hug. Father embraces me like one he has long missed, and my stepmother gives me a hearty kiss on the cheek. I am the daughter returned from court! They haven't heard of my demotion. They draw me into the paneled hall and offer me ale and cake like a guest.

"We have so much news!" Sabine declares, looking about to burst with it. She is even squeezing herself. "Ask your father to tell you."

Sitting in a room that I might call mean if I hadn't been raised to think of it as one of the grandest in our district—painted wood, pictures of Saint Catherine and Jesus, pewter ware on the sideboard—I listen. Klaus Bingen, my father, has another commission for a perspective glass. This one will be even larger than what he ground for Stellarius, and it will be part of the King's new observatorium atop the flat west tower. He is very proud of—

Sabine interrupts to announce that she is pregnant.

"Yes, Ava, you will be a sister again!" Sabine strokes her belly as if it were the subject all along, and Gerda (who I think hoped to marry Father herself) sulks as she refills our cups.

A sister. I look dubiously at my stepmother, who has always been stout and rosy but is definitely fat and glowing now, though she says she's only three months gone with child. She's forty years old if she's lived at all—rather late to be having a first baby.

"It's a miracle," Sabine pronounces, as if reading my mind.

122

"I prayed and fasted. I took a boat to the green islands and visited the house where Saint Ruta worked his miracles. There's a
lovely little shrine . . ."

"If it's a boy," Father puts in, "we'll name him Klaus Ruta."
I smile weakly.

"Won't you like having a brother?" asks Sabine. Her red
face is set; she truly expects us all to join in her joy. "You know,
in case you never marry and something—the saints forbid!—
should happen to your father. You'll have a protector."

*Yes, in case I never marry* . . . I could return here and keep
house for my brother, to whom all this naturally will belong.
If he would have me. I remember that splash of blood on the
church square and think myself more likely to find a home
among madmen. I have no right to jealousy.

I bow my head and wish them all the best.

This is enough to satisfy Sabine. "We'll see him in January,"
she says, beaming again. "Klaus Ruta Bingen." She invites
Gerda, whom she usually treats as a mere servant, to join us in
toasting the new baby.

We all draw together and drink once, twice, again. This
will be the most welcomed boy in Christendom.

When we are all a bit topply, my stepmother asks for a tale
of the court. "How I have missed your stories!" she exclaims—
she who, as far as I recall, never listened to a single one, since
she associated them mostly with my mother, who taught them
to me. "Tell us about Princess Sophia—was the wedding feast
splendid? We did feel so bad for the King and Queen, losing a
child like that . . . Was the funeral beautiful?"

She is as hungry for luxury as I once was, and she will take it in the form of words. No words about Nicolas, of course, though his secret room may well be the grandest in the palace.

"And tell about the witch's hollow in the courtyard," Father adds. "What does Stellarius think it means?"

Gerda nurses the last drops in the bottom of her wooden cup, her blue eyes bright and eager. All of them want the truth about the court. *Their* truth.

I draw a breath and steady my voice.

"I can't tell you how beautiful it was," I say, "because it was all very beautiful . . ."

I drop the words like rubies.

I remember, sometimes, the modest glory that was once my family's, back when we numbered seven. I think of it as I return to the palace: our evening prayers, our New Year's feasts. A game my father and brothers used to play with lumps of rough waste glass and a pattern chalked upon our doorstep. My hands upon my mother's knee as it pumped up and down, helping drive the wheel that spun the thread that she would later weave into a dress for me.

She was telling me a story, no doubt — something about a princess and a ring and a beast, or a princess and a glass mountain and a prince — anyway, about a princess. She was explaining the necessity of the dark forest (she also had to explain what a forest is, as there are none within a stone's throw of Skyggehavn's enchained islands), the tests of mettle, the kindness to a repellent creature who might be a fairy or a prince in disguise.

"You must keep an eye for every opportunity," she said, with the wheel whirring so fast it blurred into, I thought, a door through which I could pass from this world into the one she'd described.

I took the opportunity to stick a spare spindle into the door, to test it. I thereby broke the spindle and a spoke of the wheel.

"Bad girl, bad Ava!" my mother shouted, and she thrashed me so I wouldn't hurt myself worse the next time. She ended with a kiss on the lips so I would know I was loved none the less.

I thought her kiss tasted of forest. "I hate you!" I screamed. And just a short time after, there came the Great Sickness.

I tell myself I have an opportunity now, presented by Lord Nicolas as punishment for my crimes. I must think how to twist it to some good for us Bingens.

# Inside the Queen

OWARD the end of June, when the sun has just begun to last a little less long each night, Queen Isabel of the Lunedies lies with her knees in the air. Three men scurry intently behind, between, around as they prepare to go inside, under the heavy sheet that covers the all-important space between those soft thighs.

She waits. Gulps down deep breaths and waits.

It is now two weeks past the morning her maids expected to see blood on her sheets, and in that time she has been tired and ill, given to vomitus, weeping, and faints. So her husband has ordered her examination.

Of course, she is still in mourning. Of course, she and the King coupled only that one time. And she is thirty-nine years old. But still. It just might be that her body is cooperating in the quest for another son.

And how badly such a boy is needed! Now more than ever: For the past month, the Crown Prince has been failing. His sores are deeper than his sisters', his spirits even worse. No matter how often he is reminded that his duty is to live, he seems to be consigning himself—willfully—to a different fate: sleeping, fretting, fading slowly away. He refers to Sophia by her nickname, the Perished Lily, and has carved a clumsy version of that flower into one lion's paw of his bed. He begs to be brought down to see the witch's hollow, which still gapes obscenely in the inner yard, swallowing stones and twigs that the courtiers throw in for amusement. He says he would like to glimpse the inside of the earth that will devour his body, though he knows perfectly well that he will be entombed (if he does die, which he must not) in marble with the rest of his kin.

Isabel has worn herself out (and Countess Elinor, so devoted) with the feedings and bleedings necessary for the boy's treatment, and the constant prayers for his recovery. Her husband has prayed, too. In front of all his courtiers, he thanked her for nursing the Crown Prince, then wiped tears from his eyes and retired with stomach pains.

All of the kingdom is poised for more grief. But today Isabel and the physicians could so easily give them joy.

"You may begin," she tells them.

These are the last words it is proper for the Queen to utter; now she must pretend not to exist, even as it is her body that is explored. Two ladies — the ugly old Duchess of Marsvin and Isabel's dear, pale Elinor — pull on the strings that hoist the sheet up, and then Isabel cannot see beyond her breasts.

The men, in return, can't see her face. In this way, the niceties of social position are observed.

As Isabel breathes, the sheet swells and retreats, swells and retreats, like the sails that once bore her to these rocky islands. She turns her head to look at her favorite painting of the Virgin Annunciate. The serene surprise on Mary's face, the reassuring joy on the angel's. The puddle of light around his feet, more silver than gold.

"Her Highness will feel a stretch," Candenzius announces, as he tests her opening with his fingers. She smells the beefy tallow with which he has thoughtfully greased himself. She is grateful to him . . . and to Elinor, who gave her a dose of soothing valerian before the examination . . .

*A woman with a full stomach should be kept calm,* the Countess chanted as she held the cup to Isabel's lips, *lest emotions cause her belly harm.*

Isabel should forget, for a moment, her sick children in the nursery. She should think instead of the Virgin and the bounty of her own womb. She should pray.

*God, for I am such a young thing!* . . .

She cannot pray, because Elinor is bending down to repeat Candenzius's words.

"Your Highness will feel a stretch," Elinor whispers. She must think it delicate to pretend that Isabel can't hear what a man says when she is mostly naked, but she wants to be sure Isabel stays informed and reassured, as if the Queen has not been in this position a hundred times over. Her breath tickles Isabel's ear; it smells faintly of anise. "This will not be so bad."

Poor Elinor, childless herself. Isabel reaches for her hand. The cool white fingers slide into hers with an agreeable pressure. "Squeeze as hard as you like," Elinor says.

Duchess Margrethe offers a hand as well, but it is so

twisted with age and rheumaticks that Isabel shudders and drops it. She squeezes Elinor's soft flesh, her delicate bones. She finds strength there.

This is the first time Candenzius has served as a baby-bringer; before him, it was Venslov, and for her first two pregnancies (miscarriages), a midwife. So Isabel cannot guess how much of a stretch he means, how much pain she is going to feel. She knows only that Candenzius will examine her, and Venslov will record his findings on a wax tablet, later to be transcribed into ink and paper that will become part of the royal archives. She imagines Venslov squinting at her—all the doctors looking—stylus poised and ready. The official historian is also present, but behind a screen; he is not allowed to look directly into the royal treasures.

Candenzius's hand worms inside. It is not so bad until he pokes at the bottom of Isabel's womb; then she can't help but jump. Whether this is in pain or in shock she is unable to say, for her entrails feel at once hurt, surprised, and at the same time numb to the whole business.

With his other hand, Candenzius presses outside her belly, feeling the shape of her through the layers of fat and loose skin that have settled in her middle age. Isabel is ashamed, but kind Candenzius's voice never wavers.

"Venslov, make a note: Her Highness is somewhat larger on the right side than the left," he pronounces, and Elinor bends to repeat it.

"Larger on the right than the left." She adds an interpretation: "A good sign for a son."

The physicians surely must overhear, but they choose to ignore her. By this, Isabel concludes that they also think she's carrying a boy. Whether a man of medicine believes in the Galenic two-celled womb (one side for a prince, the other for a princess) or Paracelsus's seven-celled version (three male, three female, one in center for a hermaphrodite), it is always boys on the right, girls on the left. Isabel's wheel has spun seven times, with the seed landing only once on the right; it is high time for another boy.

She can't stop herself from smiling, at the same time as she feels an inexplicable sorrow—as if she actually wants another girl.

When Candenzius speaks now, it is in Latin. The words sound like long songs: *Placenta . . . Plaga . . . Chancre . . . Monstra . . .*

Isabel holds very still and remembers the babies that have grown inside her. How some left her body before shaping fully: bat-blind eyes, fishy little hands, snaky spines. Tiny monsters no bigger than one of Candenzius's fingers.

Elinor whispers, "I've said a prayer against witchcraft."

So often the Countess expresses the very idea in Isabel's mind. If it were proper to speak just now, she would say thank you. Instead, she smiles bravely.

As if from far away, Isabel hears snoring. The Duchess has fallen asleep on her feet.

Candenzius's hand continues to roam—very little pain now, only a dullish sense of expansion and nausea.

Isabel holds her breath and gazes at her painting till the

black-and-white floor of Mary's bedchamber tilts and throbs crazily, out of rhythm with Candenzius's probings. She wonders if she might vomit. A tear rolls out the corner of her eye, and Elinor's fingers grip her even tighter.

The room is so hot that Venslov's wax tablet must be dripping toward the floor, like the blood that Isabel feels leaking from her now. Or maybe what she feels is melted tallow. It is not the baby. Definitely not the baby.

Everyone knows she is going to have a baby, a prince, even if the doctors have not actually said the words.

"Tell me it's perfect," she says aloud, breaking the protocol that says a queen must not speak now. "Tell me it's a baby."

As one body, the three men jump away. The ladies recoil, too, as if Isabel has committed some great transgression — broken wind or made water on the other side of the sheet.

"Your Highness!" the Duchess exclaims (she whom surprise has in fact caused to wake and make water inside her skirts).

Candenzius's hand has slipped right out of Isabel's thighs. She feels its absence as a coldness accompanied by an itch.

"Perhaps the Queen would care for a draught," he suggests.

Isabel wants no such thing. "Elinor!" she calls. She tries to sit up, but of course she can't. She reaches instead for the lady's elbow, grabs a handful of satin sleeve, and pulls her down.

When Elinor's ear — shell pink, with downy white fuzz just over its opening — comes close enough, Isabel whispers fiercely, *"Make him say it's a baby!"*

She lies back, exhausted, and is unconscious before she gets her answer.

# AVA BINGEN

In our northern kingdom, the days are as endless in summer as the nights are in winter. Temptations abound at these moments of extremes, and sin runs rampant. So why have I not uncovered any useful sins in the court?

I need something to tell Lord Nicolas—some bit of news, a well-founded suspicion, anything. He may decide, after all, to have me dismissed. Above all, I don't want the other punishments that Nicolas Bullen metes out.

I feel as fragile as the sugar cherry that melted between my breasts on Princess Sophia's wedding night, as stupid as the cow to which the Countess once compared me. I am no miller's daughter; I produce nothing of value.

One afternoon as I walk 'round and 'round the inner yard, hoping to overhear something good, a pile of actual straw sparks a memory: In actuality, the miller's daughter does not turn the straw into gold herself. When the king tells her that she must spin and marry him or else fail and die, it is a hideous dwarf who transforms her rude materials and demands the first baby as reward.

I must, then, be both dwarf and daughter. As observant and as clever, if not as beautiful.

* * *

That evening with Lord Nicolas, I make my mind a blank. *Into blankness,* I think, *some story may flow, and from there to my lips.*

"Ava Mariasdatter Bingen," he says from his chair, as I wait to learn what will become of me tonight, "what news have you found for me at last?"

"Not much, my lord," I confess, and then correct myself: "The nurses and servants have been speaking of the hole in the courtyard." My back is stiff, but I can't stretch it more until I receive Nicolas's permission to move.

"Ah, that." He yawns elaborately, like an actor. "The King's engineers will have that pit shored up soon, and you'll be trotting back and forth across it before you can say *cabbage.* You must offer better than that if I'm going to keep you."

*Cabbage,* I think. That is likely to be part of the apron wearers' supper. A flavor I'll be tasting all my life.

"Some say the hollow is a sign of evil in the court," I offer. It's true; this morning as I lay in the aprons' dorter and tried to sleep, I heard a couple of ladies' maids speculating about what might have opened up that stinking hole. "I heard someone call it Satan's close-stool. As if the devil is shitting out sins."

Nicolas barks a laugh. He stretches his fingers so the ruby ring sucks up its gout of light, and he decides to use the hand to give me a pat on the head. It's as if he's rewarding a well-behaved but not particularly favorite dog. Then he yawns again.

"And what else?" he asks. "There must be more."

More, more, always more. The thought strikes me that the one way I might please Nicolas is by invention. An ornate story could win me more security and perhaps a coin, a step closer to Copenhagen and Jacob.

I use the first name that comes to mind. "There's been talk about Countess Elinor." I pause briefly to decide on her sin. "They say she's taken a lover."

This does seem to interest Nicolas. He stops twirling the ring and sits up. "Oh?"

This must be what he wants from me. "Someone . . . highly placed. He shouts the name of his dog when he has his crisis." This part comes from my father's district; the guild master was said to call for old Fido when swiving his wife.

I thought to provoke laughter, but Nicolas is not amused. He scratches himself and looks at his desk as if he has something important to do there. I imagine him writing the order to imprison a clumsy, lying nursery maid.

He asks, "Do 'they' have a reason for their suspicions?"

"She might be with child," I say desperately. "Not her husband's. Some people say it, anyway, at least one." (Myself.) "He was injured in the war—the Count was." I think of the gossip my stepmother reported about me, the rumors that damned me in the parish eyes. "Elinor vomited at Mass on Sunday."

Nicolas says, "Several ladies were ill. Saturday's chicken had gone bad."

(Only the nobles had chicken; the rest of us got lentils and leeks. We were not sick.)

I say, "The Countess heaved when the Queen took Communion." This is, in fact, true.

"That sounds more like an accusation of sin against the Queen. Do you believe that gentle Isabel should not receive Heaven's comfort?"

"I never meant that!" This is shaky ground, politics, even if Nicolas is only playing with me. Hastily I retract: "I'm sure you're right. Fowl can be dangerous in summer . . ."

"Is this a common belief?" he asks, and for a moment I am confused—everyone knows about poultry. He clarifies, "About the Countess, that is." (I hear him calling me a dolt in his mind.) "Do your set commonly believe that she's an adulteress? And do they know the identity of her lover?"

I am too anxious to notice that he is not speaking as fluidly as usual; this will occur to me only later, and I will think I probably imagined it. "I don't like to say."

"But you must say, having begun." He keeps scratching, and I think he must have worn a hole in his skin by now. "Tell me."

I don't know why the name comes so easily; perhaps because it is one name often on the lips, as people fear more arrests. As *I* fear arrest. "Sir Georg Oline, the King's Secretary."

At last, Nicolas stops scratching.

I fear I've gone too far. "But you're right—she may not be sick with a baby at all." I babble on. "There are the medicines that the Countess—and the nurses—feed to the children. It could be that they're having some effect. I've heard Doctor Candenzius say that any posset can also be a poison if administered incorrectly—"

Nicolas's face is smooth but tense, with a listening look that warns me to be careful. "Do you accuse the Countess of being a poisoner as well?"

"I—I wouldn't—I mentioned only her own illness . . . "

Nicolas stands and stretches, laughing suddenly as if this has all been a great joke. He seems willing to forget about the Countess for now.

While he seats himself again, he says, "Before you accuse the Queen's chief lady of poisoning, have a thought for your tongue."

I bite my tongue, stay standing straight, bones aching.

Nicolas uncaps a little inkwell and takes up a pen. "You may say anything you like to *me*, of course," he notes as he begins to write. "That is your duty. But be careful elsewhere, or something might *get your tongue*. A lion, perhaps, or Sir Georg's pet dog."

I think of Midi Sorte and her split tongue.

He looks up and smiles; the white teeth gleam in a manner that appears overstudied but is nonetheless effective. He is in control of himself again. I notice the clock I heard ticking on a previous visit has been removed.

# THE HEAVENS, CHRISTIAN V, AND HIS ISABEL

O one sleeps in the long-lumened nights. Prostitutes do a brisk business. The nuns of certain convents pray through the brief bluish hours, while the Queen's ladies wheel around her like stars around the earth. Christian's men suffer from headaches and wear circles under their eyes as badges of honor, proving they are worn out with duties waiting on the King. For this is a time of joy: Queen Isabel has conceived again.

After the physicians swear that it is so, Christian goes to Stellarius, the astrologer, for confirmation. Stellarius is a most talented man. On the flat west tower, now an observatory, he leads a nightly synod in which Christian and his favorites—Rafael af Hvas, Willem Braj, and always Lord Nicolas—with their assorted attendants and friends, even a dwarf or two, enjoy turns gazing through Stellarius's new perspective glass. The clever contraption has a power for picking flecks of light out of an apparently uniform sky. Even when moon and stars crowd the heavens for the brief space in which the sun is gone, Stellarius manages to scry movements among them.

"It will be a fine baby," Stellarius announces over and over. His clever machine makes him certain. He adds a further tidbit of prediction with each night's work, ensuring that he will be summoned again and again. When a week has passed, his litany has built to "A very fine baby, to be born at the end of February, probably on the day of Saint Benjamin Deacon. And see how brightly shines the heart of Sagittarius? A masculine sign, almost certainly a boy. That is, *if all goes well down here*"—he would prefer not to make an absolute promise just yet—"the heavens are in favor."

Delighted, the King and his men look through the glass, murmuring shrewdly, though none of them is *mathematicus* enough to recognize Sagittarius's heart or even whether the constellation has one. At each given moment, some star or other is pulsing to catch the eye: that, they all think, must be the one of which Stellarius speaks.

Gazing heavenward, King Christian feels a rush of tenderness for his wife.

"I will give my Isabel a gift," Christian declares. He avoids Nicolas's gaze and turns surprisingly to his historian, who is both the chief scholar of his court and the man standing closest. "*You* will find something suitable. Or have something made. A ring. She has not had a ring in a while, I think. Make it poetic, with a line of metaphor inside. Or, no—make it a book of poems. With engraved illustrations and a decorated cover."

The tall, bony scholar, not accustomed to being addressed this way, coughs delicately and begs leave to speak. "Your Majesty," he says, "the Queen is known to be deeply devout.

Perhaps, given the customary topics of poetry, you might consider a book on some religious subject instead. A book of hours or an illustrated history of female martyrs."

Christian beams at him. "An excellent idea! Visit the bookbinders' district tomorrow." He is pleased with himself for having thought of Isabel, pleased also that he will be filling her time with useful occupation.

The scholar promises this will be done. The grooms stifle yawns behind jeweled hands. Lord Nicolas stares at the moon, and a stray beam picks out the spot of silver in his beard.


The Queen lies in a night-dark chamber, fretting herself. It has become impossible for her to sleep without light, but she cannot explain this to her women. They would think her weak. So each night the shutters are closed, Isabel confined blindly inside for the health of her womb. She would like to look at her painting of the Virgin Annunciate. She would like to look at *something* other than this nasty, infernal darkness.

If the Queen were to speak truth, she'd admit that one reason she's kept watch over her children's beds in the past years is that they provide an excuse for candlelight, and she is able to doze in the soft golden glow . . . until, that is, one child or another is seized with a fit for Isabel to dose. Then she might gather them within the folds of her robe and hold them safe against her body, which gesture is also a comfort to her.

But on these nights, her own bed. The physicians have ordered her to it. It squats in the middle of her inner chamber, a relatively plain furnishing, not so elaborate or uncomfortable as the one she uses for ceremonial purposes (her husband, his awkward preferences). A maid on a pallet to each side snores faintly; Elinor, with her own pair of maids, sleeps in the small chamber adjoining.

Dear Elinor. Elinor does not snore. Elinor probably does not sleep, either. This thought is some comfort to Isabel as she follows the itch across her breasts (it travels), up her neck, and into her right ear. She digs down and comes up with a sticky little ball of wax. After experimenting with its texture awhile, she makes sure to lose it in the sheets lest anyone think it fascinates her.

The servants' dinner was plentiful in onions. The room smells nasty.

Suddenly Isabel starts to retch, and this is a relief. The maids sit up, the doors open, and Elinor floats in with a candle and a dainty embroidered towel for Isabel's mouth.

"There, there, *ma reine,*" she says, stroking Isabel's hair with her cool white fingers. "This is a good sign. It is a healthy baby that makes his mother sick."

The maids, with faces blank, scrub at the stain on Isabel's counterpane.

Christian bends again to Stellarius's perspective glass. Knees and buttocks, elbows and feet jut at angles that would be called ridiculous if he were not the King. He is very aware of Nicolas somewhere behind him and would like to appear graceful. He changes focus to gaze at his family's namesake, the moon:

*la pleine lune des Lunedie.* Already it has begun to fade as the sun swings into its place.

This marvelous device is so powerful, brings the moon so very close, that only a quarter of the face can be seen. Christian has to swivel the glass along degree by degree if he wants to study all the porous surface, the gray flecks among the luminous white. Stellarius helps him do this, mentioning casually that soon there will be an even finer device with greater and clearer magnification.

Christian longs for Nicolas to join him at the glass but does not like to ask him to approach in front of the grooms, who strictly speaking are of higher rank.

Bored, the favorites and those all-but-nameless others begin to talk. They discuss a young lady-in-waiting with a handsome nose, the palace steward's dewy wife, the talented tongue of an apron wearer. Several of Christian's men are fascinated by a Negresse who works in the nursery. "O to smack my lips upon that skin," says Willem Braj, who is famous for liking his meat burnt. He fans his mouth as if he's charred himself.

Le Fariné, Christian's broody-browed dwarf, stares at Willem with distaste. Or perhaps envy, or hatred; Le Fariné once had a black wife, small like himself, till she was given to the Dauphin of France as a gesture of goodwill.

Rafael af Hvas says the Negresse is available if any wish to try her. "She has no particular protector. When Countess Elinor first presented her to the Queen—remember, that masque about the end of the war?—she was coated in sugar crystals, with a plum in her mouth. And what could have been sweeter than the kiss of peace she gave the man who stood in for Justice? I believe, Nicolas, you were fortunate enough to be that man?"

Nicolas Bullen makes a small noise, then complains of a sore throat.

Christian looks harder at the moon, as if he might find some new part of it.

"Your Majesty," Stellarius says in a low voice. "Do you see the declivity just in the center of the moon? Let me lengthen the glass for you. There. Look. It is a sign, of course, of the growth in your wife's blessed womb . . ."

Christian adjusts his posture. He tries to lose himself in the silver slice of moon.

While King and astrologer take turns fitting their eyes to the little lens at bottom, conversation still seeps around them. The favorites declare themselves intrigued, too, by Countess Elinor herself, so unusually pale for a member of the nobility, with breasts that ride much higher than is normal in a woman of her age.

"Of course, time's stood still for her since the war began," notes a minor baron for whom Christian has no particular liking. "What with her husband off at sea so long — then his arm and leg truly off." He laughs as if this is some real witticism, as if the once-great Count of Belnát is a clown who only apes an injury.

"True," Willem Braj inserts, "who would take a maid when he might have a mistress? Or perhaps we should ask Sir

142

Georg Oline. Quite recently I've heard that he's tried them both. I heard it from a reliable source. In fact, it was—"

"Enough," says Nicolas, despite his sore throat. "Show *some* respect to the lady if not the spymaster." Chivalrous Nicolas!

But there come the predictable sniggers, the jealous pleasure one rogue takes in another's triumph.

Christian feels himself turning red. To think it is his own Secretary who is talked of in such a way! Chief secret-keeper, Christian's Groom of the Stool and official spymaster. This indignity weighs heavy on his mind, though he tells himself it does not matter. For a time the men (disobeying Nicolas) speak only of the lady's beauty, her famous icy pallor, and how a bed might turn her chill into a fever.

"No harm in a little heat, eh?"

But what secrets might the Secretary murmur under fever's influence . . .

"With a fair nurse like that at his pillow!"

Christian thinks of the hideous stumps where Count Belnát's beautiful limbs used to join his body. Christian has never cared for the Countess, though her skin is fair enough to outshine the moon and she had suitors aplenty in her day.

"We must all have a care for our hearts—and our pillows!" Willem Braj crows. Rolling onto his toes, he mimics laying his head down for a rest on the high shelf of the Countess's bosom.

Not receiving the laughter for which he'd hoped, Willem nudges the dwarf Le Fariné with a velvet-toed slipper. The small man plays along by tightening himself into a ball and tumbling till he knocks over Rafael af Hvas. Rafael rips a hole in the knee of his hose; the others laugh heartily at last. Rafael kicks Le Fariné's backside.

Nicolas makes an impatient gesture and stands up. "With your permission, Majesty, I would like to go."

The solemn night has been completely ruined. The men are making Christian's belly hurt. He prays and wishes as hard as he can that they will vanish or he will.

His wish, his dream, is granted: Christian feels himself sucked up through the perspective glass. He becomes a black speck crawling across the luminous surface.

Imagine his wife, his son, his courtiers watching him from so far below. What must they think! The black-speck part of him dares to wave its arms at Nicolas.

II.

FEAR

*There was once a princess who married a duke much older than she. At the ceremony, the girl promised her new husband the same obedience she had shown her father, the king, but she'd heard the duke whispered about and had some fears as to what he might require of her. He had already buried two wives and had no children thus far; it was said his desires were somewhat peculiar and not likely to produce offspring.*

*On the evening after her wedding, as she sat primly expectant in the great hall of the ducal palace, the princess received a visit not from her husband but from his steward, a cheerful man of flaxen hair and a ready smile.*

*He began with a bow, then asked, "Do you have anything you would like me to tell the master?" When the princess simply blinked, he clarified: "Any secrets not yet disclosed?"*

*She blinked again. "I have no secrets." In fact, she might as well have had no conscience at all, for she had never been known to commit a sin.*

*At that, the steward handed over a candle and a basket containing keys to all the rooms in the castle, with instructions to use them judiciously and only after full consideration. The princess spent the rest of the evening exploring. She found that many doors were already unlocked—the kitchens, the laundry, her own bedchamber and dressing room, where maids waited to help her change into her night shift. She decided to lock none of these essential rooms; she searched on.*

*High in the castle attics, she discovered a door, a plain door, that did not open readily.*

*Deciding that this must lead to the most important place in all the castle, the princess rummaged through her heavy basket, trying key after key. The bright ones of brass and steel were all too big, but there was one small key of dull black metal that might . . . might . . . did fit.*

*Before the princess released the latch, she remembered the steward's warning about judicious use of her new rights of entry. She also remembered a tale often told by her nurses about a locked door, a bloodstained key, a roomful of wives hanging from meat hooks and gutted like game.*

*She jiggled the black key, the works inside turned over, and the lock slid open like a bride.*

## MIDI SORTE

When they come, it be a storm day with clouds black over-head. Elinor is standing in the yard with the Queen and toss-ing rocks in to the bed of the witch, to watch the earth bubble and her toys sink. She do this for amusement, to see what the witches take and what they let float on the skin of they bad-smelling hollow-bed. A stone go down, a chip of shatter bowl from the Crown Prince's breakfast.

Elinor take the glove from the Queen's clean hand. "Now you toss something, Highness," she say, and put a pebble in Isabel palm.

Isabel close her hand upon the pebble. "No," she say, thinking aloud, "this hole is a bad omen."

The ladies rush to tell her all is well. Bridget Belskat, old Lady Drin, Duchess Margrethe, Countess Ditlevnavn, all the others given by her husband. They make a circle drawing her away.

Behind, some maids repeat the Queen's word *omen*. Whisper but not heard. They fear that wet hollow.

It be more than omen when the King's guards come through the inner gate. March, march, scuff, stop. Halberds point at cloudy sky, faces point at us; maids and ladies cross they arms and draw breath tight. No thing move then, not even Elinor. The air go quiet and the wind die. Only that stink wave up from earth's belly.

The Queen make little screamings inside her throat. She think the guard bring messages about her children.

"What do you men want?" Elinor ask with a voice like a pan-cracker, crisp but easy to break.

"Elinor Parfis," say the Marshal of Guards. "You are summoned to the King's Lower Chambers."

Queen Isabel cry out, "Elinor!" Lady Drin take her arm as if the Queen might faint.

The Countess have no look for Isabel just now. Lower Chambers be where criminals are taken and disappeared. "Explain yourself," she says quiet, and if the men do n't see the heart-pulse in her neck, they may think she taking charge as has been her right elsewhere.

The *maréchal* keep staring straight. May be he hate doing this thing. May be he owe a favor to the Countess' husband.

"My lady," he say, "I am ordered to arrest you for conspiracy and for poison."

Every one gasp, ladies and maids just the same, and they mouths make black O's in astonishment. They thought the poisoners all ready gone. They taste their breath and wonder if they be dangered too.

It be like a scene on stage, and others now come along to watch it play. Arthur Grammaticus, historian, flaps down the outside staircase like a crow who want his share of meat. He come in time to hear the charge, and I see he write it down fast.

The rain begins with big fat drops.

The Countess toss her head back and smile cold, all brave. Bosoms at her chin, hands flashing jewels: "That is ludicrous." She turn to go inside the palace, but the man stop her with one hand on her arm. She yank away and tell him, "I will speak only to the King himself. Or to Sir Georg Oline — I know *he* would never order my arrest."

The Marshal say, "Madam, come with me. No doubt you will see Sir Georg in your new quarters."

The Countess never reached her place of honor by obeying such a man. She turn to the Queen and say, "Your Highness, you can stop this."

The Queen scratch her ear and wrinkle her face to a rosebud. "Elinor!" she wail as if she make a sudden thought. "I should have a corps of my own guards!"

"Say a word, Your Highness," Elinor command. "Just one word."

The Queen's rosebud face go to a twist of straw, ready to burn at a spark. "Elinor, you must not leave me!"

But no body minds her. Elinor have spent some years making her weak, so now the Queen do n't know any thing else but weakness.

"Countess, I order you to come," say the Marshal.

And Elinor decide she 'd better. She gather her skirts up for walking. "Yes," as stern she can. "Yes, I will discuss this with the King right away."

When she walk, I see one scorch mark that nursery work have left on her fine skirts.

* * *

*Come, come,* my lover say when I describe how my heart split to see her go. *How can you, of all people, be sorrowful, when you know her better than any of the others?*

He is right, but I am in mixed feeling. First I know glee that she gone and will not slap and make me do her business— I mean that secret watching business beyond the nursery tasks. I fear for my self cause be she were my protector, of sorts, cause be she think me useful; and if a woman do n't have a friend she is lost.

I explain this in his chamber, while I turn a broken doll in my hands. This doll were once Gorma's toy but remind me now of Elinor, her half-face and clothes cover in vomitus and filth. I flake it from her belt and see yellow, green, and blue glass.

My lover pull me to him, in to the dark robe he wears, against the prickling beard at his mouth. "*You* have a friend," he says. "*We* have secrets."

This kind of secret do no special good. Inside his arms, I hug the wax doll like it belong to me before I hug him.

There be still many stories I have not told.

 messenger brings news of the arrests to Nicolas Bullen, who brings it to the King.

Christian sits on the velvet-padded close-stool in the narrow cabinet of his inner chamber, expelling the rich food that has seemed ever more reluctant to leave his body as the years stretch on. Tonight's dinner was especially heavy: beef with a sauce of pepper and cream, a sugary compote of pears, a thick wet cheese from Poland. Christian has the tense, nauseated, but bored feeling of someone waiting for particular information, and his belly has been cramping with anxiety.

"They found him?" he asks. "He went quietly? And she?"

"Quietly enough." Nicolas rocks gently on the balls of his feet, making candle shadows craze over the brightly painted paneling, the red bed drapes, the painting of the martyred Saint Sebastian; the King himself on his hollow stool. Normally it is the Secretary who attends the King here. In Georg's absence, Christian has declared that Nicolas is the only man with the right—the duty—to come here. And Nicolas is conscious of the privilege.

Thanks to widespread rumor calcified into fact, Sir Georg Oline, Christian's old friend and former—very much former—confidant, is now known to have swived and schemed with his lover, Countess Elinor Parfis, to murder the children. This creates a paradox, because he who was in charge of arrests has now been taken himself. It also creates an opportunity: there will have to be a new secretary to attend Christian at these times and to direct his net of spies. For now, for the first task, Christian has chosen Nicolas, who in many ways seems suited to the other as well. *There is no one better,* Christian thinks, *to trust with a suspicion or a secret.*

During conversation, Nicolas acquits himself admirably. He pretends not to hear the thunder coming from the royal belly, and he leaves his pomander in his breast. To do otherwise would be the worst breach of respect to the King.

And he is a discreet listener, not intruding his own opinions while the King considers the weighty questions of the court. First: What is to be done with the Countess of Belnát and her lover? Orders must be given if order is to be restored.

"No torture," Christian decides. He doesn't like to imagine his former friend Georg, or even the fish-cold Countess, writhing with the rack or the screws, though he supposes it might come to that. "Not now."

Nicolas removes a handkerchief from his sleeve and offers it to Christian, who discovers his brow has beaded with sweat. "Wise enough, Your Majesty. With some people, the worst criminals and cowards, an apparent and temporary clemency achieves greater effects than immediate action."

Christian accepts the handkerchief, grits his teeth, feels awful. He can't remember ever experiencing such pain. But this is just a recurrence of his old trouble—he knows he has not been poisoned, and certainly not by Elinor or Georg. Christian eats nothing that the tasters do not try first. Still he cannot summon a word to say next.

Nicolas speaks on smoothly, as if responding to a question. "The arrests were magnificently played, Your Majesty. Sir Georg had just docked after an excursion into the city; your guards took him as he stepped onto the pier. The Countess, meanwhile, was amusing herself by the witch's hollow. The cathedral clock struck six, and they were apprehended at the same stroke."

"Not together, then." Christian mops his own brow. "Not . . . *in flagrante.*"

"No, Majesty, they have been clever about not appearing together." Nicolas keeps his voice neutral. He steps to the table to pour out a cup of wine, adding measures of the anise juice and horehound that Candenzius has prescribed for the King's dyspepsia. The spoon clinks against the cup's glass sides; the mixture smells overpoweringly sweet. "Georg was alone except for his servants, and Elinor was with the Queen and some of the nursemaids."

The Queen. His wife, excitable in her delicate condition. Christian groans as another pain rips through him. "How did Isabel take it?" He tries to sound no more concerned than if asking how she took her latest dose of blood-strengthening medicine.

"She was dismayed, but she recognizes Your Majesty's wisdom in this, as in all matters. Naturally she appreciates your protection. As she appreciated the book of saints' lives you gave her yesterday." Nicolas hands the cup to Christian, careful to keep his fingers from brushing the King's disrespectfully.

In fact, once Elinor was well and truly gone, the Queen fell into a fit, clawing at her own hair and ears until they bled. All three physicians and her priest, Father Absolon, are with her now. But this is not the moment to share such a report with the King, who needs to feel confident in his own bold action. An action toward which Nicolas, in fact, did subtly guide him.

"Very well, then." Slowly Christian empties his medicinal cup, stares at Nicolas's nose, and thinks how fine the nostrils are, like two delicate pinpricks. It is odd, this intimacy between the two of them; for the first time, Christian feels embarrassed to be upon the stool when speaking, but nonetheless he can't imagine being there with anyone else. "We have removed a canker from the court."

He makes a gesture to show Nicolas that, for the moment, he would prefer not to speak. Nicolas is sensitive enough to understand, but in his silence there is little companionship, only an inscrutable mystery, a sense of withholding. He keeps his own counsel while the anise and horehound do their work and the new-fashioned second hand ticks its way around the chamber clock that Nicolas gave him.

*How lonely I am,* thinks the King. Then scolds himself for self-indulgence.

He counts out five minutes, ten, fifteen, punctuated by ever milder outbursts from his gut. He wonders incidentally when and how this custom was established, this keeping watch over a sovereign during his evacuations. Perhaps at some time in the past it was a service performed by a physician, who monitored the king's health by inspecting what was left behind. Or a warrior, who would protect the king at his most vulnerable moment, so he might not die on his stool like the biblical King Eglon, whose stomach was rent by a sword that disappeared in his folds of fat . . .

Christian's limbs grow eager for movement. He stands and holds up his shirt to let Nicolas finish him with a sponge upon a stick. "So," he says while this happens, "soon there will be a new official secretary." He supposes his wife will want someone for her chief lady too. "There must also be a Mistress — or Master — of the Nursery. My council will have some suggestions . . . I'll want your opinion as well," he adds as grandly as he can. "And perhaps more than that. I believe . . . I suspect you are clever with secrets."

Nicolas bows but stays silent. His dark face composed, his ruby ring pulsing as he busies himself with the sponge and a little pot of vinegar to rinse it in.

"You have thus far resisted marriage, I believe?" Christian wants to confirm.

"Yes, Your Majesty. I was betrothed once, but the lady died."

"It's just as well." Christian waits, tense, while Nicolas dries him with a linen towel. "Women do tend to gossip."

Nicolas murmurs polite agreement.

# AVA BINGEN

I am evil. At least, on the path to evil. While scheming to save myself, I have sinned and must do penance. It's useless to say, even to myself, that I didn't mean any harm — I merely told the story of Countess Elinor's adultery to satisfy Lord Nicolas lest he punish me again. I never thought she'd be accused of murder, only of wantonness.

So I make myself into an avid scrubber of nursery floors, brusher of walls, huntress of lice and bedbugs. That night, with the children in their sleeping chambers, I rub the cracks of their grandly carved daytime beds with turpentine to drive away infestations, polish them to keep the painted wood fine — things I used to do at my father's house, but unusual for even a somewhat-honored maid on a night in which the Mistress is missing. Five white wooden swans, one yellow lion, all cleansed of pests, with wormwood scattered down inside to slow the insects that creep up from the floor. No one will accuse a clean girl of lying.

The paradox is that thanks to my own efforts, there is no Mistress of the Nursery to notice what I do now. In Countess Elinor's absence, Duchess Margrethe of Marsvin has stepped in to oversee the royal children's households; but she is so old that, for her, to step in is to occupy a cushioned chair in the corner farthest from the window. She dozes in peace while the machinery of nurses, maids, and other attendants wheels around her.

The nighttime nurses don't notice me, either; they are too busy with the children. The Crown Prince and his sisters are agitated in spirit—fretful and crying out. Hungry, thirsty, tearful, itchy, with a burning in their stomachs and blisters in their mouths. Their limbs hurt, and each one of them has a soft new wound, gummy with white sap. They sob for their mother and for the Countess. Little Gorma also calls for Midi Sorte, who cannot be found here or in the dorter.

"Theriac," Candenzius pronounces, and the physicians go from room to room to dose them all with his brew of sixty-four ingredients. It has a base of Egyptian viper's milk and is the most efficient known antidote to poison. Candenzius often prescribes it "on principle."

While the physicians deliver the theriac, the nurses stand with basins and towels in case it comes back up.

One of the older women mumbles, in that way inaudible to the nobility, "Snake milk and sugar, my arse. What they need is a good lot of thistle to drain their bowels."

The new stuff smells good, at least, of that throaty spice called cinnamon. My mouth waters as if I could use an antidote myself. But I don't want to drink viper's milk . . .

I scrub harder, punishing myself with the odor of turpentine.

While the Duchess dozes, while the nurses bustle, while

the cathedral clock chimes its slow way through the hours, everyone waits for the Queen. She is said to be resting, or rather weeping, in her chambers, where Doctor Candenzius attends her when he leaves the nursery. No doubt she is bereft at the loss of her friend, betrayed by what she believes that friend has done. Or perhaps she does not believe; maybe she will order an investigation of the rumor . . .

I scrub and oil, hunt and crush, trying to craft myself a good reputation. And here is another of those paradoxes, not so minor: I who was nearly ruined by gossip have now ruined another woman by the same means. I can't help but imagine the prison — colder and nastier than that cell in which Lord Nicolas first put me, darker and smellier, tanging of torture's irons and blood. The King's Lower Chambers. Countess Elinor was no gracious mistress, but has she deserved what I've done?

I was only trying to avoid doing . . . *that* . . . again to Lord Nicolas. And so I lied.

All at once I abandon my work, to fly to the cellar where Lord Nicolas has his cabinet. I stumble through the vats and storerooms, some now packed with supplies, others emptied. Barley, wheat, beans, onions, the scurry of rats and mice. I run through the whole long series of compartments, only to come out at the far stairway without having found Nicolas or even catching a whiff of his too-perfumed scent.

He has moved on.

I collapse against the cold stone stairs. I sob. Not that I could imagine what to say if I did find him — how to explain that what I told him before was the invention of a moment, meant only to save myself and not to harm another. I don't understand how the gossip about adultery could turn to accusations of poisoning, yet I am sure I'm to blame. Another sin.

I can't even admit to him (and barely to myself) that the danger I faced was not so bad—certainly nothing to compare with what Countess Elinor faces now.

It is there, as I huddle against the cold steps, that she finds me.

At first I'm aware only of feet on the stairs, the gritty scrape of a shoe and the swish of linsey-woolsey skirts. The figure stops but says nothing; she could be a ghost. Thus, though the place is dark, I realize that my companion is Midi Sorte. But I don't look up.

In her eerie quiet, Midi plucks at my sleeve, then grabs hold of my wrist and tugs me upward.

"You want me to follow you?" I say stupidly, wondering if she might make some small voice noise of assent.

After all these weeks, I still find her silence and the thought of that forked tongue unnerving. But I realize suddenly that I don't want Midi to make a noise—if she opens her lips, the two long halves of that tongue might wind outward toward me in the dark. I imagine them wrapping around my throat and knotting tight, pulling me to Midi's sharp white teeth.

(Does she have sharp white teeth? I can't remember. I may be thinking of Nicolas's.)

I shake myself to restore my senses. I shake off Midi Sorte's hand, too. But because she is in some sense my superior, and because I don't know what else I am to do at this horrible time, I follow her up the stairs.

Midi leads me up into the courtyard, behind the sentries, and across to the southernmost of the palace buildings, one that is plain but not so plain as that which houses the aprons' dorter. Inside, Midi chooses a door very like other doors and opens it without knocking. It is heavy and silent on oiled hinges. We step in.

There is a desk, a shelf of books, a bed with faded greenish drapes. An open window by which a man has arranged himself against the pale summer night sky as if to show his profile to best advantage. He appears to be reading a map or some such document by moon- and candlelight.

If I hoped for a moment that this would be Lord Nicolas's new cabinet, I am disappointed. Not only are the furnishings much too plain, but the occupant's nose is too thick; the brow is too long, the beard too full, the man himself too tall. Bony and loose limbed. A stranger.

Midi latches the door and stands in front of it, eyes on this man.

He detaches himself from the window and steps toward the candles on the table. Now I recognize him, dimly, as someone I have seen on the fringes of events. He wears a scholar's black robe and usually, I believe, carries a tablet and stylus.

I wonder if a scholar can be an apron wearer's enemy or if enemies are only for those of high station.

He speaks. "Ava Bingen"—so he knows my true

name, not the Mariasdatter I took on with the buckets and brushes—"Health to your soul. I am Arthur Grammaticus."

He pauses as if this collection of syllables should mean something, but I am too confused to make a reply.

He explains: "Keeper of the King's chronicles."

I give him a curtsy in case this post is one of some importance. I'm not quite sure what chronicles are, if they are kept in this chamber. "Health to your soul," I say.

Arthur Grammaticus seats himself in one of the chairs and gestures as if to invite me to sit too, but I will not take a chair while Midi stands.

Sitting with knees bent upward like a stork's, Grammaticus plaits his ink-stained hands together and says, "I've noticed that you are a teller of stories."

At that, my legs give way. I find myself on a floor again, certain I will be tortured; in a posture for begging, though I struggle to defend myself. "I—but who doesn't like a story? Most people find pleasure in them. Both listening and speaking."

At the door, Midi Sorte crosses her arms. Grammaticus blinks at her.

"I have also noticed," he says, "that you have a special acquaintance with Lord Nicolas Bullen."

At that, I cannot speak.

My silence says all I need to say, for Grammaticus was sure of his information before he spoke. Grammaticus lists the dates on which I visited Lord Nicolas and the crime of which I was first accused. How silly a little needle stab seems now!

And he describes my latest meeting with Lord Nicolas as if he, Grammaticus, were a bug on the wall. I wonder how else this man could possibly have observed so much about me, when I have scarcely noticed him before.

"I know you are cunning," he says. He also knows I am the source of the gossip about Countess Elinor's dalliance with Sir Georg. *How?* He knows that Lord Nicolas planted that gossip carefully. And someone — perhaps many — watered it and let it grow until the pair had a reputation for poison. "I know it was you who put them in prison."

I look over at Midi, who once belonged to the Countess. If Nicolas has an army of angels, Elinor might have a legion of devils such as Midi to take her revenge. Perhaps this scholar is one of them. And Midi has somehow indicated to him that she hates me. (*Saa,* she certainly is not kind to me, but then she's not kind to anyone.) Midi has been spying on me . . .

Has there ever been a moment in which I was more afraid? I could fall dead and be grateful for it. Or for a good shove into a witch's oven, or a fatal spindle prick, or a pair of shoes that would dance me away from here to a hell that would surely be more friendly than Elinor Parfis's wrath.

"It was not by design — " I begin, but then, on some impulse, I stop myself. It occurs to me that I might find an advantage in appearing crafty, especially in such a way as to harm one so much more powerful than myself. I stammer out, "Lord Nicolas's orders were to report what I saw and heard."

"By design or no, you achieved what statesmen and physicians could not," Grammaticus tells me, and no longer in the easy tone of a flatterer. "You uncovered a conspiracy. You saved the royal children. You found their poisoners."

I would indeed feel wonderful at hearing this if I had not made up the rumor about Elinor and Sir Georg myself. Arthur Grammaticus appears to believe me a heroine. "I wasn't the only one who knew," I say, wishing desperately for this to be truth. "Lord Nicolas would never take my word alone. He must have . . ."

Must have what? Heard the rumor elsewhere from his secret army? I don't dare to hope it. Must have decided on his own how to use the story I gave him—*that* he most definitely did.

". . . must have a strong connection to the King if he was able to have those two arrested," I finish uneasily. "With Sir Georg having been the Secretary."

Grammaticus mulls this over, acts as if it is an observation worthy of mulling and I a person so worthy as well. I sneak a look at Midi Sorte. Still with arms folded and eyes shut tight: she hasn't moved a hair, hasn't even vented a *Shh*.

"No doubt that is true," Grammaticus concedes. He removes his lenses and rubs at the bridge of his nose. "But he is not the only person who has the King's ear. Or eye, as it were."

"What do you mean?"

"The King reads my chronicles every day," Grammaticus says proudly. "Or has them read to him in his chamber. Sometimes I am the reader." He puts his spectacles back on and blinks some more. Being my father's daughter, I want to adjust the lenses for him, perhaps try to find a new pair that might be clearer. "They keep him informed of what happens in his kingdom."

"I can't read." I wonder if this is what he's been hinting at, that I should read aloud to the King. I stay on my knees and sit on my heels. "Or, at least, not very much. And I can't write, except my name." My name, there on a page in Nicolas's vanished cabinet. *AVA*.

"You don't have to, though you might learn eventually. For now I would like to take advantage of your mouth." At his own choice of words, he flushes — and I wonder (ridiculously, at such a moment) if Arthur Grammaticus might want me. Although I'm already hot with anxious sweat, I feel myself blush. It is more likely he knows of my awful congress with Nicolas.

He corrects himself quickly: "That is, I would like you to tell *me* your stories. I'd like you to come to me with them."

"Instead of Lord Nicolas?"

"Ah" — he shifts in his seat, storky legs folding further — "I cannot order you to do that." (*So, he can order me to do some things,* I think.) "I can't even request it. But if you would like to share your stories with the King more directly, if you would like to have that hand in chronicling history . . ."

"To spy for you *and* Lord Nicolas?"

"Not to spy, no, I wouldn't call it that." His voice hoarse. "But to *report* — for the chronicles only. All I ask for is the information. So that I have many perspectives for my history. I will write everything down. It is your choice."

Now comes my turn to mull. I think of the words flowing from my lips into Grammaticus's quill, from the inked page into a reader's mouth and thus to the King's ear. (I don't believe for a minute that Christian V bothers to read for himself when he can have someone else do it; I picture him in bed with his nightcap and a cup of wine, listening.) There is something thrilling in this prospect, that my words might be marked down for both royalty and the ages.

I ask, "Are you trying to bring down Lord Nicolas? Or to become his rival?" A thought strikes me: "Do you want to be the King's new secretary?"

Grammaticus regards me as if I just leaped to the window and shouted that he's the source of Italian Fire in the court. "Good woman, I am a historian and a scholar," he says. "And the Crown Prince's tutor when he's well. I honor Nicolas Bullen as the lord of the island where I was born."

I take note of this, that he has perhaps known Lord Nicolas for many years. He is surely either a rival or a minion. I hope a rival.

"And Midi Sorte — is she already your spy?"

Grammaticus looks at Midi. She leans against the door, her skin melting into its dark wood. Of course, a mute woman can tell him nothing. Only *Shhh, shh, sh* occasionally, which she doesn't bother with now.

Grammaticus concludes, "We are all, of course, in service of the Crown and King. Who is known for being liberal with his gratitude, no matter what the rank of the creditor."

I recall something my mother used to say: *Be wary of a*

*promise without a clear price.* "How will the King be grateful to me?"

With this, I give myself away; Grammaticus's beard stretches in a smile, for he knows he has me to command. But I think it is not merely a triumphant smile; there is generosity in it, too, and earnestness—he reminds me of Jacob Lille, just a bit. "At my request, and given good reason to do it, the King could restore you to your former position in the Queen's household."

"I would be a needlewoman again?"

"If all goes well."

He is not the first man to promise me this, but what choice do I have? I grasp at straws, hoping to spin them, yes, into something. I give my newest master another curtsy.

As I leave that bookish room, with the sun cracking the sky over the bay, I think of the pearl that I watched Queen Isabel pluck from her bodice on the first day of what I now think of as my long demise. I wish I'd had the courage to pull another one off when I was so close to her. It might have given me a start in life elsewhere.

If I ever come across such wealth again, I will cut a hole in my own skin and sew the thing inside, to use in extremity. Lord Nicolas has taught me that much, at least.

# THE ITALIAN PLAY

ITTING in her prison cell, alone although never without some attendant or watcher, Countess Elinor of Belnát becomes an actor. Silently, in her mind, she runs through every play and masque she has witnessed in her too-brief career at court. Sometimes startling those attendants when she slips into the role of audience and lets a gasp or a laugh escape at a particularly moving mental performance.

Thus far, her imprisonment is not so bad. She is treated more or less like a lady. She has friends in court; she has a husband who is a count. The guards and attendants are polite, not sure whether the Countess will be restored to her old influence. Elinor herself is encouraged by the fact that she has not been tortured. Her perfect limbs and milky skin are still unbroken, except by the bug bites that plague everyone, everywhere.

The worst is the waiting. Not knowing. Unable even to launch a scheme.

And so, plays. Her favorite now is one she didn't much like when it came to Skyggehavn. It was based on an Italian poem of forty years ago: *Syphilis; or, The French Disease.* Here Syphilus, a hapless shepherd, affronts Apollo by revering his earthly lord more than the god. He is consequently sentenced to a fiery torture, all concentrated in the place one least wishes to feel a fire.

> SYPHILUS: I broke with the Sun by setting
> Altars not to him but to my King;
> And, as I tended that King's flocks,
> Apollo struck with flame and rocks;
> And vicious minions of th' angry god
> Bit blazing wounds in this shepherd's rod.

What a pretty way to describe the burning and the telltale sores that (so Elinor has heard) swarm over poxy private parts. The trembling, the blindness and madness and visions that follow after. The collapsed noses and gnawed-away fingers, the bones hollowed out and tumorous. Disease figured into poetry and rendered something fit for gods after all. And for entertainment, for royalty.

When the play was performed in the palace's great hall, it brought a flush of embarrassment to the Queen's cheeks. Thereafter it was retitled simply *Syphilis,* in deference to Isabel's French birth and delicate feelings; the disease itself was renamed Italian Fire. Nonetheless, Isabel's blush lasted over a fortnight and was said to have caused a miscarriage. Elinor, of course, nursed her through that, stirring poultices of frankincense and pennyroyal herself.

King Christian thought *Syphilis* witty in parts. No doubt he, with his sheeplike countenance, imagined his subjects setting up altars in his honor. Perhaps he himself even prayed at one. He is that vain.

Now the Countess laughs out loud, a bitter, angry laugh that ends in a cough.

"You are thirsty, my lady?" asks the sour-faced old woman assigned to Elinor today. She puts aside her busying work, a pile of stockings to be darned, and looks ready to serve, if somewhat grudging.

Elinor scratches her scalp. Her white-yellow hair is snarled and greenish in places. She accepts a cup of weak ale and dips the ends of her hair into it, trying to get them clean. She needs to look like her old self if the King or Queen sends for her.

But just then comes news that squashes hope: Sir Georg Oline, her putative lover and co-conspirator, has been found dead in his cell.

"Dashed his own brains out against the pillar he was chained to," says one attendant to another.

(Perhaps alone of her rank, Elinor understands servants' talk, hears the whispers that other courtiers take for silence.)

The sour-faced woman allows a perverse delight to rearrange her features, even as she draws the raveled edges of a hole together. "Such a shame," she breathes. "He were a handsome man."

Elinor breaks into their talk before she hears something that might convince her that Sir Georg did not take his own life, that he was killed by a dark force — cloaked in the name of justice — that might visit her too.

As if anyone still cares about Sophia or what killed her!

Of late, even Isabel had forgotten to mourn. It is easy to forget a dead pawn when there are kings and knights to play with.

"Give me your sewing," Elinor says abruptly. Snappishly, holding out one pallorous, imperious hand. "Or no, a new needle and thread. Wool thread and a canvas. I have an inclination to embroider."

She will make a cushion. A gift for the King, a gesture of appeasement; perhaps a picture of a dog or some other faithful animal. Not a sheep.

As she begins to stitch, she imagines a few more lines to the play.

SYPHILUS: Let such be the reward for loyalty —
For choice 'tween gods and royalty
Is inevitable as breath . . .

She puzzles over what the next line could be, what might best but not most obviously make a rhyming couplet.

# PERISHED LILY

N the darkness that has begun to swallow the edges of daytime, Princess Sophia climbs out of her virginal coffin and winds among the sarcophagi of her ancestors. All those dead Lunedie grandparents and great-aunts. She, the Perished Lily, knocks gently on the marble lids: already gone, or not ready yet.

It is odd to find that she is lonely. She misses her mother and father and nurses and ladies and sisters. Not so much her brother; she barely knew him, for before they all got sick, he was always off at some lesson or other, riding and fighting and Latin and history. While she learned only what she would need in order to marry Sweden. Östergötland. Where is it she was supposed to be duchess of?

At first, Sophia was surprised to find that, in death, her bones hold the same ache they did in life. Her skin still itches, and she still cannot sleep. But she finds that these things matter far less in the afterlife. Despite the discomfort, it is possible to enjoy oneself very much—to dance among the sarcophagi with the kind of abandon that is said to be the mark of a peasant, rather than with the carefully measured but immensely tiring hops and swirls that were expected of her at her wedding. She does not get tired now, not in the same way. When the monks of Saint-Peter's-on-the-Isle light candles so they can pray over the sarcophagi, Sophia dances among them without catching fire. She is reckless. She is joyful.

And she is adventurous. Rather than letting herself stay cooped up in this crypt like a chicken, she drifts out after the monks and tours their monastery: dorters, cells, kitchens, so much the same that she could be back in the old palace nursery, if it weren't for the men flogging themselves and washing out their hair shirts.

So why not visit the old nursery? The whole palace, in fact? See her mother, learn about her own death?

Sophia slides herself like a letter under a drafty door and suddenly is outside, in open air, as she can remember being only a handful of times in her life. It is cool, but she's been feeling feverish and she likes the sensation.

Even in the deep blue twilight, she sees clearly as in a summer's noon. There's the palace crouching at the bay's end, that great red sea dragon with its coppery hackles raised, its mouth gaping open to suck in and swallow the unwary. And the city beyond, a sprawling red-and-brown mass with here and there a glint of canal, a spire from a church, a chimney that pokes up so high she can make out its individual curl of smoke.

Sophia has never been out in Skyggehavn itself, only so far as the cathedral. But how to get there? She studies the green waters lapping busily at the base of the monks' island. She puts a foot into the water and sees it disappear; the water will melt her away. Will the famous mermaids help her cross?

She waits; she has no idea how long. As a child, Sophia was fretful, but as a ghost she has an endless store of patience.

And slowly, gradually, the wind picks up; the waves get infinitesimally more vigorous, and the stones of the monastery whistle. Sophia feels her skirts filling with clean, blowy wind. She holds them spread out in her hands as far as she can, and just like that, the wind sweeps up under them and behind, and it starts pushing her across the last stretch of water that separates her from everything that intrigues her: the palace, the city, Maman, Papa, her sisters. It is only a matter of time before she arrives.

Or so go some of the stories that are now told in the palace.

# AVA BINGEN

At last, fortune smiles in my direction—I have a lover! Not simply one who pumps me for pleasure and information, but a man who thinks of our life together. One who is not so nobly born as to be out of my reach, but then again not so humble that I won't feel it elevation to make a life with him. He knows my rank and still speaks softly, respectfully.

He also quotes poetry.

"'With what plant, or by what root, with which unguent or liqueur, could I succor a heart-wound that creeps bone to bone without cure?'" he asks, in that tone that indicates this is one educated man who is quoting another. "Pierre Ronsard," he adds, and then proceeds to explain the hidden artistic meaning till I want to weep. I would rather have a declaration plain and simple; I haven't listened to poetry since Jacob Lille.

But still, a suitor! A benefactor and a blessing. Arthur Grammaticus, the King's historian, has chosen me. I like him, and I am eager to fall in love—if cautious about tipping all the way into it.

I cannot help but make comparisons. Jacob was—is—much handsomer than this scholar, who is nearly thirty years old and balding under his hat. And Jacob taught me to be wary of love in all its forms, especially poetic ones.

After that first dreadful night, I seemed to see Grammaticus everywhere — certainly everywhere a royal was doing something. And his own small army, young men armed with tablets and styluses — someone is always recording events. To my surprise, he acknowledged me; he smiled and nodded. I smiled too. It was a gentle beginning to a sedate courtship; none of the excitement and passion of my first meeting with Jacob, but rather a kindness that hinted at comfort to come.

We meet in his paneled chamber or some stony corner of the courtyards. We embrace. His lips are soft, and over and over he presses them to my brows, my cheeks, my neck. My own lips.

His kisses coax the stories of my past, even my growing-up years. With just a few questions, I tell him about my mother's sweetness and my four mischievous brothers; how all of them died, one by one, during the Great Sickness when I was six. I describe the room we shared by Glasvand Kanal, in the house with the spectacled stone head; the feverish way the light jittered over the walls when we were too weak to close the shutters; and how when they'd been taken to a faraway green graveyard and only Father and I were left, that room became my bedchamber alone, and the light made me wake morning after morning to the memory of sweats and nausea and purges. I tell him about needle school and learning the stitches — satin, chain, couching, crosses, knots — and the hat I embroidered to help Father impress the King's astrologer.

"The constellations of the zodiac, with Cassiopeia, arranged to predict fortune for one born in Scorpio," I say.

"I've seen Stellarius wear it." Grammaticus nods approval. "It is fine work." He pats my fingers and assures me that soon I might hold a needle again. Soon — that means when Grammaticus has an audience with the King, who is more interested these days in reading the stars (through my father's device) than hearing the chronicles of his court that Grammaticus is compiling.

Grammaticus confides that he is composing more than one such tome. There are histories both official and unofficial — one of the court decrees and displays, and one of secrets that he keeps for himself; for as he says, secrets shape events even more than what is widely known. It is for this history of secrets and private lives that he wants my stories.

He is right about the importance of secrets. Of course I say nothing about my time with Lord Nicolas. And even as I hope to fall in love again, I hold my tongue about Jacob Lille. If he has other informants, Grammaticus probably knows that tale already and wants to hear one that hasn't already wound its way into the district mortar. Or, if I am very lucky, he doesn't know about Jacob at all, only about my liaison with Lord Nicolas: the story that I gave him, but not the rest of it, our unusual graspings and spendings. He doesn't seem to mind this part of my life. I think it intrigues him. He and Nicolas were nearly children together, on the green island where Nicolas's father had his lands. Nicolas was just enough older that when it was proposed that the two boys study together, as they were at the same stage in mathematics and languages, Nicolas refused to take lessons with him out of pride.

"Tell me about it," I say breathlessly, exhausted with my own talk and with a hammering in my heart. Grammaticus may know secrets about Nicolas that *I* can use. "Tell me about your island." I still have not seen a forest or even a large plain of grasses or a grave, only the kitchen gardens of the city.

So I find out who he is: Born to a gentleman of sorts, an estate holder married to the daughter of the old King's chamberlain, Arthur Rantzen (as he was known then) had a happy childhood. His family owned two good horses and enough money to educate their only son, who was marked out for scholarship from birth. He distinguished himself at the university of Sorö, which he finished at age seventeen (my age now!), then came to Skyggehavn to be the tutor of assorted merchants' sons and wards. His parents died somewhere along this way: his mother after childbirth, his father of apoplexy. They left debts; young Arthur was penniless.

He remembers the Great Sickness of 1561 as a time of opportunity, when he roamed the streets in his flapping black robe, writing of the various ways in which townspeople were stricken, recording their lives and deaths and the heroic prayers spoken in the chapels and cathedral. He liked the common people, respected their fears and lauded their courage. He thought a record of their thoughts would be of interest, perhaps a useful tool in governing them. So when the wave of Sickness receded, he used all his coins to bribe a guard to let him through the gates and into the presence of King Christian IV. He presented the aging King with his account and was shortly named court historian. It is a position that the current Christian has been happy to preserve and amplify, until Grammaticus achieved the distinction of a Latin name and the office of tutor to the Crown Prince (on those rare occasions when the Prince is well enough to be drilled in verbs and numbers). He has surpassed any of his family in education or influence; he believes he has even surpassed Nicolas in knowledge of the court.

I don't dare ask what he knows about Nicolas himself—another orphan (as rumor says) from that green island, the one who has recently been given the post of State Secretary. There's a bad taste in my throat when Arthur speaks of him. I ask instead for more about himself.

"But my life I know," he says modestly. "Let me have more of yours." He is ravenous for stories.

So I begin again. After months of loneliness, it is as if the episodes of my life are a hot spring; he moves one rock and lets them burst to join the flood of stories within him.

Also, he makes me wax ever more metaphoric, even though for once I'm not telling tales of witches and princesses.

"Do you wring these secrets from everyone?" I tease. "Will you use them for your chronicles?"

He says gravely, "I may," then takes my hand in his. The ink stains bleed from his fingers to mine, and I almost believe that somehow my thoughts and memories—mine, not those I observe among the courtiers or cobble together from gossip—will find their way into history.

Nicolas, meanwhile, seems to have given up his interest in me. My one tale of Countess Elinor has satisfied him—or else disgusted him; he does not send for me. Perhaps he doesn't need to, if he hears Grammaticus's reports. Or perhaps he fears what I might learn about him. He is in constant company of the King.

This should make me cautious with my suitor. It does.

At the end of each careful account, when my tongue is tired, Arthur strokes it with his tongue, presses my ribs to his ribs. But neither of us attempts to take our caresses further. We are both cautious in this way as well.

I imagine a conversation on the subject: *Why don't you make love to me as other men do?* I ask, and he answers, *I would very much like to do so.* He kisses me, and when I still hold back from passion, he asks, *Does your heart live elsewhere?* I think wistfully of Jacob Lille but hold my tongue, for don't I want — so badly — a new man, one who will not vanish? And I think it is a matter of time, then, for Grammaticus to keep courting me with poetry and metaphor, until I begin to like and trust it; and to allow himself a degree's further liberty at each meeting; until my heart expands to embrace him and my body follows, and we belong irredeemably to each other. Why not?

But this conversation does not take place. Grammaticus seems content to love me through my life's story and not its fleshy cushion.

Eventually I do ask, one evening in the courtyard, "Why don't you press for more?" and he answers, "Not till we can plan to marry."

I wonder if this is his version of a proposal. I feel a little sick. Glad, of course, but . . . Jacob. "How can we plan that?"

Grammaticus does not look at me, rubbing instead at the ink stains on his fingers. "We might plan it if I ask the King. He has to grant permission before any officer of the court is married."

"I thought that was required only for lords."

"And intimate functionaries. It would be a grave offense if I betrothed myself without asking His Majesty first, even if the bride brought me as much glory as you will." He takes an obvious pride in the thought of this potential offense, in being considered important enough to commit it. At the same time, I wonder how I'm supposed to reflect well on any man, and I worry that Nicolas has spoken to him. I am on the point of asking if he believes the reports that Nicolas killed the rest of the Bullens when Grammaticus adds, "I have to earn the right to a wife."

"Well," I say, "how can you earn it?" I think I'm more curious now than emotional; I want to know how the court works for men in his position. "What does the King want from you in particular?"

"From us," Grammaticus corrects, with an ink-smudgy tap on the point of my nose. "He wants good reports. Useful information. We must help him order his kingdom, from servants to seneschals. Make ourselves as indispensable to him as we are to each other." He hesitates, then says shyly, "You are precisely the wife I should have at court."

My practical part thinks his ambitions are too high—I can't imagine becoming indispensable to royalty, unless it is by means of information about Lord Nicolas that the man

182

himself would suppress. But I urge my more feeling side to take control, and I promise to do as my lover suggests. I allow myself to hope for that kind of power; it's the only way I'll replace the memories of Jacob Lille's spidery bed with those of another.

"Well, then," I say, "it's back to the nursery for me. I'll let you know what the children eat for dinner and how many of them vomit it back up."

"Yes." He nods earnestly. "Please do that."

Because she brought me to this man, who gives me the shimmery hint of a happy ending, I feel generous toward Midi Sorte. Perhaps I can look past her tongue to the woman inside. She seems quite nearly my age but must have seen far more in her life than I have. I think I might be her friend; she has no more friends than I do, meaning that each of us has just one and he's in common.

So, on an afternoon when we are both released from the nursery to sleep, and the early autumn chill is sharper than expected, I creep into her cot and pretend it is for coziness.

When she feels me next to her, she shudders like a caught fish. The bed straw crackles.

"It's hard to come from the nursery on a cold day," I explain chattily, "when we don't have the advantage of a fireplace here."

This is a week in which damp monthly cloths drip in a corner of the long dorter, *plink*ing into washbasins full of more rags put in to soak. It's not so cold that they freeze, though that does happen some nights.

Midi rolls onto her left shoulder, so she's perched on the very edge of the cot. She pulls up her blanket and nudges something toward me with her foot.

I look down. It's a stone, a warm one.

"How clever," I say. "You've heated a rock in the nursery fire and carried it here."

She stares at me so long, I really believe she is trying to speak to me with her eyes. I feel awkward, thinking how easy it is for me to waggle my tongue and make speech, when such a thing is impossible for her. I remember Lord Nicolas's threat—*But be careful elsewhere, or something might get your tongue*—and I ask, "Does it hurt?" I stick my own tongue out of my mouth and point to the tip. "Does it now, I mean—I'm sure it hurt when it happened . . ."

Midi Sorte sits up abruptly and pushes a long, hissing breath out of her nose. She grabs the stone from the bottom of the cot and heaves it into my hands.

"Saints and stars!" I drop the stone on the floor and blow on my palms. They have already turned a tender red.

Midi lies back and smiles. She holds up her hands, red palms toward me. Showing without words that she is not a person who lets herself feel pain.

I flee her cot for the one where I usually sleep, shared with a laundress who leaves a scent of onions and lye on the sheet but is otherwise unremarkable.

184

## MIDI SORTE

There were a time I had one tongue, and I used it to speak from red sky to red sky, a straight stream of talk that ran the length of the sun.

*Little girl, have a care,* said poison-auntie. *That tongue might tie you up in knots one day.* She give me honey to make my voice sweet, but there never were a sweetness in me. I prefer a taste of rot.

And so it happen. When poison-auntie die, and I run out the gate behind her body and wander to the docks; when the men see my oiled skin and gold arm-rings, they pounce and ask me, *What is your name? Who is your father? Where have you come from, fairy-child?*

I use my tongue to shout at them. I shout and call them names, I cry for some one to help. I cry for poison-auntie. They take the veil from my head and cram it in my mouth, and they tell me to be silent. But I think there be only danger in a silence, so I scream behind the cloth until my throat too raw for screaming. And it make no matter be cause I 'm loaded in a ship. One arm chained to the wall and the other to my feet.

I am sick for longer than I know.

And then come the sail-captain. He like to hear me scream, in the fog on the water that he say would take me to my fate. He take my bracelets. He take my clothes and lie me on his bed and roll his dirty coins over me, for he say I going to make him rich. That be *his* fate. He put coins on my eyes, in my ears, my nose, my mouth, and down below both front and back. He count them careful on the way in and out again, and hit me if they slow to return.

By time of the selling, I am use to being a coin-purse and too tired to scream. I watch him sell me; the coins are gold. I watch the next man swive me; I am too tired to feel it. He say that I taste sweet; he make me say his name. Some month later it be the last word I do say.

When his wife first hear it from me, she take out her knife. She drive it in the table between us, where I 'm shelling nuts to make a cream will beautify her skin.

"You are not to speak of him," she say.

And some thing in me, some thing small and stupid, make me say the name again.

She call her husband, have him hold my head while she take her curling tongs and pull my tongue. I cry to let her know it hurts. But this be not enough, she pick up the knife I were using. She start halfway, and she slice my tongue as if to make her dinner. I choke on blood. I vomit and it burns. I take to bed with fever and wish that it would kill me.

She seem to have some mercy then, or so her husband think. She give me salt and water to cure the wound, and

186

in one week she pull me from my bed. I return to dress her beauty.

*Now you are mine,* she say. *Now you will keep my secrets.*

It were true, he never want me after that. He look sick when ever he see me. And then he go to join the war and come back broken.

It is true too, I know her secrets now. And I never tell them, even to the ink and paper that I hide inside my bodice. But also I do n't forget how it feel to have a secret of my own, and a past, and think to shout it out with the power of poison.

Ava Mariasdatter is as the women who smile at poison-auntie while they plot to kill her. She bring a nest of hornets to my heart and I can not feel any but the sting.

But I know some things about her too. So I wrap the belt of Gorma's old wax doll around my wrist, for fortune, and I go to the King's new Secretary's closet. Some crowded, creaky wooden room in the main palace where I hand his man a paper: *There be some thing to tell you. From Countess Elinor's nurse Midi Sorte.*

There are not many people at court that can talk with out there be some one else in the room to observe. The King's Secretary, Count Nicolas Bullen, be one such person. He send out his servants and clerks so we are alone. And there is no thing for any one to hear any way, since every thing I say I must put on paper.

He do n't seem surprise to find I write. He read my words as if there be never a thing new in the world.

*Some one lie to you,* I write. My fingers jerk from hornets, and the letters wave across they page, but I get that sentence out. Then I know to wait in a way that make him ask me:

"Who? Who has lied?"

He behave as if he think this very amusing, the idea of a lie told him. But his eyebrows knit together, and his eyes burn like my father's when he trying to guess which of his wives betray him with a eunuch. I know from the Countess that he do n't like to be surprise. So there *is* some thing new after it all.

I write, *The needle you save from prison. The sewer you make a nurse.*

He do n't speak, wonder (I think) how I know all this. He can guess the name now, but I write it any way and get some pleasure: *Ava Bingen.*

Still he say no thing; he go as silent as I am. *That is fine,* I think, *I can wait as long as he for words.*

I hear a ticking in the wood upon his walls. Some thing dying with the start of autumn.

Finally he ask, "What, precisely, did she lie about?"

I smile, but inside, where he can not see. I write, *The arrest that make you Secretary. The lie that you make History. The Mistress whom you make misery.*

I wait a breath, in case he will say some thing. He do not. I write, *Ava invent her story to entertain you, but you take her for sincere. You punish the Countess, but you should punish Ava instead. She is an eel that slip through the ear and feast her self on brains.*

And now he know what I know. But he be not grateful

for it. He make some low grunt like an animal in the yard, and he grab at my skirt.

The hornets swarm my heart. I see what I have done.

I see it only, and only for one moment, cause be I do not let my self be my self while it happen. I close my eyes, I press both halves my tongue against my teeth. My hornets curl up tight.

He fuck me hard, this Secretary of the King. He do it from behind, with me on my knees like a cow. He have a lumpy thing that hurts. He spit on me to ease it in, but it go easy only for him. He do n't take the usual way, go far back instead, where I feel every knob and every tear they open in me. He want me to hurt.

Arthur tell me once that this man he knew from child hood be odd about his prick. That he sew stones inside to bring him pleasure, bring him health. Now I do believe, the nobles do mystery every day.

And now. No such mystery, more of what come all ways.

When he done, the thing be sticky in my blood, and blood drip off the lumps that move beneath his skin. It drip down over Me.

He wipe it and me off with a linen, then throw the linen in the fire with the papers I have written for him. He can not burn that smell, though. Every body who enter this room will know it.

He smile at me, sharp teeth, eyes be coals.

I straight my clothes and hate Ava Mariasdatter as if she be the devil's servant instead of the Secretary's. And as if I believe in devils.

"As far as anyone on the other side of that door knows," he tell me as he close him self up, "this was the only reason you came here today. If you let on differently, or if you cannot keep your thoughts to yourself, there will be much worse for you. You will think me gentle in comparison to your jailers."

I touch the doll belt and tell the hornets go there, leave my heart alone.

He crunch a savor-almond in his teeth and toss me one too. "Clean your breath," he say. "Your secrets have the foulest smell."

I eat. It is delicious. I hate that it is so.

# PRAYER

NE morning it comes: a miracle or a curse.
Today it is not just ladies-in-waiting
but nurses, maids, and even dwarfs who
stand at the stinking hollow's uncertain
edge. The Queen, much occupied in the
nursery, has ordered them to pray loudly enough for her to
hear; and this they do, their voices settling into the monotony
of Saint Peter's monks, till the words blur together:

*Ave-Maria-gratia-plena-Dominus-tecum-benedicta-tu-in-
mulieribus-et-benedictus-fructus-ventris-tui* . . .

They are strangely feverish, as suspenseful as they are
bored. A few of them feel something is about to happen, something more than the usual gossip of pregnancies and Italian
Fire. They grab one another's hands.

Their intuition is proved right. A skinny wench who
works in the kitchens makes a sudden movement, cries out,
and points:

There, in the center of the hollow. Something is not being
sucked away but rather spat up. Something that emerges first
as a yellow tip, then a jointed stalk, finally a silver base with a
lump of muddy green on one side. This item pops through the
surface and floats upon it full length. It spins slowly around, as
if pointing at one lady, one girl, after another.

Some of the women are struck silent with terror. Several of them shriek. Two run away. Only one, that same Negresse lately linked in rumor with Count Nicolas Bullen, dares kneel down at the edge of the hollow and reach for this slowly spinning thing.

"She will die of the attempt," whispers Lady Drin, in a mixture of horror and delight. These have been long, dull weeks, and the death of a nurse would make a change.

The Negresse snags the thing between two fingers but cannot get her balance to stand. She struggles as if she's about to be sucked away herself. A nursery maid has to haul on the Negresse's apron strings to help her stand. She does this more out of curiosity for the thing discovered than from desire to save a life.

When she is on her feet, the Negresse calmly (for this one never does anything but calmly) uses a clean spot on her apron to wipe the object dry. She holds it up and invites the women to guess at it.

"A fingertip!" exclaims the young Countess Ditlevnavn.

The women gasp. A dwarf vomits on her own skirts. It is clearly true; this is a finger removed below the second knuckle. But to whom does it belong? Perhaps the key is in the tight little ring at bottom.

"Princess Sophia?" asks Bridget Belskat, whose pock-marked lack of beauty has made her ever shy but eager to participate in events. "One of her wedding emeralds?"

Lest anyone doubt this, the Negresse turns it over.

"There is the scar from her baptism," says Lady Drin, "when she grabbed the priest's amulet and cut herself."

The maids sink to their knees, praying for heaven's protection. The ladies scatter: one to tell the Queen, another to the King, a third to Lord Nicolas Bullen.

The black nurse stands still. The yellow object lies flat across her palm; the green stone winks under a suddenly bright sky.

In the court at large, superstition takes over. Now everyone from lord to lackey is preoccupied with magic, with the idea that Sophia is coming back bit by bit. They decide there is some spell against her and all the Lunedie children. They accuse Countess Elinor Parfis not merely of a physical poisoning but of a deep magical one. Or else they believe Sophia herself is casting spells from beyond the grave. Some say she will piece herself together and destroy the court. The finger thus transforms the dead princess from an angel and a Perished Lily to a demon, a wraith, against whom all souls must protect themselves.

Now everyone with a portrait of Sophia scratches it out, plasters over the wall, and repaints to rid the house of her. Even fine gentlemen turn their shoes over at bedtime, so the spirits don't use them at night. Out on the cathedral square, there is a brisk trade in amulets and other tokens against evil.

In this, the people go too far. The King issues a proclamation of disapprobation, and he punishes any amulet sellers who seem too blatantly to evoke the Wraith Princess as a threat.

But there has always been a traffic in saints' medals, and good Catholic sovereigns cannot outlaw those; nor can the King's guardsmen examine every trinket that is for sale.

Christian V can, however, order the monks of Saint-Peter's-on-the-Isle to open Sophia's tomb and make sure a finger is missing. The three physicians—Candenzius, Venslov, and Dé—oversee the exhumation, standing tense while the monks push the marble slab off the sarcophagus.

They find the coffin filled with soup. Rotten flesh, chemicals, slivered bones and loops of entrails glistening with what might be a shining silvery insect—might be just a vision, for it flees the light and burrows into the macerated flesh.

Young Doctor Dé is aghast at what dissection has wrought. He prays aloud for his eternal soul. Old Doctor Venslov, with a sly air of self-righteousness, asks which one of them would like to put his own hand into the mess and hunt for Sophia's.

Doctor Candenzius says, "*I* believe that what was found could be the Princess's finger."

The other two agree. They order the tomb closed without touching its contents and row speedily back to the palace. The crypt will reek for months, sickening several of Saint Peter's monks unto death.

Back in their laboratory, the physicians examine the object fished from the witch's hollow. They conclude that it is indeed flesh and of Sophia's body (at the moment, they could not conclude otherwise) but that the ring is a fake—for it is not a real emerald but one made of glass, and not very well. When they announce as much, there is a general ripple of shock, that

Duke Magnus of Östergötland, mad as he once was, would give his bride a false stone. King Christian and Lord Nicolas compose a letter of sternly worded hints to Sweden. They do this without checking the treasury records that indicate all Swedish emeralds were returned; but that is not important, for Mad Magnus will not bother with the letter anyway, being much involved in celebrating the birth of an illegitimate daughter born of a longtime mistress, and in devising a clever system of nets and pulleys to trap the next mer-girl who swims into his moat.

With the identification of the finger, Queen Isabel's spirit is exhausted. She retreats to the grand bed in her state chamber and refuses to leave, claiming grief and the trials of pregnancy. But she also feels a tremendous sense of hopefulness. From the blood-red folds of drapery, she questions the Negresse who plucked the finger from the mud.

Did the sun shine in a special way? Did her head fill with heavenly voices? What gave her such strength and bravery as to collect it? Did the finger leap toward her hand? Did it feel warm or cold? Is she *sure*?

To every question, the Negresse shrugs and smiles. As far as the court knows, she has no other way to communicate. She curtsies very daintily, and the Queen scratches at her ears. Her brain is niggled by a dim memory of this girl, all but naked, coated in crystals that gave the air a sweetness . . .

The Negresse folds her hands together and turns her eyes skyward. The Queen begins to believe—dares to believe— that she is in the presence of a miracle.

Isabel orders that her scarlet taffeta underskirt, now stored in a warehouse, be found and given to this girl. On further thought, she adds, "And a white satin bodice. It will look well on her."

Of course the Queen herself is far stouter than the Negresse. But clothing can easily be remade.

Negresse forgotten, Isabel pushes up and declares herself ready to visit the nursery. "And send for a goldsmith. I will have him make a box to hold Sophia's finger." *A reliquary,* she adds to herself with pleasure. Decorated with jewels — real jewels, not the glass given Sophia by Duke Magnus. "And bring me the finger itself. I will take charge of it — not the physicians."

Isabel's maids and ladies curtsy, all of them. Furtively, the Queen takes advantage of the moment to scratch her swelling breasts, where the skin tingles with a constant itch.

Duchess Margrethe sends a lady to ask the King if he approves of this means of handling the finger. He does.

## AVA BINGEN

I was not there when the finger appeared, when Midi Sorte became a heroine and a favorite to the Queen. I seem to be present, though, whenever Midi wears the skirt that hisses like a barrel of snakes, its red shine shaming the dull russet serge of nursery workers. She likes to flaunt this evidence that the Queen now loves her. That she, Midi, has been the vehicle by which God sent Isabel a miracle. She wears it to the kitchens to eat; she wears it in the nurseries when Isabel is expected. Other times, it sits beneath her cot in a plain wooden box.

When Queen Isabel enters the nursery, she looks at Midi with a vague, kind expression usually reserved for her children themselves. The skirt gives a high howl of triumph as Midi curtsies.

The other nurses glower. If this has been a miracle, why was Midi chosen for it? Midi, with her split tongue and her prickly lack of kindness.

Much is said and not-said on this subject. I report it all to Grammaticus—Lord Nicolas still hasn't summoned me again, and anyway I would tell Arthur, my lover, anything first. I am happy to avoid Nicolas; I am glad to tarnish Midi's name.

But he isn't interested in discussing Midi. "Why should the others be jealous?" he asks, not even bothering to look up from some paper or other that he's covering with ink (my visit was unplanned). "No one would covet her reputation as you describe it. Or her life. Or herself." He scratches out a word with a penknife — cuts all the way through the page. "She is nothing. *Nothing.*"

I am confused; she was the one who brought me to him. "But the skirt —"

His ears are turning red as if in fury, though I am here only to help. "It will be destroyed soon enough in her daily chores. And you will have a prettier one someday."

He puts his pen down then and starts to kiss me with an air that I might call dutiful, but I resist. "Do *you* think it was a miracle?" I ask. "Or was it something else? The finger, I mean."

Grammaticus sighs and scratches his beard, then removes his spectacles and rubs impatiently at the red spots on the bridge of his nose. "Men far more learned than I," he says, "have spent years debating just what a miracle is. Suffice it to say that my report for the chronicles mentions only that a finger appeared and was determined to be Sophia's, and the Queen was very much pleased."

He picks up his pen again, wipes it on his sleeve as if preparing to write the observation down this very minute. I catch his hand and make my eyes large and wheedling. "You said that one day I will have a prettier skirt than Midi's. Have you any idea when I might find the occasion to wear it?"

Even a shy scholar knows quite well what I am asking.

"I can't trouble the King with my personal affairs at this moment. He is at a difficult point in his reign," he says shortly. "All Catholic sovereigns are. Just last month, the French king and his Italian mother slaughtered hundreds of Huguenot Protestants. The gutters of Paris ran red—on Saint Bartholomew's Day, no less."

I could observe that it is always the day of some saint or other, and that the French are known for their tempers, but tart remarks lessen a wife's appeal. "Why should that bother our Christian?" I ask instead, meekly, as if I am always interested in political discussion.

Grammaticus lets go of my hand to toy with his pen, rolling it lightly in his fingers. "No one wants a reputation for cruelty. Only for stern justice. If the lords of this country use the French massacre as an opportunity to denounce the corruption of the Church—and to try to seize some of the more democratic powers of Protestantism for themselves—our King could have another war to fight. There's no money in the coffers for it, and no fresh supply of soldiers and commanders . . ."

*Jacob Lille,* I think. What if the land became safe for Protestants and he came back? I recall the faint piney sweetness of amber, feel the straw and spiders beneath my knees, see the house we were to have one day . . .

I must not trade in *what ifs.* I pick up one of Arthur's big, bony hands and place it on my shoulder. I am fond of him in this moment. He is, *may* be, my salvation. But this is not the moment for caresses or fondness. Arthur has a chronicle to write. He sweeps me from his room with a flap of his long black sleeves.

\* \* \*

I step into sunshine, with a tawny slant that hints already at autumn. September. Dodge some butchers with a skinned sheep for tomorrow's eating, step around a crowd of ladies bound for chapel, enter the bustling hive that is the royal wing. And see my father.

Klaus Bingen, tall and beetling-browed, trails a robe with the charcoal smell of fresh black dye. As all of us do on early forays inside, Father has cocked his head back to gape at the frescoes, the tapestries and paintings, the ornamented ceilings, and the splendid garments of nobles who teeter about on pattens that raise them inches higher even than he is. His lenses reflect all of these splendors, while his rabbity apprentice (gawking also) sags under the weight of a leather-bound box.

Father does not recognize his only living child until I am, quite literally, on top of him. "Ava," he says mildly, as if I am barely an acquaintance. His mind is on other things. "Health to your soul."

"And to yours." I am out of sorts, smarting from rejection. "What brings you here? Are you looking for me?"

"I'm on my way to see Stellarius," Father says proudly.

"His chamber isn't in this wing; it's in —"

"*And* the King's Secretary." Klaus Bingen looks likely to burst with pleasure. "We're meeting in Lord Nicolas Bullen's apartments. To talk about the new observatorium, you know."

"For looking at the stars," the apprentice pipes up, as if I haven't known my father's business this last decade. The boy must be proud too; instead of learning the relatively simple craft of grinding lenses for spectacles, he is taking on the grander challenge of reaching the heavens.

"I have with me"—Father gestures at the box the apprentice is barely holding—"a selection of lenses for a new perspective glass. And small silvered mirrors, which I have discovered can reflect and magnify the light shed by stars . . ."

Father runs on, rehearsing the speech he will deliver to astrologer and secretary. I think how stunned and pleased he will be when he hears that I, too, have a special connection at court—not with Lord Nicolas, for I am trying to forget him, and hoping he does not connect Ava Mariasdatter with this eager artisan—but with the King's chief scholar and chronicler of all important events in the land. How Father would beam if he knew that we are to be married someday.

I lose myself in dreams of the wedding ceremony—wax tapers, a new gown, my mother's amber bracelet glowing on my wrist . . . Father and Sabine gazing on at their proudest moment, Sabine perhaps clutching the swell of her belly; for I would like the wedding to come soon, before the new heir to the Bingens pops out.

So what prevents me from sharing my good news? Why can't I bring myself to stop the churn of Father's words and toss a few well-chosen pebbles in to hear the splash? Is it the flow of court traffic around us, is it the rabbity apprentice, is it . . . something else?

Doubt. I fear that Father will doubt this betrothal, that he will expect me to be jilted again. Arthur has not explicitly proposed to me, has not even met my father, has not even asked to meet him.

And at last, I admit it to myself: *I* doubt that this marriage will really come to be. Or, rather, I still lack entire faith, which is almost the same as doubting. Faith in ink-stained Grammaticus! Who could fail to trust a scholar and a historian? But when I see my husband turning toward me in my mind, his face is not Arthur's. And it is followed by a cramp in the stomach that recalls my too-public miscarriage. And the memory of my awful hours with Lord Nicolas.

I must stop my thoughts from running away.

"How is Sabine progressing?" I ask abruptly.

I listen awhile to Father's plans for his new heir and Sabine's lying-in; until a note from the cathedral clock reminds him of his appointment, and he and the little apprentice scuttle off.

I return to the nursery's royal whimpers, to quiet them with tales told in whispers beneath the gilded branches and glass leaves; to hope to weave these stories into, again, a new future. *AVA*.

*When the duke's new wife stepped into the chamber of the black key, she found there were indeed secrets inside. Ragged, ashy secrets: they clung like bats to the rafters, crept like lizards up the walls, seeped like beetles from cracks in the floorboards.*

*As the dark things came chittering greedily toward her, the princess tried to think of a secret of her own that might shield her—but no, she was a young girl much protected, with no conscience-stricken wraith inside to do battle.*

*The duke's secrets swarmed over his bride, gnawing her soft flesh and burrowing into her most intimate parts. From here on, they would live and grow within her.*

*The princess felt all the pain of this, but she also felt a pleasure: she had come to her marriage a true innocent, and at last she, too, had something to hide.*

# COMMON PARLANCE

ERHAPS even a Negresse who was once a slave and now is known to have trafficked with the King's Secretary—perhaps especially such a person—is entitled to secrets. But one who taught her to write is also entitled; he may question her. He may stand her at the desk where he first put a pen in her hand, and he may set paper before her, and he may insist that she answer him.

In some questions, he echoes the Queen. "What *did* you think when you saw the finger emerge from the mud?"

She slits her eyes, keeps the lids smooth. She writes, *I thought there be some power at work after all.*

"'After all'?"

*After all the ugly that has happen. After all the medicine and madness and sorrow.*

"So you believed right away that this was the finger of Princess Sophia?"

*I was not who said it were Sophia's. I was not who saw it first. I only plucked it when the others were afeared.*

"You believe it might have belonged to someone other than the Princess?"

She thinks for a moment. Or, rather, wants to give the impression of thinking; she probably has her answer ready all along.

*Fate have a finger. Such is an expression of this land.* She looks up between long black lashes, a look she has used to advantage in the past. She puts down the pen.

There is one more question—unrelated, perhaps improper, but even a questioner guided by reason cannot prevent every emotion from bubbling up:

"Why did you go to the King's Secretary? Why did you seek him out? Why did you—converse with him?"

Sometimes even a man of letters betrays emotion.

At this, however, her eyes shutter down. She puts her hands behind her back as if to say she will not pick up the pen again, under any circumstances. She takes a deep breath, then two, and looks at her questioner. Her eyes are hard as stones.

He must ask: "Is this some scheme? Did Nicolas Bullen tell you to discover this object and call it Sophia's? Did he give you the ring to put on it?"

Slowly she brings her hands around to the front again. She picks up the pen. She writes, *He tell me no thing. You tell me no thing. I say no thing, but I see every thing. Every thing.*

It is impossible not to feel frustration, not to say, "But why Lord Nicolas? Midi, you knew I would have protected you—though we could obviously never marry—all your life, I would have watched over you, no matter what else became of me . . ."

She writes, *I know you. You be no better than any lord who swive among the aprons. You betray.*

With the flourish of a duchess, she gathers her red skirts around her in a knot, ready to go.

He, the scholar, accepts frustration and defeat. He gathers up the sheets on which she has written, then drops them on the brazier that heats the room.

From the doorway, she stares. The pages flare into a flame as long as an arm.

If she could speak, she would say she hates him.

If he dared speak, in spite of everything, he would voice a different feeling.

# AUTUMN

HE bells ring again in October. They ring all the way through the season of leaves falling and flowers curling into the earth, night skies beaming green swathes of light that fuddle Stellarius — what the Queen fancifully calls the River of Angels and the commoners know as fairies' flares.

The bells ring for change of season. They ring for death.

First it is Princess Amalia. Then Princess Margrethe. By Hendrika's turn, death is no longer a surprise; the princesses are perishing like the winged insects of summer. They go in the manner of Sophia, with a grand convulsion and a host of frightened witnesses; or they go quietly, mewling their way into eternal sleep, to be recognized by a single nurse who wakes from her pallet when her own bladder's full and the girl's body cold.

The princesses, never pretty in life, are hideous in death, with faces mottled red and purple. Eyes bulge and mouths gape as if astonished at what lies beyond the curtain that separates this world from the next. It is to be hoped that their spirits are granted a new beauty and vigor, that they travel that highway of northern lights into a kingdom where they will be free of pain.

First, a few final attentions to what is left behind. King Christian cannot bear to order more dissections; nor does he think them of use. Ladies prepare the bodies for display with thick layers of white lead paint and scarlet cochineal (a powdered beetle) for the lips. A nursemaid sews their lips and eyes shut with a delicate chain stitch; others wrestle them into splendid silk dresses. When the bodies are displayed in the smoky cathedral, courtiers file dutifully past and remark on the girls' loveliness, the land's loss. Among themselves, occasionally, they admit to feeling a chill when they pass the sarcophagi.

Coincidentally—eerily and alarmingly to some—there is a rash of pregnancies among the ladies. Four of the Queen's attendants announce that in a few months' time they will have to leave her service to devote themselves to their bellies. Privately they pray that *Morbus Lunediernus* will not leave a lasting impression in their quickening wombs; that the dead princesses have not taken up residence there, to burst forth with strange powers and angers.

The King, grief-struck and yet bored with grief, sends for a new doctor from Poland and, for good measure, a new astrologer from France. Both recommended by Lord Nicolas, whom Christian V is thinking of creating a count so he might sit closer at table.

King Christian orders that this time, rather than sorrowing over the losses, the court should offer up thanks that the Prince has not been taken (*or not yet,* as some mutter under their breath). Courtiers spend hours each day on their knees, praying that the boy will not pass. Some even pray for the remaining two girls, ten-year-old Beatte and little Gorma.

Christian is attacked by worsening pains in his gut. He spends much time on his close-stool. He weeps, but only in private. Lord Nicolas attends him.

Ambassadors and councillors keep busy with the mundanities of death. Letters go out on ships to Lithuania, Iceland, and Saxony: alliances by betrothal are regretfully broken, wishes expressed for continued peace and mutual benefit. The monks of Saint-Peter's-on-the-Isle keep up a constant chant that's heard at the palace when the foul-smelling wind blows west: *Dominus tecum, Dominus tecum.*

In the south wing of the royal quarters, the nursery is an echoing place. Now the silver walls and golden branches gleam around the remaining children as a menace rather than a comfort; the delicate glass leaves shatter in the slightest breath. In their suddenly enormous animal beds, young Christian, Gorma, and Beatte keep up a high, piercing whine; they fear the physicians, they fear the shards and shadows cast by falling leaves, they even (sometimes) fear each other. They wake from terrible day-dreams and are impossible to comfort.

Most of all, they fear their mother. For Queen Isabel has become a wraith herself. She haunts the nurseries, keening over the empty swan beds, which she will not have removed. She wears black and gray; she shreds her own clothing. When she kisses her children, her breath smells like the tomb. She is said to eat nothing but milk pudding, in a complicated mourning for all she has lost. Her belly grows around the newest Lunedie.

One night Isabel is discovered sleeping in Hendrika's former swan, though it is not known how she got there. When elderly Duchess Margrethe bends in to wake her, the Queen is disoriented. She seems to think the swan is in some sense her protector, that it is bearing her over the sea to a beautiful garden where she and her children will stroll amid shrubbery and paddle about in pleasure boats. She calls the poor, ugly Duchess a gargoyle spouting urine.

The King orders Isabel dosed for tranquillity and confined to her rooms for the good of the baby within. He allows her favorite physician, Candenzius, to attend her. He refuses her request to receive a visit from Elinor Parfis, whose crimes she has somehow forgiven amid so much sorrow — or whom she wishes to murder outright; no one is sure.

The Queen yields despondently to Candenzius's thick fingers. He declares (somewhat desperately, for he dreads the impending addition to the physicians' ranks) that the baby is progressing well. He spreads salve on her cracking skin.

Theories, or rather speculations, take form elsewhere. The Danish and Swedish ambassadors opine, in what they believe to be a secret conference, that the cause is purely a disease of the blood, that the Lunedies are tainted and should be eliminated from the rest of Europe's bloodlines. This conversation is reported to Christian V, who relegates the ambassadors to disgracefully low seats at the grieving feasts. Members of some secret Protestant sects believe the cause of death is papist corruption; they use the princesses' demise as pretext to scatter handbills agitating for a reformed Church. Further arrests come as a result; the prisons grow crowded.

Countess Elinor's friends (she still has a few, as well as her half-dead husband) clamor for her release, as she cannot possibly be responsible for so many poisonings from the Lower Chambers. Her enemies claim she commands a network of conspirators who carry out her orders aboveground; some again suggest that she is a witch and that her poisonings are magical rather than physical. Her attendants and her comb (the latter inexplicably) are taken away.

Some sanguine courtiers believe, still, that there is simply a chord struck wrong in the music of the spheres that wheel above the palace, and that eventually all will be put right. The husbands of the gravid ladies-in-waiting congratulate each other and speculate that someday their own offspring might take the place of one or the other of the Lunedie children.

Stellarius draws chart after chart, as if he expects to find something new in the swelling nights. He finds nothing. He is wedded to truth and cannot invent new configurations, even under threat of replacement.

The three physicians, by contrast, are trained for imagination. Working against time, they spend their nights devising new possets and unguents. They have the Queen squat over a brazier burning rhinoceros dung and nightingale livers, that the smoke might calm the baby inside her. They grind up gold and rubies and pepper, narwhal horn and dolphin bone to be mixed with myrrh and the oil of the common house cat. They plaster the concoction onto the chests of the remaining girls and boy and bind it there with linen.

The children break out in new boils, red and burning, shimmering with the hint of greasy gold. Candenzius declares that this is a healthful sign; the poisons are leaving the children's bodies. He prescribes valerian and poppy to stop their weeping.

Fewer children mean fewer duties for nurses and maids, who begin to linger voluntarily with a mix of excitement and fear around the great chancre of the witch's bed in the inner courtyard. They are waiting for new bits of Princess Sophia to appear. They believe that she climbs up through the muck at night to claim her sisters and brother; if they can catch her, they can stop the deaths. So they stand at the ready, armed with kitchen knives and hairpins. They think to be rewarded for their bravery.

Yet again the King orders his engineers to find a way to drain the hollow and pave the ground over. The hole only grows larger.

# CHRISTIAN V

ICOLAS, the man who replaced Sir Georg Oline in office and more than surpassed him in importance; the man who stands beside Christian while he grunts and sweats his hour upon the stool; the man about whom Christian has such dark dreams night after night. Nicolas, the man in whose body Christian wants to lose himself.

"Your Majesty," Nicolas asks delicately one evening, "have you considered what is to be done with Countess Elinor? Should she be *put to the question?*"

Willem Braj has dared to hint that before Elinor Parfis became Sir Georg's lover, she was Nicolas's. But surely that is impossible. Surely such a kind man would not insinuate that his former lover ought to be tortured. Although, as Christian is discovering, everything about love itself is torture.

"No," he says, firm. "I will not approve doing that to a countess." He hates the very idea, as much as he hates the thought of Nicolas coupling with that milk-white woman. "Not yet. She sent me a pillow embroidered with a cat." He waits out a pain, then adds, "I gave it to my wife."

Christian thinks over the long list of problems facing his reign: the suffering children, a Protestant colony on one of the green islands, the eternal question of Sweden. The coffers' depletion after a full summer's residence in Skyggehavn, without recourse to the remunerative hospitality of country lords. Of course, that particular problem comes of the children's illness and the Queen's insistence on caring for them herself. In the last weeks, he and Nicolas have discussed these topics until Christian is sore from sitting on what is not so comfortably padded a stool after all.

Christian says, as if continuing one of these discussions, "Isabel is a worry to me."

"Oh?" Nicolas stands slim and straight and appears genuinely curious, as if it has not occurred to him to wonder about Christian's wife. "Your Majesty?"

Christian sighs heavily and the stool shifts beneath his weight; one of the wood slats grinds against its neighbor and makes a popping sound. Nicolas waits.

At last Christian admits it: "My wife is not what she should be."

"She is with child, Your Majesty. Most fortunately for all of us."

How generous Nicolas is.

"I mean more that . . . It is true a woman with a belly is not herself, but this exceeds any explanation." Christian has an image of Isabel scratching herself, filling her fingernails with cakes of dead skin. She has no awareness of decorum. "I once did suspect she might be poisoned along with the children, but when Countess Elinor was arrested, the Queen got no better."

Nicolas gives this some thought. "Perhaps she was

poisoned, but not by the Countess. Perhaps she and Georg Oline have accomplices—as we might discover if we—"

"Perhaps there is no poison at all," Christian interrupts. "Perhaps it is only grief that infects her. She was exceedingly fond of our Sophia, as was I. And the other children, of course."

Nicolas is deferentially silent, allowing Christian to think over the idea of grief-sickness. Ultimately, he rejects it, sighs, and motions for the sponge. This time with Nicolas, helpful as it might be, is over for the evening.

Nicolas dips the sponge in the cup of vinegar water but holds it just out of reach on its stick. He smiles, a beautiful sharp smile with gleaming white teeth. "No doubt Your Majesty knows best. No one is better acquainted with the Queen than you."

Christian feels Nicolas's fingers wrapping around his wrist, pulling him upward. It is much easier to stand, even half naked, with Nicolas's strength behind him. Christian discovers a kind of pride in his vulnerability, and a great sense of hope. He remembers the motto on his coat of arms: *In tenebris lumen meum metue.* In the darkness, fear my light. With Nicolas, he feels stronger. He feels light.

## AVA BINGEN

In these strange days of dying children and troubled Queen, it is perhaps not surprising that the rest of us feel sicker than usual. I, for one, am afraid to eat anything, lest it come back up and give others the impression that I am falling sick or have a poison in me that should lead to some physician's explorations. I am afraid to speak lest words bring the same result. And I am afraid to scheme, because there's more danger than advancement in trying to bring Nicolas down, especially now. I starve in so many ways.

Not so with Midi Sorte. When I retire to the dorter one wet morning, I find her on her knees, vomiting into one of the basins in which we wash our personals. She's alone except for a scrub maid sleeping on one of the far cots, snoring as if to make a point.

Midi is not like the rest of us. I've never seen her even so much as blow her nose before. Now she chokes and gasps, tears pouring from her eyes; she is fighting it, hates this weakness in herself. Her cap has come off, and her hair is loose. I'm surprised to find it's so long; it's even supple enough to slide over her shoulders and toward the foul basin.

Midi does not like me, and I don't think so much of her. But she obviously needs help, and I cannot ignore her. I go and take her hair in my hands.

It is soft, oiled, a strange texture to someone used to combing the thin yellow strands of this country. I wind it around my hand and hold it at the base of Midi's skull, and I put my left palm against her forehead to cool it. She shudders, but she lets me help her.

When she seems to have finished heaving, I fetch a drying cloth and help her wipe her face, and I tie back her hair with a cord.

Of course, Midi does not thank me. She cannot. But she continues to accept my attentions, much as if she were one of the little princesses. Quiet, docile, childlike.

"Are you better?" I ask, since it's strange that there should be no talk at all.

She spits a little, like a man on the street. Then she nods.

I believe she's dismissing me, but I inquire to be kind, "Do you think you've eaten something bad?"

She shakes her head.

I am stroking her arm now—her sleeve's ridden up, and her skin is so soft, though dark. I am amazed that she allows this much, but she even leans a little bit against me.

"Is there something else?" I ask, as if there would be any way for her to answer me. "Something you want?"

She gets up then, pushes herself off the floor, and staggers away from me. I sit for a moment ablaze with foolishness, embarrassed at again having made a friendly gesture and being rebuffed. And tired; it is my sleeping time.

But Midi comes back. And she has a piece of paper, once crumpled but now smoothed out, and a stick of charcoal. She sits down beside me and her reeking basin, and she writes—she writes!

It takes me a long moment to sort Midi's letters into a word.

*G, R, A . . .*

A speechless Negresse, a slave and former servant of Elinor of Belnát—she can write. And I can barely parse the alphabet.

She is writing the name of the man I think of as mine.

"What about him?" I snatch the charcoal from her hand, then put it back when I remember she needs it to answer.

She leans over and vomits again, a thin, clear stream.

When she is finished and I have again wiped her face, Midi rolls the charcoal stick between her fingers. She's growing back to her stiff old self; that sly, hateful smile-that-is-not-a-smile creeps over one side of her face.

*P, O, X.*

I pull back. "What does that mean?"

*ON YOU.*

Her hand continues to move down the page, filling it up with more wavery black marks. But I refuse to look at anything she might write now; I stand and shake out my skirts and draw myself up like Countess Elinor. I even give a nudge to my bosoms. "I'm glad to see you're feeling well enough to curse me. And now I hope you'll be more careful what you eat."

I am not unaware that this could be interpreted as a threat to poison her; but I am rather proud of it. I walk away, shrug off my clothing down to my shirt, and climb into my own little cot. I close my eyes and don't watch what Midi does next. But as I tell myself to go to sleep, I see her black letters smearing across my eyelids: *G, R, A . . .*

There are many wrongs at court, it is true. One of those wrongs, surely, is that Midi Sorte can write and I cannot. And that I can guess, now, who taught her. Imagine the two of them bent over a table, passing a stylus or a pen back and forth, smiling as she mastered each letter. And when began words and sentences, perhaps something more—a kiss such as a mother gives a child who has just learned to speak, or a kiss such as Grammaticus gives me?

Does he read her stories and observations as he listens to mine?

Jealousy stabs my gut again and again, until I think I might be sick myself.

## MIDI SORTE

Sick.

I wish this to Ava Mariasdatter, who pretend kindness to capture some of me. I wish on her *pox,* and she be afraid. I smile to make her more so.

While she walk away, I am sick again. She stay gone.

I take my bowl to the jakes and leave it. This palace have plenty of scrub-maids to take it away. I go back to my cot in the room with two snoring girls, and I get in and curl up around my nasty stomach. I ask some questions of it.

First, *What are you?* And then be cause I can not stand to answer now, *What be locked in the skin of Nicolas' prick?*

The best magic come from ordinary things, like an old bone and a wax doll and a scrap of glove that together become the holy relic of a princess. Or the same finger bone that turn to a sign of evil in the court. Such a trick bring power to the one who make it.

And also danger, as with poison-auntie. Who all ways knew what should be done with a belly, what ever did make it sick.

Any body recognize what some things mean. Any body who be not stupid. To vomit, to swell in the bosom, to stop with bleeding.

*G, r, a, v, i, d.*

Pox is not the worst that 's in me.

# Hydrargyrum

T is through Nicolas that Christian finds the doctor who, at last, solves (or says he solves) the mystery of the children's ailment. And it is only because this doctor has come through Nicolas that Christian considers believing his diagnosis, not clapping the man in the darkest oubliette in the foulest corner of the prison.

His name is Josef Krolik—no Latinate moniker—and thus far he has been employed by an assortment of towns and barons, recommended by a minor lord who has thought of marrying his daughter to Nicolas.

This Krolik, whose name in Polish means "rabbit," arrives in a humble bark, in a plain black robe, with the merest of medical essentials rattling in his bag. He has a large head and thin body, a big nose and drooping eyelids. His teeth are yellow and small.

With the King, the Queen, the physicians, Count Nicolas (yes, Christian V has ennobled him further), other council members, and the usual attendants, Doctor Krolik visits the Crown Prince in the day nursery. Leaning over the wooden haunch of the lion bed, he strokes the boy's sweaty pink cheek. Young Christian's eyes open, wearily and without interest, as if a visit is being paid to someone else, not to him.

Krolik moves a finger slowly in front of the Prince's face; the brown eyes follow listlessly. Krolik lifts the princely hand and flaps the arm attached, and young Christian moans. Flakes of the boy's skin fall away like feathers; two of his toenails are missing. Krolik listens to the lark-fast beat of his heart and pronounces aloud:

*"Hydrargyrum."*

When no one reacts but the physicians (who stiffen), Krolik clarifies. "Mercury. Quicksilver. There is your poison."

"On the contrary, it . . . is our cure," says Doctor Candenzius. "It is well known to draw infection out of the body, to strengthen the blood and quicken the heart—"

"In moderation," says Krolik. "When used heavily, it is poison. What matters is the amount of the dose."

There is a collective intake of breath, then a silence. These words are recognizable to all. Candenzius, after all, has been quoting Paracelsus on this subject since he arrived over a year ago: *Every substance can be a poison; only the dose determines.*

The quiet is particularly intense among the nursery staff; the air between them seems to crackle. Each of them has touched mercury. They use it every day. It has been part of the *Morbus* protocol for a year and a half, designed by Candenzius and—

With a moan, the Queen swoons.

The King, sick with love for Nicolas, wanting and yet not wanting this physician his Count has found to be of help; thinking of his own family, his throne, and the future, says, "It cannot be so."

Doctor Krolik turns to the long-standing physicians, Candenzius, Venslov, and Dé. "Do you pretend you have not suspected it?"

The three men bow their heads.

The ladies revive the Queen with salts and bear her off to her chambers. The King dismisses all but the most essential people. With the medical staff and Lord Nicolas and the historian, he visits the two girls' beds.

*"Hydrargyrum,"* Krolik says of Beatte; and . . .

*"Hydrargyrum,"* after one look at Gorma, rocked in her swan by the dark nurse's hand.

Gorma wakes up and begins to whimper, as if she might actually understand the incantation.

The men retire to the King's inner chamber to discuss the situation amid the odors of pleasant spices and perfumes, under the suffering gaze of an ethereal painted Saint Sebastian.

"Do you agree?" Christian asks the three original physicians. "Can you possibly agree?"

Before they have a chance to answer, Krolik puts his hands behind his back, fixes his gaze on the bright-painted ceiling, and recites: "Loss of hair, nails, and teeth. Loss of vision and hearing. Aching bones. Itching, peeling skin. Rashes. Weak muscles, red lips, pink cheeks and hands, fever." He seems to develop a heart then and adds, "The youngest girl is not so badly affected." But again with the coldness of a medical man: "We have found an excess of mercury leads to blindness, madness, death. But all of this, I am sure, you know."

Christian can't bear to look at Nicolas. He turns to the trusted court physician. "Doctor Candenzius, how do you explain yourself?"

Sorrowful—fearful—lines settle into the doctor's handsome face. "This is a terrible thing, Your Majesty. But . . . I do not agree with the diagnosis."

Krolik snorts. He clearly has no respect for these fine men of medicine; he just as clearly is a vulgar man not used to royal company. "It is so obvious that any layman could see. I'll bet some of them *have* seen it—the nurses and such—only they were afraid to say it out loud."

"Mercury is a precious metal," Candenzius says, as if by way of explanation. "It is the First Matter from which all other metals are formed. It transmutes other metals into gold. It is a precious gift from God."

Christian remains stern. "Do you mean to say someone has been performing alchemy on my children? Trying to turn them into a set of golden dolls?" Though he imagines them silver, there in the silvered nursery, in their finely painted beds. Sweating little dolls that others dress and put to bed.

He means it seriously, but Krolik seems amused. His yellow teeth show in a sneer.

"Mercury *is* a medicine," Candenzius says.

"One that you administered to my children?"

Candenzius bows his head again. "Your Majesty, it was one of several substances that Her Highness and I—and these two other excellent physicians—developed into a course of treatment. It was not the cause of their original illness, which came on suddenly, if you recall, some years ago—"

Doctor Dé, made nervous by his inclusion, jumps in without asking permission. "We have used the very finest extracts from Spain. Further refined and purified in our own laboratory here in Skyggehavn. Added to other precious healing ingredients—"

"Candenzius oversaw the purification," Venslov adds. "At the Queen's orders."

*If the men know so much about this substance,* Christian wonders, *why did they never see they were overusing it?*

*. . . Of course, because Isabel approved.*

Krolik repeats, "Any substance can be a poison if incorrectly administered. Even mercury, even sugar, even the salt on the table can—"

"Ah," says Candenzius, "you are a student of Paracelsus. Like myself." He speaks as if delighted to have found a kindred spirit. But he is frightened; his eyes show it.

Christian feels sick in every limb of his body, as if some poison has affected him as well. He doesn't know what to do with his own eyes. He must appear regal, even as he feels his careful world crumbling away. Pains stab his gut, and he thinks he might shame himself in front of the others.

He looks up and sees Nicolas, whose sharp, beautiful face is arranged in an expression of sympathy.

"Will they live?" Christian asks, in a small voice; but Krolik does not answer, not right away.

Nicolas declares, "The King trusted these physicians—and his wife—to make good decisions about the children's care, even as the King made decisions about the country. The King has never made a study of medicine. No blame can fall on the King."

Doctor Krolik turns to the court chronicler (who is, of course, tucked into a corner of the room). The historian is too busy writing to answer any unspoken questions, even if he knows about substances found seeped into the cracks of that silver-painted nursery. Even if he may have recorded that information, discreetly, somewhere.

Venslov breaks into a fit of coughing. He seems very old today. "The children show other symptoms," Venslov says when he has the room's attention. "Ones that do not follow a quick-silver presentation. The boils, for example."

"Hmm," says Krolik, gazing once more at the ceiling. "We must look into those."

So it is established. *Morbus Lunediernus,* in its fatal form, is a result of overmedication. Of too much care on the part of their mother and physicians. Poison after all.

Isabel. Isabel. And Elinor.

# DIADEM

N the palace prison far beneath the ground, where marshy water coats the walls with nacreous rime, Countess Elinor Parfis of Belnát writhes in irons. Her left thumb is broken; the bottoms of her feet are scorched. Her arms are scored with delicate knife marks.

"I have nothing to say," she swears during a pause in the proceedings. "Nothing at all."

"Make your confession freely," says the man in the mask. "Or it will be wrung from you."

"Wring me, then. I hold nothing inside."

A guard with a neck like a money purse approaches. This time he holds a traitor's diadem, a jagged iron band fashioned with screws to tighten around the skull.

"You still have nothing to say?" asks the man in the mask.

Elinor presses her lips together, holds her breath to make herself dizzy. So, she thinks, she will quell her fear.

*I will not approve torture,* the King has often said. He has always left the commands to his favorites instead.

"I have *nothing,*" she insists, and closes her eyes as she feels the diadem descend.

# AVA BINGEN

"It is a bad time in the court."

"It is a bad time in the court."

We say it to each other as we go about our days and duties. *It is a bad time in the court.* No one can dispute this: Not only have four children died in under half a year, but the determination for those who have survived is bleak. Too much *hydrargyrum*—mercury—for which there is no familiar antidote, not even Candenzius's theriac, which clearly hasn't cured a single princess so far.

It is almost not to be believed. In the nursery, ladies declare that they never knew, never imagined, don't believe it even now. After all, the Queen herself helped to design this treatment! Maids whisper the same thing, then mutter even quieter spells to ward both poison and guilt away from themselves. Midi Sorte, so recently ill herself, wears a disbelieving smirk, though she is as guilty as anyone if it's true. I've seen her rub quicksilver into Beatte's and Gorma's sores myself. Following Countess Elinor's orders, of course, and the Queen's. Neither of whom has authority to command anything here anymore.

I can't even dare to hope I'll be restored to the Queen's needlework now. She is not in a position to accept more seamstresses, even if she is tearing her garments to shreds in her grief. She is in disgrace, a condition I know well. She is the object of malice and gossip, also therefore like me. I might pity her if . . . if the rumors didn't seem so true.

Here are the whispers about Queen Isabel, overheard in the yards and the dorter and the nursery itself: *She is mad, in every sense. She intended to harm her children and is glad that it is so. She came to them through a secret door and crept among them with a knife, carving the boils and rashes into their skins and filling them with poison.*

The Queen no longer visits the nursery. It is said that she's locked in her chambers, mad with grief, even as she protests the diagnosis. *Who is this Krolik?* she's shouted at her ladies. *What does he know of the Lunedies?*

But the King believes the diagnosis well enough to remake his court. This also sends a shock to the nursery.

First, the three original physicians are dismissed, though not released. They are forced to share a room in the outer wing, near the apron wearers—not exactly imprisoned, but they are told not to leave the palace either. It is said that they spend their time squabbling and inventing experiments that will prove they were right to treat the children as they did. I see them from time to time, storming out into the corridor after some argument among themselves. On one occasion, Doctor Venslov orders me to bring him a bucket of milk for some experiment. When I deliver it to the door, young Doctor Dé (who used to smile at me) looks down into it as if he'd like to spit or do worse.

The Polish doctor, Krolik, becomes Master of the Nursery, and he sets about saving the children. He does it in a way that many find peculiar, but the King is so desperate as to try anything that does not outright smack of madness.

First, the nursery is moved. No more silver walls and golden branches with glass leaves; now we occupy plain quarters in the east wing, and the other rooms are closed up, for they are believed to be poisonous themselves. The children's elaborate beds are scrubbed till much of the paint rubs away, and the Queen's seamstresses fashion new sheets and coverlets for them.

Krolik orders cattle brought in from the countryside and kept not in the town but in the outer courtyard, where they are bled and their blood brewed into a nourishing broth (and where their lowing keeps the soldiers and aprons awake). He buys gallons of viper's milk and sets up a new laboratory to brew theriac from his own recipe, which calls for over a hundred ingredients rather than the usual sixty-four. He also orders a southbound merchant ship to bring back a crate of live vipers so he can milk them himself. He fills the nursery with braziers and pots of water that make it steamier than a rock spring in summertime, for perspiration is part of his cure.

As a result, the children sweat and so do their attendants. We reek. We smell of fear as much as heat, for we're all afraid of poison, and we all expect to find it everywhere.

Rather than reassuring us that medicine has mastered the problem, Krolik has awakened new terrors. We are unwilling to touch the children—or anything that they might have touched. It is as if the surfeit of mercury might well up through their skin to gnaw wounds in us as well.

"Scrub the princesses!" Krolik orders. "Wipe the sweat away!" When we do, the girls' skin comes off in a thick scurf, and they are rawly pink beneath.

The children vomit their new theriac; we stir up more. Krolik shows the nurses how to force it down a rebellious child's throat by holding his or her nose. In the moments when the children are not dedicated to sweats, he also shows us how to paint their sores with a white paste he calls "guaiac," which is from a tree of the New World and is meant to speed the healing of certain wounds. "Like will cure like," he says.

More water boils. The guaiac steams away. The nurses paint the sores again.

Midi Sorte is particularly grave in this endeavor. Alone of all of us, she seems to have no fear; without being told, she spends extra hours with Princess Gorma, and it is most often she who treats the little girl's sores. I come to admire her dedication, although I still find her frightening as a person — even more so with this fearlessness. I have not seen her ill again.

The whispers develop into speculation about witchcraft, Sophia the Wraith Princess, the waxy finger from the witch's hollow that might be working magic now. Only Midi seems unafraid. To ward away these evils, I whisper stories of my own into the children's ears: sleeping princesses who wake to a good father's kiss, goose girls who weave muck into magic cloaks, swans who discard their skins and emerge as princes ready to dance away a dull girl's sorrows.

Oh, sometimes, fear makes me tack on the true endings, the ones my mother used to tell from her days in the forest. Nasty deaths, hurts, children who are abandoned or gobbled up by their grandmothers. These seem to come from a deeper place in me. But then I make myself start again:

"Just as the goose girl had abandoned all hope, along came a tinker with a magic pot . . ."

I hear more gossip about the future: *The Queen is being banished to the country . . . She and Doctor Candenzius are running away together to the Germanies . . .*

And when the nurses get particularly weary, the cures most outlandish, they say: *The King has lost his senses. He is in Doctor Krolik's pocket and will do whatever Krolik commands. He is in Count Nicolas's pocket and will make him a duke. He and Count Nicolas . . . Nicolas . . . Nicolas . . .*

Nicolas may have murdered his family. And the Lunedies.

"Is any of it true?" I ask Grammaticus, once I've reported every last murmur.

He answers, "What is truth?" He rolls a pen between his blackened fingers, as if he might not care about the answer.

"Truth is what you *know.*" I thump him on the chest. "In here. It is what you trust." If you trust.

He steps back from me. "I can't say."

"But you have me tell you *everything,*" I complain — for once again I've spent all night in the nursery, watching Midi Sorte swanning about with her red skirt and her white bodice and her secret skill, and though I could drop dead as a stone with weariness, I've dutifully come to deliver my findings.

His face assumes a noble expression, each hair of his beard preening like the feathers on a bird's breast. "I serve the Crown," he says (words I've heard elsewhere). "Discreetly."

"Tell me *something*," I beg. "What is the good of a pact with the King's chronicler if he doesn't help me understand my own fate . . ." Which if we marry will be his fate too — but something stops me from saying it.

I face one truth now: if ever I thought of loving Arthur Grammaticus, it was to save my skin and protect me from Nicolas Bullen.

He does kiss me (fast, on the brow) and says I should try to sleep. His mind is elsewhere and has been so for some weeks. I want to wring a promise out of him — but at the same time I feel him slipping from my grasp. Which means I must *not* grasp; I must go.

He doesn't embrace me, and I don't press him to. Instead I go, and I send my deepest wishes into the night sky. Jacob. The sea. A Lutheran city someplace where he may be free and I may be with him. If only I could determine where, I would swim all the way . . .

Walking across stones that retain their daytime heat, past a wheelbarrow full of the season's last limp greens, I grow practical again. I can scarcely imagine my life without the palace. How could I follow Jacob Lille to a green island, to shiver in the snow and watch pigs trot back and forth across a farmyard? To live apart from my father and his wife, digging in the ground for vegetables while they got on with their perspective glasses and babies? I've never even seen a farmyard, except in pictures and tapestries. I've dug for vegetables in the soggy clay of our kitchen garden, of course, but I can't imagine farming. I can't figure it for Jacob, either—his fingers would lose all the delicacy that let him craft those marvels of amber, including his masterful sphere of eternity. I wonder who has it now: His parents? The guild? Did he take it with him?

I close my eyes and see each webby golden ball holding a smaller one inside, down to a speck of lace so fine, it appears only under a magnifying glass. And even then, the tiniest hint of another sphere inside, trapped by the amber threads that embrace it . . .

Eternity: *That* was where I had planned to live—with Jacob—soaring past grim endings and into the long arc of blameless forever.

I must find a new place. Again. A dream and a plan.

## CHRISTIAN LUNEDIE
## AND ISABELLE DES RAYAUX

HEN King Christian announces that he will speak to his wife in private, his favorites speculate as to the reason.

"It's been nearly six months since they were alone," says Willem Braj, propped lazily in a window seat of the long gallery that overlooks the bay.

"After so much time, any man must be eager," says Rafael af Hvas. Upright in the seat facing Willem, he pulls apart a golden pomander and sniffs, then holds the opened sphere out in invitation. "For almost any woman."

Willem leans in for a deep inhalation. Myrrh. "Even one with a crowd already in her belly."

An untitled courtier with aspirations adds, "Even in a sleety season." For outside, the skies are heavily gray, and the rain has slowed to that viscous harbinger of winter.

The three men marvel at the King's fidelity and speculate that the portly Queen possesses some unearthly allure for him. They contemplate true love and its infamous blindness. They enjoy themselves; there have been few occasions for laughter in recent weeks.

Of course, they fall quiet when King Christian approaches.

Christian scarcely notices these now-minor favorites as he strides to his wife's apartments. Mating is not his purpose, though he is happy enough to let Willem and Rafael think so.

He is followed by Doctor Krolik and Count Nicolas, also striding purposefully. These two pause in Isabel's state chamber while Christian goes to her inner one. The ladies and maids are banished to corridors and anteroom. For this conversation, Christian needs privacy.

In the state chamber, old Duchess Margrethe, Isabel's chief lady, forces her clawed arthritic hands to embroider (long, messy stitches) while she keeps one farsighted eye on the men. Count Nicolas gives her his sly white smile; she shows him her nubbins of yellow-black teeth in return.

In Isabel's private chamber, Christian avoids looking at the bed, though it is not the one in which he has known his wife. It is nunlike, dun in color, and surrounded by pictures and statues of the Virgin. With the nursery forbidden to her, Isabel has been entertaining art dealers who produce Virgin after Virgin for her to buy. Christian thinks it a relatively harmless preoccupation. He is pleased at least to see that the book of female martyrs he commissioned for her is open on her desk. It's turned to the story of Saint Ursula, who led ten thousand virgins into slaughter for the Faith. The book's presence indicates that Isabel might be biddable, or at least that she has examples of biddability and humility close to hand.

Isabel herself is clearly nervous, standing among the statues, though dressed as magnificently as possible in these days of her expanding girth: purple mourning with a violet mantle, a double-crimped ruff and ropes of pearls, with a single pearl in each ear to match Christian's own. She wears a brown wig in the French style, but even her head has swollen; the wig and her hat seem to skate atop it.

"Your Majesty." Isabel bends nearly all the way to the ground, her skirts puddling around her. When he tells her to stand, her foot catches and she stumbles toward him, then falls backward into a chair.

Christian regards his wife with distaste. Her lack of grace has become truly appalling these last months. He remembers watching her dance with Count Nicolas (only a lord then) at Sophia's wedding—the shape of her skirts not entirely inelegant as Nicolas leaped into the air, his slim legs scissoring their way back to earth. And then she tore her gown.

"Wife," Christian says abruptly, "Countess Elinor Parfis has made a full confession."

Isabel scratches her ear. She remembers Elinor, a pale presence always at her elbow, missing the last few days. How many days? How sweet Elinor is. Suddenly, through the dimness that has clouded her mind of late, she misses Elinor fiercely.

"Confession." Her wig wobbles. She settles it askew. "Is it so close to Saint Ruta's Day? Then I must confess as well. I'll instruct Father Absolon—"

"No, not *that* sort of confession. Countess Elinor has admitted to *poisoning.*"

Isabel blinks innocent brown eyes at him, still scratching her ear. She looks as simple as a cow.

Christian twitches. "Try to understand me. *Listen.* We

know Countess Elinor was poisoning the children. She identified her accomplices as well."

He feels he hardly needs to say that Elinor swore Isabel had a hand in the poisoning; even Isabel must catch the implication. Anyway, it would not be true; according to Count Nicolas, secret-keeper, the Countess is the one person who has succeeded in holding her tongue while put to the question. In fact, Elinor's shards of teeth raked her tongue so hard that even the sternest questioner could not expect her to speak, and her hands were broken so badly that she could not write either. They had to give up on their interview and put her in a tiny oubliette to heal, or not heal, as God would decree.

But Christian knows what he knows. He and Nicolas agree that Isabel and Elinor have colluded against the children—it is the only possibility with a ring of truth. Both of them had opportunity, and both had authority and means. As to motive, Elinor's crippled husband is fifth or sixth in line for the throne, after the children; she had reason for malice against them.

Why Isabel herself might have designed poisons for her brood, the men cannot say. It must be a sign of her madness. Nicolas opines that she might simply have wanted to feel important—that she felt a rivalry with Christian's own Majesty and wanted some attention for herself, which she could get (paradoxically) only by making the children sick and pretending to care for them . . . But that is a prideful thought on Christian's part, and he blushed when Nicolas planted it— knowing himself to be so much less majestic than he should be.

"Do you hear me?" Christian stoops as if leaning over his wife, though she is several feet away. "The Countess is guilty, and *she's told us who shares her guilt.*"

Isabel sways as if she might tip out of her chair. It has no arms; she catches herself by clutching the seat.

"Poison?" she says weakly. "Elinor?" Maybe she understands Christian's more subtle meaning, maybe not.

Very well, he'll say it, the lie that can only reveal truth: "The Countess named you as chief poisoner. You prepared the unguents and potions; you ordered her to administer them—"

"Stop!" Isabel flings her hands wide in supplication. "I would never—Elinor would never—and she'd never admit—"

*Never, never, never.* Christian takes note of his wife's words, especially *admit.* This is as good as a confession itself . . .

Christian allows himself to sound cold. He will be blunt and brutal. Majestic. "The point of fact is, madam, that the children have been ailing for years under your care, and four of them have died. None of our children have ever been strong, not even at birth. Doctor Krolik has a theory—"

"Theories!" Isabel bursts out. "Your people have a *theory* that their city was built by witches!"

"It may have been." He is relieved to make a turn in the conversation; the harsh topic and the need for stern attitude are increasing the pains in his gut. "But what the land has become, since then, is quite—"

"Witches," Isabel says quietly, and she sounds madder than

ever. "And mermaids. That's where you should be looking. Look for the devil's work! Poisoning—accusing—like you and all your favorites—Yes, *you!*"

Christian feels a sharp pain. He doubles over, remembering that the vision of Saint Ursula's mission came to her in a dream; in women's secret states, so much may be revealed. "I've never hurt the children," he says.

Isabel sounds perfectly lucid for a moment: "I know more than you may realize—"

"I have always cared for the children." He stops her fast, before she can speak some words that will spread like a noxious gas in the palace. "My single mistake has been in trusting you with the heirs to my throne."

She is easily distracted by accusation. "I am their *mother*. I was at their bedsides every day."

"All the more reason for the shock—and disgust—any good soul must feel at knowing what you've done to them." He glances again at Saint Ursula. The book's margins are tangled with bodies, the Huns raping and killing the virgins who've come to beg for Cologne's freedom . . . "Your own children," he insists. "The kingdom's children. Isabel, how . . . how could you?"

He is aware of bleating, like that sheep to which he is constantly compared.

Isabel says, "Doctor Candenzius and I devised a cure: He worked the mathematics; I read the Latin herbals—"

"And you killed four children. The Countess has explained . . ."

That lovely white face swims up before Isabel, glowing with light reflected off her too-pale skin . . . and then the face darkens, mottled with blood, as the white eyes bulge and the red tongue swells outward, the skull being crushed like a grape for wine . . . That is the face of confession.

"Horrible!" Isabel whispers. "It is horrible what you have done."

Christian corrects her. "What *you* have done."

"And there will be punishment." She stares forward.

"Yes," he says, playing the stern King again, "there will. For you. You will not see the children again. You will stay in your rooms. You will have only a few servants and no access to herbals and powders."

Isabel doesn't seem to hear. She sits perfectly rigid, perfectly enormous, absorbed in a mad vision; but the chair gives a fraction of an inch with a loud sound.

Christian feels uncertain.

"You won't be entirely stripped of honor," he says on a conciliatory note. "The country still needs its Papa and Maman. You may emerge to wave at the people on state occasions. You must reassure them that all is well. We depend on the baby you are growing."

Isabel is silent.

"You won't hurt the baby, will you?" he asks—bleats again, rather.

She says resolutely, "I know your heart's desire. I know *your* punishment."

Christian feels another sudden cramp. "My desire is for

241

the good of the people," he says tightly. "And that good rests in the children, who will ensure a Lunedie sits on the throne with the best intentions at heart. If you can't promise to let this baby live—or if you try to visit any of the children again, especially the Crown Prince—you'll be tied to your bed for the duration of the pregnancy, and the children will be sent into the countryside. The green islands. Is that what you want?"

Isabel repeats in her Ursuline voice of dream and venom, "I know what *you* really want, Christian Lunedie. I know what lies inside you—"

The ache in Christian's gut becomes unbearable. As if Isabel is one of the mythical witches she claims to hate and has cast a spell to torment him. He doubles over again, clutching the place where claws are twisting among his kidneys.

"I must go." Turning hastily, turning the key: "Wife, health to your—"

Isabel shouts, "Sin! Evil! *Demon!*"

Christian steps into an outer chamber stunned into silence. Every eye is round—brown, blue, gray—all the whites showing. Even Duchess Margrethe is awake, her attempt at embroidery discarded on the floor, her ugly mouth gapped open.

"The Queen needs rest," he says, while Isabel continues to moan in impotent fury. "She would like her ladies to bring her an easeful cup of wine. You know the appropriate recipe."

With a bow, Nicolas follows the King to his cabinet.

# THE WIFE OF THE CLOUDS

*Another time, there was a wife who wanted a child very badly. She had lost something by marrying her husband, who was kind but had his head in the clouds with his work, for he was a keeper of stars and he loved them more than his own life.*

*The wife went to the Queen of Elves and asked for a baby. She was assigned three impossible tasks, and upon completing them, she was given a child. It was a child so hideous, so loud and squalling and horrible, that not even a mother could love it.*

*This was the wife's only offspring, and she left it in the hearth nook to sleep or scream as it chose.*

*One day the husband came down from the clouds and said, "Wife, you have brought me nothing I value. I will take a new bride, and it will be the one you keep in a corner." The wife saw then that the elfin baby had grown into a young girl, pretty if still ill-tempered.*

*The wife was stricken with despair, for she loved her husband, after all. Nonetheless, she offered to prepare the wedding feast.*

*That night the husband and his guests dined on a pie made of flesh so tender, it melted away at the touch of a spoon. "You have murdered my bride and served her to me to eat!" accused the husband, but when the elfin girl was summoned, she appeared—sullen at having to do someone else's bidding on the eve of her wedding.*

*Surprised, the husband went to his old wife, who had aged greatly in the last hours, and lifted her skirts. She had cut off her own legs and stewed them for the pie. "My arms will be next," she said, "and then the rest of me."*

*The new bride clapped her hands. She took an enormous slice of pie and went out to howl through the woods with her wild elf cousins.*

*And so the first wife disappeared, down to the very memory of her. The elf-bride wove her hair into a blanket to swathe her first baby. So is it with mothers and their children.*

*From time to time, the husband had a thin sensation that his life was not now what it once was, but he decided this was the effect of living mostly in the clouds.*

# The Heavens

N a single night in November, the world changes. History, astronomy, religion, and medicine must be made over: A white point has poked through Cassiopeia.

A new star.

A priest sees it first, on his way home from a deathbed; he trips and falls with a splash in a canal, to be retrieved half drowned and babbling about miracles. Twin sisters, daughters of a baker, see it from their bedroom window and feel the pangs of first menses. In a glassblower's shop where a shutter was left carelessly unlatched, the new light shatters every vessel on the shelves.

Doctor Candenzius notices it from the window of the awful little room he now shares with Venslov and Dé. Trembling with opportunity, he sends a message to the astrologer Stellarius, who later tries to claim discovery, and one to the King himself, who has his men drag a cot and a brazier up to the west tower so that he can study the new arrival too.

Christian V invites the scholars to join him. And Nicolas.

Stellarius, Candenzius, the King, the Secretary, all of them are dumbfounded. This hole in the black sieve of night, this unprecedented phenomenon, reorders a sky-scape that's never altered in recorded history. Maps, predictions, zodiacs, and expectations must be reinvented. Stellarius and his assistants busy themselves immediately with charts and pencils. The others simply tilt their heads back and wonder. This is 1572.

"A newborn star," Christian declaims in a loud voice. *"Stella Neonata."* It is as if he is Adam, naming all that surrounds him, helping in its creation. He lies on the cot, gazing upward, with Nicolas behind him. How much grander this manifestation is than a finger, even the finger of his most beloved daughter, pulled from the mud. This is the type of event that makes a man's reign.

Nicolas adjusts the pillow behind Christian's head. Christian breathes deep. He thinks that despite the smoke from the brazier, he can smell his beloved's perfume.

The King says, "This is an occasion, is it not? For once, the bells should ring for happy news."

So church bells chime through the mists of Skyggehavn, informing those who do not already know that theirs is an age of miracles, and all should leave their homes to look. Footpaths and squares crowd with burghers in cloaks and shawls; the trolls who live beneath the bridges crawl out and join them. Even those who don't know the constellations can see this star, for it is stronger and clearer than any other pinprick in the heavens, including the moon.

Indeed, for a fortnight there will be many who swear they can see the star during the shortening hours of day. Stellarius will say so himself.

"A great light," he pronounces that first night, on the flat west tower. *"Stella Magna. Stella . . . Lunediae?"*

Christian Magnus V merely grunts, considering. He orders all to fall quiet, that he might listen to the music of the spheres.

If the historian were not sworn to record events rather than shape them, he would refine the astrologer's Latin, if not the King's.

Some at the court are excited; some are afraid. The new French astrologer takes one look, decides he is in danger, and sails back to Bordeaux. Stellarius is pleased.

"*Stella Nova* is a good omen," he tells the King.

The new star is a portent; everyone agrees on that. But of what? Here the scholars disagree. Candenzius calls it a sore in the heavens; he believes it will prove Krolik's diagnosis of *Morbus Lunediernus* wrong.

"Such an intense light is a concentration of celestial poisons," he says. "You shall see, the children will sicken with its arrival." He declares that he'll find some way to lance and poultice a boil in the heavens. He orders the grinder of perspective glasses to make a device that might sweep among the astral gases and stir them to a new combination.

Krolik, however, disagrees. "It can't be any but a good sign," he says. "The children are improving."

The two men bicker famously. The King orders them to be silent when he is up on the tower, giving himself the illusion that he is alone with his thoughts. He will eventually bestow upon the star an official name (*Stella Supra?* the courtiers suggest. *Stella Christiani?*), but he waits prudently for his scholars to settle on an interpretation.

Even on a misty night or a rainy one, but not during a storm, the new star beams steadily down. Poets call it the most gorgeous sight in the heavens, the new jewel of the kingdom; they compose page after page of praises to it. Goldsmiths, glassblowers, and embroiderers try to reproduce it with their earthly materials. The people fall asleep looking at it, and their hands and feet suffer frostbite.

That star is like a toddler romping overhead; there is no telling what it might do. But there is hope that it will grow into something wonderful.

## AVA BINGEN

The new star has put all of us off balance. We've always expected things to change down below, in the canals, the streets, and so on, but the heavens have been constant in our memory. This star shines even in the daylight, as if to drive away the sun. It is so bright that it seems heavier than the rest; we have the impression that if we were to stand on tiptoes, we might touch it.

In response, we ourselves change. We grow braver, more hopeful; reckless, with girls flopping down for boys who forget, for a moment, about the beauties of the heavens as they explore the pleasures of the flesh. Excitable, with great plans laid and ambitions encouraged.

Every night now, Skyggehavn grows taller, as people add rooms onto their houses so they might view the star better. Sometimes entire buildings gather up their skirts and shift into a footpath or new street. The most fashionable item in town is a perspective glass, whether it's a proper tube as made by my father or a simple glass sphere filled with water that magnifies the light in waves. Even bare-eyed, we love to stand among the stretcherous buildings and gaze.

Not everyone views the star as a good thing. I've heard some of the maids worrying that it will launch to the ground and destroy us all. Others insist that it is Sophia, the Wraith Princess, burning with fury and waiting to strike. Still more think it a sign that the Perished Lily has become an angel.

Nothing captures the fancy like a new arrangement in the heavens.

I try to see the star as a sign of hope, but in my case it seems like an ill omen instead—yet another something pretty that brings nothing good after all. Like my position at the palace. Like my love affair with Arthur Grammaticus.

At the very least, the star makes an excuse for a scholarly man to be absent from his rooms. Surely, I tell myself, the study of this star is what occupies Grammaticus now, and why I have not seen him in days. Over and over, I tap on the boards of his door, wait for him or an apprentice to open to me. No reply. It is as if he doesn't exist—or I don't. And I need him to reassure me.

I peer through the keyhole and see only a corner of his table and a sheaf of grubby pages. I consider what I might say to him: *What does it mean that you taught Midi Sorte to write?* Now and forever, sure. Though I am certain I know.

I can't bear that my lover should have so many secrets. And that he should avoid me in this manner. And that he just might not be my lover alone, but Midi's as well. He may have been hers for years. They might have kissed right before she fetched me from the stairs and brought me to him. I was most likely a brief distraction, a sort of dalliance. And no wonder she doesn't like me either . . . She must have thought to marry him. Or at least be kept by him.

*You gave her expression in the fingers when she had none in the tongue—why?*

But this much is obvious. There is only one reason, really, a man ever wants a woman to express herself: to praise him.

Why he pretended to want me, I do not know. To make Midi jealous? I have to see if I can rescue some good from it. I will do as I did with Count Nicolas. I will tell a tale that shames the subject—but the subject will be Nicolas himself, and when the King hears the report, he will banish his friend to the Lower Chambers. And then Arthur.

I decide to wait at his room till he turns up. I sink to the floor outside his door and watch the shoes shuffling and striding by: leather, velvet, wood. I don't care if the courtiers and their servants wonder about my presence here; I don't care if they gossip. I hear maids giggling and don't bother to listen for their remarks. I have been the subject of much worse, and I will never shake the shame.

I wait an hour, then two, with an ear cocked for the bells that mark time. Still, Grammaticus does not return. Finally I give up; I have to set about my work. I go to the kitchen for a handful of coarse bread and a bucket.

This is the reason I need Grammaticus now, an important one—I am no longer a maid of the nursery. With the new star, I have become a yet more lowly scrubber, one who cleans fireplaces and floor tiles throughout the Queen's household. Doctor Krolik, as Master of the Nursery, gathered us all together and explained at some length that with fewer children in bed, there need be fewer girls to attend them. And so our duties have been reconfigured according to our talents, and this is supposed to be mine. I am told it was Duchess Margrethe who recommended me personally for this task; she recalled how hard I scrubbed the night after Countess Elinor was arrested.

Midi Sorte smirked when my new duties were announced. She, of course, remains in charge of Princess Gorma; she rocks a cradle while I slop a bucket and feel myself become invisible.

I've discovered that picking up a bucket in this place is the same as putting on a cloak knit by elves. No one wants to see a scrub maid, so no one does. I am invisible; I could go virtually anywhere, as long as there was a dirty floor or fireplace in it.

While the last children are asleep in their night beds, watched over by the night nurses, I scrub the black-and-white of their new dayroom with stinking lye. In the morning, when the children are settled into their fanciful beds, I clean their simpler night rooms the same way. These quarters were previously used by the Council Chancellor and his wife, who were not notable housekeepers. The drifts of lint and dead insects seem to regenerate nightly till I sweep and scrub them away.

As I clean, I make up speeches I will deliver to Grammaticus. *Damn you,* I will say sternly. *May Satan himself bury you in dung along with Count Nicolas.* Or, *Please love me after all.*

I do need him. I would use him.

* * *

On a Sunday I receive permission to visit the house with the stone head. We — my father and his wife and I — sit in the smoky hall and make polite conversation. Sabine is unwell, tottering with her new bulk and uncomfortably windy; she craves marzipan and cumin, and she makes water more often than a porpoise.

"It is difficult the first time," Father confides to me when she is off using the pot. "Your mother was greatly inconvenienced by you, though she was a young woman in all her pregnancies. Sabine, alas, is no longer truly young."

In fact, Sabine (not unlike the Queen herself) is so old that the neighbors must be constantly surprised the baby hasn't given up his grip and slipped away.

I cross myself to ward off the evil thought. Somewhat to my surprise, I find I'm looking forward to this baby. And I want my father and his wife to be happy . . . Which is one reason I don't tell him of my most recent crisis of fortune: I can't bear to disappoint him. I resolve to free myself of scrubbing duties as soon as I can. Maybe he'll never need to know.

"How are you, my dear?" he asks, and one resolve holds firm; but then I offer all in a hopeful rush what I had earlier vowed not to say:

"Father, a man highly placed said he loves me. He offered to marry me."

My father sits still a moment, letting silence speak for him. "Ava, my dear," he says at last, "please have a care. Remember the dangers. And remember that it is not just your reputation at risk but that of your family."

He leans forward to poke at the fire, finding a new subject. "Several of the lords, and Doctor Candenzius himself, have commissioned perspective glasses. They want them ever longer and stronger than the King's. But I"—chuckling indulgently—"I know not to do *that*."

I imagine the star snagged on an exceptionally long perspective device, dripping marzipan onto the King's sleeping entourage. They might lick themselves like a pack of cats, and Grammaticus would write it all down for the annals. And Nicolas, perhaps.

"I'm glad your business is prospering," I say politely.

"Beyond our dreams," says my stepmother, squeezing herself through the doorway. "But one does miss the chance to appear at court."

To my knowledge, Sabine has never been to the palace. But, like everyone else who's never visited, she thinks about it in a very real way. The splendors inside belong not only to the Lunedies but also to all of us, who take pride in our ruling family's wealth and in the beauty of their surroundings.

Gerda pours Sabine another cup of small ale and helps her settle into a chair.

Sabine sips as if she's a grand lady. "Ava, do tell us about the Queen." Her cup is pewter with some complicated ornament. "Is her belly progressing well?"

# The Heavens and Queen Isabel

N the lengthening nights of her incarceration, Isabel is more than usually troubled. She is wakeful and anxious. Sometimes she steps over the sleeping maids and opens her shutters and unsticks the window glass to crane her head out and look at the new star. *Stella Maris, Stella Mariae.* It is speaking to her; if only she knew how to hear it.

Isabel would like to walk beneath the stars.

Even more, she would like to visit her children again. Give them their medicine, reassure them that the new star means no harm, only good things for their family. She hears Princess Gorma is feeling nearly well; if reports can be believed, all three of the remaining little souls are improving. Isabel is glad, of course.

But she also feels just the least bit hurt that her children might be healing without her. All those hours of care and worry, draughts and consultations and treatments . . . now rewritten entirely by that hideous Polish physician . . . who cannot, cannot, *cannot* be right about Isabel . . . unless somehow he *is* right, which would mean the unthinkable. That to which Elinor, wise Elinor, sweet friend, surprisingly confessed.

The new star beams serenely down on the Lunedie Queen. The music of the celestial spheres rings inside her sensitive ears. Yes, she should see the children with her own eyes. They must need her, surely they must. She is only good.

When she demands to visit the nursery, she is given wine to drink instead.

"Is this Doctor Candenzius's formula?" she asks before she drinks, and her ladies (new ladies) tell her, "Yes." She drinks, and it makes her sleep through the day.

So at night she wakes and gazes at her star. The sleeping maids don't notice the cold air from the window, except to curl deeper into each other and their blankets.

Sometimes Isabel tiptoes to a tall oak chest where she keeps silver boxes full of relics from the children who have left her. The locks of hair and milk teeth, a few fingernail cuttings, the precious miracle of Sophia's half finger. The box rattles; there are also some bits of bone she's found here and there.

Isabel takes Sophia's finger from the box and points it at *Stella Mariae* as a navigator points an astrolabe (she thinks) toward the North Star. Surely *this* star is somehow connected to the children. Surely it can do something for them. Draw them to her, alive or dead.

When she looks toward the earth, she sees starlight wink along the surface of spreading mud in the witch's hollow. It does not sink inside. It does, however, frighten some courtiers enough that Isabel sees them sneaking over to toss down their jewels, ribbons, golden braids: offerings to some old spirit residing between the slit in the earth and the eye in the heavens. They think their sacrifices might protect them. From what? From an evil they cannot name.

"Fools." Isabel runs Sophia's finger over her belly. What would she sacrifice? Nothing, for she has already lost everything. Or almost. She clutches the finger tight, rattles the bones in their box just enough to reassure herself that they're there, not enough to wake anyone.

She imagines herself outdoors. She is leaning not over the witch's hollow but over that quicksilver pool at her uncle's castle: there, she experiences the heady feel of the moving reflection, distorting the face now this way, now that, according to the wind's direction. The sweet, dizzy air above. It was no wonder that ladies bent down to kiss their own images, to fix their loveliness in one silver second.

It is impossible to believe that something so beautiful, something that feels so good, would actually kill.

Isabel shuts the reliquary box in its cabinet and locks the door. She keeps Sophia's finger with her, though; she likes the shape of it in her fist. Sophia, her eldest, her darling.

When she climbs into bed, she feels the weight of that extra finger in her hand, pulling her down. She is falling . . . falling . . . tumbling into a quicksilver pond as round as the moon and as bright as the new star.

She lets herself sink deeply into it—descending through the exquisitely shivering metal. It is cool and soft and exciting. She may never come back. She may never want to. Quicksilver mercury-maids, kindhearted reflections of the ladies above, take her by the hands. They embrace Isabel and tell her she is safe. They spit mercury into the air until the demons and witches are driven away.

Isabel, dreaming, clutches Sophia's finger and feels the small dead thing growing warm and soft. She presses it into her belly. *Stay with me,* she begs them, the finger and the belly. *Save me.*

## CROWN PRINCE CHRISTIAN LUNEDIE

ND now, the Crown Prince dies.

There can be no words to express his parents' sorrow, for there is no sorrow like that of parents who have lost their only son. Their worst fears have been realized. Royal parents, royal son.

The bells clang; the courtiers grieve. They weep, and the salt of their tears makes a hard white frost on the floors and walls of the palace.

But all of this has happened already, it is always happening. Theirs is a kingdom of mourners. Out in the city, emotion does not run as high as it should. The people are tired of eating black bread; their black clothes are in tatters, reeking of sweat. They've made their throats sore with praying, and they have to cough new prayers out to comply with tradition.

The King orders all the palace mirrors covered in crepe, all the portraits and paintings and other pretties. He would cover the night sky in black if he could, to muffle the star that he now feels has called down doom upon the Lunedies.

The boy lies on view in the amber cathedral, decaying slowly in the chill almost-winter.

In these terrible hours, Christian leans heavily on Count Nicolas. His Secretary is the one soul who seems to understand both what Christian is feeling and what must be done. In Christian's cabinet, during his hours upon the stool, Nicolas is all sympathy and especially tender, resting a hand on Christian's shoulder while he listens to the royal laments, brushing the hair beneath the wig, removing Christian's pearl earring for bed as delicately as the King's own nursemaid.

At the grieving feast, no one weeps harder than Nicolas, seated on Christian's right; except of course the Queen, who spreads in between them. She has been allowed out of her quarters for this occasion of state. Nicolas promises it will do the nobles good to see their Queen with her full belly; she represents the future, with the Lunedies still on the throne.

But reports about Isabel overall are bad. She is crying so hard now that the courtiers can barely keep up with her; they have to dig into their thighs and wrists with the tips of their knives in order to summon enough pain for tears. She might weep her baby away.

The King is too grief-struck to weep anymore. He simply sits and lets the leek pie and battered dolphin congeal upon his plate. The peasants outside the gates will make a fine supper on his scraps, and of course the courtiers'; no one at table dares eat more than a royal, however hungry that person may be. Christian broods, watching Nicolas's fine fingers scooping up food for the Queen, the famous ruby glowing as they move.

Isabel chews as if for duty, eyes still streaming. By accident (so the King believes), she catches one of Nicolas's fingers between her teeth, giving it a sharp nip before realizing her mistake and setting Nicolas free.

Christian feels a tightness around his heart. "So now we have a Crown Princess," he says aloud. His words shatter the silence; they echo down the hall, settling like ash into the fine dishes on the table. "Eventually, perhaps, a Queen. A woman to rule our *king*dom."

Nicolas, wiping his fingers, says in the softest of voices, "Your Majesty, do not forget the present Queen's belly. We must take hope from that." He nods gallantly toward Isabel.

Petulantly, Christian decides to ignore him, though he settles back into the traditional silence. He blames his wife, of course, for this death as for those of the princesses. Once again he considers having her hands tied to her bedposts. This may be the only way to protect the child-to-be. Then again, such an arrangement might make her weep even more violently, causing more harm to the infant . . .

As if she guesses his thoughts, Isabel bursts into a loud storm of tears that rinses away the last traces of her face paint, soaks her ruff, and leaves it limp around her neck. The weary courtiers politely follow suit and soak themselves. Faces bloom with pimples and sores around the table.

"Your Highness." Krolik materializes at Isabel's side with a boldness that would not be tolerated if the situation were not so dire. As it is, Christian just ignores the Polish doctor, lets him do as he thinks best. "On behalf of your husband, I must forbid you to cry any longer. Think of the child within you.

The son." He offers her a cup of his special wine; Nicolas lifts it to Isabel's mouth. "Health to both your souls."

With the glass cold against her lips, Isabel looks hard at Christian. "We can rename the oldest girl Christina if you like. Since it is so important that every ruler must have your name." Then she is violently, expansively sick into his lap.

HAT night, a thick frost settles over the palace. It turns the rain into ice and lays a downy white fuzz on top; it dulls the outlines of stone ornaments—mermaids, crosses, crescent moons, *In tenebris lumen meum metue*—and holds the light inside itself, so the roofs glow like fairy sails and the sentries' helmets glitter. Christian's shoes leave dark, distinct prints as he steps gingerly out onto the west tower to join the heavens.

All the stars, not just the new one, hang so low that the King thinks he might grab them, even without use of the several perspective glasses that the rival scholars and nobles have set up here and use around the clock—for Christian has changed his mind about draping the heavens in crepe and ordered that at this time, above all others, the overbright new star and its neighbors must be studied and analyzed so the future may be corrected if need be.

Skyggehavn Bay is a black stretch behind the palace spires, punctuated only by a lantern moving on Saint-Peter's-on-the-Isle. The city crouches to the other side, a bumpy, tumorous mass lit here and there with some dull gold light that makes dim parody of the stars overhead.

"The world looks small tonight, what," says Christian, dully. The world is bound to look small on a night like this, a night without a son. His belly cramps in nearly unbearable pain, but he doesn't think he needs the stool now. What he needs is distraction.

His courtiers rush to agree with what he just said. Stellarius and Candenzius bow low in their dark robes, murmuring that the King honors them too greatly by visiting on this night of all nights, a night with a small world. As they speak, white frost shakes loose from their beards and drifts through the air.

Christian asks himself: *A king has unlimited honors to give, unlimited wealth, unlimited land—what does he receive in return?*

*Love. The dutiful love of his people.* The answer comes to him in his father's voice, a voice the people did love. Christian IV was handsome until the day he died from a stray splinter in a joust. Christian V is not handsome. Nor is he loved.

Christian cannot bear to look at Nicolas in this moment. He turns instead to the closest of the perspective devices (Candenzius's) and crouches to look up into it. He is pleased, once more, to be so much taller than the ordinary man that he cannot stand straight at the glass. Then again, he thinks his men should adjust their machines to his height; they could always stand on boxes, but how is the King to make himself shorter?

"Tell me what I am seeing," he says.

"Your Majesty"—Candenzius hovers deferentially at his elbow—"the streams of star poisons are visible just now. I have brought the device into particular focus."

"Hmm." Christian gazes, sees nothing—just the same stars, somewhat dimmed in the complicated system of lens, light, and metal. "How do these poisonous streams look?"

"If you'll permit me . . ." Candenzius steps to the glass, gives one of the lenses a quarter turn, checks again for himself while Stellarius watches with a dour expression.

"If Your Majesty would care to look through *my* glass," the astronomer says, "you might see an interesting configuration in Scorpio that augurs for—"

"I have it!" Candenzius cheers for himself and steps back, bowing the King forward.

Given a choice without caring to choose, Christian steps listlessly up to Candenzius's lens. He is suddenly bored with the stars, with court, with children and family and the question of succession. It is unfair that a king must spend so much of his life thinking about his own death and what will happen to his throne thereafter. But, to follow through with what he has declared he wants, he bends to the glass and looks.

And there it is. The optical trick of the glass transports him again up into the vault of sky, poking about giant spheres of brightness. And now he sees the poison streaming between them—not a milky trickle of light, as he expected, but a sort of wavering dark, like the heat that rises above a pot just before it boils. The stars are pushing this poison at each other in a raging battle. Inviting him to dive in, to crest the waves of it, like a warrior sailing off to a splendid, blinding fight.

"Beautiful," he murmurs without thinking.

He looks up and sees the face of his love, Nicolas, dark

in the starlight. The Count's lips are pressed together as if for a kiss.

"Poison, Your Majesty!" Candenzius sounds delighted. "So clearly visible!"

Christian abruptly declares that he will retire to his cabinet.

## MIDI SORTE

Poison-auntie use to say there were no sore like the wound of not having, and the worst sorrow come of not knowing whether to weep be cause there be no thing to weep over. She make some potions not for killing but against sadness, to puff a spirit light as air or fill a heart with feeling where there were no feeling before, a dream-heavy kind of happiness.

Back then, half the aunties gone mad with emptiness. They figure they selves ruined to live behind walls with other women, men made in to women, swords to cut if they do not do as told, just one husband for all of them, and he gone to conquer other lands six months the year. If they have a child that lives and they live too, then they be doubly kept, for to leave a baby be the sin that put them in a sack with a stone at they feet and the sack toss over the wall in to the bay, to make a garden of corpses till the eels come by and eat them. As happen, I believe, with my own mother, for every lady there be called my auntie, and I belong to none of they.

Some times in this narrow place there be too much to feel. Too-much live in my gut with an ache, too-much live in my fingers that poke and grope around it. A fear that smash against my heart till I cannot say what make me sick. Other than the thing inside me.

I see them girls shaking skirts when I go past; they think to shake away witch craft. I hear whisper-wonders about why I keep this position when so many children die and my first mistress be disgrace. Why I were the one to win Isabel's favor when I pulled that finger from the muck. If I could speak, I may say, *I were not the one who saw it first.* Or, *I did not kill the Prince.* Or may be I would simple let them wonder at my power, like poison-auntie did.

When I go to my box of belongs, each night I see it rearrange. But they will find no clue in there.

Truth be, if there *be* truth, I do not know why I am here. With out the scarlet skirt to remind, Queen Isabel have forgot I helped her miracle, she never ask for me. May be I have been forgot entire, or may be Nursery Master Krolik have some plan. I were not one who waited on Prince Christian in especial—that were all ways Elinor, the Prince's favorite.

Now Prince and Elinor both are gone, and there remain just a hand full of nurse and two little princess, too weak even to attend they brother's grieving feast. They snuggle in the swans and mew like kittens; they do not like that the lion sit empty. They fear the journey they will make soon, to wherever it be that dead children go.

I feel my own doom too—it is a black bat in my belly. Soon I will be dead or at very least I will be shake out of court for ever. So each night may be the last I paint they girls' wounds with guaiac from a little pot. A very little pot, a very little guaiac, I do n't put on so much as the others be cause this is another thing I do not know about.

The little girls whimper that guaiac burns, ask me for drinks and sugar treats. I murmur, *"Shhh, shh, sh,"* but when their eyes fall on Ava Mariasdatter, they forget me and clap hands.

"A story!" cry Beatte. She is now the oldest. "I want the Frog Prince!"

Gorma say, "Princess on the Glass Mountain."

I paint another of her sores and she start to weep. *"Shhh, shh, sh,"* I soothe her. I dab at wounds as if re-moving drips of guaiac, in doing this I wipe her guaiac away.

Ava Mariasdatter kneel at the fire place to do her work, but the princesses keep demanding for her. I must decide do I glare at Ava or ignore her till another nursey command her go, for she will not disappear if I order her only with my eyes.

When I wrote to Krolik, in my best language to imitate Duchess Margrethe, the letter that made Ava scrub-maid instead of nursey-maid, I did not expect she would still be in these rooms. I thought she would be in kitchens, privies, halls. But she is constant here to tend the fire place and watch from her eye-corners what the princesses be doing. She speak her stories to them when others do not see. May be she still spies for Nicolas and for Arthur. No doubt she want to call me witch.

When I think this the lump in my belly turn over and make my throat sour. I swallow hard and when I *Shhh, shh, sh,* I do it to calm the lump and not the girls.

"A story!" they whine together. "Tell us!"

Ava clang the brush in to her bucket as if she have some

big grief on the world, as if this should not be her task, ruining her fingers that have been raised up for sewing fine seams and broideries. She open her mouth. "Once—" she begin.

At her noise, another nurse do say, "Go clean elsewhere." Even with out understanding that Ava like to whisper tales of magic, or that this be what Beatte and Gorma expect when they see her.

Ava answer, "Doctor Krolik wanted special care to be taken with the fire places." She play the game of martyr-maid and keep scraping round the coals to take out ash. Her apron be black.

This other nurse put hands on hips and stand square. "You can do that after the princesses are put to their night beds."

"I want a story!" sob Beatte.

Gorma cry, too, "Stories!"

I paint another blister and wipe away the sting.

The nurses do take Ava out. As Ava pass me by, I shake my skirt. The wind stir a puff of ash that settle gray upon her face, and in this small way I have pleasure.

FTER the grieving feast, the nights fold into each other like ribs of a fan. One, two, seven, and Christian's belly grows ever tighter with pain, a knot cinched taut as a rope's ends are pulled. Tonight he sits in his latrine closet and tries to push the pain away, make himself the king he needs to be.

Who would this person be? He tries to imagine. A stalwart, most assuredly unsheeplike man, noble, brave, and strong. Who puts love of his land and people before any other matter.

An infelicitous noise escapes.

Nicolas sponges the royal brow, coughing to disguise that sound. Nicolas is always most polite about such things. Christian squelches the impulse to apologize; a king must never say he is sorry, must never be embarrassed. Because he must never do anything embarrassing or wrong.

"Could you bring me some of Krolik's wine?" he asks, as if the noise were really part of a conversation.

Nicolas's physician has invented a new elixir that eases pain. It is sweet and dreamful, and Christian takes a sip with delight: because Nicolas's middle finger brushed Christian's lip as he raised the cup. It's left behind a musky perfume and the manly tint of sweat. The air around wisps with the breath curling from Nicolas's delicate nostrils.

A chink of glass against marble: the cup returns to its table. Christian shifts. Nicolas coughs again.

"Another sip," Christian commands, and again Nicolas lifts the cup. This time his finger does not touch Christian's mouth, but Christian feels the fingers in the warmth of the silver brim.

That delicious warmth spreads through the King's belly, not exactly untying the knots but making them possible to bear. Filling in pockets of pain, smoothing over sore spots.

Christian sighs and rubs his backside on the red velvet padding. He lets himself grow careless about noises; Nicolas coughs a few more times. Dear Nicolas.

"Another sip."

Such a blessing, this wine, these fingers.

## AVA BINGEN

The night sky is a coverlet worn out and mended many times—sometimes with a spangled fabric, sometimes with a dun. In places the moon and stars shine through; in others a thick gray cloud moves swift as a rat. We get sudden showers of sleety rain, then rayed brightness as Cassiopeia is revealed with that new star outshining the moon. The air, of course, is cold. There's little left of the year.

Little left of my heart, I add with a taint of poetry that should make me sneer at myself. Once again I am abandoned; I have nothing but my buckets and a pair of hands worn raw with scrubbing. I haven't spoken with Grammaticus in some weeks. I've spied him only from a distance as he rushes from one event to another. I no longer possess the courage to wait outside his rooms.

Pitying myself, I gaze at the new star and wish hard for a rescue, a way to win Grammaticus back. No, as long as I am wishing . . . *Jacob, return to me. If you are at sea, use the bright new star to guide you . . .*

Sleet brushes my face like a sloppy kiss. A spider kiss.

Soon wishes turn to anger. I stamp a foot, and then another, feeling a crackle as frost gives way to the warmth beneath the stones. It seems intolerable that I can do nothing to bring Jacob back to me, or even Arthur Grammaticus—an unsatisfactory suitor but a suitor (of a sort) nonetheless. Though I never loved him; I loved only Jacob. How is it possible for my heart to ache so long for one person? I must stop it, squash it, turn love to hate, and make myself a happier, freer person. Like Midi Sorte, who is full of hate and quite content, who has stolen Arthur (or never relinquished him in the first place) and forever looks as if she'd like to strike me, even at those times when (I admit to myself) I have most longed to be her friend.

There's one clear way to cleanse myself of unwanted feelings: I can make a sacrifice at the witch's hollow. Of course, once the priests learned what was happening there, they forbade it; the sacrifices reeked too much of pagan superstition, though some argued that nothing was more Catholic than sacrifice. (The Church never quite decided officially about Princess Sophia's finger, either: Is it a miracle or merely an oddity? We may never know.) Throughout the murky early winter hours, it's usually possible to find some hooded figure or other muttering a charm or prayer by that muddy lip, with an object disappearing inside. The guards, bored, chase them away, then watch the tributes sucked into the muck.

A guard passes now, *én, to, én, to,* marching. Women move in rhythms of three; men always act to a beat-step of two.

The guard wishes me a good evening. I wish one back to him.

*Én, to, én, to.* I look up through my breath and see men on top of the west tower, directing perspective machines at the

274

sky. Stellarius, no doubt, and Candenzius, making use of the long darkness and my father's invention. Arthur must be with them to record whatever it is they observe.

So much of my history, and of History, in one place.

Thinking to rid myself of all memories, all past and feeling, I dig into my waist pocket. I don't know what I expect to find, but my hand gropes past my mother's bracelet, kept there for safety (the dorter's seen a theft or two lately), and comes up with Jacob's amber needle case. I have held it close out of sentiment, but it is the perfect object to sacrifice. With a prayer, of course. Walking toward the hollow, with the guard's back to me, I hold the case tight in my fist, letting the dry skin there crack. I pray . . . for a sense of tranquillity, of not-wanting, of health to my soul.

I hurl the case, needles and all, into the witch's bed.

There is a sudden flit of cloud shadow, so I can't watch it go down, don't even see the stars' reflections tremble on the mud as it sinks.

I forget to pray, and utter a curse instead. I'm suddenly afraid. But in some small way, I'm also pleased, as if I've just flung every man I've ever known into the muck.

Then I turn and scurry lest the guard come to ask what I'm about.

ICOLAS'S lips are soft, softer even than Isabel's or any other lady's that Christian has kissed in greeting or in ceremony. And how does Christian know this? Because he and Nicolas are kissing, and it is not in ceremony.

Christian could not say how it began, only that it is pleasant and easeful, occurring somehow between a sip of wine and a daring lick of Nicolas's finger. He might have been embarrassed by what would have been called flirting if it took place between a man and a woman, but he feels now that he need never be embarrassed again, there will never be anything wrong again, even his pain will vanish if he can only drink deeper of the pleasures of Nicolas's mouth. His belly quivers.

All of him quivers. Too much. He is the King.

He stands (for he has still been sitting on his stool) and lurches toward the door of the tiny cabinet. But trips and has to catch himself against the wall, breeches down, head spinning.

Nicolas reacts immediately. Christian feels it, with a combination of surprise (new circumstances) and familiarity (old actions). The sponge, the sting of vinegar, the soothing ooze of rose-scented tallow. And nimble fingers tying the breeches loosely over a royal gut that does not know whether to be increasingly excited or—yes, maybe—ashamed.

No, not ashamed. Nicolas is helping him into the bed-chamber, the chamber of Inner Presence, and closing the door on the cabinet of the stool. All Christian can think is that he wants Nicolas to turn around and kiss him some more, before they can start to realize what a sin they are committing.

Nicolas's slender fingers grip Christian's shoulders, then the sensitive sinews in the back of his neck. He gives the neck a soothing rub, removes Christian's hat, and sets it on a table.

Christian feels his eyes tickling with tears. Perhaps he has only imagined . . .

More wine? No, he will not ask for it; he cannot speak.

Nicolas touches the pearl dangling from Christian's ear, and it is astonishing how such a small sensation, a minuscule trembling in an almost invisible hole in the littlest part of the body, can make Christian's heart soar and fall and hammer so that it might burst through the fragile case of bone to embrace Nicolas entirely.

Apparently unaware of the reaction he has provoked, Nicolas removes the earring, sets it on the table; as he does every night, he reaches up to rub both of Christian's ears and smooth away any cold or sting there. The ears are in fact flaming hot. Christian is blushing. He's sure now that he only imagined the kiss; he must be drunk with wine or pain.

Then Nicolas grips Christian by the dangling lobes and guides his head down so their lips can meet again.

Christian holds his breath, lest he miss some sensation.

The delicate point of the Count's tongue snakes inside to tickle the King's teeth, then the silky underside of the King's lip. Christian opens his mouth, as he has never done with his wife, and tastes all the pleasures of this warm, musky, slightly sulfurous place inside another person.

Nicolas's tongue is velvet. It is both soft and firm, salty and sweet, wide and narrow. It reaches all the way inside Christian and massages his deepest parts, stitching them up safe and free, for once, of pain.

Christian has never experienced such a swell of well-being in his life. His whole body glows with health and good feeling. And yet he knows, somehow, that there is more to feel.

Nicolas knows this too. He guides the King gently toward the bed.

A great bubble swells within Christian — pain, pleasure, anticipation . . . love at last.

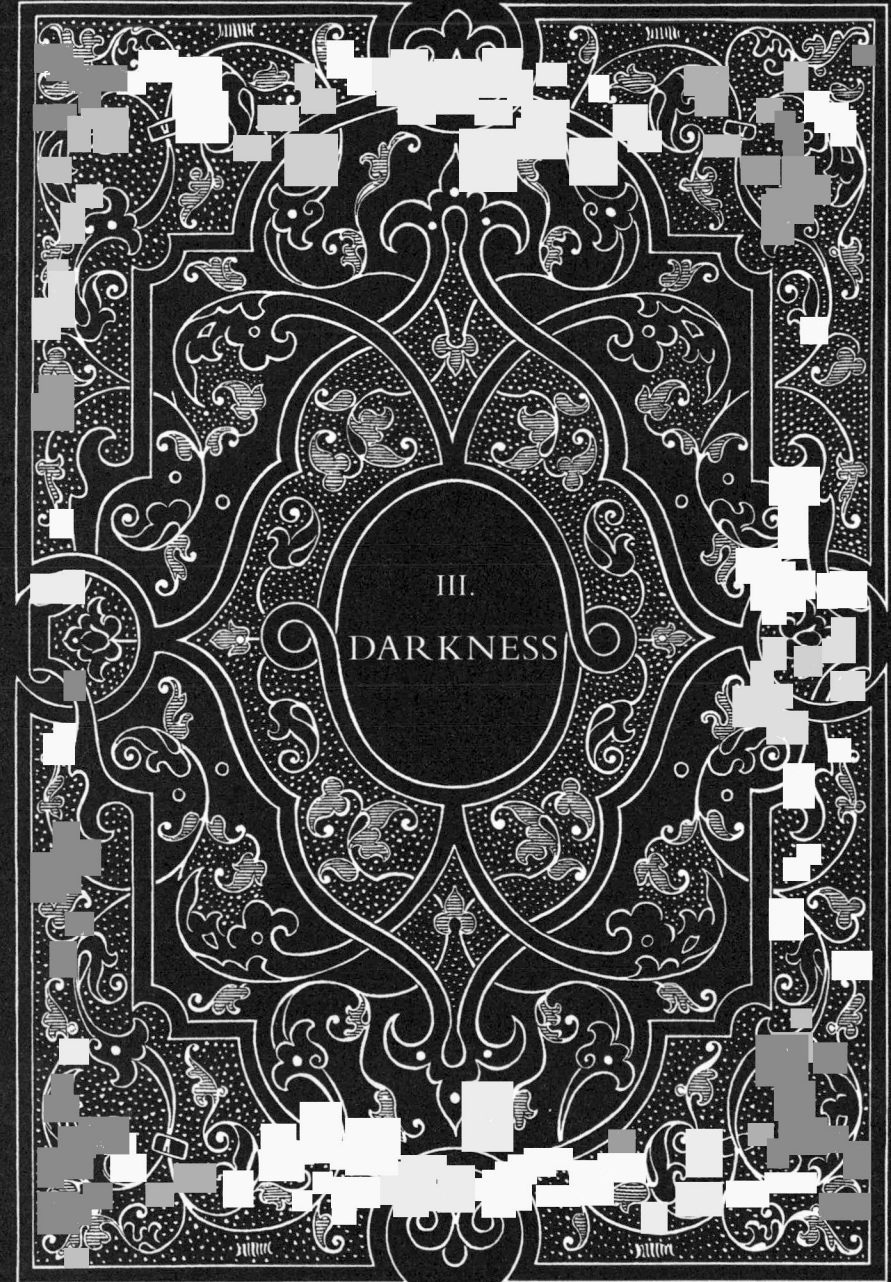

III.

DARKNESS

*There was once a princess whose land had fallen on hard times, and in order to refill the coffers and distribute charity to the poor, she had no choice but to sell herself to as many suitors as would have her during the night, at so many gold coins the hour.*

*Her father was grateful for the pile of money she deposited in his lap every morning, but he was a loving man and a suspicious one, so he ordered one of his guardsmen to follow the girl as she went to bed.*

*The guardsman discovered, of course, that rather than donning her silken nightdress upon retiring, the princess dressed in her most sparkling gowns, with her richest jewels, and painted her face in the manner fashionable at foreign courts. In this guise, and wearing the gold diadem of royalty, she rowed herself out to a ruined castle upon an island, where her suitors would line up for a chance at the favors of a woman they thought to be a fairy or a ghost, always magical in her effects.*

*These men were most often foreign ambassadors and lords of dark reputation who had made their fortunes outside the laws of the kingdom. They inevitably remarked on the girl's (or fairy's, or ghost's) resemblance to the princess and tried to tease the truth out of her. She would smile mysteriously, holding her pretty pink hands (callused with rowing) over her face, before performing in a way that no man ever expected of a true princess.*

*The guardsman, of course, fell in love with her, and he picked the pockets of the ambassadors to enjoy precious hours in her embrace.*

*And so the people enjoyed the illusion of their princess, as well as the charity that her father was able to distribute as a result of her activities. In time the king built a mighty fleet and pressed the poor into serving as its sailors. The guardsman who had followed the princess led the new navy in battles against the foreign kings whose ambassadors had behaved so shamefully on the floating island.*

*As to the princess herself, her father—who loved her very much—locked her in a tall tower, to safe-keep her and the baby who resulted from her wild island nights. There she would gaze out the window with baby at her breast, hoping to catch sight of the fleet and to hear stories of their bloody adventures wafting upward on the wind. Shut away like this, she and her offspring wasted into nothing more than a few hairs and a fine scrap of softness that the wind carried off to some unseen place.*

# AVA BINGEN

The first I know of it, a fellow scrub maid wakes me to say my stepmother is at the gates.

"She's been clanging at them ever so long," the girl says. "The guards are warning they'll arrest her for the noise, but she says she *will* see you first."

Blinking, exhausted—I fell asleep only an hour ago, after weeping as if to drown my broken heart in brine—I do up my clothes with cracked fingers and stuff messy braids under my cap. This is a cold morning; I actually consider wrapping the blanket around myself as I go out but decide it would be unseemly enough to result in my dismissal. *Which,* I think in that moment of innocent selfishness, *would not be so bad . . . Surely, Father and Sabine would be kind again . . .*

My head clears and I realize that I should worry, for if Sabine has come to the palace herself, with her belly, and she demands to see me—well, something very bad must have happened.

The guards let me pass the gates without a token, on condition that I remove the nuisance of my stepmother and return immediately.

"Bless the Virgin!" I cry when I see her.

In one glance, I understand why the guards want her gone. Sabine looks like a madwoman, sobbing wildly with her hair snaking about her face, her skin drenched in sweat despite the weather. I have never seen her so untidy before; it is as if she's given up the grand-lady pretense and acknowledged that she's a peasant in the blood.

*My* blood turns to jelly, but my bones hold strong beneath. I drag Sabine over to one of the little hollows in the cathedral facade where beggar trolls like to station themselves. It smells of urine and garbage, but no one's there now; the crowd of simples hawkers and early morning churchgoers is thin today, and the trolls have gone back to their bridges.

"Is Father sick?" This is not the season for plague, but a thousand other maladies could have claimed him, his lungs never strong. "Or has something happened to the house?" I imagine fire, collapse, any number of calamities.

"Klaus!" she wails. "My Klaus is *gone!*" Then Sabine seems to have trouble catching her breath, for her bosom swells and her face turns purple, and I can't get another word out of her for some time.

Of course I try: "Do you mean *dead*? Or has he left you?" I imagine him, madly, running off with Gerda the maid, to start life over with passion. And I imagine him lying cold in a coffin, with silver coins over his eyes. And I not given enough notice to say good-bye.

"Which is it?" I demand, and when my stepmother still cannot answer, I grab her by the shoulders and shake.

That does the trick. She turns redder than ever but manages a few words.

"This morning—the soldiers—and they knew just where to come, made straight for the house, so we had no warning at all. Klaus and his stone head with the spectacles! Wanting all the fine courtiers to find him!"

"What do you mean?" I ask with gathering dread.

"Ava, you must help. They've taken him away—they say he's *to blame!*"

The dread becomes a lump of callused fact: The worst has happened. Only I still don't know what the worst might be.

"To blame . . . for what?"

# FLUX

N the moments after Christian is stricken, Count Nicolas Bullen works fast. He tugs on his own clothes and wrestles Christian's nightshirt into order, eases Christian to the floor, and closes the bed curtains, using a corner of one to mop the sweat from his own brow. He is overheated and has lost his doublet among the sheets. No one will notice that. He grips Christian, both of them groaning now, and drags him toward the close-stool cabinet.

Hearing the groans, the King's grooms burst in. They stop to gape at the scene—Count Bullen supporting the filthy King, who moans and clutches first at Nicolas's shirt, then at his own.

"It's a flux." Nicolas, visibly upset for perhaps the first time in court history, states what appears to be obvious. Christian obliges by soiling himself again.

When the grooms rush to support him, they discover that Christian is also bleeding, like a woman in her courses. The roomful of dashing men freezes, all stupefied. This royal indignity is worse than anything they saw at war (those who went). They don't even have the strength to reach for their pomanders.

It is Willem Braj who orders, "Send for the physicians." It is a guardsman who obeys.

Christian's favorites dutifully carry him to his close-stool, but sitting is too torturous. They lay him in his bed instead, where he fouls the sheets again, obscuring the blood already soaked there. Then he drifts out of awareness, to fall into a painful shuddering sleep. As he moves, he seems to chant— perhaps a Latin prayer, perhaps a name, perhaps both.

*In tenebris lumen* . . .

Nicolas Bullen *(BullenBullenBullen)* stands to one side, thin and shivering. Naturally he is upset at having witnessed the onset of this most terrible crisis; anyone would be, even the man who should be best prepared to carry out an ailing King's wishes.

Adjusting the sheets, Rafael af Hvas hands over Nicolas's doublet without comment. Nicolas twists himself into it.

The physicians arrive, Krolik, Candenzius, Venslov, and Dé. Krolik announces that the King might choke on his own vomitus while lying on his back. The grooms turn the royal body on its side, whereupon Christian explodes again.

"How did this begin?" Dé asks Nicolas.

"I believe it is a flux," the Count repeats himself, voice ticking like the inner works of a clock.

"But when . . . how . . . ?"

Nicolas says, sweating, visibly casting about for memories and answers, "He made use of his close-stool." (This the doctors confirm, and they busy themselves studying the contents.) "And he gazed at the stars from a window." (A lie.) "And he began suddenly to—" He waves, his fine family ring an arc of red. "To be as you see him now."

Christian has lost his ovine look. He appears almost slender, noble, like the statue lying upon a sarcophagus. His breath rasps in his throat; perhaps he wants to speak. Fortunately he coughs instead, giving Nicolas more time in which to think.

The King's Secretary needs a story, a useful story. Simple collapse will not be believed; a court that thrives on suspicion requires both explanations and rumors, real and imagined causes for each mysterious effect. It is time to direct attention—deflect it—for none must guess what he and the King were doing, how they were sealing the pact between themselves forever, the pact that ripped the last fragile bit of the long-ailing King apart. That will remain the ultimate secret.

Nicolas does not believe in Fate or even in coincidence. He believes in plot. As the others work over Christian, Nicolas collects the King's garments, using the task to keep one eye on the physicians and courtiers while he schemes. He weighs the value of certain rumors: a lightning bolt, as opposed to Candenzius's celestial poison, as opposed to a more ordinary earthly toxin such as is currently believed to have sickened the children. There is something to be said for an act of God, striking down a royal sinner as he gazed through a scientific machine at what God put in the heavens to mystify man. Just such a machine is to be found in Christian's inner chamber, a contraption of metal and glass for occasional stolen minutes when Christian is seized to stare at a sky that to Nicolas looks as blank as the water on the bay.

Nicolas turns Christian's hose in his hands, putting each leg right-side out. He wonders, *Is it politic to arrest a court physician who dabbles in the stars — perhaps to acquit him later, as a favor to the Queen, who may be regent?* He should order some action; he is the Secretary, the spymaster, and he should claim his power.

He tosses the hose on the cluttered table. "Remove Doctor Candenzius," he orders. "Let him wait in the anteroom."

Candenzius's eyes are wide and frightened as he's led away.

*Or,* thinks Nicolas, tapping his lip, *what of the poisoners who have been sapping away at the children? There are plenty among the nursery workers who might be accused, as well as the Queen herself.*

Totting up advantages and disadvantages, plotting out consequences, even the slyest courtier might stumble. Nicolas looks at the clock on the King's mantel; it stopped at four, and the fancy second hand jerks forward and moves back like an itchy pendulum.

With deft swoops of the fleam and the cup, Krolik bleeds Christian from the arm, thigh, and back. Venslov and Dé assist him in every way. Their usual beakers rattle emptily; there is no point in asking the King to fill them with urine, for he has lost control of that function too, dried up like an old milch cow. Instead the doctors study cups of blood, sniffing, tasting, and heating them gently to test their qualities. They sift through basins of vomitus with their fingers, sniffing and tasting this too. They look for mandrake, wolfsbane, shards of glass. They scrape the King's tongue and dig the junk out of his ears.

None of it illuminates.

Over the next hours, Christian's skin turns a waxen yellow and retracts, making him appear more gaunt. He soils the sheets so many times that Nicolas finally orders the servants to stop changing them, as the actions pain Christian till his moans become unbearable for anyone with a heart.

At last the doctors admit what everyone knows already: The King is dying, though what the precise cause might be, they cannot tell. Rafael af Hvas sends for Father Absolon to offer final unction. Willem Braj offers to ring the chapel bells.

"Not yet," Nicolas orders. "Would you commit treason? Announce the King dead already? He might still recover." This fools no one. "Let us give the physicians time to work. Give the Queen time to wake, and give the council time to plan."

Most members of the King's council are here at his bedside, also too stunned to act. "Is his testament written?" asks one of the lords.

"Long ago," the bony court historian assures them. A scribe goes to fetch it. Sealed with a ribbon and red wax, the appearance of the scroll soothes the crowd. Nicolas, as Secretary, spreads it over a table and scans the first section.

"This was written when the Crown Prince was still alive. Before I became Secretary, even."

The rest understand: The succession is not clear. Those courtiers who bear some relation to the Lunedies, however distant, tense themselves, already stiff with plans.

Suddenly Count Nicolas is inspired. Crossing back to the bed, he pretends to hear something. He climbs onto a footstool and puts his ear to His Majesty's blue-white lips. He announces: "The King wishes to address us."

Only half the courtiers present believe this to be the case, but all of them hold their breath, hoping to hear the King's last words.

Nicolas's ear stays at the royal mouth; he nods, raises his head, murmurs into the King's ear as well. (One of the younger men present, responsible for counting royal jewels, notes that the King's earring is missing.) Then Nicolas stands up straight on that footstool as on a dais, declaring to the crowd around the bed: "His Majesty commands us to arrest the charlatan who made those sham devices for looking at stars."

It will be a start, anyway.

He bends to the King again, listens for another breathless moment. "And he wants to see his daughters," he says. "Immediately."

Rumors, traceless in origin but nonetheless clever, circulate through the tense, cold air of a dim December morning. The servants spread them without moving their lips; guardsmen and fishmongers carry them through the yards and down Skön Kanal, where lords and ladies exchange them over morning glasses of ale. And so on to merchants, craftsmen, visitors, and trolls.

For a good long while, the various stories carry equal weight. Wiry Rafael af Hvas and the chinless Baroness Reventlow are convinced that Candenzius's perspective glass conducted celestial poisons. A merchant in the bookbinders' district, however, holds Stellarius in part responsible, "for he has an identical glass and may resent the King for some reason we do not know." Willem Braj and Lord Henrik Tummler (who is sometimes rumored to be the King's half-brother, as his mother was for a time the old King's mistress) declare they will interrogate everyone who's had traffic between the nursery and the King's household, for surely there is some poison about, a ball of quicksilver or a sinister white powder carried in the hem of a garment or behind the jewel in a ring. The ancient Duke of Marsvin, when roused from sleep, instantly shouts, "Lightning!" as if he were there, or as if the word were planted in his ear during the night.

Through it all, the Queen sleeps. Count Nicolas has given orders that she is not to be disturbed.

Thus it is that a fourth rumor swells: *It was the Queen. Driven entirely mad by her confinement, she cursed the King with magic and brought on his throes.* Or, at the very least: *She had him poisoned with a special dish her cooks made for him alone.* Sometimes: *She had her physician, Candenzius, write the recipe— that's why he isn't allowed at the bedside now.*

Ugly Doctor Krolik, whose weeks at court have put flesh on his face and made his bulbous nose appear smaller, has his hands full. He must not shirk his duties as Master of the Nursery now, but he also needs to give the dying King all due attention. Following Count Nicolas's command, he orders the nurses to dress the children warmly and to carry them to the King's chamber on litters.

"Make them look well," Count Nicolas adds. "Court costume, and have them walk to the bedside."

At last he is forming a plan, an impossible one.

Krolik and the two assistant doctors bustle about with more basins and fleams, beakers and herbs, prodding the kingly flesh to see what might still be quick and what is already dead. They hope to wake him one last time, at least. They pepper his chest with leeches and lower a clean white shirt over top.

In the nursery, the attendants are beside themselves with the enormity of their task. Somehow, and swiftly, they must find grand attire for two sick children who haven't left their beds since May.

The ladies tear off their own sleeves and capelets to make bodices and skirts, pinning up hems where necessary. They donate stockings and veils, cut their collars into caps.

"Careful how you breathe," warns the Mistress of the Needle, as she puts the last pin into little Gorma's ruff. "You might get stuck."

Happily the girls' breath comes shallow, barely stirring the fabric that now swaddles them like a pair of caterpillars at summer's end. They whine and complain of the ache in their bones, the unaccustomed exertion of standing upright—until the Negresse who is their favorite nurse steps up and lays a finger over each pale pair of lips, hissing a *"Shh-sh"* through her teeth. They obey her.

The girls are bundled onto litters and carried through the corridors, then bundled off again into the hands of lords and ladies who take them by the elbows, bend at their own knees, and bear them forward.

The princesses glide to the bedside while their ladies stagger slightly behind.

Back on the footstool, Lord Nicolas nods approval. "*Et voilà,* Your Majesty," he declaims toward the royal ear. "See, your daughters are quite recovered and able to walk. They came here to wish health to your soul!" He turns the King's head toward the new arrivals.

Christian rattles the snore of the nearly dead. The courtiers stare at the girls and the ladies holding them; mentally they sketch out a future without Christian or, perhaps, any of his children. A Lunedie cousin or two slips out to begin assembling supporters.

Nicolas bends even closer to the King. He whispers a single word, the word he knows Christian has longed to hear from him. And the royal eyes open for the last time.

What *does* Christian see through the dry slits of his lids? In his condition, anything would waver before him. So chances are he does not notice the girls' glassy eyes or the too-bright pink in their cheeks, the poor fit of their clothing or the half-clad women discreetly propping them up. Does he see Nicolas, his great love? Does he gaze into the dark eyes or red ruby ring? Does he mouth the word back to him? No. He simply closes his eyes.

"Your Majesty," Nicolas prods him, "it would be best if you were to confirm your successor."

Finally Christian makes a sound in his throat.

Nicolas nods as if he understands, and he picks up the King's desiccated hand. He motions for the ladies to bring the Crown Princess closer, and they do—Beatte (Christina) appears to float upward to mattress height—and Nicolas places the King's hand where the hair grows thickest on her head.

"Your Majesty," he declaims into that dull white ear, "tradition demands that you name the next sovereign aloud."

Few of those present would swear that in the throat rasp that follows, Christian Magnus V actually pronounces the name of his ten-year-old daughter; but those closest to the bedside do see the knobby fingers contract over the girl's skull in what might be interpreted as a blessing.

So the successor is named, and the King may die. Which he promptly does, in another spout of blood—even before the attendants dip Beatte in a curtsy, even before little Gorma faints, and before Nicolas can have Christian confirm the regent who will rule until the new Queen or as-yet-unborn infant King comes of age.

Christian Magnus V is dead. Long live Queen Christina-Beatte!

At least until it is known whether the Dowager Queen's belly holds a son.

Nicolas drops Christian's hand and steps off the footstool, leaving the doctors to wipe the King's mouth, the other favorites to arrange his limbs in royal repose. He has exhausted himself.

*Everyone who dies,* he thinks, *wears a look of astonishment, as if what lies beyond this world is a great surprise.*

## MIDI SORTE

When we bring girls back to nursery, we be carrying shadows. The bodies weigh no thing: it is only clothes that make a weight. In the room we must unpin, unwind those garments to find the white-twig bodies beneath. Then rub them back to what is like their life.

Beatte cry a little, but Gorma be not even a-fret. When we rub her out of the faint, she be so tired she is silent, and so afraid she dare not tremble less it bring up sick and she die like she seen her father do.

It is a terrible thing for a girl to watch her father die, but girls must grow accustom to terrible things, be cause there will be more of them.

Beatte now is all ready gone as Beatte. To us all she become Christina. "You must call her Majesty," the ladies of the nursery teach us; then they teach her. "And, Your Majesty, you must respond as such."

For me it be so wrong to think of that thin girl as Majesty that I almost smile for sadness. This I must not do, be cause we are to keep tears in our eyes till the sun expire, to mark the King's death. So I bury my self among Gorma's things.

We nurses return clothes to ladies who wore them first. Old Lady Drin, young Mistress Belskat, Baroness Reventlow, they take but do not put these things on. It is too strange, the sleeves and ruffs have sat on sick children's bodies in a room where a King just die.

A pregnant wife remark that her cape, which Gorma had as skirt, now feel heavy "like it's full of blood," with shivers and a look round the room. "Or something worse."

We inspect. That cape have no thing on it; Gorma left none her self behind. The lady give it to her maid to wear any way. I fetch a clean chemise and a wool robe from the press and fit them on to Gorma.

Beatte, ten years aged and now a queen (may be), sit her self on the floor and scream, "I won't! I won't!" Her voice be the screech of a wet finger on a glass. No body know what it is she refuse to do.

"I thought the children were recovering," say Lady Drin, she seem to accuse us. She look through a spectacle at both princesses as if she see some breed of thing from the New World.

"They just need a rest," say Bridget Belskat. She be proud that Gorma do what we tell her, let us move her like a doll of wax.

Lady Drin send a nurse to get a sleeping draught, though time be all most noon, and she tell two nurse they must get Beatte in her bed clothes. Beatte scream the whole all-time, but her arms and legs be too tired to fight, and her nurses bend her joints and fit her in her things.

I think, *To put a Lunedie princess in to bed be like to lay some other child in a grave.* But some how we must these girls keep a-live.

So I fix the blankets round Gorma and the wooden wings of swan where paint is chipping. My body move so stiff, I see Mistress Belskat consider may be she will slap me.

"Rock the Princess to sleep," she order me instead. She like to watch other people doing things. It is often this way with ugly women.

Lady Drin stop the cradle. She give Gorma some draught. "Where is the Dowager Queen?" she ask, and some one say, "She sleeps."

Still the Queen be sleeping! With her big belly and her embroidered night gown, she sleep like a princess in a happy story.

I lean in to that swan wing, I feel the bed shudder, but my belly stay the same. I push and my arms be hard. This is be cause to imagine my Gorma and a grave be also to consider what sits in my stomach, which belong in a grave as well.

# AVA BINGEN

The Lower Chambers, the palace prisons, lie in the deepest part of the casemates. Well beneath the grand halls and bedrooms where the nobles amuse themselves, below the guardrooms and the bins for storing food and wine, they are in the muddy, murky depths, where stinging eels are more common than rats. They are forbidden to anyone but the worst prisoners and the mildewy guards who keep them.

But I go, because I am a daughter who loves her father. I descend beneath the earth and knock boldly on the heavy oaken door. A little window opens, and an eye studies me; then, because I am a woman in the russet serge of palace apron wearers, the great door swings inward.

I am greeted by one of the moldy guards. He wears the Lunedies' blue livery, but it's somehow not as sharp as the garments of those who march aboveground, and he smells of damp wool and bad eggs. He has no weapon in hand, but he is far more menacing than even the pouchy-necked lackey who held me captive for Lord Nicolas.

He leans toward me. "We don't get many girls asking to come in."

"I . . . have a message to deliver."

He looks me up and down again, takes me familiarly by the shoulders and makes me spin for him. I know he is enjoying me, or thinking of enjoyment.

He asks, "What message? Who would send one like you down here?"

I hazard, "Arthur Grammaticus. He wants me to speak with the prisoner Klaus Bingen."

The guard laughs. He leans against the door frame with his elbow high, like an apprentice flirting with a milkmaid. "And what would he have you say?"

At this, I burst into tears.

Two other guards have approached by now, staring as if I may make good sport. The first one, though, is not unkind, and he holds the others back.

"I s'pose you're his wife," he says, "or some such thing. But you're not allowed in to see the prisoners, no matter whether you know the Queen herself."

I sob on, hating myself. I do know the Queen, after a fashion, but I can't say anything about that.

The first man concludes on a note of both sympathy and dismissal, "Try the King's Secretary or the Duke of Marsvin. They're the only ones that can grant a visit now. Or a release. Or a stay of questioning."

That is all. He waits for me to retreat far enough to keep my skirts free of the closing door; when I am slow to do this, he gives me a gentle shove and shoos me like a chicken.

In the final seconds, I think I hear the start of a sharp howl, like the howling of the madmen at Holy Spirit Hospital.

I imagine my father writhing in irons—hot irons—his thumbs being crushed, his eyes plucked out. But I'm almost certain that this howling is not his. I believe I would recognize his voice, even if it were crying in a way I'd never heard before.

After my failure in the Lower Chambers, I labor up the twisted stairs to Nicolas's new apartments.

I've never visited him here before; he was done with me as soon as I gave him Countess Elinor, though I've always puzzled over why. Perhaps I had simply fulfilled my function and no longer interested him . . . or perhaps he's holding me in reserve for some task. Which terrifies but does not stop me now.

The room is plain but expensive, with a few chairs and chests of simple design, all with keyholes and locks. I wonder if this is Nicolas's true taste or if it was imposed by the King. Nicolas had such an elaborate chair in the old casemates, so many gold objects about; I wonder what he's done with them.

I stand myself in a corner. First I will observe; I will try to plan.

Other people drift in, drift out, wonder aloud where the Secretary is, and mop their eyes with handkerchiefs and sleeves in accordance with the tradition that makes citizens weep for the deceased sovereign all day. For me the tears require no effort, because my father is in prison. I sob into my apron until my eyes are sore with passing hot grains of salt.

Some people weep because we may have a queen instead, and that threatens the stability of our land. The lords, in particular, mutter about politics. They are interested in the regency, in who will rule until Beatte-Christina, or Christina-Beatte, or the swelling in Isabel's stomach comes of age. They speculate quietly about possible rebellions, other lords who might try to seize the throne.

I cry a little bit over this too. I am deeply afraid. Anyone in power might decide to kill Klaus Bingen.

Gudrun Tovasdatter, Mistress of the Needle and my step-mother's old companion, approaches. She tells me in that way of not speaking: *Your grief is excessive, Ava. You will be punished for overshowing.*

She may mean it kindly, but I turn my back on her and plug my ears. She is twice my age and growing hard of sight; I think she will soon be gone. Maybe that's why she wants to see Nicolas, to try to buy another year here.

Around midafternoon we begin to doubt Nicolas's ability to grant any favors at all. We hear that he is not officially part of the new Queen's (or unborn King's) government. According to the terms of Christian's will, the regent will be Dowager Queen Isabel.

Several of the courtiers leave at this news, heading for the Queen's rooms.

I hear speculation that Nicolas has fled the court. Some say he's raising an army to take Skyggehavn by storm; some say he won't stop till he's king himself.

I have to blow my nose. I use my sleeve. Then Gudrun gives me a handkerchief and says aloud, "Tears are a young woman's luxury. Those who need their eyes for delicate work cannot afford to sob so hard."

I blow my nose and ignore her words. I'm glad I threw away my needle case — I'm glad that part of my life is over.

I wait. It is all I know to do.

# Bay

N the dark waters of Skyggehavn Bay, Nicolas Bullen rows a boat stolen from a commoner's dock. He is alone; he rows in circles, slapping the useless water with splintery oars, pulling up fleecy shadows of seaweed, scooping handfuls of salty water, and spitting into the indifferent depths. He is a paddle-beetle that's lost a leg. He shouts and his voice is swallowed in the cacophony of the bells that proclaim the ugly death of Nicolas's only friend.

Nicolas was greatly desired, greatly loved. He knows this; it makes him furious. He could have had anything once he'd whetted the King's appetite. But he was overpatient and thus has failed. He must plan again.

He grinds willfully against the bumps in his groin until pain jolts through him like lightning. He howls, finding release in his pain.

He rows a bit farther, to feel the effort in his shoulders and wrists. He believes himself safe; he reacted well, he thinks, to the cataclysmic scene in the inner chamber—but now his steward's brain is totting up accounts and dangers, the careful moves his nascent plan will require, the risks if it fails.

The winter sun begins to set, making the water gleam like a shard of the volcanic glass found on the green island where

Nicolas was born. The surface ripples with the sound of bells; water seeps through cracks in the little boat and soaks his fine slippers.

He cannot bail and row at the same time. In fact, he has nothing with which to bail except his loose velvet hat. He chooses to row. He looks about for a destination. Island or palace? Monastery or city?

Nicolas is not a fanciful man, but when he looks toward the palace, he sees what the poets have described. As the building rises from the bay, it presents itself as a dragon crouching as it waits for tribute. The spires mark out elbows, spine, and head. Then come the scaly wings of towers and the long, low body of walls and outbuildings. The torch-lit tongue of a dock that could shake sailors loose from their ship and into the iron gates, there to swallow them whole.

For a moment, Nicolas floats. He broods.

Legend claims that the man who discovered the uses of whale oil did so after a snowstorm forced him to take refuge in a beached carcass. He burned the blubber and ate the meat, and in springtime he picked flowers to distill into perfume.

There are lessons in history, Nicolas's onetime tutor used to say. Even when the history is legend.

Nicolas wipes salt water from his face with the back of his wrist.

The oars dip; the water moves; the palace grows larger.

ROUND three o'clock, as the pale sun sinks into a sapphire sky, Isabel opens her eyes to find she has been sleeping in a cloud. Her bed hangings are now white, her covers, her tapestries, even her paintings and statues of the Virgin whisper their colors behind a snowy haze. It has all been rehung and draped in linen while she slept.

*"La Reine Blanche,"* she says. She recognizes the tradition; it is the same in France. The white queen is the queen in mourning, sequestered for forty days after the death of her husband. "Why did no one wake me?"

She realizes that all of her ladies are present, more than she thought she had. Some new ones she doesn't recognize. Their black gowns make inky blotches against the white; hands folded, faces expectant.

A stout one says, "It happened very quickly, Your Highness. Everyone thought best to let you sleep."

So it's true. Christian is gone.

No more sweating moon-face above her, no more tedious sitting next to each other at feasts and competing for tasty bits of meat and sugar. No more babies after this one.

Isabel presses against her pillows and listens to the subtle shift of feathers. Her pulse beats: *No more. No more.* She should probably ask to see her husband's body, but she is too heavy, too tired. Even the baby is asleep inside her. "Who is to rule?"

Duchess Margrethe says, with as much of a curtsy as her old knees can muster, "You are, Your Highness. You will be the regent for your daughter . . . the new Queen Apparent."

That must be the title they are using, suggested by some councillor or other.

Isabel lets the lids droop down over her eyes. Dimly, as from a great distance, she hears her ladies tell her that she is now the most powerful woman—no, the most powerful person—in the kingdom.

*You command the lords. They wait outside for your orders . . . Rafael af Hvas, Willem Braj, the Duke of Marsvin . . .*

Power. Command. From the seclusion of a white room.

A silver peacefulness descends over Isabel's vision.

"Highness. Highness." Someone is shaking her shoulder.

The white room is now lit by fire, but at the shutter edges she sees traces of darkest blue, that sort of cold color that comes of snowfall in a long twilight. Isabel has slept her way into winter. *La Reine d'Hiver.*

"Your Highness, you must rouse yourself." Some wig-less, gray-haired lady. She holds a gobletful of the bitter spiced ale that Isabel normally takes in morning. This woman is also dressed in black; even more inky ladies stand behind, watching. Their manner is as subdued as their clothing.

"Is it time for the funeral?" Isabel asks.

The baby twists in Isabel's stomach. He is awake and swimming like a hungry little fish.

"Not yet. But"—the lady seems nervous—"you have a visitor. An . . . insistent visitor."

"Beatte?" No, even as Queen Apparent, Beatte would not be able to walk so far; she would summon Isabel instead. A dim memory creates hope: "Elinor?"

"Your Highness, it is the Count of Bon. He simply appeared. He commands us to let him in."

Yes, her husband's favorite, the favorite among his favorites. Ladies say he has a way of simply appearing. Must Isabel receive him? Probably.

Isabel drains her cup, hoping it will quiet the baby so that she can think.

She must be wrapped too. Isabel's ladies bring a robe, also white—where did all these white things come from?—and a veil for her head. They seat Isabel by the fire and arrange her skirts in a white waterfall. Nobody asks if she might like something to eat. They show Count Nicolas in.

"Has it snowed?" she asks, before he even stands from his deep-kneed bow.

He treats this as the ordinary question it is. "It has, Your Highness. Last night."

Isabel studies the thin strip of lapis at her shutters. She will not see outside until her forty days are over. Even if she is allowed to attend the funeral (Does she want to?), she supposes there will be some special measures. A closed barge, a curtained box in the church of Saint-Peter's-on-the-Isle. A hood over her head.

She shivers.

"You're cold?" Count Nicolas makes a gesture as if to remove his cloak and give it to her. He seems sweaty, too hot. Her ladies think him very dashing, but Isabel has never cared much about him. Such a narrow, bony face, and he has no particular talent such as Doctor Candenzius has.

Good Candenzius—where is he now?

Isabel realizes that her ladies have left; she and this man are alone in the white-draped room. A most unusual occurrence. He must have demanded it. He is the Secretary; he can command secrecy. What does he want from her? No one visits a regent or a queen without asking a favor.

"I'm not cold, my man," she says, forgetting his name for a moment. "You may sit."

An empty chair waits very close to hers, so she knows it is proper to invite him. Anyway, it exhausts her to see him standing. So he sits, and his breeches puff around his waist like capons. This reminds her that she is hungry, but he speaks before she can ask for food.

"My lady," he says, in a quiet, deep voice that is no doubt meant to impress her, "I have come on an important errand. To preserve you."

She thinks of jellied calves' feet. "Preserve me?"

"Your life and your rule," Count Nicolas amends, with a gesture of one ringed hand. "Your children's reign. Perhaps you do not realize that at this very moment, the lords are discussing—"

"Discussing! Not with me!" she bursts out. She is suddenly petulant and achy; the baby is paddling against her bladder. "I am never consulted. I wasn't even told my husband was dying."

"Had you asked to be told?" The Count's expression is quizzical, just slightly interested, no more.

Isabel is chastened. "I might have saved him," she says in a small voice. "I have some skill with medicines."

When Nicolas does not respond, she has to admit, "No, I did not ask to be told." It seems pointless to add that this was because she did not think of such a remote and specific possibility. Just as, surely, Christian did not think of the remote possibility that he would die while she was both incarcerated and with child. The star, the star distracted him. "I did not ask."

"Perhaps that is the problem," says Nicolas. "If we are ever to get what we want, we must ask for it. And this returns us to the question of the regency." He gives her one of his plump-lipped smiles, and she catches a glimmer of what her ladies love in him. "For the moment, Your Highness, the regency belongs to you. But there are lords plotting to overtake it. To steal it from you. You must assert both your right and your desire . . ."

What would Isabel want, if she were allowed to have anything at all? Not a capon or a calf's foot, maybe a fish. She has become fond of fish in this pregnancy . . . and marzipan . . . and cherries . . .

Her eyes fall on Nicolas's famous ruby ring, the one that

has always belonged to the Bullens. She leans forward, reaches out, and tries to pull it off his finger.

"I want this," she says. She remembers Grand-mère saying over the gift of another ring, *Nothing has value till it is given away or stolen.* That sky-blue ring, now, has disappeared.

For a moment, Nicolas is still. The two of them, Count and Queen, test his claim—suggestion, rather—that it is possible to get what one wants simply by demanding it. They test, too, his declaration that he is here to benefit her.

He relaxes his finger, lets her take the ring. Then bows, in that proudly humble, irritating way he has. "I'm honored that you would allow me to make such a gift."

Isabel, delighted, slides the ruby onto the smallest of her fat fingers. It fits above the knuckle, and if she holds it in place, the red drop sucks in the light and offers it back up to her in a deeply beautiful way. It is almost, *almost,* as good as Grand-mère's ring.

"You have given me value," she says. It is the best thanks she can offer in return.

"Yes, value. I will help you preserve it. It is *your* value." His eye lingers on the ring. He must not waste time—there's no telling when a thump at the door might announce some rebel lords. "Your Highness, let me keep you in power. You must have a strategy to fight these men, and perhaps an army. I have a plan . . . I have command of informers . . ."

"A plan?" she asks, still admiring the ring, still with her air of distraction. "A plot?"

Sometimes she seems almost sane, this Queen. He will have to speak to Krolik about that.

"Perhaps something to drink?" he asks, and reaches for the silver pitcher.

"That is very kind," she says. "I so rarely get a gallant visitor these days."

"Your Highness." Nicolas gazes narrowly at her white hand, which is lifting the cup; the ring glows brighter there than it ever did on his own. "It is time that we talk about you. What you need now, in these difficult hours."

"A woman has no needs." But it is nice to get a new ring; she's had no others in a while, for her fingers have grown so fat with pregnancy that the physicians cut all her jewelry off weeks ago. That must be what happened to Grand-mère's sapphire.

Isabel says, "A woman serves her children. And the people. The Queen. Long live Beatte—Christina! Or the King in here." She puts her hands on her stomach.

But she feels her brow wrinkle; how is she to do any of it, locked in this white room? "Would you ask my daughter to visit me?" she asks.

Nicolas looks away from the ring, into Isabel's eyes. He picks up one of her words, repeats it till it sounds like the pealing of a bell: "I served Christian V. I serve the Lunedies. And I am here to serve you now."

His eyes are so pale, so penetrating—maybe she does see why her ladies like him. They are quicksilver eyes.

"Why?" she asks.

"Because the Bullens have always done so . . . Because the Lunedies are a great family."

*Are they?* Isabel wonders. Her husband, for example, looked like a sheep, and as far as she knows, he accomplished nothing for his subjects, only raised taxes to support his war. She herself is no great lady, though she has tried. And the children . . .

"Are you certain?" she asks.

"Isabel," he says in a voice very tender, *"I know."*

She blinks. "What?"

"I know how you feel."

She looks at the ruby. "I'm grateful for your gift. It is lovely."

"Not that." He shakes his head as if the precious ring means nothing; the light shines on his black curls. "I know . . . how it feels to have such responsibility. Your husband taught me that. I also know the secret pain. He taught me that too."

She would rather not hear about her husband's pain or his secrets. "We royals put aside our own wishes," she says. "But I do admire this ring."

Nicolas says more sharply, "The people won't trust your daughter as a ruler. She's too young—and a female."

Isabel looks around for her paintings of the Virgin, which are, of course, just blots of color under their white veils. She says resolutely, "I will do my duty."

"Isabel. Isabel." Nicolas makes her name sound like a song. "Why must *you* take on this enormous task? Why not rule"—drifting a hair's breadth closer, very calm—"by trusting someone very wise . . ."

"Candenzius!" A flash of happiness.

"No, not a physician," he all but snaps, and she recoils. He scratches his nose and softens his voice: "It must be a nobleman, and then you may have Candenzius's attentions for yourself. Your Highness, if only for this one time in your life, think of it. Why shouldn't you devote yourself *to yourself*—at last—and name someone to serve in your stead?" A pause, to let the idea sink in. "Appoint a new regent. You have it in your power."

His words are punctuated with a *pop!* from the fireplace.

If it weren't for that knot bursting in the flames, Isabel might decide differently; but at the sound, the baby takes a surge forward. He is a little whale inside her. He is her country's salvation. And she (the blurry Virgins beam in approval) is the country's mother.

"*I* will protect my children," Isabel says.

Various expressions flit across Nicolas's face—vexation, ambition, awareness, cunning. Isabel is not so cloudy as to miss them. Perhaps he wants her to see.

Nicolas sits up taller. He changes tone and strategy. "My queen, I must inform you. I know your secrets. All of them."

"I have no secrets," she says. "I am never alone to make secrets." Except now, with him.

"Oh, but you are clever. You guard secrets so close that not even your ladies might guess. And yet I *know.*"

Isabel gazes at the walls, where the white drapes breathe gently in and out, sometimes filling with light from the fire, sometimes flattening against the wall.

"Clever?" she asks. "Really?"

"Oh, yes." Nicolas comes another inch closer. His breath runs warm over her face—myrrh, musk, plus a pungent hint of sulfur. She thinks this proximity isn't proper, but somehow she can't tell him to back away. She doesn't quite feel she is here, with him, sitting by the fire, in her body.

"For example," Nicolas says in the thinnest, tickling whisper in the depths of her ear, "no one else knows that you're poxed."

## AVA BINGEN

Late: I'm the only one left, still hoping for some help from Nicolas Bullen. Otherwise the paneled anteroom is empty, just the chairs and tables and chests; the others have concluded that Nicolas's hour is over and are gone to curry favor elsewhere. This room seems far from the hidden treasure box where I helped Count Nicolas achieve the power he now holds. In its very simplicity, it feels sinister, even though he's no longer here to force me to comply with his wishes.

I'm curious how it feels to sit in one of these chairs, to wait like a lady instead of an apron. A chair with arms, near the fire, where I might surveil both doors: the one to this anteroom, the one to the cabinet itself. So I do.

It's so pleasant that I almost forget why I'm here. I relax against the carved back, enjoying the feel of a wooden poke here and there about the shoulders. *This is what a lady feels.*

Sitting there, it is easy to begin drifting into a story. I imagine that a girl who survives sickness and is played false by men somehow manages to save her father from death and chains and rats and is rewarded with . . . with . . . with having rescued her father, certainly, but something more, too. I push away the thought that such a tale has to end badly, with a lesson learned that proves a happy fantasy is a foolish mistake. Instead I envision a ship, a voyage, a house somewhere greenly pretty, a pair of arms that open for a welcome . . .

The dream breaks apart when Arthur Grammaticus bustles in, looking important with his furrowed brow and sheaf of papers. I have waited for him too, and recently, but he is not the person I want now.

When he stops, his robe sways as if it would like to keep going. "There you are," he says.

It's such a stupid beginning that I lose the last shreds of my fantasy. I glare at his floppy hat and his graying beard, his slightly shabby black robe and the papers in his hand. I still hate to think it: I have shared a sweetheart with Midi Sorte. And both he and Midi rejected me.

I ask, "And where have *you* been?"

"Gathering information." He waves his papers as if to demonstrate. The writing on them looks like charts of some sort, not the long accounts he normally composes. "For the chronicles. The order of succession."

"Then why are you here now?"

"I came to find you."

"Well." I stare at his bony face, the lips in the middle of his straggly beard, but he does not smile or say more. "Since these are Count Nicolas's chambers, not the servants' dorter, I think it's far more likely that you've come for a favor and that seeing me now is a surprise."

I think I've won a point, my single victory in this ugly day.

Grammaticus stays calm. "I knew you would come here when you heard about your father."

"Why would you care about my father?"

"I care," he says, "when you use my name as a passport at the prison door. You can't help yourself to it as if it's a cup of small ale. I have a *reputation*."

I feel as if I've been slapped—or stabbed. I stand. The man who once said he wanted to marry me denies me even a single use of his name! "If *your* father were still living," I say, with the hot pain starting in my eyes again, "you'd do anything possible to save his life."

"But I would be more cautious about how I used my friends to achieve my own ends."

"I only *mentioned* you—I'm sure they didn't even believe I really know you, Arthur."

"Well, then." He seems slightly mollified. He looks around the room as if he can't meet my eyes, but when he comes back to me, he's angrier than ever. "So did you mention Count Nicolas? Did they believe you know *him*? Did he promise to help you? Have you met him here often?"

"I've never been in here before," I say. I see Arthur make a mental reminder to himself; he will add this fact to his chronicle later—if humble lives like mine can be worked into that great history.

For a moment, I see no difference between him and Nicolas Bullen. They are gatherers of stories, users of women, and gobblers of hearts. I feel a flash of anger so strong, I almost forget I'm trying to persuade one of them to help me. But I do remember. And I think I may have more luck with this one than with the Count.

318

I've thought it before, many times, this afternoon: how vulnerable I will be when I ask Count Nicolas to intervene with the arrest. Grammaticus has never endangered me, even when I asked for his touch.

I put my head back to meet his hooded eyes. I try to muster some charm, though I have never felt so charmless. "I haven't seen Count Nicolas yet. And I came to him because I didn't think you would help." I try to summon my old self by running my hands over my face, feeling the heat there. "*Will* you help, Arthur?"

"I'm a historian," he says. "I cannot interfere in history, only record it."

I drop my hands. "Why do you hate me so much? What have I ever done to hurt you?" Suddenly I'm crying again. I can imagine plenty of reasons to hate me, starting with that bloody splash by the church and moving through my humiliation with Count Nicolas—but I don't see how any of them can bother *him*. Not if he doesn't love me.

"I don't hate you, Ava!" He seems shocked. It seems I've finally excited his kindlier side, the one he used to show me all the time.

He holds me at arm's length and studies my swollen eyes, my red face. "Ava, tell me about your father," he says.

I choke. "What do you mean?"

"I need everything you know about him."

"Will that help with his case?"

"In a manner of speaking."

I realize. I flinch. But I should not be surprised; I've

thought it before. "It's for your chronicle. Just for your chronicle?"

He opens his mouth, hesitates.

"Can't you do *something* to help? If I tell you everything . . . Could you help then?"

He is almost shamefaced. He is *just a historian,* with no will to better any life but his own.

And yet. And yet he is the one hope that presents itself to me now. I untie my cap and let the yellow braids fall to my waist. Jacob used to tell me my hair was one of my greatest treasures. I get down on my knees and take Grammaticus's big hand in mine. "Please?"

I wait to see if he'll accept me. My heart hammering, hoping he'll say yes, not just because I need his help but because, above all, I need to hold another soul within my arms.

# Pox

HEN Nicolas Bullen says the unthinkable, Isabel tries to swoon, but it cannot be convincing; she is too stunned. It's strange that she doesn't swoon anyway, on her own, but she doesn't.

*Poxed,* she thinks. *Pox.*

As she lurches away, Nicolas catches her wrists. His pale eyes melt into hers. "How old were you? Thirteen, fourteen, how old?"

The Italian—or *French*—Fire: half the lords who passed through her father's castle had it. They used to declare that they burned with love for beautiful Isabelle des Rayaux and her sisters; in their bedchambers, the girls joked among themselves about the true cause of the burning. They had nothing but contempt for the lords, though they could not help kissing the handsome ones from time to time. As Isabel did that time behind the tithing barn, just after her visit to Uncle Henri's château, when she longed for beauty and amours.

A branch breaks apart in the fire. Isabel says, "I came to this court as a virgin. The documents are clear."

Nicolas picks up her hand and begins to stroke the back of it, lightly tracing the scars that came of administering medicines to her children. *Not of pox.* She will not even think it lest Nicolas somehow hear her thoughts.

"Isabel," he whispers. "Isabel. How did you feel when that first red sore appeared . . . frightened, disgusted with yourself? Was it in your mouth, behind your teeth, or somewhere even more hidden? Perhaps you thought nothing of it, as the first chancre does not hurt . . . But then came the aches and the rashes and the throbbing head. Is that when you started covering yourself in mercury? Or did you wait till years later—age eighteen, nineteen?—with the boils and the white pus and the gleet . . . How you must have feared it! A sign from God—a condemnation! But you were already married and expected to produce a child. Children. Who were bound to fall ill themselves."

At his touch, Isabel is dazed. "I have always been true to my husband," she says, with the image of Candenzius's face before her, the memory of his fingers inside.

"There are many kinds of betrayal, my lady. And many people who would be interested to know you're afflicted."

The fire pops again, another shower of embers.

"Afflicted." She allows her eyes to close. That beautiful dizziness, the quicksilver mer-girls . . .

"You do know that you're quite mad," Nicolas says gently.

"Mad?" Her eyes open.

"It happens as the disease progresses." He continues to stroke her hand. Under his touch, the scars itch, which feels somehow good, even though it reminds her of those old days of the rashes on hands and feet—how she had to wear gloves even at meals, and dancing was agony. She told herself this was some little infection, not a great one, not *that* pox, and she learned to make unguents to soften the skin and soothe the burning. But there were all those nights of swiving Christian . . . then the bellies, the pains, miscarriages, the joy when her first live baby was born, followed by another and another and another . . .

Christian: he was not poxed. Was he? Should she have Candenzius investigate his corpse?

Nicolas says, "It would be a shame if this madness were to interfere with your daughter's reign. Or your son's."

Isabel shudders. She has spent her entire existence protecting some reign or other.

"I can describe how your life will be," Nicolas says, tracing a circle around the ruby newly on her finger. "Now that you have reached the age of madness, it will go and come in waves. Some days you'll feel quite clear, and others you will be exhausted unto death."

"I *am* weary," she says. Her eyes droop. "But I am not unwell." She suspects herself of lying; everybody lies.

Nicolas continues, "Many days you will not remember; these will be the good days. Other days will be painful. You will rave; you will hurt yourself. Your children, alas, can expect the same."

"The children," she murmurs. "I did not . . ." She can't bear to say more. She is admitting nothing. "Candenzius . . . the treatment . . . mercury . . ."

"Krolik." Nicolas runs a sharp fingernail down the inside

of her palm. "He's a good man. His special guaiac unguent is effective in treating the pox. Wouldn't you like to be cured, like your daughters? And he'll keep your secret. If, that is, he's appointed to a position in which he is *able* to keep secrets. Under a man to whom he vows discretion."

"My husband made him Master of the Nursery."

"Which is how he knows the truth about you. And the children."

Isabel feels dizzy, confused. Convinced, almost. She takes another sip of her special wine. "Am I really mad?" she asks.

"And will only grow madder."

In a way, this is a relief. It explains so much, and it removes a burden. The burden of deciding about things, of fighting. Now she can simply be.

Nicolas keeps stroking her palms and wrists with that long, light touch. It has become pleasurable, though she sees it's turning her skin red. "You must relax, my Queen. You must let yourself be taken care of."

"The baby," she says, wishing his hand would move toward her belly.

"The baby, of course. The baby will be taken care of too."

She looks at the ruby, now on her hand instead of his. "I may ask for what I want? I may make a condition?"

"Of course."

Recklessly: "Then I want Candenzius."

"Very well." Nicolas's expression does not change.

"I can have him?"

"You may have anything you want. You have the power

324

to elevate as you wish." He pauses, strokes the inside of her wrist. "Of course, it would all be easier if you were to designate someone to assist you. A second regent, as it were. One who would carry out your commands. One who would see to the worst business of the kingdom for you, so you can concentrate on yourself. And on your secret."

He has abandoned the idea of a substitute regent in favor of a cooperative one. Isabel feels she's won a point without arguing it; she is already victorious—though even in her madness, she knows the Count is manipulating her. "The Duke of Marsvin?" She can test Nicolas, a little, as he tests her.

He bends, breathes on her wrist in a way that warms her to the core. "Or someone else. Your most willing servant. *I*," he adds baldly.

Christian trusted him; why not Isabel?

"And you would send me Candenzius?"

"He could come to you tomorrow."

Isabel feels the first real happiness in months. "I need him to examine me. He must check on the baby."

"Whatever you wish."

*Whatever you wish*—has anyone ever said this to Isabel and meant it?

"I want the dark nurse too," she says. "The one who sees after my daughters—she can help Candenzius. Sophia always said she could soothe a stomachache. And I'm going to keep this ring," she adds, for clarity.

His eye on that red stone, Nicolas bows.

Thus the affair is settled.

## MIDI SORTE

Beatte never were so happy. She sing her self in bed whilst the maids bring arms full of fancy clothes that once belong to her sister, her mother, her cousins. They now will be made to suit an apparent queen. Every kind of gleaming thing, cloth of silk and metal, embroideries, jewels.

*What of this one, Majesty?* ask those ladies, and *What of this?* Each dress will become more rich, at least so long as she be queen. Old Lady Drin who have become chief in-waiting promise it. She thinks may be to make Beatte beautiful in this way.

Beatte hugs her self. She loves it all, she loves to be queen, she forgets to feel her pains and itches. She sing–sing–sings.

*And this one?* ask Bridget Belskat.

Beatte raise her voice to sing the louder.

The song I do not recognize. It sound like some thing to which nobles might dance, but Beatte be too weak for dancing, and any way a dance is unpermitted on the day in which every one is to weep till mid night. Beatte hums and watch the work and does not appear to know how far her life will change, for be cause she now have status of a queen she must also have more lessons to prepare her for it, and more guards to protect her from plots, and more ladies and more maids and hours with her councillors and regent. She will see the days of glass leaves and fairy stories as a kind of story in they selves, some thing that is pretty to think but not possible to believe.

Or so it seem to me, who have charge of Gorma still and am rocking her bed to soothe her tears. She weep not for her father and his dying but for the fact of not under standing how her sister be elevated and she is not. The ladies may explain till they finger tips turn purple, but they cannot make her under stand about the law of being born first, even if the birth be of a girl. The new ruler might be monster or a goat, for all the logic Gorma see.

*Give her a soothing draught,* say pocky Belskat. Another nurse go to mix it.

If I had one single tongue, I might tell Beatte about logic, how it belong only to the men and occasional lady with the power to twist and braid it. It mean no thing to the rest of the world.

"Not fair!" cry Gorma. "Not fair!" I rock the harder, till the nursey bring her cup. This time no body give me a slap. They want Gorma rocked away.

When she sees Gorma drinking, Beatte's eyes do shine. The ladies shake out a skirt of violet silk.

At last I know what she is singing, so happy she could burst. It is a funeral song of this place, sung fast.

For one moment I press my hands together like saints in church. Gorma scream at me to rock again.

# THE TROLL QUEEN'S CHILD

*A king of the Trolls wanted a child so badly that he vowed to turn his barren wife out of his palace or, at best, kill her in a way that would outpain the pangs of childbirth.*

*His queen, then, wanting nothing more than to please him, decided to present him with a child and call it their own. She combed the twigs and hollows of the forest for a suitable infant to steal but could find none; nor was there a healthy baby among the cradles of the few humans who managed to eke out a living in Troll territory. She had almost despaired of the project—and her husband was sharpening his cruel Troll fingernails, for he planned to execute her himself—when the idea struck that she did not need to find a baby in their domain after all, but might in fact go looking in another element entirely.*

*So it was that she borrowed a boat and went rowing out over the sea with a net such as is used to catch herring. She spent a day and a night and another day on the waves, until she managed to fling her net wide enough to capture a tiny, wriggling, sparkling mer-baby, a boy, who was perfect in every way except that his complexion was paler than that of the Trolls and that instead of legs, of course, his body ended in a tail.*

*These things could be disguised, at least for a time. She swaddled the child tightly and fed him from a cut in her own breast, rowing valiantly back to her husband's castle and claiming that the exertion had brought on the birth of a child she did not know sat in her belly. She pinched the baby's cheeks to a satisfying* ruddiness and praised her husband for planting such a robust creature within her.

The infant thrived on salt water and raw fish, which fortunately the Trolls found in abundance; and if he wept when he heard the keening of his kind in the distance, well, all babies cry, and this one's sobs were pleasingly melodious. The queen delighted in bathing him herself and in giving his fat cheeks those ruddying pinches.

It was only years later, when the age of swaddling was past and her husband at last saw the child's tail, that the queen discovered her first feelings of remorse. She realized that instead of netting a baby and bringing it back, she might have kept rowing until she reached a more hospitable land where she could have started her life anew.

Instead, she watched as the Troll king sliced down the center of their son's tail with one long talon, and when the bloody operation failed to produce a boy who could walk around on two legs, he ordered both the child and the queen put to death. This was swiftly accomplished, as the boy had already died from his cruelty and the queen was ready to try her luck in the afterlife.

Under the sea, the mer-people never forgot the insult, for they were capable of intense feeling too. Whenever the Trolls tried to venture beyond their own bay, the mermaids sang throaty songs to make sailors leap from their boats and drown in trying to reach them. Thus the Troll population grew ever smaller, until there were only a few descendants of that horrible king hiding in a forest that the humans had cut back, such that there was almost nothing left but rock and a few bean stalks.

329

HE noble body of Christian V, last king of the Lunedies (perhaps), lies in the amber-lined cathedral. He is watched over by monks who have rowed out from Saint Peter's, the same monks who (once Doctor Krolik made a quick, nervous inspection) washed the corpse, emptied it of certain viscera and effluvia, stitched its open parts shut, and dressed it in Christian's most splendid robes: green silk, white ermine, gold brocade; the sharp-tined crown of state and the jewel-encrusted sword of justice.

The cathedral crackles as amber walls swell and contract. It echoes. Is this one voice or many? The monks.

The monks pray for Christian's soul. They pray for his daughters, his wife, his wife's belly, his people. They praise God.

Nicolas Bullen comes every day. He prays, too, with his head in his hands, his ears ringing with the sound of his own sobs, so that he hears none of the monks' songs, none of the rustlings, creakings, and pops that show he is never alone at the corpse-side.

And Sophia the Wraith Princess is always there. She has become impish in her after-death; with her rosy skirts held high, she dances on her father's chest as she could never manage on the flat floors of life. She leads her sisters and brother in a lively galliard across the body, over the catafalque, around and around the statues who make stony partners for the dance. They creep into Nicolas's breeches and make him feel the pain of every stony boss inside. They tweak the monks' noses and blow in their ears to make them drop the notes of their prayers.

The wraith children gather up those fallen notes and fling them to the rafters, black dots of echo. They sing to Christian, *Awake, awake!*—though they are afraid of having him among them. He might save the land and spoil the party. They feast on his body, suck the eyes from between the lids, reach up his *anus* and tie what innards he has left into knots.

So runs Isabel's fancy when she remembers her husband.

## AVA BINGEN

This time, the gestures of love seem empty. Virginity is nothing and dangers feel merely sad.

Surrendering my maidenhead was not nearly as grand a gesture as I expected. A stab of pain, a quick exclamation, and then Grammaticus lay sleepy on his back. I burned for a few hours and tied on a monthly cloth, but I still felt the same inside myself.

Could *I* love Grammaticus? I ask myself while we undress as much as is necessary, while he touches and licks and rocks his way into me, loosing showers of dust from his bed curtains and exciting a creak in the bed's old wooden joints. I keep wondering till he shudders and goes still.

No, I decide then, I do not love him, and I no longer wish I did. He is now simply a fact in my life. He's the person I hope will at least preserve my father's memory in a positive light, if he will still do nothing to alter what he calls the flow of history by asking for Klaus Bingen's release. The person who provides some tiny measure of comfort as I wait for doom to lower itself over me.

No, I do not love him.

Suddenly I grasp Grammaticus tightly, fiercely, as if I am drowning and he is the only bit of flotsam left from the ship bearing me forward.

"Ava," he murmurs, sighing, with more puzzlement than affection in his voice.

This life together is not what he longs for, either; he, too, lives with disappointment. Over Midi Sorte, I suppose—she who stares coldly past the both of us if by chance she sees us together. She has been elevated to companion and personal attendant of Queen Isabel, who is said to have demanded her by name. Not even Christina-Beatte could call Midi back to the nursery; Count Nicolas, who shares the regency with Queen Isabel, has made sure of that.

I feel sick. My heart pounds. This happens not just in my hasty, secretive couplings with Arthur Grammaticus but all the time, as I eat and scrub and haul my buckets from the cisterns to the slop drains and rubbish heaps. While Midi Sorte glowers at me in the Dowager Queen's rooms and hisses if I make an unexpected noise. While I empty the Queen's chamber pot and turn the contents over to her doctors or dispose of them in the jakes; while I try, fruitlessly, to wash the stink of hard work from my hands and restore them to their seamstress softness.

It is endless, this task of cleaning rooms that never looked dirty until I started to scrub them. They now seem to be nothing but filth, so quickly does it renew itself. I think again of silver coins and how long I'll have to work to earn the rest of my passage to Denmark. Or if I'll have to spend them all to buy some comfort for my father—I cannot hope to buy his freedom, not unless some miracle spins filth into gold.

As I work, I overhear rumors, strange gossip. They concern

the man who is contracted to marry our Queen Apparent. Now that she occupies the throne, her marriage is of prime concern, and the arrangement has given rise to whispers.

*Henri of France is improper.*

*Revolting . . .*

*Delicious!*

*A sinner whose sin has no name.*

Henri is the brother of the French king who, with his mother (if reports are to be believed), killed thousands of Protestants this past August. No one mentions the family's bloodthirst, however, all being more preoccupied with determining the nature of his sin. They guess:

*Eats human flesh.*

*Does not like ladies.*

*Or what lies inside them.*

Each concludes as if he is the first to think it: *France must never marry the Lunedies again!*

"Are the rumors true?" I ask Grammaticus as we lie together one early morning. "What do they mean?"

"Why, Ava," he asks, "after all this time, are you really such a gossip?"

I leap up and gather my clothes.

Grammaticus says nothing until I'm repinning my apron. "Ava?" then, tentative.

I don't reply — I want only to be gone as fast as I can. I don't want to understand him; I don't want to feel any gentle feeling at all at this moment.

"Ava, I don't —" While I'm stuffing the braids into my cap.

"Why are you angry? Why do you care about French Henri? Did someone tell you to ask me about him?"

This is worst of all, but I still hold my tongue. If Arthur likes a silent woman, he'll get one in me—a woman who asks him nothing and tells him even less. Let him enjoy guessing my mood as I suppose he used to guess Midi's. He'll see I'm not such a gossip and that I'm not spying on his opinions.

"I didn't mean to wound you," he adds feebly as I reach the door.

As I cross the outer courtyard to the royal chambers again, I gaze beyond clouds into the winter sky and wonder how I ever found beauty in it. The darkness makes a rippling curtain whose points of light are the claw holes of an evil fate tearing its way through. It is another witch's hollow, more terrifying because we are all wallowing in it.

I think that my father would understand this, down in the dungeons of the Lower Chambers.

UT in the city, the regular busyness moves forward. Landholders must be fined for misappropriating public space, fallen bridges rebuilt. A canal that has silted up must be closed, sounded, and dredged to allow boats to pass freely to the bay.

"Wait, wait!"

The dredgers of Krydder Kanal stop work. Hans Rasmussen, young son of the poorest among the workmen, has spotted something shiny in the roil stirred up by the sounding poles. Hans has hoped all winter, while he has helped his father, to find evidence of a mermaid.

And now, here, what is it? Before his father can stop him, he hops down into the silt to see. He sinks to his knees, then his waist—grabbing around himself in the mud.

The workmen curse. Hans's father, Rasmus, takes hold of a pole, and the other men lower him carefully in to retrieve his son, who is nearly up to his neck now.

But little Hans is far too excited to care; anyway, the canal is several shades warmer than the air above it, where words break off in ice. When the men haul the two of them up (Rasmus holding tight to the scruff of the boy's neck), Hans is clutching a shiny object.

"What is it?"

The little boy's birdlike fist must be pried open; the fingers have already frozen shut.

"What is it?" Hans demands again. His teeth chatter; his lips are blue.

One dredger wraps a jacket around the boy's shoulders. Another dries off the shiny thing, blows on and inspects it. Wrenches off one end.

"It's full of needles and pins," he says, holding it carefully — for good needles are worth money. The case is made of bright metal (too much for gold, probably brass) and brown stone; it must be worth something too.

Hans's father gasps for breath, lying on the footpath beside the canal. His clothes are crackling into ice, and he will die of a cough before the month is out, leaving his family on parish charity.

"It must belong to a mermaid": quite possibly the last words little Hans will ever say.

The boy's uncle gives him a cuff across the jaw to punish him for his foolish jump; for his own certain doom and his father's; for the greedy impulse that makes the uncle itch to keep the needle case for himself. He has a family too, after all.

# Isabel Lunedie and Her Doctors

N the first day of Christmas, the Queen lies on her back. This time two sheets must be hoisted above the bloated hull of her belly so that the physicians—her own physicians, handsome Candenzius again chief among them—may evaluate the scion inside her.

This is one of the joys of being Dowager and regent: Isabel can name her doctors again and receive them in the white-hung rooms. She finds them more reticent with her now, after the terrible accusations about mercury; but they bowed quite properly when they walked in, and promised her all appropriate care, and before Candenzius began the examination, he greased himself in tallow impregnated with some sort of new flower scent that makes Isabel charmingly dizzy.

Also as regent, she can squeeze the hands of the lady to either side of her as hard as she likes, if only to show that she can squeeze hard, that she is not weak. Thus she squeezes until, she imagines, the ladies turn as white as the fabric on the walls.

On the other side of the sheets, Candenzius presses here and there, feeling inside and out. He does have a large hand, but it doesn't bother her now. The Prince—King—kicks halfheartedly at the intrusion; even he doesn't mind when it's Candenzius. Perhaps he's drunk on the tallow's perfume.

"Yes," says the good doctor, pushing through curtains of fat to feel Isabel's womb from outside as well as in, "all is progressing as it should."

*Health,* thinks Isabel. *Happiness.* A new king inside her, Candenzius in attendance . . . She has what she's wanted.

She squeezes particularly the hand of that dark nurse, her children's favorite, who stands so strong and silent beside her. A hand so tough it doesn't feel the press of Isabel's fingers, so rough its calluses cut her skin. But for all that, the woman is a fine nurse, every bit the comfort Sophia always said she was. She acts before Isabel even knows she might have a need, and so she is favored to hold the royal hand when several noble ladies jostled for that purpose.

"The people are grateful to the Dowager for this service," Candenzius said in his beautiful, raspy voice when he entered the room. "Count Nicolas particularly told me to tell you so."

*Service? Oh, yes, baby making.* She is pleased to be the object of gratitude.

The physicians confer, discuss, ask the dark nurse for a beaker of Isabel's urine. The callused hand is replaced with the soft, freckled fingers of Baroness Reventlow. Isabel squeezes all the harder. Soon after, the sheet is lowered, the Dowager Queen's privacy covered. She feels bubbles of air seeping out where Candenzius's hand was, tiny beats of a butterfly's wings. The fetal King kicks until they stop.

Before the men go, Isabel asks to speak to Candenzius. "It must be in confidence." She pushes her ladies' hands away as if they've long been irritating her.

If the sound of Isabel's voice is startling this time, it is insignificant in the general uneasiness of the room. The ladies gasp in relief, letting their hands go limp and shaking the blood back into the fingers. They retreat to a corner with the maids, assistant doctors, dark nurse, everyone else.

Isabel orders those others to sing songs in Latin. They begin, voices uncertain, humoring the mad Queen with a song to the Virgin.

Up close, Isabel whispers, "Candenzius, I must ask you a favor."

Poor man, his face looks haggard after so many weeks in disgrace. How rude of her husband to confine these good physicians or to hamper them in any way.

"*O Mother most serene,*" sing the ladies.

"Anything, Your Highness," he says.

"It requires discretion."

He repeats, "Anything."

"*Mother of mercy, suffering souls . . .*"

Isabel hoists her bulk to the left, trying to face Candenzius directly. She whispers, "You may have heard . . . the most horrible rumor."

"I beg your pardon?" The physician acts as if he's never heard a word spoken at court. In fact, his voice is so low he might almost not be speaking at all.

"*Intercessor for us all!*" The ladies sound like the monks of Saint Peter's, who are known for high and honeyed songs.

"A rumor," Isabel says, "about *Morbus Lunediernus.*"

She waits. He says nothing. The singers sing.

340

Isabel is forced to ask, "Where did it come from? The malady, I mean. Have you ever found its cause?"

Candenzius bends his handsome round head, coming as close to the Queen as is allowed during conversation. He peers at the skin on her cheek, near her ear, then gently brushes a lock of hair away to look closer. "Your Highness, you appear to have a rash."

She wonders—in her madness—if she is supposed to take this as an answer, if it means more than a simple observation by a medical man. If it is a *hint*.

"Candenzius," she says, scratching at the ear that he did not touch, "I want you . . . I want you to prove that *Morbus Lunediernus* is not . . . what people might be saying. That it is not—you understand—not *Italian* in nature."

Candenzius parts his lips, thinks better of speaking aloud, closes his mouth, and bows so that his lips are almost at her ear. "Very well." He sighs, soft as a kitten.

"You can prove it?" she whispers back.

"There might be a way." He straightens as if he would like to leave her and get started.

The other physicians stand near the veiled paintings with faces creased, watching these two confer. Young Doctor Dé holds the beaker of Isabel's urine saved from that morning.

*"Blessed art thou, blessed be all women . . ."*

Isabel gestures for Candenzius to come close again. She clutches his sleeve, forgetting to whisper. "Then, please. I beg you . . . for mercy . . . for my name . . . the Lunedies' . . . my children . . ."

"Your Highness." Candenzius gives a final bow, a sketchy one. "I'll send you a salve for that broken skin." Quickly, he leads the other physicians in departure.

Isabel lies leaking tallow and air while her ladies sing more praises to the Queen of Heaven. She expects to fall asleep but doesn't, not until she orders everyone to be quiet. Then she calls silently to the silver mer-girls, and they draw her back into dreams.

# MEDICINE

NLIKE the other two disgraced physicians, young Doctor Dé has never had control of the nursery. He has never been chief physician, never commanded the use of beakers, interior examinations, drugs from foreign lands. But he, along with the others, is suffering for having followed the mad Queen's prescription for her children.

The three doctors now share a chamber; Venslov and Dé even share a bed. They wait on the Queen, though not on her daughters, and are forbidden to venture beyond the palace gates. They fight over the right to use the chamber's single table for the various studies and experiments with which they pass the time.

Does Doctor Dé (big-eared, short, suffering repeated infestations of worms) allow himself time for self-pity? Does he despair and lie abed? He does not, or not for long.

"The Queen would like to prove a suspicion wrong," Candenzius has announced. "There will be a reward for demonstrating that the children's affliction is not . . . *Italian* in nature."

Dé is not aware that with these words Candenzius echoes the mad Queen; he does not recognize the madness of the appeal or of his own decision to volunteer. Even less does he think through the madness of the experiment that immediately springs to mind.

"I can do it," he says.

Candenzius—relieved, keen to gain permission to gaze again at the stars and diagnose them—promises a generous share of the three physicians' greatly reduced allowance. But all Dé needs is faith in God and medicine; that, and access to one of the little royal girls.

When he submits his request to Count Nicolas (discreetly, in the regent's cabinet), the man appears amused by the suggestion. His thin face twists, then he grants permission: "For a moment only."

"That's all I require," the young doctor assures him.

Maybe the expression on Count Nicolas's face was one of curiosity, not amusement; the girls' well-being is his concern now. He makes the arrangements. That very night, while the palace sleeps, the two men tiptoe through little Gorma's night nursery. Her attendants sag on their benches, probably drugged—Dé does not inquire, and Nicolas does not inform.

When it comes to dealing with Gorma herself, the Count hangs back, a sliver of deep darkness in the amber shadows. He will not even hold the candle while Dé, working with one hand, draws the thin brown hair upward to expose Gorma's neck. He unties the drawstring of her nightdress and pulls the fabric downward. He fails to find what he needs.

"She must be turned," he whispers.

No answer comes; Count Nicolas has vanished.

Courage! Taking absence as further permission, Dé grasps the Princess's shoulder and pushes—gently, just gently, for she is as light as a moth, even in her thick winter linens. He eases her onto her belly, head turned so she can breathe.

Gorma's snores grow quieter. The attendants' noises follow suit, though they do not wake.

Onward! Dé tugs the nightdress up; if Gorma were a grown woman, his action would be obscene. But this is how he finds what he needs.

"*Diable—mon Dieu,*" he whispers.

Near the cleft of her legs, on the inner roll of her skinny left thigh, Princess Gorma has a sore. Bright red at the edges, with a heart white and soft and oozing moisture.

Dé pulls the thigh to examine the little wound, its shape, its softest regions, where it might be deepest. Some force within Gorma expels another drop of nacre, and Dé congratulates himself. His experiment is perfectly designed.

Now Dé has need of one more item: that part of a man known to be most vulnerable to diseases of the Italian sort. In the best of cases, the *membrum* would be as yet untouched by woman (one's own hand does not count, not in this context); but this is rare in a court. Dé has access to just one such article, a prick as virginal as those that dangle beneath the robes of any monk in Saint-Peter's-on-the-Isle.

He parts his breeches.

If the nurses were to wake now, they would see the youngest court physician with his clothes open, his member in a soggy state shrinking from the knife poised above it. They would see Dé with the gapped smile of a zealot cutting a slit into his own most tender skin; then, finding it to be insufficiently deep, cutting again, oblivious to pain.

In another moment, the sleepers would see him wiping the blood onto his shirt. He dips a brush in Princess Gorma's sore, then rubs the brush in his own wound. He does this again and again, until the sore is inflamed and its white sap has mixed with the blood of the *membrum virile,* drying to a pinkish plaster.

As the crust tightens over his skin, they would see his smile fading to an expression of mere satisfaction, then a wrinkle of fear, uncertainty, a weak reassurance to himself—and at last bravery, for he must have faith, must be sure that in this very simple experiment, he will find the proof that the Queen seeks. And by doing so, he will also please Count Nicolas, who will reward his ingenuity and his proof that the Princess is pure.

A fat nursemaid stirs in her sleep, venting a slow belch.

Thoroughly terrified, Doctor Dé flees the Princess's bedchamber.

In the morning, Gorma wakes with a stiff neck and a deep chill, unsure how she managed to wriggle out of her nightdress as she slept. Maybe sleep turned her into an eel. Maybe in her sleep she moves freely, eel-ly, where she wishes to go, through the warm waters of gently steaming canals.

She resolves that from now on, she will try to remain awake during dreams, so she may feel this pleasure as fully as possible.

## MIDI SORTE

I am a gift again, and for the second time to Isabel. She asked for me particular. Christina-Beatte said yes, take her, the Queen Apparent be too grand to need a nursey any way. I hope at least that Gorma cry about this, some body ought to mourn my years beside the cradle.

It is ten days since the last King die and Isabel were locked again inside her chamber. The place be all white as a sugar-treat. The Queen be whited too, as if she made of snow that fall in this place, or of lime, or of mandrake.

Now she has me sleep upon her floor and clean between her legs and fetch her drinks and a pudding made of blood that she dictate the recipe to me. She do not think it strange that I can write, or that I add some herbs from what I learned with poison-auntie, or that I do not speak.

"A vow of silence," explain Isabel to her ladies, may be to her self as well. "This dear woman is very holy. Which is why I will trust no one else to touch me in this private way."

And so I touch her, every way she wishes it. Her bed be the new cradle that I rock, and she the baby with demands just some what more ornate than others'. I know she be not strong enough to order any torment, may be she cannot endure her own as the baby in her belly kicks the hurt in to her brain. I keep her out of pain so much I can.

One day she call me Elinor.

When she does, this all most cause no shock. I think may be she wishing, may be she simply more mad than before. No body know for certain how mad she is, she 've been most strange since the King die. She have asked for Countess Elinor so much, may be she convince her self that Elinor have come be cause she be wanted. Elinor with a vow of silence, Elinor all most a nun. That Countess of torment!

And when she say *Elinor,* she smile some creases to her face and call me to her side.

"You have been so good to me in this illness," she say, while hold my hand in hers that wear Nicolas' ruby. "From now forward, you must share my bed."

This be a great honor in the court, even the real Elinor did not sleep beside the Queen.

The ladies bob they knees and murmur *Countess.* This be the maddest thing of all, but I play the part of madness too. When I hear the word, I hoist my bosom to my chin like Countess did. I be Elinor reborn from pain.

I wonder could I be mad too, if I have caught delusion like a *Morbus* from the Queen. I am treated different. Differently from different, I am Elinor. Strange even to my self.

I get new clothes. They use to be the Queen her self's and she has the ware house to open so they can be found. This is much more than one red silk skirt, finer and so many of it. Her seamstresses remake seams for I am short, and the dyers dye the garments black as most every other noble's at this court. The clothing make my skin more dark. A shiny skirt, a bodice tight upon my belly that still carry a visitor inside. No apron. A hat like ladies wear, with black wings and a white veil that float behind. Slippers and pattens that *clack-clack* on the floor and make me tip.

When I wear so much, Nicolas who visit every day looks so as if he do not remember the time he were in me. He acts that I am the lady who should wear these clothes. I ask inside what this can mean, he all ways have some meaning.

May be he mad him self, I have all ways thought since he first come see the Countess in her chamber, for who could lie with such a woman and be sane? He come each day or two to discuss governing, and she lets him have his way in matters. While I fetch her pudding and a spoon to feed her with, she explain she must take care for her self, that she have wore out from seeing to others.

Nicolas bend to her hand and say that she is wise. He turn and say to me the Queen must have what ever she want to swallow or to touch. "For she knows best in what's regarding her."

I wonder what I know. I wonder if the lump in me will know its father. I wonder who that father be.

When Nicolas is here, the lump do not move, even though it have reached the age of start to shimmer. It stay just a lump. He were only in behind any way, but I have heard of babies made as such. My aunties told me, my father did it.

Poison-auntie say a baby made with love be impossible to

chase away. Out of all the men, I did love Arthur, so I might quicken for him and not the others.

But the lump do not move for Arthur, either. It just sit inside while all the rest of me sinks low and try not to be seen.

Yes, Arthur once my lover follow the Count Nicolas every where. He will not look at me; he will not bow or greet me. I wonder will history write that Elinor Parfis did return from prison as a dark nursey with a big belly.

History! By Arthur Rantzen Grammaticus.


Now I write receipts, now I have ideas. I too have paper and some goosey pens, and all the ink I wish for. So some times I write these pages when the others sleep, and I hide them in my skirts. And another day I write commands for Isabel's pudding, with clove to make blood strong.

That same time I write a draught I will not give her. A recipe from poison-auntie, some thing to end the matter up of who be father to the lump in me and when will it quicken. I think this must be reason for my mad change in to a pretend Countess, it is the one power ever granted me.

Here is what I need:

    tansy

    pennyroyal

    catnip

    rue

    worm fern

    hellebore

savory

sage

There would be more if I could know the names that they wear here. And if I found some ants that be not dead with winter, I would crush and mix them too, with the whiskers of a large cat. Instead I grind these plants in oils and waters as they require.

The air around goes bitter, I blow it at the fire.

"What are you doing, my dear?" ask the Queen in her bed. "I'd like for you to read to me."

I hoist my bosom. I bring her wine and she ask no more for reading. She sleep like a chicken full of egg, she cluck but will not open eyes. She does not wish to wake now if not for her physicians.

I write for beakers and a brazier, and they come to me.

Finally I steep my pastes in water from a clean well, make it simmer to a sauce that clings to spoons and knifes I dip in it. I fear the portions, worry that the leaves be too dry for strength, that I should add more or less of some things. I make my best deductions.

Do the ladies shush that I 'm a witch? No, they think I follow Isabel's command. Or may be they hope I do some evil, may be it 's why I be here.

On the eve before the King is tombed, Candenzius come to see the Queen again. Count Nicolas have sent him, to check the progress of the heir inside. She yields to his big fingers, she holds my hand and that of Reventlow, squeeze till pain in us is dull and constant. She seem content.

"It will be a fine boy," she says, though not suppose to speak. She mad enough think she is physician in full now and ready to judge her own condition. "He'll save the Lunedie succession and the realm. You must assure the Count of this."

On they side of sheets, Venslov and Candenzius wipe their hands. Young Dé do a wiggle. As if they did not hear, they confer about her urine and taste it for the salts and sweets.

The ladies of the corners sing the high headache songs the Queen likes at these times.

Before those three wise men go, Candenzius lead me to a corner where he bow, call me Countess, and slip in to my hand a jar of dull red paste he say I am to rub upon the Queen each night from this one forward. On her belly and her privacy.

"While the others sleep," he say, and look as if he wish they be sleeping now. The ladies fuss on Isabel, they pretend they do not see us. "In secrecy. For the good of us all."

I push hands together as in church, hide the red jar between. What more can I do? For I know there be no *good* with in this jar. It is not guaiac, it is not theriac, it is poison.

Candenzius is Nicolas' creature now and have turn against Queen Isabel. He mean for me to kill the heir inside Isabel if not in fact her self. For I think this must be why Nicolas have allowed me to live these days as Elinor—if I refuse to do as this man say, I will be punish worse than the real Countess. More pain, more pain, more pain than ever I have thought.

And then that history will be writ done.

Death crawling through the womb, a terrible path. But terrible for me instead if I do n't shove Isabel down it.

So that night, while all the others sleep, I gulp the drink that I have made and also fill my cleft with what the doctor gave to me. I take care that Isabel do not taste the brews or even smell them, what happen to her belly will be no done thing of mine. I will not poison her, though what I do now most like to mean death for me as well as the lump.

I drop the jars in to the jakes, they will fall in to canals and wash they selves from harm.

As I walk back full at both my ends and in between, I hope for death, to both my lump and my person. For there be no purpose in to stay alive if I am told to kill a Lunedie, and no purpose if I keep the size in my own belly.

So am I elevate to Countess just to die.

# ISABEL LUNEDIE

HEN Isabel first hears the cannons boom across the bay, her heart rattles like a clam in its shell.

It is the morning of her husband's funeral. The cannons mean that Christian's barge has reached the isle of Saint Peter's and he is about to be entombed among his ancestors. There to decay in lush velvet darkness.

For as long as she can remember (fourteen days now), Isabel has been sitting in her white-draped bedchamber, *La Reine Blanche* by candlelight, lately trying to embroider something pretty for the baby. This is the sort of task she's given in these days of confinement, a way to whittle off the few hours in which she doesn't doze. She uses silver threads, couching them with silk on linen. But she has no talent for it, not anymore; her eyes are weak and her hands shake. She runs a needle through a bit of thick skin on a fingertip, and it sticks there without drawing blood.

Despite the smoky heat of hearth and braziers, Isabel feels cold. She wonders if she's wet her chair.

Or perhaps she misses her husband. That could be possible. It is often sad when people die.

The cannons fire again. The windowpanes rattle and a picture crashes to the floor behind the white linen draping.

This time Isabel feels the rumble deep in her belly. Suddenly, for the first time in weeks, she is sick. It splatters the front of her white mourning gown and ruins the bit of nothing she was making for the heir.

A few of the ladies stir sleepily. The room is stenchful, and Isabel knows that something must be wrong; this is not her usual vomitus.

"Where is my Elinor?"

## MIDI SORTE

Morning.

I wake from pain. More pain than ever I could dream, though I were asleep for it.

I thought that I would die by now, but my belly's hard beneath my hand and though I soaked my skirts it were n't with blood, just every else liquid that might soak a skirt instead. And I still breathe.

The ladies finally now are wakened, for there come a crash of cannons on the bay that shake the room. They yawn and blink and sniff, it is disgusting what I 've done.

"The fire's gone out," say Baroness Reventlow, she never were much clever.

"How long were we asleep?" ask Lady Drin.

The Queen say, "Where is my Elinor? Someone must wipe me clean."

I try to go, it be my instinct to obey. But I 'm a snail who can 't escape his curl.

We forgot Isabel in a chair, or may be she heave her self there over night. She has a needle and a scrap in her hand, a candle at her side. She may have sewed all night. I see that even from my nook I 've soiled her gown, that fleece that wrap the thing that she is brooding. But they all think she wear her own sickness and that I be merely so asleep as they have been.

How can she be sick when I took her poison for myself?

"Countess," say Lady Drin to me, and in a way that make me real, "will you not help the Dowager Queen as she asks?"

I curl the tighter, close my eyes. I am not Elinor, I am no nursey in this moment. I cannot stand. But Isabel calls again.

"Here, Elinor, come to me." She throw her embroidery to the floor, it fall plop at my shoulder. "And you others, leave us. Elinor will care for me."

My stomach clench and I try to not groan, but it escape me. No thing more do escape, though, be cause I am dry now inside. I try to rise, for if I am to live there be no other way to do so than in the service of the Queen and who command her.

I cannot rise.

So surprise, I do not tend to her, it is she who do for me. When all the rest have gone with sleep-blink eyes, she shove up from her chair, she have to twist to free of its arms, and come to pant above me.

"Elinor," she say, all tender as to her own children, "how you are suffering. Get into bed and I will make you a posset."

So suddenly, I feel the Lump inside me move. It turns as if it recognize at last the one who made it.

N her gleaming purple mourning gown, with a circlet of pearls and a brown wig over her patchy hair, Christina-Beatte sees only beauty as her attendants carry her into the palace's great hall for her father's grieving feast. She notes that every soul in the room is instantly on his or her feet—except her sister, Gorma, whose litter is just behind Christina-Beatte's and who therefore cannot stand as others do.

The musicians raise their trumpets and the courtiers bow; all in silence, of course. Still the air is alive: the whine of silk against silk, the shush of velvet, the creaks of knees and hips worn out with bowing. Count Nicolas, the friend of Christina-Beatte's father, grips a gilded chair in which the Queen Apparent is to sit.

Christina-Beatte claps as she would clap for actors performing a particularly charming play. After so many months in a sickbed, isolated from the court, she cannot believe this obeisance is for her. Then again, isn't it what's promised in every story told to children? A cure, acclaim, a feast. At least at first.

Christina-Beatte likes being Queen Apparent. This means she must be glad her father is dead, which is a terrible thing but only what happens in the natural course of life. Resolutely, she shutters the memory of his dying from her mind; it must have been a dream, or a horrid tale told by a maid. She won't think about tombs either, or Saint Peter's, or any other ugliness such as a little brother about to be born to take her place.

Such fun to have a new name, such pleasure to be someone else, someone not as sickly as Beatte Lunedie.

Attendants hoist the Queen Apparent and her young sister into their chairs. The women pant, for the room is warm and the Lunedie daughters are gaining in substance. Hurrah for the health of the Queen Apparent and the First (last) Princess!

But something is not right.

Christina-Beatte considers the women who carried her. Their upper lips are moist, and one of them smells. Onions, sweat, a cheesy odor of unchanged linen.

The Queen Apparent does not need to tolerate such an insult. "You are dismissed!" she cries, pointing one thin finger at the smelly bearer. "Off to the prisons!"

The result is most gratifying. The girl goes away crying, and Gorma looks awestruck—enormous brown eyes in a pinched white face.

Count Nicolas, settling himself in between the two girls, touches his forehead and bows. He says to Christina-Beatte, "You are developing into a formidable woman."

She feels herself growing warm.

*Power,* thinks little Gorma, with a surge of that old sickness. *Pleasure.*

* * *

The feast itself is boring. The courtiers gaze at their plates rather than at Christina-Beatte, and she must sit between Count Nicolas and the doddering Duke Harald of Marsvin. She fidgets with her heavy rope of pearls. The courtiers think she doesn't notice that they amuse themselves by counting the tears that flavor the sauces, betting on who can water a plate enough to make the herring swim across it again. Turning her father's death into a joke. Her father, who always had a gentle word on his tours through the nursery.

Christina-Beatte is sharing a silver charger and a glass goblet with the Duke while Gorma shares with Nicolas. This sharing is both an honor for Marsvin and his due as the current highest-ranking man in the land. But the Duke disgusts her, worse even than that dismissed attendant. His hands are bumpy with veins, and food has crusted around his ragged fingernails. The few teeth that do remain to him are orange, and he slurps his food; his lips are so greasy that Christina-Beatte cannot see the etching along the glass's rim. Instead she sees a layer of lard.

Politely, the Duke offers her some morsels. Christina-Beatte refuses to eat. She will be ill if she eats from those horrible hands. But she cannot send the Duke of Marsvin to the prisons; this much she understands about rank and court.

Christina-Beatte glares at the Duke's wife, seated down the dais. The Duchess should tidy up her husband, but Christina-Beatte knows the old woman will say nothing because she is snoring on a dampened chair. Those two have been married as long as Christina-Beatte remembers, longer even than Maman and Christina-Beatte's father. They are both anciently hideous, but it has been said that the Duchess was scarcely more than Christina-Beatte's age when they married.

From somewhere comes a memory, a sentence from a story perhaps: *A man might know all kinds of love for a woman, if he raises her up from a child to a wife.* For some reason, this sentence makes her flush warm all over.

The Queen Apparent makes a decision. "When I am twelve," she says, very loudly, "I'm going to marry an elf. All my children will be changelings."

As if pulled tight by a cord, the diners all around the hall sit up tense and straight. The dwarfs hide their faces in their hands, and the aprons stare forward expressionlessly. Too late, the Queen Apparent remembers this is to be a feast of silence, even for her.

But Willem Braj, whose rank has him seated far down the table, leans daringly in to make a comment.

"Perhaps Your Majesty Apparent would prefer a merman." He waves at the tapestries of state history that have been hung on the walls. "In keeping with the history of your realm. One with a mighty tail, of course."

A few of the ladies titter at this.

Christina-Beatte imagines what they are laughing at, herself next to a man with a long, flowing beard and a fat, scaly tail. Floundering in the bay.

"I can't swim!" she admits.

She is confused when the table bursts into loud laughter and applause, as if they think this very funny.

Christina-Beatte sobs in fury. The beauty of the occasion is lost.

*When I'm Queen in full,* she vows, *I'll send them all to be tortured.*

## ISABEL AND ELINOR

HE poor thing, poor dear Elinor, has turned quite black with illness. Only now does Isabel see it: Her skin glistens; her eyes are glassy; she has an obvious fever that cannot be attributed to her position in the hearth nook, for the fire has all but gone out. And she has broken her vow to silence, for how she groans! Though she is steadfast enough (dear valiant Elinor) not to form the groans into words.

"There, there," says Isabel, as soothingly as she can. She bends awkwardly, off balance, tipping a cup in the direction of her friend's lips and spilling a good bit down her own front as she does. The day's rule of silence does not apply to Isabel. "Have a sip of this draught. It is exactly the same as what I take myself. And when you are stronger, you may have some blood pudding."

Elinor's eyes are first round with wonder, then slitted in pain. After a single mouthful of Isabel's good spiced wine, she vomits. The cup goes flying and clatters against a chest somewhere out of the candlelight.

"Never you mind," says Isabel, looking down at what's become of her gown. "I'll say it's all mine. Everyone knows you haven't been sick a day in your life."

Isabel bustles around Elinor's corner, wishing the heir would not get in her way. She can't hoist Elinor (though Elinor is small) into bed herself; she will need help for that. It will be much easier to tend Elinor once she lies among the mattresses.

"It's not good to be ill in this court," Isabel confides. "A suffering soul is easily dismissed."

Elinor's throat makes a little sound, half whimper and half growl. Her eyes are nearly blue with pain.

"*Shhh, shh, sh,*" murmurs Isabel. "Do not fret, a maid shall come."

## AVA BINGEN

*One, two, three,* and almost done.

To say that I'm surprised by what I find when summoned to the Queen's chamber would be to underdress my feelings. There is the Queen, on her feet but about to tumble over any moment, bent down and tugging at a figure on the floor—Midi Sorte!—who I realize quickly is the one who's matted the rushes and carpets with a marshy substance fouler than anything I remember from the Great Sickness. It's spattered down the Queen's gown, too, and the bed curtains; it sizzles against the bricks of the fire nook.

"I have been unwell," Isabel announces with what I might call pride. "Do you see how terrible it's been? Poor Elinor is quite overwhelmed with looking after me."

*Elinor.*

I stare at Midi Sorte, and she refuses to stare back. Indeed, I wonder if perhaps she can't; she does appear very sick indeed, so sick that I break etiquette and ask a question of Midi.

"Should I fetch one of the physicians?"

Midi manages some sort of grunt that could mean yes or no. Her answer doesn't matter; Isabel decides, "Oh, good-ness, we have everything we need here, don't we, Elinor? I understand her better than any doctor. Unless"—she sacrifices some measure of pride—"Elinor would like Candenzius to examine her."

This time Midi's grunting is clearly refusal; violent refusal. One might almost suspect Candenzius of having been the lover who jilted her, she is so opposed to having him summoned.

Isabel beams. She's proud to be chosen over a man (both her favorite and, in this case, her rival) trained by the great academies to the south. And maybe she really can understand Midi Sorte's strange noises. Who but one madwoman could make sense of another?

"Help me lift her," Isabel commands, and at her direction I hoist Midi by the armpits and drag her toward the bed, never mind the pain in my own bones. The Queen follows behind, carrying the hat that Midi has been wearing as Elinor.

Midi moans. I ease her down to the floor again, where she clutches her belly. The dye from her silk dress has melted in her perspiration and stained my hands a sticky black. I dart a look at the Queen to see what I'm to do next.

Isabel drops the hat and holds out her arms in a cross. "You need to undress us. Both of us. We need a washing and fresh linens."

It's clear that she expects me to do everything by myself, but nonetheless I ask, "Should I tell the ladies to come in and wait on Your Serene Highness?"

"*Pas de besoin.* There is no need. After you're done, Elinor and I will take care of each other." She looks pleased at the idea.

Of course this is ridiculous, but the last thing I should do now is to argue with the Dowager. So I wait on them both: I strip away the filthy clothes—the fabric tears where it's been soaked—and swipe my rags across their naked skins.

Which is how I discover what's made Midi so ill.

The belly that she tries to shield is swelling outward, round and hard as a ripening plum. Just enough to make herself look stocky, which is how she managed to keep the secret from her dorter-mates and then, later, from the ladies who also wait on the Dowager. She cowers from me.

*Four months,* I think, *or maybe five.* I remember that time in the dorter when I held her head, and I feel stupid for not realizing it then. Particularly when she started writing Grammaticus's name.

A stab of jealousy makes me hot and sick myself—thinking of what Arthur gave to Midi instead of me, and at a time when he still spoke of marriage to me. He gave her a baby; he gave her his heart. But in the Queen's presence, I force myself to keep wiping and rinsing, squeezing the rags instead of Midi's neck. Then I get to the space between her legs, and my cloth comes back red. A strange red, not the metallic slick-ness I know so well from the monthlies; more a gluey streak that stays on the rag's surface.

And . . . I close my eyes.

. . . I'm on the square of Helligánds Kirke, awash in the howls of the madmen and the hiss of the sword swallower. The pain, my pain. The neighbors' whispers swept along by the red flood that left its stain on the stones of the square . . . A stain that was of my body, not some foreign paste that a desperate girl might use.

With the tears pricking at my eyes, I discover an unexpected well of pity in myself. What else is there for Midi to do? She has even less recourse than I did.

So I perform a small kindness, take care to hide the greasy rags from Isabel. I toss them into the fire, which I build up to a blaze in order to warm the two women I've somehow managed to tuck together into the white-curtained bed, Midi with a wad of dry linen between her legs. I wonder if a pregnancy as far along as hers will miscarry slowly or if there will be a sudden rush that reveals her secret.

Isabel puts her arms around Midi, or as close to around as she can manage, cuddling her as a mother does a child. "Bring us some wine," she orders me. "We need refreshment."

I don't even begrudge Midi this service. In fact, I make both a prayer and a wish for her as I curtsy. I pour a cup and hold it to each pair of lips in turn.

When I present the cup to Midi, however, she won't open her mouth to drink. She pushes her face into the pillow.

Far from noticing, Isabel seems to think all's taken care of. "Very well," she says, relaxing against her true friend. "You may clean the room now."

## ISABEL

HILE the maid works, they lie together, Isabel and Elinor, whispering secrets. Or Isabel whispers and Elinor listens; the poor Countess needs distraction, to lead her mind away from the demons of illness.

"When I was young," Isabel begins, "at the court of my uncle Henri, there was a beautiful fountain . . ."

As she speaks, her belly presses into Elinor's. She feels the heir move—something he has not done for several days. To Isabel, this is proof that she is right to look after Elinor and is doing it in the best way.

"All silver," she continues, "and quick. Alive. Our faces trembled in the surface reflection, and the falling drops dizzied us with beauty . . ."

Isabel, hearing nothing but the slosh of the maid's cloths and buckets, takes a breath and confides shyly into the delicate darkness of Elinor's ear, "Pleasure is that way, perhaps you know. It is the closest one ever comes to death."

# MIDI SORTE

All this, and the Lump still with in me.

HEN Count Nicolas Bullen brings the latest sheaf of papers to Queen Isabel's room on Epiphany, the last day of Christmas, the day her husband was entombed, he finds her abed with the upstart crow who has replaced Elinor Parfis in her household. For the first time in some days he is nonplused.

First, the Dowager is alive. Next, the other woman looks pale, if Negresses can be said to look pale. Old Queen Isabel, on the other hand, even seems to have found a new freshness; her skin glows with health, as if she has been sucking it from her friend's veins. Isabel is feeding her black Elinor some kind of concoction from a bowl, spooning it up as if to nurse a foundling kitten. The Negresse (or Greek, as some call her) sips feebly. Her lips have turned whiter than those of a native Skyggehavner.

"I am saving Elinor's life!" Isabel announces with a good deal more cheer than the courtiers have seen from her in recent months. "Poor, dear lady—worn out with looking after me. Now it's my turn!"

Nicolas recovers and says, perhaps by reflex, "But, Your Highness, you must remember to make your own well-being your chief concern." He watches another spoonful go to the

Negresse's mouth and adds, "I hope you are remembering to take your own remedies too."

"Of course." Isabel allows herself to show mild irritation. "But I've always found the best remedy for my ills is caring for someone less fortunate, as the ancient Christians used to do. Father Absolon will say so too."

The Queen's confessor, at the east wall with her small altar, bows his agreement. He looks uneasy.

"Charity, you see," says Isabel. "Love. This is the basis of our faith."

There is a crackle as Nicolas grips his papers tighter. "The child inside you—"

Isabel smiles, touching her belly. "He moves with Elinor. He responds to her."

The courtiers behind Nicolas cough. No one is at ease in the presence of madness.

Count Nicolas says smoothly, "I'm sure you know best, Your Highness . . . Which is why I know you'll be pleased— you must be—at the news I've brought." He makes a gesture dismissing the rest of his attendants and Father Absolon, who go willingly; but he cannot clear away the sleeping dark Elinor without the assistance of at least a strong servant or two. He decides it is safe to speak, since he knows that, whether awake or asleep, she cannot.

He puts a hard cushion on the floor and climbs onto it so he can tower over Isabel. "Let us discuss this matter of importance," he says in his soft, rich voice, "as one regent to another."

## MIDI SORTE

My eyes stay close, but my lashes let through sight.

Nicolas bows so little he can and still show respect. He sound and look like that virtue which he played when I were a sugar-gift with a plum in my mouth. Justice. And this today be a masque as that last one were.

He say, "Your Grace, I seek my fellow regent's blessing for a special project." Now wait for Isabel response, but she say no thing, she look bored. Probably she want to feed me more.

Count Nicolas speak quick. "Here is my plan to save Skyggehavn and the rest of the land from possible invaders: I aspire to marry the Queen."

If I be not abed all ready, I might fall down. Marry the Queen! She still be pregnant, and old, and no man's willing choice. The Lump kick hard against my lung.

Isabel's body is flush hot. "So soon?" I feel her move to look him straightly, feel her draw together as if she try to recall the girl she once were.

Nicolas admit, "It is early, perhaps, but we need to establish a strong political union through a prudent marriage." He nod at the door behind where lords and pages and officers all wait. "The French betrothal proved unpopular with the council. They insist it be annulled."

Isabel is confuse. "Betrothal? To France? I . . . King Christian is barely in the grave . . ."

Now she stop. She is the Mad Queen, but she be not stupid.

Nicolas' voice goes gentle in a fancy way. "Your Eminence," he say, as if he feel truly sorry to hurt another heart, "the Queen to whom I refer is Christina. Or Beatte, as she used to be called."

Isabel tremble all cold now like white pudding. "She's ten years old!" Then a pause, as if to wonder, *Is she?* I feel her count fingers.

Nicolas speak even gentler. "And so she is vulnerable, very vulnerable to foreign rulers and to schemers at home. As is her reign. Both must be protected." I hear a teardrop swell in each his pale eye. He must work hard to summon tears, a snake do not make them easily. "The wedding will not take place, of course, for two or three years—as soon as she gets her courses."

He do not flinch to talk this part of womanhood. He who may have stop *my* courses with his sloppy cruelness.

He make his case through those skinny tears. He say that at last he have found little Beatte *a consort who will secure the realm, father new kings, bring the government out from the curse left by that evil new star, promote a prosperity throughout the land,* and countless other thing that may be true but which I forget as I remind me:

This person is him self. He want to marry my Beatte, whom I have save from death. He will use on her that awful thing beneath his belly that can have planted a horrible thing in mine.

He say, "She has no father, no uncles, no brothers. She is a lamb in a land of wolves. But as her betrothed—in time her husband—I am prepared to do all that's required to keep her safe. And happy. And free from suffering of any sort, whether it be from intrigue . . . or disease."

At that, Isabel who have remain silent, make a whimper sound but no words. I peek one eye and see her twist the red ring to frame the stone between the knuckles. Then twist again to hide it.

Nicolas' smile get wider. He look his usual rat-snaky self. He say like a saint with a sacred vow, "Your Eminence, I shall destroy all enemies of the Crown. As her mother, surely you want this for Christina-Beatte. As her regent, you must desire it for the good of the land. I have the contracts here; they require the regents' signatures."

"Say it again?" Isabel ask. She scratch at her ear like to dig the madness out. "You must say it all again."

So Nicolas repeat him self. His voice stay slither-smooth and he mention disease once more at the end, cause be "Queen Christina-Beatte will not suffer weakness of any sort, from any source, now that she is fully under my care. Do you understand? I will protect her against *all* enemies. I have especial methods against disease."

There be silence. Even were I truly Countess Elinor, I would not be notice at this moment unless I run at Nicolas screaming with a knife in my fist. Queen Isabel is caught by some word in Nicolas' speech that have her wiggling like a moth stuck with a pin.

"I can't think!" she cry at last. "May I see her? My Beatte. I would ask her wishes."

All this make a fine fit to Nicolas' plan.

"Your Eminence," he say, "you *must not* think. You may have recovered a bit of health — for now — today — for which we thank the Lord and your excellent physicians. But thought is taxing to the complexion, and another bout of illness might send you . . ."

We hold breath till he go on, with out a threat, "The Queen Apparent is yet young, it's true. So her wishes are prone to caprice, and her advisers must make decisions for her. The council seeks the assurance of your blessing now. Today. The people must know the future of their monarch is secure if the Lunedie bloodline is to be protected."

"But the King." Her voice shake, she hold her belly, she worry on her health and future. "There will soon be a strong, beautiful King."

"Yes, Your Eminence, there will be."

I guess his face to wear a smirk, may be round the eyes where he think no one might notice. Nicolas never have seen a man he think more handsome than he, and if he be not so strong in body as some, he be clever enough to make others think he is so. Now he wait, smug like a spider, standing on a cushion. It is the cushion that read *CHATTE,* I saw it when he took it from the bed. A cat.

Isabel make a choking sigh. She let Nicolas put his pen in her hand.

"Your Eminence, sign here." He hold the contract which be laid upon a tablet such as Arthur use.

Isabel surrender. Her name scratch weak upon the paper. She say, "You are picking my children to pieces, Nicolas."

I believe he answer, very soft, "They are in pieces already." Or may be that is just my thinking.

# AVA BINGEN

Betrothal! Even if I didn't know Count Nicolas as I do, the news would make me sick now. Christina-Beatte is far too young to bleed, and still suffering from *Morbus,* no matter what ugly Krolik says. But of course Nicolas feels he will be safe from all disease, thanks to the magic stones he carries in that ornamented scepter of his breeches.

If anyone else is enraged at the announcement that Nicolas makes as he leaves the Dowager's chamber, that person is wise enough to smother all emotion for the time being. All, that is, but for the polite pleasure that must be expressed as they congratulate him, not only for his prudent decisions but also for his willingness to sacrifice himself for the Crown in this new way.

There is a sour taste in my mouth, even as I observe from very far away. With my bucket and my rags of invisibility.

Nicolas is gracious in accepting his friends' attention. His face is strained, but he has managed a spectacular feat and is well aware of the fact. He thanks his congratulators with a weary smile and requests that Rafael af Hvas make plans for a betrothal feast.

In the far yards, my fellow aprons grumble: *Sweat of Saint Peter* this and *God's collops* that. The city's larders are near exhausted; sweet makers will have to make do with honey rather than sugar, and there won't be more than a bullock or two within sailing distance, especially at this season; but still they must do their best, for their (our) lives depend upon making a good show. This is a celebration. Of love.

Nicolas glides around the palace like a black swan, appearing and disappearing as if by magic, always somehow everywhere.

Run the nobles' whispers in his wake, those rumors he's planted carefully: *A man might know all kinds of love for a woman, if he raises her up from a child to a wife.*

And eventually, very quiet, comes one that he did not invent: *What love will she know by raising him from a count to a king?*

There is no answer to that question.

## MIDI SORTE

When Count Nicolas is gone, Isabel sit still. She weeps. I think to pat her hand, to do what ladies do when they console each other. Even if I be not a lady and there for not allowed to touch before I am touched.

Isabel did save my life. That I do believe. If it were worth the saving, that is what we 'll see.

I achieve one pat. It is strange, our skins are near the same color now but not quite, never will be. I feel some stronger from touching her my self, she the Queen and I a black slave nursey.

Isabel take her hand away to wipe her nose and then she swing her self from bed.

"I have something to show you."

She cross to the chest that is a cabinet, a small room of many drawers and doors. She have a tiny key for each one. She open several, fill her hand with little things that tick-tick against the others. She bring them back to me.

"You see," she say, "these are my children. The pieces that remain."

Then she shows. The finger of Sophia, that I remember be cause I crafted it my self though I cannot remember why unless to make some meanness—I drop it in the witch-bed one morn and pull it up by slender thread that noon. I did not know how to shout another way and to be seen. Queen Isabel be mighty fond this finger, she kiss it fore she put it in my palm. For one time I feel ashamed my self.

Isabel also have knuckles and a toe here-there, and some bones the dogs have left. Five teeth, I do not know of whom. Finger nails and bits of hair and an eye that dried to stone. It look like the eye of a sheep.

"Relics," she explain, as if she have been trying to remember the word. "God and the Virgin sent them so I would never lose my children entirely."

She make her gown to a pocket over where her lap would sit if she did have one, and she hold these scraps inside and drop tears as if to stitch them up again.

I think first that others must be right all along, the old Queen have lost her sense entire, to keen over slivers of bone and wax. But then I think how some times the women of my father's house did fall in to a mind-mud from which they could not lift, just lie upon a couch or bed or floor and moan as they struggle with they selves. This happen most often when an auntie had no visit from the husband, or when dry months ended in a bloody rush, or if a child that was hers in special did die.

Poison-auntie had a cure for such a grief, and it were not so different from what Isabel have begun. She would gather bits of herb and candle-wax, and she sang as she stirred them all together in a brew with some hairs and other remainings. She would form the wax in to a manikin and made the suffering woman to attach the token of the child as best she could to make the wax a living form. If the woman could not manage, poison-auntie did it for her.

With this idea I fight my self to sit straight. I may vomit again, that sticky paste still gobs between my legs. But I have a candle near by, and I reach and pour its wax in to my palm, knead like bread with spit to keep supple. My fingers gain some strength this way. I ease back till I am close to crying Isabel.

"*Shhh, shh, sh,*" I whisper, and I hoist my bosoms to give her Elinor. She let me squeeze her hand and take a relic out, a round bone she says were missing from inside the dead Prince Christian's right foot. "And thus he couldn't find his way through life with us."

It all makes sense to her.

I pick this up and some other shard of bone and dip them in the wax. Then Isabel moan as if I be killing children, not merely touch their remainings. She try to grab the morsel out my hand.

I put my finger to her lips. Then take her hand. I set that wax in to her palm, and I put the bones together and nest them in her palm as in a woman's womb.

At last she under stands, give me the bones so she can heave up, and she wobble to her cabinet for more candles.

Together we fashion it, a sorrow-child.

We take the pieces Isabel have found, and we put them in a shape she like. That first finger of Sophia make the spine,

382

and the dried eye which I think be of a sheep go to the belly. The tiny bits make arms, legs, ears. There is hair. Isabel prick her finger and paint wax red for lips. She pluck black buttons to make eyes, but they look too much and she pull them out again.

"The little fellow needs his sleep," she say.

When we finish, it is big as Isabel's hand and heavy. She hold it on her breast and sing:

*Oh, God! For you are a sweet little thing . . .*

Perhaps there be some sanity here.

Or could be I have let the madness win.

## AVA BINGEN

All day Isabel and Midi have refused to let the aprons in to clean or feed them, but now at last Isabel has shouted, "Come!"

When the door opens, she points to me and says, "Only her."

I tremble. Perhaps she's about to reward me for my service yesterday; perhaps Father will have his freedom within the hour. Or she could as easily have taken a whim to call me a cow and slap me down.

I walk into a room with a sweet-reeking rotten smell and an odor of something warm and even summery, though I cannot think what it is. Secrecy.

My mother had a saying, *If kindness truly had the power to kill, the Virgin would rule over Hell.* By this I once thought she meant that I should be more sweet and giving to others, for she feared I had a selfish disposition. The extremity of her expression — the Virgin in Hell! — proved that she also believed I could learn only by acute example.

This is an acute situation. I cannot say just yet, but every hair on my body prickles with warning.

I did not fully understand the meaning of my mother's phrase for myself until that day, long after she died, when I visited Holy Spirit Hospital to look for Jacob. As I passed my bits of cake to the madmen who insulted me for my troubles, then gagged on the good things I'd brought them, I realized this: Virtue is its own jail; kindness, a danger whether one displays or receives it; madness, a mere expression of a soul's real thoughts and longings, its ravings perhaps neither true nor untrue.

"I'd like you to mix a new pitcher of wine," Isabel says, more as if I'm a lady than the lowliest maid in her household. Well, she has been confusing identities and ranks for some time . . . and now no one disputes her madness.

I blame Count Nicolas (or else I should thank him). Amid the flurry of preparations for his gruesome betrothal, he has decided to leave these two to drive each other the rest of the way to distraction. And both appear as distracted as Nicolas would have wished. When I watch over them this afternoon, I see women who are in peril of being slain with crazy kindness—and I am not quite sure which will be the murderess and which her victim. Both have lost their senses, it seems; and there is no sight more strange than the two of them, one so slight and dark, the other as big and pale as the swelling moon, lying side by side in bed and passing cupfuls of potions to each other with the greatest air of solicitousness. Both, of course, growing babies inside, though at different stages in their breeding.

(Babies, babies, babies. My forlorn stepmother, too, is sitting on an egg, and Isabel recently dismissed an unwed in-waiting for getting herself with child while in service. Why such a plague of pregnancy in this kingdom? I count back to my own last monthlies and am uneasy. Others in the dorter have started washing their cloths already.)

The Dowager seems to have no sense of Midi's body, even though yesterday it was her one concern. Instead, today there's a mystery between them, an object that they slide about beneath the counterpane and tuck among the pillows. Now and then I catch a glimpse of something yellow-white and odd-shaped, a pale little frog with bristles on its back.

I want to see. I have to see. The room is dark; most of the candles have burned out. To do my duty to light the Dowager's day (and satisfy my curiosity), I rummage in a chest until I find more candles, some so old they've bent and cracked.

"What are you doing?" asks the Queen.

*Looking for a shame to save my father,* I want to say, but I get no further than the first word before she interrupts: "Very well."

I bite down on my tongue. Surely my moment will come. With light restored, I bundle away their dirty sheet — no vomitus this time, I see, and very little of anything else except streaks of a crunchy yellow-white that I recognize as wax. Isabel and Midi tuck their secret in their sleeves, then trade it back and forth when I undress them for their washing. I discover wax, too, under their fingernails, and spattered on the bed curtains and the small table near the bed that holds Isabel's special pitcher of wine. I pick at the wax on the table, around the outline of the jug that clearly stuck there till it was prized free. Something to do with their secret?

I crouch and reach about beneath the bed, which is usually the resting place of all secrets.

I come up with the stubs of a few candles, the bare black wicks of them crumbling over my fingers. A few harder pieces, splinters that catch in my skin and that seem to be, when I pull them out in the filmy light, thorns of some plant collected in the New World.

"Midi, what have you done?" I exclaim, forgetting that I must not speak before the Queen. I sense the presence of magic — witchcraft — forbidden by the Church. I drop to my knees as if to pray. "Begging pardon, Your Highness."

To my surprise, Isabel takes no offense. "Where are you, my dear?" she asks sleepily from the shadows of the bed. "We need you."

Slowly I rise.

The Queen's little brown-prune eyes wink at me in the shadows. "You're a seamstress, aren't you?"

I could fall to the floor again, I'm so surprised she remembers. That bloom of blood beneath my needle . . . "Yes, Highness."

"We need a new gown."

What could be the occasion? Does she intend to dance at her daughter's betrothal?

Isabel fumbles about in the bed, and my spine shivers bone by bone.

She pulls out a sickly thing, that secret she and Midi have been keeping. As yellow-gray as the candles around it, lumpy with crustations I can only guess at, speckled with dried flowers and dust. A horrid little shape such as witches make to pass curses. Carefully the Queen puts it in my hands.

"He needs a dress," she says. "Something warm—velvet, I think. And linen underthings." Seeing the way I hold the . . . frog-manikin, she adds, "Remember to support his head—newborn necks are very fragile. But don't worry too much, dear, he's strong."

I curtsy, speechless. Isabel is not too mad to read the horror on my face, even if she mistakes its cause. She thinks I simply fear of a lack of materials, for she adds, "You may use whatever you need from my rooms. Take the bed curtains, take the carpets. Whatever keeps him safe."

I look to Midi, at the gleam of white between her shadowed lashes. She pretends to sleep, but I see her nod. And because I am a seamstress, with cracked fingers itching to take up the needle again, I obey them both.

"I can make a little dress," I whisper, lest anyone outside hear me. "I'll use the canopy over your bed. And I can make a cloak from the table carpet."

The Dowager beams at me. "I knew you were the right one."

*After this,* I think, *I will certainly have the right to beg a favor.* But will I want it from a woman who's not just mad but witching?

ND so Christina-Beatte is to be a bride as well as a queen! Although she is not betrothed to an elf (as would still be her preference), the Queen Apparent claps her hands and dances about her inner chamber. Count Nicolas is handsome, by far the most elfin of all the court in appearance, and he pays her lovely compliments; she is his *treasure,* his *heart's desire.* He has sent her a gift, a glittering little dagger with which, he says in a beautifully scripted note, "You may defend yourself against any who would try to harm your precious person." And he is teaching her to use it.

Christina-Beatte is woman enough to love the bright jewels on the handle, queen enough to love the blade's sharp edge. It is mostly ornamental, not so sharp as a sword or even a carving knife, and it bears her father's famous motto ("In the darkness, fear my light"), and it is still capable of cutting quite a slit in a mattress when it is tested (which she is child enough to do). Count Nicolas has shown her how to pull it from her belt and make a threatening sweep to impress her enemies and protect her *virtue,* the meaning of which word he had Lady Drin explain to her.

She also loves the polished blade in which she can see herself reflected, eyes and lips gleaming, skin powdered so white that the ugly scars and blotches of *Morbus Lunediernus* are hidden.

"The rubies make a pattern of hearts and love knots," that chinless, pock-freckled Reventlow points out, every time Christina-Beatte removes it from its sheath. Reventlow loves love.

Christina-Beatte waves the blade at the Baroness for daring to comment on this object that is hers and hers alone.

She remembers a time when she was so annoyed with her little sister, Gorma, that she seized Gorma's wax doll and broke it to bits against the neck of her carved swan bed, even weak from *Morbus* as they both were. Elinor Parfis pinched Beatte hard in punishment but kept the secret, and Gorma was too afraid of another pinch to tell Maman.

Christina-Beatte studies her dagger again, sliding it in and out of its gilded leather sheath to taunt Reventlow, whose hips wiggle with the itch of fear. Christina-Beatte understands that a queen must not go about stabbing people, or even dogs, without cause. But she would like to test this blade on something more than her feathery bed.

She remembers there are dark places in the palace, rooms she has never visited but about which the legends fly like bats. Blood, chains, torture. This is where, she has heard, Elinor Parfis now resides.

"The Lower Chambers," Christina-Beatte declares, so suddenly as to mystify anyone who cannot guess her private thoughts. "I want them opened. I want to see inside."

Baroness Reventlow blanches. Without asking permission, she runs to tell Count Nicolas that the Queen Apparent is making plans.

IV.

DEATH

*There was once a princess whose parents sent her to town with a coin and the instructions to bargain with it for bread. They thought in this way to build the sort of practical character in her that would attract a husband, for she was sadly lacking in beauty.*

*Along the way, she crossed paths with a hideous crone carrying a covered basket. The princess steeled herself for a test: Should she give the crone her coin, as she would surely be asked to do, and perhaps receive some magical reward? Or should she keep the coin and follow her parents' orders strictly?*

*To her surprise, the old woman asked for nothing but gave her a piece of advice: "Whatever you do, my girl, you must not interpret a coincidence such as meeting me to be a sign of anything. It may in fact be one, but the meaning is not necessarily for you. So you'd best forget all about me." She turned to the muddy road and hobbled on her way.*

*The princess was disappointed, for as the crone had guessed, she ever tried to find meaning in the small incidents of her life. She would have liked to feel she was participating in a grand plot of adventure, not simply trudging into town for bread that a servant could just as easily have brought back. Still, she went forth on her errand, bargaining well and heading home by a less muddy path with a brown loaf steaming under each arm.*

*She was just in time to see the crone knocking on the door of a hut all but hidden among the trees. She noticed that the old woman had uncovered her basket and that it was full of trinkets, ribbons, and apples, the last of which were perfectly formed and such a bright red that they might have been made of glass. But they were not glass, they were real apples, and the pretty dark-haired girl who opened the door grabbed one gleefully and took a big bite.*

*The smell of apple juice spread heavy and sweet through the air. The princess felt faint with longing, for her parents believed that fruit was an indulgence she would have to deny herself, since she would be unlikely to attract the sort of husband who would give her such things.*

*But then the pretty, dark-haired girl fell to the ground, the apple still between her lips; for it was poisoned. When the crone saw what she had done, she cackled and, suddenly spry, took off running with her rags flapping behind her.*

*The princess trembled in fear, but she guessed that this might be the test she was expecting: She must go to the fallen girl and see if she could help. Yet when she leaned over the motionless form, there was no breath; neither could she feel a pulse when she loosened the girl's bodice.*

*As she worked, the princess noticed a pair of jeweled combs in the dark hair. Surely these were too fine to adorn the head of a mere peasant!*

*Realizing that this coincidence must have meaning for her after all, the princess plucked the gleaming combs from the dead girl's hair and slid them into her own mousy locks. The jewels' reflected light made her braids much finer, and she walked with her head high and tossing to make them flash.*

*The bread was cold by the time she got home, but her parents were so pleased with her clever acquisition that they gave her an apple of her own. Much later, the combs became part of her bridal crown when she married a prince as crafty as herself.*

## AVA BINGEN

In the morning, I wake to find that fortune's wheel has spun again.

Gudrun, Mistress of the Needle, comes to fetch me from the dorter herself. She shakes me out of an hour's sleep and informs me that I am to replace old Nidia Stinesdatter and work the under-linens again—for both Queens, she adds darkly, as if this double service is more onus than honor. "The Dowager and the Apparent. And little Princess Gorma, of course."

"But why?" I blink, try not to yawn in her face. "Who ordered this?"

I've been a maid so long now that I can't believe in good luck, even after hard work. And I am fearful, still, of my day with Isabel and Midi—of course I never asked a favor; I fled as soon as they released me from my task.

"It wasn't me." Gudrun waves her hands as if to dispel a bad odor, then leaves me to push off my pallet and make ready to keep seamstresses' hours.

I stuff my hair into a nest beneath my cap, my face greasy but rubbed with a petticoat to dull the sheen. If I don't make haste, I'll lose my chance. Then I discover it's my monthly time after all, as for most of the sleepers who follow the cycles of the moon. I lose precious minutes to grab a still-damp cloth from the drying racks and pin it to a little girdle beneath my clothes, and I'm out of the dorter before most of the other daytime aprons have stirred.

While I'm scurrying across the outer yard, I hear about the Lower Chambers.

Again, Fate is spinning. And so is my head.

The prisons will open this evening, runs the talk as men unload carts and women haul baskets of laundry away. And then the Chambers will be emptied, for tomorrow Nicolas and little Christina-Beatte plan to celebrate their union with multiple executions, cleansing the palace of sin and crime.

"*All* the prisoners?" I ask of the skirts and jackets switching around me. "Even without trial?"

Not a single answer comes. Perhaps there is no answer; perhaps nobody knows, or the way in which I've asked has removed me from the circle of inaudible whispers. But most likely the answer is yes: for the Queen Apparent's pleasure, every prisoner, including my father, will be killed without the formality of even the simplest trial. Every soul in the Lower Chambers is now considered guilty.

I ask, standing still, "How? Will . . . will it be hanging?" I see Father's tongue protruding, blue, his eyes bulging in a purple face. "Or beheading?" His thinning pate rolling on a blood-damp floor. I can't bear to think of other possibilities: stoning, drawing and quartering, slaughter by a thousand arrows—terrible, agonizing earthly deaths for a man who lived aspiring to the stars.

No answer. The busyness of the palace goes on, as cold

breezes twine our bodies and ice forms a creaky skin on the bay. I hear only some murmur about it taking more than one dose to make an old biddy die. So I go on too, numbly, past the guards and the carts and the bubbling witch's bed that still fills the inner yard with the smell of sulfur. I have a position to keep. And a little, desperate time to pray.

Gudrun sets me first to hemming alongside other needle-women. Pale blue silk, an embroidered underskirt for the little Queen's betrothal costume, which is being made over from the defunct Princess Sophia's day-after-wedding dress. The hem is to be scalloped and tacked with nun-made lace; it will take the six of us all day.

"But if you finish in good time," says Gudrun, with an eye on my chapped fingers, "you all may visit the Lower Chambers when they are opened. The regents want everyone to see."

The others in the cozy paneled room breathe in as one. As if they're thrilled to think of peering at the wretched souls driven desperate by conscience, confinement—injustice . . .

"Count Nicolas says the Chambers will make a useful lesson," Gudrun finishes, "for any who are tempted to stray from duty. But of course, *this* duty, ours, comes first, being more important than most. The young Queen's got to dress well for her ceremony. So none of you will leave this room until we finish . . ."

As one, we thread our needles. Or try to.

I wish for the lenses my father assembled for me long ago, now utterly lost in my months of keeping the Queen's house. The dress for that awful waxen thing was easy enough to make, a matter of cutting fabric with scissors the Dowager gave to me, then tying threads by feel. Now, however, without spectacles, I get the thread into the needle by sheer chance, and then I can barely see where to plant the sharp end. I quickly fall behind the other women; what's more, my hands have grown stiff and clumsy, unused to such fine work, and cracked calluses pull up threads until the crevices bleed. This may not have mattered when I clothed the gruesome doll, but it will be noticed now.

My fellow seamstresses keep looking over, frowning at my lack of speed and fineness, no doubt asking themselves how I re-elevated so suddenly. As I still wonder too. So for a while I dig blindly into the soft blue blur, trying to hide my mistakes and pricking my fingers over and over. I don't care about blood, I don't care about anything in this room, not even the Virgin and Saint Anna watching sternly over me from the wooden wall. I think of my father. And Jacob. And Queen Isabel and Midi Sorte, the horrible things I saw last night . . . and my false sense of relief as I stumbled back to the dorter under my father's star.

No more than an hour passes before Gudrun yanks me away. She doesn't have to tell me why. I even start for the door. Nonetheless, she takes me to a corner and says, shortly, "You can't compare with the others."

I curtsy. "Apologies, mistress—" I might be glad to go back to buckets and brushes.

Gudrun interrupts. "So. Instead of doing fine work,

you will finish up a nightdress that Nidia began for the old Queen. Her Eminence's grown too large for everything she has now—in fact, she ruined her last good garment yesterday. So in this case the quality of the stitching matters less than the speed. You can make yourself useful after all."

I'm stunned. "Health to your soul," I say by reflex; and, "Health to yours," Gudrun replies, nodding like a fine lady as she sends me to my new task.

The world, the wheel, it spins and spins. I'm glad to sit again, even in a corner with a lapful of white lawn.


Morning, noon, and after have no meaning here, with candles burning and fingers flying. The others make nimble work of the blue silk; they go on to other parts of Christina-Beatte's costume, each working as silent as the nuns who blinded themselves knotting the silver lace they use for trimming. No one asks me for one of the old stories I used to tell, and I don't offer any.

When the palace bells ring five, we are finally allowed to stand and flex our fingers. Shake our shoulders, blink our eyes, take deep breaths, and unwind the serpents of our spines. I had almost forgotten these myriad little pains of seamstressing.

And here is one result of taking such pains: the Queen Apparent's dress is the loveliest thing I have ever seen. Spring-sky shades mingle with pearls and silver netting to give an impression of dawn upon the bay . . . It's almost impossible to think this is pieced from scraps and dyed (as a poet would say) with the spirit of her dead sister.

My sister needlewomen gaze upon the dress with clear pride, though I imagine that some of them, at least, feel tinges of regret as they contemplate a sickly child being linked to the demon-lover who will never let her go. Or perhaps they take Nicolas at old King Christian's assessment and think the sun rises and sets upon him.

As to my labors, the Dowager's nightdress is almost finished too, even though I've been the only one working its ells of thin lawn and added a stain with every stitch. It is ugly but sufficient, a covering for the secrets of which I know too many. Instead of lace, I've trimmed it with applications of embroidery: a lily, a swan, and a moon that the departed Nidia must have worked to someone's orders, for we never devise such designs on our own. (No carnation; that was once my special design.) The last part of the embroidery needs tacking down, but Gudrun says I may leave it to join the others when they take their tour through the Lower Chambers.

"It is not a choice," she says crisply, watching me fold the unfinished nightdress slowly. "Everyone has to go, by order of the young Queen. Even we essential staff."

I suppose everyone will also attend the executions, which must be considered even more instructive to essentials.

We stop first at the latrines and then at the kitchens for our allotment of bread and beer, for we have not eaten all day. I can't swallow; I think I feel the others staring at me, though I can't say precisely why. Those who were here with me before know me as Ava Bingen; but it's a common-enough name, so they might not think of my father. Or maybe they wonder what I'll do next. At the very least, I know they're asking why I've been allowed to stay in the sewing room with my ruined hands.

"I don't know," I say baldly, and they skitter away like roaches.

So, like roaches, we head for the prisons and the last rags of humanity there. In the military yard, we find a crowd not unlike the one that filled the cathedral at Sophia's death. A line of souls reverent not for the Perished Lily but for the spectacle of sin, as sick as they are excited. And up in the wide window of the soldiers' hall stands Count Nicolas, the Queen Apparent's intended, gazing down with torchlight playing over his black velvet and white teeth, while a drummer keeps rhythm and a herald reads the names of the prisoners we will see:

"Henrik Asgar . . . François Ebbelkraft . . . Ehrengard Nattogdag . . ."

Where is Christina-Beatte? Perhaps she is considered too young to participate now.

"Lars Valise . . . Anna Callioux . . ."

Through it all, Nicolas says nothing. His face looks narrower than ever, his clothing darker, his teeth more bright. He has completed his transformation into some sharp and cutting creature. The strong light behind him rims his black hair with luminescence, making his face hard to read—except for those teeth bared in a smile.

"Aurore Lavransdatter . . . Ludvig Rummel . . ."

I shuffle forward, waiting to hear my father's name, though as excitement mounts, the herald's voice is being lost in the sound of the crowd.

"... Klaus Bingen ..."

There it is. By reflex, I cross myself and begin to pray.

*Please, God; please, Virgin—please, any spirit who might help* ... I could almost make a pact with the Devil if he would do what I need.

For all my fervent wishes, I feel nothing. No answering glow, no sense even that my thoughts are anything more than a wet bubble of hope broken against a needle.

My mother also used to say this: *If God wanted us all to live, he wouldn't have created work or childbed.*

*Or,* I'd add now in my own voice, *wishes and questions.* If only Father had managed to leave the skies alone.

When it's my turn to enter the Lower Chambers, I do it with the normal trepidation, skidding on stones that seem placed deliberately so as to trip people up. I see the same guards as before, the one who was kind to me and the ones who were not, standing watch over the first set of gates with their halberds at the ready. I wonder if they'll have work tomorrow or if empty prisons will mean empty barracks for a while. How quickly will the prisons fill after Nicolas and Christina-Beatte empty them?

This has been Father's home for almost a month now. The narrow passages are warmer than the air aboveground, either because the breeze is less or because so many visitors are pressed together. Nonetheless, there's a special fishy feeling under the earth; the whitewashed walls feel like wet scales, and here and there a drop of water rolls its slow way to the floor.

All of this excites the grand ladies and gentlemen. They stagger giddily about on their pattens, holding their silks and furs above the stones, bumping into one another and venting soft squeals of naughtiness. To them, prison is a novelty and a pageant—as long as they aren't the ones locked away. They are mixed in with us now, as the space is too small to separate properly. So when we all get to the cells, it's impossible to see prisoners because noble hats are blocking every view, especially the tiny grates that mean a prisoner is being punished harshly by a very small oubliette.

"You were looking for someone in particular, mistress? I seem to recall."

It's the young guard. He's at my elbow, has changed places with someone to come to me. I'm surprised.

"You remember?" I ask.

"Like I said, we don't get many girls asking to come in. Not until today. You know," he explains awkwardly, "good girls."

I wonder if he is flirting with me or just curious or maybe kind. Anyway, speaking to him gives me a sudden surge of unburst hope—I'm a good girl; I haven't lost everything of myself. I give the young man an overpowering smile of gratitude (overpowering to me; I doubt he can see it in the half dark) and dive deeper into the crowd without further answer.

I don't dare say Father's name aloud, here where there are those who might toss me in next to him. But Klaus Bingen is not so hard to find. Of course he's drawn a large set of viewers as the man who summoned the stars' poisons to murder King Christian. The space before his cell is packed like a barrel of salt herring, and even though guards are shouting, "Move along, please, with all respect, move along, the Count and Queen Apparent wish it," I have to wiggle and pinch and pry my way between them to look.

I peer over a lady's shoulder. Father is all dignity (or as much as can be mustered in this situation), well lit with torches and chained to a little stool such as peasants use for milking; his back straight and his face and hair as clean as he can make them, gazing forward at the floor while people around him swear inventively.

My father. Who made delicate contraptions for mastering the heavens and who kissed my mother every morning upon waking up.

I notice for the first time how little he and I resemble each other. Both thin and pale, but there the likeness ends. His eyelids are longer, his frame larger, the shape of his face heavier toward bottom than top.

I might not dare to say Klaus Bingen's name, but plenty are voicing it around me, in the silent way of aprons and the noisy one of nobles. They demand to know what he did to the King, why he did it, if the effects can be reproduced again or reversed. They ask if he is a Protestant or a witch. They ask if his wife is an enchantress as well, and if the baby she's just borne him (Just borne! 'Swounds, can it be true?) is the child of trolls or of mermaids.

Quite naturally, he doesn't answer any of it; to speak could only bring his execution closer. He continues to stare, as if into some new vision of stars and planets that will save him from this earthly mess. Perhaps he's realizing, as I am, the importance of that idle whisper—if it's even true—that he has another child, an infant, who will grow up without defenses.

"*Lille far*," I whisper. Little father. For he seems very small to me in this moment.

At those two words, which he cannot possibly hear, he does look up. Without hesitation, he finds me in the gawping throng, and his blue eyes meet mine. Now his are cloudy; he's lost his light.

Then he blinks and looks down again, and that is all. Our good-bye, our I-have-failed-you.

So.

I shuffle blindly past the other poor souls imprisoned, thinking only of that one glimpse of my father. The dimming of his hopes and heaven: strangely, I feel closer now to his heart than I ever did when we were whole.

## MIDI SORTE

I think, *This be the tale, the tale, the tale. Of a time poison-auntie magic failed.*

I thought to pull Isabel out of madness, not make her happier in it. But now I watch her squeeze her breast to bring the milk, as she have seen the wet nurse do. She make a kissing noise to her self and she do n't hear the sorrow-child makes none.

"Is he not beautiful?" she ask. "Just what I've wished for."

I say no thing, wonder how long I can pretend to sleep while I think what must happen next and if poison-auntie had any cure for such deep madness. Except the obvious, which be death, which I have once refuse to give Isabel.

Nicolas will soon give me death as a trade, for failing him. I wonder will it hurt, how will he do it, how much will I mind. It would be better if I died from my own poison, but that is one more failing.

Isabel coo at her baby, she sing it a song about sweetness and youth. I try to breathe to the bottom of my lungs, a trick for thinking better.

All at once Isabel squirm and lose the baby mouth so she can poke me. She have remember some thing.

"Do you think it can pass through milk?" she asks. "The Fire, I mean. The . . . Italian disease."

I shrug. I do not know and it does not matter.

"Elinor," she whine, soft so she do not wake the waxy child, "Elinor, help me!"

To answer, I pinch her breast and guide it back to baby's mouth. *"Shhh, shh, sh."* I can think of no thing else, but Isabel is content.

"I'm losing my fat," she confide while the baby mouth cup her nipple. "I've heard that's why poor women are always skinny, they feed their own children. I'll be as slim as the Virgin before you know it!"

Some place in this palace, I know, Nicolas gloats all ready too. He will marry his apparent queen and later kill the darlings.

Kiss, kiss, kiss. The sorrow-child seem happy enough in his way too.

The Lump bubble within me.

## AVA BINGEN

Outside the Lower Chambers, Gudrun pulls me away from the crowd and the gossip about prisoners and sentences. We go far across the yard, into the shadow of a pillar where the torch has snuffed but where I can still watch visitors emerging from the prisons like spangled ghosts, gleaming in the darkness.

"Time for more work?" I ask, numb and dumb with it—another piece of my heart has broken and fallen away.

"Tomorrow . . ." she says, and hesitates.

Tomorrow? Of course, tomorrow. There is always work tomorrow. I hunch like a shrub and wait for tomorrow.

Gudrun takes a breath, then presses a cold bit of something into my hand and holds it there till it becomes warm. "Tomorrow," she says, as if still searching for words, "when you finish the Dowager's nightdress . . ."

I wait.

"We all serve the Crown," she interrupts herself; words I recognize. Suddenly my heart quickens, and with it the rush of blood between my legs. "Our duty, yes, by God's wounds, our duty is to the Crown rather than any one head under it. So—to serve. Tomorrow, when you finish, after you have starched and ironed it, the nightshift—yourself, you have to do it yourself, that's very clear—and fold it up and wait till the rest of us are gone, then you must sprinkle this powder inside, all of it. Then iron the whole thing again, to let the powder bond with the cloth."

I look down, try to open my fingers, but Gudrun keeps them curled.

"It's in a glass vial," she whispers. "Don't let the vial break. When you cut the seal around the stopper, make sure you don't breathe in. Don't let the powder touch your skin, either. And don't let it settle in the cracks in your hands. Wrap the nightdress in a fresh piece of linen before you deliver it to the inner chamber."

I understand. "Poison." With another surge of blood: "You want me to poison the Queen."

Gudrun doesn't confirm it; she doesn't have to. She holds my hand the harder. "Make sure that her in-waiting, that Negresse she calls Elinor, puts her in the nightdress right away. It had best be the Negresse."

"But—why? Why does Isabel have to be poisoned?"

Gudrun shifts; if it were possible the night could get darker, I'd say she's pulling it around her like a cloak. "We serve the Crown," she repeats.

I want to throw the vial away, dash it against the stones of the yard, but Gudrun keeps me still as if she can read me through my fist. "Remember," she says, and once again it's as if she's repeating some speech heard elsewhere, "we are working for the good of the Crown. For the land under the Crown. And your family—so they can stay part of that land."

This takes me a moment to puzzle out.

"Are you saying my father will go free if I do this?"

Far off, the courtiers flit through smoky torchlight.

Despite the cold, Gudrun's hand is sweating. "That isn't in my power to offer. But I do have something you've long desired—"

Briefly I see Jacob's face in the eyes of my mind, before I interrupt Gudrun to accuse her: "You're part of the angel army. Count Nicolas's spy. And that's why you brought me back to the sewing room—he told you to."

Again she says neither yes nor no, simply applies pressure to my hand.

"You used to be a good girl, Ava," Gudrun says. "You sewed the most beautiful seams and white-work. Wouldn't you like to be in the Queen's—the *new* Queen's—needle room forever? Someday you might be Mistress of the Needle yourself. I could put in a word when I am ready to leave."

At one time in my palace life, this was all I could have dreamed of. I still want it, more than I first imagined—when something is within my grasp, I have always found I always want it all the more, right until the moment that I touch it. So if the prison guard hadn't just called me a good girl an hour ago, I might be more easily swayed. Instead I answer resolutely, "If I could have one reward, I would choose my father's freedom."

"I told you, that isn't in my power." Gudrun seems truly sorrowful; or else being part of that special army has trained her to be an actor too. "We, none of us, hardly get to choose."

# CONTRACTING

HE cannons at the palace speak to cannons at Saint Peter's: *Grum! Grum! Grum!* The contracts have been signed and witnessed, Christina-Beatte is dressed in her finest, and the betrothal—it is now. *Long may they prosper!* cry the guns. *Long may they rule!*

It seems the city has forgotten about the Dowager's belly and its potential to change history. Christina-Beatte spares it not a single thought as she walks—yes, walks!—slowly up the aisle of the glowing cathedral, past the Stations of the Cross worked in amber, over the sunken tomb of Saint Ruta. Hundreds of eyes upon her, and the light of thousands of jewels. Clouds of incense, and so much beauty. It weighs her down.

Churchly formality is usually reserved for a wedding. A betrothal, Christina-Beatte knows, might take place in some room at the palace, and she herself would not normally need to be present. She is only ten and cannot marry till she has her woman's courses. But. There is Count Nicolas, his sharp face smiling at her, his clever eyes alight at the very sight of her—oh, yes, she feels a tingle that might well mean she's to be womaned soon. She is wearing the ornamental dagger that he gave her at her belt, and she likes its gentle weight bouncing lightly on her blue-padded loins.

If only it weren't so exhausting, walking this far. She has Lady Drin to support her on one side, but Duchess Margrethe is no help tottering on the other. The Duchess smells dreadfully of urine but must be there as Christina-Beatte's closest relative besides Maman.

Thinking of this, Christina-Beatte stumbles, and in a moment her mood changes, for feeling weak makes her feel cross. She blames Margrethe. The Queen Apparent wants to stick a pin in the old witch. And her starchy ruff has begun to itch unbearably; she would love to take out *all* its pins and drive them into the leaky cushion of her father's cousin's flesh.

But. Again. There is her husband-to-be, her betrothed, stepping down to take her hand and all but lift her up to a place beside him; whereupon he immediately drops to his knees, so he is her height, and kisses her hand as if it's a holy relic. He emanates warmth; he beams. He whispers, "Remember what is to come next, Your Highness — our heart's desire."

So Christina-Beatte, ten years old and bred to be sick, allows herself to sink into that warmth and think, *This is love, this is love.*

When the cannons boom their deep-bellied message, Isabel feels it in her belly too. A vibration, a pain. She can ignore that sensation for a time, as everybody knows the cannons have disturbed her stomach in the past and nothing much happened from it then.

Reventlow, the chinless ugly baroness, sleeps on a bench in the window, hips wiggling to each thrum of the guns.

She took a draught of something Krolik recommended for a minor female complaint, and she hasn't risen since. Elinor, too, is asleep: beside Isabel, recovering from her own illness.

The cannons are nothing to those two, so they should be nothing to Isabel, either. She dares to reach among the pillows for the dear white baby that dark Elinor has explained must be hidden when any but the two of them are present. The poor little thing must be hungry.

But as she reaches, her belly ripples. Isabel observes it: a wave moves through the fatty flesh after each cannon fire; and after fifteen years and around thirteen births (some live, some not), Isabel recognizes certain signs. Even if they vary a little bit from the usual. (What is "usual"?) Even if she already has a baby in bed beside her.

Of course. She remembers Candenzius's fingers and the three physicians' talk of cells in the womb. It is possible she's held more than one child within, that the wheel of her womb has spun and another cell is opening. It's time to see what sits inside, beyond the undulations of pain.

Isabel reaches for her easy baby, the one she and her dark Elinor birthed together. Poor little boy born of bones and fingernails.

"I am ready to die," she announces bravely into the firm pink lips. Or she thinks she says it; words are hard to form amid the subtle tearings and bruisings inside.

Elinor has heard her; she wakes. Brown eyes blinking, then wide and frightened in her deep brown face. She reaches for the baby and plucks him from Isabel's arms.

*I am ready to die.* How could Isabel have said that? She is not ready; no one is ever ready. She grasps for her baby again, and Elinor holds him out of reach.

*Grum. Grum. Grum.*

Somewhere, amid the booming cannons and the pain, while Elinor hides the sorrow-child, Isabel's daughter is being contracted to a man whom Isabel dislikes. She thinks of this as the tearing pains ebb into squeezing ones.

"It *is* better that I die," she says. Pain is making her mind remarkably clear. "Better than to let this baby die. A boy must rule instead of Beatte. Beatte is . . ." Clamping for a pain. "Beatte—isn't—"

But what Beatte is or isn't will have to wait until after Isabel vents a groan, giving in to her pain, letting it engulf her and drive away thoughts of anything but it, the pain.

Elinor, stronger than she's seemed for days, clamps a black hand over Isabel's mouth, helping her be silent.

Reventlow sleeps on, tumbled into slumber by her drug.

Isabel thinks: *What is Beatte? A girl, a child. What isn't she? Kind or clever. Queen or adult.* Of course, she has been ill, and illness warps the mind as well as bodies. All bodies.

It's certain now, another body's moving within Isabel—or her body is moving around it, as this one seems at heart as still as his brother, that sweet waxen thing that Isabel fears is being crushed as she struggles against her pain. Strains against it. The pain is too great, too insistent, to allow her to protect any fragile being in its way.

Her eyes promise quiet, and Elinor leaves her for a

414

moment, to tie one end of the sheet to a bedpost and put the other in Isabel's hand, so she has something to pull against and squeeze. Isabel would prefer to squeeze the warm, living, fragile flesh of her dear dark Elinor's hand, but Elinor is doing other things. She is shaking Reventlow awake and giving her a note describing some errand that will take her away and grant the Queen her privacy.

Both of them know, instinctively, that they must be alone to face what comes next. There is nothing but danger in the next hours.

Dear Elinor. If Isabel dies, Elinor should be regent. She who so recently escaped death herself.

The pain surges and Isabel pulls her sheet, like a sailor tugging his oar against the ocean. She allows herself to groan again. Elinor stuffs a clean handkerchief into her mouth; Isabel nods her gratitude.

The Countess gropes the Queen, feels the storm within her belly. She lifts the sheets and Isabel's nightdress and wrestles her massive legs up and apart to investigate. She does this with the soothing silence that made her an excellent Mistress of the Nurseries. She says only, *"Shhh, shh, sh."* She touches around Isabel's privacy in a way the Queen has not been touched before, even by Candenzius.

Isabel relaxes, just a little. Elinor touches one last spot.

And suddenly it's done. Isabel's flabby old womb is loose and practiced, the inside walls easily breached. She feels a slick shoot of early flesh barely pausing at any point, so eager does the thing feel to be out.

Isabel waits excitedly for the first cry. It does not come.

Elinor must not know she has to suck the mucus from the baby's nose and throat. She has never had children of her own, Isabel remembers. With her own heart buzzing like a hive of bees, Isabel can't hear if the baby breathes at all. She moans, trying to give instructions; twists and sees that Elinor is staring at something in her hands. Something red against dark fingers.

Isabel feels the usual fluids leaking out, feels her womb contract again to expel the mother-cake. Already. Gone.

Her tongue works the sodden gag from her mouth. "Show me!"

She has to say it several times before Elinor gathers up the sheet and shows her, nestled inside, this thing that is her own. Blood and a newborn's yellow meal cling about its creases, though Elinor has given its face, if that is its face, a cursory swipe.

Isabel allows herself to faint.

## MIDI SORTE

So Isabel be not so mad as to think she can not be quiet. This were a good thing, for if she give voice to feeling we may both be dead all ready.

There were a time at my father's house I did see another mad woman give a birth. She were a simple one not so much older than Beatte now, not right in the head, and not sure why she felt this wriggling inside her, no matter how many time the aunties try to explain. When her pains came she were a lost creature, senseless and screaming so to shake the palace walls; my father sent a man to order her to silence. But on she howled like some wild thing, and when the baby were presented, she screamed as at a stranger.

The baby were a simple one, too, and drowned in a pool meant for bathing. His mother never notice, for she never did recognize him her own.

No more will Isabel know this one. This thing that might kill us both if it is discover. This *monster*. That I should not look on less it turn my own Lump in to its likeness—in this land as well as mine, a woman with a belly is kept from animals and horrors, less they shape the baby.

Here it is, the first moment I think to protect the Lump. Such a moment!

When if the thing be seen, I will surely to be murder, for some one will swear I witched the Queen in to monstrous birth.

The drumming come now for executions. The first ones shall begin, this is all ways the sign. I know Arthur must be sharpen his stylus to write events upon his tablet of wax. With his apprentice-boys all around, repeating words so to endure beyond this night.

I want to endure. I want my Lump and I want my life.

Isabel sleeps, like any woman after childbed. Deep and still a-bleeding.

So I wrap the monster in a fur and put him in a chest, that way he will not be cold. I think this as if he be alive and dead at one time. (But he cannot be alive, no such thing could live.) I tuck the mother-cake beside him, it is so small as a sheep's kidney.

May be I can hide every thing. For a time at least, a time I shall have with the Lump.

I clean the Queen as much I can. I wash and wash. I burn the linens wet with blood. It takes a long while, first they must dry behind the fire and then be pull to the front and I watch them go. Wispy smoke of blood, the stains and also the broideries upon the edge. All in flowers of ash, smell of meat.

Isabel wakes up. I think it be the drums, *bumpbumpbump-bumpbump.* "How much?"

I show seven fingers, I do n't know what she meant exactly but this baby were inside her so many months.

418

"Too much," she says, and, "I must not eat more fish." She fade to sleep again.

That much be true, she were ever fond of fish and ate a dolphin entire at one meal. May be this explain the baby shape.

Now panic. I need water. I have used all in here, and all the wine, and every other wet thing I could find to make Isabel as she were this morning. Yet there is still blood between her legs, and in time Reventlow will return from watching deaths to report on real Elinor, and then she will inquire about this blood. She will summon Krolik to search the signs that Isabel have been a mother once again. And then I will be witched.

I open a shutter to gobble air. Down the yard, beneath the window, that muddy witch-bed bubble and beckon.

"Elinor!" Isabel whine awake, a-drafty. "Elinor, come here!" She have her Queen ways again, the command in the voice and the anger if her thoughts be not anticipated. "The Prince and I grow cold." Her waxen boy.

This is my choice, death below the window or a life above uncertain, with a great secret and madness but one step away. My choice which I have faced recently with what should have been death in the bottom of a salve jar—but even then I faced not real choice but fate, for the Lump would not depart.

"Elinor! Come, the Prince needs reswaddling. He mustn't soil his overdress. Is it not pretty?"

That soft thing that Ava Bingen sewed quick as a shroud so she could depart our strangeness. It is pretty, yes, a little velvet sack for the sorrow-child I helped create.

"And close that shutter!" she finish. "You know moon-light's dangerous for a newborn."

I close it loose and I return. I slide in to the bed beside her as she like me to do. I hold my Lump and fuss with her lump's dress. I am glad now for the Queen's madness. She have accept the wax child for the real one and do not ask about her stillbirth.

"You are so warm," she tell me happily. "Like a coal in a fire. Put your arms around us."

I do this. I worry I may melt her sorrow-child, but for now I am content to clutch some flesh. I am afraid and even one mad woman be company for me.

"Ah, dear Elinor." Happy at last, and she goes to sleep.

I lie while the Lump bubbles up my belly. He tickles my throat and say he is not going to leave. He want to make me speak for him now if not for my self.

He tell me, *You are Elinor.*

I jump from the bed and return to that burning.

# AVA BINGEN

I have noted before that while serving my time as a scrub maid, I discovered one important object, a magic talisman that renders the bearer invisible. A bucket. Whether it is made of wood or leather, whether it holds water, slops, or simply brushes, no one looks beyond the bucket to the person carrying it. To be truthful, no one really looks at the bucket, either; the mere fact of its presence works some enchantment to create an unseeable space, especially in the beautiful rooms where courtiers are playing their lutes and sniffing their pomanders, flirting in the window nooks and generally pretending that filth does not exist. The dwarfs notice only when a careless bucket is about to strike them in the head, and then they're likely to upend its contents on the bearer's skirt.

None of these people, of course, are present as I march grimly toward Queen Isabel's chambers, gripping the bucket in which I have stowed her new nightdress. The gorgeous rooms are all but empty, as everyone from slave to dwarf to duchess has gone to witness first the betrothal ceremony, then the executions that are now following it. Only a few dozy guards remain, and they lounge on the otherwise forbidden benches. Their armored eyes barely blink as I pass.

But the tapestries sway lightly. The woodwork of the ceilings braids into a net waiting to drop; the gods painted among it point and chide. The palace is gathering itself against me.

I am doing a terrible thing.

Yes, I chose my father over Queen Isabel, even considering that many more might die as a result. I am about to kill the Queen. What other choice, really, does a daughter have?

I am a murderess. A regicide. But not a patricide.

The night cracks open my wishes.

I still hunger for the beautiful part of the story, the part with the wedding or the wealth or the lover un-beasted, the family restored, before the trials and sadness that follow into another story. I want the life of the princess just starting out on her adventures, the kind of tale I used to tell when it was my turn to speak at night in the seamstresses' dorter, or while we were at work in the needle room. I want to save my father and then to be reunited with my vanished love . . . or at the very least to gain independence, with a shop and a house of my own. And I still, even now, I *still* think I might earn these things, if I complete a few more trials correctly.

Far off, I hear cheering, and I know a prisoner is being brought out. Then there is the slowing *bump-bump-bump* of drums; then silence, during which Nicolas might make a speech and a priest might take final confession. I imagine Grammaticus (once my suitor, later my lover) writing all this on a tablet. Then more cheering—I believe the ax has fallen.

As I have noted, persons of the highest status are executed by losing their heads. Those lower down are hanged. I wonder which will be my father, noble or humbled — that is, if he dies, which will happen if I don't finish my task: to kill quickly and in the most royal way, with poison.

And here is the Dowager's outer chamber, which I have cleaned so often and so thoroughly that the dirt of it still stains the cracks of my hands. Today the room bristles with more than the usual number of guards; as I walk in, they stand straight and gaze sternly ahead of themselves, rattling their various weapons.

I tremble, sure I'm sweating out guilt in waves; but I'm surprised. Either the bucket truly is magical or Nicolas and his angel army have already given orders, for the guards let me pass without question. I simply walk (trembling) up to the door of the inner chamber, grasp the cold iron handle, and push against the tapestry flap. Then I am within.

If being able to enter was a surprise, being inside is a shock.

The odor of blood is strong here, despite the cold air pouring through a half-opened shutter. Maybe the blood of prisoners is already so thick in the military yard that any crack will let in a slaughterhouse reek. I imagine blood flooding the stones outside, the nobles first slipping in it and then, as it thickens and freezes, stuck in place like statues.

But there's no time for fancies. Something has gone direly wrong right here, I can see it at once. Midi Sorte crouches by the fire with a wild look in her eyes, hair burst out of her ladylike headdress and skin shining with sweat; and Queen

Isabel, a mound of a woman gone so pale as to be translucent, snores amid disordered bedclothes.

I set my bucket down. Then pick it up again—I'm here for a purpose.

"I—does the Queen need a change of linen?" I ask. Then force myself to be firmer: "I was sent with . . ."

Midi doesn't seem to hear me. Still crouching catlike, she wipes at the sweat running into her eyes. I get the impression she's about to spring.

My own sweat turns to ice. "Wh-what are—What is wrong?" Witches can sense thoughts, substances, everything: Midi must have detected the poison in the nightdress. I expect her to kill me straight out, right now, as my father is approaching the executioner. I regret the kindness I showed her when she was ill with the first weeks of pregnancy. No one is fiercer than a woman protecting her young.

Midi puts her finger to her lips, ordering me and my thoughts to be silent. Then, as if they operate with a separate will, the two parts of her tongue creep out around that finger and lick the sweat from her lip.

She growls. Her hand stretches toward me.

# EXECUTION

T is a slow business, execution. Who would have expected so much ceremony? Certainly not Christina-Beatte, sitting stiffly (as she must, because of her unforgiving silver-bay gown) in a gilded chair on the carpeted dais facing the platform that has been erected so that sparkling courtiers may watch the grubby prisoners die, in a few weak hours of light on a January afternoon.

Why must there be so much *confession*? Each one to be killed has his moment with the priest, and his moment of offering forgiveness and a coin to the black-draped executioner. And then, only then, comes the heavy thwack of the ax and the thump as the head drops away. There is more slow ceremony, too, in the way the guards collect the body and the head and carry them away, as if these corpses deserve as much honor as any other dead.

Thus far, there have been only two deaths: a manservant accused of helping to poison her sister Sophia, and a girl said to be his lover. Neither one said anything memorable, and Nicolas shielded the girl's eyes at each actual death blow, which was most annoying.

Christina-Beatte barely remembers Sophia, for whose sake these people are officially being punished. She is tired and hungry. But there is a whole prison left to go, and she is the royal Lunedie who commanded all this bloodshed, so she endures.

She schemes.

The next one, she will watch. She will slip from Nicolas's hand, peel her eyes open, and see everything.

In a moment of gleeful anticipation, Christina-Beatte takes time to pity the last sister who remains to her. Poor little Gorma, back in the nursery, missing the day's riches! How jealous she'll be when Christina-Beatte describes to her, in gruesome detail, just how each one perished!

That selfsame tiny princess, meanwhile, leans into her pillows and listens to the drums. The cheering courtiers. The various noises that accompany history as it pushes forward into her sister's reign.

Gorma picks at the flakes around her nails, then digs inside her nose. She repeats the process, thinking of her sister and Count Nicolas. Married now, or all but married. In the smoldering amber cathedral, they promised to be as one body forever and ever and ever, amen. Someday.

Gorma wonders when she will be well enough to join them at events like the one in progress. Christina-Beatte is only five years older, but she forbade the youngest princess to attend the rest of the day's events. Only for adults and those of highest rank, she said. Showing off her older-sisterliness, her queen-apparentness. But Count Nicolas gave Gorma several kindly looks as she stood in the cathedral propped up among the ladies-in-waiting, and once he even winked.

Gorma wonders if someday he might marry her as well. When the nurses tell their stories, his is always the face Gorma imagines for a dark and handsome man.

And now, as if she's summoned him, here comes the *shuffle-shuffle* of leather-clad feet and the *stir-stir* of heavy cloth.

But it is not Count Nicolas. The *tink* of glass, the smell of pain.

It is the physician, the young one, Doctor Dé. He looks so sad lately, with brown eyes that puff underneath. He carries a box of vials and powders and beakers and fleams.

She shrinks from him into the feathery pillows, as if they are wings to enfold and protect her. Wings—how she longs for the public bed in the shape of a swan! So many little nooks in a swan, so many places to cling and elude grasping hands. (Has she only imagined that some of those hands were black? The gentlest hands, with the gentlest lips whispering, *"Shhh, shh, sh."*) Ever more frightened, Gorma slides toward the far side of the bed, which is just inches from the wall.

She is trapped, and she knows it.

## MIDI SORTE

Ava Bingen, it is all ways Ava Bingen. Wants to make some noise, wants to know some question that can 't have answer. I tell her to *Grrr, grr, gr.*

But she come close any way. "I've brought a new garment," she say. "I don't think I can put it on her alone. Is she asleep?"

So slow, I nod. Queen Isabel be snoring in her bed, her sorrow-child inside her arms in the monster-child's stead.

Hard to remember that for some this be a day of normal duties. Hard to believe Ava do not recognize some awefulness have happened here in this room and do not run away from it. I want to shove Ava Bingen in the fire place to burn with the rags of sheet.

Yet when I look close, I see. She does know awefulness, though it be not the awe of this room.

"I-if you won't help me," she stammer, "I will have to order you to leave."

I pull my self tall. I am still in the guise of Countess Elinor, though I have left off the pattens and slippers and am some shorter than Ava. My filthy silk make a rustle. My paillettes shine. I will not take any command from a Bingen.

But I worry about when Reventlow might return and find us.

In a flash I have an idea. A lightning, a lightening! But I hold it to my self a moment to be sure.

Ava Bingen say, and her sweat reek of fear, "Midi, I know we have had some — dispute in the past, but you would do yourself a kindness as well as me if you were to leave now . . ."

I use my idea. I put a finger to her mouth, so she smell the blood there. I pull her sleeve from the fire place to the chest beside it. Her bucket bumps the wood.

When I take out my key, I am a lady again and unlock the lock and lift the lid. Then I pick up the monster and put him in her arms. I peel away the fur that wrap his face.

So fast, I clap my bloody hand over her mouth to stop her scream.

And so I make her my accomplice.

HE gasps, the throaty noises as if someone is about to choke — they do not belong in this silvered world of sleep. Isabel opens her mouth to complain and dismiss, but then it floods with silver too, and she cannot speak.

She has summoned someone. A hand slides into each of her hands; long soft tresses twine with her own. It is the silver mer-girls, come to welcome her.

Or is this punishment? For although she makes herself as heavy as she can, they pull her upward with a stroke of their tails, steering the way with their long fingers and pointy mer-noses. Again Isabel tries to speak, to beg them to let her sleep in this beautiful bottom of dreams, but the quicksilver fills her lungs, and though she does not suffocate, she cannot muster the breath to whisper.

# AVA BINGEN

I dropped my bucket.

That is the first thought I have after a long time of undiluted horror: *Dropped the bucket.* And thus dropped my task, dropped my mind, let everything else fall away. I dropped my jaw also, and with it all power of speech. For I am holding a demon.

In this moment, I remember certain things: the messy but relatively easy births of my four brothers, the bits and pieces left over once they were cleaned and my mother emptied. Their bloodless but difficult deaths in the Great Sickness, there in the house with the stone head that belongs to my father. The red splash that fell from my skirts and the stain it left before the church on Helligánds Plads. The howls of the madmen in Helligánds Hospital as if in witness to my sin, the rats and gulls sniffing around that stain as if there might be something left that my stepmother hadn't scooped into her apron as my father carried me away.

I think, *Evil.* That is the smell beyond blood that is baking in the Queen's inner chamber. Evil born into this world and held in my arms, which are somehow unable to let it go. They have clamped around and will not release, no matter the horror.

I must explain.

The little demon bears a sad face, a melancholy one. Its skull is covered in black hairs, like the hairs of the fur in which Midi wrapped it; its single eye puckers half open, one little fist pressed to the hole where its nose and mouth should be. In place of those ordinary human parts, the demon has a mass of red jellied bulbs, not quite eyelike; one of them protrudes farther than the rest and looks distinctly like a leg, complete with tiny foot and toes.

Midi, holding a candle now, unfolds the fur the rest of the way. I see the body.

A chest, two arms, and on the stomach, around the stub of cord, a shape that might almost be the real face. It has lips, a nose, and a brow pressing against the skin. Below that, evidence that the creature is definitely male, with a boy's tackle (or is this another leg?) hung above the thicker single limb that dips in the center and barely manages to distinguish itself into two feet at the end, less well shaped than the one that protrudes from the mouth.

It is a demon, yes. But is it —

"Dead?" I ask.

Midi nods: *Yes, dead.*

I hand the thing back to her and spit into my apron. Midi makes a sound of exasperation and puts the creature back in its chest. While I wipe my mouth, holding my apron like a wine sack, she points from the chest to the sleeping Queen. At last, I understand.

This is the long-awaited heir to the Lunedie throne. This

devil, blessedly dead. Of course it could not be Midi's baby; she is far too early in her pregnancy for that, and this thing is far too pale.

*Oh, Isabel,* I think, pitying her. *Some terrible magic has been worked against you.*

I shrink from Midi Sorte, though she would hardly have shown me the monster if one of her spells had produced it. Nor would she have much reason to do a similar magic against me, however little she might like me. I don't even have a belly now, only trickling monthly blood, thank the stars.

Midi clucks in her throat, pushing some rags into the fireplace flames. Isabel snores, and for a mad moment, the scene becomes almost cozy.

I wonder if I am still supposed to kill the Dowager, even though the baby is born and is in no way capable to rule. She should be dead already; how could anyone birth that hideous worm and live? I wonder how to convey the news to Nicolas. Through Gudrun, obviously, but I'm afraid—

And then I realize: *I must not tell anyone of this,* for the mere fact that I am alone, with the Queen and a black nurse disguised as a countess. We are the only three who have seen and touched this baby, and this fact both involves me in the birth and makes me likely to be blamed for it. Midi and I will be called witches together. We will be hanged or burned, and everything I have lived will become nothing.

*Jacob Lille.* My one love, and I never found him again.

*Grammaticus.* Lost to both of us.

These thoughts race through in less than a minute, so fast

does my mind work in its panic. I hear the drums far away: another prisoner to be killed. My father? I wonder what to do with my dirty apron. I begin to weep, from fear and frustration and all the plans of everything I was once going to do.

This is when Isabel awakes. The oaken bed shudders; its linen drapings stir like ghosts.

Isabel coughs, clearing her throat of some mad dream.

"Can I trust you to keep a secret?" she asks, looking up at the hole I cut in her bed's canopy when I was dressing her doll, and then, without waiting for an answer from either Midi or me, "What are we going to *do*?"

# MIDI SORTE

A secret. I write it here a dozen times to show I know how to keep and how to express: a secret, a secret, a secret, a secret, a secret, a secret, a secret, a secret, a secret, a secret, a secret, a secret. It will keep on the page, and I will hide the page beneath some floorboard or in the hole of some bedclothes or my bodice. It is too big for my heart to hold alone.

Here be the secret things that happen next:

Ava Bingen weeps and chatter words in a language that might be her own. Isabel in her bed stay patient as a saint in church, waits for us to end our madness like a saint wait for visions. As if some how she have of a sudden lost her own madness and be wiser than us all.

I touch Ava on the shoulder to say well, it is all well some how, though I do not know how. I showed her the creature to make her my ally, not my burden. I try drinking strength from her tears. I clasp harder, till I feel her bones inside, and this calm her sobbing. Then I cross to the bed to speak with the Queen.

By now Isabel have found the waxen sorrow-child in her bed. She holds it to her chest again, but this time as one holds some thing familiar that can provide small comforts, not one that is in its self a being to be comforted. To her it is no baby any more, it is a prayer bead.

She looks to Ava, who heaves still with the tears that pour over her long white face. Isabel say, "You have come to kill me."

Ava wipe her eyes and nod. That is how she confess, so simple. She be too afraid for lies. "I have no choice."

Isabel ask, "Poison?" and again Ava wipe. Nod.

"Count Nicolas?"

Ava nod one time more.

Isabel strokes the head of the sorrow-child where we did put the bones of Hendrika (I believe). She gives the head a kiss. "It will happen one way or another, soon enough. I'm surprised no one's tried before now."

I wait for more, but there be no more. Except the awe that a queen can accept such fate. She seem so willing as if she willed it her self. And she do not consider that if she is killed, so shall we others be.

May be this the gravest maddery of all.

Isabel point to the pitcher on the table as if she tell Ava, *Go on, put the poison there and I will drink it.* She does not know that pitcher be empty, I have emptied it in trying to clean away her shame.

Ava will not look up, just snuffle and scrub at her tears as if she cry for her own death instead, which in fact she shall do soon.

Those two women, so happy to be murders! I clap my hands to wake them. I have not lived so much to die be cause of this monster-child or the wax one. So I grab the sorrow-baby from Isabel's arms and hold it away from her. I rock it back and forth, back and forth, in to her dreams and out of them again.

"You give that back," she say clear. I think she recognize me. Not her Elinor any more, the dark nursey again. She seem so irritated as if I play, not speak in the way that I can. The sorrow-child be my shouting.

I hold that waxy baby up to the candle. He do not smell of blood like the other, he smell of bees. A drop fall from his head to sputter on the flame.

Ava Bingen stare as if she be gone so mad as Isabel's reputation. But she under stand me. She say to the Queen, "You need a baby."

And Isabel simples a yes. She will die with out one, she will likely die with one too, but chances are better the other way. She reach for the sorrow-child.

Ava announce, "*I* have a baby. A new one."

We look to her stomach.

She put her hands there. "I mean, my stepmother does. In — two miles from here, the glassmakers' district. She has a baby, or so I've heard. A rumor only . . . but perhaps a boy."

Isabel sit up alert, of interest and of jealousy. She keep one eye for the sorrow-child, one eye for Ava.

Cunning Ava Bingen. I feel the hornets buzz my heart and also I feel grateful — be cause may be we have hope.

"We could . . . switch them," Ava say slow, for she know she might lose her head for this suggestion as easy as for having part in the monster-child. "That is, we might dispose — respectfully — of the . . . miscarriage, then bring the live baby here."

"And you would not kill me?" ask Isabel, as if this be the part of the dream she cannot believe.

Ava shudder. "N-no . . . Your Eminence." But this may be her trick.

When Isabel turn back to the wax child, Ava add, "The baby would be yours. We would present it as your own flesh-and-blood baby. Or we could try, at least. The new king, so Count Nicolas won't rule through Beatte."

Isabel ask with the air of great sense, "But how?"

# AVA BINGEN

*Saa.* There it is.

Midi Sorte and I are allies.

And we are walking outside the palace walls, along the great Skön Kanal of Skyggehavn. Edging our way between shoulders and hips, along the spaces opened up for entertainments. We are together.

The crowds make a stew of murmurous anticipation. On foot and in boats, they cheer when the nobles cheer. I reach back among Midi's soft skirts and clasp her arm. Not merely so we won't be pulled apart amid the shifting and the bumping; she also seems to need it. She wears her noble pattens for walking on muddy footpaths and stony squares, but she's clumsy as a pig in a ditch and almost stumbles into one. She's tired and unwell; her fingers are like ice. No cloak, because she hasn't needed one in the Queen's chambers, and she's unused to cold.

Yes, this version of Elinor Parfis, Countess of Belnát, needs me to hold her up. She needs me to find her way. She has not been among common Skyggehavners in years, if she ever did walk through them; more likely, she took a boat with the real Elinor everywhere the Countess went. She recoils from trolls who beg for money, even from sellers of nuts and ribbons who call out that some color would enliven her gown.

*"Nej, nej, nej,"* I say, arm out to ward them off. No, no, no.

In time, the people start to fall away. They dip knees to Midi's strangeness, to her silks and glittering paillettes. They speculate.

*Must be an entertainment from the palace.*

*Look again. Entertainment don't wear silk.*

*I've heard of this one. She's the Dark Countess who waits on the Queen.*

*She's Queen of Night herself.*

My father's star, once brighter than the sun, has paled to the light of an ordinary torch. Night is growing nightlier.

So Midi and I stumble on together, beside the great canal, toward the house with the stone head. Following my plot.

At first, I could not think of a *how.* The *how* was too hard to imagine. I knew only that I had to speak and please the others.

So I began to gibber another fairy story, one I made up as I spoke. About an evil king with a bloody crown, two little princesses he demanded to take as brides, a mother who saved them by casting a spell.

And as I spoke, an idea grew in me, so when I stopped the story (with what some would call a bad end), I was ready. I had a plan.

As I should have expected, Midi and Queen Isabel found my scheme as difficult to believe in as the magical tale I had just told them. But perhaps the tale prepared the way for action, because here we are embarked upon what I suggested. My scheme. My madness.

In Isabel's chamber, I pointed at Midi. "She's the only one of us who can pass the gates unchallenged. You can't, Your Highness, because you're the Queen; and I can't because I'm a servant. But that one can go wherever she likes, as long as she's dressed as the Countess and is known to have your favor."

Midi looked down at her once-glorious gown, streaked now from Isabel's miscarriage. I could tell it had never occurred to her, this idea that she might simply walk out and thereby escape her bonds. She is so accustomed to being a slave that she would never think of running away.

"No one will see the blood on your skirt, now there's no sun," I assured her, even as I remembered uncomfortably that I had to change my soggy monthly cloths for clean ones. "You'll pass the guards as a countess. They'll let you do anything you want tonight."

I could see Midi wavering, almost daring to believe, but Isabel fretted. "I cannot lose my Elinor again!" she wailed— though she retained enough sense to hold her wailing to a whisper, so only Midi and I heard.

At that, Midi touched her gently on the shoulder. I realized then that some change had come over her, as if she'd developed a true friendship for Isabel, and one more tender than the real Elinor's ever was.

"Midi—Elinor—will come back," I said, somewhat uncertainly; for why would she, once having tasted freedom? "If perhaps . . . Your Highness might offer her some reward?"

Of course, I was seeking a reward for myself as well. I held my request ready. But Isabel focused on Midi, brown eyes on brown eyes.

"Elinor, if you do this, *I will grant your heart's desire.*" The words from a fairy tale.

In reply, Midi spread her hands. What would anyone want in her position? What would anyone dare to want? Even when told she could do it for herself, she sought permission to go.

"Yes," Isabel resolved. "If you do this for me, I'll give you . . . complete liberty." She seemed to understand in that moment that Midi is a slave—though in some sense we are all slaves to our sovereigns. "Then you may do exactly as you please. You may join Count Belnát on the green islands or go wherever else you like." Then again, it was as if she didn't understand after all who Midi is. "Or" (wistfully) "you could remain with me . . . If you would like to, *I* would like you to. And you"—she turned to me at last—"what do you want?"

For a moment, with the words *heart's desire* echoing in the anxious bell of my brain, I saw Jacob Lille's face and the legendary solid streets of Copenhagen into which he's vanished. But I say instead, "I want freedom too. For Klaus Bingen, who has been unfairly imprisoned."

I still have some doubts as to whether Isabel can really grant this wish, given Nicolas's tight hold on the present government; but a mad queen seemed more likely to keep a promise than a cruel regent, and so I decided.

I never wanted to kill her, anyway. I prefer not to be a

murderess. It is a relief to shake off that role—one impossible task I need not complete.

"He'll go free," Queen Isabel vowed. Her lips were white from the effort of speaking and plotting and trying to remain un-mad. "My daughter will do it. My son. Bring me a baby and you'll have what you wish for, and money besides. But here . . ." Her right hand struggled with her left, tugging at the little finger until she pulled something off. "Take this. A baby cannot come cheap."

I dared step to her loose-clasped fingers and dig into their nest. I emerged with a most precious egg: the famous ruby ring of the Bullen family.

I carry the ring in my pocket now.

It is surprisingly heavy, the first real jewel I've held without a backing of cloth or a casing of skin. No, not surprising; a jewel should have a certain heft. Especially a ruby. And one of such importance.

At first, I took pleasure at feeling this weight upon *my* hand, rubbing against *my* fingers. Then Isabel, for what seemed like the last time possible, called me away from pleasure and back to duty. "Go quickly, both of you."

And when we looked at each other, uncertain—for accompanying Midi was not part of my plan—Isabel added, "She'll never find the way on her own."

Midi pointed to the chest where the miscarriage was stored. But I thought, with that selfish scheming part of me, that it was better to leave the demon there for now; because the demon keeps pressure on Isabel to honor her promises. While I mouthed something about it being easier to dispose of after the new baby is in place, Isabel interrupted impatiently:

"Then go on, go quickly, together. You can leave me alone for once in my life. Everyone considers me dead, anyway."

So here we walk on the other side of the gates, among crowds who treat Midi as noble; on an errand for a dead Queen, to save a man who may be dead already himself. It is the one constant of our lives: We push against Fate, driven forward by the limpest of hopes, that Chance will intervene and save us.

# The Beloved Princess

*There was once a princess whose portrait so enchanted a foreign king that he sailed across the sea to behold her beauty for himself. When he arrived, he found her every bit as lovely as her painted version, and as a result he ran her father through with a sword and swallowed every ornament on the dead king's body.*

*Fed by those treasures, a magnificent golden crown grew from the bones of the wicked king's skull. That crown was so sharply tined that the birds who attempted to alight and feed upon its bright jewels were instantly speared, and blood ran down into the evil king's eyes. He left it there, for it made him ever more fierce and terrifying. And now he announced that he would marry the princess immediately.*

*If the girl did not agree, he said, he would murder her and marry her sister, who was nearly as fair; and if neither of them did as he required, he would murder them both in the most horrible way and then kill their mother, who was already ill with grief at what had happened.*

*Under this threat, the queen discovered a strength in herself and resolved to save the two girls. Sick as she was, she marched them to the docks and tied a rock around each one's neck and pushed them into the sea, where they drowned. Or rather, they appeared to drown, because the rocks were in fact magic stones that put the girls to sleep.*

*The two princesses were caressed by feathery seaweeds and tended by creatures of the sea, while, above water, the evil king* conducted a campaign of vengeful destruction. The land was laid waste, its riches gathered in the hull of his great black-sailed ship, which bobbed at anchor above the sleeping objects of his rough courtship. Golden statues, bushels of wheat, paintings of saints, clocks that chimed for the passing minutes: All went to this evil king, whose crown was now so bloody that even the jewels did not shine anymore; it was instead the skulls of dead songbirds that glowed red in testimony to his power.

In those days, every baby born in the land was a monster, for the evil king had corrupted its wombs. Their skins were like lizards'; their eyes were like goats'. Infanticide became common.

The queen wept, and the princesses kept sleeping.

## MIDI SORTE

I am Elinor.

After every thing that have happen in my life, here be the first thought that cause me deep upset. *I am Elinor.*

When I crack the door and leave the inner chamber and pass through the rooms and nooks and down the stair . . . all the palace see me as she. They let me pass, they bow to my skirts. And though they might stare, they require no thing of me — no paper or permission — be cause while I be Elinor, I am one who give such permission, not get it. And Ava is the one who knew it could be so. Why did I never think it? Why did n't Arthur say so? If he ever had a kind feeling for me . . .

Outside where the night smell too sweet and feel too cold, I nod at guards and hoist my bosoms. They bow and dip they halberds. So they also let me pass, and Ava with me. To the gate, and then they ope the gate. And at last I am Outside.

*I am Elinor.*

*I walk in the city.*

It is a terrible place.

Three steps beyond the palace, on the square of the cathedral, filth begin. Heaps of trash and dirt and cats crawling every where, eating trash. Dogs snapping at the cats. They eat trash, too, and fight each other.

Some thing catch my skirt with it jaws. I fall, Ava catch me. From then after she hold my arm while our breath make snow in the air and broken people ask for money. One balance a knife upon his nose and then push it down his throat to ask that people pay. I refuse, though he speak around the knife and call me a *grande dame* and say that I be beautiful.

We have no money any way. We have just a ring to buy a baby. A tiny child who have no opinion for his own price and who will become a coin-purse for the Lunedies.

Ava have said may be we will not need to pay, a baby with such a future may come free. If he even exist. But I know she will make sure to use the ring some way and mold me to her plan, and so she grip my arm so tight as an eel she'll eat for her dinner.

We trace the canal they call Beautiful, and though I see great houses that I know belong to some of the court, I see also more filth heaps between them, streams of garbage leak to the big water. The canal is choked of boats, and in between there swim rats who seek out trash and careless skirts to nibble. The tall, cold people of this place point to me and stare as we pass by, while rats tear shreds from off they clothes to make their beds.

They speak. They talk some stories, they think they know me. Outside the palace, even.

So here is what I think as Ava Bingen pull me down an alley that end with a bridge: *There can be no more freedom Outside than in the palace.*

## SOLITUDE

OR the first time in her life, Isabel experiences solitude. Savors it, rolls it over her senses, and gets its flavor. Sweet, bitter, slightly charred, with the metallic tang of sacrifice . . . She is alone, without a lady-in-waiting or a maidservant, a fellow regent or a husband or a physician or a sister or a friend: she is alone.

Isabel Lunedie, formerly Isabelle des Rayaux.

It is a strange sensation to be by herself, and Isabel feels the rush of heat and color returning to her fingers and face while she considers how to put it into words. Funny how she can name flavors but not feelings. To be alone today is to be weak, certainly, but that is because of the — No, she will not think about whatever-it-is she glimpsed before dark Elinor tucked it away.

Instead, she studies the glob of wax that Elinor finally returned to her, once they agreed to the plan put forth by that sharp-faced maid. The wax has gone soft in her clasp, easy to reshape. She works on it earnestly for a while. First she gives it a pointy fish-nose, then rubs that down to almost nothing. With the nose flattened, the cheeks become wider, giving the little thing the appearance of a sheep. That cannot be allowed either, so she works on the cheekbones, giving them more definition, making them look less like a baby's and more like Grand-mère's when she gave young Isabelle the sapphire ring that vanished when her fingers swelled for this last child.

*Nothing has value,* said Grand-mère, *until it is given away or stolen.* Isabel does not know what's become of the ring since then.

She rounds down the cheekbones again.

The sorrow-child's waxen face is getting grubby, gray and pink. And yet it also grows translucent, glowing like amber, hinting at what's underneath — nubbins of bone, fine strands of hair twining around themselves in order to grow.

Isabel's breasts ache. She feels a burning itch and a trickle in the part of her that just split open. She remembers that she is diseased. She thinks, also, that there is something wrong with that sharp-faced maid, something familiar — if only she can name it.

When Lady Isabelle des Rayaux arrived in Skyggehavn, she was fourteen years old: fresh, beautiful. Excited.

Already she felt it. From the moment that the lips of the bay closed around the French ship's hull, as she passed rocky islets too inhospitable for even a clump of moss or a stray ant, she knew this place was her destiny in a way that she hadn't imagined back at her father's sun-drenched court. Gulls swooped around the ship and left their pearly droppings as the palace materialized through wisps of mist. It was a dragon crouching, kneeling (she thought) in submission. The spires were elbows, spine, and head. Then came the towers and the long, low body of walls. The gates gaping like an open mouth. Skyggehavn was taking her in, and she realized she needed to be swallowed, wanted, courted, and coveted in just this way.

Her long dark hair whipped in the sea wind. Her soft red heart fluttered in her chest. She knew that, in surrendering herself, she would conquer.

"My lady." Attendants brought Isabelle below deck to braid her hair. She gazed into a mirror and knew that she looked lovely.

She went up on deck again when her ship anchored in the bay. The royal barge glided out to meet her. She was helped on board and presented to her almost-husband, a thin and sallow lad with sad eyes. Curtsied to his stout mother, exchanged pretty speeches in French as the barge maneuvered around to the long pier.

"*Merci,*" she said several times. "*Grâce à vous et au bon Dieu . . . J'admire votre beau paysage et votre belle ville principale . . .*"

(*God, she thought, for I am such a young thing!. . .*)

In the middle of such a sentence, Isabelle's father-in-law-to-be—much taken with her, some said to an unseemly degree—swept her into his arms and leaped from the barge onto the pier, where she sank very properly to her knees and thanked him for arranging her marriage.

He bent down and whispered in her ear, tickling words incomprehensible in the accent of this place although they came in her native tongue.

The courtiers applauded.

*She will have the most beautiful children,* they agreed.

Isabel, alone, is growing weaker. She has some notion that she should heave herself out of bed and hide this heavy sorrow-child, but she cannot.

She hears cheering outside.

Her last moments, and she is not so alone after all. The court, at least; that vague glistening thing—it will always be with her.

## MIDI SORTE

Ava explain that this city be all ways in change, that she have
not stepped out in it for months and so it be a-stranged to her.
A bridge have fallen here and a new house were built there.
Much of our walking is returning to a place where Ava knows
some other way to go. Untangling also the moon which move
her self in journey over the roofs.

After some time we come up on a long stone bridge that
lead to a church. There the walls moan *No Hope* and wind
turn to whistles in the spire. Filths fall from Elinor's shoes
while we cross toward it, garbage drop to the water and feed
the rats that swim.

No body share the footpath here. They all may be in the
palace crowd or in the moaning tower and this be ever a dark
place. Ava know her way now.

The moaning grow stronger, then it fade.

We walk through filth again to the house that Ava have
sought, tall but not taller than the neighbors, dark and with a
tear of black cloth that blow from a high window. A head of
stone hangs sculptured by the door, with yellow wires twisted
round the neck and bits of glass in shatters on the ground.

This be Ava Bingen's home.

She tries the door and it is locked. Ava look up at that black cloth and breathe quick in greater fear, but she make a fist and pound upon the door.

"Gerda!" she shout. "Sabine!" Though I should guess that persons with a house marked out by broken glass will not come for shouting.

When Ava knock the door, the head shake as if it warning go away. There come more shouting too, from the place of howls that we just passed; so all the neighborhood does caution us.

Ava make a noise inside her throat.

She jumps up to grab the head. It is the leap of a mad woman. Last embrace of our last hope.

## AVA BINGEN

When I fall, the stone head falls with me. We crash bruisingly
to the footpath.

Midi stares round-eyed. She clutches her ribs, panting;
she can't believe that meek Ava Mariasdatter—Ava Bingen—
has torn a rock from its mooring.

More than that, now I heave the thing up with both my
arms and bash it at the door handle. Bash, dash, crash again:
the door groans open. I drop the stone head (let it shatter, I
don't care) and shoulder my way in, shoving against a chest
and a chair set there to delay intruders. There's not much in
the chest, and even I can easily lever my way inside.

As I am about to step over the threshold, I reach back for
Midi. I pull her in after, lest the Dark Countess change her
mind and abandon me here.

"Come along—you helped hatch this plan too."

We walk in together, fingers wrapped in fingers.

The hall is murky; nothing's lit. It's also cold. I shush Midi
(who never needed shushing before) and whisper not to rattle
her teeth; Sabine might think she's gnashing to make a fight.

At the sound of my voice, there comes a noise above. A
cry, stifled. Of a woman or a child? I remember the black cloth
hanging from the old third-story window.

I pray that the sound is a baby, a live baby, as I head for the narrow stairs, dragging Midi behind me.

"Sabine? Gerda?" I call them again, though they didn't answer when I stood in the street. Maybe they'll recognize my voice indoors. "It's Ava."

I hear no specific reply, but the sounds do grow louder as we squeeze up the narrow stairs, winding ourselves around the central spindle and tangling Midi's fine skirts thereby.

"I'm Ava!" I fairly shout, and hear it echo up and down the house.

There's not much but a name left to the place, I discover as I tug Midi into the second-floor chamber. Where once Sabine and my father occupied a room full of bridal furniture and a tall, thick-hung bed, there lie now a few heaps of junk and a straw pallet by the fireplace, where a thick woman huddles beneath the scraps of a bed hanging that must have been too tattered to redeem against Father's debts.

My heart sinks. Nothing of Father left in here; perhaps nothing at all.

The grate holds the feeblest of embers, and the room's so cold I can see my breath in the orange light. I don't bother to stop Midi from knocking her teeth anymore. We approach the heap by the hearth.

There we find not one woman but two, when Gerda detaches herself from my stepmother and sits, holding the old bed curtain protectively over both herself and Sabine's gray head. She peers through the smoky light. "Is it really you, then?"

*The place must be too dark for her to be sure,* I think at first — then realize that with Midi beside me, gleaming blackly, I might appear like some attendant in the company of Death herself.

I leave Midi, kneel down. I'm afraid of what I might find out. I touch Gerda's arm. "Is Sabine dead?"

"No." Gerda doesn't move, either to embrace or to flinch away. She keeps both eyes on Midi, who stands as still as if she really is some dark, silent angel of mortality. "Weak."

"I —" I hesitate, reluctant to make it seem we came only for the baby; but then I realize a good stepdaughter would inquire after a half-sibling, anyway. "I heard she had her child."

"She did."

"Is the baby well?" This and a thousand other questions crowd my tongue. It's ominous that I haven't heard a cry or coo since coming in. "Did she have a boy or a girl?"

Gerda clutches the curtain closer to herself. She's shivering like a minnow. "A boy. Klaus, named as planned for his father, though the name might well doom him to the same fate. And us along with him," she ends grimly, looking from Midi to me at last. "We hung the mourning cloth from the window so's the neighbor boys would think the master dead and leave us alone. Not but what he'll be dead soon enough — we hear the gossip coming from the street . . ."

Gerda rambles on, detailing her fears for the future, which

are also my own. Midi hasn't moved in so long that Gerda must have decided she's just an apparition, an oddity of my life at the palace.

*So,* I think, *I have a half-brother, another Klaus.* One of the four who died was, of course, a Klaus as well. But this one—I pray he not be dead. "Where is he? Is he safe?"

"He's here." Gerda indicates the heap beside her. "Was whining till he heard you bash the door in, then for some reason he stopped. The mistress must've stuffed him with her nipple—though she's not moving much these hours and don't have any milk. We've been feeding your brother what sugar there's left in the crannies of bags."

I clear my throat, delicate as a lady, and peel back the coverings. Cowering beneath the old drape lies Sabine, still blood-streaked and only half awake despite her fear, cupping her hand protectively over a curve that I must take to be a skull. It has been wrapped in a crude form of swaddling, with linen that was probably white in recent past.

"Health to your soul, Sabine," I whisper as I reach a finger toward that little head. "And to tiny Klaus's. Health and prosperity." I touch the linen; it is cold. "I've come with a proposal."

"OU need a *goûter*," he says, acknowledging her fatigue at last. "You'll feel stronger once you get something inside you."

Nicolas must have recognized long ago that Christina-Beatte has no strength left, is surviving only because her ladies and the bones in her gown are holding her up. There may be another princess waiting in the royal nursery, but this one is most likely to mature soon and grant him all he wants. So despite his own delight in prison blood, he will preserve her.

Christina-Beatte murmurs "Yes" with lips that have gone white beneath their coat of red cochineal. She has witnessed two complete executions now—the actual severings of head from body, the scarlet squirts from arteries protesting the loss of what they spent their lives braiding into—but even her bloodthirstiness has slaked in the favor of a greater, overwhelming weakness that might be consoled with pigeon pie.

She allows her new betrothed to bear her away to the great hall, where minstrels and dwarfs are ready to entertain while serving men circulate with platters of food and pitchers of wine. There is ever more cheering as the courtiers find their spots at table and lift their glasses to celebrate the couple now married in symbol if not in fact.

Christina-Beatte's temples pound. It is like the old days of the nursery and the mercury, the guaiac and antimony and other remedies pressed into the sad voids of children's bodies. She is going to return to that sickroom, she is sure of it; she will be locked away.

Lord Nicolas eschews as much ceremony as possible in order to feed his bride. He passes her scraps of meat under the table, and she nibbles them as she once nibbled at pessaries and licked at spoons presented by Maman and Doctor Candenzius.

Once, when she looks down to accept a shred of chicken, Christina-Beatte meets the eyes of Le Fariné, one of her father's favorite and most grotesque dwarfs, staring gravely from beneath the cloth.

Christina-Beatte chokes. But quietly, swooningly, without being sick. She wipes her mouth on her sleeve. Count Nicolas pretends it hasn't happened, and the two of them make the speeches and murmurs appropriate to a joyful occasion, the ones that Nicolas has written. An in-waiting whispers the words in the Queen Apparent's ear, and the Queen Apparent declaims them in her reedy voice.

Yes, Christina-Beatte is growing into her queenhood, and she has some sense of how to behave in public now. Happily; no matter how painfully.

Count Nicolas kicks Le Fariné away, and the ugly dwarf is not seen for the rest of the festivities.

"Drink deep! Eat heartily, good friends!" Nicolas urges the diners. "The executions will recommence once we've restored our strength. And, of course, we'll resume the rites of betrothal this evening, after the prisons have been purged."

*Rites? What more can there be?* Christina-Beatte wonders wearily as she begins to refill her stomach, choosing mild foods such as sallet and dolphin from the plate she shares with her betrothed. She contemplates the second death she witnessed, that of a Lord Tummler, whose neck was stronger than the executioner's ax. It took two thwacks to break the part of his spine that ran to his skull, and when that was over, the head dropped with a sound that accented the hollowness beneath the platform's boards.

Once he was dead, Lord Tummler's face rolled to greet Christina-Beatte's, to bid her farewell. He bore a surprised expression. She watched as the eyelids twitched and the orbs below them glazed fast over, as the soul departed from the body and what lay before her became only flesh, nothing more.

*It is* that, she thinks as she forces herself to swallow the dolphin (which is not so mildly spiced after all), *it is* that moment *in which magic lies.*

She takes a sip of wine. She feels stronger. *Formidable.*

## MIDI SORTE

Ava Bingen may speak "proposal" to her father's wife, but the wife be fast to say that what Ava wants is not for her to choose but for the man of the house, who at this time be but a baby.

A baby who be too thirsty to cry any more.

Ava say yes, what her stepmother think be true in normal circumstance. But since the child can not speak for him self, this Sabine must speak for him, and she must make her decision out of love.

At this the woman start to weep but with out tears. I think that if we wait some short time we will not have to ask for the child but may simply take him, for she will be dead. It seem simple to me, but I am no part of any family.

And this idea make me weak, as do the whole reason of our errand, and I am weak any way.

The serving woman, Gerda, hop up in the pallet and put her arms in front of the woman and her baby. "Every mother loves her child!" she cry. I clutch my gut, the Lump is swimming to the sound of that voice.

I cannot listen more, I who my life will belong to my Lump and even it may die at any moment, and this time I'd be miserable. So I tip toe back ward on the fronts of my pattens and do not trip on old rushes that blunt my noise or on my skirts that rustle, and I find the stair and wind my way back down.

The bottom of the house be even more cold with its windows to the street, but I can be here alone and think as I could never do up the stairs. Also, in this plain home I might under stand how it be that a person with no money can find comfort, if this may some how be possible for me. I wonder, *How could the Lump and I live?* So I blow the light in to a stub of candle from the last ember down here, and I study this narrow room with no table or chair or cabinet or chest except the one that did block the door and that I open now to find some dried mouse droppings and an under shirt with brown beneath the arm pits.

I hold it up. This is the shirt that I would have as a poor woman. I would wear a long time be cause linen be strong, much more strong than silk which shatter at a sudden move. And I would not see the brown marks be cause I would have no choice about them.

I feel the filth up on me. I think to find some wet and use this shirt to scrub me clean of Isabel. So I ope the one door that do not lead out front, and then I am in a strange place.

It is a big room of glistens and shines. Hooks on the walls to hang wires and a table for circles of glass. They stand tucked between ridges and facing the door. One row, two row, a dozen, more than I can count. And more on some shelf upon the wall. They wink the candle's little light like a hundred yellow eyes, like a counting-room of coins. Like some poison-auntie magic. But they just be spectacles like such that Arthur wear.

I hear a cat at the window, first with claws and then miaow. Just one. I once had four that were my own, in that palace made of turquoise. I see her nipples swollen, she be another nursing mother.

I unhook the shutter and let it in, and the cat streak past in black and white to leap at the loops of wire up on the wall. The night air come in with a moon light that makes the glass circles look more faint, like the ghosts of old ideas.

# AVA BINGEN

"Why don't *you* stay?"

It is Gerda who suggests this, not Sabine, though I know Sabine would want the same if she were well enough to say so. I am the daughter of the house. As such I bear responsibility to look after the other women in it.

Gerda wraps the shred of curtain a little snugger around Sabine. "You and your friend, that dark person — you could both stay, and then there'd be a family here again. Of sorts."

I hear the dry, feeble smack of lips on Sabine's teat.

"He'll die if I don't take him," I say. "He's failing. But at the palace he'll have milk. He'll have everything. He'll be the king."

"Unless he's killed when you try to put him in the Queen's bed," Gerda points out.

I try to *"Shhh-shh-sh"* her, the way Midi would do. (I wonder incidentally why Midi isn't doing this herself.) The last thing that might help the baby or the Bingens just now would be an upset to Sabine's emotions.

"Poor little thing," and I could mean Sabine or my brother. "Let me hold him," extending my arms to touch the chilly heap of flesh the three of them make. "I'd like to hold the new Klaus Bingen."

I want this very much, a chance to hold a new-created infant who is not a demon. The hunger in me must show.

Sabine comes alive again and pulls away. "He's mine!" She clutches the baby so hard, I think she might strangle him. At last, he wails and proves his lungs are strong. "He's all I have!"

"What about my father?" I remind her above the sound of the baby. "He is your husband." I hesitate, for this is a delicate suggestion. "If you save his life, he could give you other children. And just think," I conclude, "what a wonderful fate you would be giving this child. *Your own child,* Sabine, would rule over all of us."

She says nothing.

I wonder if a story might help the situation, persuade Sabine as it persuaded Queen Isabel. Not the same story, but one of substitution and happy endings . . .

"You see"—I am brave—"it is like with the wife who so longed for a child that she went to the Queen of the Elves—"

Before I can get far, however, Gerda asks suddenly, "Where's your dark companion? Has she deserted us?"


I thunder downstairs, slipping on uneven angles of stone. In order to succeed, the bargain Isabel and I have struck requires two chief elements: the baby and Midi Sorte, who will get the three of us into the palace again. I can't say that I've secured the one yet, only that the other must not abandon us.

I mutter a prayer to the Virgin, then an incantation: "Midi Sorte, of all the witches! If you are in the house at all, I order you to materialize!"

I'm relieved to see the shadow of Midi stepping quietly out of my father's shop. There is the faintest shimmering sound around her, as of actual magic.

"I—I'm sorry," I stammer. "I thought you'd gone. I'm sorry I called you—that."

She gives one of her famous shrugs, which is the darkness moving against itself, accompanied by more of that shimmering sound. At this point, I think perhaps she likes to be thought a witch, someone with powers rather than someone enslaved. And it seems that she is, after everything, loyal to Isabel and the plan we've concocted. A far better person than I am. A friend.

A cat yowls from somewhere inside the house, though we've never had a cat before. It is a ghostly sound. I shiver and clutch myself, preparing to return to that cold chamber and demand that my stepmother hand over her child.

But in the time that I've been gone, it's happened: Gerda's set aside her own fears and managed to persuade Sabine for me, or else she's given up persuasion and plucked the baby from his mother's arms. For she appears at the bottom of the steps and holds him out, blocking the stairs with what frail bulk she has left.

"Take him. Save him. Do your best for us all." She says it simply, with a bend in her knees as she deposits young Klaus in the crook of my left arm, the one that does not hold the candle.

My body assumes the curled-over posture learned from carrying other baby brothers over a decade ago. I make a shell around young Klaus Bingen. He feels surprisingly light, just a crisp atom of newborn child, in dire need of warmth and good milk.

I realize, quite suddenly, that Gerda has not brought him to me from an instinct of self-preservation, or even because she once loved my father. She is doing it because she loves this baby and wants to give him his best chance at life. And as I draw back his swaddling and gaze for the first time at those weak, blindly pleading infant eyes, I know that for all the strangenesses and plottings of the last hours, I love him too.

I'm struck as dumb as Midi Sorte.

Mute—for I confess I'd hoped with some part of me to keep it for myself, to start a new life or at least a quest—I slip the ring from my pocket and give it to Gerda. And so simply, the famous ruby of the Bullens becomes the secret wealth of the Bingens.

# FÊTE

T is the moment of wildest entertainment, with the prettiest dwarfs dancing the most exuberant dances on the deck of a ship fashioned from one of the gilded swan beds. Everyone is laughing and banging spoons against the table to show enthusiasm; the minstrels must blow and strum all the harder, popping veins in their foreheads and arms, in order to give the dwarfs their music. Even Duchess Margrethe manages to stay awake for this. She laughs with the others — it is such joy to laugh after so much grieving.

"I didn't even make a joke," whispers Lillegry, a golden-haired dwarf, to the others. She is new and uncertain.

"But now I will." An old favorite, Wantonesse, prepares to lift her skirts above her head.

Champignon, with silvered hair and silvered mask, does a handspring to clear her path. He ends upside down on the betrothed couple's table, causing Duchess Margrethe to shriek and Count Nicolas to glower.

It is at this moment that Christina-Beatte collapses into the plate she shares with her almost-husband. Her head wobbles several seconds (measured by the Great Hall clock's expensive extra hand) under the weight of her tiara, which is tethered to an even heavier wig; and then, waist stiff with the whalebones that have held her up so long, she falls face-first into the assortment of soft vegetables and meats that she and her intended have been slowly depleting. Her tiara upsets a salt cellar. Then, off balance and board straight, her body begins an ungainly slide to the floor.

Count Nicolas catches the girl before she disappears beneath the cloth. He hoists her upward to prop as if she's sitting on her own. Ignores the smears of food upon her lead-pale face and behaves as if no one else could possibly notice them, either.

"My betrothed is eager for her bed," he declares. "We will rearrange our celebration anon, according to her needs."

He is not ordinarily the type of man to use a word like *anon;* but this is a special night, and anyway he must get accustomed to high verbiage in his new position.

"The executions will resume after the *couchement,"* he concludes.

The courtiers sit still, not sure whether they are meant to cheer for this or not.

After the slightest hesitation, the dwarfs exchange a flurry of kisses aboard their golden swan ship, and then it is clearly acceptable to applaud.

# MIDI SORTE

I fall.

On a short bridge all most to the *palais,* where we hear all ready the voices of more celebration in the street, I trip on Elinor skirt and pitch to a side. I twist to land on my hip, not my belly. Not my Lump. My legs half over the edge. I feel the circles I took from Ava's glass shop; they crack beneath like bones. Some bones.

The mama cat have been following us. And she have friends, and they circle my head like if to take my breath. Ava fight through them and with her hand that do not hold her brother, she hauls me to sit. One of my patten fall plunk in to the water.

Ava rub my wrist between her fingers. "When was the last time you ate?"

She ask, "Have you slept at all?" and "Have you been careful?"

Ask, "Does Grammaticus know you're pregnant?"

The cats surge against me. How do Ava know? But then the signs be there to any who wish to read them. Even now I feel my bosoms squeeze with ache against my bodice; the stays press my belly, and the smell of filths on the bridge and under it rise fast to my nostrils.

I turn my head.

"So it *is* true, then," she say, in a tight voice that make me think she clutch her brother the harder. "You are having *his* baby. Grammaticus's. Arthur's."

If fortune smile; if it do not kill me. If I have not kill my self all ready. If the Lump belong not to Nicolas.

Ava reach her free hand to touch my belly, feel it top and bottom. The moon shine on her big brow and she frowns.

"I had four brothers before this one," she say. "And it's too early for yours to sit so low. Have you swallowed any-thing meant for Queen Isabel?" She sound worried in a true way.

The two parts my tongue twist tight together, fill my throat. I cannot admit it were my own hand that make me sick and not some accidentish poison. I cannot move my head for yes or no. I let the cats to rub my cheeks.

"You should tell Grammaticus," Ava say finally. "He would want to know. Maybe—maybe there's a way for him to marry you." But she do not sound hope full or pleased.

She make me kick away my last patten and walk in filth beside her. With cats.

# SUCCESSION

LONE, alive, awake.

Isabel receives a visit from her children the Wraith Prince and Princesses, whom Sophia has at last persuaded across the water from Saint Peter's. They've tired themselves out with tweaking noses and pressing bladders at their sister's betrothal feast; after the failure of Sophia's brilliant plan to smother Beatte with dampening spirits, there was no more fun to be had. And so they have come, as an afterthought, in their afterlife, to see Maman, the gray dame who fed them bitter draughts with words of love on her lips.

Words of love! Feeling them gather around at the moment of her death, Isabel addresses them all: "I would surrender this child" (she means the ball of wax and relics), "for the chance to touch you . . . even just one of you . . . in the flesh again. If I could have that" (she sobs), "I would never need any other gift."

She waits.

"I am sorry if I made you ill," she says timidly, or she thinks it. "I had the best intentions. I loved you all—I still love you!"

She waits again.

"At least show yourselves to me!"

She feels them whirl around her. She feels their whispers: *Maman, Maman, we love you! Maman, come to us!* One of the girls (Is it Hendrika? Amalia?) loosens a shutter and lets it rattle, teasing Maman with the possibility of seeing stars. Others poke at the monstrous brother hidden in the chest and leave bruises where his flawed flesh begins immediately to rot. They sit, all five in a row, astride Maman's enormous body, and they push the air out of her. *If you want to see us, come to the other side!*

Isabel's breathing grows labored. The waxen lump of sorrow-child congeals as her hands grow colder. No one would recognize it as a baby anymore, but she bears it a strange gratitude. It preserved her long enough to birth the monster and to regain some mind. To realize that this court where she has tried so hard to belong, this court that once seemed her destiny, it is not her home after all. And to know that, one way or some other, she is going to die, and she doesn't mind, and she has been loved after all.

The shutter flies open and in wash the stars.

*Maman, come to us! Come now!*


Just as she's slipping away, into the arms of her eager, naughty, fretful wraith children, Isabel hears the door open. A different kind of light enters, more brilliant than the stars: two women—one pale and wrapped in a shawl, one dark and carrying a candle—step in. They close the door and lock it (though the guards on the other side have the same key) and drop the flap over the opening so that the gray tatters of linen surround Isabel and her children, who start swinging on the strips and playing tricks with the wind.

Isabel is afraid her little wraiths will fall out the window, that she'll never see them again. But she's also curious about what these two women have brought. Her heart begins to beat again; her breasts ache with the return of life.

The woman with the candle sets it on the table that holds Isabel's medicines and wines. She lights other candles from its flame, too, and in the swelling glow she seems to grow darker herself. She looks bad—dirty and tired and in need of one of the draughts that Isabel used to prescribe for her children. She even sounds broken, like shards of herself scrape and tinkle on each other.

*Come, Maman! This may be your last chance!*

The other woman approaches. She is pale and tousled but sturdy looking, like all the Elinors born on these shores. She allows the shawl to slip from her shoulders as she draws near the bed. She has her arms wrapped around some bundle and wears an amber bracelet, a set of cheap beads that distract Isabel's eye as the woman climbs onto a cushion by the bed.

"Your Highness," whispers this too-familiar woman, whose sharp features stir a special memory in Isabel's dying mind. "Your Highness, may I present your son, the King."

At first Isabel smiles, just hearing the words "your son." Then follows doubt. This is the third son in as many days. And finally pure joy, as the sharp Elinor leans in gently to nestle a baby, a real living creature, among the pillows holding Isabel in place.

A little nose pokes gently in the direction of Isabel's bosom as the tiny creature whimpers. With the last ounce of her strength, Isabel frees the unused bag of her tit from the blankets, and she fits the swollen grub of her nipple to the tiny mouth. He feeds.

It is the most marvelous, miraculous feeling Isabel has ever experienced, one she'd never thought to be allowed, given her husband's insistence on wet nurses. She has milk. The feeding tugs her spine out through her dug and into the ravenous little creature whose bones will now be nurtured with her bones.

In the mingled pain and pleasure of it, Isabel fails to notice when and how her wraith children disappear. She allows herself to float away on a dizzy river of swelling, miraculous life.

She wakes, perhaps weeks later, to a voice whispering in her ear.

"Your Highness, you will have to scream."

Isabel blinks. Someone has been waving a vial of terrible-smelling stuff beneath her nose, a salty odor that reminds her of a part of the palace she'd rather forget. The outside. She coughs, and her nipple falls out of the child's mouth.

"Scream?" she asks, wondering if one of the others will replace the nipple or if this baby, too, will now be taken away for someone else to feed. She feels a pang of loss for the wraith children.

"To represent childbirth," says the woman she now thinks of as Light Elinor. "You have to scream to simulate the pain. If anyone is going to believe that this is your baby—and they have to believe, that's our plan . . ."

"But . . ." Isabel thinks the plan is not complete; there is some part or parts missing. "For childbirth . . ."

"With your permission." The woman holds up a handful of bloody cloths. They look like the linen strips that Isabel has scarcely ever used, the kind that women need when they aren't pregnant. "Your Highness, you are still leaking some blood yourself, which Midi—your Elinor—which we can stop once we have the proper herbs. But it is not enough. We'll spread this along your thighs and rub it on the sheets. We'll produce these cloths as yours. We have the mother-cake still in the chest from before . . . We can make the birth look real," the woman concludes with what even Isabel recognizes as doubt that tries to convince itself. "But we will need you to scream."

"The baby?" Isabel asks.

"He's sleeping, Your Highness." The woman picks him up, with care for his neck; she runs her finger down his cheek. "His name is Klaus. At least, that has been his name thus far. Of course, you have the right to give him a new one."

It is the expression of tenderness on girlish sharp features that convinces Isabel. All at once she remembers the story, the scheme, the possibility that she might save her daughters and herself by embracing this baby. A baby brought from elsewhere, one untainted by any sickness of her own blood. A Lunedie baby. Who deserves her love. Isabel reaches out. She will give that love.

And yet the woman's face is troubled.

"My dear," Isabel says gently to this Light Elinor, "what seems to be mattering you?"

# AVA BINGEN

And then I do it. In front of Queen Isabel and Midi Sorte, clutching my brother in my arms, I pour out the whole sorry tale of my life, from the Great Sickness and my father's certainty that if we alone had survived, we must be destined for greatness; to falling in love with Jacob Lille and abandonment and pregnancy, a miscarriage that will always be suspected of being something more.

"They know I fornicated—they think I aborted — they shamed me . . ."

And, finally, these last dirty months of doing Nicolas's bidding, first directly through him, then as commanded by intermediaries such as Candenzius.

I sob it all out, my disgrace, my horribleness. The way I can't help feeling little Klaus belongs to me, and yet I cannot figure *how.* How to claim him and abandon my father. How to justify the life this baby would have as my child rather than the Queen's. I even confess that, for a while, for selfish hope, I stole a man from Midi and that it was no more fair than anything else that happens under the sun and stars.

"And I am sorry, Midi, I truly am," I babble. "Arthur Grammaticus doesn't love me and I don't love him. But he is worth a thousand courtiers—even Count Nicolas, with the jewels in his prick."

Midi stares at me. So does the Queen. I guess at the cause of their astonishment—or I choose the cause least awful to address.

"Yes, Count Nicolas has sewn pearls and turquoise and—oh, I don't remember exactly what else—in his manhood. He says they protect him from disease and give him wealth wherever he goes, in case he encounters a desperate situation."

Midi still stares, but Queen Isabel speaks.

"My dear, are these your sins? All of them?"

I nod. But then I add, "Until tonight, with the ring that we gave in exchange for my brother. I considered keeping it. So I'm guilty of greed as well."

Isabel scratches her ear, looks longingly at the baby. We are all greedy for him; perhaps she thinks she must persuade me to give him over.

"It strikes me," she says, not unkindly, "that what you need is absolution."

*Absolution?* I shudder, and little Klaus whimpers. Religion, a priest, a silly ritual—when priests are the worst gossips of all, if they've had enough holy wine in them. Absolutism.

Isabel's voice pulls my gaze upward. "Forgiveness," she says, as if *absolution* must be too complex for my understanding. "You need to be forgiven."

"I have never trusted priests."

Isabel gestures me closer, till Klaus is in reach. "I have my own confessor, Father Absolon." She strokes my brother's skull with fingers drained of blood; it seems a miracle she can move at all. I let her do it. "But I don't tell him everything. If I were to advise you . . . as I might advise my own daughter . . . I would say a priest might give you penance, but for absolution, you must look within yourself."

While I wait, gap-mouthed, for her to continue, she smiles some secret melancholy smile, the kind that says its owner is thinking of her own past.

Queen Isabel says, "Such things as you describe . . . sad things . . . happen to all of us, you know. They are not part of some great plan."

She reaches out for Klaus, and I give him to her, mute-struck. She beams down at him.

"I don't believe in Fate," she says. "After this past month, I'm not sure I believe in sin. How can there be sin in love?" She kisses Klaus. "And disease, even the Great Sickness— our Lord has not devised it as a weapon for meting out justice. It is earthly. It strikes to remind us that we are mortal, not that our sins or our abilities are any greater than someone else's." Her voice gathers strength as she speaks; she seems to have contemplated this topic to the fullest. "It makes us humble. It makes us kind."

I am transfixed, unable to believe the Queen herself is offering me not just advice but also compassion. And not a Catholic compassion—a new sort that alters every notion I have had of her as rigid, selfish, mad. Has Klaus done this?

"And as to those other things you speak of," (she still

strokes my brother) "passion and all that—well, we have all dreamed of poetry. And you aren't the first woman to have lost a child, or to have been blamed for it, or to have acted desperately in order to save herself and the ones she loves."

I hear a sound, a growl, from Midi, but I ignore it. Isabel lets her hand fall on that great loose belly. Now I know she's talking not just of me but of something that to her seems much greater. Perhaps our Queen is a philosopher. Perhaps she never was mad at all.

Mumbling now, she speaks into the bundle tucked against her breast, "If you are pure of heart, a priest's absolution means nothing, and neither does general opinion. If you know your heart is good and guiltless, you can grant yourself absolution. I believe the Virgin would say it so. If you fear the father, she has always said, turn to the mother." Her eyes go to her shrouded paintings.

She draws a deep breath. "You must decide, I think, where your loyalty lies. Is it to me? To the Crown? *Nicolas?*" (She can't keep the loathing out of her voice with that name.) "Or will you be loyal to your . . . self? Your heart's desire."

There comes a long pause that I would call pregnant if the word were not so laden. I look at Midi. She looks back at me, eyes liquid, feeling her own pain. She is crying, silently.

"Do you understand?" Isabel asks me.

Nodding, I wipe my eyes, though in fact I hardly comprehended a word of what she just said.

She seems to guess this, too. "Bend down a little," she

says. With great difficulty, she lifts the hand that once bulged around the Bullens' ruby ring. She reaches it toward me until her palm covers my skull.

"For any crime you intended against me, I forgive you," she says softly. "You are absolved."

I look up, and my eyes meet Midi's. In the flush of knowing Arthur loves her, I can see in their black depths that she, too, forgives me; just as I forgive her.

*This* is how it must feel to dive into the Troll Kingdom and come back dragging their king by the beard.

I can quite nearly forgive myself now.

# ISABEL

ITH her hand still on Light Elinor's head, Isabel gathers her strength. She screams.

Light Elinor screams too, in surprise. The baby wails. Dark Elinor makes a *"Shhh, shh, sh"* noise, but there is no time. Of a sudden, after an absolution in which she gave herself forgiveness also, Isabel is desperate to save this baby and the rest of her fleshly family. And herself. So where once she used all her strength to keep from screaming, now she uses all she has to scream as loudly as she can.

A knock comes on the door, a pounding. "Your Eminence!" shouts some man or other.

The girls move swiftly. Light Elinor goes to the door while Dark Elinor busies herself between Isabel's legs, with gestures that feel familiar. Light Elinor murmurs something that Isabel can't hear above the sound of her own screaming. Boots pound as guards go to fetch something, someone.

The baby's cries grow in volume. High, piercing, like needles diving into the Queen's ears and puncturing her again and again. Isabel clutches him tight. She screams louder, and in her shapeless sounds she is telling him, *Hold fast and trust.* She screams, *You belong to me.* She tells him, *All is forgiven. All will be well.*

# COUCHEMENT

HE belongs to him now. Or at least that is what she's told, what the words spoken by the councillors (in French) and priests (in Latin) mean. And now, this gesture, this putting the two of them in bed together, in their nightclothes, with his hairy dark leg touching her thin, soft, bruised one, where the white paint can't cover the dark marks of veins and sores: somehow, this gesture—with his thirty-six-year-old body touching her ten-year-old one in this way—signifies an irrevocable possession.

Christina-Beatte has spent most of her life in bed, and in her fatigue she expects that the rest of it will be passed in much the same way. Lying down, ministered to. But *possessed*? She is a Lunedie princess! She is the Queen Apparent!

All around the room, courtiers are clapping. Some smirk, as if at a sort of joke that they won't allow themselves to speak aloud.

Once the image of these two in bed has taken hold in so many minds, the smelly old Duke and Duchess of Marsvin begin unsteadily to roll the sheet away again.

Christina-Beatte gets angrier and angrier. Her body will be revealed before all her courtiers, not just her ladies, in its undignified reediness, for she is still as thin and ill-formed as a sapling on a cliff side.

"Stop," she whimpers; but amid all the clapping, no one can hear her.

*Christina-Beatte is Queen.* She has inherited her father's discretion and her mother's sleight of hand. So it is only the dwarfs, who are used to looking closely, who notice as she reaches for her pillow, while the courtiers' applause grows louder and more of Count Nicolas's chest comes into view.

He has left his shirt untied, the slit exposed. Both Christina-Beatte and the dwarfs notice the prickles where hairs have started to grow back after their morning shave. They also notice that the Duke and Duchess are now having some difficulty, that the ceremonial sheet appears to be caught on something just below the Count's waist.

It is at this moment, as the glittering courtiers can't help a laugh encouraged by the proud smile on Nicolas's lips, that Christina-Beatte strikes. Just as he taught her to do, just as the nursery stories have suggested. Anyone who dishonors her, who holds her up to ridicule, who seeks to *possess* her—such a person deserves immediate punishment.

She knows what the thing below his waist is. It is disgusting.

But she is resourceful. She pulls the pillow out from under her head and boffs him across the face with it, to knock the smile away. And then, as delighted laughter shakes the very bricks and stones of the palace, and the Duke and Duchess lose their balance in freeing the sheet, Beatte springs up and plunges into that thing that has caused Nicolas such pride.

She plunges her dagger. The one that he gave her. Into his thigh.

The flesh yields more easily to the blade than she ever imagined, perhaps because she has put more weight into the cutting than ever before. In fact, she did not mean, she is sure she did not mean, to stab him so hard—she fell on him. And now falls against the thorns of his chest. She thinks he will probably tickle or—*puhha*—embrace her now. She does not expect him to make her wet.

## The Beloved Princess, Concluded

Once the evil king had robbed the lovely princess's land of everything of value, and once he had departed with his shipload of treasure, the heavens sent a miracle: The tiny monsters who had survived his reign transformed into the children they were meant to be—healthy, beautiful children who laughed and played and hopped into the sea to pull starfish and mussels off the two princesses sleeping under the waves. The children swam the princesses back onto solid ground, where they joined their mother and brother in returning the land to prosperity.

Yes, there was a brother. He was a brave boy and a clever one, but when he was young, according to the custom of the place, he had been sent to live with another family, who raised him well. When he returned to the palace, he proved a most just and wise ruler. He brought the country back to prosperity, found suitable husbands for both his sisters and his mother, and married a virtuous princess himself.

As to the evil king: On the voyage back to his homeland, a relentless sun melted the crown that he'd conjured from his skull. The evil king choked on molten gold, and the jewels transformed into beetles that fed on his eyes. The songbirds formerly impaled on the crown's bony tines regained their plumage and sang praises of the true royal family, before flying home on fresh wings.

## AVA BINGEN

The guards and messengers have done their job well—too well. Before we can get my blood (the blood of my pure heart) and Isabel's properly spread about, the room is nearly full. Isabel's ladies, Beatte's ladies, even a councillor or two. They rush toward the bed and then halt. Appalled, astonished, puzzled? For there Isabel is calmly nursing my brother, with a dreamy smile on her face and hardly a care that the court is now packing her chamber like herrings.

"*Shhh, shh, sh.* There's a baby," Isabel says, quietly, but somehow everyone seems to hear. "*My* baby. A boy. Your King."

They fall silent. Staring. At the lips tugging away at the red royal nipple. At the nipple itself, which has so grown in color and size as to resemble a duke's gouty thumb. Mostly, I think, they stare at the light that glows through my brother's skin as he feeds, naked now and sprawled on the Queen's great chest, with his chilly blue pallor replaced by a swell of rosy-gold.

He is a beautiful child. We are all beautiful in his light.

All at once, the women in the front—Baroness Reventlow, Lady Drin, Mistress Belskat—spread their skirts and fall to their knees, heads bent. As each cluster of courtiers behind them realizes what has happened, they follow suit, rustling and clanking into place. Their curtsies crowd against the others in the room, push the aprons and the guards to the edges and even out the door.

In the absence of Duchess Margrethe, the Countess of Ditlevnavn is the highest-ranking lady here. She utters the thought in every spinning head:

"Welcome, King Christian VI."

"Christian Klaus," Isabel says.

Many things happen in the next minutes; any momentary peace dies away as soon as Isabel allows her ladies to stand. Some enter, some exit, all of them wheel about the bed to admire the baby and to wonder, truly, how a Queen so gross and mad could produce such a perfect specimen.

Lady Drin turns my brother over in her horny hands. "The cord is neatly cut," she observes, as Isabel demands to have her son back. "The end is already crusting over."

Reading in this statement a question—which in fact is there; the court ladies rarely speak in simple declaratives— Midi squeezes to the linen chest where so much is stored. She produces a pair of scissors, conveniently stained red. Also a mother-cake, a small one, wrapped in linen. She unwraps it and lays it at the foot of the bed.

We have provided proof.

"'Swounds," the courtiers murmur in astonishment.

"But—when?" asks the pockmarked, chinless Baroness Reventlow.

I clear my throat. No one must speak to this but I; even

sane as she seems now, Isabel cannot be trusted to answer questions. "During the ceremony," I say as bravely as I can. I imagine myself as Midi, suddenly given a whole tongue and a wily brain with which to pass on a false tale. "The cannons, I believe it was, brought on Her Highness's labor. She requested Countess Elinor"—I curtsy in Midi's direction—"and me to attend her. She said she did not wish to disturb her daughter's betrothal while the length and outcome of her labor were uncertain."

I think how Nicolas will react when he hears my words repeated. He will curse himself, thinking that if only he'd delayed the betrothal, he might have managed to get Isabel properly murdered.

No: he will curse me. And he will make his curse come true, in the way most bloody and painful to myself. But, strangely, I feel almost calm as I think of this. I believe I can withstand torture, even. *I have been absolved.*

Queen Isabel smiles ecstatically, like one of the Virgins whose faces show ghostly through the linen drapings. "How proud my husband would have been," she says. "We have a prince—even better, a king!"

For that, Nicolas will kill me and anyone else he ordered to poison Isabel. Still, I am not as terrified as I might have thought. Death—it is only death. I can meet it with a clean heart.

"Christian the Sixth," Isabel continues in her dreamy voice. "Christian VI. *Vi*—you know, in the language of the common people, it means 'we.' *Nous.* He will be the people's king."

These words, I know, will be printed in the history books—and not because they are particularly clever. They will be written down because Arthur Grammaticus has slipped into the chamber, with his wax tablets and sheaves of paper.

I look for Midi. I see just the gleam of her eyes and her dirty skirts; she is holding herself up by a bedpost.

Consider what an event this is, to bring the court historian to the Dowager's private apartments. He left Christina-Beatte's bridal bed to come record what must seem to most a miracle. Nicolas will be angry about that too, unless he ordered Grammaticus here to twist the truth as he witnesses it, to disprove the wondrous birth and finish off the Queen.

*Sainted lice and blowflies,* as Nicolas himself once exclaimed—I somehow have myself believing that this baby really is Isabel's, that she birthed him herself.

Midi sets the mother-cake down on top of the chest. Two physicians have arrived, Candenzius and Venslov, and it is their duty to determine the truth, at least as it is currently configured.

Most of the ladies leave while the two men poke at the bit of gray *morkage,* fuzzy with its linen threads. I wish Midi had found some other place to put it; but then again, as long as the men are performing their investigation on the lid of the chest, they can't be lifting it to see what's inside.

"Seems rather dry," says old Venslov.

Grammaticus writes this down.

"And undersized," adds Candenzius.

They both look at the baby, blissfully feeding. Isabel has

491

switched him to her other nipple; she has no lack of milk. And the boy himself is of good vigor.

"He must have come early?" Venslov suggests, almost as if it's a question. "By my calculations, at least. Perhaps he ate the rest of what sat in the womb? Or there might be something left inside . . ."

Candenzius approaches the Queen. "Begging permission, Your Highness." He coughs delicately and gets her attention. "We should—it is our duty—to ensure your health. We will need to examine you once more. To see that all is as it should be."

Isabel smiles so wide, her face might crack. "Certainly," she says with an air of haughty grandeur. "You may assure yourselves. In fact, as regent, I command you to do so."

She must know that this is another test, to see whether in fact a baby did lately pass between her thighs. I'm sure she thinks her greatest moment's just about to come.

"*Donc,* give me my ladies," she says. "Elinor and Drin. Reventlow will hold the baby. And that maid there" (she points to me, so recently a seamstress again), "let her tidy up meanwhile."

## MIDI SORTE

Ava do n't know it, Isabel do n't, but I feel it. Some thing gone wrong.

For one, my love have enter the same room as I and do not take notice. Write-write-write a stack of papers, his back in my direction and his fingers bleeding ink.

But this be not what's wrong in a big sense. The ladies and the men of court did not run in be cause of some report a king were born. This is a surprise and a distraction. They gape at him but also have some other shock in minds. Threads of mood stretch short to pluck like overstrung lutes.

Yes, some thing's a-rotted, more than the corpse. Which I hope Ava will have sense to move some place more safe as the rest of us be occupied.

While the physicians dive between Isabel legs, I hold one hand and Drin the other. Both my hands be shaking but Isabel's hold steady. We wait for men to make decisions one last time. Quiet Ava gathers rags in to a slop-bowl, tries to dab around here-there, does n't have courage to open the chest and dispose of what really need be gone. I wish we did not leave the first child sleeping there so long, but who could guess we 'd succeed this far? I expect to have die my self some time in the hours just past.

The Lump shift an inch lower down. My body be about to break. I must clench to Isabel to drain force from her if I am still to stand.

I wonder where is my special cat, the one of black fur and white fur and a broken tail. Have she returned to her kittens.

I wonder too where is Count Nicolas. He should be feared of any news that Isabel have produce a living infant.

In sum, I wonder when we shall die, the three of us who dare to make this plan.

"The Queen is in good health," those physicians say on their far side of the sheet. Their voices tick like a clock, be cause they have some worry.

The physicians pack Isabel wounds with they own linen. They predict the Queen will soon thrive as much her baby do all ready.

Isabel hum a little song. The baby cries on Reventlow's hip, to make for sound lost when he were too weak to cry.

"Send for Doctor Krolik," Isabel say in her new grand manner. "We should have his examination too, since this concerns the new King. I am sure Count Nicolas will want the assurance."

Doctor Candenzius come around the sheet and give her a hurt expression, for she were once greatly taken with him and needed no opinion more than his. Then he say, "Doctor Krolik must be with Count Nicolas now. There has been . . ."

He pause as actors do when they wish to develop interest in the next words. ". . . a sort of accident."

494

T takes a moment for the courtiers to realize what has happened. At first they think this some sort of childish game.

The dwarfs understand it first. They scurry under the bed, to roll together on the tiles. There they hear crepitations in the mattress; they sense the redistribution of weight. For Count Nicolas's body is emptying its mass into the feathers and straw that support him.

Atop the mattress and through Count Nicolas's nightshirt, a red fountain bubbles from the linen covering that part of him. By chance or by luck, Christina-Beatte has struck deep inside her betrothed, a vein (or artery, a physician will later correct the misapprehension) that surges with the force of his vital spirits and then collapses to let life trickle away.

Or nearly so. As the courtiers gasp, as the councillors recoil, as the dwarfs feel the first splashes of blood upon their poor tortured faces, Count Nicolas murmurs what sounds like a proverb: "*Alors*, the worm will turn." Or perhaps: "*Encore*, a Rome will burn."

His breath hisses as blood loss snakes him to a place beyond words. His face appears . . . blank.

The lords and ladies, maids and menservants, cluck like a butcher's backyard. They back away, still unsure what's happening, unsure whether they will claim in the future that they were present at the moment when Christina-Beatte stabbed her husband-to-be; unsure, most of all, whether it is she who will be punished or Count Nicolas, for aspiring too high. Or themselves, somehow, for being within reach. What they are sure of: They don't want to watch him actually die beside his ten-year-old bride. That duty must fall to some other soul, someone willing to be held accountable. They vanish.

Christina-Beatte breathes in deep. The blood from Nicolas's wound is spreading so fast, she can taste it on the air. She rolls off the Count and onto her pillowless side of the mattress, banging her skull against the massive headboard. Her wig cushions the blow. She still clutches the dagger her betrothed gave her himself, with its blade's elegant inscription (*In tenebris lumen meum metue*) now clouded with his blood, the jewels on the hilt still glowing clear through her fingers.

O the minutes when he taught her how to use it! How he wooed her with bloodthirst! The quality that bound them most closely together. How strange and how smelly to be in the presence of a familiar life leaking away . . . She wonders when Count Nicolas will assume that expression of surprise she noticed on the executed Lord Tummler's face. For the moment, he merely looks tired, with that wrinkle between his eyebrows still cut deep as if he's puzzling out some great problem.

Christina-Beatte thinks, *Another worm will turn. A lover's Rome will burn.*

Duchess Margrethe, still here and curiously unafraid, lays a papery hand on the little girl's forehead. Christina-Beatte had all but forgotten her. "You may have a fever, my dear," the old woman says, with as much deliberation as Maman used to show in the nursery. She takes the dagger from Christina-Beatte's hand and lets it drop to the floor, then nudges it under the bed with one damp shoe. "I think perhaps you are ill."

Count Nicolas, if he hears at all, must hear these words as in a dream. The spotty Duke of Marsvin is padding his groin with the sheet. Everyone assumes that someone else has sent for a physician and that a physician will be willing to come. Or perhaps no one wants a physician at all, certainly not Krolik.

Underneath the great bed of state, the dwarfs, like puppies, clean the blood from one another's faces.

ISTENING to Candenzius, Isabel is over-come with pride. Not just with herself for having produced an heir, a male heir and a healthy one, a boy who was indisputably born while the rest of the court was at cer-emony and whom she fed from the breast for the first hour of his court life—though she is proud of that, and even of the pains that still mark another child's exit, while the greater bur-den of pain has moved upward and flowed out of her nipples and into his satisfied belly—

Yes, she is proud of herself . . .

But she is also proud *of her daughter,* not typically a category of creature about whom royalty can feel this way. Isabel's daugh-ter, fierce little Beatte, has brought down the terrible beast who tempted and prodded the Lunedies almost into extinction. For Beatte has all but killed Count Nicolas Bullen! Who knows, by the time Candenzius has finished telling the tale with his shapely chin a-wagging, Nicolas might already be dead.

"He suffers terribly, Your Highness," Candenzius says on a note of conclusion. He politely pretends not to see the smile of glee on Isabel's face, or else he ascribes it to her delight in her son, now being swaddled by the dark nurse who has taken Countess Elinor's place.

When Isabel says nothing (speechless with pleasure), Candenzius continues: "But you will be relieved to know that the Queen Apparent — that is, Princess Beatte — is not presently being blamed for the accident. The Duke and Duchess of Marsvin say it resulted from some sort of game they played during their courtship. The dagger being one that he gave her himself, Your Highness, in order to protect her virtue until her wedding night. She may simply have misunderstood the circumstances . . ."

"Are you accusing my daughter of stupidity?" Queen Isabel asks with something like sharpness of tongue, a quality that has not been noted in her since the children began to appear. "Of *course* she was preserving her virtue — this was *not* her wedding night, and she should not have been put to bed with that man."

"I'm sure Count Nicolas had no intention of consummating — not with the entire court there to observe. It was ceremonial only. But if you would allow me" (Candenzius seeks escape from a conversation beyond his diplomacy), "I may bring in Your Highness's councillors, who will explain far better than I can . . ."

"Yes," Isabel says, serene again, holding out her arms for Baroness Reventlow to fill with the child, now neatly swaddled and sobbing himself scarlet in the face. "Yes, do send in my councillors, all of them. We must prepare decrees clarifying the succession and excusing Beatte from that ridiculous betrothal. Perhaps we should arrest Count Nicolas as well. Yes, send the councillors and —"

"Your Highness!" Doctor Venslov, old and jaded as he must be, and disappointed in his own career in court intrigue, breaks into her stream of words. He has just tightened the sheet over the royal parts again and feels he must speak, if only to protect the Dowager from her own ambitions. "Count Nicolas is bleeding heavily. Our messenger tells us that the Duke has had trouble stanching the flow. It is a most terrible wound, and there is no saying what may happen. At the very least, the Count will lose the use of his leg."

"But I have a solution," says Isabel. Once again she has popped her nipple into the little boy's mouth, and even the physicians who know her body so intimately are forced to look away out of a mixture of decorum and, truth be told, ill feeling at the unseemliness. So no one is able to read Isabel's face when she says, "Yes, I have a solution. That black nurse there"—and she seems to gesture toward the woman known sardonically for some weeks now as the Dark Countess—"send her to Nicolas. She will know how to take care of him."

In the puzzled silence, the baby's lips smack on the Queen's teat.

"That woman was the children's favorite. She always did know how to quiet them, even when they were having the most dreadful fits," concludes Isabel. "She will do the same with Count Nicolas."

Let it be recorded that upon hearing these words, the dark nurse curtsies toward the bed, behind which the chronicler hides and watches every movement on her face.

## AVA BINGEN

The nights in this month are not longest of all; that consuming darkness belongs to days before Christmas. But at any season, some nights feel eternal. And now, as I watch Midi march out of the Queen's inner chamber to succor Count Nicolas, I am inevitably led to the everlasting night that follows the brief sun rays we call our lives. How will I spend it? Who will be beside me?

Not, I hope, the monstrous little worm in his wrapping of fur, the creature it is my task somehow to spirit away while Midi restores Nicolas's health and Grammaticus makes his last notes on the state of the Queen's womb. And yet, at the moment, this demon seems my most likely companion: for when I am caught with him, we shall both be destroyed as evidence of sin, crime, witchcraft—whatever the councillors who control the Queen will call it. Is there any hope of saving Father, much less myself? Dubious, but still I might pray that complicated Fate will step in, so I continue with the plan we've begun.

While the room is astir, I go to the monster's chest. I open it. I make a show of searching out clean linens and soiled ones, placing what's dirty and monstrous in the bucket in which I carried the poisoned nightdress destined for poor Isabel and setting aside something clean for making the Queen's bed yet again.

But where is that nightdress? Perhaps I've taken the wrong bucket—though this is the only one within sight. My bucket might have rolled under the bed? I try bending casually to look. The last thing I want is to be found an aspiring poisoner, in addition to a spiriter-away of demon births, but I can't dig too deep without raising suspicion.

Already Grammaticus is watching me, his cold blue eyes appraising my gestures. I bite down firmly on my tongue to repress an urge to babble, make up some silly story that will smack of impossible magic. I am a servant; I do not speak. I need to muster possible magic, and that I can do with my leather bucket and a few more bloody cloths. At the very least, I can remove myself from this room and drink down a lungful of fresh air before I head into the prisons.

"Ultimates," I say to the guard by the door. "For the privy."

He merely glances at the red rag I've laid over the bucket (one of my own, freshly between my legs). Men may savor the blood they spill in battle, but a woman's blood is always something sick to them. "Have the physicians given their approval?" he asks, loudly enough that the physicians may hear and decide whether to respond.

"Yes, let her go—go," Candenzius dismisses me. He and doddering Venslov are back to examining the mother-cake, wondering again what relation its puny dryness has to the lusty boy draining the Queen's breasts.

Isabel has no eyes for any of us now, just the new King Christian Klaus, whose eyes have opened and are gazing into hers with rapt attention as she nurses him.

"There is a terrible reek in this place," says Candenzius, sniffing again at what he calls the *placenta*. "I can't tell one odor from another. We might be advised to open a window fully."

"Certainly not!" Venslov retorts heatedly. "The infant is just making his transition out of the womb."

I leave as the two doctors enter a debate about the virtues of bloodless outdoor air versus the stale but comforting fug of indoors.

The last words I hear are Isabel's: "Open all the shutters— let the King see the moon and stars. He claims his father's star now, you know."

Outer chamber, waiting space, women's hall. I trudge with a burden heavier than it should be, for the awful miscarriage is dense. I try to make the bucket swing like a much lighter thing, ever conscious of how I might appear to watchers.

Because I am being watched. Even a bucket can't grant invisibility at this strange hour. A man is following me.

For a while I try to pretend it isn't so, or that he will ignore me and go past, but his black robes *swish-swish* behind until my last patience is split and I turn to demand, "Arthur, isn't it time to leave me alone?"

"Ava." He stops, a good five feet away from me and out of any guard's sight—treating me warily, like an escaped pig that wants to kill the man who'd butcher it. "I need your report on this birth. For the chronicles," he adds, as if I might accuse him of idle gossip. "There weren't many present, and the birth of a king—"

I clutch the bucket so tightly the rope handle might fray in two, if my sweat doesn't melt it away. "I'm on an errand," I say with an attempt at bravado. "My only reason to speak with you would be to find out if my father's still alive or how he died. I gather from the gossip that he wasn't one of the four murdered today. As for childbed, ask Queen Isabel to tell you. Or Midi Sorte. You could have her write it down for you and save yourself some trouble. She writes a lot, you know. Busy fingers always running all over the page . . ."

Grammaticus is tensing away from me, as if the pig has shown its tusks. "I would think you'd be glad to be part of history," he says in his lofty way. And then smiles, a wee bit timidly, as if he still hopes to please me somehow.

The bucket seems to grow heavier by the second; the demon inside is converting words to flesh. "I *am* part of history, whether anyone knows it or not," I say, too tired to fight him anymore. "All of us are. But you really should ask Midi for her writings. She has pages and pages tucked away in the Queen's inner chamber. Some in her own clothes, even. And that's not all she's hiding from you."

He reaches as if to touch me, crumpling the pages he himself carries. "Why are you speaking in riddles? It's unlike you not to say what you mean."

"Check Midi Sorte's belly, and there's your answer!" I fairly shout. Then, knowing he truly does love a riddle and won't follow farther once he's started puzzling it, I take to my heels and run before the devil-baby can grow too heavy for me to carry.

## MIDI SORTE

He lie there in his fine bed, with pictures of the kingdom wove in thread upon the walls, his fat bandage upon his thigh, his fever sweating on his brow and armpits. He look please with him self none so less. As if it be enough to him to have reach this bed and these sheets and tapestries, and he do n't mind that he him self bear the wound of it.

But he is sleeping; Doctor Krolik's sleep. Of course he have powers now to make pain a pleasure, give the right powders. I curse inside, I did hope there would be no men of medicines.

At least there are no courtiers. The Duke and Duchess have carried Beatte away.

Krolik stand with Dé by a candle, shakes a beaker full of yellow. "How dark would you say that is?" ask the ugly old doctor. The more dark the urine, the quicker he must pack his bags to hie back to Poland.

"Not so very," say little Dé. The one who all ways were kindest to my girls. "I don't believe the blood has entered his voiding channel yet. Maybe it is a superficial wound only."

But the bed be so bloody as if Nicolas did deflower a dozen girls, not just go through a ritual with one of them.

And still he smile that weird smile, which I wonder now be a smile of death pulling at the face to make a joke of him at the last. But no, his chest rise and fall, and his lips part enough to make a whistle while he breathes.

"He is a lucky man?" Dé says, unsure, he will make no opinion till Krolik give it him.

"He might well survive this insult," Krolik agree with him.

They neither one cast a look at me. They can 't think of functions for a black countess in a dirty gown and gloves, so they do not see her.

Thus it be easy for me to cross to that bed and do my own inspection. I feel Count Nicolas' brow and neck, both wet with sweat but cold any way. I lift his arm and drop it, plop, to see how limp it fall against the mattress. At this I think his eyes blink at me and ope to slits that stare like house windows on a damp day when every body be at church.

This the doctors do not see. "The new King is a healthy boy," say Krolik, "or so the messengers have told it. They say also that the Queen's regained her senses. We should ascertain for ourselves before we go further."

Dé nods, he seem too terrified to speak. He must wonder were he wrong to come to Nicolas and not Isabel when these events did happen.

"The question is," say Krolik, "would it be best to leave one of us behind to watch over the Count, or should we pay homage to the new King together?"

"We can't leave him alone," say Dé. "Can we?"

They both turn now and do look at me. I drop Nicolas' other hand, plop, against the feather bed. I smile.

"Did you send for her?" Krolik ask. Dé shake his head.

I make the gestures for Queen Isabel—tall, round body, and a crown—and for rocking a baby, then touch my mouth for speech and point to Nicolas. I make them under stand. They know me as dark nursey long before Dark Countess.

"Well, if the Dowager Queen ordered it . . ." Krolik say with some relief.

"We would not be deserting our post," say Doctor Dé.

"There are guards outside the door . . ."

"And we must pay our respects to the King."

So they bundle off to see which side of this day's bread have more butter on it. They leave so fast the tapestries do shake, so a tide wash the mermaids' water and a wind blow the air round the witches and the priests and the man who lived his winter in a whale. They stir the bed-curtains too, and the curls on Nicolas' brow, and his beard, and they coax a tickle more of blood from out his wound.

My Beatte, murderess! I wonder can I go to her. I wonder what the lords will do if this man dies. What Nicolas will do if he live and he realize he have one more princess left who be younger and more docile. This were suggest in Ava's story, he have more than one chance for a Lunedie wife. Gorma, who all ways were most tender.

So this be what decide me.

I lean in to see his wound. The bandage blood be mostly black by now, except that one red spot in center. I poke with my glove on and the wound do not give way so much, just flakes of blood upon the leather tip. He looks like to heal. But to be sure, I take a fleam from the physicians' kit and cut away the cloth where it is dry, and then I yank it off at one rip and see the wound exposed.

Nicolas wake up then, to yell in pain. Fortunate that I have clap my hand over his mouth, and that in the hand I hold the night dress which he did order Ava to poison for the Queen. I had precautioned to hide it wrapped with in my underskirt.

He take a deep breath in of all that powder in the cloth—and then he cannot shout, for he cannot release the breath.

He look at me, I look him back. Some small blood flow from that place in his thigh, but more goes to his face, where it turn to purple and I feel his tongue come out his mouth like a dog's that will lap water, but there be no water to lap, there be only my hand. And he could not swallow any way.

Mandrake, I guess. The most cruel of all the poisons.

When this have happened, I take the night dress away and fold it many times to make a strip, and this I wind about the hole in his thigh and over his hips, so if his poison do not go in the one end, it will in the other, and perhaps two streams shall meet in the middle and kill him dead. I fasten this neat with pins left from his ruff, and I remove my gloves and watch while his face go more purple and then black.

Yes, I 've decide. He had me once, and he may have my Lump (I am not certain, only tired), but he shall not take both my girls. My princesses.

For pleasure I slap his dying face with Elinor gloves and let them fall, like a noble man who challenge an other to a duel. This makes his mouth rictus in to smile again, and for the last second of his life, he and I are laughing together.

# The Organic of Death and Life

T is a night of mysteries. Every mind at court, at least each mind that matters, is impenetrable, even to a chronicler expert at peering around corners and listening through walls.

The greatest mystery lies in the chamber of Count Nicolas Bullen, regent and bridegroom, who sags abed with an injury and no one to tend him but a royal baby nurse. The two of them are smiling. She laughs her throaty version of laughter.

She does not stop when she sees a new actor enter; and Count Nicolas cannot bother himself to turn his head, merely continues to smirk at the rafters with his eyes slitted draftily. The two of them are locked in some occult intimacy.

An ordinary man would not be blamed for abandoning such a scene; discretion and courtesy would be expected of him. But a man who is charged with recording major court events, including and especially its secrets: this man must steel himself to stay.

He plants his feet; he draws himself tall. He arranges his various papers, wax tablet, and stylus so as to be ready for chronicling when a noteworthy fact is revealed.

But the children's nurse merely stares at him with lips gone sullen, and the Count continues to gaze heavenward, as if History is not present.

Thus the scholar might be forgiven if he does more than merely observe but rather asks a question directly, to clarify what he's heard elsewhere. Forgiven by History, that is, if not by the person to whom he addresses his question.

He says, "What in the name of devils and saints are you doing now?"

Her response is predictable: she presses her lips together, then licks the top one with the two tips of her forked tongue. History knows by long practice that this can be a sign of either confusion or rebellion.

"Is he—" The historian gestures. "Is that man *still* your lover?"

In answer, she bursts with a laugh, a different sort of laugh, that sprays drops from her nose and lips over Count Nicolas. He does not react. She gives a few further heaves of violent mirth, then clutches her belly with an expression of pain wrinkling her face like a walnut.

History must not be thought to have a heart. Impartial, cold, detached—this is what History must be, though where this woman is concerned, he has often slipped. When a woman holds her stomach in that particular way, the reflex has only one meaning, and the meaning sends a jolt through the historian's entrails.

*Check Midi Sorte's belly, and there's your answer!* So Ava Bingen had warned him.

Any reader of this chronicle will remember the slave's quiet first appearance as attendant to Countess Elinor, then the part she played in the magnificent masque that marked the end of the Seven Years' War. Glittering with white sugar, a candied purple plum between her lips, the sweetest possible kiss offered to the lord who stood in for Justice and who now lies here weak from blood loss but smiling up at her with pride. And this chronicle contains the account of terrible rumors about her liaison with this very lord in recent months, and how she yielded to him when she was loved by another. That other who taught her to write so she could express her feelings for him as he did for her.

That other stands before her now, moved by her pain and gaping at its cause—and unsure, after some arithmetic, whether it be his responsibility or that of the man in the bed.

He asks, "Is it—?"

She catches herself on the bedpost, braces herself on the high mattress. Her face has broken into sweat. Still her bed-bound lover does not speak, either to defend or dismiss her. In this way, History knows that the occupant of the ceremonial *letto matrimoniale* has died.

The historian should make a note of the time and the man's expression, but he does not. He goes around the bed to take Midi's elbow and guides her to the carved-arm chair in the corner. He helps ease her down and puts the tablet and stylus in her hands.

"Now," he says, and he is proud of voicing it without anger or judgment, "what would you like me to know? What *should*

I know? For example . . . a small example . . . How should I describe this man's death?"

She takes a few more gulps of air, then picks up the stylus and writes on wax, *Misadventure*.

That is all.

Sitting, the curve of her stomach is more pronounced than before, when the belly was hidden in her skirts. She could have been harboring this atom a long time, in which case it is (most likely) the product of History's seed, not the Count's.

But that is not what he asks her next. He asks, "What did he promise you?"

In answer, she gives one of her maddening shrugs and removes hands from her belly long enough to hold them up empty.

True, the Count is a master of not-promising.

"Did he say anything to you just now?"

She shakes her head.

"Did you kill him?"

Finally, she looks at Arthur Grammaticus. It is a look for which poets would have a thousand comparisons — her eyes like black stones, the twin tips of a murderous lance, the mushroom caps beneath which wicked fairies prepare their poisons. None of these would be adequate expression for the anger she bores into him. Her feeling makes him both recoil and long to kiss her.

"A few moments ago," he says instead, "Ava Bingen instructed me to do two things. I should look to your belly and I should ask for your writings, as you have been keeping a history of your life at court and most particularly with the Queen. I suppose"—he cannot help himself, he stares at that rounded belly and must keep speaking—"the secret of your baby is revealed there too?"

He lets his heart run ahead of History, which is a grievous offense when he should be doing his best to secure those papers. And, yes, to determine what has happened to Nicolas Bullen, the companion of his youth who managed such a rise to prominence.

In answer, his dark love reaches into the bosom of her tattered finery and draws forth a handful of scraps. She shoves them at him, but so carelessly as to let them fall about their ankles. The ink is smeary with her sweat, tears, rain, something—but he sees a word here and there: *story, lick, turquoise, Queen, Gorma.*

Of a sudden, he sees the danger. Not just in these words that he is scrambling to collect before others see them—but in the entire situation: Midi, the dead Count, and himself alone in this chamber. The words have made him know it. He might stuff the pages inside his own shirt and hope to prevent other eyes from finding them, but how is he to extricate his darling, who is perhaps to bear his child, from a situation that will surely warrant her death?

And with that question, he knows something else: He does not mind so much whether she carries his child or the Count's, only that she survives somehow. Some truths do not matter.

"You can't stay here," he tells her, still stuffing the crackly sheets into his own clothes. She rolls her eyes at him. "*Here,* I mean, in the palace—in Skyggehavn. You must go away. Whether you've killed Count Nicolas or not."

He is fairly certain that she has killed him. Whatever may have happened earlier tonight, somehow when Nicolas was left alone to die, she made sure that die he did.

"You will be blamed, not Princess Beatte," says the historian. "Everyone knows Queen Isabel ordered you to tend to the Count. The physicians left you with him. My dear, you have to flee. Take a ship far away—the guards will let you pass tonight, at least until his death is known." He stops and watches that forked tongue press against her upper lip again. Beloved tongue. He reaches into his pocket and finds only two silver shield coins and some brass, no more. His little bit of wealth lies pathetic on his palm. Not enough for a single passage, let alone two, and no time to return to his chambers in the far quarters. And Midi Sorte wears no jewelry, even in her costume as the Countess. She has no way to bargain for her safety.

Poor doomed love. He should have married her, never mind public or royal opinion.

But she wastes no time gazing at him with a sense of all they've lost together. It is as if in shedding the written words, she has found a new strength in herself. She walks briskly to the bed, where she picks up a little knife the physicians left behind. He can only stare, numb, counting his few coins, as she pulls the sheet away from Nicolas's injury and grabs that part of him that has caused so much trouble in the court's desires. Shoving a bandage aside with her knife, she stretches his manhood to its fullest length. The flesh is still elastic, but beginning to congeal in knots beneath the skin.

With two hard strokes, she cuts it off his person.

The whole affair takes less than a minute. It leaves very little blood. But History feels the coins slip through his fingers and tinkle against the floor.

Midi stuffs that part of the Count into her bosom and wipes her hands upon the sheet. She does not bother to cover Count Nicolas again—let the whole world behold his new wound, she seems to say, it means nothing to her—and is about to open his door and leave when the historian comes to his senses and stumbles over to catch her arm.

"You cannot go alone. Let me at least show you some secret ways of leaving that I've learned over the years."

She pulls herself up into the posture of Elinor Parfis, hoists her bosoms in the manner of that lady, and nods her head with its hair flying wild about her. As if permission is her favor to grant. She no longer seems unwell; she seems, truly, like a countess.

With every moment, his terror of her grows. He dares not ask why she's chosen to steal Nicolas's manhood, though there is a part of him that's pleased to see her take revenge this way.

In this fear, he has discovered a greater love than ever imagined. It cannot be compared to anything; it is only itself.

But Beatte will not sleep. She refuses! Until she notices that the candlelight shining through her lids gives the same impression of story unfurling that she found in the dagger that Nicolas gave her. She can watch herself stabbing him over and over, watch the ruby blood spurt from the slit in his thigh. She can stab at the wraith siblings too, stab away everything, anything, even the parts of herself she doesn't like.

So instead of fighting sleep, Beatte presses her eyelids down as hard as she can, to make them bloom with red. She thinks very hard to remember every detail. She will send it all as story-pictures into Gorma's dreams. She will terrify Gorma and the wraith sisters with what she, Beatte, has done.

# Beatte

HE has been washed and returned to bed, her old bed—tucked in next to Gorma, in fact, who shrinks away from her in fear, although none of their attendants have made mention of any of the night's events. Beatte knows there is a fierceness about herself now, the air of a woman—a woman!—who will do anything to please herself, a warrior who loves blood for blood's sake.

She does not know what happened to her dagger. She wishes for it. That beautiful jeweled dagger in which the bottom of every ruby told a story, tiny figures acting out complicated tales of violence depending on how the hilt was turned. A thousand stories for Beatte to enact herself, once she gets her dagger back. She will demand it in the morning. She will have herself declared Queen in full.

For now, the little girls have been dosed with valerian, and Beatte's lids are heavy. She feels the nurses standing 'round, some ladies too, watching anxiously till she and little Gorma tumble into dreams and cause the grown women no more worry.

And she feels the presence of the wraith children, her sisters and brother, who have come to watch over her. When she sleeps, they will pull her down into their savage world.

## AVA BINGEN

My heart is a hammer cracking my ribs. I wish and pray and wish for a swift dispatch of my duty — I should be glad to have dispatched Grammaticus, at least, but now I am alone with a demon growing heavier by the second, and I don't know how long I can carry it before my body splits and my very soul pours out.

I am a jelly, there is nothing else inside me. Just the sensations of fear and the chill, pliant flesh remembered on my fingers.

When I transferred the thing from its fur wrapping to the leather bucket, its boneless body curled easily inside, as if longing for a familiar shape. I got a closer look at the one-eyed tumorous head, the long stalk hardly marked out for belly or legs, tiny stumps of arms that bent neatly to fit against the bubbling eggs where a mouth belonged. A monster from a fairy tale, a figure from a nightmare. Worse than either one; this was life. And the creature must be disposed of.

Somehow I march through four rooms, five rooms, six.

I'm not heading to the privy, of course, or any other place I'd name to Grammaticus. Imagine if a devil were found floating in the pits the next day! The inquiries, the talk of witchcraft. No, I have to deposit this mistake in a much more permanent spot.

By the time I reach the courtyard, I'm gasping. I lean against the outside wall and gulp down cold air till my throat is coated with the airy sweetness that floats there. My arms ache as if I've carried the bucket a great distance. But I put my head back and pass another final pair of sentries as if this is an ordinary errand, then slide across the cobblestones to the portal of the dock. I hope there will be fewer guards posted here than at the square, especially as so many must have rushed to the twin poles of Nicolas's chamber and the Queen's.

It is so quiet I can hear my own breath, pounded out below my heart. I hear the vapors of the earth steaming up from the muddy crack of the witch's hollow.

When I follow the steam upward, I see that all clouds have gone and we have a completely clear sky with a moon and stars shining in a great bubble over the palace. My father's star is dimming into gold, but it—no more than any of the others—does not waver while I stare.

It is at this moment that the chapel bells start ringing, then the bells of the cathedral. Announcing a birth. Almost immediately it seems that bells ring all over the city, and in their clanging tongues I hear the rush of feet—as if every pair in the palace is headed now not for Nicolas or Isabel but for me, for this particular spot I occupy.

With that, I end my decline into madness. I skate the last few yards to the witch's hollow and upend the bucket.

Queen Isabel's miscarriage tips onto the ooze. I throw the bucket after it.

For a moment, as the bucket itself sinks, the little demon

floats like the bloated corpses of the Great Sickness. The single milk-skinned eye stares upward at the mystery of the heavens as it rotates gently. A sleet of sugar and star-shine clings to its skin.

I close my eyes; I cross myself. It's as if I'm bidding farewell to everyone I've already lost: mother, brothers, Jacob Lille. Father. And, of course, the baby I once carried inside and that I lost when it was far less shaped, even, than the horrible creature I've been carrying tonight. I say good-bye to my life.

God's wounds. When my eyes open again, the fetus is still there.

I fear it will be the one object that cannot sink into the hollow, that its unholy nature will keep it floating on the sulfurous mud. I prepare to turn my heels and flee.

But then the slow spin arrests itself, and I can't look away. A rumble comes from deep beneath my feet, and a gulping sound that makes the stones vibrate. The hungry spirits of the center of the earth—mud-witches, muck-maids, whatever they are—reach up to pluck my offering, and the ground swallows the poor demon-child.

# The Dwarfs

HUS the dwarfs beneath Count Nicolas's bed are left in sole possession not only of the truth but also of the jeweled dagger that killed him. Neither they nor the dagger will be seen again.

## MIDI SORTE

I am running and it runs too. That slug part of Nicolas, eel part of him, will not rest. Its blood mixes to my sweat, and the eel swim down tween my bosoms in a wake of slime.

Arthur has me by the arm and he hurries me, but gentle, down a passage that he think he have invented him self, he is so proud to know the way.

He have said again that he loves me. In spite of all he 've seen. And I did not think there were ever such a person as he. All this, his love, in pay for sheets of broken language.

The eel of Nicolas reach my belly and stop on the Lump. I feel the Lump a-kicking. To clear that thing away, may be, or else say *Bonjour* to its *papa*.

I think it as we scurry underneath the moon: *For this Arthur had me hold his pen. This is why I can write his language.* I hope the Lump be of him, all though he be about to send me far from here.

Far, but where? And do it matter, if I go with out him?

So sudden, I believe there is love. I love Arthur.

My thinking makes me deaf as I am mute, be cause I do not hear the bells till Arthur speak of them.

"It means we have very little time," he says, but yet he stop to listen while the palace vibrate round us.

I know in this moment that he have no plan, even the lessons of history have taught no thing of this situation. A black mistress who have changed a good infant for a bad and who carry a baby inside with out surety of the father, and also who have helped to kill one man that might have planted seed in her. *And* who have cut away that evil part of him and carry it with her, Arthur do not know why.

For a time I wish for one tongue, so I might explain it fast . . .

But I am wrong. This is not why Arthur have stopped his hurry. He stops be cause he sees Ava.

*Ava. Arthur.* The snake find another inch to slither. Love turns on me to hiss.

Then Arthur be dragging me toward her. My knees lock and feet do n't move, but they ride rough over the yard stones toward that place she stand in a cloud that lurch from the earth. She has a bucket. She throws it at the witch that sleep in that muddy bed of many tricks.

Now Arthur halt again. I fall against him, my knees are soft. I am tired. I think may be his plan is throw me after the bucket. So he and Ava can be together so long they like, with Ava's brother on the throne and her father free and no me to remind of what they did.

So swift, I lose belief. I regain fury.

The hornets clog my throat with wings and stings. I could spit rage. I could spit *words* before I die.

I growl.

Arthur shush me. I push him, though I be weak. Ava turn now and see us.

Her eyes are white in the moon. "D-did you see?" she ask.

"I saw," whisper Arthur.

I am having pain above the Lump. I cannot breathe. I hate them.

Arthur say, "I saw it blink."

Ava wail in her throat then, she makes sounds like mine. "It can't—" She does not finish.

They are not discussing me.

"I saw a blink," Arthur say. ". . . Or I thought I did."

Ava cover her face in her hands. She is of heart to confess. "It was born days ago. Yesterday? I've lost count—only Midi knows for certain. She was there. It could not live. It's the Queen's baby, you might as well know . . ."

Arthur turn to ask what I know, and he notice now that I feel pain. My belly have brought me to knees, and I swim dizzy in the sparkled heavens.

He kneel beside me.

## AVA BINGEN

"I shall," he promises with an equal mix of pride and humility—only a scholar could manage it—"I *will* take care of History."

He says this as a sort of plea, there by the witch's bed. With one arm he supports Midi. His love. Who is staring at me with her usual deep-boring eyes, but this time, perhaps with a little less hatred than usual and a bit more . . . yes, pleading. Her belly is causing her pain; that much is obvious.

"We have to leave this place," I say, also obvious; uneasy about who else might spot us here and whether the demon-baby will fight his way up, if he's as alive as Grammaticus seems to think. "Go to the dorter—maybe pretend to sleep . . ."

"You have to leave the palace altogether," he says. "Both of you. Right away—there's danger, awful danger."

Just as I think I don't know how to feel more fear, now comes another wave of it. "What do you mean? Has Isabel confessed? Has Nicolas discovered the switch? Has he taken my brother?"

"Ava, please." Grammaticus is gathering Midi into his arms—arms that have rarely carried more than a book or two.

"I suppose Midi's told you who the baby in Isabel's room really is." My poor brother, who did nothing to create this situation but exist.

Whether she has or hasn't, Grammaticus considers the baby's identity a trivial matter. "No one will take him away," he vows dismissively. "Certainly not Nicolas." He staggers under Midi's weight to the arched gallery that rings the inner yard. "The Queen wants that boy—everyone wants him—a good, healthy king." He pants. I trail along behind, hands empty.

Grammaticus says, "I'll make sure the baby's entered into the annals that way, as the Dowager's birth. But you'll have to leave."

"Why?" Relief followed by dismay nearly topples me over, just as Grammaticus lays Midi carefully on the ground. He covers her in his black robe; he looks skeletal and frail without it, like something I shouldn't see. "Arthur, everything is falling into place—I can watch over little Klaus as he grows up. I'll make his clothes. I'd like my father to see him—if Father is alive, Queen Isabel promised to free him no matter what Count Nicolas says . . ."

"You must watch over Midi instead," he says, rubbing her hands between his own. "She is the vulnerable one now. And she cannot stay here. She has done—something."

At the same moment, I feel blood escape my cloth again. "To Nicolas?" I guess.

"She finished what Beatte began," says Arthur. "She killed him."

I cannot describe how this news makes me feel. Elated—

I could sing and feel the stars and the seas would sing with me. Also ashamed, as if I had a hand in his death, because I wished so hard for it. And, finally, suspicious: What if Midi and Arthur have settled on me to take blame, as one of the murderous Bingens? I feel another rush of blood. I take a step backward. Where will I attain absolution now?

"Tell me," I say, "*is* my father alive?"

With that, it seems, the cats who followed Midi and me discover us once more. They stream darkly to her fallen body, curling and rubbing on it both as if they wish to eat her and as if they might keep her warm.

"Please"—Grammaticus arrests me as he tries to shoo the animals—"won't you help us? Take her away? I'll fix History so neither of you appears at all. You'll simply vanish from the record. Come, you have always said you wished to travel . . ."

*Travel.* Sail away from Skyggehavn, from my brother and Sabine (who may have died or else is rich with Nicolas's ruby); even from my father, whom I have just rescued, if Isabel keeps her bargain.

It will be a kind of rescue for me too, though one that brings an exile. In the company of Midi Sorte.

"Where?" I ask cautiously. "How?" Without the ruby, I have no wealth at all, just the handful of silver coins left behind in the dorter to which I cannot return.

"A boat," he says. "We'll find one on the quay used by the laundresses. You can reach one of the green islands, at least . . ."

"A rowboat won't get us that far." A plan, a wish, is bubbling in my mind already. Do I dare?

We argue back and forth a few quick minutes, while Midi slows her breath to recover strength; but it is clear to all of us that in the fullness of time (and sooner than I'd like), Midi and I will be in a boat rowing into the bay.

Meanwhile, the inner yard grows more populated, with people running back and forth bearing news and demands; and bells all over the city have taken up the cathedral's cry.

"I must return to my duty," Grammaticus insists, cowering behind a pillar. "It's expected. If I'm not in one place or the other, all of us could lose everything."

"But what do we *have*?" I ask practically. (I mean to ask what *I* have.) "I can't row a sick woman all the way . . . to Copenhagen."

If Arthur and Midi are shocked by my daring to name a destination, they do not show it. Why not Copenhagen, after all? We understand the language, and it is one of the great cities of the world. They don't need to know about Jacob and what I hope to find there.

"True, you'll need passage on a ship," he acknowledges. I hear a jingle. Grammaticus has a small handful of coins to press into my palm. "This won't get you far," he admits, "but it is something . . ."

That is when Midi stirs. She draws a deep breath and gestures at her bosom. I think, too late, that since she is in the costume of Countess Elinor, she is probably wearing stays, and I should have loosened them to help her breathe. I do it now, propping her up while Grammaticus looks anxiously around, fearing discovery. I unlace the back of her dress and then the whalebones beneath it.

Midi is still gesturing at her chest. There is something stoppering her breath. I reach into that curiously wet, warm crevice and find an unexpected handful of flesh.

I don't know how I know exactly what this is, but I do. I've touched it several times, after all, though in a different condition. I feel no horror, only pleasure; now I have the luxury of pulling my hand away.

"We will be fine," I tell Arthur. "We can get to Copenhagen."

"Your father is alive," he says. "And I will do my best to keep him so."

So it is that the first purple inkling of dawn finds us down on the laundresses' quay, loading Midi into the sturdiest of the rowboats tied up at the water gate. I balance in the center, moving backward as I take her weight from him. She helps as best she can, but she is exhausted at last; I think that if we were not moving now, she might allow herself simply to fade into death. We settle her in the bottom of the boat. Grammaticus wraps her securely in his woolen robe and gives her a kiss upon the brow — not the lips, I notice with some interest. Her lips are wrapped already in black wool.

"Take care," he cautions me needlessly, as I sit on the rough plank seat and take up the oars. Or rather, he cautions us both. We are taking many cares away with us.

I nod — why speak now? — and begin to row.

I am not good at rowing. Even with all the buckets I've hoisted lately, it's a matter of minutes before I feel wet blisters rising on my palms. But I move doggedly on, pulling from sore shoulders, nearly exhausted enough myself to curl up against Midi and doze away into death.

I look up and see we've traveled perhaps twenty feet. Grammaticus is still on the quay, near the servants' portal, watching anxiously. He raises a bony hand in farewell. And I notice also that cats are following, stepping delicately on the quay and jumping over ropes to stay parallel to us.

We are some small distance toward the silvering bay when a terrible thought fills my mind: What if Nicolas lied all along? What if those bumps that I — and Midi — felt, are not jewels after all but some deformity? I remember the sight of the demon-child, poor monster, spinning in the witch's bed and am struck by terrible doubt.

I stop rowing. "Take it out," I order Midi. "We need to see it, make sure of what's inside."

She understands immediately; she has always been a suspicious person. Weakly she rummages around beneath Grammaticus's robe and pulls out that lump of flesh, puts it in my hand. It shrinks slightly in the cold air.

I feel tension from the quay — Grammaticus eager to see us gone, the cats wondering what we're about. The bells are deafening; I imagine yowling and shouting, but we can't hear it echoing off the water.

In the slowly growing light that ushers in a brief winter

day, Midi and I study the squat little thing in my hand. The bumps are barely visible now. We have to press hard, squeezing out a drop or so of blood, to locate those hard places that Nicolas used to count off for me like a rosary: *emerald, turquoise, ruby, pearl* . . . I can't even remember what all he promised I would find. I have a vivid memory in which he explains how wise it is always to carry some wealth about one's person where others cannot reach it. But we must reach it.

I feel inside my pocket. Nothing. My seamstress tools are gone.

Midi guesses my intent and moves. I hear again that tinkling sound of magic. But this time I recognize it as glass.

And when I reach into *her* pocket—and cut my finger—and remove a crescent shard, I recognize this too: a lens carefully ground in my father's shop.

I use it as Father never expected it to be used. I cut—so we can see. When I feel the scrape of something hard, I set down the lens and squeeze.

A stone pops out. Yes! Clotted in blood. I spit in my palm and rub it to wash it—rub fast lest it become an icicle—and there we are. It is round, small, the size of a pea; luminous. A pearl. I rub its surface against my front tooth and feel the slight roughness that is a sign of authenticity.

Midi and I, both tired beyond belief, smile at each other. Because, at last, we have something in which to believe.

We decide we will finish the job, unpack Nicolas's legacy right here, so that whatever obstacles still await us and whatever favors we must ask, at least we are not carrying a nobleman's mutilated manhood when we do it. Grammaticus jumps and shouts while together we cut and press and pop the stones out, and with each one we crow with glee. We are wealthy. We are filthy and criminal and floating in a rowboat, but we have wealth beyond imagining.

And when we are done, there's the thing itself. We both feel (Midi may not speak it, but I know she feels it) the need for a Gesture. We cannot simply cast the prick upon the waters and let it sink or swim.

Midi, of course, has the right idea. She takes it back from me and struggles herself upright, then uses what last strength she has to hurl it toward the quay.

The cats are still waiting, though the boards must be trembling with bell sounds beneath their paws. A scrawny black-and-white specimen with a broken tail leaps up above the others and catches Nicolas in its mouth, then streaks off to enjoy the prize, the others tumbling after her.

Let Nicolas at last nourish the strays. It will be his charity.

And so. There is enough light, now, to see Saint-Peter's-on-the-Isle and the great ships at anchor near the mouth of the bay. There is enough hope, now, for me to take up the oars again and set to work with a purpose.

The palace eases away, and Grammaticus with it, as the sun heaves up from the water. An early ray picks out white swirls of sandstone against the scaly red bricks (a little redder now than I've seen before). It reveals the ornamental moon, the mermaid, the Latin motto that have made the palace famous. *In tenebris lumen meum metue:* In the darkness, fear my light.

Gray winter sunlight touches the bristling copper spires and lingers on the stark black teeth of the gates.

It almost misses the single figure running—running!—down the quay, as if chasing the cats who've disappeared. A figure clutching, as always, a sheaf of white papers in his hand, but without the twinkling glass over the eyes that might allow him to see far and distinguish, in this tiny boat drawing steadily toward the sea, two women: one dark and not natively of this place, one so fair as to be invisible, both grabbing for the oars as if they might row back to receive some declaration from the dark folds of a heart that appears loving after all. He waves as if to call us back, as if he's found some new solution to our troubles.

But it is no use. The mermaids have hold of the little boat now, and they are driving it forward with strokes of their muscled tails. We are borne toward the ships and the sea and adventure.

And this, in its own way, makes a pleasant-enough end to the story.

So we go, and so we end.

AFTERWORD

*"That cannot be the end!" cries the youngest among the listeners, and for once her sisters agree— the one who will rule, the one who will poison, the one who insists that Truth is Magic. None of them accept this conclusion.*

*And indeed, even a dwarf born to entertainment has to acknowledge that a story told true never ends in hope. There must be something bitter to make the sweetness; for there is no happiness without contrast, just as there is no substance that is not poison, no delicacy without the capacity for harm. Only the dosing makes the difference.*

*The story must obey; the story continues.*

*Perhaps it goes on in this way:*

*By full daylight, the hole in the courtyard has knit itself together again, with ground as firm as any in that city, the bare earth cold and smelling no worse and no sweeter than any other patch in the environs. This healing of what was long wrong in the court is interpreted as a blessing from the angels and a favorable omen that portends happy fortunes to those so often battered by Fate. They welcome their Christian VI.*

*Delighted by this outcome, the truthful princesses speculate: What if . . .*

*It's possible that the two women, the seamstress and the slave, survive a long journey at sea to reach Copenhagen. They will certainly find it's a bigger city than the one from which they came, with a warren of streets no less complicated and far more extensive* than in *Skyggehavn, though the ground is stable and less prone to change.*

*When they step off the ship, the women are quite well and healthy, round of limb and waist; but they have somehow failed to calculate the difficulties both of understanding a new inflection in the tongue they know best, and of finding one Lutheran among an entire nation practicing that faith.*

*It is likely that they take a room in a neighborhood of travelers, where a Negresse is uncommon but not unimagined, not necessarily enslaved. It is probable that they make a series of inquiries, that they spend their wealth as carefully as possible and keep the reserve hidden within their persons, lest their room be searched while they are gone. Experience has been their best teacher in this matter.*

*But teachers are many. During summer's long light hours, the dark mute of the forked tongue shows pen and paper to the pale girl who speaks — too much — of locating the heart's desire that led them here. Slowly the seamstress learns to prick out a story not just in threads but also in words. They come to understand each other at last. When the Negresse gives birth, the seamstress catches the baby (a dusky girl) and sews up the tears in maternal flesh. When infection sets in, poison-auntie's niece writes a list of useful plants and the stargazer's daughter goes to market to buy them, then follows the recipe for a cure. The new mother recovers. Her baby is slender and prone to giggles.*

*Together, throughout the year, they read the letters sent regularly through official mail by Skyggehavn's court historian. He assures them that the chaos of the palace has settled into a tranquil*

*routine, much as the earth around the witch's bed has healed itself.*
*He is now appointed tutor to King Christian VI and is a member*
*of the Dowager's council. He also oversees the education of the two*
*young princesses, who have been sent to the green islands to live*
*free of miasma and under the strict guidance of Duchess Margrethe.*

*Most significant, the historian reports that on the first day*
*of spring, the lengthy process of closing the prisons is concluded.*
*While Count Nicolas and his former betrothed intended to execute*
*all prisoners, the Dowager and the people have been clamoring for*
*their release. The people have been especially inspired by an event*
*that they see as a miracle akin to the sudden manifestation of Saint*
*Ruta's bones in the cathedral a century ago: Some fishermen trawl-*
*ing the bay have netted, along with a glittering catch of herring,*
*an actual mer-baby — somewhat nibbled by the fish but luminous*
*in its beauty. The surprising find has restored their belief not only*
*in the diversity of God's creatures but also in the myth of their own*
*origins; in the amber-lined cathedral, a special Mass celebrates the*
*marriage of sea and land. After entombment beside the bones of*
*Saint Ruta, the mer-baby's image is woven carefully into a history*
*tapestry that commemorates the birth of Christian VI.*

*So, in May, the last of Christian V's prisoners step into the*
*military yard half blind with darkness and with pain, wincing at*
*the sun and staggering on shrunken legs. They are led out the gates*
*to freedom.*

*Among those are the most notorious prisoners of all: the man*
*accused of murdering the old King with magic and the woman who,*
*some claim, confessed to poisoning that first poor princess on her*
*wedding night.*

*Countess Elinor Parfis is so broken in body that she has no choice but to join her husband in his sickbed on one of the far islands, there to live out her few last days in an agony of spirit that might have led her to a nunnery, if fever didn't catch her first.*

*The ambitious astronomer, meanwhile, vanishes into the labyrinth of the city. The star once said to have obeyed his bidding has now vanished too, having faded slowly from yellow to orange to red to nothing. By the time of his release, it is as if the star never existed at all.*

*Perhaps he reaches his old house to find strangers living within; perhaps his wife has remarried, thinking him dead. It is likely that he does not stay in the city but departs for some other land, one where he might climb a mountain and gaze at skies with naked eye. His whereabouts are unknown, but all agree he's made a fortunate escape.*

*There has been another strange disappearance, that of the wicked Count who nearly brought down the Lunedies. When the physicians returned to his bed, they found it empty, bloodstained, with a discarded bandage nearby. It is conjectured, and recorded, that Count Nicolas wandered in a delirium from his sickbed, to take refuge in some hidden nook behind the wall of a fireplace or window seat. Though his body is not recovered, for some months the palace is plagued with a sickly sweet odor of rot.*

*Soon a year has passed and both of the traveled women, established ladies now, are out of funds; for Copenhagen is a costly city. Thus it is that she who has long believed in the quest is finally convinced, by sheaves of argument that stain twenty fingers coal-black and feed the fireplace for weeks, to stop hoping.*

*Neither of them, writes the new mother, shall see a lover again.*

*The two take their baby, now a sturdy girl with green eyes and white teeth and nearly black hair, to an island—for they are most comfortable on islands—where they find a cottage and a meadow yielding several useful herbs and a certain spider whose webs are useful for stoppering wounds. Here they set themselves up as wise women. They provide cures for many another woman's ills, from broken heart to leaky womb to the painful gleet of Swedish Fire. Their child plays along the shore, bringing home pockets full of pebbly treasures: black rocks ringed in white, amber droplets, shards of brick or glass polished soft; strands of a brown seaweed that the three of them call mermaid hair and that can be boiled into simples that villagers believe will summon lost love home.*

*And so run their lives, peaceful and not entirely unhappy.*

*But if one day there should appear a man, no longer in his first youth but retaining a certain weary charm; a man who knows Copenhagen well and may not listen much to rumors but cannot overlook the clues that Fate plants regularly in his path . . . and if this man should speak in a rusty accent and smell pleasantly of piney clarified amber, and stride with purpose over pebbles and sand to the cottage of the two wise women . . . and if that man were to knock upon the cottage door and ask to be driven mad with love again—would there be any harm in a happy ending? Who could regret such a conclusion?*

*Certainly not a princess, who must applaud for heart's desire.*

## A Note on the History

ONCE there was a teenager who wanted to live in the Renaissance. She loved Shakespeare and historical novels and books with recipes for antiquated foods. She was lucky enough to be half Danish and to feel a loyalty to the kings and queens she studied in obscure history books, and to the fairy tales of Hans Christian Andersen and Isak Dinesen. She sewed authentic costumes for her Barbies (with which she played till a very late age) and had them act out elaborate historical plots. She tried wearing a corset. She also read up on magic, and she wrote a novel in a spiral notebook while traveling back and forth on the school bus. It was about three geeky girls who develop magic powers.

Her classmates thought she was strange. They called her a witch.

That teenager, of course, grew into me—who still loves everything in that list (including Barbie), though corsets are truly dreadful. I still have that passion for the beauties of the Renaissance, triumphs of art, architecture, and literature. But as I grew up and Fate batted me around in its sharp-clawed paws, I became more interested in the nasty side of life: diseases and poisons and everyday cruelty. Here was the unseen dark side of the gleaming golden objects and elaborate royal portraits I found in the castles of my mother's native land.

Beauty, darkness, light, and fear . . . Once again I've written a novel about three girlish women on the margins of their society: the seamstress Ava Bingen, the slave Midi Sorte, and Queen Isabel. To give them a home, I combined fairy tales and my research into Real History to imagine what life might be like in the city of Skyggehavn. (The name means "Shadows' Harbor" and is pronounced Skü-geh-hown, to rhyme with *down*.) This book took seven years to write — a great fairy-tale number — which strikes a chord with the seven years of war that Scandinavia endured from 1563 to 1570. For them, it was Sweden against everybody else. For me, it was seven years of reading books and taking trips to Scandinavia and writing at least nine separate drafts.

When people asked what I was working on, I would answer, "A fairy tale about syphilis." I got nervous smiles in return. I am still considered weird.

Fairy tales are the first stories we remember; the first book I owned was *Rumpelstiltskin,* which I read to my mum while she was sick. They give us a template for organizing our lives, preparing for the trials of puberty, marriage, and carving a path through the muddled forest of Life. The heroines we recognize — Cinderella, Gretel, Beauty, Snow White — come from an oral tradition of tale-telling that spreads across continents and dates back before the Bible. Their stories are elastic; when a raconteur told a tale, she or he could alter it to suit the audience.

The fairy tales we know now come in tidy little packages, with modern ideas of a beginning, middle, and end. But the earliest print versions are often ragged little things; the endings we recognize aren't really endings but trail off into more adventures, many of them even more unpleasant than what we see as the "main story." For example, in the Sleeping Beauty tale recorded by Charles Perrault in 1695, there is no "happily ever after." Once the ring is on the heroine's finger, she has a mother-in-law to deal with—and the woman wants to eat Sleeping Beauty's babies.

That's how Life really works: Just when you think you've reached your darkest hour, you black out completely. And so those ragged tales are the stories by which Ava and other characters understand their world—and they explain why Ava is so desperate to pause at a pleasant moment, giving herself the kind of ending that we have come to expect in the era of happily ever after.

In 1572 syphilis was a world-shattering disease, one of the worst trials a person might have to endure. Imagine the sudden appearance of an illness that brought painful bony calluses, burning, itching, insanity, blindness, and death. It was relatively new to Europe, having appeared first when French soldiers invaded Naples, Italy, in 1494/1495. It was known as "the French disease" or "the Italian disease" until 1530, when Italian poet-physician Girolamo Fracastoro wrote an epic poem about a shepherd named Syphilus, who defies Apollo in the way described herein.

There are two camps when it comes to determining the disease's origin. One side says it came back from the New World with Columbus; this is the theory that Doctor Krolik espouses and the reason he uses sap from an American tree in his attempt at a cure. The other side (less interesting) says it already existed in Europe but wasn't really noticed until the French invaded Naples that year and came down with the nasties. I've recently heard yet another hypothesis: It was a relatively harmless disease among South American llamas, who were used as handy sexual outlets by their herders. The herders passed it on to their women, and the women passed it to European explorers. The remedies that physicians tried then, including mercury, were usually poisonous and brought their own set of deadly symptoms. (Good news, though— syphilis is now easily cured with penicillin.) Famous sufferers include Karen Blixen (who wrote under the name Isak Dinesen), who caught it from her husband; Denmark's mad King Christian VII; and Adolf Hitler. There really was a doctor in the early centuries who decided to prove syphilis was not a venereal disease by experimenting on his own penis. Of course, he proved himself wrong instead and died an unpleasant death.

The medicine practiced by physicians in 1572 may sound terrible. That's because it was. But the drugs and methods that those doctors used were the most sophisticated available, whether they were followers of the ancient Galen (active until about 200 C.E. and still the primary theorist for Renaissance medicine) or of the radical Paracelsus, a sixteenth-century mystic with some decidedly odd ideas. The notions that I've presented—his belief that disease is caused by poison flowing between the stars, a seven-chambered womb with one chamber being reserved for a hermaphrodite—are just the tip of an enormous and bizarre iceberg.

As strange as these theories seem to us now, *they worked at the time*—at least as well as anything people could hope for. Renaissance physicians would probably be horrified by modern medicine . . . even though treatments such as chemotherapy for cancer prove Paracelsus's idea that all things are poisonous in some quantity and that one poison may cure another.

Poisons were, knowingly or not, used to treat a variety of ills. Caustic antimony, which might eat away your flesh—and mercury, which could drive you crazier than syphilis itself—and all the lists of herbs and flowers that might serve either to make the womb ready for a baby or else to expel one if the woman wasn't ready for a child. Abortion was a crime in 1572, but it was also a necessity that might save a woman's life or ensure she didn't have more mouths to feed than she had gruel to put in them. Wisdom about abortifacient substances and birth control has been passed down as long as humans have been in existence.

Every medicine, remedy, and procedure I've presented here was used in the way described. Nicolas applies the medicinal properties of gemstones in an unusual way, but why not?

Poor Queen Isabel. Who wants to have a pelvic exam attended by so many doctors, servants, and ladies? I was somewhat merciful to her, though, as it was not unheard of to have male officers of the court present as well. There was simply no privacy for a royal in those days (and precious little of it now).

You were never supposed to leave a king or queen alone for a minute — no telling what some enemy might do if the queen were caught by herself, for example. Hence the practice of having maids and ladies sleeping in bed with the queen and on the floor around her.

And hence the custom of having an adviser and confidant watch the king in his most private moments on the toilet. No one knows how that tradition began, whether with a doctor who was supposed to monitor health or with a soldier who was supposed to prevent attacks. By the time of England's Henry VIII, however, it was an established routine and a great honor for the lucky lord appointed to be Groom of the Stool. Given how much Henry ate, I imagine he spent much more time on his stool (which I've seen at Hampton Court Palace) than Christian Lunedie — even though Christian has a disease of the bowels that causes him much pain and precipitates his death. Depending on how much you want to see him hurt, you might imagine this mysterious ailment as an abscessed fistula or as chronic Crohn's disease, from which Abraham Lincoln probably also suffered.

Christian and Isabel have separate households with different officers. This arrangement was normal in Europe at the time because the king and queen weren't always together — and they usually weren't with their children, either. The same protectiveness that meant a total lack of privacy also meant it was considered best to split up the family and farm the children out to lords and ladies in the countryside. That way no one could attack and kill them all at once. In Skyggehavn, disease has kept the family together longer than was typical.

As to the other family in the novel, the Bingens—it is unfortunate that relatively little is known about "ordinary" lives, because I find them the most fascinating of all. How would *I* have lived in 1572? Neither my father's ancestors, who were Slovenian tavern keepers, nor my mother's Danish fisher people were nobility (though my grandmother did know Isak Dinesen).

And the girl without a family, Midi Sorte, is one of several slaves who were transported to northern Europe. While kidnapped people like Midi were bought and sold, other persons of non-European origin were able to live more or less independently; one African became a prominent scholar in Holland. Non-Europeans were often seen as exotic pets, like parrots or monkeys, though they suffered even crueler treatment than an animal stolen away from its forest. Think of the American Indians who languished and died at the court of Queen Elizabeth I of England. And Midi doesn't even have a name for the country where she was born, as before she ran away she lived a secluded and all but orphaned life in her father's harem. One of the most urgent questions for me as I wrote this novel was how she would see this cold kingdom and the treatment she got at Elinor's hands . . . and later, Isabel's.

In recent decades, scholars have turned more and more to cultural history—basically, the story of how people lived on a regular day as well as during the big events of wars, plagues, and so on. I've spent hours in Copenhagen's National

Museum looking at remnants of material culture (objects used). A knitted boot or a needle case shaped like a baby can say so much more than even the best-chosen words, though I obviously love the words too. There's nothing like seeing the things people actually touched: a lacelike ivory puzzle-ball that holds infinite smaller versions of itself inside; worn-down paintbrushes made of horsehair; rusted spectacles kept in a wooden carrying case.

Telescopes—or perspective glasses as they were called long ago—did not wait for Galileo's invention. His telescope was just another refinement of a series of devices that scholars had long been working on to bring the sky closer. Even in classical times, people used globes filled with water as magnifiers, and lens grinders experimented with contraptions made of glass and steel, eventually mirrors. The first mostly modern telescope was invented by spectacle makers in the England of the 1580s. So it's thanks to what we'd call optometrists that we're able to study the moon and stars.

On November 2, 6, or 11 (accounts vary), 1572, Europeans were astonished to find a supremely bright star shining in the night sky. We know it now as Tycho Brahe's supernova; Brahe was a Danish astronomer who gave the most thorough known account of the star's appearance and gradual demise, though of course everyone was able to see it. The new star changed forever the way people thought of the heavens and even of religion, as the skies had previously been thought to be unchanging. So the effect on Skyggehavn is an accurate depiction of scholarly and popular response. The supernova grew fainter as months passed, and it eventually disappeared sometime in 1574 . . . but it revolutionized astronomy.

The new star was hard to explain, though plenty of people tried, with a wide spectrum of ideas. Many of them involved magic. Virtually every European—in fact, every soul around the world—believed in what we would call magic. For example, Duke Magnus of Östergötland really was known as Mad Magnus because he jumped out of Vadsted Castle's window to try to catch a mermaid he'd glimpsed in the moat. (Honestly, some of this stuff no novelist would dare to make up!) He did end up a raving lunatic, but in 1572 his madness was in remission, partly because others believed in mermaids too. You can't be insane unless other people paste the label on.

Whether it concerned a saint's biography or a fairy tale, a way of reading Fate in the stars or a cure in a rhinoceros horn, the most devout Christians and learned scientists believed in things we'd consider impossible. They just did—in the same way as we now believe in quantum physics, though very few of us have seen proof that it really explains the world. We follow whatever theory works for our era.

So, back to that syphilitic fairy tale. Does Isabel really have the disease, and is she responsible for passing it on to her children? I'm not quite sure myself. What I do know is that she's highly impressionable, due in part to a lifetime of prescription drug taking, and that the theory of Italian Fire makes a compelling explanation for her sorrows.

History is whatever we believe; history itself is a fairy tale. Story and truth can be anything we dream of.

In the end (this ending), any philosophy of truth is like a fountain flowing with mercury, a quicksilver distraction that reflects whatever the individual wants to see in it. It is intoxicating and it is dangerous, and it goes beyond concrete facts to lift us out of ourselves.

And, yes, Renaissance lords really did create fountains that ran with quicksilver. They did so because the mercury was beautiful.

# GRATITUDE

A peasant who spends seven years upon a story cannot finish without the help of a village, and I thank them seven ways:

Sugared cherries, cheeses, and plums to my oldest friends, who've never forgotten or flagged: Leslie Hayes, Stanley Walens, Marjorie Darraugh, Steve Darraugh, and Trixie Rummell.

Amber beads to my first readers, who generously advised and prodded: Tom Fahy, Colleen Curran, Fred R., and Virginia Pye. The amber must hold insects and flowers for two final fairy godmothers, Gretchen Comba and Gigi Amateau, whose insights set the heart beating.

A seaweed garland to each cousin of the needle, sword, and pen: Sherrie Page Najarian, Kristin Swenson, Julie Anderson, Jo Park, Siouxie Lee, Mindy Daniels, Donna Sanna, Emyl Jenkins, Lee S., Panthia K. Buck, John Vernon, and the members of James River Writers.

Buckets of herring to colleagues at VCU who have supported oddities and ruins, especially Nick Sharp, Richard Fine, Bryant Mangum, Sachi Shimomura, Kathleen Graber, Margaret Vopel, Ginny Schmitz, Katherine Bassard, and James Coleman.

Perspective glasses for my tour guides through light and darkness: Gunver Hasselbalch never tires of palaces (or never admits to it); Ole Hasselbalch showed me my first witch's hollow. James Ker did all the clever Latin, though any mistakes are mine-all-mine. Participants in a springtime writers' workshop grew preoccupied with STDs and led me gently toward syphilis—thanks, y'all. I'm grateful to Robin Selby and Lydia Morris, and they know why.

A quicksilver crown to my longtime friend and magical editor, Liz Bicknell, who makes a point of popping up every few years to turn my straw life into gold. Her like-minded familiars should get a swan each: Erin DeWitt, Nicole Raymond, Andrea Tompa, Kathryn Cunningham, Sherry Fatla, Angie Dombroski, Hannah Mahoney, Martha Dwyer, and Pier Gustafson.

Finally, simple gratitude to Weatherford.

Health to your souls!

*For information about the history and culture of 1572 Scandinavia, plus information and reflection on fairy tales and writing in general, please visit susanncokal.net.*

The font used throughout this book
is Bembo, which was designed in
late fifteenth-century Venice.

To reflect the mystique and mystery
of foreign influences in the Kingdom,
the decorative elements were adapted from
sixteenth-century French and Italian
printers' motifs and bindings.

The initial capitals are from
a sixteenth-century version of the
thirteenth-century French poem
*Le Roman de la Rose.*